Nineteenth-Century
Literature Criticism

Guide to Gale Literary Criticism Series

For criticism on	Consult these Gale series
Authors now living or who died after December 31, 1959	*CONTEMPORARY LITERARY CRITICISM (CLC)*
Authors who died between 1900 and 1959	*TWENTIETH-CENTURY LITERARY CRITICISM (TCLC)*
Authors who died between 1800 and 1899	*NINETEENTH-CENTURY LITERATURE CRITICISM (NCLC)*
Authors who died between 1400 and 1799	*LITERATURE CRITICISM FROM 1400 TO 1800 (LC)* *SHAKESPEAREAN CRITICISM (SC)*
Authors who died before 1400	*CLASSICAL AND MEDIEVAL LITERATURE CRITICISM (CMLC)*
Black writers of the past two hundred years	*BLACK LITERATURE CRITICISM (BLC)*
Authors of books for children and young adults	*CHILDREN'S LITERATURE REVIEW (CLR)*
Dramatists	*DRAMA CRITICISM (DC)*
Hispanic writers of the late nineteenth and twentieth centuries	*HISPANIC LITERATURE CRITICISM (HLC)*
Native North American writers and orators of the eighteenth, nineteenth, and twentieth centuries	*NATIVE NORTH AMERICAN LITERATURE (NNAL)*
Poets	*POETRY CRITICISM (PC)*
Short story writers	*SHORT STORY CRITICISM (SSC)*
Major authors from the Renaissance to the present	*WORLD LITERATURE CRITICISM, 1500 TO THE PRESENT (WLC)*

ISSN 0732-1864

Volume 59

Nineteenth-Century Literature Criticism

Criticism of the
Works of Novelists, Poets, Playwrights,
Short Story Writers, Philosophers, and Other
Creative Writers Who Died between 1800
and 1899, from the First Published Critical
Appraisals to Current Evaluations

Denise Evans
Mary L. Onorato
Editors

GALE

DETROIT · NEW YORK · TORONTO · LONDON

STAFF

Denise Evans and Mary L. Onorato, *Editors*

Dana Ramel Barnes, Jelena O. Krstović, James E. Person, Jr., *Contributing Editors*
Gerald R. Barterian, *Associate Editor*
Amy K. Crook, Michelle Lee, *Assistant Editors*

Aarti D. Stephens, *Managing Editor*

Susan M. Trosky, *Permissions Manager*
Kimberly F. Smilay, *Permissions Specialist*
Sarah Chesney, *Permissions Associate*
Kelly A. Quinn, *Permissions Assistant Co-Op*

Victoria B. Cariappa, *Research Manager*
Laura C. Bissey, Julia C. Daniel, Tamara C. Nott, Michele P. LeMeau,
Tracie A. Richardson, Cheryl Warnock, *Research Associates*
Alfred A. Gardner, *Research Assistant*

Mary Beth Trimper, *Production Director*
Deborah L. Milliken, *Production Assistant*

Sherrell Hobbs, *Macintosh Artist*
Randy Bassett, *Image Database Supervisor*
Mikal Ansari, Robert Duncan, *Imaging Specialists*
Pamela A. Reed, *Photography Coordinator*

This book is printed on acid-free paper that meets the minimum requirements of American National Standard for Information Sciences—Permanence Paper for Printed Library Materials, ANSI Z39.48-1984.

Library of Congress Catalog Card Number 84-643008
ISBN 0-8103-7106-5
ISSN 0732-1864
Printed in the United States of America

10 9 8 7 6 5 4 3 2 1

Contents

Preface vii

Acknowledgments xi

Preface

Since its inception in 1981, *Nineteenth-Century Literature Criticism* has been a valuable resource for students and librarians seeking critical commentary on writers of this transitional period in world history. Designated an "Outstanding Reference Source" by the American Library Association with the publication of its first volume, *NCLC* has since been purchased by over 6,000 school, public, and university libraries. The series has covered more than 300 authors representing 29 nationalities and over 17,000 titles. No other reference source has surveyed the critical reaction to nineteenth-century authors and literature as thoroughly as *NCLC*.

Scope of the Series

NCLC is designed to introduce students and advanced readers to the authors of the nineteenth century, and to the most significant interpretations of these authors' works. The great poets, novelists, short story writers, playwrights, and philosophers of this period are frequently studied in high school and college literature courses. By organizing and reprinting commentary written on these authors, *NCLC* helps students develop valuable insight into literary history, promotes a better understanding of the texts, and sparks ideas for papers and assignments. Each entry in *NCLC* presents a comprehensive survey of an author's career or an individual work of literature and provides the user with a multiplicity of interpretations and assessments. Such variety allows students to pursue their own interests; furthermore, it fosters an awareness that literature is dynamic and responsive to many different opinions.

Every fourth volume of *NCLC* is devoted to literary topics that cannot be covered under the author approach used in the rest of the series. Such topics include literary movements, prominent themes in nineteenth-century literature, literary reaction to political and historical events, significant eras in literary history, prominent literary anniversaries, and the literatures of cultures that are often overlooked by English-speaking readers.

NCLC continues the survey of criticism of world literature begun by Gale's *Contemporary Literary Criticism (CLC)* and *Twentieth-Century Literary Criticism (TCLC),* both of which excerpt and reprint commentary on authors of the twentieth century. For additional information about *TCLC, CLC,* and Gale's other criticism series, users should consult the Guide to Gale Literary Criticism Series preceding the title page in this volume.

Coverage

Each volume of *NCLC* is carefully compiled to present:

- criticism of authors, or literary topics, representing a variety of genres and nationalities
- both major and lesser-known writers and literary works of the period
- 5-8 authors or 4-6 topics per volume
- individual entries that survey critical response to an author's work or a topic in literary history, including early criticism to reflect initial reactions, later criticism to represent any rise or decline in reputation, and current retrospective analyses.

Organization

An author entry consists of the following elements: author heading, biographical and critical introduction, list of principal works, excerpts of criticism (each preceded by a bibliographic citation and an annotation), and a bibliography of further reading.

- The **Author Heading** consists of the name under which the author most commonly wrote, followed by birth and death dates. If an author wrote consistently under a pseudonym, the pseudonym will be listed in the author heading and the real name given in parentheses on the first line of the biographical and critical introduction. Also located at the beginning of the introduction to the author entry are any name variations under which an author wrote, including transliterated forms for an author whose language uses a nonroman alphabet.

- The **Biographical and Critical Introduction** outlines the author's life and career, as well as the critical issues surrounding his or her work. References are provided to past volumes of *NCLC* in which further information about the author may be found.

- Most *NCLC* entries include a **Portrait** of the author. Many entries also contain reproductions of materials pertinent to an author's career, including manuscript pages, title pages, dust jackets, letters, and drawings, as well as photographs of important people, places, and events in an author's life.

- The list of **Principal Works** is chronological by date of first publication and identifies the genre of each work. In the case of foreign authors with both foreign-language publications and English translations, the English-language version is given in brackets. Unless otherwise indicated, dramas are dated by first performance, not first publication.

- **Criticism** in each author entry is arranged chronologically to provide a perspective on changes in critical evaluation over the years. All titles of works by the author featured in the entry are printed in boldface type to enable the user to easily locate discussion of particular works. Also for purposes of easier identification, the critic's name and the publication date of the essay are given at the beginning of each piece of criticism. Unsigned criticism is preceded by the title of the journal in which it appeared. Publication information (such as publisher names and book prices) and some parenthetical numerical references (such as page and line references to specific editions of works) have been deleted at the editors' discretion to provide smoother reading of the text. Footnotes that appear with previously published pieces of criticism are reprinted at the end of each essay or excerpt. In the case of excerpted criticism, only those footnotes that pertain to the excerpted text are included.

- A complete **Bibliographic Citation** provides original publication information for each piece of criticism.

- Critical excerpts are prefaced by **Annotations** providing the reader with a summary of the critical intent of the piece. Also included, when appropriate, is information about the critic's reputation, individual approach to literary criticism, and particular expertise in an author's works, as well as information about the relative importance of the critical excerpt. In some cases, the annotations cross-reference excerpts by critics who discuss each other's commentary.

- An annotated list of **Further Reading** appearing at the end of each entry suggests secondary sources on the author. In some cases it includes essays for which the editors could not obtain reprint rights.

Cumulative Indexes

■ Each volume of *NCLC* contains a cumulative **Author Index** listing all authors who have appeared in Gale's Literary Criticism Series, along with cross-references to such biographical series as *Contemporary Authors* and *Dictionary of Literary Biography*. Useful for locating authors within the various series, this index is particularly valuable for those authors who are identified with a certain period but who, because of their death dates, are placed in another, or for those authors whose careers span two periods. For example, Fyodor Dostoevsky is found in *NCLC*, yet Leo Tolstoy, another major nineteenth-century Russian novelist, is found in *TCLC* because he died after 1899.

■ Each *NCLC* volume includes a cumulative **Nationality Index** which lists all authors who have appeared in *NCLC*, arranged alphabetically under their respective nationalities.

■ Each new volume in Gale's Literary Criticism Series includes a cumulative **Topic Index**, which lists all literary topics treated in *NCLC, TCLC, LC 1400-1800*, and the *CLC* Yearbook.

■ Each new volume of *NCLC*, with the exception of the Topics volumes, contains a **Title Index** listing the titles of all literary works discussed in the volume. In response to numerous suggestions from librarians, Gale has also produced a **Special Paperbound Edition** of the *NCLC* title index. This annual cumulation lists all titles discussed in the series since its inception. Additional copies of the index are available on request. Librarians and patrons have welcomed this separate index: it saves shelf space, is easy to use, and is recyclable upon receipt of the following year's cumulation. Titles discussed in the Topics volume entries are not included in the *NCLC* cumulative index.

Citing *Nineteenth-Century Literature Criticism*

When writing papers, students who quote directly from any volume in Gale's Literary Criticism Series may use the following general forms to footnote reprinted criticism. The first example pertains to material drawn from periodicals, the second to material reprinted from books:

[1]T.S. Eliot, "John Donne," *The Nation and Athenaeum*, 33 (9 June 1923), 321-32; excerpted and reprinted in *Literature Criticism from 1400-1800*, Vol. 10, ed. James E. Person, Jr. (Detroit: Gale Research, 1989), pp. 28-9.

[2]Clara G. Stillman, *Samuel Butler: A Mid-Victorian Modern* (Viking Press, 1932); excerpted and reprinted in *Twentieth-Century Literary Criticism*, Vol. 33, ed. Paula Kepos (Detroit: Gale Research, 1989), pp. 43-5.

Suggestions Are Welcome

In response to suggestions, several features have been added to *NCLC* since the series began, including annotations to excerpted criticism, a cumulative index to authors in all Gale literary criticism series, entries devoted to criticism on a single work by a major author, more illustrations, and a title index listing all literary works discussed in the series.

Readers who wish to suggest authors, single works, or topics to appear in future volumes, or who have other suggestions, are cordially invited to write: The Editors, *Nineteenth-Century Literature Criticism*, 835 Penobscot Bldg., 645 Griswold St., Detroit, MI 48226-4094; call toll-free at 1-800-347-GALE; or fax to 1-313-961-6599.

Acknowledgments

The editors wish to thank the copyright holders of the excerpted criticism included in this volume and the permissions managers of many book and magazine publishing companies for assisting us in securing reproduction rights. We are also grateful to the staffs of the Detroit Public Library, the Library of Congress, the University of Detroit Mercy Library, Wayne State University Purdy/Kresge Library Complex, and the University of Michigan Libraries for making their resources available to us. Following is a list of the copyright holders who have granted us permission to reproduce material in this volume of *NCLC.* Every effort has been made to trace copyright, but if omissions have been made, please let us know.

COPYRIGHTED EXCERPTS IN *NCLC,* VOLUME 59, WERE REPRODUCED FROM THE FOLLOWING PERIODICALS:

Critical Inquiry, v. 12, Winter, 1986. Copyright © 1986 by The University of Chicago. Reproduced by permission.—*Diacritics,* v. 12, Summer, 1982. Copyright © Diacritics, Inc., 1982. Reproduced by permission of The John Hopkins University Press.—*Emerson Society Quarterly,* v. 50, 1968, First Quarter. Copyright © 1968, Kenneth Walter Cameron. Reproduced by permission.—*Encounter,*v. XIV, February, 1960 for "The Anglo-Jewish Writer" by Brian Glanville. © 1960 by the author. Reproduced by permission of the author.—*Essex Institute Historical Collections,* v. C, July, 1964; v. CVIII, July, 1972. Copyright © 1964, 1972, by the Essex Institute, 132-134 Essex Street, Salem, MA 01970. Both reproduced by permission of the publisher.—*The French Review,* v. LXVI, April, 1993. Copyright 1993 by the American Association of Teachers of French. Reproduced by permission.—*The London Mercury,* v. XII, July, 1925. Reproduced by permission.—*Orbis Litterarum,* v. 41, 1986. Reproduced by permission.—*The Sewanee Review,* v. LXXIX, Winter, 1971. Copyright © 1971 by Robert Penn Warren. Reprinted by permission of William Morris Agency, Inc. on behalf of the author.—*Signs,* v. 15, Summer, 1990. © 1990 by The University of Chicago. All rights reserved. Reproduced by permission.—*Studies in Romanticism,* v. 34, Summer, 1995. Copyright 1995 by the Trustees of Boston University. Reproduced by permission.—*Studies in Scottish Literature,* v. XIV, 1979. Copyright © G. Ross Roy 1979. Reproduced by permission of the editor.—*Studies in the American Renaissance,* 1993. Copyright © 1993 by Joel Myerson. All rights reserved. Reproduced by permission.—*Studies in the Novel,* v. XXVI, Fall, 1994. Copyright 1994 by North Texas State University. Reproduced by permission of the publisher.—*Tulsa Studies in Women's Literature,* v. 2, Fall, 1983. © 1983, The University of Tulsa. Reproduced by permission.—*Victorian Poetry,* v. 28, Summer, 1990 for "Alexander Smith and the Poetry of Displacement" by Richard Cronin. Reproduced by permission of the author.—*The Yale Journal of Criticism,* v. 2, Fall, 1988. Reproduced by permission of The Johns Hopkins University Press.

COPYRIGHTED EXCERPTS IN *NCLC,* VOLUME 59, WERE REPRODUCED FROM THE FOLLOWING BOOKS:

Driscoll, Joan. From "Theophile Gautier's 'Voyage en Italie': The Description of Experience, or the Experience of Description," in *Words of Power: Essays in Honour of Alison Fairlie*. Edited by Dorothy Gabe Coleman and Gillian Jondorf. The University of Glasgow Publications in Language and Literature, 1987. Copyright © of papers by individual authors. Reproduced by permission of authors.—Ellis, Kate. From "Monsters in the Garden: Mary Shelley and the Bourgeois Family," in *The Endurance of Frankenstein: Essays in Mary Shelley's Novel.* Edited by George Levine and U. C. Knoepflmacher. University of California Press, 1979. Copyright © 1979 by The Regents of the University of California. Reproduced by permission.—Feldman, Jessica R. From *Gender on the Divide: The Dandy in Modernist Literature.* Cornell, 1993. Copyright © 1993 by Cornell University. All rights reserved. Used by permission of the publisher, Cornell University Press.—George, Albert J. From *Short Fiction in France: 1800-1850.* Syracuse University Press, 1964. Copyright © 1964 by Syracuse University Press. All rights reserved. Reproduced by permission.—Gilbert, Sandra M., and Susan Gubar. From *The Madwoman in the Attic: The Woman Writer and the Nineteenth-Century Literary Imagination.* Yale University Press, 1979. Copyright © 1979 by Yale University. All rights reserved. Reproduced by permission of Feminist Studies.—Homans, Margaret. From *Bearing the Word.* University of Chicago Press, 1986. © 1986 by The University of Chicago. All rights reserved. Reproduced by permission.—Knoepflmacher, U. C. From "Thoughts on the Aggression of Daughters," in *The Endurance of Frankenstein: Essays in Mary Shelley's Novel.* Edited by George Levine and U. C. Knoepflmacher. University of California Press, 1979. Copyright © 1979 by The Regents of the University of California. Reproduced by permission.—Mellor, Anne K. From *Mary Shelley: Her Life, Her Fiction, Her Monsters.* Methuen, 1988. Copyright © 1988 by Methuen, Inc. All rights reserved. Reproduced by permission.—Murphy, Richard. From "Alexander Smith on the Art of the Essay," in *If by Your Art: Testament to Percival Hunt.* Edited by Agnes Lynch Starrett. University of Pittsburgh Press, 1948. Copyright 1948 by University of Pittsburgh Press. Reproduced by permission.—New, Melvyn. From an introduction to *The Complete Novels and Selected Writings of Amy Levy, 1861-1889.* Edited by Melvyn New. University Press of Florida, 1993. Copyright 1993 by the Board of Regents of the State of Florida. All rights reserved. Reproduced by permission.—Wagenknecht, Edward. From *Daughters of the Covenant: Portraits of Six Jewish Women.* Amherst: The University of Massachusetts Press, 1983. Copyright © 1983 by Edward Wagenknecht. All rights reserved. Reproduced by permission.—Richardson, Joanna. From *Theophile Gautier: His Life & Times.* Max Reinhardt, 1958. © Joanna Richardson 1958. Reproduced by permission of the author.—Schick, Constance Gosselin. From *Seductive Resistance: The Poetry of Theophile Gautier.* Rodopi, 1994. © Editions Rodopi B. V. Reproduced by permission.—Smith, Albert B. From *Theophile Gautier and the Fantastic.* Romance Monographs, Inc., 1977. Copyright © 1977 by Romance Monographs, Inc. Reproduced by permission.

PHOTOGRAPHS AND ILLUSTRATIONS APPEARING IN *NCLC*, VOLUME 59, WERE RECEIVED FROM THE FOLLOWING SOURCES:

The Broomielaw, Glasgow, looking West, Glasgow, Scotland, photograph of an illustration. Archive Photos, Inc. Reproduced by permission.—Gautier, Theophile, drawing. French Cultural Services.—Gautier, Theophile, photograph of an illustration. Archive Photos, Inc. Reproduced by permission.—Glasgow Cathedral, photograph of an illustration. Archive Photos, Inc. Reproduced by permission —The Irongate, Glasgow, photograph of an illustration. Archive Photos, Inc. Reproduced by permission.—Karloff, Boris and Mae Clarke (in the 1931 motion picture "Frankenstein"), photograph. The Kobal Collection. Reproduced by permission.—Karloff, Boris (in

Théophile Gautier

1811-1872

French poet, novelist, short story writer, critic, travel writer, and dramatist.

For further information on Gautier's works and career, see *Nineteenth-Century Literature Criticism*, Vol. 1.

INTRODUCTION

One of the most highly respected literary figures of his time, Gautier played a prominent role in the Romantic movement of the 1830s. Although primarily a poet and a novelist, Gautier made many other contributions to nineteenth-century literature. He was a leader in the "art for art's sake" movement, and his preface to *Mademoiselle de Maupin* (1835-36) stands as the manifesto of this doctrine, which claims that art has no other aim and no other morality than the creation of beauty. Gautier also wrote highly praised travel books, ballets, and plays, and was an influential critic of literature and the arts.

Biographical Information

Born in 1811 in southwestern France, Gautier moved with his family three years later from Tarbes to Paris, where he would live for the rest of his life. While a student at the Collège Charlemagne, Gautier met his lifelong friend, French poet Gérard de Nerval. It was Nerval who introduced him to Victor Hugo, a French novelist who had a great influence on Gautier's life and work. During this time Gautier gave up his early ambitions as a painter and began writing poetry. He became part of the Petit Cénacle, a group of artists and writers—which included Nerval, Pétrus Borel, and Auguste Maquet—who delighted in shocking the middle class. Gautier earned his scandalous reputation during this period with the publication of his first novel, *Mademoiselle de Maupin*, which not only celebrates a pagan ideal and an ambiguous morality, but contains erotic elements as well. Gautier soon found that the income from his creative writing could not support his lifestyle, and he turned to journalism for financial help. Even though he was never happy as a journalist, his theater and art columns at the *Presse* and the *Moniteur Universel*, among others, placed him among the most influential critics of the period. Also, it was as a journalist that Gautier was able to travel throughout Europe. These journeys not only gave him the inspiration to write his highly praised travel books, but also pro-

vided material for his poetry and fiction. Gautier's downward spiral began in 1870, during the political and civil strife caused by the Prussian siege of Paris. The combination of financial problems, professional uncertainties, domestic displacements, and deteriorating health all contributed to Gautier's death in 1872.

Major Works

Gautier wrote during a time marked by inventive diversity. Many authors were experimenting with different genres, and Gautier stood out among them. He wrote travel literature, criticism, and dramas in addition to his fictional works (which included novels, novellas, and short stories) and poetry. His most unusual achievement was *Giselle, ou les Wilis* (1841), one of the most popular ballets of all time. Gautier wrote *Giselle* for the dancer Carlotta Grisi, in whom he saw both the perfect dancer and the perfect woman. However, like most of the heroes in his fictional works, he never gained her affection or realized his ideal. The conflict between the ideal and reality is a recurring theme in

Gautier's writing. His heroes are constantly reaching for the unattainable, but reality stands in the way of their goals. In his first novel, *Mademoiselle de Maupin*, D'Albert seeks an ideal beauty, while Madelaine de Maupin seeks the ideal of unswerving love. The story ends unhappily, with both characters failing to achieve their ideals. This theme also plays out in Gautier's "fantastic" works, which depict the intrusion of supernatural phenomena into a fictional universe. The fantastic beings in Gautier's works often serve as symbols of his heroes' ideals. For example, in "Arria Marcella" (1852), the hero finds himself in love with a ghost, the beautiful Arria Marcella, who died in Pompeii during the eruption of Vesuvius. Although Gautier had many achievements in a variety of genres, it is his poetry that created a niche for him during his own time. His famous poem "L'art" (1857) became the creed of the Parnassian poets, and his most celebrated volume of poetry, *Emaux et camées* (1852), went through an exceptional six editions in twenty years.

Critical Reception

Early critics were slow to recognize Gautier's works. In fact, he gained little recognition until the controversy over the immorality of his series of articles (later to be collected in *Les Grotesques*, 1844) and the success of his first novel, *Mademoiselle de Maupin*, brought him into the spotlight. Once there, Gautier began to earn a reputation based purely on literary merit. His writing attracted praise from his peers; Charles Baudelaire, in his dedication of *Les Fleurs du mal* (1857), revealed the veneration in which Gautier the poet was held: "To the impeccable poet, to the perfect magician in letters, to my dear and revered master and friend Théophile Gautier, with the deepest humility I dedicate these sickly flowers." As a journalist, Gautier acquired an even greater reputation as one of the major critics of his day. It was this combination of success as journalist, novelist, and poet that positioned him as a key figure in mid-century France. Today, however, Gautier is one of the least read of all the great nineteenth-century French writers. He has been criticized for neglecting plot and character, and many commentators have felt his use of extensive description often caused his narratives to lack cohesion. André Gide has asserted that Gautier's poetry had no depth and was "blind to everything but the exterior world." William C. Mead has similarly argued that Gautier had no originality and "contented himself for the most part with other peoples' ideas, and in particular with the ordinary 'romantic' ideas." However, not all modern critics agree with such assessments. Many scholars have claimed that Gautier is undervalued and that his work possesses an intrinsic and historical significance. Marcel Voisin, for example, has contended that Gautier deserves a place among the major authors of French literature, stating, "Thanks to his literary achievements, Théophile Gautier, by revealing himself to us, all of

himself, speaks to us about ourselves, our anxieties and our hopes, about human beings eternally divided between the sunlight and the night.

PRINCIPAL WORKS

Poésies (poetry) 1830

Albertus, ou l'âme et le péché (poetry) 1833

Les Jeunes-France, romans goguenards, suivis de contes humoristiques [*The Young-France, Stories in a Jesting Manner*] (satire) 1833

Mademoiselle de Maupin (novel) 1835-36 [*Mademoiselle de Maupin*, 1890]

L'Eldorado (novella) 1837; also published as *Fortunio*, 1838 [*Fortunio*, 1915]

La Comédie de la mort [*The Comedy of Death*] (poetry) 1838

**Une larme du diable* [*A Tear Shed by the Devil*] (short story) 1839

Giselle, ou les Wilis [with Vernoy de Saint-Georges] (ballet scenario) 1841

Tra los montes (travel essay) 1843; also published as *Voyage in Espagne*, 1845 [*Wanderings in Spain*, 1853]

Les grotesques (criticism) 1844

España (poetry) 1845

Nouvelles (novellas) 1845

Zigzags (travel essays) 1845; also published as *Caprices et zigzags* (enlarged edition), 1852

Emaux et camées [*Enamels and Cameos*] (poetry) 1852

Italia (travel essay) 1852; also published as *Voyage en Italie* (enlarged edition), 1875 [*Journeys in Italy*, 1902]

***Un Trio de romans* (novel and novellas) 1852

Constantinople (travel essay) 1853 [*Constantinople of Today*, 1854]

Les beaux-arts en Europe (criticism) 1855

Avatar (novel) 1857

Jettatura [*The Evil Eye*] (novel) 1857 [*Jettatura*, 1888]

Romans et contes (novels and short stories) 1857

Le roman de la momie (novel) 1858 [*The Romance of the Mummy*, 1882]

Histoire de l'art dramatique en France depuis vingt-cinq ans (criticism) 1858-59

Le Capitane Fracasse (novel) 1863 [*Captain Fracasse*, 1880]

Spirite, nouvelle fantastique [*Spirite: A Fantasy*] (novel) 1866

Voyage en Russie (travel essay) 1867 [*A Winter in Russia*, 1874]

Histoire du romantism (unfinished critical essay) 1872 [*A History of Romanticism*, 1900]

Théâtre (drama) 1877

The Works of Théophile Gautier. 24 vols. (novels, short stories, travel essays, criticism, drama, novellas, and poetry) 1900-03

The Romantic Ballet (criticism) 1908
Nouvelles (novellas) 1923
Poésies complètes. 3 vols. (poetry) 1932
Contes fantastiques (short stories) 1962

*This volume includes the material in *Poésies*.
**This volume also includes "La Morte amoureuse" ["The Dead Leman"].
***This volume contains "Arria Marcella."

CRITICISM

F. C. de Sumichrast (essay date 1902)

SOURCE: "Theophile Gautier," in *Captain Fracasse*, by Theophile Gautier, translated by F. C. de Sumichrast, P. F. Collier & Son, 1902, pp. v-xxii.

[*In the following essay, de Sumichrast examines Gautier's use of beauty, wit, picturesqueness, and realism in his works, particularly as seen in his novel* Captain Fracasse. *The critic also argues that although Gautier is perhaps one of the least recognized members of the Romanticist school, he is in fact "the soundest Romanticist and also the most typical Frenchman of them all."*]

It is probable that to the average reader of French literature, whether in the original or in translations, the name of Théophile Gautier would not at once occur were he to recall the important members of the great Romanticist school that made the beginning of the last century so illustrious and interesting. Chateaubriand, the founder of the school, the creator and exponent of the melancholy hero who so long dominated both the novel and the drama; Lamartine, the sweet singer in the new Israel of letters; De Musset, the lightsome, daring, pert, and independent spoiled child of the band; De Vigny, the one serious thinker; Dumas the elder, the brilliant and dashing novelist, whose books still command, *pace* René Doumic and other modern critics, the close interest and excite the lively admiration of thousands upon thousands of readers; Sainte-Beuve, the arbiter of taste and the champion of that wondrous sixteenth-century literature, until then so unjustly disdained and unread—these are the names that first recur to the memory; and, above all, the name of the famous chief, of the standard-bearer, Victor Hugo, poet, novelist, dramatist, critic, philosopher—in his own peculiar way—the writer who, above and beyond all, made the school what it became and who linked its fortunes so closely with his own.

Yet, in many respects, Théophile Gautier is the soundest Romanticist and also the most typical Frenchman of them all. Endowed with a very marked and striking individuality, he is more than the "sonorous echo" Victor Hugo so accurately described himself as being. He

never attained to the splendour of lyricism so easily reached by his chief, but never did he fall into such bathos as one regretfully comes upon in the dramas, the novels, and the verse of the singer of "The Legend of the Ages." He has not the peculiar melody of Lamartine nor that poet's spiritual uplifting, but he is truer to Nature as it really is, and when he expresses the emotions of suffering man, it is with an intensity of humanity and a sobriety of speech that is more virile than much that Lamartine has done in this way. He is never as lightsome as Musset, yet he, too, can be bright, engaging, and daring to degree. Neither *Namouna* nor *Mardoche* surpasses, in this respect, the audacious preface to **Mlle. de Maupin,** which recalls in certain ways that memorable preface Beaumarchais wrote for his *Figaro.* Unquestionably he is not the peer of Alfred de Vigny as a thinker; reflection was not the forte of Romanticist writers, and Vigny was neither fully appreciated nor fully understood in his own day; he trusted, and rightly, to posterity to give him the rank he merited. But Gautier is a thinker of value, if not on matters philosophical, which he has rarely touched upon, at all events on matters of art in all its forms and manifestations.

And here is the characteristic of the man, what makes him so truly and completely a Frenchman, and gives him so conspicuous and important a place in nineteenth-century literature. It is his deep, all-pervading feeling for art, his devotion to it, through good and evil report, at all times and in all places. There is not a single subject treated of by him in which this is not plainly evident. His preface to **Mlle. de Maupin,** already alluded to, and yet more the novel itself, are a violent expression of his worship of Beauty, which appears to him uncomprehended of the vulgar, a class, in his view, comprising a far larger number of people than is generally supposed. And as his first, so his last important work, **Enamels and Cameos,** is a vindication of beauty. He touches nothing but he communicates to it the sense and feeling, outward as well as inward, of beauty. She is his goddess; the object of a cult to which he was never for one moment unfaithful. He is neither a Christian nor a pagan; he is an artist, and remains one to his dying breath; an artist capable of perceiving all that was new, all that was perfect in the common things around him as well as in the masterpieces of painter, sculptor, goldsmith, writer, or musician. In this he is thoroughly and truly French; a member of the race in which the feeling for art and the power of expressing it are more widely spread and more deeply rooted than in any other contemporary nation.

French again by his common sense, obscured though that quality may appear to be at times by Romanticist exaggeration or youthful indiscretion and lack of proportion. Gautier is a sensible man, and no one can read his works without recognising the fact. He becomes excited at times, not infrequently, perhaps, but he never allows himself to be so extravagantly carried away as does Victor Hugo, whom it is often impossible to follow in his flights into the mysterious and incomprehensible. The best proof of Gautier's common sense is that he contributed more largely, in all probability, than any other writer of his day to bring the public he addressed to a realizing sense of the genuine beauties contained in Romanticism and in the art of other nations and other ages; and he attained this result not by frantic denunciations of the *bourgeois* or wild exaggerations of the value of Romanticism, but by steady demonstration of the soundness of his views, by persistent explanation and illustration, by patient teaching of the masses whom he reached through the medium of those innumerable *feuilletons* and articles that, as he has declared himself, would, if reprinted in collected form, fill more than three hundred volumes.

French again in his lighter moods. His wit is essentially the *esprit gaulois* which, in recent years, has taken the place of charity as a covering for a multitude of sins. He can scarcely be termed a brilliant wit; rather is he one of those whose perception of the *spirituel* is somewhat commonplace; not, however, to the same extent as with a Homais or a Victor Hugo. His wit is not forced; indeed, it often is spontaneous enough, but it is conventional. His jokes and his allusions in the way of pleasantry are exactly of the kind that the genuine *bourgeois* loves, a fact that would have been most unpleasant to Gautier in his younger and more hotheaded days, though it none the less remains a fact.

French once more in his use of prose in infinitely larger measure than verse. It is quite true that he was compelled to the use of prose by the necessities that drove him into the slavery of the press, as he somewhere calls it; but verse was not to him the all imperious need which it was to Victor Hugo, to Leconte de Lisle, or, to go back farther, to Racine. To Gautier, it was the delight, the satisfaction of the writer; it was not an absolute necessity. He has written much verse, some of it beautiful exceedingly, yet the poet in him reveals himself fully as much in his wonderful prose descriptions as in the earlier or the later rimes he gave to the world. It would be idle to discuss here the question whether poetry is not in its essence a gift really bestowed upon the French. The long line of singers sufficiently answers the doubt to which expression has at times been given; but it is plain that the disappearance of poetry from the national literature in the preceding age, and the substitution of prose, ever clearer and ever terser, did hamper the writers of the nineteenth century, who at first strove to express themselves in the language of the gods, whose chief charm, as Musset said, is "that the world hears it, and understands it not." Gautier's prose is poetical, though he would thank no man for saying so; poetical in that it is filled and instinct with the feeling of the ideal and the beautiful, that it is rhythmic and cadenced, and that it conveys so

much more than the mere dry words comport. A poet he is and always was, because he was an artist to the very marrow, and must therefore express himself poetically and not prosaically. But none the less the more French in that he made prose the chief vehicle of the expression of his thoughts.

Gautier has written on many subjects, many of them very wide apart, and this was, to a certain extent, due to the calls made upon him by the press he served. This fact, and the other fact that led him into the career of the journalist, was of incalculable service to him in that it removed him gradually, and more completely than he probably had any idea of, from the exclusiveness of the Romanticists and protected him from the danger of himself falling into the mistake of separating himself from human interests and needs, an almost unavoidable consequence of the exaggeration and misapplication of the famous doctrine of "Art for Art's sake," which he maintained, and which others after him applied in such wise as to lose much of the beneficial influence they might have exercised upon thought and conduct. There was peril that the absurd detestation of the bourgeois and all his works, so characteristic of artists at all times and in all places, but especially of the Romanticists in the heyday of their success, would lead Gautier to forget the world around him and to use his talents more for the gratification of a select circle, as has been the case recently with the Symbolist school, than for the greater advantage of the large mass of the public. The very necessity for addressing that public, a necessity the rigour and oppressiveness of which were so irksome to him at first, compelled him to become the teacher of the Beautiful to an audience who had indeed great need of such lessons. An artist, and therefore a man endowed with peculiar gifts; a trained artist—that is, a man who had been taught to *see* and not merely to glance at things— Gautier was admirably adapted to carry out the mission which Fate imposed upon him. His influence in the way of opening the eyes of the blind public was enormous; nor was it less great upon his fellows. His reputation as a wild-haired, thorough-paced Romanticist, which do what he would, clung to him through life, gave the greater weight to his eloquent praise of writers, painters, sculptors, composers, who were abandoning pure Romanticism, and, preserving what it had of true and useful, were working out a new form of art and entering upon the study of the realistic. The great critic had become broad-minded with the passing years, and could in later life admire as freely and enjoy as fully Greek art as Byzantine, the architecture of the days of Louis XIV as that of Gothic times, the music of Wagner as that of the composers who had hitherto claimed the undivided allegiance of musical circles.

Bursting upon the reading world as the author of the most daring novel, as it has since been considered, that even a full-fledged Romanticist could write, Gautier speedily showed that novel-writing was not to be his one sole occupation. He excelled in it, although he does not rank perhaps with Dumas the elder, George Sand, or Victor Hugo. Yet three of his works have held their place in France without any diminution of popularity: *Mlle. de Maupin, Fortunio,* and *Captain Fracasse.* But it is not as a novelist alone, nor even as a poet and a novelist, that he made his great reputation, and is still read with such delight by lovers of good literature. He is unmatched, or at least unsurpassed as a writer of travels. Whatever may be urged against his *Spain,* his *Italy,* and his *Russia,* to name the more famous only of his works in this line, as lacking a study of the manners, of the customs, of the life of the people of the different countries he has visited and described, the fact remains patent to all dispassionate readers that Gautier has a power rarely equalled of bringing vividly before one the scenes he paints. There are whole passages, in any one of the three works above named, that are absolutely perfect in their way, and that convey the most vivid and truthful idea of the land. And to indicate one other, *Constantinople,* who that has read that fascinating work but will concede that the impression of Orientalism, of strangeness, of unlikeness to European civilization is more strongly brought out by Gautier than by any other writer on the same subject? Constantinople becomes a living Turkish city in his pages, even though he does not dwell upon the manners of the inhabitants or enlarge upon statistics of one kind and another.

Nor is this the last of the manifestations of his busy brain. Poet, novelist, writer of travels, he is also a critic, and a good one. Not a morose, sour, vicious carper at everything done or said by those around him, by the men who have attained fame, or by the younger generation that seeks to win it; but a kindly critic, too kindly, say some, disposed to encourage rather than to drive to despair, to see what is praiseworthy rather than that only which is faulty and blamable. But withal a critic with a very clear insight into the merits and demerits of the work he is examining, and a power of expressing graphically whatever he observes. His very kindliness, which has by some been made a reproach to him, is justified of the sympathetic articles he has written upon the great François Villon, upon lesser poetic lights of the sixteenth and the earlier seventeenth century, upon modern authors, whose excellences he dwelt upon more lingeringly than he did upon their faults. Because he is inclined to deal gently with the writers that he passes in review, he succeeds in bringing out of their works much that is truly good and might perchance be forgotten by later generations or by a contemporary public that has neither the knowledge nor the inclination to find it out for itself.

It is curious to note, alongside of this kindheartedness, manifesting itself not in criticism only, but in many another way, sometimes subtly, sometimes plainly, a

certain apparent cold-bloodedness. He takes a positive delight in the spectacle of the bull-fight, and travels miles for the sole purpose of witnessing an exhibition that strikes most people as barbarous and disgusting. The efforts of the baited animal to rid itself of its persecutors interest him in the highest degree, and the rush of the maddened bull, its flanks bristling with barbed darts, its blood streaming, its mighty chest panting, impart to him something of the ferocious exultation that marked the ancient Romans in the Coliseum and that even now is characteristic of the Spaniard. It is a joyous sight, that combat between one animal and many armed men; a sight that awakens the liveliest emotions in his soul, and for which he longs even when back in that France that had not then sought, as it has done in these latter days, to emulate and surpass Iberian lust for blood. The reason no doubt is to be found in his Southern temperament, for while he became a true Parisian in every sense of the word, he never lost the traits of the Southerner, though they were in a measure tempered and softened by the North in which he lived; also, in the bull-fight, as in the sight of the ruins wrought by the fires of the Commune in Paris, Gautier discerned a form of beauty. This is evident from the points in the spectacle on which he lays most stress; he is struck by the picturesqueness of the whole scene; the vast crowd of spectators, the brilliancy and variety of the colours, the splendid array of chulos, picadors, and matadors, the train of mules, all adorned with tassels and bells, the shining coats and muscular frames of the bulls, the splendid curving horns, the dazzling azure of the sky that forms the roof of the amphitheatre. At bottom, these are the things which appeal to him, just as on the Neva, in the depth of winter, it is the picturesqueness of the moujik's sleigh with its wild, shaggy horses that outrace the trained steeds of the wealthier nobles; just as when the innumerable crows return to roost in the evening it is the endless stream of dark cohorts that strikes his imagination.

Victor Hugo, it has been well said, thought in pictures, in images, rather than in ideas. Gautier thinks in ideas but sees the pictures that are scattered thickly about him. He beholds them so plainly that he describes them convincingly, and we see them in our turn. He does not compose and invent them; he shows them. He possesses a word-palette that is as rich and varied in hues as the palette of the greatest colourist among painters. And this fact has greatly contributed to the influence he has exercised upon writers. Professor Norton once said that it would be an interesting study to make a series of extracts from modern French prose writers who have described landscapes and to compare these with the innumerable masterpieces of their brethren of the brush. Were this done, it is to Gautier that much of the praise of having developed word-painting would be unquestionably assigned. Of course Chateaubriand would occupy a foremost place in the list of landscape painters in words, and Victor Hugo would figure advantageously among them, but to no one would so much praise fall due as to Gautier himself. This for the simple reason that he was at once painter and writer, that the resources of both arts were equally familiar to him, and that no writer has, to anything like the same extent, introduced admirable and true paintings into his prose.

Closely connected with this remarkable quality in him is the power of evocation. Not that he attempts to bring up the far-distant past, the vanished civilizations on so large a scale as has been done by Victor Hugo and Flaubert, to name two well-known examples. His **"Aria Marcella"** and his *Romance of a Mummy* fall very far short of Flaubert's *Salammbô,* and Hugo's *Notre-Dame* in the extent and completeness of the evocation of bygone days. But if he has done nothing that may be compared with the marvellous view of Paris in the fifteenth century or the swarming camp of the mercenaries round Carthage, he has been singularly successful in bringing back in life-like manner the period of Louis XIII. This was always a favourite period of his; its architecture, its costumes, its mode of life, its love of adventure, its duels and love-affairs appealed very strongly to the Romanticist in him. His first novel, **Mlle. de Maupin,** is plainly set in the days of the melancholy monarch, although it might, so far as any precise indication goes, have prefixed to it the delightful direction on the opening page of Rostand's *Les Romanesques:* "The scene is wherever one pleases; only let the dresses be dainty." And more than one of his tales has reminiscences of that age which so strongly captivated his imagination.

Captain Fracasse is clearly set in that period. There are innumerable references to the new plays of the day, such as Corneille's *Illusion comique,* to the tremendous success of the *Cid,* which made such a sensation that the stage itself was invaded by the spectators, to authors whose reputation was at its height under Richelieu's rule, while the minute description of the dresses worn by the chief characters leaves no doubt as to the time of the action.

Precisely because the period is one of picturesqueness, or has been made so by the novelists and historians who have written about it, the novel itself is one of the most picturesque composed by Gautier. It is also his longest, and, in many respects, his most important one. It has not the daring of **Mlle. de Maupin,** but it has a briskness and a vivacity of action that are lacking in the other, where such qualities are not of equal importance, since it is rather an analysis of feelings and a hymn to beauty than a novel in the ordinary sense of the word. In **Captain Fracasse,** on the contrary, the action is important, and the dangers that threaten the loves of Sigognac and Isabella form the real interest of the book. It is a novel in the style of those that happen

to be so popular at the present day, and in which an unconquerable hero triumphs over difficulties of all sorts with a skill and resourcefulness that are not often met with in real life. A novel in which, equally of course, the heroine is a persecuted paragon of virtue and a pattern of fidelity, no matter how great the temptations to which she is exposed. It is melodramatic to a considerable degree, as works of that class must necessarily be; it has the due mingling of the comic and the tragic; the suitable proportion of fighting, hair-breadth escapes, and love-making without which the reader and lover of this class of fiction would feel himself defrauded and ill-used. There is the needed abundance of titled persons to give the proper aristocratic fillip so dear to the heart of the French bourgeois—and his transatlantic congener. There are the descriptions of splendid homes and gorgeous palaces, as well as of humbler abodes; in a word, it contains all the ingredients necessary to the success of a story that is to win and retain popularity with the bulk of the reading public, but it has other elements that make it a piece of good literature and insure its inclusion among classics of romance.

Among these a certain charm which is far more readily felt than defined; there is, as has been said, a good deal of the melodramatic in the work—it was apparently impossible for a Romanticist to escape that—but there is a great deal more of that humanity which commends the book it pervades to the affection of the reader. There is no overpowering character in the novel, none that monopolizes the attention, but a number of characters that are interesting in themselves, and, above all, that are human, ordinarily human, instead of being eccentric or monstrous or impossible, or even improbable, as is the case so generally with the characters in Hugo's works. There is an element, an air of probability, of verisimilitude about the greater part of the adventures that befall the hero and the heroine; not about them all, it must be granted, but about most of them. The arrival at Poverty Hall of the company of strolling players, the privations and sufferings they undergo, the death of the Hector of the troupe—to whom one takes a liking from the moment he comes on the scene— the attack on Sigognac on the Pont-Neuf by the professional bravo, the carrying off of Isabella by Malartic and his followers, all these are just such adventures as the memoirs and accounts of the day tell us were of almost daily occurrence. The personages themselves are interesting outside of their Romanticist garb. Sigognac, the hero, is the most romantic of them all. He is patterned after the well-known and well-worn line of heroes that begins with Rousseau's Saint-Preux, and is continued through Chateaubriand's René and Eudore, and Victor Hugo's Hernani and Ruy Blas. He has something of the valiant and amazing personages that swagger and stride through the novels of the elder Dumas, though he lacks their resourcefulness. As first presented to the reader, he is essentially a "man of no account," and it is difficult to feel any sympathy for him in his distressed circumstances, unless one is convinced, as were the French aristocrats of the ante-Revolution days, that it was better for a noble to starve than turn his hand to handicraft or business in order to retrieve his fortunes. Gautier appears to have been conscious of the little enthusiasm such a figure would excite in the breasts of his readers, and he has judiciously improved Sigognac by giving him a realizing sense of his own uselessness in the world and inspiring him with the wish to do something for himself. The assumption of the part of the Hector, in the strolling players' troupe, after the most unhappy and dramatically told death of the original lanky holder of the part, is the wisest thing Sigognac could do both to better his fortunes and to attach the reader to the tale of his love and his adventures.

For it goes without saying that love has been the compelling power, and that it is to the heroine, with her silken hair and soft blue eyes, that we are indebted for the advantageous change in the forlorn hero. Now a Romanticist heroine needed no particular force of character; all-sufficient was it for her to be dowered with good looks by her Creator. This is the case with Isabella, but she does possess some decision of character and some clear ideas of duty, together with the power of sticking firmly to what she believes to be the right course for her to pursue. In so far she is an improvement on the general run of women in the drama and the novel of the Romanticist school; she is neither a perfect nonentity nor a deep-dyed and at the same time splendidly beautiful wretch. Indeed, there is plainly a striving after an adequately human and realistic depicting of character on the author's part. There are no great figures, as has been said, in the collection, brought together by chance and the author's will, but at least there is something genuinely true about all of them, even about the wicked Duke of Vallombreuse, whose sudden conversion to the paths of peace and righteousness is perhaps the weakest part of the composition. The women and the men alike who form the strolling company are delightfully drawn, and if all this be something of a reminiscence of Scarron's *Roman comique,* it is a reminiscence which has its own originality and its own peculiar savour.

Captain Fracasse, then, is a novel that unquestionably comes within the class of Romanticist work. But it presents this difference, that it is free from the exoticism characteristic of the earlier tales, whether in prose or verse, produced by the writers of that school. Chateaubriand wholly neglected the opportunities that lay to his hand in France itself. Filled with the spirit of Jean-Jacques Rousseau, he had gone abroad both for the subjects and the scenes of his stories: *Atala* and *René* and *The Natchez* were American; *The Last of the Abencerrages* was Spanish, and if in *The Martyrs* he laid the action partly in ancient Gaul, it was mostly in

Greece and Italy that he loved to dwell. Mme. de Staël had neglected France, and Victor Hugo had preferred the tropics and Norway for his first efforts. But Gautier was attracted in this case by the France of Louis XIII and Richelieu, and without attempting a restoration of the history of the times, after the free and easy, but so captivating manner of Dumas the elder, he was satisfied to evoke the manners and customs of a period of the national life that always had a very great attraction for him, as witness his literary studies of the writers of that particular epoch. The picturesqueness of those days is undeniable, and this element appealed very strongly to him. He has brought it out in its full strength and charm; he has made the times real to his readers; he has passed by the Court life and Court intrigues that have since been worked so steadfastly, and chosen rather to give a view of a class not often thought of by novelists, but in whose habits and whose pursuits he felt satisfied there were numerous opportunities for dramatic effects and striking scenes. There was something also in the possibilities of imbroglio offered by the presence among the company of a young and impoverished aristocrat, and in the mystery of the young girl's birth that drew him willingly, for he loved the involved drama of that early part of the seventeenth century, when Corneille had not yet imposed himself as a master and exemplar, when the law of the Three Unities was not only not yet accepted universally, but was indeed fiercely resisted or contemptuously set at naught; a time of freedom of action and methods, of individuality and independence which, if it produced no great rivals to the rising genius of the author of the *Cid,* had at least the merit of enabling all manner of talents to follow their own bent unchecked and undisturbed by a supremacy that erelong was, in conjunction with the national trend and the authority of theoreticians and critics, to force all dramatists to work along certain lines whether they would or not.

Captain Fracasse, again, is free from the wilder form of exaggeration that so often spoils Romanticist work. It is sufficient to recall the work of that Petrus Borel, of whom Gautier has spoken so frequently and so sympathetically, and some of the more notable novels of the great chief of the school. Gautier indulged in this form of excess at times; his **Fortunio** is a proof of it, and that book is still one of his most popular tales. But **Captain Fracasse** might have been written at the beginning of this twentieth century, and does not greatly differ in its plan and episodes from many a story that is at this time winning popular favour. There is this difference, however, between the novel of adventure now so much the fashion and Gautier's entertaining story, that the former almost invariably lacks literary style, while the French writer's work is eminently good literature. And this is the main reason why **Captain Fracasse** has attained to the rank of a classic, and is not only republished with great regularity in its own native land, but has been and is being translated again and again for the benefit of English readers.

It has a large touch of the realism that was even then making its way steadily into French literature and that was presently to displace Romanticism in the favour of the public. It does not go the lengths which will soon be reached by the writers of the new school, but it does contain many a homely scene, admirably rendered, with a care for sober truth which is most welcome after the florid and extravagant performances of the men he had so long been associated with. It is almost completely a piece of real life, as completely as could be expected of a poet trained in the highest ideals of Romanticism. An interesting fact in connection with this view is told by the author's daughter and the writer of a notice of the opera that was later founded on the novel. It is that Gautier intended the novel to end in very different fashion from what it does. The present *dénouement* is a purely commonplace one; it is expected by the reader, but that does not lift it out of the class of similar endings to similar works. It is logical enough, if one is not too particular about the quality of the logic, but it compels the writer to a weakness in his work that otherwise would not have been present: the sudden conversion of the Duke of Vallombreuse, already referred to. That is undoubtedly feeble; the whole description of the man's character and habits, of his modes of thought, of his ways of looking at women, make it difficult to reconcile his later conduct with his previous actions. It may be urged that one should not be too particular in a work of fiction, but since the days of **Captain Fracasse** we have learned to insist upon greater verisimilitude, as the men of the seventeenth century were accustomed to it in the masterpieces of their dramatists. Gautier's original ending of the story would not have been such pleasant reading, that goes without saying, but the picture of Sigognac, slayer of his love's brother, wasting his life in grief and solitude in his Castle of Hunger until, having lost his only companions, old Peter, Miraut his dog, Beelzebub his cat, and Bayard his horse, he himself died in loneliness and misery, would have been truer in many ways and certainly more dramatic. But the public of that day was not yet ripe for such realism, and probably the present-day reader will share the feeling of satisfaction of the French *bourgeois* and rejoice that all ends well with the pair of lovers.

Horatio E. Smith (essay date 1917)

SOURCE: "The Brief-Narrative Art of Théophile Gautier," in *Modern Philology*, Vol. 14, No. 11, March, 1917, pp. 135-52.

[*In the following essay, Smith compares the narrative processes of Gautier's short fiction to those of the short stories of Poe and of the nineteenth-century German nouvelle.*]

When Maxime Du Camp affirms[1] that Gautier is less of a *romancier* than a *conteur,* he is attempting to distinguish between these as between invention and imagination, arguing that whereas a *roman* is composed objectively, upon a deliberate plan, a *conte* or a *nouvelle* is subjective and spontaneous. This distinction, carried to its logical consequences, means that in novels the writer guides the narrative, in brief tales the narrative guides the writer, a reduction to the absurd even if limited to Gautier. For the structural unity of **"la Morte amoureuse"** is as voluntary as that of **le Capitaine Fracasse,** and vastly superior to that of such novels as *Partie carrée.* Du Camp is manifestly correct in assuming that many of Gautier's briefer tales are the result of musing over adventures, generally erotic, of which the author imagines himself the hero, and there is a degree of reason in his remark that "c'est parce qu'elles ont été un épisode de sa vie intellectuelle que ses nouvelles sont simples, presque sans incidents, émues néanmoins et communiquant l'émotion dont elles palpitent."[2] But this subjectivity is not in itself an adequate explanation of the peculiar singleness of effect of some of the stories, and the question remains by what narrative methods Gautier achieved this.

The ultimate solution should include an appraisal of Gautier's importance in the development of brief fiction in France, but this can be attempted only after such a survey of the entire field as no one has yet made. My immediate purpose is to examine Gautier's tales for themselves and to discover whether he evolved a type or types of any narrative distinction.

In a group of the earlier stories, notably in **"la Morte amoureuse"** (1836), his methods are comparable to Poe's, although there is no likelihood that at this period Gautier was acquainted with the writings of the American.

Whoever analyzes **"la Morte amoureuse"** will perceive that it fulfils the short story requirements later expounded by Poe and so diligently studied by his followers and his critics.[3] Gautier chooses for a theme the *liaison* of a priest and a female vampire and sets out, as the short-story adepts now do, "to produce a single narrative effect with the greatest economy of means that is consistent with the utmost emphasis."[4] His devices for procuring complete harmony are legion. The point of view is constant, for the whole experience is related in the first person by the victim. The initial sentences tend to the outbringing of the preconceived effect, to sounding that note of the uncanny which is constantly to be maintained: "Vous me demandez, frère, si j'ai aimé; oui. C'est une histoire singulière et terrible, et, quoique j'aie soixante-six ans, j'ose à peine remuer le cendre de ce souvenir."[5] The entire first paragraph, summing up the indelible impression made upon the priest, is in the same key, and throughout the tale the note rings out, ever lugubri-

Like other writers of his time, Gautier experimented with several different genres.

ous.[6] Except for supernumeraries entirely inconspicuous, there are only three characters, the vampire, the priest Romuauld, and a brother-priest whose attempts to offer guidance form an essential part of the action. In the matter of descriptions, tabooed in the short-story as foreign to its essence, Gautier, who is notoriously fond of the picturesque, has restrained himself to an unusual degree. The events are simple and decisive, and at turning-points in the story attention is fastened upon the stage of development reached by a terse summarizing phrase.[7] Suspense is brought skilfully to a head by the cumulation of manifestations made to the priest by Clarimonde. When Romuauld is summoned to the unfamiliar château, the promptness with which he realizes that he is to see his lady is not only natural but a factor—one of a score—in securing swift progress. The ending is as direct as the beginning: the *liaison* is broken, Clarimonde bids the priest farewell, "elle se dissipa dans l'air . . . et je ne la revis plus."[8] There follows a paragraph of a few lines which sound for the last time the note of the awfulness of the experience and is simply long enough to save the termination from being brusque, to put the needed period to the whole.

"La Morte amoureuse" was prepared for Balzac's *Chronique de Paris*,[9] and Balzac himself had written a little earlier[10] several tales of salient short-story characteristics, yet neither he nor Gautier in any way suggest that they were aware of the temporary similarity of their narrative processes. A similarity there is, however, and not in the case of **"la Morte amoureuse"** alone; other stories written by Gautier within a few years preceding 1836 approach the same standard and may be considered tentative efforts at the form finally achieved in 1836.

The first of these is **"la Cafetière"** (1831). A young man, Théodore, staying at a country house, has a singular adventure during the night, and, like the priest Romuauld, he tells of the experience himself. Objects in his room come to life, a porcelain coffee-pot thumps its way from table to hearth, portraits become animated and dance, and the youth, perceiving a charming girl without a partner, joins her. At dawn the spell is broken, the girl falls to the floor, and Théodore, rushing to pick her up, finds only the pieces of the coffee-pot. The exposition is of the briefest, the narrative progress is swift, the attention is focused, first upon the weird group of figures in the room and then, sharply, upon the principal figure. Angéla.[11] A single tone, suggesting the weird and the tragic, prevails as in **"la Morte amoureuse,"** and is last sounded in the final words of the tale when the hero expresses his—somewhat callow—despair with the remark: "Je venais de comprendre qu'il n'y avait plus pour moi de bonheur sur la terre!"[12] In a tentative version of the first part of the story, reproduced from the manuscript by Lovenjoul,[13] there are copious descriptions of no narrative value, and a more cumbersome exposition, and in the fact that this version was rejected there may be a sign of a conscious move to attain a higher degree of unity.

"Onuphrius" (1832) consists of a series of adventures of a young man who gradually becomes insane. The events are related with remarkable imaginative power and are somewhat varied, too varied no doubt to admit classification of the story with the Poe type. But the basic unity is complete. **"Onuphrius"** has something in common with *le Horla* by Maupassant, a tale worthy of Poe at his best, resembling it closely enough to prove short-story characteristics, differing sufficiently to indicate short-story defects. The experiences in *le Horla* are as diversified, but there results a high degree of unity from the fact that the illusion of the patient is a single one, while that of Onuphrius, except for the recurring hallucination of the demon with the ruby on his finger, varies. The climacteric development in *le Horla* is superior, and the attention is more completely focused on the man and his obsession. *Le Horla* is told in the first person, whereas with Gautier, although the point of view is constant, the third person is used, with consequent diminution, it may be argued, of intensity.[14]

Three other products of the years immediately preceding **"la Morte amoureuse"** merit a word. Two of them are hardly more than anecdotes. The first, published by Lovenjoul,[15] who without vouching altogether for its authenticity thinks it may be the first piece of fiction ever composed by Gautier (March 24, 1831), is the account of the experience of a young Frenchman in Egypt, compelled to seek the hospitality of a Bedouin camp and discovering that he has eaten of a gazelle roasted over blazing mummies. The next is the story, covering some eight pages in **"Sous la Table"** (1833),[16] concerning a youth and a *grisette*. The episode is too trivial to warrant serious consideration, yet, its essential narrative structure alone considered—and it is sufficiently developed to be said to have a structure—the singleness of effect is achieved by a process comparable to Poe's. In the third, **"Omphale"** (1834), the narrative current is swift and steady. Omphale is a lady portrayed on an old piece of tapestry in a young man's room. She comes to life and loves him, but the affair is interrupted by the young man's uncle, who removes the tapestry. The account of the subsequent effort of the youth to regain the tapestry is not, however, acceptable from the short-story point of view, and, a more vital matter, the chief interest is in the picturesque setting, as the subtitle, *histoire rococo*, suggests.

These of course do not constitute all of the brief tales written by Gautier between 1831, at the beginning of his career, and 1836, but the others are nondescript, and some of them, such as **"le Bol de punch,"** a picture of a revel, and **"Daniel Jovard,"** a character sketch, are narrative only in name. The point is that during this period Gautier wrote one genuine short-story and other pieces approaching the type. As has been suggested, it is not safe to posit in this group any influence of Poe, who was only beginning to write at this period and who was not known in France, at least in translation, until the forties.[17] The truth seems to be that Gautier is one of several authors who were at that time creating in France, independent of foreign models, a type the identity of which with Poe's is at once fortuitous and complete[18]—and which I label short-story for want of authority to call it anything more distinctive. But after 1836 Gautier writes no more narratives of this form; his methods continue to develop, and, oddly enough, by the time it may be assumed that Gautier was well acquainted with Poe, he is producing stories of a stamp distinct from the American's.

The prime difference is in degree of compression. Superlative concision, the *sine qua non* of the Poe type, is no longer achieved or sought. What this means in actual practice will become evident upon inspection of the significant examples.

The tendency is already manifest in **"Une Nuit de Cléopâtre"** (1838). A young Egyptian, so enamored

of Cleopatra that he dares penetrate to her bath, is there discovered by the capricious queen, who accepts him as her lover with the condition that the next morning he shall die. At daybreak he pays the penalty. This would be an admirable nucleus for a short-story, and it is not difficult to imagine how the theme would be treated. The bounds of the above summary would be respected, the action would hardly begin before the capture of the youth at the bath, and would cease with the administration of the poison. In the latter case Gautier has, unconsciously, met the short-story requirement; his termination, according to that convention, is impeccable, possessing even that unexpected twist so sought after by the American twentieth-century writer, often with a resultant artificiality—though the turn which Gautier gives the narrative development is altogether probable as well as interesting: at the crucial moment Cleopatra wavers and considers preventing her lover from drinking the potion, when the unlooked-for announcement of the arrival of Mark Antony precipitates the catastrophe. The story at this point moves as rapidly as Poe's followers say it must. But here only. Gautier does not introduce the episode of the bath until he reaches the fifth of the six chapters. His preparation is leisurely. In the first chapter we learn that Cleopatra is bored, in the second this theme is elaborated and we have a first glimpse of the lover, in the third the lover becomes active to the extent of sending Cleopatra a message by an arrow, in the fourth we learn that Cleopatra is no longer bored and that the youth contemplates further activity. This easy-going preliminary, the frequent changes in viewpoint and in place, and above all the copious descriptions, are quite contrary to short-story practice.

In the case of **"le Roi Candaule"** (1844), Gautier appears to have been of two minds. He was evidently tempted at the outset to yield to the charm of the picturesque, and then became interested in the development of the action and gave over the static for the kinetic. An admirable narrative is developed about a central point the inspection of the queen's beauty. The author seems to have taken, for structural purposes, the point of view of Gyges.[19] At the beginning it is not apparent that the young captain is to play an important rôle, for the first chapter consists almost entirely of an elaborate description of the marriage of King Candaules and Nyssia, but, as the story moves on, more and more light is centered upon Gyges, the descriptions which, from the point of view of narration, obstruct, become less and less frequent, and after an extremely leisurely start the action becomes rapid. The preparation for the climax is adroit. It is necessary to explain concisely, when the crisis approaches, how it happens that Candaules wishes to have another man behold his wife's charms, and this is the more easily done since it has already been casually developed that he is a person of uncommon stamp and especially that his appreciation of beauty may be that of the artist as much as that of the lover. The keenness of vision which enables Nyssia to discover the eyes of Gyges as he looks into the chamber from his hiding-place is suggested early in the story. Surely such arrangement of details demonstrates what Maxime Du Camp would deny, the exercise of inventive powers by the *conteur*.[20] The termination of the story, after cleverly maintained suspense, is swift; climax and end are almost simultaneous. The murder done, the problem solved, a brief final paragraph gives a last glance at the central theme: "le nouveau roi se maintint sur le trône de Lydie, qu'il occupa pendant de longues années, vécut heureux et ne fit voir sa femme à personne, sachant trop ce qu'il en coûtait."[21]

Somewhat parallel in structure is **"Arria Marcella"** (1852).[22] A young Frenchman, at a museum in Naples, is moved by a relic of Pompeii, a mass of ashes which has hardened about the form of a beautiful woman perishing in the destruction of the city. With imagination stirred by a daylight inspection of the ruins he returns there the same night, finds the conditions of eighteen hundred years ago restored, encounters the lady in question, and is welcomed by her, when her Christian father steps in, berates his daughter, and destroys the hallucination.[23] **"Arria Marcella"** is composed with no regard for the short-story principle that "the narrative must move, move, move furiously each action and every speech pointing directly toward the unknown climax,"[24] yet it is carefully organized in the interest of unity, with graduated and skilful focusing of the attention upon the heroine and artful alternation of suspense and swift advance. The exposition and the action proper are amalgamated by the author's conception that Arria is already acquainted with the passion of the young man and knows, by a weird interchange of the centuries, that he has admired her in the museum.[25]

Common to these later stories is a feature already observed in **"la Morte amoureuse,"** the deliberate insertion of forward-pointing remarks which serve to emphasize the central theme. The ultimate and sinister achievement of Gyges is already faintly suggested, at the very outset of **"le Roi Candaule,"** in the musings of the young captain: "il songeait aux enivrements de la toute-puissance, au bonheur . . . de poser le diadème sur la tête de la plus belle," "en effet, c'était bien sur ce front [de Nyssia] qu'il eût voulu poser le diadème," "l'amour qu'il éprouvait pour Nyssia lui causait une secrète terreur."[26] The strange adventure of the hero of **"Arria Marcella"** is foreshadowed in the searching glance of his companion, and in his own first impressions: "Octavien . . . semblait plus touché que ses insouciants compagnons du sort de ces trépassés de deux mille ans," "Les phrases banales du guide causèrent une vive émotion à Octavien."[27] Occasional emphatic sentences, such as the statement in **"Une Nuit de Cléopâtre,"** "il s'était juré . . . qu'il serait l'amant

de Cléopâtre . . . ne fût-ce qu'une nuit . . . dût-il lui en coûter son corps et son âme,"[28] are at once a prophecy and a summary, and the progress of a story is often epitomized, with a resultant and deliberately attained narrative unity, as in Gyges' résumé of the course of events: "Un hasard lui avait fait connaître sa beauté murée à tous les yeux, entre tant de princes et de satrapes elle avait épousé précisément Candaule, le roi qu'il servait, et, par un caprice étrange qu'il ne pouvait s'empêcher de trouver presque fatal, ce roi venait faire, à lui Gygès, des confidences sur cette créature mystérieuse que personne n'approchait. . . ."[29]

These features become less conspicuous in three narratives of later date, much longer than those so far under discussion and yet possessed of a similar unity distinct from that of the novel. The evolution appears to be steady, from a narrative organization strictly limited, with unity consciously emphasized, to one of broader scope.

The theme of *Avatar* (1856) is a reincarnation and its consequences. Octave de Saville almost despairs at the hopelessness of his love for the Countess Labinski, who adores her husband. Thanks to the occult science of an uncanny physician, Octave's soul is transferred to the husband's body, and the husband's soul is incorporated in his. But the lover finds success as impossible as before, and the souls at his behest are being retransferred when his flies off into space, and the doctor occupies his body. The progress of the story is as steady and unhurried as that of **"Arria Marcella,"** but the attention is not equally concentrated. In **"Arria Marcella"** the single interest is in the relations of the youth and the girl of Pompeii; in *Avatar* the interest is for a considerable period in the relations of Octave and the lady, but later, when this situation is solved, much space is devoted to the resultant fate of the young man. And since, in the nature of the situation, the reader would be almost as interested in the effects of the reincarnation on the husband as in its effects on the lover, there is a considerable discussion of this. The remark of Gautier, summing up the case for Octave, "Ame obscurément sublime, il ne savait qu'aimer et mourir,"[30] may be regarded as the nucleus of the tale, yet when the interest turns away from Octave the author does not hold it in check, he does not impose an adventitious unity. The theme of **"Arria"** calls for development within a small circle, that of *Avatar* occupies a relatively large one.[31]

Avatar is promptly followed by another story of the same order, *Jettatura* (1856). Here Gautier unfolds the consequences of the Neapolitan superstition of the evil eye when it fastens itself upon a young foreigner in love with a girl threatened with tuberculosis. At every point, in composing the tale, he has kept this situation in mind. His methods as usual are leisurely, but the narrative is held true to its course. The technique is remote from that of the short-story. The beginning, where, before the hero is introduced, there are five pages of easy-going description of the approach to Naples and some humorous animadversions on British travelers, recalls the lack of restraint of the novel.[32] Yet there is a deliberate and successful attempt to secure singleness of effect. Step by step the theme of the evil eye of Paul d'Aspremont is developed. The thought that there is a peculiar and pernicious power in his gaze is kept constantly before the reader. At first there are only mild suggestions. Then disasters which take place in the presence of Paul and which, the reader is gradually persuaded, may be due to the peculiar power of his eye, accumulate. At length, at a point where his gaze seems to produce catastrophes in rapid succession, Paul first hears the epithet *jettatore!* His concern over his strange situation and especially over its possible consequences for Alicia grows rapidly until the climax. Preparation for the one critical situation and the development of that situation, or in other words a climacteric elaboration of the power of Paul's eye and then an account of the result when this power is concentrated upon Alicia, such is Gautier's method.[33]

Spirite (1865), one of his last pieces of fiction, closes the series of distinctive tales I am here considering. It is of particular interest in that it was written under the influence of Poe,[34] with whose work the author was now thoroughly familiar,[35] and yet, as regards structure, is closer to the *Avatar* type than to **"la Morte amoureuse"**.

Once more, maximum compression is not sought. The essential theme, the relations of Guy de Malivert and the spirit of a woman who had already loved him in the flesh, without his knowing it, is given due prominence, yet Gautier does not refrain from dealing with the immediate ramifications. In addition to Malivert and Spirite two characters play rôles of some importance, Madame d'Ymbercourt, the flesh-and-blood rival, and the Baron de Feroë, a mystic who is able to explain to Guy the manifestations of his intangible mistress. Both are required in Gautier's manipulation of the subject, the first as a foil, the second as an interpreter. The scene is allowed to shift, the point of view changes. The fourteenth chapter, wherein the main issue waits while the jealousy of Madame d'Ymbercourt is healed by Spirite, would be considered by Poe an unpardonable interpolation.[36] Even from a more liberal point of view certain features may be considered to clog the narrative, for example the long description by Spirite, who is recounting her mortal life, of the ball where she did not dance with Malivert.[37] On the other hand, it is clear that Gautier felt the need of a certain degree of narrative concision: when the situation becomes critical the story is made to move rapidly, the writer comes promptly to the essential,[38] and once he remarks: "Il est inutile de

décrire avec détail les impressions de voyage de Malivert; ce serait sortir du cadre de ce récit."[39]

This note of conscious construction is rare in Gautier, either in his stories or in his critical writing. If we now examine the latter, it will become evident that he can hardly be said to have, in the case of fiction, any doctrine.

Even as regards terminology he is careless. He called *Spirite* a *nouvelle*. *Avatar* and *Jettatura* first appeared as *contes*,[40] but they are the longest stories, and stand at the head, in the subsequent collection entitled *Romans et Contes* (1863). In his autobiography, referring to his activities in the field of fiction, he writes: "Sans être romancier de profession je n'en ai pas moins bâclé, en mettant à part les nouvelles, une douzaine de romans: *les Jeunes-France, Mademoiselle de Maupin, Fortunio, les Roués innocents, "Militona," la Belle Jenny, Jean et Jeannette, Avatar, Jettatura, le Roman de la momie, Spirite, le Capitaine Fracasse*."[41] Here is a list which includes novels, tales that approach the short-story type, and tales that bear another stamp; they have in common merely the fact that they are relatively long. There is apparently no distinction between *roman* and *nouvelle*, unless it be one of length, in the following remark: "Il y a douze ou quinze ans, M. Jules Janin publia, dans *la Revue des Deux Mondes,* une nouvelle d'une centaine de pages—on n'avait pas encore inventé, en ce temps-là, les romans qui n'en finissent pas—une nouvelle, disons-nous, intitulée *le Piédestal*."[42] And certdainly little difference between *nouvelle* and *conte* is recognized by Gautier when he uses the two words in the same sentence of the same story.[43]

A specific problem of narration is discussed by him to some purpose in his article on Karr. Of the digressions in the novels of the latter he writes:

> Un mot fait éclore un chapitre, et malgré toutes leurs folles brindilles éparpillées à droite et à gauche, ces digressions n'en tiennent pas moins à la tige commune par des filaments et des nervures invisibles. Relevez le feuillage de la main, et vous verrez la branche qui s'attache solidement au tronc; toute action, si elle a réellement une portée philosophique, fait lever une moisson de pensées sous lesquelles il lui arrive quelquefois de disparaître comme la terre aride du sillon sous le manteau d'or des épis.—Lequel vaut mieux de l'épi ou du sillon, de la feuille ou de la branche?[44]

No doubt the principle was applied by Gautier himself, although with modifications and a limited *portée philosophique,* and perhaps the remark is the inspiration of Du Camp when he says of Gautier's workmanship: "Le sujet . . . est toujours d'une extrême simplicité, mais l'écrivain a su le parer et l'envelopper, parfois jusqu'à le faire disparaître, d'une forme élégante et touffue."⁴⁵ Similar praise of inherent unity, deserving of quotation in a discussion of Gautier's own procedure, is found in his encomium of Fenimore Cooper:

> Les plus beaux romans de Cooper sont composés avec des éléments d'une simplicité extrême. . . . Les personnages n'apparaissent que comme des points blancs et rouges sur le fond d'outre-mer des lointains, ou sur le vert sombre et dur des ébéniers centenaires. Cependant, malgré leur petitesse relative, par leur énergie et leur résolution, ils dominent cette gigan-tesque nature, et c'est là la source de l'intérêt sublime et profond qui s'attache au *Dernier des Mohicans, à la Prairie.* L'orgueil humain est inti-mement flatté de cette victoire et s'en réjouit par esprit de corps. Cette disposition rendait Fenimore Cooper plus propre que tout autre à réussir dans le roman maritime. . . . L'idée qui éclate à chaque page est celle exprimée par le proverbe breton: "Ma barque est si petite et la mer est si grande!" De là vient tout l'intérêt.⁴⁶

But these acute bits of criticism stand almost alone. An able practitioner, Gautier, as I have said, was not given to theorizing about fiction.

It is therefore upon the examination of the structure of his stories that conclusions must largely be based. Two types appear to have been evolved, a form exceedingly compact, best represented by **"la Morte amoureuse,"** and another less restrained but still highly unified, of which **"Arria Marcella"** and *Jettatura* are characteristic examples. The one develops out of the other; the first group is the result of an early tendency culminating in 1836, the second includes some of the best work of the author's maturity.⁴⁷

Needless to say, many of his narratives do not yield to this classification. Some are not primarily narrative but descriptive;⁴⁸ some are genuine novels;⁴⁹ some, within a narrower compass, retain the characteristic structural complexity of the novel.⁵⁰ Even such a tale as **"le Chevalier double,"** in spite of its strongly emphasized central theme, might be considered a novel *in parvo*, were it not unreasonable to apply modern narrative standards to a story which aims at and achieves the characteristics of an ancient legend.⁵¹ **"La Toison d'or"** is an intermediate form. The story is an organic whole; the central theme is the quest of Tiburce, a youth who, having admired womankind only from the point of view of a connoisseur of the fine arts, only in painting and sculpture, determines to seek a flesh-and-blood mistress and, inspired by Rubens, goes to Flanders. At the beginning the interest is fastened upon the question whether Tiburce will find a blond maiden, then it is deflected to the infatuation of Tiburce for Rubens' Magdalene, and ultimately to that development of the character of Gretchen which results in the final solution, with the affections of Tiburce satisfied and his power as an artist revealed. In other words, the atten-

tion is not focused. It is not difficult to imagine the expansion of **"la Toison d'or"** into a full-sized novel, where the character development, no longer compressed into a few lines, would be vastly more convincing; on the other hand, the story could hardly be given a unity comparable to that of **"le Roi Candaule"** or of *Avatar* without fundamental revision.

But from the whole mass of works of fiction published by Gautier, the brief tales analyzed here, from **"la Morte amoureuse"** to *Spirite,* emerge as structurally unique.

The credit is probably due to Gautier alone. The likeness of some of the earlier stories to the tales Poe was producing at about the same time in America⁵² does not warrant inferences, it has been observed, as to the influence of Poe. Equally fortuitous and no less interesting is the parallel between the later products of Gautier and the nineteenth-century German *Novelle.*

A purely casual remark of the author in **"Arria Marcella"** that he is presenting "le simple récit d'une aventure bizarre et peu croyable, quoique vraie,"⁵³ is nearly identical with Goethe's famous definition: "Was ist eine Novelle anders als eine sich ereignete unerhörte Begebenheit?"⁵⁴ *Aventure* may be set off against *Begebenheit, bizarre et peu croyable* against *unerhörte, vraie* against *sich ereignete, simple* against *eine.* Indeed, Gautier's statement, put alongside of Goethe's, illuminates the later, which, "the quintessential result of an investigation . . . conducted intermittently for over thirty years,"⁵⁵ is cast in somewhat oracular form. There is a meager possibility that Gautier was acquainted with this definition. It is a fact that he knew the *Wahlverwandtschaften,*⁵⁶ which includes the story of *Die wunderlichen Nachbarskinder,* the first of Goethe's narratives to be presented to the public under the express title *Novelle.* But there is not the requisite evidence to substantiate a belief that Gautier was inspired by the German, and the remark which so neatly corresponds to Goethe's appears to be a felicitous accident.

In practice, the epithet *vraie* is not equivalent to Goethe's *sich ereignete.* For obviously the adventure in **"Arria Marcella,"** or that in *Avatar,* is not true, could not actually happen, in the same sense as the events of *Der Prokurator* or of *Ferdinand.* Closer to Goethe in this respect are *Jettatura* and **"Une Nuit de Cléopâtre,"** although these sin against a principle enunciated by one of Goethe's spokesmen: "Ich leugne nicht, dass ich die Geschichten nicht liebe, die unsere Einbildungskraft immer in fremde Länder nötigen. Muss denn alles in Italien und Sizilien, im Orient geschehen? Sind denn Neapel, Palermo und Smyrna die einzigen Orte, wo etwas Interessantes vorgehen kann?"⁵⁷ As regards unity and novelty, however, Gautier's stories fully meet the German's requirements. Likewise,

Gautier's leisurely expositions find a counterpart in such stories as *Die wunderlichen Nachbarskinder* and *Der Prokurator,* his occasionally appended codas a corresponding feature in *Ferdinand.*

Two other definitions, by Tieck and by Paul Heyse, stand out in the ponderous mass of German criticism, and both of these have their application here. Tieck, writing in 1829, insists with Goethe upon unity and novelty and develops independently the theory that the prime requisite is a single turning-point "von welchem aus sie [die Geschichte] sich unerwartet völlig umkehrt, und doch natürlich, dem Charakter und den Umstanden angemessen, die Folge entwickelt. . . . ."[58] Apparently Tieck would give his entire approval to **"le Roi Candaule,"** where the action turns upon the discovery by the queen that Gyges is inspecting her beauty, and to **"Une Nuit de Cléopâtre,"** developed about the compact which Cleopatra makes with the young Egyptian. In some of the other Gautier tales, such as *Avatar* and *Spirite,* there is no prominent *Wendepunkt,* but perhaps the theorist would be liberal in his interpretation, for he states that each of the *Novelas exemplares* of Cervantes possesses such a turning-point, yet investigation of these shows, I think, that it is frequently not easy to determine which decisive act shall be so denominated.[59]

More specific and of special application to Gautier is the definition made by Paul Heyse in order to set a standard for his *Deutscher Novellenschatz:*

> Im allgemeinen . . . halten wir . . . an der Regel fest *der* Novelle den Vorzug zu geben, deren Grundmotiv sich am deutlichsten abrundet und . . . etwas Eigenartiges, Spezifisches schon in der blossen Anlage verrät. Eine *starke Silhouette*—um . . . einen Ausdruck der Malersprache zu Hilfe zu nehmen—dürfte dem, was wir im eigentlichen Sinne *Novelle* nennen, nicht fehlen, ja wir glauben, die Probe auf die Trefflichkeit eines novellistischen Motivs werde in den meisten Fällen darin bestehen, ob der Versuch gelingt, den Inhalt in wenige Zeilen zusammenzufassen, in der Weise, wie die alten Italiener ihren Novellen kurze Überschriften gaben, die dem Kundigen schon im Keim den spezifischen Wert des Themas verraten.[60]

This is close to Gautier's conception of brief-narrative unity as exemplified in the series of stories under discussion,[61] the last of which was published five years before the promulgation of Heyse's theory (1871). That is to say, here again are narrative methods parallel and independent.[62]

Probably Gautier was not the only Frenchman to produce during this period stories comparable in form to the *Novelle.* This structural method would seem sufficiently elastic to lend itself—perhaps with results not so lurid and of deeper literary import—to the purposes of authors in power and doctrine quite different from him.

For Gautier, in any case, one point remains to be made. His critics,[63] maintaining that he is above all a poet and a painter, like to stress either the lyric or the pictorial element in his stories, and grant him small skill in sheer narration. Without doubt their view that fiction was of secondary interest to him is correct. Yet he accepted its conditions more whole-heartedly than they think. There is a suggestion of this truth in his letter to Sainte-Beuve: "Si j'avais possédé la moindre fortune personnelle, je me serais livré uniquement à *l'amour du vert laurier;* mais dans la prose où je suis tombé, j'ai toujours défendu les intérêts de l'art. . . ."[64] And the evidence proves that the structure of many of his tales is far from being either haphazard or spontaneous, that the degree of unity he sometimes attains is the result of deliberate plan, that after all, as a narrator, he is no mean figure.

Notes

[1] *Théophile Gautier* (Paris, 1890), pp. 147-52.

[2] *Ibid.,* p. 149.

[3] For an abridged short-story bibliography, cf. my article on "Balzac and the Short-Story," *Modern Philology,* XII, 71, note 3. The famous statement of Poe, part of which is quoted in that note, was written in 1842. The short-story character of *"la Morte amoureuse"* has already been pointed out by Professor Baldwin, *American Short Stories* (New York, 1909), Introduction, p. 33. In the present article I shall use the term "short-story" only in the restricted American sense.

[4] Hamilton, *Materials and Methods of Fiction* (New York, 1908), p. 173.

[5] *Nouvelles* (Paris, 1871), p. 261.

[6] Observe the repetition of the idea of a nightmare (*ibid.,* pp. 266, 275, 289); of the apostrophe of Clarimonde: "Malheureux! qu'as-tu fait?" (pp. 267, 268, 295); of the motif of a single fatal glance: "un seul regard . . . jeté sur une femme" (p. 261), "pour avoir levé une seule fois le regard sur une femme" (p. 274), "ne regardez jamais une femme . . . il suffit d'une minute" (p. 295).

[7] Pp. 263, 268, 288.

[8] P. 295.

[9] Lovenjoul, *Histoire des œuvres de Théophile Gautier* (Paris, 1887), No. 130. The story was divided between two issues of the *Chronique de Paris.* Apparently Gautier had no thought of the advantage which, according to Poe, results from a single, uninterrupted presentation.

[10] Cf. p. 136, note 1.

[11] In 1852 the story was published under the title *Angéla* (Lovenjoul, *op. cit.,* No. 45).

[12] *Les Jeunes-France* (Paris: Charpentier), p. 261. In this edition the story is dated, erroneously, 1833.

[13] Louvenjoul, *op. cit.,* I, pp. 16-20.

[14] The ending of the first edition, quoted by Lovenjoul, *op. cit.,* No. 56, is more abrupt and less artistic than that of the *Jeunes-France* volume.

[15] *Op. cit.,* I, pp. 8-11.

[16] *Les Jeunes-France,* pp. 11-18.

[17] According to Retinger, *le Conte fantastique dans le Romantisme français* (Paris, 1909), p. 33, note, *The Murders in the rue Morgue* appeared anonymously as early as 1841. Cf. Lauvrière, *Poe* (Paris, 1904), p. 644, note 2; p. 276; Morris, *Cooper et Poe d'après la critique française du dix-neuvième siècle* (Paris, 1912), pp. 80, 203.

[18] Professor Baldwin, *op. cit.,* Introduction, p. 33, pointing to the dates of *"la Morte amoureuse"* (1836) and of *Berenice* (1835), says: "Remarkable as is the coincident appearance in Paris and in Richmond of a new literary form, it remains a coincidence." Cf. Canby, *Study of the Short Story* (New York, 1913), p. 45; "The work of their [the American writers'] French contemporaries . . . represents a parallel, not a derivative movement."

[19] The following is a summary of the chapters from this angle: (i) it transpires that Gyges, by a rare chance, has seen the queen unveiled before her marriage; (ii) Gyges is the chosen confidant of the king as regards her beauty; (iii) Gyges sees her in the chamber; (iv) he is summoned to the queen to avenge her; (v) he wins her.

"Le Roi Candaule" is clearly enough an adaptation of Herodotus' story of Gyges (i. 8-12), itself an excellent example of narrative economy; the principal incidents in Gautier are those related by the Greek, and several items of the conversation between Gyges and Candaules and of that between Gyges and the queen are almost exactly reproduced. But Gautier's elaboration of the theme remains his own.

[20] Cf. Taylor, "The Short Story in France, 1800-1900," *Edinburgh Review,* July, 1913, p. 144: "Mérimée, Gautier, Flaubert, exercised, however covertly, an art of composition; they disposed their incidents in due order of sequence; they arranged their figures with an aesthetic sense of perspective, prepared and suspended their crises, and held the balance of accent and emphasis."

[21] *Nouvelles,* p. 419.

[22] Lafcadio Hearn (*One of Cleopatra's Nights,* etc. [New York: Brentano, 1906], pp. 385-88) thinks that Gautier may have found the inspiration for *"Arria Marcella"* in an old Greek ghost story, and quotes Michelet's version of this. In any case it is clear that Gautier's narrative methods are his own.

[23] Observe how frequently the basic plot of a *liaison* interrupted by a third person recurs (*"Omphale," "la Morte amoureuse," "le Pied de momie,"* even, in a sense, *"Une Nuit de Cléopâtre"* and *"le Roi Candaule"*).

[24] Canby, "Free Fiction," *Atlantic Monthly,* July, 1915, p. 61. Professor Canby urges his compatriots not to be fettered by such rules.

[25] The period to the story, the final sentence, deftly enhances the unity.

[26] *Nouvelles,* pp. 364, 365, 365, respectively.

[27] *Romans et Contes* (Paris: Charpentier), pp. 272, 280, 282, respectively.

[28] *Nouvelles,* p. 345.

[29] *Ibid.,* p. 387.

[30] *Romans et Contes,* p. 126.

[31] The twelve sections of the story, as it appears in book form, are presumably the twelve units of its serial publication (cf. Lovenjoul, *op. cit.,* No. 1400). Here, as well as elsewhere, Gautier deals successfully with the exigencies of the *feuilleton* system; his division into short chapters is highly logical and his final sentences sometimes epitomize with the succinctness of the short-story termination, sometimes point forward to the next stage of the tale in a way that welds the sections together.

[32] There are other suggestions of novel technique. Cf. p. 161, where Gautier returns to the exposition by relating events that antedate the action of the story. Such retrogression is rare in tales where a high degree of unity is the desideratum (although it is found in Stevenson's *Dr. Jekyll and Mr. Hyde*). Cf. pp. 252-55, where the author introduces supernumerary characters of somewhat meager interest as exemplifying the idiosyncrasies of the British and of almost no usefulness in advancing the narrative.

[33] Gautier started to cast *Jettatura* in verse, and several fragments of his work exist (cf. Lovenjoul, *op. cit.,*

No. 2306). The beginning of the narrative is more direct, the tone more sinister, than in the prose form.

[34] Cf. Retinger, *op. cit.,* pp. 61, 77. Gautier mentions Poe in the course of the story (pp. 4, 33-34).

[35] I find no reference by Gautier to Poe earlier than 1858 (cf. *Portraits contemporains* [Paris, 1898], p. 52). From this time forward allusions are frequent, as if Gautier had suddenly become aware of the American, perhaps through Baudelaire's translations (1856). In his article on Baudelaire, Gautier quotes, without comment, a remark by Poe which contains in essence the latter's short-story theory (*Portraits et souvenirs littéraires* [Paris, 1892], p. 191).

[36] Furthermore, Gautier has not, in the Poe manner, "deliberately preconceived" the whole story, to judge from the following (*Vacances du Lundi* [Paris, 1907], p. 75): "nous voilà installé au sein d'un doux et charmant loisir, cherchant sous les grands marronniers la fin de *Spirite.*"

[37] Perhaps the explanation at the close of this description may be considered faintly apologetic (*Spirite* [Paris, 1907], p. 134).

[38] Cf. *ibid.,* p. 138.

[39] *Ibid.,* p. 218. Observe, however, that a page of description follows.

[40] Lovenjoul, *op. cit.,* Nos. 1400, 1421.

[41] *Portraits contemporains,* p. 13.

[42] *Histoire de l'art dramatique en France* (Paris, 1859), VI, 5. *Le Piédestal* was published in 1832, not in the *Revue des Deux Mondes* but in the *Revue de Paris.* Janin, in the course of the story, makes a significant distinction between *nouvelle* and *roman* (XLIII, 103): "Ici si je faisais un roman et non pas une histoire, j'aurais un bien beau sujet de développments de mœurs. J'arrangerais à loisir mon récit, le conduisant en habile écuyer à travers toutes les difficultés du terrain, changeant souvent ma voie. . . .

"Mais il n'en est pas de la *nouvelle* comme du roman. La nouvelle, c'est une course au clocher. . . . On va toujours au galop, on ne connaît pas d'obstacles; on traverse le buisson d'épines, on franchit le fossé, on brise le mur, on se brise les os, on va tant que va son histoire." In performance, Janin proves somewhat irresponsible. His composition is lax. But the metaphor brings out effectively the essential directness of the *nouvelle* type, and, although Gautier passes it over in silence, suggests the economy of the short-story art at which he himself was trying his hand in 1832.

[43] *Histoire de l'art dramatique,* I, 254, 299; Lovenjoul, *op. cit.,* No. 830.

[44] *Portraits contemporains,* p. 17.

[45] Du Camp, *op, cit.,* p. 151.

[46] *Souvenirs de théâtre, d'art et de critique* (Paris, 1904), pp. 21-22. This is part of a page of criticism of Cooper which occurs in an article on Eugène Sue first published in the *Chronique de Paris* in 1836. It is not listed by Professor Morris, *op. cit.*

[47] In addition to the stories discussed, *la Chaîne d'or* (1837) and especially *la Mille et deuxième nuit* (1842) belong to the second group.

[48] *Le Pied de momie, le Pavillon sur l'eau,* even *Fortunio,* which is a cross-section of a peculiarly sumptuous and voluptuous life with the central figure hardly a man but a personification of a picturesque lavishness.

[49] *Le Capitaine Fracasse, le Roman de la momie,* etc. The plot of the second is relatively simple. Cf. the simplicity of plot of *la Croix de Berny,* written by Gautier in collaboration with Mme de Girardin, Sandeau, and Méry.

[50] *Militona, le Berger,* etc. So also *les Roués innocents,* and *Jean et Jeannette,* although in each case the elaborations develop from a single nucleus.

[51] Other legends and fairy-stories by Gautier approach more closely, in narrative simplicity and concentration of attention, the types under discussion. Cf. the exquisite *Enfant aux souliers de pain* and *Nid de rossignols,* and the mediocre *Oreiller d'une jeune fille.*

[52] It may also be affirmed that there is a resemblance to Hawthorne in some of Gautier's work. In fact, the following criticism of Hawthorne, by Robert Louis Stevenson (*Essay on Hugo,* p. 20), is applicable, in its entirety, to the author of *Jettatura:* "There is a unity, an unwavering creative purpose, about some at least of Hawthorne's romances, that impresses itself on the most indifferent reader; and the very restrictions and weaknesses of the man served perhaps to strengthen the vivid and single impression of his works." Gautier was acquainted with the fiction of Hawthorne (cf. *Portraits contemporains,* p. 157) and had been particularly impressed by the conception of a garden of poisonous flowers in *Rappacini's Daughter,* a story kindred in structure to *Jettatura, Avatar,* etc. (cf. *Histoire du Romantisme,* p. 353; *Fusains et eaux-fortes* [Paris, 1907], pp. 308-11).

[53] *Romans et Contes,* p. 273.

[54] *Gespräche mit Eckermann,* January 29, 1827.

[55] Mitchell, "Goethe's Theory of the Novelle," *Publications of the Modern Language Association,* XXX, 236. This article and Professor Mitchell's thoroughgoing study, *Heyse and his Predecessors in the Theory of the Novelle* (Frankfurt, 1915), are the principal source of the following remarks on the German definitions.

[56] *Histoire de l'art dramatique,* I, 193; IV, 337.

[57] Goethe, *Werke,* Weimarer Ausgabe, XVIII, 190, quoted by Mitchell, *Heyse and his Predecessors,* p. 25.

[58] *Schriften* (Berlin: Reimer, 1829), XI, p. lxxxvi. The theory is discussed by Mitchell, *op. cit.,* pp. 33 ff.

[59] Closest to the *Novelle* type are *La Gitanilla* and *El Celoso Extremeño.* In the *Coloquio de los Perros* are one or two comments on problems of narration; cf. especially where Cipion urges Berganza to refrain from digressions (p. 340 of the Leipzig, 1869, edition): "Quiero decir que la sigas [la novela] de golpe, sin que la hagas que parezca pulpo, segun la vas añadiendo colas." Gautier refers several times to Cervantes' stories, but not critically (cf. *Voyage en Espagne* [Paris, 1899], pp. 118, 299; *Guide au Louvre,* p. 274).

[60] *Deutscher Novellenschatz* (München, 1871), Einleitung, pp. xix-xx.

[61] Heyse quotes, for illustration of his theory, Boccaccio's abstract of the ninth *Novella* of the fifth day: "Federigo degli Alberighi ama e non è amato; e in cortesia spendendo si consuma, e rimangli un sol falcone, il quale, non avendo altro, dà a mangiare alla sua donna venutagli a casa: la qual ciò sappiendo, mutata d'animo, il prende per marito e fàllo ricco."

Gautier's stories may be summed up quite as succinctly. Cf. the abstracts given in the course of this article. Cf. also the lines of Swinburne which epitomize *"Une Nuit de Cléopâtre"* (*Poems* [London, 1904], III, 64):

> And that great night of love more strange than
> this,
> When she that made the whole world's bale
> and bliss
> Made king of all the world's desire a slave,
> And killed him in mid kingdom with a kiss.

[62] Speculation about the reasons for these resemblances between Gautier's work and the short-story and the *Novelle* types remains idle until more is known about the French field. Apparently the conditions of modern literature tend to develop two forms of brief tale, as in English where we have not only the close-knit "short-story," but the more loosely woven—and clumsily named—"long short-story."

[63] Faguet, Sainte-Beuve, Lafcadio Hearn, *et al.*

[64] Lovenjoul, *op. cit.,* Introduction, p. xx.

T.S. Omond compares Gautier and Hugo:

Next to Hugo, Gautier is the ablest craftsman, the hardest worker, of the school. He tries experiments, not freakishly like Musset, but gravely and purposefully. He shares Hugo's delight in sound, his love of words for themselves. He ransacks the dictionary for striking expressions, and revels in reviving obsolete phrases. He carries pictorial description to its height, and his pages literally glow with colour. Like Hugo, too, he sometimes cares more for the music of a line than for its sense: take care of the words, and the meaning will take care of itself. In all this, he was Hugo's right-hand man, his ablest lieutenant, striving and fighting, and ready to accept any task. But in *Émaux et camées* he is the perfect artist come to his own, expressing his idea with the apparent ease of victory.

T.S. Omond, in The Romantic Triumph,
William Blackwood and Sons, 1900.

Aaron Schaffer (essay date 1928)

SOURCE: "Theophile Gautier and *l'art pour l'art,*" in *The Sewanee Review,* Vol. XXXVI, No. 4, October, 1928, pp. 405-17.

[*In the following excerpt, Schaffer examines the aesthetic influence of the fifteenth- and sixteenth-century French poets on Gautier's poetry.*]

Gautier's first work of real significance was a narrative poem—*Albertus, ou l'âme et le péché: légende théologique*—in the ultra-Romantic vein, wherein is manifest the influence of Part One of *Faust,* of the works of Byron, and of the early poems of Musset. Albertus was a painter torn between his love for his own art and his interest in poetry and music: in his choice of subject-matter for his pictures, he is a true Romanticist, for his studio contains, among others, canvases of Bürger's Lenore, of Macbeth and the sorceresses, of the children of Lara, and of Marguerite (Faust's Gretchen) at prayer. Albertus succumbs to the charms of an entrancing woman who is actually a hideous witch in disguise and who, after a session of most frenetic cohabitation, regains, in the very arms of her lover, her original form. The painter is carried off on a broomhandle to a witches' sabbath, plainly a mere reproduction of the Faustian Walpurgisnacht, and in the morning is found dead on the Appian Way. The poem is, from beginning to end, derivative; indeed, it might be an interesting pastime to cull passages borrowed directly from other authors. Gautier's apostrophe to love: **"Amour, joie et fléau du monde",**[1] can hardly be less than an unabashed lifting from Musset's "Don Paez",[2] where we find the verse: "Amour, fléau du monde, exécrable folie." Likewise, the line: "Comme emparadisés dans les brase l'un de l'autre,"[3] is a word-for-word translation of Milton's "Imparadised in one another's arms."[4] Despite the slightly hyperbolical assertion with which Gautier begins the concluding stanza of his poem: **"Ce poème homérique et sans égal au monde"**, *Albertus* is interesting solely as a typical example of the Byronic influence in France and for the light it casts on the poet's ever-present attachment to painting, his first love among the arts.

This predilection is revealed in numerous poems contained in later collections of Gautier's verse. It even assumes a tone of bitterness in such poems as **"la Diva"**, where we read:

> Pourquoi, découragé par vos divins tableaux,
> Ai-je, enfant paresseux, jeté là mes pinceaux,
> Et pris pour vous fixer le crayon du poète?
> . . . . .
> Pourquoi, lassé trop tôt dans une heure de
>   doute,
> Peinture bien-aimée, ai-je quitté ta route?
> Que peuvent tous nos vers pour rendre la
>   beauté?
> . . . . .
> Ah! combien, je regrette et comme je déplore
> De ne plus être peintre.[5]

The poem **"A une jeune tribun"** is a veritable tirade against the "useful" arts and bourgeois morality. We read:

> Il est dans la nature, il est de belles choses,
> Des rossignols oisifs, de paresseuses roses,
> Des poètes rêveurs et des musiciens
> Qui s' inquiètent peu d'être bons citoyens,
> Qui vivent au hasard et n'ont d'autres
>   maximes,
> Sinon que tout est bon pourvu qu'on ait la
>   rime;
> . . . . .
> Qui s'enivrent de vers comme d'autres de vin
> Et qni ne trouvent pas que l'art soit creux et
>   vain.
> . . . . .
> Qui donc dira cela, que toute chose belle,
> Femme, musique, ou fleur, ne porte pas en
>   elle
> Et son enseignement et sa moralité?[6]

It would be supererogatory to call attention to the similarity of this passage to some of the oft-quoted lines of Keats. In **"Pensées de minuit"**,[7] Gautier bewails the fact that the high enthusiasm of his youth had been replaced by a sceptical disillusionment due, in part at least, to his readings in the literature of Romanticism.

> J'ai lu Werther, René, son frère d'alliance;
>   Ces livres, vrais poisons du cœur,
> Qui déflorent la vie et nous dégoûtent d'elle,
> Dont chaque mot vous porte une atteinte
>   mortelle;
>   Byron et son Don Juan moqueur.

A final point of interest in the first volume of Gautier's *Poésies complètes* is worthy of at least passing notice. A great many of the poems of the volume are capped by quotations drawn from a host of poets, native as well as foreign. A large number of these, naturally enough, are from the works of Gautier's fellow-Romanticists of France, England, and Germany: Musset, Joseph Delorme (Sainte-Beuve), Gérard de Nerval, Ulric Guttinguer, Pétrus Borel, Byron, Goldsmith, Bürger; but just as many, and this is significant, are taken from the preclassical French poets. Virtually the entire Pléiade is thus honored, as are the *Roman de la Rose,* Alain Chartier, Villon, du Bartas, and Desportes. Gautier, for one, was convinced of the æsthetic kinship of the Romanticists with the French poets of the fifteenth and sixteenth centuries.

In the year 1836, Gautier, for monetary reasons exclusively, took a step which resulted in his enslavement for the remaining thirty-six years of his life and which he never ceased lamenting. He became the *feuilletoniste* of the Paris journal, *la Presse,* and later passed, in the same capacity, to *le Moniteur universel* and *le Journal officiel,* and was rescued from this cordially hated hackwork, to which he clung because it was the sole possible "gagne-pain" for one to whom any other profession but that of letters was unthinkable, only by his death in 1872. Week-in, week-out, Gautier must needs have his article—chiefly dramatic reviews and art-criticisms—ready for the greedy maws of the printing-presses. In a feverish chase after "copy", he took trips to Spain, Italy, Constantinople, and Russia, all of which were recounted in travel-essays later published in volume form. Whatever leisure he was able to wrest from his detested vocation he applied to the composition of poetry and prose fiction. His tour of Spain found poetic echo in a slender book, *España* (1845); his finest verses were collected into a volume upon which his permanent reputation as a poet will rest: *Emaux et camées* (1852). The poems contained in the second volume of the *Poésies complètes*[8] are a continuous "lamento" against the fate that had chained him to the Ixion-wheel of the *feuilleton.* In **"Sur un album"** he complains:[9]

> Ma poésie est morte, et je ne sais plus rien
> Sinon que tout est laid, sinon que rien n'est bien.

And again:

> O poètes divins, je ne suis plus des vôtres!
> On m'a fait une niche, où je veille tapi,
> Dans le bas du journal comme un dogue
>   accroupi.

In **"Dans la sierra"** he exclaims:[10]

> J'aime d'un fol amour les monts fiers et
>   sublimes!
>
>   . . . . .
>
> Ils ne rapportent rien et ne sont pas utiles;
> Ils n'ont que leur beauté, je le sais, c'est bien
>   peu.

His admiration for pure poetry, in the person of Victor Hugo, is set down in **"A Jean Duseigneur, Sculpteur:"**[11]

> Tout est grêle et mesquin dans cette époque
>   étroite
> Où Victor Hugo, seul, porte sa tête droite
> Et crève les plafonds de son crâne gêant.

Of the remaining poems in the volume, very few are deserving of attention. *La Comédie de la mort*[12] (1838) is a macabre composition that may not have been without influence upon Baudelaire; in it, the poet seeks, after the fashion of Ecclesiastes, to discover the meaning of life. This he does by consulting, in turn, Faust, the ardent seeker after knowledge; Don Juan, whose life was an uninterrupted quest for the ideal love; and Napoleon, who had staked his all upon the achievement of military glory. The poet concludes with Solomon that "all is vanity", and looks forward longingly to the release afforded by death.

Gautier, it has been asseverated, believed with firm conviction that art is its own justification, and that such art as is employed to serve as handmaiden to morals, ethics, religion, sociology, is thereby prostituted. This theory took its most concrete form in his **Emaux et camées,** the volume of verse which might well have inspired the poet to echo the Horatian "Exegi monumentum". In the prefatory poem, Gautier compares himself to Goethe, who amidst the fracas of the imperial wars, had composed the *West-östlicher Divan;* similarly, he (Gautier) had written the verses of which his volume was composed during the stormy days of the *coup d'état* of 1851.

> Sans prendre garde à l'ouragan
> Qui fouettait mes vitres fermées
> Moi, j'ai fait *Emaux et camées.*

In this collection of poems, Gautier had scrapped all the remnants of the Romantic folly and pseudo-philosophy evident in **Albertus** and **la Comédie de la mort;** he has become the complete master of his tools, and he has used these tools for the creation of poems which, for sheer perfection of artistic finish, have seldom been surpassed. The poems are truly "enamels and cameos"—clear-cut gems, exquisitely painted miniatures. For subject-matter Gautier has drawn upon all the beautiful, ostensibly useless things his eyes might anywhere have encountered: the hands or the azure eyes of a woman, the first smile of spring, a pink gown, the smoke issuing from a peasant's hut, fountains, tea-roses, clouds, flowers, turtle-doves. **"Transpositions d'art"** abound; a **"Poème de la femme"** has as its sub-title **"Marbre de Paros";** there are a **"Symphonie en blanc majeur", "Contralto", "Lied", "La Fellah—sur une aquarelle de la Princesse M."** Chinese porcelains, Spanish guitars, music-boxes, butterflies, Russian furs, myosotis-flowers, dragon-flies, jewels—of such dainty ephemera has Gautier carved and chiseled his poetic Tanagra-marbles. The noteworthiness of this achievement becomes even more amazing when it is recalled that all the poems in the volume, with the exception of the last three, are written in the same metrical form, and that one of the simplest conceivable, the octosyllabic quatrain with alternating rhyme. The last of the **Emaux et camées** is a veritable pæan to the durability of art. Its final stanzas read:

> Tout passe.—L'art robuste
>   Seul a l'éternité.
>   Le buste
> Survit à la cité.
>
> Et la médaille austère
>   Que trouve un laboureur
>   Sous terre
> Révèle un empereur.
>
> Les dieux eux-mêmes meurent
>   Mais les vers souverains
>   Demeurent
> Plus fort que les airains.
>
> Sculpte, lime, cisèle;
>   Que ton rêve flottant
>   Se scelle
> Dans le bloc résistant.

This doctrine was a far cry from the Romanticism of 1830; not for a Lamartine or a Musset, a Hugo or a Vigny was the cold, patient kneading of impalpable nothings into immortal works of art. Indeed, Romanticism, long before its official interment in the failure of Hugo's last play, *les Burgraves* (1842), had become a house divided against itself. Out of the schism sprang the Parnassians. The generation that had come to life just before or during the stirring decade from 1820 to 1830 (Flaubert, Bouilhet, Fromentin, Leconte de Lisle, Théodore de Banville) had carried all through its youth a profound veneration for the giants of the epoch.[13] The link between the two generations was Théophile Gautier, the perfect poet of *Emaux et camées.* Though loyal all his life to the Romantic attachment of his youth, Gautier had traveled his own road. "Comme Alfred de Musset," says Maxime du Camp,[14] "il entendit garder son indépendance et il la garda jusqu'à la dernière heure, conservant son individualité intacte et ne se laissant pas entamer, malgré la dévotion qu'il professait pour Victor Hugo." And again: "Il resta ce quil voulut être, le chevalier errant de la littérature nouvelle, sans autre attache que l'admiration pour le général en chef et la sympathie pour le corps d'armée; mais il marcha isolé, n'accepta aucun joug, pas même celui de Victor Hugo." It was under the ægis of Gautier, the champion of poetry as a "pure" art comparable to music, painting, and sculpture, that the Parnassians were to launch their artistic strivings upon an indifferent world; for the practice of "art for art's sake" by no small number of the artists of our own day, we are indebted to the precept and example of Théophile Gautier.

Notes

[1] Stanza XLVII (*Poésies complètes,* Vol. I, p. 146).

[2] *Premières poésies,* p. 19. The poem is undated but it is printed between one dated 1828 and another 1829, and must have been written in one or the other of these years, as it is only the fifth poem in the volume. *Albertus,* on the other hand, is dated 1831.

[3] Stanza LV.

[4] *Paradise Lost,* Book IV, line 506.

[5] *Poésies diverses* (*Poésies complètes,* 1833-38, Vol. I, p. 229).

[6] *Ibid.,* pp. 246-52.

[7] *Ibid.,* pp. 256-61.

[8] Which includes all his poems written after 1838, with the exception of those comprising the volume of *Emaux et camées.*

[9] *Poésies diverses,* 1838-45 (*Poésies complètes,* Vol. II, pp. 53-54).

[10] *Ibid., España,* p. 133.

[11] *Ibid., Poésies nouvelles, poésies inédites, et poésies posthumes,* 1831-72, p. 167.

[12] *Ibid.,* pp. 3-49.

[13] An interesting statement of the attitude is to be found in Maxime du Camp's *Souvenirs littéraires* (2 vols., Paris, Hachette, 1906, Vol. I, Chaps. 4 and 5).

[14] *Théophile Gautier,* p. 129.

15 *Ibid.,* p. 130.

Joanna Richardson (essay date 1958)

SOURCE: Afterward in *Theophile Gautier: His Life & Times,* Max Reinhardt, 1958, pp. 278-90.

[*In the excerpt below, Richardson maintains that since Gautier "was an artist and a poet, not a conventional journalist or critic . . . he gave journalism a new significance and a new status" by making his criticism "a work of literary art."*]

Gautier's criticism is indeed (in Brunet's phrase) an organ of revivification; and it not only revivifies the drama, art and literature of the past but, as Gautier anticipated, it is a vast source of information about the arts, celebrities and events of the nineteenth century. Gautier's dramatic criticism reflects the French theatre from Marie Dorval to Sarah Bernhardt, from Hugo to Sardou. His music criticism embraces the performances of Chopin and of Liszt, the struggles of Berlioz and Wagner, the early work of Verdi. His criticism of art begins at a time when artists are still reacting from the neo-classicism of David, and it discusses the full flush of Realism. Gautier's literary criticism covers French literature from Béranger to Mistral. His topical reporting records, among much else, the great exhibitions of mid-century, the growing understanding between England and France, the coming of the railways, the interest in air travel, the Siege of Paris. And his journalism, taken as an all-embracing whole, is a source of information for any study of aesthetic thought in nineteenth-century France, for a study of almost any figure in the contemporary French artistic world.

It helps, more particularly, to refute Emile Montégut's strange statement that Gautier declined as a poet when he established himself in journalism.[1] No student of *Emaux et Camées* would maintain that these poems, nearly all of them written in mid-career or late in life, were inferior in technique to the poet's early work; while if journalism imposed life-long frustration on Gautier, poetry is born of sorrow, weariness and anger as well as joy, and a study of his career confirms that his regrets brought new elements into his work. Besides, some of Gautier's verse was in all probability inspired by his prose; and growing ideas for poems, and echoes of poems completed, may be found in his journalism. It is also quite possible that frequent descriptive practice helped to change Gautier's poetry: that his critical work helped to make this determined

Romantic the master of the Realists of the Second Empire. And he himself was not unaware of such benefits. When Murger, after years as a journalist, won instant fame with *la Vie de Bohême,* Gautier wrote: 'Let Murger not repent this broadcast scattering of the intellect from which, whatever people say, the poet gains more than he loses. . . . Journalism has this advantage, that it mingles you with the crowd, and saves you from the stupidities of solitary pride; it is fencing which breaks you in and makes you supple.'[2]

Gautier's journalism is not only a guide to some of his poetry; it is also a precious source of information for a study of his character and career. It is, in the first place, abundantly clear from his aesthetic sympathies and dislikes, from his attitude to life itself, that he was no Parnassian. He was, instead, and unmistakably, a born Romantic of 1830. Whatever he told the Goncourts about repressing himself in his work, whatever he told Engénie Fort about his impersonality, it proved impossible, naturally enough, to conceal himself from his readers for some forty years; nor did Gautier desire to do so. Repeatedly he chose, in Romantic fashion, to express his own unhappiness and frustration; inevitably he revealed his hopes and his pleasures. And he published, in his journalism, a considerable amount of autobiography, both open and concealed.

And here it may be remarked that Gautier's business correspondence does much to destroy Flaubert's contention that Gautier was the victim of his editors. 'Make it quite clear,' Flaubert advises Feydeau, who is about to write a biography, 'make it quite clear that he was exploited and victimized in all the papers he wrote for; Girardin, Turgan and Dalloz were torturers to the poor man. . . . When you write the biography of a friend, you should do it from the point of view of his *vengeance.* . . . Be serious, be pitiless.'[3] It is clear from Gautier's journalism that he knew financial hardship, felt himself oppressed by editors and by the discipline of his profession. It also seems evident that the editors and publishers suffered considerably from Gautier's lack of discipline, his recurrent vagaries, his frank, indeed publicized distaste for much of his work.

And it is this very distaste for journalism that explains Gautier's distinction and achievement as a journalist and critic. He did not consider himself a man of letters; he considered himself an artist.[4] It was to his early training in Rioult's studio that he claimed to owe his taste for art and his feeling for beauty; and all his life, regretting that he had abandoned painting, he transposed it into literature. *'Anch'io son pittore!'* he said in 1867. 'I've regretted all my life I abandoned my first career. Since then I've done nothing but make transpositions of art.'[5]

In his *Pages de Critique et de Doctrine* Paul Bourget indicates, perceptively, the connection between the Gautier of ***Mademoiselle de Maupin*** and the Gautier of this three-dimensional journalism, quoting the words of d'Albert: 'My pictures are only coloured bas-reliefs. For I like to touch what I've seen and to follow the curves of contours into their most hidden folds. I consider everything from every aspect, and I turn about it, a light in my hand.' Here again is Gautier the artist; here again is a key to his journalism. For Gautier the critic confirms Bourget's suggestion that Gautier makes, with words, the gesture of d'Albert. To write is, for him, 'to follow the curves of contours into their most hidden folds.'[6]

So it is that Gautier, the pupil of Rioult, sets out as a dramatic critic not only to criticize but to produce 'a daguerrotype of the theatre'; and in his dramatic criticism, at its best, we are given not only aesthetic considerations, but three-dimensional figures re-enacting their parts. It has been suggested that Gautier's plastic criticism of the theatre is defective; that he has painted the scenery instead of analysing the plays. Plastic criticism, if exclusive, might indeed be inadequate; but in Gautier's work it lends charm to ephemeral performances, preserves (as he had hoped) many fine ones, and both explains and enhances his literary considerations. Gautier himself told Lovenjoul that he considered this plastic criticism highly important.[7] He went further: he considered it a philosophy.[8]

Gautier's devotion to the visual arts inspired not only his writing on the theatre but his happiest writing about music: the portraits of Liszt at the piano, the imaginative commentary on Weber; and it inspired, most significant of all, his brilliant, constant, influential use of correspondences. Gautier sought to create the plastic criticism of music, and his chief contribution to music criticism was happily indicated by Ernest Reyer: 'He spoke about it like a poet, translated the pleasure it had given him into language rich with imagery.'[9]

The artist who wrote plastic criticism of the theatre and music achieved his highest successes as a writer on literature when he recreated, visually, his great and lesser contemporaries, or revivified, in visual language that sometimes touched the height of a prose-poem, the impressions that poetry had made upon him.

And, naturally and deliberately, Gautier created the plastic criticism of art. And here one might recall the perceptive appreciation with which he declared himself so satisfied: 'Art criticism, the manner in which he practises and understands it, is one of the innovations and special gifts of Théophile Gautier [wrote Sainte-Beuve in 1863]. . . . Every painting and fresco seems to appear in the light in which he describes it, and one sees not only its project and disposition, but its effect, its tone and line. Gautier's system of description is a system of transposition, an exact, equivalent reduction rather than a translation. Just as a symphony is reduced for piano, so he *reduces* a picture to an *article*. It is not ink he uses, but lines and colours; he has a palette and pencils. . . . These accounts speak and live. In art, perhaps the most useful form of criticism is to show rather than judge.'[10] And the words of Sainte-Beuve are confirmed and enhanced by those of an artist, Baudry: 'The description of my pictures enchants me. No writer performs or will perform, like you, this miracle of transposition and crystallization, as Stendhal called it (though Stendhal only applied the term to love). It is true you love painting as men love women. . . . When time has faded my paintings something at least will remain in the magnificent veil you cast about them. It is the story of the mummies of which, when life is gone, the body almost vanished, only perfumes remain. . . .'[11]

'They often call me *fanciful,*' said Gautier to Sainte-Beuve, 'and yet, all my life, I have only tried to see properly, to study nature, draw, interpret, paint it, if I could, just as I saw it.'[12] He did not merely observe outward appearances; yet throughout his work one finds the constant preoccupation with the visual, the plastic and the three-dimensional, and time and time again one recalls his comment to the Goncourts: 'I am a man for whom the visible world exists.'[13]

Gautier was not, however, only an artist. He was also a poet; and he constantly reminded his readers of the 'poor poet diverted from his art'. They were reminded more happily of his vocation by the germs of poetry scattered throughout his work, by the poems published in and out of articles, and by the echoes of poems resounding in his criticism. They were reminded of his poetry, too, in numerous improvisations and asides; for the journalist, so he told them blandly, 'is a hybrid animal, half critic and half improviser'.[14] A comment on the farewell of Taglioni, on the transience of dramatic art, on the funeral of Decamps, may lift his prose to the level of a prose-poem; a sterile week in the theatre will allow him to improvise engagingly on the winter or the spring.

It is at such moments that Gautier's poetry touches his prose. Gautier's poetic (and Romantic) feeling is found in his love of colour and history, his affection for the exotic: the Spanish, Egyptian, Chinese and Japanese; it is found in his veneration for all religions and for the supernatural, even for superstition, it is found in his eager interest in the prospects of ballooning, in the prosaic notes he made on the undiscovered world of astronomy. It is found in the experiments with hashish, recalled in **"le Club des Hachichins,"**[15] in which he attempted to discover new dimensions of experience. And Gautier the poet is reflected not only in his love of the remote and strange. He is reflected (and here the poet and the artist meet) in the principle which guides his work, indeed his very life: in his evident and abiding search for beauty.

'I adore above all things the beauty of form,' he had written in **Mademoiselle de Maupin**. 'Beauty, for me, is visible divinity, it is palpable happiness, heaven descended on earth. . . . Who could not kneel before thee, pure personification of the thought of God?' And again: 'I ask only for beauty, it is true, but it must be so perfect, that I shall probably never encounter it.' Those few sentences hold much of the philosophy that informed his work.

One finds there what René Lauret defined as the Romantic longing for the impossible.[16] Yet if, as Lauret suggests, 'the thirst for the impossible is the mark of powerlessness,' it is still this very striving after the unattainable, this very regret of human inadequacy, that gives dignity to Gautier's philosophy, and to the criticism it inspires. 'The delights for which he yearns,' writes Lauret of Gautier, 'are esthetic; he wants them so fervently, his love of beauty is so candid that it ennobles his very insensibility, and sets him above the lovers of nameless beauty.' A study of Gautier underlines the contradiction: Gautier cannot be both fervent and insensible. Nor is he (as Lauret implies) a superior dilettante; nor can he be dismissed (as Lauret dismisses him) for 'his too ardent need of beauty'. The need of beauty cannot be too ardent; the religion of beauty, which Gautier professed, raises him far above the amateur of art, and gives him not only his fervour as poet and as artist but his distinction as a critic. Antoine-Orliac much more nearly understands Gautier's philosophy[17] when he sees it as the Platonic cult of beauty and relates it to 'the Greek dream which moves towards the divine through beauty of form'.

Yet Antoine-Orliac sees Gautier's plastic ideal, his worship of form, as his consolation for 'metaphysical disquietude'; and Gabriel Brunet reaches much the same conclusion: 'Gautier discovered the balm for every grief: consolation by the contemplation of appearance.'[18] Gautier may indeed have consoled himself for the disappointments of life by the contemplation of beauty in art and nature. But it must be emphasized yet again (and his writing makes it abundantly clear) that though he could not, to his sorrow, accept all the tenets of Catholicism, he was a devoted pantheist. When he declares in **Mademoiselle de Maupin:** 'Christ did not die for me. I am as pagan as Alcibiades and Phidias', he is declaring himself a pantheist as much as a pagan. He worships beauty, so he tells us himself in his novel and throughout his work, as the visible form of divinity. He worships the beauty of nature and the beauty of art. As he wrote once, himself, of Diderot: 'If he did not see God at a particular place in the heavens, he saw Him everywhere in the beauty of the universe.'[19] And as Emile Montégut so well expressed it: 'The pleasures of dilettantism, usually so superficial, attain, in Gautier, the power and nobility of the pleasures of mystic ecstasy. His eyes turn towards the sun of art with the same burning desire as the eyes of a Christian monk who seeks the invisible sun of morality; his whole being is absorbed in the contemplation of beauty, undistracted by any preoccupation foreign to the vision that possesses him, and never was Brahmin, lost in his search for the place occupied by intelligence, more separate from earth than Théophile Gautier by the ravishment into which he is thrown by a Renaissance canvas and a fragment of Greek art.'[20]

So it is that Gautier recognizes the work of an artist as an act of devotion; so it is he maintains what all critics should maintain: the ideal purpose and unattainable standards, the sovereign independence and sacred nature of art. So it is that Gautier professes his belief in Art for Art's Sake from his earliest criticism, from the moment he writes so nobly, so sincerely: 'In art we have no religion but the religion of art itself.'[21]

Critics have long indicated one of the obvious distinctions of Gautier's journalism. Victor Fournel observed that 'criticism for him was only a pretext for pictures, and, frankly, he was not asked for anything else'.[22] 'Nostalgia for the picturesque,' added Pontmartin, 'dominates his talent and his life.'[23] And Zola rightly confirmed: 'His constant effort was to reduce written thought to the material nature of the painted form. Théophile Gautier had, in brief, a painter's eye, and that was his dominant quality.'[24] Hugo indicated the other major characteristic of Gautier's criticism when he thanked him for an article on *Ruy Blas*. 'What a master you are, dear Théophile! What poetic prose! . . . Your criticism has the power of creation.'[25] Yet none of these critics remarked that Gautier's distinction came from his dual nature: from the fact that he was artist and poet together. It is Sainte-Beuve who touches the heart and sums the significance of Gautier's criticism when he writes: 'After all, he is only a displaced artist and poet.'[26]

Here lie both the weakness and the extraordinary strength of Gautier's work for the Press. His love of art and poetry, it is true, often led him to be undisciplined, to indulge in his own prose-pictures, his own imaginings, instead of critical comment; to delegate the tasks he found unrewarding; to permit occasional plagiary; to be, throughout his career of some forty years, the desperation of is punctual editors. Artist and poet born, he must have been one of the most rebellious, least predictable contributors to any paper since journalism began. And there is, perhaps, another weakness in Gautier's love of art and poetry: an inherent weakness which he recognized. We cannot look to him for academic judgments, we cannot look to him for reasoned surveys, documented explanations. We must not expect him to explore a problem deeply, bring a vast weight of erudition to his theme. For Gautier is not an intellectual; he is, perhaps, by nature, the least critical of critics. He had written, once, of Diderot: 'He thinks with his heart as much as with his head.'[27] He himself appreciates the arts with his heart and soul rather than his intellect.

And yet, is this a weakness? When all is said, the arts, in their purest form, are inspired by emotion rather than intellect, and it is through the heart that they should be comprehended, and with the heart that they should be loved and described. It is, perhaps, the distinction of Gautier the critic, not his weakness, that he approached the arts in a loving, not an academic, spirit. His devotion to art and poetry may explain some of his failings; but it gave him, also, an intimate and unusual understanding. It gave him a broad and lofty conception of the arts and a superlative visual style: made his writing, at its best, a living record and a work of literature. Gautier tried, persistently, throughout his long career of some forty years, to make his daily work embrace both art and poetry, both the vocations he felt he had abandoned. And as we consider his journalism we often recall the theory he expressed in the early years of his career: 'Every art has its weakness, whence derives a part of its beauty. The measureless struggles of the poet who lacks a plastic form, the artist who lacks a succession of ideas, the sculptor who lacks movement, the composer who lacks words, have produced the most wondrous works of the human spirit.'[28]

Gautier's journalism suggests one surely inescapable conclusion: that Gautier was an artist and a poet, not a conventional journalist or critic; and precisely because he was far more than a journalist or critic, he gave journalism a new significance and a new status. He made it, at its best, when poet and artist took over the common task, a work of literary art. And he did more: he wrote it with the eagle-eyed view of his time, the religion of art, the ideal and constant standards that alone can give criticism its value and its permanence. In an age when superficial values were too readily accepted and public taste was too frequently gratified, he maintained in his criticism the importance of the ideal, the permanent values of civilization. Coppée described him as 'the great and exquisite poet who has consented, in the interest of the Cause of Art, to become the first of contemporary critics'.[29] If Gautier's journalism and criticism are given their distinction by his artistic and poetic nature, they are also given their dignity by his militant, unswerving, religious devotion to art and beauty. It was with truth that he wrote to Sainte-Beuve: 'If I had possessed the least personal fortune I should have devoted myself entirely to *the love of the green laurel*; but in the prose into which I have fallen, I have always defended the interests of art and proclaimed the name of the sacred masters with my whole heart and soul.'[30]

Notes

[1] *le Moniteur universel,* 6 March 1865

[2] *La Presse,* 26 November 1846

[3] Flaubert: *Corr.,* VI, 448/9

[4] *L'Artiste,* 14 December 1856

[5] Primoli, op. cit., p. 345

[6] Bourget: *Pages de Critique et de Doctrine,* I, 66 sqq.

[7] Lovenjoul: *Histoire,* I, 124

[8] Sarcey: *Quarante Ans de Théâtre,* 91 sqq.

[9] Reyer: *Notes de Musique,* 408 sqq.

[10] *Le Constitutionnel,* 30 November 1863

[11] Chantilly: C 491 ff. 322/3

[12] *Causeries du Lundi,* XIV, 73

[13] Goncourt *Journal,* I, 141/2

[14] *La Presse,* 12 May 1851

[15] Reprinted in *Romans et Contes*

[16] *Mercure de France,* 16 May 1911

[17] Ibid, 15 August 1928

[18] Ibid, 15 October 1922

[19] *le Moniteur universel,* 7 January 1854

[20] *le Moniteur universel,* 17 January 1865

[21] *Le Cabinet de Lecture,* 19 March 1836

[22] Fournel: *Figures d'Hier et d'Aujourd'hui,* 47

[23] Pontmartin: *Causeries littéraires,* 303

[24] Zola: *Documents littéraires,* 140

[25] Hugo: *Corr. gén.,* III, 306

[26] *Le Constitutionnel,* 30 November 1863

[27] *le Moniteur universel,* 7 January 1854

[28] *La Musique,* 262

[29] Chantilly: C 492 ff. 582/3

[30] Lovenjoul, op. cit., I, xix/xx

Works Cited

Bourget, Paul, *Pages de Critique et de Doctrine* (Dentu 1885) *Etudes et Portraits* (Lemerre 1889)

Brunet, Gabriel, 'Sur la Critique' (*Mercure de France,* 15 April 1922) 'Théophile Gautier, poète' (*Mercure de France,* 15 October 1922)

Feydeau, Ernest, *Théophile Gautier. Souvenirs intimes* (Plon 1874)

Flaubert, Gustave, *Œuvres complètes. Correspondence.* Nouvelle édition augmentée (Conard 1926 sqq.)

Fournel, Victor, *Figures d'Hier et d'Aujourd'hui* (Calmann Lévy 1883)

Gautier, Théophile, *Emaux et Camées.* Introduction de Jean Pommier, Notes et Lexique de Georges Matoré (Genève. Droz 1947)

———. *Mademoiselle de Maupin* (Charpentier 1922)

———. *Romans et Contes* (Bibliothèque-Charpentier. Fasquelle s.d.)

Goncourt, Edmond & Jules de, *Journal* (Flammarion. Fasquelle 1935-6)

Hugo, Victor, *Correspondance générale* (Albin Michel. 1947 sqq.)

Lauret, René, 'L'âme romantique de Théophile Gautier' (*Mercure de France,* 16 May 1911)

Lovenjoul, Vicomte de Spoelberch de, *Histoire des Œuvres de Théophile Gautier* (Charpentier 1887)

———. *Les Lundis d'un Chercheur* (Calmann Lévy 1894)

Montégut, Émile, *Nos Morts contemporains.* 2e série (Hachette 1884)

Orliac, Antoine, 'Essai sur le Pessimisme chez les Parnassiens' (*Mercure de France,* 15 August 1928)

Primoli, J. N., 'La Princesse Mathilde et Théophile Gautier' (*Revue des Deux Mondes,* 1 November 1925, pp. 47-86; and 15 November 1925, 329-66)

Reyer, Ernest, *Notes de Musique* (Charpentier 1875)

Sainte-Beuve, C. A., *Portraits littéraires* (Garnier 1862-4)

———. *Premiers lundis* (Michel Lévy 1874-5)

————. *Nouveaux lundis* (Michel Lévy 1863-70)

————. *Les grands écrivains français*. Etudes des Lundis et des Portraits classées selon un ordre nouveau et annotées par Maurice Allem. XIXe siècle. Les poètes. II. Victor Hugo-Musset-Théophile Gautier (Garnier 1926)

————. *Correspondance générale*. Recueillie, classée et annotée par Jean Bonnerot (Stock 1935 sqq.)

Sarcey, Francisque, *Quarante ans de théâtre. Feuilletons dramatiques*. (Bibliothèque des annales politiques et littéraires 1900)

Zola, Emile, *Documents littéraires. Etudes et Portraits* (Charpentier 1881)

Albert J. George (essay date 1964)

SOURCE: "The Second Generation," in *Short Fiction in France: 1800-1850*, Syracuse University Press, 1964, pp. 166-204.

[*In this excerpt, George offers a thematic and stylistic analysis of Gautier's short fiction and praises him for raising the standard of the genre.*]

The *petits romantiques,* the second generation of romantics, boasted fewer distinguished names than the original group, but they made up for this lack in devotion to a cause. Their faith in their destiny flamed even higher than that of the founders of the movement; they developed an overpowering sense of the sanctity of their mission. Tragically, most of them possessed a modicum of talent but no genius, with the result that their work scarcely outlived them. Most were devout poets who, like their predecessors, turned reluctantly to the brief narrative as it became an accepted mode of literary expression. Yet some of them, Gautier, for instance, would help raise short fiction to a level where it could stand unashamed alongside any of the other genres.

. . . . .

Like Mérimée, Théophile Gautier brought a sense of art to the short narrative; like him, he stood out from his contemporaries in his sure knowledge of the possibilities of brief fiction. Whenever the crushing necessity to earn a living permitted, he could produce works with perspective, balanced in emphasis, and cleverly constructed. Though inclined to verbosity and easily enticed into long descriptions from the intoxication of reading his own words, he had a sense of form known to few of his fellow romantics.

Life, however, generally refused him the leisure to polish his narratives. Like Balzac, he struggled incessantly to satisfy a horde of nagging creditors. For a good thirty years, while others were building major reputations, Gautier worked like a hack to liquidate his debts. He debased his large talent by grinding out *feuilletons* because of the legal paper that regularly snowed down on him. Thus, one of his special crosses was a constant need to sacrifice a strong sense of integrity for monetary gain. For example, from April to December, 1848, he produced at least ninety *feuilletons* for *L'Evènement, Le Journal,* and the *Revue des Deux Mondes,* approximately four volumes in eight months.

Under the pressure of time and need, Gautier made everything grist for his mill, but mostly he drew on himself and his friends. His heroes are generally Gautier in disguise, characters drawn from the environment he knew well, or contemporary stereotypes. His protagonists recall the companions of the *Jeune-France* group, slightly eccentric and passionately dedicated to the pursuit of love and beauty. The autobiographical content runs high in many of his stories, which also contain his dreams and hopes. Harried as he was, he still managed to cling to the belief in the dignity of artistic creation he so eloquently defended in the preface to **Mlle de Maupin**.

. . . . .

In his first story, **"La Cafetière,"** published in *Le Cabinet de lecture* on May 4, 1831, Gautier showed a sense of public taste when he took advantage of current interest in phantoms and the possibility of return from death. As with many of his tales, the story was told in the first person. After a trip to Normandy the sleepless hero was terrified when, as the clock struck eleven, a Falstaffian man stepped from a tapestry and released the other figures. The narrator leaped from bed to waltz with a beautiful girl who called him by name. He lost track of time until his partner fell to the floor at dawn and he, too, fainted. His friends found him dressed in the garments of his host's grandfather and clutching some broken porcelain. Later he moodily began to sketch a coffee pot that stood in the room, producing instead a portrait of his host's sister, Angela, who had died two years before. "Je venais de comprendre qu'il n'y avait plus pour moi de bonheur sur terre!"

In **"La Cafetière,"** Gautier had written in the temper of his age. Like Nodier and many subsequent imitators, he passed from the real to the hallucinatory to stress the actuality of the dream substance. He arranged his story to provide a logical explanation, a tired man having a nightmare in a strange chateau. Gautier firmly believed in spiritism and the occult. A tapestry come alive, a coffee pot turned beautiful girl, were only devices to introduce the land of the ever present dead. Angela remained faceless because Gautier wished to deal only with the love of a man for a phantom. Consequently, instead of explaining the vision rationally, he introduced the ancient clothing and the portrait of the host's sister. The romantic theme of love forever lost and never enjoyed ended the story.

"La Cafetière" represents an important point both in Gautier's career and in the history of short prose fiction, despite its trite and conventional nature. He joined Mérimée in moving toward a conception of brief fiction that recalls Poe's definition of the formal short story. The plot was organized toward a single effect, the sudden, sorrowful comprehension of the lover's plight. The dream itself constituted the major portion of the fantasy, economically structured although slightly commonplace. More important, however, he had turned his back on the contemporary habit of padding a story with moralizing digressions.

For more that a year Gautier neglected brief fiction; then, in August, 1832, he published in *La France littéraire* a take-off on Hoffmann, **"Onuphrius ou les Vexations fantastiques d'un admirateur d'Hoffmann."** However joking the title, Gautier had the serious intention of reproducing the attitudes of a man verging on schizophrenia. As Balzac normally did, he began *in medias res:* Onuphrius, a full-fledged member of the lunatic fringe of romanticism, arrived late at a rendezvous with the excuse that all the clocks said he was early. When he took Jacintha to his studio to finish a portrait, he found his painting decorated with a pair of moustaches; as he tried to finish the work, a blow jiggled his elbow, though nobody was present. The next day, four toughs dressed as harlequins threw an unidentified white object under his horse. Onuphrius went to bed, to slip into a nightmare in which he was nailed into a coffin and buried. In the grave, he composed poetry about "la vie dans la mort." Thenceforth Onuphrius lived with his hallucinations. When asked to recite some verse at a salon, he found an ironical young man catching the lines and swallowing them before they could be heard. As his mind slipped, Jacintha cared for him, but Onuphrius persisted in thinking that the devil had made off with his body. He wandered into the world of fantasy and never returned.

While he was writing **"Onuphrius,"** Gautier's own memory was working well. The plot smacks of *Le Mort réssuscité,* published in the *Mercure de France du XIXe siècle* in 1829; Gérard de Nerval had used the idea of the revived corpse in *La Métempsychose* in 1830. Hugo, Chamiso, Gavarni, Daumier, all provided material; Hoffmann furnished the scene in which Onuphrius recited his poetry; and Gautier even borrowed from his own *Albertus*.

Within a structure similar to that of **"La Cafetière,"** Gautier stitched these bits and pieces into a coherent whole. As he told Mélanie Waldor on July 26, 1832, "Il y a une idée philosophique dessous." Gautier wanted

to describe a man so concerned with watching himself live that his imagination pulled him away from reality. "A force d'être spectateur de son existence, Onuphrius avait oublié celle des autres, et depuis bien longtemps il ne vivait plus qu'au milieu de fantômes. . . . Il aurait pu être le plus grand des poètes, il ne fut que le plus extraordinaire des fous."

Gautier introduced this *romantique forcené* lost in mystical poetry and the study of sorcery at the moment Onuphrius' mind first began to totter. Somewhat of a misanthrope, he fled into the past, into the mystic, the marvelous and the occult, which led him to attribute life's small annoyances to hostile supernatural forces. Gautier intervened to vouch for the nightmare, slipping from the facts to the hallucinations that his friend had described to him. He repeated an idea used in **"La Cafetière"** when Onuphrius imagined his own funeral, symbolically the death of his mind, to celebrate which he composed *La Vie dans la mort.* The last scene portrayed his divorce from reality, and his insanity took the form of satanic persecution involving the loss of his body. And young Gautier could not refrain from pointing out cynically that Jacintha a year later could not recall his name.

"Onuphrius" led Gautier into the sketch of a young man who took a ridiculously exaggerated romanticism so seriously that he made it a way of life. He continued working in this vein by creating the portrait of **"Elias Wildmanstadius ou l'Homme moyenâge,"** prepared as a text for an English engraving of Saint Sebald Square in Nuremberg (1832). The portrait, patterned on Célestin Nanteuil, a friend from the time of the *petit cénacle,* drew on memories of the carefree days of the rue d'Enfer and *Le Camp des Tartares.* For the benefit of "friend reader," Gautier drew up a list of the varieties of *Jeune-France: artiste, viveur,* Byronian, with or without beards. Of them all, the type *moyenâge* was most numerous, as, for example, his friend, Elias, presently deceased. Elias had been born too late (an unfortunate historical accident). He lived apart from his fellow man in medieval style, surrounded by medieval furniture, dressed in medieval clothes, sometimes even clanked around the house in armor. He enjoyed a lonely splendor, in which he could sculpt or make miniatures, leaving home only to visit the cathedral. He died two years before Gautier wrote the story, at the same hour lightning struck the church.

Elias Wildmanstadius, like Onuphrius, had lost contact with the world, but he took evasive flight into the supposed simplicity of the past. He had judged his society and, much like Gautier himself, found it repulsive. He was as "dépaysé qu'un sauvage des bords de l'Orénoque dans un cercle de fashionables parisiens." His plight was sketched in a manner reminiscent of Balzac, describing his habits, his home, and the attitudes of a man trying to turn back the clock.

In August of the following year, 1833, Gautier continued exploiting the promising vein of his recent past by publishing the ***Jeunes-France, romans goguenards,*** composed of six stories and preface. Of these, **"Onuphrius"** and **"Elias Wildmanstadius"** had already appeared and were now retouched for the present publication. To them he added **"Celle-ci et Celle-là,"** **"Sous la table,"** **"Le Bol de punch,"** and **"Daniel Jovard."**

The deliberate satirization of his recent companions seems surprising at first glance. However, two of the stories in this *décameron fashionable* had been intended for the *Contes du bousingo,* a collective enterprise the *petit cénacle* never completed. "Onuphrius Wphly," **"Elias Wildmanstadius,"** Gérard de Nerval's *Main de gloire,* and probably some of Pétrus Borel's *Champavert* had also been intended for the abortive joint effort. Now Gautier's two entries were revised for the ***Jeunes-France*** in a manner that gave the collection a sharp satiric edge. Superficially, they are humorous tales about the posture of extreme romanticism that mirror the attitude of contemporary literary rebels toward virtue, the social conventions, and bourgeois snobbery. However, Gautier had outgrown his carefree rebellion by 1833. The decline of romanticism into a fad seized on by a lunatic fringe had frightened the bourgeoisie to the point where the conservative *Figaro* launched an attack on what it considered the socially delinquent. Then the great promise of the *petit cénacle* turned into a snare and a delusion as most of its members faded into oblivion, frustrated, never fulfilling their first bold promise. The leader, Pétrus Borel, wildest of them all, would even abandon lycanthropy for a career in the civil service. Others, faddists and extroverts without the seriousness of purpose that distinguished this first Bohemia, were discrediting the romantic movement with their extravagance. Hence, to protect his friends, his memories, and the dignity of his artistic principles, Gautier tinged the sketches with overtones of satire. He was decidedly not joining the bourgeoisie, but he could not stomach the antics of the eccentrics he listed in **"Elias Wildmanstadius."**

Gautier used a sense of humor rare among the romantics in the fashion he had learned from Sterne. He claimed to have written the book because "il est indécent aujourd'hui de ne pas avoir fait un livre, un livre de contes tout au moins." Like Daniel Jovard, he had been converted to the doctrine of the *Jeunes-France.* "Je parle art pendant beaucoup de temps sans ravaler ma salive, et j'appelle bourgeois tous ceux qui ont un col de chemise." The sneer broadened. He hoped to make a mattress of his mistress's hair: "Il ne me manque vraiment que d'être bâtard pour que je sois parfait." Mocking the latest literary trends, he swore that his book contained neither myth nor allegory; in fact, it contained no ideas.

Each of the four added tales dealt with some aspect of life among the imitators of the *bousingos.* Their morality, for example, provided the material for **"Sous la table, dialogue bachique sur plusieurs questions de haute morale,"** in which Gautier captured a moment in the night life of Roderick and Théodore: At 2 A.M. both lay drunk under a table, where they solemnly discussed virtue, of which they disapproved. Roderick complained of the purity and coldness of his mistress, Théodore criticized the insatiable fire of his own. Before they fell asleep, they agreed to exchange mistresses, but one month later, under the same table, they chorused "Au diable les femmes!"

To the picture of the *Jeunes-France* who escaped into superstition and madness, and of those who fled into the past, Gautier added comments on their easy cynicism, tomcat morality, and evasion through alcohol. The result remains a sketch, despite the story-within-a-story of Roderick's adventure with a poor working girl, satiric in intent, interesting as a glimpse at the antics of the gilded youth of the age. The narrative was drawn out, a fact apparent even to the author: "Les détails sont tout, sans les détails, il n'y a pas d'histoire. D'ailleurs c'est de la couleur locale." The concision, the organization of the first stories, had been sacrificed because Gautier was writing the kind of portrait Balzac favored in satiric vindication of his friends. **"Le Bol de punch,"** another sketch of the lunatic fringe, recalled the famous "orgies" of *Le Camp des Tartares* which had frightened conservative neighbors and contributed to the legend of the *bousingos.* Gautier described the tale as a "conte panthéistique et palingénésique," a jibe at poor Ballanche, his own particular bête noire. "Notre ami Philadelphe" lived amidst bric-a-brac, broken furniture, a stuffed peacock, a yatagan, and a missal. His friends sported beards ranging from the carefully tended to the deliberately wild. When the *Jeunes-France* decided to honor Théodore's house with a party, the costumed young men loudly disagreed on proper procedure. The over-happy guests noisily indulged in horseplay by throwing a girl out the window, and the next morning the police led them away to preserve the peace and security of a middle-class world.

The sketch was intended to interest the morbidly curious in the mythical high life of the *avant-garde.* The irony deepened to include the reader in "ce conte véridique." Recalling Paul de Musset's *Table de nuit,* Gautier discussed with the reader such points of craftsmanship as the correct use of dialogue and local color. He punctured the legend of Bohemian life by revealing the weakness of his own stomach in a tale more loosely woven than his earlier works; his purpose had shifted from gentle humor to an attack on the genre itself. While the characters were exposed as shoddy imitators of hard-working artists, the author busily pulled the leg of the bourgeois reader by debating with

Albert and Théodore over how to conduct an orgy. In this tale the digressions stood forth as more important than the plot itself.

In **"Celle-ci et Celle-là ou la Jeune-France passion-née,"** Gautier deflated another misconception of the proper romantic with the tale of a young man who decided to celebrate his majority by having "une passion . . . volcanique." Full of wine and high purpose, Rodolphe decided to seek an affair with a lady he saw at the Tuileries. Alone with Madame one morning, Rodolphe moved quickly. Closing the door to avoid a draft, he began kissing her passionately, putting his hand on her breast; Madame succumbed as Rodolphe quoted wildly from *Antony* and *Hernani*. Gautier interrupted here with an irrelevant offer of an engraving of Rodolphe's hand to purchasers of the 19th edition. He claimed that the chastity of the French language prevented his describing the seduction in detail but promised to append the omitted scenes to the next printing so that his lady readers could more easily find them. Rodolphe played out his part by trying to make the lady's bald husband jealous; he even proposed that his friend Albert court Madame so that he might discover the treachery and stab them both. When Rodolphe returned home to find Mariette, his maid, packing to leave, he suddenly discovered his ideal, and Albert entered to explain the moral of the tale: "Il faut être bien fou pour sortir de chez soi dans l'espoir de rencontrer la poésie. La poésie . . . est en nous." Rodolphe apparently heeded his advice, for "Mariette, le lendemain, n'eut qu'un lit à faire."

Gautier called his tale an "histoire libertine, écrite pour l'édification des petites filles." To mock a contemporary critical fad, he solemnly added an explanation of his "myth" for the benefit of a reader whom he called "garde national." Rodolphe represented the human soul in its youth; Madame was classical poetry, brilliant and false; Monsieur stood for coarse common sense, "la prose bête"; Mariette symbolized true poetry, and Albert reason, "la prose fine et délicate."

"Celle-ci et Celle-là" contains a great many literary reminiscences: Mérimée's *Double Méprise,* Paul de Musset, Walter Scott, and Hugo are well represented, though Gautier showed a fine sense of organization in reshaping these disparate elements. The story follows a common pattern: search for an ideal, deception, and the discovery of the true ideal. Similarly, the plot was structured around old themes: the quest, the pursuit of happiness, the great passion, the eternal triangle, and home is where the heart is.

But Gautier set these out of focus with an irony that threatened the form he practiced. He had almost as little love for prose as Musset, and the current vogue for short fiction annoyed the poet who understood how seriously the popularity of prose was affecting the

reception of poetry. Moreover, he was continuing his exposure of the adolescent and untalented imitators of his hard-working friends in a satire as acid as that of the preface of *Mlle de Maupin*. This intent led Gautier to end each scene in ridicule. Thus, Rodolphe the romantic met his ideal wearing a bourgeois night cap. In great shame he leaped off the Pont Royal. As he flew toward the water, he gloated that his death would push the sales of his poems to twelve, but when he rose to the surface he swam to the bank, hat and all. The seduction ended peacefully in a discussion of Racine; and even when he tried to betray himself, the husband laughed and beat him at cards. Rodolphe was a sorry imitation of Don Juan who lived in a dream world fashioned from the untrustworthy matter of books.

The interruptions Gautier set at the end of each scene demonstrate how lightly he took the narrative. He discussed Rodolphe's morals with the lady reader, commented on Mariette, no better than she ought to be, and reviewed the love habits of the French. As an unreconstructed advocate of male supremacy, he proposed an Oriental role for women, "à la maison et au lit." Gautier had as little fondness for his characters as for his plot. Rodolphe constantly smashed his nose against reality: Madame refused to behave in the volcanic manner he expected; Albert would not agree to woo Madame so that he might be stabbed. Rodolphe could not even commit suicide with dignity; he was a perfect example of futility.

Yet the portrait of the inept hero revealed as much of Gautier as of Rodolphe. He was striking at sham, at shoddy recipe literature. Albert spoke for the author when he said, "La poésie . . . est en nous." For him the honest and faithful Mariette *did* represent true poetry. The edge to his complaint came from the deeply wounded feelings of the most vocal representative of art for art's sake, the defender of young poets who resented the fact that a middle-class society was erecting a system of values that excluded them.

This mood carried over into **"Daniel Jovard ou la Conversion d'un classique,"** the last portrait in his gallery. Daniel, a conservative young Voltairian and an excellent lotto player, went one evening to the Comédie Francaise to perfect his diction. From a *merveilleux,* he learned a new art which so enflamed him that Daniel burned his classics, threw away his conservative clothes, and called his father "garde national." Daniel began to write for the little magazines and drew attention to himself with violent clothes and a wild beard. Since he had a novel and a long poem in preparation, his literary name appeared in catalogues: M . . . us KWpl. . . . He was, as Gautier pointed out, on his way to becoming a publicly recognized talent.

This last story pointed up the reason for Gautier's bitterness. The *petit cénacle* had been hard-working, serious, and committed to artistic integrity, but now he saw Johnnies-come-lately, self-appointed geniuses, reducing others' theories to clichés. Daniel Jovard (the name is a pun on *jobard,* a sucker), metamorphosed from an ordinary citizen into a shaggy literary radical, an obscenity in the eyes of an honest writer. Matters had come to a sorry pass when a beard and an unpronounceable name substituted for real ability.

After the *Jeunes-France,* Gautier turned perforce to other subjects. Satire might satisfy his soul, but he had a precarious living to make. How much the pressures of haste and need would affect his work was revealed in 1833 when he published **"Laquelle des deux? Histoire perplexe,"** the story of a man unable to decide which of two sisters he loved. The tale lacks the concision of his satirical portraits; inconsequential in plot, it depends primarily on a strange dilemma for interest. The interruptions to chat with the reader, to defend the peculiar story, and to offer asides to *Madame* indicate that, like Balzac, Gautier was falling victim to a salable formula.

Soon, however, his growing interest in the unusual and his professional's sense of appeal led him to an ancient and honorable theme, the work of art come alive. **"Omphale ou la Tapisserie amoureuse, histoire rococo"** took him into the world of fantasy he had entered in **"La Cafetière."** Told as autobiography, the story concerned the adventures of a boy fresh from a *collège* who came to live in his uncle's pavilion while he learned the trade of *conteur fantastique.* On his wall hung a tapestry representing Hercules at the feet of Omphale. That night the lady left the tapestry to seduce the lad; she returned every evening thereafter until the boy's listlessness moved the uncle to pack away the tapestry and order the youngster home. Years later, the author found the tapestry in an antique shop, and when it was bought by an Englishman, he bowed his head in a moment of silent pity for the unsuspecting purchaser.

In **"Omphale,"** Gautier used the technique of the dream, common currency at the time, to describe a boy's education. The anecdote revealed characteristics that would become hallmarks of his brief narratives. The irony is still there, but gentler: the uncle's taste in literature was limited to *L'Epître à Zétulbé,* while the boy aspired to become a hack writer. Omphale herself preceded a long line of worldly women whom Gautier delighted in portraying in their boudoirs, dressing, undressing, or bathing. His penchant for long descriptions was now becoming more evident. The uncle's house, the pavilion, the tapestry, and the insatiable lady lent themselves to an attempt to create word pictures that could match paintings, a transformation of one medium into another.

This marriage of the bizarre and the occult with plastic prose reappeared in his next tale, **"La Morte amoureuse"** (1836). For three years a country priest named Romuald had lived a dual life, by day a conscientious curate, by night a worldly rake—even though he never left the presbytery. Romuald led a separate existence with the beautiful vampire, Clarimonde, whom he had raised from the dead with a kiss. The country pastor struggled unsuccessfully to escape Clarimonde until the abbé Sérapion disinterred her body. When holy water finally turned her corpse to dust, "une grande ruine venait de se faire audedans de moi."

"La Morte amoureuse" came close to what Poe would define as a short story, with all details arranged to produce "a single narrative effect with the greatest economy of means that is consistent with the utmost emphasis." Baudelaire, who counted this tale among Gautier's masterpieces, noted "le vertige et l'horreur du néant," an end toward which the themes converged. To this purpose the familiar figure of the country priest was transformed into the *Doppelgänger* and Romuald committed sacrilege by succumbing to the traditional *coup de foudre* at the moment of ordination. The abbé Sérapion, acting as Romuald's conscience, furnished the standard against which the priest was measured, a latter-day Tiberge, the voice of doom and the constant friend. The inevitable dream assumed the texture of a nightmare when a mysterious negro servant summoned Romuald and they flew over a desolate plain to his downfall. The themes of the schizoid personality recurred as the hero fell into the uncertainty of not knowing whether he was priest or hellion. Even the solution maintained the tone of horror as, at the witching hour, the two priests dug up the corpse and destroyed it with ritual incantation. And, true to form, Clarimonde's ghost returned to bid Romuald a sorrowful adieu.

Gautier's conception of the story as a letter from a priest to his brother involved him in the problem of handling space and time on different planes. Romuald never left the church, yet traveled over large expanses of the earth; not only a split personality, he led two lives, the drama of which took place in his mind. Hence he faced the necessity of deciding what was dream and what reality. Since Gautier believed they touched, he had to surmount the same artistic difficulties Flaubert would later handle so well in the legend of Saint Julien. But Gautier never satisfactorily solved the problem of how to express simultaneity of action or to show motion over timeless space; he had at his command only the techniques elaborated over the past, none of them suitable. Both Balzac's solution of the flashback and the romantic devices used in nightmare and horror literature proved inadequate for creating the illusions involved in shifts from the clear outlines of time to the vague, distorted shape of fluid dreams. He narrated chronologically in blocks: the *coup de foudre,* the first meeting, the fall, and the rescue, separating the sections as stages of the action. The dream quality he indicated by reiterated explanatory statements and strange events. It would be too much to expect him to solve these problems without the benefit of prior experimentation.

His drift toward exotic subjects led him to publish *Fortunio* in 1837. Musidora, a blond courtesan of great reputation, fell in love with the mysterious Fortunio, spent an idyllic day with him at his country estate, then was jilted for Soudja-Sari, a slave girl bought for three oxen.

Gautier might write to earn a living, but he did not have to like "romans à grandes prétentions," or his own brief narratives, for that matter. In a facetious preface he declared that "*Fortunio* ne prouve rien. . . . *Fortunio* est un hymne à la beauté." Gautier obviously meant to enjoy the story as he deliberately slowed the action by inserting an irrelevant section on Musidora's cat and by arguing constantly with the reader. When the courtesan capitulated almost instantaneously to the hero's well-described charms, Gautier felt it necessary to explain away any objections. Yet he complained of the long, peripatetic novels, with their great platonic passions, duels, and abductions. With his lady reader in mind, he discoursed on clothing, furniture, feminine emotions, even corsets, adding teasing comments on feminine virtue. To her he offered all the popular irrelevancies he thought she would like, even at Fortunio's expense: "Nul héros n'est plus incommode."

Actually, *Fortunio* represented an attempt by Gautier to escape from a world hostile to his conception of poetry and to the manner in which he projected his mind into the fictional world of his daydreams. The belligerent preface of *Mlle de Maupin* had not long been off the presses with its fierce condemnation of modern society. Fortunio lived the life of which Gautier approved. He had been raised in India so permissively that at fifteen he had a harem of 500 slaves. His home near Paris was luxury itself, boasting a private lake on which he and Musidora floated in amorous dalliance. Fortunio lived as his weird humor dictated, even whimsically setting Musidora's house afire and killing her servant; he was subject to no law but the exclusive ownership of what he wanted. When he finally decided to blow up his palace and return to India, he castigated France as poor, Paris as dirty. Bourgeois dress, bourgeois music, newspapers, and railroads he loathed as fit only for the undiscriminating. Gautier even included a satire on the learned savants of the Institut. When Musidora found Fortunio's papers written in a strange language, she consulted a bemused professor who thought the visiting courtesan was a duchess enamored of him after reading his treatise on Manchu punctuation.

With mockery the overriding consideration, the construction of the story suffered from a plot that consisted of a string of unrelated episodes interspersed with sarcastic irrelevancies. Moreover, Gautier indulged a taste for long plastic descriptions. The courtesans were described like Titians, the negro servant like a Veronese. Not too long out of classes under the painter Rioult, he enjoyed noting color and line, literally painting his characters with the meticulous art of his beloved Flemish artists. He lingered over Musidora rising and Musidora bathing. Fortunio's estate, Eldorado, fascinated him, though when he came to the love scene, he used one of his old tricks: "Il ne nous est plus permis de rester dans le petit salon."

His days as an angry young man were obviously fast fading. Not that he approved of the world, but life no longer permitted him the privilege of complaints. He had to write fast and often to relieve the pressure of stifling debts, but he could at least fulfill some of his wishes in stories like **"Une Nuit de Cléopâtre,"** in which a queen bored by royal loneliness was pursued by the love-struck Méïamoun. "Assurément je vais t'aimer," she greeted him. "Je te ferai tuer demain; ta vie pour une nuit."

"Une Nuit de Cléopâtre" illustrates the kind of structure Gautier came to favor: two or more almost independent scenes, each with possibilities for plastic portrayal. In his successful works he achieved a unity of effect, but the needy Gautier also made the disastrous discovery that he could attain a narrative of the desired length by stringing together a series of such segments. Thus in **"Cléopâtre"** he portrayed the queen on the Nile, in her bath, and at Méïamoun's last banquet. These pictures formed the key points of the story and permitted full descriptions of the river, the royal barge, Méïamoun, Cleopatra naked, and an Oriental feast. He gave himself full license to describe settings, customs, and clothes, particularly the last. "Nos lectrices seront peut-être curieuses. . . ."

The plot offered Gautier as much of an escape from reality as he had planned for his readers. Like Stendhal, he held in high esteem the powerful of the past who lived life fully, even violently. An arrogant elite untroubled by the petty annoyances that beset the nineteenth century, they seized great pleasures avidly. As he wrote wistfully on the grandeur of life in the ancient East, he contrasted the poverty of constitutional monarchs and the "néant de l'uniformité" to the "existences énormes" of the Pharaohs. The giants had disappeared in France, where it had become impossible even to imagine an orgy. The narrative constituted for him a kind of primitivism, a vision of happy people in happier times who could bargain for perfect happiness, even for a night, though it cost them their lives. Méïamoun shot into the queen's chamber an arrow that carried a declaration of love, then swam the Nile to escape the guards; Méïamoun prowled the grounds until he found an entrance to the palace through a water conduit that led to Cleopatra's bath. In a way, Gautier was also advising the ladies of the nineteenth century on how to act.

His desire to transpose into prose the techniques of the painter and his yearning for a great, if fictional, love led him to publish **"La Toison d'or"** (1839): Tiburce, an artist, journeyed to Antwerp where he was thunderstruck by Rubens' "Descent from the Cross," particularly the portrait of Mary Magdalene. When sixteen-year-old Gretchen fell in love with him, her heart was broken when she heard him talk to Rubens' picture. Tiburce continued to dream of Magdalene until, one day, dressing Gretchen in sixteenth-century costume, he saw a *tableau vivant*. Tiburce promptly forgot Mary Magdalene and married the young girl.

The **"Toison d'or"** was a variation of an oft-used Gautier plot. The tale rested on the quest theme, with the moral that of **"Celle-ci et Celle-là"** the treasure sought afar may be right at home. The narrative consisted of a discussion of Belgian art and architecture unhappily wedded to a love story. Tiburce, an original if lazy artist, did not find nature "true," and began a search for blond beauty which permitted Gautier to present a kind of guidebook. The love story, appended to justify the art criticism, contained all Gautier's usual mannerisms. He challenged his own choice of Gretchen. "Est-ce bien l'héroine qui convient à notre héros?" Unlike the heroines of most contemporary novels, she could not play the piano; she was not thirty years old, nor a princess. Tiburce conformed to the romantic pattern when he followed Gretchen to her door, dropped a note, and sent flowers. Gautier lectured his hero, as he had Rodolphe, on paying attention to the beauty at hand; he solved the inevitable misunderstanding with a stroke of his pen.

By 1839 Gautier had apparently given up any idea of treating short fiction respectfully. It could not measure up to the magic of poetry and it gave him only the solace of withdrawal from an angry world, a means of expressing complaints or seeking wish-fulfillment. **"L'Ame de la maison ou la Vie et la Mort d'un grillon"** (1839) reveals how badly Gautier felt life was treating him. Not only had he lost his original purity, but his illusions had vanished as practical men tramped over his soul. He retreated into daydreams of better days, to the kitchen of his uncle, a canon with whom he had lived. In this story, on winter nights he and little Maria sat by the fire listening to a cricket that conversed with them. Unfortunately, one day Jacobus Pragmater, the schoolmaster, pulled a leg off the cricket. After the canon left on a trip, no one heard of him for months until, one night, Jacobus watched the priest slide down a moonbeam into the library. The boy learned afterwards that his uncle had been killed in a fall; Maria died soon, then the cricket and Pragmater. Years later, the lad felt that he, too, had become a wounded cricket as he wrote verse and thought of Maria and what might have been.

In this short sketch, the theme of retrospective love was transformed into a kind of fairy tale. In the world of the youngsters, the cricket symbolized the soul of the house, stolen by Jacobus Pragmater. Gautier, who believed in the spirit world, introduced the uncle's ghost not only to maintain the illusion of the fairy tale but because he considered its appearance possible. Skepticism and adult cruelty, intruding on the innocence of a child's dreams, brought disaster to an entire household by destroying a happiness founded on simple belief.

The fable, however, has another meaning when read as a witness of Gautier's bitterness toward life. Gautier blamed the middle class for his having missed the glory acquired by Hugo and other members of the *cénacle*. Jacobus Pragmater, cast in the role of fatality for the fairy tale, was, as his name indicates, the materialistic bourgeois, the exponent of Voltairian doctrines who set contemporary values. A schoolmaster, Pragmater had the matter-of-fact attitude toward the magic of poetry which had brought disaster to Gautier and his friends. It was the coincidence of these two stories that gave the narrative a consistent tone, a mood of sadness that carried overtones of the frustration and disappointment that had been Gautier's lot. Like little Maria, he had lost a dream, that of leading a great poetic movement. Told in a straightforward manner, the melancholy reminiscence indicated what Gautier might have done if he had consistently taken his work seriously.

A growing compulsion to escape, a preoccupation with the occult and the mysterious, led to **"Le Chevalier double"** (1840), the story of a young knight with a split personality who finally conquered the incubus that dwelt within him. That same year, he published a *conte étranger*, titled **"Le Pied de momie,"** a first-person narration of a young man's love for the daughter of the Pharaoh Xixouthros, dead thirty centuries. Two years later, with unconscious irony, the great enemy of the middle class published **"La Mille et deuxième nuit"** in **"the Musée des familles,"** a mass-medium family magazine. "Once upon a time" young Mahmoud-Ben-Ahmed, a lazy poet, became the lover of the beautiful *péri* Ayesha, who promised to protect him from all harm. In all three tales he could turn his back on the industrial present, fly to medieval France or the East, court a Pharaoh's daughter, or be protected by a lovely fairy. In any case, the hero lived happily ever after.

He used his great skill at evoking the past when, in 1844, he returned to the serious exploitation of antiquity in **"Le Roi Candaule."** Five years after the Trojan War, King Candaule married Nyssia, daughter of the satrap Mégabaze. Candaule became so fascinated by his wife's charms that he embarrassed Gygès, captain of his guards, by discussing conjugal delights, and even ordered him to peep through the keyhole as Nyssia undressed. Unfortunately, the horrified queen saw his eyes shine and resolved to wreak vengeance for the ocular adultery. Nyssia drugged Candaule and the captain stabbed him; later, after the Delphic oracle conveniently picked him for the new ruler, Gygès married Nyssia, but nobody ever saw his wife's face.

As on other occasions, Gautier had borrowed the main lines of his narrative. Berthoud's *L'Ami de mon oncle Bertrand* had used the Candaule legend; Boissard had exhibited a *"Roi Candaule"* in the Venetian style in the salon of 1841. The combination of pictorial and written sources admirably suited Gautier's aim to transpose one art form into another. Just as the beauty of Ctésias had been a major factor in determining the direction of the plot of **"La Chaîne d'or,"** just as the hero's love for painted beauty formed the basis of **"La Toison d'or,"** now the intrigue of **"Le Roi Candaule"** pivoted on the loveliness of a queen. The regression into the distant past gave his imagination great latitude for the major scenes: the marriage, Nyssia's beauty, the betrayal, the queen's anger, her bargain with Gygès, and the murder. Of these, all but the fourth were constructed to let Gautier exercise his considerable descriptive talents. The background, the people in the streets, the wedding procession, the statuary, the palace, all received full treatment. Nyssia fascinated Gautier as much as she did Candaule. He described her preparations for bed with such obvious relish that the well-exposed Nyssia commented ironically that Gygès would soon tire of seeing her disrobe.

The plot received far less attention than the descriptions, with the characters, except for Nyssia, subordinated to the author's passion for creating effects normally produced by the visual arts. Thus, the story was fitted between a series of major descriptions, some of them expanded far beyond proportions useful to the plot. Crowd scenes, regal splendor, strange rituals, Nyssia's strip-tease, all enticed Gautier away from his purpose though they did contribute to reviving the ancient grandeur and exotic aura of the legend. Actually, the facts of the story needed this kind of prop since they consisted of such worn devices as love at first sight, a palace plot based on ambition and jealousy, and a woman's revenge.

Gautier wrought so well that the tale held together despite his readiness to play with words or indulge in irrelevant humor. He remarked on modern tragedy when Candaule decided to seek a confidant, discussed women's feet as Gygès stared goggle-eyed at the naked Nyssia. Furthermore, unlike the normal romantic hero, the captain rushed off to take a cold tub after peeping at the queen. But Gygès fell victim to events he could not control when the king forced him into the ridiculous posture of voyeur. In this world of barbaric

violence, two views of life, that of the cultured and sophisticated Candaule and that of the cloistered but savage Nyssia, created tragedy because neither could adapt to the other. Spartan aggression destroyed culture when pride in the possession of artistic perfection led Candaule to commit unpardonable blunders.

When Gautier reluctantly returned to his own times, it was only to publish **"Le Club des Hachichins"** (1846), a reminiscence of the romantics' experiments with drugs. The dream sequence not only appealed to contemporary interest in mental states, but also exploited bourgeois convictions on the conduct of artists. The participants were conveniently described as bearded men of strange behavior who arrived on the Ile Saint-Louis one foggy night to pursue their search for an artificial paradise. The initial descriptions set the atmosphere for the subsequent hallucinations and irrational states so dear to the romantics. Gautier wrote of a world without logic, beyond thought, where color and sound merged, where forms shifted fluidly in a universe without temporal or spatial references. In fact, the visions persisted until a monster released the clock hands he had immobilized.

After the **"Hachichins,"** Gautier forsook the inspiration of personal experience and hid in the long ago, the far away, or the occult. In September, 1846, he published **"Le Pavillon sur l'eau,"** a tale of the love of a Chinese boy and girl, "a quelle époque, c'est ce qu'il importe peu de savoir, les contes n'ont pas besoin d'une chronologie bien précise." Three years later, in 1849, he followed this with a children's story, **"L'Enfant aux souliers de pain."** "Ecoutez cette historie que les grand'mères d'Allemagne content à leurs petits enfants."

The old touch was missing from these tales, obviously potboilers, but it reappeared in **"Arria Marcella, souvenir de Pompeï"** (1852), a curious story involving the same kind of retrospective love he portrayed in **"La Cafetière"** and **"Omphale."** Young Octavien had gone to Pompeii in search of a dream. As he wandered in the moonlight, a delighted Octavien slipped back through time to 79 A.D. to find a beautiful girl whose voluptuous bosom convinced him she was the woman he sought. Invited to Arria Marcella's home, he made passionate love until the girl's father, bearing a cross, made her vanish as the Angelus rang out. Octavien later returned to Pompeii, but never found Arria again.

Gautier cleverly adapted the device of the story within a story to present a young tourist at Pompeii where, as Octavien explained, the truly passionate could make the dead relive outside of time and space. "Dans ce monde où je flotte invisible. . . . En effet, rien ne meurt, tout existe toujours." The world about him was filled with phantoms: "La figuration matérielle ne disparaît que pour les regards vulgaries, et les spectres qui s'en détachent peuplent l'infini." A belief in spirits and the ultimate conquest of time bound the inner story to the outer.

The last days of Pompeii, during the reign of Titus, seemed happy ones to Gautier: *Hic habitat felicitas.* The colorist in him took over in the three sections that constitute the inner story: Pompeii alive, Arria at the play, Arria on her couch. Inspired by the picture of the city which Guérin had exhibited in the Salon of 1841, Gautier painted in prose; incidents were pushed aside in favor of descriptions, and the plot moved along hastily once the picture possibilities had been exhausted. The world into which Octavien passed grew out of Gautier's emotional primitivism. Long ago and far away people lived grandly, loved passionately, and respected the arts. The moral of his fable pointed out that Christianity had ruined a perfection the modern age could not even imagine. The theme of the fated love, the quick invitation more quickly accepted, the instant seduction, the conventional old man with his more conventional curse, all these clichés mattered little to Gautier; he wanted only to establish the dimensions of an era into which he could have fitted. The plot served only to provide space for his mural, while the characters remained faceless stereotypes.

As his debts piled up, Gautier forced an overworked pen to write *Avatar* and *Jettatura* (1856), his last two tales, which he expanded into *feuilletons* by complicating the plot. He abandoned any thought of form for a narrative adjusted to the space requirements of a newspaper. Full of *feuilletoniste* tricks, dreams, superstitions, and improbable events, these tales became a succession of "chapters" arranged like the traditional "cliff-hanger." It was a sad close to a career in short fiction that had once seemed so promising.

Gautier's success in brief fiction came despite his religion of verse and, paradoxically, because of it. The poet in him could not have cared less for plots or character delineation. His heroes resemble Gautier or his friends, projections that provided ready-made personalities. Generally speaking, they represented his own sentiments, were satisfied with a restricted life, and dreamt of a great love. The stories coalesced around the descriptions, and his plots became a succession of loosely connected scenes, each of which provided plastic possibilities. The major portion of his work, then, depended on color, not controlled form; he worked with silhouettes rather than in clearly defined relief, translating the visual into the written. As a result, most of his narratives lack proportion and concision. Technical distinctions seemed to mean little to him, since *Avatar* and *Jettatura* were first labeled *contes,* later *romans.* Despite this, Gautier stands forth as one of the earliest to construct a formal short story. In the **"Nuit de Cléopâtre," "La Cafetière,"** and **"Le Roi Candaule,"** he arranged episode with a sense of perspective and carefully regulated tone and emphasis; in

"Arria Marcella" he came to an understanding of the potentialities and limitations of short fiction. Along with Mérimée and, to some extent, Musset, Gautier helped short fiction shed its burden of moralizing. The implicit took over from the explicit and the genre was permitted to speak for itself. Content helped shape form, with the result that, once again, after Mérimée, he pointed out that the brief narrative might function as more than a frame for an anecdote. It could, his work indicated, serve to create the sketch, the portrait, and, most important of all, the formal short story.

Arthur Ransome praises Gautier's art:

When [Gautier] is at his best; when he is not projecting young men with a mathematical freedom of morals into a Western society; in those moments, strung like rare beads along the life of an artist, when he is most himself, we hear clipped feathers beat against the bars. . . . As the Christian fingers his crucifix and is able to kneel upon the footsteps of the throne, so Gautier found talismans to help his dreams to their desires. A mummy's foot, a marble hand took him to the times he loved, or half revealed the perfections that reality refused. A curiosity shop was a postern-gate to Heaven, and a merchant of antiquities held St. Peter's keys.

His art is that of making his dreams come true. He is not an observer of life, like Richardson, Fielding, or De Maupassant. He does not copy the surface of contemporary existence; but cuts away all but passion, and clothes that in symbols whose strangeness disentangled it and helped him to make it real.

Arthur Ransome, in Stories by Théophile Gautier, *translated by Lafcadio Hearn, T.C. & E.C. Jack, 1908.*

Albert B. Smith (essay date 1977)

SOURCE: "The Function of the Fantastic," in *Theophile Gautier and the Fantastic,* Romance Monographs, Inc., 1977, pp. 118-38.

[*In the excerpt that follows, Smith explores the fantastic in Gautier's works, including his use of various phenomena such as impossible events, dreams and hallucinations, and heightened expressivity.*]

The fantastic in most of Gautier's works is based upon the assumption of two worlds, reality and an "other" order: Heaven, the after-life, a fairy kingdom. *Spirite* posits, in opposition to the ordinary world, what is variously called "l'extramonde," "le monde des esprits," "le monde invisible," and "l'autre vie." Clarimonde, in **"La Morte amoureuse,"** returns among the living from the world of the dead (*Contes fantastiques,* pp. 103-104). In *La Comédie de la mort,* the speaker journeys into the after-life, where he converses with the spirits of famous literary and historical personages. The peris exist in their fairy paradise, invisible to ordinary human perception, coming from time to time to mingle among mortals. The narrator of **"Arria Marcella"** suggests the existence of an ideal universe outside time and space, where all that has ever existed lives on, waiting to be evoked by sensitive men: "En effet, rien ne meurt, tout existe toujours; nulle force ne peut anéantir ce qui fut une fois. Toute action, toute parole, toute forme, toute pensée tombée dans l'océan universel des choses y produit des cercles qui vont s'élargissant jusqu'aux confins de l'éternité. La figuration matérielle ne disparaît que pour les regards vulgaires et les spectres qui s'en détachent peuplent l'infini. . . . Quelques esprits passionnés et puissants ont pu amener à eux des siècles écoulés en apparence, et faire revivre des personnages morts pour tous" (*CF,* pp. 245-246).

This concept of two worlds serves Gautier in several ways. Whatever the specific character of the other reality in a given work, it usually functions as an opposition to the ordinary reality in which the hero exists, and it shows itself to be a desirable opposite in his view. Venice in **"La Morte amoureuse"** is the diametric contrary of Romuald's country parish, representing all of the material pleasures in life which the priestly order cannot provide. The Muslim paradise shown at the end of **"La Péri"** symbolizes the final satisfaction of Achmet's desires for happiness through ideal pleasures. Behind the hero are the walls of his prison, the last earthly obstacle to his felicity, itself a thoroughly appropriate emblem of the tangible world. Similarly, the extrahuman sphere evoked in *Spirite* represents the happiness enjoyed by the spiritually oriented individual who has broken free of materialism. Spirite describes her passage into this Heaven thus:

> 'Des mots humains ne peuvent rendre la sensation d'une âme qui, délivrée de sa prison corporelle, passe de cette vie dans l'autre, du temps dans l'éternité et du fini dans l'infini. Mon corps immobile et déjà revêtu de cette blancheur mate, livrée de la mort, gisait sur sa couche funèbre . . . et j'en étais aussi détachée que le papillon peut l'être de la chrysalide, coque vide, dépouille informe qu'il abandonne pour ouvrir ses jeunes ailes à la lumière inconnue et soudainement révélée. A une intermittence d'ombre profonde avait succédé un éblouissement de splendeurs, un élargissement d'horizons, une disparition de toute limite et de tout obstacle, qui m'enivraient d'une joie indicible. Des explosions de sens nouveaux me faisaient comprendre les mystères impénétrables à la pensée et aux organes terrestres. Débarrassée de cette argile soumise aux lois de la pesanteur, qui m'alourdissaient naguère encore, je m'élançais avec une alacrité folle dans l'insondable éther'. (p. 159)[2]

The conception of two different orders also functions to accentuate the strength or the quality of the hero's desire. The difficulty of passage from one world to the other is overcome only as his desire is sufficiently strong. Clarimonde, for example, emphasizes that she met almost insurmountable obstacles as she returned from the dead; if it had not been for Romuald's intense longing for her, she would not have succeeded in crossing back into life (*CF,* p. 104). Arria Marcella relates directly to the strength of Octavien's love her ability to overcome the great distance that separates her world from his: "'Oh! lorsque tu t'es arrêté aux Studii à contempler le morceau de boue durcie qui conserve ma forme . . . et que ta pensée s'est élancée ardemment vers moi, mon âme l'a senti dans ce monde où je flotte invisible pour les yeux grossiers; la croyance fait le dieu, et l'amour fait la femme. On n'est véritablement morte que quand on n'est plus aimée, ton désir m'a rendu la vie, la puissante évocation de ton cœur a supprimé les distances qui nous séparaient'" (*CF,* p. 245). That this resurrection of a desired object is the only success which Octavien enjoys in a long history of attempts further confirms the strength of his passion at the moment of his visit to Pompeii. His inability afterwards to revive Arria Marcella again suggests that something has weakened his desire. One is led to see that force as the gloomy Christianity which, according to the story, pervades modern morality.

Elsewhere the other reality serves to emphasize the dangers of certain approaches to happiness. The underwater kingdom in **"L'Ondine et le pêcheur"** is, implicitly, a place where the fisher will be destroyed (*Poésies Complètes,* II, 244-245). The spirit world of the *wilis* in **"Giselle,"** which symbolizes full surrender to the imagination, is also a dangerous place. Despite the charms which Duke Albert sees in it—because of Giselle—the reader understands that to enter there means to lose one's sanity.

The world of the dead in *La Comédie de la mort* symbolizes not only physical death but also the death of men's hopes and expectations. It and its inhabitants give material form to a disenchantment depicted in the poem as universal. Gautier's narrator explicitly invites such an understanding of the afterlife in the poem. Before introducing Faust, Don Juan, and Napoleon, he emphasizes that death is manifold:

> Il est des trépassés de diverse nature:
> Aux uns la puanteur avec la pourriture,
>   Le palpable néant,
> L'horreur et le dégoût, l'ombre profonde et
>   noire,
> Et le cercueil avide entr'ouvrant sa mâchoire
>   Comme un monstre béant;
>
> Aux autres, que l'on voit sans qu'on s'en
>   épouvante
> Passer et repasser dans la cité vivante
>   Sous leur linceul de chair,
> L'invisible néant, la mort intérieure

Que personne ne sait, que personne ne pleure
   Même votre plus cher.

. . . . .

Toute âme est un sépulcre où gisent mille
   choses;
Des cadavres hideux dans des figures roses
   Dorment ensevelis.
On retrouve toujours les larmes sous le rire,
Les morts sous les vivants, et l'homme est à
   vrai dire
   Une Nécropolis. (*PC,* II, 23-25)

The three figures whom Gautier introduces represent both types of death. Each of the three is dead physically and spiritually. Their laments are concerned with their respective failures to reach particular goals in which they envisioned happiness and with the impossibility of changing what was. Even the service which they now perform in speaking from the grave is vain; all they can do is exemplify the inevitable death of the body and profess a sad lesson on the prospects of human expectations. The fantastic element—spirits addressing man from beyond the tomb—serves this purpose adequately. Faust, Don Juan, and Napoleon could not perform their function with equal effectiveness if they were speaking from another condition.

Another category of phenomena includes various kinds of impossible or strange events. Closely related to the concept of two worlds are events characterized by displacement in time and space. Some heroes, like the narrator of **"Le Pied de momie,"** are mysteriously transported back to a period in antiquity. What they find is a culture far superior to their own, chiefly because of its view of life. The paganism discovered by Octavien in **"Arria Marcella"** and by Konrad in **"La Statue amoureuse"** is infinitely more attractive than the real world from which they have come. The fantastic journey functions, then, to put the protagonist into a situation where he can have the immediate experience of an ethos radically different from that which prevails in his own day. The voyage allows Gautier to contrast the two worlds in such a way that he can economically favor antiquity while emphasizing the shortcomings of modern Western culture. It furthermore gives him a means of suggesting the great distance which separates the two outlooks. The hero is able to bridge the gap only by a miraculous upset in natural law; yet his ability to prolong or to repeat his visit to the ancient world is severely restricted. Though the protagonist may not understand fully, the reader recognizes, by Gautier's exploitation of fantastic event, that escape to a better world is in the long run impossible.

The fantastic journey in other works serves to suggest psychological distance. Albertus' voyage with Véronique from Leiden to the witches' sabbath in Rome implies the moral deterioration that has taken place within him. Not only do we see in the demons of the celebration the nightmarish aspects of sensuality and of the knowledge that physical beauty is ephemeral; but we see also that Albertus' return to Leiden is impossible. His submission to material pleasures has cut him off irrevocably from the satisfactions offered by art. In **"La Morte amoureuse"** the journeys which Romuald repeatedly makes to Venice underscore the distance which separates his desires from his duty. Venice is at a great distance from his parish, as the life which he enjoys with Clarimonde is radically different from his barren life as a priest.

The requirements which Gautier sets for travel from one order to another always have meaning. Both in **"La Péri"** and in *Spirite,* unreal beings from invisible worlds outside the material universe descend to reveal themselves to the respective heroes. The latter, on the other hand, are for a time incapable of rising to the domain of the spirits. Gautier states clearly the reasons for this frustrating weakness in his protagonists: both are weighed down by their materiality. Attachment to matter thus shows itself to be a major obstacle to the enjoyment of ideal pleasures. Moreover, the radical means which Gautier shows to be necessary to achieve this goal only accentuate the difficulty which he recognizes is involved in severing one's ties to the materialistic disposition.

Dream and hallucination also figure among the fantastic events which Gautier employs symbolically. Despite Caillois' and others' discontent with the inclusion of such phenomena within the fantastic, these are common not only in Romantic literature but also in later examples of the fantastic. Gautier introduces both dreams and hallucinations caused by drugs into a number of works. Both are related to the concept of two worlds and to displacement in time and space. In dreams, protagonists find themselves transported to a state substantially different from—and preferable to—reality which is their ordinary field of perception. They may find themselves transplanted in time, as in **"Le Pied de momie,"** or in space, as in **"La Morte amoureuse"**. What is important is that they experience in their dream state pleasures which ordinary reality does not afford them. When, in his dream, Romuald flees to Venice with the resurrected Clarimonde, he expresses his delight unequivocally: "Jamais je n'avais éprouvé un bonheur aussi vif. J'avais oublié tout en ce moment-là, et je ne me souvenais pas plus d'avoir été prêtre que de ce que j'avais fait dans le sein de ma mère" (*CF*, p. 108). Achmet's opium dream gives him precisely the perception that he has desired and that reality cannot grant him (*Théâtre: mystère, comédies et ballets,* p. 385). These pleasures do not, it is true, necessarily depend upon the fact that they are dreamed. It is their character that is important.

In **"Omphale,"** the narrator's satisfactions are mainly erotic, while in *Spirite* they are of a noumenal nature. Nevertheless, the dream appears as an effective device for representing these superior pleasures and especially for contrasting preferred and actual realities.

Dreams also underscore aspects important for a better understanding of the problems encountered by certain heroes. In **"La Morte amoureuse"**, Romuald's allusions to dream point up the seriousness of his emotional state. He recognizes that Clarimonde's first visit to him is a dream (*CF,* pp. 102, 106). Afterwards, however, he is unable to distinguish between his life as a priest and the pleasurable existence which he leads in Venice: "A dater de cette nuit, ma nature s'est en quelque sorte dédoublée, et il y eut en moi deux hommes dont l'un ne connaissait pas l'autre. Tantôt je me croyais un prêtre qui rêvait chaque soir qu'il était gentilhomme, tantôt un gentilhomme qui rêvait qu'il était prêtre. Je ne pouvais plus distinguer le songe de la veille, et je ne savais où commençait la réalité et où finissait l'illusion" (*CF,* p. 108). It is plain that he is near insanity, and the change in his perception of his dreams indicates just how far out of touch with reality he has gone.[3]

In addition to the brief but important opium-dream episode in **"La Péri"**, Gautier presents two cases of hallucinations caused by drugs: **"La Pipe d'opium"** and **"Le Club des hachichins"**. It might appear from a superficial reading that these reports of perceptions experienced under the influence of hallucinogens are gratuitous, without any function. Closer study reveals that they, like the dream accounts, serve a clear purpose. The ghost in **"La Pipe d'opium"** is scarcely a random impression. She is what she is—the spirit of an adolescent who desires to return to life—because she symbolizes a particular brand of materialism and because, by pointing up her youth, Gautier can make us regret more deeply the uncertainty of existence. His account is but another form of the *carpe rosam* theme.

The character and the order of the hallucinations which the narrator of **"Le Club des hachichins"** experiences invite the inference that this narrative, too, is more than the simple inventory of images perceived under the influence of a drug. Once we have understood what the expectations regarding the hallucinogen are, we see that the account has meaning. It is the function of the digression on the Old Man of the Mountain to emphasize the particular pleasure promised by the drug: such a sense of delight in release from corporality that one can scarcely bear to return to reality and is even willing to commit the most violent crimes to acquire the means for another escape (*CF,* pp. 192-193). If the narrator himself is seeking such ideal pleasures, he gains, according to **"Le Club des hachichins"**, only brief satisfaction. We have already considered the forms assumed by the images in his state of hallucination: he

becomes trapped in that very matter from which he is attempting to escape. The particular imagery functions to convey a message: the pursuit of ideal pleasures by means of drugs is ultimately unproductive, because these do not after all deliver the release which the idealist requires.

Another kind of fantastic event is the heightened ability to express oneself or to communicate with others. The ghost in **"La Pipe d'opium"** speaks in verse of marvelous beauty and expressivity; and, when words no longer serve to render her thought, she adds music (*CF,* p. 130). The narrator of **"La Cafetière"** enjoys perfect communication without the need of words: "Je comprenais ce que nul homme ne peut comprendre, les pensées d'Angéla se révélant à moi sans qu'elle eût besoin de parler; car son âme brillait dans son corps comme une lampe d'albâtre, et les rayons partis de sa poitrine perçaient la mienne de part en part" (*CF,* p. 19). The soul of the dead child in **"L'Enfant aux souliers de pain"** communicates its sadness to the mother through dreams (*Romans et contes,* pp. 379-380, 380-381).

In fact, it is for the most part during dreams that cases of superior communication and perception take place.[4] In **"Le Pied de momie,"** the narrator establishes a clear relationship between dream and intellectual illumination: "mon obscurité intellectuelle s'éclaira, les songes commencèrent à m'effleurer de leur vol silencieux" (*CF,* p. 155). Similarly, the narrator of *Spirite* emphasizes the superior perception which comes with sleep, though he is quick to state that even sleep does not afford one the release form materiality necessary for perfect apprehension of the spirit world. Before *Spirite,* then, dream represents one of several paths to full happiness. In the context of Gautier's *nouvelle fantastique* it is situated low on the scale of means for the enjoyment of ideal pleasures.

A further justification lies in the conditions under which superior communication, perception, and expressivity are possible. One recognizes, in considering Gautier's fantastic works, that heightened mental capacity never occurs when the protagonist is carrying on his ordinary affairs. He is always in a special state of release from his surroundings. This condition underscores a fact with which we are already acquainted, that ordinary reality is incapable of yielding the ingredients of happiness. In addition, the brevity of the moments of release calls attention to yet another condition of life which prevents happiness, the limited capability of the imagination to provide extended pleasure.

Superior expressivity usually belongs to spirits, and this also has meaning. While the case of Carlotta in **"La Pipe d'opium"** is ambiguous, the justification for Spirite is plain. Her ability to express the ineffable is directly attendant on her spiritualization. Malivert gains in expressive capacity as he becomes more spiritualized. We can scarcely read these cases as anything other than indications that expressive genius as well as heightened perceptiveness is intimately bound to the degree of one's spirituality.

In several instances, communication is possible between protagonist and spirit, but contact cannot readily be achieved. Duke Albert is unable to seize and hold the ghost of Giselle. Likewise, Achmet can perceive the peri; yet, when he attempts to touch her, he fails. Malivert, too, can see Spirite and communicate with her, but he cannot join her in the supra-natural world. How we are to understand this problem is explained by Spirite: she emphasizes that Malivert is unable to reach her because he is still bound to the real world. In the end, we see that he must give up all materiality in order to be united with her in Heaven.

The doubling of a character's existence or personality occurs in several of Gautier's fantastic works. Romuald leads two lives, each standing in sharp contrast to the other. Count Oluf, in **"Le Chevalier double,"** has a double character, his evil side represented as a physically powerful twin. Doctor Cherbonneau in *Avatar,* makes it possible for Octave de Saville's soul to reside in the body of Olaf Labinski. Guy de Malivert, once he is introduced to ideal realities, leads a double life, perfunctorily meeting the demands of society while privately attentive to his spiritual development.

Dédoublement serves a variety of functions. It may emphasize the need for a proper approach in the pursuit of happiness. Romuald loses Clarimonde because he cannot make a decisive choice in her favor. We understand in reading the account of his condition that its double nature is a clear sign of his lack of single-mindedness. Malivert's double life, on the other hand, represents progress in spirituality. His is a dynamic *dédoublement.* At the beginning of his story, we see him unaware of the spirit world. Later, when he is convinced of its existence and is seeking to come closer to it, his double life begins. But its components never reach a state of intolerable deadlock such as characterizes Romuald's condition. As Malivert gives less and less attention to the real world, he grows spiritually, so that in the end, with his death and full spiritualization, he achieves abundant felicity. It is this very shift from materialism to spirituality that constitutes the basic action of Gautier's *nouvelle fantastique.*

Count Oluf, in **"Le Chevalier double,"** cannot have Brenda's promise of marriage until he has overcome his twin. His victory over the Knight of the Red Star marks his suppression of the malevolence in his personality. The message of the story is that happiness depends upon psychological unity. *Dédoublement* functions to characterize graphically the antagonistic factors which split Count Oluf's soul and which threaten his chances to be happy.

In *Avatar,* a peculiar kind of *dédoublement* is evident in Octave de Saville's disguise. Rather than appearing as two characters in one person, he maintains his essential nature despite the change in his physical form. His violent passion, deriving from his soul, continues to show in his eyes. Prascovie recognizes immediately that the personality moving her husband's body is bent solely on physical pleasure, which is a profanation (*RC,* pp. 97-98). Her rejection of the disguised Octave confirms that the approach which he takes to happiness is misguided.

Dédoublement sometimes serves to suggest the gravity of the hero's mental state. Taken in a strictly clinical sense, Romuald's double existence reflects a very serious psychic condition. He reports in retrospect that he had reached a point where, in fact, he was no longer able to distinguish reality from illusion. A bit more time and he would have been schizophrenic. Gautier's representation of the pain which Romuald experiences in liberating himself from his intolerable situation likewise indicates its seriousness. Father Sérapion's destruction of Clarimonde has the desired result of separating Romuald from his worldly twin, but for the young priest the experience is shattering. As Gautier has him describe the event, he felt a great inner collapse: his materialism was thus profound, and the tone of his narration suggests that, after years, he questions whether salvation was worth the price he paid.

Count Oluf's struggle to overcome his evil twin is not dissimilar. He feels not only the blows which the Knight of the Red Star inflicts on him but also those which he himself strikes. By this combat between Oluf and his double, Gautier accentuates what pain accompanies any effort to achieve psychological unity.

Fantastic beings encountered by Gautier's protagonists are no less important for meaning than the impossible events which occur. Gautier introduces a variety of such personages: figures from paintings and tapestries, statues, decorative objects, literary characters, all of which become inexplicably animated; persons resurrected from the dead; unreal beings—Satan and other demons, ghosts, Heavenly spirits, fairies—which appear among men; vampires; and a *jettatore,* a possessor of the evil eye. It is not necessary to study each case; a few examples will serve to demonstrate how Gautier uses these personages for symbolic purposes. I take examples from each of the categories listed above.

It is chiefly the nature of the figures animated that has importance. In **"Omphale,"** the likeness which steps down from the tapestry in the narrator's room is the Marquise Antoinette de T***, a beauty from the time of the Regency. Even in the tapestry her physical charms are exciting, and her pose hints that her character has equal appeal: "Vraiment elle était charmante! Sa tête se rejetait en arrière d'un air de crânerie adorable; sa bouche se plissait et faisait une délicieuse petite moue; sa narine était légèrement gonflée, ses joues un peu allumées; un *assassin,* savamment placé, en rehaussait l'éclat d'une façon merveilleuse . . ." (**CF,** p. 67). One expects from the original of this facsimile a self-confident woman, sure of her beauty and of her magnetic power over men. As Omphale, she cannot fail to subjugate even the strongest male. She in no way betrays the promise of the tapestry. She easily charms the adolescent narrator, who is delighted to submit (**CF,** p. 71).

In the main, it is her character that makes her attractive. When she speaks, the narrator is struck immediately by the delicate *grasseyement* affected by Regency society. The delicately teasing nature and the elegant manner of the upper class during the early eighteenth century are evident in her conversation. Her need for social exchange is plain in her account of the efforts which she has made to capture the young man's attention. Finally, her nonchalant sophistication in matters of love captivates the narrator so thoroughly that he can think of nothing beyond their nocturnal meetings (**CF,** pp. 70-74, et passim).

The action of "**Omphale**" takes place in a century-old *pavillon* belonging to the narrator's uncle, so that everything in the encounter between the youth and the Marquise de T*** has a relationship to the Regency. We see in Antoinette the charm of the Regency spirit. Her function is to personify that spirit, a highly refined and sophisticated form of materialism. The narrator's reactions to the attractive woman guide our own. With him we are led to appreciate the attractiveness of the Regency outlook; and with him, too, we are directed to regret the irrevocable loss of that spirit, due to the changes in attitude and morality brought about in the course of time and symbolized by the uncle's removal of the tapestry to the attic storeroom.

Similar to the figures animated are personages resurrected from the dead: Angéla, in "**La Cafetière**"; Clarimonde; Princess Hermonthis, in "**Le Pied de momie**"; and Arria Marcella. The four women who seem to come back to life all symbolize a reality which the protagonist finds far more alluring than the world in which he exists. Angéla, like Omphale, has a relationship to the Regency, though in "**La Cafetière**" the connection is not emphasized. More important appear the attraction which the narrator feels toward her because of her delicate beauty and the correspondence which he senses between them. The sense of release from the real world which constitutes a major part of his happiness suggests the sharp division between the kind of pleasures which Angéla represents and the limited potential of the reality around him. The grief which

he experiences on learning that he cannot be reunited with the source of his joy confirms the antagonism. Angéla defines and at the same time gives an affective charge to both sides of this opposition.

It is not necessary to go into detail concerning Clarimonde, Hermonthis, and Arria Marcella. Each functions like Angéla, to personify a particular kind of reality represented as preferable to that in which the protagonist is constrained to exist. We need only to recognize again the point emphasized in regard to "**Omphale,**" that these resurrected women symbolize not merely beauty but also a *spirit,* an outlook on life which unquestionably reflects attraction to physical charm but which is far broader. The value of each one lies partly in her adequacy as a symbol of all the elements which make up the particular spirit which she represents.

Equally important is the fantastic character of each woman. Without the invention of Arria Marcella, for example, Gautier would not have been able to express so fully and so dramatically as he did the satisfactions conceived in paganism. Nor would he have been able to show so graphically and so palpably the futility, in the contemporary world, of seeking to resurrect the pagan spirit.

The fantastic manner in which two of these heroines are resurrected shows particular expressive value. Both Clarimonde and Arria Marcella come back to life because of the strength of the respective protagonists' desire. Given new life by Romuald's kiss, the courtesan explains to him that she died from despair that he would never come to her (**CF,** p. 99), and she emphasizes that her resurrection is directly attributable to his love (**CF,** p. 104). Arria Marcella is no different: Octavien's passion, like Romuald's, brings her back to life (**CF,** p. 245). She begs him to embrace her and to envelop her in his warm breath, because she is cold for having remained so long without love (**CF,** p. 246). We may also include here the Venus of "**La Statue amoureuse,**" who represents a special case. She at first appears as a statue; but, as Konrad's passion increases, she takes on life, brought out of her cold oblivion by love. When it is at last evident that Konrad has fallen back under the influence of Christianity, she gradually resumes her inanimate form: "Vénus, qui n'est plus aimée, pâlit; le marbre la reprend, elle devient immobile et l'ermite arrache de son doigt pétrifié l'anneau que Konrad lui avait donné dans un moment de folie et d'amour" (Emile Bergerat, *Théophile Gautier: entretiens, souvenirs et correspondance,* préface de Edmond de Goncourt, 1879, p. 221). The fantastic manner in which these spirits exist and are resurrected thus also has symbolic value. Representing them as having lived on, in a state of cold suspension, Gautier suggests that, while they have the potential to regain their former prestige, Western men have for the most part forgotten the spirit which they represent. Yet, when a modern experiences a strong enough love for that spirit, they can be resurrected. Their survival is brief, however; an ascetic form of Christianity now prevails, ever on guard to see that modern materialists do not enjoy the satisfactions which they seek. The fantastic form by which each woman loses her life a second time is a commanding invitation to view with regret the vulnerability of a certain kind of materialism and the power of those modern forces which seek to counteract its allurements.

Though vampirism and evil eyes are not frequent among Gautier's fantastic personages, the few cases which we find are particularly appropriate. Gautier might have chosen to depict Clarimonde, for example, simply as an extraordinarily beautiful woman resurrected by Romuald's desire. Yet he made her also a vampire. A reasonable explanation is that he wished to indicate by this element of her nature the very physical threat which attends the pursuit of sensuality and worldliness. She will slowly but surely drain away Romuald's blood. She represents the increasing physical demands placed upon the individual seeking full sensual pleasure.[5]

Clarimonde's nature as a vampire functions further to demonstrate the intensity of Romuald's passion. Though he recognizes immediately the mortal dangers of remaining with her, he is willing, nay, eager to give his very life to preserve her health and vitality. His is scarcely a faint passion. Not only does it cause him for a time to abandon his chances for salvation; it also causes him to forego his physical well-being, sure sign that desire has for a time taken full control of his reason.

Gautier's representation of an evil eye in *Jettatura* is no more gratuitous than his use of the vampire motif in **"La Morte amoureuse."** Paul d'Aspremont's nature, too, must be seen as symbolic. The evil-eye here represents the short-coming of the visual orientation—and, more broadly, of materialism in general—as a means to achieve happiness. When d'Aspremont himself at last recognizes that his eyes are causing Alicia Ward to decline, he gladly gives up his sight to save her, but not before enjoying a last—and mortal—look at his fiancée. He loses her forever, all because he cannot resist the power of his desire to see. In *Jettatura*, the eye is indeed evil. D'Aspremont's subjection to sight demonstrates the error of materialism in the pursuit of happiness which, if we understand Alicia Ward's nature correctly, is spiritual in character.

Gautier introduces a variety of unreal beings in his fantastic works; devils, ghosts, and fairies, to mention the most frequent. These, as well as certain "real" personages, may have miraculous powers. The peri, for example, bridges the gap which separates her fairyland from the real world. The rat-catcher in *Le Preneur de rats de Hameln* is able, with his musical ability, to control the actions of humans and animals. Santa-Croce, in *Gemma,* has the skill to magnetize others, while Doctor Cherbonneau, in **Avatar,** possesses the Indian formula which gives him power over human souls. In addition, certain unreal beings may carry objects which possess magic virtues. Whenever Achmet kisses the star in the magic bouquet left him by the peri, he can cause her to re-appear. Venus, in **"La Statue amoureuse,"** uses her magic cestus to hold Konrad, while her adversary, the priest, employs a rosary to draw the artist under his Christian influence.

Personages, whether real or un-real, and objects may function for the good or harm of the protagonist. The *wilis* in "Giselle" lead unsuspecting men to their death. Spirite, on the other hand, seeks to guide Malivert to everlasting felicity in Heaven. Cherbonneau is eager to serve the cause of Octave de Saville's passion for Prascovie Labinska.

Such personages, with their extraordinary powers, also function symbolically in Gautier's fantastic works. Each has his own purpose. Véronique, as we know, is an ugly witch in the service of Satan. To lead men to perdition, she magically assumes incomparable beauty. So, in **"Albertus,"** appearances are deceptive. The hero unfortunately discovers this truth too late. By the time he recognizes Véronique for what she really is, he has lost all chances for salvation. We learn, too, that beauty is ephemeral. No sooner has Albertus reached the most intense erotic satisfaction with Véronique than he sees her resume her natural ugliness. The witch thus serves a double function: to underscore the transitoriness of beauty, and to emphasize the dangers of sensuality.

It would have been difficult for Gautier to express in fictional form the desirability of the spiritual orientation in the pursuit of happiness other than by introducing such a fantastic personage as he does in *Spirite*. He might have found other means, but their affective value would have been inferior. In her dictation to Malivert, Spirite reports her passage from the real world into the realm of the spirits. She first realizes that she is absolutely free, released from all restraints. She immediately gains a new, intuitive comprehension of phenomena, Heavenly and earthly, so that she understands the universal harmony and the presence of the Divinity in man. She feels only delight: "'Je lisais à livre ouvert dans ce poème de Dieu qui a pour lettres des soleils. Que ne m'est-il permis de vous en expliquer quelques pages! mais vous vivez encore parmi les ténèbres inférieures, et vos yeux s'aveugleraient à ces clartés fulgurantes'" (p. 162). She is able to enjoy such delights, according to the narrative, only because she is a spirit. Malivert, on the other hand, must wait, until he too can die. We know what satisfactions are in store for him, however, because Spirite has already enjoyed them. Gautier uses his heroine both to suggest the happiness to be enjoyed through the spiritual orientation and to indicate what this orientation requires: full abandonment of materialism and materialistic instincts.

Certain individuals connected with Christianity also possess powers not explicable on empirical grounds. Father Sérapion of **"La Morte amoureuse"** knows what miraculous means are necessary to destroy vampires and he employs them zealously to save Romuald. After opening Clarimonde's tomb, he sprinkles holy water over her body and her coffin, then makes the sign of the cross. No sooner has he performed these acts than her body turns to dust (*CF*, p. 116). In **"Arria Marcella,"** Arrius Diomèdes pronounces an exorcistic formula which reduces his daughter to ashes (*CF*, pp. 248-249). The hermit in **"La Statue amoureuse"** uses a miraculous rosary to dominate Konrad. Just as the artist is about to surrender wholly to paganism, the priest arrives, encircles Konrad in the rosary, and leads him back into an outlook tolerable to the Church and to modern men.

It is immediately evident that the three works have common features. The protagonists discover sources of happiness which, in their appeal to materialism, are inadmissible to the Church as represented in the fantastic works. The representatives of the Christian outlook view the materialistic approach to happiness as the work of Satan, and they are willing to take extreme measures to save the heroes' souls. By the miraculous means which they employ they succeed in separating the protagonists from the sources of their happiness forever. The Christians represent a force which stands in opposition to that materialism which seeks happiness through immediate pleasure in the senses.[6] In depicting them as unsympathetic, at times terrifying, Gautier leads us to see Christianity as offensive. The regret which we experience at each hero's loss is thus accompanied by a feeling of antipathy toward the force frustrating his happiness.

The representatives of Christianity, then, like the women who promise happiness, have symbolic value. They stand for an outlook that receives little favor in Gautier's fantastic works. It is not without significance that, even in *Spirite*, Christianity has no place. Gautier chooses as Malivert's spiritual guide not a priest but the Baron de Féroë, a man who has no ties to the institutional Church and who seeks rather in Illuminism the satisfactions which his soul requires.

Notes

. . . . .

[2] Gautier uses the "other" world in the opposite way in *"La Pipe d'opium"* Death to the ghost of the young dancer represents an immobile eternity, while life holds a treasure of satisfactions waiting to be enjoyed (*CF*, p. 130). Here the accent is on material pleasures, so it

is natural that Gautier has the ghost attempt to re-enter the real world.

[3] Though "Onuphrius" does not, in my opinion, figure among Gautier's fantastic works, the use of dream in this narrative deserves mention. The purpose of the long dream sequence is clear: after a particularly upsetting experience which he views as the work of the devil, Onuphrius returns home and collapses on his sofa: "son sommeil était agité; le cauchemar lui avait mis le genou sur l'estomac. Il fit une multitude de rêves incohérents, monstrueux, *qui ne contribuèrent pas peu à déranger sa raison déjà ébranlée*" (*CF*, p. 40; italics mine). The nightmare serves not only to unhinge Onuphrius further but also, already at an early stage in the narrative, to emphasize that he, too, is fast losing whatever grip he has had on reality up to this time.

Certain elements in the dream serve, in addition, a picaresque purpose. At one point in the nightmare, Onuphrius' soul, detached from his body, floats through Paris, visiting different houses: "'je montai, je montai, regardant aux vitres des mansardes des grisettes qui se levaient et faisaient leur toilette, me servant des cheminées comme des tubes acoustiques pour entendre ce qu'on disait dans les appartements. Je dois dire que je ne vis rien de bien beau, et que je ne recueillis rien de piquant'" (*CF*, p. 46). Noticing a painting exhibition at the Louvre, he enters. His comments on the middle-class spectators reveal them to be dull-witted and uninformed. He is delighted to find one of his own painting hanging there, but his pleasure quickly turns to rage, for the signature belongs to one of his friends, turned thief now that Onuphrius is dead (*CF*, p. 47). Later, at the Théâtre de la Porte Saint-Martin, he learns that the same friend has also signed a play which Onuphrius wrote and is receiving enthusiastic acclaim which should rightfully go to the dead author. To cap his upsets, Onuphrius discovers his fiancée Jacintha sharing with the same friend his stolen success (*CF*, p. 48).

The nightmare thus serves a double purpose. It gives Gautier an opportunity to satirize both public and artists; and it affords him yet another chance to demonstrate the seriousness of Onuphrius' madness. The protagonist's dream clearly reflects some of his obsessions and fears.

[4] This indicates that Gautier readily saw the literary possibilities of the Romantic myth that in dreams, freed from the inhibitions of logical thought, one enjoys superior mental capacity.

[5] There is a hint that Arria Marcella is also a vampire. During the dinner which she has had prepared for Octavien, she does not eat: "mais elle portait souvent à ses lèvres un vase myrrhin aux teintes opalines remplis d'un vin d'une pourpre sombre comme du sang figé; à

mesure qu'elle buvait, une imperceptible vapeur rose montait à ses joues pâles, de son cœur qui n'avait pas battu depuis tant d'années . . ." (*CF,* p. 245). Since Gautier does not emphasize her vampirism, we have no justification for pursuing the question.

[6] It is clear in "Arria Marcella," especially, that Christianity dominates the whole modern mentality.

Rosemary Lloyd (essay date 1986)

SOURCE: "Rereading *Mademoiselle de Maupin,*" in *Orbis Litterarum*, Vol. 41, No. 1, 1986, pp. 19-32.

[*Here, Lloyd examines the "underlying structures, the associated contrasts and parallels, and the cultural allusions" in Gautier's novel,* Mademoiselle de Maupin, *contending that traditional readings of the work which compare Gautier and d'Albert overlook the novel's complexity and tension.*]

For Sainte-Beuve 'la Bible du romantisme', described by R. Jasinski in 1929 as an 'œuvre plus célèbre que connue', considered by P. Albouy 'le roman de la contradiction, de toutes les contradictions', seen by A. Bouchard as an 'ouvrage pour le moins composite, qui a d'emblée déconcerté la critique', judged by M. Crouzet a 'roman misogyne et misoandre', and appearing to at least one of its readers as 'ce roman, ce conte, ce tableau, cette rêverie continuée avec l'obstination d'un peintre, cette espèce d'hymne à la beauté', *Mademoiselle de Maupin* has not been neglected.[1] Indeed, Penguin has recently published Joanna Richardson's translation of the novel, with a brief, mainly biographical introduction; Georges Poulet has drawn on it both for his exploration of the myth of 'la blonde aux yeux noirs' in Gautier and Nerval, and for his study of Piranesi in Romantic thought; P. Albouy has sought in it clues to the image of the androgyne and hermaphrodite in mid-nineteenth-century thinking; A. Bouchard, in a sensitive appreciation of what she terms 'une œuvre exceptionnelle', looks at its use of mirrors and masks; Ross Chambers reveals the extent to which the work is marked by the 'complexe de Pygmalion'; and A. Schnack, through a study of images of water and depths, reaches the conclusion that 'si Gautier [. . .] est le poète de la beauté extérieure, il y a tout lieu de penser qu'il l'est par peur des profondeurs intérieures'.[2] Yet I would suggest that there are areas where accepted critical views could be called into question, and aspects of this scintillating, puzzling, at times irritating novel which could be explored afresh.

It could well be salutary to begin by setting aside three common preconceptions, one of which, dating from the days of biographical criticism, has survived remarkably intact: that of assuming that Gautier and d'Albert are identical, and that d'Albert's opinions on women,

beauty, paganism and so forth are necessarily those of his creator.[3] The assumption that since the publication of **Albertus** d'Albert became 'un surnom de Gautier'[4] begs too many questions to be taken seriously: along such lines one might claim—perhaps with more justification—that Théo[dore] = Théo[phile] and that on those grounds Mademoiselle de Maupin herself is more likely to speak for Gautier. It is part of the novel's challenge to the reader that it abounds in hints that Gautier, through gentle mockery and irony, is distancing himself and us from the male protagonist and using the novel to debate questions of love and aesthetics, rather than to set down a fixed code. D'Albert, after all, is a 'poète manqué', one on whose uncut volume his mistress falls asleep (**Mademoiselle de Maupin,** 132), who lacks 'la moitié des termes indispensables' to paint female beauty (**MM,** 264) or the torments of love (**MM,** 317),[5] whose audience consists of 'toutes les femmes de l'assemblée qui ne disent plus leur âge, et les quelques petites filles que l'on n'a pas invitées à danser' (**MM,** 273), and who is forced eventually to accept 'cette poésie sublime de la réalité' (**MM,** 318). It is to his pen that we owe the amusing mixed metaphor, made just before d'Albert claims yet again that he is a poet: 'dans quel flot d'ineffables extases, dans quels lacs de pures délices doivent nager ceux qu'il a atteints au cœur d'une de ses flèches à pointe d'or, et qui brûlent des aimables ardeurs d'une flamme mutuelle' (**MM,** 148). The narrative voice mocks him as a 'digne personnage' (**MM,** 161), with an epithet we might associate more with honest burghers than with Romantic poets. Above all, however, the gap between what d'Albert perceives to be the truth (in regard to Rosette, to Madeleine and to himself) and what the reader sees to be the truth is too great for there to be any possibility that d'Albert speaks constantly and consistently for Gautier.

Secondly, there is the assumption that the character of Rosette is inconsistent. According to G. van den Bogaert, for example, 'coquette et sans cœur au début du livre, Rosette se révèle ensuite une amoureuse que consume une passion sans espoir'.[6] Noting that if Rosette pleased d'Albert initially by having 'ni tante revêche ni frère spadassin' she does eventually aquire precisely these attributes, Jasinski draws the conclusion that "visiblement il y a plusieurs Rosettes'.[7] Two points should be borne in mind here. Firstly, if Rosette appears 'coquette et sans cœur' when we first meet her, it is because she is presented through the eyes of d'Albert's cynical friend; and secondly, if she is later found to possess a deep mystery and at least a 'frère spadassin' and an aunt who is 'revêche' only in so far as being elderly, this is all part of Gautier's insistence on d'Albert's blindness, his failure to interpret correctly the clues provided by the external world, and therefore his inability to be a great poet before he has undergone the *éducation sentimentale* that Madeleine provides.

Thirdly, there is the belief that to explore the motives of one character, one can draw indiscriminately on the self-analysis of another. Thus Schnack, seeking the reasons for Madeleine's flight at the end of the novel, is content to quote in support of his thesis a letter written by d'Albert.[8] Connected with this assumption is the conviction that Gautier was unable, or unwilling, to differentiate between his characters. Certainly on the level of style there is little effort to discriminate between the letters of d'Albert and those of Madeleine, particularly in comparison with the consummate skill of Laclos in *Les Liaisons dangereuses,* but I shall argue that from the point of view of imagery and substance, if not of register, Gautier constantly suggests differences, and that these points of conflict are an essential part of the novel's tone and of its purpose.

With these preconceptions set aside, we can explore three main areas: the underlying structures, the associated contrasts and parallels, and the cultural allusions, in an attempt to reach a clearer understanding of the text.

Gautier's best prose fictions reveal a remarkable consistency in their underlying structures, despite the apparent change in emphasis from the materialism of the early works to the spiritualism of *Spirite* (a change already adumbrated in the development of d'Albert). *Mademoiselle de Maupin* not only contains a fleeting salute to **"Omphale, ou la tapisserie amoureuse"** of 1834—'lorsque j'étais petite, je n'entrais guère dans une chambre tapissée sans éprouver une espèce de frisson' (***MM,*** 287)—it also frequently points forward to the central themes of later tales: thus there are references to the fate of the man who loves a woman who died centuries before (***MM,*** 319: cf. **"Arria Marcella"**); to the psychological reasoning behind Cleopatra's habit of executing her lovers after a single night (***MM,*** 228: cf. **"Une nuit de Cléopâtre"**); to the motif of the exchange of bodies by a lover determined to possess his beloved by fair means or foul (***MM,*** 112, 152 etc.:cf. *Avatar*); and to the image of a man loved by a spirit and rejecting wordly pleasures in his longing to unite with her after death (***MM,*** 80, 82, 98, 99, 131, 144, 169, 194, 203, 248, 319, 324-5, 345: cf. *Spirite*). This last image appears with such obsessive frequence in *Mademoiselle de Maupin* that it casts a particularly ambiguous light on Madeleine's epigramme: 'bien souvent le sens de la vie c'est que ce n'est pas la mort' (***MM,*** 315).[9]

The underlying coherence of these works, moreover, is increased by two recurrent schemata which, paradoxically, lose their surface banality by dint of repetition, and to which we might apply C. Mauron's phrase 'mythes obsédants': that of the impossibility of happiness, and that of the triangular relationships which place that happiness beyond reach. Indeed, however, frequently Gautier draws on the double, that stock element of the fantastic code, the most common structure in the short stories is the triangle in which the hero's chance of happiness is destroyed by a substitute father.[10] And, like many of the short stories, Mademoiselle de Maupin is dominated by a system of triangles in which the character who represents for another 'la réalité du rêve' destroys a third person's chance of happiness. Here perhaps we should recall the comic triangle of *As You Like It,* the play acted out by Rosette and her guests and on which Gautier draws so frequently in his novel: Rosalind, disguised as the youth Ganymede, attracts the unwelcome attentions of Phœbe, who is loved by Sylvius. In *Mademoiselle de Maupin,* d'Albert is first faced with a choice between Rosette and a 'dame en blanche'[11]: but for him 'le bonheur est blanc et rose' (***MM,*** 139), and in choosing Rosette he is left constantly wondering not only if the choice itself were right, but also whether either woman alone could fulfil his expectations of perfect happiness. Other triangles are more central: both Rosette and the disguised page Isnabel vie for Madeleine's attentions, in a triangle which mirrors the predicament of Rosette and d'Albert both loving Madeleine yet having to make do with each other. It is of course the sexual duality of Madeleine that gives these triangles their complexity and explains Gautier's frequent recourse to masks and mirrors, and to references in the text to man's duality in general (see for example ***MM,*** 306) and to the Hermaphroditus myth in particular. Thus, on seeing Madeleine dressed as Rosalind for the play, both d'Albert and Rosette are forced to 'se demander s'il était bien possible que ce fût lui, Théodore de Sérannes, [. . .] et s'il était parfaitement sûr qu'il ne fût pas sa sœur jumelle' (***MM,*** 265). Moreover, when Rosette attempts to seduce Madeleine, it is the myth of Hermaphroditus's encounter in the lake with the waternymph Salmacis that determines Gautier's choice of imagery: 'Son corps, facile et souple, se modelait sur le mien comme de la cire, at en prenait tout le contour extérieur aussi exactement possible:—l'eau ne se fût pas insinuée plus précisément dans toutes les sinuousités de la ligne' (***MM,*** 303).[12] In addition, Madeleine's image of a state of perfect love is one which enables the lovers to 'se doubler en se donnant', to 'fondre et mêler [leurs] âmes de façon à ne plus savoir si vous êtes vous ou l'autre' (***MM,*** 344). To underline the impossibility of such a love, Gautier sets up a complex series of oppositions between Madeleine and d'Albert, using his triangular structures to give the novel tension and direction. Clearly that tension would be weakened if the authorial voice fused too frequently with one or other of the three central characters.

Much of the tension in the novel arises from a surprisingly modern stress on the ambivalence of human sexuality. D'Albert is told he dresses 'd'une manière trop effeminée' (***MM,*** 101), finds himself looking on Rosette as 'un joli camarade avec lequel on couche' (***MM,*** 105), and confesses that he has longed to be a woman 'pour connaître de nouvelles voluptés' (*MM,* 156). In an attempt to convince himself of the reality of his love for Rosette he attempts to fuse his body with hers, 'comme l'antique Salmacis, l'amoureuse du jeune Hermaphrodite' (*MM,* 113), and on discovering his love for Madeleine, at the stage when he thinks she is Théodore, confesses: 'je doute si je suis un homme ou une femme' (*MM,* 195). Rosette, compliantly conforming to traditional female roles in her relationship with d'Albert, assumes the masculine role of active wooer and would-be seducer in her love for Madeleine. Indeed, the misogyny so frequently attributed to Gautier by those who simply see d'Albert as Gautier's *porte-parole* is doubly undermined: firstly, by the *éducation sentimentale* that d'Albert undergoes, and secondly, by a complex scheme of counterpoints between d'Albert and Madeleine. The crass young d'Albert of the early letters, who proclaims: 'je n'ai jamais demandé aux femmes qu'une seule chose—c'est la beauté; je me passe très volontiers d'esprit et d'âme' (*MM,* 149), is forced to acknowledge that one of the most attractive of Madeleine's characteristics is 'un esprit très vif et très étendu' (*MM,* 159). It is this keenness of mind that gives a particular bite to the many issues in which she and d'Albert take opposing points of view. D'Albert, that 'Romantique à tous crins', rushes frenziedly from pillar to post in the belief that love awaits precisely where he is not, while Madeleine knows that 'c'est une chose qui vous leurre et vous trompe que de penser que toutes les aventures et tous les bonheurs n'existent qu'aux endroits où vous n'êtes pas' (*MM,* 344-5). The narcissistic d'Albert spends his days exploring his 'âme au microscope' (*MM,* 98), while the analytical Madeleine sets out to 'étudier l'homme à fond, l'anatomiser fibre par fibre avec un scalpel inexorable' (*MM,* 221). And while d'Albert asks of women only physical beauty and sensorial pleasure (*MM,* 98 etc.), Madeleine asserts: 'ce que je demandais avant tout, ce n'était pas la beauté physique, c'était la beauté de l'âme' (*MM,* 344).[13] Finally, if d'Albert believes that happiness would be provided by a 'sérail fantastique' (*MM,* 210), Madeleine is aware that a single woman can create 'un sérail complet' (*MM,* 309).[14]

Indeed, if, in the debate on the theatre, it is Rosette who takes the opposite view from d'Albert, seeking a 'vérité *vraie*' while d'Albert wants to 'laisser le champ tout à fait libre à l'auteur', allowing 'la fantaisie' to 'régner en souveraine', it may well be that Madeleine speaks for Gautier in preferring 'une vérité de convention et d'optique' (*MM,* 252). Certainly one can only feel relieved that the *mièvrerie* of d'Albert's theatre (*MM,* 243-4) although present in 'Premier sourire de printemps' in *Emaux et Camées* does not dominate *Mademoiselle de Maupin*.

The dynamics of the triangle depends not just on tensions and oppositions, but also on attractions and connections. Between d'Albert and Madeleine there are, of course, points of contact, although even these tend to underline the superior intelligence of Madeleine. D'Albert gropes towards an awareness of the weakness of the human will, seeing the problem in purely personal terms: 'je crois que ce qui m'empêche d'avoir une maîtresse c'est que j'ai résolu d'en avoir une' (*MM,* 77); Madeleine goes beyond the personal to make a general point: 'c'est le propre des plans que l'on a de n'être point exécutés et c'est là que paraissent principalement la fragilité de la volonté et le pur néant de l'homme' (*MM,* 342). There are points of contact, too, between Madeleine and Rosette, firstly on the banal level of the names Rosette and Rosalind, secondly in the nexus created by the description of 'sainte prostituée' (*MM,* 170) applied to Rosette and the traditional images associated with the name of Madeleine. And if there is 'author de Rosette une atmosphère de prose dans laquelle une idée poétique ne peut vivre' (*MM,* 96), what d'Albert finds in Madeleine is 'cette poésie sublime de la réalité' (*MM,* 318). Moreover, the clearsightedness that marks Madeleine's judgement is also present in Rosette's analysis of d'Albert. He is convinced that Rosette is unaware of his doubts and worries about his love for her and if he does occasionally suspect her of play-acting, he reassures himself in the following way: 'si grandes comédiennes que soient naturellement les femmes, j'ai peine à croire qu'elles le soient à ce point-là; et, au bout du compte, toutes les démonstrations de Rosette ne sont-elles que l'expression exacte de ses sentiments pour moi?' (*MM,* 141-2). Rosette, however, is not only seeking in d'Albert a substitute for Madeleine, but she is lucidly aware of his hesitations. She tells Madeleine calmly: 'si je ne l'aide pas, il est capable de s'ennuyer consciencieuse-ment avec moi jusqu'au jour du jugement dernier, et même audelà' (*MM,* 166).

One more structural device should be explored: that of the microcosm, which Ross Chambers analyses so well in regard to the theatre motifs in *Mademoiselle de Maupin* and Hoffmann's *Prinzessin Brambilla*. Gautier draws his reader's attention very clearly to the function of the play within the novel in suggesting meanings accessible only to an initiated élite: 'c'est en quelque sorte une autre pièce dans la pièce, un drame invisible et inconnu aux autres spectateurs que nous jouions pour nous seuls, et qui, sous des paroles symboliques, résumait notre vie complète et exprimait nos plus cachés désirs' (*MM,* 276). In Gautier's writing, it is often desire that holds the key to the enigmatic microcosm: Madeleine's vision of love, for example, is a state in which 'ma prunelle est un ciel, ma bouche est un paradis plus souhaité que le véritable' (*MM,* 293: cf. 317). But there is a further microcosm in *Mademoiselle de Maupin* where images of erotic and artistic desire meet and coincide. The *locus* of this meeting is the tapestry which, together with the painting, holds a privileged position in Gautier's thinking:

the tapestry and the painting freeze time, circumvent decay, overcome death (as Mallarmé saw Gautier himself doing through his poetry) and at the same time seem to promise love—hence the references to women stepping out from a painting or a tapestry—thereby combining the 'hantise de la mort' that Poulet sees in Gautier with the causal longing for permanent love that Chambers discerns in him.[15]

The tapestry analysed in **Mademoiselle de Maupin** is of a hunting scene, reminiscent of many of the scenes of Ovid's *Metamorphoses* and offering as the result of time and artifice several minor metamorphoses: the faded colours create 'de bizarres transpositions de nuances', flesh resembles wood, the pistils of flowers look like 'des aigrettes de paon' (**MM,** 286). The scene that most attracts Madeleine's attention is of 'une chasseresse' whose arrow eternally pursues a bird flying on 'ailes immobiles'. But because the tapestry meets a corner at that point, the arrow is on another angle of the wall from the huntress, who therefore cannot see it, and waits eternally for her prey to fall without ever knowing if her aim were true.[16] Madeleine, who elsewhere compares herself to Diana the Huntress (**MM,** 367), draws from this scene a general interpretation (the arrow doomed never to reach its target symbolizes human destiny) and a specifically aesthetic one (the huntress represents a poet dying before achieving his masterwork). But by insisting on a symbolic reading of the tapestry and, by extension, of the novel as a whole, the passage draws attention to the erotic symbolism: the arrow itself, gold-tipped as are Cupid's (cf. **MM,** 148), and the description of the purple bird about to be 'percé de part en part' like the emblem of a heart pierced by desire, are evident sexual symbols.

Equally characteristic of the novel as these structural devices, and combining as they do the erotic with the aesthetic, is the rich texture of cultural and literary allusions. In his sensitive reading of **Spirite,** Ross Chambers asserts that 'toutes les allusions culturelles du livre [sont] en liaison avec le réseau thématique du texte.'[17] In **Mademoiselle de Maupin** the proliferation of literary allusions is such that one suspects its young author of delighting in this *étalage d'érudition,* a casting of handful upon handful of pearls to his dazzled audience. Yet that delight is bound up with an enthusiasm which Gautier succeeds in making highly contagious, and which reveals a deeper purpose. The doffing of the cap to Horace (**MM,** 102) and the allusion to Catullus in the phrase 'addition de baisers catulienne' (**MM,** 206) lead up to a wonderful pastiche where d'Albert compares himself to 'un mauvais poète du temps d'Auguste'. Yet this light-hearted weaving of variations on the theme of 'Hâtez-vous, Cinthia; la plus petite ride peut servir de fosse au plus grand amour' (**MM,** 207), also performs the more serious function of contrasting love which is essentially physical with 'les poésies érotiques faites depuis l'ère chrétienne' in which

'une âme [. . .] demande à une autre âme de l'aimer, parce qu'elle l'aime' (**MM,** 206). When he really experiences love, d'Albert, too, will find himself unable to speak with 'la voix brève et dure du maître qui tâche de s'adoucir en parlant à l'esclave' (**MM,** 206) and will be forced instead to long for that kind of relationship in which 'un lac azuré et souriant [. . .] invite un ruisseau à se fondre dans son sein' (**MM,** 206: cf. 322). It may well be that allusions to *Amadis de Gaule* (MM, 95, 141, 178) and to Cazotte's *Le Diable amoureux* (**MM,** 271, 323) are little more than a salute to Gautier's close friend Nerval, but they, and the references to *L'Astrée* (**MM,** 123, 334, 335), *Orlando furioso* (**MM,** 102, 273)[18] and *Les Liaisons dangereuses* (**MM,** 211)[19] are designed to lock the novel into a long tradition of physical explorations of human sexuality and through such intertextual references add weight and resonance to Gautier's own findings. The most important literary allusions however spring from three main sources: Ovid, Hoffmann, and Shakespeare. All three have in common the theme of metamorphosis. It is far from extraneous to the text that the cabin to which Rosette takes Madeleine is decorated with 'les scènes les plus galantes des *Métamorphoses* d'Ovide' (**MM,** 299: cf. 282, 320): the power of love to transform lover or beloved is central to the novel, as it is of course in Ovid's masterpiece, and the myth Ovid recounts of Hermaphroditus and Salmacis is echoed throughout the work, not only in the whole *topos* of the androgyne but also in the frequent use of water imagery.[20] The allusions to Hoffmann are also concerned with metamorphosis, and the tales concerned are those which chart the progress of a clumsy, pretentious young man who becomes a sensitive poet and lover. There are, I would suggest, two references to *Der goldne Topf* (in which, it will be remembered, there are frequent transformations of an archivist into a salamander and a young girl into the emerald-coloured snake Serpentina): these allusions can be found in the question: 'qui métamorphosait les feuilles mortes en topazes, les feuilles vertes en émeraudes' (**MM,** 118), which is reminiscent of the passage where 'trois petits serpents diaprés de vert et d'or' move so quickly through the leaves that 'on croyait voir le sureau étinceler de mille émeraudes'[21]; and in the mention of the 'petites perruches [qui] finiront par vous crever gentiment les yeux' (**MM,** 251), which recalls both the mocking birds 'au plumage somptueux' that tease Anselmus in the conservatory, and the parrot that plucks out the cat's eyes in the decisive battle of good against evil.[22] There are also references to *Prinzessin Brambilla*, the work Baudelaire was to call 'un catéchisme de haute esthétique.'[23] The allusion to the net in which d'Albert feels he is entrapped recalls that in which Giglio, transformed into a bird, is captured by the ladies of the Pistoja Palace[24] and Madeleine's description of her page as being so delicate that she 'la voudrai[t] enfermer dans une boîte de coton et la porter suspendue à [s]on cou' (*MM,* 354) is very like Brambilla's longing to carry her prince in a tiny box.[25]

Most importantly, of course, Gautier draws frequently and ingeniously on Shakespeare, in whose characters d'Albert sees the playwright personifying 'sa joie, sa mélancolie, son amour et son rêve le plus intime sous les apparences les plus frivoles et les plus dégagées' (*MM,* 247). Gautier seems to have found inspiration in *As You Like It* not just for the debate on the theatre and the double *travestissement* of Madeleine: after all, he could have used *Cymbaline* or *Twelfth Night* if he had merely needed a play in which a girl dresses as a boy. *As You Like It,* in addition to its attractive glimpse of the utopian life in the forest of Arden—'many young gentlemen flock to [the old Duke] every day and fleet the time carelessly as they did in the golden world' (I, i)—offers a vision of an intimate friendship between two girls—'never two ladies loved as they do' (I, i) and 'wheresoe'er we went, like Juno's swans / Still we went coupled and inseparable' (I, iii). It also provides the picture of a woman, dressed as a man, hearing her sex abused: 'I thank God I am not a woman, to be touched with so many giddy offences as he hath generally tax'd their whole sex withal' (III, ii), and the image of a bad poet hanging on trees sonnets, some of which 'have in them more feet than the verses would bear' (III, ii: cf. *MM,* 270).[26] Moreover, it specifically depicts the theatre as microcosm in the famous line: 'All the world's a stage' (II, vii). Certainly the play is not simply introduced as a kind of *deus ex machina* to reveal the true nature of Madeleine, but has been woven into the texture of the novel through the multiple references to the theatre and to acting. D'Albert, for example, has been told he is more like a 'comédien' than a man (*MM,* 101), and presents himself in the affair with Rosette as having passed 'de l'état de simple spectateur à celui d'acteur' (*MM,* 102), the park around the chateau resembles 'des coulisses d'une décoration de théâtre' (*MM,* 136), when someone sighs it is 'pareil au soupir d'un acteur qui est arrivé au bout d'un long couplet' (*MM,* 219), and the setting sun is compared to 'le lustre d'un théâtre qu'on abaisse quand la représentation est finie' (*MM,* 225). And of course all these references to artifice, to pretence and to metamorphosis point to the enigmatic nature of the human psyche.[27]

Despite the pirouettes and jokes of *Mademoiselle de Maupin,* despite the self-indulgently lengthy passages analyzing the Romantic soul (and the degree of parody and pastiche, particularly in d'Albert's letters, should not be overlooked), Gautier does have important points to make. Firstly, he emphasizes the confining nature of sexual stereotypes: if, in the wake of Laclos, he laments women's condition and education (*MM,* 217, 222) and reveals the emptiness of d'Albert's dream of happiness (*MM,* 210-1), it is above all to explain and deplore the fact that, as Madelaine puts it so succinctly,

'il n'y a pas le moindre lien intellectuel entre les deux sexes' (*MM,* 221). Secondly, he reveals the animality of man, a theme brought out through the proliferation of images comparing man to the animal world. D'Albert sees himself as a 'coquillage', a 'grillon' (*MM,* 62) and a 'cloporte' (*MM,* 110); Rosette is likened to 'une couleuvre' (*MM,* 332) and a 'tigresse' (*MM,* 334); human passions are 'comme les bêtes d'une ménagerie' (*MM,* 64)[28] and desires are 'une nuée d'oiseaux qui tourbillonnent et voltigent sans but' (*MM,* 174). More importantly, Gautier is anxious to explore the nature of love, of pleasure and of desire, which he presents as three separate emotions. Love is merely 'cette molle passion qui a tant de prise sur les rêveurs et les mélancoliques' (*MM,* 292), a rather predictable novel (*MM,* 70, 102, 103, 296) whose dominant tone is less of lyricism than of prose, even if it is 'prose poétique' (*MM,* 296), and a commodity on a level with money (*MM,* 107, 201, 272, 275). Pleasure, however, is a 'vin capiteux' destroying the individual's power of reason (*MM,* 332), or a 'feu dévorant qui fond les rochers et les métaux de l'âme et les fait retomber en pleurs' (*MM,* 110).[29] Desire, for its part, is far more intense than either of these and of far briefer duration, as d'Albert realizes when the 'baiser équestre' is interrupted 'à point, au moment où, par son intensité même, il allait devenir une douleur ou s'affaisser sous sa violence' (*MM,* 115). As Madeleine explains in her final letter, using a formulation which underlines the constant fusion in *Mademoiselle de Maupin* of the erotic and the aesthetic: 'en amour, comme en poésie, rester au même point, c'est reculer' (*MM,* 375). It is desire, moreover, which reveals most clearly the power of the physical side of human nature: thus, Madeleine asks, in a passage whose import and imagery point forward to Proust: 'la voix du corps parle-t-elle plus haut que la voix de l'esprit? [. . .] une odeur de feuillage qui vous arrive des champs [. . .], une ancienne chanson d'amour qui vous revient malgré vous [. . .]. Alors la jeune fille ouvre ses bras au premier laquais avec qui elle se trouve seule; le philosophe laisse sa page inachevée, et, la tête dans son manteau, court en toute hâte chez la plus voisine courtisane' (*MM,* 238).

Possibly the triangle of Rosette, d'Albert and Madeleine corresponds to that of love, pleasure and desire, with Madeleine's abrupt departure underlining the fact that desire will last only if it is not fulfilled. More importantly, however, Gautier seems to be attempting in *Mademoiselle de Maupin* the creation of a modern myth in which beauty, poetic inspiration and love can coincide only in a being who is both Apollo and Aphrodite (*MM,* 320), appealing to both sexes and exciting both the senses and the intellect, a being who manifests herself only long enough to leave an indelible impression of unattainable perfection. It is an extremely ambitious first novel, witty, ironic, parodic, not without flaws, but one which lies at the heart of nineteenth-century aesthetic thinking.

Notes

Abbreviations used in this article are: MM = *Mademoiselle de Maupin* (Paris, Garnier-Flammarion, 1966).

[1] Sainte-Beuve, quoted by M. Crouzet, "Mademoiselle de Maupin" ou l'Eros romantique', *Romantisme,* 8 (1974), 2-21 (p. 6); R. Jasinski, *Les Années romantiques de Th. Gautier* (Paris, 1929), p. 283; P. Albouy, *Mythographies* (Paris, 1976), p. 328; A. Bouchard, 'Le Masque er le miroir dans "Mademoiselle de Maupin"', *Revue d'histoire littéraire de la France,* 72, No. 4 (July-August 1972), 583-99 (p. 584); Crouzet, art. cit., p. 15; Baudelaire, *Œuvres complètes,* II, edited by C. Pichois (Paris, 1976), p. 111. Anyone writing on *Mademoiselle de Maupin* can sympathise with d'Albert's problem of nomenclature: 'Théodore,—Rosalinde,—car je ne sais de quel nom vous appeler' (*MM,* 317). I refer to her throughout as *Madeleine.*

[2] G. Poulet, *Trois essais de mythologie romantique* (Paris, 1966); P. Albouy, op. cit.; A. Bouchard, art. cit, p. 599; R. Chambers, 'Gautier er le complexe de Pygmalion', *Revue d'histoire littéraire de la France,* 72, No. 4 (July-August 1972), 641-58; A. Schnack, 'Surface et Profondeur dans "Mademoiselle de Maupin"', *Orbis Litterarum,* 36 (1981), 28-36 (p. 34).

[3] Among recent critics who make this assumption are R. Benesch, *Le Regard de Théophile Gautier* (Zurich, 1969), p. 15; M. Crouzet, art. cit., p. 9; E. Hartman. 'Théophile Gautier on Progress in The Arts', *Studies in Romanticism,* 12, No. 2 (Spring, 1973), p. 546, note 22; A. Schnack, art. cit., p. 31.

[4] M. Crouzet, art. cit., pp. 8-9.

[5] Compare Baudelaire, op. cit., p. 108: '[Gautier] ajouta *"que l'écrivain qui ne savait pas tout dire,* celui qu'une idée si étrange, si subtile qu'on la supposât, si imprévue, tombant comme une pierre de la lune, *prenait au dépourvu et sans matériel pour lui donner corps, n'était pas un écrivain."*

[6] In her preface to the edition from which I am quoting, p. 15: compare Jasinski, op. cit., p. 293: 'se ressemble-t-elle toujours?'.

[7] Jasinski, op. cit., p. 293.

[8] Schnack, art. cit., p. 31.

[9] On the theme of death in Gautier, see G. Poulet, *Etudes sur le temps humain* (Paris, 1949), pp. 278-307 and Chambers, *'Spirite' de Théophile Gautier: une lecture* (Paris, 1974).

[10] See P. G. Castex, *Le conte fantastique en France* (Paris, 1962), R. Girard, *Mensonge romantique et vérité romanesque* (Paris, 1961) and I. Bessière, *Le Récit fantastique* (Paris, 1974).

[11] A. Delmas and Y. Delmas, *A la recherche des 'Liaisons dangereuses'* (Paris, 1964), pp. 76-8, assert that the choice is between Rosette and Mme de Thémines, whom, in fact, d'Albert instantly rejects. The 'dame en blanche', significantly, is never named.

[12] See Ovid, *Metamorphoses,* book IV, lines 285-388.

[13] This image of love is in part determined by Madeleine's assessment of male ugliness: see for example *MM,* 346.

[14] Fortunio, too, discovers in Musidora—temporarily at least—a replacement for his entire seraglio: see Gautier, *Nouvelles* (Paris, 1882), pp. 144-6.

[15] See G. Poulet, *Etudes,* ed. cit. and Ross Chambers, *Spirite,* p. 60: 'modifions donc [. . .] l'énoncé de Poulet: ce qui domine, chez Gautier, est bien la hantise de la mort, mais ce qui domine à son tour cette hantise, c'est l'amour'.

[16] Impossible not to think here both of Proust's use of the interplay of the contours of the room and the magic lantern's image in *Combray,* and of Keats's response to a moment frozen by art in his 'Ode on a Grecian Urn'.

[17] R. Chambers, *Spirite,* p. 7. Joanna Richardson, however, considers that the allusions in *Mademoiselle de Maupin* have no bearing on the text: see her introduction to her translation (Harmondsworth, 1983).

[18] It is however possible that the Orlando of *As You Like It* has reminded Gautier of the eponymous hero of Ariosto's masterpiece.

[19] For a full study of the influence of *Les Liaisons dangereuses* on *Mademoiselle de Maupin* see A. and Y. Delmas, op. cit. I suspect that the focus they have adopted here has led to an overstating of similarities. Certainly the characters of Gautier's novel lack both the cynicism of the major characters in *Les Liaisons dangereuses* and that kind of intelligence that seeks to manipulate others.

[20] A. Schack, art. cit., refers to the abundance of water imagery, but does not suggest any parallels with the myth.

[21] Hoffmann, *Contes* (Paris, 1979), p. 248: compare p. 361. For the influence of Hoffmann in France see E. Tiechmann, *La Fortune d'Hoffmann en France* (Paris, 1961); P. Whyte, *The 'Conte fantastique'* (Unpublished thesis, Cambridge, 1967); and my *Baudelaire et Hoffmann* (Cambridge, 1979).

[22] See Hoffmann, *Contes,* pp. 295-7 and 346-7.

[23] Baudelaire, *op. cit.*, p. 547.

[24] Hoffmann, *Späte Werke* (München, 1969), p. 318.

[25] Ibid., p. 241: compare also the reference to 'cette ombre adorable' (*MM*, 319) and Hoffmann's 'Ombra adorata' in *Kreisleriana Nro 1-6*. Gautier expresses his admiration for the *Kreisleriana* in an article reproduced in Ma, 456-61.

[26] The reference to Orlando's line quoted in *MM*, 269 may be either to III, ii: 'Fair youth, I would I could make thee believe I love' or to v, ii: (Orlando) 'Why blame you me to love you?' (Rosalind, as Ganymede) 'Why do you speak so too "Why blame you me to love you"?'.

[27] Space does not allow me to explore the interesting emphasis Gautier places on rendering nature artificial: see for example *MM* 284, 286-7.

[28] Both here and in his interest in woman's condition one may detect the influence of Fourier: see P.S. Hambly, 'Théophile Gautier et le fouriérisme', *Australian Journal of French Studies*, 11, No. 3 (September-December 1974), 210-36; and for an amusing response to his reading of Fourier, Gautier's article in *La Presse*, 3 January 1837.

[29] The sexual implications of this image are evident and no doubt deliberate although elsewhere the post-Freudian reader may well detect a latent meaning of which Gautier himself may have been unaware: see for example *MM*, 202, 360-1. The metamorphosis of jewels to liquids is also an important image in the novel and could be further explored. In addition there is a close parallel between the description of pleasure as 'cette chaine de diamant' (*MM*, 110) and d'Albert's image of himself 'enchaîné avec des fers de diamant sur une roche chenue' (*MM*, 321).

Joan Driscoll (essay date 1987)

SOURCE: "Théophile Gautier's *Voyage en Italie*: The Description of Experience, or the Experience of Description," in *Words of Power: Essays in Honour of Alison Fairlie*, edited by Dorothy Gabe Coleman and Gillian Jondorf, The University of Glasgow Publications in Language and Literature, 1987, pp. 139-61.

[*In the essay that follows, Driscoll discusses Gautier's detailed descriptions in his travelogue,* Voyage en Italie, *and attempts to distinguish between the two voices of the narrator—the journalist and the poet.*]

In its earliest version, Gautier's account of his travels in Italy appeared in instalments in *La Presse*, beginning in September 1850, while Gautier himself was

Raymond Giraud examines the effect of classical antiquity on Gautier's writing:

Despite his occasional protests, Gautier was a man of his own time; indeed the very sense of living in an age to which one does not belong was confessed or vaunted by most of his most sensitive contemporaries. His understanding of classical antiquity developed in the context of archeological findings, historical and esthetic thought of the early nineteenth century. The Greece he regretted not having been born in was in fact a fabrication of modern imagination and scholarship. Gautier had, of course, a direct knowledge of Greek sculpture; he haunted the Greek collection in the Louvre and had many times made what Heine had mockingly called his "pilgrimage to Notre Dame de Milo." But in those statues, as in the texts he read, he found inevitably something of what he himself sought in them. They were "the most sublime expression of human genius" and, more particularly, they were a gallery of forms of beauty—the beauty of the undraped human body—on which he would draw, throughout his literary and journalistic career, whenever he attempted to evoke the beauty of living or fictional persons.

Raymond Giraud, "Winckelmann's Part in Gautier's Perception of Classical Beauty,"
Yale French Studies, *Vol. 38, May 1967.*

still absent in Venice.[1] At first sight, the **Voyage en Italie** seems to represent a relatively simple literary enterprise: the author visits Italy and describes, for his readers at home in France, what he sees there.

It is evident, however, from the moment of Gautier's entry into Italy, that this simplicity is more apparent than real; and, throughout Gautier's **Voyage,** we find him reflecting, not only upon the character of Italian life and scenery, but also upon that of the language which he must use to represent them.

> 'Le caractère des montagnes, que l'on croirait devoir devenir plus doux et plus riant en approchant de l'Italie, prend au contraire une âpreté et une sauvagerie extraordinaires. On dirait que la nature s'est fait un jeu des prévisions . . . Ce renversement est très-curieux: c'est la Suisse qui est italienne et l'Italie qui est suisse dans cette étonnante route du Simplon'
>
> (pp. 22-3).[2]

The fiction of a mischievous Nature who, by a paradoxical reversal of the faces of Switzerland and Italy, makes play with our normal expectations concerning the relationship between words and the things they represent, provides a fitting starting point for our own investigation. Following the author in his travels, we shall try, without too assiduously avoiding the temptation to share Gautier's own pleasure in the paradox and the *boutade,* to examine some of the ways in which the text encourages us to examine our own assumptions about the nature and purposes of description.

The notion that nature or 'reality' is the model, and that the value of descriptive language lies quite simply in its power to provide a faithful mirror-image of that model is, of course, naive; and the theory itself is not one to which Gautier himself would have subscribed. Nevertheless, the **Voyage en Italie** is, at least in its role as a work of popular journalism, a travelogue: and the reader who read it in the expectation that it would provide him with an accurate account of a series of places which had an objective existence in the external world, and which he could himself visit, would not be making an altogether unreasonable assumption.

Moreover, Gautier's own observations concerning the purpose and the character of the text suggest that we may at least begin from this premise. He states his intention of bringing to his reader a more complete account of Italian life and scenery than those which he had found in the works of his predecessors: 'en lisant les récits des voyageurs, il nous est arrivé de souhaiter des détails plus précis, plus familiers, plus tracés sur le vif, des remarques plus circonstanciées sur ces mille petites différences qui avertissent qu'on a changé de pays . . . Nous avons fait notre butin de tout cela, et décrit des maisons, des cabarets, des rues, des traguets' (p.295). He suggests, indeed, that his concern for accuracy, even photographic accuracy, was greater than his concern for the formalities of literary composition: 'ce sont des croquis faits d'après nature, des plaques de daguerréotype, de petits morceaux de mosaïque recueillis sur place, que nous juxtaposons sans trop nous soucier d'une correction et d'une régularité qu'il n'est peut-être pas possible d'obtenir dans une chose aussi diffuse que le vagabondage à pied ou en gondole d'un feuilletoniste en vacance' (p.273).

However, Gautier himself stresses the fact that the **Voyage** is not a guide, but a series of impressions: in other words, it is not a work of reference, to be dipped into or consulted on occasion but, albeit within the limitations of the *feuilleton,* a literary text, where the detailed description which 'conviendrait plutôt à un guide spécial qu'à un recueil d'impressions de voyage' (p.120) has no proper place. Moreover, as he observes, the very act of writing such a text imposes conditions which conflict at times with the demands of accurate and faithful description. Indeed it is, paradoxically, the journalist's very desire to minimise the role of the writer and to relax the formality of literary composition, so that all the variety, and even the incoherence, of Italian life and scenery may be presented directly to the reader as it is experienced in reality, which leads Gautier to reintroduce into his text the figure of the author— the author who, if his account is to be readable at all, must first solve the problems of composition and give

at least a minimum of coherence to his narrative. 'Nous ne sommes pas de ceux dont la joie ou la tristesse importe au monde, et, si nous usons quelquefois de notre personnalité dans ces notes de voyage, c'est comme moyen de transition et pour éviter des embarras de formes' (p.143).

The decision to broaden the scope of the existing *récit de voyage,* and to include not only the splendid and the monumental but also the detail of everyday life, is of course in itself the decision of a writer who is conscious of the literary framework within which he works, and of the limitations which existing conventions may place upon innovation or faithful representation.

The very nature of things, and our multiple experience of them, seems to defy the assumption that they can be represented without distortion within the bounds of a text which is coherent enough to be readable; and Gautier remains to the end of his **Voyage** uncertain of his ability to combine successfully the assessment of artistic treasures, the description of architectural monuments, the presentation of historical and geographical information, the notation of the details of everyday life, and the representation of the varied scenery through which he travels. 'L'architecture nous a souvent entraîné, et nous avons souvent abusé, en dépit du précepte de Boileau, du feston et de l'astragale . . . Les mœurs de la société vénitienne ne tiennent peut-être pas assez de place dans ces esquisses, et le tableau y a souvent le pas sur l'homme' (pp.295-6): the written text demands a polish, a unity, and a balance of its different elements which is at variance with the complexity and even the confusion of the things to be described.

Moreover, as Gautier more than once has cause to observe, the reader himself makes other demands which conflict at times with the avowed purpose of the text— to bring to the public at home a faithful description of the places which the author has visited.
In the description of the art treasures of Venice, Gautier finds himself confronted with a veritable *embarras de richesses.* Eager as he is to omit nothing of significance, and even to restore the reputation of some of the minor artists who are more usually overlooked, he remains mindful of his reader's limited endurance: 'nous sentons malgré nous s'allonger cette nomenclature; mais à chaque pas un chef-d'œuvre nous tire par le basque de notre habit quand nous passons, et nous demande une phrase. Le moyen d'y résister! nous allons, ne pouvant tout dire, laisser travailler votre imagination' (p.129).

It is in fact a weakness of Gautier's text that the distinction between the guide (in which comprehensiveness and accuracy of reference are of prime importance) and the more literary series of 'impressions de voyage' (where techniques of selection and suggestion might more successfully convey the quality of the author's own experience) is not always sufficiently respected. Aware though he is of his reader's limited patience, and of the greater potential of suggestion as opposed to statement, Gautier does not always resist the temptation of enumeration or accumulation, and offers, in his account of the splendours of the Doges' Palace for example, not a persuasive picture of the riches of the place as a whole, but a mere list of the names of the many artists whose works he has no space to describe: 'comme architectes, Palladio, Scamozzi, Sansovino, Antonio da Ponte, Pierre Lombard; comme peintres, Titien, Paul Véronèse, Tintoret, Carlo Cagliari, Bonifazio, Vivarini, J. Palma, Aliense, Contarini, Le Moro, le Vicentino . . .' (p.130). The catalogue continues.

The techniques of communication and persuasion themselves differ from those of accurate notation and description. As Gautier well knew, it is not enough that something should be real, it must seem to be real. Even with the object before us, we may remain unconvinced of its authenticity—like that of the famous porphyry columns of the 'palais Vendramin Calergi' which 'paraissent fausses, quoique de la vérité la plus incontestable' and disappoint because their appearance belies the reality of their great value: 'elles sont placées devant une porte, et font aussi peu d'effet que les lapis-lazuli du salon Serra à Gênes, qu'on croirait volontiers peints et vernis, et qui ressemblent, à faire peur, à du moiré métallique bleu' (p.278-9).

The persuasiveness of any representation, and the writer's descriptions are no exception, derives as often from art, or even artifice, as from accuracy or strict authenticity. Dürer's map of medieval Venice seems as real as the contemporary city itself to the author of the **Voyage;** and this impression is achieved, not by total fidelity to the detail of the city, but by a skilful combination of mathematical precision and free fantasy: 'ce grand artiste, à la fois si fantastique et si exact, qui introduisit la chimère dans les mathématiques, a retracé la ville d'or, la *città d'oro*, comme la nomme Pétrarque, telle qu'elle était à cette époque avec une minutie scrupuleuse et un caprice étrange' (p.125)

The ostensible purpose of Gautier's descriptions, if not the *raison d'être* of the **Voyage** itself, may lie in the accuracy with which they mirror the reality of Italian life and scenery. Nevertheless, there are numerous indications in the text of the fact that the real business of the writer lies just as much in the reinforcement of common preconceptions concerning the nature of that reality, and indeed in the flattery of the reader's own preference for the unreal or the artificial, rather than the real or the natural.

The interest of the travelogue might well be expected to lie in the fact that it creates for the Frenchman at home an impression of a country which is strange, exotic, and different from his own. It was, after all, Gautier's intention to bring to his reader 'tous les détails caractéristiques de ces mille et une différences presque imperceptibles, mais qui vous avertissent à chaque instant qu'on a changé de pays' (p.197).

However, Gautier's own text reveals the extent to which language, as a means of communication, remains inimical to the precise description of things which are truly foreign or exotic. His account of his visit to the 'hôpital des fous' on the island of San Servolo demonstrates the degree to which the artist's powers of representation are limited by the necessity of using forms of expression which are familiar to both artist and spectator, to writer and reader alike. In short, the abnormal can only be represented by means of the conventional.

The fresco painted by the mad monk of San Servolo might be regarded as the counterpart of the frescoes of St Mark's, the latter with their 'monde d'anges, d'apôtres, d'évangélistes, de prophètes, de docteurs' (p.109), representing the triumph of reason and enlightenment, the former 'une ménagerie de l'extravagance la plus effrénée . . . des bêtes sans forme et sans nom, dont l'équivalent ne se trouve guère que dans le monde microscopique ou les cavernes des dépôts diluviens' (pp.245-6), the triumph of unreason and obscurity.

The madman's fresco is as empty of real significance for the spectator as the frescoes of St Mark's are rich in meaning. However, if the figures which the mad monk represents have no reality for the spectator, this is not because he is mistaken in his belief that they are copied faithfully from nature (many of the figures in the frescoes of St Mark's have themselves no equivalent in the world of everyday reality), but because of the absence, in the case of the monk's painting, of the shared cultural convention which permits both Gautier and his reader to recognise the figures depicted in the frescoes of St Mark's as elements of the languages of a number of different religions or creeds. The difficulty of describing works so rich and varied as the frescoes of St Mark's within the brief space of the **Voyage** is indeed great: but the difficulty of representing forms so strange and singular as those of the madman's imagination within the common currency of language is much greater. Gautier himself can only communicate the outlandish nature of the monsters of the madman's painting by referring his readers to a series of very well-known works and genres: 'les animaux héraldiques . . . les monstres chinois . . . la fantaisie des songes drôlatiques de Rabelais . . . peuvent seules en donner une idée' (p.246). The very familiarity of these references, which were already part of the stock repertoire of the French writers of the 1830's, threatens to render the unknown commonplace.

In the *Voyage* as a whole, the description of landscape very often involves the transmutation of the strange or the exotic into a type of scenery which corresponds closely with the Frenchman's own preconceived ideas of the picturesque. The use of such points of reference as Canaletto's Venetian painting from the Louvre provides a compromise between the known and the unknown, lending an authentically Italian air to the description without disturbing that sense of familiarity which permits both writer and reader to 'recognise' a landscape with which they are not yet acquainted: 'nous reconnûmes sur-le-champ la Salute, d'après le beau tableau de Canaletto, qui est au Musée' (p.71). More often, however, Gautier describes the scenery of both Switzerland and Italy by using references to the paintings of his own countrymen or to works of other origin which were well known to them—creating in this way a series of picturesque impressions which belong, not so much to the Swiss or Italian countryside itself, as to the artistic repertoire of the French. The landscape of Lake Geneva is compared with those of Isabey, Wyld, Bonington and Decamps, those of Venice with the work of Bonington, Joyant and Wyld—repetition in these different contexts of similar patterns of references itself gives emphasis to the affinities between the landscapes of the different countries rather than to their exotic or unique character.[3]

Throughout his travels in Switzerland and Italy, Gautier rediscovers those picturesque or poignant scenes which he and his Romantic contemporaries had earlier discovered much closer to home; and the predominance of references in the text of the *Voyage* as a whole to works which enjoyed their greatest vogue in the Romantic 1830's itself seems to belie Gautier's expressed intention to bring a greater immediacy and realism to the description of Italian scenery. The settlement on the shores of the Rhône as it leaves Lake Geneva: 'tout cela, vermoulu, fendillé, noirci, verdi, culotté, chassieux, renfrogné, caduc, couvert de lèpres et de callosités à ravir un Bonnington ou un Decamps' (p.5), offers a picture of neglect and decay very similar to that which Gautier had evoked in his early poem, 'Pan de mur', a reminiscence of the house in the Marais district of Paris where he had spent his youth and which would, he observed, have provided Boulanger or Bonington with a characteristically picturesque motif.[4] The landscape of Fusina on the Venetian lagoon: 'sur le bord des canaux, le nénuphar déploie ses larges cœurs visqueux, et soulève ses fleurs jaunes, la sagittaire fait trembler son fer de lance au vent' (p.191), has much in common with those which the poets and painters of the 1830's discovered on the outskirts of Paris, and which Gautier himself evoked in 'Le Marais': 'C'est un marais dont l'eau dormante / Croupit, couverte d'une mante / Par les nénuphars et les joncs'.[5]

Even when, in order to discover the real Venice behind the magnificent façade, Gautier penetrates the mysteri-ous Jewish quarter, less often pictured and described by previous travellers, we seem to find ourselves within the familiar territory of Victor Hugo's *Notre-Dame de Paris:* 'ce quartier fétide et purulent, cette Cour des Miracles aquatique' (p.284), or of the Dutch interiors whose popularity with Gautier's own countrymen dates again from the 1830's: 'nous remarquâmes, dans cette synagogue, un grand nombre de lustres en cuivre jaune avec des boules et des bras tortillés d'un goût hollandais, comme on en voit souvent dans les tableaux de Gérard-Dow ou de Mieris, notamment dans le tableau de la *Paralytique,* que la gravure a rendu populaire' (pp.284-5).[6]

The quest for an accurate exchange of information between writer and reader almost seems to preclude the exchange of accurate information, and leads at times to a mere repetition of the commonplaces and platitudes which render the foreign familiar and the exotic banal. Nor does this tendency appear simply as a weakness of descriptive language, in which the demands of communication conflict with those of faithful representation, but as a fundamental characteristic of our perception of things. The desire for the reinforcement of the familiar cliché is often stronger than the willingness to acknowledge the change and flux which is an essential part of our true experience. So much so, that what Gautier seeks to acclaim as the truly Italian style of dress survives in fact in the village of Sesto-Calende only on market days, and is only discovered by chance: 'c'était jour de marché. Circonstance favorable pour un voyageur; car un marché fait venir du fond des campagnes une foule de paysans caractéristiques qu'il serait fort difficile de voir sans cela' (p.39). The modern, urban Italian hastens to abandon his Italian dress in favour of a mode which is indistinguishable from that of his French neighbour: the characteristic Italian of the traveller's folklore survives in present reality only as an untypical exception.

Gautier observed, and the paradox certainly amused him, that the commonplaces of popular exoticism, far from being discredited by the real experience of the traveller, at times persuade reality itself to conform, so that the stereotype becomes more true than the living reality. The domination of the cliché is a little sinister in the décor of Venice: 'la Venise monumentale, espèce de décoration d'opéra féerique' (p.142), 'ce masque monumental que chaque cité se pose sur le visage pour dissimuler ses laideurs et ses misères' (p.281), more comical in the persons of its singers, the gondoliers, who preserve traditional local colour by reviving their forgotten songs for the tourist: 'comme les filles d'Ischia, qui ne revêtent leurs beaux costumes grecs que pour les Anglais, ils ne déploient leurs mélodies qu'à bon escient et avec accompagnement de guinées' (p.178).

Although the performance of the gondoliers is now self-conscious and artificial where once it was natural and spontaneous, the repetition of the platitude remains unavoidable for the author of the travelogue: 'c'est un de ces lieux communs de voyage qu'il est plus maniéré peut-être d'éviter que d'accepter' (p.178).

Far from being a simple enterprise, the writing of the travelogue reveals the complexity of the relationship between words and the things they represent, a relationship in which the word reflects the object, while the object, itself at least in part a creation of language, reflects or even seems to guy the word.

· · · · ·

So far, we have considered the *Voyage en Italie* as a travelogue. However, Gautier was of course not only a journalist but also a poet; and the *Voyage* is, like much of his writing, the work of both the journalist and the poet.

In the preface to **Albertus** of 1832, Gautier deplored the prevalent confusion between the poetic or aesthetic mode of language and its prosaic or practical mode, indicating the danger of the erosion of the former by the latter.[7] The dangers of this confusion are nowhere more apparent than in Gautier's own work than in the series of **Voyages,** journeys which the poet makes only by courtesy of the journalist's copy.

Of the *Voyage en Italie* itself it might be said that the text contains, not one single homogeneous account, but two different versions of the same journey, recounted by two different narrators, playing two different roles and serving two very different ends. Gautier knew all too well the difficulties of combining the roles of the journalist and of the poet, difficulties which were no doubt responsible, to some extent, both for the richness of this text as a source of observations by the writer upon the practice of his craft, and for its characteristic weakness, which Gautier himself noted— imperfection in the balance and distribution of the material and a lack of coherence in the composition.

The overall shape of the *Voyage* itself suggests some uncertainty as to the role of the narrator and the character of the written text. The *Voyage en Italie* was based upon a real journey which took Gautier through Switzerland into Italy, to Milan, Venice, Padua, Ferrara and on to Florence, Rome and Naples, ending with the author's expulsion from Naples in the Autumn of 1850. As a journalist, Gautier apparently intended to follow the outline provided by this itinerary closely; and indeed the articles which appeared as regular *feuilletons* in Parisian newspapers contain accounts of the visits to Geneva, Milan, Venice, Padua, Ferrara and Florence.

However, the form of the *Voyage* as it was published first by Lecou in 1852 and subsequently in the augmented edition of Charpentier, suggests that its author

was influenced by something other than the journalist's concern to bring to his public an accurate account of the principal stages of his journey. The text of the *Voyage* as we have it ends with the account of the visit to Florence: there is no mention of the visits to Rome and Naples. Moreover, the predominance of the Venetian episode, to which twenty of the twenty-nine chapters of the *Voyage* are devoted, confirms the impression that the writer, if not the traveller, had reached his true destination in Venice and was reluctant to continue.[8] This, together with the richness and abundance of references to the works of the French writers and painters of the 1830's and to those of other periods and origins which enjoyed a particular vogue at that time, points to the dual nature of the text as, not merely a journalist's account of his own present travels, but also a more poetic recapitulation of the familiar artistic and literary theme of the 'voyage en Italie', in which the visit to Venice traditionally played a major part, as it does in the earlier versions which Gautier sketched in his own first Romantic works.[9]

Throughout the *Voyage,* the journalist and the poet (if we may continue to use these convenient labels to distinguish between the two voices of the narrator) display very different priorities and reveal very different attitudes to the use of language as a means of representation—and, indeed, to the nature of the subject to be represented.

The distinction between the two approaches is particularly apparent in the Venetian episode itself. The journalist, equating reality with realism, sets out to observe the characteristic details of Venetian life. The chapters devoted to such matters as 'la vie à Venise' (XII), 'détails familiers' (XIII) and 'détails de mœurs' (XXVI) testify to his intention. In this respect, the failure of language to embrace completely the reality of the traveller's experience may be seen as an involuntary failure, and the fiction of a mischievous Nature, who repeatedly defies the attempts of language to encapsulate her fickle moods within the confines of its conventional formulae, holds good.

By contrast, in the poet's version, the failure to seize the realities of Italian life and scenery is not really failure at all, but the result of the writer's own deliberate refusal to identify truth with the detail of everyday life. In direct contravention of the principles on which the travelogue is ostensibly based, Gautier observes more than once in his reflections on the works of fellow artists, both writers and painters, that realism in art is of little value in his eyes—a position to which he repeatedly returned, as the basis for both his criticism and his own creative writing. Although his task as the author of a travelogue took him into the backstreets of Venice, he found that the true atmosphere of the city was most perfectly captured in the magnificence of Veronese's vast architectural compositions which had, as he himself acknowledged, little to offer to 'les amateurs de la vérité vraie' (p.221). The sight of the marionettes which entertained him in Domo d'Ossola at the outset of his journey through Italy had already caused him to reflect that truth is more often to be found in the unreality of art than in the so-called realities of everyday life.[10]

The journalist seeks the reality of Venice in its present, and bases his account upon close, direct observation of the lives of its inhabitants and their immediate surroundings. The poet, on the other hand, prefers to view the city from the height, and the distance, of the campanile of St Mark's. From this aesthetic distance, characteristically represented in many of Gautier's works by the view of the city from the height of a tower, the poet discovers, or rediscovers, a landscape which is revealed by the intuition or the imagination of things distant in time and space.[11] The buildings of Venice, with their 'milliers de cheminées rondes, carrées, évasées en turban'. Their domes and roofs which offer 'l'effet de ces armures de chevaliers mystérieux dans les tournois du moyen-âge' (p.83) seem to be inhabited still by the Oriental potentates and the medieval knights who peopled the world of the Romantic past.

The journalist attempts, if he does not always succeed in his aims, to widen the scope of the existing *récit de voyage* by uncovering, behind the magnificent façade of conventional representation, the minutiae and even the misery of contemporary Venetian life. The poetic vision on the other hand, free from the limitations imposed upon the journalist by the necessity for direct observation, gives to the travelogue its own new dimension by the very means of recollecting and even repeating the procedures and practices of its author's predecessors in the literary and artistic tradition to which this version of the **Voyage en Italie** belongs. Gautier's account of the ascent of the campanile and the view over the rooftops of Venice echoes Hugo's ascent of the cathedral of *Notre-Dame de Paris,* from whose towers the modern city appears transfigured by the memory of its more glorious past. Moreover, the Venice of the **Voyage** markedly resembles the half-medieval, half-oriental city which Gautier had himself evoked in the poem which he entitled 'Notre-Dame' and dedicated to the master.[12]

The contrast between observation and imagination is reinforced in the text of the **Voyage** by the opposition between daylight and darkness. Venice by day belongs to the journalist, Venice by night to the poet.

Arriving in Venice by night, the journalist strives in vain to find his bearings by means of the landmarks made familiar by the versions of previous travellers: 'des deux côtés, la lagune, avec ce noir mouillé plus sombre que l'obscurité même, s'étendait dans l'inconnu . . . on ne pouvait distinguer ni le ciel, ni l'eau, ni le pont' (p.67).

In the light of morning, he is reassured to recognise the church which Canaletto had represented with such meticulous accuracy: 'nous reconnûmes sur-le-champ la Salute, d'après le beau tableau . . .'; and it is as though, despite all their apparent exoticism, his travels do not after all take him outside the formal galleries of the Louvre with its well-known masterpieces.

The darkness, which masked the familiarity of the Venetian scenery for the journalist, illuminates the links between the forms of the poet's own imagination and those created by the artists and writers whom he recognises as his precursors in the Romantic tradition: 'nous croyions circuler dans un roman de Maturin, de Lewis ou d'Anne Radcliff, illustré par Goya, Piranèse et Rembrandt' (p.69).[13] The poet accepts with pleasure the hazards of a journey in which darkness opens up perspectives almost beyond the reaches of the imagination, and where reality, in defiance of all preconception, apes unreality: 'certes, ce n'était pas ainsi que nous avions rêvé notre entrée à Venise; mais celle-ci dépassait en fantastique tout ce que l'imagination de Martynn eût trouvé de mystérieux' (p.67), 'jamais la réalité n'a moins ressemblé à elle-même que ce soir-là' (p.69).[14]

In the eyes of the journalist, the reality of Venetian life becomes most intelligible when the things which he describes conform most perfectly with the simple logic of cause and effect. The 'marchand de fritures', who peddles some of the most tempting morsels of Venetian local colour, lends himself obligingly to the demonstration of the principle of the influence of climate upon character: 'la sobriété est une vertu méridionale qui se complique aisément de paresse, et il se fait peu de cuisine dans les maisons. On envoie chercher à ces officines en plein vent des pâtes, des beignets, des bras de poulpe, des poissons frits' (p.155).

In the eyes of the poet, truth is more often glimpsed when Venice rediscovers the freedom of its imagination. In the hours of darkness, the Venetians are revealed in their true light, regaining a verve and a passion which serves the more mysterious purposes of melodrama: 'l'ombre lui rend le mystère dont le jour la dépouille, remet le masque et le domino antiques aux vulgaires habitants, et donne aux plus simples mouvements de la vie des allures d'intrigue ou de crime. Chaque porte qui s'entre-bâille a l'air de laisser passer un amant ou un bravo' (p.70).

The journalist observes in the conduct of the present inhabitants of the city the sad realities of a life which is dominated by the consequences of their historical position. He remarks upon the response of the Venetians to the celebrations in honour of the Austrian emperor: 'ce peuple qui faisait le mort tandis que ses oppresseurs exultaient de joie, cette ville qui se supprimait pour ne pas assister à ce triomphe' (p.239).

The poet on the other hand discovers the true heritage of the Venetians in the survival of an artistic tradition which liberates them, under cover of darkness, both from subjection to an alien regime and from conformity to the conventions of realism: 'tout le mélodrame et la mise en scène romantique de l'ancienne Venise nous revenait malgré nous en mémoire . . . cette impression, qui semblera peut-être exagérée, est de la vérité la plus exacte, et nous pensons qu'il serait difficile de s'en défendre, même au philistin le plus positif; nous allons même plus loin, c'est le vrai sens de Venise qui se dégage, la nuit, des transformations modernes' (p.69). Fantasy has its own strange truth; and human nature finds a more spontaneous expression in the contrived inventions of melodrama than in the apparently artless observations of the journalist.

In the poetic version of the **Voyage,** the Venetian episode is not a description of a real city but the evocation of an ideal place whose importance stems from the position which it occupies, not in geography or history, but among the states of the mind: 'chaque homme, poëte ou non, se choisit une ou deux villes, patries idéales qu'il fait habiter par ses rêves, dont il se figure les palais, les rues, les maisons, les aspects, d'après une architecture intérieure . . . Pour notre part, trois villes nous ont toujours préoccupé: Grenade, Venise et le Caire' (pp.65-6). The landscape of Venice is defined here, not as the journalist had tried to define that of Italy, by opposition with that of Switzerland, but by analogy with the two other images of the ideal city which occupy a place of privilege in the poet's mind, representing the area where his imagination, finding itself at home, and not abroad, may freely move.

The poetic version brings about a reversal of the values on which that of the journalist was apparently based. Much of the humour of the travelogue arises from the author's observation of the ways in which direct experience banishes his preconceptions and illusions. With a smile, Gautier recalls the idea which he had formed of the city of Geneva: 'une idée enfantine . . . nous fait toujours imaginer les villes d'après le produit qui les rend célèbres . . . ainsi Bruxelles est un grand carré de choux . . . Nuremberg une boîte de jouets, et Genève une montre avec quatre trous en rubis' (p.3). The imaginary city is picturesque, enchanting: 'nous nous imaginions une vaste complication d'horlogerie, roues dentées, cylindres, ressorts, échappements, tout cela faisant tic-tac et tournant perpétuellement' (p.3).

The reality is drab, monotonous: 'Eh bien! ce rêve s'est envolé comme les autres. . . . La courbe et l'ellipse sont proscrites comme trop sensuelles et trop voluptueuses: le gris est bien venu partout, sur les murailles et sur les vêtements (pp.3, 4). Accurate description is associated with the use of a language stripped bare of its colour and charm, whose questionable virtue lies in its power to banish the frail but fertile visions of the imagination in favour of the more robust but arid observations of the external eye.

The imaginary vision is denounced as false in this context because it upsets the logical basis of the realistic description, reversing cause and effect, taking the product of the city for the city which produced it, and allowing the character of the object to be determined by that of its representation.

In the Venetian episode, by contrast, the imaginative vision becomes powerful, legitimately, by virtue of its fidelity to the true character of the writer's experience, which is revealed to be more closely associated with the nature of his previous responsiveness to other forms of representation, both visual and verbal, than with that of the objects of the external world themselves: 'qui jette les fondations de cette ville intuitive? . . . Les récits, les gravures, la vue d'une carte de géographie, quelquefois l'euphonie ou la singularité du nom, un conte lu quand on était tout jeune' (p.66). The preconception loses its comic naiveté now, to emerge, in place of the landscape of the external world, as the subject to be represented, or re-presented, to the mind's eye by means of a poetic evocation whose theme is, this time, not the dominance of present realities, but the continuing strength of the images of past experiences which the creative mind receives and builds upon: 'nous ne connaissons encore Venise que par cette image tracée dans la chambre noire du cerveau, image souvent si arrêtée que l'objet même l'efface à peine' (p.66).

However, the recognition of the poetic qualities of these images sometimes becomes so closely bound up with the familiar pattern of the writer's thinking that he is tempted to forget the real origins of their significance— to be found in the chance encounters which have left their indelible impressions upon his own imagination, with the forms of an engraving or the sound of a word. He tries to redefine their meaning by allowing himself to glimpse a promise of the authenticity of the image in the appearance, within external reality, of figures which closely reflect the forms of his ideal. Knowingly led astray in his pursuit, through the backstreets of Venice, of the young girl whose fate it is to represent the incarnation of the poet's ideal of feminine beauty—she is cast in this role because she possesses, naturally, all the elegance and dignity achieved by the art of the actress Mlle Rachel in the performance of classical tragedy—Gautier protests his innocence with less than perfect good faith: 'entre toutes les suppositions que put faire cette pauvre enfant, attaque galante, séduction, enlèvement, elle ne s'imagina certainement pas qu'elle était suivie par un poëte plastique qui donnait une fête à ses yeux' (p.164).

The poet's error, the converse of that denounced in the journalist's account of his attempt to impose the picturesque character of the preconceived image upon the drab reality of the city of Geneva, is revealed when the version of the artist is betrayed as a mere copy of a real model rather than an expression of the ideal of his imagination. The imperfection of the ideal vision is apparent, not when Gautier fails to find it realised in the person of the young girl whom he follows through the backstreets of Venice and who constantly eludes him, but when the paintings in which he thought he had glimpsed its perfection prove to be too perfectly matched, or indeed surpassed, by the beauties who parade in the public parks: 'après une promenade aux jardins publics, on ne s'étonne plus de la splendeur dorée de l'école vénitienne; ce qu'on croyait un rêve de l'art n'est que la traduction quelquefois inférieure de la réalité' (p.162).

. . . . .

Surprised to find blue hydrangeas growing on the shores of Lake Maggiore, Gautier had himself indicated that the culmination of artistic endeavour, if not of all human endeavour, lay not in the cultivation of the perfections of existing reality, but in the creation of those which were absent from it: 'ces hortensias bleus nous ont beaucoup frappé, car le bleu est la chimère des horticulteurs, qui cherchent sans les trouver la tulipe bleue, la rose bleue, le dahlia bleu' (p.36).

The abundance of literary and pictorial references in the *Voyage,* as in Gautier's writing as a whole, itself indicates the extent of his own preoccupation with the processes of artistic creation and the perfection of artistic expression. The subject of the conflict between the interests of the journalist and those of the poet brings us naturally to that of the rivalry between the poet and the painter, and to a reinterpretation, proposed by Gautier himself in the *Voyage,* of the familiar theme, in which Gautier has so often been thought to give the upper hand to the painter. In his attempt to capture the splendours of the Piazzetta viewed from the sea: 'ce tableau sans rival au monde, et le seul peut-être que l'imagination ne puisse dépasser' (p.75), he himself seems to envy the painter and the musician their superiority in the representation of the landscapes of the external world: 'car le poëte, moins heureux que le peintre et le musicien, ne dispose que d'une seule ligne; le premier a toute une palette, le second tout un orchestre' (p.78).

Nevertheless, by another of the quirks of language, the expression of impotence may serve to mark what the consummate artist knows to be a *tour de force;* and Gautier himself offers a felicitous account of the failings of language in the representation of those things which language is apparently unable to represent: 'comment exprimer ces tons roses du palais ducal, qui semble vivre comme de la chair; ces blancheurs neigeuses des statues . . . ? Qui peindra cette atmosphère vague,

lumineuse, pleine de rayons et de vapeurs, d'où le soleil n'exclut pas le nuage?' (p.77).

Moreover, in his account of the beauty of Lake Geneva, though he borrows the conventions of pictorial perspective or, to be more accurate, the terminology of the painter, to define the principal outlines of the scene, he indicates the superiority of language over pictorial means in the suggestion of those aspects of the subject which seem to lie beyond the scope of artistic representation:

> Voilà à peu près les linéaments grossiers du tableau; mais ce que le pinceau serait peut-être plus impuissant encore à rendre que la plume, c'est la couleur du lac . . . le cobalt, l'outre-mer, le saphir, la turquoise, l'azur des plus beaux yeux bleus, ont des nuances terreuses en comparaison. Quelques reflets sur l'aile du martin-pêcheur, quelques iris sur la nacre de certaines coquilles peuvent seuls en donner une idée.

> (pp.14-15)

Gautier's acknowledgement of his own impotence is no doubt well founded. The power of poetic evocation is not in direct proportion to the abundance of the imagery; and the apparent virtuosity of Gautier's writing does not always disguise an underlying sterility, which is betrayed by the repetition of stock patterns of images, recurring in different contexts, and indicating a preference for the well-tried formula rather than a perfect sensitivity to the most telling or the most appropriate form of expression. In the rehearsal of the different analogies, the immediacy of the impression of the colours of the lake is all too easily lost: the rarity of nature's gems is itself commonplace. Nevertheless, the fleeting aspects and the subtle hues are perhaps, as Gautier himself indicates, more easily captured by the writer's images, themselves no more than a series of suggestions, than by the substitution of another and possibly inferior colour from the painter's limited palette. If the scope of the artist's work is to be restricted to the direct representation of the visible aspects of the external world, the painter may just have the edge. However if, as Gautier's own reflections on the image of the ideal city of Venice suggest, the real aim of the artist is to recapture the impressions and associations with which the mind gives meaning to the things the eye perceives, then the poet may well regain the upper hand.[15]

Throughout the *Voyage* there is both confusion and distinction between statement and suggestion, description and evocation. These are, after all, different versions of the same journey, a journey in which the traveller addresses himself as much to the processes of literary creation as to the landscape of Italy itself. The voices of the different narrators belong to different modes of the same language, in which, through the constant shifting in the relationships between words and the things they represent, the pursuit of meaning is both frustrating and fertile. If the text of the **Voyage** speaks explicitly of the difficulties of adapting the existing forms of language to the description of the unfamiliar landscapes of the external world, it speaks implicitly, though none the less essentially, of the riches of the creative imagination which can be revealed in the patterns of poetic evocation.

Notes

[1] Twenty-eight articles appeared in *La Presse* between September 24, 1850 and November 15, 1851. The version published by Lecou in 1852, with the title *Italia*, contained in addition to these the text of one article devoted to Ferrara and previously published in *Le Pays* for January 11, 1852. The first Charpentier edition of 1875 took the title *Voyage en Italie* and included the text of one further article, devoted to Florence and first published in *Le Pays* for January 13, 1852.

[2] Page references in the text indicate the Charpentier edition of the *Voyage en Italie* (Paris, 1876), reprint of the edition of 1875.

[3] Eugène Isabey (1803-1886), Wiliam Wyld (1806-1889), Richard Parkes Bonington (1801-1828), Gabriel Decamps (1803-1860) and Jules Joyant (1803-1854) were influential in the development of the new school of French landscape painting which emerged in the early 1830's.

[4] Théophile Gautier, *Poésies complètes,* ed. Nizet (Paris, 1970), I, 97.

[5] Ibid., I, 9.

[6] See *Notre-Dame de Paris* (first published 1831), Book II, chapter vi, 'La cruche cassée'. Gérard Dow (also known as Gerrit Dou), 1613-1675, and Franz van Mieris the Elder, 1635-1681, were among the Dutch painters of the seventeenth century whose influence was frequently acknowledged by the French writers and painters of the 1830's and whose works were popularised by engraving.

[7] 'En général, dès qu'une chose devient utile, elle cesse d'être belle.—Elle rentre dans la vie positive, de poésie, elle devient prose, de libre, esclave.' *Poésies complètes,* I, 82.

[8] As Jean Richer points out in his *Etudes et recherches sur Théophile Gautier,* ed. Nizet (Paris, 1981), Part II, ch. iv, 1, 'Venise imaginée', the chapters devoted to Venice represent 65% of the text as it stands and, had Gautier completed his itinerary, giving similar atten-

tion to Rome and Naples, the *Voyage* would have occupied several volumes.

[9] See, for example, *Albertus* (*Poésies complètes,* I, 127), the Romantic poem to end all Romantic poems, in which, as my study of *Transposition d'art in the poetry of Théophile Gautier* (diss. Cambridge, 1972) has shown, Gautier makes abundant use of a range of pictorial and literary references which are very similar to those of the *Voyage en Italie.*

[10] See p. 32: 'C'est un spectacle étrange et qui prend bientôt une inquiétante réalité, qu'une représentation de marionnettes. . .'.

[11] Pierre Citron discusses Gautier's preference for this aesthetic viewpoint in *La Poésie de Paris dans la littérature française* (Paris, 1961), II, 5.

[12] See *Notre-Dame de Paris,* III, i, 'Notre-Dame', and ii, 'Paris à vol d'oiseau', and Gautier, *Poésies complètes,* II, 147.

[13] These were again familiar references for the author of *Albertus* and for his contemporaries.

[14] Christopher Thompson discusses the influence of the work of the English painter John Martin (1789-1854) upon Hugo's early poetic evocations of vast and fantastic architectural visions—see *Victor Hugo and the Graphic Arts* (Geneva, 1970), pp.74-95.

[15] Sainte-Beuve's Joseph Delorme had already drawn a similar lesson from his own meditation upon the relationship between poetry and painting: 'les couleurs naturelles des choses sont des couleurs sans nom; mais, selon la disposition d'âme du spectateur, selon la saison de l'année, l'heure du jour, le jeu de la lumière, ses couleurs ondulent à l'infini, tout en paraissant copier. Les peintres vulgaires ne saisissent pas ces distinctions . . . Mais, sous ces couleurs grossièrement superficielles, les Bonington, les Boulanger, devinent et reproduisent la couleur intime . . .', *Vie, poésies et pensées de Joseph Delorme,* ed. Gérald Antoine (Paris, 1957; first edition, 1830), p.148. See also Baudelaire: 'Si tel assemblage d'arbres, de montagnes, d'eaux et de maisons, que nous appelons un paysage, est beau, ce n'est pas par lui-même, mais par moi, par ma grâce propre, par l'idée ou le sentiment que j'y attache', "Salon de 1859, vii, Le Paysage", *Oeuvres complètes,* ed. de la Pléiade (Paris, 1976), II, 660.

Melanie C. Hawthorne (essay date 1988)

SOURCE: "Dis-Covering the Female: Gautier's *Roman de la momie,*" in *The French Review,* Vol. LXVI, No. 5, April, 1993, pp. 718-29.

[In the following essay, originally presented in 1988 at the Southeast Conference on Foreign Languages and Literatures at Rollins College, Florida, Hawthorne analyzes the inaccuracies found in the prologue of Gautier's Le Roman de la momie *and exposes the gender bias inherent in his descriptions.]*

Théophile Gautier's **Le Roman de la momie,** once a canonical text of the French secondary school literature curriculum, is now seldom read, and then only as an illustration of aspects of Gautier's work developed elsewhere.[1] I do not intend to take up here the politics of the rise and fall of the novel's stock, which are tied to the rising and falling stock of orientalism and sentimental fiction; rather, I shall argue that a text which at one moment seems irredeemably sexist deserves a closer look because of the message written in its margins. I shall focus on the margins by discussing only the Prologue, a framing device that establishes the context of the main narrative.[2] It recounts the discovery of a female mummy, together with a manuscript describing an anomaly: how a woman came to be buried in the Valley of the Kings.

I would have said that this prologue appears sexist *at first glance,* except that historically, those readers who have given the text *a first glance*—and even a second—seem not to have noticed any particular narrative point of view at all. The novel, and especially the descriptive prologue, drew praise precisely because of its "accuracy." Indeed, for some critics, the work is so minutely detailed as to be tiresome in its subordination of narration to description.[3]

Part of the reason that accuracy became an issue, no doubt, was that when **Le Roman de la momie** first appeared in twenty-one episodes of the *Moniteur* between 11 March and 6 May 1857, Théophile Gautier had yet to set foot in Egypt. Unlike his celebrated literary contemporaries Nerval and Flaubert, Gautier had to describe what he had never seen. On the one hand, this was perhaps not a disadvantage. Orientalism always was—and still is—more a matter of the way the West has dealt with, and indirectly represented, itself; it is not about how accurately it renders the "other" of the Orient. As Edward Said has noted, "[t]he things to look at [in the Orientalist text] are style, figures of speech, setting, narrative devices, historical and social circumstances, *not* the correctness of the representation nor its fidelity to some great original" (21).

On the other hand, despite an increasing, problematization of the notion of "accuracy," for over a century, those who have written about **Le Roman de la momie** have been lured into discussing not the meaning of accuracy in this context, but the degree of accuracy to be found in the work. Gautier borrowed materials on Egyptology from his friend Ernest Feydeau (the father of the more well-known Georges), and the consensus is that he did rather well with them. Gautier's immediate contemporaries marvelled at his precision (Boschot, *Théophile* 89). Writing somewhat later, toward the turn of the century, George Saintsbury observes that "*Le Roman de la momie* is scarcely more than one long translation, into Gautier's exquisite literary language, of the results of discovery as to the manners, customs, and furniture of the ancient Egyptians" (232). Indeed, so accurate is the rendering that Saintsbury finds the style "tedious." Jean-Marie Carré undertook a scrupulous check of all Gautier's Egyptian sources in 1932, and described Gautier's method in **Le Roman** as "des transcriptions presques [sic] littérales de passages empruntés aux ouvrages archéologiques . . . qui copient, avec une fidèle minutie, les bas-reliefs et les peintures murales reproduits dans les planches de Champollion, Belzoni, Prisse d'Avennes, etc." (151).[4] Writing in the 1960s, Adolphe Boschot summarizes the more recent critical judgment:

> La valeur littéraire de *La Momie* est évidemment ce qui importe le plus dans un roman. Mais son exactitude archéologique fut reconnue par plus d'un égyptologue. A part quelques inadvertances, quelques vétilles topographiques, quelques menus détails que l'érudition, depuis un siècle, n'a pas manqué d'éclaircir ou de préciser, le scrupuleux Gautier a fidélement mis en œuvre les documents dont il disposait. (Introduction xxxvi)

This consensus has continued into the present without substantial challenge.[5]

In praising Gautier for his ability to enable the reader to experience the discovery of a mummy so vividly, critics have minimized those "slips, trifles, and details" that Boschot also dismissed as insignificant. But as Serge Fauchereau points out in an essay on Gautier, "l'intéressant, c'est *l'erreur* qui est faite dans la lecture d'un texte, d'un auteur" (133). In other words, Gautier's ability to create an illusion is less interesting when it works than when it breaks down. When **Le Roman de la momie** is read, Laurence Lévy-Delpla suggests, "en fonction de ses blancs, de ce qu'il ne dit qu'en creux" (152), a different aspect of the work emerges. I want to (mis-)take Virginia Woolf's suggestion that "we think back through our mothers," and think back through one mummy in particular to "flesh out" the literary implications of accuracy and its failures by focusing on the example of the discovery of a mummy, that is, the uncovering and display of the female body.

The discovery and unwrapping of a female mummy in the prologue of **Le Roman de la momie** constitutes a kind of strip-tease. The epithet "well preserved" is often euphemistically used of older women who retain their sexual attractions, but in the case of Tahoser's mummy, the literal and euphemistic meanings coincide. The literally well-preserved mummy appears beneath the veil of the suggestive language, making the description of archaeological discovery a vehicle for equally thinly-veiled pornography.

The prologue describes the arrival in Egypt of Lord Evandale, a philanthropic aristocrat and amateur archaeologist, and Dr. Rumphius, a German scholar. Together they contact a Greek guide named Argyropoulos to help them locate an undefiled tomb. Their mission is presented as a pure and altruistic quest for knowledge, and the gendered aspect of their search is not at first explicit: they seek any tomb that has not already been plundered. But the sexual politics of their venture soon emerge in a series of sexualizing metaphors that suggest that a female body will best meet their needs. Their goal is "une tombe inviolée" with "ses richesses intactes et son mystère vierge" (151). The use of the adjective "inviolé" indicates that their intention is not only violence and violation, but rape (in French, "violer"), preferably of a *virgo intacta*. Their guide, who assumes the role of procurer, quickly realizes that "vulgar curiosities" will not "seduce" his clients, and thus offers them a site he has been saving for a special occasion.

The vocabulary of sexual conquest continues to permeate the description of the expedition as the party proceeds further into the "ventre" of the hillside. When the funeral chamber is finally reached, Lord Evandale's privilege earns him "la virginité de la découverte" (172). The first to "penetrate" this sacred chamber, he feels a little horrified "en violant" (174), but is reassured when the room is lit "pour faire jouir." The light reveals walls painted" d'une fraîcheur virginale, d'une pureté inouïe." Finally, they examine the sarcophagus and learn that the mummy is that of a woman, a fact they initially surmise from the absence of the ritual phallic beard, but later confirm by more empirical means. They are surprised by this revelation, but the reader attentive to the descriptive language which frames the discovery (a narrative voice audible to the reader-witnesses of the adventure, but not to the participants) has received numerous hints.

Although still "clothed" in its funereal wrappings, the mummy is provocative because the viewer, seeing here through the eyes of Evandale and Rumphius, senses the "corps gracieux et jeune" hidden underneath, and glimpses the "contour ferme et pur de deux seins vierges" (180). As the preservative bands are gradually stripped from the body, however, so too the loose fabric of objective description slowly unravels as Rumphius decides quite arbitrarily that the mummy is young, thereby also adding a note of paedophilia. Finally, the corpse is revealed:

> la jeune femme se dessina dans la chaste nudité de ses belles formes, gardant, malgré tant de siècles écoulés, toute la rondeur de ses contours, toute la grâce souple de ses lignes pures. Sa pose, peu fréquente chez les

momies, était celle de la Vénus de Médicis, comme si les embaumeurs eussent voulu ôter à ce corps charmant la triste attitude de la mort, et adoucir pour lui l'inflexible rigidité du cadavre. L'une de ses mains voilait à demi sa gorge virginale, l'autre cachait des beautés mystérieuses, comme si la pudeur de la morte n'eût pas été rassurée suffisamment par les ombres protectrices du sépulcre. (186)

It would seem that Tahoser's premonition that her tomb will not be sufficient to protect her modesty is vindicated by the treatment of her discoverers. The scene climaxes when the last bands are finally removed, and both men "ejaculate" verbally in admiration (186).

A close reading of these passages may lead the reader to wonder how such description could seem "almost of the nature of a moral tonic" (Saintsbury 229). A first reaction to this thinly-disguised rape might be indignation at Gautier's sexist objectification of women. Pointing out such textual bias has been an important first step in feminist criticism, but increasingly such awareness is only the first step and raises more questions than it answers. In thinking through how such description, clearly intended to titillate, could be read as objectivity for over a century, there is a need to examine first reactions more closely. As Lillian S. Robinson has stated, the most important question for feminist criticism to ask is "so what?"[6] Feminist criticism has already exploded the myth of objectivity, both in general terms that describe the objectification of women and stress the gendered nature of the viewer's response (Berger, Booth, Miller), and also in specific contexts such as those of nude painting or the male gaze (Garrard, Mulvey, Robinson).[7] The treatment of Tahoser's mummy could serve as a textbook example of these phenomena, but is there anything else, anything new, to be said? Disinterested, neutral objectivity is a rhetorical fiction. So what?

The first clue that there may be more to be discovered, more to the mummy than meets the eyes of Evandale and company, is that Gautier himself was well aware of the distortion in his text. That is to say, he was aware of the divergence between his description of the mummy in the prologue and the real appearance of ancient mummies, and he draws the reader's attention to this in the prologue itself. He emphasizes Tahoser's unusually well preserved condition by pointing out that most mummified corpses become blackened over time; although not subject to decomposition, they nevertheless do not resemble living bodies (187). Yet in the same paragraph as he makes this generalization, he describes a mummy which has preserved "l'élasticité de la chair, le grain de l'épiderme et presque la coloration naturelle" (187). As Richer notes, an excessive fidelity to sources would produce (textual) "dryness," whereas Gautier introduces "life" into his material (102). These metaphors, while never specifically applied to the description of the mummy, nevertheless summarize the point of departure in Gautier's text: the mummy that should be dehydrated is instead vivid and life-like, even lubricious.

After completing *Le Roman de la momie,* Gautier also witnessed the unwrapping of a real mummy during the Universal Exhibition. His written account of that event provides an interesting comparison—albeit retroactive—with the description in *Le Roman de la momie,* and confirms the extent to which his depiction of Tahoser's mummy diverges from any realist pretensions. The unwrapping of the mummy of Nes-Khons at the Universal Exhibition provoked the following reflection:

> Etait-elle après tout jeune ou vieille, belle ou laide, cette Nes-Khons. . . . C'est à quoi il est difficile de répondre. Ce n'est plus guère qu'une peau enveloppant des os, et comment retrouver dans ces lignes sèches et raides les sveltes contours des femmes égyptiennes telles qu'on les voit peintes dans les temples, les palais et les tombeaux.
>
> (*L'Orient* II 108)

Gautier lists in this meditation the very parameters he uses in the description of Tahoser: she is more than just "skin and bones," for in *Le Roman de la momie* the skin, or epidermis, was elastic, and the "lignes sèches et raides" were pure and supple; Gautier succeeded in envisioning the "contours" he knew from paintings and supplied from imagination what was lacking in fact. In contrast to the vision he presented of Tahoser's body, when viewing a real mummy, Gautier found it impossible to determine whether the subject was young or old, beautiful or ugly.

It is difficult to believe, then, that Gautier could not have supplied a more accurate description of Tahoser, the heroine-mummy, had he chosen to. That he chose not to creates a significant rupture in the text, not quite an error (to use Fauchereau's term), but "une ouverture fantastique que le roman va dédaigner" (Lévy-Delpla 19). It is this opening, this window of vulnerability in a text highly determined by the availability of rich source materials which invites the reader to take a second look.

The fantastic is the irruption of a repression. The fantastically well-preserved mummy illustrates Freud's thesis that the uncanny (and by extension, the fantastic) stems from the return of the repressed sight of the mother's genitals. In this text, the mummy's genitals are fantastically and spectacularly re-discovered, but the excavation of the unconscious also turns up some other buried thoughts.

The unwrapping of Tahoser's mummy is not only a fantastic moment buried in an otherwise tediously realistic text; it also represents a moment of fantasy.

When the reader identifies with the viewer, the female body is displayed voyeuristically and the pleasures associated with the gaze are evoked and indulged. But if the reader does not adopt this perspective, then, like the bored patron at the porn flick, the reader's eyes may start roving around the darkened chamber in which the spectacle is being projected and begin to notice other things. It is in this sense that a feminist perspective becomes relevant, for in so far as the gaze is a gendered construct, a reader "reading as a woman" is less likely to identify with Tahoser's violators and more likely to adopt a position of critical distance in which the element of fantasy itself becomes readable.[8]

Recognizing that the protagonists are not neutral in their response to the female body leads to the recognition that they are not neutral in their entire archaeological project. The "ouverture fantastique" serves thus as an overture, an introduction to the main work (much as the prologue functions in relation to the main narrative). The sexual investments operating in the discovery of the mummy are matched by economic and epistemological investments in other aspects of the project. When the last veil is removed from the mummy, the veil of objectivity is lifted from the text itself, and what is revealed first and most dramatically by the team's reaction to the mummy then also becomes readable elsewhere.

Based on the individual interests at work, the main characters may be viewed as allegorical, rather like the scenes decorating the tomb walls, "où l'on distinguait vaguement une suite de scènes allégoriques" (166). An amateur archaeologist, a graduate of Cambridge, and a caricature of the colonial English aristocrat (literally the kind who goes out in the mid-day sun), Lord Evandale is the personification of social and economic privilege (152-53). He uses his fortune in socially responsible ways like his real-life counterpart Lord Elgin to enrich the nation. His privilege is thus protected by its superficial altruism from scrutiny and criticism, although his appropriation of the cultural heritage of another country is here implicitly compared to the exploitation of the female body.

On this occasion, Evandale's philanthropy supports the worthy research of the erudite archaeologist Dr. Rumphius, who, as a German, embodies the ideal of the objective, scrupulous, and to the French mind excessively pedantic, quest for truth and pure knowledge. Together these two figures depict pseudo-scientific Objectivity and Privilege cloaked in philanthropy working side by side. The third figure in this allegorical trinity is the Greek Argyropoulos, the middleman who serves knowledge and tolerates privilege in the interest of turning a profit. His incarnation of Capitalism is suggested not only by his actions, but by his eloquent articulation of the laws of supply and demand:

j'espère retirer un bon prix de ma découverte; chacun vit, en ce monde, de sa petite industrie: je déterre des Pharaons, et je les vends aux étrangers. Le Pharaon se fait rare, au train dont on y va; il n'y en a pas pour tout le monde. L'article est demandé, et l'on n'en fabrique plus depuis longtemps. (157)

His claim that everyone has to make a living serves to insulate him from any moral responsibility attached to his activities, and he never questions the principle that distribution of a rare resource should be based purely on who can afford to pay most. His justifications are underscored stylistically by the passive constructions and use of the impersonal "on," which make the economic laws appear natural and without any individual originator or even perpetrator.

As though there could be any doubt about the text's intention to comment on its own production and reception, the prologue reiterates the importance of interpreting signs by presenting archaeology as a matter of reading. First, the guide must interpret the signs in the landscape which indicate the presence of tombs:

> Argyropoulos . . . s'était dit qu'à une certaine place, derrière des rochers dont l'arrangement semblait dû au hasard, existait certainement l'entrée d'une syringe masquée avec un soin tout particulier, et que sa grande expérience en ce genre de perquisition lui avait fait reconnaître à mille indices imperceptibles pour des yeux moins clairvoyants que les siens. (156)

The inexperienced reader would miss the clues indicating an opening in the text of the landscape and would attribute the arrangement to chance, but Argyropoulos sees clearly and his experienced eyes perceive not just one clue, but thousands. The tombs were deliberately disguised in a conscious attempt to confuse the ordinary person. As Argyropoulos mutters darkly, "Ces damnés Egyptiens étaient si rusés pour cacher l'entrée de leurs terriers funèbres! ils ne savaient que s'imaginer afin de désorienter le pauvre monde" (168). Already, then, the text announces the theme of a hidden entry visible only to those with experience at reading the signs. When the entrance to the undisturbed tomb is finally revealed, the metaphor shifts from interpreting landscape to hieroglyphs. The reader is now Rumphius, "un déchiffreur d'inscriptions" (154), who confirms that they are on the right path (163).

Having discovered the opening to the tomb, and suspecting that it contains the treasures that they seek, the intrepid explorers must find their way through the labyrinthine tunnels and chambers, with its deliberately deceptive trails and dead ends. They succeed by hypothesizing that the tomb will try to mislead them. The alluring strip-tease act offered by Tahoser's mummy functions analogously as such a diversion to those exploring the text. Gautier was aware that the prurient,

those prone to censor, would be distracted from attending to the redeeming features of a work of art by nudity, as he commented in the preface to *Mademoiselle de Maupin:* "S'il y a quelque nudité dans un tableau ou dans un livre, ils y vont droit comme le porc à la fange, et ne s'inquiètent pas des fleurs épanouies ni des beaux fruits dorés qui pendent de toutes parts" (Preface 26). Treasure-hunters, those who would pick the golden apples awaiting harvest, must thus mis-read the directions and ignore the "signs" given by the tomb in order to overcome its defenses. The strategy applies both to the readers of landscape and hieroglyphs as well as to the readers of Gautier's text. Fortunately, with this key and some basic skills, success is virtually guaranteed: "avec de l'insistence on entre partout" remarks Rumphius (170). This causal tribute to perseverance as the key to forced entry echoes the violation of the mummy, but also connects that central scene to the entry of the tomb, a metacritical comment on the mode of entry into the text itself in which the mummy scene suggested an "opening."

Thus, like numerous other texts which appear superficially to be about the geographically or temporally distant, the prologue of *Le Roman de la momie* reveals itself instead to be very much about the contemporary. A common way of deflecting criticism at any time, this strategy holds special appeal during periods of severe repression and censorship. France in the 1850s has been described as just such a period, when novelists employed "oppositional strategies" to disguise their critiques, strategies which often remained unreadable to the novelists' contemporaries (Chambers 22-27). Gautier's incentive to adopt such a mask becomes evident when it is remembered that *Le Roman de la momie* was published in 1857, that is to say, in the midst of this most repressive era emblematized by the prosecution of Flaubert's *Madame Bovary* and Baudelaire's *Les Fleurs du mal.* As one whose career as a journalist flourished during the Second Empire, Gautier could hardly have ignored the impact of censorship on his profession. Although the "art for art's sake" movement founded by Gautier made a point of rejecting politics, such a rejection was hardly apolitical itself (Chambers, "1851" 711).[9] Moreover, while Gautier may have repudiated political involvement, he was neither politically naive nor unaware of the connection between art and politics. In the preface to *Mademoiselle de Maupin* he drew attention to an (inverse) connection between pleasure and civil rights, stating "[j]e renoncerais très joyeusement à mes droits de Français et de citoyen pour voir . . . une belle femme nue" (45-46). In *Le Roman de la momie,* he gives his readers a similar choice: those who choose to see" une belle femme nue" do so at the expense of certain rights; the text uses pleasure as a distraction from the right to question the objectivity of the text itself.

To find a rich meaning that has not already been explored, picked over, and raided by the censors, the reader must, then, be skilful and must search beyond the obvious. The reward for this trouble is a hidden indictment of objectivity in general, and of business, philanthropy and science in particular. Argyropoulos is clearly the least disinterested party, since his financial gains are immediate and obvious to all, but his role in procuring the mummy also places him in the position of pimp. This implied analogy between procurement and trade challenges Argyropoulos's disavowal of responsibility (quoted above), and suggests that the desire to make a living does not *ipso facto* render ethics irrelevant.

Because he is independently wealthy, Evandale appears financially disinterested in the venture: he seems to represent a relatively benign form of privilege, an enlightened leader from whom much can be expected because much has been given him. Yet Gautier shows that nothing compels his generosity and that he is as capable of selfish interest as any churl: Evandale does not in the end share his latest treasure with the nation as he had proclaimed he would. He decides not to donate the sarcophagus to the British Museum as intended (190) because he has fallen in love with Tahoser. There is nothing, therefore, that compels those with sufficient power and privilege (such as Emperors?) to fulfill their promises, to be fair and just. Their privilege may be tolerated because it is offset by philanthropy, but good intentions can change on a whim, with no recourse for those who find themselves disenfranchised as a result. Gautier hints that such self-interest carries its own punishment, however, for the same motivation behind Evandale's selfish act causes him to die without offspring: "il n'a jamais voulu se marier, quoiqu'il soit le dernier de sa race" (342). His perverse love for Tahoser condemns his entire race to die out, suggesting an unspoken curse upon the gold-digging aristocracy of the Second Empire that Gautier would never have dared proclaim publicly.

Finally, there remains the figure of Rumphius, whose neutrality, claimed in the name of pure knowledge, appears at first the most untarnished. Of course, it is understood that Rumphius stands to gain personally from the expedition—he will publish an erudite dissertation that will place him among the foremost scientists (151)—but fame seems the natural reward for someone who advances the public good through science. After all, Rumphius intends to share his knowledge, and it is of only minimal financial advantage. But Rumphius's rewards are in inverse proportion to those of Argyropoulos: less material and immediate, but more abstract and lasting. The power of knowledge seems destined to extend literally beyond the tomb, and to make its owner immortal and all-powerful in a way Argyropoulos, would scarcely dream of. As Rumphius himself states "les uns cherchent l'or, les autres la vérité, les deux choses les plus précieuses du monde" (167). As one who controls discourse (the "symbolic"), Rumphius will be able to shape truth itself, thus his hidden motives are the most powerful of all.

Once again, it is the reaction to Tahoser's mummy that reveals the breakdown of Rumphius's objectivity. For him the pleasure of undressing the mummy is clearly only an incidental reward, a minor victory in a larger battle for control of discourse:

> Oh! les Egyptiens, dit Rumphius en souriant, étaient de prodigieux architectes, d'étonnants artistes, de profonds savants; les prêtres de Memphis et de Thèbes auraient rendu des points même à nos érudits d'Allemagne, et pour la symbolique, ils étaient de la force de plusieurs Creuzer; mais nous finirons par déchiffrer leurs grimoires et leur arracher leur secret. Le grand Champollion a donné leur alphabet; nous autres, nous lirons couramment leurs livres de granit. En attendant, déshabillons cette jeune beauté. (184)

Although the works of the Egyptians are literally written in stone, indeed in granite, Rumphius foresees a time when another civilization will succeed in appropriating their symbolic power. In this endeavor, although insistence may be the key, the use of force is more explicit. The adversarial language of competing Egyptian and German scholars, the matching of intellectual "forces," and the triumph of snatching the enemy's secrets, all reveal that knowledge is not a collaborative and cumulative process, but a violent fight for control. Tearing off the mummy's clothes is an immediate gratification while awaiting the later satisfaction of being able to dominate a culture recognized as intellectually equal. Such incidental rape and pillage is the reward of the troops who wage such wars, a reward Rumphius claims casually "en attendant."

When the battle for control is won, Rumphius will have more power than money could buy, although financial resources are necessary to gain access to what he seeks. This state of indebtedness is represented by the dedication of his *magnum opus* to Evandale, underscoring symbolically that this supposedly "pure" knowledge is in fact quite "interested." But money is a means, not an end, for Rumphius, since control of truth will give him more power than control of wealth. In addition to publishing his erudite dissertation, Rumphius will also become a translator. A papyrus text is discovered along with Tahoser's mummy, and Rumphius undertakes to translate and publish the hieroglyphs that tell Tahoser's story. It is thus Rumphius who makes the text available to the reader and who is able to shape history even after his own death through his retelling of an episode of Egyptian history. This role reveals even more clearly the extent of his control. Rumphius mimics the role of an author (he, not Gautier, we are to believe, is responsible for the text we are about to read), but the basis of his narrative power is an appropriation of the voice of the very subject he has dominated in his quest for knowledge.

Thus, Argyropoulos, Evandale, and Rumphius all reveal their vested interests when reacting to the divestment of Tahoser. Those who focus on the strip-tease may neglect to notice that these emperors, rather than having no clothes, instead wear particular uniforms. By reading Gautier's text the same way as the explorers "read" the signals of the landscape and tomb, by deliberately "reading against the grain," I have suggested that **Le Roman de la momie** calls into question the possibility of pure knowledge when the search for truth is indebted to privilege and mediated by the profit motive.[10] However, this broad indictment of objectivity only becomes readable when a perspective that challenges the neutral objectivity of the male gaze is employed. The "ouverture fantastique" of the mummy's dis-covery then reveals several hidden treasures. For Argyropoulos, Evandale, and Rumphius, the principal rewards come in the form of money, love, and power; for the reader, the most precious discovery is not a papyrus, but a palimpsest which reveals its message only when the more visible text is deliberately ignored.

Notes

[1] Earlier versions of this paper were presented at the Southeast Conference on Foreign Languages and Literatures at Rollins College, Florida in 1988 and at the Women's Festival at the University of Arkansas in 1990. I am also indebted to Jane Gallop for her insightful and probing comments in the course of a summer seminar made possibly by the NEH, and to Joe Golsan for his helpful suggestions.

[2] I am not the only one to give more weight to this part of the narrative; moreover, the prologue has played a significant role in arguments about Gautier's accuracy. Of the three examples of Gautier's accuracy cited by Boschot, two are from this introductory part of the novel. The first is the description of the descent into the mummy's tomb, "la transcription littérale d'un plan publié par Feydeau" (xxxvii). The second is the description of the mummy found there, based on an engraving and a description by Passalacqua. According to Geneviève van den Bogaert, "[l]a description de la momie de Tahoser reproduit fidèlement celle que Passalacqua avait donnée de la morte inconnue" (14). Describing specifically the unwrapped mummy, Carré notes the many details Gautier borrows—"Gautier n'a même pas inventé sa pudique et charmante attitude" (156)—and implies a lack of imagination on Gautier's part. The description of the mummy itself, then, described in terms of literalness and faithfulness, represents one of the key pieces of evidence in the argument for Gautier's accuracy.

[3] For Jean-Marie Carré it is merely "une suite de tableaux" (157), while for Marc Eigeldinger "[l]'ensemble du roman s'organise comme une succession d'images et de tableaux, privilégiant la représentation" (255).

[4] For further discussion of sources, see Bogaert's introduction and bibliography.

[5] For Jean Richer, writing in 1981, Gautier as a historical writer brings "un souci de vérité" to the genre (99), and in the case of *Le Roman de la momie*, "[Gautier] n'a presque rien inventé" (100). Eigeldinger, on the other hand, acknowledges in his 1985 preface that *Le Roman de la momie* n'apparaît en aucune manière comme une représentation de la rélité historique vécue dans un temps déterminé de l'ancienne Egypte" (5) but goes on to state that the novel attempts to appear "objective" (8-9) as part of its narrative strategy.

[6] The remark is reported by Judith Newton and Deborah Rosenfelt (xv).

[7] An example that deals specifically with the theme of strip-tease can be found in Sheila Rowbotham's description of watching the Beatles's film *Magical Mystery Tour,* an experience which reveals both how pervasive such identification is and how frequently it passes unnoticed. Rowbotham notes that at one point in the film, the "boys and girls" are separated, with the viewer following the perspective of the boys, who go to a strip-tease. Rowbotham is surprised to realize that she identified so easily with the male persepctive constructed by the film: "I had caught myself going to watch another woman as if I were a man. I was experienceing the situation of another women stripping through men's eyes" (41).

[8] I have borrowed Culler's phrase to stress that it is not enough (or even necessary) to be female to "read as a woman." As Judith Fetterly has shown, women are used to reading as men, and therefore the "double vision" necessary to read differently may be more readily acquired; however, the active resistance necessary to acquire such vision may not be the exclusive purview of women.

[9] The Parnassian movement, with which Gautier was later associated, has similar political implications. For example, Barbara Johnson has suggested that "Parnassianism can be seen as a critique of the dominance of the concept of need" (744-45).

[10] Science was co-opted by the state in France as early as the seventeenth century. Erica Harth explains that Jean Chapelain advised Colbert concerning the founding of the Académie des Sciences in 1666, and recommended that professional rather than court scientists be selected, since they were more distinterested and less personally ambitious, and therefore could more easily

be manipulated into furthering the interests of the state (231).

Works Cited

Berger, John. *Ways of Seeing*. Harmondsworth: Penguin, 1972.

Bogaert, Geneviève van den. Préface. *Le Roman de la momie*. By Théophile Gautier. Paris: Garnier-Flammarion, 1966. 10-23.

Booth, Wayne C. "Freedom of Interpretation: Bakhtin and the Challenge of Feminist Criticism." *Critical Inquiry* 9.1 (September 1982): 45-76.

Boschot, Adolphe. Introduction. *Le Roman de la momie*. By Théophile Gautier. Paris: Garnier, 1963. i-xxxviii.

———. *Théophile Gautier*. Paris: Desclée de Brouwer, 1933.

Carré, Jean-Marie. *Voyageurs et écrivains français en Égypte*. Le Caire: Imprimerie de l'Institut Français d'Archéologie Orientale, 1932.

Chambers, Ross. *Mélancolie et opposition: les débuts du modernisme en France*. Paris: Corti, 1987.

———. "1851, 2 December: Literature Deterritorialized." *A New History of French Literature*. Ed. Denis Hollier. Cambridge: Harvard UP, 1989. 710-16.

Culler, Jonathan. *On Deconstruction: Theory and Criticism After Structuralism*. Ithaca: Cornell UP, 1982.

Eigeldinger, Marc. Preface and Afterword. *Le Roman de la momie*. By Théophile Gautier. Paris: Librairie Française Générale, 1985. 5-11; 239-64.

Fauchereau, Serge. *Théophile Gautier*. Paris: Denoël, 1972.

Fetterly, Judith. *The Resisting Reader: A Feminist Approach to American Fiction*. Bloomington: Indiana UP, 1978.

Garrard, Mary, and Norma Broude, eds. *Feminism and Art History: Questioning the Litany*. New York: Harper and Row, 1982.

Gautier, Théophile. *L'Orient*. Paris: Charpentier, 1877. 2 vols.

———. Preface. *Mademoiselle de Maupin*. 1835. Paris: Garnier-Flammarion, 1966.

———. *Le Roman de la momie*. 1857. Paris: Garnier, 1963. Harth, Erica. *Ideology and Culture in Seventeenth-Century France*. Ithaca: Cornell UP, 1983.

Johnson, Barbara. "1866: The Dream of Stone." *A New History of French Literature*. Ed. Denis Hollier. Cambridge: Harvard UP, 1989. 743-48.

Lévy-Delpla, Laurence. *Le Roman de la momie de Théophile Gautier*. Paris: Larousse, 1980.

Miller, Nancy K. "Rereading as a Woman: The Body in Practice." *Poetics Today* 6.1-2 (1985): 291-99.

Mulvey, Laura. "Visual Pleasure and Narrative Cinema." *Women and the Cinema*. Eds. Karyn Kay and Gerald Peary. New York: Dutton, 1977. 412-28.

Newton, Judith, and Deborah Rosenfelt. Introduction. *Feminist Criticism and Social Change: Sex, Class, and Race in Literature and Culture*. New York: Methuen, 1985. xv-xxxix.

Richer, Jean. *Etudes et recherches sur Théophile Gautier prosateur*. Paris: Nizet, 1981.

Robinson, Lillian S., and Lise Vogel. "Modernism and History." *Images of Women in Fiction: Feminist Perspectives*. Ed. Susan Koppelman Cornillon. Bowling Green, OH: Bowling Green U Popular P, 1972. 278-307.

Rowbotham, Sheila. *Woman's Consciousness, Man's World*. Harmondsworth: Penguin, 1973. Said, Edward. *Orientalism*. New York: Vintage, 1979.

Saintsbury, George. "Théophile Gautier." *Essays on French Novelists*. 1891. Folcroft, PA: Folcroft Library Editions, 1974. 225-62.

Terdiman, Richard. "1852, 2 December: Bonapartism." *A New History of French Literature*. Ed. Denis Hollier. Cambridge: Harvard UP, 1989. 717-22.

Woolf, Virginia. *A Room of One's Own*. 1929. New York: Harcourt, 1957.

Jessica R. Feldman (essay date 1993)

SOURCE: "Paroles Hermaphrodites: Gautier's Dandy," in *Gender on the Divide*: *The Dandy in Modernist Literature*, Cornell, 1993, pp. 25-53.

[*In the excerpt that follows, Feldman discusses Gautier's exploration of dandyism and gender in his novel* Mademoiselle de Maupin.]

CELLE-CI ET CELLE-LÀ: GAUTIER CONSIDERS CATEGORY

Théophile Gautier (1811-1872) came of age as a Romantic artist not when he fought the battle of *Hernani* in 1830 but when he realized that, by its principles

---

William C. Mead discusses Gautier's style:

It is quite true that Gautier was not the impassive, patient and delicate tinkerer one might hastily have supposed. One learns that when he wrote, words flooded out from his pen, which rarely ever hesitated or went back to change anything it had put on paper. . . . But along with this, one also learns that Gautier did have a perfectly consistent set of aesthetic principles which he applied almost everywhere in his work with perfect consistency; ultimately classical by instinct and inclination, he believed in the *beau ideal* and considered its attainment largely a matter of style and form, of word-choice, imagery, harmony and rhythm. And as for the rest, [Emile] Faguet, who wrote so unkindly about so many notable writers, seems to have been right in saying that Gautier *had no ideas.* Gautier, who had intellectual and artistic tastes which were very much his own, and of a fairly high order, contented himself for the most part with other peoples' ideas, and in particular with the ordinary "romantic" ideas, from the *vague des passions,* one might say, through the *danse macabre,* accompanied by the usual gnashing of teeth and xylophone obligato. He obviously believed that the beauty of the forms he used was his only serious responsibility. The forms themselves, their source and, above all, what their use might customarily imply, or what readers might imagine they implied—all this was a matter of sovereign indifference to Gautier himself.

William C. Mead, in Medieval Epic to the "Epic Theater" of Brecht, *edited by Rosario P. Armato and John M. Spalek, University of Southern California Press, 1968.*

---

of energy and change, Romanticism required its own transformation. As a member of *le petit cénacle,* a second-generation circle of Romantic artists, Gautier seized on satire as a transforming device. In 1833 he published *Les Jeunes-France: Romans goguenards,* a collection of stories that mock *la vie bohème,* from its fanciful costumes and erotic practices to its artistic productions and pretensions.[1] Among his targets was dandyism, for the phenomenon that had been imported from London some fifteen years earlier had been naturalized in part by the Jeunes-France, young Romantic artists, themselves.[2]

A celebration of the elegance and aloofness of the wealthy English "sporting" gentleman, dandyism does not initially appear a useful form for the French Romantic poet or painter. Yet one aspect of dandyism—its principled rejection of the vulgarity of middle-class life—appealed to Gautier and his circle. For this was the era of Louis-Philippe, and the dandy's antibourgeois posture attracted the artists of the day.[3] Retrospectively, Gautier sees the Jeunes-France as followers of the high priest of the dandies, Lord Byron:

Nous admirions fort les prouesses du jeune lord [Byron] et ses bacchanales nocturnes dans l'abbaye de Newstead. . . . Ces banquets où circulait, pleine d'une sombre liqueur, une coupe plus blanche que l'ivoire, effleurée par des lèvres de rose avec un léger sentiment d'effroi nous semblaient la suprême expression du dandysme, par l'absolue indifférence pour ce qui cause l'épouvante du genre humain.

(*Histoire du Romantisme* 50)

We strongly admired the prowess of the young lord [Byron] and his nocturnal bacchanals in the abbey of Newstead. . . . Those banquets where circulated, full of a somber liquid, a chalice whiter than ivory, and touched by rosy lips with a slight feeling of fear, seemed to us the supreme expression of dandyism, by the absolute indifference to what causes fear in the human species.

In *Mademoiselle de Maupin,* Gautier's novel of 1835, he radically expands the notion of the dandy as merely a stylishly dressed, wealthy, and blasé man. Gautier begins with dandyism as a social pose and ends with a dandyism so aestheticized that it can be expressed only in works of art. He begins with the dandy as character—and here the cavalier d'Albert, that snob, aesthete, fop, comes to mind—but he leads us to enlarge our view of dandyism by presenting us with d'Albert's mirror image, Madeleine, who shares with d'Albert the dandy's mask. . . . It is a process of feminizing art in order to challenge the very distinctions commonly made between male and female.

Gautier's dandyism grows beyond its embodiment in both sexes: he presents us with a dandyism not just of character but of novelistic texture itself. *Mademoiselle de Maupin* is a novel of and about metamorphosis; its issues are those of structure and flux. In metamorphosis we may seek the etiology of that mythical creature, the dandy, the figure who has transformed himself. Gautier leads us to look beyond even metamorphic texture, to seek the dandy in an allegory of aesthetic belief. Gautier's dandy impersonates the Parnassian aesthetic credo as he takes his place in a modernist analogical universe: historical figure, fictional character, narrative technique, aesthetic belief all reveal one another, once the dandy appears to our eyes as the figure in the carpet. Because dandies are always fictional (both in books and on the avenue, where they create the fiction of themselves), they present special problems for critics. Stalking the dandy, we find him hovering between myth and history, among the incidents and coincidences of plot, the hazes and particularities of character, the echoes of allusion.

Gautier's story **"Celle-ci et celle-là"** ("This One and That One," included in the *Jeunes-France* collection of 1833) can provide us with a map of the at first bewildering landscape of *Mademoiselle de Maupin*. It locates us in the dandy's world; it asks us to pay special attention to narrative technique; and it instructs us in the art of reading allegory. Rodolphe, the dandy-hero of the tale, who consults the mirror as his first act of the day, passes the time in leisured ennui. Although he is a poet, he appears never to write, and his most blissful hours are those in which he and his friend Albert design an especially enchanting *gilet* (waistcoat). Rodolphe seeks a grand passion; but to his credit as a dandy it is "non une passion épicière et bourgeoise, mais une passion d'artiste, une passion volcanique et échevelée" (*Les Jeunes-France: Romans goguenards* 98; not a shopkeeper's or a bourgeois's passion, but an artist's passion, a volcanic and frenzied passion); furthermore he wants it primarily "pour compléter sa tournure, et le poser dans le monde sur un pied convenable" (*JF* 98; in order to complete his image and present him to the world on a proper footing). The plot of the story grows out of Rodolphe's vain and shallow character: he finds the woman of his dreams, but in reality she cannot conform to the ideal. The lady, "celle-là" or Madame de M***, is willing, but Rodolphe fails repeatedly to raise the affair to a level of drama commensurate with his idealized version of himself. At last his pretty maidservant-mistress Mariette, "celle-ci," rebels, demanding that he replace his cold and artificial lover with her own honest and sweetly natural self. Rodolphe accepts her happy ending.

This is the tale of a dandy who gives up falsity to become a man without masks, loved for himself and capable of loving others. Yet, as the title announces, the story has another point to make, one about categories and relations between them. Gautier presents three principal sets of relations—man over woman, human over animal, master over servant—in order to upset them. These hierarchical relations recognized, the story then offers itself in three versions: Rodolphe's interpretation of the events diverges utterly from the narrator's and ours. Our thick hero learns that his power over women is superficial and that a good woman will exercise a beneficial power over him. Animals—Rodolphe's cats appear frequently, especially when he is discouraged or sad—instruct him in the evil artificialities of "society." Likewise, Mariette teaches him that social hypocrisy blinds people to true virtue and true love. The narrator, however, undercuts each of these lessons, mocking the didacticism in art which Gautier will soon attack head-on in the preface to *Mademoiselle de Maupin*. By his unrelenting tone of ridicule, the narrator prevents us from believing in the possibility of Rodolphe's psychological or moral growth. From the narrator's cynical point of view, Rodolphe has merely traded one falsity (social power) for another ("natural" love). By the story's end Rodolphe, soon to become, we suspect, a dull husband, is no longer much of a dandy; the narrator, who has taken hold of our values and given them a sharp twist, *is*. He is particularly so because we have nothing but his tone upon which to pin our denunciation of Rodolphe. The narrator is a dandy in his masks—superior to Rodolphe certainly, but superior to the very act of telling the tale, given to satiric asides, parody, preaching, always with his elbow in our ribs. The narrator's persona is one of manic wit, defying us to take anything in the story seriously, especially and paradoxically defiance itself. The pose, then, is one of distance, impertinence, world-weary cynicism.

For the reader, the choice between Rodolphe's naiveté (*ci*) and the narrator's cynicism (*là*) seems a thematic red herring. Rather than a narrative that brings some truisms home, **"Celle-ci and celle-là"** presents as its uncomfortable burden *the necessity of questioning the very distinctions we make between ci and là, whatever the issue*. Gautier scrutinizes relations in general, particularly those that clearly involve power. If one should love the humble servant rather than the shallow society woman, perhaps it is equally true that one should love the humble cats rather than the humble servant. After all, Rodolphe often strokes his favorite (male) cat and Mariette simultaneously. And if one can entertain the notion of loving "celle-ci" rather than "celle-là" or both of them equally, perhaps Rodolphe should love his intimate friend Albert rather than his servant or his cats. If this were to come to pass, perhaps he could love women, cats, and men at once, and go beyond the bounds not just of propriety and morality but of control itself. The story's pat conclusion denies itself, leaving us with the faint but echoing promise of anarchy: personal, social, universal.

Added to the tale, as if to stem the tide of disorder, is a second ending, an allegorical interpretation of its characters and events: "Il y a un mythe très-profond sous cette enveloppe frivole: au cas que vous ne vous en soyez pas aperçu, je vais vous l'expliquer tout au long" (*JF* 199; There is a very profound myth underneath this frivolous envelope: in case you haven't noticed it, I will explain it to you at length). Here Gautier plays with the idea of personifying aesthetic ideas:

> Madame de M*** représente la poésie classique, belle et froide, brillante et fausse, semblable en tout aux statues antiques. . . . Mariette, c'est la vraie poésie, la poésie sans corset et sans fard, la muse bonne fille qui convient à l'artiste . . . qui vit de la vie humaine, etc.
>
> (*JF* 199)

> Madame de M*** represents classical poetry, beautiful and cold, brilliant and false, similar in all respects to ancient statues. . . . Mariette is true poetry, poetry without a corset and without makeup, the well-behaved muse appropriate to the artist . . . poetry that lives on human life, etc.

While the narrator here nonchalantly offers us some near-nonsense (what *is* poetry that "vit de la vie humaine"?), he is also rehearsing a set of allegorical relations that extend throughout the tale: cold statue/warm flesh, classical/romantic. Gautier mocks aesthetic allegory in this "roman goguenard" but finds it important enough to repeat, on a grander scale, in *Mademoiselle de Maupin*. In the novel as in the story, Gautier disembodies the dandy as he stands in his favorite position, contemplating his mirror image. He examines category and relation, especially those of gender. Erotic interest vivifies aesthetic statement. Thus Gautier forms the complex contours of modernism's dandy: figure, texture, aesthetic creed.

"UN AIR DAMOISEAU": CROSSING THE GENDER LINE

Critics have analyzed at length the many doublings, mirrorings, echoes, and masks of *Mademoiselle de Maupin*.[4] The novel is indeed a vast *mise en abyme;* all characters operate within a system of mirrors. Among these mirrors, that of the dandy—the glass before which he poses, first to create and then to judge himself—reflects the greatest urgency. There he expects to see both self and not-self; only the purest paradox of identity will suffice. In *Mademoiselle de Maupin,* Gautier places before the dandy's mirror the cavalier d'Albert. We watch d'Albert scrutinizing his image, finding it perhaps a bit too effeminate, certainly not beautiful enough, obviously the most interesting image in the wide world. It is only gradually that Gautier lets us see the image staring back at him: that of Madeleine. Like Rodolphe, who fails as a dandy from the first paragraph of his tale, when he looks into his mirror "pour se constater à lui-même qu'il n'était pas un autre" (*JF* 96; to prove to himself that he was not someone else), d'Albert seems to fall short of some unspecified standard. Like Rodolphe, d'Albert cannot accept the paradox of the mask in which *je* is always *un autre;* Madeleine thrives upon it. D'Albert is finally an egotist and an aesthete, but he lacks power, will, superiority, grace—the attributes which Madeleine certainly possesses. Yet, without d'Albert's yearnings and disquisitions, without his concentrated stare into the glass, Madeleine is but an amusing lady swashbuckler. Let us begin, as Gautier means us to, with d'Albert's dandyism, and then seek its translation in Madeleine. Just as French dandies translate the English code of dandyism into their native tongue, creating a language neither French nor English ("les happy few," "le sportsman," "le fashionable," etc.), so Gautier translates a male into a female figure, seeking a third way for the dandy. It is the act of translation, not the "arrival" at the female, which interests Gautier. His dandyism begins in the space between d'Albert and Madeleine, between male and female; it is from the first neither *celle-ci* nor *celle-là,* but instead a challenge to polarized thinking.

Gautier withholds his title character and opens the novel with an epistolary self-portrait of the cavalier d'Albert. D'Albert moves strangely in and out of focus as a dandy. Certainly his daily life would qualify him for the role; wholly free of economic pressures, his daily task appears to be the graceful conquering of empty hours. He suffers from ennui, takes pains with his costume and coiffure even though he is aware that people find him effeminate:

mes cheveux étaient bouclés et lustrés avec plus de soin qu'il ne convenait; que cela, joint à ma figure imberbe, me donnait un air damoiseau on ne peut plus ridicule . . . je ressemblais plus à un comédien qu'à un homme.

(*Mademoiselle de Maupin* 112)

my hair was curled and shined with more care than was seemly; and that, together with my beardless face, gave me the most ridiculous air of a young pageboy. . . . I resembled more an actor than a man.

An actor more than a man, d'Albert admits to his correspondent Silvio what he would never, as a dandy, admit publicly—that he desires a mistress. The publicly self-satisfied fop is privately the insecure male: "Une maîtresse pour moi, c'est la robe virile pour un jeune Romain" (*MM* 79; A mistress for me is as the virile toga for a young Roman). Yet as a dandy he does not seek out or encourage women, because they fall short of his vision of pure beauty. Furthermore, he fears that his own lack of beauty and his limited wealth preclude an ideal love affair. Although he may appear to possess a dandy's *froideur*—"j'ai la réputation d'un jeune homme tranquille et froid, peu sensible aux femmes et indifférent aux choses de son âge" (*MM* 76-77; I have the reputation of being a cold and tranquil young man, little interested in women and indifferent to the trappings of his age)—in fact his coldness hides from the world a richly smoldering emotional life.

Slowly we take our bearings in d'Albert's verbiage. Gautier gives us enough clues to enable us to identify d'Albert: he is dandylike in his vanity, foppishness, lethargy, nonchalance, and ennui. Short of living in Paris, he is a dandy on the pattern of the comte d'Orsay; a lesser, provincial version, perhaps, but a dandy nonetheless. Yet Gautier floods us with much more information about his character than the type seems to require. Nothing that we learn about d'Albert disqualifies him as a dandy; rather, it complicates and deepens the very concept of dandyism. Gautier re-creates through d'Albert the psychological history which would lead a man to join the ranks of the dandy-brotherhood. As Gautier writes a novel, he creates a mythic being: the dandy who is also aesthete and would-be artist. D'Albert's self-appointed task, throughout the novel, is to find and possess the ideal mistress, but he serves as well Gautier's *programme,* to claim the dandy as a type of the modern aesthete. The model is no longer to be the British sporting gentleman, shallowly self-satisfied, but the prisoner of his own consciousness, the martyr of his own complicated sensibility. Chief among the dandy's complications are those of gender. Gautier tags the gender of his dandy-aesthete with a question mark, and then distributes between d'Albert and Madeleine his meditations upon that very act. Thus in Gautier begins the artist's argument with himself on the subject of gender, an argument that is to characterize the literature of dandyism throughout the nineteenth century.

Although d'Albert rails against the solitude and ennui that trap him in himself, he lacks neither the beauty nor the funds necessary for approaching women. Instead, d'Albert describes himself as simply estranged from society in general, "une goutte d'huile dans un verre d'eau" (*MM* 122; a drop of oil in a glass of water), or as slowly hardening, "la volupté même . . . ce feu dévorant qui fond les rochers et les métaux de l'âme . . . n'a jamais pu me dompter ou m'attendrir" (*MM* 122; sensual delight, even . . . that devouring fire that melts the rocks and metals of the soul, . . . never could subdue me nor soften me). Although women initially promise a focus outside himself, he cannot melt in their presence because he really wishes to borrow or, better, to possess their beauty for his own. He begins by claiming to seek an ideal of female beauty, but the movement toward another is, in his mind, always one in which he will engulf the other, take on her beauty, rather than merge with her:

> J'ai aimé les armes, les chevaux et les femmes: les armes, pour remplacer les nerfs que je n'avais pas; les chevaux, pour me servir d'ailes; les femmes, pour posséder au moins dans quelqu'une la beauté qui me manquait á moi-même.
>
> (*MM* 166-67)
>
> I loved arms, horses, and women: arms, for replacing the nerve I did not have; horses, for giving me wings; women, in order to possess in at least one of them the beauty that was lacking in myself.

Albert perceives himself, like a woman, to lack nerve. He loves women because he can, by possessing them, hope to take on their beauty. The statement presents a characteristic blend of vanity and defensiveness; in it d'Albert imagines himself swift, sure, and beautiful, but the accent falls on the wish to repair deficiencies rather than the image of power. What this statement lacks, to render it the wholly characteristic statement of a dandy, is impertinence. While it insults women by placing them on a par with animals and objects, d'Albert probably means it as complimentary. A dandy's impertinence must be at least wielded as a weapon, if not received as a blow.

From the inability to possess a mistress because he wants in some sense to incorporate female qualities, it is but a brief step to the dandy's preference for women depicted in art rather than possessed in the flesh:

> je me suis rejeté sur les tableaux et les statues;—ce qui, après tout, est une assez pitoyable ressource quand on a des sens aussi allumés que les miens. Cependant il y a quelque chose de grand et de beau à aimer une statue, c'est que l'amour est parfaitement désintéressé, qu'on n'a à craindre ni la satiété ni le dégoût de la victoire, et qu'on ne peut espérer raisonnablement un second prodige pareil à l'histoire de Pygmalion.
>
> (*MM* 167)
>
> I fell back on paintings and statues;—which, after all, is a relatively pitiful resource when one has senses as inflamed as mine. However, there is something grand and beautiful in loving a statue, in that the love is perfectly disinterested, in that one need fear neither the satiety nor the disgust of conquest, in 'that one may not reasonably hope for a second wonder equal to the story of Pygmalion.

For the dandy, physical love is vulgar and ugly. Erotic victory disgusts him, because it means losing a vital, composed isolation. If the dandy is cold and pure, why not "mate" with his own kind: a statue. The statue will not metamorphose into life, because the dandy's imperturbability freezes all movement. Yet a certain kind of change does occur. When *volupté* does not melt him, when he cannot find a living woman who will complete his own beauty and prove herself worthy of the possessing, he can claim these failings as victories, seek only "l'amour désintéressé" (disinterested love), and cultivate his sangfroid. Such is the maneuver of the dandy, who traditionally lives out his day in the wholly male society of club, restaurant, and private gambling circle. Women are publicly ignored; the dandy's womanizing occurs with the utmost discretion. A real woman is someone to hide, and Gautier tells us why this is so. As a dandy, d'Albert seeks a center within himself, turning away from life and toward art, cultivating internally his darker self, externally a posture of superiority and disdain.

D'Albert relentlessly pursues love, even as, dandylike, he denies its place in his life. While Gautier carefully displays the vanity involved in this desire, its centrality to the plot and the vast number of pages dedicated to its explororation throw it into a kind of prominence that appears to belie the dandy's asexual pose. D'Albert even goes so far as to take the second-best Rosette as a mistress and to leave society for the pleasures of her company alone. For all his egotism, he looks longingly outward and upward, seeking the incarnation of his vision of perfect beauty. He never ceases to pursue that vision, even when he half believes Madeleine to be a man. Gautier appears to close d'Albert out of the kingdom of the dandies, by virtue of his most unseemly lust for beauty.

We gradually recognize, on the contrary, that d'Albert's yearning for Madeleine strengthens his image as a dandy. He sees in her the embodiment of his vision of beauty because she is his mirror image. Not merely Echo to his Narcissus, Madeleine complements d'Albert's strengths and reverses his weaknesses. The novel demands that we consider the two characters together, as versions of each other. The figure of the dandy multiplies and blurs.

The similarities between the two characters begin with the very substance of the novel: they write the letters of which it is primarily constructed. Furthermore, the recipients of their letters, Graciosa and Silvio, are doubles. Both d'Albert and Madeleine dislike social hypocrisy and the social institutions of courtship and marriage followed inevitably by adultery. Both vow to travel in search of a better kind of love. They share a Platonic view of love, although d'Albert has only imperfectly grasped Diotima's wisdom and Madeleine has emphasized perhaps too heavily the moral element in love. Both stage events and view their lives in dramatic terms. Both succumb to Rosette's sexual charms while denying the possibility of loving and living with her on into the future. D'Albert sees in Madeleine "[l]a beauté de l'ange, la force du tigre, et les ailes de l'aigle" (*MM* 166; the beauty of an angel, the force of a tiger, and the wings of an eagle); in possessing her, d'Albert would be able to claim for himself her strength, nerve, birdlike speed, and beauty.

Madeleine's undeniable personal beauty, her power and elegance in sword fighting, her mask, and her disdain for vulgar, hypocritical men make her, as well, a dandy. Her very being contradicts but completes d'Albert: he searches for beauty, she for truth. She glories in power, he flounders in sensibility. He wishes to become, like Tiresias, a woman, but the desire is shallow and fleeting. Madeleine's wish to "become" a man for the purpose of educating herself in the ways of love spurs her to cross-dress and set in motion the plot of her own life. Her search for a man worthy of her life and her continual disappointment (not to mention her frequent attempts to disentangle herself from the webs of others' lustful attractions to her) lead her not into despair, but into a sense of increasing distance from the erotic fray. Her penultimate act in the novel is to lose her virginity, but her ultimate act is to disappear. After dividing a night of love between Rosette and d'Albert, she leaves forever, preventing erotic victory from degenerating into the futility of repetition, the vulgarity of satiety.

Both Madeleine's gender and her masquerade make her defensive, but she transforms that defensiveness into superiority, just as dandies on the avenue transform lack of exalted social standing, imperfect beauty, and laziness into a dramatic persona which either hides these failings or claims them as victories. Madeleine's defensive duel with Alcibiades and her continued du-

eling thereafter are emblematic of her ability to turn threats against her person and her persona into triumph. Such a triumph, and not erotic triumph, is the dandy's goal, even if he duels with pointed words more often than with swords. Not that Madeleine lacks the dandy's verbal acuity. Her speech, spilling over with double entendres and verbal feints, enables her to evade the erotic clutches of those who believe her to be male and those who know her to be female.

Madeleine arrives in d'Albert's life not to fulfill his desire but to echo it. She impersonates the dandy's desire because she cannot or will not find a resting place in any human breast. Her ambiguous gender and her bisexuality suggest that her needs are too great for social fulfillment: the social taboos that cluster about her character represent the radical disjunction of personal needs and social fulfillment. Like the dandy's strolling, her picaresque story will not admit of conclusion. Both accept the impossibility of closure. Embodying a total, voluptuous yearning, a sinking into the self treasured for its very masochistic intensity, Madeleine gives the lovelorn Rosette a dandy's counsel:

> Hélas . . . la meilleure partie de nous est celle qui reste en nous, et que nous ne pouvons produire.— Les poètes sont ainsi.—Leur plus beau poème est celui qu'ils n'ont pas écrit.
>
> (*MM* 180)

> Alas . . . the best part of us is that which remains in us, and that we cannot produce.—Poets are thus.— Their most beautiful poem is the one they have not written.

Both love and creation must be a yearning toward the impossible, an accepted, even cherished, sterility. The other alternative for the dandy in the throes of love or creative yearning is the attraction to the dark realm, here suggested by homoeroticism, a strand taken up several decades later by the dandy's descendants, the decadents. Decadent love and creation, by virtue of their twisted tableaux of dangerous possibilities, act as an antidote to society's sentimental farce of vulgar sexual and pseudoartistic activities.

Madeleine's transvestism allows Gautier to express his view of dandyism as revolutionary. After dressing as a man in a self-initiated rite de passage, Madeleine sees the world turned, not upside down, but back to front.[5] What is usually hidden from women during courtship— men sniggering at the very women they court—takes its place on the stage of her drama; backstage all the temporarily eclipsed forms of sentimentality and polite sexual posturing proceed without director or audience. Madeleine sees the debased side of men, but instead of sharpening her skills in choosing a good man for a husband (her initial plan) she learns that husbands and marriage are, for her, impossible. Indeed, her female identity itself is now called into question:

> j'étais un homme, ou du moins j'en avais l'apparence: la jeune fille était morte. . . . il me sembla que je n'étais plus moi, mais un autre, et je me souvenais de mes actions anciennes comme des actions d'une personne étrangère auxquelles j'aurais assisté, ou comme du début d'un roman dont je n'aurais pas achevé la lecture.
>
> (*MM* 238)

> I was a man, or, at least, I had the appearance of a man: the young girl was dead. . . . it seemed to me that I was no longer myself, but someone else, and I remembered my former actions as a stranger's actions that I'd witnessed, or like the beginning of a novel I'd yet to finish reading.

If rites de passage are intended as experiences of monstrosity, in which the initiate learns to see, understand, and value the structures of society, this rite de passage has failed.[6] Instead, Gautier has created a figure who, in finding herself constitutionally unable to reenter the categories of gender, will call those categories themselves into question. A dandy in privilege, beauty, will, superiority, aloofness, Madeleine, we begin to recognize, is perhaps more a dandy for her paradoxical gender status: a woman dressing as a man who feels herself to be neither male nor female. She achieves this state first by forgetting for long periods of time that she is female:

> j'oubliais insensiblement que j'étais femme;—mon déguisement me semblait mon habit naturel . . . je ne songeais plus que je n'étais au bout du compte qu'une petite évaporée qui s'était fait une épée de son aiguille.
>
> (*MM* 310)

> I forgot imperceptibly that I was a woman;—my disguise seemed to me my natural dress. . . . I no longer thought that I was, all things considered, only a little scatterbrain who'd made a sword of her needle.

She no longer believes herself to be a "petite évaporée," a bit of nothingness, but she chooses to be a nobody, pure incognito, if personhood must involve gender.

And it is this last claim which Gautier explores with special care. First, he offers us d'Albert, a dandy manqué, an effeminate male who wishes to possess feminine Beauty. Next, he displays d'Albert's double, a woman whose mask of superiority and powers of self-creation reveal her as a dandy not so manqué. Then Gautier has Madeleine question the concept of gender. While d'Albert is "un peu éffeminé" (a little effeminate), Madeleine/Théodore de Seranne's effeminate

appearance hides, paradoxically, a person who is no longer, by "her" own account, either male or female: *"Je ne suis plus une femme, mais je ne suis pas encore un homme"* (*MM* 319, emphasis added; I am no longer a woman, but I am not yet a man). Madeleine has learned what every dandy of my study announces: gender is a creation of self-presentation and social attribution, not of god-given or genetically fixed biological "fact."[7]

Finding herself outside the categories of gender, Madeleine responds sexually to both men and women, but her marginal position causes her always to hold back, to assess, to judge. She becomes the spectator of her own sexual experience, the reader of the novel that is her life. She is simultaneously novelist and critic, consciousness and self-consciousness, hedonist and strict moralist. She may be physically expansive, but she must always control herself. Gautier, in creating Madeleine's problematical gender, imagines not just a sexual, but an aesthetic, stance toward the world. Cool without and volcanic within, coldly judgmental and open to sense impression, the double being of the dandy-aesthete here is born in an extended sexual conceit which will serve Gautier, Barbey, and Baudelaire equally well.

From the point at which she recognizes the strange status of her gender, Madeleine's letters read as a dandy's daybook. She gives up her plan to seek a good man, recognizing that the fulfillment of her desire is impossible. She raises this understanding to a law of human nature: "c'est le propre des plans que l'on a de n'être point exécutés, et c'est là que paraissent principalement la fragilité de la volonté et le pur néant de l'homme" (*MM* 358; it is the nature of the plans that one makes not to be carried out, and it is therein that appears chiefly the fragility of the will and the pure nothingness of man). The dandy may have a daily routine, but never a plan. The dandy's will may be strong, but directed inward; the kingdom of the self may perhaps be ruled, but the outer world of nature and public affairs, symbolized by the mob, never. Language must be divorced from emotion, once hope of realizing desire is abandoned; Madeleine notes that her epigrams "brillaient par un mérite d'exactitude" (*MM* 360; shone with the merit of exactitude) because her invective, in contrast to that of men, is unmixed with love.

Mademoiselle de Maupin is not, however, the tale of a transsexual, a woman "becoming" a man. It is a novel about "crossing over" in which Madeleine's gender masquerade stands for change in general, especially change within pairs of opposing terms: human/animal, self/other, masked/naked, object/image, day/night, artificial/real. The novel is saturnalian; the festivities merely begin with the upsetting of sexual arrangements. A glorious disorder gradually emerges. At its center stands the dandy, perfectly attired, superciliously smiling, and ready to explode.

Notes

[1] I translate *roman* as "story" or "tale," because these fictions are not novels. In titling the volume *Romans goguenards* (mocking novels), Gautier mockingly inflates their genre; they fall somewhere between *conte* (story) and *roman* (novel).

[2] For histories of dandyism, see Moers, Carassus, and Matoré.

[3] For a still valid analysis of the relation between dandyism and the Jeunes-France, see Creed, especially the chapter "Le dandysme transplanté" (7-18). She further discusses Gautier and his circle in "Le costume" (60-80).

[4] The critical literature on the subject is well developed but limited; it does not address the topic of d'Albert and Madeleine as the masked and mirrored dandy, nor does it analyze the novel's style and rhetoric as textual dandyism.

For detailed surveys of the novel's masks and mirrors, see, for example, Bouchard and Savalle.
Albouy, in an extremely useful article, links the novel's sexual doubling to aesthetic issues, arguing that Madeleine's "false androgyny" reveals Gautier's willingness to dwell in ambiguity and to entertain opposing notions of aesthetic idealism and Parnassian materialism. Lloyd ("Speculum Amantis," 86-87) joins Albouy in questioning earlier interpretations of the novel as "mimetically reproducing the life of an actual individual," corroborating my view that the dandy in literature must be read allegorically. Lloyd's focus on the novel as a "web of cracks," a *"mise en abyme"* that breaks down the barriers between the real and the artificial, supports both her view of the novel's "duplicity" and my notion of dandyism as paradoxical in nature.

[5] For a useful anthropological account of the phenomenon of "the world turned upside down," see Babcock, especially the introduction (13-36), and Davis (147-90).

[6] For a discussion of rites de passage and their importance in conserving cultural values, see Turner.

[7] . . . I allude here to an argument which I base on the work of Kessler and McKenna. . . .

Works Cited

Albouy, Pierre. "Le myth de l'androgyne dans *Mademoiselle de Maupin*." *Revue d'Histoire Littéraire de la France* 72 (1972): 600-608.

Bouchard, Ann. "Le masque et le miroir dans *Mademoiselle de Maupin*." *Revue d'Histoire Littéraire de la France* 72 (1972): 583-99.

Carassus, Emilien. *Le mythe du dandy*. Paris: Armand Colin, 1971.

Creed, Elizabeth. *Le dandysme de Jules Barbey d'Aurevilly*. Paris: Librairie Droz, 1938.

Davis, Natalie Zemon. "Women on Top." In *The Reversible World: Symbolic Inversion in Art and Society*, edited by Barbara A. Babcock, 147-90. Ithaca: Cornell University Press, 1978.

Gautier, Théophile. "Celle-ci et celle-là: Ou la Jeune-France passionnée." In *Les Jeunes-France: Romans goguenards*, 96-200. Paris: Bibliothèque Charpentier, 1900.

————. *Mademoiselle de Maupin*. Edited by J. Robichez. Paris: Imprimerie Nationale, 1979.

Kessler, Suzanne J., and Wendy McKenna. *Gender: An Ethnomethodological Approach*. Chicago: University of Chicago Press, 1978.
Lloyd, Rosemary. "Speculum Amantis, Speculum Artis: The Seduction of Mademoiselle de Maupin." *Nineteenth Century French Studies* 15 (Fall-Winter 1986-87): 77-86.

Matoré, Georges. *Le vocabulaire et la société sous Louis-Philippe*. Geneva: Librairie Droz, 1951.

Moers, Ellen. *The Dandy: Brummell to Beerbohm*. 1960. Lincoln: University of Nebraska Press, 1978.

Savalle, Joseph. *Travestis, métamorphoses, dédoublements*. Paris: Librairie Minard, 1981.

Turner, Victor. "Betwixt and Between: The Liminal Period in *Rites de Passage*." In *The Forest of Symbols*, 93-111. Ithaca: Cornell University Press, 1967.

Constance Gosselin Schick (essay date 1994)

SOURCE: "Introduction: Facing Textuality," in *Seductive Resistance: The Poetry of Théophile Gautier*, Rodopi, 1994, pp. 1-7.

[In the excerpt below, Schick examines the aesthetics of Gautier's poems, noting that "Gautier's concept of poetry stresses the preeminence of words, of craft and of beauty."]

Poetry afforded Théophile Gautier his greatest pleasure as a writer. He repeatedly expressed his delight in what he referred to as a sculpturing in verse:

Les esprits qu'on est convenu d'appeler pratiques . . . n'auront pas connu leur [the poets'] pur enchantement: contempler la nature, aspirer à l'idéal, en sculpter la beauté dans cette forme dure et difficile à travailler du vers, qui est, comme le marbre de la pensée, n'est-ce pas là un noble et digne emploi de ce temps qu'on regarde aujourd'hui comme de la monnaie?[1]

Expressing the opinion that writers of poetry were superior to writers of prose, he explains: "Un chanteur sait parler, mais un orateur ne sait pas chanter. Les oiseaux volent et marchent; les chevaux, si fringante et si fière que soit leur allure, ne peuvent que courir . . . la double nature du poète tient de celle de l'hippogriphe."[2] He claimed that poetry was his destiny "J' tais né pour faire des voyages et écrire des vers," [3] and often spoke of it as the salvation of his life. In the preface to **Albertus ou l'Ame et le Péché,** he says that even if his poetry were to remain completely unnoticed, he would not regret "la peine qu'il a prise . . . ces vers lui auront usé innocemment quelques heures, et l'art est ce qui console le mieux de vivre."[4] He was to repeat this sentiment in a letter to Maxime du Camp, written in December of 1850: "Je me sens mourir d'une nostalgie d'Asie Mineure et si je ne faisais quelques vers, je m'abandonnerais aux asticots, quoique je trouve la mort plus hideuse encore que la vie."[5]

His literary fortune, however, has not supported this predilection. Most readers of Gautier do not turn to his poetry for their textual pleasure. The admiration professed by Baudelaire and by Mallarmé, by Ezra Pound and by T.S. Eliot, by the Russian formalists and the Latin American *modernistas* remain exceptions.[6] In fact, they are exceptions that many literary critics and historians explain and discard as either polite flattery or the flattering projection of greater genius onto lesser talent. The dominant canonic opinion regarding Gautier's poetry is that voiced by Jules Supervielle for whom Gautier provides an example of minor poetry, one lacking in mystery; and that of André Gide for whom Gautier is a writer plagued by "cécité" for all that is not exterior and visible.[7] Admitting that Gautier occupies "une place considérable" in French literature, Gide adds: "c'est seulement fâcheux qu'il la remplisse si mal" (162).

In fact, the role and place attributed to the poetry of Gautier is considerable. It is pivotal to Art-for-Art's Sake poetry, a gratuitous, aesthetic poetry whose finality is beauty rather than any moral or social purpose. Furthermore, this aesthetics is wide-reaching. In Gautier's poetry we find the Romantic aesthetic for dark, mysterious gothic beauty, for the affective beauty of nature, and for the evocative and mimetic beauty of local color. We also find the Parnassian aesthetic which seeks impersonal, exotic, and monumental beauty; the ephemeral, sentient, and modern beauty of the Impressionists; the elitist, refined and amoral beauty of Dan-

dyism; the artificial, immoral and exacerbated beauty of Decadence; and the spiritual, evocative, and suggestive beauty of Symbolism. . . . Baudelaire found yet another form of beauty in Gautier's writing: "la *beauté du diable,* c'est à dire la grace charmante et l'audace de la jeunesse, il contient le rire, et le meilleur rire" (683). In the article on Gautier which he wrote in 1859, Baudelaire summarizes: "Or, par son amour du Beau, amour immense, fécond, sans cesse rajeuni . . . Théophile Gautier est un écrivain d'un mérite à la fois *nouveau* et unique" (689).

The writer for whom "le monde visible existed" is also an important key in the development of realist poetry, a poetry which is said and says itself to be more concrete, objective and prosaic; one which focuses on visuals and objects, on deictic matter-of-factness rather than on sentiment, philosophy and rhetoric. Finally, Gautier's poetry is seminal to "la poésie pure," or to autonomous poetry, a poetry whose poeticity is said to be constituted by and according to linguistic and formal elements rather than by referential or signifying ones.

To a certain extent, it may be because of the importance of its place and role that Gautier's poetry is so rarely read with pleasure. It is read as a case of literary history, as an illustrative space of that canonic break between Romanticism and post-Romanticism. Gautier's literary output is usually summarized in terms of being Romantic-turned-something else (usually sour or Parnassian, the two being almost synonymous for many readers). His poetry is thus made to be the locus of a fault, both in the sense of a break and in the sense of a defect. It is looked at as marginal, an outer border to the predecessors, contemporaries and successors who represent a particular spirit or movement more centrally, and therefore, by implication, more successfully. The admission of Gautier's influence and importance is usually accompanied with a pejorative acknowledgement that he is not a Hugo, not a Baudelaire, not a Mallarmé.

A review of the reception which his poetry has occasioned reveals this marginality in interestingly contradictory ways. It is a poetry which is said to be too Romantic to be objective, yet too impersonal and disengaged to be Romantic; too fanciful to be Parnassian yet too concrete to be Symbolist. It is judged, often simultaneously, as too discursive and too formalist, too escapist and too conformist, too self-conscious and too mimetic, too overstated and too understated. Its innovations are recognized, yet it is still dismissed as conventional and commonplace.

It seems to me that such contradictions suggest that there may be more mystery in Gautier's poetry than Supervielle accords it. The "poëte impeccable," the "très-vénéré maître"[8] deserves better consideration. Gautier's poetry merits attentive close readings which, while not necessarily being "pour un Gautier" (as Ponge did *Pour un Malherbe*), at least respect the criteria that are in keeping with its textuality.[9] Gautier's concept of poetry stresses the preeminence of words, of craft and of beauty, yet it is most often evaluated according to referentiality and/or signification: its (and the *its* is really a euphemism for *his*) honesty, its sincerity, its truth, be this personal, philosophical, phenomenal, social, moral, or symbolic truth. A corollary to these referential and signifying criteria is the criterion of originality, both of style or form and of content. Questions regarding poetry's ability to distance itself from, or better yet to discard commonplaces and convention are really questions regarding its sincerity and its commitment to a personal and/or a contemporary reality. Yet Gautier asserted repeatedly that message or content and originality were secondary in poetry, as they were in art in general. "L'art, c'est la beauté, l'invention perpétuelle du détail, le choix de mots, le soin exquis de l'exécution,"[10] and by invention, Gautier meant making: "Le mot poète veut dire littéralement *faiseur:* tout ce qui n'est pas bien *fait* n'existe pas."[11] As for originality, that is only "la note personnelle ajoutée au fonds commun préparé par les contemporains ou les prédécesseurs immédiats."[12] Molière, Shakespeare, and all the greats, he insists, never worried about originality any more than Michelangelo worried about the illusion of reality.[13]

When Taine once expressed a preference for Musset over Hugo, Gautier responded:

> Demander à la poésie du sentimentalisme . . . ce n'est pas ça. Des mots rayonnants, des mots de lumière . . . avec un rythme et une musique, voilà ce que c'est que la poésie. . . . Ça ne prouve rien, ça ne raconte rien. . . . Ainsi, le commencement de *Ratbert* . . . il n'y a pas de poésie au monde comme cela. C'est le plateau de l'Hymalaya. Toute l'Italie blasonnée est là . . . et rien que des mots.[14]

Poetry is not what is said, that is an *énoncé,* but rather it is a saying, an *énonciation* which allows words to radiate, which makes them disseminate their light/their meanings in all directions according to and by means of a rhythm, a music.[15] The referent of *Ratbert* may well be Italy, but it is an Italy so blazoned, so heralded that it is first and foremost an other-wordly poetry, evoking, for Gautier, Himalayan heights as well as its Italian referent. It is poetry because it is a radiation onto multiple signifieds constituted solely and purely by and of words. Regarding *Les Fleurs du Mal,* Gautier wrote:

> Les mots ont en eux-mêmes et en dehors des sens qu'ils expriment une beauté; une valeur propre, comme les pierres précieuses qui ne sont pas encore taillées. Il y a des mots diamant, saphir, rubis, émeraude, d'autres qui luisent comme du phosphore quand on les frotte, et ce n'est pas un mince travail que de les choisir.[16]

It is necessary to recognize, therefore, that for Gautier, poetry is writing which "ne prouve rien, ne raconte rien." Whatever rhetoric, narration or reference it may possess or produce, these are not what define or constitute its poeticity. In *Spirite,* Gautier describes a reader/reading which would be in touch with his writing:

> Il ne faut pas toujours prendre au pied de la lettre ce que dit un auteur: on doit faire la part des systèmes philosophiques ou littéraires, des affectations à la mode en ce moment-là, des réticences exigées, du style voulu ou commandé, des imitations admiratives et de tout ce qui peut modifier les formes extérieures d'un écrivain. Mais, sous tous ces déguisements, la vraie attitude de l'âme finit par se révéler pour qui sait lire; la sincère pensée est souvent entre les lignes, et le secret du poète . . . se devine à la longue; l'un après l'autre les voiles tombent et les mots des énigmes se découvrent. (94)

While I don't propose to be the realization of the ideal Lavinia/Spirite reading and understanding her beloved poet, I do propose that a deviant reading, that is, one which accepts the disguise of Gautier's writing, its displacement and its artifice, in short, its textuality, is in order. What is perhaps most striking about Gautier's poetry (and in fact all his writing) is its textuality, which, of course, is also an intertextuality. It exhibits its borrowings, its literary and cultural repetitions, its codes and conventions. It puts on display its literariness, that is, its existence as cultural artifact. It does so at times serenely, at times theatrically, at times playfully and humorously, at times ironically, at times obsessively.

Many have previously noted this artificiality. Michel Crouzet discussed it as Gautier's reproduction of the false and as his "creative problem." In "Théophile Gautier, poète," Gabriel Brunet saw "le type d'esprit qui ne perçoit le monde que sous l'aspect d'un ensemble de formes artistiques et ne cherche à le juger que par rapport à l'art créé par les hommes" (331). More recently, M. C. Schapira wrote: "Ce qui intrigue dans ses récits, c'est moins le non-dit que ce qui le masque en tout lieu: c'est l'artifice séduisant et trompeur de son écriture qui me parut très vite s'imposer comme le centre de toute réflexion sur son oeuvre" (8). What needs to be done for Gautier is to acknowledge this artifice and/or this artificiality not as something negative, something that goes against or prevents "good," "authentic" poetry, but as an essential constituent of poeticity. Rather than seeing artificiality and artifice as false and deceptive, I propose to accept them for what Gautier himself saw them to be: elements which are inherent and true to poetry, to writing and to art.

There are perhaps no verses of Gautier which are more widely known and quoted than those which conclude his poem **"L'art"**: "Sculpte, lime, ciselle; / Que ton rêve flottant / Se scelle / Dans le bloc résistant!" (***Poésies complètes*** III: 130). It may be that what readers have often resisted in Gautier's poetry is its manifestation of the resistance of the block, that is, the resistance of poetic language to what it would keep outside of it, namely time and therefore reality, as well as its resistance to that which it would have be within it, namely the *rêve flottant. Résistant,* the final word of Gautier's *art poétique,* is usually interpreted as signifying his commitment to a firmly defined formal poetry which would thereby possess the "hardness" to endure. One should note, however, that such an interpretation ignores, or is resistant to, that concomitant aspect of resistance by which the block is also impervious to the dream. It ignores, or is resistant to, the fact that Gautier himself modified the monosemic resistance which was expressed in the original variant of the poem: "Scelle ton rêve, afin / Qu'il dure / Tant que le monde ait fin!"[17]

The artificiality, the perceived and perceptible nearsightedness or lack in Gautier's poetry may be the honest, sincere, and lucid manifestation of poetry's inherent otherness to what is otherwise and elsewhere floating dream, as well as to its other "otherwise and elsewhere," reality. In fact, dream and block are mutually exclusive, as are dream and reality; they can coexist only rhetorically. The sealing of a floating dream is an oxymoron, a resistant, linguistic block or artifact defying realization and thus, paradoxically, assuring the continued existence of the *rêve flottant* in that realm outside or without textuality. Gautier's *art poétique* concludes with the purely figural and rhetorical exhortation ("Sculpte, lime, ciselle") that poetry be the simulation of a seal, the simulation of a tomb and/or of an imprint, both only traces of or monuments to the thereby absent and still floating dream. These verses which are usually cited in order to typify all that is solid in the textual artifact that Gautier would have be poetry, actually manifest a poetics that is a complex play of deviance and simulation.

Gautier's poetry is not deceptive, however, precisely because it acknowledges and exhibits its duplicity. It does not delude. It makes visible its artifice both as prosodic legerdemain and as monumentality or blazonry. In a sense, the canonic opinion of this poetry as excessive surface and as lacking in mystery is justified. Gautier's poetry does reveal itself to be a textual surface which is only a supplement to what is absent. It is made up of an excess of what is not essential and exhibits a lack of what is essential. This, however, does not necessarily negate or impede poetry; rather it informs it and constitutes it. In his study of Genet, Sartre proposes that beauty is the triumph of the nothingness of appearance over the nothingness of the real, whereas

"le non-être poétique se révèle dans l'échec . . . il est moins donné que pressenti, qu'espéré" (351). Poetry is Mallarmé's admission that "rien n'a eu lieu que le lieu." Gautier's poetry makes its readers aware of this gratuitousness, makes them aware of poetry's failure by making manifest the void of its exteriority. In Gautier's poems, beauty's triumphs are shown to be hollow because they are made superficial, that is, they are made manifestly textual. His poetry is a chiseled, polished surface which reveals its hollowness and inadequacy. It effects perceptible borders, gaps, and instabilities which reveal the limits of the poetic, textual surface. Its very superficiality allows, invites and seduces the reader to go "entre les lignes" and perceive the mystery, not of what is present and revealed, and therefore not mysterious, but of the absent.

Notes

[1] "Les progrès de la poésie française depuis 1830," *Histoire du romantisme* in the *Oeuvres complètes* XI: 359. Future references to the *Oeuvres complètes* will be abbreviated to OC.

[2] *Fusains et eaux-fortes,* OC III: 49. . . .

[3] Quoted by Ernest Feydeau in his *Théophile Gautier, souvenirs intimes* 47.

[4] *Poésies complètes,* ed. R. Jasinski I: 84. Unless otherwise noted, all my citations of Gautier's poetry will be taken from this edition which I will refer to as PC.

[5] *Correspondance générale 1849-1851* IV: 273. Gautier here reaffirms the same dual need for travel and for writing poetry which he expressed in the above statement cited by Feydeau. This need can be seen to reflect a desire for evaporation: a dispersal of the *moi;* and for condensation: a realization of the *moi* in the *non-moi.*

[6] Serge Fauchereau lists these admiring readers of Gautier at the conclusion of his study, *Théophile Gautier,* 114-121. P.E. Tennant also concludes his book, *Theophile Gautier,* with an interesting sampling of views on Gautier (116-122).

[7] Supervielle, in Robert Mallet's *Les incertitudes du langage—entretiens à la radio avec Robert Mallet* 264; Gide, *Incidences* 161.

[8] These are the well-known attributions given to Gautier in Baudelaire's dedication of *Les Fleurs du Mal.*

[9] Christopher Prendergast's "Questions of Metaphor: Gautier's 'La Nue'" in *Nineteenth-Century French Poetry* is one such reconsideration. Jacques Lardoux has also suggested that rereadings in a more contem-

porary mode yield appreciative insights into Gautier's poetry ("Quelques hypothèses sur la modernité poétique de Théophile Gautier").

[10] *Revue des Deux-Mondes,* April 1, 1841.

[11] *Revue des Deux-Mondes,* April 1, 1841.

[12] *Histoire du romantisme,* OC XI: 299.

[13] *Histoire de l'art dramatique en France depuis vint-cing ans,* 169; *Fusains et eaux-fortes,* OC III: 138-140.

[14] Preface to Emile Bergerat's *Théophile Gautier: entretiens, souvenirs et correspondance* vii-viii.

[15] The plasticity of Gautier's poetry is often unjustly used to negate its musicality. . . .

[16] Gautier's introduction to *Les Fleurs du Mal* (Paris: Calmann-Lévy, 1925) xlvi.

[17] This version appeared in *L'Artiste,* September 13, 1857 and is cited in Claudine Gothot-Mersch's edition of *Emaux et Camées* 275. Gautier's poem, as has often been noted, was a response to Théodore de Banville's "Odelette" which itself manifests a particularly strong sense of poetic resistance: "Car il faut qu'il [the poet] meurtrisse, / . . . Un métal au coeur dur," "Les strophes, nos esclaves / Ont encore besoin / D'entraves," and "Les pieds blancs de ces reines / Portent le poids réel / Des chaînes . . ." (Gothot-Mersch 275-276).

Works Cited

Banville, Théodore de. *Mes souvenirs.* Paris: Charpentier, 1883.

Baudelaire, Charles, trans. "La genèse d'un poème." *Histoires grotesques et sérieuses de Edgar Poe.* Paris: Michel Lévy, 1865.

————. *Oeuvres complètes.* Paris: Gallimard, 1961.

Bergerat, Emile. *Théophile Gautier, entretiens, souvenirs et correspondance.* Avec une Préface d'Edmond de Goncourt. Paris: Charpentier, 1880.

Brunet, Gabriel. "Théophile Gautier poète." *Mercure de France* 159: 162 (October 15, 1922), 289-332.

Crouzet, Michel. "Gautier et le problème de créer." *Revue d'histoire littéraire de la France* 72.4 (July-August 1972): 659-687.

Eliot, T.S. "Baudelaire." *Selected Essays.* N.Y.: Harcourt, Brace, 1950. 371-381.

————. *Selected Poems.* N.Y.: Harcourt, Brace Jovanovich, 1964.

Fauchereau, Serge. *Théophile Gautier.* Paris: Denoël, 1972.

Gautier, Théophile. *Correspondance générale.* Ed. Claudine Lacoste-Veysseyre. 8 vols to date. Genève-Paris: Droz, 1985-1993.

————. *Emaux et Camées.* Ed. by Claudine Gothot-Mersch. Paris: Gallimard, 1981.

————. *Oeuvres complètes.* 11 vols. Geneva: Slatkine Reprints, 1978.

————. *Poésies complètes.* Ed. René Jasinski. 3 vols. Paris: Nizet, 1970.

————. *Spirite.* Paris: Flammarion, 1970.

Gide, André. *Incidences.* Paris: Gallimard, 1924.

Lardoux, Jacques. "Découvrir les poésies libertines." *Bulletin de la Société Théophile Gautier* 13 (1991): 61-84.

Mallarmé, Stéphane. *Oeuvres complètes.* Paris: Gallimard, 1945.

Mallet, Robert. *Les incertitudes du langage.* Paris: Gallimard, 1970.

Ponge, François. *Pour un Malherbe.* Paris: Gallimard, 1965.

Pound, Ezra. "The Approach to Paris." *Selected Prose 1909-1965.* Ed. William Cookson. N.Y.: New Directions, 1974.

Prendergast, Christopher. "Questions of Metaphor: Gautier's 'La Nue.'" *Nineteenth-Century French Poetry.* Ed. Christopher Prendergast. Cambridge: Cambridge University Press, 1990. 138-156.

Sartre, Jean-Paul. *Saint Genet, comédien et martyr. Oeuvres complètes de Jean Genet.* Paris: Gallimard, 1952.

Schapira, M.-C. *Le regard de Narcisse.* Lyon: Presses Universitaires de Lyon, 1984.

Tennant, P.E. *Théophile Gautier.* London: Athlone Press, 1975.

FURTHER READING

Biography

Grant, Richard B. *Théophile Gautier.* Boston: Twayne Publishers, 1975, 179 p.

Gives a broad overview of Gautier's life and works, while examining a few of his texts in detail.

Snell, Robert. *Théophile Gautier: A Romantic Critic of the Visual Arts.* Oxford: Clarendon Press, 1982, 273 p.

Offers an account of Gautier's career by trying "to arrive at an inside view of the man," in part by viewing him through a historical perspective.

Tennant, P.E. *Théophile Gautier.* London: Athlone Press, 1975, 149 p.

Biographical account of Gautier which also includes a critical evaluation of his works.

Criticism

Driscoll, Irene Joan. "Visual Allusion in the Work of Théophile Gautier." *French Studies* 27, No. 4 (October 1973): 418-28.

Examines the value of visual allusion in Gautier's literary works and challenges the assumption that Gautier "judged reality according to aesthetic standards alone."

Easton, Malcolm. "Shocking the Burghers." In *Artists and Writers in Paris: The Bohemian Idea, 1803-1867*, pp. 57-72. London: Edward Arnold, 1964.

Discusses Gautier's involvement with the *petit cénacle*, a group of Romantic artists and writers.

Gide, Andre. *Incidences.* Paris: Gallimard, 1951.

Criticizes Gautier's work on the grounds that it was "blind to everything but the exterior world."

Hamrick, Lois Cassandra. "Artists, Artisans and Artistic Discontinuity: Baudelaire and Gautier Speak Out." In *Discontinuity and Fragmentation*, edited by Freeman G. Henry, pp. 67-79. French Literature Series, Vol. XXI. Atlanta: Rodopi, 1994.

Addresses Gautier's and Baudelaire's contrasting responses to the artistic discontinuity of the mid-nineteenth century.

Lowrie, Joyce O. "The Question of Mimesis in Gautier's *Contes Fantastiques*." *Nineteenth Century French Studies* 8, Nos. 1-2 (Fall-Winter 1979-80): 14-29.

Analyzes the two domains that exist in fantastic fiction—the real and the unreal—as they apply to Gautier's works.

Mickel, Emanuel J., Jr. "Opium and Hashish in the Literature of French Romanticism." In *The Artifical Paradises in French Literature: I. The Influence of Opium and Hashish on the Literature of French Romanticism and "Les Fleurs Du Mal,"* pp. 81-126. Studies in the Romance Languages and Literatures, No. 84. Chapel Hill: The University of North Carolina Press, 1969.

Traces the relationship between Gautier's "dream fiction" and his occasional experiences with opium and hashish.

Palache, John Garber. *Gautier and the Romantics.* New York: The Viking Press, 1926, 186 p.

Discusses Gautier's importance as a theorist and as a member of literary society.

Prendergast, Christopher. "Questions of Metaphor: Gautier's 'La Nue'." In *Nineteenth-Century French Poetry: Introductions to Close Reading*, edited by Christopher Prendergast, pp. 138-56. Cambridge: Cambridge University Press, 1990.

Challenges the current view of Gautier as a "minor poet" and his poetry as "emotionally and intellectually sterile."

Riffaterre, Hermine. "Love-in-Death: Gautier's 'morte amoureuse'." In *The Occult in Language and Literature*, edited by Hermine Riffaterre, pp. 65-74. New York: New York Literary Forum, 1980.

Attempts to explain the myth of "morte amoureuse" or "the dead woman in love" which repeatedly surfaces in Gautier's works.

Schick, Constance Gosselin. "A Case Study of Descriptive Perversion: Théophile Gautier's Travel Literature." *Romantic Review* 78, No. 3 (May 1987): 359-67.

Examines the use of precision and exactness of detail in Gautier's travelogues and claims that "description for Gautier was not perverse; it was simply poetic."

——. "Théophile Gautier's Poetry as *Coquetterie Posthume*." *Nineteenth Century French Studies* 20, Nos. 1-2 (Fall-Winter 1991-92): 74-84.

Discusses the theme of life and death in Gautier's poem "Coquetterie Posthume."

Smith, Albert B. "Gautier's *Mademoiselle de Maupin*: The Quest for Happiness." *Modern Language Quarterly* 32, No. 2 (June 1971): 168-74.

Studies the relationship between desire and its fulfillment in Gautier's *Mademoiselle de Maupin*.

Spencer, Michael Clifford. *The Art Criticism of Théophile Gautier.* Geneva: Librairie Droz, 1969, 124 p.

A historical review of Gautier's art criticism.

Voisin, Marcel. *Le Soleil et la nuit: L'Imaginaire dans l'oeuvre de Théophile Gautier.* Brussels: Editions de l'Université de Bruxelles, 1981, 375 p.

Asserts that Gautier is a distinguished author who deserves a place among the major literary figures of French literature.

Additional coverage of Gautier's life and career is contained in the following sources published by Gale Research: *Nineteenth-Century Literature Criticism*, Volume 1, *Dictionary of Literary Biography*, Volume 119, *Short Story Criticism*, Volume 20, and *DISCovering Authors Poets Module.*

Amy Levy

1861-1889

English novelist, poet, short story writer, and essayist.

INTRODUCTION

Levy's brief but impressive career has received increasing critical attention in recent years, with discussion focusing in particular on the author's fictional
and poetic treatment of feminist themes, bourgeois
Jewish culture, nineteenth-century urban life, and the
motif of suicide. Levy's oeuvre includes three short
novels, three collections of poetry, and noted contributions of short fiction and essays to such major nineteenth-century periodicals as *Temple Bar,* the *Gentleman's Magazine,* and the *Jewish Chronicle.* Noted in
particular for her portrayal of Jewish life in her novel
Reuben Sachs (1888), Levy is also recognized for her
depiction of independent, entrepreneurial women in
such works as *The Romance of a Shop* (1888). Levi's
poetry is characterized by her facility with a variety of
forms, though most critics emphasize her skill as a
lyric poet.

Biographical Information

Born in Clapham in 1861, Levy was the second daughter of Lewis Levy and Isobel Levin. Levy's writing
career began early, her poem "Ida Grey" appearing in
the journal the *Pelican* when she was only fourteen.
Levy became the first Jewish woman admitted to
Newnham College of Cambridge University in approximately 1879. The following year, *Dublin University
Magazine* published what many critics consider among
her most significant poems, "Xantippe"; her first story,
"Mrs. Pierrepoint" appeared in *Temple Bar* later that
same year. Levy's literary career continued to progress
during her college years, with her first collection of
poetry, *Xantippe and Other Verse*, appearing in 1881.
During the next few years, she published several short
stories as well as a second collection of poetry, *A Minor
Poet and Other Verse* (1884). In 1886, Levy began
writing a series of essays on Jewish culture and literature for the *Jewish Chronicle*, including "The Ghetto
at Florence," "The Jew in Fiction," "Jewish Humour,"
and "Jewish Children." Publishing sentimental stories
in *Temple Bar* in 1888 and 1889, Levy also contributed to Oscar Wilde's journal, *Woman's World.* Levy's
first two novels, *The Romance of a Shop* and *Reuben
Sachs,* were published in 1888. Her second volume of
poems, *A London Plane-Tree*, was published the following year. Deeply depressed by causes still conjec-
tural, Levy committed suicide in 1889, shortly before
her twenty-eighth birthday.

Major Works

Considered Levy's major work, the novel *Reuben
Sachs* represents the author's most direct treatment
of the theme of Jewish values and culture. Focusing
on the upper-middle-class Jews who were becoming
increasingly present in all walks of English society
during the nineteenth century, the novel comments
on what Levy perceived as the materialistic values
and cultural insularity of the English Jewish bourgeoisie. The presence of negative stereotypes in the
novel's characterizations suggests authorial ambivalence toward the Jewish subject matter—a problem
which has been the focus of much critical discussion
of Levy's oeuvre. Linda Hunt comments: "[*Reuben
Sachs*] is a novel whose stance is so slippery—the
relationship between narrator and narrative so shifting—the reliability of the narrative voice so questionable . . . that the reader is not at all sure where Levy
stands." Feminist themes are also important in Levy's
fiction and poetry. Cited by many critics as an example
of Levy's feminism, the poem "Xantippe," for example,
is written from the perspective of Socrates' wife. *The

Romance of a Shop also explores a woman's perspective through its depiction of four sisters who experience the pleasures and hardships of running a business in London during the 1880s. Women are also the focus of the posthumously published short story "Wise in Her Generation" (1890), which presents a cynical view of the "marriage game" that dominated the activities of many Victorian women. Commenting on the style of Levy's fiction, Edward Wagenknecht observes: "All are direct, simple, straightforward narratives, avoiding all unnecessary complications, and paying no heed to the sophisticated, self-conscious considerations of 'method' which were coming more and more into vogue." As a poet, Levy is best known for her lyric verse, much of which reveals a brooding, pessimistic tone. Critics have commented on her facility with the ballad form, and her penchant for assuming a variety of narrative voices and perspectives in her verse. Suicide is a prominent motif in such poems as "Felo De Se," as it is in much of Levy's fiction. The short story "Sokratics in the Strand" (1884), for example, depicts a depressed poet's conversation with a successful, optimistic attorney—an experience which further disheartens the poet and blights his prospects for a bearable life.

Critical Reception

With the exception of early praise by E. K. Chambers, who placed Levy's works in the tradition of modern pessimism, most recent critical discussion of Levy's works has been concerned with her status as a Jewish writer. Although widely regarded as an accomplished artist, Levy is considered a problematic figure by many because her depictions of Jewish culture (particularly in *Reuben Sachs*) often suggest stereotypes and anti-Semitic sentiments. While praised by such critics as Oscar Wilde for its "directness, its uncompromising truth, its depth of feeling," *Reuben Sachs* was rejected by many contemporary Jewish readers as anti-Semitic, stereotypical, and hostile. Some contemporary critics, however, such as Melvyn New and Deborah Epstein Nord, have emphasized the feminist, rather than ethnic, motifs of the work. Nord, for instance, notes that it is a feminine consciousness that comes to dominate the narrative: "[Levy] allows herself to imagine without disguise the chilling position of the unmarried woman cornered into lifelong celibacy or a loveless marriage." Arguing for a general reassessment of Levy's status as a writer, New comments: "It seems possible that Levy's Jewishness has gotten in the way of a valid assessment of her achievements, most particularly as a feminist voice." New's 1993 anthology of Levy's writings brought into print several works which had been largely inaccessible, potentially contributing to the growth of critical attention to Levy's work.

PRINCIPAL WORKS

Xantippe and Other Verse (poetry) 1881
"Between Two Stools" (short story) 1883
A Minor Poet and Other Verse (poetry) 1884
"Sokratics in the Strand" (short story) 1884
"The Ghetto at Florence" (essay) 1886
"The Jew in Fiction" (essay) 1886
"Jewish Humour" (essay) 1886
"Jewish Children" (essay) 1886
The Romance of a Shop (novel) 1888
Reuben Sachs (novel) 1888
A London Plane-Tree and Other Verse (poetry) 1889
Miss Meredith (novella) 1889
A London Plane Tree (poetry) 1889
"A Slip of the Pen" (short story) 1889
"Wise in her Generation" (short story) 1890

* This work was published posthumously

CRITICISM

The Literary World (review date 1889)

SOURCE: Review of *The Romance of a Shop* and *Reuben Sachs*, in *The Literary World*, Vol. XX, No. 8, April 13, 1889, p. 123.

[In the following review, the anonymous critic offers a favorable assessment of Levy's novels The Romance of a Shop *and* Reuben Sachs.*]*

The critic who takes up a new novel, by a new and unknown writer, in these days when the number of novels is legion, may be forgiven if he does not look forward to much pleasure from its perusal. There is such a painful amount of "meritorious mediocrity" in print today that there are nine chances out of ten against the new novel being worth reading. But this wearisome sameness, this monotonous dead level of current fiction, forms an excellent contrasting background for real merit. Great is the satisfaction then, after taking up a novel from which one expects nothing, to find that the writer actually has power and possibilities. It is with this keen kind of satisfaction that we lay down **The Romance of a Shop**. It is not a great novel, but it is distinctly above the average and shows that the writer must be a woman of intellect and insight. It has evident faults of construction, but its pages are lit up with touches of pathos and glimpses of human life which astonish us with their truth and beauty.

The story is of four sisters left orphans, who attempt to support themselves in London by photography. The different characters of the four sisters and the various ways in which their new life affected their dispositions are admirably described. The strong-minded Gertrude, the conventional Fanny, the industrious Lucy, and the beautiful Phillis win their own places in our affections, and are very real persons to us before we close the book. The writer does not content us by merely picturing the outer lives, but she lets us see the hopes and fears, the temptations and sorrows, which came to each sister individually while they lived together.

Besides these character sketches the writer gives us a delightful picture of Bohemian London and the artist life. She takes us to picture exhibitions and studio receptions, and with an artist's love of contrast presents us often to a representative of conventional middle-class London life in the shape of the sisters' rich but disapproving Aunt Caroline. Bohemian London with all its fascinations is of course full of perils for young unchaperoned girls. In the sad story of poor little Phillis's life and death we are shown the dangerous side of what otherwise would be the most charming society in the world—a society made up as Gertrude says of "picked individuals."

Miss Amy Levy has the ability to tell a story well, the power of creating characters who talk cleverly, and a poetical imagination which keeps her realism from being bare and dry. What she has not is dramatic power. She lets admirable situations pass without using them to any purpose. *The Romance of a Shop* is moreover put together awkwardly. The wheels of the machinery creak. But aside from these flaws the story is original and suggestive; it holds our attention from the beginning to end; and the writer has the most important gift for a novelist to possess, what James Russell Lowell calls the "divine faculty"—that is, she "*sees* what everybody can look at."

Reuben Sachs is but a sketch by the side of the novel we have been noticing. It shows, however, an advance in power. It is a book which will probably call forth some indignant protests from Miss Levy's compatriots of the Jewish race in London and elsewhere. The picture it gives in outline of the modern descendants of Jacob is the complete opposite in many respects of George Eliot's in *Daniel Deronda*. "I have always been touched," says one of the characters here, "at the immense good faith with which George Eliot carried out that elaborate misconception of hers. . . . We are materialists to our fingers' ends. . . . We have outlived from the nature of things such ideals as we ever had." *Reuben Sachs* is not a pleasant book to read; it has too much of the bitterness of reality in it. But we should advise Christians to be slow in reproaching Jewish society because of it; Mammon is a very popular god in all civilized lands.

After enjoying *The Romance of a Shop* it is pleasant to learn from Mrs. Moulton that Amy Levy is the daughter of a London editor, a mere girl, but one whom Oscar Wilde calls "a girl of genius." She brought out

several years ago a volume of very pretty verses. If this be, as we suppose, her first full novel we shall look forward to her literary future with pleasant anticipation.

E. K. Chambers (essay date 1892)

SOURCE: "Poetry and Pessimism," in *The Westminster Review*, Vol. CXXXVIII, July-December, 1892, pp. 366-76.

[*In the following assessment of Levy's career. Chambers places Levy in the context of late nineteenth-century literary pessimism.*]

In the mind of a student of humanity, if he be also a reader of books, intellectual problems are apt to crystallise around individual personalities. A single poet, a single novelist, comes to stand to him for a whole complex of thought, a web of vague ideas and tendencies which are elsewhere, as we say, in the air, but which first become palpable when compelled by an artist's hand into the rigidity of the written word. This is especially the case with poets, for poetry, by its very nature, strikes to the heart of things and sets them before us in their naked essence, stripping away the vesture of irrelevant detail that, in the novel no less than in life, often veils and obscures them. It is by its poignancy, its directness of presentment, that poetry claims to be, as a medium of ideas, what Aristotle called it, most akin to philosophy.

The analysis, for example, of modern pessimism can scarcely be dissociated from the study of that gifted writer whose work it permeates and informs, Amy Levy. Two little volumes of her poems, in a dainty green-and-white binding, lie on my table, and have fascinated me for hours together. Vividly personal as they are, the pent-up sufferings of hundreds of souls throb through them, launching one on wide seas of melancholy speculation. Of Amy Levy's short and sad life I have no knowledge. She was, it would seem, by birth a Jewess, but one for whom the faith of her fathers had become an impossible thing. Gifted with brilliant intellectual powers, she spent a short time as a student at Cambridge, and then entered upon the perilous ways of literary life. It was not long before success appeared to be within her reach, but she was not destined to reap the fruition of it. A haunting shadow had fallen upon her path; she came to find the burden of life intolerable; and while still a girl was contented to yield up her share therein. Throughout all her work, prose and poetry alike, hand in hand with a sincere devotion to art, there runs a note of invincible sadness.

Such is the dominant impression that one gets from reading these volumes. Looked at purely as literature, they have a remarkable charm. They possess all the subtle workmanship, the delicacy of finish, the innumerable scholarly touches, which are so characteristic of the minor verse of our day. If they are somewhat full of echoes, there also they do not stand alone. But far beyond their merely artistic value, is their interest as the record of a soul. They are, indeed, a human document at least as rich with suggestion as the much discussed diary of Marie Bashkirtseff. And a document, one would think, far more legible; for Marie, even in her most secret moments, was always and inevitably a *poseuse,* whereas Amy Levy is throughout absolutely genuine and sincere. How could it be otherwise? Utterly disenchanted with the world, why should she try to keep up a brave show before it? Her verse mirrors her thought, and its *leit-motif,* recurring with constant sad iteration, is the consciousness of pain.

I suppose that the philosophical attitudes which we call optimism and pessimism are generally less the result of mental conviction than of individual temperament. They are moods, not systems. Life in itself is iridescent with pleasure and pain: to one the richer hues, the lurking purples and leaping crimsons alone are visible; another is spiritually colour-blind, and can see only the browns and drabs, the dusky shadows and more sombre depths of existence. Personality is a selective force, choosing from the vast mass of what is, by some subtle magnetism, just those elements which are most akin to its own nature. For all who attract pleasure, life is a triumph; for the rest, a pilgrimage. This, no doubt, has been a universal law, no less true when the world seemed vanity to the author of *Ecclesiastes,* than it is now. Yet it will hardly be denied that, for whatever cause, pessimism is in an especial degree characteristic of our own time and our own stage of development.

Our splendid literature is invested with melancholy. Tennyson and Browning, indeed, are optimists, but their optimism is grave, not buoyant; they walk by faith, not by sight. Browning twists an assurance for the future out of the failures of the present, while Tennyson, in no less doubtful a strain, bids us "stretch lame hands of faith" to a dimly felt Providence, and "faintly trust the larger hope." So, too, with the rest. George Meredith saves himself from pessimism by a strong will and an austere philosophy. Matthew Arnold and A. H. Clough are openly and profoundly despondent; for them the light of the past is quenched, the future is beset with clouds; they are for ever "wandering between two worlds, one dead, the other powerless to be born." Even in the Neo-Romantic poets, who least express the spirit of their age, the same tone may be discerned. Rossetti, though a lover, walked in Willow-wood all the days of his life. Morris, in youth, sought a refuge from the century's stress in the groves of an earthly Paradise, a dream-world of Greek and northern and mediæval legend. But his attempt was not all a success: the blitheness of Hellas was beyond recapture;

the violin-note of modern feeling rang incongruously through Arcadia, and in the end—

> he could not keep,
> For that a shadow lour'd on the fields,
> Here with the shepherds and the silly sheep.

He translated his ideals from the past to the future, and the "idle singer of an empty day" became the busy herald of a visionary hope. And if this sadness haunts the great poets of the age, still more is it noticeable in the lesser singers. Look at the pages of Mr. Miles's *Poets and Poetry of the Century.* There is a literature surcharged with tears, whose sure touch is on the pathetic, whose lyre sounds in groves that are shaded by cypresses and poplars, among roses that weep their petals.

When one turns from letters, the reflex of life, to life itself, the outlook is equally drear. We moderns find the world a very serious matter. Fifty years of individualism, of free thought, and unrestricted competition, have bitten their mark deep into our civilisation. The suffering which inevitably accompanies the struggle for existence is not less, but greater, for organisms upon a high level of self-consciousness. Flesh is ever but a transparent veil to spirit, and of this suffering we bear the plain sign upon our brows. It needs no wide knowledge of art to realise that the faces which Gainsborough painted differ notably in character and expression from those which fill the walls of a modern picture-gallery. The new type is as beautiful perhaps, more deeply intellectual, but certainly far more sad. It is scarcely fantastic to suggest that Leonardo's ironically named *La Gioconda,* an alien to our great-grandmothers, is curiously at home among the women of our own generation. By the same spirit our philosophy is coloured. Mr. Alexander, in his thoughtful book on *Moral Order and Moral Progress,* has singled out, as a central point in current ethical conceptions, the growing sense of the significance of pain. Pleasure was the loadstar of the earlier Hedonist; his modern successor, less exigent, would barter hopes of positive felicity to be quite sure of escaping suffering. This tendency to dwell on pain manifests itself among many who are by no means Hedonists. In it are rooted both strong and weak elements in our social organisation, the self-sacrifice of genuine philanthropy, as well as the excesses of sentimental humanitarianism.

It is difficult to analyse the causes which have made pain and pessimism so aggressive nowadays. Perhaps they are not really new dwellers among us, but only now for the first time becoming articulate, after long silent years in the heart of humanity. Partly they may be the outcome of fundamental changes in the religious consciousness. I do not mean the spread of unorthodoxy, but the disappearance of what George Eliot called "other-worldliness," that facile optimism which held this world as a vale of tears, to be compensated for by an eternity of pleasures in the next. More and more the conception that "I myself am heaven and hell," with all that it implies, is coming to be a fixed and abiding mode of belief. In part, also, a reason may be found in the intensity of our intellectual life, in the constant feverish speculation, the besetting desire to know. We are "sicklied o'er with the pale cast of thought." Only the superficial, the unreflecting, can dare to echo in all soberness the famous words of Mr. Pole; "No one has said the world's a jolly world so often as I have. It's jolly!" Given a temperament exceptionally sensitive to pain, and set in a modern environment, the result will be yet farther conditioned by individual characteristics. In the sympathetic, for whom the sufferings of others are no less real, no less vivid than their own, it will generally be devotion, in some one of its many forms, to the cause of humanity. In the self-centred, who have no safety-valve, it can hardly be other than a life of brooding misery. And such a life, faithfully presented, one would think, but at any rate with poignancy, is revealed to us in these poems of Amy Levy's. On opening them one's eye falls upon some such passage as this, lines in which the stored-up bitterness of the heart seems forcing itself into expression:

EPITAPH

ON A COMMONPLACE PERSON WHO DIED IN BED.

This is the end of him, here he lies:
The dust in his throat, the worm in his eyes,
The mould in his mouth, the turf on his
    breast;
This is the end of him, this is best.
He will never lie on his couch awake,
Wide-eyed, tearless, till dim daybreak;
Never again will he smile and smile,
When his heart is breaking all the while;
He will never stretch out his hands in vain,
Groping and groping—never again;
Never ask for bread, get a stone instead,
Never pretend that the stone is bread;
Never sway and sway 'twixt the false and
    true,
Weighing and noting the long hours through;
Never ache and ache with the choked-up
    sighs:
This is the end of him—here he lies.

One turns instinctively to the portrait facing the title-page to see what manner of woman she was who could write thus, but the secret is hardly revealed. There is a face of no special beauty, the brow and eyes burdened with a weight of thought, the lips set as if in some reticence of sorrow. Baffled rather than satisfied, one goes back to the poems, anxious if possible to win the mystery from themselves. They are not many. A few lyrics and fragmentary snatches of verse, and a

Browningesque monologue, *A Minor Poet,* clearly in some measure autobiographical. Brief as these records are, it is yet possible to decipher in them some image of the personality by which they were dictated. Amy Levy was in her way a passionate idealist. She entered upon life full of hope and strength and self-confidence, conscious of unbounded capacities for happiness and intensely eager to realise them. In the person of the Minor Poet she cries:

I want all, all;
I've appetite for all: I want the best,
Love, beauty, sunlight, nameless joy of life.

Moreover, she was modern to the core, keen in relish of the pleasures of æsthetic and philosophical speculation; sensitive, as only moderns can be, to the thousand charms and phases of Nature, in her infinite variety; blessed with rich potentialities for friendship and love; thirsting, like Tennyson's Ulysses, to "drink life to the lees." But it is part of the irony of things that those who have most power to enjoy are often those whom joy visits most rarely. Little by little, disillusion crept upon her; overlooked by love, cheated in friendship by death and misprision, she discovered in girlhood that the universe was hollow, and life, for her at least, "a circle of pain," more terrible than death itself, although, or perhaps because, death bore no promise of a hereafter. As her capacity for joy had been deep, so her actual sufferings were intense; they find some expression in these volumes, with their pitiful mottoes from Omar Khayyam, filled with poems of which each is a wail, only more penetrating for the artistic charm which makes of it a carven shrine for grief. The keynote of them all is struck in a half-serious, half-ironic imitation of Swinburne, by the lines:

I am I—just a Pulse of Pain—I am I, that is
    all I know.
For Life, and the sickness of Life, and Death,
    and desire to die:
They have passed away like the smoke, here
    is nothing but Pain and I.

And this dominant sense of a besetting personal pain is never far away, coming at last to bear the aspect of a fate, disastrous to all hope and all effort, a watcher at the threshold, of whose presence she is ever conscious, with bitterness, or with resignation, or with a half surprise, all alike unavailing. Desolation and solitude add a pang:

The people take the thing of course,
    They marvel not to see
This strange unnatural divorce
    Betwixt delight and me.

Only most rarely, in the swing of a waltz, in some spiritual day of April or Midsummer, in the presence of an elect soul, does a moment of gladness come to her; never is it more than a moment, and in most of her moods, even the intimations of beauty, moral and physical, are powerless. They speak to a deaf ear, and the heart regardeth them not:

> Is it so much of the gods that I pray?
>   Sure craved man never so slight a boon!
> To be glad and glad in my heart one day—
>   One perfect day of the perfect June.
>
>   . . . . .
>
> I would hold my life as a thing of worth;
>   Pour praise to the gods for a precious thing.
> Lo! June in her fairness is on the earth,
>   And never a joy does the niggard bring.

More cruel than all else is the contrast between what is and what might have been, between the aspiring idealism of the past and the sorry levels of the present. This is the burden of a striking little poem called *The Old House:*

> In through the porch and up the silent stair;
>   Little is changed, I know so well the ways;
> Here the dead came to meet me, it was there
>   The dream was dreamed in unforgotten days.
>
> But who is this that hurries on before,
>   A flitting shade the brooding shades among?
> She turned—I saw her face—O God, it wore
>   The face I used to wear when I was young.
>
> I thought my spirit and my heart were turned
>   To deadness; dead the pangs that agonise.
> The old grief springs to choke me—I am
>   shamed
>   Before that little ghost with eager eyes.
>
> O turn away, let her not see, not know!
>   How should she bear it, how should
>   understand?
> O hasten down the stairway, haste and go,
>   And leave her dreaming in the silent land.

Among thoughts such as these it is only natural that the image of death, in its varied aspects, should be a familiar visitant, presenting itself now as a strong deliverer, now as a terrible veiled shape, inscrutable, and therefore to be feared. As a matter of theory, Amy Levy in her strenuous rejection of the religious standpoint can only look upon death as the goal of existence and ultimate barrier between human souls. And so, when one whom she had loved passes away, the blank sense of loss is unrelieved by any hope. Every link is shattered:

> There is no more to be done,
> Nothing beneath the sun.
> All the long ages through
> Nothing—by me for you.

> *All's done with* utterly,
> *All's done with.* Death to me
> Was ever death indeed:
> To me no kindly creed
>
> Consolatory was given
> You were of earth, not heaven.

This for her friends. But for herself death seems all the more a gracious thing in its finality. Annihilation might yield a rest unknown to sentience; the whirl of life might vanish for ever in a "poppied sleep." The thought of death makes strange disturbance in her heart, becoming at last an imperious summons not to be disregarded. It obtrudes itself, in unexpected places, at inappropriate moments, striking across every vein of reflection with ironic self-assertiveness, waiting at the close of every avenue of conversation.

> It is so long gone by, and yet
>   How clearly now I see it all!
> The glimmer of your cigarette,
>   The little chamber, narrow and tall,
>
> Perseus, your picture in its frame
>   (How near they seem and yet how far!)
> The blaze of kindled logs: the flame
>   Of tulips in a mighty jar.
>
> Florence and Spring-time: surely each
>   Glad thing unto the spirit saith,
> Why did you lead me in your speech
>   To these dark mysteries of death?

And so the days pass by, and life becomes more intolerable, and the thought of the end more alluring, until the second volume of poems—of which, the publishers tell us, the proofs were corrected by the author about a week before her death—closes upon the ominous words:

> On me the cloud descends.

The first effect of such a record as this upon the mind is purely an emotional one. "Sunt lacrimæ rerum et mentem mortalia tangunt." The pity, the infinite pity of it, resists all attempts to draw a moral. But before long the inevitable problem asserts itself. What help is there? By what philosophy, what direction of will is a soul smitten with this *welt-schmerz,* this modern disease of pessimism, to shake off the paralysis, and get back into touch with the normal and saner aspect of things? Many answers have been given and merit consideration; but it must frankly be admitted that they are none of them very cogent. Theories that challenge refutation when set forth in an essay or from the pulpit have a terrible way of shrivelling up and ceasing to convince when brought face to face with the concrete facts of an individual human life. Ideals are so often ineffectual from the mere lack of dynamic force. To the present difficulty both the moral philosopher and the plain man, influenced more or less consciously by centuries of Christian tradition, would probably offer the same very obvious reply. Pessimism, they would say, is rooted in self-absorption. Constant inward gazing upon the bare self can only beget a sense of emptiness and vanity. Fruition, and happiness therewith, can alone be attained by contact with the other than self, by entering into some form of sympathetic union with the universal life wherein each person is only a unit. And this is perfectly true, as an ethical maxim. But it does not meet the case of those who have not the gift of sympathy. "He that loseth his soul, the same shall find it." But there are those whose temperament does not permit them for one instant to lose their souls. Take Miss Levy. What are the ways by which the individual mingles with the universal? Love, Friendship, Religion, the passion of Art, the passion of Humanity. For her, it would seem, all these avenues were irretrievably closed. Friendship and love she had grasped at, but they had proved bitter and elusive—apples of Sodom in the mouth. Religion she held an unmeaning thing. "Both for me and you, you know," she cries, "there's no Above and no Below." Hers indeed was the saddest of all spiritual states upon the earth, that of an awakened Israelite, cheated of the hope of Israel. So, too, with Art: once she might have striven to find a vocation in some mode of creative effort; but little by little her early ambitions had been nipped by a chilling sense of impotence, until all faculty of absorbing herself in them was gone. There remains the service of Humanity, in which, no doubt, under its various forms, many have found the consolation for which they had sounded the depths of their own personality in vain. Yet one reads a confession in *A Minor Poet,* which shows how little this could ever have appealed to her:

> Then, again,
> "The common good," and still "the common
>   good,"
> And what a small thing was our joy or grief
> When weighed with that of thousands. Gentle
>   Tom,
> But you might wag your philosophic tongue
> From morn till eve, and still the thing's the
>   same,
> I am myself, as each man is himself—
> Feels his own pain, joys his own joy and
>   loves
> With his own love, no other's. Friend, the
>   world
> Is but one man: one man is but the world.
> And I am I, and you are Tom, that bleeds
> When needles prick your flesh (mark, yours
>   not mine).
> I must confess it; I can feel the pulse
> A-beating at my heart, yet never knew

> The throb of cosmic pulses. I lament
> The death of youth's ideal in my heart;
> And, to be honest, never yet rejoiced
> In the world's progress—scarce indeed
>   discerned.

Ah no! it is idle to preach philanthropy to those who have not the genius for sympathy. At bottom it is a matter of temperament. "We are as the Fates make us." In spite of all gospels, the self-centred will be self-centred still to the end of time, and must spin their threads of interest from within, or not at all. And on this rock of the essential difference between centripetal and centrifugal natures, the Christian answer to the pessimistic problem necessarily founders.

The neo-paganism of the nineteenth century has also attempted its answers to this same problem. In the end these reduce themselves more or less directly to the idea of harmony with Nature. All alike preach self-surrender, acceptance of the inevitable, and a strenuous cultivation of the consciousness that only by his attempt to transcend Nature, and to live his life on another plane than hers, does man vex and fret himself away. One side of this philosophy addresses itself to the emotional correspondences between Nature and man. Nature is the universal Mother, the infinite comforter, consoling her lovers with subtle spells of forest and cloud and meadow, yielding to whoso will take it the cup of Lethe, the soporific that lulls doubt and destroys sorrow. It is in Wordsworth that this teaching first became articulate, and in virtue of it he has been enabled to dominate a whole century of poetry. It is the burden of his most inspired moods, of *Lucy,* of the lines on *Tintern Abbey,* of the *Ode on Immortality.* Matthew Arnold, with his accurate critical instinct in such matters, has touched this central point in Wordsworth's attitude to life and has in some measure learnt the lesson of it.

> He found us when the age had bound
> Our souls in its benumbing round;
> He spoke and loosed our heart in tears.
> He laid us as we lay at birth
> On the cool flowery lap of earth.
> Smiles broke from us and we had ease;
> The hills were round us, and the breeze
> Went o'er the sunlit fields again;
> Our foreheads felt the wind and rain,
> Our youth returned, for there was shed
> On spirits that had long been dead,
> Spirits dried up and closely furl'd,
> The freshness of the early world.

Transfigured and stamped with the impress of a wayward genius, the same ruling ideal appears in the Nature-poetry of George Meredith. For him the man who has attained is Melampus, the eyes open and ears unsealed for every secret of bird and beast and flower, in whom insight has been born of love.

> Through love exceeding a simple love of the
>   things
> That glide in grasses and rubble of woody
>   wreck.

Only in the "Woods of Westermain" may the riddle of life be read. Those who can walk there undismayed find all the joys of life and lose its hungers. Beauty and the meaning of beauty, passion and the seeds of passion, are made manifest to them; they become interpreters and know themselves "kin of the rose" and of all delicious things. But not for every one is such transfiguration possible: it is reserved for those of a right heart and a right temper, those who are by nature "servile to all the skyey influences," who can give an absolute confidence, an absolute self-surrender. At a single hint of mistrust, the spell of the woods is broken, terrible shapes possess them.

> Thousand eyeballs under hoods
>   Have you by the hair!

And this is why, for all its magic, the Nature-philosophy is no panacea against pessimism. Like the ethical gospel, it is only true for certain temperaments that have already a faculty of detachment from self, and can greet the physician in his own spirit. And such are not the stuff of which pessimists are made. Those on whom the burden of the world presses most heavily are yet most strongly drawn to it; they are linked to it for ever with adamantine fetters. So it was with Amy Levy. The peace of Nature was to her merely an Arcadia, a languid bower of bliss, impotent to satisfy her restless perturbed spirit. "Fain would I bide," she moans, among the lavender and lilies of a summer garden—

> Fain would I bide, but ever in the distance
>   A ceaseless voice is sounding clear and low:
> The city calls me with her old persistence,
>   The city calls me—I arise and go.
>
> Of gentler souls this fragrant peace is
>   guerdon;
>   For me, the roar and hurry of the town,
> Wherein more lightly seems to press the
>   burden
>   Of individual life that weighs me down.

But there is another aspect of the neo-pagan creed, Stoic rather than Epicurean, in which the harmony to be set up between Nature and man finds a basis not in the emotions, but in the intellect. Of this, too, Meredith in certain moods is the best representative. He conceives of life as a constant struggle between natural law rigid and invincible and the idealism which strives to overleap law. So long as the unequal battle lasts, the issue for the idealist must be disastrous, tragic alternately and comic. Only when man wins himself "more brain," and by coming to understand the laws of Nature comes also willingly to submit to them, can he look for any semblance of happiness. But rarely will he bring himself to this. Love, for example, will yearn for immortality, forgetful that change is the one fixed principle in things, although the annual process of the seasons might so easily have taught the lesson:

> "I play for Seasons, not Eternities!"
> Says Nature, laughing on her way. "So must
> All those whose stake is nothing more than
>   dust."
> And lo, she wins, and of her harmonies
> She is full sure! Upon her dying rose
> She drops a look of fondness, and goes by,
> Scarce any retrospection in her eye;
> For she the laws of growth most deeply
>   knows,
> Whose hands bear here a seed-bag, there an
>   urn.
> Pledged she herself to aught, 'twould mark
>   her end!
> This lesson of our only visible friend
> Can we not teach our foolish hearts to learn?

And then, like all philosophers sooner or later, Meredith points us to the flaw in his own doctrine. The idealist cannot accept law; he would not be an idealist if he could. Emotion, after all, is the strongest thing in man. Theories cannot quell it, nor syllogisms subdue. From the ruins of them it arises craving and unassuaged.

> Yes! yes!—but oh, our human rose is fair.
> Surpassingly! Lose calmly Love's great bliss,
> When the renewed for ever of a kiss
> Sounds through the listless hurricane of hair.

Christianity, then, and paganism alike attempt to provide the pessimist with an antidote against his secret sickness, nor can either claim to have effected a cure. One last alternative remains, that "which Cato gave and Addison approved." Is the remedy for life to be found in the will not to live, the high goal of man's hopes and possibilities to be reached in his annihilation? Such, no doubt, is the official teaching of pessimism. And some such dream haunts line after line of Miss Levy's verse. But to defer the difficulty is not to solve it. Long ago a great dramatist taught us that in the supreme creation which has tasked the wits of three centuries. To Hamlet, most modern of Elizabethans, the pessimist problem presented itself. He, too, looked lovingly upon the white poppy of death. "'Tis a consummation devoutly to be wished." And yet the thought of what might be beyond stayed his hand. Let us not be too hasty to ring down the curtain, for how if the gods do not applaud? Better to wait and strive and, if it may be, pray; for what is, is, and not even Zeus, as Agathon tells us, can make it as though it were not. It were idle to suppose that the razor's edge or a drop of dark liquid in a phial could erase the past, or cut the thread of continuity with the future. And the pity of it is that in her strong moments Amy Levy knew this well. How should the argument against suicide be better put than in the farewell words of Tom Leigh over the deathbed of the Minor Poet:

> Nay, I had deemed him more philosopher;
> For did he think by this one paltry deed
> To cut the throat of circumstance, and snep
> The chain which binds all being.

Excerpt from an 1889 letter from Olive Schreiner to Edward Carpenter:

[Dear Edward:]

I should have written yesterday but I had had a blow that somewhat unfitted me. My dear friend Amy Levy had died the night before. She killed herself by shutting herself up in a room with charcoal. We were away together for three days last week. But it did not seem to help her; her agony had gone past human help.

The last thing I sent her was the 'Have Faith' page of *Towards Democracy*. She wrote me back a little note, 'Thank you, it is very beautiful, but philosophy can't help me. I am too much shut in with the personal.' You need not refer to all this when you write. I only tell you that you may know why I didn't write sooner. . . .

Olive

Olive Schreiner, in Olive Schreiner Letters, Volume 1: 1871-1899, *edited by Richard Rive, Oxford University Press, 1988.*

Brian Glanville (essay date 1960)

SOURCE: "The Anglo-Jewish Writer," in *Encounter*, Vol. XIV, No. 2, February, 1960, pp. 62-4.

[In the following essay, Glanville views Levy's works as a product of Anglo-Jewish alienation.]

There are Anglo-Jewish writers; there is no such thing as Anglo-Jewish writing. As for the writers, the two things that strike one about them are their scarcity, and their relative lack of distinction. The great bulk of Anglo-Jewry shares with American Jewry its origins in Eastern Europe, where a mass exodus began after the passing of the Russian May Laws, in 1881. But where American Jewry has produced an astonishing crop of writers and poets—Saul Bellow, Lionel Trilling, Karl Shapiro, Nelson Algren, Arthur Miller, and the rest—English Jews can point only to a handful of minor figures.

This was forcibly made clear to me when the *Jewish Chronicle* recently asked me to conduct a series of interviews with "younger Jewish writers." One found, in the event, half a dozen, but of these, not one could remotely be called a major literary figure, while three were in that amorphous category known as "young and promising." A category from which Arnold Wesker has since emerged.

One more characteristic of Anglo-Jewish writers instantly comes to mind. They don't, on the whole, write about English Jews, though Wolf Mankowitz, the chief exception, has made a name with highly competent whimsy about an East End Jewish world which no longer exists, presented in terms of a tradition which was built up and died in Eastern Europe. Bernard Kops, a young playwright, has written plays in the same romantic *genre,* but it is really a question of blowing on the embers of a fire which went out with the death of Israel Zang-will.

These facts—the scarcity of Anglo-Jewish writers, their general lack of stature, and their apparent disinclination to write about Jewish life—seem to me to be intimately connected.

For a complex of reasons, the Anglo-Jewish writer is inclined to be much less identified with his group than his American counterpart. In the first place, this can be partly explained in terms of sheer numbers. The Jews in America can be counted in millions; there are some three million in New York alone. The English Jews amount to roughly four hundred thousand. This means that the Jewish community in Britain cannot be physically so all-embracing as it is in the U.S.A.

Secondly, where the tendency in America has been for the national group to remain intact and self-contained, in Britain the trend is towards assimilation. Lip-service may be paid in the States to an American, initially Anglo-Saxon, culture, but in practice Jews, Greeks, Italians, Germans, tend to stick together; certainly to a far greater degree than they do here.

Thirdly—and as a consequence of both these factors—there is in America a definite Jewish intellectual life, centred on New York. In Britain, there is none; if the young second- or third-generation Jew wants intellectual activity, he knows very well that he must go outside the group. There, he will very probably meet other young Jews, but it will not be within a Jewish context. Cultural attempts within the Anglo-Jewish group are almost always half-hearted, promoted and patronised by the second-rate, with no organic life of their own.

This leads to the nature of Anglo-Jewish society itself. I have the impression that it differs from American Jewry in no radical sense, but only in so far as it possesses no intelligentsia. Thus, a self-perpetuating process has arisen, whereby, for lack of such a stratum, the intellectual goes outside the group, the group is deprived of intellectual "leaven," and the writer loses contact with the group, as possible material.

The Anglo-Jewish community is recent, wealthy, and isolated. Though various Jewish families have been settled in Britain for several hundred years, few of them play much part in Jewish society, which is overwhelmingly made up by descendants of the immigrants of 1881-1910. To the materialism of Western society, British Jews have brought the traditional Jewish characteristic of living through, by identifying themselves with, their children, and the result is a community polarised around materialism and possessive love. These qualities both interact and reinforce one another, and the result is a society in which the artist has no place. Though middle-class English society may not have a great deal more respect for him, the important difference is that it hasn't the same intense pressure towards conformity.

The response to my *Jewish Chonicle* interviews with young writers was, as one should have expected, on the whole violent, emotional, and confused. The mild remarks made by Mr. Wolf Mankowitz produced an almost hysterical attack from a rabbi in Westcliff-on-Sea, and the paper itself cautiously prefaced the series with a leader which reaffirmed most of the preconceptions of its readers.

These were stated with less restraint in the subsequent correspondence. What clearly hurt most of all was that none of the interviewees subscribed to the Jewish religion, though it was significant that Peter Shaffer, the only writer to show deep concern with religious issues, aroused more spleen than anybody else. The general line of attack—or perhaps defence would be a better word in the context—was to accuse the six of "lack of Jewish knowledge." It was a stout stick with which to beat the dog, but none of the correspondents followed the editorial in realising that this should be viewed as an alarming symptom, rather than a useful defence mechanism. A letter, almost obsessional in tone, affirming the validity of salvation through ritual, showed how wide the gap between Mr. Shaffer's near mysticism and the orthodox wing of the Jewish church can be.

A deep horror and fear of assimilation also became clear—and with it, a further gap between the six young Jewish writers, none of whom would endorse such prejudices, and the community, still living in a ghetto which is moral where it isn't geographical.

The series concluded with the reactions of four younger members of the Jewish establishment, which emphasised better than any outside criticism could have done the poverty and complacency of its thought. One young rabbi deplored the lack of interest shown by the intellectual in religion, and the religious in modern thought, but he was alone in his concern. Reading the other replies, it became perfectly clear that English Judaism has little hope of reclaiming its lost sons.

The community, however, shows a corresponding indifference to its writers; its slender link with modern fiction has been the novels of the late Louis Golding, to which a complete evening was devoted in the course of the recent Anglo-Jewish book week.

Thus, the Jewish writer in Britain does not stay long enough within his community to produce much more than a novel of protest. Of these, there have been several: the first—*Reuben Sachs,* by Amy Levy—was published in 1888.

Reuben Sachs (whose author committed suicide at the age of twenty-eight) is a poor, stilted, self-conscious piece of work, full of the knowing self-congratulation of the "educated" child of *nouveaux riches* parents. What interest it retains lies in the extraordinary similarity of the monied, Bayswater Jewish society it depicts, at a time when the East Europe immigrants had yet to emerge from the East End—and their descendants in London to-day. There is the same ostentation, the same social intolerance, the same overt materialism, the same breach with Jewish traditions, uncompensated by a real identification with those of England.

Nearly fifty years later, Gerald Kersh and Willy Goldman similarly attacked the Jews of the East End. Kersh wrote a bitter novel, *Jews Without Jehovah,* which was withdrawn after libel proceedings. Goldman endorsed it, describing the East End Jews, in an essay, as "a scattered backwash of a people, shorn of its tradition of learning." When any young man wanted to become an artist, he wrote, every possible obstacle was put in his way, and he was urged to go into business, which meant finding any means he could of "crooking a living." If he succeeded, the very people who opposed him were the first to acclaim him as a Jew. Both Kersh and Goldman struck a slightly hysterical note. Yet neither created the controversy caused by *Reuben Sachs*. This was equally true of Kersh's *The Thousand Deaths of Mr. Small,* a novel published in 1950, sprawling, bitter, undisciplined, and often brilliantly comic, in which he returned to his former whipping boys.

The explanation was simple enough: the new Anglo-Jews had by this time moved out of the East End into North-West London, and could afford to regard their parents and themselves when poorer with a certain indulgence.

The fact that my own novel, *The Bankrupts* (1958), caused a commotion among them similar to **Reuben Sachs'** was because of its immediacy, rather than its alleged malice; *The Thousand Deaths of Mr. Small* makes it seem almost a eulogy by comparison, but it hasn't the sting of contemporaneity.

For the most part, the chief Anglo-Jewish writers have been recognised on the basis of work which has nothing to do with Jews, or Jewish problems. I have tried to explain the reasons for this; a corollary of one of them—the tendency towards assimilation—is that Jewish writers want to *belong;* not to the Jewish community, but to England itself. If they feel separate, this is a source of embarrassment, rather than strength, and there is no tradition of Anglo-Jewish letters to fortify them.

Thus, Peter Shaffer's recent play, *Five Finger Exercise,* presents the classical Anglo-Jewish family situation of wealthy, ignorant, adoring parents, and cleverer, assimilating son, who doesn't want to "go into the business." The play, however, makes the family an English one. There's no doubt that such problems can perfectly well exist in English households, but it is significant that Mr. Shaffer should have felt the need to disguise his material.

As for the better-known Jewish novelists, Alexander Baron made a name with his novels and short stories about British infantry in World War II, and although he has published a novel with a Jewish theme, it was neither as successful as his earlier work, nor did it appear as grateful to him as a subject. Marghanita Laski has not dealt with Jewish themes at all.

The misfortune of this is that Jewish writers are cutting themselves off from the best of their material. Anglo-Jewish middle-class life may be strident, materialistic, and culturally barren; it is still far more vivid and vigorous than its English counterpart, which produces so much competent, bloodless, mediocre writing, year by year. In addition to this, the Anglo-Jewish writer tends to turn away from his problems and conflicts as a Jew, another rich potential source of literature. There has been no English equivalent of Bellow's *The Victim* or Arthur Miller's more talented if equally obsessional novel, *Focus.*

Nor will there be. The Anglo-Jewish writer has attached himself to a culture which no longer can provide him with material, even if he successfully assimilates its traditions. Yet he can hardly be blamed for turning his back on a community where he is so patently unwelcome.

Edward Wagenknecht (essay date 1983)

SOURCE: "Amy Levy," in *Daughters of the Covenant: Portraits of Six Jewish Women,* Amherst: The University of Massachusetts Press, 1983, pp. 55-93.

[*In the following essay, Wagenknecht provides a survey of Levy's life and career, characterizing her as "a child, albeit a belated, disappointed, and disillusioned child, of the Romantic Age."*]

Like many Americans, I first encountered the name of Amy Levy in the fine poem "Broken Music" Thomas Bailey Aldrich wrote about her after her tragic death.

> A note
> All out of tune in this world's instrument.
> AMY LEVY

> I know not in what fashion she was made,
>   Nor what her voice was, when she used to speak,
> Nor if the silken lashes threw a shade
>   On wan or rosy cheek.

> I picture her with sorrowful vague eyes
>   Illumed with such strange gleams of inner light
> As linger in the drift of London skies
>   Ere twilight turns to night.

> I know not; I conjecture. 'Twas a girl
>   That with her own most gentle desperate hand
> From out God's mystic setting plucked life's pearl—
>   'Tis hard to understand.

> So precious life is! Even to the old
>   The hours are as a miser's coins, and she—
> Within her hands lay youth's unminted gold
>   And all felicity.

> The winged impetuous spirit, the white flame
>   That was her soul once, whither has it flown?
> Above her brow gray lichens blot her name
>   Upon the carven stone.

> This is her Book of Verses—wren-like notes,
>   Shy franknesses, blind gropings, haunting fears;
> At times across the chords abruptly floats
>   A mist of passionate tears.

> A fragile lyre too tensely keyed and strung,
>   A broken music, weirdly incomplete;
> Here a proud mind, self-baffled and self-stung,
>   Lies coiled in dark defeat.

The "Book of Verses" referred to here was her second collection, *A Minor Poet and Other Verse,* which, to judge by the date written with his name on the inside of the front cover of his copy (which is now in the Houghton Library at Harvard), Aldrich had owned since its publication in 1884.

As to the "fashion" in which "she was made" we know a little more than Aldrich knew. The great Shakespeare scholar, Sir Edmund K. Chambers, probably after Aldrich her most illustrious admirer,[1] found in the face shown in her photograph "no special beauty, the brow and eyes burdened with a weight of thought, the lips set as if in some reticence of sorrow," but Harry Quilter thought he "had rarely seen a face which was at once so interesting, so intellectual, so beautiful, and alas! so unhappy." She was "a small dark girl of unmistakably Jewish type, with eyes that seemed too large for the delicate features, and far too sad for their youthfulness of line and contour."[2] The only photograph I have seen shows an oval-shaped face, rather large dark eyes, arched eyebrows, a fairly large nose, dark hair parted on the right side, and a straight but sensitive mouth. I should call her face sensitive and intelligent rather than either beautiful or plain.

There remains the act which Aldrich found "hard to understand" and which still puzzles us. The most authoritative comment here comes from Richard Garnett, who based his account of her in the *Dictionary of National Biography* on "private information."

> No cause can or need be assigned . . . except constitutional melancholy, intensified by painful losses in her own family, increasing deafness, and probably the apprehension of insanity, combined with a total inability to derive pleasure from the extraneous circumstances which would have brightened the lives of most others. She was indeed frequently gay and animated, but her cheerfulness was but a passing mood that merely gilded her habitual melancholy, without diminishing it by a particle, while sadness grew upon her steadily, in spite of flattering success and the sympathy of affectionate friends.

To this the unsigned obituary in Oscar Wilde's magazine, the *Woman's World,* to which Amy Levy had been a contributor, added that "she was never robust; not often actually ill, but seldom well enough to feel life a joy instead of a burden."[3]

She was born, the second daughter of Lewis and Isabelle (Levin) Levy, in Clapham, on November 10, 1861, and died at 7 Ensleigh Gardens, London, on September 10, 1889, just two months short of her twenty-eighth birthday.[4] She studied for a time at Newnham College, Cambridge, where, if we may trust the testimony of her poem **"Alma Mater,"** she was unhappy, but she afterwards remembered the city with affection.[5] She was well read in English literature and at home with both

French and German and she translated the *Comme quoi Napoléon n'a jamais existé* of Jean Baptiste Pérès. She traveled in Europe and probably also knew some Italian. There is one Latin quotation in **The Romance of a Shop.** Whether the Medea piece which she called a "fragment" after Euripides (it is not exactly that but rather a brief play in the classical manner, complete in itself) implies a knowledge of Greek is not clear, but **"Sokratics in the Strand"** has an epigram in Greek, and she quotes a line of Greek in **"The Poetry of Christina Rossetti."**[6]

At the time of her death she had published three novels: **The Romance of a Shop** (1888), **Reuben Sachs** (1888), and **Miss Meredith** (1889). Her first collection of poems, a thirty-page volume called **Xantippe and Other Verse,** was published at Cambridge in 1881. The title poem had already appeared in the *Universal Magazine* in May 1880 and was taken up into her first substantial collection, **A Minor Poet and Other Verse,** in 1884. She corrected the proofs of her final collection, **A London Plane-Tree and Other Verse** (1889), only a week before her death.

So little has been recorded concerning Amy Levy's life that, with her as with Shakespeare, we are dependent for our knowledge of her personality almost wholly upon what she reveals or what can be inferred from her own writings, a method of procedure which leaves us with more questions than answers. But questions can be illuminating, the effort is worth making, and her work is eminently worth examining. Her circumstances being what they were, she is certainly a minor late Victorian writer, but her accomplishment was impressive for one who died in her twenty-eighth year, and one cannot but believe that she might have developed into a really important writer if she had lived.

Since the three novels are less rich in self-revelation than the poems, we may well consider them first.[7] All are direct, simple, straightforward narratives, avoiding all unnecessary complications, and paying no heed to the sophisticated, self-conscious considerations of "method" which were coming more and more into vogue. **Miss Meredith** is a first-person narrative by the name character; both the other novels employ the omniscient author. For a Victorian, Amy Levy exercises considerable restraint in the matter of direct authorial comment, and what does occur infrequently is not particularly intrusive. Chapters, like the novels themselves, are short. The **Shop** has both chapter titles and epigraphs à la Walter Scott while **Reuben Sachs** has epigraphs only and **Miss Meredith** only titles.

The tone of the novels is much less melancholy, more bracing than that of the poems. Though the dark side of life is not ruled out, there is never any serious apprehension that the characters who speak for the author will be overwhelmed by it, and both the **Shop** and

Miss Meredith have happy endings. The only unmistakable resemblance between the poems and the stories is that both are obviously the product of a sensitive and highly literate mind. And though both *Miss Meredith* and the *Shop* are distinctly "light," it should be stated with emphasis that there is never any suggestion of anything approaching the trifling or the vulgar which so generally disfigures this kind of fiction.[8] In the contrast it indicates between English and Italian marriage customs, *Miss Meredith* suggests the international novels which found their flowering in the work of James and Howells, neither of whom Amy Levy admired.

Gertrude Lorimer, the heroine of *The Romance of a Shop,* is "not a beautiful woman, . . . but a certain air of character and distinction clung to her through all her varying moods, and redeemed her from a possible charge of plainness." She writes, and among her unpublished manuscripts is a five-act tragedy about Charlotte Corday. Gertrude is twenty-three. Her sister Lucy, twenty, is "fair, slight, upright as a dart, with a glance at once alert and serene." Upon her Gertrude can always rely. Frances (Fanny), their half-sister, is "a stout, fair woman of thirty, presenting somewhat the appearance of a large and superannuated baby. She had a big face, with small, meaningless features, and faint, surprised-looking eyebrows. Her complexion had been charmingly pink and white, but the tints had hardened, and a coarse red colour clung to the white cheeks." Phyllis is "the youngest, tallest, and prettiest of the sisters; a slender, delicate-looking creature of seventeen, who had outgrown her strength, the spoiled child of the family by virtue of her youth, her weakness, and her personal charms." At the beginning of the book the already motherless sisters have just lost both their father and their fortune, and they set up a photographic studio. Phyllis dies of consumption, and the others all find husbands.

Their friends and acquaintances and the men they finally marry are all satisfactorily characterized. The most interesting among them is Aunt Caroline, who is perhaps a literary descendant of Lady Catherine de Bourgh. She is "a handsome person of her age, notwithstanding a slightly equine cast of countenance, and the absence of anything worthy of the adjectives graceful or *sympathique* from her individuality," for she "belonged to that mischievous class of the community whose will and energy are very far ahead of their intellect and perceptions."

I should say that *The Romance of a Shop* skirts melodrama and suggests that the author may have felt that she needed more incident than the normal lives of her protagonists could supply only when Phyllis elopes with a worthless, married artist and is brought back from his rooms by Gertrude. There is also at one point a report that Lucy's fiancé has been killed in Africa, but this turns out to be false.

Elsie Meredith leaves England at the beginning of her novel to teach English and music to the eighteen-year-old daughter of the Marchese Brogi at Pisa. The girl, wary at first, becomes very fond of Miss Meredith, and she herself is soon conscious of a "silent sympathy" with the old and withdrawn Marchese. But the Marchesa, "with her glib talk, her stately courtesy, was in truth the chilliest and the most reserved of mortals." The older son, Romeo, who obviously has his drawbacks as a husband, has a fat, friendly wife, Annunciata, who is often in tears. The younger son, Andrea, the rebel of the family, had cleared out in a huff, and the beginning of the book finds him in America. When his return is announced, the family promptly invites Costanza Marchetti, his hand-picked wife-to-be, to come to stay with them. "She was no longer in her first youth—about twenty-eight, I should say—but she was distinctly handsome, in a rather hard-featured fasion"; she is also distinctly bad tempered. Of course, Andrea—who looks enough like the Bronzino portrait of one of his ancestors in the family gallery so that when Miss Meredith first encounters him, she almost believes that the portrait, which has already fascinated her, has come to life—falls in love with her and she with him. The Marchesa tells Elsie that her son is "extremely susceptible" and no doubt honestly fancies himself in love with her. He will certainly "never take back his word, on that you may rely. But be sure of this, his life will be spoiled, and he will know it." Elsie's pride and her sense of honor force her to break the engagement, but when Andrea counters by announcing that if he cannot wed Miss Meredith, he will write off the appointment he has just accepted in England and return to America, his generally passive father intervenes. "My son, can you persuade this lady to remain with us? . . . You must forgive us if we are slow to understand the new spirit of radicalism which, it seems, is the spirit of the times. Once before our wishes clashed; but, my son, I cannot bear to send you away in anger a second time. As for this lady, she knows how deeply we all respect her. Persuade her to forgive us, if indeed you can." Perhaps the warmest admirer of *Miss Meredith* has been Harry Quilter, who found its art equivalent to Josef Israël's in painting and wrote of it with penetration and charm.

I have disturbed the chronology of the novels to take up *Reuben Sachs* last, for it is by all means the most significant of the three, and the only one that has been reprinted in our own time. It is also the only one which concerns itself with Jewish matters or affords any evidence that the author was herself a Jew. Her attitude toward Jews and Judaism I shall take up later in another connection, but the other aspects of the book fall for consideration here.

"Reuben Sachs," so the book begins, "was the pride of his family." He is a rising barrister with a fine scholastic record who might have aspired to the woolsack, but he prefers a political career and is elected to Parliament in the course of the novel. "Out-door sports he detested; the pleasures of dancing he had exhausted long ago; the practice of philanthropy provided a vent for his many-sided energies."

The novel begins as if it might be on the way to become something like a Jewish *Forsyte Saga,* picturing the Sachses, their relatives and friends, in a kind of cross section of the prosperous Jewish community in London. There are so many characters that here, as at the beginning of *The Forsyte Saga,* though the author has them all clearly in mind and differentiates their characteristics with ease, the reader must make an effort to keep them straight. But the author was right to use the subtitle "A Sketch," for she soon directs her attention and ours away from the clan to center it upon the ill-fated love affair between Reuben and Judith Quixano.

James Branch Cabell used to argue that a book which is named for a character has not been named at all; he broke his rule only with *Jurgen,* which he wished to call "The Pawnbroker's Shirt" but yielded to his publisher's objection. With Amy Levy's novel the label she used is clearly inept, for Judith is at least as important a character as Reuben, and though the action revolves around him, the reader comes to know her much better, getting inside her to a much greater extent, probing her passion for Reuben and suffering with her through its frustration. Indeed, during the second half, Reuben practically disappears from the scene. After she has lost him, Judith marries, not for love, a rather futile, silly Englishman, Herbert (Bertie) Lee-Harrison, who has been converted to Judaism.

The death of Reuben, reported to Judith by her imperceptive husband at the end, is one of the rare successful uses of surprise in fiction. Amy Levy had prepared for it by dropping various hints about Reuben's health and his overworking, but none of these has been heavily stressed. There has been just enough preparation so that we accept what she tells us but we still get the shock she intended, and it is necessary that we should have this in order fully to savor Judith's reaction. The whole incident is managed admirably.

What now, then, of the mind revealed in the poetry, with reinforcement, wherever it appears, from other sources?

The obvious thing had better be said at the outset, though it must be documented more fully later. Amy Levy was, of course, as Chambers perceived, "a passionate idealist," a child, albeit a belated, disappointed, and disillusioned child, of the Romantic Age; this was her glory, and this was also importantly involved in

what Aldrich called her "dark defeat." Only the disappointed idealist can suffer such disillusionment as consumed her; the "realist" has never expected very much; one must have asked a great deal of life to be as crushed as Amy Levy was by the best that life can give. She herself supplies us with an essential clue when she prefixes to one of the sections of her final collection what is at once the most idealistic and the most disillusioned quatrain in *The Rubáiyát of Omar Khayyám:*

> Ah Love! could you and I with Him conspire
> To grasp this sorry scheme of things entire,
>   Would we not shatter it to bits—and then
> Remount it nearer to the Heart's Desire!

Literature, art, and music—beauty in all its forms—spoke to her more clearly than anything else, but since the most obvious and omnipresent form of beauty is the beauty of nature, we must not omit this aspect, especially since, in her case, there is an important qualification to be entered.

She was a city girl, and she never forgot it; to the *Plane-Tree* volume she prefixed an epigram from Austin Dobson:

> Mine is an urban Muse, and bound
> By some strange law to paten ground.

And in the title poem, **"A London Plane-Tree,"** the author obviously feels a kinship with the tree she praises:

> Green is the plane-tree in the square,
>   The other trees are brown;
> They droop and pine for country air;
>   The plane-tree loves the town.
>
> Here from my garret pane, I mark
>   The plane-tree bud and blow,
> Shed her recuperative bark,
>   And spread her shade below.
>
> Among her branches, in and out,
>   The city breezes play;
> The dun fog wraps her round about;
>   Above, the smoke curls grey.
>
> Others the country take for choice,
>   And hold the town in scorn;
> But she has listened to the voice
>   On city breezes borne.

Other poems in the same collection reinforce this one. One of Amy Levy's few really light-hearted poems, **"Ballad of an Omnibus,"** is written from the point of view of "a wandering minstrel, poor and free," who is contented with his lot.

The scene whereof I cannot tire,
The human tale of love and hate,
The city pageant, early and late
Unfolds itself, rolls by, to be
A pleasure deep and delicate.
An omnibus suffices me.

Judged by the frequency with which she invokes them, the poet must have loved Gilbert and Sullivan, and I think we may be sure that her wandering minstrel was a legitimate son of Nanki-Poo. But we must not overlook **"London in July"**:

The London trees are dusty brown
  Beneath the summer sky;
My love, she dwells in London town.
  Nor leaves it in July.

And who cries out on crowd and mart?
  Who prates of stream and sea?
The summer in the city's heart—
  That is enough for me.

Yet nature cannot be completely escaped even in the city.

Between the showers I went my way.
  The glistening street was bright with
  flowers;
It seemed that March had turned to May
  Between the showers.

Nor is it always gentle. The east wind can make the town look grey even when it has a blue sky over it.

'Tis the wind of ice, the wind of fire,
Of cold despair and of hot desire,
Which chills the flesh to aches and
  pains,
And sends a fever through all the veins.

Nevertheless the last stanza of **"A March Day in London"** is cheerful:

And o'er, at last, my spirit steals
A weary peace; peace that conceals
Within its inner depths the grain
Of hopes that yet shall flower again.

Poems like **"Out of Town"** frankly acknowledge the beauty of the country:

Out of town the sky was bright and blue,
  Never fog-cloud, lowering, thick, was seen
  to frown;
Nature dons a garb of gayer hue,
      Out of town.

Spotless lay the snow on field and down,
  Pure and keen the air above it blew;
All wore peace and beauty for a crown.

For all that, the call of the city will not be stilled:

London sky, marred by smoke, veiled from
  view,
  London snow, trodden thin, dingy brown,
Whence that strange unrest at thoughts of you
      Out of town?

And it is much the same in **"The Village Garden,"** which, since it is dedicated to "E.M.S." probably refers to an actual garden and an actual friend.

Fain would I bide, but ever in the distance
  A ceaseless voice is sounding clear and
  low;—
The city calls me with her old persistence,
  The city calls me—I arise and go.

Of gentler souls this fragrant peace is
  guerdon;
  For me, the roar and hurry of the town,
Wherein more lightly seems to press the
  burden
  Of individual life that weighs me down.

I leave your garden to the happier comers
  For whom its silent sweets are anodyne.
Shall I return? Who knows, in other summers
  The peace my spirit longs for may be mine.

We must not, however, conclude that Amy Levy was unresponsive to the charms of nature. In the dedication to the *Plane-Tree* volume, the consolations which abide after all others have failed are the fair days of summer

            and more fair
The growths of human goodness here and
  there.

"The Old Poet" resolves

I will be glad because it is the Spring;
  I will forget the winter in my heart—
Dead hopes and withered promise; and will
  wring
  A little joy from life ere life depart.

The poem ends:

So once it was with us, my heart! To-day
  We will be glad because the leaves are
  green,
Because the fields are fair and soft with May,
  Nor think on squandered springtimes that
  have been.

Similarly, **"On the Wye in May"** begins:

> Now is the perfect moment of the year.
>   Half naked branches, half a mist of green,
> Vivid and delicate the slopes appear;
>   The cool, soft air is neither fierce nor keen.

On this point too the reinforcing testimony of the novels is relevant. Gertrude Lorimer, the "inveterate cockney" of *The Romance of a Shop,* though fascinated by "the humours of the town" and "the familiar London pageant," longs for the country when she is under strain and finds her courage strengthened by the laburnum tree and other wonders of the April morning, and Elsie Meredith in Italy longs "with all my soul and body for the country" when spring comes on and loves the "great ilex tree" in the Brogi garden, "its massive green trunk old and gnarled, its blue green foliage casting a wide shadow. Two or three cypresses, with their broomlike stems, sprang from the overgrown turf, which, at this season of the year, was beginning to be yellow with daffodils, and a thick growth of laurel bushes ran along under the walls."[9]

In the last analysis, however, we must conclude that, however Amy Levy may have responded to nature, it did not suffice, as with Wordsworth, for example, to supply her with a religion that was mighty to save. In **"In September"** we read

> The sky is silver grey; the long
>   Slow waves caress the shore,—
> On such a day as this I have been glad,
>   Who shall be glad no more.

In **"The Birch-Tree at Loschwitz"** she comes closer to pagan or Romantic nature worship than anywhere else.

> I lean against the birch-tree,
>   My arms around it twine;
> It pulses, and leaps, and quivers,
>   Like a human heart to mine.

But even this does not satisfy.

> One moment I stand, then sudden
>   Let loose mine arms that cling,
> O God! the lonely hillside,
>   The passionate wind of spring!

And I think final, conclusive testimony on this point may well be drawn from the poem **"A Dirge"** in which she describes nature and its charms more fully than anywhere else in her work.

> *"Mein Herz, mein Herz is traurig*
> *Doch lustig leuchtet der Mai."*

> There's May amid the meadows,
> There's May amid the trees;

> Her May-time note the cuckoo
> Sends forth upon the breeze.
> Above the rippling river
> May swallows skim and dart;
> November and December
> Keep watch within my heart.

> The spring breathes in the breezes,
> The woods with wood-notes ring,
> And all the budding hedgerows
> Are fragrant of the spring.

> In secret, silent places
> The live green things upstart;
> Ice-bound, ice-crown'd dwells winter
> Forever in my heart.

> Upon the bridge I linger,
> Near where the lime-trees grow;
> Above, sweet birds are circling,
> Beneath, the stream runs slow.

> A stripling and a maiden
> Come wand'ring up the way;
> His eyes are glad with springtime,
> Her face is fair with May.

> Of warmth and sunward sweetness
> All nature takes a part;
> The ice of all the ages
> Weighs down upon my heart.

It is time to pass on from nature to art. The references to literature in Amy Levy's work, both poetry and prose, are so numerous that only a few samples can be given here. Her references to the Bible (both the Old Testament and the New) show an easy familiarity, and English literature is omnipresent. Shakespeare and Goethe are the writers of whom the **"Minor Poet"** in the monologue of that title takes his fondest leave, though he also mentions Theocritus and Heine,[10] adding "I've grown too coarse for Shelley lately." Miss Meredith, however, had not done this; for her the charm of Pisa was greatly increased by its association with the Romantic poets. The **"Minor Poet"** also pays special tribute to

> one wild singer of to-day, whose song
> Is all aflame with passionate bard's blood
> Lash'd into foam by pain and the world's
>   wrong.
> At least, he has a voice to cry his pain;
> For him, no silent writhing in the dark,
> No muttering of mute lips, no straining out
> Of a weak throat a-choke with pent-up sound,
> A-throb with pent-up passion. . . .

The "wild singer" is not named, but Swinburne, of whom Amy did a good imitation in **"Felo de Se,"** would seem a reasonable guess. Browning was, how- ever, in her monologues, the most obvious strong in- fluence upon her, though the only English poets whom she honored with complete essays were apparently James Thomson and Christina Rossetti.[11]

She thought that "a woman poet of the first rank is among those things which the world has yet to pro- duce," for even Sappho's lyrics had "few strings" and "few notes," and Mrs. Browning achieved real excel- lence only in *Sonnets from the Portuguese* and "Great God Pan." She liked Christina Rossetti best when she was least "mystic, least involved— . . . simplest, most direct, most human," and her own tone being what it is, it seems odd that she should have found in her "that youthful exaggeration of sadness, that perverse assump- tion of the cypress." On the other hand, her reference in passing to Felicia Hemans as "a sweet singer, un- dervalued in our day as she was overpraised in her own" shows a refreshing independence of judgment and an intelligent realization that the latest opinion is not necessarily definitive.

The essay on James Thomson is especially interesting because of the author's obvious temperamental sympa- thy with her subject. Though she admits Thomson's "minor" quality, she finds him "a poet of wonderful originality and power" and responds eagerly to his "passionate, hungry cry for life, for the things of this human flesh and blood life; for love and praise, for more sunlight and the sun's warmth." **"The City of Dreadful Night"** is a poem that "goes to the very heart of things; it is for all time and all humanity." She admits Thomson's lack of refinement and tells us hon- estly that he is reported to have drunk himself to death, yet he remains for her "the image of a great mind and a great soul thwarted in their development by circum- stances; of a nature struggling with itself and Fate; of an existence doomed to bear a twofold burden." Whether or not she was wholly right in these judg- ments, one cannot but respond to her generosity, nor, in view of her own fate, can one read unmoved such a statement as "for, if one comes to think of it, it is appalling what infinite and exquisite anguish can be suffered by a single human being who is perhaps sit- ting quietly in his chair before us, or crosses our path on the sunny street and fields."

I get the impression that Amy Levy cared more for Thackeray than for Dickens, though she was not im- pressed by either as portrayer of Jewish character. When Elsie Meredith plans her trip to Italy, her sister Rosalind fears she will be captured by an Italian Mr. Rochester, but Elsie reminds her that she herself will have some- thing to say about that and adds that she has "always considered Mr. Rochester the most unpleasant person that ever a woman made herself miserable over." In *Reuben Sachs,* Leo Leuniger expresses the opinion that Bertie Lee-Harrison must have been shocked by

finding the Sachses and the Leunigers "so little like the people in *Daniel Deronda,*" and we know that his creator shared this opinion, for though she gave George Eliot due credit for generosity and good intentions and praised her as a novelist, she disliked "the labored jocoseness" and "the straining after pompous epigram" which characterized her "later manner," and she did not think the novelist knew very much about Jews. "We have, alas! no M. Daudet among us. His mingled brilliance and solidity; his wonderful blending of pic- turesqueness and fidelity, have no counterpart among our own contemporary novel-writers."[12]

The principal influence from the classics in Amy Levy's work appears in her **"Medea"** in the *Minor Poet* vol- ume. This little drama opens after Jason has deserted Medea for Kreon's daughter Glauké, who attracts him because of his ambition to succeed her father on his throne. Medea laments:

> For this indeed is woman's chiefest curse,
> That still her constant heart clings to its love
> Through all time and all chances; while the
>   man
> Is caught with newness. . . .

By her children she sends poisoned garments to Kreon and Glauké; then she kills the children. Jason decrees

> Let no man seek this woman; blood enough
> Has stained our city. Let the furies rend
> Her guilty soul; not we pollute our hands
> With her accursèd body.

At the end she goes forth "Into the deep, dense heart of night—alone."

The most interesting references to art occur in the novels. The Lorimer photographic studio is decorated with "a little cheap Japanese china" and pictures from Dürer, Botticelli, Watts, and Burne-Jones, all impor- tant in "aesthetic" Victorian circles. Judith Quixano's brothers are "two little dark-eyed, foreign-looking chil- dren—children such as Murillo loved to paint." The passion of the Slade school for Titian-colored hair is mentioned at the beginning of *Miss Meredith,* and I have already noted the Bronzino in the Brogi picture gallery, a work

> of considerable beauty, representing a young man,
> whose charming aspect was scarcely marred by his
> stiff and elaborate fifteenth century costume. The dark
> eyes of this picture had a way of following one up
> and down the gallery in a rather disconcerting manner;
> already [thinks Elsie] I have woven a series of little
> lessons about him, and had decided that he left his
> frame at night, like the creatures in "Ruddygore," to
> roam the house as a ghost where he had once lived
> as a man.

The reference to *Ruddigore* may provide a convenient transition to music. Leo Leuniger hums Schumann's "Ich grolle nicht" under his breath, and though **"Lohengrin"** is not essentially a poem about music, it takes its point of departure from Wagner's opera. Music causes sadness in **"The Piano-Organ,"** where a student, settling to work behind a garret window, is disturbed by an organ grinder in the street below.

> Grind me a dirge or a requiem,
>   Or a funeral march sad and slow,
> But not, O not, that waltz tune
>   I heard long ago.
>
> I stand upright by the window,
>   The moonlight streams in wan:—
> O God! with its changeless rise and fall
>   The tune twirls on and on.

But perhaps the most interesting reference to music is in **"A June-Tide Echo (After a Richter Concert),"** where the poet longs

> For once, for one fleeting hour, to hold
> The fair shape the music that rose and fell
> Revealed and concealed like a veiling fold;
> To catch for an instant the sweet June spell.

Dancing is of course closely connected with music, and Elsie Meredith's first waltz with Andrea was "one of the intensely good things of life which cannot happen often even in the happiest careers; one of the little bits of perfection which start up now and then to astonish us." **"The First Extra"** is called "A Waltz Song," and in **"A Wall Flower"** perfect waltzing is praised and longed for, but this poem is quickly turned into an exercise in déjà vu.

> Somewhere, I think, some other where, not
>   here,
> In other ages, or another sphere,
> I danced with you, and you with me, my dear.

I should say these pieces provide all the evidence we need to be sure that Amy Levy enjoyed dancing, but the only reference of any kind I have found to games is in **"A Game of Lawn Tennis"**. That she had friends we know from Richard Garnett's testimony, from what has been recorded of her contacts with Olive Schreiner, Vernon Lee, and Clementina Black, and the poems she dedicates by initials to what must have been persons she knew and valued.

Did she have any extrapersonal interests, any views upon public affairs? Clearly the bent of her mind was liberal and humane. Her first published poem appeared when she was thirteen in a short-lived suffrage magazine, the *Pelican,* and in 1879 the *Victoria Magazine* carried another (reprinted in the **Xantippe** collection)

about a gypsy woman and her baby who were "Run to Death" by hunting nobles in France. "Wise in Her Generation" has references to blue-books, poor law reports, and Toynbee Hall, and we know that in 1886 Amy was secretary of the Beaumont Trust, of which Lewis Levy was president, and which was soliciting funds to erect a "People's Palace for East London," which should embrace a concert hall, library, technical schools, and other features. As for her ethical standards, **"Eldorado at Islington"** is a touching little story about a poor family with one child crippled. They believe for a day that the father has inherited a fortune from a long-estranged brother, but when he returns from the lawyer's office they find he has rejected it as "the fruit of cruelty and extortion; it was wrung from the starving poor. It is money that no honest man can touch." Surely her creator must have agreed with Gertrude Lorimer of the *Shop,* who, when asked for her idea of good society, defines it as "a society not of class, caste, or family—but of picked individuals."[13]

If there is any one cause with which Amy Levy identified herself, it is female emancipation. From Aunt Caroline's point of view the way the Lorimer sisters set themselves up in a business which necessitates their going out into the world and meeting men upon equal terms goes beyond verging upon the improper, and it is interesting that most of their customers think they ought to charge less than male photographers do. The heroine of **"Wise in Her Generation"** knows how hard it is for a woman to make her way alone "unless she happens to be Patti, or Lady Burdett-Coutts, or Queen Elizabeth," and in **"Women and Club Life,"**[14] Amy Levy herself sees the development of clubs as a response to the demand of women for emancipation from "the narrowest of grooves which have hitherto confined them." Though she can spare a sigh of regret for the old-fashioned woman at her best, she considers her too expensive a luxury for the times and even adds that she sees no reason to suppose that club women will develop the selfishness of their husbands and brothers!

Amy Levy's principal feminist document, however, is the Browningesque dramatic monologue, **"Xantippe,"** one of her most ambitious poems, which attempts to rehabilitate the generally unadmired wife of Socrates. Xantippe had "high thoughts" and "golden dreams," a "soul which yearned for knowledge," and a tongue

> That should proclaim the stately mysteries
> Of this fair world, and of the holy gods,

but in the position in which she finds herself, she feels that her "woman-mind" had gone astray in thinking what are not "woman's thoughts."

Her marriage to Sokrates (as the poet spelled it) was an arranged marriage. He did not satisfy her dreams of "a future love, / Where perfect body matched the perfect soul," but she reached and strained "until at last / I caught the soul athwart the grosser flesh." She learned much after their marriage.

> But that great wisdom, deeper, which dispels
> Narrowed conclusions of a half-grown mind,
> And sees athwart the littleness of life
> Nature's divineness and her harmony,
> Was never poor Xantippe's.

Her husband (who is dead by the time we meet her) did not plan it thus:

> 'Twas only that the high philosopher,
> Pregnant with noble theories and great
>   thoughts,
> Deigned not to stoop to touch so slight a
>   thing
> As the fine fabric of a woman's brain—
> So subtle as a passionate woman's soul.
> I think, if he had stooped a little, and cared,
> I might have risen nearer to his height,
> And not lain shattered, neither fit for use
> As goodly household vessel, nor for that
> Far finer thing which I had hoped to be.

Once her wrath flared as he held forth to his disciples— Plato with "narrow eyes and niggard mouth" and Alkibiades,

>   with laughing lips
> And half-shut eyes, contemptuous shrugging
>   up
> Soft, snowy shoulders, till he brought the gold
> Of flowing ringlets round about his breasts.

Sokrates expatiated upon woman's frailty, how

> "Her body rarely stands the test of soul;
> She grows intoxicate with knowledge, throws
> The laws of custom, order, 'neath her feet,
> Feasting at life's great banquet with wide
>   throat."

But Xantippe's protest met only blank incredulity and incomprehension.

> Then faded the vain fury; hope died out;
> A huge despair was stealing on my soul,
> A sort of fierce acceptance of my fate,—
> He wished a household vessel—well, 'twas
>   good,
> For he should have it.

Thereafter Xantippe devoted herself to spinning.

There is not a great deal of this kind of thing, however, for essentially Amy Levy was a Romantic lyric

poet and such are necessarily largely committed to the expression of personal interests and emotions. There are several dramatic monologues in the **Minor Poet** volume, but the later **Plane-Tree** collection is almost wholly lyrical. In **"The Last Judgment,"** the speaker, a man grown old, approaches the judgment seat troubled because others bring

> Gold and jewels and precious wine;
> No hands bare like these hands of mine.
> The treasure I have nor weighs nor gleams;
> Lord, I can bring you only dreams.

Amy Levy's poetic imagination made it easy for her to think of herself as a man and old besides. **"The Old House,"** whose use of the *Doppelgänger* motif suggests a familiarity with German poetry, ends with

> But who is this that hurries on before,
>   A flitting shade the brooding shades
>   among?—
> She turned,—I saw her face,—O God, it wore
>   The face I used to wear when I was young!

Nevertheless, it must always be remembered that she was still young when she died and to this extent entitled to youth's emotions, aspirations, depressions, and dreams. If she was fond of calling her most ambitious enterprises fragments, her life was a fragment too.

But what then was the cause of the despair that finally engulfed so intelligent and so high-minded a woman just when her career was going so well? As we saw at the outset, Aldrich puzzled over it; so do we; so apparently did the writer herself.

> O is it Love, or is it Fame,
>   This thing for which I sigh?
> Or has it then no earthly name
>   For men to call it by?
>
> I know not what can ease my pains,
>   Nor what it is I wish;
> The passion at my heart-strings strains
>   Like a tiger in a leash.

Basically, of course, it was the true Romantic, self-tormenting melancholy, asking more of life than life can give. Though this was perhaps more characteristic of French and German than of English romanticism, it casts its shadow over a whole generation and more, and its diagnosis is too complicated a matter to be undertaken here. It will be remembered that Garnett says Amy Levy feared insanity; I do not know whether there was any basis for such fear, but Beth Zion Lask, who apparently knew more about her uncollected writings than anybody else, points out that, though she was a prolific magazinist, she does not seem to have published anything during 1887. In the poem called **"In the Black Forest"** she wonders whether her sadness has been caused by "the sloth and the sin and the failure" of the past, but this view is quickly rejected:

> They had made me sad so often;
>   Not now they make me sad;
> My heart was full of sorrow
>   For the joy it never had.

This seems essentially in harmony with the words of the suicidal hero of **"A Minor Poet"**:

>   I lament
> The death of youth's ideal in my heart;
> And, to be honest, never yet rejoiced
> In the world's progress—scarce, indeed,
>   discerned;
> (For still it seems that God's a Sisyphus
> With the world for stone).

Nevertheless, it is clear that the speaker here has no faith in "progress," and it may well be that the poet had none either.

Suicide is the logical outcome of such depression, but human beings are not always strictly logical, whether for good or for evil. In **"Sokratics in the Strand,"** the ethics and the advisability of suicide are debated between Horace, a writer who finds a flaw in his machine and is inclined to try melting down the good material he believes it contains into the general crucible, and Vincent, a barrister who advises against flying in the face of nature, because she has "a little way of avenging herself." There is a first-person epilogue in which the circumstances of Horace's death are left obscure. "Poets and those afflicted with the so-called 'poetic temperament,' although constantly contemplating it, rarely commit suicide. They have too much imagination."

Probably Amy Levy herself knew well the ambivalence she described so well in **"The Two Terrors"**:

> Two terrors fright my soul by night and day;
> The first is Life, and with her come the years;
> A weary, winding train of maidens they,
> With forward-fronting eyes, too sad for tears;
> Upon whose kindred faces, blank and grey,
> The shadow of a kindred woe appears.
> Death is the second terror; who shall say
> What from beneath the shrouding mantle nears?

> Which way she turn, my soul finds no relief,
> My smitten soul may not be comforted;
> Alternately she swings from grief to grief,
> And poised between them, sways from dread
>   to dread.

> For there she dreads because she knows; and here
> Because she knows not, inly faints with fear.

In **"The Promise of Sleep,"** however, death lures as a comforter:

> All day I could not work for woe,
>   I could not work nor rest;
> The trouble drove me to and fro,
>   Like a leaf on the storm's breast.

> Night came and saw my sorrow cease;
>   Sleep in the chamber stole;
> Peace crept about my limbs, and peace
>   Fell on my stormy soul.

> And now I think of only this—
>   How I again may woo
> The gentle sleep—who promises
>   That death is gentle too.

And surely the last poem in the *Plane-Tree* volume, **"To E,"** is melancholy enough, coming as it does from a poet who killed herself a week after correcting her proofs. Here the speaker recalls her intercourse with two other people "three years gone by."

> Our Poet, with fine-frenzied eye,
> You, steeped in learned lore, and I
>   A poet too.

> Our Poet brought us books and flowers,
> He read us *Faust;* he talked for hours
> Philosophy (sad Schopenhauer's),
>   Beneath the trees.

But the poem ends ominously:

> On you the sun is shining free;
> Our Poet sleeps in Italy,
> Beneath an alien sod; on me
>   The cloud descends.

In the lovely **"June,"** on the other hand, in which the poet laments an absent lover, she looks forward to a long life:

> O many Junes shall come and go,
>   Flow'r-footed o'er the mead;
> O many Junes for me, to whom
>   Is length of days decreed.

And in **"Twilight,"** the speaker, though brooding over a recent death, reports that

> I leaned against the stile, and thought
>   Of her whose soul had fled,—
> I knew that years on years must pass
>   Or e'er I should be dead.

Finally, when Tom Leigh finds the "Minor Poet" dead, he muses quite in the manner of Vincent in **"Sokratics in the Strand"**:

> Nay, I had deemed him more philosopher;
> For did he think by this one paltry deed
> To cut the knot of circumstance, and snap
> The chain which binds all being?

The testimony of the novels supports this point of view. Both Miss Meredith and the Lorimer sisters face their problems bravely (even the weak Phyllis boasts justly at the end that she does not funk). Gertrude Lorimer often walks at a swinging pace around Regent's Park "exorcising her demons—she was obliged, as she said, to ride her soul on the curb, and be very careful that it did not take the bit between its teeth." She never permits herself to forget that there is "only a plank" between herself and her sisters "and the pitiless, fathomless ocean on which they had set out with such unknowing fearlessness; into whose boiling depths hundreds sank daily and disappeared, never to rise again," and she feels sure that "to do and do and do . . . is all that remains to one in a world where thinking, for all save a few chosen beings, must surely mean madness." Yet she does not regret having been forced to face life as it is, for, "fastidious and sensitive as she was, she had yet a great fund of enjoyment of life within her; of that impersonal, objective enjoyment which is so often denied to her sex." *Reuben Sachs* is much sterner than the other novels, yet at the end we leave Judith, crushed by Reuben's death and married to a man she does not love, with "the germ of another life" within her, "which shall quicken, grow, and come forth at last. Shall bring with it no doubt, pain and sorrow, and tears; but shall bring also hope, and joy, and that quickening of purpose which is perhaps as much as any of us should expect or demand from life."

It may be that Gertrude Lorimer was the kind of woman her creator would have liked to be rather than what she knew she was; it may be that she included herself among those to whom "impersonal, objective enjoyment of life had been denied"; it may even be that if, like Judith, she could have known "the germ of another life" quickening within herself, her fate might have been different. One must wonder then whether frustrated or disappointed love played any part in her tragedy. She herself wrote of Judith that "there is nothing more terrible than this ignorance of a woman of her own nature, her own possibilities, her own passions."

In the absence of biographical information about Amy Levy, it is impossible to answer such questions, and it may be that even to raise them, however sympathetically, comes under the head of unlovely prying. As a poet, surely, she was immensely concerned with love, but that is true of lyric poets in general. As a poet too she concerns herself more with aborted than fulfilled love (even Gertrude Lorimer, at the beginning of the *Shop*, had lost a lover who was obviously not worth holding, a fair-weather friend," who had deserted her in her family's time of trouble). But here again we must remind outselves that poets in general have been more preoccupied with the sorrows than the joys of love; the great German Lieder and the imbecilities of Tin Pan Alley join their testimony upon this score. And though it is difficult to believe that Amy's love poems could have been written by a writer who had never been in love, the fact that, like many female poets, she could express the man's point of view quite as well as the woman's must make us wary of attempting to trace a close correspondence between her work and her life.

The stories too are relevant here. The heroine of **"Wise in Her Generation"** wonders "sometimes, that we do not go oftener to the bad, we girls of the well-to-do classes." When such a girl is thrown into the swim of social life and contacts with the men encountered there, she mistakes "the natural promptings of her modesty . . . for resistance to this unknown force, which is drawing her to itself as inevitably as the magnet draws the needle. With her little prudent defences, she believes herself equipped for any fray; she feels strong, and O God, she is so weak!" **"Between Two Stools"** is the story of a young woman who did not know her own mind. She rejects Stephen Brooke because she fancies herself in love with Reginald Talbot, but when he has been won, she discovers that Brooke is the man she really cares for and so must reject Talbot too. "Mrs. Pierrepoint," more culpable, sold herself to a rich, unloved old man who lived only six months. A year after his death, she attempts to return to the lover she had declined, Philip Quornham, now a curate in Whitechapel, who rejects her.[15]

But the poems are, if possible, sadder. The lover in **"To Sylvia"** says,

> I scarcely knew your hair was gold,
> Nor of the heavens' own blue your eyes.
> Sylvia and song, divinely mixt,
>   Made Paradise.

But he also tells her,

> You've robbed my life of many things—
> Of love and hope, of fame and pow'r.
> So be it, sweet. You cannot steal
>   One golden hour.

In **"At Dawn"** love's fulfillment comes only in dreams:

> In the night I dreamed of you;
> All the place was filled

With your presence; in my heart
  The strife was stilled.

All night I have dreamed of you;
  Now the morn is gray,—
How shall I arise and face
  The empty day?

In **"New Love, New Life"** the brown nightingale who symbolizes love is waking and singing within the poet's heart again, but the prognosis is not good:

Love blest and love accurst
  Was here in days long past;
This time is not the first,
  But this time is the last.

And in **"Impotens"** love makes the other dissatisfactions of life seem worse rather than better:

The pitiless order of things,
  Whose laws we may change not nor break,
Alone I could face it—it wrings
  My heart for your sake.

In **"On the Threshold"** the poet dreams that the beloved is dead.

                    I had crept
Up to your chamber-door, which stood ajar,
And in the doorway watched you from afar,
Nor dared advance to kiss your lips and brow.
I had no part nor lot in you, as now;
Death had not broken between us the old bar;
Nor torn from out my heart the old, cold sense
Of your misprison and my impotence.

Except that in the novel the death is real, this might almost be the utterance of the heroine of *Reuben Sachs*. With this poem it is interesting to compare **"In the Mile End Road,"** which of all Amy Levy's poems seems to me most like Hardy:

How like her! But 'tis she herself,
  Comes up the crowded street,
How little did I think, the morn,
  My only love to meet!

Whose else that motion and that mien?
  Whose else that airy tread?
For one strange moment I forgot
  My only love was dead.

"A Greek Girl," too, in her dramatic monologue, mourns for a man who has really died:

Alas, alas, I never touched his hand;
And now my love is dead that loved not me.

And again:

For if indeed we meet among the shades,
How shall he know me from the other
    maids?—
Me, that had died to save his body pain!

Whatever else may be thought of Amy Levy's love poems, there can be no question that hers was a very chaste muse. The frankest expression of passion I have found anywhere is in the monologue **"Christopher Found"**:

This time of day I can't pretend
With slight, sweet things to satiate
The hunger-cravings. Nay, my friends,
I cannot blush and turn and tremble,
Wax loth as younger maidens do.

Yet

Till the world be dead, you shall love but me,
Till the stars have ceased, I shall love but
    you.

But much more characteristic—and even more touching—is the very Browningesque **"In a Minor Key,"** which is written from the point of view of a lover who is not sure he still loves:

And yet—and yet—ah, who understands?
We men and women are complex things!
A hundred times Fate's inexorable hands
May play on sensitive soul-strings.

This poem closes as follows:

I paced, in the damp, grey mist, last night
In the streets (an hour) to see you pass:
Yet I do not think I love you—quite;
What's felt so finely 'twere coarse to class.

And yet—and yet—I can scarce tell why
(As I said, we are riddles and hard to read),
If the world went ill with you, and I
Could help with a hidden hand your need;

But ere I could reach you where you lay,
Must strength and substance and honour
    spend;
Journey long journeys by night and day—
Somehow, I think I should come, my friend!

If we do not know whether or not unhappy love played a part in Amy Levy's disillusionment and unhappiness, there can, I think, be no doubt that religion did. But before proceeding directly to this consideration, we must return for a moment to *Reuben Sachs*.

As has already been noted, this is Amy's only Jewish novel, but though such chapters as the one describing the Day of Atonement at the synagogue have clearly been written by an insider, it would hardly be an exaggeration to describe the general impression of Jewish character which emerges from this book as hostile. If Reuben and Judith are, with reservations, sympathetically portrayed, the Jewish community in general appears as clannish, self-righteous, and ingrown, shamelessly devoted to the main chance, and much given to gambling for high stakes. Sensitive to criticism from others, its denizens are divided from each other by "innumerable trivial class differences" and "acute family jealousy."[16]

Old Solomon Sachs, the head of his family, is "blest with that fitness of which survival is the inevitable reward. . . . If report be true [he] had been a hard man in his dealings with the world, never overstepping the line of legal honesty, but taking an advantage wherever he could do so with impunity." Reuben's mother "was an elderly woman, stout and short, with a wide, sallow, impassive face, lighted up by occasional gleams of shrewdness from a pair of half-shut eyes" and his sister Adelaide "a thin, dark young woman of eight or nine-and-twenty, with a restless, eager sallow face, and an abrupt manner. She was richly and very fashionably dressed in an unbecoming gown of green shot silk, and wore big diamond solitaires in her ears. She and her mother indeed were never seen without such jewels, which seemed to bear the same relation to their owners as his pigtail does to the Chinaman." As for the Leunigers, though they begrudge no money for food, clothes, furniture, or theater tickets, they regard every shilling spent on books as an extravagance. Except that he would not have considered it respectable to permit his niece Judith to marry a Gentile, old Israel Leuniger is "a thorough-going pagan"; "you need only marry a Jew and be buried at Willesden or Ball's Pond; the rest would take care of itself."[17]

As I say, Reuben and Judith are more sympathetically portrayed, but only up to a point. Judith is beautiful, and certainly the reader is expected to feel with her in her ordeal, but even here we must be told that her figure was "distinguished for stateliness rather than grace." She is also a "thorough-going Philistine" and "conservative in strain," and though she had enjoyed Shakespeare and Tennyson in school, she needs to settle down in Leo's room and read some of his books in order to realize that there was "something to be said for feelings which had not their basis in material relationships." Her religion she has accepted unthinkingly, and it has no strong hold on her. "These prayers, read so diligently, in a language of which her knowledge was exceedingly imperfect, these reiterated praises of an austere tribal deity, these expressions of a hope whose consummation was neither desired nor expected, what connection could they have with the personal

needs, the human longings of this touchingly ignorant and limited creature?" She had been brought up to marry for interest, not love, and when she has lost Reuben or thinks she has and feels no choice available to her except that of Bertie Lee-Harrison, her mother is pleased to hear that she does not like him; indeed she would be a little shocked if she did. "No girl likes her intended—at first."

As for Reuben, honorable though he is, "from his cradle he had imbibed the creed that it is noble and desirable to have everything better than your neighbor; from the first had been impressed on him the sacred duty of doing the very best for yourself," and though he cares for Judith, at least as much as he is capable of caring for anybody, he fails to propose to her because he does not believe that a marriage with her would advance his career. When he is snubbed, he always proceeds to wipe out the insult by making a conquest of the snubber. "Persons less completely equipped for the battle of life," writes the author tartly, "have been known to prefer certain defeat to the chances of such a victory."

One curious aspect of Amy Levy's portrayal of Reuben Sachs relates to his physical make-up. He was "of middle height and slender build. He wore good clothes, but they could not disguise the fact that his figure was bad, and his movements awkward; unmistakably the figure and movements of a Jew." And if we blink at this, we shall find as we read on that it is not accidental, for elsewhere his creator generalizes about "the ill-made sons and daughters of Shem." This was evidently a settled conviction of hers, for in what is perhaps her most significant short story, **"Cohen of Trinity,"**[18] she gives her villain-hero "a curious figure; an awkward, rapid gait, half slouch, half hobble." And in *Reuben Sachs* itself she tells us that "the charms of person which a Jew or Jewess may possess are not usually such as will bear the test of being regarded as a whole.'

The best Jews in the novel are Leo Leuniger and Judith's father, who has been working for years on a monograph on the Jews in Spain which is obviously never going to be finished. His daughter regards him rightly as "one of the pure spirits of the world," but she knows too that he does not count; he is quite ignored at the dinner of the clan that they attend together. "He was one of the world's failures; and the Jewish people, so eager to crown success in any form, so determined to laying claim to the successful among their number, have scant love for those unfortunates who have dropped behind in the race." Leo's devotion is to classical scholarship and his violin, and he is hopelessly in love with a Gentile girl, Lord Norwood's sister. Leo almost hates his people, who, "so far as he could see, lived without ideals, and were given up body and soul to the pursuit of material advantage." Even their religion, he tells Reuben, is "the religion of materialism. The corn and the wine and the oil; the multiplication of the seed; the conquest of the hostile tribes—these have always had more attraction for us than the harp and crown of a spiritualized existence." Reuben, who admits that the Jewish religion no longer remains a vital force in the lives of those Jews who have been enlightened by Western thought, attempts to make a stand for "our self-restraint, our self-respect, our industry, our power of endurance, our love of race, home and kindred, and our regard for their ties," but all Leo will yield to him is that "our instincts of self-preservation are remarkably strong; I grant you that."

"**Cohen of Trinity**" is the most important of the author's other writings about Jews, but it is not the only one; "**Euphemia, A Sketch,**" which appeared in the *Victoria Magazine* as early as August 1880, has a half-Jewish, half-Gentile heroine. Cohen himself is a rather loathsome character, but though he feels out of place at Trinity, his difficulties seem more attributable to his personal deficiencies than to his race. He has "a glowing face" and an "evil reputation," with a "strange suggestion of latent force" about him, and the narrator says that "his unbounded arrogance, his enormous pretensions, alternating with and hampered by a bitter self-depreciation, overflowing at times into self-reviling, impressed me, even while amusing and disgusting me." He came to Cambridge on a scholarship but gave such a disappointing performance there (his own view was that the portion of his brain which had enabled him to win the scholarship had ceased to function) that he was dropped. Afterwards he astonished everybody by writing an able and successful book, but his success brought him so little satisfaction that he died a suicide. When he was reproached with crying for the moon, he defended himself by replying that after all the moon was the only thing worth having, and the narrator's final question about him is challenging: "Is it, then possible that, amid the warring elements of that discordant nature, the battling forces of that ill-starred, ill-compounded entity, there lurked clear-eyed and ever-watchful, a baffled idealist?" The *Gentleman's Magazine* gave "**Cohen of Trinity**" the place of honor in the issue in which it appeared, and the distinction was richly deserved.

Amy Levy's nonfiction writings about Jews seem to have appeared mainly in the *Jewish Chronicle,* and though in one of them she fears that she is not a very good Jew, they are marked by uncompromising honesty and an unyielding demand for intelligence, wisdom, and sincerity. In "**The Jew in Fiction,**" which has already been cited, she asks for a truthful picture of "the Jew, as we know him today, with his curious mingling of dramatically opposed qualities; his surprising virtues, and no less surprising vices; leading his eager, intricate life; living, moving, and having his being both within and without the tribal limits. . . ." But "**Jewish Children, By a Maiden Aunt,**"[19] is even more significant, a wise, humane, and keen-sighted

essay which, incidentally, shows that in some respects Jewish character, as manifested in family relations, has not changed very much in the last hundred years. Many marriages among Jews are still arranged, says the author, and "domestic affection" seems stronger among Jews than "romantic passion." "Love of offspring might, indeed, be described as our master-passion, stronger than our love of money, than our love of success." Jewish children, consequently, stand in considerable danger of being both killed with kindness and forced into a dangerous precocity. As a result, "the rate of mental and nervous diseases among Jews is deplorably high," and "there is scarcely a Jewish family which does not possess its black sheep."

One can hardly believe, then, that Amy Levy found much spiritual nurture in Judaism, nor, though there is much religious coloring in her writings, in Christianity either. The sisters in *The Romance of a Shop* go to church on Sunday morning, and *Miss Meredith* opens "about a week after Christmas"; later the beauty of the cathedral at Pisa plays a large part in Elsie's surrender to the charm of Italy. Somewhat more surprising is one of Reuben Sachs's meditations over Judith: "If he had happened to be a doctor, Judith might have developed scientific tastes, or if a clergyman, have found nothing so interesting as theological diversion and the history of the Church." One story deals with psychic matters,[20] but it is impossible to say whether or not this indicates any belief in such things on the author's part.

There is a difference, of course, between a poem and a confession of either personal belief or unbelief; neither must the possibility of dramatic utterance ever be overlooked. It is "**Magdalen,**" not the poet, who tells us:

> Death do I trust no more than life,
> For one thing is like one arrayed,
> And there is neither false nor true;
> But in a hideous masquerade
> All things dance on, the ages through,
> And good is evil, evil good;
> Nothing is known or understood
> Save only Pain. I have no faith
> In God or Devil, Life or Death.

Nevertheless, when similar notes are struck again and again in poems in which no obvious dramatic necessity appears, we are surely justified in suspecting that the ideas expressed were of some importance to the writer. In the *Minor Poet* volume, for example, we find "**A Cross-Road Epitaph,**" with its grim German epigraph: *Am Kreuzweg wird begraben / Wer selber brachte sich um,*"

> When first the world grew dark to me
> I call'd on God, yet came not he.
> Whereon, as wearier wax'd my lot,
> On Love I called, but Love came not.

When a worse evil did befall,
Death, on thee only did I call.

In "**Impotens**" the poet tells us that if she were "a woman of old" she would pray all sorts of prayers for her beloved but that now her "pitiful tribute" is "not a prayer, but a tear." And in the same *Plane-Tree* collection which contains this poem we encounter such utterances as

Our hopes go down that sailed before the
    breeze;
Our creeds upon the rock are rent in twain;
Something it is, if at the last remain
One floating spar cast up by hungry seas.

The secret of our being, who can tell?
To praise the gods and Fate is not my part;
Evil I see, and pain; within my heart
There is no voice that whispers: "All is well."

All's done with utterly,
All's done with. Death to me
Was ever Death indeed;
To me no kindly creed

Consolatory was given,
You were of earth, not Heaven. . . .
This dreary day, things seem
Vain shadows in a dream.

Your grave, I'm told, is growing green;
And both for you and me, you know,
There's no Above and no Below,
That you are dead must be inferred,
And yet my thought rejects the word.[21]

But I think the most cogent testimony to Amy Levy's unbelief—and to her agony—comes from **"A Ballad of Religion and Marriage,"** which was privately printed by some unknown printer at an unknown date in an edition of twelve copies, of which one is in the Houghton Library:

Swept into limbo is the host
    Of heavenly angels, row on row;
The Father, Son, and Holy Ghost
    Pale and defeated, rise and go.
The great Jehovah is laid low,
    Vanished his burning bush and rod—
Say, are we doomed to deeper woe?
    Shall marriage go the way of God?

Monogamous, still at our post,
    Reluctantly we undergo
Domestic round of boiled and roast,
    Yet deem the whole proceeding slow.
Daily the secret murmurs grow;
    We are no more content to plod

Along the beaten paths—and so
    Marriage must go the way of God.

Soon, before all men, each shall toast
    The seven strings unto his bow,
Like beacon fires along the coast,
    The flames of love shall glance and glow,
Nor let nor hindrance man shall know,
    From natal bath to funeral sod;
Perennial shall his pleasures flow
    When marriage goes the way of God.

Grant, in a million years at most,
    Folk shall be neither pairs nor odd—
Alas! we shan't be there to boast
    "Marriage has gone the way of God!"

English poetry has achieved no more desolating summary of the late nineteenth-century religious disillusionment. But we shall read this terrible poem very superficially if we permit it to convince us that Amy Levy's was fundamentally an irreligious spirit. It is not the pagans who feel that if God is lost, all is lost. They live quite comfortably without Him. Whatever they may think they "believe," they are the only real atheists.

In his sympathetic but highly critical essay on Amy Levy, Harry Quilter wrote that she had "perception and knowledge and intuitive feeling, sufficient to perceive [the world's] incongruities, to estimate its difficulties, and to gauge its sorrows" but that "she does not seem to have arrived at that further stage which renders such an experience possible despite its sadness—the stage in which the recognition of sorrow and pain turns freely, if not gladly, to action, which seeks to lighten the one and decrease the other." This suggests Gamaliel Bradford's remark about Henry Adams, when, weary of probing Adams's psyche for his own portrait of him, not long after he had made a similar study of the pioneer New England female educator Mary Lyon, he wrote, "Mary Lyon would have seemed to this wide seeker for education very humble and very benighted; but all Mary Lyon cared to teach her pupils was that 'they should live for God and do something.' If she could have communicated some such recipe to Henry Adams she might have solved his problem, though she would have robbed the world of many incomparable phrases."[22]

Coming as I did to Amy Levy fresh from my study of Lillian Wald, I find myself asking whether that indomitable spirit, who saw so much more of the world's evil than Amy did but was never defeated by it, could have helped her, but I pull myself up sharp with the realization that, no more than with Mary Lyon and Henry Adams, could she have done anything of the kind unless she had been able to make her over into something like herself. Whatever Amy Levy's responsibility or lack of responsibility for her final failure of nerve may have been, she surely paid a higher price for it than her severest critic could have desired. Neither Amy Levy nor Lillian Wald, nor Henry Adams nor Mary Lyon, put themselves together, and it is better to be grateful for what each has left us than to attempt to sit in judgment upon any of them.[23] As Goethe tells us,

> Eines schickt sich nicht für alle:
> Sehe jeder wir er's treibe,
> Sehe jeder wie er bleibe,
> Und wer steht, dass er nicht falle!

Notes

[1] E. K. Chambers, "Poetry and Pessimism," *Westminster Review* 138 (1892): 366-76. Chambers admitted that Amy Levy's poems "have fascinated me for hours together. Vividly personal as they are, the pent-up sufferings of hundreds of souls throb through them, launching one on wide seas of melancholy speculation." Regarded as literature, "they have a remarkable charm. They possess all the subtle workmanship, the delicacy of finish, the innumerable scholarly touches, which are so characteristic of the minor verse of our day. . . . They are indeed a human document at least as rich with suggestion as the much discussed diary of Marie Bashkirtseff."

[2] Harry Quilter, "Amy Levy: A Reminiscence and a Criticism," in his *Preferences in Art, Life, and Literature* (Swan Sonnenschein & Co., 1892).

[3] *Woman's World* 3 (1890): 51-52.

[4] She left her papers and her copyrights to her friend Clementina Black, the dedicatee of *A London Plane-Tree*. By her own choice, she became the second Jew and the first Jewish woman to be cremated in England.

[5] See also "Cambridge in the Long." Warwick James Price, "Three Forgotten Poetesses," *Forum* 47 (1912): 361-76, makes her a Clapham factory girl; not only is there no confirmation of this elsewhere but it is hopelessly irreconcilable with what we know of her life.

[6] *Cambridge Review* 5 (1883-84): 163-64; *Woman's World* 1 (1888): 178-80.

[7] Short stories and criticism, published only serially, will engage us later in connection with various points they may help to illuminate.

[8] The only suggestion of anything of the kind I have observed anywhere in Amy Levy's writing is in the passage in the *Shop* where she has Gertrude working "like a nigger."

[9] Harry Quilter gives an account of Amy Levy's contacts with nature in Cornwall and of her intercourse with a woman who took care of her when she came there after an illness, which incidentally shows that she could charm. "Out of This World," *London Society* 49 (1886): 53-56, is dated from Cornwall. But even here she writes, "Much as I admire the superior peace, simplicity and beauty of a country life, I know that my own place is among the struggling crowd of dwellers in cities" and compares herself to Browning's "icy fish" in "Caliban upon Setebos."

[10] Heine's influence upon Amy Levy was considerable from the time of her first published poem, "Ida Grey." Her most interesting comments on him are in "Jewish Humour," *Jewish Chronicle*, n.s. 908, August 20, 1886, pp. 9-10, where she sees him as the typical Jewish humorist. "The poet stretched on his couch of pain; the nation whose shoulders are sore with the yoke of oppression; both can look up with rueful humourous eyes and crack their jests, as it were, in the face of Fortune. . . . True humour, we are told, has its roots in pathos; there is pathos and to spare, we think, in the laughter that comes up from the Paris lodging, or which surges up to us through the barred gates of the Ghetto." But "there is a limit to human power of suffering no less than to human endurance; sensibilities grow blunted and the finer feelings are lost. A tendency to 'debase the currency' by turning everything into a joke, never to take oneself or one's neighbour quite *au sérieux,* is, perhaps, one of the less pleasing results of our long struggle for existence."

[11] "The Poetry of Christina Rossetti," *Woman's World* 1 (1888): 178-89; "James Thomson: A Minor Poet," *Cambridge Review* 4 (1882-83): 240-41, 257-58.

[12] See "The Jew in Fiction," *Jewish Chronicle*, n.s. 897, June 4, 1886, p. 13; "Jewish Children," ibid., n.s. 919, November 5, 1886, p. 8.

[13] For "Wise in her Generation," see *Woman's World* 3 (1890): 20-22; for "Eldorado at Islington," ibid. 2 (1889): 488-89. There are notices of the Beaumont Trust in *Jewish Chronicle*, n.s. 896, May 28, 1886, p. 4, and elsewhere.

[14] *Woman's World* 1 (1888): 364-67.

[15] "Between Two Stools," *Temple Bar* 69 (1883): 337-50; "Mrs. Pierrepoint," ibid. 59 (1880): 226-36.

[16] The *Cambridge Review* found *Reuben Sachs* written in vitriol, but Beth Zion Lask, who regarded Amy Levy as the greatest Jewess England had produced, reminds us that the characters represent "Kensington and Bayswater Jewry, who in their own material success had ceased to care for the spiritual welfare, or even the material welfare, of their less fortunate brethren. It is a matter of the

deepest regret that [Amy Levy] did not know that section of Jewry which, despite its worldly poverty, was imbued then as now with the ideals of Judaism that make every thinking Jew proud of his spiritual heritage." To this writer the novel is an important study of "that portion of Anglo-Jewry that had set up Mammon in place of the God of Israel," a prophetic utterance, and "a cry of protest."

[17] In view of the alleged connection between Scott's Rebecca and Rebecca Gratz, the following comment by Amy Levy is interesting: "Generally speaking, the race instincts of Rebecca of York are strong, and she is less apt to give her heart to Ivanhoe, the Saxon knight, than might be imagined."

[18] *Gentleman's Magazine* 266 (1899): 417-24.

[19] *Jewish Chronicle*, n.s. 919, November 5, 1886, p. 8.

[20] "The Recent Telepathic Occurrence at the British Museum," *Woman's World* 1 (1888): 31-32. A dying woman reveals the secret of her love for a man who had evidently cared more for her than he had ever admitted even to himself by manifesting to him at his desk in the reading room of the Museum.

[21] The three poems quoted from are the dedication to Clementina Black, "Last Words," and "Contradictions." The punctuation at the end of the second line of the second stanza of "Last Words" is the author's; nothing has been omitted.

[22] Bradford, *American Portraits, 1875-1900* (Houghton Mifflin, 1922), pp. 56-57.

[23] In this connection there is an interesting passage in the poem "Lohengrin." The first part describes the departure of Lohengrin and the reappearance of Elsa's "young, lost brother" as in the opera. Then comes:

> God, we have lost Thee with much
>   questioning.
> In vain we seek Thy trace by sea and land,
> And in Thine empty fanes where no men sing.
>   What shall we do through all the weary days?
>   Thus wail we and lament. Our eyes we raise,
> And, lo, our Brother with an outstretched hand!

Who or what is "our Brother" in the context of the poem? If mankind is indicated and the service of mankind recommended, we have here something pretty close to Comte's religion of humanity which interested George Eliot. I may add that personally I find the most convincing testimony to Amy Levy's idealism in the one literary article in which I disagree with her radically, her attack on Howells and James in "The New School of American Fiction," *Temple Bar* 70 (1884): 383-89. "Nothing is too trivial, too sordid, or too far-fetched to engage the attention of these 'fine-art' writ-

ers." James, she declares, is to Thackeray as Alma Tadema is to Rembrandt. We know Beatrix Esmond better than Isabel Archer and Colonel Esmond better than Ralph Touchett. James "makes us see a great many things, but we should see them better if we could feel them as well," and Howells's books are like photographs: "no artistic hand has grouped the figures, only posed them very stiffly before his lens." The "moral standard" of both writers "is a low one. It is with the selfish record of selfish people that [they] chiefly occupy themselves. There is never a spark of ideality (Mr. James used to give us occasional flashes), the whole thing is of the earth, earthy." They are "terribly finite," without "a touch of the infinite. . . . And in this finiteness lies the germ of decay." How any critic with Amy Levy's intelligence could see no more than this in James and Howells is beyond my understanding. But my point here is that her own high and lofty ideal of what fiction can and should do is equally impressive.

Deborah Epstein Nord (essay date 1990)

SOURCE: "'Neither Pairs nor Odd': Female Community in Late Nineteenth-Century London," in *Signs*, Vol. 15, No. 4, Summer, 1990, pp. 733-54.

[In the essay below, Nord explores how Levy's poetry and fiction reflect the social realities of London in the 1880s.]

[Amy Levy] dealt the most directly with her single state and her urban existence; she was also the most overtly ambivalent about the sexual identification of her public persona. Her Jewishness made her more thoroughly and permanently an outsider in English society than either [Beatrice] Webb or [Margaret] Harkness: theirs was at least in part a willed marginality; Levy's was inherited and indelible. Still, in her poetry she writes of her alien status only obliquely, and in her novel *Reuben Sachs* she signals a marked ambivalence about her ties to her own people. She was the only member of this group who had been to university—she was educated at Newnham—and her experiences at Cambridge might well have heightened her feminist sensibilities while, at the same time, binding her to certain male traditions of learning and literature. Her second volume of poems, *A London Plane Tree,* published posthumously in 1889, contains two illustrations: the first is a frontispiece drawing of a plane tree next to a church and the second shows a young woman seated hand-on-brow at a desk, surrounded by papers that cover and spill off the desk onto the floor. Placed in front of an open window through which the spires and tops of city buildings can be glimpsed, she is the quintessential woman writer alone with her work in a London garret.[1] A quotation from Austin Dobson opposite the frontispiece reads, "Mine is an urban Muse, and bound / By some strange law to paven ground." The first poems in the collection celebrate urban life, chronicle the omnibus ride and the newspaper seller's cry, and summon up the poet's view from behind "garret-pane." In these poems, Levy chronicles her own experience of the city. In **"The Village Garden"** she expresses her sense that for burdened souls like hers the city is preferable: "For me, the roar and hurry of the town, / Wherein more lightly seems to press the burden / Of individual life that weighs me down." In **"Ballad of an Omnibus"** she writes of her untiring enjoyment of seeing the human pageant unfold from the top of a bus. In more

cases than not, however, this personal experience is noticeably camouflaged by the use of male persona.

In **"London in July"** the poet, taking a lovesick man's voice, wonders "That all the people in the street / Should wear one woman's face," and in numerous other lyrics in the collection, the beloved, usually an unresponsive one, is imagined as a woman. In these poems Levy uses conventional forms, among them the ballad, as if practicing as an apprentice the traditional modes of her poet's trade.[2] Somewhat paradoxically, the lyric enabled her to achieve impersonality, to use another's voice—a man's voice—while other, more impersonal forms—dramatic monologues and verse plays—allowed her to speak as a woman, to express private feeling in a veiled way. There are a couple of interesting exceptions to this. In the poems entitled **"Philosophy"** and **"To E.,"** the poet speaks more personally of relations with men that are tensely, and perhaps misguidedly, platonic: "Proudly, we sat, we two, on high, / Throned in our Objectivity; / Scarce friends, not lovers (each avers), / But sexless, safe Philosophers." Her most powerful expressions of female passion, resentment, and longing, however, are not to be found among her lyric verses but in her first volume of poems, *A Minor Poet,* in the dramatic modes she learned from Tennyson and the Brownings.[3]

"Xantippe" and **"Medea,"** in which she inhabits the personae of two classical antiheroines, are Levy's most memorable and original poems and they are also, not coincidentally, her most feminist poems.[4] In form they take after the works of her Victorian forefathers, but in perspective they look forward to the "Helen" and "Eurydice" of H. D. In **"Xantippe,"** the rejected and ridiculed wife of Socrates, famous for her legendary shrewishness and slow wit, reveals what it was like to be married to the "high philosopher" who "Deigned not to stoop to touch so slight a thing / As the fine fabric of a woman's brain." Socrates saved his love and learning for "this Athenian city and her sons" and failed to teach Xantippe what as a bride she yearned to have, a "tongue / That should proclaim the stately mysteries." Her "tender language wholly misconceived," she becomes to all the world a "household vessel," untutored and ill-tempered, ignorant and bitter. In **"Medea,"** written as a fragment of a play rather than as a dramatic monologue, we have the plaint of another ill-used, apparently monstrous woman. Medea rails against her husband's treachery and betrayal and accuses him of duplicity and ungratefulness, but it is, above all, her sense of foreignness, of being a lusty Colchian in the midst of cold Corinthians, that dominates the poem. A citizen of Corinth declares that he likes not "your swart skins and purple hair; / Your black fierce eyes where the brows meet across" and asks instead for "gold hair, lithe limbs and gracious smiles." Levy, the anomalous, Jewish woman, surely stands behind the alien and enraged Medea, the stranger in a strange land who is marked in physical type as in temperament.

In her two novels, *The Romance of a Shop* and *Reuben Sachs,* Levy found it possible to express more directly her own personal experience of marginality. Levy's first novel, which anticipates Gissing's *The Odd Women,* tells the story of four orphaned, unmarried sisters who are left virtually penniless by a brilliant but reckless father and determine to make their livings as something other than governess or teacher.[5] Unlike Gissing's Madden sisters, however, they have a skill, photography, which they have learned from their father, and they undertake to set up a photographer's shop in Baker Street. Gertrude Lorimer, the sister who seems closest to Levy herself, finds the idea of business appealing: it is "progressive" and "a creature capable of growth," the "very qualities in which women's work is dreadfully lacking."[6] In their zeal for the world of business and in their belief that it is a means to independence, the sisters prefigure Gissing's Rhoda Nunn and Mary Barfoot rather than Alice, Gertrude, and Monica Madden.

The Romance of a Shop succeeds at conveying how difficult and yet how exhilarating it was to be women alone in London in the 1880s. Like the unprotected women imagined in Woolf's *The Pargiters,* another work that Levy's novel anticipates, the Lorimer sisters are made so convincingly vulnerable that the oldest sister, Fanny, prudish and old-fashioned in her instincts, feels them to be as "removed from the advantages and disadvantages of gallantry as the withered hag who swept the crossing near Baker Street Station."[7] The shop, quite realistically, is always on the verge of failure, and even the sisters' friends expect cheap photographs from female photographers. Still, as Lucy Lorimer says when she sees the studio and rooms in Baker Street that Gertrude has rented, "This is work, this is life." Gertrude, referred to as the most "inveterate cockney" of the lot, regrets not at all that she has been "transported from the comparative tameness of Campden Hill to the regions where the pulses of the great city could be felt distinctly as they beat and throbbed," and she harbors a "secret, childish love for the gas-lit street, for the sight of the hurrying people, the lamps, the hansom cabs, flickering in and out of the yellow haze, like so many fire-flies."[8]

Levy's first novel shares the urban sensibility of her *London Plane Tree* poems but combines it with a self-consciously female one. We most often see Gertrude gazing longingly and lovingly at the street from her window, able truly to relish the "London pageant" only in the safe position of voyeur (the sisters first get to "know" their neighbor Frank Jermyn by watching him out the window, so that when he finally appears at their flat, they feel a certain justifiable familiarity with him). She cannot occupy the city streets as men do: she must enjoy its public life from a largely private vantage point. Gertrude identifies with the kinds of scorned and tortured heroines Levy used for her dramatic poems: when the novel begins she has been writing a play about Charlotte Corday, and she refers to herself repeatedly as "Cassandra." Levy's failure in the novel, however, is precisely that she does not know what to do with her independent, idiosyncratic heroines—particularly Gertrude—and opts for killing off the beautiful, "fallen" sister and marrying off the remaining ones. Lucy's fiancé, Frank, has gone off to cover the Boer War as an illustrator and is reported dead; but he makes a miraculous reappearance and saves Lucy from spinsterhood. Even Gertrude, who in the final pages of the novel still believes that she will continue to pay "the penalty, which her sex always pays one way or another, for her struggles for strength and independence," is reunited at the very last minute with the older, distinguished Lord Watergate, a man she has earlier rejected.[9] More serious than these marital dei ex machina is the thrust of the entire last third of the novel: it begins to resemble a cheap *Pride and Prejudice*—all four sisters searching for the appropriate mate—and ceases to foreshadow *The Odd Women* (although that too owes something to Austen's novel, more as a subversion, perhaps, than as a repetition). After the struggle for independence is essentially won in the novel, Levy cannot sustain it, at least in part because she understands that independence is painful, precarious, and exhausting and because, as a fledgling novelist, she shies away from writing the kind of book that will tell an uncomfortable truth.

Levy's second novel, *Reuben Sachs,* confronts directly that aspect of herself that she so obliquely expressed in her Medea poem, her Jewishness. She tells the story of middle-class London Jewry, initially from the point of view of a man. The novel's eponymous hero Reuben, who suffers from a nervous condition and unlimited ambitions, turns his back on the poor Jewish woman he loves in order not to thwart a budding political career. The novel exposes the crassness of the Sachs family in terms that understandably earned Levy the disapproval of some of her coreligionists: "I think," says a cynical member of the family about a Gentile friend in the novel, "that he was shocked at finding us so little like the people in [George Eliot's] *Daniel Deronda. . . .* Ours [is] the religion of materialism. The corn and the wine and the oil; the multiplication of the seed; the conquest of the hostile tribes—these have always had more attraction for us than the harp and crown of a spiritualized existence."[10] If Margaret Harkness tried to capture the nature of interactions between classes, Levy sought to pillory the upper middle class through her portrait of London Jewry. That Eleanor Marx translated the novel is not surprising, for its indictment of upper bourgeois life—in this case, Jewish life—is scathing.[11] *Reuben Sachs* can indeed be seen as a latter-day *Daniel Deronda,* a revision from inside the Jewish community and, ultimately, as we shall see, from a woman's point of view.

Something interesting happens about two-thirds of the way through the novel: it ceases to be written from the perspective of Reuben Sachs and shifts its focus to Judith Quixano, the woman he loves but rejects. It becomes a novel about the choices a poor but genteel woman must make rather than one about the vexed ambitions of a young man; the novel emerges as a *Daniel Deronda* that puts Mirah rather than Daniel at its center and imagines a fate for her quite different from that of Eliot's eclipsed Jewish heroine. From the moment of Reuben's rejection of Judith it is her consciousness that dominates the narrative. It is as if Levy ceases to throw her voice, as she had done in so many of her poems, and allows herself to imagine without disguise the chilling position of the unmarried woman cornered into lifelong celibacy or loveless marriage. As a result of her sorrow and disappointment Judith is awakened from a kind of willed ignorance about the ways of the world, but her fate is to be a soul grown "frozen and appalled." She marries a man she does not love (he is rich, Gentile, and finds her exotic), and as the novel closes we leave her absorbing the news of Reuben's premature death and anticipating the birth of a child. The chilling sense of limited possibilities that Levy avoided in the conclusion of her first novel here dominates the ending. The aspirations of middle-class manhood and womanhood alike have been utterly thwarted.

Notes

[1] Amy Levy, *A London Plane-Tree and Other Verse* (New York: Frederick A. Stokes, 1890). The two illustrations were done by J. Bernard Partridge, who appears in Levy's novel, *The Romance of a Shop* (Boston: Cupples & Hurd, 1889), as the artist Frank Jermyn.

[2] It is possible that Levy addressed such poems to women because she was a lesbian, but her conventional love lyrics do not at all give that impression. These poems seem rather like exercises, often spirited ones, in which she carries convention to the point of taking a male poet's voice. Rather than revealing intimate feeling, they seem instead to be burying it almost completely.

[3] Amy Levy, *A Minor Poet and Other Verse* (London: Unwin, 1884).

[4] Ibid., 15-30, 31-58.

[5] I can find no evidence that Gissing read *The Romance of a Shop*, but in his diary he does mention taking *Reuben Sachs* out of the library in April of 1892, a very few months before he started to write *The Odd Women*. See *London and the Life of Litera-*

ture in Late Victorian England: The Diary of George Gissing, ed. Pierre Coustillas (Hassocks: Harvester, 1978), 276.

[6] Levy, *The Romance of a Shop*, 10.

[7] Ibid., 100.

[8] Ibid., 61, 113.

[9] Ibid., 294.

[10] Amy Levy, *Reuben Sachs* (London: Macmillan, 1888), 115-17. For response to the novel, see Richard Garnett's entry on Levy in the *Dictionary of National Biography*, 11:1041.

[11] Yvonne Kapp notes that Marx must have translated *Reuben Sachs* immediately after its publication (the German edition also appeared in 1889) and that it was the only work she is known to have translated out of, rather than into her native tongue, which was English. See Kapp, *Eleanor Marx* (New York: Pantheon, 1976), 2:258.

Melvyn New (essay date 1993)

SOURCE: Introduction to *The Complete Novels and Selected Writings of Amy Levy, 1861-1889*, edited by Melvyn New, University Press of Florida, 1993, pp. 1-52.

[*In the following essay, New provides an overview of Levy's life and writings, maintaining that Levy is impressive for "the depth of her commitments, the versatility of her talents, the breadth of her learning."*]

Amy Levy was born in Clapham in 1861 and died by charcoal gas inhalation in 1889, two months before her twenty-eighth birthday. In taking her own life, she not only raised numerous questions about the despairs of an educated Jewish woman in late Victorian England but also put an end to a promising literary career. In her twenty-seven years she had been the first Jewish woman admitted to Newnham College, Cambridge; had published three short novels and three slim collections of poetry; and had become a contributor to several major literary magazines, including *Temple Bar* and *The Gentleman's Magazine*, as well as to the "leading and almost universally read weekly newspaper among British Jews,"[1] *The Jewish Chronicle*. Oscar Wilde's obituary notice in *Woman's World* (which he founded in 1888, and to which Levy contributed poems, short stories, and essays) took particular notice of this promise cut short:

> The gifted subject of these paragraphs, whose distressing death has brought sorrow to many who knew her only from her writings . . . was Jewish, but she . . . gradually

ceased to hold the orthodox doctrines of her nation, retaining, however, a strong race feeling.... ["**Xantippe**" is] surely a most remarkable [poem] to be produced by a girl still at school [and] is distinguished, as nearly all Miss Levy's work is, by the qualities of sincerity, directness, and melancholy . . . and no intelligent critic could fail to see the promise of greater things. . . .

Miss Levy's two novels, *The Romance of a Shop* and *Reuben Sachs,* were both published last year [1888]. The first is a bright and clever story, full of sparkling touches; the second is a novel that probably no other writer could have produced. Its directness, its uncompromising truths, its depth of feeling, and, above all, its absence of any single superfluous word, make it, in some sort, a classic. . . .

To write thus at six-and-twenty is given to very few. . . .[2]

Yet today Amy Levy is by and large unknown and unread. Christopher Ricks includes two of her poems ("**Epitaph**" and "**On the Threshold**") in *The New Oxford Book of Victorian Verse;*[3] and in 1973 AMS Press published a facsimile edition of *Reuben Sachs,* but it has gone out of print.[4] Her other novels are exceedingly rare (indeed, the only copy of the first edition of *The Romance of a Shop* in the United States is in the Library of Congress and is considered too rare and fragile to lend or photocopy); and her volumes of poetry are equally difficult to secure. The only full-length modern discussion is by Edward Wagenknecht in *Daughters of the Covenant* (1983), a work I found useful, though somewhat dated in its interests and judgments.[5]

Gail Kraidman, in her entry on Levy for the *Encyclopedia of British Women Writers,* suggests one possible reason for this obscurity:

Active in radical and feminist organizations such as the Men and Women's Club, Levy was politically controversial. This and the negative feelings engendered in some quarters [i.e., in the London Jewish community] by *Reuben Sachs* and "**Cohen of Trinity**" may explain why her writing, which has such artistic merit, has been suppressed. Her inclusion in the *DNB* is testimony to the degree of excellence of her work but her exclusion from anthologies and republication lists is even more significant.[6]

One need not completely share so suspicion-laden a thesis to agree with its upshot: Amy Levy's work deserves a modern audience it does not presently have.

This collection is designed above all to rectify the unavailability of Levy's writings by offering a very generous selection of her works—all three short novels; more than half her poetry, including several of her longer works; seven short stories; and seven essays. Not all this writing is of equal quality, but I will take some pains in this introduction to explain the rationale

behind individual selections. In choosing to represent Levy across the wide spectrum of her genres and interests, and ranging chronologically from writings that are late-adolescent efforts to materials written just days or weeks before her suicide, I have made an obvious decision to weigh Levy's historical significance equally with whatever perception I might have as to her literary merit. At the same time, let it be noted that her poetry and fiction sparkle for me with moments of great intensity and insight on the one hand, spirited humor and satire on the other; and, more important, that I find my own best sense of her achievement in the mass rather than in the minutiae. Taken together, the Levy canon impresses me immensely with the depth of her commitments, the versatility of her talents, the breadth of her learning. I would be hard-pressed to name a Romantic or Victorian writer we read today with whom she was not familiar; and she was conversant as well with German literature (Goethe, Heine, and Schopenhauer seem to have been her favorites), sufficiently skilled in French that Richard Garnett asked her to translate Jean Baptiste Pérès's famous parody of the "higher criticism," *Comme quoi Napoléon n'a jamais existé,*[7] and well-read in classical literature, both Greek and Latin.

Levy's world is clearly the world of books, although she also seems comfortably familiar with the visual arts (including, as demonstrated in *The Romance of a Shop,* the relatively new art of photography) and with the broader social and political issues of her everyday world. Still, when her heroine in *Reuben Sachs,* Judith Quixano, faces the critical moment of her life, the scene is unfolded primarily through her encounter with books. First she rejects, as empty of consolation, her favorite books up to this time, books Reuben had given her, Blackmore's *Lorna Doone,* Carlyle's *Sterling,* Macaulay's *Essays,* Kingsley's *Hypatia, The Life of Palmerston,* a *Life of Lord Beaconsfield;* instead, she turns to Leo's library:

Leo was an idealist—poor Leo!

There were books on a table near, and she took them up one by one: some volumes of Heine in prose and verse; the operatic score of *Parsifal;* Donaldson on the *Greek Theatre;* and then two books of poetry . . . [Swinburne's] *Poems and Ballads,* and a worn green copy of the poems of Clough.

It is, finally, in Swinburne's "Triumph of Time" that Judith finds her own situation and her own moment of Jamesian insight. Judith Quixano is not, unfortunately, a character as richly developed as is Isabel Archer, but she does make one sorely regret the twenty or thirty years Levy did not allow herself to ripen as a writer.

The most extensive biographical and bibliographical discussion of Amy Levy remains a long essay by Beth

Zion Lask, presented to the Jewish Historical Society of England in 1926 and published two years later. Lask opens with a glance at the same political "conspiracy" posited by Kraidman some sixty years later, what she calls the "wilful neglect on the part of her co-religionists":

> Indeed, the extent of this neglect may be gauged from the fact that at a recent lecture on "Jewish Women Writers in England," the name of our greatest contributor to English literature was not even mentioned, while other writers, less able, less poetic, rather inclined to the prosiness that makes the early Victorian novel such a nightmare to the present generation, were praised.[8]

Amy Levy, the second daughter of Lewis Levy and Isobel Levin, was born on November 10, 1861, at Clapham and received her early education at Brighton. The Levys later moved to 7 Endsleigh Gardens, where Amy took her own life on September 10, 1889;[9] it is interesting to note that the first address suggests separation from the Jewish community, while the second is in the heart of Bloomsbury, where middle- and upper-class Anglo-Jews settled in large numbers during the 1860s and 1870s. This district lies within a few blocks of the University of London on Gower Street and the former site of Jews' College in Tavistock Square—that is, near the two centers of higher learning for Anglo-Jews in the Victorian era.[10]

Levy attended Newnham College, Cambridge (established in 1875 and incorporated in 1880), probably between 1879 and 1881. As with so many aspects of her life, she was breaking quite new ground, both as a Jew and as a woman. The so-called local examinations by which one could qualify for Cambridge were not opened to women until 1865; for Oxford, until 1870. Before 1871, Jews could matriculate at Cambridge but not proceed to degrees; at Oxford, professing Jews could not even matriculate until after the University Tests Act of 1871.[11] At both universities, women could not proceed to degrees well into the twentieth century.

Levy seems to have dedicated herself to a writing career very early; a poem, **"Ida Grey,"** appeared in a short-lived journal, *The Pelican,* in 1875 when she was only fourteen, and **"Run to Death,"** which I have included in this collection, in *The Victoria Magazine* four years later.[12] In 1880, she published what may be her most successful poem, **"Xantippe,"** in the *Dublin University Magazine,*[13] and her story **"Mrs. Pierrepoint"** appeared in *Temple Bar* in June of that year. While that story seemed to me too weak overall to be included here, the protagonist—a twenty-two-year-old woman who has married for money and now relishes the death of her husband because it frees her to propose to her former young lover—is a surprisingly perceptive portrait for a writer not yet twenty years old. Here is Mrs. Pierrepoint retiring to her room after the funeral:

She would stay there alone that evening, and would not dine. Not that, as a rule, she was indifferent to delicate cookery—on the contrary, there was a good deal of the epicure in her nature; it was this very epicureanism which kept her fasting tonight. She had a subtler, more exquisite feast in store for herself; she would not spoil the effect of either banquet by indulging in both at the same time.[14]

The sharpness of observation and moral pessimism exhibited in this passage are hallmarks of Levy's later writing; in this instance, she unskillfully blunts her own insight by having the young lover, an idealistic clergyman, reject Mrs. Pierrepoint's offer.

Levy's first collection of verse, *Xantippe and Other Verse,* was published in 1881 in Cambridge. The title poem is a dramatic monologue in blank verse of almost three hundred lines; the speaker is Socrates' shrewish wife, Xantippe, and the poem attempts, quite imaginatively, I think, to see the world through her eyes. Her early awareness of the inappropriateness of being an intellectual woman is well stated:

> Then followed days of sadness, as I grew
> To learn my woman-mind had gone astray,
> And I was sinning in those very thoughts—
> For maidens, mark, such are not woman's
>   thoughts—
> (And yet, 'tis strange, the gods who fashion us
> Have given us such promptings).

In joining herself to Socrates, she had hoped to share his world of ideas, but soon discovers his limitation:

> . . . the high philosopher
> Pregnant with noble theories and great
>   thoughts,
> Deigned not to stoop to touch so slight a
>   thing
> As the fine fabric of a woman's brain—

The subtlety of Levy's poetry is suggested by the word "Pregnant," which plays effectively against her suggestion of the homoeroticism within the Socratic circle, especially Alcibiades, with his "laughing lips / And half-shut eyes, contemptuous shrugging up / Soft snowy shoulders, till he brought the gold / Of flowing ringlets round about his breasts." Xantippe's own personality is shaped in response to the exclusivity of this male society (but also, in a splendidly cruel insight, to the way in which it does open itself to one woman, the beautiful Aspasia, mistress of Pericles; "wives need not apply!"); and in the poem's finest image, the domestic life at the loom becomes an emblem of her bitterness:

> I spun until, methinks, I spun away
> The soul from out my body, the high thoughts

From out my spirit; till at last I grew
As ye [her maids] have known me,—eye exact
    to mark
The texture of the spinning; ear all keen
For aimless talking when the moon is up,
And ye should be a-sleeping; tongue to cut
With quick incision 'thwart the merry words
Of idle maidens.

Of this poem, Lask writes: "It bears the impress of the Feminist movement, the ideals of which were then agitating so many women of intellect. A note of passion surges through the poem, touches of tragic intensity, of the thwarting of youth's dreams. The treatment is strong, the versification finished—a mature production that is indeed surprising when one remembers she was yet in her teens" ("Amy Levy," p. 170). I believe that is a fair assessment.[15]

From this first collection I have also included **"A Prayer,"** a love poem that gives us our first glimpse of the lyric voice that will eventually dominate Levy's poetry. Her use of the short trimeter line, rhyme, and a variety of rhythmic forms are all characteristics of her later work; and the brooding tone is one we must finally accept, if only because of its unrelenting presence in the canon and the final fate of the author: "To live—it is my doom—/ Lonely as in a tomb."

The poem **"Felo De Se"** (i.e., self-murder) is offered by Levy "With Apologies to Mr. Swinburne" and is a splendid parody of his characteristic style in, say, "Hymn to Proserpine" or "Hymn to Man." Swinburne had, of course, brilliantly parodied himself in "Nephelidia"; we might compare, for example, the opening line of that poem, "From the depth of the dreamy decline of the dawn through a notable nimbus of nebulous noonshine," to some of Levy's more successful parodies: "I was weary of women and war and the sea and the wind's wild breath," or "Repose for the rotting head and peace for the putrid breast," or, my favorite, "Could fight fierce fights with the foe or clutch at a human hand; / And weary could lie at length on the soft, sweet, saffron sand." At the same time, this poem is Levy's first encounter with a dominant topic of her writing, suicide, and perhaps offers one of her best statements of the pessimism that is at once so characteristic of the final decades of the nineteenth century and yet so uniquely personal a voice in her own work.[16] What separates Levy, however, from the mere cries of anguish of poetasters is her constant attention to form and to style, her self-discipline as a poet, most especially in her diction and ever-present self-ironies. Note also that the poem is *not* an attack on Swinburne but a self-conscious play with his style as a means of approaching her inaccessible subject; it is the lesson of much of Swinburne's own poetic experimentations, and Levy seems to have grasped it well.

Levy also tried her hand at the sonnet, and I have included one example from *Xantippe,* reprinted in Unwin's second edition of *A Minor Poet and Other Verse* (1891); it might be said to encapsulate almost all the themes of her later poetry. The final poem selected from *Xantippe* is **"Run to Death,"** which is subtitled "A True Incident of Pre-Revolutionary French History." In this narrative poem, Levy uses long heptameter lines, often rhymed, to tell the story of a hunting party of French noblemen who chase down and kill a Gypsy woman and her child in the absence of better game. A volume that begins with **"Xantippe"** and ends with **"Run to Death"** is a feminist treatise before its time, whatever other purposes Levy might also have tried to fulfill; we shall probably never fully understand how she could reach so angry and anguished a perspective on her society at so early an age, but one might suspect that we have here an avid reader, whose family placed no restrictions on her books.[17] The spadework of two generations of nineteenth-century feminists encountered in Amy Levy a most fertile soil.

I have included two efforts published in 1883: the short story **"Between Two Stools,"** which appeared in *Temple Bar,* and an important critical effort, **"James Thomson [B.V.]: A Minor Poet,"** in *The Cambridge Review.* Lask's analysis of the latter is quite perceptive:

> Indispensable to any study of the work of Amy Levy is [this essay]. . . . James Thomson . . . is the poet of that phase of life which in its morbid mental suffering, in its "pain inane," resultant of modern life and conditions acting adversely on a hyper-sensitive being, makes him cry aloud for "the pain insane." . . .

> To Amy Levy, already conscious and resentful of that unevenness of life which helps to preserve the world's balance, James Thomson appeared as a martyr to his unhappy lot, a moody being at the mercy of his temperament, ". . . a passionate[ly] subjective being, with intense eyes fixed on one side of the solid polygon of truth, and realising that one side with a fervour and intensity to which the philosopher with his bird's-eye view rarely attains." ("Amy Levy," p. 172)

James Thomson (B.V.) (1834-1882) is rarely read today, but he did attract a following in his own day, including George Eliot and George Meredith. For Levy, he was almost surely a primary intellectual influence, for reasons she is able to define with sympathy and self-prescience:

> "The City of Dreadful Night" [Thomson's major work, published in 1874], his masterpiece, as it is a poem quite unique in our literature, stands forth as the very sign and symbol of that attitude of mind which we call Weltschmerz, Pessimism, what you will; *i.e.,* the almost perfect expression of a form of

mental suffering which I can convey by no other means than by the use of a very awkward figure—by calling it "grey pain," "the insufferable inane" which makes a man long for the "positive pain."

This is precisely the subject matter of **"Felo De Se"**: Thomson experiencing in life what the suicide of that poem discovers is the ultimate agony of death—the total inability to respond to the "Circle of pain" in which one continues to find oneself. Levy argues that Thomson has "caught the spirit of his spiritual kinsmen Heine and of Leopardi, as no other poet has succeeded in doing"; she reveals in this statement the source of her own appreciation, since one might well argue that they are her "spiritual kinsmen" as well.[18] Levy's commentary makes the reader want to look again at Thomson's work; nothing more complimentary can be said about literary criticism.

"Between Two Stools" is a clear illustration of Levy's antidote to her own "mental suffering" and tendency to dwell on her own "pains." The protagonist, Miss Nora Wycherley, now living in the Bayswater section of London, writes to her college friend, Miss Agnes Crewe, Newnham College, about her readjustment to "philistine" society after life at Cambridge, where they "puzzled over Plato on the lawn, and read Swinburne on the roof in the evenings." One cannot read two paragraphs of Nora's correspondence without appreciating Levy's self-parody of intellectual pretensions, her recognition of and amusement over the incipient snobbery and self-importance that almost surely accompanied a career as successful as hers gave promise of being. In the best Swiftian style, for example, she makes use of the well-placed lacuna:

> Oh, what a relief to get back to solitude, even when solitude means the old terrible pain, the old awful longings! Yet is it not something to have "known the best and loved it"?—to have seen what is noblest, highest, and purest in the world, and to have felt it to the depth of one's being? . . .

To be sure, Nora is sufficiently educated so that her views are perhaps not far removed from Levy's; she recognizes, for example, that a woman in her circle "is held to have no absolute value; it is relative, and depends on the extent of the demand for her among members of the other sex. The way the women themselves acquiesce in this view is quite horrible." It is clear to the reader, however, that she has already fallen in love with one of the philistines and that the tug of acquiescence is hard upon her. It is precisely this self-blindness that makes **"Between Two Stools"** one of Levy's better short stories.

One additional story that appeared in 1883, **"The Diary of a Plain Girl,"** has not been included here, but it does introduce several ideas that emerge in Levy's

work, most specifically the relationship between physical appearance and happiness. In this story, as elsewhere, Levy's protagonist, Milly, is the "plain" sister, a young woman who attributes her loneliness and moodiness to her looks—and to competition with a dazzling beauty, her sister. On the one hand, the subject seems quite mundane, the stuff of fairy tales and adolescent romances; on the other hand, it is so pervasive in Levy's writings that one is tempted to pursue it as a clue. The surviving portrait of Levy does not suggest plainness, but there seems to be enormous sympathy between herself and Milly in such a passage as this:

> I don't think the saddest music ever composed can be half so sad as waltz music when you're not waltzing, only looking on at other people. . . . It is torture music, and the happy people dancing round are torturers, exquisitely cruel torturers.[19]

In her fiction, Levy always provides an indication of the "attractiveness" or "unattractiveness" of her characters as part of her initial description, and always condemns those who judge by appearances or who live by such judgments. The women with whom we are to be sympathetic are almost always described as "below" the standard of beauty, the contrast often being between beautiful and interesting. There is, in short, an awareness of the foolishness of the commodity-driven mentality behind these judgments, as well as a perhaps surprising inability to escape them. In *The Romance of a Shop,* Levy's weakest moment may be the seduction and killing off of the beautiful sister, an act of "revenge," perhaps, quite unjustified, as Oscar Wilde points out, by the tone of the story itself.[20]

I do not mean to imply that Levy necessarily saw herself as the "plain" sister. An equally plausible scenario might be written in which she plays the attractive but painfully sympathetic observer of a sister's misery—and one might well assume much difficulty for the sister of an "overachiever" like Levy.[21] The point is that in any commodity-driven society, appearance seems to increase in importance and thus serves well to indicate social hollowness and the failure of human relations—for Levy, it is clearly one aspect of the "Circle of pain" into which she plunges both herself and her characters.

The story **"Sokratics in the Strand"** appeared in 1884, as did Levy's second collection of poetry, *A Minor Poet and Other Verse,* published by T. Fisher Unwin.[22] In both story and title poem, James Thomson (B.V.) is still clearly on her mind.[23] **"A Minor Poet"** is a long dramatic monologue of 207 iambic pentameter lines; the speaker, who has failed in his first two attempts at suicide, succeeds in his third. The setting is Faustian, and almost certainly Goethe is the primary presence in the poem. Levy strikes her own pessimistic note, however, in true late-nineteenth-century fashion:

I lament
The death of youth's idea in my heart;
And, to be honest, never yet rejoiced
In the world's progress—scarce, indeed,
   discerned;
(For still it seems that God's a Sisyphus
With the world for stone).

A specific tribute to Thomson would seem to occur in the middle of the poem as the poet surveys his library, regretting the authors to be left behind—Shakespeare, Goethe, Heine,

And one wild singer of today, whose song
Is all aflame with passionate bard's blood
Lash'd into foam by pain and the world's
   wrong.[24]

On the other hand, quite clearly the poet himself is also Thomson, Levy melding together the idea of suicide with Thomson's fatal alcoholism. Here, for example, is a portion of her essay on Thomson:

. . . all through the work . . . we hear one note, one cry, muffled sometimes, but always there; a passionate hungry cry for life, for the things of this human, flesh and blood life; for love and praise, for mere sunlight and sun's warmth.

And here is its poetic rendition:

Out on you! Resign'd?
I'm not resign'd, not patient, not school'd in
To take my starveling's portion and pretend
I'm grateful for it. I want all, all, all;
I've appetite for all. I want the best:
Love, beauty, sunlight, nameless joy of life.

Levy also offers her first strong social criticism in this poem, suggesting her contact at this time with more radical thinkers in London; the unfair distribution of the world's goods is offered as the primary reason for the poet's despair: "One man gets meat for two, / The while another hungers." This is certainly not one of Levy's better efforts, but within the joint contexts of the life, poetry, and sad death of Thomson on the one hand, and Victorian optimism on the other, it does achieve a certain dramatic power.[25]

"Sokratics in the Strand" revisits the same scene, a depressed poet whose entire conversation is about suicide; in this instance, his audience is a successful friend (an attorney) whose optimism and good health only depress the poet further. What makes the story of particular interest, however, is that its tone is ultimately closer to that of **"Between Two Stools"** than to that of Levy's previous writings on suicide and poetic despair. That is to say, Levy here once again holds an ironic

mirror to her own most deeply held visions, exorcising what she perhaps feared were affectations of pain and anguish rather than the "thing itself." Horace, her protagonist, is, after all, a bit of a poseur, a point she rather unnecessarily underscores in her intrusive conclusion:

The circumstances of poor Horace's death are, by now, too well-known to need recital. Opinions differed, as we know, on the subject, but my own belief is, that however much his mode of life may have tended to hasten it, he did nothing by any individual act to bring about the final catastrophe. Poets, and those afflicted with the so-called "poetic temperament," although constantly contemplating it, rarely commit suicide; they have too much imagination.

It is Levy's capacity to approach the same issue from a variety of often conflicting and contradictory perspectives that seems to me to elevate her achievement above the commonplace. And, needless to say, her own suicide provides especial poignancy to this passage, written only five years before the event.

Other poems from *A Minor Poet* include **"Sinfonia Eroica,"** a skillful lyrical play of the senses of sound and sight as strains of concert music intertwine themselves with the lover's observation of "Sylvia" in the audience:

Then back you lean'd your head, and I could
   note
The upward outline of your perfect throat; . . .
      And I knew
Not which was sound, and which, O Love,
   was you.

This is beautifully rendered, with even a slight foreshadowing of Yeats, but it is also marred by five intervening lines that I here omit. Still, it is one of Levy's most carefully conceived poems.

Three of the poems from *A Minor Poet* are translations, one from Heine and two from Nikolaus Lenau (1802-1850), perhaps Austria's greatest lyric poet and a partaker of the tradition of *Weltschmerz*, in which Heine and Leopardi were the most successful voices. The rhymed quatrain becomes a favorite form for Levy and is used in all three poems with quiet effectiveness. Translation is perhaps always a good discipline for poets, but in Levy's case it seems to bring forth some of her best, most disciplined poetry. In **"A Farewell,"** for example, she changes the setting to Cambridge ("Sweetest of all towns") and her own leave-taking, but the poem is carefully controlled by rhyme, parallelism, the short line, and repetition; the sublime simplicity and ironic conclusion are reminiscent of Heine, and Levy skillfully captures much of his complex tone.[26]

Also in *A Minor Poet* is her **"Medea, a Fragment of Drama after Euripides."** Although Lask praises the work highly ("Amy Levy," pp. 174-75), and at least one modern reader, Isobel Armstrong, singles it out for comment, it does not seem to me to rise much beyond an exercise and I have not included it. Armstrong's comment is perhaps worth recording, however: "Every poet I mention here," she writes, "deserves a modern edition of her work—Adelaide Anne Proctor, Dora Greenwell, Jean Ingelow, Augusta Webster, Mathilde Blind, Amy Levy. . . . Levy deconstructs feminine roles . . . in poems such as 'Medea' (1884), where Medea's fury and destructiveness questions [sic] conventional paradigms."[27] There will come a time, I hope, when interest in Levy demands a complete edition of her poetry and prose; when that occurs, the weaker works will be valued for the light they cast on the stronger and will not diminish the author's status. Now, however, it seems most important to establish Levy's claim for consideration, and I have tried to make her case by putting forward her best face. The anthologizer is always subject to criticism (and especially so when Alexander Pope is his favorite English poet), but I believe that Levy's poetic voice is very often too derivative and insubstantial to warrant reprinting until such time as every scrap and fragment belonging to her becomes of interest. Hence, the omission of **"Medea"** and some thirty other poems from the present collection.

"Magdalen" is a return to dramatic monologue, but Levy's form changes to iambic tetrameter couplets (with a few variations). The speaker is a dying prostitute, Levy's only engagement with this common Victorian subject; as we have seen in her other work, the wish is for death, the lament for a world of meaningless pain, more directly stated, perhaps, than heretofore:

> For one thing is like one arrayed,
> And there is neither false nor true;
> But in a hideous masquerade
> All things dance on, the ages through.
> And good is evil, evil good;
> Nothing is known or understood
> Save only Pain. I have no faith
> In God or Devil, Life or Death.

What is compelling in this poem is the woman's lament that the man who "ruined" her knew the consequences; conversely, she argues, had she known that her love would destroy him she would have had the "strength" to turn away: "Ay, tho' my heart had crack'd with pain— / And never kiss'd your lips again." The same strength enables her to conclude with an assertion of her freedom from her lover "through all eternity."

The final poems selected from this volume are **"To Lallie"** and **"Epitaph (On a commonplace person who died in bed)."** The first is a humorous experiment with form, six-line stanzas (but presented as tercets) rhymed *aabaab;* the couplets are iambic tetrameter, the third and sixth lines are dimeters with feminine endings. The effect is similar to that achieved by Robert Burns in "To a Louse," although his six-line stanza rhymes *aaabab,* with the fourth and sixth lines being short. Once again, Levy seems bemused by her own existence:

> You look'd demure, but when you spoke
> You made a little, funny joke,
>   Yet half pathetic.
>
> Your gown was grey, I recollect,
> I think you patronized the sect
>   They call "æsthetic."

Given the sadness of most of Levy's poetry, this little *jeu d'esprit* is all the more welcome in her canon.

"Epitaph," on the other hand, returns us to the more recognizable Levy: "This is the end of him, here he lies: / The dust in his throat, the worm in his eyes, / The mould in his mouth, the turf on his breast; / This is the end of him, this is best." It recalls **"A Minor Poet"** both in tone and in the theme of despair over life's unfairness; recognizing this, perhaps, Levy makes it the final poem of the collection.[28]

One additional work appeared in 1884, an essay in *Temple Bar,* **"The New School of American Fiction,"** which attacks, with wonderful abandon, Henry James and his "school." As with Johnson's attack on *Lycidas,* one might wish it had not been written, and yet one also delights in the iconoclasm of it all:

> what may fairly be complained of is that intense self-consciousness, that offensive attitude of critic and observer, above all that aggressive contemplation of the primrose [Dr. Johnson indeed!] which pervades all his work. He never leaves us alone for an instant; he is forever labelling, explaining, writing; in vulgar phrase, he is too clever by half.

In contrast, Levy offers Thackeray: "Might not a novel of Thackeray's and a story of Mr. James' be respectively compared to a painting of Rembrandt's and a study of Mr. Alma Tadema's?" This is patently unfair, but her dismissal of Howells strikes me as at least worth entertaining: "Mr. Howells is a person of considerable shrewdness and some humour, who has taken to writing novels; he believes moreover that there is one infallible recipe for novel-making, and that he and Mr. James and M. Daudet have got hold of it." And in her final comments, she strikes several telling chords, not the least because her formulations will come to haunt her own novel-writing. There can be no question but that she understands quite fully what James was doing; she simply disagrees with the aim: "Some of us take a certain melancholy pleasure in reflecting that we live in a morbid and complex age; but do the most complex of us sit tense, weighing our neighbour's turn of head, noting the minute changes in his complexion?" Or again, she exhibits a fine turn of phrase, a critical sense of the jugular: "For all their cosmopolitanism, it is an eminently provincial note which the new musicians have struck." Surely this is the only time that Henry James has ever been accused of provincialism, but what a clever charge against him, especially if one is seeking to draw blood.[29] And finally, her conclusion:

> Shall we be allowed, without exciting ridicule, to say that what is wanting to these novels is a touch of the infinite? For all the fragmentary endings, they are so terribly finite. And in this finiteness lies the germ of decay. This is the heaviest charge we make against the new literature; it is a literature of decay.

This is, I suggest, a profound insight, not merely into Henry James, but into all of modern literature, which so often confuses wholeness with closure. The difficulty, of course, is the attempt in a secular, finite-laden age to introduce even "a touch of the infinite"; almost needless to say, it is a trap Levy herself will never quite be able to negotiate. Finally, and I hope I am not belaboring the point, let us keep in mind that this criticism of Henry James was written by a person twenty-three years old, one who, moreover, was unable—being a woman—to receive a degree from Cambridge University.[30]

After this record of publication, one almost breathes a sigh of relief that 1885 was by and large a dry year.[31] However, in 1886 Levy took a somewhat new direction, a series of essays in *The Jewish Chronicle,* the primary weekly newspaper for Britain's sixty thousand Jews. Her first essay, indicating that she was abroad perhaps for much of 1885 and the beginning of 1886, was **"The Ghetto at Florence,"** a touching though understated account of awakening to her Jewish heritage: "We ourselves, it is to be feared, are not very good Jews; is it by way of 'judgment' that the throng of tribal ghosts haunts us so persistently tonight?" Lask identifies other impressions from Italy in the 30 April and 28 May issues;[32] and in the 4 June issue **"The Jew in Fiction"** appeared. Despite its interesting title, I have not included it in this volume; it makes only one significant point, to be repeated in *Reuben Sachs,* that Eliot's presentation of Jews in *Daniel Deronda* is not as positive as Jews (and Christians) wanted to believe:

> . . . which of us will not acknowledge with a sigh, that the noble spirit which conceived Mirah, Daniel and Ezra, was more royal than the king? It was, alas! no picture of Jewish contemporary life, that of the little group of enthusiasts, with their yearnings

after the Holy Land. . . . As a novel treating of modern Jews, *Daniel Deronda* cannot be regarded as a success; although every Jew must be touched by, and feel grateful for the spirit which breathes throughout the book.

> There has been no serious attempt at serious treatment of the subject; at grappling in its entirety with the complex problem of Jewish life and Jewish character. The Jew, as we know him today, with his curious mingling of diametrically opposed qualities; his surprising virtues and no less surprising vices; leading his eager, intricate life; living, moving, and having his being both within and without the tribal limits, this deeply interesting product of our civilisation has been found worthy of none but the most superficial observation.[33]

In *Reuben Sachs,* Levy picks up the same argument against Eliot, when a Christian convert to Judaism seems disappointed that the company is so "little like the people in *Daniel Deronda":*

> "Did he expect," cried Esther, "to see our boxes in the hall, ready packed and labelled *Palestine?"*

> "I have always been touched," said Leo, "at the immense good faith with which George Eliot carried out that elaborate misconception of hers."

Indeed, in *Reuben Sachs* one might suspect that Levy was trying to produce precisely the study of modern Jewish culture she calls for in the essay; from the point of view of her contemporary Jewish community she failed rather dismally.[34] Significantly enough, however, Israel Zangwill seems to have heard the call; his most recent biographer suggests that here and in her next piece for *The Jewish Chronicle,* on "Jewish Humour," she "laid out the program and themes [he] would attempt to implement six years later in *Children of the Ghetto.*"[35]

"Jewish Humour" offers several perceptive insights into a subject that was probably far more original in 1886 than it might appear today. Typically enough, Levy's primary example of "Jewish humour" is from literature, Heine in particular: "In general circles the mention of Jewish Humour is immediately followed by that of HEINE; nor is this a *non-sequitur.*" Her two-line illustration from his poetry ("Sun and moon and stars are laughing; / I am laughing too—and dying") does seem to reach to the heart of the phenomenon; interestingly, she melds the poet and the Jew together in "this tough persistence in joke-making under every conceivable circumstance; this blessed power of seeing the comic side of things, when a side by no means comic was insisting so forcibly on their notice." As I have tried to indicate about such stories as **"Between Two Stools"** and **"Sokratics in the Strand,"** this is the gesture that for me most defines Levy's own literary career.[36]

I have included one essay from *The Jewish Chronicle* that I have not elsewhere seen attributed to Levy, **"Middle-Class Jewish Women of To-Day,"** which appeared on 17 September 1886. It is signed simply "By a Jewess," but in tone, content, and diction the voice strikes me as Levy's. Whether actually by her or not, it casts valuable light on her fiction:

> In the very face of statistics, of the unanswerable logic of facts,[37] [the young Jewish woman] is taught to look upon marriage as the only satisfactory termination to her career. . . . If, in spite of all the parental efforts she fail, from want of money, or want of attractions, in obtaining a husband, her lot is a desperately unenviable one.

While one might argue that this was the condition of all Victorian women, Jew or Christian, the essay several times makes the point that while British society was changing, Jewish society was not: "It must be frankly acknowledged, that for all [his] anxiety to be to the fore on every occasion, the Jew is considerably behind the age in one very important respect." In that everything in this essay seems to us today an irrefutable picture of late-nineteenth-century Britain, it is perhaps worth noting that it was riposted one week later, with considerable vituperation, "By Another Jewess" (*The Jewish Chronicle*, 24 September 1886, p. 7), including the citing of Proverbs 31:10ff. If I am correct in assigning "Middle-Class Jewish Women" to Levy, it provided her an ample foretaste of what would happen when she resumed and broadened her attack in *Reuben Sachs*.[38]

The final essay from the *Chronicle*, which appeared on 5 November 1886, is **"Jewish Children,"** by a "Maiden Aunt." Levy makes an illuminating contrast between the stress in classical cultures on filial piety and in Jewish culture on the affection of parents for children, including Jacob, whom she impertinently labels "that most pathetic and most injudicious of fathers." The core of the essay, however, has to do with parents' ambitions for their children and the "delicate and elaborate" organism on which these ambitions are practiced. Levy returns again to the interrelationship she perceives between Jews and the urban experience: "the Jewish child, descendant of many city-bred ancestors . . . is apt to be a very complicated little bundle of nerves indeed"; and surely there is some consideration of her own health in her remark that the "rate of mental and nervous diseases among Jews is deplorably high." One might be tempted to read this essay as Levy's closest approach, except in her poetry, to self-revelation.

Lask calls 1887 a "barren year," but while Levy's appearance in print might have been minimal, her productivity was monumental; at year's end she would have only twenty-two more months to live, but in that span she published, at the least, three short novels, her largest collection of poetry (containing more than fifty new poems), more than a half-dozen short stories, and several essays. In many ways, this final period was Amy Levy's *annus mirabilis*.

Whether or not Levy was acquainted with Oscar Wilde before 1887 we do not know, but she contributed to the first issue of his new journal, *Woman's World* (1888), and Wilde continued to publish her material in 1889 and 1890. In the one surviving letter of his correspondence with her, he writes: "I hope you will send me another short story. I think your method as admirable as it is unique" (October 1887).[39] In the obituary notice already cited, he singles out several short stories for praise, including those reprinted here for the first time, **"Cohen of Trinity," "Wise in her Generation,"** and **"The Recent Telepathic Occurrence at the British Museum,"** about which he adds:

> This last is a good example of Miss Levy's extraordinary power of condensation. The story occupied only about a page of this magazine, and it gives the whole history of a wasted and misunderstood love. There is not so much as a name in it, but the relation of the man and woman stands out vivid as if we had known and watched its growth.[40]

Wilde published **"Wise in her Generation"** posthumously in 1890. It is Levy's clearest look at female cynicism, a product of the "marriage game" that seems to have engaged so many Victorian women, Jew and non-Jew alike. The bourgeois London society is clearly the one on which she had begun to focus with increasing hostility: "For it must be owned that we were that night a distinctly middle-class gathering, a great mixed mob of Londoners; no mere Belgravian birds of passage, but people whose interests and avocations lay well within the Great City." There is something so jaded, so exhausted, about the protagonist, Virginia Warwick, that one thinks more of the 1920s than the 1880s, of Scott or Zelda Fitzgerald, not a Victorian "authoress." Here, for example, is Virginia's dismissal of Sir Guy: "[he] is very strong on all social questions. He is also an Agnostic, and a Socialist of an advanced type. He regards the baronetcy conferred on his father, a benevolent mill-owner at Darlington, in the light of a burden and an indignity." And here she is on a woman's plight: "how often is woman doomed to ride pillion on a man's hobby-horse!" That the story's ending stuggles to return a modicum of the ideal to life seems to me the trap Levy never quite circumvents. Surely, however, Virginia's final thought, rejecting her previous endorsement of the "survival of the fittest or toughest," expresses a very special pain in the light of Levy's own life: "Better be unfit and perish, than survive at such a cost."

In contrast to her work for Wilde,[41] the stories published in *Temple Bar* in 1888 and 1889 are far more optimistic, "sentimental" if you will. **"Griselda,"** at some thirteen thousand words, is more than half the length of the separately published *Miss Meredith* (which first appeared, it should be noted, in magazine serial form); both involve the courtship of a governess and hence make rather self-conscious reference to the ur-story of the genre, *Jane Eyre*. One feels here, more than elsewhere perhaps, the limits not so much of Levy as of her audience; clearly she is generating material for which readers—and hence publishers—were willing to pay. Yet it may also be said that Levy is beginning to develop some distinction of style to accompany her clarity and exquisite observations— "Griselda," despite a modern reader's efforts to resist its appeal to the heart, proves quite effective as narrative.

"A Slip of the Pen," on the other hand, justifies itself by its clever little hinge, what we have now learned to call a "Freudian slip." Levy handles the occasion with understated Jamesian humor. One might be set to wondering just how many thousand stories similar to this were published for Victorian readers, but Levy is developing a stronger hand than many. Her transition between sections 3 and 4 of this story, for example, is certainly worthy of applause:

> Sick with shame, hot and cold with anguish, poor Ethel sat cowering in the great drawing-room like a guilty thing.

> 4.

> Ethel astonished her family at dinner that evening by enquiries as to the state of the female labour-market in New Zealand.

"A Slip of the Pen" is clearly a period-piece, but like the other examples of her short-story writing, it helps us to understand better the audience for her longer fiction—as, indeed, for all her writings. The stories also offer windows into aspects of her unknown life that we will perhaps never be able to approach otherwise.

This is certainly the case with "Cohen of Trinity," which appeared as the lead story in *The Gentleman's Magazine* for May 1889. Except for the major explosion of *Reuben Sachs*, it is Levy's only mature creative work in which she examines "Jewishness." That several of the characters appear in both works suggests a linkage in her own mind; and surely Cohen's fate, to write a book that meets with acclaim and then to take his own life, has something to do with Levy's own fate.

In a small way, one might profitably think of Cohen as the negative of Griselda; despite her conditions, her every word and action bespeak a secure sense of birth and position precisely in their unaffected simplicity;

Cohen, on the other hand, has manners that "were a distressing mixture of the *bourgeois* and the *canaille,* and a most unattractive lack of simplicity." One senses here the conflict I have mentioned earlier, what I take to be Levy's own private dilemma: unable to be "simply" happy or "simply" depressed, her happiness is always crossed by ambitions, her depression by the self-suspicion of posturing.[42] And as is so often the case with Levy, her character best defines himself by quoting poetry, in this instance from Browning's "Caliban upon Setebos":

>   icy fish,
> That longed to 'scape the rock-stream where
>   she lived,
> And thaw herself within the lukewarm waves,
> O' the lazy sea . . .
> Only she ever sickened, found repulse
> At the other kind of water not her life, [. . .]
> Flounced back from bliss she was not born to
>   breathe,
> And in her old bonds buried her despair,
> Hating and loving warmth alike.[43]

Surely this is self-analysis on Levy's part, generally of her life, specifically of the instinct for self-immolation that underlies many aspects of *Reuben Sachs*.

Before turning to that novel, however, it would be useful to say something about her first extended fiction, *The Romance of a Shop,* published by Unwin in October 1888.[44] Perhaps because it was so shortly overshadowed by *Reuben Sachs* and Levy's death, it has never received very much attention. In his obituary for Levy, Wilde calls it "bright and clever . . . full of sparkling touches," Garnett simply mentions its existence, and Lask is brusquely dismissive: "The writing is light and easy; the theme does not impress itself on the reader as convincing. It is original in conception, but otherwise the least interesting of Amy Levy's books" ("Amy Levy," pp. 179-80). Wagenknecht also seems quite uninterested in the work.

I would like to make some small claims for its value, and not merely as a historical artifact. Much is made of *Reuben Sachs* because the work caused a stir, particularly among Jewish readers (and when Levy is mentioned today it is most often in studies of Anglo-Jewish literature). If, however, we follow the lead of her poetry and short stories, we might sense and imbalance; and indeed, it is worth pointing out that *The Romance* is almost twice as long as *Reuben,* far and away Levy's most sustained effort. It seems possible that Levy's Jewishness has gotten in the way of a valid assessment of her achievements, most particularly as a feminist voice. Editorial decorum suggests that such arguments should not be made in the introduction to an edition of her works, where it can only sound like special pleading. Suffice it to say that even a cursory glance at a feminist study such as Elaine Showalter's *Sexual Anarchy* discloses ideological matrixes that seem to me obviously contained within Levy's **Romance;** for example:

> The 1880s and 1890s, in the words of the novelist George Gissing, were decades of "sexual anarchy," when all the laws that governed sexual identity and behavior seemed to be breaking down.

Or again:

> The 1880s were a turbulent decade in English history. The making of vast industrial fortunes was balanced by the organization of trade unions and the founding of the British Labour party. . . . Even while the age of imperialism was at its height, there were also fears of degeneration and collapse.

Or finally:

> In the 1880s . . . feminist reform legislation . . . began to dismantle England's time-honored patriarchal system. . . . Women also challenged the system of higher education, and their efforts to gain admission to university lectures at Oxford and Cambridge were met with strong opposition. . . . There were riots at Cambridge.[45]

It is perhaps not entirely fortuitous that Showalter is one of the very few modern feminist critics to call upon Levy to support her argument, citing Levy's most obscure work, "**A Ballad of Religion and Marriage,**" in which Levy "predicted a future in which the concept of universal marriage and domestic drudgery would decline along with religious faith" (Showalter, *Sexual Anarchy,* p. 26).[46]

One other critic who has approached Levy in this manner is Deborah Epstein Nord.[47] In her sustained and useful essay she explores Levy's association with the Men and Women's Club; with Beatrice Potter Webb, Margaret Harkness, Eleanor Marx, and Olive Schreiner; and with particular questions concerning women, marriage, and work, fundamental aspects of *The Romance*. Nord finds in the work an expression of Levy's "experience of marginality" and puts her finger on what I would agree is its primary achievement:

> *The Romance of a Shop* succeeds at conveying how difficult and yet how exhilarating it was to be women alone in London in the 1880s. Like the unprotected women imagined in Woolf's *The Pargiters,* another work that Levy's novel anticipates,[48] the Lorimer sisters are made so convincingly vulnerable that the oldest sister, Fanny, prudish and old-fashioned in her instincts, feels them to be as "removed from the advantages and disadvantages of gallantry as the withered hag who swept the crossing near Baker Street Station." ("Female Community," pp. 749-50)

Nord also honestly confronts what certainly most modern readers would see as the fault of the work:

> Levy's failure . . . is precisely that she does not know what to do with her independent, idiosyncratic heroines—particularly Gertrude—and opts for killing off the beautiful, "fallen" sister and marrying off the remaining ones. ("Female Community," pp. 750-51)

Nord sees the work deteriorating in its last third into a "cheap *Pride and Prejudice*," as the sisters seek and find their "proper mates"; she cannot justify this but does offer extenuation: "in part . . . [Levy] understands that independence is painful, precarious, and exhausting and . . . as a fledgling novelist, she shies away from writing the kind of book that will tell an uncomfortable truth" ("Female Community," p. 751).

With Showalter and Nord in mind, one can read, with far more appreciation for Levy's sensitivity to the "revolution" she is portraying, the scene in which Frank[49] engages the sisters to take photographs in his studio:

> Gertrude explained that they were quite prepared to undertake studio work. Frank briefly stated the precise nature of the work he had ready for them, and then ensued a pause.

> It was humiliating, it was ridiculous, but it was none the less true, that neither of these business-like young people liked first to make a definite suggestion for the inevitable visit to Frank's studio.

And hence, when Lucy and Frank leave the shop to cross the street to his studio, "a solemn young man and a sober young woman," we do begin to sense the real upheaval Levy is conveying, the drama of the social experiment, however muted her style and tone. Later, when Gertrude is called upon to defend herself, we can feel the march of history behind her simple expressions: "Aunt, how shall I say it for you to understand? We have taken life up from a different standpoint, begun it on different bases. We are poor people and we are learning to find out the pleasures of the poor, to approach happiness from another side."

Gertrude, who is "not a beautiful woman" although "a certain air of character and distinction" redeems her from a "charge of plainness," is the character with whom Levy most identifies (Gertrude is, in fact, a writer, her first accepted poem being "Lawn Tennis," which Levy republished in her final collection, *A London Plane-Tree, and Other Verse*). Nord makes much the same point, citing Levy and Gertrude's shared interest in tormented women: Xantippe and Medea in Levy's case; Charlotte Corday (the subject of her rejected play) and Cassandra, with whom she often compares herself, in Gertrude's. However, the parallel ought not be pushed too far. Levy has an interesting capacity to sink herself into several roles, often conflicting ones, in her fiction. No better example can be offered than her use of the tag "the world's a beast, and I hate it!": in *The Romance* it is given to a minor character, Conny (a pleasant enough portrait of a family friend who need not work for her money); in "**Cohen of Trinity**" it is Cohen's "battle-cry."[50] In both instances, one senses a sentiment often on Levy's own mind but also a self-conscious wavering of attitude about such despair.[51]

The last third of the work, which Nord so strongly deplores, does have certain strengths. No matter how much one might wish for a novel that does not "marry off" its women, *something* must be done to redefine male-female relationships in a book redefining women's role in society. Gertrude's recognition of this is perfectly reasonable, to my mind:

> Heaven forbid that her sisterly solicitude should lead her to question the "intentions" of every man who came near them; a hideous feminine practice abhorrent to her very soul. Yet, their own position, Gertrude felt, was a peculiar one, and she could not but be aware of the dangers inseparable from the freedom which they enjoyed; dangers which are the price to be paid for all close intimacy between young men and women.

Nord's complaint is that of an academic; Gertrude's (Levy's) position, that of a proletarian, one aware that the working world is not a college classroom. It is, I believe, this awareness that drives the last third of *The Romance,* as Levy studies the effect of work on the other roles a woman might be required to undertake in the course of her life. The sense of "labor" is very powerful in the closing pages of the book, whether the labor is of the lover, the mother (Lucy's maternalism vis-á-vis Frank), the sister (Gertrude's "rescue" of Phyllis), or the shopkeeper; all are workers: "To do and do and do; that is all that remains to one in a world where thinking, for all save a few chosen beings, must surely mean madness." The consistent appearance of such thoughts, even when they accompany the usual pairings of romance and romantic comedy, raises *The Romance of a Shop* (the paradox of which is embedded in its title) to a higher level.

It would perhaps be best to discuss *Miss Meredith* here, for although it was published after *Reuben Sachs,* it is certainly closer in concept to *The Romance of a Shop,* and one is tempted to guess that it was indeed an earlier composition. It first appeared in a serialized form in *The British Weekly,* which started publication in November 1886 and reached a circulation of one hundred thousand within the decade.[52] In 1887, the magazine serialized a novel by Annie S. Swan; in 1888, Ellen Fowler's *Concerning Isabel Carnaby;* and from 19 April to 28 June 1889, Levy's *Miss Meredith.* As was the publisher's practice, the work, really a novella of slightly more than

twenty thousand words, was then issued in book form; an undated edition (but presumably 1889 or 1890) was published in Montreal by John Lovell and Son.

Unfortunately, Nord seems unaware of the existence of *Miss Meredith,* referring to Levy's "two novels," and Wagenknecht is content with a one-page summary of its plot. Lask, however, is quite enthusiastic in her evaluation, calling it a "perfect gem, a charming tale, slight and simply told. . . . The theme is that of *Jane Eyre,* with the difference of a peaceful calm spring day . . . compared with a summer storm" ("Amy Levy," p. 184). The greatest accolades, however, are found in Harry Quilter's "Amy Levy: A Reminiscence and a Criticism." Quilter was an art critic and editor of the *Universal Review,* archetypally late Victorian, perhaps, but fascinating in his interweaving of literature and art criticism:

> [*Miss Meredith* is] good, delicate, sincere, artistic work—marked with strong originality, and full of nascent knowledge, and perception which was rather hidden than displayed. . . . Throughout, the work is slight, but the slightness is that of intention, not of laziness nor incompetence. . . . To write in such a [detailed] manner . . . and yet to preserve the more ideal portion of the story, and render it in no way trivial or commonplace, denotes very high art, and is equivalent in fiction to such work as that of [Josef] Israels in painting—work which is apparently homely in subject, and simple in execution, but yet containing many elements of beauty and pathos, and really the result, from a technical point of view, of a complete mastery over its material and its method.[53]

I quote Quilter at some length because I believe his is the sort of commentary Levy would have liked to hear about her work; that is, it provides a good indication of the precepts and values by which Levy would have judged herself.

It is difficult to be quite so enthusiastic one hundred years later, but as with *The Romance of a Shop, Miss Meredith* is a book well worth examining, particularly as a reflection of late-nineteenth-century European culture. The most repeated word in the work is, I suspect, *enervation* and its various forms. While perhaps a reflection of Levy's own condition, this emphasis seems to suggest a certain cultural exhaustion as well—and indeed, the only energy in the work is provided by Andrea, the younger son who has declared his independence from Italian nobility by going off to America. The narrator, Elsie Meredith, is a plain, *middle* sister who sees in that position an emblem of her self-confessed "mediocrity"; since she leaves her family, she leaves out of her narrative whatever energy her more "talented" sisters might possess. And while we might want to compare Elsie Meredith to Jane Eyre, her own view of the matter completely blocks us: "I have always considered Mr.

Rochester the most unpleasant person that ever a woman made herself miserable over." Shakespeare's Rosalind is more to her liking: "men have died from time to time, and worms have eaten them, but not for love."[54]

And yet Elsie does undertake the governess role, does travel on her own to Pisa, does respond to the sunlight of Italy. The transition from enervation to strength, from chill to warmth, from "mediocrity" to passion is the substance of this short tale, and if it lacks, as it surely does, the profundity of Henry James on the same themes, it is nevertheless recognizably his arena. What Levy can add is a feminist perspective, as, for example, in her description of the English associations of Pisa:

> Here Shelley came with his wife and the Williams', and here it was that they made acquaintance with Emilia Viviani. . . . Byron had a palace all to himself. . . . Leigh Hunt lingered here . . . and Landor. . . . Claire Clairmont, that unfortunate mortal, who where'er she came brought calamity, vibrated discontentedly between here and Florence, and it seemed that sometimes I saw her, a little, unhappy, self-conscious ghost, looking from the upper windows of Shelley's palace.
>
> And here, too, after the storm and the shipwreck in which their lives' happiness had gone down, came those two forlorn women, Mary Shelley and Jane Williams.

There is a pleasant emphasis here on the women of Romanticism that perhaps balances the self-indulgence of the passage. At the same time, there is, I think, an identification with them that Levy perceives as "enervating": "I was not unhappy, but I grew thin and pale, and was developing a hitherto unknown mood of dreamy introspection."

The clash of class values toward the end of *Miss Meredith,* and indeed the entire romance between Elsie and Andrea, are dealt with in a rushed manner that suggests Levy lost interest in her subject. Part of the problem is that she shifts the responsibility for recognition and understanding from Elsie to the Brogi family: "You must forgive us if we are slow to understand the new spirit of radicalism which, it seems, is the spirit of the times." And in part, the problem is Levy's own cautious surrender to a conservative resolution; that Elsie is packing her bags in the face of the family's opposition strikes me as an awkward failure to bring her character into the realm of awareness that is necessary if we are to take pleasure in her narrative.

The telling of *Miss Meredith* reenacts in many ways the struggle between convention and difference that is the story's subject; ultimately the social and literary conventions under which Levy was trying to earn her wages in late Victorian England triumphed.

That cannot be said about the novel for which she is most noted, *Reuben Sachs*, published at the very end of 1888.[55] With George Eliot's patronizing attitude still heavy on her mind, Levy sets out to draw a "realistic" portrayal of the Jews she knew—the upper-middle-class Anglo-Jews who had escaped the East End and were making their way into every walk of English society. For Oscar Wilde, the result was to be praised for its "directness, its uncompromising truth, its depth of feeling . . ."; and he goes on to suggest that its "strong undertone of moral earnestness . . . prevents the satiric touches from degenerating into mere malice."[56] Contemporary Jewish readers saw it quite differently, and "malice" was for them the mildest of epithets. And years later, the portraits in *Reuben Sachs* cannot convince many readers that Eliot's condescensions[57] are not more palatable than Levy's stereotypes. Writing almost forty years after the book appeared, Lask is still obviously uncomfortable:

> It will be remembered that in her article ["The Jew in Fiction"] . . . she had regretted that "there had been no serious attempt at serious treatment of . . . Jewish life and Jewish character." Amy Levy sought to grapple with it, but succeeded only in grappling with one portion of Jewry—that of Kensington and Bayswater Jewry, who in their own material success had ceased to care for the spiritual welfare, or even the material welfare, of their less fortunate brethren. It is matter for the deepest regret that she did not know that section of Jewry which, despite its worldly poverty, was imbued then as now with the ideals of Judaism that make every thinking Jew proud of his spiritual heritage. ("Amy Levy," p. 180)

What is interesting in this is that Lask reveals a way of thinking about Jewishness that probably was not available to Levy, namely, that the eastern European Jews represented a spirituality against which the social critic could measure the perversities of assimilated Jews. While the migration of these Jews was getting under way in the 1880s, it does not play a role in *Reuben Sachs,* as it would, for example, in Zangwill's fictions just a few years later.[58] At most, Levy might observe a nascent fear among Anglo-Jews that their hard-won gains in British society would be affected by a deluge of the "unwashed"; but even that feeling was by and large masked in the 1880s by charity, by resettlement projects, and simply by the as yet small number of immigrants. Hence, Levy had no "Jewish" norm by which to alleviate her satire of Anglo-Jews; her norms are all external to them, having to do with her own political and social ideas of secular justice, her own idealistic value system, her own pain at her inability to escape the promptings of ambition and success, which, I believe, she found the hallmarks of her own "Jewish" life.

One hundred years after publication, some parts of *Reuben Sachs* still rankle. Wagenknecht, for example, is sensitive to one aspect of the work for which I have already tried to provide some context, Levy's obsession with physical appearance:

> One curious aspect of [her] portrayal of Reuben Sachs relates to his physical make-up. He was "of middle height and slender build. He wore good clothes, but they could not disguise the fact that his figure was bad, and his movements awkward; unmistakably the figure and movements of a Jew." And if we blink at this; we shall find as we read on that it is not accidental, for elsewhere his creator generalizes about "the ill-made sons and daughters of Shem." This was evidently a settled conviction of hers.[59]

What is actually Levy's settled conviction is the distinctiveness of the Jews as a "race," a term she and her contemporaries used freely, without any foreknowledge of what some in the twentieth century would make of the usage. One of the most interesting discussions of the novel occurs between Leo (who usually speaks for Levy) and Reuben, whose words, especially when grandiloquent, must be taken with caution:

> "There is one good thing," cried Leo, taking a fresh start, "and that is the inevitability—at least as regards us English Jews—of our disintegration; of our absorption by the people of the country. . . . You and I sitting here, self-conscious, discussing our own race-attributes, race-position—are we not as sure a token of what is to come as anything well could be?"

> "Yours is a sweeping theory," said Reuben. . . . "It may be a weakness on my part, but I am exceedingly found of my people. If we are to die as a race, we shall die harder than you think. . . . Jew will gravitate to Jew, though each may call himself by another name."

Reuben demonstrates in his relationship with Judith the hollowness and hypocrisy of his "idealism" here; while, interestingly enough, we are told that Leo will, as he grows older, find more to admire in his Jewishness.[60] As with any good writer, Levy explores not her convictions but her uncertainties.[61]

Perhaps the most enthusiastic modern evaluation of the work is Bryan Cheyette's, who believes it "transformed the Victorian Anglo-Jewish novel," stimulating a "dozen popular Anglo-Jewish novels of 'revolt' over a twenty-year period. . . ." In particular, Cheyette believes it is a mistake to dismiss Levy as "bigoted,"[62] quoting Zangwill in her defense: "'She was accused, of course, of fouling her own nest; whereas what she had really done was to point out that the nest was fouled and must be cleaned out.'"[63] Both he and Nord make a similar point, namely, that Levy's criticism of the bourgeois Jewish society was perhaps as much the result of her political associations as of any religious feelings; as Nord remarks, "That Eleanor Marx translated the novel is not surprising, for its indictment of upper bourgeois life—in this case, Jewish life—is scathing" ("Female Community," pp. 751-52). And Nord goes on to suggest the strong feminist orientation of the work as its interest shifts from Reuben to Judith:

> From the moment of Reuben's rejection of Judith it is her consciousness that dominates the narrative. It is as if Levy ceases to throw her voice, as she had done in so many of her poems, and allows herself to imagine without disguise the chilling position of the unmarried woman cornered into lifelong celibacy or loveless marriage. . . . The aspirations of middle-class manhood and womanhood alike have been utterly thwarted. ("Female Community," p. 752)

Surely this is a more useful reading of *Reuben Sachs* than one that condemns its author as self-loathing or anti-Semitic.

The work itself, it might be noted, is subtitled "A Sketch," and in many ways it is just that; thirty-three thousand words are not sufficient to develop the family saga that one seems headed into when in the opening pages we are introduced to three generations and five different families. What they have in common is kinship in the Sachs family (through birth or marriage), the city of London, and a variety of unpleasant characteristics. As in "Jewish Children," Levy makes much of the urban environment as a cause of certain "Jewish" tendencies; almost all the women are "sallow," two of the men are mentally damaged (Kohnthal and Ernest Sachs),[64] and Reuben himself has just returned from a time abroad to treat "a case of over-work, of over-strain, of nervous break-down." Levy's observant eye is everywhere apparent in these opening pages, as is a certain cruelty of observation, a clear desire to distance herself from her creations. This is especially true of Reuben, the darling of his family and the obvious romantic interest of her heroine; for Levy, he holds little charm: "[His] was a pleasant voice; to a fine ear, unmistakably the voice of a Jew . . ."; and again, "unmistakably the figure and movements of a Jew"; and a third time, "And his features, without presenting any marked national trait, bespoke no less clearly his Semitic origin." What makes all this negative from Levy's perspective is that Reuben's public efforts and private ambitions all seem terribly bent toward assimilation, a denying of his origins despite lip service to them.

Amidst all these distancing devices, and immediately after being told that one of the cousins, Esther Kohnthal, is "the biggest heiress and the ugliest woman in all Bayswater," we are introduced to Judith Quixano, "in the very prime of her youth and beauty; a tall, regal-looking creature, with an exquisite dark head . . . [and a] hue of perfect health." The name Quixano represents, in addition to perhaps a literary allusion, Judith's Sephardic (actually Marrano) background[65] as opposed to the Ashkenazi origins of the Sachses; it thus indicates a position of impoverished aristocracy in the Jewish community, the wealth and power of which had by and large been transferred to Anglo-Jews of central European origin by the middle of the nineteenth century. Interestingly, Judith seems poised in these early pages to serve as a measure of the crass values of those around her; it is a mark of Levy's growing maturity as a writer—and of the fact that her interests are feminist as well as ethnic—that she soon begins to distance herself from her heroine, who fails to achieve self-understanding until far too late:

> But the life, the position [as companion to her wealthy cousin, Rose], the atmosphere, though she knew it not, were repressive ones. This woman, with her beauty, her intelligence, her power of feeling, saw herself merely as one of a vast crowd of girls awaiting their promotion by marriage.

It is not that Levy lacks sympathy with Judith: "it is difficult to conceive a training, an existence, more curiously limited, more completely provincial than hers." The result is a "conservative" habit of mind, a "sensibleness," that leads her to place all her own aspirations in the hands of a man, Reuben, who proves unworthy and leaves her no satisfactory alternative outlet. It is this surrender to the male, especially its borderline condition between unconsciousness and hypocrisy, that Levy condemns. To be sure, Reuben is far more culpable than Judith; he fully recognizes the situation and finds that the dalliance between them "added a charm to existence of which he was in no haste to be rid."

One particularly valuable aspect of **Reuben Sachs** is its reconstruction of Anglo-Jewish life in the 1880s as a geographical, physical, social reality. The expansion of Jews into the Bayswater, Kensington Gardens, and Maida Vale sections is astutely chronicled, with the relative currency of each address established. Similarly, the division of the family on Yom Kippur into four different synagogues mirrors a reality of the time, especially the new Reformed synagogue in Upper Berkeley Street, with its "beautiful music, and other innovations."[66] Equally pertinent is the status of Samuel Sachs, the "unsuccessful member of his family," who is exiled to Maida Vale and a Polish wife; the healthiness of this wayward branch is in stark contrast to the pale enervations of success. Levy's attitude toward "the hundred and one tribal peculiarities which clung to them" is complex; on the one hand, she seems honestly to deplore their insularity: "They had been educated at Jewish schools, fed on Jewish food, brought

up on Jewish traditions and Jewish prejudice." In an age where barriers are everywhere coming down, they continue to live within the "tribal pale"; and the thirteen-year-old Bernard, with "inordinately thick lips and a disagreeable nasal twang," is clearly a distasteful portrait. But surely the snobbery of his young cousins is designed to evoke our sympathy; and indeed, the entire presentation leaves us divided in attitude—a reflection, I believe, of Levy's own divided mind.

The most powerful episode Levy ever created—one replete with promise for her future—is the climactic scene of **Reuben Sachs,** where Reuben symbolically "deflowers" Judith:

> There were some chrysanthemums like snowflakes in her bodice, scarcely showing against the white, and as she turned, Reuben bent towards her and laid his hand on them.

> "I am going to commit a theft," he said, and his low voice shook a little. Judith yielded, passive, rapt, as his fingers fumbled with the gold pin.

The scene anticipates, in its overt sexuality, the adjusting of the cattleyas in Marcel Proust's *Swann's Way,* and when Reuben drops and tramples the flowers upon hearing the cry of the "Special Edition," that Ronaldson is dead, we are provided in one dramatic image the remainder of the story.

Judith's solitary reflections upon the evening, a tradition of self-examination that perhaps begins with Austen's Emma Woodhouse and reaches its finest moments (*pace* Levy's criticisms) in Henry James, tell us much about the way in which Levy's feminist interests were overriding all other concerns. I do not want to use this introduction to push one particular critical interpretation, but surely we can agree that Levy confronts Judith with the meaninglessness for her of that "reality" she has allowed a patriarchal society to impose: "There is nothing more terrible, more tragic than this ignorance of a woman of her own nature, her own possibilities, her own passions." This is a cry of real anguish from the character and, perhaps, from Levy herself; that it is an insight Judith cannot live with is a measure of the radicalness of the perception, the revolution it entails, the unbearable disruption of a patterned life that perhaps no one embraces except by chance and accident. There is a cynical, pessimistic, hard edge to the conclusion of **Reuben Sachs,** but it is one that must always be measured against Levy's radical idealistic perspectives, her strong belief—or was it merely hope—that the world could not continue to worship "the great god Expediency."

As good as I believe **Reuben Sachs** to be, I am glad it was not Levy's last word. According to a flyleaf in **A London Plane-Tree,** she corrected proofs of her third slim volume of poetry "about a week before her death." The collection of fifty-one poems, almost all of them new lyrics, is prefaced with a couplet from Austin Dobson—"Mine is an urban Muse, and bound / By some strange law to paven ground"—and a dedicatory poem to Clementina Black, Levy's friend and some-time traveling companion. The poems are divided into four groups: **"A London Plane-Tree,"** in which Levy does indeed exercise an "urban Muse"; **"Love, Dreams, and Death,"** a series of love lyrics; **"Moods and Thoughts,"** in which the dominant themes seem to be exhaustion and suicide; and **"Odds and Ends,"** including three lyrics from what seems to have been a projected new volume of poetry, *The New Phaon,* and three additional poems, one of which, **"A Game of Lawn Tennis,"** had been published in ***The Romance of a Shop.*** In selecting poems from this volume I have tried to represent each section fairly; to avoid reprinting—as noted above—what I consider weak poems (significantly, I have chosen to reprint all six poems from the final section, evidence perhaps that Levy's fourth collection would have been even better than her third); and to represent some of the themes and concerns I have traced in the course of this introduction to her entire canon.

In one of her *London Society* pieces describing her pastoral vacation in Cornwall, Levy's persona writes to her London friend:

> I think I see you smile ironically as you read. 'And this Cockney is deceiving herself, and thinks to deceive me!' you are saying; 'this person, who has a confessed preference for chimney-tops to tree-tops, is pretending to enjoy herself in a rustic solitude in the heart of October.' No, dear, frankly, I am not playing at Wordsworth, not trying to 'get at one with nature,' as one used to in the old days, before one had come to recognize one's limits.[67]

And she concludes the piece with a sentence that speaks much about her life and writings: "Much as I admire the superior peace, simplicity, and beauty of a country life, I know that my own place is among the struggling crowd of dwellers in cities." Her "London" poems all speak to this role of the city in her own life, striking a note at once busy and crowded, yet sad and isolated. As with so many fellow poets of her day (perhaps Swinburne, most particularly), she seems fascinated by the interplay of formal restrictions and innovative subject matter; the rhymed quatrain with alternating tetrameter and trimeter lines is one of her favorite forms, but she also experiments with couplets, roundels, and ballades.[68] This last form seems to me to work especially well for her, providing lyric intensity to such unpoetic subjects as the omnibus and newspaper headlines (which, as evidenced in ***Reuben Sachs*** and elsewhere, was a subject that pressed itself upon her mind). Of her three roundels,[69] I have chosen **"Out of Town"**

as the most successful, with its strong scenic contrast between country and city. The last two poems selected from this section offer street scenes intertwined with the poet's vocation. I am particularly impressed by the sonnet **"London Poets,"** a return to the world of **"A Minor Poet"** and Levy's best statement of her perpetual blending of pain and self-irony: "The sorrow of their souls to them did seem / As real as mine to me, as permanent. / Today, it is the shadow of a dream, / The half-forgotten breath of breezes spent."[70]

Of Levy's love lyrics, **"On the Threshold"** and **"Borderland"** seem to me the most important, both in their linking of her declared subjects, "Love, Dreams, and Death," and in their carefully crafted obscurity. One might imagine the fictional Judith Quixano reciting them in relation to Reuben, but their lyric form and concealments strongly suggest personal involvement; the concluding passage of **"Threshold"** is particularly rife with mystery: "Death had not broken between us the old bar; / Nor torn from out my heart, the old, cold sense / Of your misprision and my impotence." The monosyllabic penultimate line and self-consciously awkward music of the last indicate to me Levy's increasing skills as a poet. They also indicate, as do all the poems in this section, the enormous influence of Heinrich Heine (and German lyric poetry more generally) on her lyricism. In such clear-voiced poems as **"The Birch-Tree at Loschwitz"** and **"At Dawn"** one hears the whisper of a new voice for Levy, the result of intertwining English and German traditions—Swinburne and Heine, to put it as reductively as possible. It is a voice I might just begin to associate with Emily Dickinson's, although fully aware that she is company Levy cannot often aspire to. Still, as one example, this stanza from **"A Reminiscence,"** set in Florence, seems comparable, especially in its not quite buried sexuality:

> Perseus; your picture in its frame;
> (How near they seem and yet how far!)
> The blaze of kindled logs; the flame
> Of tulips in a mighty jar.

A similar voice is heard in **"In the Mile End Road,"** although Wagenknecht (p. 84) is probably also correct in believing that he hears Thomas Hardy in its tight little drama.

The section **"Moods and Thoughts"** is headed with lines from the *Rubáiyát of Omar Khayyám:*

> I sent my Soul through the Invisible
> Some letter of that After-life to spell;
>   And by and by my Soul returned to me,
> And answered, "I Myself am heaven and
>   Hell."[71]

The poems here were difficult to select, so often does the voice seem to me to lapse into undisciplined (and hence unpoetic) lament and self-pity, but the section also contains several of her very best efforts. The confrontation with childhood in **"The Old House,"** a subject so easily rendered maudlin, is redeemed by several fine touches, including "that little ghost with eager eyes" and "leave her dreaming in the silent land."[72] Similarly, it would seem almost impossible to say anything fresh about charity, but **"Lohengrin"** manages to convert the Wagnerian scene quite imaginatively into a mandate:

> God, we have lost Thee with much
>   questioning.
> In vain we seek Thy trace by sea and land,
> And in Thine empty fanes where no men sing.
>   What shall we do through all the weary
>   days?
>   Thus wail we and lament. Our eyes we
>   raise,
> And, lo, our Brother with an outstretched
>   hand![73]

This is as close as Levy gets in her poetry to her social and political concerns, concerns we can infer from her associations and prose writings.

The most complex poem by far in this group is the sonnet **"To Vernon Lee."** In many ways it is Levy's most beautiful love poem, particularly the exchange of flowers in the first half of the sestet. That "Vernon Lee" was the penname for Violet Paget (1856-1935), a prolific author and scholar and, it would seem, a friend of Levy and possible companion on her travels, raises a question that has surrounded Levy ever since her death. Nord, commenting on Levy's use of the male voice in several of her love lyrics, adds in a footnote: "It is possible that Levy addressed such poems to women because she was a lesbian, but her conventional love lyrics do not at all give that impression. These poems seem rather like exercises, often spirited ones, in which she carries convention to the point of taking a male poet's voice. Rather than revealing intimate feeling, they seem instead to be burying it almost completely" ("Female Community," p. 748).[74] With the exception of this poem and **"To E.,"** I tend to agree with Nord's evaluation; these two, however, constitute a serious challenge to the usual "conventionality" of Levy's persona.

The poems I have chosen from Levy's **"Odds and Ends"** strike a quite different tone, from the rhythmic experimentation of **"The First Extra"** to the typically self-critical **"Philosophy,"** which replays, to some extent, her story **"Between Two Stools"**: "Dear Friend, you must not deem me light / If, as I lie and muse tonight, / I give a smile and not a sigh / To thoughts of our Philosophy."[75] And finally, she concludes with a quite mysterious poem, **"To E."** I have not identified "E.," who seems to have joined a threesome with the

poet, perhaps on her travels "three years gone by." The poem is highly structured into ten quatrains, each with a tetrameter triplet and a dimeter last line that rhymes with the dimeter of the next stanza—a typical Victorian experiment with sapphic form. The subject, as in **"Philosophy,"** is the intellectual life, the time of reading Faust and Schopenhauer,[76] although this time two women are in the company of a man. The nostalgic, elegiac mood of the poem is helped by echoes from eighteenth-century poets like Gray and Collins ("Thrice-favoured bard! to him alone / That green and snug retreat was shown, / Where to the vulgar herd unknown, / Our pens were plied."), but the tone changes abruptly in the last two stanzas, recalling the irony of **"Philosophy,"** and, even more, the conclusion of **"To Vernon Lee,"**[77] the division of life between "Hope unto you, and unto me Despair," with the male companion "beneath an alien sod." It is painfully sad to note that Levy's last lyric utterance consists of five ominous words:

>   on me
> The cloud descends.

Amy Levy died before *A London Plane-Tree* could be published. The speculations of her contemporaries—and indeed of later critics—about causes seem to me somewhat idle. Better to end with the voice of another of Levy's friends, a woman whose observations concerning the era's sense of itself have withstood the test of time far better than most. Beatrice Webb, a month after the event, made the following observation in her diary:

> The very demon of melancholy gripping me . . . my imagination fastening on Amy Levy's story, a brilliant young authoress of seven-and-twenty, in the heyday of success, who has chosen to die rather than stand up longer to live. We talk of courage to meet death; alas, in these terrible days of mental pressure it is courage to *live* we most lack, not courage to die.[78]

By her own wish, Amy Levy was cremated and her ashes interred at Balls Pond Cemetery; *The Jewish Chronicle* hastened to inform its readers that while the corpse was removed from the coffin for the cremation of Mr. Camillo Roth the year before, "in the case of Miss Levy the body remained in the coffin."[79]

Notes

[1] V.D. Lipman, *A History of the Jews in Britain since 1858* (Leicester: Leicester University Press, 1990), p. 31.

[2] *Woman's World* 3 (1890): 51-52.

[3] Christopher Ricks, ed., *The New Oxford Book of*

Victorian Verse (Oxford: Oxford University Press, 1987), pp. 529-30; I have included both poems in this collection. The original edition, edited by Arthur Quiller-Couch (Oxford: Clarendon Press, 1922), included three of Levy's poems, "A London Plane-Tree," "New Love, New Life," and "London Poets" (pp. 814-15); the first and last are included in this volume.

A particularly interesting reprinting of some Levy poems is Thomas B. Mosher's in *The Bibelot* (July 1901). Mosher published pamphlets of poetry and prose from "scarce editions and sources not generally known" every month for twenty years (1895-1914), eventually binding them together as annual volumes. The Levy entry includes fourteen poems and the elegy by Thomas Bailey Aldrich, reprinted on pages 53-54 of this volume. In his brief introductory comment, Mosher singles out "In the Mile End Road" as "a flawless little jewel: for the moment it lifts and leaves us at the level of greater singers." Among the authors reprinted along with Levy in 1901 were Henley, Symons, Morris, Swinburne, Dobson, and R. L. Stevenson—excellent company, indeed, for Amy Levy. One additional Levy poem, "A London Plane-Tree," was reprinted by Mosher in vol. 18 (1912) to introduce three essays by James Douglas.

[4] Bryan Cheyette, "From Apology to Revolt: Benjamin Farjeon, Amy Levy and the Post-Emancipation Anglo-Jewish Novel, 1880-1900," *Jewish Historical Studies* 29 (1988): 265, n.37, indicates that Virago Press was at that time planning a reprint edition of *Reuben Sachs.*

[5] Edward Wagenknecht, *Daughters of the Covenant: Portraits of Six Jewish Women* (Amherst: University of Massachusetts Press, 1983), pp. 55-93.

[6] *Encyclopedia of British Women Writers,* ed. Paul and June Schlueter (New York: Garland, 1988), pp. 294-95.

[7] Levy's translation was published as *Historic and Other Doubts; or, the Non-Existence of Napoleon Proved* (London: E. W. Allen, 1885). Garnett provided the introduction to the text (which, according to the title page, is edited by "Lily") and informed his readers that the translation "is the work of a young lady not unknown in literature." Levy's anonymity in this instance may be the result of some reluctance to associate herself publicly with what was, after all, a famous apology for revealed religion, but most specifically, for Christianity.

Garnett authored Levy's *DNB* entry, a very fine homage.

[8] Beth Zion Lask, "Amy Levy," *Transactions of the Jewish Historical Society of England* 11 (1928): 168. An unpublished Oxford University dissertation, "Amy Levy: The Woman and Her Writings" by S. A. Levy,

was completed in 1989; I have not been able to procure a copy, but one may assume it contains information not available to Lask.

[9] Obituary, *The Jewish Chronicle,* 13 September 1889, p. 6.

[10] A very useful brief survey of Levy's Jewish environment is provided by Vivian D. Lipman, "The Anglo-Jewish Community in Victorian Society," in *Studies in the Cultural Life of the Jews in England,* ed. Dov Noy and Issachar Ben-Ami (Jerusalem: Magnes Press, 1975), pp. 151-64. Perhaps the most important point is that this was a time of great solidification and advancement for the sixty thousand Jews of Britain (forty thousand in the London area), just prior to the disruptive wave of immigration from eastern Europe after the assassination of Czar Alexander II in March 1881.

[11] Philippa Levine, *Victorian Feminism: 1850-1900* (Tallahassee: Florida State University Press, 1987), pp. 27, 36, 55; Lipman, *History,* p. 30. Cf. Ralph Loewe, "Jewish Student Feeding Arrangements in Oxford and Cambridge," in *Studies in the Cultural Life of the Jews in England,* ed. Noy and Ben-Ami, pp. 168-69: "The sons (and very few daughters) of the older-established, upper-middle-class Anglo-Jewish families . . . began to go to the older universities [but] the number . . . probably never exceeded 25, and will often have been less." Certainly it was in the 1880s.

[12] In *Xantippe and Other Verse,* Levy dates this poem 1876, which means she may have written it (or at least a version of it) as early as age fifteen; it is a remarkably precocious performance.

[13] In his obituary for Levy, Oscar Wilde dates the composition of this poem as 1878.

[14] "Mrs. Pierrepoint: A Sketch in Two Parts," *Temple Bar* 59 (1880): 227. Levy also published in 1880 a story entitled "Euphemia," in two installments in *The Victoria Magazine.* It is an inartistic effort to tell the story of a young girl who outgrows her early stage career; that she is the illegitimate child of a Jewish mother seems irrelevant to the story. Perhaps the most significant aspect of the effort is the clue its epigraph (from Goethe) provides as to Levy's state of mind: "The common burdens of humanity, which we have all to bear, fall most heavily on those whose intellectual faculties are developed early."

[15] Richard Garnett calls the poem "in many respects her most powerful production, exhibiting a passionate rhetoric and a keen, piercing dialectic, exceedingly remarkable in so young a writer. It is . . . only short of complete success from its frequent reproduction of the manner of the Brownings" (*DNB*). One might, of course, consider that imitation the source of the poem's strength rather than a weakness.

Deborah Epstein Nord, "'Neither Pairs Nor Odd': Female Community in Late Nineteenth-Century London," *Signs* 15 (Summer 1990): 748-49, is one of the very few modern critics to comment on Levy's poetic achievement:

> Her most powerful expressions of female passion, resentment, and longing, however, are not to be found among her lyric verses but in her first [sic] volume of poems, *A Minor Poet,* in the dramatic modes she learned from Tennyson and the Brownings.
>
> "Xantippe" and "Medea," in which she inhabits the personae of two classical antiheroines, are Levy's most memorable and original poems and they are also, not coincidentally, her most feminist poems. In form they take after the works of her Victorian forefathers, but in perspective they look forward to the "Helen" and "Eurydice" of H.D.

One does wonder if Nord's view would be modified in any way had she realized that "Xantippe" (which Levy reprinted in *A Minor Poet*) was written when the author was in her teens. In this regard, Nord's desire to associate Levy and Medea as two alienated women seems to me particularly overwrought.

[16] One of the most sensitive tributes to Levy appears in an 1892 essay by the Shakespearean scholar E. K. Chambers, "Poetry and Pessimism," *The Westminster Review* 138 (1892): 366-76. He admits to being "fascinated" by her poetry: "the analysis . . . of modern pessimism can scarcely be dissociated from the study of that gifted writer whose work it permeates and informs." He singles out these lines from "Felo De Se" as the "keynote" for her poetic canon: "I am I—just a Pulse of Pain—I am I, that is all I know. / For Life, and the sickness of Life, and Death, and desire to die: / They have passed away like the smoke, here is nothing but Pain and I" (pp. 366, 370).

[17] After Levy's suicide many rumors about her family life naturally followed; her friend, Clementina Black (to whom Levy dedicated her last volume of poetry, *A London Plane-Tree, and Other Verse*), tried to put some of them to rest in *The Athenaeum,* 5 October 1889, p. 457. Among her several comments is this observation: "Her parents were justly proud of her; it was impossible to be more uniformly indulgent, more anxious to anticipate her every wish than they were." Black (1855-1923) was a novelist and labor organizer, and Levy's sometime traveling companion, probably in 1885.

[18] In addition to evidence of Heine's influence in the poems themselves, and direct statements of Levy's interest in him, it should be noted that *Xantippe and Other Verse* is headed by an epigraph from him: "Aus meinen grossen Schmerzen / Mach' ich die kleinen Lieder" ("Out of my own great woe / I make my little songs"; trans. E. B. Browning).

[19] "The Diary of a Plain Girl," *London Society* 44 (1883): 297. Cf. Levy's poem "A Wall Flower," pages 399-400 of this volume.

[20] *Woman's World* 2 (1889): 224: "It is so brightly and pleasantly written that the sudden introduction of a tragedy into it seems violent and unnecessary. It lacks the true tragic temper, and without this temper in literature all misfortunes and miseries seem somewhat mean and ordinary."

[21] Clementina Black (see above, n. 17) comments that Levy's "sister was with her on the afternoon before her death, and from her also she parted affectionately." Black is responding to rumors of a family quarrel as the cause of Levy's suicide.

[22] This was just two years after the firm was established, but already Unwin was gaining a reputation for publishing young writers at the start of their careers. One Unwin author at the time was Violet Paget, whose novel *Ottilie: An Eighteenth-Century Idyll* also appeared in 1883. Paget, who published under the name Vernon Lee, was obviously acquainted with Levy and is the subject, under that name, of one of her finest lyric efforts (see p. 398). Edward Garnett would join Unwin as its first reader in 1887, but whether he read for the firm at this time is not known. Olive Schreiner also published with Unwin, but not until 1890.

Unwin published a second edition of *A Minor Poet* in 1891, with the addition of a sonnet from *Xantippe and Other Verse* and the translation of a love poem by the German lyric poet Emanuel Geibel (1815-1884). As with *A London Plane-Tree,* published two years earlier, it was a volume in Unwin's "Cameo Series"; other volumes for 1891 included Ibsen's *The Lady from the Sea* and William Watson's *Wordsworth's Grave, and Other Poems.*

[23] Levy subtitles her essay on Thomson "A Minor Poet" and emphasizes the status in her second paragraph; it is a tribute to her critical acumen that she does not push a larger claim.

[24] Wagenknecht, *Daughters,* p. 70, suggests Swinburne.

[25] I have also included the prefatory poem of the collection, "To a Dead Poet," which is undoubtedly dedicated to Thomson. Levy had ended her Thomson essay with these words: "But his few friends speak of the genial and loving spirit; the wit, the chastity, the modesty and tenderness of the dead man. To us, who never saw his face nor touched his living hand, his image stands out large and clear, unutterably tragic: the image of a great mind and a great soul thwarted in their development by circumstance. . . ." The poem is a polished, elegant restatement of these sentiments.

[26] Levy published several additional translations in Katie (Lady) Magnus's *Jewish Portraits* (London: Routledge,

1888), and I have included two in this collection, both of Jehudah Halevi, the great medieval Jewish poet and philosopher. Levy worked with German translations rather than with the original Hebrew, but the result is two good poems, one a love lyric, the other a tribute to Jerusalem; there is a surprising intensity of feeling in the latter that I would not have associated with Levy, at least not vis-à-vis her Jewishness. Perhaps good translators can capture the intensity of their originals without the underlying emotion, but I rather suspect not.

27 Isobel Armstrong, "Victorian Poetry," in *Encyclopedia of Literature and Criticism,* ed. Martin Coyle et al. (London: Routledge, 1990), pp. 291-93. See also Nord, "Female Community," p. 749.

28 Wilde writes of this second collection that it has "no single superfluous line in it. The two epitaphs with which it closes [only the last is included in this volume], and the dedication 'to a dead poet' with which it opens, are perhaps the most perfect and complete things in it; these, if they stood alone, would be enough to mark their writer as a poet of no mean excellence" (*Woman's World* 3 [1890]: 52). Frankly, I am not able on many occasions to deduce Wilde's standards of approbation.

Chambers, "Poetry and Pessimism," p. 369, quotes "Epitaph" in full to illustrate the "life of brooding misery" and the "stored-up bitterness of the heart" that seems to force itself into expression in Levy's poetry.

29 Of course, James would also have smarted at the comparison with Sir Lawrence Alma-Tadema (1836-1912), whose immense popularity in midcentury was in serious decline by the 1880s; the general charge was a total lack of substance behind the breathtaking ornamentation and detail of his work. It was a most apt comparison from Levy's viewpoint and a good indication of her currency in the arts.

30 Wagenknecht, *Daughters,* p. 179, n.23, is far less sympathetic with this essay: "How any critic with Amy Levy's intelligence could see no more than this in James and Howells is beyond my understanding."

31 Lask, "Amy Levy," p. 175, notes one contribution to *London Society,* "Eastertide in Tunbridge Wells," a very lightweight effort. It should be noted, however, that Levy often published anonymously and that I have not made a concerted effort to survey the periodicals for additional work.

32 The datelines are Rome and Turin, respectively; I have some difficulty hearing Levy's voice in either piece—and both are unsigned. The newspaper obviously had many "foreign correspondents."

33 "The Jew in Fiction," *The Jewish Chronicle,* 4 June 1886, p. 13. For a similar view, a century later, of

Eliot's portrayal of Jews in *Deronda,* see Deborah Heller, "Jews and Women in George Eliot's *Daniel Deronda,*" in *Jewish Presences in English Literature,* ed. Derek Cohen and D. Heller (Montreal: McGill-Queens University Press, 1990), esp. pp. 86, 95.

34 Even her obituary writer for *The Jewish Chronicle* (13 September 1889) cannot leave her in peace: "she wrote a novel of Jewish life . . . in which she by no means flattered Jews. Curiously enough, Miss Levy herself wrote an article . . . on 'Jews in Fiction,' in which she expressed views that were scarcely carried out in her own 'Reuben Sachs'" (p. 6). Needless to say, this is a matter of opinion, but one might at least credit Levy with believing that she was offering a realistic depiction of the conflicts of assimilation (Jews to English society, but also, more generally, spiritual values to a secular era), rather than an assault on Anglo-Jewish life per se.

35 Joseph H. Udelson, *Dreamer of the Ghetto: The Life and Works of Israel Zangwill* (Tuscaloosa: University of Alabama Press, 1990), pp. 55-56. I would like here to acknowledge Udelson's brief discussion of Amy Levy, pp. 54-58, which roused my own interest in her writing and led directly to this present collection. As I suggested about Levy's essay on Thomson, criticism that makes us want to read the author under discussion seems to fulfill its function.

36 Equally perceptive in this fine essay is Levy's association of Jewish humor with the urban experience. And her discussion of the "Jewish" habit of judging by appearance casts considerable light on the issues I raised earlier about this theme in her writing.

37 Levy addresses a problem noted by many Victorian feminists and modern scholars alike, namely, the dearth of men in late nineteenth-century Britain. Cf. "Griselda" (reprinted in this collection), the title character of which laments "these days of surplus female population"; describes the dancers as "two dozen shortskirted, perfumed young women, a dozen warm young men. . . . In consequence of the overwhelming female majority, many of the young ladies are dancing with one another, making valiant efforts to look as if they enjoyed it"; and, in a third reference, praises her escort for supplying not only her wants at dinner but those of "half-a-dozen cavalierless young women."

38 It is also possible that an essay in the 3 September 1886 issue of *The Jewish Chronicle,* p. 9, "Some Aspects of Our Social Life," is also Levy's; it too casts important light on the world depicted in *Reuben Sachs.*

39 *The Letters of Oscar Wilde,* ed. Rupert Hart-Davis (New York: Harcourt, 1962), p. 208. The story he is referring to must be "The Recent Telepathic Occur-

rence at the British Museum."

40 *Woman's World* 3 (1890): 52. Wilde also praises "Eldorado at Islington," which he published in 1889 but which I found slight, and "Addenbrooke," which I was unable to locate.

41 Levy also published two essays in *Woman's World,* both in 1888. The first, "Women and Club Life," has been included because of its social and historical information and insight, especially its acute perception into the usefulness of "networking" and the need for women to establish a counterbalance to the dominant "old-boy network." Levy does not, of course, use these popular modern terms, but her discussion leaves no doubt that she has fully anticipated this particular contemporary feminist issue. Elaine Showalter, *Sexual Anarchy: Gender and Culture at the Fin de Siècle* (New York: Viking, 1990), quotes from the essay in her brief discussion of clubs, pp. 12-13, but only Levy's digressive lament that a men's club had voted to continue its exclusion of women—certainly not the main thrust of the essay. The second essay, "The Poetry of Christina Rossetti" (*Woman's World* 1 [1888]: 178-80), I decided, after some deliberation, not to include. It is an appreciative exercise rather than a study and adds nothing to our understanding of Rossetti or Levy—as opposed, for example, to her essay on Thomson, which adds to our understanding of both poet and commentator. The Victorian practice of criticism by adjectives (still in use among contemporary poets for patting the backs of fellow poets) is not very useful: e.g., "the quaint yet exquisite choice of words; the felicitous *naïveté,* more Italian than English; the delicate, unusual melody of the verse; the richness, almost to excess, of imagery" (p. 178). Suffice it to say that Levy recognized the talents of another woman poet—albeit with reticence: "of Christina Rossetti let it be said that if she is not great, at least, artistically speaking, she is good" (p. 180).

42 Late in the story, Cohen encounters the narrator, whose response is particularly telling: "'Do you know what success means?' he asked suddenly, and in the question I seemed to hear Cohen the *poseur,* always at the elbow of, and not always to be distinguished from, Cohen starknakedly revealed." And see also his comment a few lines later: "I was struck afresh by the man's insatiable demands, which looked at times like a passionate striving after perfection, yet went side by side with the crudest vanity, the most vulgar desire for recognition." I believe this is not necessarily an accurate portrayal of Levy's character but rather an indication of fears about herself and how she might appear to the world.

43 Lines 33-43. Levy drops several lines and slightly misquotes the passage, perhaps from memory (e.g., "waves" should read "brine" and "bonds" should read "bounds"). The entire poem provides an interesting gloss

not only to "Cohen of Trinity" but to Levy's own alienation as well.

44 My text is set from a copy published in Boston by Cupples and Hurd ("The Algonquin Press") in 1889. As far as I have been able to ascertain, Cupples and Hurd had an agreement with Unwin and simply reissued Unwin's text with a new title page.

45 Showalter, *Sexual Anarchy,* pp. 3, 4, 7. Perhaps her quotation from the presidential address of Dr. William Withers Moore to the British Medical Association in 1886 makes the point most clearly; educated women, he warned, would become "more or less sexless. . . . [Such women] have highly developed brains but most of them die young" (p. 40). One could, I am certain, assemble in short order an encyclopedia of such attitudes among Levy's contemporaries.

46 Twelve copies were printed "for private circulation," without date, publisher, or place of publication; the *British Library Catalogue* conjectures 1915.

47 Nord, "Female Community," pp. 733-54. Nord obviously worked closely with Showalter and shares many of the same materials.

48 Nord argues the influence of *The Romance* on Gissing's *The Odd Women,* although she cannot establish direct borrowings. Gissing did check out *Reuben Sachs* from the library (Nord, "Female Community," p. 748 and n. 48).

Woolf makes clear in *The Pargiters* (later, *The Years*) that young women of the 1880s "could not visit friends, walk in the park, or go to the theater unaccompanied. . . . Indeed, at the universities, women students were not permitted to attend lectures at the men's colleges unchaperoned . . ." (Showalter, *Sexual Anarchy,* p. 119). One might note that in "A Slip of the Pen" the heroine does walk by herself in Regents Park.

49 In a note, Nord informs us that the two illustrations in *A London Plane-Tree* are by J. Bernard Partridge, who "appears in . . . *Romance* . . . as the artist Frank Jermyn" ("Female Community," p. 748, n. 44). While the specificity of identification argues its validity, one still might wish that scholars had not lost the habit of documenting their assertions.

50 The sentence is borrowed from W. S. Gilbert's farce *Tom Cobb* (1875), from which Levy also borrows one of the epigraphs to "Sokratics in the Strand." The play is about a young man contemplating suicide, but only so far as Gilbert could reduce such contemplations to inanity.

51 There is also something of Cohen in the villain of *The Romance,* Sidney Darrell; Gertrude pierces "to the

second-rateness of the man and his art. Beneath his arrogance and air of assured success, she read the signs of an almost craven hunger for preeminence; of a morbid self-consciousness; and insatiable vanity." These are, I suspect, the dreadful fears of a driven "minor poet," Cohen or Darrell or Amy Levy.

52 See the entry for "Hodder and Stoughton, Ltd." (by Dorothy W. Collin) in *Dictionary of Literary Biography,* vol. 106, *British Literary Publishing Houses* (Detroit: Gale Research, 1991), pp. 143-44.

53 Harry Quilter, *Preferences in Art, Life, and Literature* (London: Swan Sonnenschein, 1892), pp. 139-40.

54 *As You Like It,* IV.i.106-8.

55 *Reuben Sachs* was published by Macmillan and Company, with a "second edition" (actually a second printing) appearing in July; in that printing, the first-edition date has been changed to "January 1889." Eleanor Marx translated *Reuben Sachs* into German; and it is the only one of Levy's works to be reprinted in this century (in 1973, by AMS Press).

56 *Woman's World* 3 (1890): 52.

57 One cannot help but suspect that Levy is satirizing Eliot in the figure of Bertie Lee-Harrison, the Christian convert to Judaism, who is agog with the "local colour" of the Jews, who "stares and wonders" but is "completely out of touch with these people," and who gives up "with considerable reluctance his plan of living in a tent" to celebrate the Feast of Tabernacles. Levy may be severe on her Jewish compatriots, but she is absolutely vicious toward Christian condescension.

58 One might almost feel certain that Zangwill's Esther Ansell in *Children of the Ghetto* (1892), who writes a novel "which castigates the double standards and insincerity of Anglican Judaism," is a reflection of Amy Levy.

59 Wagenknecht, *Daughters,* p. 87. He goes on to comment on Cohen's appearance, the "awkward, rapid gait, half slouch, half hobble," but interestingly avoids the most offensive description: "the full, prominent lips, full, prominent eyes, and the curved beak of the nose with its restless nostrils."

Harry Quilter, who was so favorably impressed by *Miss Meredith,* finds *Reuben Sachs* "a disappointing book" despite its "power and originality": "The divorce of sympathy between the author and the characters depicted, is complete and manifest, and is forced upon us at every turn in the narrative." He particularly condemns her habit

of setting down any unamiable peculiarity of one of her characters . . . as a tribal peculiarity or Jewish characteristic, or some similar phrase which drives home, as it were, against her own people, the general accusation, by means of the individual instance. Throughout the narrative is kept up this continual harping on the unamiable, vulgar or sordid traits of the Jewish race, till at last one feels inclined to say pettishly, "Why can't the woman leave her 'people' alone?. . . ." Not that the author's accusations . . . strike us as much exaggerated or unjust, but that so evidently she was not the right person to say them. (Quilter, *Preferences,* pp. 146-47)

Such criticism, from a "friend," suggests how steep a path Levy was trying to climb, both in portraying the Jewish community she knew and in believing that Eliot's approach was ultimately more damaging to the Jew than her own.

60 "The time was yet to come when he should acknowledge to himself the depth of tribal feeling, of love for his race, which lay at the root of his nature. At present he was aware of nothing but revolt against, almost of hatred of, a people who, as far as he could see, lived without ideals, and was given up body and soul to the pursuit of material advantage." Clearly Levy admires Leo, and perhaps assigns to him her own awakening; whether love had yet overcome hatred would be a matter of how we come to interpret *Reuben Sachs.*

61 A present-day Anglo-Jewish novelist, Brian Glanville, discovers a much different Levy behind the work: "*Reuben Sachs* . . . is a poor, stilted, self-conscious piece of work, full of the knowing self-congratulation of the 'educated' child of *nouveaux riches* parents. What interest it retains lies in the extraordinary similarity of the monied, Bayswater Jewish society it depicts . . . and their descendants in London today. There is the same ostentation, the same social intolerance, the same overt materialism, the same breach with Jewish traditions, uncompensated by a real identification with those of England" ("The Anglo-Jewish Writer," *Encounter* 14 [1960]: 63). Glanville seems a sad instance of an "angry young man" of one generation failing to recognize an "angry young woman" of another. To my mind, no description of Levy could be further from the truth than "self-congratulating."

62 In contrast to Linda Gertner Zatlin in *The Nineteenth-Century Anglo-Jewish Novel* (Boston: Twayne, 1981), p. 97. Zatlin suggests that Levy "foreshadows the quality of Jewish self-hatred . . . in which the accultured Jew is alienated from Judaism and Jewish society and may even identify with the oppressor" (pp. 104-5).

63 Cheyette, "From Apology to Revolt," p. 260.

64 Levy may also be making a charge of excessive inbreeding by these instances: "'There is always either a ne'er-do-weel or an idiot in every Jewish family!' Esther Kohnthal had remarked in one of her appalling bursts of candor."

[65] Judith's father, from a Portuguese family of doctors and scholars, "had been stranded high and dry by the tides of modern commercial competition" and is now a Casaubon, gathering materials "for a monograph on the Jews of Spain and Portugal" that we know will never be written. Although Levy defines him as "one of the pure spirits of this world," he plays no real part in the narrative and hence is, at best, a vague and indistinct hint of a Jewish measure by which to judge the faults of Levy's world.

[66] A useful discussion of Jewish neighborhoods and synagogues is to be found in Lipman, *History,* pp. 52-54; Levy brings his lists to life.

One is tempted to imagine that in the naming of Montague Cohen, Reuben's social-climbing brother-in-law, Levy satirized one of the most important of Victorian Jews, Samuel Montagu, whose original name, Montagu Samuel, somehow got reversed and remained permanently so by his choice; see Eugene C. Black, *The Social Politics of Anglo-Jewry, 1880-1920* (Oxford: Basil Blackwell, 1988), pp. 14-19.

[67] "Out of the world," *London Society* 49 (1886): 54-55. Levy goes on to describe a peaceful rustic scene and then asks, "but do you know what happened to me? I thought I heard a distant newsboy calling out Special Editions and terrible catastrophes!"

[68] The ballade (not a ballad, as Nord, "Female Community," p. 748, believes) is a lyric composed of three stanzas of eight or ten lines each and a concluding envoi. Each stanza ends with the same refrain, and only three or four rhymes are used in the entire poem. Dobson, Swinburne, and W. E. Henley all experimented with it, but Levy indicates she has in mind Andrew Lang's collection *Ballades in Blue China.*

[69] Levy is here imitating Swinburne, whose *A Century of Roundels* appeared in 1883. The eleven lines are divided into three stanzas rhyming *abaR bab abaR, R* being the refrain, repeating the first words of the poem.

[70] Wagenknecht, *Daughters,* pp. 64-69, discusses Levy's urban poetry with a strange fear of having to conclude that she was "unresponsive to the charms of nature." It seems to me, however, that some of her weakest writing is indeed just that in which she attempts to force a response to natural scenes; and she speaks to the issue with great insight, I think, in "Jewish Humour," when she reminds us how long it is since the Jew "gave up pasturing his flocks and 'took (perforce) to trade'; he hardly has left, when all is said, a drop of bucolic blood in his veins." In this regard, her urban poetry might be considered a contribution to Anglo-Jewish writing in a way that the bulk of her poetic effort is not. I do not, by the way, endorse her stereotype but only suggest she believed it.

[71] Stanza 66. The second section, "Love, Dreams, and Death," is headed by stanza 99: "Ah Love! could you and I with Him conspire / To grasp this sorry Scheme of Things entire, / Would not we shatter it to bits—and then / Re-mould it nearer to the Heart's Desire!" Wagenkencht labels it the "most disillusioned quatrain" in the *Rubáiyát* and an "essential clue" to Levy's own disappointed idealism (*Daughters,* p. 64).

Cf. Chambers, who speaks of the "pitiful mottoes from Omar Khayyám" and of each Levy poem that follows them being "a wail, only more penetrating for the artistic charm which makes of it a carven shrine for grief" ("Poetry and Pessimism," p. 370).

[72] Chambers, "Poetry and Pessimism," p. 371, quotes it in full, as "a striking little poem" that illustrates Levy's obsessive contrast "between what is and what might have been, between the aspiring idealism of the past and the sorry levels of the present."

[73] Levy seems to have enjoyed Wagner; as noted earlier, among Leo's books in *Reuben Sachs* is the score of *Parsifal.*

[74] For one aspect of contemporary gossip surrounding Levy's death, see Ruth First and Ann Scott, *Olive Schreiner* (New York: Schocken, 1980), p. 87; and Yvonne Kapp, *Eleanor Marx* (New York: Pantheon Books, 1976), 2:259-60.

[75] In a letter Olive Schreiner wrote immediately after Levy's suicide, she recounted her inability to raise Levy from depression: "her agony had gone past human help. The last thing I sent her was the 'Have Faith' page of [Edward Carpenter's] *Towards Democracy.* She wrote me back a little note, 'Thank you, it is very beautiful, but philosophy can't help me. I am too much shut in with the personal'" (*Letters,* ed. Richard Rive [Oxford: Oxford University Press, 1988], 1:157).

[76] They also read about the German-Jewish socialist Ferdinand Lassalle, but whether in Helene von Dönniges's biographical version or in George Meredith's novel *The Tragic Comedians* (1880), we cannot tell.

[77] The closeness between these two poems might suggest that the other woman in "To E." is indeed, Violet Paget. On the other hand, the one "E." we know among Levy's friends was Eleanor Marx, and she is equally possible.

[78] Quoted in Deborah Epstein Nord, *The Apprenticeship of Beatrice Webb* (Amherst: University of Massachusetts Press, 1985), p. 134.

[79] *The Jewish Chronicle,* 20 September 1889, p. 7.

Linda Hunt (essay date 1994)

SOURCE: "Amy Levy and the 'Jewish Novel': Representing Jewish Life in the Victorian Period," in *Studies in the Novel*, Vol. XXVI, No. 3, Fall, 1994, pp. 235-53.

[*In the following essay, Hunt examines Levy's novel* Reuben Sachs *as a critique of prevailing representations of Jewish life in Victorian literature.*]

In the last month of 1888 Macmillan brought out what was to become a controversial novel within the Jewish community on both sides of the Atlantic. Amy Levy, a twenty-seven-year-old Jewish woman who had already made something of a name for herself as a writer of poetry, non-fictional prose, and fiction, was the author of this book, **Reuben Sachs**. It was her first published work of fiction about Jewish life. The question of how to represent Jews in fiction had evidently been on her mind for a long time, for in 1886 Levy had published in the weekly *Jewish Chronicle* an article, **"The Jew in Fiction,"** in which she had criticized the treatment of Jewish characters by a number of different novelists.

In this article Levy takes jabs at Dickens' unpleasant Fagin but is no more pleased by his idealized Jew, Riah (in *Our Mutual Friend*); she reminds us that Thackeray too has Jewish characters who are entirely negative; and she speaks disparagingly of a now-forgotten novelist, a Mr. Baring-Gould, who, she charges, "follows the old Jew-baiting traditions" in his novel *Court Royal*. She dismisses Lord Beaconfield's (Disraeli's) idealized Jewish characters as unmemorable, and, with considerable emotion, complains that another novel of the day, L.L. Clifford's *Mrs. Keith's Crime* (1885), is "offensive" in its "condescending" depiction of Jewish people (a reading of this book reveals that its Jewish characters, while likeable, are minor and used only for comic relief).[1] What is perhaps surprising is that Amy Levy includes in her critique the Jews in George Eliot's "Jewish novel" *Daniel Deronda* (1876); Eliot's book had been hailed by most literary Jews of the time and many since, as a model for how to treat Jewish people in fiction.[2]

In **Reuben Sachs**, Levy followed up on her 1886 critique of George Eliot by explicitly satirizing the idealized depiction of Jews in *Daniel Deronda,* and, in doing so, rejected a way of representing Jewish life that had become one of the conventions for treating Jews available to the Victorian novelist, especially the Anglo-Jewish novelist. Dispensing with this convention allows her to raise the question of what it means to be a Jew and to probe the moral nature of the Anglo-Jewish community. At the same time, she uses George Eliot's last book to widen the significance of her own Jewish novel, and she relies on the resonance created by the intertextual relationship between the two books to make the novel accessible to the mostly gentile reading public. Moreover, as we shall see, Levy's dissatisfaction with George Eliot's approach to the representation of Jews in fiction, together with her criticisms of other novels with Jewish characters, may have led her to depart in **Reuben Sachs** from what is now often called "classic realism."

In **"The Jew in Fiction,"** Levy had called for a serious treatment of Jewish life and character. Like most literary critics today, she admires the impulse behind the idealized portraits of the important Jewish characters in Eliot's novel but finds them impossibly virtuous; therefore she asks rhetorically, "[W]hich of us will not acknowledge with a sigh, that the noble spirit which conceived Mirah, Daniel, and Ezra, was more royal than the king?"

Toward the end of her article Levy asserts, "No picture of English 19th century life could be considered complete without an adequate representation of the modern son of Shem." The point which emerges (albeit implicitly) is that the Jews are an intrinsic part of British society and must therefore be neither romanticized nor trivialized in British fiction. Seeing the Jews as thoroughly English although singular in many ways, she dismisses *Daniel Deronda* as "no picture of Jewish life, that of the little group of enthusiasts, with their yearnings after the Holy Land and dreams of a *separate nation*" (emphasis mine).[3]

George Eliot's saintly Jews are in tune with what British critic Bryan Cheyette calls the "apologetic" tradition of nineteenth-century fiction about Jews. He uses this term to refer to novels written by British Jews who, he explains, throughout the nineteenth century, particularly in the years preceding the appearance of **Reuben Sachs,** tended to write fiction in which Jewish characters were pictures of perfection. These Anglo-Jewish novelists first chose "to portray Jews as particularly moral in character so that they could be considered 'deserving' of emancipation"[4] (Jews, that is, of course, Jewish men, were emancipated—given full political rights—in 1859) and later created idealized portraits in order to show that England need not fear the flood of Eastern European Jewish immigrants coming to its shores.[5]

Cheyette gives Levy credit for transforming the Victorian Anglo-Jewish novel in the direction of "revolt" while acknowledging that Levy was not the only Anglo-Jewish writer to eschew apology in the late 1880's. He points out that Julia Frankau's *Dr. Phillips: A Maida Vale Idyll* (1887) offered "a negative discussion of Jewish 'realities'" and that Cicely Ullman Sidgewick's (Mrs. Andrew Dean's) *Isaac Eller's Money* (1889) "had an explicitly conversionist message" which concludes that Jews could only become "good citizens by marrying into the English upper classes." His description of *Dr. Phillips* does not convey the virulence of Frankau's portrait of Jewish life.[6]

As in *Isaac Eller's Money* (and in **Reuben Sachs,** as we will see), the Jewish community in *Dr. Phillips* is crude and materialistic, but Frankau's protagonist, a Jewish physician, is a monster who ends by experimenting with his patients, "maiming men and unsexing women." Because his qualities of character are explicitly linked to his "Hebraism," the novel is a demonizing fable which belongs in the long tradition of anti-Semitic writing.

The Jewish Chronicle lumped the work of Frankau, Sidgewick, and Levy together, complaining in its review of *Isaac Eller's Money* (the last of the three novels just mentioned to appear), that "the clever ill-natured fiction of Jewish life has now reached a high stage of development. Can nothing be said in favour of Jews that is not hard fact?" It is surprising—given that, among other things, Levy does not recommend the demise of the Jewish community—that the unsigned reviewer asserts that Sidgwick's novel is "less intentionally offensive" than **Reuben Sachs.**[7] In fact, in **Reuben Sachs** Levy paints a much more balanced picture of the life of her people than do the other two women writers under discussion. It is true that her Jews like money and things, and they are people who value, to an unhealthy degree, individualistic competition, yet she is attempting to do what her article, "The Jew in Fiction" had asked for: to represent the "Jew . . . with his curious mingling of diametrically opposed qualities, his surprising virtues and no less surprising vices."

There is no denying that the overall impression of life within the Anglo-Jewish community that one gets from this novel is not pretty. When the story opens, Reuben, a rising young lawyer with political ambitions, has just returned from the antipodes where he had gone to recover from a nervous breakdown. His father, we are told, died years before, and the narrator makes it clear that his death was premature since longevity runs in this family. In fact, as the various characters are introduced, the Jewish ones all being members of Reuben's extended family, we find that nearly all the men are defective, sick, or nervous. His brother, "a hopeless n'er-do-weel . . . had . . . been relegated to an obscure colony,"[8] and his cousin Esther's father is in a madhouse.

Ernest Leuniger, Reuben's cousin, is an important example: "[I]t would be unfair to say that he was an idiot. He was nervous, delicate; had a rooted aversion to society" (p. 204). He spends his time obsessively playing a game of solitaire, which involves a board, marbles, and a little glass ball. Near the end of the novel, he finally is triumphant at this game, the meaninglessness of which is signified by the condescension

of Judith, the female protagonist, who is "vaguely" kind but unimpressed by his success.

Even though the game is solitary, it symbolically represents the competitive individualism to which Reuben, and, to a lesser extent, nearly all of the male Jewish characters in this novel, dedicate their lives and to which Reuben ultimately sacrifices so much. Reuben betrays his love for his cousin Judith because his ambition requires that he marry a wealthy woman; the night after he rejects her "there was a withered, yellow look about him," and his mother thinks, "He is not well" (p. 264). By the novel's end, he is dead. Judith is told by Bertie Lee-Harrison, a convert to Judaism, "It seems that his heart was weak; he had been overdoing himself terribly, and cardiac disease was the immediate cause of his death—cardiac disease" (p. 290). The redundancy of Bertie's wording emphasizes the metaphoric significance of how Reuben died. In **Reuben Sachs,** the Jewish way of life, with the drive that it requires and its false values, takes a severe toll.

The Jewish women are ambitious in a different way, involved in a different form of competition: Judith sees "herself merely as one of a vast crowd of girls awaiting their promotion by marriage" (p. 209). Such marriages are not love matches; indeed, Judith's mother says quite frankly, "No girl likes her intended—at first" (p. 279). Conventional to the core, though passionately in love with Reuben, Judith obediently makes a socially-advantageous marriage to Bertie for whom she feels no love, and in the novel's last pages we are told "she knew now more clearly than before . . . the nature and extent of the wrong which had been perpetrated; which had been dealt her; which she in her turn had dealt herself and another person" (p. 288). The language here—the use of the passive voice, except when describing Judith's own behavior—emphasizes Judith's victimization while acknowledging she was not without agency.

The other women in the novel, Reuben's sister and his Aunt Ada, for example, do not, in fact, give the impression that their affection for their husbands has grown over time. His mother and aunt are described in such a way that their very appearance speaks of the price they have paid for material wealth: we read of Mrs. Sachs's "wide, yellow expanse of . . . face, with its unwholesome, yet undying air, lighted up by the twinkling diamonds on either side of it, looking agitated and alarmed" (p. 242) and of Aunt Ada's "dejected, untidy figure, with the load of diamonds on the fingers, the rich lace round neck and wrists, the crumpled gown of costly silk" (p. 279). Levy makes the ubiquitous diamonds worn by the matrons an emblem of their pathos, and she reinforces the sense that the female characters have little control over their lives by associating the women with a pattern of drug imagery: for instance, Judith in love is "like a hashish-eater" (p. 222); having lost Reuben, she has "the false calmness which narcotic drugs bestow" (p. 262); and Esther, one of the cousins, likes to say that "marriage was an opiate" (p. 284).

Finally, the narrator makes overt Levy's belief that the women of the Jewish community have the worst share of existence by having the narrator comment that for Jewish men "pride of sex is a characteristic quality" and quote the notorious Judaic daily prayer, "'Blessed art Thou, O Lord my God, who hast not made me a woman'" (p. 214); Esther, who is rich, ugly, bitter, and cynical, tells Judith that as a child she revised that prayer, writing, "'Cursed art Thou, O Lord my God, Who hast had the cruelty to make me a woman'" (p. 265).

But Levy said in her 1886 article that fiction should write of the Jew's virtues as well as of his vices, and she does. There can be little question that Reuben has an attractive vitality, which we see in the following portrait:

> He was back again; back to the old, full, strenuous life which was so dear to him; to the din and rush and struggle of the London which he loved with a passion that had something of poetry in it.
>
> With the eager curiosity, the vivid interest in life, which underlay his rather impassive bearing . . . he returned with unmixed delight to his own haunts; to the work and the play; the market-place and the greetings in the marketplace. (p. 200)

Reuben Sachs' extraordinary energy, if not his joy, is matched by that of his mother, who is described as having an "air of intense, but subdued vitality"; the narrator also tells us she is "an old lady it would be difficult to kill" (p. 198). His cousin Leo, a Cambridge student, is almost equally passionate in his commitment to music and in his romanticization of university life and the aristocratic friends he has made there; his youthful condemnation of his own people is also ardent.

In comparison, the only two gentiles whom Levy characterizes (others are mentioned) are conspicuously lacking in fire. We are given a brief sketch of Lord Norwood, Leo's friend, as possessing a "refinement of mind and soul and body, and . . . delicate strength of . . . character" (p. 246). The other gentile is Bertie, whose desire to convert seems ludicrous at least in part because he is too polite and vapid to seem capable of an intense spiritual quest.[9]

The most attractive thing about the members of Reuben and Judith's extended family is that they love each other to an almost remarkable, though always credible, degree. When Reuben returns from his sea voyage at the novel's opening, he can hardly wait to see his cousins, the Leunigers, and the other kin that live with them or frequent their home. When he enters, his little cousins throw themselves at him adoringly, and he responds to them with affection. When Judith is tossed aside by Reuben, her cousin Rose, a "good natured, high spirited" girl, gives her advice and affection which, if restrained, is nonetheless sincere.

Reuben's mother, whom we might expect to dislike Judith out of fear that Reuben would make a materially disadvantageous marriage to her, feels just the opposite: "She admired the girl immensely, and at the bottom of her heart was fond of her" (p. 215). Reuben feels tender towards his cousin Leo even though they disagree on everything and even though Reuben's recognizes that Leo "regards me at present as an incarnation of the sevenSachs deadly sins" (p. 219). Of old Solomon, the family patriarch, we are told that "the ties of race, of family, were strong with him. His love for his children had been the romance of an eminently unromantic career" (p. 215). Amy Levy is able to evoke all this familial affection without ever slipping into sentimentality, truly an achievement in a Victorian novel.

Indeed, the way in which Jews are drawn toward one another is a major part of the substance of Reuben's moving attempt to answer his cousin Leo's attack on Jews and Judaism. Reuben refers with pride to "our love of race, home, and kindred, and regard for their ties," and goes on to say about his people:

> "[I]f we are to die as a race, we shall die harder than you think . . . That strange strong instinct which has held us so long together is not a thing easily eradicated . . . Jew will gravitate to Jew, though each may call himself by another name . . . If all the world, metaphorically speaking, thought one thought and spoke one language, there would still remain unspeakable mysteries, affinity and—love." (p. 240)

As if in proof of Reuben's prophecy, at the end of the book, Judith, married to the convert (who remains an outsider), feels "a strange fit of homesickness, an inrushing sense of exile." Her inner life is evoked powerfully by the narrator who speaks for her in the third person: "Her people—oh, her people!—to be back once more among them!" (p. 289). No longer part of the Jewish community, she is in alien space, and this is rendered emblematically by the fact that the scene is almost entirely framed by two references to the gold cross above the Albert Memorial outside her window.

What then does Levy suggest as possible answers to the questions: What does it mean to be a Jew? What is the moral nature of the Anglo-Jewish community? It would seem that, for her, some Jews and "Jewesses" possess a unusually powerful appetite for life. Even more important, the novel posits the idea that to be Jewish is to be a communal creature, part of a people. The Jewish community represented in *Reuben Sachs* is corrupt, however, and the novel is in a sense a jeremiad, a lamentation for a people that has sold its soul for money and power, that has maltreated its women, that demands from its men a diseased and even suicidal style of life. These people love each other for the most part, but, as we have seen, that does not keep Reuben from betraying Judith—and himself. His treachery becomes a figure for a disturbing strain in Jewish life, seriously dimming, without entirely erasing, the hypothesis that the affection which holds these people together is enough to be redemptive.

The Jewish press on both sides of the Atlantic, responded, for the most part, negatively. The review in the *American Hebrew* is revealing:

> The story [*Reuben Sachs*] tells is that of an Englishman who is in love with a poor girl. His political ambition is about to be crowned with success in the shape of a seat in Parliament. The necessities of the situation require that he marry a rich woman, and renders [sic] it necessary that he give up the poor girl. Now the fatal blunder that Amy Levy makes is that she makes this Englishman a Jew as well, for no earthly reason whatsoever. She must know of course that there are Episcopalians and Dissenters in England who would have acted exactly as Sachs did and with as little, if not with less compunction. In fact, there are a number of other people in the book called Jews, for no evident reason than to say ill-natured things about them. It is a Jewish novel only in that sense that the characters are ostentatiously labelled with the name of their race.

It goes on to say, "An antipodal ethnological student reading Miss Levy's novel . . . would think that Thackeray and Dickens had either maligned the English people or that they had all since then become transformed perfect angels compared with the Jews."[10]

This reviewer makes a good point in recognizing that Levy's plot and the values which it attacks are squarely in the tradition of the English novel. One need only think of Thackeray and Dickens, as he does, and remember that, in *Vanity Fair*, George Osborne brings on his father's wrath by marrying poor Amelia Sedley, or that in, *Great Expectations*, Pip humiliates and rejects Jo, the good simple man who has been a father to him, because he is now higher than Jo in the class hierarchy. He would have been even more on target if he had thought of George Eliot's *Daniel Deronda*, as Levy asks her readers to do by twice referring to Eliot's novel in *Reuben Sachs*.

Toward the end of a dinner party that takes place at the home of the family patriarch on the Day of Atonement, the younger members of Reuben's extended family jokingly wonder about what the (at that point) would-be convert, Bertie, thought of the religious service he had attended and the dinner that broke the day's fast. Leo says, "'I think . . . that he was shocked at finding us so little like the people in *Daniel Deronda*.'" His cousin Esther replies, "'Did he expect . . . to see our boxes in the hall ready packed and labelled *Palestine?*'" Leo replies ironically, "'I have always been touched . . . at the immense good faith with which George Eliot carried out that elaborate misconception of hers'" (p. 238).

This exchange serves several purposes. It reminds us that Levy does not believe Jews should be represented as paragons of virtue—she rejects the "apologetic" tradition that the *American Hebrew* reviewer would prefer—and that she regards England's Jews as natives who will remain in what is their own country. And, as indicated above, these remarks, together with a later allusion to George Eliot's Gwendolen Harleth and Grandcourt, signal the reader to bear *Daniel Deronda* in mind.

Two recent commentators on *Reuben Sachs,* Bryan Cheyette and Deborah Nord,[11] do exactly that although only Cheyette indicates an awareness that he is responding to Amy Levy's cue.[12] Both Cheyette and Nord recognize the many parallels between Levy's novel about Jewish life and the "English part" of *Daniel Deronda,* understanding that Levy's Jews, with their corrupt values and way of life, are a microcosm of the larger society (Cheyette, more than Nord, grasps that what is distinct about them is also the subject of the novel).

Both books attack a society given over to materialism and exaggerated individualism expressed through an obsession with competition. Again, this situates them squarely in the tradition of nineteenth-century British fiction, but the societies that George Eliot and Levy evoke are especially brutal. Levy uses two symbols that correspond to the gambling den depicted at the beginning of *Daniel Deronda*. We have already taken note of the game of solitaire that Ernest pursues so relentlessly, and another of Levy's symbols is the cardplaying that goes on whenever the Leuniger-Sachs clan gathers.

In developing the character and the plight of Judith Quixano, the character whose story rather surprisingly comes to dominate *Reuben Sachs,* Levy gestures to the narrative of Gwendolen Harleth repeatedly and with force. It is not that the two young women resemble each other in personality. Gwendolen is arrogant, narcissistic, and, at least superficially, daring; Judith is unassuming, not particularly self-absorbed, and conventional. Also, Gwendolen has a peculiar propensity for extreme nervousness in certain situations while Judith is distinguished by her calm demeanor (even if this composure comes to be questioned as a kind of narcotic).

Nevertheless, what the two female protagonists have in common is noteworthy. For one thing, each is the heroine of a novel named after the male protagonist, yet (in different ways) each takes over the narrative. Most readers find the story of Gwendolen Harleth more artistically satisfying and therefore more emotionally powerful than the Daniel Deronda narrative;[13] as for **Reuben Sachs**, about two-thirds of the way through the novel it shifts its focus to Judith Quixano, and the previously secondary feminist theme becomes prominent.

Both Gwendolen and Judith are poor relations living close to or with affluent kin: Gwendolen was not cast in this dependent role until her stepfather died, and even then does not feel its full force until her mother's money is lost through reckless financial speculation, while Judith, the daughter of an unworldly Sephardic scholar, came to live with her affluent relatives at an early age and grew up knowing she must marry expediently because she would have only a small dowry. These diverse histories explain Gwendolen's sense of entitlement and Judith's relative diffidence.

After Reuben's rejection, Judith sees no option other than marrying upper-class Bertie Lee-Harrison even though he is culturally alien to her and she is emotionally indifferent to him. After she accepts his proposal, Levy's narrator says, "Bertie, as Gwendolen Harleth said of Grandcourt, was not disgusting. He took his love, as he took his religion, very theoretically" (p. 282). This remark is surely intended to strike fear in the heart of Levy's readers because Grandcourt's cold and distant manner, which allows Gwendolen to think she will be able to tolerate him, turns into psychological sadism after the wedding. In fact, Bertie never does display any behavior more chilling than emotional remoteness and excessive politeness, but Amy Levy apparently wants the reader to link Judith with Gwendolen and be afraid for her.

One of Levy's major themes in **Reuben Sachs** is the vulnerability of women to commodification by the marriage market, particularly when their families are not financially sound. Gwendolen's uncle, a clergyman, makes no pretense about why he wants her to marry Grandcourt: "You are quite capable of reflecting, Gwendolen . . . You have a duty both to yourself and your family."[14] He goes on to say that she holds in her hands "a fortune . . . which almost takes the question out of the range of mere personal feeling, and makes your acceptance of it a duty."[15] Levy's Judith, in contrast, does not require such overt pressure; once Reuben is lost to her, she knows the script and performs her role. But Levy's explicit and implicit allusions to *Daniel Deronda* seem intended to remind us

that women in British society, whether Jewish or gentile, are often sold to (and are expected to sell themselves to) the highest bidder.

Of course, the commodification of young women had been a theme in the British novel from the inception of the genre; a moment's reflection will bring to mind Richardson's *Clarissa,* the fate of Charlotte Lucas in Austen's *Pride and Prejudice,* and the pitiful ironmonger's daughter, whose misfortune it was to be married off to Crawley the baronet in *Vanity Fair*. Levy wants her reading public to place her novel in this context, and, like George Eliot in *Daniel Deronda*, gives this theme an even more central position than it has in most Victorian novels.

To make sure the reader notices the intertextual relationship she has created, Levy not only cites George Eliot directly; she also makes the analogues to *Daniel Deronda* particularly evident and numerous, and occasionally she allows herself to echo specific words and phrases. For example, the narrator of *Daniel Deronda* observes that "Of course, marriage was social promotion"[16] while Judith is said to be "awaiting promotion by marriage" (p. 209)

Perhaps the most important similarity between the two women is their narrowness of vision both in relation to their own possibilities and in regard to the world outside of themselves. Gwendolen Harleth's narrowness, as so many critics have noted, is her most distinguishing characteristic. George Eliot evokes it powerfully through her brilliant use of imagery, perhaps most memorably by Gwendolen's dread of wide spaces: "Solitude in any wide scene impressed her with an undefined feeling of immeasurable existence aloof from her, in the midst of which she was helplessly incapable of asserting herself."[17] The result is a crippling of the imagination, a total blindness to the needs of the world outside herself, so that while she has the desire to play a leading role and win the admiration of others, "such passions . . . dwelt among strictly feminine furniture, and had no disturbing reference to the advancement of learning or the balance of the constitution."[18]

Levy's Judith inhabits a world so limited that the perimeters of her imagination do not even permit an exaggerated sense of her own importance. The blinders that society has imposed on her make her unaware of her own uniqueness and value: "This woman, with her beauty, her intelligence, her power of feeling, saw herself merely as one of a vast crowd of girls" (p. 35). Amy Levy wants the reader to see the resemblance to Gwendolen but also to recognize a unique human being, one who, she believes, could only be produced by the particularities of Anglo-Jewish attitudes toward women which, **Reuben Sachs** suggests, are even more repressive than those of the larger society.[19]

The narrator says that Judith's "outlook on life was of

the narrowest; of the world, of London, of society beyond her own set, it may be said she had seen nothing at first hand" (p. 210). The lack of a sufficiently wide view of existence is a major element in the oppression Gwendolen and Judith have experienced as women: both George Eliot and Amy Levy acknowledge that society's devaluation of women not only unfairly restricts them but also inhibits their potential, stunting their development as full human beings.

Another link between Gwendolen Harleth and Judith Quixano is that both are, to an important degree, constructed by the men with whom they are in love (but cannot marry) and by whom they are mentored. In many respects, George Eliot is using a convention in women's fiction that goes back to the eighteenth century: Fanny Burney's Camilla, for example, must undergo a painful reeducation under the guidance of her male mentor.[20] Gwendolen goes to Daniel for spiritual guidance after her marriage, and he counsels her patiently, trying to widen her horizons. Finally in her last note to him, she paraphrases his advice: "I have remembered your words—that I may live to be one of the best of women, who make others glad that they are born."[21] By allowing her heroine to accept a direction for her life that is highly conventional—these words could be the motto of Coventry Patmore's paradigmatic "angel in the house"—and by allowing a man who is much wiser than she to define that direction, George Eliot can hardly be said to be a feminist.

The relationship between Judith and Reuben can be seen as a bow to the young woman/male mentor convention, but Levy departs from Eliot and other predecessors by taking a negative attitude toward the role of the mentor. In significant counterpoint, Reuben does not provide an antidote to Judith's narrowness. Instead, his relationship with her is understood to be one of the reasons for her limitations. The paragraph quoted above about Judith's narrowness concludes: "[I]t may be said that she had seen nothing at first hand; had looked at it all, not with her own eyes, but with the eyes of Reuben Sachs" (p. 210). Levy shows us that Reuben has not done Judith a favor by shaping her development through directing her reading, lending her books, and exposing her to his ideas.

It is only after she has lost him that she begins to think for herself (even if she never is able to *act* unconventionally), coming to understand that, regardless of what Reuben and nearly everyone else in her world believes, "there was something to be said for feelings which had not their basis in material relationships. They were not mere phantasmagoria conjured up by silly people, by sentimental people, by women" (p. 269). After being prodded to think about *Daniel Deronda* throughout the reading of *Reuben Sachs,* readers are likely to note the contrast when Levy strikes out on her own in a more feminist direction.

Some of the reviews of *Reuben Sachs,* together with the Macmillan reader's report on the novel, enable us to see why Amy Levy needed the relationship her book bore to *Daniel Deronda* in order to expand its implications and make its themes more resonant for the gentile reader. The Jews in late-Victorian England were marginalized in the sense that even though they were tolerated and many doors were open to them[22] they were thought of as alien and, by many, repugnant.

We see this in George S. Street's turn-of-the-century "Essay on Jews," which focuses on *Reuben Sachs* and some other fiction, and concludes in response to their representation of Jewish life: "I am left partly in the accounts of these books repelled, partly attracted, but wholly baffled by a mystery."[23] The reviewer for *The Academy* says the Jews "are a people of whom the outside world knows but little."[24] The sense of Otherness that the Macmillan reader feels in relation to the life Levy represents is revealed by his opening remark: "A rather curious little book." It has "cleverness," but his lack of confidence in it—"I don't suppose the little book would achieve much popularity"—seems to stem from concern that the material is *outre* and distasteful.

His confidence that Levy's portrait of Jewish life is a "most effective bit of narrow and close photography" reflects an assumption, shared by other reviewers, that the novel exposes only negative truths about Jewish life and that this bleak portrait is the result of Levy's verisimilitude and not an interpretation on her part. He says that "The people are not made at all *excessively* [emphasis mine] disagreeable; but are painted just (I should think) as they really are in the synagogue, shopping at Whitely's, dining, and so on."[25] His parenthetical remark indicates his own lack of sufficient first-hand knowledge, but this does not shake his confidence in his convictions.

The reviewer for the *Academy,* who asserts that the majority population is not familiar with Jewish life, seems unfamiliar with the less attractive aspects of gentile society and the vast body of fiction which represents Englishmen engaged in a race for worldly goods and prestige. He states matter-of-factly and, one feels, smugly, "Miss Levy is apparently conscious of a certain soullessness and absence of ennobling ideals in the national character and deplores her kinsmen's sordid devotion to material interests and lack of any yearning for a higher life."[26] He also ignores everything in the novel that does not fit in with his preconceptions about Jewish people, the most obvious omission being Leo Leuniger's idealistic yearnings for transcendence.

Deborah Heller, in "Jews and Women in *Daniel Deronda,*" shows that George Henry Lewes and George Eliot herself were concerned that the Jewish dimension of *Daniel Deronda* would not be well-received, hurting the acceptance of the novel as a whole. Heller cites in evidence letters to Eliot's publisher, John Blackwood, written both before and after *Daniel Deronda* came out, and Blackwood's replies. The letters written after the novel was published reveal that their anxiety was well-founded. One could argue that the gentile reading public did not respond well to the Jewish half for aesthetic reasons, but both the Leweses and Blackwood assume a lack of sympathy on the part of the public toward Jews. In one letter, dated November 22, 1876, Blackwood remarks: "'The Jews should be the most interesting people in the world, but even *her* [George Eliot's] magic pen cannot *at once* make them a popular element in a Novel.'"[27]

This correspondence about *Daniel Deronda* provides some possible insight into why Amy Levy was slow to publish fiction dealing with Jews and Jewish themes even though she had written at least one fine story about a Jew at Cambridge while still a Cambridge student herself between 1879 and 1881. This unpublished story, scribbled in a school notebook, is about a Leo Leuniger who is very much the same person he is in ***Reuben Sachs,*** and it includes two other characters who play a minor role in that book.[28] The appearance of these characters seven or eight years later in her published novel suggests a long preoccupation with them, together with a hesitancy to bring this material to the public eye.

Perhaps Levy needed artistic maturity to figure out how to amplify her Jewish material so that the public would want to hear it and would be able to understand its implications for Jewish life and for the society as a whole. Apparently she was more successful with her Christian audience than her Jewish one, the gentile reviews being quite favorable despite the fixation on the strangeness of Jewish society of some of the reviewers and the inability of many of them to see parallels with gentile life.

It is true that most non-Jewish reviewers saw the novel as a harsh condemnation of Jews and Judaism. Yet the reviewer for the *Literary World* is not alone in being able to recognize that the Jewish world of ***Reuben Sachs*** is no worse than the larger society which contains it. He writes that "***Reuben Sachs*** is not a pleasant book to read; it has too much of the bitterness of reality in it. But we should advise Christians to be slow in reproaching Jewish society because of it; Mammon is a very popular god in all civilized lands."[29] One feels that Levy, in referring to *Daniel Deronda* in a variety of ways, hopes to legitimize the concern her novel has with questions pertaining to the Anglo-Jewish community and to enable her readers to receive ***Reuben Sachs*** as more than a foreign curiosity; her method relies in large part on triggering just such a recognition of how much Jews and gentiles have in common.

Daniel Deronda may have been useful to Levy in another and rather paradoxical way too; the pres-

ence of Jewish characters who are *not* noble-minded and handsome—who are unappealing in ways conventionally associated with Jews—may have prompted her to create a novel which suggests a range of responses to sensitive questions regarding Jewish matters but which offers them in an unresolved, polyphonic way.

Deborah Heller is one of the few critics who takes note of the fact that George Eliot's last novel contains some unfavorable "representatives of Judaism whose unattractiveness is inextricably tied to their conformity to familiar Jewish stereotypes."[30]

In this regard, she mentions or discusses several figures: the vulgar Jewish pawnbroker, Ezra Cohen, and his young son;[31] Mr. Wiener, the Leubrun dealer, to whom Gwendolen sells her turquoise necklace at the novel's start; Daniel's long-lost father, a moneylender and banker; and Lapidoth, Mirah and Mordecai's detestable thief of a father who was planning to sell his own daughter into concubinage for profit. She realizes that "the evident purpose of these unattractive Jews is to balance and therefore give credibility to the more ideal Jews" but remains troubled because "their unattractiveness is automatically presented as having a particularly Jewish flavour."[32]

Levy's unpublished story about Leo Leuniger at Cambridge indicates a pained awareness of anti-Semitism, as does one of her letters written when she was in high school[33]: she is unlikely to have missed the kind of negative stereotyping (in the case of Lapidoth, even demonization) Heller talks about. An article Levy wrote for the *Jewish Chronicle*, **"Jewish Children,"** provides evidence that she was indeed disturbed by the minor Jewish characters in *Daniel Deronda*. Levy reminds us that young Jacob Alexander Cohen, the pawnbroker's son, wears "red stockings and velveteen knickerbockers," and she quotes a passage (which Heller also cites) that describes his voice as "'hoarse in its glibness, as if it belonged to an aged commercial soul, fatigued with bargaining for many generations.'"

In her article, Levy also calls our attention to the way that George Eliot describes the remaining progeny of Ezra Cohen, thus revealing her sensitivity to nuances of stereotyping that Heller ignores. Jacob's sister, Adelaide Rebekah, has "'monumental features,'" a "'miniature crinoline,'" and, Levy paraphrases, a "Sabbath frock of braided amber." The baby, Eugenie Esther, "'carries on her teething intelligently'" and "looks about her with such precocious interest." Levy's choice of these remarks indicates an understanding that George Eliot's Jews, when they are not poetic, are drawn from a received stock of ideas which include lack of physical charm, preternatural intelligence, and a penchant for overdressing and loud colors.

Levy registers her discomfort when she comments,

"[T]hese three little persons are drawn . . . with an absence of tenderness which we should hardly have expected from the creator of Tottie, of Eppie, of Tom and Maggie Tulliver," and goes on to say, "The rather laboured jocoseness . . . seem[s] singularly out of place in her description of the young Cohens".[34]

Levy's recognition that stereotyping of Jews abounds even in a novel which was written in part to counter anti-Semitic ideas[35] may have led her to an important apprehension. *Reuben Sachs* can be read as suggesting that Levy had come to grasp that however well-intentioned and "realistic" a writer tried to be, British culture harbored so many deeply-held notions about Jews—so many un-examined ideological assumptions—that even the most gifted and serious of writers could only produce an interpretation built, at least for the most part, on received ideas. Such insights seem to have prompted her to depart from classic realism: *Reuben Sachs* shows Levy's recognition that the language of fiction has a complex and problematic relationship to any preexisting referents.

Aware that a writer's ability, including her own, to imagine the world and produce meaning is limited and defined by the belief-system which she receives from the systems of representation that the society makes available, Levy writes her Jewish novel in such a way that "truth" is hard to pin down. *Reuben Sachs* is a text whose stance toward the sector of Jewish society it seeks to represent is far from resolved. Epistemologically experimental, it lacks what Penny Boumelha, in a theoretical discussion of classic realism, calls "a controlling 'truth voice.'"[36]

Levy makes her novel polyphonic in the Bakhtinian sense by experimenting with narrative technique. It is important to note that the narrative voice functions inconsistently, sometimes calling attention to its omniscience and at other times undercutting its own authority. We see the former when the narrator shows off by predicting the future, telling us about young Leo, so eloquent in his hostility to his own people: "The time was yet to come when he should acknowledge to himself the depth of tribal feeling, of love for his race, which lay at the root of his nature" (p. 229).

At other moments, the narrator distances herself (assuming it is a she) from authority, as in the conclusion when, instead of closure, she offers a question: "Is life indeed over for Judith, or at least all that makes life beautiful, worthy—a thing in any way tolerable?" (p. 292). The chill of this possibility is only slightly mitigated by the news that Judith, unbeknownst to herself, is with child. The novel's last sentence predicting that the child shall bring both sorrow and happiness and a "quickening of purpose" still leaves the reader feeling that Judith's future is indeterminate.

Even when the narrator confidently predicts the future, as with Leo in the passage quoted above, the effect is to emphasize the fluidity of truth because the glimpse we get of a more mature Leo undermines the notion of a unitary self. The notion of a coherent self is subverted specifically in relation to attitudes towards the Jews and Judaism. Similarly, when the narrator tells us that Reuben "understood perhaps more of Leopold's state of mind than any one suspected, of the struggles with himself, the revolt against his surroundings which the lad was undergoing" (p. 219), the hint of a different, younger Reuben who felt negatively about being a Jew suggests that the reliably correct stance on what might be called the "Jewish Question" is not easily arrived at.

The authority of the narrator is again called into question by a remark she makes in the chapter about Yom Kippur, the Day of Atonement. Esther, Reuben's highly sarcastic cousin, does not go to synagogue, having had a fight with her mother. We are told: "She, poor soul, was of those who deny utterly the existence of the Friend of whom she stood so sorely in need" (p. 230). At this point the reader is likely to wonder: just who is this voice telling the story?

There has been no previous indication that the universe is watched over by a caring, or indeed, any other kind of God. In fact, religion has been devalued as when the narrator speaks mockingly of Yom Kippur, a day when observant Jews fast and spend the entire day in the synagogue:

> [F]rom an early hour, in all quarters of the town, the Chosen People—a breakfastless band—might have been seen making their way to the synagogues . . . if traces of depression were discernible on many faces, in view of the long day before them, it is scarcely to be wondered at. (p. 228)

Given this satiric attitude toward Judaism, who is this "Friend" the narrator is talking about? It doesn't seem likely that this God is a Jewish deity. Is Levy suggesting Judaism is an inadequate religion? Another thought comes to mind: is the narrator a gentile? Then one wonders about certain observations of the narrative voice which link the physical unattractiveness of the characters to their Jewishness and other remarks that make a connection between the fact that they are Jews and their materialism and obsession with success.

Reuben is described early on: "He wore good clothes, but they could not disguise the fact that his figure was bad, and his movements awkward; unmistakeably the figure and movements of a Jew" (p. 201). Another illustration of the narrator's assumption that Jews are unpleasant to look at should suffice: at a party in the home of the Leunigers, the narrator remarks that "some quite commonplace English girls and men who were here tonight looked positively beautiful as they moved about among the ill-made sons and daughters of Shem" (p. 251). Among the many statements made by the narrative voice which assume that Jews are excessively worldly in their values is the following: "[T]he Jewish people, so eager to crown success in any form, so determined to lay claim to the successful among their number, have scant love for those unfortunates who have dropped behind in the race" (p. 235).

One wonders if comments of this sort are not made from the perspective of an outsider, a non-Jew, who is simply revealing her own anti-Semitism. This hypothesis is supported by the fact that sometimes what the characters say and do undercuts the narrator's negative generalizations about Jews. The most dramatic illustration of this is the narrator's statement: "If there is a strong family feeling among the children of Israel, it often takes the form of acute family jealousy" (p. 249). The tone here is snide, suggesting that the narrator is not friendly toward the Jewish people; moreover, we see no signs of the jealousy of which she speaks. Instead, her generalization is patently belied by the close and loving ties which bind the Leunigers, the Sachses, and the Quixanos (the only exception would been the sneering attitude Reuben's relatives have toward the less assimilated and less affluent Samuel Sachses from vulgar Maida Vale).

The relationship between narrator and narrative is certainly unstable. In some important respects, the characters do confirm remarks made by the narrator that strike the reader as anti-Semitic. Reuben himself acts, speaks, and thinks at times in ways that compel one to see Jewish life as oriented toward the single-minded pursuit of self-interest and ambition.

On the other hand, while he sometimes brings to mind stereotyped notions about Jews, most notably when he puts ambition ahead of his love for Judith, he is rendered with so much specific and contradictory detail—through what he does, what he says, and the access we are given to his inner life (by means of free indirect style)—that he never *becomes* a stereotype. When Leo charges that one doesn't find idealists among Jews, using the mythic King Cophetua as an example, Reuben responds with acute perception: "King Cophetua had an assured position. It isn't everyone that can afford to marry beggar-maids" (p. 237).

Reuben's self-conscious ability to understand the relationship between his values and his status as an outsider in English society enhances his three-dimensionality. It also provides motivation for his later decision to put ambition ahead of love, suggesting that his behavior is more than a reflex resulting from something innate in Jewishness. Finally, the many reminders of the corrupt gentile world of *Daniel Deronda* create a context that makes the negative side of Jewish life in *Reuben Sachs* look ordinary instead of appalling.

The result is a novel whose stance is so slippery—the relationship between narrator and narrative so shifting—the reliability of the narrative voice so questionable—the stereotypical ways in which some of the characters act maybe only a representation of the culturally dominant image of the Jew (or perhaps merely of late-Victorian bourgeois manhood)—that the reader is not at all sure where Levy stands.

Levy's use of narrative technique in *Reuben Sachs* allows her to tell a story, the meaning of which is unstable but suggestive of multiple possibilities. Read carefully, *Reuben Sachs* offers such a hotly contested ideological terrain that it becomes evident that Levy understood that "a serious attempt at serious treatment" of "the complex problem of Jewish life and Jewish character"[37] required going beyond apology, demonization, or "laboured jocoseness" in the direction of epistemological innovation.

Notes

[1] George Eliot's effort to write a book sympathetic to the Jews has been appreciated by them; in 1948 she had a street named after her in Tel Aviv, and there are now streets named after her in all of Israel's major cities. See Edgar Rosenberg, *From Shylock to Svengali: Jewish Stereotypes in English Fiction* (Stanford, CA: Stanford Univ. Press, 1960), p. 184; for a study of the Jewish response to *Daniel Deronda* see Shmuel Werses, "The Jewish Reception of *Daniel Deronda*," *Daniel Deronda: A Centenary Symposium*, ed. Alice Shalvi (Jerusalem: Jerusalem Academic Press, 1976), pp. 11-47.

[2] It is interesting to note that not all Jews found the treatment of Jews in *Mrs. Keith's Crime* objectionable. An anonymous columnist praises it while glancing at a number of recent novels which have Jewish characters. See *The American Hebrew* (23 Aug. 1889): 36; Levy's standards were evidently higher or at least different.

[3] Amy Levy, "The Jew in Fiction," *The Jewish Chronicle* (4 June 1886): 13.

[4] Bryan Cheyette, "From Apology to Revolt: Benjamin Farjeon, Amy Levy and the Post Emancipation Anglo-Jewish Novel," *Jewish Historical Society of England Transactions* (Jan. 1985): 253-65. During the Victorian period gentile novelists faced with the task of creating Jewish characters tended either toward one-dimensional demonization or idealization (what Cheyettte calls "apology").

[5] Cheyette, "'from Apology to Revolt,'" p. 256.

[6] *Ibid.*, p. 262. In a more recent essay Cheyette explains that in writing *Dr Phillips* Frankau was influenced by French naturalism, observing that she "internalized a racial discourse about Jews" and that in Zola's fiction "semitic motifs appeared frequently": see "The Other Self: Anglo-Jewish Fiction and the Representation of Jews in England, 1875-1905," *The Making of Modern Anglo-Jewry,* ed. David Cesarani (Oxford: Basil Blackwell, 1990) pp. 103-04.

[7] Review of Mrs. Andrew Dean's *Isaac Eller's Money, Jewish Chronicle* (2 August 1889): 12.

[8] Amy Levy, *Reuben Sachs, A Sketch* (London and New York: Macmillan and Co., 1888; rpt. *The Complete Novels and Selected Writings of Amy Levy, 1861-1889,* ed. Melvyn New (Gainesville: Univ. Press of Florida, 1993) p. 199; (all further page references to *Reuben Sachs* will be cited within the text).

[9] Reuben's family does not take Bertie's conversion seriously for other reasons as well; as Reuben says "he has a taste for religion," having started out High Church, "flirted with the Holy Mother" and "joined a set of mystics . . . somewhere in Asia Minor" before getting interested in Judaism (p. 205). Also, the younger members of this family are not themselves interested in the religious dimension of their Judaism.

[10] Review of *Reuben Sachs, The American Hebrew* (5 April 1889): 142.

[11] See Deborah Epstein Nord, "'Neither Pairs Nor Odd': Female Community in Late-Nineteenth Century London," *Signs: A Journal of Women in Culture and Society* 15 (1990): 733-54, for an interesting discussion of three late-Victorian "New Women," one of them Amy Levy.

[12] Cheyette, p. 261.

[13] For the most famous devaluation of the "Jewish part" of *Daniel Deronda* see Frank R. Leavis, "George Eliot's Zionist Novel," *Commentary* XXX (1960): 317-25.

[14] George Eliot, *Daniel Deronda* (Great Britain: Penguin Books, Ltd., 1973), p. 178.

[15] *Ibid.*, p. 179.

[16] *Ibid.*, p. 68.

[17] *Ibid.*, pp. 94-95.

[18] *Ibid.*, p. 69.

[19] Levy's narrator refers to Jewish "orientalism" as an explanation for the inferior position of women within Jewish society on p. 210. Levy develops this idea in interesting detail in her article, "Middle-Class Jewish Women of Today," *The Complete Novels and Selected Writings of Amy Levy, 1861-1889,* pp. 525-27.

[20] For a discussion of the young woman/male mentor motif in eighteenth- and nineteenth-century British women's literature, see Linda Hunt, *A Woman's Portion: Ideology, Culture, and the British Female Novel Tradition* (New York & London: Garland, 1988), p. 43.

[21] Eliot, p. 882.

[22] For a discussion of the position of Jews in late-Victorian England see Todd Endelman, *Radical Assimilation in English Jewish History 1656-1945* (Bloomington: Univ. of Indiana Press, 1990), pp. 97-99.

[23] G. S. Street, "An Essay on Jews," *Pall Mall Magazine* 21 (1900): 288.

[24] Review of *Reuben Sachs, Academy* (16 February 1889): 109.

[25] Macmillan reader's report, British Library, BM Add.ms. 5541; pp. 146-47.

[26] Review of *Reuben Sachs, Academy* (16 Feb. 1889): 109.

[27] Deborah Heller, "Jews and Women in *Daniel Deronda,*" *Jewish Presences in English Literature,* eds. Derek Cohen and Deborah Heller (Montreal & Kingston: McGill-Queen's Univ. Press, 1990), p. 78.

[28] Amy Levy's unpublished story about a Jew at Cambridge is entitled "Leo Leuniger: a Study," and it is part of the collection of Amy Levy papers owned by Camellia Plc., London, England.

[29] Review of *Reuben Sachs, Literary World* (13 April 1889): 123.

[30] Heller, p. 85.

[31] Deborah Heller, in her essay cited above, finds Ezra Cohen a stereotype, describing him as "a mildly repulsive portrait of Jewish vulgarity and self-satisfaction" (p. 85). William Baker, in contrast, appears quite satisfied with the way his character is drawn; see William Baker, *George Eliot and Judaism* (Salzburg: Austria: Institut fur Englische Sprache und Literatur, 1975), pp. 223-26.

[32] Heller, p. 86.

[33] "Leopold Leuniger: A Study," cited above, is about Leo's deep sense of social inferiority in relation to

the aristocratic friends he has made at Cambridge; the climax comes when he overhears them making anti-Semitic remarks. Levy's undated letter to her sister Katie was written when she was a student at the Brighton High School for Girls (between 1876-1879); she reports on the anti-Semitic remarks made by a classmate, expressing hurt and dismay.

[34] Amy Levy, "Jewish Children," *The Complete Novels and Selected Writings of Amy Levy, 1861-1889,* p. 528.

[35] Heller, p. 81.

[36] Penny Boumelha, "On Realism and Feminism," *Realism,* ed. Lilian R. Furst (London and New York: Longman, 1992), p. 320: this essay provides a good discussion of what is meant by the term "classic realism." For the most explicit explanation of the concept, see Catherine Belsey, *Critical Practice* (London, 1980), pp. 67-84, 112-17.

[37] Amy Levy, "The Jew in Fiction."

FURTHER READING

Criticism

Modder, Montagu Frank. "The Old Order Changeth." In *The Jew in the Literature of England to the End of the 19th Century,* pp. 317-24. Philadelphia: The Jewish Publication Society of America, 1939.

Includes discussion of Levy's portrayal of the Jewish community in *Reuben Sachs* and "Cohen of Trinity."

Price, Warwick James. "Three Forgotten Poetesses." *The Forum* 47 (March 1912): 361-76.

Includes discussion of Levy's poetry, emphasizing the tone of longing and sadness that characterizes her verse.

Udelson, Joseph H. "Amy Levy." In his *Dreamer of the Ghetto: The Life and Works of Israel Zangwill,* pp. 54-58. Tuscaloosa, Alabama: The University of Alabama Press, 1990.

Offers a survey of Levy's career and comments on the major thematic interests of her fiction and poetry.

Frankenstein; or, The Modern Prometheus

Mary Wollstonecraft Shelley

The following entry presents criticism of Shelley's novel *Frankenstein* (1818). For a discussion of Shelley's complete career, see *NCLC*, Volume 14.

INTRODUCTION

When Mary Shelley wrote of Victor Frankenstein and his monster, she brought to life a story that would fascinate audiences through the ensuing centuries. Although the story seems "classic" to readers and movie-goers at the end of the twentieth century, Shelley's novel was something of an anomaly when she published it anonymously in 1818. The genre of science fiction did not yet exist, and novels themselves were often looked upon as "light" reading that did not rank with serious literature. In the twentieth century, however, *Frankenstein* has gained recognition as a pioneering effort in the development of the novel and as a progenitor of science fiction.

Biographical Information

Frankenstein was Shelley's first major literary production, completed when she was not yet twenty. Her life up to that point had been shaped by the presence of powerful intellectual figures: her father, political philosopher and novelist William Godwin; her mother, one of the earliest advocates of women's rights, Mary Wollstonecraft; and her husband, Romantic poet Percy Bysshe Shelley. Mary grew up without a formal education—a situation typical for girls in her era—but with the formidable training of her parents' writings and the many classics available to her in her father's library. Because Wollstonecraft had died ten days after Mary's birth, Godwin raised her and her half-sister alone at first, then with a stepmother who apparently cared very little for the two girls. Mary escaped her home life in July 1814, when she eloped with Percy Shelley, who deserted his wife in order to be with her. With little money at their disposal, the pair travelled the continent, living primarily in Switzerland, Germany, and Italy. At the time Mary began writing *Frankenstein* in 1816, the couple's financial difficulties were exacerbated by personal loss: there were suicides in both of their families, and three of their children died in infancy. The one child who would survive was born in 1819, just three years before Percy Shelley drowned in Italy.

After her husband's death, Shelley struggled to support herself and her son, Percy Florence, often writing in order to earn money. A small stipend from Percy

Shelley's father, Sir Timothy, brought with it some financial security, but also the condition that Shelley not publish under her married name. Consequently, her five novels and other publications all appeared anonymously. Sir Timothy increased the allowance again in 1840, enabling Shelley and Percy to live with a greater degree of comfort. Shelley died in 1851, after several years of illness.

Plot and Major Characters

Shelley wrote *Frankenstein* as a series of framing narratives: one narrator's story told within the framework of another narrator's story. The events described by the creature (which Shelley composed first) appear within Victor Frankenstein's narrative, which in turn appears in a letter written by Captain Robert Walton—an explorer who met Frankenstein in the North Pole—to his sister. Consequently, the reader's experience begins at the end of the drama, when Frankenstein and his monster have removed themselves from human society and are pursuing each other in perpetuity across the tundra. Walton then relates Frankenstein's story, which returns to his childhood, when Victor developed his initial interest in science. Some years later, Victor's planned departure for University is delayed when his mother dies; Frankenstein's interest in science simultaneously turns to the possibility of reanimating the dead. Working in comparative isolation at the University, Frankenstein pursues his obsession until he succeeds—bringing to life a pieced-together body. He immediately flees his creation in horror.

Entirely isolated, fully grown but without any guidance in its social and intellectual development, the creature makes its own way in the world; his story, told in the first-person as related to Victor some time later, occupies the center of the novel. The reader witnesses the gradual degradation of what began as an apparently good and loving nature. Because the creature's monstrous appearance inspires horror wherever he encounters humans, his potential for goodness falters, especially when Frankenstein fails to supply him with the companionship of a mate. Turning vindictive, the creature sets out to recreate for Victor the isolation of his own circumstances, gradually killing the members of his family, including Elizabeth, the beloved adopted sister who has just become Victor's wife. The two characters finish "wedded" to one another, or to the need to destroy one another, in the emptiness of the arctic tundra.

Major Themes

The issue that occupies *Frankenstein* most prevalently and explicitly is that of creation, manifested in a variety of forms. Shelley signalled the significance of this to her reader from the start with her subtitle and her epigraph: the one referring to the classical myth of Prometheus, and the other, taken from Book Ten of Milton's *Paradise Lost*, referring to the Genesis story: "Did I request thee, Maker, from my clay / To mould me Man? Did I solicit thee / From darkness to promote me?" (*Paradise Lost* X, ll.743-45). The three characters invoked by these allusions—Prometheus, Lucifer, and Adam—share a history of rebellion, of a desire to "steal" some of the godly fire of life or knowledge for themselves. Shelley reflects the many layers of this mythology in her own rendering with the temptation and power Frankenstein finds in knowledge, as well as the danger that surfaces once it becomes apparent that he has either misused his knowledge or overstepped his bounds in acquiring it.

With the rise of feminist and psychoanalytic literary criticism late in the twentieth century, another aspect of the creation theme surfaced: reproduction. Viewed in this light, Frankenstein has usurped the prerogative of creation not from god, but from woman, and has thus tampered with the laws of nature and social organization. Generally, this approach to the novel critiques traditional gender roles and the bourgeois family as depicted in *Frankenstein*. The novel abounds in depictions of different familial relationships, particularly when read in light of Shelley's family history: woman's relationship to childbirth, daughter's relationship to mother, daughter's relationship to father. Fundamental to the novel's two main characters, despite the extreme differences in family relationships, are the stories of their intellectual and emotional development, which resonate deeply within the era in which Shelley wrote. The nature of the human individual, the nature of that individual's development, the basic issue of inherent goodness or evil, concerned many artists and thinkers of the Romantic age.

Critical Reception

Frankenstein immediately became popular upon its publication, when it fit neatly into the current fashion for the Gothic novel, a genre abounding in mystery and murder. It would be some time before critics would look at Shelley's novel—or any novel—as a serious work of literature; initial critical attention often reduced *Frankenstein* to an aside to the work of her husband and the other Romantic poets. The first significant shift in critical reception occurred in the middle of the twentieth century, when major critics like Harold Bloom and M. A. Goldberg took it up with enthusiasm, exploring its Promethean and Miltonic echoes. Readers generally understood the novel as an evocation of the modern condition: man trapped in a godless world in which science and ethics have gone awry.

While most *Frankenstein* criticism has stressed the importance of Shelley's biography as a reflection upon the work, the approach has been central to psychoanalytic and feminist critics. The latter led a resurgence in Shelley criticism in the early 1980s, discovering in her work not only one of the earliest literary productions by a woman author, but also a source of rich commentary on gender roles and female experience at the beginning of the nineteenth century. At first, the biographical emphasis tended to reduce Shelley's creative and intellectual achievement to an effect of postpartum depression, experienced when she lost one of her babies immediately after giving birth. Later critics explored more and more aspects of Shelley's familial relationships, often considering her novel as a reflection of complex oedipal conflicts, or finding in her an early and rich feminist voice.

CRITICISM

Mary Wollstonecraft Shelley (essay date 1831)

SOURCE: "Appendix A," in *Frankenstein or the Modern Prometheus: The 1818 Text*, edited by James Rieger, The University of Chicago Press, 1982, pp. 222-29.

[*When a third edition of* Frankenstein *was produced in 1831, Shelley wrote a new introduction, reprinted below with James Rieger's notes. Shelley briefly recounts her biography, with an emphasis on her intellectual development and the events that led to the "waking dream" in which she first envisioned Victor Frankenstein and his creature.*]

The Publishers of the Standard Novels,[1] in selecting *Frankenstein* for one of their series, expressed a wish that I should furnish them with some account of the origin of the story. I am the more willing to comply, because I shall thus give a general answer to the question, so very frequently asked me—"How I, then a young girl, came to think of, and to dilate upon, so very hideous an idea?" It is true that I am very averse to bringing myself forward in print; but as my account will only appear as an appendage to a former production, and as it will be confined to such topics as have connection with my authorship alone, I can scarcely accuse myself of a personal intrusion.

It is not singular that, as the daughter of two persons of distinguished literary celebrity, I should very early in life have thought of writing. As a child I scribbled; and my favourite pastime, during the hours given me for recreation, was to "write stories." Still I had a dearer pleasure than this, which was the formation of castles in the air—the indulging in walking dreams—the following up trains of thought, which had for their subject the formation of a succession of imaginary incidents. My dreams were at once more fantastic and agreeable than my writings. In the latter I was a close imitator—rather doing as others had done, than putting down the suggestions of my own mind. What I wrote was intended at least for one other eye—my childhood's companion and friend;[2] but my dreams were all my own; I accounted for them to nobody; they were my refuge when annoyed—my dearest pleasure when free.

I lived principally in the country as a girl, and passed a considerable time in Scotland. I made occasional visits to the more picturesque parts; but my habitual residence was on the blank and dreary northern shores of the Tay, near Dundee. Blank and dreary on retrospection I call them; they were not so to me then. They were the eyry of freedom, and the pleasant region where unheeded I could commune with the creatures of my fancy. I wrote then—but in a most common-place style. It was beneath the trees of the grounds belonging to our house, or on the bleak sides of the woodless mountains near, that my true compositions, the airy flights of my imagination, were born and fostered. I did not make myself the heroine of my tales. Life appeared to me too common-place an affair as regarded myself. I could not figure to myself that romantic woes or wonderful events would ever be my lot; but I was not confined to my own identity, and I could people the hours with creations far more interesting to me at that age, than my own sensations.

After this my life became busier, and reality stood in place of fiction. My husband, however, was from the first, very anxious that I should prove myself worthy of my parentage, and enrol myself on the page of fame. He was for ever inciting me to obtain literary reputation, which even on my own part I cared for then, though since I have become infinitely indifferent to it. At this time he desired that I should write, not so much with the idea that I could produce any thing worthy of notice, but that he might himself judge how far I possessed the promise of better things hereafter. Still I did nothing. Travelling, and the cares of a family, occupied my time; and study, in the way of reading, or improving my ideas in communication with his far more cultivated mind, was all of literary employment that engaged my attention.

In the summer of 1816, we visited Switzerland, and became the neighbours of Lord Byron. At first we spent our pleasant hours on the lake, or wandering on its shores; and Lord Byron, who was writing the third canto of Childe Harold, was the only one among us who put his thoughts upon paper. These, as he brought them successively to us, clothed in all the light and harmony of poetry, seemed to stamp as divine the glories of heaven and earth, whose influences we partook with him.

But it proved a wet, ungenial summer, and incessant rain often confined us for days to the house. Some volumes of ghost stories, translated from the German into French, fell into our hands. There was the History of the Inconstant Lover,[4] who, when he thought to clasp the bride to whom he had pledged his vows, found himself in the arms of the pale ghost of her whom he had deserted. There was the tale of the sinful founder of his race,[5] whose miserable doom it was to bestow the kiss of death on all the younger sons of his fated house, just when they reached the age of promise. His gigantic, shadowy form, clothed like the ghost in Hamlet, in complete armour, but with the beaver up, was seen at midnight, by the moon's fitful beams, to advance slowly along the gloomy avenue. The shape was lost beneath the shadow of the castle walls; but soon a gate swung back, a step was heard, the door of the chamber opened, and he advanced to the couch of the blooming youths, cradled in healthy sleep. Eternal sorrow sat upon his face as he bent down and kissed the forehead of the boys, who from that hour withered like flowers snapt upon the stalk. I have not seen these stories since then; but their incidents are as fresh in my mind as if I had read them yesterday.

"We will each write a ghost story," said Lord Byron; and his proposition was acceded to. There were four of us.[6] The noble author began a tale, a fragment of which he printed at the end of his poem of Mazeppa. Shelley, more apt to embody ideas and sentiments in the radiance of brilliant imagery, and in the music of the most melodious verse that adorns our language, than to invent the machinery of a story, commenced one founded on the experiences of his early life. Poor Polidori had some terrible idea about a skull-headed lady, who was so punished for peeping through a key-hole—what to see I forget—something very shocking and wrong of course; but when she was reduced to a worse condition than the renowned Tom of Coventry,[7] he did not know what to do with her, and was obliged to despatch her to the tomb of the Capulets, the only place for which she was fitted.[8] The illustrious poets also, annoyed by the platitude of prose, speedily relinquished their uncongenial task.[9]

I busied myself *to think of a story,*—a story to rival those which had excited us to this task. One which would speak to the mysterious fears of our nature, and awaken thrilling horror—one to make the reader dread to look round, to curdle the blood, and quicken the beatings of the heart. If I did not accomplish these things, my ghost story would be unworthy of its name. I thought and pondered—vainly. I felt that blank incapability of invention which is the greatest misery of authorship, when dull Nothing replies to our anxious invocations. *Have you thought of a story?* I was asked each morning, and each morning I was forced to reply with a mortifying negative.[10]

Every thing must have a beginning, to speak in Sanchean phrase;[11] and that beginning must be linked to something that went before. The Hindoos give the world an elephant to support it, but they make the elephant stand upon a tortoise. Invention, it must be humbly admitted, does not consist in creating out of void, but out of chaos; the materials must, in the first place, be afforded: it can give form to dark, shapeless substances, but cannot bring into being the substance itself. In all matters of discovery and invention, even of those that appertain to the imagination, we are continually reminded of the story of Columbus and his egg. Invention consists in the capacity of seizing on the capabilities of a subject, and in the power of moulding and fashioning ideas suggested to it.

Many and long were the conversations between Lord Byron and Shelley, to which I was a devout but nearly silent listener. During one of these, various philosophical doctrines were discussed, and among others the nature of the principle of life, and whether there was any probability of its ever being discovered and communicated.[12] They talked of the experiments of Dr. Darwin, (I speak not of what the Doctor really did, or said that he did, but, as more to my purpose, of what was then spoken of as having been done by him,) who preserved a piece of vermicelli in a glass case, till by some extraordinary means it began to move with vol-

untary motion. Not thus, after all, would life be given. Perhaps a corpse would be re-animated; galvanism had given token of such things: perhaps the component parts of a creature might be manufactured, brought together, and endued with vital warmth.[13]

Night waned upon this talk, and even the witching hour had gone by, before we retired to rest. When I placed my head on my pillow, I did not sleep, nor could I be said to think. My imagination, unbidden, possessed and guided me, gifting the successive images that arose in my mind with a vividness far beyond the usual bounds of reverie. I saw—with shut eyes, but acute mental vision,—I saw the pale student of unhallowed arts kneeling beside the thing he had put together. I saw the hideous phantasm of a man stretched out, and then, on the working of some powerful engine, show signs of life, and stir with an uneasy, half vital motion. Frightful must it be; for supremely frightful would be the effect of any human endeavour to mock the stupendous mechanism of the Creator of the world. His success would terrify the artist; he would rush away from his odious handywork, horror-stricken. He would hope that, left to itself, the slight spark of life which he had communicated would fade; that this thing, which had received such imperfect animation, would subside into dead matter; and he might sleep in the belief that the silence of the grave would quench for ever the transient existence of the hideous corpse which he had looked upon as the cradle of life. He sleeps; but he is awakened; he opens his eyes; behold the horrid thing stands at his bedside, opening his curtains, and looking on him with yellow, watery, but speculative eyes.

I opened mine in terror. The idea so possessed my mind, that a thrill of fear ran through me, and I wished to exchange the ghastly image of my fancy for the realities around. I see them still; the very room, the dark *parquet,* the closed shutters, with the moonlight struggling through, and the sense I had that the glassy lake and white high Alps were beyond. I could not so easily get rid of my hideous phantom; still it haunted me. I must try to think of something else. I recurred to my ghost story,—my tiresome unlucky ghost story! O! if I could only contrive one which would frighten my reader as I myself had been frightened that night!

Swift as light and as cheering was the idea that broke in upon me. "I have found it! What terrified me will terrify others; and I need only describe the spectre which had haunted my midnight pillow." On the morrow I announced that I had *thought of a story.* I began that day with the words, *It was on a dreary night of November,* making only a transcript of the grim terrors of my waking dream.

At first I thought but of a few pages—of a short tale; but Shelley urged me to develope the idea at greater length. I certainly did not owe the suggestion of one incident, nor scarcely of one train of feeling, to my husband, and yet but for his incitement, it would never have taken the form in which it was presented to the world.[14] From this declaration I must except the preface. As far as I can recollect, it was entirely written by him.

And now, once again, I bid my hideous progeny go forth and prosper. I have an affection for it, for it was the offspring of happy days, when death and grief were but words, which found no true echo in my heart. Its several pages speak of many a walk, many a drive, and many a conversation, when I was not alone; and my companion was one who, in this world, I shall never see more. But this is for myself; my readers have nothing to do with these associations.

I will add but one word as to the alterations I have made. They are principally those of style. I have changed no portion of the story, nor introduced any new ideas or circumstances.[15] I have mended the language where it was so bald as to interfere with the interest of the narrative; and these changes occur almost exclusively in the beginning of the first volume. Throughout they are entirely confined to such parts as are mere adjuncts to the story, leaving the core and substance of it untouched.

M.W.S.
London, October 15, 1831.

Notes

[1] Henry Colburn and Richard Bentley (London).

[2] Isabel Baxter (later Mrs. David Booth), the daughter of W. T. Baxter of Dundee. . . .

. . . . .

[4] "La Morte Fiancée."

[5] "Les Portraits de Famille." Despite her assertion that these stories remain "fresh in my mind," Mrs. Shelley does not recall them accurately.

[6] There were five of them, if one includes Claire Clairmont. In his Preface (p. 7) Shelley omits both Claire and Polidori.

[7] "Peeping Tom," who watched the ride of Lady Godiva, was struck blind.

[8] There is no evidence that Polidori ever planned such a story. In the Introduction to his realistic *Ernestus Berchtold; or, The Modern Oedipus* (1819), he claims that the "tale here presented to the public is the one I began at Coligny, when Frankenstein was planned, and when a noble author having determined to descend from his lofty range, gave up a few hours to a tale of terror, and wrote the fragment published at the end of Mazeppa."

[9] Shelley may not have attempted "the platitude of prose" at all. The following doggerel fragment, editorially dated 1816, may be part or all of his contribution to the contest:

> A shovel of his ashes took
> From the hearth's obscurest nook,
> Muttering mysteries as she went.
> Helen and Henry knew that Granny
> Was as much afraid of Ghosts as any,
>   And so they followed hard—
> But Helen clung to her brother's arm,
> And her own spasm made her shake.

[10] It is unlikely that it took Mary Shelley all this time "to think of a story." Byron seems to have proposed the contest on 16 June, when Polidori was laid up with a sprained ankle and the Shelley party slept overnight at Villa Diodati. They would not ordinarily have done so, for their own house was a few minutes' walk away. Shelley's Preface recalls cold, rainy evenings when "we crowded around a blazing wood fire," but the sixteenth seems to have been the *only* day on which, in Mary's words, "incessant rain . . . confined us . . . to the house." In any case, Polidori noted in his *Diary* for 17 June: "The ghost-stories are begun by all but me." This date is independently supported by that on Byron's "A Fragment" . . .

[11] An allusion to the political theory of Sancho Panza, the commonsensical squire in Cervantes' *Don Quixote de la Mancha* (II.xxxiii).

[12] Polidori's *Diary* for 15 June records a conversation between himself and Shelley "about principles,—whether man was to be thought merely an instrument." This is almost certainly the discussion Mary Shelley recalls as "many." Polidori had just published his thesis on the psychosomatic aspects of sleepwalking (*Disputatio Medica Inauguralis, Quaedam de Morbo, Oneirodynia Dicto, Complectens* [Edinburgh, 1815]). He was therefore far more expert than Byron was on such questions as the discovery and communication of "the principle of life." The conversation apparently took place the day before Byron suggested the story contest, not, as recollected here, some time afterwards. . . .

[13] Galvanism—here, the application of electricity to dead tissue—had given spectacular "token of such things" in 1803, when Galvani's nephew, Giovanni Aldini (1762-1834), induced spasms in "the body of a malefactor executed at Newgate." Cf. Byron, *Don Juan*, I (1819), 1034: "And galvanism has set some corpses grinning . . . ."

[14] Shelley contributed more than his widow recalls here. . . .

[15] Another misstatement of fact. . . .

U. C. Knoepflmacher (essay date 1979)

SOURCE: "Thoughts on the Aggression of Daughters," in *The Endurance of Frankenstein: Essays in Mary Shelley's Novel*, edited by George Levine and U. C. Knoepflmacher, University of California Press, 1979, pp. 88-119.

[*In the essay that follows, Knoepflmacher contends that "Frankenstein is a novel of omnipresent fathers and absent mothers," a situation he relates explicitly to Shelley's own family history and the repressed anger at her father that appears to surface in the novel.*]

> Parental affection, indeed, in many minds, is but a pretext to tyrannize where it can be done with impunity.
>
> —Mary Wollstonecraft, *A Vindication of the Rights of Woman* (1792)

> I will keep a good look out—William is all alive—and my appearance no longer doubtful—you, I daresay, will perceive the difference. What a fine thing it is to be a man!
>
> —Mary Wollstonecraft to William Godwin, 10 June 1797

> There never can be perfect equality between father and child . . . the ordinary resource is for him to proclaim his wishes and commands in a way sometimes sententious and authoritative and occasionally to utter his censures with seriousness and emphasis. . . . I am not, therefore, a perfect judge of Mary's character. . . . [She] shows great need to be roused.
>
> —William Godwin to William Baxter, 8 June 1812

> I learned from your papers that you were my father, my creator; and to whom could I apply with more fitness than to him who had given me life?
>
> —Mary Wollstonecraft Godwin Shelley, *Frankenstein* (1818)

On the first page of *Frankenstein,* beneath the title and subtitle, appears a three-line quotation from *Paradise Lost,* X.743-45: "Did I request thee, Maker, from my clay / To mould me Man, did I solicit thee / From darkness to promote me?" The following page contains an inscription that seems far more tame and submissive: "To WILLIAM GODWIN Author of Political Justice, Caleb Williams, &c. / These Volumes / Are respectfully inscribed / By / The Author."

Major Media Adaptations: Motion Pictures

Frankenstein, 1910. Edison. Cast: Charles Ogle.

Frankenstein, 1931. Universal. Director: James Whale. Producer: Carl Laemmle Jr. Cast: Boris Karloff, Colin Clive, Mae Clarke, Dwight Frye, John Boles.

The Bride of Frankenstein, 1935. Universal. Director: James Whale. Producer: Carl Laemmle Jr. Cast: Boris Karloff, Elsa Lanchester, Colin Clive, Valerie Hobson.

Son of Frankenstein, 1939. Universal. Director and Producer: Rowland V. Lee. Cast: Basil Rathbone, Bela Lugosi, Boris Karloff.

The Curse of Frankenstein, 1957. Warner Brothers. Director: Terence Fisher. Producer: Anthony Hinds. Cast: Peter Cushing, Christopher Lee, Hazel Court.

Young Frankenstein, 1974. Twentieth-Century Fox. Director: Mel Brooks. Producer: Dalia di Lazzaro, Monique Van Vooren, Joe Dallesandro.

Victor Frankenstein, 1975. Films Around the World. Director and Producer: Calvin Floyd. Cast: Leon Vitali, Per Oscarsson, Nicholas Clay, Stacy Dorning.

Frankenstein '80, 1979. Director: Mario Mancini. Cast: John Richardson, Gordon Mitchell, Leila Parker, Dada Galloti, Marisa Travers.

Frankenstein, 1982. Director: James Ormerod. Cast: Robert Powell, Carrie Fisher, David Warner, John Gielgud.

Mary Shelley's Frankenstein, 1994. TriStar. Director: Kenneth Branagh. Producers: Francis Ford Coppola, James V. Hart, John Veitch. Cast: Kenneth Branagh, Robert De Niro, Helena Bonham Carter, Aidan Quinn, John Cleese.

Major Media Adaptations: Television

Frankenstein, 1973. ABC. Director: Glenn Jordan. Producer: Dan Curtis. Cast: Robert Foxworth, Susan Strasberg, Bo Svenson, Willie Ames.

Frankenstein, 1993. Director: David Wickes. Cast: Patrick Bergin, Randy Quaid, Lambert Wilson, Fiona Gilles.

The bitterness of Milton's Adam is intensified in *Frankenstein* by the companionless Monster: "I remembered Adam's supplication to his Creator; but where was mine? he had abandoned me, and, in the bitterness of my heart, I cursed him."[1] Though recognizing "Satan as the fitter emblem of my condition," the Monster also seems to remember Adam's fit of rebellion in Book Ten of *Paradise Lost* when it sarcastically reproaches its own indifferent maker: "Oh truly, I am grateful to thee my Creator for the gift of life, which was but pain" (p. 115). In the speech from which Mary Shelley takes her novel's epigraph, Adam revolts against that same Spirit of Creation earlier described "brooding on the vast Abyss" and making "it pregnant" (I.20-22). When Adam considers that he can only increase and multiply his own progeny's "curses," Eve invites him to abjure creation, to remain the first and last Man. In Mary Shelley's revenge story, the Adamic Monster who has turned into a Satan forces its neglectful father-creator to experience its own desolation; in Milton's paternal universe, however, the rebellious child Adam must be forced to accept his own role as parent, even if parenthood does convert him into a death-bringer, the father of Cain and Abel. Adam's revolt is short-lived. To deny God's design would be tantamount to submission to a far more terrifying "Universe of death" and to a banishment into the Satanic abode of "many a frozen Alp"—so like the ice-scapes into which the Monster lures its creator—a region where "all life dies, death lives, and Nature breeds / Perverse, all monstrous, all prodigious things / Abominable, inutterable, and worse, / Than Fables yet have feign'd, or fear conceiv'd, / *Gorgons* or *Hydras,* and *Chimeras dire*" (II.622, 624-28).

If the three lines quoted on the title page of *Frankenstein* thus evoke a locus for the "anger and hatred" that so irreconcilably separate the Monster from its father and creator, the novel's dedication seems to stem from quite opposite an intention. The "Author," who so "respectfully" aligns herself with that other "Author" she will not publicly address as her father, assumes a stance that is as dutiful and self-effacing as that adopted by the exemplary Elizabeth Lavenza, the orphan whom Alphonse Frankenstein cherishes as "his more than daughter, whom he doated on with all the affection a man feels, who, in the decline of life, having few affections, clings more earnestly to those that remain" (pp. 195-96). In her 1831 introduction to the revised version of *Frankenstein,* Mary Shelley speaks of herself "as the daughter of two persons of distinguished literary celebrity." Her 1818 dedication, however, pays tribute only to the father who had been her mentor in the decline of his life; it ignores the famous mother whose conflicts with a tyrannical father had helped shape her first published work, a pamphlet entitled *Thoughts on the Education of Daughters.* Had Mary Shelley forgotten the rebellious mother who had written that "respect for parents is, generally speaking, a much more debasing principle" than marriage and who had insisted that the "father who is blindly obeyed is obeyed from sheer weakness, or from motives that degrade the human character"?[2]

Before I attempt to answer that question, let me point out that the quotation from *Paradise Lost* and the dedication to Godwin have a connection that is so obvious that it can easily be missed. In each passage, a father is addressed by the offspring he has "moulded." And, what is more important, in each passage the father addressed is that offspring's only parent. Like Adam, and like the Monster who calls himself "an abortion to be spurned at" (Walton's last letter, p. 219), Mary Shelley never knew a mother's nurture.

Frankenstein is a novel of omnipresent fathers and absent mothers. It is no coincidence that after killing the child who boasts of his powerful "papa," the Monster should stop to gaze at "the portrait of a most lovely woman" and be momentarily calmed by her maternal beauty, only to remember angrily and ruefully that "I was for ever deprived of the delights that such beautiful creatures could bestow" (p. 139). Nor is it a coincidence, I think, that the Monster's previous "rage of anger," the "kind of instanity in my spirits" that leads him to burn down the De Lacey cottage and to seek "redress," is the direct result of his realization that he will never be accepted as a member of the family of "the old man"—the blind father whose hand he had seized in his unsuccessful plea for affection and kinship (pp. 134-35, 136).

Frankenstein resurrects and rearranges an adolescent's conflicting emotions about her relation both to the dead mother she idealized and mourned and to the living, "sententious and authoritative" father-philosopher she admired and deeply resented for his imperfect attempts at "moulding" Mary Wollstonecraft's two daughters. Fanny "Godwin" emulated the mother who had twice attempted to commit suicide. Her hardier half-sister attempted to master guilt and hostility in the "voyage of discovery" begun by Walton the mariner. As she tries to explain in her 1831 introduction—written after she had completed *Valperga, The Last Man, Perkin Warbeck,* and nearly a dozen short stories—*Frankenstein* is unique among her productions. It differs from her other works because in it she refused to "exchange the ghastly image of my fancy for the realities around" (p. 228). The adolescent mother and wife could confront "frightful" fantasies—destructive and aggressive thoughts—which the matured professional writer still entertained, yet carefully defused and disguised in most of her subsequent fictions.

Critics have inevitably ventured into biographical speculations in their attempts to come to terms with *Frankenstein.* In the preceding essay in this collection, Ellen Moers demonstrates the significance for this novel of the death of Mary Shelley's first (unnamed) "female child" in 1815, of the birth of the son she named after her father in 1816, and of the death by suicide, later in that same year and when *Frankenstein* was well under way, of Mary's half-sister Fanny, whom Godwin had described in 1812 as possessing "a quiet, modest, unshowy disposition," quite the reverse of his own daughter's "singularly bold, somewhat imperious" manner.[3] Like Professor Moers, I tend to read *Frankenstein* as a "phantasmagoria of the nursery," a fantasy designed to relieve deep personal anxieties over birth and death and identity. Yet I prefer to stress the importance of an earlier nursery—of the nurture denied to Mary herself when her mother died of a retained placenta eleven days after her birth and of the highly inad-

Boris Karloff and Mae Clarke in the 1931 motion picture Frankenstein.

equate substitute for a nursery which she found in her remarried father's household.

Since in my reading of **Frankenstein** William Godwin may appear almost a villain, it ought to be acknowledged that he was genuinely solicitous about the care and welfare of Mary Wollstonecraft's two daughters. (Indeed, his very solicitude contributed to Mary Shelley's conflicting emotions of allegiance and resentment; had he been more like her maternal grandfather, Edward John Wollstonecraft, a drunkard and a bully, Mary might have found it easier to emulate her mother's rebellious detachment.) Godwin himself had been "brought up in great tenderness" as a child. Just as, in a passage added to elaborate on Victor Frankenstein's happy youth, Victor describes "the ardent affection that attached me to my excellent parents" (p. 31), so did Godwin gratefully remember his own parents. He claimed that his mother had "exercised a mysterious protection over me" and yet, significantly, he never could bring himself to forgive her for sending him away from home while an infant "to be nourished by a hireling."[4] This personal understanding of the need

for mothering must have been decisive in Godwin's stubborn quest for a second wife to act as surrogate mother for the two orphans in his care. Still, as every biographer has pointed out, Mrs. Clairmont was hardly a Mary Wollstonecraft. Vulgar, mundane, preoccupied with the welfare of her own two children, she failed to establish a good relationship with her two stepdaughters. Rather than compensating Mary for her deprivation, as Godwin had intended, she actually helped activate in Mary a lifelong desire to compensate her father for the loss of his exquisite first wife and their short-lived marital happiness. The situation was hardly improved when, in 1803, before Mary's sixth birthday, the new Mrs. Godwin presented her husband with the son he had actually expected in 1797 when he and the pregnant Mary Wollstonecraft, strangely overconfident of the sex of the child she was carrying, had repeatedly promised themselves a "little William" in their letters.[5]

Professor Moers hints that the Monster's wanton destruction of little William in the novel is an expression of a young mother's anxieties over the precarious health of her own baby William. The speculation is not entirely new. Back in 1928, Richard Church also thought he detected a "miserable delight in self-torture" and a prophetic "anticipation of disaster" in Mary Shelley's decision to depict the fictional murder of "that fair child" who bears the name of her actual son:

> At the time that she was writing this book, the baby William was in the tenderest and most intimate stage of dependent infancy. The mite five months of age was passionately tended—but not very knowledgeably or hygienically—by both his parents. It is almost inconceivable that Mary could allow herself to introduce a baby boy in her book; deliberately call him William; describe him in terms identical with those in which she portrays her own child in one of her letters [in which she alludes to the real boy's identical blue eyes in similar rhapsodic terms]—and then let Frankenstein's monster waylay this innocent in a woodland dell and murder him by strangling.[6]

Church's clue is valid, as we shall see; but his surmise remains as incomplete as Muriel Spark's added suggestion that the murder of the boy who bears the name of "the child Mary loved more than any" is symptomatic of a split between feeling and intellect that led her "automatically" to identify the threatened child with her own threatened emotions.[7]

Church, Spark, and Moers are undoubtedly correct in linking the Monster's first murder to Mary Shelley's fears for her second child. Yet these fears, which proved so sadly justified when William died in 1819, also stemmed from deeper and more primal associations. For, in addition to her own son, there were two other "little Williams" who played a crucial role in the fantasy life of Mary Shelley's formative years. The first of these was none other than Mary herself, the little William expected in 1797 who turned into a little girl responsible for her mother's death and father's grief. The second was the half-brother born to Mary's stepmother, William Godwin the Younger, whose arrival she must have regarded as a threat to her relationship with a father to whom she so desperately wanted to make amends.

Even after the birth of this rival man-child, Mary eagerly tried to repair her father's loss both of the philosopher-wife he had worshipped and the philosopher-son he had hoped for from his first union. In the same 1812 letter in which Godwin contrasts Mary's imperiousness to Fanny's passivity, he notes approvingly that, unlike her half-sister, his daughter had shown herself true to her parental stock by responding to his teachings: "Her desire for knowledge is great, and her perseverance in anything she undertakes almost invincible." It seems fairly obvious that this extreme eagerness to learn was related to Mary's even greater eagerness to please the father for whom she had, as she later would put it, from very early on entertained an "exces-

sive and romantic passion." Still, her deep thirst for knowledge and her active identification with his own learning, so like the impulse that binds the Monster and Walton to the more deeply studied and "philosophical" Victor, seems to jar both with Mary's lifelong insistence on her ignorance, timidity, and "horror of pushing" and with Percy Shelley's self-justificatory, yet believable, description in "Epipsychidion" of an unresponsive and indifferent wife. Indeed, visitors who came to the Godwin home detected no real distinction between Mary and the torpid and unambitious Fanny; Coleridge, for instance, found "the cadaverous silence of Godwin's children quite catacombish."[8]

This discrepancy is crucial to **Frankenstein** and to Mary Shelley's self-divisions into aggressive and passive components, a raging Monster and a "yielding" Elizabeth. But the discrepancy itself is easy enough to reconcile. In 1838, two years after Godwin's death, Mary Shelley was finally able to voice her disappointment in the exacting father-tutor she had tried to please:

> My Father, from age and domestic circumstances, could not "*me faire valoir.*" My total friendlessness, my horror of pushing, and inability to put myself forward unless *led, cherished, and supported*—all this has sunk me in a state of loneliness no other human being ever before, I believe, endured—except Robinson Crusoe.[9]

It is clear from this account that Mary could, when "led, cherished, and supported," be the active and responsive, even "somewhat imperious," child described by Godwin in his 1812 letter; but like "Lucy," who lost her mother as an infant and whose case history is described in Erna Furman's *A Child's Parent Dies: Studies in Childhood Bereavement,* she could also resort to the defence of withdrawal and passivity whenever thwarted in this acute need for support.[10]

Mary Shelley's identification with the total isolation of Robinson Crusoe is significant. By 1838 she might have allowed another fictional analogue to characterize her sense of desertion. Yet the qualifying use of the adjective "human" prevents an identification with the Monster: the motherless creature who clings to the blind De Lacey to plead for affection and support is pointedly distinguished by its "un-human" features. What is more, the Monster is aggressive. As a male, albeit a male who wishes a female complement to subdue its "evil passions," it can find an outlet for hatred not permissible for nineteenth-century daughters. Fearful of releasing hostilities which—without a maternal model—she regarded (or wanted to regard) as exclusively male attributes, Mary Shelley could resort only to passivity as a safer mode of resistance. Again like "Lucy," Mary experienced a depressive crisis at the age of fifteen in the same year in which her father had hailed her "invincible" drive for knowledge. Noting that his "bold" daughter had suddenly become so listless that she showed "a great need to be roused," Godwin sent the teenager to the Baxters in Scotland, where she observed a happy family nucleus for the first time in her life. Recalled from Scotland by her father two years later (is it sheer coincidence that Victor Frankenstein should destroy the female monster in the Hebrides?), she soon became reacquainted with Shelley, the anti-authoritarian son of Sir Timothy. It was during their honeymoon at Marsluys that Shelley, perhaps to help her weather the bitterness of her father's disapproval, encouraged Mary to write her first piece of fiction. The title of that story, now lost, was "Hate."[11]

Yet, unlike Shelley the iconoclast, she was not cast for the role of rebel. Even her elopement could not be construed as an act of open defiance. The poet, after all, had presented himself as her father's eager disciple, as one who would—and could—put into practice the principles of the "inestimable book on 'Political Justice.'" It is not too fanciful therefore to suppose that the young girl who pledged her love to Shelley over her mother's grave at St. Pancras Churchyard hoped to revive or resurrect the short-lived union between her own parents. Shelley had been betrayed, Mary was willing to believe, into a marriage with one inferior and unsympathetic to his genius. Had she not seen her father debased by just such a union with her stepmother? She would nobly rescue Shelley from her father's fate, and, in the process, repair the damage done by her own birth. Through her, the "little William" her parents had expected could be born again, and, by giving it the nurture she had herself lacked as a child, she would be able to assume her dead mother's identity and role. Yet the child once again was a female, and again the bond between mother and daughter was short-lived; after recording her successful nursing of the baby for three consecutive days, Mary Shelley laconically wrote: "Find my baby dead. Send for Hogg. Talk. A miserable day. In the evening read 'Fall of the Jesuits.' Hogg sleeps here."[12] The unemotional, seemingly indifferent tone of this and subsequent entries (the next one ends: "Not in good spirits. Hogg goes at 11. A fuss. To bed at 3") is broken when she records her dream, on 19 March 1815, "that my little baby came to life again; that it only had been cold, and that we rubbed it before the fire, and it lived."[13]

As Professor Moers observes, this dream is linked to the fantasy of animation that underlies *Frankenstein*; yet it could hardly have been Mary Shelley's first wishful "dream" of making the dead come alive. Before, a child had wished to restore a mother; now, a mother wished to restore a child. The restoration again became a possibility after the birth of a male "babe" in January of 1816.[14] By naming her first male child after her father, Mary could signify the reparation she had so long intended. The offering was as deferential as the dedication of her first literary offspring to the

"Author" of *Political Justice,* of *Caleb Williams,* and of herself. But, like that dedication, it was also double-edged.

By 1816, the surrogate life with Shelley had already been sorely tested. No "little William" could breach the sense of loneliness and desertion she once more intensely experienced. Not only her father, but also her father's substitute, had been found wanting.[15] The integration that she, like the Monster, had yearned to find through a mate who might take the place of a rejecting father seemed impossible. Although she clung tenaciously to her second child, the rebelliousness and self-pity she had previously stifled began to surface. Like the Malthusian Adam of Book Ten who resents his own birth and decides to resist his Father by not procreating, she resented her role as perpetuator of a male line.

The 1831 introduction makes much of the "hideous" thoughts that went into the making of *Frankenstein*. As if to deny that these thoughts germinated within her, Mary Shelley overemphasizes her passivity, the defense to which she had previously resorted to her father's (and to Shelley's) chagrin. She insists that she had no control over her revenge story: "My imagination, unbidden, possessed and guided me." If this tactic recalls Coleridge's own distancings from an "unhallowed" and possibly demonic imagination, it also strongly resembles both Victor Frankenstein's trance-like activities and the Monster's repeated claim that its vengeful crimes are solely attributable to the neglect of, and contempt for, all its eager efforts to please.

At least in the early stages of its growth and education in the ways of "man" (Mary Shelley deliberately seems to eschew the words "humanity" or "mankind") the Monster is a most willing student. Not only does it quickly master the lessons intended for Safie (whose name means "wisdom"), but it is eager to please the De Laceys by anonymously performing the most menial tasks. Like a child who reveres grownups, it looks upon the family "as superior beings, who would be the arbiters of my future destiny." The Monster fantasizes "that it might be in my power to restore happiness to these deserving people," particularly to "the venerable blind father" whose losses have been greater than his children's (p. 103). De Lacey first wins the Monster's "reverence" by the soul-stirring music of his violin. Significantly, the ugly Monster and the beautiful Agatha respond identically to the "sweet mournful air." Indeed, when the Monster later kneels at De Lacey's feet, it hopes to win the same recognition earlier accorded to De Lacey's kneeling daughter:

> He played a sweet mournful air, which I perceived drew tears from the eyes of his amiable companion, of which the old man took no notice, until she sobbed audibly; he then pronounced a few sounds

and the fair creature, leaving her work, knelt at his feet. He raised her, and smiled with such kindness and affection, that I felt sensations of a peculiar and overpowering nature.... I withdrew from the window, unable to bear these emotions [Pp. 103-4]

Frankenstein clearly draws on Mary Shelley's recollection of her vain attempts to win "notice" and approval as her father's pupil. (Indeed, after her elopement she remained most interested in the "conduct" of the second "little William" being "moulded" in her father's house.[16]) In her 1831 introduction she depicts herself as "a devout but nearly silent listener" to Byron's and Shelley's discourses on "the principle of life." She deliberately belittles both her "tiresome unlucky ghost story" and her ideas, which, she says, required "communication with [Percy's] far more cultivated mind." But the belittlement can hardly conceal her ready appropriation of the subject discussed by the two poets and "poor Polidori." Their conversation about the piece of flesh that twitched "with voluntary motion" may well have evoked, in her mind, the piece of flesh that caused her mother's death. But it was clearly their speculation that perhaps a "corpse would be reanimated" that attracted and repelled her so powerfully.

Mary could not acknowledge to her 1831 English readers that the topic which the three men had so casually touched upon was integral to a private fantasy she had by 1816 long cherished and recently despaired of—the fantasy of restitution that would reconcile the apparently antagonistic aims of resurrecting a mother and regaining a father's undivided love. In the 1831 introduction it is Shelley, and not his wife, who soon starts a story "founded on the experiences of his early life." Although Mary Shelley dwells on her own early life in Scotland (an "eyry of freedom" in which she was "not confined to my own identity"), she ostensibly dwells on this past only to suggest her subsequent acquisition of a greater sense of "reality." The wife of a husband "anxious that I should prove myself worthy of my parentage" thus wants above all to stress her maturation. She has outgrown "the indulging of waking dreams" and must apologize for the "so very hideous" production of a "young girl." Nonetheless, it is noteworthy that the introduction should depict her Scottish fantasy life as wholly "pleasant" and thus in no way connected to the "ghastly image" that overwhelmed her in 1816 when forbidden and ugly material had, like the Monster itself, come to life.

That "hideous progeny," Mary Shelley insists in 1831, is her very own. Though she acknowledges Shelley's "incitement," she stresses her originality with unaccustomed forcefulness: "I certainly did not owe the suggestion of one incident, nor scarcely of one *train of feeling,* to my husband" (p. 229; italics added). Indeed,

there is a faint note of resentment at the two "illustrious poets" who, "annoyed by the platitude of prose, speedily relinquished their uncongenial task" (p. 225). The seed they have so carelessly implanted in Mary (and "poor Polidori") becomes a burden that is hers alone. It is she who has to give birth to a "hideous progeny," because she can better understand the pains of abandonment. Like the Monster, the author has been deserted. And, if we are to trust her account, she began her story neither with Walton's frame or Victor's account of his idyllic youth, but with the scene of desertion in chapter 4, with a father who rejects the stretched-out hand ("seemingly to detain me, but I escaped") of the "miserable monster whom I had created" (p. 53). Victor's repulsion of "the demoniacal corpse I had so miserably given life" will unleash antagonistic emotions that Mary Shelley had resisted and would stoutly continue to resist.

Yet the Monster does not become truly demoniacal until it murders little William and thereby causes the death of the guiltless Justine. As it explains to its creator, "I was benevolent and good; misery made me a fiend." Unlike the "fallen angel" he professes to have become, the Monster insists that evil need not be its good: "Make me happy, and I shall again be virtuous" (p. 95). The words recall another male demonist created by a female imagination, Emily Brontë's Heathcliff, who asks Nelly to "make me good." Yet Mary Shelley was far less willing than her Victorian successors to acknowledge her attraction to the anarchic and the destructive. Her violent figures are inevitably males; she could not have depicted a Jane Eyre who bloodies a boy's nose or a Maggie Tulliver who mutilates her dolls. And, whereas Emily Brontë quickly passes over the particulars of Heathcliff's early deprivation, Mary Shelley lingers over the Monster's painful degradation before she will depict it as an enraged murderer and fiend.

By the time the Monster does strangle little William our sympathies have so fully shifted from Frankenstein to the Monster that the action almost seems justifiable. Like little William, the Monster has been an innocent more sinned against than sinning. Though no "darling of a pigmy size," it is a genuine Wordsworthian child who has been able to "wander at liberty" and to derive intense "pleasure" in the natural world. It is as delighted by "the bright moon" and "the little winged animals" (p. 98) as any Romantic child of a feminine Nature.[17] But unlike Wordsworth's asocial children, this grown-up child desires socialization, human contact. On observing the De Laceys, who are exiled from society and yet remain self-sufficient as a family unit, the Monster discovers that its "heart yearned to be known and loved by these amiable creatures" (p. 127). It is from them that it—like the Mary Shelley who observed the Baxter family—learns the rudiments of kinship:

The youth and his companion had each of them several names, but the old man had only one, which was *father*. The girl was called *sister*, or *Agatha*; and the youth *Felix, brother*, or *son*. I cannot describe the delight I felt when I learned the ideas appropriated to each of these sounds, and was able to pronounce them. I distinguished several other words, without being able as yet to understand or apply them; such as *good, dearest, unhappy*. [Pp. 107-8]

The absence of a "mother" in this paragraph (which ends on the word "unhappy"!) is conspicuous. Less apparent, I think, is the strange fact that Agatha is called "sister" but never "daughter," even though "brother" Felix, who will tear away the old man with the single name of "father," is accorded the name of "son."

It is its own exclusion from such a system of relations that later leads the Monster to maintain that both the killing of little William and the execution of the innocent Justine have been a warranted retaliation, the outcome of "the lessons of Felix, and the sanguinary laws of man" (p. 140). Felix had removed his father from the Monster's reach after mistaking its Agatha-like feelings for the contrary emotions of hatred and violence. That the creature should still so vividly remember this potential brother's action after the deaths of William and Justine seems rather poignant. For, in its way, the murder of William was a delayed fratricidal act.

After it has burned the De Lacey cottage the Monster manages to reassert its softer nature. On entering "a deep wood," it blesses the sun and "dared to be happy." But its "hatred" for its "unfeeling, heartless creator" is soon reactivated when it is accidentally cast in a life-giving role like that of its own deserting father. Just as Victor had animated the corpse from which he created the Monster, so the Monster tries "to restore animation" to a young girl it has rescued from drowning. But again a gesture of kinship is rewarded with a wound— a literal injury this time—from the "ball" shot by "the man" who, like Felix, misreads an expression of the benevolent side of the Monster's divided personality as an act of aggression. Unlike a Mary Shelley who desperately clung to her Agatha- or Elizabeth-self, the Monster now yields to its destructive impulses and vows "eternal hatred and vengeance."

Yet the Monster wavers still one more time when it sees, not an adult male rival, but a "beautiful child, who came running into the recess I had chosen with all the sportiveness of infancy" (p. 138). The vague syntax almost seems designed to confuse us momentarily— does "the sportiveness of infancy" refer to little William or to the Monster? Assuming "this little creature" to be as "yet unprejudiced," the larger creature is "seized" by the idea to "seize him, and educate him as

my companion and friend." The child, however, displays Victor's own adult horror: "monster! ugly wretch! you wish to eat me, and tear me to pieces—You are an ogre—Let me go, or I will tell my papa" (p. 139). Significantly, the scene both reverses and matches the earlier encounter with Felix: whereas the threatened little boy invokes his father to protect him, Felix tried to protect his own father from the Monster's threat. In both cases, however, this threat is only imaginary: just as the Monster has revoked its vows of "eternal hatred" on seeing the harmless child, it had earlier "refrained" from strangling Felix. But when little William utters the name of his father, the oath of revenge is remembered. Assuming that "M. Frankenstein" and his own creator are one and the same, the Monster has found its "first victim": "Frankenstein! you belong then to my enemy" (p. 139). The murder is a delayed act of revenge, not only against a father but also against a father's rival son, like Felix a brother-figure. A huge and alienated Cain kills an Abel who can be sure of his father's support and secure in that father's identity.

If, as Church was the first to suggest, the fictional little William were no more than an analogue for Mary Shelley's real-life "baby boy," then the sympathetic, almost exculpating, attention devoted to all the psychic wounds inflicted on the Monster before it commits the murder would be distracting and illogical, as well as inartistic. The Monster's first choice of "victim" derives its fitness as much from the unattainability of a father as from fraternal slights. Little William possesses the birthright the Monster longs for. Only a course of aggression can obtain for the Monster the parental recognition it desires. And that course will prove irreversible—despite the Monster's pleas for a restraining female counterpart. It will also prove self-destructive.

Frankenstein is a fiction designed to resist that potential self-destruction. The destruction of little William can obviously be related to Mary Shelley's own muted hostility toward her younger half-brother: unlike herself, the younger William Godwin possessed a mother and, as a male, had received his father's identity and approbation. Simultaneously, however, the Monster's murder of the little boy must also be recognized as a self-mutilation which the novel as a whole tries to resist and conquer. Just as Mary Shelley must have feared that the possible death of her own little William might damage her identity, so does the death of the fictional boy mark the irreparable loss of the "benevolent" or feminine component of the Monster's personality, making it indistinguishable from Victor Frankenstein, similarly alienated from his feminine self—a self represented both by his dead mother and by the wife who dies on his wedding night.

I have said that *Frankenstein* is a novel of fathers and absent mothers, and it is time to examine this statement more closely. The book's central relationship is obviously that between father and child. After his mother's death, the secluded Frankenstein pursues feminine Nature "to her hiding places" to appropriate for himself the maternal role and the blessings of a new "species" created without a mother's agency: "No father could claim the gratitude of his child so completely as I should deserve theirs" (p. 49). After the destruction of its female complement ("a creature of another sex, but as hideous as myself"), the Monster becomes father to the man and relentlessly imposes on its creator the same conditions of dependency and insecurity that it was made to suffer.[18] Once able to identify with Agatha, the daughter, and to respond so powerfully to the "benign divinity" of little William's and Victor's mother, the Monster culminates its revenge by depriving Victor of Elizabeth. This contest between males divorced from female nurturance is framed by a series of forbidding fathers—the father whose "dying injunction" forbade Walton to embark on a sea-faring life; Henry Clerval's father, who insists that his son be a merchant rather than a poet; the "inexorable" Russian father who tries to force his daughter into a union she abhors; the treacherous Turkish father who uses Safie to obtain his freedom yet issues the "tyrannical mandate" that she betray Felix.

There are kinder fathers in the novel, to be sure, but their kindness is tainted: as Kate Ellis shows on pp. 129-130 below, the "proud and unbending disposition" of Beaufort leads him to seek an exile that results in his loyal daughter's total degradation; the "Italian gentleman" who is Elizabeth's father in the 1818 version (in 1831 she is the daughter of an imprisoned patriot and a German lady who "had died on giving her birth") decides, on remarrying, that it would be preferable to have her educated by her uncle and aunt rather than have her "brought up by a step-mother"— a decision that, in reversing William Godwin's own choice, may be construed as an act of kindness, but nonetheless involves an abdication of parental responsibility. De Lacey and Alphonse Frankenstein are impaired by an impotence and lack of discrimination that Mary must often have regretted in a father who "from age and domestic circumstances could not '*me faire valoir.*'" De Lacey can welcome Safie as a daughter but cannot respond to the Monster's need for affection; Alphonse Frankenstein values Elizabeth as a replica of Caroline Beaufort yet cannot believe in the innocence of Justine Moritz. A rationalist, like Godwin, the elder Frankenstein rather cruelly chastens his son's youthful imagination; his disparagement of Cornelius Agrippa actually may have produced, according to Victor, "the fatal impulse that led to my ruin" (p. 33). The 1818 version of the novel is even harsher on the old man whose heart is finally broken by Elizabeth's death. In a contradiction which Mary Shelley emended in her 1831 revisions, Alphonse is also blamed for leading his son to science when he conducts a Franklin-

like experiment and draws some electrical "fluid" down from the clouds (p. 35). The Monster's confusion of Alphonse with Victor, when he encounters William, thus seems quite warranted. When, after Clerval's murder, the calm but "severe" magistrate, Mr. Kirwin, informs Victor that a "friend" has come to visit him, the prisoner believes that the visitor is the Monster: "I know not by what chain of thought the idea presented itself that the murderer had come to mock me at my misery." Surprised, Mr. Kirwin rejoins: "I should have thought, young man, that the presence of your father would have been welcome, instead of inspiring such violent repugnance" (p. 177). To the reader, however, the "chain of thought" seems quite intelligible: Alphonse, Victor, and the Monster have all become manifestations of the same truncated male psyche.

Frankenstein questions the patriarchal system (see Kate Ellis on this, pp. 135-136), yet the novel is more than an indictment of fathers as potential monster-makers. If in his parental neglectfulness Victor resembles William Godwin (as well as Percy Shelley), his obsessive "desire for knowledge" and "perseverance" are the very same qualities displayed by the younger Mary Shelley when she wanted to signify her oneness with her father. The novel's attack on a male's usurpation of the role of mother therefore goes beyond a daughter's accusation of a father who could not "*me faire valoir.*" It is also an expression of Mary Shelley's deep fears about an imbalance within herself—the imbalance of a personality that had developed one-sidedly, without a feminine or maternal model. Karen Horney points out that a "girl may turn away altogether from the female role and take refuge in a fictitious masculinity" in order to assuage "disappointments in the father" or "guilt feelings towards the mother."[19] It seems obvious that the young woman who addresses the readers of *Frankenstein* (including the "Author" to whom the book is dedicated) through three male speakers acquired such an attitude in her own childhood. Yet *Frankenstein* represents a desperate attempt to recover "the female role." Despite its use of male masks and its emphasis on male aggression, the novel tries to exorcise a sadistic masculinity and to regain the female component of the novelist's threatened psyche.

Just as the novel oscillates in its sympathies between Victor and the increasingly demonic monster, so does it oscillate in the sexual characterization of these two antagonists. At first, though nurtured by loving women, Frankenstein is phallic and aggressive, capable of torturing "the living animal to animate the lifeless clay" (p. 49). Conversely, the Monster—purposely not called a "he" in this discussion—initially displays feminine qualities. It identifies with both Agatha and Safie and is respectful of that same Wordsworthian and feminine Nature whose "recesses" its creator is so eager to "penetrate" (p. 42).[20] These sexual associations, however, shift with the Monster's first act of aggression, the "mischief" that leads it to plant the portrait of maternal "divine benignity" into one "of the folds of [Justine's] dress" (p. 140). The Monster now assumes Victor's phallic aggression; and Victor becomes as tremulous and "timid as a love-sick girl" (p. 51).

Victor's desire to marry Elizabeth is presented as a pathetic and hopeless attempt to reenter the broken circle of affection over which his dead mother had presided. Conversely, the Monster's similar yearning for a female companion is treated as highly dangerous. Victor's marriage to Elizabeth evokes the image of a debilitated patient in need of a nurse (an image corroborated in James Whale's film *The Bride of Frankenstein,* which implies that the newly wed "Henry" Frankenstein is far too frail to consummate his marriage to the voluptuous Elizabeth). The Monster's desire for a mate, however, raises the specter of "a race of devils" to be "propagated on the earth" (p. 163). Even an unconsummated union holds dangers: Victor fears that the female monster might "turn with disgust from [the Monster] to the superior beauty of man" or that the Monster's own aggression (so far limited to the murder of William and the death of Justine) might be exacerbated upon his beholding his own "deformity" in "female form" (p. 163).

But above all Victor fears the possibility of a female creature not only more aggressive than the novel's remarkably passive female characters, but also capable of surpassing the sadistic and "unparalleled barbarity" of the killer of little William: "she might become ten thousand times more malignant than her mate, and delight, *for its own sake,* in murder and wretchedness" (p. 163; italics added). The implications are clear. Victor seems to acknowledge that the Monster's aggression has been partly justified, but a female who might delight in sadism "for its own sake" is a horror he cannot contemplate. Mary Shelley may well intend to have her readers see the speciousness in Victor's rationalizations—his decision is made when he "had not sufficient light" for his "employment." Still, Victor's terror seems also to be Mary Shelley's. The specter of female sadism is resisted by the novelist who fears her own aroused anger and desire for revenge. Victor rejects the Monster when he destroys the half-formed shape of its female companion; Mary Shelley, too, distances herself from the demonic figure at the casement, whose "ghastly grin" proclaims the retaliations that will follow: the deaths of Clerval, Alphonse Frankenstein, and Elizabeth. Only after the death of Victor will the Monster turn its aggression on itself. In a parody of the self-sacrificing Son, the feminine principle of compassion in *Paradise Lost* who balances the exacting justice of God the Father, the Monster will immolate itself to save humanity from its own violence.

The only surviving male speaker of the novel, Walton, possesses what the Monster lacks and Frankenstein

denies, an internalized female complementary principle. Walton begins his account through self-justificatory letters to a female ego-ideal, his sister Margaret Saville (the British pronunciation of her name sounds like "civil"). The memory of this civilizing and restraining woman, a mother with "lovely children," helps him resist Frankenstein's destructive (and self-destructive) course. Frankenstein and the Monster are the joint murderers of little William, Justine, Clerval, Alphonse Frankenstein, and Elizabeth; Walton, however, refuses to bring death to his crew. In a skillful addition to the 1831 version, Mary Shelley has Walton remind his sister that a "youth passed in solitude" was offset by "my best years spent under your gentle and feminine tutelage."

Mary Shelley, who likened her own "state of loneliness" to that of Robinson Crusoe, lacked the "feminine tutelage" that rescues Walton. Bereft of a maternal model that could teach her how to acknowledge and channel her own aggression, fearful of the unleashed aggression that consumes both Victor and the Monster, she turned to passivity as a stabilizing force. In her story **"The Sisters of Albano"** (published in *Keepsake* for 1829), the young nun Maria sacrifices herself for her more passionate sister Anina (who then becomes herself a nun). In *Frankenstein* the falsely accused Justine Moritz meets her degradation and death with "an air of cheerfulness"—in total contrast to the Monster's rage at the injustices it is forced to suffer (p. 84). In **"The Sisters,"** Anina, "her only wish to find repose in the grave," delays this death-wish (so like both Fanny Imlay's and that of Richardson's Clarissa) until the death of her own "miserable father," whose loss she tries to repair through constant "filial attentions";[21] in *Frankenstein,* Justine can die peacefully since she, "the favourite of her father" until the day of his death, has no such amends to make (p. 60).

This equation of femininity with a passivity that borders on the ultimate passivity of death is, in *Frankenstein* and in Mary Shelley's own life, associated with a dead mother. Caroline Beaufort Frankenstein, who nurses her dying father "with the greatest tenderness" and is the perfect daughter-wife to Alphonse Frankenstein, is a model accepted by Justine and by Elizabeth yet rejected (or forgotten) by the Monster and by Victor. Caroline is found by the elder Frankenstein near her father's coffin; on her own deathbed, she enjoins the "yielding" Elizabeth to take her place as mother and "supply my place to your younger cousins" (p. 38). It is significant that both she and Elizabeth are invoked in Victor's dream just after he has seen "the dull yellow eyes of the creature" to which he has given life. Presumably one of Victor's objects in finding "a passage to life" is to restore his mother and "renew life where death had apparently devoted the body to corruption" (p. 49); but his dream only underscores his rejection of the maternal or female model.

In the dream, Victor embraces Elizabeth, about whom he had said that she and he "were strangers to any disunion and dispute" (p. 30); when Elizabeth turns into the "corpse of my dead mother" (p. 53) the startled dreamer awakes and beholds "the miserable monster whom I had created." The conjunction of dream and reality, both equally frightening to Victor, forces us to link the four personages, the two females and the two males. The relation between Caroline and Elizabeth is one of fusion: although Elizabeth, like Mary Shelley, is the accidental agent of the mother's death, the "amiable woman"[22] harbors no resentment and insists that Elizabeth take her place. The relation between Victor and the two female corpses and the relation between Victor and the Monster are both based on "disunion"; his reaction is identical in each case: he recoils from the association.

But what is the relation between the two female corpses and the Monster? Like the Elizabeth of the 1831 version, the Monster is an orphan; like the young woman whose single remonstrance in the entire novel is her regret "that she had not the same opportunities of enlarging her experience, and cultivating her understanding" (p. 151) as her male friends, the Monster is denied a formal education. It is customary by now to discuss Frankenstein and the Monster as the feuding halves of a single personality. Yet the beautiful and passive Elizabeth and the repulsive, aggressive Monster who will be her murderer are also doubles—doubles who are in conflict only because of Victor's rejection of the femininity that was so essential to the happiness of his "domestic circle" and to the balance of his own psyche.[23]

Victor's dream, then, can be read as an intrapsychic conflict that has its roots in Mary Shelley's deprivation of a maternal model. Though Frankenstein is the dreamer, it is Caroline, Elizabeth, and Monster who dramatize this conflict. The Elizabeth whose mother died on giving her birth in the 1831 version and whose father deserted her in the 1818 version can find a feminine model in Caroline, and inherit her place. The motherless Monster deserted by its father finds this model in the picture of Caroline, only to be triggered by it into a course of revenge that ends with Elizabeth's death. Victor's dream thus contains an ominous warning. Though male, ugly, and deformed, the Monster is a potential Elizabeth (indeed, what if Frankenstein had created a little Galatea instead of a heroic male of Brobdingnagian proportions?). Yet Victor fails to recover the feminine ideal of nurture represented by Caroline, that sentimentalization of a forgiving Mary Wollstonecraft. By rejecting his child as a Monster, he will also be responsible for the death of Elizabeth, that less monstrous, yet also unduly passive, component of Mary Shelley's personality.

Death remains the only reconciler in *Frankenstein,* as the dream of Elizabeth's corpse and the reality of the corpse turned Monster foreshadow. For not only Victor and the Monster, but also the Monster and Elizabeth fuse through death into a single personality. Like Keats and Percy Shelley, but for rather different reasons, Mary Shelley was half in love with easeful death. The demise of Caroline so early in the novel suggests that Mary Shelley could endorse this escape from a world of fathers, brothers, husbands, and male justices and identify it with the repose found by her own mother.[24] There is strong empathy, too, with the grief the Monster feels as it hangs "over the coffin" of its dead parent, a scene that parallels Caroline Beaufort's own grief by her father's coffin. The Monster's lament ("Oh, Frankenstein! generous and self-devoted being! what does it avail that I now ask thee to pardon me?") may seem out of character, as Walton rather self-righteously points out, but Walton of course fails to understand that the Monster has also recovered that softer, feminine side that enabled it before to identify with Agatha and Safie. Indeed, as we shall see in the next section, the very phrasing of the Monster's tribute to Victor resembles the speeches of penitent daughters in *Mathilda* and "The Mourner."

The conclusion of *Frankenstein* exorcises aggression. With the death of Victor, the Monster turns its hatred against itself. "You hate me" it tells Walton, "but your abhorrence cannot equal that with which I regard myself" (p. 219). These words echo the expression of Mary Shelley's own revulsion, in her 1831 introduction, over the "hideous" embodiment of anger she had allowed herself to create. The Monster now sees justice in destroying its own "miserable frame"; its sadism has turned into self-pity: "I, the miserable and the abandoned, am an abortion, to be spurned at, and kicked, and trampled on." Sadism becomes masochism, the outlet for self-inflicted anger: "Polluted by crimes, and torn by the bitterest remorse, where can I find rest but in death?" (p. 220). Rest rather than restitution. The Monster must welcome the death so eagerly embraced by many of Mary Shelley's female penitents, figures often far more guiltless than it has been.

One such figure is that other victim of "injustice," the ironically named Justine Moritz. Mary Shelley asks us to regard the revengeful Monster and the passive Justine who is falsely accused of the murder of little William as exact opposites. Yet are they? If the child's murder can be construed as a fratricidal act on the part of the Monster, why are we told shortly before the murder that Madame Moritz has accused poor Justine of "having caused the deaths of her brothers and sisters"? (p. 61). The accusation is as false as the later indictment: it comes from one who—like Mrs. Clairmont in the Godwin household—clearly prefers the other children to this Cinderella and "neglected daughter." But why is the detail inserted? We must trust the novel rather than the novelist, and the suggestion that Justine may harbor thoughts as aggressive as the Monster's is corroborated by her willingness to confess to the murder. "Threatened and menaced" by her father confessor, charged "with the blackest ingratitude" for killing the child of the woman who had adopted her, Justine tells Elizabeth that she "almost began to think that I was *the monster* that he said I was" (p. 82). And so she dies for the Monster's crime. She is an innocent—and yet so is the Monster. She is its associate: her passive death becomes almost as much a retaliation against injustice as its murderous passion. She can also cause pain: her self-deprecating speeches are as agonizing to Victor as the Monster's later accusations. And Elizabeth, by identifying with Justine's death-wish ("I wish," cried she, "that I were to die with you; I cannot live in this world of misery" [p. 84]), also manages, ever so sweetly, to sharpen Victor's guilt and pain over William's death. Passivity, used correctly, as Mary Shelley knew but could not admit, can be as powerful a weapon as rage.

Novels, as we all know, are relations based on relations: narratives based on the interconnection of characters as well as on the links between these characters and their creator. In a famous illustration in *Vanity Fair*, Thackeray drew his own mournful and timid face peering out behind the removed mask of laughing jester; in a celebrated passage in *Middlemarch*, George Eliot, who had privately claimed that Casaubon was based on no other "original" but herself, rejected the notion that Dorothea's mummified husband ought to be regarded as a heartless monster: "some ancient Greek," the narrator volunteers, must have "observed that behind the big mask and the speaking-trumpet, there must always be our poor little eyes peeping as usual and our timorous lips more or less under anxious control."[25] In *Frankenstein*, too, the lifting of a monstrous mask produces a startling unveiling: beneath the contorted visage of Frankenstein's creature lurks a timorous yet determined female face.

The unveiling should not really surprise us. For *relatio*, as Percy Bysshe Shelley seemed to remember in his distinction between poetry and logic, once simply meant evocation: the recalling or bringing back of forgotten or dormant associations that the conscious will must then rearrange and recombine. The fluidity of relations in *Frankenstein*, which converts each character into another's double and makes a male Monster not only a counterpart of Victor and Walton but also of little William, Agatha, Safie, Caroline, Justine, and Elizabeth, stems from common denominators that can be traced back, as I have tried to show, to Mary Shelley's childhood and to her threatened identity as an adult daughter, wife, and mother. Yet this fluidity of relations, which makes *Frankenstein* so powerful as an exploration of the very act of kinship and relation, is absent in the novelist's later fictions, even though these later works are equally obsessed with the same intrapsychic conflicts. The later

Mary Shelley, who suffered severe new shocks through the deaths of her own William, her daughter Clara, and Shelley himself, seemed no longer capable of the imaginative strength that had enabled her to relate her own adolescent deprivations to the Monster's development and education. Whereas only a matured George Eliot, could, after much experimentation, have produced *Middlemarch*, maturity for Mary Shelley involved a loss of the powers she had been able to tap in her first novel. Her gradual acceptance of her father's deficiencies, her Amelia Sedley-like cult of the dead Shelley, and her devotion to little Percy Florence, permitted her to domesticate the daemon within and to advocate, in fiction as in life, the renunciatory virtues of an Elizabeth-Justine.

To be sure, there was one more important imaginative outburst and it came, not unexpectedly, after William died in Rome in June 1819. Mary had been able to bear the deaths of her first female child in 1815 and of the year-old Clara in 1818, but the loss of the little boy overwhelmed her as powerfully as the death of the fictional little William had unsettled Frankenstein. Life (or death) threatened to imitate art as the grieving mother indulged the same death-wish to which Justine had yielded. Writing to Amelia Curran three weeks after the burial, Mary Shelley asked to hear about the child's tomb, "near which I shall lie one day & care not—for my own sake—how soon—I shall never recover that blow—I feel it more now than at Rome— the thought never leaves me for a single moment— Everything has lost its interest to me."[26] But again, life and creativity came to the rescue: she had been pregnant since March, and Percy Florence was born in November 1819; angered by a new affront from her father and increasingly alienated from Shelley, she was "roused" once more into writing a fiction that might master these turbulent emotions, the novella *Mathilda*, on which she worked feverishly in August and September.

Shelley had written to Godwin to ask him to "soothe" Mary "on account of her terrible state of mind." Instead, the philosopher (who could not remember his grandson's age) wrote to berate Shelley and to ask for more money to help him fight a litigation. A second letter to Mary proved equally insensitive; instead of consolation for the loss of the boy she had named after Godwin, Mary found herself threatened once more with the withdrawal of her father's love: "Remember too," wrote Godwin, "though at first your nearest connections may pity you in this state, yet that when they see you fixed in selfishness and ill humor, . . . they will finally cease to love you, and scarcely learn to endure you."[27] That this bullying accusation of selfishness was taken seriously by Mary Shelley is evident in *Mathilda*, her most autobiographical piece of fiction, the writing of which must have been almost as therapeutic as the birth, after its completion, of her new male child.

Unlike *Frankenstein,* with its three male narrators, *Mathilda* is told by a twenty-two-year-old woman (Mary Shelley's own age in 1819). And unlike Walton who successfully repels the death that consumes Victor and the Monster, this narrator is engulfed by death: in one version of the manuscript, she is a penitent soul in limbo who addresses herself to a female listener who (unlike Walton's sister) is also dead, possibly after committing suicide on suffering a "misfortune" in Rome that reduced her "to misery and despair."[28] Elizabeth Nitchie, the critic most extensively concerned with *Mathilda,* has stressed the biographical implications of the novella's second half in which the lonely Mathilda meets a deprived young poet called Woodville and tries to cajole him into a suicide pact (in the days before their elopement, it had been Shelley who suggested to Mary that they both commit suicide). Nitchie is undoubtedly correct when she reads this second half as a self-castigation on Mary's part for her estrangement from Shelley: "*Mathilda* expresses a sense of estrangement from, even of physical repulsion toward, one whom she had deeply loved, a realization of her own selfish, petulant, and unreasoning absorption in her grief."[29] But in the first half of the narrative Mathilda's guilt and grief are traced to their source in her relationship to her father.

Like Mary Shelley, Mathilda is the daughter of a beautiful, intelligent, and adored woman who dies a few days after Mathilda's birth; like Godwin, her father is crushed by his loss. Although, unlike Godwin, he does not remarry, he leaves his child in the care of a stern and unsympathetic foster mother and (like De Lacey) becomes an exile. Again like Mary Shelley—who in the 1831 preface to *Frankenstein* speaks of living "in the country as a girl" and of passing a "considerable time in Scotland"— Mathilda grows up in the Scottish countryside. Her sole "pleasures," like the Monster's, "arise from the contemplation of nature alone; I had no companion."[30] At this point Mary Shelley begins to invert the fictional parallels: whereas she was recalled from Scotland by her father, Mathilda's father visits her in Scotland when she is sixteen; whereas Mary found herself as neglected as before by Godwin after her return, Mathilda's father tries to compensate for his earlier desertion by lavishing attentions on his daughter; and, lastly, while Mary gave up her "excessive and romantic" attachment to Godwin when she eloped with Shelley, Mathilda discovers, to her horror, that her father's love for her is incestuous. After she repels him, he leaves her a letter in which he acknowledges that he had hoped to find in her a substitute for his beloved dead wife. She dreams that she pursues him to a high rock, and her dream (like Frankenstein's) is prophetic: she finds her father's corpse in a cottage on a cliff. Guilt-stricken, she withdraws from society until she meets Woodville, himself a guilty mourner.

This melodramatic fable obviously displays in a different fashion the passive and aggressive impulses I have examined in *Frankenstein*. Mathilda's passive withdrawal clearly stems from parricidal wishes which the narrative conveys and yet never fully dares to acknowledge. Just as the Monster protests that it has not willed its crimes, so is Mathilda absolved from wishing her father's death—an event she dutifully tries to prevent. Why, then, should she feel such inordinate guilt over the death of the incestuous lecher who can love her only after she has become a fully developed woman? Though far less artistic than *Frankenstein,* the story must be read as a pendant to the novel, as still another self-exploration and confrontation with acknowledged hatred and wishful self-destruction; moreover, by dispensing with the protective masks of male protagonists, the story places Mary Shelley's marital difficulties at her father's doorstep.

How could Mary Shelley have had the temerity to send the manuscript of *Mathilda* to Godwin? She asked Maria Gisborne to take the manuscript to London, show it to her father, and obtain his advice about publishing it. When Maria demanded its return, Godwin held on; he told her that he did "not approve of the father's letter" in the story and that he found the entire subject "disgusting and detestable."[31] Had Mary Shelley finally succeeded in unsettling the revered "Author" of *Political Justice?* Was he finally forced to recognize what was so much more elliptically presented through Victor's rejection of the disgusting and detestable Monster? Godwin made sure that *Mathilda* would never be published. But when his daughter sent him *Valperga* to help him defray new debts and expenses, he gladly saw this new novel to press. Begun in 1820, yet not published until February of 1823, well after Shelley's death, *Valperga* had again anticipated an actual disaster, as Mary recognized: "it seems to me that in what I have written hitherto I have done nothing but prophecy [sic] what has [? arrived] to. Mathilda foretells even many small circumstances most truly—and the whole of it is a monument of what now is."[32]

What "now" was in 1823, however, was the death of Shelley and not the death of the father, who calmly wrote his daughter early that year that he had "taken great liberties with [*Valperga*], and I am afraid your *amour propre* will be proportionately shocked."[33] He need not have worried. The wife who had deferred to Percy's "far more cultivated mind" while composing *Frankenstein* did not resent her father's editorial tampering with *Valperga*. Yet the old conflicts could not be exorcised, and they would continue to surface in her fictions—particularly in her short stories.

In **"Transformation"** (1831), perhaps her best short story, a monster—this time a deformed Satanic dwarf— must be killed before an "imperious, haughty, tameless" young man, who has shown sadistic traits and whose thirst for revenge against his beloved's father leads him to exchange bodies with the monster, can win his Elizabeth-like bride: by mutilating himself on his enemy's huge sword while feebly plunging in his tiny dagger, Guido the rebel can regain his manly shape, marry the kind Juliet, and be henceforth known as "Guido il Cortese." If **"Transformation"** is a fantasy in which the aggression and monsterhood induced by two fathers—Guido's "generous and noble, but capricious and tyrannical" father and Juliet's "cold-hearted, cold-blooded father"—can be overcome, **"The Mortal Immortal"** (1834) reverses the emphasis. In this story, which George Eliot must have read before writing her own horror tale "The Lifted Veil" (1859), the alchemist's apprentice Winzy (another ironic name suggestive of the Pyrrhic victories of "Victor" and "Lavenza") becomes responsible for the death of Cornelius Agrippa (the youthful Frankenstein's own mentor) when he drinks the elixir of life the old master had prepared for himself; he thus not only becomes a parricide of sorts who is forced to see his "revered master" expire before his eyes, but also a passive victim of his own longevity as he watches the gradual deterioration of his beloved Bertha into a "mincing, simpering, jealous old" hag. Nursing her until her death "as a mother might a child," Winzy, like the Monster, seeks some place where he might end his life-in-death.[34]

It is the tale called **"The Mourner"** (1830), however, which most pronouncedly allegorizes the self-division first manifested in *Frankenstein*. The story's narrative interest is itself split between a grief-stricken Mathilda-figure called Ellen (her real name turns out to be Clarice) and the Guido-like narrator Neville, a young man whose impetuosity is checked by Ellen much in the way that Walton is restrained by the feminine fosterage of his sister. Neville's rebellious feelings toward education and parental authority are carefully contrasted to Ellen-Clarice's feelings about her own dead father and tutor. At Eton Neville has only met "a capricious, unrelenting, cruel bondage, far beyond the measured despotism of Jamaica" (p. 87); his outrage and sense of "impotence" reach their apex when he is abused by a tutor. He rebels and, like the Monster, gives in to a "desire of vengeance." After the departure of the De Laceys, the Monster is "unable to injure any thing human" and turns its "fury towards inanimate objects" (*Frankenstein,* p. 134); Neville too wants to leave a "substantial proof of my resentment," and, like Proust's Marcel who destroys the hat of Charlus, he tears his tutor's belongings to pieces, "stamped on them, crushed them with more than childish strength," finally dashing a "time-piece, on which my tyrant infinitely prided himself" (*Stories and Tales,* p. 88). Neville flees to Ellen's cottage, sure that his violent outburst has forever alienated him from his father, but she persuades him that he will be forgiven.

Ellen-Clarice may be able to reclaim Horace Neville from exile and monsterhood, but she cannot overcome her own self-loathing as a female monster; her alienation can be conquered only through a withdrawal into death. Like so many of Mary Shelley's fictional orphans, Ellen-Clarice is the daughter of a widower who, after the "deadly blight" of his wife's death, leaves his surviving "infant daughter" to be reared by others (p. 96). He returns when Clarice is ten and devotes himself to her education. Their relationship, totally unlike that between Mathilda and her returning father, is ideal and she quickly becomes "proficient under his tutoring": "They rode—walked—read together. When a father is all that a father may be, the sentiments of filial piety, entire dependence, and perfect confidence being united, the love of the daughter is one of the deepest and strongest, as it is the purest passion of which our natures are capable" (p. 96). This wishful harmony between parent and child is disrupted by an incident that links Clarice's passivity to Neville's aggression much as Justine-Elizabeth are linked to the Monster. During a raging storm, Clarice's father deposits her in a lifeboat in which there is room for but one more passenger. He dies, fighting the waves and battling "with the death that at last became the *victor*" (p. 100) and leaves Clarice haunted by the idea of "self-destruction." Neville's attempts to dispel her "intense melancholy" ("what do I not owe to you? I am your boy, your pupil") are fruitless. Unable to bear her guilt, sure that no young man would ever want "to wed the parri—," she wills her death (p. 106), joins her "father in the abode of spirits" (p. 105), and leaves Neville to tell her story to his own bride.

Mary Shelley's deep ambivalence about William Godwin informs most of her works of fiction. While thesis-novels such as *The Last Man* (1826) show the impress of her father's philosophical tutorship by incorporating some of his ideas on institutions and government, *Frankenstein* and tales like those discussed above reveal the impact of a very different legacy.[35] The philosopher who had so strongly inveighed against "coercion" of any sort, who had written that all "individuals" ought to be left "to the progress of their own minds,"[36] clearly failed to apply his precepts during the early development of his daughter. His effect on her was as inhibiting as that which James Mill, another rationalist prescriber of felicity, was to have on the emotional life of his son.

When Godwin died in April 1836 at the age of eighty, Mary Shelley was at work on her last piece of fiction, *Falkner* (1837), a novel about remorse and redemption. The fact that she wrote no more novels or stories in the fifteen years after his death can be attributed to a variety of reasons, among them, no doubt, her greater financial independence. Still, the fact remains intriguing. Intriguing, too, is her decision to postpone the edition of Godwin's manuscripts and the composition of his biography. Like George Eliot's Casaubon, Godwin had left her a message adjuring her not to allow his papers "to be consigned to oblivion." Yet, very much like the Dorothea Brooke who no longer could think that the "really delightful marriage must be that where your husband was a sort of father, and could teach you even Hebrew, if you wished it,"[37] Mary Shelley now stoutly resisted the hold of the dead hand. She had once wanted "little William" to be recognized by her father. Now she could adduce her maternal solicitude for another boy as a foil to "the sense of duty towards my father," whose "passion for posthumous fame," so like Victor Frankenstein's eagerness to receive the blessings of future generations, she no longer professed to share: "With regard to my Father's life," she wrote Trelawny, "I certainly could not answer it to my conscience to give it up—I shall therefore do it—but I must wait. This year I have to fight my poor Percy's battle—to try to get him sent to College without further dilapidation of his ruined prospects."[38] To see Percy Florence reinstated in the graces of Sir Timothy Shelley, that other forbidding father, had become more important than to make amends for guilty thoughts and feelings. Aggressive at last in a sanctioned way, she had become a militant mother rather than a daughter penitent for not being a son. Godwin had squelched the publication of *Mathilda* in 1820; when Mary Shelley died in 1851, the promised biography consisted of only a few manuscript pages, largely about Godwin's relation to Mary Wollstonecraft. "Little William" had been revenged at last.

Notes

[1] *Frankenstein; or, The Modern Prometheus,* ed. James Rieger (Indianapolis and New York, 1974), chap. 7, p. 127. All future references in the text are to this edition of the 1818 version of the novel.

[2] Mary Wollstonecraft, "Duty to Parents," *A Vindication of the Rights of Woman, with Strictures on Political and Moral Subjects* (New York, 1833), chap. 11, p. 167.

[3] Quoted in C. Kegan Paul, *William Godwin: His Friends and Contemporaries* (London, 1876), II:214; the letter was written to an "unknown correspondent" who had inquired about Godwin's theories of education.

[4] *Ibid.,* I:7; see also Ford K. Brown, *The Life of William Godwin* (London and Toronto, 1926), p. 3.

[5] See *Godwin and Mary: Letters of William Godwin and Mary Wollstonecraft,* ed. Ralph M. Wardle (Lawrence, Kansas, 1966), pp. 80, 82, 88, 92, 102; the passage used as the second epigraph to this essay ("William is alive") occurs on p. 94.

[6] Richard Church, *Mary Shelley* (London, 1928), pp. 54-55.

[7] Muriel Spark, *Child of Light: A Reassessment of Mary Wollstonecraft Shelley* (Southend-on-Sea, Essex, 1951), p. 138.

[8] Quoted in Edna Nixon, *Mary Wollstonecraft: Her Life and Times* (London, 1971), p. 248.

[9] *Mary Shelley's Journal,* ed. Frederick L. Jones (Norman, Oklahoma, 1947), p. 205; the entry occurs on 21 October 1838.

[10] *A Child's Parent Dies: Studies in Childhood Bereavement* (New Haven and London, 1974), p. 176; see also pp. 194-95.

[11] For a fuller account of Mary's early life with Percy see Peter Dale Scott's discussion on pp. 178-183, below.

[12] *Journal,* p. 39; 6 March 1815.

[13] *Ibid.,* p. 41; 19 March 1815.

[14] Mary Shelley's journal for May 1815-July 1816 is lost; since it would have contained entries about the first six months of her "little William's" life, it is possible that she herself destroyed it after the boy's death in 1819.

[15] Why had Mary Shelley called for Hogg immediately after the death of her first child? In her letter to Shelley of 27 July 1815 she pleads that he "attend to" and "comply with" her feeling that they "ought not to be absent any longer": "We have been now a long time separeted [*sic*]" (*The Letters of Mary Shelley,* ed. Frederick L. Jones [Norman, Oklahoma, 1944], I:16-17).

[16] *Journal,* p. 15; 16 September 1814. As a male child, the younger William Godwin was permitted to go away to school: from 1811 to 1814 he went to the Charterhouse, from 1814 to 1818 to a school in Greenwich run by the younger Dr. Burney. Described as "wayward and restless" as a youth, he became a successful journalist and wrote a novel called *Transfusion.* He died of cholera at the age of twenty-nine, leaving a wife but no children (Mary's Percy Florence thus was William Godwin's only grandchild). In 1818, Godwin described his son as "the only person with whom I have been any way concerned in the course of education, who is distinguished from all others by the circumstance of always returning a just answer to the questions I proposed to him"; this habit of mind apparently seemed more important to Godwin than the boy's "very affectionate disposition" (Paul, *William Godwin,* II: 258). After his son's death, Godwin published the

novel he had left behind and added, in Paul's words, a "gravely self-restrained Memoir" (II:321).

¹⁷ Juliet Mitchell points out that in the conditions established by "patriarchal human history," the growing girl learns "that her subjugation to the law of the father entails her becoming the representative of 'nature'" ("A Woman's Place," *Psychoanalysis and Feminism* [New York, 1974], p. 405).

¹⁸ Frankenstein describes himself as "passive" in the arrangements of his return to Geneva immediately after he has agreed to the Monster's dictates; when, "trembling with passion, [he tears] to pieces the thing on which I was engaged," the Monster soon forces him into passivity again (pp. 145, 164). By the time the two reach Walton's ship, the presumed aggressor, Victor, is clearly the victim of the Monster he thinks he is pursuing.

¹⁹ "Inhibited Femininity," *Feminine Psychology* (New York, 1967), p. 79; see also, in the same volume, "The Flight from Womanhood": "the desire to be a man is generally admitted comparatively willingly and . . . once it is accepted, it is clung to tenaciously, the reason being the desire to avoid the realization of libidinal wishes and fantasies in connection with the father" (p. 66).

²⁰ The contrast between the two figures, in fact, resembles that between "Man of Science" and poet developed by Wordsworth in his 1800 "Preface": the scientist "seeks truth" in "solitude," while the creative poet carries "everywhere with him relationship and love."

²¹ *Tales and Stories by Mary Wollstonecraft Shelley,* ed. Richard Garnett (London, 1891), p. 19.

²² Mary Shelley seems to have had difficulties choosing the right adjective to describe the mother who is infected by Elizabeth; "amiable" was originally "admirable," but in the 1831 edition the novelist had apparently become less hesitant about identifying Caroline with her own mother: "this amiable woman" now becomes "this best of women."

²³ In a way, it is Mel Brooks, in his script for the comic *Young Frankenstein,* who has been the most acute reader of the novel when he reunites the Monster, not with Victor, but with Elizabeth; Brooks also recognizes the novel's fluid interchanges when he has young Frahnkensteeeeen become endowed with the Monster's brain.

²⁴ It may not be necessary to remind the reader that in both males and females the longing for death is associated with the longing for a reunion with the mother; in women, however, this death-wish seems to be free

of the fears which lead men to paint a destructive *femme fatale* who brings death rather than life into the world.

²⁵ *Middlemarch,* ed. Gordon S. Haight (Cambridge, Mass., 1956), p. 297.

²⁶ 29 June 1819, *Letters,* I:74.

²⁷ Quoted in Spark, *Child of Light,* p. 62.

²⁸ *Mathilda,* ed. Elizabeth Nitchie (Chapel Hill, 1959), p. 90. The Bodleian notebook simplifies the implausibility of a dead narrator by having Mathilda write out her story just before her death. The fullest account of the bibliographical and biographical history of the manuscript is to be found in the third appendix of Elizabeth Nitchie's *Mary Shelley: Author of "Frankenstein"* (New Brunswick, N.J., 1953), pp. 211-17.

²⁹ Nitchie, *Mary Shelley,* p. 212.

³⁰ *Mathilda,* p. 10.

³¹ Quoted in Nitchie, *Mary Shelley,* p. 214n.

³² Mary Shelley to Maria Gisborne, 2-6 May 1823, *Letters,* I:224; by a coincidence, a stern portrait of Godwin faces the pages from which this passage is taken.

³³ February 1823, quoted in Paul, *William Godwin,* II:277.

³⁴ *Tales and Stories,* p. 161; future references to stories in this collection will be given in the text.

³⁵ A study of the ways in which *Frankenstein* and some of the other novels enlist, yet also subvert, Godwinian ideology is beyond the scope of this essay. Such an investigation, however, I am convinced, would yield fruitful results. It would show, for instance, that the Monster I have called a Wordsworthian child of Nature is also a Godwinian child whose freedom from social institutions paradoxically proves as injurious as Justine's degradation at the hands of the legal system, which Godwin pronounced to be "an institution of the most pernicious tendency" (*An Enquiry Concerning Political Justice and Its Influence on General Virtue and Happiness,* edited and abridged by Raymond A. Preston [New York, 1926], II:210). It would also show that in her rebellious moods Mary Shelley sided with the idea of Godwin's former disciple, T. R. Malthus, against her father, who, by 1818, was preparing his reply to the *Essay on Population.*

³⁶ *An Enquiry Concerning Political Justice,* II:27.

³⁷ *Middlemarch,* p. 8.

[38] To Edward John Trelawny, 27 January 1837, *Letters,* II:119.]

Kate Ellis (essay date 1979)

SOURCE: "Monsters in the Garden: Mary Shelley and the Bourgeois Family," in *The Endurance of Frankenstein: Essays on Mary Shelley's Novel,* edited by George Levine and U. C. Knoepflmacher, University of California Press, 1979, pp. 123-42.

[*In the essay that follows, Ellis reads* Frankenstein *alongside the paradigms of the bourgeois family—its idealized structure, its separation of public and private, and its division of social roles according to gender difference.*]

> Nature has wisely attached affections to duties, to sweeten toil, and to give that vigour to the exertions of reason which only the heart can give. But, the affection which is put on merely because it is the appropriate insignia of a certain character, when its duties are not fulfilled, is one of the empty compliments which vice and folly are obliged to pay to virtue and the real nature of things.
>
> —Mary Wollstonecraft, *A Vindication of the Rights of Woman*

The 1818 Preface to *Frankenstein* tells us that the author's "chief concern" in writing the novel had been limited to "avoiding the enervating effects of the novels of the present day and to the exhibition of the amiableness of domestic affection, and the excellence of universal virtue." Perhaps Percy Shelley's statement was simply one of those ritual declarations of moral intent that we find in prefaces written before the novel became a respectable genre. But if Shelley meant to be descriptive, he was certainly reading *Frankenstein* selectively. It is true that each of the novel's three interconnected narratives is told by a man to whom domestic affection is not merely amiable but positively sacred. Yet each narrator also has been denied the experience he reveres so highly, and cannot, because of this denial, transmit it to a future generation.

The three narratives are thematically linked through the joint predicament of those who have and those who have not the highly desirable experience of domestic affection. The recurrence of this theme suggests that Mary Shelley was at least as much concerned with the limitations of that affection as she was with demonstrating its amiableness. She is explicit, moreover, about the source of these limitations. It is not domestic affection but the context in which it manifests itself that brings death into the world of her novel. And that context is what we have come to describe as the bourgeois family.

In her analysis of domestic affection Mary Shelley carefully sifts the degree to which members of the various families in the novel accede to the separation of male and female spheres of activity characteristic of the bourgeois family. Historically, this separation of spheres had an economic base as factory production replaced cottage industry and as wealth increasingly represented by capital eroded old ties of economic interdependency, not only between landlords and tenants but also between husbands and wives.[1] Female wage laborers were rarely paid even subsistence wages; middle-class wives, on the other hand, welcomed their separation from paid work, now done exclusively by their husbands, as a sign of bourgeois status. Pursuits once restricted to the aristocracy were thus opened to a much larger class of women. Accordingly, considerable attention was paid, by many a writer, to the "nature" of the female sex, the education best suited to its cultivation, and the duties arising from its new relationship to the masculine world of production. An important contributor to this debate was Mary Wollstonecraft, who saw domestic affection undermined by an exaggerated separation between female charm and social usefulness. The success with which she transmitted this view can be seen in both the narrative method and the content of her daughter's first novel.

The structure of *Frankenstein,* with its three concentric narratives, imposes upon the linear unfolding of the plot the very sort of order that Mary Shelley is commenting on in the novel as a whole: one that separates "outer" and "inner," the masculine sphere of discovery and the feminine sphere of domesticity. Moreover, the sequence in which the reader encounters the three narrators gives the plot line a circular as well as a linear shape. It begins and ends with Walton, writing to his English sister from the outer periphery of the civilized world, the boundary between the known and the unknown. From there we move inward to the circle of civilization, to the rural outskirts of Geneva, birthplace of the Protestant ethic, the spirit of capitalism. Then, in the physical center of the novel, accessible only if one traverses many snowy mountains, we come upon the limited Paradise Regained of the De Lacey family. Here males and females learn together, role distinctions are minimal, and domestic bliss is eventually recovered, largely through the initiative of Safie, a young woman who comes from a world outside the sphere of Western Protestantism. Yet we are not allowed to end with this fiction of the isolated triumph of domestic virtues. Elizabeth Bennett can remove herself to Pemberley away from her family's pride and prejudice; but we follow the dispossessed Monster back into the outer world, witness his destruction of the remnants of Victor's harmonious family circle, and finally behold Walton's defeated attempt to discover in the land of ice and snow a Paradise beyond the domestic and the familiar.

The circularity of *Frankenstein* underscores Mary Shelley's critique of the insufficiency of a family structure in which the relation between the sexes is as uneven as the relationship between parents and children. The two "outside" narrators, Walton and Frankenstein, are both benevolent men whose exile from the domestic hearth drives them deeper and deeper into isolation. Neither, however, can see that his deprivation might have been avoided through a better understanding of the limits of the institution into which he was born. Even the De Lacey family, where these limits are meaningfully transcended, is basically innocent of what Mary Wollstonecraft, in the title of chapter 9 of her *Vindication of the Rights of Woman,* had called "the pernicious effects which arise from the unnatural distinctions established in society." The "rational fellowship"[2] of this family nucleus has been enforced by necessity. De Lacey's blindness, combined with the primitive conditions in which his family must create a refuge from the world's injustice, simply makes rigid roles impractical, if not impossible to maintain. Safie has asserted her independence from her Turkish father in the belief that she will be able, in a Christian country, "to aspire to higher powers of intellect, and an independence of spirit, forbidden to the female followers of Mahomet."[3] She has no idea, in other words, that what she has done would be unthinkable to Elizabeth Lavenza and her virtuous nineteenth-century middle-class counterparts. She and Felix learn from Volney's *Ruins of Empires* "of the division of property, of immense wealth and squalid poverty; of rank, descent, and noble blood" (p. 120). But they do not read *A Vindication of the Rights of Woman,* where Mary Wollstonecraft connects the "pernicious effects" of these divisions with the tyranny of husbands over wives and parents over children in the middle-class home.[4]

This leaves only the Monster to articulate the experience of being denied the domestic affections of a child, sibling, husband, and parent. In his campaign of revenge, the Monster goes to the root of his father's character deformation, when he wipes out those who played a part, however unwitting, in fostering, justifying, or replicating it. If we view his violent acts as components of a horror story, the novel can be read either as a warning against uncontrolled technology and the ambition that brings it into being, or as a fantasy of the return of the repressed, a drama of man at war with alienated parts of himself, variously identified.[5] But an additional meaning emerges if we also take the violence in the novel to constitute a language of protest, the effect of which is to expose the "wrongs" done to women and children, friends and fiancés, in the name of domestic affection. It is a language none of the characters can fully decode because they lack the perspective on bourgeois domesticity that Mary Shelley had learned, principally from her mother's writings, and which she assumed, perhaps naively, in her readers.

To grasp the subversiveness of Shelley's critique of the family we need to look more closely at her depiction of the various domestic groupings in the novel. Each of the families in the outer two narratives illustrates a differently flawed model of socialization, ranging from the "feminine fosterage" of Walton's sister and the "silken cord" employed by Victor's parents, to the wrongheaded class pride of Caroline Beaufort's father and the overt tyranny of Mme. Moritz. None of these arrangements provides the younger generation with adequate defences against powerful forces in the outside world, forces that can neither be controlled nor escaped through the exercise of domestic affection.

Mary Shelley makes clear that Robert Walton's career has been nourished and shaped by conflicting cultural artifacts. From his uncle's travel books he learned that his culture confers its highest praise on those who endure great personal hardships to bring "inestimable benefits" to all mankind. This knowledge, he tells us, "increased the regret which I had felt, as a child, on learning that my father's dying injunction had forbidden my uncle to allow me to embark on a seafaring life." The fact that he was told this before he began to read suggests that his contact with his father, if any, had taken place very early in his life. There is no mention of a mother, only of the sister whose influence upon him he so persistently acknowledges:

> A youth passed in solitude, my best years spent under your gentle and feminine fosterage, has so refined the groundwork of my character that I cannot overcome an intense distaste for the usual brutality exercised on board ship. [P. 20]

Walton's brief account of his "best years" parallels in two particulars the more lengthily elaborated early life of Victor. The parental injunction (which he transmits without any explanation) has the same effect on him that Alphonse Frankenstein's cursory dismissal of the work of Paracelsus and Cornelius Agrippa has on the youthful Victor. The other similarity is between the brother-sister relationship he values so highly and the ersatz sibling bond between Victor and Elizabeth. Lacking a Clerval among his friends, the orphaned Walton regards his sister as his better, because more refined, self. He is markedly uncomfortable in the presence of men who have not been similarly "fostered" by women like his sister. His lieutenant's "endowments," he notes, are "unsoftened by cultivation." In telling his sister the "anecdote" of the sailor's generosity in bestowing his "prize-money" on a rival suitor of the "young Russian lady" who spurned him, Walton suggests that such disinterestedness is nonetheless tainted: "'What a noble fellow!' you will exclaim. He is so; but then he has passed all his life on board a vessel, and has scarcely an idea beyond the ship and the crew."

Walton's stance prevents him from acknowledging that his lieutenant possesses a natural generosity that is instinctive (not unlike that of the Monster). The sailor, he notes, had amassed sufficient wealth to buy himself the hand of the woman he loved. But on discovering that her heart belonged to another, he relinquished his entire fortune to an impoverished rival—thus enabling the lovers to conform to the prevailing social definition of marriage as an economic transaction. The realization that domestic affection may be simply a commodity to be purchased on the marketplace has apparently left the lieutenant highly disenchanted.

Walton, too, possesses sufficient wealth to have made him the target of some real-life Mr. Harlowes and Mrs. Bennetts. "My life might have been passed in ease and luxury," he tells his sister, "but I preferred glory to every enticement that wealth placed in my path" (p. 17). His quest for glory alienates him from the crew whose physical work is necessary to the success of his venture. Although, unlike nineteenth-century factory owners, Walton does not plan to enrich himself at the expense of his seafaring "hands," he is as baffled by their lack of commitment to his "glorious expedition" as factory owners were by their workers' unwillingness to subordinate their needs to the higher cause of industrial expansion. Determined to find for himself and all mankind a substitute for the domestic affections, Walton nonetheless cannot exorcise the effects of his sister's "gentle and feminine fosterage." The drastic separation of home and workplace enforced on the Arctic explorer cannot be maintained. Walton must behold the "untimely extinction" of the "glorious spirit" that had driven him into the land of ice: "My tears flow; my mind is over-shadowed by a cloud of disappointment. But I journey towards England, and may there find consolation."

In Walton we see a benevolent man made incapable of happiness by the very forces that make him an exemplary, self-denying bourgeois male. Since Victor is caught in the same double bind, it is not surprising that similar forces shape his early life, especially those that separate domestic life from work. The Frankensteins have been, Victor recounts, counsellors and syndics for many generations, distinguished members of the bourgeoisie of Calvinist Geneva, and respected servants of the state as public office holders. Victor's father "had passed his younger days perpetually occupied by the affairs of his country . . . nor was it till the decline of life that he became the husband and father of a family." Although eager to bestow "on the state sons who might carry his virtues and his name down to posterity," Alphonse Frankenstein retired from public life entirely in order to pursue this self-perpetuation. The very first paragraph of Victor's narrative thus presents the same dichotomy between public service and domestic affection already exemplified in an extreme form by Walton's career—a dichotomy, moreover, which will widen for Victor himself as his narrative progresses.

After describing his father's retreat from public life, Victor supplies a second example of such a removal, though not into felicity. Beaufort, Alphonse Frankenstein's friend, was a merchant who, "from a flourishing state, fell, through numerous mischances, into poverty" (p. 31). Fortunately for him, his motherless daughter follows him into exile, where she descends voluntarily into the working class to support them so that her father may be spared a humiliation his male pride could not have endured. Caroline Beaufort's self-sacrifice says a good deal about her conception of domestic affection. De Lacey in the Monster's narrative is blind, and thus actually disabled from sharing the burden of maintaining the family economy. But we are told nothing from which to conclude that Beaufort was unable to work. In the face of misfortune he is passive, a characteristic of other males in the novel, and condones, by that passivity, the exploitation of his daughter.

It is in this nobly submissive attitude that Victor's father finds his future bride, weeping by the coffin of her dead father. This, it would seem, was her finest hour, the shadow of her future idealization and just the kind of scene sentimental nineteenth-century painters loved. Victor's father rescues her from the painful fate of working-class womanhood, bringing her back, after a two-year courtship, by the only route that women can return, that is, through marriage. Yet Beaufort's response to economic reversal, and the success of one friend in finding him, act as a comment on the relationship between class and friendship that one exceptional act does not negate. All of Beaufort's other friends have apparently conformed to the usual pattern of bourgeois behavior when one of their number drops over the economic edge. Given the economic turbulence that marked capitalist development in the later eighteenth and early nineteenth centuries, the experience of being "ruined" was even more common in life than in novels. Yet in the fiction of the same period it is rare to find the victims of that upheaval sustained by friendship made in better days. Class solidarity was not large enough, it would seem, to encompass misfortune.

Of course Beaufort's personality has not helped the situation. He was, says Victor, "of a proud and unbending disposition, and could not bear to live in poverty and oblivion in the same country where he had formerly been distinguished for his rank and magnificence" (p. 31). Still, his self-removal into oblivion, which his fellow merchants would have imposed had he remained where he was, implies that he is not unique but rather disposed to view a loss of money in much the same way the others do, that is to say, as a fall from grace. Like Robert Walton, Beaufort has internalized an ideology which, though painful to him and his daughter, advances the interests of his class as a whole by purging it of its failures. Domestic affection may be heavily taxed, but it is the one source of self-esteem left to him once he and his neighbors have collaborated in his emotional "ruin."

At the center of this ideology is the belief that material prosperity and social recognition are conferred on superior merit, and thus the lines that divide the bourgeoisie from the rest of humanity reflect worth, not birth. Nevertheless, this view, while often expressed in the public sphere without shame,[6] was difficult to reconcile with other Christian teachings. One popular fictional device that obfuscates this ideological contradiction is that of the "noble peasant" and his various fairy tale counterparts, male and female. Caroline Beaufort's devotion to her father is the glass slipper that gives her entrée to her new role as child bride. For her, this role involves revisitations to the fallen world of poverty from which she had been so fortuitously rescued. Her son explains:

> This, to my mother, was more than a duty; it was a necessity, a passion—remembering what she had suffered and how she had been relieved—for her to act in turn the guardian angel to the afflicted. [P. 34]

Like her husband, Caroline rejects the harsher side of an ideology that views poverty as a problem to be solved only through hard work on the part of those afflicted. Motherless herself, she attempts to alleviate social injustice by becoming a "good mother" to those for whom no Prince Charming is likely to appear. Yet when she finds one who clearly does not belong where fate has placed her, Caroline's response is to single out this exception and give her more than periodic bounty. In fact, she gives Elizabeth everything she had: a bourgeois father, a mother who dies young, a Prince Charming, and a view of the female role as one of constant, self-sacrificing devotion to others.[7] What is more, she remains dependent, as Elizabeth will be, on male energy and male provision. When Victor tells us that "My father directed our studies, and my mother partook of our enjoyments," he unwittingly suggests much about Caroline's reduced sphere of action.

To say that domestic affection, extended into the public sphere, is an inadequate remedy for the ills of an industrial society would be to fly in the face of an idea that gained immense popularity in the Victorian era, both in England and in the United States. But to say that Elizabeth's early death, like her adopted mother's, was a logical outgrowth of the female ideal she sought to embody, is a radical statement indeed. Mary Shelley may well have thought she was going too far in this direction when she revised her account of Caroline's death from the following:

> Elizabeth had caught the scarlet fever; but her illness was not severe, and she quickly recovered. During her confinement, many arguments had been urged to persuade my mother to refrain from attending upon her. She had, at first, yielded to our entreaties; but when she heard that her favorite was recovering, she could no longer debar herself from her society, and entered her chamber long before the danger of infection was past. On the third day my mother sickened. . . .[8]

In 1831 Mary revised this ironic passage. It is precisely because Elizabeth "was in the greatest danger" that Caroline now

> had, at first, yielded to our entreaties; but when she heard that the life of her favorite was menaced, she could no longer control her anxiety. She attended her sick-bed—her watchful attentions triumphed over the malignity of the distemper—Elizabeth was saved but the consequence of this imprudence were fatal to her preserver. On the third day my mother sickened. . . . [Pp. 42-43]

In the revision Caroline's death is tragic, but not gratuitous. Her motherly touch would seem to have been crucial, whereas in the first version it kills her without benefiting anyone else.

The revised Caroline becomes a heroine in death, but her daughter's self-effacing behavior throughout the novel is singularly ineffectual in actual crisis situations. Her most dramatic public act is her attempt to save Justine, yet all she seems able to do is to display her own goodness, her willingness to trust the accused, to have given her the miniature of her mother, had Justine but asked for it. Yet feminine sweetness does not win court cases. It may captivate male hearts, and even elicit "a murmur of approbation" from those in the courtroom. But making a convincing argument before a male judge and jury requires skills that Elizabeth hardly possesses.

Elizabeth seems unaware of her ineffectuality. She hopes that Victor "perhaps will find some means to justify my poor guiltless Justine." Still, like Alphonse Frankenstein, who believes in Justine's guilt, Elizabeth is uninterested in pursuing the truth: that the "evidence" that convicts Justine has been planted. The description of Justine's apprehension makes this oversight seem truly incredible. Ernest, Victor's younger brother, tells the story:

> He related that, the morning on which the murder of poor William had been discovered, Justine had been taken ill, and confined to her bed for several days. During this interval, one of the servants, happening to examine the apparel she had worn the night of the murder, had discovered in her pocket the picture of my mother, which had been judged to be the temptation of the murderer. The servant

instantly showed it to one of the others, who, without saying a word to any of the family, went to a magistrate; and, upon their deposition, Justine was apprehended. [P. 79]

This act on the part of two servants is certainly one that might reasonably arouse suspicion on the part of their employers, but the Frankensteins appear to view their inability to suspect anyone as one of their greatest virtues. Furthermore, for a murderer to keep such a damning piece of evidence on her person is at least questionable, yet none of the bereaved family even thinks of raising the issue in Justine's defence. Instead, believing in the power of domestic affection unaided by deductive reasoning, they follow the lead of the elder Frankenstein, who urges his family to "rely on the justice of our laws, and the activity with which I shall prevent the slightest show of partiality."

Elizabeth's passivity, however, goes beyond a suspension of the need to find little William's true murderer. On hearing of the boy's death, she immediately blames herself for having given him the miniature to wear. And if this is her response, when no finger is pointing at her, how much less able to defend herself is Justine, whose very confusion is interpreted as a sign of her guilt. Both Justine and Elizabeth have learned well the lessons of submissiveness and devotion to others that Caroline Beaufort epitomized for them. Their model behavior similarly lowers their resistance to the forces that kill them.

Of the education Justine received in the Frankenstein household we know only that it was "superior to that which [her mistress] intended at first," and that Justine thought this second mother of hers to be "the model of all excellence, and endeavoured to imitate her phraseology and manners" (p. 65). We know a lot more about Elizabeth's education, particularly from the second edition of the novel, where Mary Shelley expanded two sentences that appear in her husband's handwriting in the original manuscript. In the original,

> I delighted [says Victor] in investigating the facts relative to the actual world; she busied herself in following the aerial creations of the poets. The world was to me a secret, which I desired to discover; to her it was a vacancy, which she sought to people with imaginations of her own.[9]

Here we see the crucial difference in the respective educations of the two figures: Victor translates his interest in science into a career aspiration, while Elizabeth translates her interest into a substitute for experience, a way of filling a void created by her lack of contact with the outside world.

In her 1831 revision, Shelley lays even greater stress on the domestic harmony that formed the context of the early education of Elizabeth, Victor, and their friend Clerval. She develops the division of the realm of masculine knowledge between Victor and Clerval, connecting (in Clerval's case especially) their studies and their future aspirations:

> It was the secrets of heaven and earth that I desired to learn; and whether it was the outward substance of things, or the inner spirit of nature and the mysterious soul of man that occupied me, still my enquiries were directed toward the metaphysical, or, in its highest sense, the physical secrets of the world.

> Meanwhile, Clerval occupied himself, so to speak, with the moral relations of things. The busy stage of life, the virtues of heroes, and the actions of men, were his theme, and his hope and his dream was to become one of those whose names are recorded in story, as the gallant and adventurous benefactors of our species. [P. 37]

Elizabeth's literary studies, on the other hand, have been dropped rather than developed. She is now shown to spend her entire time shining "like a shrine-dedicated lamp in our peaceful home." To whom, one may ask, is this shrine dedicated? Both editions remark that Elizabeth and Victor "were strangers to any species of disunion or dispute." But in the first they learn Latin and English together so that they "might read the writings in those languages," while in the second her participation in the studies of the other two is quite different:

> She was the living spirit of love to soften and attract: I might have become sullen in my study, rough through the ardour of my nature, but that she was there to subdue me to a semblance of her own gentleness. And Clerval—could aught ill entrench on the noble spirit of Clerval?—yet he might not have been so perfectly humane, so thoughtful in his generosity—so full of kindness and tenderness amidst his passion for adventurous exploit, had not she unfolded to him the real loveliness of beneficence, and made the doing good the end and aim of his soaring ambition. [P. 38]

What Mary Shelley spells out, in these additions, is Elizabeth's role in maintaining the atmosphere of continual sunshine in which Victor claims he spent *his* best years.

One might argue that Elizabeth was not harmed by having her mind filled with these exclusive demands, that she was in fact happy with the "trifling occupations" that took up all her time after Victor and Clerval left their common schoolroom, occupations whose reward was "seeing nothing but happy, kind faces around me" (p. 64). Or one might say that she was being excessively modest, that keeping others happy generally and softening the "sometimes violent" temper and "vehement passions" (p. 37) of two male students in particular, is no trifling occupation. Thomas Gisborne, whose extensive treatment of *The Duties of the Female Sex* was first published in 1797, was one of the many debaters on the nature of women who held this latter view. He posited three general categories of female duties, "each of which," he insisted, "is of extreme and never-ceasing concern to the welfare of mankind." The second of these sets of duties entails "forming and improving the general manners, dispositions, and conduct of the other sex, by society and example." Female excellence, he observed, was best displayed in "the sphere of domestic life," where it manifests itself

> in sprightliness and vivacity, in quickness of perception, fertility of invention, in powers adapted to unbend the brow of the learned, to refresh the over-laboured faculties of the wise, and to diffuse throughout the family circle the enlivening and endearing smile of cheerfulness.[10]

But Mary Wollstonecraft, debating from the other side, had very different views on the kind of education Elizabeth receives in the second version of *Frankenstein*. For her "the only way to make [women] properly attentive to their domestic duties" was to "open" political and moral subjects to them. "An active mind," she asserts, "embraces the whole circle of its duties and finds time enough for all."[11] Victor praises his adopted sibling for her charms and graces, for which "everyone loved" her. But her education has no content, and she does not live long enough for Victor to test Wollstonecraft's assertion that "unless the understanding be cultivated, superficial and monotonous is every grace." What is not evident to Victor is certainly evident to the reader, however. Elizabeth is not a real force in the novel: she is too superficial and monotonous.

The division into roles that takes place in the Frankenstein schoolroom corresponds roughly to the divisions described in Plato's *Republic*. There the citizens learn in earliest childhood a "myth of the metals" which divides them into groups according to whether intellect, courage, or neither predominates in their makeup. The purpose of the indoctrination is to eliminate friction in the kingdom. But in *Frankenstein* the division has the opposite effect: Victor, divided from his courageous, moral self as well as from his ability to subdue his own vehement passions, sets in motion a chain of events that will destroy those parts of a potentially whole human psyche that he has already partly lost through his conflict-free upbringing.

There is in Victor much that could not find expression without disrupting the tranquility of his happy home. On leaving that home he indulges at first "in the most melancholy reflections." But, he continues,

> as I proceeded my spirits and hopes rose. I ardently desired the acquisition of knowledge. I had often, when at home, thought it hard to remain during my youth cooped up in one place, and had longed to enter the world, and take my station among other human beings. [P. 45]

Unfortunately for him, these other human beings turn out all to be male, their sisters and daughters being busied with "trifling occupations" within the safety of the domestic circle. Only males, in the world of the novel's second narrator, are seen acting upon their longings to acquire knowledge, to leave a home that coops them up, and to take their places in the world.

Thus Victor discovers a flaw in the wall that keeps his hearth untouched by evil from the outside: you cannot take its protective magic with you when you leave. For Elizabeth's power "to soften and attract" does him little good if he must leave it behind when he goes "to take [his] station among other human beings." He may be devoted to preserving her innocence, grounded in passivity, and revere her for her self-denying dedication to the happiness of others. But since these qualities cut her off from any active engagement in his life, and thus deprive him of a real companion, her supposed perfection only intensifies his isolation. Unable to detect any flaws in his mother's and Elizabeth's unreproaching dependency, he creates in the Monster a dependent child who does reproach him for his neglect. Furthermore, by making this child ugly he can justify his neglect by appealing to a prejudice shared by all the characters in the novel: resentment toward (and cruelty to) an ugly helpless creature is perfectly appropriate human behavior. Indignation is aroused in the novel only by cruelty to beautiful children like Elizabeth and William. Thus Victor can vent on his Monster all the negative emotion that would otherwise have no socially acceptable object and remain unaware of the transference he has made from his child bride to his "child."

From Victor's remarks about spending his youth "cooped up in one place," we may surmise that his feelings of resentment, for which the Monster becomes an uncontrollable "objective correlative," had their first stirrings while the would-be scientist-hero was still blissfully lodged in the womb of domesticity. But resentment in Paradise, for Victor no less than for Satan himself, leads to an expulsion that intensifies the resentment. Outside the home, there is nothing to prevent that feeling from growing until it reaches literally murderous proportions. Had Victor not been so furtive about his desire to astound the world, he might have allowed himself time to make a creature his own size, one who mirrored the whole of him, not just the part of himself he cannot bring home. But to do that he would have had to be a whole person outside the home and a whole person within it.

Repeatedly throughout the novel Shelley gives us examples of the ways in which the insulated bourgeois family creates and perpetuates divided selves in the name of domestic affection by walling that affection in and keeping "disunion and dispute" out. We have noticed already that those whose role is to embody domestic affection cannot go out into the world. "Insiders" cannot leave, or do so at their peril. At the same time Shelley dramatizes, through the experiences of Victor's creature, that "outsiders" cannot enter; they are condemned to perpetual exile and deprivation, forbidden even from trying to create a domestic circle of their own. This point is emphasized by the fate of Justine, who succeeds in imitating to perfection the similarly rescued Caroline Beaufort, but who is abandoned at the first suggestion of rebellion. By having Justine abandoned first by her own jealous mother, Shelley is making her most devastating indictment of bourgeois socialization: another family cannot, as Milton put it, "rectify the wrongs of our first parents."

The Frankenstein family fails Justine because its response to her at a time of crisis was passivity. Yet here the distinction between "outsiders" and "insiders" breaks down: the Frankensteins respond to one another, when crises come, in the same way, adjuring one another to repress their anger and grief for the sake of maintaining tranquility.

Their repressed emotions, especially anger, are acted out by others. We can see this in the behavior of the jurors at Justine's trial: they are ruled by the spirit of vengeance that the family members themselves refuse to admit into their consciousness. Of course the Monster is the example *par excellence* of this process of projection, and his victims come from within the family circle as well as outside it. Their only crime is that they participated (voluntarily) in the process of self-division that left Victor incapable of being a loving father, passive in the face of crises, and content to let other people complete him.

The one murder that does not seem to fit into this scheme is that of "little William." What we know of him comes only from Elizabeth, who notes his beauty and his precocious interest in domestic affection in its traditional form:

> When he smiles, two little dimples appear on each cheek, which are rose with health. He has already had one or two little *wives,* but Louisa Biron is his favorite, a pretty little girl of five years of age. [P. 66]

Ernest Frankenstein is drawn to a life of adventure and a career in the foreign service, though he does not have, Elizabeth reports, Victor's powers of application. Thus William, preparing to be just like his "papa," is the one on whom Victor can indirectly visit, through the agency of the Monster, a resentment against a childhood spent in domestic role-playing.

The hothouse atmosphere in which Victor and later William play with their "pretty little" child brides stands in contrast to the mutually supportive, matter-of-fact life of Felix and Agatha De Lacey. Nor is this the only point on which the De Laceys contrast with the other families in the novel. They are the only family that perpetuates itself into the next generation, largely because no one in it is striving for the kind of personal immortality that propels Victor and Walton out of their respective domestic Edens. De Lacey *père,* like Beaufort and Frankenstein the elder, was once a prosperous member of the bourgeoisie. He was exiled and stripped of his fortune and place in the social order because his son, motivated by benevolence, impulsively aided in the escape of a Turk who was a victim of French racism and political injustice. But his idealistic impulse precipitates events in "the world" that are beyond his control, events that bring down ruin on his whole family.

The De Laceys exhibit a great deal less rigidity, however, when coping with misfortune than either of the two Genevese families who are called upon to deal with ruin or bereavement. Not that they are entirely happy. Although the father encourages "his children, as sometimes I found that he called them, to cast off their melancholy" (p. 112), his blindness prevents him from seeing that there is often not enough food for himself and them too. But if the land nurtures them meagerly even with the help of the Monster, it is at least a resource for meeting real needs. The relationship of the De Laceys to nature significantly differs from that of Victor, for whom nature can only provide occasions for the repeated display of a histrionic sensibility.

Furthermore, the social exile of the De Laceys is involuntary; they did not choose it, nor do they blame Felix and exile him as a punishment for the fate they must all share. Victor's family is incapable of such action. Returning home after his first encounter with the Monster as a speaking creature, he notes:

> My haggard and wild appearance awoke intense alarm; but I answered no question, scarcely did I speak. I felt as if I were placed under a ban—as if I had no right to claim their sympathies—as if never more might I enjoy companionship with them. [P. 149]

One might almost think this was the Monster speaking of his relationship with the De Lacey family. Victor's refusal, or inability, to be an accepting father to his creature, and to give him a companion who would share his sorrows as well as his joys, is a repetition of his own father's refusal to accept or give to him. His exile, as he portrays it in this passage and elsewhere, is largely self-imposed. He "answered no question," but questions were asked. Nevertheless, everything we have seen about the Frankenstein family's mode of dealing with the disturbing reality outside their circle indicates that Victor is right to keep quiet, that his revelations might provoke a response even more damaging than alarm: they might pretend he had never spoken.[12]

The deficiencies of Victor's family, dramatized in his inability to bring the Monster home (openly, that is), to deal with evil in the outside world, or to own the repressed impulses that others are acting out for him, stem ultimately from the concept of domestic affection on which the continuing tranquility of the family depends. The root of this evil lies in the separation of male and female spheres for purposes of maintaining the purity of the family and the sanctity of the home. The effect of domestic affection on both Victor and Walton is "an invincible repugnance to new countenances" that leads them toward the solitary pursuit of glory, which paradoxically disqualifies them for domestic affection. Once touched by the outside world, they cannot reenter the domestic circle without destroying its purity. Victor's rejection of the Monster also makes it impossible for him to embrace Elizabeth without destroying the purity that is her major attraction in his eyes.

Scholarly interest in the bourgeois family, the target of Mary Shelley's critique of domestic affection, has received a good deal of impetus in the last ten years from the feminist movement's attempts to name and trace the origins of what Betty Friedan has called "the problem that has no name."[13] Shelley seems to suggest that, if the family is to be a viable institution for the transmission of domestic affection from one generation to the next, it must redefine that precious commodity in such a way that it can extend to "outsiders" and become hardy enough to survive in the world outside the home. It is not surprising that a woman should be making this point. Eradicating the artificial gulf between the work of the world and the work of the home is of greater concern to women than men since they experience in almost every aspect of their lives the resultant "unnatural distinctions established in society" against which Mary Wollstonecraft protested almost two hundred years ago. If we can imagine a novel in which a woman scientist creates a monster who returns to destroy her family, the relevance to women of the problem that Mary Shelley has imagined becomes more immediately apparent.

The one character who clearly exemplifies such a redefined notion of domestic affection is Safie, the daughter of a Christian Arab woman who, "born in freedom, spurned the bondage to which she was now reduced" upon her marriage to the Turk. Safie's father had res-cued his wife from slavery, just as Victor's father had rescued Caroline Beaufort from poverty. But instead of translating her gratitude into lifelong subservience and sporadic charity, this woman taught her daughter "to aspire to higher powers of intellect, and an independence of spirit forbidden to the female followers of Mahomet" (p. 124). Safie's lucid perception of the rightness of her mother's views was doubtless only confirmed by her father's selfish duplicity in encouraging her union with Felix when it served his purposes while at the same time he "loathed the idea that his daughter should be united to a Christian."

Although Safie is, like Mary Shelley, motherless when she must put her early training to the test, she applies her mother's teachings in a way that is intended to contrast, I believe, with the behavior of the passive Elizabeth, equally influenced by her adopted mother's teachings and example. Safie discovers that her mind is

> sickened at the prospect of again returning to Asia, and being immured within the walls of a harem, allowed only to occupy herself with infantile amusements, ill suited to the temper of her soul, now accustomed to grand ideas and the noble emulation of virtue. [P. 124]

In consequence, she not only refuses to wait for the possibility that her lover will miraculously find her, but actively seeks Felix out, traveling through Europe with only an attendant for protection. Had Elizabeth been encouraged "to aspire to higher powers of intellect, and an independence of spirit," she might have followed Victor to Ingolstadt and perhaps even have insisted that he provide the Monster a companion for his wanderings. As it is, Victor cannot conceive of involving Elizabeth in his work on any level; both are petrified in fatally polarized worlds.

In her essay, Ellen Moers observes that *Frankenstein* "is a birth myth, and one that was lodged in the novelist's imagination . . . by the fact that she was herself a mother" (p. 79). But women are daughters before they are mothers, and daughters of fathers as well as mothers, as U. C. Knoepflmacher points out. The kind of family that Shelley is describing shapes us still: its most distinctive feature is that of the dominant yet absent father, working outside the home to support a dependent (or underpaid), subservient wife and children, all roles circularly functioning to reinforce his dominance. *Frankenstein* is indeed a birth myth, but one in which the parent who "brought death into the world, and all our woe" is not a woman but a man who has pushed the masculine prerogative past the limits of nature, creating life not through the female body but in a laboratory.

Victor's father seems to be the exception that proves the rule. He is an absent father for Victor not because he leaves home every day but because he does not. He is so uninvolved in matters that do not pertain directly to the domestic tranquility that he does not act to guide Victor's interest in science—an interest he shared with his son in the first version of the novel but not the second. Likewise, Victor is alienated from his "child" not by his work but by his desire to flee to the shelter of domesticity, which gives a further twist to the already novel image of a man giving birth and then escaping his parental responsibility. The price paid for the schisms that are encouraged behind the pleasant façade of "domestic affection" may be higher than even Mary Shelley could imagine. The modern world can create worse monsters.

Notes

1 See Alice Clark, *Working Life of Women in the Seventeenth Century* (London, 1968), p. 12 and *passim.*

2 Mary Wollstonecraft, *A Vindication of the Rights of Woman,* ed. Carol H. Poston (New York, 1975), p. 150.

3 Mary Shelley, *Frankenstein, or The Modern Prometheus,* ed. M. K. Joseph (New York, 1971), p. 124; future references to this edition will be given in the text.

4 *A Vindication,* chaps. 9-11, pp. 140-57.

5 See George Levine on pp. 15-16, above.

6 See, in this connection, Sidney and Beatrice Webb, *English Poor Law History* (Hamden, Conn., 1963); Ivy Pinchbeck and Margaret Hewett, *Children in English Society* (London, 1969), vol. I; J. J. Tobias, *Urban Crime in Victorian England* (New York, 1972).

7 In his discussion, U. C. Knoepflmacher draws numerous parallels between Mary Shelley and her characters. The links between Mary and both Caroline Beaufort and Elizabeth Lavenza are reenforced in other ways: Mary's mother also died young, leaving her orphaned daughter with a father who "passed his younger days perpetually occupied in the affairs of his country; a variety of circumstances had prevented his marrying early, nor was it until the decline of life that he became a husband and father of a family." If both Caroline and Elizabeth are retrieved by Alphonse Frankenstein, a Prince Charming also rescued Mary (or so she at first thought) from the family with which she could not be happily accommodated.

8 *Frankenstein, or The Modern Prometheus,* ed. James Rieger (New York, 1974), p. 37.

9 *Ibid.,* p. 30.

10 Thomas Gisborne, *An Enquiry into the Duties of the Female Sex* (London, 1798), pp. 20-21.

11 *A Vindication,* p. 169.

12 Examples of this mode of paternal interaction, and of the schizophrenia it elicits, may be found in R. D. Laing and A. Esterson, *Sanity, Madness, and the Family* (Middlesex, England, 1970).

13 Betty Friedan, *The Feminine Mystique* (New York, 1965). For an overview of recent scholarship on the family, see Christopher Lasch, "The Family and History," *New York Review of Books,* November 13, 1975, pp. 33-38. For a feminist view of this material see Barbara J. Harris, "Recent Work on the History of the Family: A Review Article," in *Feminist Studies,* vol. 3, nos. 3-4 (spring-summer 1976): 159-72.

Sandra M. Gilbert and Susan Gubar (essay date 1979)

SOURCE: "Horror's Twin: Mary Shelley's Monstrous Eve," in *The Madwoman in the Attic: The Woman Writer and the Nineteenth-Century Literary Imagination,* Yale University Press, 1979, pp. 213-47.

[In the following excerpt, Gilbert and Gubar view Frankenstein *not so much in terms of Shelley's relationship to her own father as in her relationship to literary patriarchy in general, figured in John Milton's* Paradise Lost. *Noting that Shelley read Milton's poem before writing her novel, the critics assert that Shelley adopted the misogyny of* Paradise Lost *into her own "pained ambivalence toward mothers."]*

Many critics have noticed that *Frankenstein* (1818) is one of the key Romantic "readings" of *Paradise Lost.*[14] Significantly, however, as a woman's reading it is most especially the story of hell: hell as a dark parody of heaven, hell's creations as monstrous imitations of heaven's creations, and hellish femaleness as a grotesque parody of heavenly maleness. But of course the divagations of the parody merely return to and reinforce the fearful reality of the original. For by parodying *Paradise Lost* in what may have begun as a secret, barely conscious attempt to subvert Milton, Shelley ended up telling, too, the central story of *Paradise Lost,* the tale of "what misery th' inabstinence of Eve / Shall bring on men."

Mary Shelley herself claims to have been continually asked "how I . . . came to think of and to dilate upon so very hideous an idea" as that of *Frankenstein,* but it is really not surprising that she should have formulated her anxieties about femaleness in such highly literary terms. For of course the nineteen-year-old girl who wrote *Frankenstein* was no ordinary nineteen-year-old but one of England's most notable literary heiresses. Indeed, as "the daughter of two persons of distinguished literary celebrity," and the wife of a third, Mary Wollstonecraft Godwin Shelley was the daughter and later the wife of some of Milton's keenest critics, so that Harold Bloom's useful conceit about the family romance of English literature is simply an accurate description of the reality of her life.[15]

In acknowledgement of this web of literary/familial relationships, critics have traditionally studied *Frankenstein* as an interesting example of Romantic mythmaking, a work ancillary to such established Promethean masterpieces as Shelley's *Prometheus Unbound* and Byron's *Manfred*. ("Like almost everything else about [Mary's] life," one such critic remarks, *Frankenstein* "is an instance of genius observed and admired but not shared."[16]) Recently, however, a number of writers have noticed the connection between Mary Shelley's "waking dream" of monster-manufacture and her own experience of awakening sexuality, in particular the "horror story of Maternity" which accompanied her precipitous entrance into what Ellen Moers calls "teen-age motherhood."[17] Clearly they are articulating an increasingly uneasy sense that, despite its male protagonist and its underpinning of "masculine" philosophy, *Frankenstein* is somehow a "woman's book," if only because its author was caught up in such a maelstrom of sexuality at the time she wrote the novel.

In making their case for the work as female fantasy, though, critics like Moers have tended to evade the problems posed by what we must define as *Frankenstein's* literariness. Yet, despite the weaknesses in those traditional readings of the novel that overlook its intensely sexual materials, it is still undeniably true that Mary Shelley's "ghost story," growing from a Keatsian (or Coleridgean) waking dream, is a Romantic novel about—among other things—Romanticism, as well as a book about books and perhaps, too, about the writers of books. Any theorist of the novel's femaleness and of its significance as, in Moers's phrase, a "birth myth" must therefore confront this self-conscious literariness. For as was only natural in "the daughter of two persons of distinguished literary celebrity," Mary Shelley explained her sexuality to herself in the context of her reading and its powerfully felt implications.

For this orphaned literary heiress, highly charged connections between femaleness and literariness must have been established early, and established specifically in relation to the controversial figure of her dead mother. As we shall see, Mary Wollstonecraft Godwin read her mother's writings over and over again as she was growing up. Perhaps more important, she undoubtedly read most of the reviews of her mother's *Posthumous Works,* reviews in which Mary Wollstonecraft was attacked as a "philosophical wanton" and a monster, while her

Vindication of the Rights of Woman (1792) was called "A scripture, archly fram'd for propagating w[hore]s."[18] But in any case, to the "philosophical wanton's" daughter, all reading about (or of) her mother's work must have been painful, given her knowledge that that passionate feminist writer had died in giving life to *her,* to bestow upon Wollstonecraft's death from complications of childbirth the melodramatic cast it probably had for the girl herself. That Mary Shelley was conscious, moreover, of a strangely intimate relationship between her feelings toward her dead mother, her romance with a living poet, and her own sense of vocation as a reader and writer is made perfectly clear by her habit of "taking her books to Mary Wollstonecraft's grave in St. Pancras' Churchyard, there," as Muriel Spark puts it, "to pursue her studies in an atmosphere of communion with a mind greater than the second Mrs. Godwin's [and] to meet Shelley in secret."[19]

Her mother's grave: the setting seems an unusually grim, even ghoulish locale for reading, writing, or lovemaking. Yet, to a girl with Mary Shelley's background, literary activities, like sexual ones, must have been primarily extensions of the elaborate, gothic psychodrama of her family history. If her famous diary is largely a compendium of her reading lists and Shelley's that fact does not, therefore, suggest unusual reticence on her part. Rather, it emphasizes the point that for Mary, even more than for most writers, reading a book was often an emotional as well as an intellectual event of considerable magnitude. Especially because she never knew her mother, and because her father seemed so definitively to reject her after her youthful elopement, her principal mode of self-definition—certainly in the early years of her life with Shelley, when she was writing *Frankenstein*—was through reading, and to a lesser extent through writing.

Endlessly studying her mother's works and her father's, Mary Shelley may be said to have "read" her family and to have been related to her reading, for books appear to have functioned as her surrogate parents, pages and words standing in for flesh and blood. That much of her reading was undertaken in Shelley's company, moreover, may also help explain some of this obsessiveness, for Mary's literary inheritance was obviously involved in her very literary romance and marriage. In the years just before she wrote *Frankenstein,* for instance, and those when she was engaged in composing the novel (1816-17), she studied her parent's writings, alone or together with Shelley, like a scholarly detective seeking clues to the significance of some cryptic text.[20]

To be sure, this investigation of the mysteries of literary genealogy was done in a larger context. In these same years, Mary Shelley recorded innumerable readings of contemporary gothic novels, as well as a program of study in English, French, and German literature that would do credit to a modern graduate student. But especially, in 1815, 1816, and 1817, she read the works of Milton: *Paradise Lost* (twice), *Paradise Regained, Comus, Areopagetica, Lycidas.* And what makes the extent of this reading particularly impressive is the fact that in these years, her seventeenth to her twenty-first, Mary Shelley was almost continuously pregnant, "confined," or nursing. At the same time, it is precisely the coincidence of all these disparate activities—her family studies, her initiation into adult sexuality, and her literary self-education—that makes her vision of *Paradise Lost* so significant. For her developing sense of herself as a literary creature and/ or creator seems to have been inseparable from her emerging self-definition as daughter, mistress, wife, and mother. Thus she cast her birth myth—her myth of origins—in precisely those cosmogenic terms to which her parents, her husband, and indeed her whole literary culture continually alluded: the terms of *Paradise Lost,* which (as she indicates even on the title page of her novel), she saw as preceding, paralleling, and commenting upon the Greek cosmogeny of the Prometheus play her husband had just translated. It is as a female fantasy of sex and reading, then, a gothic psychodrama reflecting Mary Shelley's own sense of what we might call bibliogenesis, that **Frankenstein** is a version of the misogynistic story implicit in *Paradise Lost.*

It would be a mistake to underestimate the significance of **Frankenstein**'s title page, with its allusive subtitle ("The Modern Prometheus") and carefully pointed Miltonic epigraph ("Did I request thee, Maker, from my clay / To mould me man? Did I solicit thee / From darkness to promote me?"). But our first really serious clue to the highly literary nature of this history of a creature born outside history is its author's use of an unusually *evidentiary* technique for conveying the stories of her monster and his maker. Like a literary jigsaw puzzle, a collection of apparently random documents from whose juxtaposition the scholar-detective must infer a meaning, **Frankenstein** consists of three "concentric circles" of narration (Walton's letters, Victor Franken-stein's recital to Walton, and the monster's speech to Frankenstein), within which are embedded pockets of digression containing other miniature narratives (Frankenstein's mother's story, Elizabeth Lavenza's and Justine's stories, Felix's and Agatha's story, Safie's story), etc.[21] As we have noted, reading and assembling documentary evidence, examining it, analyzing it and researching it comprised for Shelley a crucial if voyeuristic method of exploring origins, explaining identity, understanding sexuality. Even more obviously, it was a way of researching and analyzing an emotionally unintelligible text, like *Paradise Lost.* In a sense, then, even before *Paradise Lost* as a central item on the monster's reading list becomes a literal event in **Frankenstein,** the novel's literary structure prepares us to confront Milton's patriarchal epic, both as a sort of research problem and as the framework for a complex system of allusions.

The book's dramatic situations are equally resonant. Like Mary Shelley, who was a puzzled but studious Miltonist, this novel's key characters—Walton, Frankenstein, and the monster—are obsessed with problem-solving. "I shall satiate my ardent curiosity with the sight of a part of the world never before visited," exclaims the young explorer, Walton, as he embarks like a child "on an expedition of discovery up his native river" (2, letter 1). "While my companions contemplated . . . the magnificent appearance of things," declares Frankenstein, the scientist of sexual ontology, "I delighted in investigating their causes" (22, chap. 2). "Who was I? What was I? Whence did I come?" (113-15, chap. 15) the monster reports wondering, describing endless speculations cast in Miltonic terms. All three, like Shelley herself, appear to be trying to understand their presence in a fallen world, and trying at the same time to define the nature of the lost paradise that must have existed before the fall. But unlike Adam, all three characters seem to have fallen not merely from Eden but from the earth, fallen directly into hell, like Sin, Satan, and—by implication—Eve. Thus their questionings are in some sense female, for they belong in that line of literary women's questionings of the fall into gender which goes back at least to Anne Finch's plaintive "How are we fal'n?" and forward to Sylvia Plath's horrified "I have fallen very far!"[22]

From the first, however, **Frankenstein** answers such neo-Miltonic questions mainly through explicit or implicit allusions to Milton, retelling the story of the fall not so much to protest against it as to clarify its meaning. The parallels between those two Promethean overreachers Walton and Frankenstein, for instance, have always been clear to readers. But that both characters can, therefore, be described (the way Walton describes Frankenstein) as "fallen angels" is not as frequently remarked. Yet Frankenstein himself is perceptive enough to ask Walton "Do you share my madness?" at just the moment when the young explorer remarks Satanically that "One man's life or death were but a small price to pay . . . for the dominion I [wish to] acquire" (13, letter 4). Plainly one fallen angel can recognize another. Alienated from his crew and chronically friendless, Walton tells his sister that he longs for a friend "on the wide ocean," and what he discovers in Victor Frankenstein is the fellowship of hell.

In fact, like the many other secondary narratives Mary Shelley offers in her novel, Walton's story is itself an alternative version of the myth of origins presented in *Paradise Lost.* Writing his ambitious letters home from St. Petersburgh [*sic*], Archangel, and points north, Walton moves like Satan away from the sanctity and sanity represented by his sister, his crew, and the allegorical names of the places he leaves. Like Satan, too, he seems at least in part to be exploring the frozen frontiers of hell in order to attempt a return to heaven, for the "country of eternal light" he envisions at the

Pole (1, letter 1) has much in common with Milton's celestial "Fountain of Light" (*PL* 3. 375).[23] Again, like Satan's (and Eve's) aspirations, his ambition has violated a patriarchal decree: his father's "dying injunction" had forbidden him "to embark on a seafaring life." Moreover, even the icy hell where Walton encounters Frankenstein and the monster is Miltonic, for all three of these diabolical wanderers must learn, like the fallen angels of *Paradise Lost,* that "Beyond this flood a frozen Continent / Lies dark and wild . . . / Thither by harpy-footed Furies hal'd, / At certain revolutions all the damn'd / Are brought . . . From Beds of raging Fire to starve in Ice" (*PL* 2. 587-600).

Finally, another of Walton's revelations illuminates not only the likeness of his ambitions to Satan's but also the similarity of his anxieties to those of his female author. Speaking of his childhood, he reminds his sister that, because poetry had "lifted [my soul] to heaven," he had become a poet and "for one year lived in a paradise of my own creation." Then he adds ominously that "You are well-acquainted with my failure and how heavily I bore the disappointment" (2-3, letter 1). But of course, as she confesses in her introduction to *Frankenstein,* Mary Shelley, too, had spent her childhood in "waking dreams" of literature; later, both she and her poet-husband hoped she would prove herself "worthy of [her] parentage and enroll [herself] on the page of fame" (xii). In a sense, then, given the Miltonic context in which Walton's story of poetic failure is set, it seems possible that one of the anxious fantasies his narrative helps Mary Shelley covertly examine is the fearful tale of a female fall from a lost paradise of art, speech, and autonomy into a hell of sexuality, silence, and filthy materiality, "A Universe of death, which God by curse / Created evil, for evil only good, / Where all life dies, death lives, and Nature breeds, / Perverse, all monstrous, all prodigious things" (*PL* 2. 622-25).

Walton and his new friend Victor Frankenstein have considerably more in common than a Byronic (or Monk Lewis-ish) Satanism. For one thing, both are orphans, as Frankenstein's monster is and as it turns out all the major and almost all the minor characters in *Frankenstein* are, from Caroline Beaufort and Elizabeth Lavenza to Justine, Felix, Agatha, and Safie. Victor Frankenstein has not always been an orphan, though, and Shelley devotes much space to an account of his family history. Family histories, in fact, especially those of orphans, appear to fascinate her, and wherever she can include one in the narrative she does so with an obsessiveness suggesting that through the disastrous tale of the child who becomes "an orphan and a beggar" she is once more recounting the story of the fall, the expulsion from paradise, and the confrontation of hell. For Milton's Adam and Eve, after all, began as motherless orphans reared (like Shelley herself) by a stern but kindly father-god, and ended as beggars rejected by God (as she was by *God*win when she eloped).

Thus Caroline Beaufort's father dies leaving her "an orphan and a beggar," and Elizabeth Lavenza also becomes "an orphan and a beggar"—the phrase is repeated (18, 20, chap. 1)—with the disappearance of her father into an Austrian dungeon. And though both girls are rescued by Alphonse Frankenstein, Victor's father, the early alienation from the patriarchal chain-of-being signalled by their orphanhood prefigures the hellish fate in store for them and their family. Later, motherless Safie and fatherless Justine enact similarly ominous anxiety fantasies about the fall of woman into orphanhood and beggary.

Beyond their orphanhood, however, a universal sense of guilt links such diverse figures as Justine, Felix, and Elizabeth, just as it will eventually link Victor, Walton, and the monster. Justine, for instance, irrationally confesses to the murder of little William, though she knows perfectly well she is innocent. Even more irrationally, Elizabeth is reported by Alphonse Frankenstein to have exclaimed "Oh, God! I have murdered my darling child!" after her first sight of the corpse of little William (57, chap. 7). Victor, too, long before he knows that the monster is actually his brother's killer, decides that his "creature" has killed William and that therefore he, the creator, is the "true murderer": "the mere presence of the idea," he notes, is "an irresistable proof of the fact" (60, chap. 7). Complicity in the murder of the child William is, it seems, another crucial component of the Original Sin shared by prominent members of the Frankenstein family.

At the same time, the likenesses among all these characters—the common alienation, the shared guilt, the orphanhood and beggary—imply relationships of redundance between them like the solipsistic relationships among artfully placed mirrors. What reinforces our sense of this hellish solipsism is the barely disguised incest at the heart of a number of the marriages and romances the novel describes. Most notably, Victor Frankenstein is slated to marry his "more than sister" Elizabeth Lavenza, whom he confesses to having always considered "a possession of my own" (21, chap. 1). But the mysterious Mrs. Saville, to whom Walton's letters are addressed, is apparently in some sense *his* more than sister, just as Caroline Beaufort was clearly a "more than" wife, in fact a daughter, to her father's friend Alphonse Frankenstein. Even relationless Justine appears to have a metaphorically incestuous relationship with the Frankensteins, since as their servant she becomes their possession and more than sister, while the female monster Victor half-constructs in Scotland will be a more than sister as well as a mate to the monster, since both have the same parent/creator.

Certainly at least some of this incest-obsession in *Frankenstein* is, as Ellen Moers remarks, the "standard" sensational matter of Romantic novels.[24] Some of it, too, even without the conventions of the gothic thriller, would be a natural subject for an impressionable young woman who had just spent several months in the company of the famously incestuous author of *Manfred*.[25] Nevertheless, the streak of incest that darkens *Frankenstein* probably owes as much to the book's Miltonic framework as it does to Mary Shelley's own life and times. In the Edenic cosiness of their childhood, for instance, Victor and Elizabeth are incestuous as Adam and Eve are, literally incestuous because they have the same creator, and figuratively so because Elizabeth is Victor's pretty plaything, the image of an angelic soul or "epipsyche" created from his own soul just as Eve is created from Adam's rib. Similarly, the incestuous relationships of Satan and Sin, and by implication of Satan and Eve, are mirrored in the incest fantasies of *Frankenstein,* including the disguised but intensely sexual waking dream in which Victor Frankenstein in effect couples with his monster by applying "the instruments of life" to its body and inducing a shudder of response (42, chap. 5). For Milton, and therefore for Mary Shelley, who was trying to understand Milton, incest was an inescapable metaphor for the solipsistic fever of self-awareness that Matthew Arnold was later to call "the dialogue of the mind with itself."[26]

If Victor Frankenstein can be likened to both Adam and Satan, however, who or what is he *really*? Here we are obliged to confront both the moral ambiguity and the symbolic slipperiness which are at the heart of all the characterizations in *Frankenstein*. In fact, it is probably these continual and complex reallocations of meaning, among characters whose histories echo and re-echo each other, that have been so bewildering to critics. Like figures in a dream, all the people in *Frankenstein* have different bodies and somehow, horribly, the same face, or worse—the same two faces. For this reason, as Muriel Spark notes, even the book's subtitle "The Modern Prometheus" is ambiguous, "for though at first Frankenstein is himself the Prometheus, the vital fire-endowing protagonist, the Monster, as soon as he is created, takes on [a different aspect of] the role."[27] Moreover, if we postulate that Mary Shelley is more concerned with Milton than she is with Aeschylus, the intertwining of meanings grows even more confusing, as the monster himself several times points out to Frankenstein, noting "I ought to be thy Adam, but I am rather the fallen angel," (84, chap. 10), then adding elsewhere that "God, in pity, made man beautiful . . . after His own image; but my form is a filthy type of yours. . . . Satan had his companions . . . but I am solitary and abhorred" (115, chap. 15). In other words, not only do Frankenstein and his monster both in one way or another enact the story of Prometheus, each is at one time or another like God (Victor as creator, the monster as his creator's "Master"), like Adam (Victor an innocent child, the monster as primordial "creature"), and like Satan (Victor as tormented overreacher, the monster as vengeful fiend).

What is the reason for this continual duplication and reduplication of roles? Most obviously, perhaps, the dreamlike shifting of fantasy figures from part to part, costume to costume, tells us that we are in fact dealing with the psychodrama or waking dream that Shelley herself suspected she had written. Beyond this, however, we would argue that the fluidity of the narrative's symbolic scheme reinforces in another way the crucial significance of the Miltonic skeleton around which Mary Shelley's hideous progeny took shape. For it becomes increasingly clear as one reads *Frankenstein* with *Paradise Lost* in mind that because the novel's author is such an inveterate student of literature, families, and sexuality, and because she is using her novel as a tool to help her make sense of her reading, *Frankenstein* is ultimately a mock *Paradise Lost* in which both Victor and his monster, together with a number of secondary characters, play all the neo-biblical parts over and over again—all except, it seems at first, the part of Eve. Not just the striking omission of any obvious Eve-figure from this "woman's book" about Milton, but also the barely concealed sexual components of the story as well as our earlier analysis of Milton's bogey should tell us, however, that for Mary Shelley the part of Eve *is* all the parts.

On the surface, Victor seems at first more Adamic than Satanic or Eve-like. His Edenic childhood is an interlude of prelapsarian innocence in which, like Adam, he is sheltered by his benevolent father as a sensitive plant might be "sheltered by the gardener, from every rougher wind" (19-20, chap. 1). When cherubic Elizabeth Lavenza joins the family, she seems as "heaven-sent" as Milton's Eve, as much Victor's "possession" as Adam's rib is Adam's. Moreover, though he is evidently forbidden almost nothing ("My parents [were not] tyrants . . . but the agents and creators of many delights"), Victor hints to Walton that his deific father, like Adam's and Walton's, did on one occasion arbitrarily forbid him to pursue his interest in arcane knowledge. Indeed, like Eve and Satan, Victor blames his own fall at least in part on his father's apparent arbitrariness. "If . . . my father had taken the pains to explain to me that the principles of Agrippa had been entirely exploded. . . . It is even possible that the train of my ideas would never have received the fatal impulse that led to my ruin" (24-25, chap. 2). And soon after asserting this he even associates an incident in which a tree is struck by Jovian thunder bolts with his feelings about his forbidden studies.

As his researches into the "secrets of nature" become more feverish, however, and as his ambition "to explore unknown powers" grows more intense, Victor begins to metamorphose from Adam to Satan, becoming "as Gods" in his capacity of "bestowing animation upon lifeless matter," laboring like a guilty artist to complete his false creation. Finally, in his conversations with Walton he echoes Milton's fallen angel, and

Marlowe's, in his frequently reiterated confession that "I bore a hell within me which nothing could extinguish" (72, chap. 8). Indeed, as the "true murderer" of innocence, here cast in the form of the child William, Victor perceives himself as a diabolical creator whose mind has involuntarily "let loose" a monstrous and "filthy demon" in much the same way that Milton's Satan's swelled head produced Sin, the disgusting monster he "let loose" upon the world. Watching a "noble war in the sky" that seems almost like an intentional reminder that we are participating in a critical rearrangement of most of the elements of *Paradise Lost,* he explains that "I considered the being whom I had cast among mankind . . . nearly in the light of my own vampire, my own spirit let loose from the grave and forced to destroy all that was dear to me" (61, chap. 7).

Even while it is the final sign and seal of Victor's transformation from Adam to Satan, however, it is perhaps the Sin-ful murder of the child William that is our first overt clue to the real nature of the bewilderingly disguised set of identity shifts and parallels Mary Shelley incorporated into *Frankenstein.* For as we saw earlier, not just Victor and the monster but also Elizabeth and Justine insist upon responsibility for the monster's misdeed. Feeling "as if I had been guilty of a crime" (41, chap. 4) even before one had been committed, Victor responds to the news of William's death with the same self-accusations that torment the two orphans. And, significantly, for all three—as well as for the monster and little William himself—one focal point of both crime and guilt is an image of that other beautiful orphan, Caroline Beaufort Frankenstein. Passing from hand to hand, pocket to pocket, the smiling miniature of Victor's "angel mother" seems a token of some secret fellowship in sin, as does Victor's postcreation nightmare of transforming a lovely, living Elizabeth, with a single magical kiss, into "the corpse of my dead mother" enveloped in a shroud made more horrible by "grave-worms crawling in the folds of the flannel" (42, chap. 5). Though it has been disguised, buried, or miniaturized, femaleness—the gender definition of mothers and daughters, orphans and beggars, monsters and false creators—is at the heart of this apparently masculine book.

Because this is so, it eventually becomes clear that though Victor Frankenstein enacts the roles of Adam and Satan like a child trying on costumes, his single most self-defining act transforms him definitively into Eve. For as both Ellen Moers and Marc Rubenstein have pointed out, after much study of the "cause of generation and life," after locking himself away from ordinary society in the tradition of such agonized mothers as Wollstonecraft's Maria, Eliot's Hetty Sorel, and Hardy's Tess, Victor Frankenstein has a baby.[28] His "pregnancy" and childbirth are obviously manifested by the existence of the paradoxically huge being who emerges from his "workshop of filthy creation," but even the descriptive language of his creation myth is suggestive: "incredible labours," "emaciated with confinement," "a passing trance," "oppressed by a slow fever," "nervous to a painful degree," "exercise and amusement would . . . drive away incipient disease," "the instruments of life" (39-41, chap. 4), etc. And, like Eve's fall into guilty knowledge and painful maternity, Victor's entrance into what Blake would call the realm of "generation" is marked by a recognition of the necessary interdependence of those complementary opposites, sex and death: "To examine the causes of life, we must first have recourse to death," he observes (36, chap. 4), and in his isolated workshop of filthy creation—filthy because obscenely sexual[29]—he collects and arranges materials furnished by "the dissecting room and the slaughterhouse." Pursuing "nature to her hiding places" as Eve does in eating the apple, he learns that "the tremendous secrets of the human frame" are the interlocked secrets of sex and death, although, again like Eve, in his first mad pursuit of knowledge he knows not "eating death." But that his actual orgasmic animation of his monster-child takes place "on a dreary night in November," month of All Souls, short days, and the year's last slide toward death, merely reinforces the Miltonic and Blakean nature of his act of generation.

Even while Victor Frankenstein's self-defining procreation dramatically transforms him into an Eve-figure, however, our recognition of its implications reflects backward upon our sense of Victor-as-Satan and our earlier vision of Victor-as-Adam. Victor as Satan, we now realize, was never really the masculine, Byronic Satan of the first book of *Paradise Lost,* but always, instead, the curiously female, outcast Satan who gave birth to Sin. In his Eve-like pride ("I was surprised . . . that I alone should be reserved to discover so astonishing a secret" [37, chap. 4]), this Victor-Satan becomes "dizzy" with his creative powers, so that his monstrous pregnancy, bookishly and solipsistically conceived, reenacts as a terrible bibliogenesis the moment when, in Milton's version, Satan "dizzy swum / In darkness, while [his] head flames thick and fast / Threw forth, till on the left side op'ning wide" and Sin, Death's mother-to-be, appeared like "a Sign / Portentous" (*PL* 2: 753-61). Because he has conceived—or, rather, misconceived—his monstrous offspring by brooding upon the *wrong* books, moreover, this Victor-Satan is paradigmatic, like the falsely creative fallen angel, of the female artist, whose anxiety about her own aesthetic activity is expressed, for instance, in Mary Shelley's deferential introductory phrase about her "hideous progeny," with its plain implication that in her alienated attic workshop of filthy creation she has given birth to a deformed book, a literary abortion or miscarriage. "How [did] I, then a young girl, [come] to think of and to *dilate* upon so very hideous an idea?" is a key (if disingenuous) question she records. But we should not overlook her word play upon *dilate,* just as we should not ignore the anxious pun on the word *author* that is so deeply embedded in *Frankenstein.*

If the adult, Satanic Victor is Eve-like both in his pro-creation and his anxious creation, even the young, prelapsarian, and Adamic Victor is—to risk a pun—*curiously* female, that is, Eve-like. Innocent and guided by silken threads like a Blakean lamb in a Godwinian garden, he is consumed by "a fervent longing to pen-etrate the secrets of nature," a longing which—ex-pressed in his explorations of "vaults and charnel-houses," his guilty observations of "the unhallowed damps of the grave," and his passion to understand "the structure of the human frame"—recalls the crimi-nal female curiosity that led Psyche to lose love by gazing upon its secret face, Eve to insist upon consum-ing "intellectual food," and Prometheus's sister-in-law Pandora to open the forbidden box of fleshly ills. But if Victor-Adam is also Victor-Eve, what is the real significance of the episode in which, away at school and cut off from his family, he locks himself into his workshop of filthy creation and gives birth by intellec-tual parturition to a giant monster? Isn't it precisely at this point in the novel that he discovers he is not Adam but Eve, not Satan but Sin, not male but female? If so, it seems likely that what this crucial section of *Fran-kenstein* really enacts is the story of Eve's discovery not that she must fall but that, having been created female, she *is* fallen, femaleness and fallenness being essentially synonymous. For what Victor Frankenstein most importantly learns, we must remember, is that he is the "author" of the monster—for him alone is "re-served . . . so astonishing a secret"—and thus it is he who is "the true murderer," he who unleashes Sin and Death upon the world, he who dreams the primal kiss that incestuously kills both "sister" and "mother." Doomed and filthy, is he not, then, Eve instead of Adam? In fact, may not the story of the fall be, for women, the story of the discovery that one is not in-nocent and Adam (as one had supposed) but Eve, and fallen? Perhaps this is what Freud's cruel but meta-phorically accurate concept of penis-envy really means: the girl-child's surprised discovery that she is female, hence fallen, inadequate. Certainly the almost gro-tesquely anxious self-analysis implicit in Victor Frankenstein's (and Mary Shelley's) multiform rela-tionships to Eve, Adam, God, and Satan suggest as much.

The discovery that one is fallen is in a sense a discov-ery that one is a monster, a murderer, a being gnawed by "the never-dying worm" (72, chap. 8) and therefore capable of any horror, including but not limited to sex, death, and filthy literary creation. More, the discovery that one is fallen—self-divided, murderous, material—is the discovery that one has released a "vampire" upon the world, "forced to destroy all that [is] dear" (61, chap. 7). For this reason—because *Frankenstein* is a

story of woman's fall told by, as it were, an apparently docile daughter to a censorious "father"—the monster's narrative is embedded at the heart of the novel like the secret of the fall itself. Indeed, just as Frankenstein's workshop, with its maddening, riddling answers to cosmic questions is a hidden but commanding attic womb/room where the young artist-scientist murders to dissect and to recreate, so the murderous monster's single, carefully guarded narrative commands and con-trols Mary Shelley's novel. Delivered at the top of Mont Blanc—like the North Pole one of the Shelley family's metaphors for the indifferently powerful source of creation and destruction—it is the story of deformed Geraldine in "Christabel," the story of the dead-alive crew in "The Ancient Mariner," the story of Eve in *Paradise Lost,* and of her degraded double Sin—all secondary or female characters to whom male authors have imperiously denied any chance of self-explana-tion.[30] At the same time the monster's narrative is a philosophical meditation on what it means to be born without a "soul" or a history, as well as an exploration of what it feels like to be a "filthy mass that move[s] and talk[s]," a thing, an other, a creature of the second sex. In fact, though it tends to be ignored by critics (and film-makers), whose emphasis has always fallen upon Frankenstein himself as the archetypal mad sci-entist, the drastic shift in point of view that the name-less monster's monologue represents probably consti-tutes *Frankenstein*'s most striking technical *tour de force,* just as the monster's bitter self-revelations are Mary Shelley's most impressive and original achieve-ment.[31]

Like Victor Frankenstein, his author and superficially better self, the monster enacts in turn the roles of Adam and Satan, and even eventually hints at a sort of di-gression into the role of God. Like Adam, he recalls a time of primordial innocence, his days and nights in "the forest near Ingolstadt," where he ate berries, learned about heat and cold, and perceived "the bound-aries of the radiant roof of light which canopied me" (88, chap. 11). Almost too quickly, however, he meta-morphoses into an outcast and Satanic figure, hiding in a shepherd's hut which seems to him "as exquisite . . . a retreat as Pandemonium . . . after . . . the lake of fire" (90, chap. 11). Later, when he secretly sets up house-keeping behind the De Laceys' pigpen, his wistful observations of the loving though exiled family and their pastoral abode ("Happy, happy earth! Fit habita-tion for gods . . ." [100, chap. 12]) recall Satan's mingled jealousy and admiration of that "happy rural seat of various view" where Adam and Eve are emparadised by God and Milton (*PL* 4. 247). Eventu-ally, burning the cottage and murdering William in demonic rage, he seems to become entirely Satanic: "I, like the arch-fiend, bore a hell within me" (121, chap. 16); "Inflamed by pain, I vowed eternal hatred . . . to all mankind" (126, chap. 16). At the same time, in his assertion of power over his "author," his mental conception of another creature (a female monster), and his implicit dream of founding a new, vegetarian race somewhere in "the vast wilds of South America," (131, chap. 17), he temporarily enacts the part of a God, a creator, a master, albeit a failed one.

As the monster himself points out, however, each of these Miltonic roles is a Procrustean bed into which he simply cannot fit. Where, for instance, Victor Frankenstein's childhood really was Edenic, the monster's anxious infancy is isolated and ignorant, rather than insulated or innocent, so that his groping arrival at self-consciousness—"I was a poor, helpless, miserable wretch; I knew and could distinguish nothing; but feeling pain invade me on all sides, I sat down and wept" (87-88, chap. 11)—is a fiercely subversive parody of Adam's exuberant "all things smil'd, / With fragrance and with joy my heart o'erflowed. / Myself I then perus'd, and Limb by Limb / Survey'd, and sometimes went, and sometimes ran / With supple joints, as lively vigor led" (*PL* 8. 265-69). Similarly, the monster's attempts at speech ("Sometimes I wished to express my sensations in my own mode, but the uncouth and inarticulate sounds which broke from me frightened me into silence again" (88, chap. 11) parody and subvert Adam's ("To speak I tri'd, and forthwith spake, / My Tongue obey'd and readily could name / Whate'er I saw" (*PL* 8. 271-72). And of course the monster's anxiety and confusion ("What was I? The question again recurred to be answered only with groans" [106, chap. 13]) are a dark version of Adam's wondering bliss ("who I was, or where, or from what cause, / [I] Knew not. . . . [But I] feel that I am happier than I know" (*PL* 8. 270-71, 282).

Similarly, though his uncontrollable rage, his alienation, even his enormous size and superhuman physical strength bring him closer to Satan than he was to Adam, the monster puzzles over discrepancies between his situation and the fallen angel's. Though he is, for example, "in bulk as huge / As whom the Fables name of monstrous size, / *Titanian,* or *Earth-born,* that warr'd on *Jove,*" and though, indeed, he is fated to war like Prometheus on Jovean Frankenstein, this demon/monster has fallen from no heaven, exercised no power of choice, and been endowed with no companions in evil. "I found myself similar yet at the same time strangely unlike to the beings concerning whom I read and to whose conversation I was a listener," he tells Frankenstein, describing his schooldays in the De Lacey pigpen (113, chap. 15). And, interestingly, his remark might well have been made by Mary Shelley herself, that "devout but nearly silent listener" (xiv) to masculine conversations who, like her hideous progeny, "continually studied and exercised [her] mind upon" such "histories" as *Paradise Lost,* Plutarch's *Lives,* and *The Sorrows of Werter* [*sic*] "whilst [her] friends were employed in their ordinary occupations" (112, chap. 15).

In fact, it is his intellectual similarity to his authoress (rather than his "author") which first suggests that Victor Frankenstein's male monster may really be a female in disguise. Certainly the books which educate him—*Werter,* Plutarch's *Lives,* and *Paradise Lost*—are not only books Mary had herself read in 1815, the year before she wrote ***Frankenstein,*** but they also typify just the literary categories she thought it necessary to study: the contemporary novel of sensibility, the serious history of Western civilization, and the highly cultivated epic poem. As specific works, moreover, each must have seemed to her to embody lessons a female author (or monster) must learn about a male-dominated society. Werter's story, says the monster—and he seems to be speaking for Mary Shelley—taught him about "gentle and domestic manners," and about "lofty sentiments . . . which had for their object something out of self." It functioned, in other words, as a sort of Romantic conduct book. In addition, it served as an introduction to the virtues of the proto-Byronic "Man of Feeling," for, admiring Werter and never mentioning Lotte, the monster explains to Victor that "I thought Werter himself a more divine being than I had ever . . . imagined," adding, in a line whose female irony about male self-dramatization must surely have been intentional, "I wept [his extinction] without precisely understanding it" (113, chap. 15).

If *Werter* introduces the monster to female modes of domesticity and self-abnegation, as well as to the unattainable glamour of male heroism, Plutarch's *Lives* teaches him all the masculine intricacies of that history which his anomalous birth has denied him. Mary Shelley, excluding herself from the household of the second Mrs. Godwin and studying family as well as literary history on her mother's grave, must, again, have found in her own experience an appropriate model for the plight of a monster who, as James Rieger notes, is especially characterized by "his unique knowledge of what it is like to be born free of history."[32] In terms of the disguised story the novel tells, however, this monster is not unique at all, but representative, as Shelley may have suspected she herself was. For, as Jane Austen has Catherine Morland suggest in *Northanger Abbey,* what is woman but man without a history, at least without the sort of history related in Plutarch's *Lives*? "History, real solemn history, I cannot be interested in," Catherine declares " . . . the men all so good for nothing, and hardly any women at all—it is very tiresome" (*NA* I, chap. 14).

But of course the third and most crucial book referred to in the miniature *Bildungsroman* of the monster's narrative is *Paradise Lost,* an epic myth of origins which is of major importance to him, as it is to Mary Shelley, precisely because, unlike Plutarch, it does provide him with what appears to be a personal history. And again, even the need for such a history draws Shelley's monster closer not only to the realistically ignorant female defined by Jane Austen but also to the archetypal female defined by John Milton. For, like the monster, like Catherine Morland, and like Mary Shelley herself, Eve is characterized by her "unique knowledge of what it is like to be born free of history," even though as the "Mother of Mankind" she is fated to "make" history. It is to Adam, after all, that God and His angels grant explanatory visions of past and future. At such moments of high historical colloquy Eve tends to excuse herself with "lowliness Majestic" (before the fall) or (after the fall) she is magically put to sleep, calmed like a frightened animal "with gentle Dreams . . . and all her spirits compos'd / To meek submission" (*PL* 12. 595-96).

Nevertheless, one of the most notable facts about the monster's ceaselessly anxious study of *Paradise Lost* is his failure even to mention Eve. As an insistently male monster, on the surface of his palimpsestic narrative he appears to be absorbed in Milton's epic only because, as Percy Shelley wrote in the preface to **Frankenstein** that he drafted for his wife, *Paradise Lost* "most especially" conveys "the truth of the elementary principles of human nature," and conveys that truth in the dynamic tensions developed among its male characters, Adam, Satan, and God (xvii). Yet not only the monster's uniquely ahistorical birth, his literary anxieties, and the sense his readings (like Mary's) foster that he must have been parented, if at all, by *books;* not only all these facts and traits but also his shuddering sense of deformity, his nauseating size, his namelessness, and his orphaned, motherless isolation link him with Eve and with Eve's double, Sin. Indeed, at several points in his impassioned analysis of Milton's story he seems almost on the verge of saying so, as he examines the disjunctions among Adam, Satan, and himself:

> Like Adam, I was apparently united by no link to any other being in existence; but his state was far different from mine in every other respect. He had come forth from the hands of God a perfect creature, happy and prosperous, guided by the especial care of his Creator; he was allowed to converse with and acquire knowledge from beings of a superior nature, but I was wretched, helpless, and alone. Many times I considered Satan as the fitter emblem of my condition, for often, like him, when I viewed the bliss of my protectors, the bitter gall of envy rose within me. . . . Accursed creator! Why did you form a monster so hideous that even *you* turned from me in disgust? God, in pity, made man beautiful and alluring, after his own image; but my form is a filthy type of yours, more horrid even from the very resemblance. Satan had his companions, fellow devils, to admire and encourage him, but I am solitary and abhorred. [114-15, chap. 15]

It is Eve, after all, who languishes helpless and alone, while Adam converses with superior beings, and it is

Eve in whom the Satanically bitter gall of envy rises, causing her to eat the apple in the hope of adding "what wants / In Female Sex." It is Eve, moreover, to whom deathly isolation is threatened should Adam reject her, an isolation more terrible even than Satan's alienation from heaven. And finally it is Eve whose body, like her mind, is said by Milton to resemble "less / His Image who made both, and less [to express] / The character of that Dominion giv'n / O'er other Creatures . . ." (*PL* 8. 543-46). In fact, to a sexually anxious reader, Eve's body might, like Sin's, seem "horrid even from [its] very resemblance" to her husband's, a "filthy" or obscene version of the human form divine.[33]

As we argued earlier, women have seen themselves (because they have been seen) as monstrous, vile, degraded creatures, second-comers, and emblems of filthy materiality, even though they have also been traditionally defined as superior spiritual beings, angels, better halves. "Woman [is] a temple built over a sewer," said the Church father Tertullian, and Milton seems to see Eve as both temple and sewer, echoing that patristic misogyny.[34] Mary Shelley's conscious or unconscious awareness of the monster woman implicit in the angel woman is perhaps clearest in the revisionary scene where her monster, as if taking his cue from Eve in *Paradise Lost* book 4, first catches sight of his own image: "I had admired the perfect forms of my cottagers . . . but how was I terrified when I viewed myself in a transparent pool. At first I started back, unable to believe that it was indeed I who was reflected in the mirror; and when I became fully convinced that I was in reality the monster that I am, I was filled with the bitterest sensations of despondence and mortification" (98-99, chap. 12). In one sense, this is a corrective to Milton's blindness about Eve. Having been created second, inferior, a mere rib, how could she possibly, this passage implies, have seemed anything but monstrous to herself? In another sense, however, the scene supplements Milton's description of Eve's introduction to herself, for ironically, though her reflection in "the clear / Smooth Lake" is as beautiful as the monster's is ugly, the self-absorption that Eve's confessed passion for her own image signals is plainly meant by Milton to seem morally ugly, a hint of her potential for spiritual deformity: "There I had fixt / Mine eyes till now, and pin'd with vain desire, / Had not a voice thus warn'd me, What thou seest, / What there thou seest fair Creature is thyself . . ." (*PL* 4. 465-68).

The figurative monstrosity of female narcissism is a subtle deformity, however, in comparison with the literal monstrosity many women are taught to see as characteristic of their own bodies. Adrienne Rich's twentieth-century description of "a woman in the shape of a monster / A monster in the shape of a woman" is merely the latest in a long line of monstrous female self-definitions that includes the fearful images in Djuna Barnes's *Book of Repulsive Women,* Denise Levertov's "a white sweating bull of a poet told us / our cunts are ugly" and Sylvia Plath's "old yellow" self of the poem "In Plaster."[35] Animal and misshapen, these emblems of self-loathing must have descended at least in part from the distended body of Mary Shelley's darkly parodic Eve/Sin/Monster, whose enormity betokens not only the enormity of Victor Frankenstein's crime and Satan's bulk but also the distentions or deformities of pregnancy and the Swiftian sexual nausea expressed in Lemuel Gulliver's horrified description of a Brobdignagian breast, a passage Mary Shelley no doubt studied along with the rest of *Gulliver's Travels* when she read the book in 1816, shortly before beginning *Frankenstein.*[36]

At the same time, just as surely as Eve's moral deformity is symbolized by the monster's physical malformation, the monster's physical ugliness represents his social illegitimacy, his bastardy, his namelessness. Bitchy and dastardly as Shakespeare's Edmund, whose association with filthy femaleness is established not only by his devotion to the material/maternal goddess Nature but also by his interlocking affairs with those filthy females Goneril and Regan, Mary Shelley's monster has also been "got" in a "dark and vicious place." Indeed, in his vile illegitimacy he seems to incarnate that bestial "unnameable" place. And significantly, he is himself as nameless as a woman is in patriarchal society, as nameless as unmarried, illegitimately pregnant Mary Wollstonecraft Godwin may have felt herself to be at the time she wrote *Frankenstein.*

"This nameless mode of naming the unnameable is rather good," Mary commented when she learned that it was the custom at early dramatizations of *Frankenstein* to place a blank line next to the name of the actor who played the part of the monster.[37] But her pleased surprise was disingenuous, for the problem of names and their connection with social legitimacy had been forced into her consciousness all her life. As the sister of illegitimate and therefore nameless Fanny Imlay, for instance, she knew what bastardy meant, and she knew it too as the mother of a premature and illegitimate baby girl who died at the age of two weeks without ever having been given a name. Of course, when Fanny dramatically excised her name from her suicide note Mary learned more about the significance even of insignificant names. And as the stepsister of Mary Jane Clairmont, who defined herself as the "creature" of Lord Byron and changed her name for a while with astonishing frequency (from Mary Jane to Jane to Clara to Claire), Mary knew about the importance of names too. Perhaps most of all, though, Mary's sense of the fearful significance of legitimate and illegitimate names must have been formed by her awareness that her own name, Mary Wollstonecraft Godwin, was absolutely identical with the name of the mother who had died in

giving birth to *her.* Since this was so, she may have speculated, perhaps her own monstrosity, her murderous illegitimacy, consisted in her being—like Victor Frankenstein's creation—a reanimation of the dead, a sort of galvanized corpse ironically arisen from what should have been "the cradle of life."

This implicit fantasy of the reanimation of the dead in the monstrous and nameless body of the living returns us, however, to the matter of the monster's Satanic, Sin-ful and Eve-like moral deformity. For of course the crimes that the monster commits once he has accepted the world's definition of him as little more than a namelessly "filthy mass" all reinforce his connection with Milton's unholy trinity of Sin, Eve/Satan, and Death. The child of two authors (Victor Frankenstein and Mary Shelley) whose mothers have been stolen away by death, this motherless monster is after all made from dead bodies, from loathsome parts found around cemeteries, so that it seems only "natural" for him to continue the Blakeian cycle of despair his birth began, by bringing further death into the world. And of course he brings death, in the central actions of the novel: death to the childish innocence of little William (whose name is that of Mary Shelley's father, her half-brother, and her son, so that one can hardly decide to which male relative she may have been alluding); death to the faith and truth of allegorically named Justine; death to the legitimate artistry of the Shelleyan poet Clerval; and death to the ladylike selflessness of angelic Elizabeth. Is he acting, in his vile way, for Mary Shelley, whose elegant femininity seemed, in view of her books, so incongruous to the poet Beddoes and to literary Lord Dillon? "She has no business to be a woman by her books," noted Beddoes. And "your writing and your manners are not in accordance," Dillon told Mary herself. "I should have thought of you—if I had only read you—that you were a sort of . . . Sybil, outpouringly enthusiastic . . . but you are cool, quiet and feminine to the last degree. . . . Explain this to me."[38]

Could Mary's coolness have been made possible by the heat of her monster's rage, the strain of her decorous silence eased by the demonic abandon of her nameless monster's ritual fire dance around the cottage of his rejecting "Protectors"? Does Mary's cadaverous creature want to bring more death into the world because he has failed—like those other awful females, Eve and Sin—to win the compassion of that blind and curiously Miltonic old man, the Godlike musical patriarch De Lacey? Significantly, he is clinging to the blind man's knees, begging for recognition and help— "Do not you desert me in the hour of trial!"—when Felix, the son of the house, appears like the felicitous hero he is, and, says the monster, "with supernatural force [he] tore me from his father . . . in a transport of fury, he dashed me to the ground and struck me violently with a stick . . . my heart sank within me as with bitter sickness" (119, chap. 15). Despite everything we have been told about the monster's physical vileness, Felix's rage seems excessive in terms of the novel's overt story. But as an action in the covert plot—the tale of the blind rejection of women by misogynistic/ Miltonic patriarchy—it is inevitable and appropriate. Even more psychologically appropriate is the fact that having been so definitively rejected by a world of fathers, the monster takes his revenge, first by murdering William, a male child who invokes his father's name ("My papa is a syndic—he is M. Frankenstein— he will punish you") and then by beginning a doomed search for a maternal, female principle in the harsh society that has created him.

In this connection, it begins to be plain that Eve's— and the monster's—motherlessness must have had extraordinary cultural and personal significance for Mary Shelley. "We think back through our mothers if we are women," wrote Virginia Woolf in *A Room of One's Own*.[39] But of course one of the most dramatic emblems of Eve's alienation from the masculine garden in which she finds herself is her motherlessness. Because she is made in the image of a man who is himself made in the image of a male creator, her unprecedented femininity seems merely a defective masculinity, a deformity like the monster's inhuman body.[40] In fact, as we saw, the only maternal model in *Paradise Lost* is the terrifying figure of Sin. (That Eve's punishment for *her* sin is the doom of agonized maternity—the doom of painfully becoming no longer herself but "Mother of Human Race"—appears therefore to seal the grim parallel.) But all these powerful symbols would be bound to take on personal weight and darkness for Shelley, whose only real "mother" was a tombstone—or a shelf of books—and who, like all orphans, must have feared that she had been deliberately deserted by her dead parent, or that, if she was a monster, then her hidden, underground mother must have been one too.

For all these reasons, then, the monster's attitude toward the possibility (or impossibility) of finding a mother is unusually conflicted and complex. At first, horrified by what he knows of the only "mother" he has ever had—Victor Frankenstein—he regards his parentage with loathing. Characteristically, he learns the specific details of his "conception" and "birth" (as Mary Shelley may have learned of hers) through reading, for Victor has kept a journal which records "that series of disgusting circumstances" leading "to the production of [the monster's] . . . loathsome person."[41] Later, however, the ill-fated miniature of Caroline Beaufort Frankenstein, Victor's "angel mother," momentarily "attract[s]" him. In fact, he claims it is because he is "forever deprived of the delights that such beautiful creatures could bestow" that he resolves to implicate Justine in the murder of William. His reproachful explanation is curious, though ("The crime

had its source in her; be hers the punishment"), as is the sinister rape fantasy he enacts by the side of the sleeping orphan ("Awake, fairest, thy lover is near— he who would give his life but to obtain one look of affection from thine eyes" [127-28, chap. 16]). Clearly feelings of rage, terror, and sexual nausea, as well as idealizing sentiments, accrete for Mary and the monster around the maternal female image, a fact which explains the later climactic wedding-night murder of apparently innocent Elizabeth. In this fierce, Miltonic world, *Frankenstein* says, the angel woman and the monster woman alike must die, if they are not dead already. And what is to be feared above all else is the reanimation of the dead, specifically of the maternal dead. Perhaps that is why a significant pun is embedded in the crucial birth scene ("It was on a dreary night of November") that, according to Mary Shelley, rose "unbidden" from her imagination. Looking at the "demoniacal corpse to which I had so miserably given life," Victor remarks that "A *mummy* again endued with animation could not be so hideous as that wretch" (43, chap. 5). For a similarly horrific (and equally punning) statement of sexual nausea, one would have to go back to Donne's "Loves Alchymie" with its urgent, misogynistic imperative: "Hope not for minde in women; at their best / Sweetnesse and wit, they are but / *Mummy* possest."

Interestingly, the literary group at Villa Diodati received a packet of books containing, among other poems, Samuel Taylor Coleridge's recently published "Christabel," shortly before Mary had her monster-dream and began her ghost story. More influential than "Loves Alchymie"—a poem Mary may or may not have read—"Christabel"'s vision of femaleness must have been embodied for the author of *Frankenstein* not only in the witch Geraldine's withered side and consequent self-loathing ("Ah! What a stricken look was hers!") but also in her anxiety about the ghost of Christabel's dead mother ("Off, wandering mother! Peak and pine!") and in Christabel's "Woe is me / She died the hour that I was born." But even without Donne's puns or Coleridge's Romanticized male definition of deathly maternity, Mary Shelley would have absorbed a keen sense of the agony of female sexuality, and specifically of the perils of motherhood, not just from *Paradise Lost* and from her own mother's fearfully exemplary fate but also from Wollstonecraft's almost prophetically anxious writings.

Maria, or the Wrongs of Woman (1797), which Mary read in 1814 (and possibly in 1815) is about, among other "wrongs," Maria's search for her lost child, her fears that "she" (for the fantasied child is a daughter) may have been murdered by her unscrupulous father, and her attempts to reconcile herself to the child's death. In a suicide scene that Wollstonecraft drafted shortly before her own death, as her daughter must have known, Maria swallows laudanum: "her soul was calm . . . nothing

Sketch of Shelley, c. 1814.

remained but an eager longing . . . to fly . . . from this hell of disappointment. Still her eyes closed not. . . . Her murdered child again appeared to her . . . [But] 'Surely it is better to die with me, than to enter on life without a mother's care!'"[42] Plainly, *Frankenstein's* pained ambivalence toward mothers and mummies is in some sense a response to *Maria's* agonized reaching—from beyond the grave, it may have seemed—toward a daughter. "Off, wandering mother! Peak and pine!" It is no wonder if Coleridge's poem gave Mary Wollstonecraft Godwin Shelley bad dreams, no wonder if she saw Milton's "Mother of Human Race" as a sorrowful monster.

Though *Frankenstein* itself began with a Coleridgean and Miltonic nightmare of filthy creation that reached its nadir in the monster's revelation of filthy femaleness, Mary Shelley, like Victor Frankenstein himself, evidently needed to distance such monstrous secrets. Sinful, motherless Eve and sinned-against, daughterless Maria, both paradigms of woman's helpless alienation in a male society, briefly emerge from the sea of male heroes and villains in which they have almost been lost, but the ice soon closes over their heads again, just as it closes around those two insane figure-skaters, Victor Frankenstein and his hideous offspring. Moving

outward from the central "birth myth" to the icy perimeter on which the novel began, we find ourselves caught up once more in Walton's naive polar journey, where Frankenstein and his monster reappear as two embattled grotesques, distant and archetypal figures solipsistically drifting away from each other on separate icebergs. In Walton's scheme of things, they look again like God and Adam, Satanically conceived. But now, with our more nearly complete understanding of the bewildered and bewildering perspective Mary Shelley adopted as "Milton's daughter," we see that they were Eve and Eve all along.

Nevertheless, though Shelley did manage to still the monster's suffering and Frankenstein's and her own by transporting all three from the fires of filthy creation back to the ice and silence of the Pole, she was never entirely to abandon the sublimated rage her monster-self enacted, and never to abandon, either, the metaphysical ambitions *Frankenstein* incarnated. In *The Last Man* she introduced, as Spark points out, "a new, inhuman protagonist," PLAGUE (the name is almost always spelled entirely in capitals), who is characterized as female and who sees to it that "disaster is no longer the property of the individual but of the entire human race."[43] And of course PLAGUE's story is the one that Mary claims to have found in the Sibyl's cave, a tale of a literally female monster that was merely foreshadowed by the more subdued narrative of "The Modern Prometheus."

Interestingly, PLAGUE's story ends with a vision of last things, a vision of judgment and of paradise nihilistically restored that balances *Frankenstein's* vision of first things. With all of humanity wiped out by the monster PLAGUE, just as the entire Frankenstein family was destroyed by Victor's monster, Lionel Verney, the narrator, goes to Rome, that cradle of patriarchal civilization whose ruins had seemed so majestically emblematic to both Byron and Shelley. But where Mary's husband had written of the great city in a kind of ecstasy, his widow has her disinherited "last man" wander lawlessly about empty Rome until finally he resolves, finding "parts of a manuscript . . . scattered about," that "I also will write a book . . . [but] for whom to read?—to whom dedicated? And then with silly flourish (what so capricious and childish as despair?) I wrote,

DEDICATION
TO THE ILLUSTRIOUS DEAD
SHADOWS, ARISE, AND READ YOUR FALL!
BEHOLD THE HISTORY OF THE LAST MAN.[44]

His hostile, ironic, literary gesture illuminates not only his own career but his author's. For the annihilation of history may well be the final revenge of the monster who has been denied a true place in history: the moral is one that Mary Shelley's first hideous progeny, like

Milton's Eve, seems to have understood from the beginning.

Notes

. . . . .

[14] See, for instance, Harold Bloom, "Afterword," *Frankenstein* (New York and Toronto: New American Library, 1965), p. 214.

[15] Author's introduction to *Frankenstein* (1817; Toronto, New York, London: Bantam Pathfinder Edition, 1967), p. xi. Hereafter page references to this edition will follow quotations, and we will also include chapter references for those using other editions. For a basic discussion of the "family romance" of literature, see Harold Bloom, *The Anxiety of Influence.*

[16] Robert Kiely, *The Romantic Novel in England* (Cambridge, Mass.: Harvard University Press, 1972), p. 161.

[17] Moers, *Literary Women,* pp. 95-97.

[18] See Ralph Wardle, *Mary Wollstonecraft* (Lincoln, Neb.: University of Nebraska Press, 1951), p. 322, for more detailed discussion of these attacks on Wollstonecraft.

[19] Muriel Spark, *Child of Light* (Hodleigh, Essex: Tower Bridge Publications, 1951), p. 21.

[20] See *Mary Shelley's Journal,* ed. Frederick L. Jones (Norman, Okla.: University of Oklahoma Press, 1947), esp. pp. 32-33, 47-49, 71-73, and 88-90, for the reading lists themselves. Besides reading Wollstonecraft's *Maria,* her *Vindication of the Rights of Women,* and three or four other books, together with Godwin's *Political Justice* and his *Caleb Williams,* Mary Shelley also read parodies and criticisms of her parents' works in these years, including a book she calls *Anti-Jacobin Poetry,* which may well have included that periodical's vicious attack on Wollstonecraft. To read, for her, was not just to read her family, but to read *about* her family.

[21] Marc A. Rubenstein suggests that throughout the novel "the act of observation, passive in one sense, becomes covertly and symbolically active in another: the observed scene becomes an enclosing, even womblike container in which a story is variously developed, preserved, and passed on. Storytelling becomes a vicarious pregnancy." "'My Accursed Origin': The Search for the Mother in *Frankenstein,*" *Studies in Romanticism* 15, no. 2 (Spring 1976): 173.

[22] See Anne Finch, "The Introduction," in *The Poems of Anne Countess of Winchilsea,* pp. 4-6, and Sylvia Plath, "The Moon and the Yew Tree," in *Ariel,* p. 41.

[23] Speaking of the hyperborean metaphor in *Frankenstein,* Rubenstein argues that Walton (and Mary Shelley) seek "the fantasied mother locked within the ice . . . the maternal Paradise beyond the frozen north," and asks us to consider the pun implicit in the later meeting of Frankenstein and his monster on the *mer* (or *Mère*) *de Glace* at Chamonix (Rubenstein "'My Accursed Origin,'" pp. 175-76).

[24] See Moers, *Literary Women,* pp. 99.

[25] In that summer of 1816 Byron had in fact just fled England in an attempt to escape the repercussions of his scandalous affair with his half-sister Augusta Leigh, the real-life "Astarte."

[26] Matthew Arnold, "Preface" to *Poems,* 1853.

[27] Spark, *Child of Light,* p. 134.

[28] See Moers, *Literary Women,* "Female Gothic"; also Rubenstein, "'My Accursed Origin,'" pp. 165-166.

[29] The *OED* gives "obscenity" and "moral defilement" among its definitions of "filth."

[30] The monster's narrative also strikingly echoes Jemima's narrative in Mary Wollstonecraft's posthumously published novel, *Maria, or The Wrongs of Woman.* See *Maria* (1798; rpt. New York: Norton, 1975), pp. 52-69.

[31] Harold Bloom does note that "the monster is . . . Mary Shelley's finest invention, and his narrative . . . forms the highest achievement of the novel." ("Afterword" to *Frankenstein,* p. 219.)

[32] James Rieger, "Introduction" to *Frankenstein,* (*the 1818 Text*) (Indianapolis: Bobbs-Merrill, 1974), p. xxx.

[33] In Western culture the notion that femaleness is a deformity or obscenity can be traced back at least as far as Aristotle, who asserted that "we should look upon the female state as being as it were a deformity, though one which occurs in the ordinary course of nature." (*The Generation of Animals,* trans. A. L. Peck [London: Heinemann, 1943], p. 461.) For a brief but illuminating discussion of his theories see Katharine M. Rogers, *The Troublesome Helpmate.*

[34] See de Beauvoir, *The Second Sex,* p. 156.

[35] Adrienne Rich, "Planetarium," in *Poems: Selected and New* (New York: Norton, 1974), pp. 146-48; Djuna Barnes, *The Book of Repulsive Women* (1915; rpt. Berkeley, Calif., 1976); Denise Levertov, "Hypocrite Women," *O Taste & See* (New York: New Directions, 1965); Sylvia Plath, "In Plaster," *Crossing the Water* (New York: Harper & Row, 1971), p. 16.

[36] See *Mary Shelley's Journal,* p. 73.

[37] Elizabeth Nitchie, *Mary Shelley* (New Brunswick, N.J.: Rutgers University Press, 1953), p. 219.

[38] See Spark, *Child of Light,* pp. 192-93.

[39] Woolf, *A Room,* p. 79.

[40] In "The Deluge at Norderney," Isak Dinesen tells the story of Calypso, niece of Count Seraphina Von Platen, a philosopher who "disliked and mistrusted everything female" and whose "idea of paradise was . . . a long row of lovely young boys . . . singing his poems to his music." "Annihilated" by her uncle's misogyny, Calypso plans to chop off her own breasts with a "sharp hatchet." See *Seven Gothic Tales,* pp. 43-51.

[41] Marc Rubenstein speculates that as a girl Shelley may actually have read (and been affected by) the correspondence that passed between her parents around the time that she was conceived.

[42] *Maria,* p. 152.

[43] Spark, *Child of Light,* p. 205.

[44] *The Last Man,* p. 339.

Barbara Johnson (essay date 1982)

SOURCE: "My Monster/My Self," in *Diacritics,* Vol. 12, No. 2, Summer, 1982, pp. 2-10.

[*In the landmark essay below, Johnson presents* Frankenstein *not just as a complex fictionalization of Shelley's autobiography, but more explicitly as a commentary on the nature of female autobiography.* "Frankenstein," *Johnson contends,* "can be read as the story of the experience of writing* Frankenstein.*"*]

To judge from recent trends in scholarly as well as popular literature, three crucial questions can be seen to stand at the forefront of today's preoccupations: the question of mothering, the question of the woman writer, and the question of autobiography. Although these questions and current discussions of them often appear unrelated to each other, it is my intention here to explore some ways in which the three questions *are* profoundly interrelated, and to attempt to shed new light on each by approaching it via the others. I shall base my remarks upon two twentieth-century theoretical studies—Nancy Friday's *My Mother/My Self* and Dorothy Dinnerstein's *The Mermaid and the Minotaur*—and one nineteenth-century gothic novel, ***Frankenstein; Or, the Modern Prometheus,*** written by Mary Shelley, whose importance for literary history has until quite recently been considered to arise not

from her own writings but from the fact that she was the second wife of poet Percy Bysshe Shelley and the daughter of political philosopher William Godwin and pioneering feminist Mary Wollstonecraft.

All three of these books, in strikingly diverse ways, offer a critique of the institution of parenthood. *The Mermaid and the Minotaur* is an analysis of the damaging effects of the fact that human infants are cared for almost exclusively by women. "What the book's title as a whole is meant to connote," writes Dinnerstein, "is both (a) our longstanding general awareness of our uneasy, ambiguous position in the animal kingdom, and (b) a more specific awareness: that until we grow strong enough to renounce the pernicious forms of collaboration between the sexes, both man and woman will remain semi-human, monstrous" [p. 5]. Even as Dinnerstein describes convincingly the types of imbalance and injustice the prevailing asymmetry in gender relations produces, she also analyzes the reasons for our refusal to abandon the very modes of monstrousness from which we suffer most. Nancy Friday's book, which is subtitled "A Daughter's Search for Identity," argues that the mother's repression of herself necessitated by the myth of maternal love creates a heritage of self-rejection, anger, and duplicity that makes it difficult for the daughter to seek any emotional satisfaction other than the state of idealized symbiosis that both mother and daughter continue to punish themselves for never having been able to achieve. Mary Shelley's ***Frankenstein*** is an even more elaborate and unsettling formulation of the relation between parenthood and monstrousness. It is the story of two antithetical modes of parenting that give rise to two increasingly parallel lives—the life of Victor Frankenstein, who is the beloved child of two doting parents, and the life of the monster he single-handedly creates, who is immediately spurned and abandoned by his creator. The fact that in the end both characters reach an equal degree of alienation and self-torture and indeed become indistinguishable as they pursue each other across the frozen polar wastes indicates that the novel is, among other things, a study of the impossibility of finding an adequate model for what a parent should be.

All three books agree, then, that in the existing state of things there is something inherently monstrous about the prevailing parental arrangements. While Friday and Dinnerstein, whose analyses directly address the problem of sexual difference, suggest that this monstrousness is curable, Mary Shelley, who does not explicitly locate the self's monstrousness in its gender arrangements, appears to dramatize divisions within the human being that are so much a part of being human that no escape from monstrousness seems possible.

What I will try to do here is to read these three books not as mere *studies* of the monstrousness of selfhood, not as mere *accounts* of human monsterdom in general, but precisely as autobiographies in their own right, as textual dramatizations of the very problems with which they deal. None of the three books, of course, presents itself explicitly as autobiography. Yet each includes clear moments of employment of the autobiographical—not the purely authorial—first person pronoun. In each case the autobiographical reflex is triggered by the resistance and ambivalence involved in the very writing of the book. What I shall argue here is that what is specifically feminist in each book is directly related to this struggle for feminine authorship.

The notion that **Frankenstein** can somehow be read as the autobiography of a woman would certainly appear at first sight to be ludicrous. The novel, indeed, presents not one but *three* autobiographies of men. Robert Walton, an arctic explorer on his way to the North Pole, writes home to his sister of his encounter with Victor Frankenstein, who tells Walton the story of his painstaking creation and unexplained abandonment of a nameless monster who suffers excruciating and fiendish loneliness, and who tells Frankenstein *his* life story in the middle pages of the book. The three male autobiographies motivate themselves as follows:

> *Walton (to his sister):* "You will rejoice to hear that no disaster has accompanied the commencement of an enterprise which you have regarded with such evil forebodings. I arrived here yesterday, and my first task is to assure my dear sister of my welfare." [p. 15]

> *Frankenstein (with his hands covering his face, to Walton, who has been speaking of his scientific ambition):* "Unhappy man! Do you share my madness? Have you drunk also of the intoxicating draught? Hear me; let me reveal my tale, and you will dash the cup from your lips!" [p. 26]

> *Monster (to Frankenstein):* "I entreat you to hear me before you give vent to your hatred on my devoted head." [Frankenstein:] "Begone! I will not hear you. There can be no community between you and me [. . .]" [Monster places his hands before Frankenstein's eyes]: "Thus I take from thee a sight which you abhor. Still thou canst listen to me and grant me thy compassion . . . God, in pity, made man beautiful and alluring, after his own image; but my form is a filthy type of yours, more horrid even from the very resemblance." [pp. 95, 96, 97, 125]

All three autobiographies here are clearly attempts at persuasion rather than simple accounts of facts. They all depend on a presupposition of *resemblance* between teller and addressee: Walton assures his sister that he has not really left the path she would wish for him, that he still resembles *her*. Frankenstein recognizes in

Walton an image of himself and rejects in the monster a resemblance he does not wish to acknowledge. The teller is in each case speaking into a mirror of his own transgression. The tale is designed to reinforce the resemblance between teller and listener so that somehow transgression can be eliminated. Yet the desire for resemblance, the desire to create a being like oneself—which is the autobiographical desire par excellence—is also the *central* transgression in Mary Shelley's novel. What is at stake in Frankenstein's workshop of filthy creation is precisely the possibility of shaping a life in one's own image: Frankenstein's monster can thus be seen as a figure for autobiography as such. Victor Frankenstein, then, has twice obeyed the impulse to construct an image of himself: on the first occasion he creates a monster, and on the second he tries to explain to Walton the causes and consequences of the first. *Frankenstein* can be read as the story of autobiography as the attempt to neutralize the monstrosity of autobiography. Simultaneously a revelation and a coverup, autobiography would appear to constitute itself as in some way a repression of autobiography.

These three fictive male autobiographies are embedded within a thin introductory frame, added in 1831, in which Mary Shelley herself makes the repression of her own autobiographical impulse explicit:

> The publishers of the standard novels, in selecting **Frankenstein** for one of their series, expressed a wish that I should furnish them with some account of the origin of the story. [. . .] It is true that I am very averse to bringing myself forward in print, but as my account will only appear as an appendage to a former production, and as it will be confined to such topics as have connection with my authorship alone, I can scarcely accuse myself of a personal intrusion. [p. vii]

Mary Shelley, here, rather than speaking *into* a mirror, is speaking *as* an appendage to a text. It might perhaps be instructive to ask whether this change of status has anything to do with the problem of specifically *feminine* autobiography. In a humanistic tradition in which *man* is the measure of all things, how does an appendage go about telling the story of her life?

Before pursuing this question further, I would like to turn to a more explicit version of surreptitious feminine autobiography. Of the three books under discussion, Nancy Friday's account of the mother/daughter relationship relies the most heavily on the facts of the author's life in order to demonstrate its thesis. Since the author grew up without a father, she shares with Frankenstein's monster some of the problems of coming from a single-parent household. The book begins with a chapter entitled "Mother Love," of which the first two sentences are: "I have always lied to my mother. And she to me" [p. 19]. Interestingly, the book carries the following dedication: "When I stopped seeing my mother with the eyes of a child, I saw the woman who helped me give birth to myself. This book is for Jane Colbert Friday Scott." How, then, can we be sure that this huge book is not itself another lie to the mother it is dedicated to? Is autobiography somehow always in the process of symbolically killing the mother off by telling her the lie that we have given birth to ourselves? On page 460, Nancy Friday is still not sure what kind of lie she has told. She writes: "I am suddenly afraid that the mother I have depicted throughout this book is false." Whose life is this, anyway? This question cannot be resolved by a book that sees the "daughter's search for identity" as the necessity of choosing *between* symbiosis and separation, *between* the mother and the autonomous self. As long as this polarity remains unquestioned, the autobiography of Nancy Friday becomes the drawing and redrawing of the portrait of Jane Colbert Friday Scott. The most truly autobiographical moments occur not in expressions of triumphant separation but in descriptions of the way the book itself attempts to resist its own writing. At the end of the chapter on loss of virginity, Nancy Friday writes:

> It took me twenty-one years to give up my virginity. In some similar manner I am unable to let go of this chapter. [. . .]
>
> It is no accident that wrestling with ideas of loss of virginity immediately bring me to a dream of losing my mother. This chapter has revealed a split in me. Intellectually, I think of myself as a sexual person, just as I had intellectually been able to put my ideas for this chapter down on paper. Subjectively, I don't want to face what I have written: that the declaration of full sexual independence is the declaration of separation from my mother. As long as I don't finish this chapter, as long as I don't let myself understand the implications of what I've written, I can maintain the illusion, at least, that I can be sexual and have my mother's love and approval too. [pp. 331-333]

As long as sexual identity and mother's judgment are linked as antithetical and exclusive poles of the daughter's problem, the "split" she describes will prevent her from ever completing her declaration of sexual independence. "Full sexual independence" is shown by the book's own resistance to be as illusory and as mystifying an ideal as the notion of "mother love" that Friday so lucidly rejects.

Dinnerstein's autobiographical remarks are more muted, although her way of letting the reader know that the book was written partly in mourning for her husband subtly underlies its persuasive seriousness. In her gesture of rejecting more traditional forms of scholarship, she pleads not for the validity but for the urgency of her message:

> Right now, what I think is that the kind of work of which this is an example is centrally necessary work. Whether our understanding makes a difference or not, we must try to understand what is threatening to kill us off as fully and clearly as we can. [. . .] What [this book] is, then, is not a scholarly book: it makes no effort to survey the relevant literature. Not only would that task be (for me) unmanageably huge. It would also be against my principles. I *believe* in reading unsystematically and taking notes erratically. Any effort to form a rational policy about what to take in, out of the inhuman flood of printed human utterance that pours over us daily, feels to me like a self-deluded exercise in pseudomastery. [pp. viii-ix]

The typographical form of this book bears out this belief in renouncing the appearance of mastery: there are two kinds of footnotes, some at the foot of the page and some at the back of the book; there are sections between chapters with unaligned right-hand margins which are called "Notes toward the next chapter." And there are bold-face inserts which dialogue with the controversial points in the main exposition. Clearly, great pains have been taken to let as many seams as possible show in the fabric of the argument. The preface goes on:

> I mention these limitations in a spirit not of apology but of warning. To the extent that it succeeds in communicating its point at all, this book will necessarily enrage the reader. What it says is emotionally threatening. (*Part of why it has taken me so long to finish it is that I am threatened by it myself.*) [p. ix; emphasis mine]

My book is roughly sutured, says Dinnerstein, and it is threatening. This description sounds uncannily like a description of Victor Frankenstein's monster. Indeed, Dinnerstein goes on to warn the reader not to be tempted to avoid the threatening message by pointing to superficial flaws in its physical make-up. The reader of **Frankenstein,** too, would be well advised to look beyond the monster's physical deformity, both for his fearsome power and for his beauty. There are indeed numerous ways in which *The Mermaid and the Minotaur* can be seen as a modern rewriting of **Frankenstein**.

Dinnerstein's book situates its plea for two-sex parenting firmly in an apparently twentieth-century double bind: the realization that the very technological advances that make it possible to change the structure of parenthood also threaten to extinguish earthly life altogether. But it is startling to note that this seemingly contemporary pairing of the question of parenthood with a love-hate relation to technology is already at work in Mary Shelley's novel, where the spectacular scientific discovery of the secrets of animation produces a terrifyingly vengeful creature who attributes his evil impulses to his inability to find or to become a parent. Subtitled "The Modern Prometheus," *Frankenstein* itself indeed refers back to a myth that already links scientific ambivalence with the origin of mankind. Prometheus, the fire bringer, the giver of both creation and destruction, is also said by some accounts to be the father of the human race. Ambivalence toward technology can thus be seen as a displaced version of the love-hate relation we have toward our own children.

It is only recently that critics have begun to see Victor Frankenstein's disgust at the sight of his creation as a study of postpartum depression, as a representation of maternal rejection of a newborn infant, and to relate the entire novel to Mary Shelley's mixed feelings about motherhood.[1] Having lived through an unwanted pregnancy from a man married to someone else only to see that baby die, followed by a second baby named William—which is the name of the Monster's first murder victim—Mary Shelley, at the age of only eighteen, must have had excruciatingly divided emotions. Her own mother, indeed, had died upon giving her birth. The idea that a mother can loathe, fear, and reject her baby has until recently been one of the most repressed of psychoanalytical insights, although it is of course already implicit in the story of Oedipus, whose parents cast him out as an infant to die. What is threatening about each of these books is the way in which its critique of the *role* of the mother touches on primitive terrors of the mother's rejection of the child. Each of these women writers *does* in her way reject the child as part of her coming to grips with the untenable nature of mother love: Nancy Friday decides not to have children, Dorothy Dinnerstein argues that men as well as women should do the mothering, and Mary Shelley describes a parent who flees in disgust from the repulsive being to whom he has just given birth.

Yet it is not merely in its depiction of the ambivalence of motherhood that Mary Shelley's novel can be read as autobiographical. In the introductory note added in 1831, she writes:

> The publishers of the standard novels, in selecting *Frankenstein* for one of their series, expressed a wish that I should furnish them with some account of the origin of the story. I am the more willing to comply because I shall thus give a general answer to the question so very frequently asked me—how I, then a young girl, came to think of and to *dilate upon* so very hideous an idea. [p. vii, emphasis mine]

As this passage makes clear, readers of Mary Shelley's novel had frequently expressed the feeling that a young girl's fascination with the idea of monstrousness was somehow monstrous in itself. When Mary ends her introduction to the re-edition of her novel with the words: "And now, once again, I bid my hideous prog-

eny go forth and prosper," the reader begins to suspect that there may perhaps be meaningful parallels between Victor's creation of his monster and Mary's creation of her book.

Such parallels are indeed unexpectedly pervasive. The impulse to write the book and the desire to search for the secrets of animation both arise under the same seemingly trivial circumstances: the necessity of finding something to read on a rainy day. During inclement weather on a family vacation, Victor Frankenstein happens upon the writings of Cornelius Agrippa, and is immediately fired with the longing to penetrate the secrets of life and death. Similarly, it was during a wet, ungenial summer in Switzerland that Mary, Shelley, Byron, and several others picked up a volume of ghost stories and decided to write a collection of spine-tingling tales of their own. Moreover, Mary's discovery of the subject she would write about is described in almost exactly the same words as Frankenstein's discovery of the principle of life: "Swift as light and as cheering was the idea that broke in upon me" [p. xi], writes Mary in her introduction, while Frankenstein says: "From the midst of this darkness a sudden light broke in upon me" [p. 51]. In both cases the sudden flash of inspiration must be supported by the meticulous gathering of heterogeneous, ready-made materials: Frankenstein collects bones and organs; Mary records overheard discussions of scientific questions that lead her to her sudden vision of monstrous creation. "Invention," she writes of the process of writing, but her words apply equally well to Frankenstein's labors, "Invention . . . does not consist in creating out of the void, but out of chaos; the materials must, in the first place, be afforded: it can give form to dark, shapeless substances but cannot bring into being the substance itself" [p. x]. Perhaps the most revealing indication of Mary's identification of Frankenstein's activity with her own is to be found in her use of the word "artist" on two different occasions to qualify the "pale student of unhallowed arts": "His success would terrify the *artist*" [p. xi], she writes of the catastrophic moment of creation, while Frankenstein confesses to Walton: "I appeared rather like one doomed by slavery to toil in the mines, or any other unwholesome trade than an *artist* occupied by his favorite employment" [p. 55].

Frankenstein, in other words, can be read as the story of the experience of writing *Frankenstein.* What is at stake in Mary's introduction as well as in the novel is the description of a *primal scene of creation. Frankenstein* combines a monstrous answer to two of the most fundamental questions one can ask: where do babies come from? and where do stories come from? In both cases, the scene of creation is described, but the answer to these questions is still withheld.

But what can Victor Frankenstein's workshop of filthy creation teach us about the specificity of *female* authorship? At first sight, it would seem that *Franken-*

stein is much more striking for its avoidance of the question of femininity than for its insight into it. All the interesting, complex characters in the book are male, and their deepest attachments are to other males. The females, on the other hand, are beautiful, gentle, self-less, boring nurturers and victims who never experience inner conflict or true desire. Monstrousness is so incompatible with femininity that Frankenstein cannot even complete the female companion that his creature so eagerly awaits.

On the other hand, the story of Frankenstein is, after all, the story of a man who usurps the female role by physically giving birth to a child. It would be tempting, therefore, to conclude that Mary Shelley, surrounded as she then was by the male poets Byron and Shelley, and mortified for days by her inability to think of a story to contribute to their ghost-story contest, should have fictively transposed her own frustrated female pen envy into a tale of catastrophic male womb envy. In this perspective, Mary's book would suggest that a woman's desire to write and a man's desire to give birth would both be capable only of producing monsters.

Yet clearly things cannot be so simple. As the daughter of a famous feminist whose *Vindication of the Rights of Women* she was in the process of rereading during the time she was writing ***Frankenstein,*** Mary Shelley would have no reason to believe that writing was not proper for a woman. Indeed, as she says in her introduction, Mary was practically born with ink flowing through her veins:

> It is not singular that, as the daughter of two persons of distinguished literary celebrity, I should very early in life have thought of writing. (. . .) My husband (. . .) was from the first very anxious that I should prove myself worthy of my parentage and enroll myself on the page of fame. [pp. vii-viii]

In order to prove herself worthy of her parentage, Mary, paradoxically enough, must thus usurp the parental role and succeed in giving birth to *herself* on paper. Her declaration of existence as a writer must therefore figuratively repeat the matricide that her physical birth all too literally entailed. The connection between literary creation and the death of a parent is in fact suggested in the novel by the fact that, immediately after the monster's animation, Victor Frankenstein dreams that he holds the corpse of his dead mother in his arms. It is also suggested by the juxtaposition of two seemingly unrelated uses of italics in the novel: Mary's statement that she had *thought of a story* (which she inexplicably underlines twice) and the monster's promise to Frankenstein, *I will be with you on your wedding night,* which is repeatedly italicized. Both are eliminations of the mother, since the story Mary writes is a tale of motherless birth, and the wedding night marks

the death of Frankenstein's bride, Elizabeth. Indeed, Mary herself was in fact the unwitting murderous intruder present on her own parents' wedding night: their decision to marry was due to the fact that Mary Wollstonecraft was already carrying the child that was to kill her. When Mary, describing her waking vision of catastrophic creation, affirms that "His success would terrify the artist," she is not giving vent to any ordinary fear-of-success syndrome. Or rather, what her book suggests is that what is at stake behind what is currently being banalized under the name of female fear of success is nothing less than the fear of somehow effecting the death of one's own parents.

It is not, however, the necessary murderousness of any declaration of female subjectivity that Mary Shelley's novel is proposing as its most troubling message of monsterdom. For, in a strikingly contemporary sort of predicament, Mary had not one but *two* mothers, each of whom consisted in the knowledge of the unviability of the other. After the death of Mary Wollstonecraft, Mary's father William Godwin married a woman as opposite in character and outlook as possible, a staunch housewifely mother of two who clearly preferred her own children to Godwin's. Between the courageous, passionate, intelligent, and suicidal mother Mary knew only through her writings and the vulgar, repressive "pustule of vanity" whose dislike she resented and returned, Mary must have known at first hand a whole gamut of feminine contradicitons, impasses, and options. For the complexities of the demands, desires, and sufferings of Mary's life as a woman were staggering. Her father, who had once been a vehement opponent of the institution of marriage, nearly disowned his daughter for running away with Shelley, an already married disciple of Godwin's own former views. Shelley himself, who believed in multiple love objects, amicably fostered an erotic correspondence between Mary and his friend Thomas Jefferson Hogg, among others. For years, Mary and Shelley were accompanied everywhere by Mary's stepsister Claire, whom Mary did not particularly like, who had a child by Byron, and who maintained an ambiguous relation with Shelley. During the writing of ***Frankenstein,*** Mary learned of the suicide of her half-sister Fanny Imlay, her mother's illegitimate child by an American lover, and the suicide of Shelley's wife Harriet, who was pregnant by a man other than Shelley. By the time she and Shelley married, Mary had had two children; she would have two more by the time of Shelley's death, and would watch as all but one of the children died in infancy. Widowed at age 24, she never remarried. It is thus indeed perhaps the very hiddenness of the question of femininity in ***Frankenstein*** that somehow proclaims the painful message not of female monstrousness but of female contradictions. For it is the fact of self-contradiction that is so vigorously repressed in women. While the story of a man who is haunted by his own contradictions is representable as an allegory of monstrous doubles, how indeed would it have been possible for Mary to represent feminine contradiction *from the point of view of its repression* otherwise than precisely in the *gap* between angels of domesticity and an uncompleted monsteress, between the murdered Elizabeth and the dismembered Eve?

It is perhaps because the novel does succeed in conveying the unresolvable contradictions inherent in being female that Shelley himself felt compelled to write a prefatory disclaimer in Mary's name before he could let loose his wife's hideous progeny upon the world. In a series of denials jarringly at odds with the daring negativity of the novel, Shelley places the following words in Mary's mouth:

> I am by no means indifferent to the manner in which whatever moral tendencies exist in the sentiments or characters it contains shall affect the reader; yet my chief concern in this respect has been limited to (. . .) the exhibition of the amiableness of domestic affection, and the excellence of universal virtue. The opinions which naturally spring from the character and situation of the hero are by no means to be conceived as existing always in my own conviction; nor is any inference justly to be drawn from the following pages as prejudicing any philosophical doctrine of whatever kind. [pp. xiii-xiv]

How is this to be read except as a gesture of repression of the very specificity of the power of feminine contradiction, a gesture reminiscent of Frankenstein's destruction of his nearly-completed female monster? What is being repressed here is the possibility that a woman can write anything that would *not* exhibit "the amiableness of domestic affection," the possibility that for women as well as for men the home can be the very site of the *unheimlich*.

It can thus be seen in all three of the books we have discussed that the monstrousness of selfhood is intimately embedded within the question of female autobiography. Yet how could it be otherwise, since the very notion of a self, the very shape of human life stories, has always, from St. Augustine to Freud, been modeled on the man? Rousseau's—or any man's—autobiography consists precisely in the story of the difficulty of conforming to the standard of what a *man* should be. The problem for the female autobiographer is, on the one hand, to resist the pressure of masculine autobiography as the only literary genre available for her enterprise, and, on the other, to describe a difficulty in conforming to a female ideal which is largely a fantasy of the masculine, not the feminine, imagination. The fact that these three books deploy a *theory* of autobiography as monstrosity within the framework of a less overtly avowed struggle with the raw materials of the authors' own lives and writing is perhaps, in the final analysis, precisely what is most autobiographically fertile and *telling* about them.

Notes

[1] See Ellen Moers, "Female Gothic," and U. C. Knoepflmacher, "Thoughts on the Aggression of Daughters," in *The Endurance of Frankenstein,* ed. Levine and Knoepflmacher (Berkeley: University of California Press, 1979). Other related and helpful studies include S. M. Gilbert and S. Gubar, "Horror's Twin," in *The Madwoman in the Attic* (New Haven: Yale University Press, 1979) and Mary Poovey, "My Hideous Progeny: Mary Shelley and the Feminization of Romanticism," *PMLA,* 95 (May 1980).

Devon Hodges (essay date 1983)

SOURCE: "Frankenstein and the Feminine Subversion of the Novel," in *Tulsa Studies in Women's Literature,* Vol. 2, No. 2, Fall, 1983, pp. 155-64.

[*In the following essay, Hodges focuses on the literary originality of* Frankenstein, *arguing that, in opposition to the conventions set by a powerful lineage of male authors, Shelley uses the novel form "to change structures of narrative as well as to introduce new topics of discussion."*]

Mary Shelley's **Frankenstein** has long been labelled a "woman's book." Ellen Moers describes **Frankenstein** as a female "birth myth" which depicts Shelley's ambivalence about motherhood;[1] Kate Ellis interprets **Frankenstein** as a critique of the bourgeois family and the separation of male and female spheres;[2] Sandra Gilbert and Susan Gubar write that the book describes a "woman's helpless alienation in a male society,"[3] and Mary Poovey calls it a "myth of female powerlessness" which justifies the female writer's uncontrollable desire for self-expression.[4] All these interpretations rightly insist that Shelley is concerned about the position of women in a patriarchal culture, but their thematic emphasis does not enable us to see how the female themes of the novel are given particular efficacy because of Shelley's ability to subvert patriarchal narrative conventions. Shelley's text works to change structures of narrative as well as to introduce new topics of discussion.

The novel, as the genre most obviously in the service of social and material reality, necessarily recreates patriarchal culture and ideology. Nonetheless, it is the form to which women readers and writers have always been most devoted. This devotion is not surprising since feminine authority itself is deeply connected to the rise of the novel. In a recent essay, Nancy Armstrong has insisted on the relation of the feminine to the novel while arguing that the femininity of the novel is not the product of "female nature nor even female culture, strictly speaking . . . but of ideology and cultural myth."[5] As Armstrong explains it, the well-documented split between the economic and domestic spheres that took place in the eighteenth and early nineteenth centuries created a female provenance that reproduced not some essential femininity but rather "old patriarchal traditions of pre-industrial England."[6] The female voice, because it seemed naturally connected to the domestic sphere and to traditionally paternal tastes and values, served the interest of patriarchy by hiding the contradiction between old and new forms of patriarchy brought about by disruptive patriarchal capitalism. In other words, women were allowed to write precisely at the moment when their writing was a "feminine power that preserves the system of primogeniture."[7] Armstrong's compelling discussion of the novel as a form in service of patriarchal culture traces the ambivalence of women's writing to the very codes that structure it.

Several modern theorists have looked at the narrative conventions of the novel and located there a grammar which works to create a seemingly natural sequence of events and a powerful sense of closure as a way of securing masculine identity and speech, of making male dominance seem inevitable. The paternal premise of the novel, as Edward Said has pointed out, *depends* on the novelistic conventions of sequence, finality, and integrity.[8] The form of the novel is not neutral.[9] Nor is language itself: feminists have long been aware that the woman's voice is muted in a patriarchal culture. To explain this all too familiar equation of the feminine with silence, many have adopted the influential work of Jacques Lacan which describes the female's relation to this symbolic order as one characterized by lack.

No wonder, then, that feminist interpretations of women's writing have increasingly concerned themselves with the woman writer's effort to speak within the language and codes of her society without being appropriated by them. Her problem might be stated this way: the woman writer desires to take advantage of opportunities to express herself, yet the language and codes of patriarchal culture impose yet another silence on her. As Mary Jacobus writes, "access to a male-dominated culture may be felt to bring with it alienation, repression, division—a silencing of the 'feminine,' a loss of women's 'inheritance.'"[10] What then is a woman writer to do? Her most utopian option is to write in a new language, but who is going to be able to read this language? She can also refuse to speak, but such a protest offers no challenge to the patriarchal order. Her other option is to deform, to transgress literary structure from within—demonstrating the inadequacy of the paternal narrative by opening it up to what it excludes.

If the feminine novel is the creation of a patriarchal culture, we must look, as Nancy Armstrong suggests, to disruptive effects, to "discontinuities" that work

against the "novel's traditional gestures toward closure" in order to find how women writers communicate a feminine position within writing.[11] Of course, it is precisely such discontinuities that may make the woman writer seem less able than her male counterparts. Shelley's *Frankenstein,* for example, though praised as a rich ground of thematic interpretation, has been widely criticized as a flawed novel. One critic says that it is "radically uneven and awkward,"[12] and another notes its "lack of causal sufficiency."[13] *Frankenstein,* we are told, is a narrative "not fully elaborated into rational, sequential art."[14] These judgments, based on the assumption that art must obey the conventions of patriarchal narrative—sequence, finality, integrity—implicitly announce that Shelley's text does not exist entirely within the conventional literary framework.

Frankenstein's violation of literary propriety does not mean that Mary Shelley deliberately privileges the feminine. In the "Author's Introduction" she writes that she is "very averse to bringing herself forward in print."[15] And through much of the novel she adopts a male voice while assigning her self-effacing female characters (appropriately described as exotic, as outsiders) to a marginal position. In this way, her novel reproduces the traditional opposition of masculine and feminine, speech and silence, that makes so paradoxical the position of the woman who writes: if speech is associated with masculinity, then a woman must lose her identity in order to make self-expression possible. But perhaps in adopting a male voice, the woman writer is given the opportunity to intervene from within, to become an alien presence that undermines the stability of the male voice.

The identity of the self, the authority of the narrative "I," lends coherence to the traditional novel's structure and provides an anchor for its meanings. It is a unifying device that needs transformation if women are to speak. As one feminist puts it, "To change the system, we have to change the speaking subject."[16] In other words, the subject must be free to define itself in new ways. Mary Shelley acknowledges the power of fiction to allow for a more flexible identity in her "Author's Introduction." Here she describes the pleasures of childhood dreaming in which she was not "confined to my own identity" (p. viii). In *Frankenstein,* the unity of the subject is subverted by the presence of multiple narrators. The story is narrated by three men: Robert Walton, Victor Frankenstein, and the monster. Each of these men is an image of the others—all are wandering creatures who are in some way deviant. Walton is embarked on a voyage to the northern pole which has been prohibited by his father, and in Victor Frankenstein he finds "the brother of his heart" (p. 26). Frankenstein, described by Walton as a "creature" whose eyes "expressed madness" while he "gnashed his teeth," is an image of the monster he pursues, and he explicitly tells his story to reveal to Walton the madness he and Walton share. The monster, Frankenstein's offspring, eventually recapitulates Walton's movements and becomes even more obviously a figure of Walton's prohibited desires.

Such doubling and dislocation are produced by the non-identity of the self to itself (the self is found in the Other), a mechanism that Shelley does not employ without ambivalence. While an apparently fixed order of things is shown to be the basis for oppression—in the monster's story, for example—the transgression of this order not surprisingly leads to fear, since cultural assumptions have long maintained that fixed roles protect men and women from dangerous anti-social impulses. This fear is articulated several times in the novel when the "artist" Frankenstein regrets his decision to defy propriety and employ "exploded systems and useless names" (p. 45) in order to create a new species. But at the same time, Shelley knows that to obey the law and stay at home is no good either. The hearth is the abode of "angels of the house" whose repose is "akin to death" (p. 43), and in her text the law dramatically victimizes the innocent Justine. So Shelley has it both ways: she decenters man by using multiple narrators who question the symbolic order while, at the same time, she insists that changing the shape of man can only result in the creation of monstrosity.

Shelley's ambivalence, recorded in her plot, does not compromise her narrative practice. Shelley challenges the place of women plotted by the traditional novel by disrupting narrative sequence. Her characters do not escape traditional female destinies—to be mother, wife, dead, or some combination of the three—but the novel subverts the *form* of female destiny by defamiliarizing narrative sequence, making it seem unnatural, inadequate. Robert Walton, the narrator of the letters that frame the novel, pronounces the unreliability of his story when he writes that letters are a "poor medium of communication" (p. 18). His uncertain narrative is interrupted by the accidental arrival of Victor Frankenstein, whose narrative displaces Walton's. Frankenstein's story is also insufficient since it is broken by faints, fevers, dreams, inexplicable silences that dislocate narrative sequence. (Why doesn't Frankenstein speak to save the innocent Justine who is accused of killing his brother? Why doesn't he understand the monster's threat: "I will be with you on your wedding night"?) Further, the accuracy of his account is put into question by the monster, whose story displaces Frankestein's narrative in the middle of the novel— and who is the source of the disruption recounted in it. And this figure of disruption, like the novel itself, is never fully contained: the monster's death by fire and ice remains only a promised and deliberately improbable conclusion. To contribute further to the novel's lack of unity, dependent upon a resolution that provides a sense of closure, Shelley directs the novel it-self toward a woman reader, Mrs. Saville, who is located both in and outside the text, and provides the narrative with an uncertain destination.

One obvious explanation for the narrative's refusal of a fixed identity and its subversion of the conventions of narrative sequence and unity is that it is a dream text. In her introduction to the book, Mary Shelley states that her novel is the "transcript of the grim terrors" of a "waking dream" (p. xi). What dislocates the narrative might simply be the irrational logic of the dream, of the unconscious. Yet dream logic may be in the service of a woman writer's critique of prevailing structures. Dreams, as Edward Said has pointed out, "are interventions in the ongoing course of things, not additions to it. Where once stood a *pater familias,* or an unfolding plot, or a single image . . . we have a break in the sequence."[17] Dreams allow something to speak which is not normally present in the patriarchal course of things. Through the agency of dream, this order confronts something it cannot fully account for, something it has excluded or repressed. Such a bringing to the surface of a troubling otherness, sometimes explicitly connected to the unconscious, has been described as an effect of women's writing. "A feminine text," writes Hélène Cixous, "can't be predicted, isn't predictable, isn't knowable, and is therefore very disturbing."[18] It is disturbing because it exposes the inadequacy of the symbolic order, the limits of its knowledge.

The dream form of *Frankenstein,* then, might be seen as a transgression of the boundaries of patriarchal order. A similar act of transgression occurs on the thematic level of the novel. In the story, Victor Frankenstein, the bearer of the qualities of god-like power and knowledge that characterize the masculine position in culture, discovers the limits of his mastery. He intends to create a "new species" that will flatter his ego: "No father," he imagines, "could claim the gratitude of his child so completely as I should deserve theirs" (p. 52). And he gives his creature an especially large frame as if to insure that it will reflect him at twice his size— and thus become the flattering mirror men often expect women to be. Frankenstein's desire for domination and his expectation of submission are captured in the pose he takes before his inanimate creature: Frankenstein stands erect above its prone body, a position that has been called the classical spectacle of male power and female powerlessness in a patriarchal society.[19]

The proof of Frankenstein's mastery, however, depends on the aesthetic unity of his creation—and Frankenstein's monster is anything but a perfect form. The monster is a haphazard collection of parts. This incoherent structure, because it exposes the limitations of Frankenstein's power and knowledge, contaminates Frankenstein. On viewing the animated creature, Frankenstein becomes "discomposed" and his disrupted state appears in the language of the passages following his act of creation:

> I started from my sleep with horror; a cold dew covered my forehead, my teeth chattered, and every limb became convulsed; when, by the dim and yellow light of the moon, as it forced its way through the window shutters, I beheld the wretch—the miserable monster whom I had created (p. 57).

This sentence is typical of the style of these passages, accurately described as "spasmodic, juxtapositive, and repetitive."[20] The disruption of mastery thus has an effect on the formal structure of the narrative.

Other feminist critics have written about this moment not as demonstrating the limits of male authority through a distinctive textual practice, but rather as depicting female authorship as a "frightful transgression." My own discussion of Shelley's ambivalence suggests this element too. Shelley's novel challenges the privileged position of the male in a patriarchal system—most particularly by challenging narrative conventions that powerfully articulate the fiction of man as the locus of truth, identity, knowledge—but it also records the anxiety of a woman participating in an alien system: the symbolic order belongs to the fathers. Perhaps the conditions of patriarchal culture insist that women's writing must necessarily sustain these two positions: woman has no place in writing yet can subvert male identity and truth by destabilizing narrative, making it uncertain about its patriarchal message. In the preface, Percy Shelley constructs an apologia for **Frankenstein** that attempts to blur the contradiction between the text's transgression of and adherence to the familiar opposition of masculine and feminine. He insists that the text functions to show the virtue of the domestic sphere—a place for women that has been largely defined by men:

> [M]y chief concern . . . has been limited to the avoiding of the enervating effects of the novels of the present day, and to the exhibition of the amiableness of domestic affection, and the excellence of universal virtue. The opinions which naturally spring from the character and situation of the hero are by no means to be conceived as existing always in my own conviction . . . (p. xiv).

Of this disclaimer, Barbara Johnson writes: "How is this to be read except as a gesture of repression of the very specificity of the power of feminine contradiction?"[21] Another critic, Virginia Woolf, suggests that contradiction is a necessary condition of women in a patriarchal culture since that culture is an "ill-fitting form."[22]

It is Shelley's monster, of course, who articulates the misery of being neither fully inside nor outside cul-

ture. The monster does not desire to be a rebel; he wants to be assimilated into society. As a spectator looking on society from the outside, he discovers language and the wonderful power of communication it makes possible: "I found that these people possessed a method of communicating their experience . . . this was indeed a godlike science, and I ardently desired to become acquainted with it" (pp. 107-08). His success at acquiring language is manifest in the eloquence of his narrative, an eloquence even Frankenstein acknowledges: the monster is "eloquent and persuasive," he tells Walton, "but trust him not" (p. 198). The monster cannot be trusted because, though he ably performs in an alien language, he never fully inhabits it. As a result, his language always seems to be a disguise for something terrifying that remains unspoken.

The monster is the character in the novel who makes the reader most selfconscious about language as a foreign medium. And since Mary Shelley's style as a whole seems artificial, she seems to share the monster's problem: for her too, language is an "ill-fitting form." Her prose style has been the object of criticism because, as one critic says, it is "inflexibly public and oratorical even in its most intimate passages."[23] Her style, in other words, pushes language into the foreground as an impersonal form, as unreal, as lacking a "natural" relation to its speaker and to the objects it names. Her style thus insists that language is an artificial cultural production, a view best articulated by the monster. Describing the cottagers, he says: "Their pronunciation was quick and the words they uttered, not having any apparent connection with visible objects, I was unable to discover any clue by which I could unravel the mystery of their reference" (p. 107). Of course a style of writing which uncovers the unnaturalness of language can turn against the author rather than the culture that produces it, and the public nature of Shelley's prose can thus be viewed not as a critique of patriarchal discourse, but as a sign of artistic failure. Shelley herself is apologetic about her work. In her "Introduction," she remarks that while her husband could "embody his ideas and sentiments in the radiance of brilliant imagery and in the music of the most melodious verse that adorns our language," she is capable only of finding the "machinery of a story"— a phrase that points again to the artificial quality of literary production.

By not valuing a transgressing mode of writing which produces a work that Shelley herself calls her "hideous progeny," Shelley seems to accept a subordinate place in culture. She is a "good" girl who writes because her parentage makes the desire to write "natural," and even more emphatically, because her husband and his friends want her to. This portrait of feminine virtue is underlined in Percy Shelley's description of the text as portraying the "amiableness of domestic affection." Yet these assertions of the conventionality of the text recall the monster's words to Frankenstein: "I will not be tempted to set myself in opposition to thee. I am thy creature" (p. 95). Like Shelley herself, the monster asserts his desire to conform to the expectations of society—his inner core is basically good. His problem is that he is defined from the outside as evil, alien, other: "my life has been hitherto harmless and in some degree beneficial; but a fatal prejudice clouds their eyes, and where they ought to see a good and kind friend, they behold only a detestable monster" (p. 128). And his monstrousness *is* projected on him. The monster represents, as we have seen, the limits of Frankenstein's own knowledge. But this is precisely what Frankenstein does not want to admit. In order to maintain his position of mastery, he represses the existence of the monster: "I avoided explanation and maintained a continual silence . . . supposed I had a persuasion that I should be mad" (p. 177). He refuses to create a mate for the monster in the name of the social order, the "whole human race" (p. 159). What is repressed by society cannot be included on any terms without causing its maddening dislocation, or more positively, without causing its transformation.

Shelley's text has such disruptive power. In spite of her disclaimers, *Frankenstein* strays from propriety because it does not support a patriarchal system of representation. The "I" is loosened from its moorings; the chain of events becomes incoherent, the textual order violated. This disruption of novelistic conventions is the violent gesticulation of a repressed femininity pushing against a patriarchal form that privileges male identity and speech and victimizes even obedient women. Shelley both appropriates the form and disrupts it: her narrative technique provides a model for a more flexible discourse, but Shelley accepts conventional standards and calls that discourse "hideous."

The monster, not Shelley's stereotypic female characters, is the figure of this deformed and deforming text. He articulates the possible options of the woman who writes in order to express herself but finds that her culture imposes, in its very codes, an obstacle to feminine self-expression. One of her options, already mentioned, is to find a new language. The monster embraces this option only when he finds that he simply cannot be assimilated into society. He asks Frankenstein to create a new form of woman. With her, the monster plans to build a new society in which he can be in "communication with an equal" (p. 140). This utopian hope is denied realization by Frankenstein in the name of a cultural order threatened by the monster, and, Frankenstein imagines, "ten thousand times" more threatened by a female monster. So the monster is left to express his desires by unsettling the order which frustrates them: he makes Frankenstein undergo his own experience of incoherence and exile—what the monster calls the "miserable series" of his being (p. 297). In this, he is the figure of feminine textuality.

Like the monster, woman in a patriarchal society is defined as an absence, an enigma, mystery, or crime, or she is allowed to be a presence only so that she can be defined as a lack, a mutilated body that must be repressed to enable men to join the symbolic order and maintain their mastery. As Baudelaire puts it, "woman is different, that is to say, abominable." Her difference places her outside culture, and her abominable presence places her within it. Mary Shelley, because she writes from this paradoxical position, has been accused of artistic failure: "Mary Shelley is not inside or outside enough" writes one male critic.[24] But her representation of the liminal position of women—and the relation of that position to sexual categories of a patriarchal culture—is precisely her achievement.

Frankenstein is a novel suspended in an indefinite space. The shifts in narrative voice, the narrative's violation of causal sequence, its refusal of a definite conclusion, its public style, are strategies that destabilize narrative form so that it communicates the monstrous burden of female difference as it is defined by patriarchal culture. At the same time, the novel challenges the authority of the cultural order by making it feel the pressure of something it has tried to exclude and repress. Shelley, then, is a woman writer who uses the resources of fiction to transgress literary structure from within.

"It is an odd feeling," writes Virginia Woolf, "writing against the current: difficult entirely to disregard the current."[25] Difficult too for the current not to feel a woman's resistance as she pushes against the stream of patriarchal culture—interrupting, disturbing, deforming it—encouraging us to see that what seems continuous, inexorable, natural, contains within it other possibilities, other ways of imagining the order of things.

Notes

[1] Ellen Moers, "Female Gothic," *The Endurance of Frankenstein,* ed. George Levine (Berkeley, Los Angeles, London: University of California Press, 1979), p. 79.

[2] Kate Ellis, "Monster in the Garden: Mary Shelley and the Bourgeois Family," *The Endurance of Frankenstein,* pp. 128-42.

[3] Sandra Gilbert and Susan Gubar, *The Madwoman in the Attic* (New Haven: Yale University Press, 1979), p. 246.

[4] Mary Poovey, "My Hideous Progeny: Mary Shelley and the Feminization of Romanticism," *PMLA,* 95 (1980), 332-46.

[5] Nancy Armstrong, "The Rise of Feminine Authority

in the Novel," *Novel: A Forum on Fiction,* 15 (Winter 1982), 138.

[6] Armstrong, 129.

[7] Armstrong, 141.

[8] Edward Said, *Beginnings: Intention and Method* (New York: Basic Books, 1975), p. 163.

[9] My understanding of feminine textuality has greatly benefitted from discussion with Janice Doane about her unpublished dissertation, "Silence and Narrative: The Early Novels of Gertrude Stein," SUNY Buffalo, 1981.

[10] Mary Jacobus, "The Difference of View," *Women Writing and Writing About Women* (London: Barnes and Noble Books, 1980), p. 10.

[11] Armstrong, 142.

[12] George Levine, "The Ambiguous Heritage of *Frankenstein*," *The Endurance of Frankenstein,* p. 3.

[13] Phillip Stevick, "*Frankenstein* and Comedy," *The Endurance of Frankenstein,* p. 227.

[14] Stevick, p. 230.

[15] Mary Shelley, "Author's Introduction," *Frankenstein or The Modern Prometheus* (New York and Scarborough, Ontario: New American Library, 1965), p. vii. All citations from *Frankenstein* are from this text.

[16] Alice Jardine, "Introduction to Kristeva," *Signs,* 7 (1980), 11.

[17] Said, p. 172.

[18] Hélène Cixous, "Castration or Decapitation," trans. Annette Kuhn, *Signs,* 7 (1980), 53.

[19] See Mary Ann Doane, "Gilda: Epistemology as Striptease," *Camera Obscura,* No. 10 (Spring, 1982).

[20] Paul Sherwin, "*Frankenstein:* Creation as Catastrophe," *PMLA,* 96 (1981), 895.

[21] Barbara Johnson, "My Monster/My Self," *Diacritics,* 12 (Summer 1982), 9.

[22] Virginia Woolf, *Three Guineas* (New York: Harcourt, Brace, and World, Inc., 1966), p. 105.

[23] George Levine, p. 3.

[24] Paul Sherwin, 901-02.

[25] Virginia Woolf, from her diary as noted by Michele Barret in her introduction to *Virginia Woolf: Women and Writing* (New York and London: Harcourt Brace Jovanovich, 1980), p. 4.

William Veeder (essay date 1986)

SOURCE: "The Negative Oedipus: Father, *Frankenstein*, and the Shelleys," in *Critical Inquiry,* Vol. 12, No. 2, Winter, 1986, pp. 365-90.

[*In the essay that follows, Veeder emphasizes the significance of Shelley's relationship with her father, examining less its latent aggressiveness than its latent desire. In order to make his argument, Veeder invokes Freudian psychoanalysis, describing Shelley and Godwin's relationship through the structure of a negative oedipal complex.*]

> It was Grandfather's and when Father gave it to me he said, Quentin, I give you the mausoleum of all hope and desire. . . . I give it to you not that you may remember time, but that you might forget it now and then for a moment and not spend all your breath trying to conquer it.
>
> —Quentin Compson, in WILLIAM FAULKNER, *The Sound and the Fury*

> A son can never, in the fullest sense, become a father. Some amount of amateur effort is possible. A son may after honest endeavor produce what some people might call, technically, children. But he remains a son. In the fullest sense.
>
> —DONALD BARTHELME, *The Dead Father*

Defining the role of father in Mary Shelley has been both fostered and impeded by recent criticism. Feminist theory with its recognition of the importance of *mother* has prevented any overrating of father. In the context of Kleinian arguments by Nancy Chodorow and Dorothy Dinnerstein that Freud's neglect of the pre-oedipal years caused him to seriously undervalue the maternal role in child development, literary critics such as Sandra Gilbert and Susan Gubar, Mary Jacobus, Mary Poovey, Marc A. Rubenstein, and Janet M. Todd have established convincingly the importance of Mary Wollstonecraft for Mary Shelley.[1] Feminist readings can, however, go too far in this direction. Mother can achieve such prominence that father is cast into shadow. Poovey's chapters are the best overall appraisal of Mary Shelley's novelistic career that I know, but I cannot agree that "in Mary Shelley's own youth and in *Falkner* (and, in a slightly different sense, in *Frankenstein*) the motherless daughter's relationship with the father carries the burden of needs originally and ideally satisfied by the mother; in a sense, the relationship with each father is only an imaginative substitute for the absent relationship with the mother."[2] Mary Shelley in fact insisted upon the superiority of a father's tuition for daughters, devoted much of her fiction to father-directed emotions and events, confessed privately to untoward affection for Godwin, and expressed this affection so shockingly in *Mathilda* that her father suppressed the novel.

A second approach to Mary Shelley, that of the psychoanalytic critics of *Frankenstein,* does give prominence to father, since the oedipal model presupposes generational conflict. Preeminence, however, is once again accorded to mother. The primary object of Frankenstein's affection is presumed to be his mother Caroline, and the primary object of his scientific labors is presumed to be the discovery of a principle of life which would bring her back from the dead. Despite unquestionably valuable insights by J. M. Hill, Gordon D. Hirsch, Morton Kaplan and Robert Kloss, Rubenstein, U. C. Knoepflmacher, and others, the oedipal model has tended to occlude deeper levels of the psyche where Mary Shelley moves beyond mother love.[3] Here Freud's "negative" Oedipus provides a more useful paradigm, because here the son desires to murder *mother* in order to get to *father.*[4]

My study of Mary Shelley and father includes her husband because Percy Shelley's obsessions with patriarchy, with "'GOD, AND KING, AND LAW,'" influenced profoundly Mary's [Referring to the Shelleys is difficult. "Mary and Shelley" is obviously sexist; calling her "Shelley" is particularly confusing in an essay which mentions the poet frequently. I will therefore use "Mary" and "Percy" throughout.] art and life. Percy's idealizations of father in *The Revolt of Islam* and *Prince Athanase* indicated ways of resolving familial antagonisms which Mary adopted and developed in her later fiction. Percy's relationship with *Frankenstein* is still more intricate. Recognizing that her husband's obsessions with father and self-creation were contributing to the deterioration of their marriage, Mary represents these obsessions (among many others, including her own) in Victor Frankenstein—partly to vent in art the anger which would have further damaged the marriage, and partly to show Percy before it was too late the errors of his ways. It was too late. Percy responded to *Frankenstein* in *Prometheus Unbound* and *The Cenci* with a reaffirmation of sonship which has been largely unrecognized by scholars.

Father looms so large for both Mary and Percy Shelley that no one critical approach can account for him fully. At their most idealistic—and thus most traditional—the Shelleys encourage a critical methodology which integrates the traditional disciplines of biographical and close textual analyses. By taking this approach to Mary's later fiction and to Percy's *The Revolt of Islam,* I can not only confirm the prominence of father for the Shelleys but also establish the ideal against which their most subversive and important art was created. Reading this indirect, overdetermined art in light of the negative Oedipus will help answer important questions about *Frankenstein, Prometheus Unbound,* and *The Cenci* and will, I hope, add to our understanding of the vexed role of father in the Romantic period and in subsequent generations whose children we are.

1. The Ideal

In a biographical nexus as amazing as the persons involved, Percy's intricate conflicts with father are illuminated by Mary's incestuous attractions to father. Mary's admiration for Mary Wollstonecraft, unquestionable though it is, cannot match the intensity of what she called "my excessive and romantic attachment to my Father."[5] Mary, like her Mathilda, "clung to the memory of my parents; my mother I should never see, she was dead: but the idea of [my] unhappy, wandering father was the idol of my imagination." The primacy of father is confirmed by Mathilda's knowledgeable steward: "'You are like her [your mother] although there is more of my lord in you.'"[6] Although she reveres Mary Wollstonecraft as a theorist of pedagogy, Mary Shelley insists upon the advantages of a father's tuition. "There is a peculiarity in the education of a daughter, brought up by a father only, which tends to develop early a thousand of those portions of mind, which are folded up, and often destroyed, under mere feminine tuition."[7] In her last novels Mary continues to insist how much fathers love daughters. *Perkin Warbeck* features the heroic mariner De Faro who "could not prevail on himself to leave his lovely, unprotected girl behind"; *Falkner* attests that "no father ever worshipped a child so fervently" as the title character does his Elizabeth.[8] Mary never gets over Godwin's coldness. She is forty-one years old when she says "My Father, from age and domestic circumstances, could not '*me faire valoir.*'"[9] Even in middle age, Mary can bring herself to this terrible admission only by insulating the reality in French phrasing (when English would suffice), in italics (which she does not always apply to foreign expressions), in quotation marks (which are unnecessary), and by atoning for the aggression by capitalizing "My Father" (which she by no means always does).

Percy too makes father paramount. The intensity of his feelings—which finds negative expression in *The Mask of Anarchy*'s rage at "'GOD, AND KING, AND LAW'"[10] and at his father, Sir Timothy—expresses itself positively in Percy's lifelong search for lawgivers. After Dr. James Lind, who taught science, occult lore, and the right to be different, comes Thomas Jefferson Hogg. "I [Percy] took you for one who was to give laws to us poor beings who grovel beneath."[11] Then Percy finds Godwin. The older man's enormous authority comes in part from his confirming what the young philosopher needs to believe—that reason can control passion and assure perfection. But Godwin also answers the needs of a rebellious son. Jean Overton Fuller has it backward when she says that "from the time he [Shelley] read this [*Political Justice*], he regarded the circumstances of his birth as shaming, and only possible to live down by the dedication of his mind and position to the elevation of those less endowed."[12] Percy's rebelliousness predates his reading of *Political Justice* because his anger was father-directed before it was political. Godwin thus serves less to generate rebellion than to legitimize it. He lessens the guilt while encouraging the crime.[13] Godwin allows the son both to have *him* as new father and to have a nonpsychological and thus largely guiltless rationale for rejecting the old father.

Mary can see so accurately into Percy because she shares with him more than an obsession with father: daughter and son here desire the same man, William Godwin.

Percy and Mary both project their desires for father onto the screen of art. Seeing how desire is satisfied ideally there will help us to understand both why such satisfactions prove impossible in the Shelleys' marriage and how their dissatisfactions are figured forth in *Frankenstein*. A convenient starting point is the passage in Percy's *Revolt of Islam* where Laon sees Cythna's corpse hanging from a tree:

> A woman's shape, now lank and cold and blue,
>   The dwelling of the many-coloured worm,
> Hung there; the white and hollow cheek I drew
>   To my dry lips . . .
>   . . . . .
>   —in the deep
> The shape of an old man did then appear,
> Stately and beautiful; that dreadful sleep
>   His heavenly smiles dispersed, and I could
>   wake and weep.
>   [*The Revolt of Islam*, ll. 1333-36, 1347-50]

Union with the father can occur in *The Revolt of Islam* only after woman is removed. Kissing hanged Cythna's "hollow cheek" (*I*, l. 1335) cannot relieve Laon's physical and spiritual dessication, but the Hermit as good father is androgynous enough to be female as well as male. His "solemn" voice is "sweet"; his "giant" arms nurse Laon tenderly (*I*, ll. 1357, 1364). First the physical dessicaton is relieved ("my scorched limbs he wound, / In linen moist and balmy" [*I*, ll. 1365-66]), then the spiritual. "That aged man, so grand and mild, / Tended me, even as some sick mother seems / To hang in hope over a dying child" (*I*, ll. 1401-3). Since the Hermit is equally effectual in the manly arts—he controls the intellectual discussion as decisively as he "ruled the helm" of the ship—he could prove overbearing (*I*, l. 1380). In fact, Laon initially feared "it was a fiend" (*I*, l. 1383). But the Hermit does not play the heavy father. Like his model Dr. Lind who defended Percy against Sir Timothy, the Hermit can cut the Old Ones down to size with "a glance as keen as is the lightning's stroke / When it doth rive the knots of some ancestral oak" (*I*, ll. 1466-67).

Up to this point Percy has been following the precedent of Wordsworth's *Excursion*: Youth-in-need-of-Wisdom finds all-wise-aged-Man. But *The Excursion* fails, as Percy (in effect, if not consciously) sees it, to recognize that discipleship is only half the battle. No matter how devoted a pupil the son is, he can never achieve full manhood and thus can never get beyond the natural, inevitable emotions of aggression and alienation. *The Excursion* offered the son no way out because it confined him to a single-staged relationship with an elder who dispensed wisdom in propositional statements ("'the good die first'"[14]) and in exemplary tales ("The Ruined Cottage"). Thus the best the younger man could do was to acknowledge and embrace the elder's wisdom.

From such permanent dependence Percy finds an escape by insisting that the father-son relationship be two-staged. Although his Hermit does address Laon's problems, Percy presents no propositional statements and no exemplary tales. In fact he allows the Hermit no dialogue at all at this point in *Islam*. The elder's role here is largely maternal: he creates a nurturing ambience in which the young man's psyche heals itself. Then stage two can begin. The son takes over the role of Wordsworth's seer and provides the elder with ideas and the "power" to effect them.

> I have been thy passive instrument
>   . . . . .
>   thou has lent
> To me, to all, the power to advance
> Towards unforeseen deliverance.
>   [*I*, ll. 1549, 1551-53]

Likening Laon's tongue to "a lance" (*I*, l. 1566), the Hermit confirms the son's phallic manhood by crediting him with that transition from language to action which the father could never make.

Son also surpasses sire in *Prince Athanase* where the Wordsworth situation is again reversed:

> The youth, as shadows on a grassy hill
> Outrun the winds that chase them, soon outran
> His teacher, and did teach with native skill
>
> Strange truths and new to that experienced
>   man;
> Still they were friends.
>   [*PA*, ll. 176-80]

This last line is crucial for *Islam* as well as for *Prince Athanase*. In surpassing the father, the son must not generate a guilt that would blight his flowering manhood. In the bloody battle against tyranny in *Islam,* Laon "in joy . . . found, / Beside me then, firm as a giant pine / Among the mountain-vapours driven around, / The old man whom I loved" (*I,* ll. 2416-19). The Hermit's progress from ruined tower (*I,* ll. 1415-16) to towering pine does not indicate any maturation on his part. The growth is Laon's. The phallic pine's association with father establishes that Laon is now confident enough of his own powers to recognize the manhood of his father and of every other male. A benign coda is now possible. The Hermit's glorious death in battle can complete the generational transfer because father and son have achieved the only equality possible to creatures bound upon the wheel of time. Each is assured the dignity of his place in the generational cycle.

The problem of Mary's "excessive and romantic attachment" to Godwin finds in her later fiction a resolution which is as idealized and conventional as Percy's in *Islam.*

> On a bed of [forest] leaves lay an old man [a Hermit]: his grey hairs were thinly strewn on his venerable temples, his beard white, flowing and soft, fell to his girdle; he smiled even in his sleep a gentle smile of benevolence. I knelt down beside him; methought it was my excellent father.[15]

All her life Mary as well as Percy is the child in the fairy-tale who wanders through the psychic forest seeking father. He materializes in *Valperga* as he did in *Islam,* to fulfill through art the fantasy denied in life. Like Percy's Hermit, Mary's is all-sufficient because androgynous. "Soft . . . gentle . . . benevolence" signal his feminine capacity to nurture, while the role of "father" as spiritual guide assures his masculine authority. "Venerable" characterizes this "excellent father" as it did Percy's surrogate father in "The Coliseum"; a smile associated with sleep establishes the benignity of both *Valperga's* Hermit and *Islam*'s. The conjunction here of "temples" and "knelt" reflects the willingness of both Shelleys to revere properly androgynous paternity.

The quest for father recurs in virtually all of Mary's novels. Besides the patently incestuous *Mathilda* where the mother's death frees daughter and father for untoward desires, there is *Falkner,* where the mother's death impels Elizabeth toward a foster father; *Lodore,* where the mother's abandonment of her daughter assures Ethel's dependence upon "the only parent she had ever known" (*L,* 2:80); *Perkin Warbeck,* where motherless Monina returns to her manly father after intervals of (platonic) devotion to Perkin; and *Valperga,* where Euthanasia considers her bond with father "the dearest tie she had to earth" (*V,* 1:167) and where orphaned Beatrice venerates both "my excellent father" the Hermit and "my good father, the bishop" (*V,* 3:70). The abundance of motherless heroines in nineteenth-century fiction indicates the appeal of this situation to the culture: how much more strongly does it affect Mary Godwin whose situation it actually is.

Fathers in Mary's later fiction satisfy ideally a daughter's need for physical, psychological, and intellectual support, but there are also more intensely charged emotions which must be defused. The repetition of "she idolized her father," "her idolized father," and "her father whom she idolized" seems particularly obsessive because three different heroines are involved: Ethel in *Lodore* (*L,* 1:37), Elizabeth in *Falkner* (*Fa,* 1:125), Clara in *The Last Man.*[16] The obsession is Mary Godwin's. She insists, however, that incestuous feelings are reciprocal. Whereas it is the daughter in *Falkner* who "felt herself bound . . . by stronger than filial ties" (*Fa,* 1:110), the father is the one who knows "more than a father's fondness in *Lodore* (*L,* 1:42).[17] Such fondness makes him the aggressor, "penetrating the depths of her soul" with his "dark expressive eyes" (*L,* 1:62), while it is the "rapturous" daughter in *Falkner* whose "thrilling adoration . . . dreamt not of the necessity of a check, and luxuriated in its boundless excess" (*Fa,* 1:67). When Elizabeth exclaims "'God preserve you, my more than father,'" Mary Godwin is speaking (*Fa,* 1:120).

Feelings more than daughterly are frequent in nineteenth-century fiction, but incest is not. The traditional way to channel untoward emotion is followed by Mary Shelley in her fiction after *Mathilda.* Suitors replace sires. In a century when bridegrooms were admonished endlessly to carry on the parental guidance of the weaker vessel, Neville is told by Falkner "'You must compensate to my dear child for my loss—you must be father as well as husband'" (*Fa,* 2:309). Neville can replace Falkner so smoothly because he is in fact the same character. Similar physically (dark, olive, craggy) and psychologically (prone to macho rage but open to feminine influence), both men live under the same cloud, "the mysterious wretchedness that darkened the lives of the only two beings, the inner emotions of whose souls had been opened to her" (*Fa,* 1:156). Although Elizabeth encourages Neville in the quest for his mother's killer which eventually brings Falkner to trial, Elizabeth's endeavors are therapeutic, not punitive. Only after Falkner has publicly confessed his part in Alithea's death can he be forgiven by Neville and be reconciled to him. Only *then* can the triangle of Elizabeth-Neville-Falkner be assured permanence. The conventional marriage which resolves the love plot thus provides an unconventional wish fulfillment. *Falkner* ends not with the wedding of Ethel and Neville but with the cemented bond between Neville and Falkner because only the union of suitor and father assures that the daughter can at last consummate the passion which has driven Mary's heroines. And herself.

Why does Mary not find with Percy the resolution of complexes and the completeness of union which Ethel achieves with Neville? Mary certainly tries to put *Falkner* into practice—to move from father to suitor by recreating the elder man in the younger. "Until I met Shelley I [could?] justly say that he [Godwin] was my God."[18] Mary abandons herself to Percy with the most orthodox completeness. "Perhaps [I] will one day have a father till then be every thing to me love" (*LMS*, 1:4-5, 28 October 1814). Mary of course remains deeply concerned with Godwin, but she makes Percy her god—investing "everything" in him and expecting as much in return. If she has gotten beyond father ties and united permanently with Percy, why can't he get beyond father problems and unite exclusively with her? *Islam* seems to second Mary's espousal of the "normal" teleology of relationships. After the Hermit's death, Cythna—who, it turns out, is not actually dead—reenters the plot and is united with Laon in ecstatic congress.

Why art and life don't reflect each other for Percy will become clearer if we turn back to *Islam* and see that beneath its apparently idealistic surface are subversive forces at work. Why does Percy put himself in the awkward position of having to resurrect Cythna? Why hang her in the first place? If Laon needs to be alone with the Hermit to achieve solidarity, Cythna's capture and abduction at this point in the plot are convenient enough. The very unnecessariness of Cythna's hanging indicates how necessary it must be to Percy. Especially since her corpse is presented so gruesomely, the assassination of woman—as opposed to her absence—seems a precondition of male solidarity for Percy.

Islam reverses *Falkner* by paralleling it too exactly. Percy as well as Mary is seeking father *as end*. The ostensibly similar teleologies of daughter going beyond father to suitor and son going beyond father to beloved involve, in fact, quite different processes. While the woman has only to change the object of her affection, the man must change the gender of his. That a male is the object of Percy's desires is indicated not only in the Hermit scenes of *Islam* but in much of his life. If we compare the duration and intensity of Percy's bonds with men and with women, we may well agree with various scholars that the paramount figures of his emotional life are Hogg, Byron, Edward John Trelawny, and Edward Williams. Men are also the paramount objects when rage is the prevailing emotion. Inadequate fathers—Sir Timothy, Godwin, Wordsworth, Rousseau—obsess the poet-son to the end, to *The Triumph of Life*. Either way, rage or affection, the lesson is the same. Either solidarity with father is achieved, and woman is superfluous; or solidarity is denied, and the son's continued search for father keeps woman secondary.

Islam proves subversive in a different way if we view it in light of the Erotic desire for self-union which is a paramount theme of Percy Shelley and of *Frankenstein*.[19] Is even a father-son bond possible? Male solidarity obviously constitutes a threatening alternative to self-union because the father becomes a rival who must be extirpated. But solidarity is even more threatening than that. It *fosters* death. Initially the son's escape from mother and body may be directed toward father and mind, but soon he recognizes that father is not only *as* mortal as mother and thus as incapable of assuring the son's immortality, father is *more* mortal. Uniting with him involves death as a precondition rather than simply as a consequence. Equality means mortality, since the son can ascend to the father's place upon the wheel of time only if he acknowledges the elder's humanity and thus accepts the inevitability of his own descent to death. Father is the ultimate threat to self-union because he provides a model so attractive that the son may accept mortality to achieve it.

There is something else about father, however, something promising for Eros. Father *in death* seems to offer an escape from mortality that mother, dead or alive, can not. So important is this aspect of father-son relations that it informs the major literary productions of both Mary and Percy Shelley.

2. Subversion and the Oedipus

I want to begin my discussion of Victor and his father Alphonse in what may seem an unlikely place—the Arab Maid of Shelley's *Alastor*. Mary in the opening frame of *Frankenstein* establishes her position on father-son conflicts by having Margaret Saville agree with Mr. Walton about the foolhardiness of Robert's seaborne quests. Since no one in the central frame of *Frankenstein* can succeed Margaret as arbiter, Mary proceeds more indirectly. In *Alastor,* the Arab Maid does what Mary considers natural and what she herself did for Percy—steals away from the father and tends upon the beloved. Woman's reward in *Alastor* is abandoment. "Self-centred seclusion" (*CP*, p. 15) makes the male too obsessed with his "antitype" to bond with his complement.[20] *Frankenstein* recapitulates the Arab Maid scenario, twice. "The Arabian," Safie, leaves her father and travels to Felix's home. Her reward is felicity. Elizabeth travels from her father to Frankenstein's home. Her reward is murder. The contrast between Felix's and Victor's treatments of woman signals that something is seriously wrong with Victor's relationship with father.

Felix, despite many hardships, feels no apparent antagonism toward a father excellent like the best old men in Mary's and Percy's art. Like the blind seer in Percy's "The Coliseum," M. De Lacey responds positively to the wanderer who comes seeking knowledge and love; like the Hermits in *Islam* and *Valperga,* he is served devotedly by an excellent daughter. With this ideal father, Felix achieves the solidarity which allows him, like Neville, to go on to complementary union with the beloved. Why can't Victor do the same with Alphonse and Elizabeth?

Critics in recent years have found oedipal tensions in the Victor-Alphonse relationship. They note that the son is hurt by his father's belittling Agrippa; that Victor consequently fears to share with Alphonse his new readings in alchemy and his later experiments in monster-making; that Victor feels exiled from the family when he is sent to Ingolstadt; that he associates Alphonse with the monster after Henry's murder; that he feels bound to his parents "by a silken cord" and includes "seemed" in his description of their love for him.[21] These and other pieces of evidence fit so readily into psychoanalytic patterns that we can forget we are dealing with a character, not a patient. Especially since the text is a *narrator's* account, we must ascertain the *author's* intent. "When I would account to myself for the birth of that passion . . . I find . . ."[22] Victor is accounting to himself. What "I find" is self-justification. Events which some psychoanalytic readers have taken as factual evidence may be convenient pretexts, as Kaplan and Kloss demonstrate with Victor's initial horror at the creature.

> Why should Frankenstein react in this astounding way? . . . because the creature is ugly in appearance! At least this is the only explanation Frankenstein gives us.

> But what an achievement is here. Ugly or not, it moves, breathes, lives! . . . With the description he gives, he might just as easily, and more realistically, have marvelled that the resemblance to a man was so close.

> If we are to understand him, and the novel as well, we must presume that this terror, having its origin in other causes, is transferred to a convenient pretext.[23]

Convenient pretexts are Victor's stock-in-trade. Particularly in passages defining the reasons for his behavior, Frankenstein's reactions often seem inordinate, the effects disproportionate to the causes. As we seek underlying motives, we must look carefully at Victor's placement of the blame upon Alphonse, and also at Levine's less extreme judgment that "fathers and sons are almost equally responsible and irresponsible."[24] We must, in other words, remain alive to distinctions between narrator and author, between Victor's assertion and our experience of it.

Take, for example, Alphonse's remark about Agrippa:

> My father looked carelessly at the title-page of my book, and said, 'Ah! Cornelius Agrippa! My dear Victor, do not waste your time upon this; it is sad trash.'

> If, instead of this remark, my father had taken the pains to explain to me, that the principles of Agrippa had been entirely exploded, and that a modern system of science had been introduced . . . , I should certainly have thrown Agrippa aside. [*F*, pp. 32-33]

Victor is correct: Alphonse should explain, not simply dismiss. But just as unquestionably, the *magnitude* of Alphonse's failure is relevant too. Is our experience really that "a rationalist, like Godwin, the elder Frankenstein rather cruelly chastens his son's youthful imagination" ("AD," p. 104)? Alphonse's "'my dear'" is neither rationalistic nor cruel, as Godwin's chastenings of Mary show. She could easily have made Alphonse's dismissal of Agrippa seem cruel enough to warrant Victor's reaction. Instead what we experience is a minor mistake. What parent has not missed by at least this much the proper tone in a random moment? (And random the moment is: on vaction, on a rainy day indoors, with a child who has never before evinced an interest in science.)

That Victor is finding convenient pretexts is signaled in his admission that "if, instead of this remark, my father had taken the pains to explain . . . I . . . should probably have applied myself to the more rational theory of chemistry which has resulted from modern discoveries. It is even possible, that the train of my ideas would never have received the fatal impulse that led to my ruin" (*F*, p. 33). Is it really? "Probably" and "possible" foster suspicions which are confirmed when Alphonse *does* explain about modern science.

> The catastrophe of this tree [hit by lightning] excited my extreme astonishment; and I eagerly inquired of my father the nature and origin of thunder and lightning. He replied, 'Electricity;' describing at the same time the various effects of that power. He constructed a small electrical machine, and exhibited a few experiments; he made also a kite, with a wire and string, which drew down that fluid from the clouds.

> This last stroke completed the overthrow of Cornelius Agrippa. [*F*, p. 35]

Is our experience of this passage actually that the "1818 version of the novel is even harsher on the old man" than the substantially revised 1831 text, or that "Alphonse is also blamed for leading his son to science when he conducts a Franklin-like experiment" ("AD," pp. 104-5)? Alphonse can't win for trying. Here he does all that Victor faulted him for omitting before: he is patient; he explains; he even demonstrates. How does Mary treat him harshly here? Or rather, what does it mean that "the 1818 version of the novel" treats him harshly? Is the treatment attributable to the author or to the narrator? That *Victor* is trying to implicate Alphonse in his youthful swerve toward destructive studies is clear. But we must distinguish between

Victor's attempt and Mary's, between Victor's attempt and our response.

After the Franklin-like experiment, Victor "by some fatality . . . did not feel inclined to commence the study of any modern system" (*F*, p. 35). In its vagueness, "some fatality" carries on from "probably" and "possible," but it goes beyond these words as the clearest signal yet that the prime force operating upon Victor is not Alphonse. The 1818 edition introduces at this point a lecture course which "some accident" prevents Victor from attending "until the course was nearly finished. The lecture . . . was entirely incomprehensible to me" (*F*, p. 36). Accidents are convenient pretexts for Victor so often that we are not inclined to see external forces operating strongly here, and this interpretation is confirmed by Mary's revision in the 1831 edition of *Frankenstein*. The lecture course is deleted, Alphonse is replaced as Victor's electricity mentor by "a man of great research,"—and still the boy does not go on to study modern science (*F*, p. 238).

> By some fatality the overthrow of these men [Agrippa, Albertus Magnus, Paracelsus] disinclined me to pursue my accustomed [scientific] studies. It seemed to me as if nothing would or could ever be known. All that had so long engaged my attention suddenly grew despicable. By one of those caprices of the mind . . . In this mood of mind I betook myself to the mathematics . . .
>
> Thus strangely are our souls constructed . . . Destiny was too potent, and her immutable laws had decreed my utter and terrible destruction. [*F*, p. 239]

By repeating the word "fatally" which begs the question that it seems to answer, Mary directs us away from Alphonse and toward Victor. "It seemed to me" . . . "suddenly" . . . "caprices of the mind" . . . "mood of mind" . . . "strangely" . . . "Destiny" . . . "Laws had decreed." Victor does not understand what is happening inside him and does not want to. Mary, I believe, tries to avoid in 1831 exactly what Dussinger faults her for—"indecisiveness" about Alphonse's role in 1818 ("KG," p. 42). Having initially established that Victor's "family was not scientifical," Mary needed the boy familiarized with modern science and she chose Alphonse as the handiest teacher—forgetting that he was not scientifical (*F*, p. 34). Later, in the Thomas copy, she caught her mistake and reminded herself in the margin "you said your family was not scientifical." In 1831 she corrects the mistake by keeping Alphonse consistently nonscientifical and inventing, clumsily, the man of great research who teaches Victor what she wants him to know. Mary never, I feel, intended a rivalry between Alphonse and Victor as scientists, never intended the father to have any large role in the son's disastrous move toward monster-making. Father and son do not seem almost equally responsible and irresponsible. Instead the son absolves himself of irresponsibility by making the father responsible.

To appreciate Victor's motivation here, we must, I feel, heed a distinction present in Freud and important in recent psychoanalytic work—a distinction between the Oedipus as a fantasy projected by the son upon the innocent father and the Oedipus as a son's correct perception about the father. Psychoanalytic critics have tended to assume that the latter is the case in *Frankenstein*, whereas I incline to the former. Victor blames Alphonse for sending him to Ingolstadt, for example.

> When I had attained the age of seventeen, my parents resolved that I should become a student at the university of Ingolstadt. I had hitherto attended the schools of Geneva; but my father thought it necessary, for the completion of my education, that I should be made acquainted with other customs than those of my native country. My departure was therefore fixed at an early date.
>
> [*F*, p. 37]

'I' *attain* seventeen, but the family does the rest. "My parents resolved" . . . "my father thought" . . . "my departure was therefore fixed." The son is already feeling himself driven from home and mother by his rival the father (and may also be feeling, as the plural "parents" indicates, that mother is siding with father) when suddenly Caroline Frankenstein dies. What ensues is analyzed well by Dussinger. Victor first blames his mother's death on his father's banishing of him; then Alphonse's continued insistence upon Victor's departure makes the son see things the opposite way—that the father blames *him* for Caroline's death and is punishing him with banishment. "The narrator, it would be possible to say, wants to lessen his guilt involved in his secret rebellion against the enervating domestic order by attributing the decision to leave to his father" ("KG," p. 43). Victor's word "early" supports Dussinger by indicating not only that the date is soon, but that the son feels it is too soon, feels he is being forced to leave early. This is not how we take it, however. That sons become "acquainted with other customs than those of . . . [their] native country" is a traditional goal of fathers. Particularly in Mary's fiction, sons repeatedly practice the wisdom preached in *Lodore*: "'At seventeen years many their fortunes seek'" (*L*, 3:158). At "seventeen" Lodore goes off to Oxford (*L*, 1:82); Lionel, admonished by Adrian in *The Last Man* to "begin life . . . you are seventeen," sets off for "the necessary apprenticeship" in a foreign land.[25] And barely a month before her seventeenth birthday, Mary Godwin elopes with Percy Shelley.

The contrast between Victor's reluctance and the eagerness of Castruccio, whose "fervent desire" as "he entered his seventeenth year" was "to quit what he thought a lifeless solitude," shows how closely Victor resembles Percy Shelley (*V*, 1:37). Percy, who at various times suspected Sir Timothy of seeking to exile him to a madhouse and the Peninsular Wars, sees the inevitable need to go away to school as a father-generated plan of banishment. *He* responds by setting a washroom fire which could have consumed his home.

The parallels with Percy's life and the analogues in Mary's fiction confirm our sense that Alphonse is not malevolent, especially since he sympathetically postpones Victor's departure after Caroline's death. Victor downplays the sympathy by mitigating Alphonse's agency. "I obtained from my father a respite of some weeks" (*F,* p. 38). The emphasis is upon "I." That what I do is to "obtain" and "a respite" stresses the son's subservience and his struggle to wrest a concession from father. The truly domineering father in *Frankenstein* is M. Clerval, who for a long time forbids Henry to attend Ingolstadt. Why would Mary portray Henry's father this way except to highlight Victor's father? Instead of the psychological pattern which Frankenstein implies—that Alphonse's traditional goal and sympathetic postponement of it screen his "real," oedipal design—we experience the well-intentioned plan of a father properly ambitious for his gifted son.

Where does Victor get an "oedipal" sense of father-son relations nearly a century before Freud? The obvious answer—that sons have ever felt abused by fathers—is bolstered by a more historiographic source. Gothic fiction, as Judith Wilt argues, makes paternal abuse a major theme. "The son must die so that the old man may live."[26] This paradigm, which recurs from *The Castle of Otranto* through *Dracula,* is prominent in Godwin's *Caleb Williams* and *St. Leon.* In *Frankenstein,* however, the son's oppression by the father informs not the plot of the novel but the mind of the protagonist: Victor interprets life as though it were a gothic novel. Mary Shelley dramatizes not the oedipal paranoia of the gothic tradition but the dangers of such paranoia, the dangers of approaching complex realities with the self-justifying convenience of a paradigm. *Frankenstein* is, in this sense, antigothic. It is orthodoxy's counterattack against the dark tradition which had exposed the self-deceived convenience of its own sentimental paradigms. In another sense, however, Mary's very skepticism about gothic paranoia is very gothic. Monk Lewis, Charles Maturin, James Hogg, Thomas Lovell Beddoes, as well as Brown, Edgar Allan Poe, Nathaniel Hawthorne, and Herman Melville all share her distrust of the son's self-justifying rage, even as they, like her, make oedipal emotions central to their art. Mary Shelley's critical examination of all paradigms, gothic and sentimental, is what drives her and her readers beyond Victor's self-justifying explanations to the darker teleology of him and Percy.

3. The Negative Oedipus

What is the nature of the antagonism toward Alphonse which Victor expresses in oedipal terms? Psychoana-

lytic critics have rightly seen Victor's philanthropic rationale for monster-making as a convenient pretext. The claim that he is creating life in order to save mankind from death screens Frankenstein's deeper desire to resuscitate his dead mother. Readers can, however, recognize this second level and still sense another, even deeper motive. Victor's devotion to woman is not all it might be. He kills woman. As a wish fulfillment, Victor's famous nightmare is manifestly *not* oedipal because the nightmare kiss functions not to awaken the mother from death, as in "Sleeping Beauty," but to reduce Elizabeth to Caroline's moribund state. Victor is then free to move beyond woman to father. In Freudian terms, Victor's feelings are not oedipal (kill the father to possess the mother) but negative oedipal (kill the mother to possess the father).

Why father? The answer, as we have seen, cannot lie in any illusion of paternal immortality. In fact one reason why Percy rages against old men is that he too is aging, and prematurely. When he says "I have lived to be older than my father," he is reflecting not only upon his superior wisdom but upon his graying hair and wasted body (*LMS* 1:189, 27 August 1822). Confronted with the danger of becoming *like* his father, Percy determines to *become* his father.

This determination is proclaimed, quite amazingly, on the title pages of his first two books of verse. *Original Poetry* is authored by Victor (Percy) and Cazire (Elizabeth Shelley); *Posthumous Fragments of Margaret Nicholson* is "edited" by John Fitzvictor. Victor and Fitzvictor. What Shelley desired ultimately is not what *Islam* idealized, not that place upon the wheel of time which allows to both son and father the dignity of all roles from birth to death. Victor and Fitzvictor, father and son: Shelley desires to become his own father because as Victor-Fitzvictor he can sire himself.

How this promises immortality is dramatized in *Prometheus Unbound.* Demogorgon is eternal. Like Percy, he is older than his father, but unlike Percy, he is not threatened by age. This son who kills the father lives forever. Demogorgon who descends as Killer-Son with Jupiter in act 2 emerges by himself as Eternity in act 4. He is no longer "son" because he no longer has a father. Even as fantasy, however, Demogorgon seems unsatisfying: since Shelley is not eternal, how can he take Demogorgon for his model? The answer to this question lies in Percy's understanding of myth. Demogorgon's association with Eternity comes not from Thomas Love Peacock or John Milton but from Boccaccio. In *The Genealogy of the Pagan Gods,* Demogorgon is the principle of force who cohabits with the Witch of Eternity. Shelley takes this union of male and female and combines the two principles into one character. Demogorgon ingests the female principle of eternity. If Shelley can do likewise, if he can contain both masculine and feminine as self and antitype, he can become self-sufficient.

Like the snake swallowing its tail, the male can provide both the phallus and its receptacle. Siring oneself assures immortality by closing the generative cycle and thus precluding death. Victor-Fitzvictor. For this most perversely solipsistic version of his antitype idea, Percy finds sanctioning precedents in both Romantic satanism and orthodox Christianity. One of the things which attracts the Romantics to Milton's Satan is his daring claim to self-generation. This parodies the Christian notion that "the Father pours himself out into the son; the son, knowing himself separate, makes the astonishing choice to curve that stream of being back toward the progenitor."[27] Victor's discovery of the secret of life abolishes Alphonse by supplanting the very biological process which made the father a father. Rather than curve the stream of being back to Alphonse, Frankenstein as the only begetter of a new system of begetting curves it into himself.

Although Frankenstein's desire to become Fitz-victor is achieved partially by giving birth to himself as monster, he remains a son so long as he, like Demogorgon, has a father. Alphonse must die. Mary's *Frankenstein* and Percy's life and art thus feature early in the nineteenth century a motif recurrent in western culture and particularly central to literature and biography for the next hundred and fifty years—sons desiring to extirpate fathers and to sire themselves. Both the desire and its consequences are summed up in Freud's essay on Dostoyevski: "You wanted to kill your father in order to be your father yourself. Now you *are* your father, but a dead father."[28] Recent critics have found this motif in novelists as diverse as Melville ("behind these [Pierre's] strategems lies the desire to be one's own father") and Joyce ("Stephen is the son-type in the process of fathering himself"). In Dickens, Thackeray, and Faulkner, this process is made still more intricate by the son's attempt to recreate himself through language. Pip, "the metaphorical writer-as-son . . . attempts to give birth to himself in writing, to beget or engender himself without the help of fathers"; Esmond, "the fatherless son[,] is allowed, in a sense, to be father himself through the first-person narrative"; and Quentin can become in effect the sire of Jason Sr. if he can articulate the Compson history and thus "seize his father's authority by gaining temporal priority." Mary Shelley agrees emphatically with all these writers about "the lunacy of attempting . . . to engender the self," but the most relevant context for her masterpiece remains Percy Shelley.[29] He provides Mary with an immediate example of that "poetic will," that reaction against father and that concern with self-generation which characterize the next two hundred years and which have been called by Harold Bloom "an argument against time, revengefully seeking to substitute 'It is' for 'it was.' Yet this argument always splits in two, because the poetic will needs to make another outrageous substitution, of 'I am' for 'It is.' Both parts of the argument are quests for priority."[30]

In the analysis which follows I will often discuss Victor in terms of works written by Percy *after* 1818. Two considerations warrant this. As Percy's "handwriting was very early formed and never altered," so the artistic products of that hand show remarkable consistency.[31] The dismissal of the living Godwin as dead in the 1820 "Letter to Maria Gisborne" repeats the 1815 dismissal of Wordsworth which I will discuss soon. More important, the psychological moves I will define in *Prometheus Unbound* and *The Cenci*—the dual need to assassinate and to deny responsibility for the act—repeat at the highest levels of art what Percy had been doing at least since he introduced plagiarism into *Original Poetry* and then blamed Elizabeth Shelley for it. Victor in 1818 can anticipate Percy's moves in 1819 because Mary has learned through grim experience her husband's instinctual responses. In the intricate literary interaction between *Frankenstein* and *Prometheus Unbound* and *The Cenci,* it is as though Percy learns from Mary what he had taught her. Or rather, he reaffirms in 1819 what she had urged him in 1818 to repudiate.

Fundamental to the Greek myth of Prometheus is father-killing. Jupiter destroyed his sire, Saturn, and was in turn threatened by his own offspring. Attractive as this situation is to the Erotic Percy, it does not lead to the absolute annihilation he requires. "The *Prometheus Unbound* of Aeschylus supposed the reconciliation of Jupiter with his victim . . . I was averse from a catastrophe so feeble as that of reconciling the Champion with the Oppressor of mankind" (*CP*, p. 205). Reconciliation was the theme of *Islam* and *Prince Athanase,* but father, like almost everything else with Percy, evokes contradictory responses. While *Islam* revealed the ideal acceptance of paternal manhood which Agape encourages, other poems express the Erotic son's attack upon the manhood of sires who have failed to measure up. Percy finds it difficult to discover limitations in an authority figure and still acknowledge that man's masculinity. Wordsworth is a "moral eunuch" in *Peter Bell the Third,* "an unsexual man" (ll. 314, 551). Percy cannot face directly the sexuality of that ultimate elder, Sir Timothy, so he strikes back by claiming superior maturity. "'I have lived to be older than my father, I am ninety years of age'" (*LMS,* 1:189); "'The life of a man of talent who should die in his *thirtieth year,* is, with regard to his own feelings, longer than that of a miserable priest-ridden slave.'"[32] Although Percy credits himself here with that experiential wisdom which Laon and Prince Athanase acceded to, his life cannot achieve what *Islam* and *Prince Athanase* enacted—the friendship between younger and older male which assures their equality and manhood.

Unable to be reconciled to Wordsworth or Godwin or Sir Timothy, Percy Shelley never resolves his obsession with fathers. Instead he extirpates them.

> Deserting these [truth and liberty], thou
>   leavest me to grieve,
> Thus having been, that thou shouldst cease to
>   be.
> ["To Wordsworth," ll. 13-14]

Needless to say, Wordsworth is very much alive in 1815. But not to Percy. Unlike *Islam* where the limitations of the elder male could be acknowledged and accepted, "To Wordsworth" tolerates no deviation from the ideal. Once Wordsworth acts as he should not, he ceases to be. The same happens to Godwin. With a switch of verb tense and a switch to neuter gender, Percy can switch off a man whose life has failed to measure up:

> [In London] . . . You [the Gisbornes] will see
> That which was Godwin . . .
>
>   . . . . .
>
> You will see Coleridge—he who sits obscure.
> ["Letter to Maria Gisborne," ll. 196-97, 202]

And Sir Timothy? Again Percy finds it hardest to deal with his real father, but again he manages to make his point. The need to defeat rather than to bond with father shapes both of Percy's greatest long works.

As *Islam* idealized the reconciliation advocated by Agape, *Prometheus Unbound* effects the extermination required by Eros. Percy transforms father from loving Hermit to Jupiter, the quintessential evil. The son's response to him is not the guilt-producing one of a patricide but the noble one of an assassin.[33] What might seem self-indulgent becomes obligatory: the world must be redeemed from Evil.

This change cannot preclude guilt entirely, so Percy further justifies assassination by aligning himself with two of the canonical traditions of his time. As Romantic, he models his rejection of reconciliation upon the heroic defiance of Satan in *Paradise Lost*. Satan is, however, hardly a model to all readers (or to Percy as erstwhile Christian), so the poet acknowledges the "ambition, envy, revenge" of Milton's character and makes Jesus Christ another of his own party (*CP*, p. 205). "Christ the benevolent champion, falsely identified with the Son of God, must destroy the notion of the Father in the mind of Man in order to vindicate his own humanity and goodness."[34] Since guilt still remains a possibility so long as killing remains the theme, Percy makes the ultimate gesture and declares Prometheus perfect—"the type of the highest perfection of moral and intellectual nature, impelled by the purest and the truest motives to the best and noblest ends" (*CP*, p. 205).

An apparently insuperable dilemma now confronts Percy: either someone perfect cannot kill, or a killer cannot be perfect. The way out of this dilemma is explained by Mary herself. "According to the mythological story . . . the offspring of Thetis . . . was destined to be greater than his father. . . . Shelley adapted the catastrophe of this story to his peculiar views. The son greater than his father . . . was to dethrone Evil" (*CP*, p. 272). In Percy's "peculiar" view, the "son" is *two* men who reflect his contradictory responses to father. Prometheus is Percy the son who, though oppressed by fathers, remains as perfect in love as they are sunk in evil. Then, since the "son" in the Greek myth is not Prometheus, the actual offspring of Thetis can express homicidal rage. Demogorgon does what Percy-Prometheus cannot and what Percy-Assassin must. Demogorgon does the dirty work and keeps Prometheus' hands clean.

Deflection of guilt occurs in a different way in *The Cenci*. Father is again made so monstrously evil that no substantial sympathy can devolve to him, and the agent of assassination is again removed sufficiently from Percy (Beatrice is female and modeled from life) to prevent his direct implication.[35] To make all the more certain that guilt cannot surface, Percy resorts to another characteristic expedient—indignation. He criticizes the woman who does his bidding, as he blamed his sister Elizabeth for his plagiarism in *Original Poetry*.

> Undoubtedly, no person can be truly dishonoured by the act of another; and the fit return to make to the most enormous injuries is kindness and forbearance, and a resolution to convert the injurer from his dark passions by peace and love. Revenge, retaliation, atonement, are pernicious mistakes. If Beatrice had thought in this manner she would have been wiser and better. [*CP*, p. 276]

My point is not to contest the moral stance taken in the *Cenci* preface ("turn the other cheek" is impeccably Christian), or to belabor the fact that Percy did not always turn the cheek when his was the one struck (as in the Rhine boat incident of 1814, the Rome Post Office fight of 1819, and the Pisa fracas of 1822). My point is the priggish inflexibility of the preface's attitude toward Beatrice. A man who assures a woman that rape does not really touch her essence and that she must submit to whatever degradations lie ahead—this man should employ warier rhetoric. The lack of syntactic complication in "if Beatrice had thought in this [my] manner, she would have been wiser and better" contrasts with the manifold complications of Beatrice's actual situation. She cannot escape the house; no one would shelter her anyway; and her father will unquestionably carry out his threat to rape her again and again. Percy's sentence, however, is not badly written. Its syntactic stiffness and righteous tone are the inevitable consequences of its therapeutic—as opposed to its rhetorical—purpose. Its function is not only, or at least not primarily, to persuade us that Beatrice acted wrongly, but also to convince Percy that he feels properly. Percy guiltily uses the preface to insist upon the proper attitude toward patricide, after his unconscious has already used the play to satisfy homicidal desires. Readers of the play empathize consistently with Beatrice because the Erotic Percy enjoys her patricide.[36] She is, after all, destroying Sir Timothy, and Godwin, and Wordsworth, and . . .

That Alphonse evokes comparable conflicts in Victor is revealed in the conflict between Victor's surrogate, the monster, and Alphonse's youngest son, William.

> "Hideous monster! Let me [William] go; My papa is a Syndic—he is M. Frankenstein . . ."

> "Frankenstein! You belong then to my enemy . . . you shall be my first victim." [*F,* p. 139]

William is doomed only when he is identified as a son; murder was not inevitable or apparently even intended before that. Victor's first strike at Alphonse is thus through his beloved son. (This son in turn warrants punishment as a sibling rival for the father's affection, and for the mother's love too, since William is in possession of Caroline's portrait. Emblematic of Victor's sense of domestic exclusion is the fact that when word of William's death calls him back to Geneva, "the gates of the town were already shut" [*F,* p. 70].) The traditional association of "little brother" and penis emphasizes the castrating intent of striking at the father through his offspring. As an indirect move, it saves Victor from having to lay a guilt-fostering hand upon the father. Since the act *is* indirect, however, since little William is only a stand-in for Alphonse, a second attack must be launched against the now vulnerable sire. Frankenstein must assassinate Alphonse to become a true victor.

The guilt and awe generated by patricide continue to require that the son proceed indirectly, so Victor resorts to both of the tactics practiced by Shelley in his long poems. As Shelley displaced his dark deeds upon another (Demogorgon, Beatrice Cenci, and Elizabeth Shelley), Victor has created the monster to enact his murderous will against his family. His hands remain legally as clean as Prometheus'. In fact the monster does not even dirty *his* hands with Alphonse's blood. The creature could have swum across the lake and throttled the unsuspecting sire before Victor reached Geneva to warn him, but this would have brought patricide too close to home. The most fiendish thing about the sequence of events generated by Frankenstein's Erotic unconscious is that it results—in effect—in Alphonse's suicide. By succumbing to grief, the old man dies of natural causes, and lets Victor off Shelley-free. The son does remain conscience-ridden,

however. "An apoplectic fit was brought on" (*F,* p. 196). *By whom,* the sentence cannot admit. The question of responsibility, of agency, need not even have come up, had not guilt at killing by indirection prompted the self-indicting Victor to forego the active construction ("he died of an apoplectic fit") which would have acquitted him entirely.

To emphasize his innocence, Victor further deflects guilt through indignation. Like Percy in the *Cenci* preface, he vilifies his surrogate. In face-to-face encounters, he accuses the monster of having "'diabolically murdered'" innocent "'victims'" (*F,* p. 94); and in a retrospective move like that of Percy's preface, he concludes that the creature "shewed unparalleled malignity and selfishness" (*F,* p. 215). Since this is society's reaction (everyone abhors the monster), and since this would surely be Alphonse's reaction (you have slaughtered my children), Victor's indignation testifies to his orthodoxy as Percy's indignation did in the *Cenci* preface.

Even if Victor's need for clean hands precludes the monster's throttling Alphonse, grief over little William and Justine (and Caroline) could have caused Alphonse to die conventionally from sorrow *before* Elizabeth's murder. The unconvincing thing about fictional deaths-from-sorrow is precisely that they can occur whenever the novelist requires. Why does Mary Shelley require so many corpses, and why is Alphonse's death the last?

William   Justine   Henry   Elizabeth   Alphonse

The deaths proceed in terms of increasingly important relationships for Victor: a tie with a child, then with a peer, then with the closest male peer, then with the still closer female peer, and finally the ultimate bond with father.[37] With each increase of intimacy, there is a greater threat to the self-union which promises immortality. And, as we have seen, father is the supreme threat because solidarity with him is an alternate ideal. "'Whose death,' cried I, 'is to finish the tragedy? Ah! my father, do not remain in this wretched country'" (*F,* p. 180). Victor's covert message—"'to finish . . . my father'"—solves the problem it poses: "'the tragedy . . . my father.'" Victor at some deep level knows the teleology that he will not acknowledge. Mary stresses Alphonse's climactic placement in the family fatalities by having Victor say in 1831 "I turned to contemplate the deep and voiceless grief of my Elizabeth. This also was my doing! And my father's woe" (*F,* p. 246). Victor knows. After Elizabeth's "voiceless" death by strangulation comes the father's death from "woe."

But there is more. As the last fatality, Alphonse fits not only into a scale of increasing intimacy but also into a reversal of alphabetical order.

W—J—H—E—A

Whether Mary consciously intended to reverse alphabetization—and for an author attentive to names to do it accidentally seems unlikely to me—the fact of the reversal reflects her reaction to self-union. The reversal establishes that Victor's motion to father is regressive. "Regressive" can mean two things. Insofar as Victor-Percy is capable of the intimacy and solidarity of Agape, regressive has the positive associations of the term in Freud's clinical papers (particularly "Remembering, Repeating, and Working-Through"[38]) and in more recent discussions of transference (particularly by Jacques Lacan and Heinz Kohut). The analysand cannot simply be *told* what is the matter; s/he must work back to the original trauma and either reexperience it or experience a comparable moment through the transference. If this were what Victor was attempting, if he were returning to his childhood relationship with Alphonse in order to understand and relive it, then "regression" would mean that the son was making that peace with the parent which is essential if psychological and social maturity is to match biological development. Particularly if we see the father in light of *Totem and Taboo* and the work of Lacan, Phallus as Law is what the son should be oriented to. Victor's pursuit of the monster could then signal a therapeutically male orientation. But since Victor pursues the monster with unnatural attraction and homicidal rage, and since his own father is ultimately absent because Victor has killed him, "regressive" has the negative connotations of ordinary parlance.

W—J—H—E—A. After "A" there is nothing else. It is the beginning as end, Alpha as Omega of I AM.[39] Suppose Mary had named Victor's father Bartholomew or Benedict or Bardolph. Suppose, in other words, that after Mother—Caroline—and Father—Bardolph—there remained *A*. Son would have some role beyond, before family. But Father is the end of the line. Beyond Mother there is Alphonse, but beyond Alphonse—Alpha—there is only silence. In his desire to become Victor-Fitzvictor, in his determination to predate his predecessor and sire himself, Frankenstein has regressed from society to preexistence, to the letterless wordless tundra of the phallic Pole's self-centred seclusion.

Notes

[1] See Nancy Chodorow, *The Reproduction of Mothering: Psychoanalysis and the Sociology of Gender* (Berkeley and Los Angeles, 1978); Dorothy Dinnerstein, *The Mermaid and the Minotaur: Sexual Arrangements and the Human Malaise* (New York, 1976); Sandra M. Gilbert and Susan Gubar, *The Madwoman in the Attic: The Woman Writer and the Nineteenth-Century Literary Imagination* (New Haven, Conn., 1979); Mary Jacobus, "Is There a Woman in This Text?" *New Literary History* 14 (Autumn 1982): 117-41; Mary Poovey, *The Proper Lady and the Woman Writer: Ideology as Style in the Works of Mary Wollstonecraft, Mary Shelley, and Jane Austen* (Chicago, 1984); Marc A. Rubenstein, "'My Accursed Origin': The Search for the Mother in *Frankenstein,*" *Studies in Romanticism* 15 (Spring 1976): 165-94; and Janet M. Todd, "Frankenstein's Daughter: Mary Shelley and Mary Wollstonecraft," *Women and Literature* 4, no. 2 (1976): 18-27.

[2] Poovey, *The Proper Lady,* p. 168.

[3] See J. M. Hill, "Frankenstein and the Physiognomy of Desire," *American Imago* 32 (1975): 332-58; Gordon D. Hirsch, "The Monster Was a Lady: On the Psychology of Mary Shelley's *Frankenstein,*" *Hartford Studies in Literature* 7 (1975): 116-53; Morton Kaplan and Robert Kloss, "Fantasy of Paternity and the Doppelgänger: Mary Shelley's *Frankenstein,*" *The Unspoken Motive: A Guide to Psychoanalytic Literary Criticism* (New York, 1973); and U. C. Knoepflmacher, "Thoughts on the Aggression of Daughters," in *The Endurance of "Frankenstein": Essays on Mary Shelley's Novel,* ed. George Levine and Knoepflmacher (Berkeley and Los Angeles, 1979), pp. 88-119. All further references to this essay, abbreviated "AD," will be included in the text.

[4] Freud's fullest discussion of the "negative" Oedipus occurs in chapter 3 of *The Ego and the Id, The Standard Edition of the Complete Psychological Works of Sigmund Freud,* ed. and trans. James Strachey, 24 vols. (London, 1953-74), 19:28-39; it also permeates his analysis of the Wolf-Man (*From the History of an Infantile Neurosis, Standard Edition,* 17:7-122).

[5] *The Letters of Mary W. Shelley,* ed. Frederick L. Jones, 2 vols. (Norman, Okla., 1946), 2:88, 17 Nov. 1834. All subsequent references to this work, abbreviated *LMS* and with volume and page numbers, will be included in the text.

[6] Mary Shelley, *Mathilda,* ed. Elizabeth Nitchie (Chapel Hill, N. C., 1959), pp. 11, 24. Although written in 1819, this novel was first published in 1959.

[7] Mary Shelley, *Lodore,* 3 vols. (London, 1835), 1:29. All further references to this work, abbreviated *L* and with volume and page numbers, will be included in the text.

[8] Mary Shelley, *The Fortunes of Perkin Warbeck,* 3 vols. (London, 1830), 2:178; *Falkner: A Novel,* 2 vols. (London, 1837; rpt. Folcroft, Pa., 1975), 1:300. All further references to this work, abbreviated *Fa* and with volume and page numbers, will be included in the text.

[9] *Mary Shelley's Journal,* ed. Jones (Norman, Okla., 1947), p. 205, 21 Oct. 1838.

[10] Percy Bysshe Shelley, *The Mask of Anarchy, The Complete Poetical Works of Percy Bysshe Shelley,* ed. Thomas Hutchinson (London, 1943), 1. 37. All further references to Shelley's prose taken from this work, abbreviated *CP,* will be included in the text. All further poetry references, also taken from this edition, will be identified by line number in the text. *The Revolt of Islam* will be abbreviated *I* and *Prince Athanase, PA.*

[11] *The Letters of Percy Bysshe Shelley,* ed. Jones, 2 vols. (London, 1964), 1:171, 10 Nov. 1811.

[12] Jean Overton Fuller, *Shelley: A Biography* (London, 1968), p. 45.

[13] I am speaking here of how Godwin's philosophy operated upon Percy psychologically. Godwin's actual advice was that the young heir reconcile himself with his wealthy father. If Godwin was dispassionately concerned with patching up the hallowed relation of parent and child, he was also passionately aware how much Percy's financial gifts depended upon the son's access to the father's purse.

[14] William Wordsworth, *The Excursion, The Poetical Works of Wordsworth,* ed. Hutchinson and Ernest de Selincourt (London, 1936), 1. 300.

[15] Mary Shelley, *Valperga; or, The Life and Adventures of Castruccio, Prince of Lucca,* 3 vols. (London, 1823), 3:92-93. All further references to this work, abbreviated *V* and with volume and page numbers, will be included in the text.

[16] Mary Shelley, *The Last Man* (London, 1826; rpt. Lincoln, Nebr., 1965), p. 280.

[17] Elsewhere in *Lodore,* Ethel's "affection for her father gathered strength from the confidence which existed between them. He was the passion of her soul, the engrossing attachment of her loving heart" (*L,* 1:235). Probably most revealing—in the extreme care with which it is phrased—is the continuation of this passage.

> Her heart was bent upon pleasing him, she had no thought or pursuit which was not linked with his participation.

> There is perhaps in the list of human sensations, no one so pure, so perfect, and yet so impassioned, as the affection of a *child* for its parent, during that brief interval when *they* are leaving childhood, and have not yet felt love. There is something so *awful* in a father. His words are laws, and to obey them happiness. Reverence and a desire to serve, are mingled with gratitude; and duty, without a flaw or question, so second [sic] the instinct of the heart, as to render it imperative. Afterwards we may love, in

spite of the faults of the object of our attachment; but during the interval alluded to, we have not yet learnt to tolerate, but also, we have not learned to detect faults. All that a parent does, appears an emanation from a diviner world. [*L,* 1:235-36; my italics]

[18] Quoted from an unpublished letter in the Abinger collection in Nitchie, *Mary Shelley: Author of "Frankenstein"* (New Brunswick, N.J., 1953), p. 89.

[19] Eros and Agape are terms which I apply to the homicidal and the loving sides of Percy Shelley and of Victor Frankenstein. For the terms themselves, I draw upon Anders Nygren, *Agape and Eros,* trans. Philip S. Watson (Philadelphia, 1953; rpt. Chicago, 1982); Denis de Rougemont, *Love in the Western World,* trans. Montgomery Belgion (New York, 1940; rev. ed. New York, 1956); and M. C. D'Arcy's *The Mind and Heart of Love, Lion and Unicorn: A Study in Eros and Agape* (Cleveland, 1956). From the ancient mystery rites through Platonism, Neo-Platonism and Gnosticism, to the troubadours and the Tristan story of Wagner, Eros seeks "the deliverance of the soul from the prison-house of the body and the senses, and its restoration to its original heavenly home" (Nygren, p. 167). This Eros is essentially antisocial. "It despises the law-abiding and reasonable morality—marriage for example" (D'Arcy, p. 114). Agape, on the other hand, is based upon the Incarnation, and thus seeks not to escape from time into the absolute but "[to make] the best of time and of the present" (D'Arcy, p. 39). Marriage and love of neighbor are espoused because "the symbol of love is no longer the infinite *passion* of a soul in quest of light, but the *marriage* of Christ and the Church" (de Rougemont, p. 169).

[20] In his essay "On Love," Shelley says, "There is something within us which from the moment that we live, more and more thirsts after its likeness. . . . We dimly see within our intellectual nature a miniature as it were of our entire self yet deprived of all that we condemn or despise, the ideal prototype. . . . The discovery of its antitype . . . is the invisible and unattainable point to which Love tends" (*The Complete Works,* ed. Roger Ingpen and Walter E. Peck, 10 vols. [New York, 1965], 6:201-2). Shelley's word "antitype" seems to suggest complementarity by assuming the oppositeness, the "anti-ness" of the beloved, but Nathaniel Brown is correct that antitype in Shelley means "responding 'as an impression to the die'" (*Sexuality and Feminism in Shelley* [Cambridge, Mass., 1979], p. 36). The power of the lover, not the equality

of the beloved, is what Shelley's vision of the antitype establishes.

²¹ John A. Dussinger is probably hardest on Alphonse ("Kinship and Guilt in Mary Shelley's *Frankenstein*," *Studies in the Novel* 8 [Spring 1976]: 42-47; all further references to this essay, abbreviated "KG," will be included in the text). See also Hill, "Physiognomy of Desire," pp. 345-46; Hirsch, "The Monster Was a Lady," p. 128; Knoepflmacher, "AD," pp. 104-5; and George Levine, "*Frankenstein* and the Tradition of Realism," *Novel* 7 (Fall 1973): 20. Christopher Small goes too far in the opposite direction, asserting that Frankenstein "never shows anything for his father but pious regard" (*Ariel Like a Harpy: Shelley, Mary, and "Frankenstein"* [London, 1972], p. 193). There are unquestionably oedipal aspects to Victor's behavior. John V. Murphy emphasizes these elements in Shelley's early work. The father who ruins a young man's mother appears in *Zastrozzi* and in "Revenge." Even here, however, one needs caution. Father-killing in *Zastrozzi* is, Murphy says, "a simple matter and actually takes place outside the story's action" (*The Dark Angel: Gothic Elements in Shelley's Work* [Lewisburg, Pa., 1975], p. 29). The very fact that the killing occurs offstage precludes its being a simple matter. Shelley's more mature work features the father as blighter of his children's lives. In "Rosalind and Helen" (1818), the lovers reach "the altar stair, / When my father came from a distant land, / And with a loud and fearful cry / Rushed between us suddenly" (ll. 290-3). *The Cenci*, of course, allows Shelley unlimited expression of antipaternal sentiment. "Such merriment again / As fathers make over their children's graves . . . tortured me from my forgotten years, / As parents only dare" (1.3.124-25; 3.1.72-73). Judith Wilt wisely rejects any simple oedipal interpretation of such materials. "A Freudian might see in the whole progress of Frankenstein . . . a wish to join his dead mother in the grave: but . . . the Gothic adds an extra dimension, a profound resentment of the sources of one's being, especially the female sources, stemming from the desire to be one's own source—and goal" (*Ghosts of the Gothic: Austen, Eliot, and Lawrence* [Princeton, N.J., 1980], p. 39).

²² Mary Shelley, *Frankenstein; or, The Modern Prometheus (The 1818 Text)*, ed. James Rieger (Indianapolis, 1974; rpt. Chicago, 1982). All further references to this work, abbreviated *F*, will be included in the text.

²³ Kaplan and Kloss, "Fantasy of Paternity," pp. 122-23.

²⁴ Levine, "The Tradition of Realism," p. 21.

²⁵ Mary Shelley, *The Last Man*, pp. 24-25.

²⁶ Wilt, *Ghosts of the Gothic*, p. 29.

²⁷ Ibid., p. 14.

²⁸ Freud, "Dostoevsky and Parricide," *Sigmund Freud: Collected Papers*, ed. Ernest Jones, The International Psycho-Analytical Library, 5 vols. (New York, 1959), 5:232.

²⁹ Régis Durand, "'The Captive King': The Absent Father in Melville's Text," in *The Fictional Father: Lacanian Readings of the Text*, ed. Robert Con Davis (Amherst, Mass., 1981), p. 70; Jean-Michel Rabaté, "A Clown's Inquest into Paternity: Fathers Dead or Alive in *Ulysses* and *Finnegans Wake*," in Davis, *The Fictional Father*, p. 88; Dianne F. Sadoff, *Monsters of Affection: Dickens, Eliot, and Brontë on Fatherhood* (Baltimore, 1982), p. 38; Richard Barickman, Susan McDonald, and Myra Stark, *Corrupt Relations: Dickens, Thackeray, Trollope, Collins, and the Victorian Sexual System* (New York, 1982), p. 169; John T. Irwin, *Doubling and Incest / Repetition and Revenge: A Speculative Reading of Faulkner* (Baltimore, 1975), p. 119; Sadoff, *Monsters of Affection*, p. 45. Useful for understanding fathers is Ernest Jones, "The Phantasy of the Reversal of Generations," *Papers on Psycho-Analysis* (Boston, 1961), pp. 407-12. For self-generation in Shakespeare see C. L. Barber's "'Thou That Beget'st Him That Did Thee Beget': Transformation in 'Pericles' and 'The Winter's Tale,'" *Shakespeare Survey* 22 (1969): 59-67. Among other authors concerned with self-generation, Dickens has elicited particularly good analyses; see Lawrence Jay Dessner, "*Great Expectations*: The Ghost of a Man's Own Father," *PMLA* 91 (May 1976): 436-49; Albert D. Hutter, "Nation and Generation in *A Tale of Two Cities*," *PMLA* 93 (May 1978): 448-62; Branwen Bailey Pratt, "Dickens and Father: Notes on the Family Romance," *Hartford Studies in Literature* 8, no. 1 (1976): 4-22. For fathers in nineteenth-century American literature see Eric J. Sundquist, *Home as Found: Authority and Genealogy in Nineteenth-Century American Literature* (Baltimore, 1979).

³⁰ Harold Bloom, "Freud's Concepts of Defense and the Poetic Will," in *The Literary Freud: Mechanisms of Defense and the Poetic Will*, ed. Joseph H. Smith, M.D., Psychiatry and the Humanities, vol. 4 (New Haven, 1980), p. 6. Bloom's most extended discussion of Shelley and origins is "Shelley and His Precursors," in *Poetry and Repression: Revisionism from Blake to Stevens* (New Haven, Conn., 1976), pp. 83-111. See also *The Anxiety of Influence* (New York, 1973), and *A Map of Misreading* (New York, 1975). Self-generation in Shelley is discussed by Leslie Brisman in *Romantic Origins* (Ithaca, N.Y., 1978).

³¹ Medwin, *Shelley*, p. 375.

³² Ibid., p. 434.

³³ In his persuasive study of the psychological forces shaping *Prometheus Unbound*, Leon Waldoff sees

Shelley caught between oedipal rage at father and guilt at that rage. Shelley's solution, according to Waldoff, is to give hate "guiltless expression through moral assertiveness" ("The Father-Son Conflict in *Prometheus Unbound:* The Psychology of a Vision," *Psychoanalytic Review* 62 [1975]: 92). Aggressive feelings merge and then emerge as moral superiority. A related psychology is at work, Irwin notes, in Thomas Sutpen. "The son tries to overcome the mastery of the personal father while maintaining the mastery of fatherhood—a mechanism in which the personal father dies without the son's having to kill him" (*Doubling and Incest*, p. 99).

[34] William H. Marshall, "The Father-Child Symbolism in *Prometheus Unbound*," *Modern Language Quarterly* 22 (Mar. 1961): 45.

[35] Interestingly, Shelley's first poetic persona, the Margaret Nicholson whose poems "Fitzvictor" supposedly edits in Percy's second volume of verse, is another woman from the past who expresses homicidal inclinations toward authoritative males. She is, Shelley tells us, "that noted Female who attempted the life of the King in 1786" (*CP*, p. 861).

[36] For various recent viewpoints on *The Cenci* (and bibliographies of earlier work) see Sara Mason Miller, "Irony in Shelley's *The Cenci*," *University of Mississippi Studies in English* 9 (1968): 23-35; Earl R. Wasserman, *Shelley: A Critical Reading* (Baltimore, 1977), pp. 84-128; Stuart Curran, *Shelley's "Cenci": Scorpions Ringed with Fire* (Princeton, 1970); Justin G. Turner, "*The Cenci*, Shelley vs. the Truth," *American Book Collector* 22 (Feb. 1972): 5-9; Arline R. Thorn, "Shelley's *The Cenci* as Tragedy," *Costerus* 9 (1973): 219-28; P. Jay Delmar, "Evil and Character in Shelley's *The Cenci*," *Massachusetts Studies in English* 6, no. 1, 2 (1977): 37-48; Fred L. Milne, "Shelley's *The Cenci*: The Ice Motif and the Ninth Circle of Dante's Hell," *Tennessee Studies in Literature* 22 (1977): 117-32; Ronald L. Lemoncelli, "Cenci as Corrupt Dramatic Poet," *English Language Notes* 16 (Dec. 1978): 103-17; James D. Wilson, "Beatrice Cenci and Shelley's Vision of Moral Responsibility," *Ariel* 9 (July 1978): 75-89; James B. Twitchell, "Shelley's Use of Vampirism in *The Cenci*," *Tennessee Studies in Literature* 24 (1979): 120-33.

[37] The one critic to notice that the deaths proceed in the order of increased intimacy is Frank H. McCloskey ("Mary Shelley's *Frankenstein*," in *The Humanities in the Age of Science*, ed. Charles Argoff [Rutherford, N.J., 1968], p. 137). David Seed suggests that "since he is ultimately responsible for all their deaths we could see Frankenstein progressively killing off more and more humanizing aspects of his self" ("*Frankenstein*—Parable of Spectacle?" *Criticism* 24 [Fall 1982]: 332). Seed does not, however, go on to explain how Alphonse

as the last of the family fatalities might be the most humane aspect of Victor's self. Martin Tropp argues that Frankenstein is destroying rivals for his parents' love (*Mary Shelley's Monster: The Story of "Frankenstein"* [Boston, 1977], pp. 20-27). David Ketterer, moving out from Tropp, suggests, I think quite incorrectly, that sibling rivalry explains why Alphonse is *not* murdered. "He dies 'naturally' of grief" (*Frankenstein's Creation: The Book, the Monster, and Human Reality*, ELS Monograph Series, no. 16 [Victoria, B.C., 1979], p. 64). Ketterer goes on to recognize Victor's "ambivalence" toward Alphonse, but does not see the father killed by the son. More generally, Paul A. Cantor maintains that "something in Frankenstein wants to kill anyone who comes close to him so that he can maintain his willful isolation" ("The Nightmare of Romantic Idealism," in *Creature and Creator: Myth-making and English Romanticism* [New York, 1984], p. 118).

[38] See Freud, "Remembering, Repeating, and Working-Through (Further Recommendations on the Technique of Psycho-Analysis 2)," *Standard Edition* 12: 145-56.

[39] "A" names are an important feature of Gothic fiction and an odd fact of nineteenth-century life. "A" names in Gothic fiction are discussed by Eve Kosofsky Sedgwick in "The Character in the Veil: Imagery of the Surface in the Gothic Novel," *PMLA* 96 (Mar. 1981): 261. In a Gothic novel which Mary Shelley knew well, *The Monk*, "A" names proliferate obsessively. Besides the two main characters, Ambrosio and Antonia, there are Agnes, Sister Agatha, d'Albornos, Alonzo, and Alphonso d'Alsarada. How "A" names function in nineteenth-century life is a large vexed topic which I have only begun to explore. In the Gothic family in which the Gothic master Ambrose Bierce grew up, for example, all thirteen children received "A" names. This was in keeping with a family tradition which went back to the seventeenth century and which gave "A" names to every male from the original settler Austin to Ambrose's father Marcus Aurelius. Part of Bierce's rage at his family may be reflected in his refusal to give his own children "A" names.

Margaret Homans (essay date 1986)

SOURCE: "Bearing Demons: *Frankenstein*'s Circumvention of the Maternal," in *Bearing the Word*, University of Chicago Press, 1986, pp. 100-19.

[*In the following chapter from her* Bearing the Word, *Homans uses the tools of feminist psychoanalytic theory to study* Frankenstein *as a parallel between writing and mothering. In this view, Shelley becomes a champion of maternal nurturing, and the novel an indictment of the male desire to reject or excise the maternal role altogether.*]

Married to one romantic poet and living near another, Mary Shelley at the time she was writing *Frankenstein* experienced with great intensity the self-contradictory demand that daughters embody both the mother whose death makes language possible by making it necessary and the figurative substitutes for that mother who constitute the prototype of the signifying chain. At the same time, as a mother herself, she experienced with far greater intensity . . . a proto-Victorian ideology of motherhood, as Mary Poovey has shown.[1] This experience leads Shelley both to figure her writing as mothering and to bear or transmit the words of her husband.[2] Thus Shelley not only practices the daughter's obligatory and voluntary identification with the literal, as do Dorothy Wordsworth and Charlotte and Emily Brontë, but she also shares with George Eliot and Elizabeth Gaskell (and again with Charlotte Brontë) their concern with writing as literalization, as a form of mothering. It is to Shelley's handling of these contradictory demands, and to her criticism of their effect on women's writing, that my reading of *Frankenstein* will turn.

Frankenstein portrays the situation of women obliged to play the role of the literal in a culture that devalues it. In this sense, the novel is simultaneously about the death and obviation of the mother and about the son's quest for a substitute object of desire. The novel criticizes the self-contradictory male requirement that that substitute at once embody and not embody (because all embodiment is a reminder of the mother's powerful and forbidden body) the object of desire. The horror of the demon that Frankenstein creates is that it is the literalization of its creator's desire for an object, a desire that never really seeks its own fulfillment.

Many readers of *Frankenstein* have noted both that the demon's creation amounts to an elaborate circumvention of normal heterosexual procreation—Frankenstein does by himself with great difficulty what a heterosexual couple can do quite easily—and that each actual mother dies very rapidly upon being introduced as a character in the novel.[3] Frankenstein's own history is full of the deaths of mothers. His mother was discovered, as a poverty-stricken orphan, by Frankenstein's father. Frankenstein's adoptive sister and later fiancée, Elizabeth, was likewise discovered as an orphan, in poverty, by Frankenstein's parents.[4] Elizabeth catches scarlet fever, and her adoptive mother, nursing her, catches it herself and dies of it. On her deathbed, the mother hopes for the marriage of Elizabeth and Frankenstein and tells Elizabeth, "You must supply my place to my younger children" (chap. 3). Like Shelley herself, Elizabeth is the death of her mother and becomes a substitute for her. Justine, a young girl taken in by the Frankenstein family as a beloved servant, is said to cause the death of her mother; and Justine herself, acting as foster mother to Frankenstein's little brother, William, is executed for

his murder. There are many mothers in the Frankenstein circle, and all die notable deaths.

The significance of the apparently necessary destruction of the mother first emerges in Frankenstein's account of his preparations for creating the demon, and it is confirmed soon after the demon comes to life. Of his early passion for science, Frankenstein says, "I was . . . deeply smitten with the thirst for knowledge" (chap. 2). Shelley confirms the oedipal suggestion here when she writes that it is despite his father's prohibition that the young boy devours the archaic books on natural philosophy that first raise his ambitions to discover the secret of life. His mother dies just as Frankenstein is preparing to go to the University of Ingolstadt, and if his postponed trip there is thus motivated by her death, what he finds at the university becomes a substitute for her: modern scientists, he is told, "penetrate into the recesses of nature and show how she works in her hiding-places" (chap. 3). Frankenstein's double, Walton, the polar explorer who rescues him and records his story, likewise searches for what sound like sexual secrets, also in violation of a paternal prohibition. Seeking to "satiate [his] ardent curiosity," Walton hopes to find the "wondrous power which attracts the needle" (letter 1). Frankenstein, having become "capable of bestowing animation upon lifeless matter," feels that to arrive "at once at the summit of my desires was the most gratifying consummation of my toils." And his work to create the demon adds to this sense of an oedipal violation of Mother Nature: dabbling "among the unhallowed damps of the grave," he "disturbed, with profane fingers, the tremendous secrets of the human frame" (chap. 4). This violation is necrophiliac. The mother he rapes is dead; his researches into her secrets, to usurp her powers, require that she be dead.[5]

Frankenstein describes his violation of nature in other ways that recall what William Wordsworth's poetry reveals when read in conjunction with Dorothy Wordsworth's journals. Of the period during which he is working on the demon, Frankenstein writes,

> The summer months passed while I was thus engaged, heart and soul, in one pursuit. It was a most beautiful season; never did the fields bestow a more plentiful harvest or the vines yield a more luxuriant vintage, but my eyes were insensible to the charms of nature. . . . Winter, spring, and summer passed away during my labours; but I did not watch the blossom or the expanding leaves—sights which before always yielded me supreme delight—so deeply was I engrossed in my occupation. (chap. 4)

Ignoring the bounteous offering nature makes of itself and substituting for it his own construction of life, what we, following Thomas Weiskel, might call his own reading of nature, Frankenstein here resembles

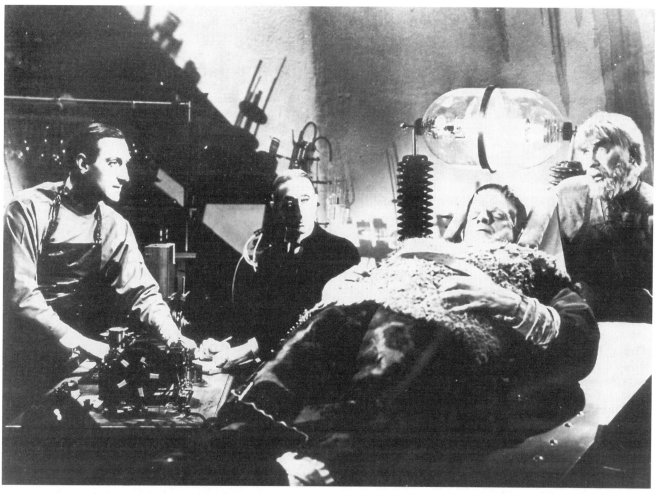

Basil Rathbone and Bela Lugosi examine Karloff, as the monster, while a scientist looks on. From Son of Frankenstein, *1939.*

William Wordsworth, reluctantly and ambivalently allowing himself to read nature, to impose on nature apocalyptic patterns of meaning that destroy it. Dorothy Wordsworth herself makes an appearance in the text of **Frankenstein,** if indirectly, and her presence encodes a shared women's critique of the romantic reading of nature. Much later in the novel, Frankenstein compares his friend Clerval to the former self William Wordsworth depicts in "Tintern Abbey," a self that he has outgrown but that his sister remains. Shelley quotes (with one major alteration) the lines beginning, "The sounding cataract / Haunted him like a passion" and ending with the assertion that the colors and forms of natural objects (rock, mountain, etc.) were

> a feeling, and a love,
> That had no need of a remoter charm,
> By thought supplied, or any interest
> Unborrow'd from the eye.[6]

If Clerval is like Dorothy, then Frankenstein is like William, regrettably destroying nature by imposing his reading on it.

When, assembled from the corpse of nature, the demon has been brought to life and Frankenstein has recognized—oddly only now that it is alive—how hideous it is, Frankenstein falls into an exhausted sleep and dreams the following dream:

> I thought I saw Elizabeth, in the bloom of health, walking in the streets of Ingolstadt. Delighted and surprised, I embraced her, but as I imprinted the first kiss on her lips, they became livid with the hue of death; her features appeared to change, and I thought that I held the corpse of my dead mother in my arms; a shroud enveloped her form, and I saw the grave-worms crawling in the folds of the flannel. I started from my sleep with horror. (chap. 5)

He wakes to see the demon looking at him, hideous, but clearly loving. The dream suggests that to bring the demon to life is equivalent to killing Elizabeth, and that Elizabeth dead is equivalent to his mother dead. Elizabeth may have been the death of the mother, but now that she has replaced her, she too is vulnerable to whatever destroys mothers.[7] And, indeed, the dream is prophetic: the demon will much later kill Elizabeth, just as the demon's creation has required both the death of Frankenstein's own mother and the death and violation of Mother Nature. To bring a composite corpse to life is to circumvent the normal channels of procreation; the demon's "birth" violates the normal relations of family, especially the normal sexual relation of husband and wife. Victor has gone to great lengths to produce a child without Elizabeth's assistance, and in the dream's language, to circumvent her, to make her unnecessary, is to kill her, and to kill mothers altogether.

Frankenstein's creation, then, depends on and then perpetuates the death of the mother and of motherhood. The demon's final, and greatest, crime is in fact its murder of Elizabeth, which is, however, only the logical extension of its existence as the reification of Frankenstein's desire to escape the mother. The demon is, to borrow a phrase from Shelley's *Alastor*, "the spirit of" Frankenstein's "solitude." Its greatest complaint to Frankenstein is of its own solitude, its isolation from humanity, and it promises that if Frankenstein will make it a mate, "one as hideous as myself. . . . I shall become a thing of whose existence everyone will be ignorant" (chap. 17). That is, no longer solitary, the demon will virtually cease to exist, for its existence is synonymous with its solitude. But, on the grounds that "a race of devils would be propagated upon the earth," Frankenstein destroys the female demon he is in the process of creating, thus destroying yet another potential mother, and the demon promises, "I shall be with you on your wedding-night" (chap. 20). If the demon is the form taken by Frankenstein's flight from the mother, then it is impossible that the demon should itself find an embodied substitute for the mother, and it will prevent Frankenstein from finding one too.

The demon's promise to be present at the wedding night suggests that there is something monstrous about Frankenstein's sexuality. A solipsist's sexuality is monstrous because his desire is for his own envisionings rather than for somebody else, some other body. The demon appears where Frankenstein's wife should be, and its murder of her suggests not so much revenge as jealousy. The demon's murder of that last remaining potential mother makes explicit the sequel to the obviation of the mother, the male quest for substitutes for the mother, the quest that is never intended to be fulfilled. Elizabeth suggests in a letter to Frankenstein that his reluctance to marry may stem from his love for someone else, someone met, perhaps, in his travels or during his long stay in Ingolstadt. "Do you not love another?" she asks (chap. 22). This is in fact the case, for the demon, the creation of Frankenstein's imagination, resembles in many ways the romantic object of desire, the beloved invented to replace, in a less threatening form, the powerful mother who must be killed.[8]

This imagined being would be an image of the self, because it is for the sake of the ego that the mother is rejected in the first place. Created right after the death of the mother to be, as Victor says, "a being like myself" (chap. 4), the demon may be Adam, created in God's image. Indeed, this is what the demon thinks when it tells Frankenstein, "I ought to be thy Adam, but I am rather the fallen angel" (chap. 10). But it is also possible, as Gilbert and Gubar suggest, that the demon is Eve, created from Adam's imagination.[9]

When the demon takes shelter in the French cottager's shed, it looks, repeating Milton's Eve's first act upon coming to life, into the mirror of a "clear pool" and is terrified at its own reflection: "I started back" (chap. 12). Here is the relevant passage from Milton, from Eve's narration in book 4 of her memory of the first moments of her creation.[10] Hearing the "murmuring sound / Of waters issu'd from a Cave and spread / Into a liquid Plain," Eve looks

> into the clear
> Smooth Lake, that to me seem'd another Sky.
> As I bent down to look, just opposite,
> A Shape within the wat'ry gleam appear'd
> Bending to look on me, I started back,
> It started back, but pleas'd I soon return'd . . .
> (4.453-63)

But the disembodied voice instructs her, "What there thou seest fair Creature is thyself" (468), and tells her to follow and learn to prefer him "whose image thou art" (471-72). Christine Froula argues that the fiction of Eve's creation by a paternal God out of the flesh of Adam values the maternal and appropriates it for the aggrandisement of masculine creativity.[11] Frankenstein revises this paradigm for artistic creation: he does not so much appropriate the maternal as bypass it, to demonstrate the unnecessariness of natural motherhood and, indeed, of women. Froula points out that in this "scene of canonical instruction," Eve is required to turn away from herself to embrace her new identity, not as a self, but as the image of someone else.[12] Created to the specifications of Adam's desire, we later learn—"Thy likeness, thy fit help, thy other self, / Thy wish, exactly to thy heart's desire" (8. 450-51)—Eve is, like Frankenstein's demon, the product of imaginative desire. Milton appropriates the maternal by excluding any actual mother from the scene of creation. Eve is the form that Adam's desire takes once actual motherhood has been eliminated; and in much the same way, the demon is the form taken by Frankenstein's desire once his mother and Elizabeth as mother have been circumvented. These new creations in the image of the self are substitutes for the powerful creating mother and place creation under the control of the son.

That the demon is, like Eve, the creation of a son's imaginative desire is confirmed by another allusion both closer to Shelley and closer in the text to Elizabeth's question, "Do you not love another?" Mary Poovey has argued that the novel criticizes romantic egotism, specifically, Percy Shelley's violation of the social conventions that bind humans together in families and societies. As the object of desire of an imaginative overreacher very like Percy Shelley himself, the demon substitutes for the fruitful interchange of family life the fruitlessness of self love, for what Frankenstein loves is an image of himself. The novel was written when Percy Shelley had completed, of all his major works besides *Queen Mab,* only *Alastor,* the archetypal poem of the doomed romantic quest, and it is to this poem that Mary Shelley alludes.[13] Just before Frankenstein receives Elizabeth's letter, just after being acquitted of the murder of his friend Clerval, Frankenstein tells us, "I saw around me nothing but a dense and frightful darkness, penetrated by no light but the glimmer of two eyes that glared upon me" (chap. 21). This is a direct allusion to a passage in *Alastor* in which the hero, who has quested in vain after an ideal female image of his own creation, sees

> two eyes,
> Two starry eyes, hung in the gloom of
>   thought,
> And seemed with their serene and azure
>   smiles
> To beckon him.
>
> (489-92)

In *Alastor,* these eyes belong to the phantom maiden, the "fleeting shade" whom the hero pursues to his death, a beloved who is constructed out of the poet's own visionary narcissism. The girl he dreams and pursues has a voice "like the voice of his own soul / Heard in the calm of thought" (153-54), and like him, she is "Herself a poet" (161). In the novel, the starry eyes become glimmering, glaring eyes, alternately the eyes of the dead Clerval and the "watery, clouded eyes of the monster, as I first saw them in my chamber at Ingolstadt" (chap. 21). This conflation of the eyes of the poet's beloved with the eyes of the demon suggests, even more surely than the allusion to Eve, that the demon is the form, not only of Frankenstein's solipsism, of his need to obviate the mother, but also of the narcissism that constitutes the safety of the ego for whose sake the mother is denied. The monster is still the object of Frankenstein's desire when Elizabeth writes to him, just as its creation was the object of his initial quest.[14] It is this monster, the monster of narcissism, that intervenes on the wedding night, substituting Frankenstein's desire for his own imagining for the consummation of his marriage, just as the visionary maiden in *Alastor* takes the place both of the dead Mother Nature of the poet's prologue and of the real maiden the hero meets, attracts, and rejects in the course of his quest.

That the demon is a revision of Eve, of emanations, and of the object of romantic desire, is confirmed by its female attributes. Its very bodiliness, its identification with matter, associates it with traditional concepts of femaleness. Further, the impossibility of Frankenstein giving it a female demon, an object of its own desire, aligns the demon with women, who are forbidden to have their own desires. But if the demon is really a feminine object of desire, why is it a he? I would suggest that this constitutes part of Shelley's exposure of the male romantic economy that would substitute for real and therefore powerful female others a being imagined on the model of the male poet's own self. By making the demon masculine, Shelley suggests that romantic desire seeks to do away, not only with the mother, but also with all females so as to live finally in a world of mirrors that reflect a comforting illusion of the male self's independent wholeness. It is worth noting that just as Frankenstein's desire is for a male demon, Walton too yearns, not for a bride, but for "the company of a man who could sympathize with me, whose eyes would reply to mine" (letter 2).[15]

It may seem peculiar to describe the demon as the object of Frankenstein's romantic desire, since he spends most of the novel suffering from the demon's crimes. Yet in addition to the allusions to Eve and the "fleeting shade" in *Alastor* that suggest this, it is clear that while Frankenstein is in the process of creating the demon, he loves it and desires it; the knowledge that makes possible its creation is the "consummation" of his "toils." It is only when the demon becomes animated that Frankenstein abruptly discovers his loathing for his creation. Even though the demon looks at its creator with what appears to be love, Frankenstein's response to it is unequivocal loathing. Why had he never noticed before the hideousness of its shape and features? No adequate account is given, nor could be, for as we shall see, this is what most mystifies and horrifies Shelley about her own situation. Frankenstein confesses, "I had desired it with an ardour that far exceeded moderation; but now that I had finished, the beauty of the dream vanished, and breathless horror and disgust filled my heart" (chap. 5). The romantic quest is always doomed, for it secretly resists its own fulfillment: although the hero of *Alastor* quests for his dream maiden and dies of not finding her, his encounter with the Indian maid makes it clear that embodiment is itself an obstacle to desire, or more precisely, its termination. Frankenstein's desire for his creation lasts only so long as that creation remains uncreated, the substitution for the too-powerful mother of a figure issuing from his imagination and therefore under his control.

To return to the terms with which we began in chapter 1, we might say that the predicament of Frankenstein, as of the hero of *Alastor,* is that of the son in Lacan's revision of the Freudian oedipal crisis. In flight from the body of the mother forbidden by the father, a maternal body that he sees as dead in his urgency to escape it and to enter a paternal order constituted of its distance from the mother, the son seeks figurations that will at once make restitution for the mother and confirm her death and absence by substituting for her figures that are under his control. Fundamentally, the son cannot wish for these figurative substitutes to be embodied, for any *body* is too reminiscent of the mother and is no longer under the son's control, as the demon's excessive strength demonstrates; the value of these figurations is that they remain figurations. In just this way, romantic desire does not desire to be fulfilled, and yet, because it seems both to itself and to others to want to be embodied, the romantic quester as son is often confronted with a body he seems to want but does not.[16] Thus Frankenstein thinks he wants to create the demon, but when he has succeeded, he discovers that what he really enjoyed was the process leading up to the creation, the seemingly endless chain of signifiers that constitute his true, if unrecognized, desire.

Looking at *Alastor* through *Frankenstein*'s reading of it, then, we see that the novel is the story of a hypothetical case: what if the hero of *Alastor* actually got what he thinks he wants? What if desire were embodied, contrary to the poet's deepest wishes? That Shelley writes such a case suggests that this was her own predicament. In real life, Percy Shelley pursued her as the poet and hero of *Alastor* pursue ghosts and as Frankenstein pursues the secrets of the grave. That he courted the adolescent Mary Godwin at the grave of her mother, whose writing he admired, already suggests that the daughter was for him a figure for the safely dead mother, a younger and less powerfully creative version of her. Yet when he got this substitute, he began to tire of her, as he makes quite explicit in *Epipsychidion*, where he is not embarrassed to describe his life in terms of an interminable quest for an imaginary woman. Mary starts out in that poem as one "who seemed / As like the glorious shape which I had dreamed" (277-78) but soon becomes "that Moon" with "pale and waning lips" (309). The poet does not seem to notice that each time an embodiment of the ideal turns out to be unsatisfactory, it is not because she is the wrong woman, but because the very fact of embodiment inevitably spoils the vision. Emily, the final term in the poem's sequence of women, remains ideal only because she has not yet been possessed, and indeed at the end of the poem, the poet disintegrates and disembodies her, perhaps to save himself from yet one more disappointment. Shelley was for herself never anything but embodied, but for Percy Shelley it seems to have been a grave disappointment to discover her substantiality, and therefore her inadequacy for fulfilling his visionary requirements. *Frankenstein* is the story of what it feels like to be the undesired embodiment of romantic imaginative desire. The demon, re-

jected merely for being a body, suffers in something of the way that Shelley must have felt herself to suffer under the conflicting demands of romantic desire: on the one hand, that she must embody the goal of Percy's quest, and on the other, his rejection of that embodiment.

Later in the novel, when the demon describes to Frankenstein its discovery and reading of the "journal of the four months that preceded my creation," the discrepancy between Percy's conflicting demands is brought to the fore. The demon notes that the journal records "the whole detail of that series of disgusting circumstances" that resulted in "my accursed origin," and that "the minutest description of my odious and loathsome person is given, in language which painted your own horrors and rendered mine indelible" (chap. 15). This summary suggests that while Frankenstein was writing the journal during the period leading up to the demon's vivification, he was fully aware of his creature's hideousness. Yet Frankenstein, in his own account of the same period, specifically says that it was only when "I had finished, the beauty of the dream vanished, and breathless horror and disgust filled my heart" (chap. 5). If Frankenstein is right about his feelings here, why should his journal be full of "language which painted [his] horrors"? Or, if the account in the journal is correct, if Frankenstein was aware from the start of his creature's "odious and loathsome person," why does he tell Walton that the demon appeared hideous to him only upon its awakening? If the text of this journal is, like *Alastor*, the record of a romantic quest for an object of desire, then the novel is presenting us with two conflicting readings of the poem—Frankenstein's or Percy's and the demon's or Shelley's—confirming our sense that Shelley reading *Alastor* finds in it the story of Percy's failure to find in her the object of his desire, or the story of his desire not to find the object of his desire, not to find that she is the object.

A famous anecdote about the Shelleys from a few days after the beginning of the ghost story contest in which *Frankenstein* originated lends support to this impression of Shelley's experience. Byron was reciting some lines from Coleridge's *Christabel* about Geraldine, who is, like the demon, a composite body, half young and beautiful, half (in the version Byron recited) "hideous, deformed, and pale of hue." Percy, "suddenly shrieking and putting his hands to his head, ran out of the room with a candle." Brought to his senses, he told Byron and Polidori that "he was looking at Mrs. Shelley" while Byron was repeating Coleridge's lines, "and suddenly thought of a woman he had heard of who had eyes instead of nipples."[17] If disembodied eyes are, in *Alastor*, what are so alluring to the hero about his beloved, eyes in place of nipples may have been Percy's hallucination of the horror of having those ideal eyes reembodied in the form of his real lover. This is an embodiment that furthermore calls attention to its failure to be sufficiently different from the mother, whose nipples are for the baby so important a feature. An actual woman, who is herself a mother, does not fit the ideal of disembodied femininity, and the vision of combining real and ideal is a monster. Mary's sense of herself viewed as a collection of incongruent body parts—breasts terminating in eyes—might have found expression in the demon, whose undesirable corporeality is expressed as its being composed likewise of ill-fitting parts. *Paradise Lost, Alastor,* and other texts in this tradition compel women readers to wish to embody, as Eve does, imaginary ideals, to be glad of this role in masculine life; and yet at the same time, they warn women readers that they will suffer for such embodiment.

It requires only a transposing of terms to suggest the relevance of this reading of **Frankenstein** to the myth of language we traced in chapter 1 in its form as the romantic quest. The demon is about the ambivalent response of a woman reader to some of our culture's most compelling statements of woman's place in the myth. That the mother must vanish and be replaced by never quite embodied figures for her is equivalent to the vanishing of the referent (along with that time with the mother when the referent had not vanished) to be replaced by language as figuration that never quite touches its objects. Women's role is to be that silent or lost referent, the literal whose absence makes figuration possible. To be also the figurative substitute for that lost referent is, Shelley shows, impossible, for women are constantly reminded that they are the mother's (loathed, loved) body, and in any case, "being" is incompatible with being a figure. The literal provokes horror in the male poet, or scientist, even while he demands that women literalize his vision.

That Shelley knew she was writing a criticism, not only of women's self-contradictory role in androcentric ontology, but also of the gendered myth of language that is part of that ontology, is suggested by the appearance of a series of images of writing at the very end of the novel. Once again, the demon is the object of Frankenstein's quest, pursued now in hate rather than in love. Frankenstein is preternaturally motivated in his quest by an energy of desire that recalls his passion when first creating the demon, and that his present quest depends on the killing of animals recalls his first quest's dependence on dead bodies. Frankenstein believes that "a spirit of good" follows and directs his steps: "Sometimes, when nature, overcome by hunger, sank under the exhaustion, a repast was prepared for me in the desert that restored and inspirited me. . . . I will not doubt that it was set there by the spirits that I had invoked to aid me" (chap. 24). He says this, however, directly after pointing out that the demon sometimes helped him. Fearing "that if I lost all trace of him I should despair and die, [he] left some

mark to guide me," and Frankenstein also notes that the demon would frequently leave "marks in writing on the barks of the trees or cut in stone that guided me and instigated my fury." One of these messages includes the information, "You will find near this place, if you follow not too tardily, a dead hare; eat and be refreshed." Frankenstein, it would seem, deliberately misinterprets the demon's guidance and provisions for him as belonging instead to a spirit of good: his interpretation of the demon's marks and words is so figurative as to be opposite to what they really say. The demon, all body, writes appropriately on the body of nature messages that refer, if to objects at a distance, at least at not a very great distance ("you will find near this place . . ."). Frankenstein, however, reads as figuratively as possible, putting as great a distance as possible between what he actually reads and what he interprets. His reading furthermore puts a distance between himself and the object of his quest, which he still cannot desire to attain; figurative reading would extend indefinitely the pleasure of the quest itself by forever putting off the moment of capture. Just at the moment when Frankenstein thinks he is about to reach the demon, the demon is transformed from a "mark," as if a mark on a page, into a "form," and Frankenstein seeks to reverse this transformation. One of Frankenstein's sled dogs has died of exhaustion, delaying him; "suddenly my eye caught a dark speck upon the dusky plain"; he utters "a wild cry of ecstasy" upon "distinguish[ing] a sledge and the distorted proportions of a well-known form within" (chap. 24). Frankenstein's response, however, is to take an hour's rest: his real aim, which he does not admit, is to keep the demon at the distance where he remains a "dark speck," a mark on the white page of the snow, his signification forever deferred.[18]

At the same time that **Frankenstein** is about a woman writer's response to the ambiguous imperative her culture imposes upon her, it is also possible that the novel concerns a woman writer's anxieties about bearing children, about generating bodies that, as we have seen with reference to *Jane Eyre* and *Wuthering Heights,* would have the power to displace or kill the parent. Ellen Moers first opened up a feminist line of inquiry into the novel by suggesting that it is a "birth myth," that the horror of the demon is Shelley's horror, not only at her own depressing experience of childbirth, but also at her knowledge of the disastrous consequences of giving birth (or of pregnancy itself) for many women in her vicinity.[19] The list is by now familiar to Shelley's readers. First, Mary Wollstonecraft died eleven days after she gave birth to Mary; then, during the time of the writing of the novel, Fanny Imlay, Mary's half-sister, drowned herself in October 1816 when she learned that she was her mother's illegitimate child by Gilbert Imlay; Harriet Shelley was pregnant by another man when she drowned herself in the Serpentine in December 1816; and Claire Clairmont, the daughter of the second Mrs. Godwin, was, scandalously, pregnant by Byron, much to the embarrassment of the Shelleys, with whom she lived.[20] Illegitimate pregnancy, that is, a pregnancy over which the woman has particularly little control, brings either death to the mother in childbirth (Wollstonecraft) or shame, making visible what ought to have remained out of sight, the scene of conception (Claire), a shame that can itself result in the death of both mother (Harriet Shelley) and child (Fanny).

At the time of the conception of the novel, Mary Godwin had herself borne two illegitimate children: the first, an unnamed girl, died four days later, in March 1815; the second was five months old. In December 1816, when Harriet Shelley died and Shelley had finished chapter 4 of the novel, she was pregnant again. With but a single parent, the demon in her novel is the world's most monstrously illegitimate child, and this illegitimate child causes the death of that parent as well as of the principle of motherhood, as we have seen. Read in connection with the history of disastrous illegitimacies, the novel's logic would seem to be this: to give birth to an illegitimate child is monstrous, for it is the inexorable life of these babies, especially those of Mary Wollstonecraft and of Harriet Shelley, that destroys the life of the mother. Subsequently, as Marc Rubenstein argues, the guilty daughter pays for the destruction of her own mother in a fantasy of being destroyed by her own child.[21]

In *Jane Eyre* and *Wuthering Heights*, we saw that the image of childbirth is associated with the uncontrollability of real things. Once a conception has taken objective form, it has the power to destroy its own source, to transform the mother herself into the literal. In the Brontës' novels, childbirth is structurally equivalent to (and indeed also often situated in) the coming true of dreams, which has, like childbirth, an ironic relation to the original conception. Shelley's 1831 introduction to her novel makes a comparable equation of giving birth, the realization of a dream, and writing. As many readers have pointed out, this introduction to her revised version of the novel identifies the novel itself with the demon, and both with a child.[22] She tells of being asked every morning if she had thought of a story, as if a story, like a baby, were necessarily to be conceived in the privacy of the night. And at the close of the introduction she writes, "I bid my hideous progeny go forth and prosper," and she refers to the novel in the next sentence as "the offspring of happy days." The genesis of the novel, furthermore, is in a dream that she transcribes, a dream moreover that is about the coming true of a dream. One night, she says, after listening to conversation about the reanimation of corpses, "Night waned upon this talk. . . . When I placed my head on my pillow I did not sleep, nor could I be said to think. My imagination, unbidden, possessed and guided me." Then follows her account of the famous dream of "the pale student of unhal-

lowed arts kneeling beside the thing he had put together," the "hideous phantasm of a man" stirring "with an uneasy, half-vital motion," and the "artist" sleeping and waking to behold "the horrid thing . . . looking on him with yellow, watery, but speculative eyes." Waking in horror from her dream, she at first tries "to think of something else," but then realizes that she has the answer to her need for a ghost story: "'What terrified me will terrify others; and I need only describe the spectre which had haunted my midnight pillow.' . . . I began that day with the words, 'It was on a dreary night of November,' making only a transcript of the grim terrors of my waking dream." Making a transcript of a dream—that is, turning an idea into the "machinery of a story"—a dream that is about the transformation of a "phantasm" into a real body, is equivalent here to conceiving a child. She makes it very clear that her dream takes the place of a sexual act ("Night waned. . . . When I placed my head on my pillow . . . I saw the pale student."), just as the book idea she can announce the next day substitutes for a baby. The terrifying power of the possibility that her dream might be true encodes the terrifying power of conception and childbirth. In Deutsch's language, "she who has created this new life must obey its power; its rule is expected, yet invisible, implacable."[23]

Despite Ellen Moers's delineation of the resemblance of the demon to the apprehensions a mother might have about a baby, it is the introduction that supplies the most explicit evidence for identifying demon and book with a child. Mary Poovey has demonstrated that this introduction has a significantly different ideological cast from the original version of the novel (or even from the revised novel). Written in 1831, fourteen years after the novel itself and following the death of Percy Shelley (as well as the deaths of both the children who were alive or expected in 1816-17), the introduction takes pains to distance itself from the novel, and it aims to bring the writing of the novel further within the fold of the conventional domestic life Shelley retrospectively substitutes for the radically disruptive life she in fact led.[24] Referring obliquely to her elopement with Percy and its effect on her adolescent habit of inventing stories, for example, she writes, "After this my life became busier, and reality stood in place of fiction." Echoed later by Robert Southey's remark to Charlotte Brontë, that "literature cannot be the business of a woman's life," Shelley's busyness refers largely to her responsibilities as a mother and wife. When she describes her endeavor to write a ghost story she repeats this term for family responsibility: "I busied myself *to think of a story.*" This echo suggests that her busyness with story writing is somehow congruent with, not in conflict with, her "busier" life as a wife and mother. It makes the novel, "so very hideous an idea," seem somehow part of the busy life of a matron. It is this effort, to domesticate her hideous idea, that may be at the bottom of her characterizing it as a "hideous progeny." If the novel read in this light seems, like *Jane Eyre* and *Wuthering Heights,* to be full of a horror of childbirth, that may only be the result of the impossibility of changing the basic story of the 1817 novel, the result of assembling mismatched parts.

Thus the novel may be about the horror associated with motherhood, yet this reading seems unduly influenced by the superimpositions of the introduction, and furthermore it ignores the novel's most prominent feature, that the demon is not a child born of woman but the creation of a man.[25] Most succinctly put, the novel is about the collision between androcentric and gynocentric theories of creation, a collision that results in the denigration of maternal childbearing through its circumvention by male creation. The novel presents Mary Shelley's response to the expectation, manifested in such poems as *Alastor* or *Paradise Lost,* that women embody and yet not embody male fantasies. At the same time, it expresses a woman's knowledge of the irrefutable independence of the body, both her own and those of the children that she produces, from projective male fantasy. While a masculine being—God, Adam, Percy Shelley, Frankenstein—may imagine that his creation of an imaginary being may remain under the control of his desires, Mary Shelley knows otherwise, both through her experience as mistress and wife of Percy and through her experience of childbirth. Shelley's particular history shows irrefutably that children, even pregnancies, do not remain under the control of those who conceive them.

Keats writes that "the Imagination may be compared to Adam's dream—he awoke and found it truth."[26] In *Paradise Lost,* narrating his recollection of Eve's creation, Adam describes how he fell into a special sleep— "Mine eyes he clos'd, but op'n left the Cell / Of Fancy my internal sight" (8. 460-61)—then watched, "though sleeping," as God formed a creature,

> Manlike, but different sex, so lovely fair,
> That what seem'd fair in all the World,
>   seem'd now
> Mean, or in her summ'd up.
>   (8. 471-73)

This is "Adam's dream." But what of "he awoke and found it truth"? Adam wakes, "To find her, or for ever to deplore / Her loss" (479-80), and then, "behold[s] her, not far off, / Such as I saw her in my dream" (481-81), yet what Keats represses is that the matching of reality to dream is not so neat as these lines suggest.[27] Eve comes to Adam, not of her own accord, but "Led by her Heav'nly Maker" (485), and as soon as he catches sight of her, Adam sees Eve turn away from him, an action he ascribes to modesty (and thus endeavors to assimilate to his dream of her) but that Eve, in book 4, has already said stemmed from her preference for her image in the water. Though designed by

God for Adam "exactly to thy heart's desire" (8. 451), Eve once created has a mind and will of her own, and this independence is so horrifying to the male imagination that the Fall is ascribed to it.

It is neither the visionary male imagination alone that Mary Shelley protests, then, nor childbirth itself, but the circumvention of the maternal creation of new beings by the narcissistic creations of male desire. While Keats can gloss over the discrepancy between Adam's dream and its fulfillment, Shelley cannot. As Frankenstein is on the verge of completing the female demon, it is for her resemblance to Eve that he destroys her. Just as Adam says of Eve, "seeing me, she turn'd" (8. 507), Frankenstein fears the female demon's turning from the demon toward a more attractive image: "She also might turn with disgust from him to the superior beauty of man" (chap. 20). Also like Eve, who disobeys a prohibition agreed upon between Adam and God before her creation, she "might refuse to comply with a compact made before her creation," the demon's promise to leave Europe. Frankenstein typifies the way in which the biological creation of necessarily imperfect yet independent beings has always been made to seem, within an androcentric economy, monstrous and alarming. Although Mary Wollstonecraft would in any case have died of puerperal fever after Mary's birth, her earlier pregnancy with Fanny and the pregnancies of Harriet Shelley, Claire Clairmont, and Mary Godwin would have done no harm had they not been labeled "illegitimate" by a society that places a premium on the ownership by a man of his wife's body and children. The novel criticizes, not childbirth itself, but the male horror of independent embodiment. This permits us to speculate that the horror of childbirth in *Jane Eyre* and *Wuthering Heights* stems from the Brontës' identification with an androcentric perspective. To a certain extent, as a writer in a culture that defines writing as a male activity and as opposite to motherhood, Shelley too must share the masculine perspective, with its horror of embodiment and its perennial reenacting of Adam's affront at Eve's turning away. For whatever reason, however, perhaps because of her direct experience of the mother's position, Shelley is able to discern the androcentrism in her culture's view of the relation of childbearing to writing, and thus she enables us to interpret her own painful exposure of it.

At the site of the collision between motherhood and romantic projection another form of literalization appears as well. While it is important how Shelley reads texts such as *Alastor* and *Paradise Lost,* it is also important to consider, perhaps more simply, that her novel reads them. Like the Brontës' novels, whose gothic embodiments of subjective states, realizations of dreams, and literalized figures all literalize romantic projection, Shelley's novel literalizes romantic imagination, but with a different effect and to a different end. Shelley criticizes these texts by enacting them, and because enactment or embodiment is both the desire and the fear of such texts, the mode of her criticism matters. Just as the heroes of these poems seem to seek, but do not seek, embodiments of their visionary desires, these poetic texts seem to seek embodiment in "the machinery of a story." For in the ideology of postromantic culture, it is part of a woman's duty to transcribe and give form to men's words, just as it is her duty to give form to their desire, or birth to their seed, no matter how ambivalently men may view the results of such projects. In the same passage in the introduction to the novel in which Shelley makes the analogy between the book and a child, between the conception of a story and the conception of a baby, and between these things and the coming true of a dream, she also identifies all these projects with the transcription of important men's words. Drawing on the ideology of maternity as the process of passing on a male idea, Shelley describes her book-child as the literalization of two poets' words:

> Many and long were the conversations between Lord Byron and Shelley to which I was a devout but nearly silent listener. During one of these, various philosophical doctrines were discussed, and among others the nature of the principle of life, and whether there was any probability of its ever being discovered and communicated. . . . Perhaps a corpse would be reanimated; galvanism had given token of such things: perhaps the component parts of a creature might be manufactured, brought together, and endued with vital warmth.

Directly following this passage appears her account of going to bed and vividly dreaming of the "student of unhallowed arts" and the "hideous phantasm," the dream of which she says she made "only a transcript" in transferring it into the central scene of her novel, the dream that equates the conception of a book with the conception of a child.

Commentators on the novel have in the past taken Shelley at her word here, believing, if not in her story of transcribing a dream, then certainly in her fiction of transcribing men's words.[28] Mario Praz, for example, writes, "All Mrs. Shelley did was to provide a passive reflection of some of the wild fantasies which, as it were, hung in the air about her."[29] Harold Bloom suggests that "what makes *Frankenstein* an important book" despite its "clumsiness" is "that it contains one of the most vivid versions we have of the Romantic mythology of the self, one that resembles Blake's *Book of Urizen*, Shelley's *Prometheus Unbound*, and Byron's *Manfred*, among other works."[30] It is part of the subtlety of her strategy to disguise her criticism of such works as a passive transcription, to appear to be a docile wife and "devout listener" to the conversations of important men. Indeed, central to her critical method is the practice of acting out docilely what these men tell her they want from her, to show them the consequences of their desires. She removes herself beyond reproach for "putting [her]self forward," by formulating her critique as a devout transcription, a "passive reflection," a "version" that "resembles." She inserts this authorial role into her novel in the form of a fictive M. S., Walton's sister, Margaret Saville, to whom his letters containing Frankenstein's story are sent and who silently records and transmits them to the reader.

Now that we have assembled the parts of Shelley's introductory account of the novel's genesis, we can see that she equates childbearing with the bearing of men's words. Writing a transcript of a dream that was in turn merely the transcript of a conversation is also giving birth to a hideous progeny conceived in the night. The conversation between Byron and Shelley probably represents Shelley's and Byron's poetry, the words, for example, of *Alastor* that she literalizes in her novel. That the notion of motherhood as the passive transcription of men's words is at work here is underscored by the allusion this idea makes to the Christ story. "Perhaps a corpse would be reanimated" refers initially, not to science's power, but to that occasion, a myth but surely still a powerful one even in this den of atheists, when a corpse was reanimated, which is in turn an allusion to the virgin birth. Like the creations of Adam and Eve, which excluded the maternal, Christ's birth bypassed the normal channels of procreation. It is this figure, whose birth is also the literalization of a masculine God's Word, who serves as the distant prototype for the reanimation of corpses. And within the fiction, the demon too is the literalization of a word, an idea, Frankenstein's theory given physical form. As Joyce Carol Oates remarks, the demon "is a monster-son born of Man exclusively, a parody of the Word or Idea made Flesh."[31] The book-baby literalizes Shelley's and Byron's words, the words of their conversation as figures for Shelley's words in *Alastor*, just as the demonbaby literalizes Frankenstein's inseminating words. Christ literalizes God's Word through the medium of a woman, Mary, who passively transmits Word into flesh without being touched by it. Literalizations again take place through the medium of a more recent Mary, who passively transcribes (or who seems to), who adds nothing but "the platitude of prose" and "the machinery of a story" to the words of her more illustrious male companions who for their own writing prefer "the music of the most melodious verse." And yet, as we will see again with Eliot's *The Mill on the Floss*, it is precisely the adding of this "machinery," which would seem only to facilitate the transmission of the ideas and figures of poetry into the more approachable form of a story, that subverts and reverses what it appears so passively to serve.

The demon literalizes the male romantic poet's desire for a figurative object of desire, but it also literalizes the literalization of male literature. While telling Frankenstein the story of its wanderings and of its education by the unknowing cottagers, the demon reports having discovered in the woods "a leathern portmanteau containing . . . some books. I eagerly seized the prize and returned with it to my hovel" (chap. 15). The discovery of these books—*Paradise Lost,* Plutarch's *Lives,* and *The Sorrows of Werther*—is followed in the narrative, but preceded in represented time, by the demon's discovery of another book, Frankenstein's "journal of the four months that preceded [the demon's] creation."[32] Both **Frankenstein,** the book as baby, and the demon as baby literalize these books, especially *Paradise Lost*—the demon is Satan, Adam, and Eve, while Frankenstein himself is Adam, Satan, and God— as well as a number of other prior texts, among them, as we have seen, *Alastor,* but also the book of Genesis, Coleridge's "Rime of the Ancient Mariner," Aeschylus's *Prometheus Bound,* Wordsworth's "Tintern Abbey," William Godwin's *Caleb Williams,* and many others. At the same time and in the same way, the demon is the realization of Frankenstein's words in the journal of his work on the demon, a journal that is in some ways equivalent to (or a literalization of) *Alastor,* since both record a romantic quest for what was "desired . . . with an ardor that far exceeded moderation." The demon, wandering about the woods of Germany carrying these books, the book of his own physical origin and the texts that contribute to his literary origin, embodies the very notion of literalization with which everything about him seems to be identified. To carry a book is exactly what Mary Shelley does in bearing the words of the male authors, in giving birth to a hideous progeny that is at once book and demon. Carrying the books of his own origin, the demon emblematizes the literalization of literature that Shelley, through him, practices.

I pointed out earlier that Mary Shelley, unlike the Brontës, would not see childbirth itself as inherently threatening apart from the interference in it by a masculine economy. Likewise, writing or inventing stories is not inherently monstrous—witness her retrospective account in the introduction of how, before her life became "busier," she used to "commune with the creatures of my fancy" and compose unwritten stories out of doors: "It was beneath the trees of the grounds belonging to our house, or on the bleak sides of the woodless mountains near, that my true compositions, the airy flights of my imagination, were born and fostered." Like both Cathys in *Wuthering Heights* in their childhood, indeed, probably like the young Brontës themselves, Mary Shelley's imagination prior to the fall into the Law of the Father—in her case, elopement, pregnancy, and marriage—is at one with nature and also does not require to be written down. The metaphor of composition as childbirth—"my true compositions . . . were born and fostered"—appears here as something not only harmless but celebratory. It is only when both childbirth and a woman's invention of stories are subordinated to the Law of the Father that

they become monstrous; it is only when such overpowering and masculinist texts as Genesis, *Paradise Lost,* and *Alastor* appropriate this Mary's body, her female power of embodiment, as vehicle for the transmission of their words, that monsters are born. When God appropriates maternal procreation in Genesis or *Paradise Lost,* a beautiful object is created; but through the reflex of Mary Shelley's critique, male circumvention of the maternal creates a monster. Her monster constitutes a criticism of such appropriation and circumvention, yet it is a criticism written in her own blood, carved in the very body of her own victimization, just as the demon carves words about death in the trees and rocks of the Arctic. She is powerless to stop her own appropriation and can only demonstrate the pain that appropriation causes in the woman reader and writer. As we turn now to Eliot's *The Mill on the Floss,* which takes up like **Frankenstein** the question of a woman writer's—and her heroine's—literalization of powerful masculine texts, we will see that Eliot shares much of Shelley's sense of the necessity and the high cost of a woman's literalization, as well as of its power as a criticism of that which appropriates.

Notes

[1] Mary Poovey, *The Proper Lady and the Woman Writer* (Chicago: University of Chicago Press, 1984), 114-42. Hereafter I will refer to Mary Shelley as Shelley (except where her unmarried name is necessary for clarity) and to her husband as Percy.

[2] Sandra Gilbert and Susan Gubar's reading of the novel focuses on its "apparently docile submission to male myths" and identifies it specifically as "a fictionalized rendition of the meaning of *Paradise Lost* to women" (*The Madwoman,* pp. 219, 221). Although my interest in Shelley as a reader of prior, masculine texts, as well as some of my specific points about the novel's reading of Milton, overlaps with theirs, I am putting these concerns to uses different from theirs.

[3] For example, Robert Kiely writes that Frankenstein "seeks to combine the role of both parents in one, to eliminate the need for the woman in the creative act, to make sex unnecessary" (*The Romantic Novel in England* [Cambridge: Harvard University Press, 1972], p. 164). Marc Rubenstein remarks on "the series of motherless family romances which form the substance of Frankenstein's past" ("'My Accursed Origin': The Search for the Mother in *Frankenstein,"* *Studies in Romanticism* 15 [1976], 177). The general argument of his psychoanalytic reading of the novel is that the novel represents Shelley's quest for her own dead mother. U. C. Knoepflmacher, in the course of arguing that the novel portrays a daughter's rage at her parents, mentions "the novel's attack on a male's usurpation of the role of mother" ("Thoughts on the Aggression of Daughters," in *The Endurance of Frankenstein: Es-*

says on *Mary Shelley's Novel,* ed. George Levine and U. C. Knoepflmacher [Berkeley: University of California Press, 1979], p. 105). Mary Jacobus writes that "the exclusion of woman from creation symbolically 'kills' the mother" ("Is There a Woman in This Text?" p. 131). Barbara Johnson suggests that the novel focuses on "eliminations of the mother" as well as on "the fear of somehow effecting the death of one's own parents" ("My Monster/My Self," *Diacritics* 12 (1982): 9). Christine Froula's argument about the maternal in Milton, although it focuses on the author's appropriation of the maternal for masculine creativity (as differentiated from its circumvention or elimination) helped to stimulate my thinking. See Froula, "When Eve Reads Milton," pp. 321-47.

4 I am following, in this reading, the 1831 revised text of the novel; in the 1818 version, Elizabeth is Frankenstein's cousin. All quotations from the novel will be from the Signet edition (Mary Shelley, *Frankenstein, Or The Modern Prometheus* [New York: NAL, 1965]), which prints the text of 1831. Future references will be cited in the text by chapter number or by letter number for the letters that precede the chapter sequence. See also James Reiger's edition of the 1818 version, with revisions of 1823 and 1831 (Chicago: University of Chicago Press, 1982).

5 Rubenstein notes the sexual nature of Walton's quest, as well as the maternal associations of those aspects of nature on which Frankenstein carries out his research ("My Accursed Origin," pp. 174-75, 177). Kiely notes the necrophilia of the passage from *Alastor's* invocation to Mother Nature (discussed here in chapter 1), and suggests its similarity to Frankenstein's "penetrating the recesses of nature" (*The Romantic Novel,* pp. 162-63).

6 Quoted p. 149; Frankenstein quotes lines 76-83 of the poem, altering the original "haunted *me* like a passion" to fit a third person.

7 In the context of arguing that the novel critiques the bourgeois family, Kate Ellis shows that Frankenstein's mother passes on to Elizabeth her "view of the female role as one of constant, self-sacrificing devotion to others," and she suggests that "Elizabeth's early death, like her adopted mother's, was a logical outgrowth of the female ideal she sought to embody" ("Monsters in the Garden: Mary Shelley and the Bourgeois Family," in *The Endurance of Frankenstein,* p. 131). My argument would explain why what created this "female ideal" also determined the interchangeability of mother and daughter.

8 Harold Bloom suggests the resemblance between the demon and Blake's emanations or Shelley's epipsyche, in his afterword to the Signet edition of the novel, p. 215. The essay is reprinted in *Ringers in the Tower*

(Chicago: University of Chicago Press, 1971), pp. 119-29. Peter Brooks makes a similar point when he writes, "fulfillment with Elizabeth would mark Frankenstein's achievement of a full signified in his life, accession to plenitude of being—which would leave no place in creation for his daemonic projection, the Monster" ("Godlike Science/Unhallowed Arts: Language and Monstrosity in *Frankenstein,*" *New Literary History* 9 [1978]: 599). Ellis also suggests, though for different reasons, that the demon is a representative for Elizabeth ("Monsters in the Garden," p. 136). Jacobus writes that Frankenstein "exchang[es] a woman for a monster," and she discusses Frankenstein's preference for imagined over actual beings ("Is There a Woman in This Text?" p. 131).

9 Gilbert and Gubar suggest first that "the part of Eve *is* all the parts" and then discuss at length the demon's resemblance to Eve (*The Madwoman,* pp. 230, 235-44. However, in describing this resemblance, they focus primarily on the patriarchal rejection of women's bodies as deformed and monstrous, as well as on Eve's motherlessness, but not, as I do here, on Eve as Adam's imaginative projection. Joyce Carol Oates also suggests the demon's resemblance to Eve, also using the scene I am about to discuss, in "Frankenstein's Fallen Angel," *Critical Inquiry* 10 (1984): 547.

10 Quotations from *Paradise Lost* are from *Complete Poems and Major Prose of John Milton,* ed. Merritt Hughes (Indianapolis: Bobbs-Merrill, 1957), and are cited in the text by book and line numbers. Other critics have noted Shelley's allusion to this Miltonic scene; see, for example, Brooks, "Godlike Science," p. 595.

11 Froula writes, "Through the dream of the rib Adam both enacts a parody of birth and gains possession of the womb by claiming credit for woman herself." Milton, she goes on to argue, reenacts Adam's solution to his "womb envy" by analogously repressing female power in his account of the origin of his poem: "The male Logos called upon to articulate the cosmos against an abyss of female silence overcomes the anxieties generated by the tension between visible maternity and invisible paternity by appropriating female power to itself in a parody of parthenogenesis" ("When Eve Reads Milton," pp. 332, 338; and see passim pp. 326-40).

12 Ibid., pp. 326-28.

13 All quotations from Shelley's verse are from the Reiman and Powers edition of his works.

14 Gilbert and Gubar also discuss narcissistic love in the novel, although with reference only to the potentially incestuous relation between Frankenstein and Elizabeth, not with reference to the demon (*The Madwoman,* p. 229). My reading would suggest that

Frankenstein's relation to Elizabeth is far less narcissistic than his relation to the demon; in his descriptions of Elizabeth, he focuses on her difference from him, which is what I believe makes her like the mother and therefore threatening.

[15] Jaya Mehta pointed out to me the significance of this aspect of Walton, in a seminar paper at Yale in 1984.

[16] Kiely discusses "the sheer concreteness" of the demon, though his concern is with the mismatching between ideal and real in the novel (*The Romantic Novel*, p. 161).

[17] *The Diary of Dr. John William Polidori*, ed. W. M. Rossetti (London: Elkin Matthews, 1911), pp. 128-29, entry for 18 June 1816. Cited also by Rubenstein, who reads it as a story about "maternal reproach" and connects it with Frankenstein's dream of his dead mother ("My Accursed Origin," pp. 184-85). I am grateful to Marina Leslie for her discussion of this episode in a seminar paper at Yale in 1984.

[18] Peter Brooks's essay on *Frankenstein* also connects the plot of desire with the plot of language in the novel, but to a somewhat different effect. Brooks argues that the demon's acquisition of the "godlike science" of language places him within the symbolic order. Trapped at first, like any baby, within the specular order of the imaginary, the demon is first judged only by its looks; it is only when it masters the art of rhetoric that the monster gains sympathy. But, Brooks continues, despite the promise that the symbolic seems to hold, the monster's failure to find an object of love removes its life from the signifying "chain" of human interconnectedness and makes of it instead a "miserable series," in which one signifier refers always to another with "no point of arrest." Thus Brooks sees the monster as a dark and exaggerated version of all life within the symbolic, where desire is never satisfied and where there is no transcendental signified. Although I agree with much of what Brooks writes, I would argue that in its materiality and its failure to acquire an object of desire, the demon enters the symbolic primarily as the (dreaded) referent, not as signifier. The negative picture of the demon's materiality is a product of its female place in the symbolic, and not of any lingering in the realm of the imaginary (which Brooks, with other readers of Lacan, views as tragic). I would also argue that the novel presents, not a vision of the condition of human signification, but a targeted criticism of those in whose interests the symbolic order constitutes itself in the ways that it does.

[19] Ellen Moers, *Literary Women* (New York: Doubleday, 1977), p. 140.

[20] Ibid., pp. 145-47.

[21] This is the general tendency of Rubenstein's argument, carrying the material Moers presents into a psychoanalytic frame.

[22] See Rubenstein, "My Accursed Origin," pp. 168, 178-81; Poovey, *The Proper Lady*, pp. 138-42.

[23] Deutsch, *Motherhood*, p. 215.

[24] One of the central tenets of Poovey's argument concerns Shelley's endeavor in her 1831 revisions to make the novel more conservative, more in keeping with a proto-Victorian ideology of the family (see *The Proper Lady*, pp. 133-42). Poovey argues, however, that both versions of the novel oppose romantic egotism's assault on the family.

[25] Gilbert and Gubar assert as part of their argument that everyone in the novel is Eve that "Frankenstein has a baby" and that as a consequence he becomes female (*The Madwoman*, p. 232). I would argue, to the contrary, that Frankenstein's production of a new life is pointedly masculine, that it matters to the book that he is a man circumventing childbirth, not a woman giving birth.

[26] Letter of 22 November 1817 to Benjamin Bailey, in *Letters of John Keats*, ed. Robert Gittings (London: Oxford University Press, 1970), p. 37.

[27] I am indebted to Suzanne Raitt for her discussion of this point in a seminar at Yale in 1984.

[28] Rubenstein also argues that Shelley deliberately created the impression that she merely recorded Percy and Byron's conversation as part of a project to make her creativity seem as passive and maternal as possible. He discusses at length the analogy she sets up between conceiving a child and conceiving a book, and he specifically suggests that the men's words in conversation are like men's role in procreation, which was, in the early nineteenth century, thought to involve the man actively and the woman only passively: "She is trying to draw for us a picture of her imagination as a passive womb, inseminated by those titans of romantic poetry" ("My Accursed Origin," p. 181). I would agree with everything Rubenstein says, although I am using this idea for a somewhat different purpose: he is using it to show how the novel is about Shelley's effort to make restitution for her dead mother.

[29] Mario Praz, *The Romantic Agony*, trans. Angus Davidson (London: Oxford University Press, 1933), p. 114. Cited by Moers and also by Rubenstein in support of his argument discussed in note 28 above.

[30] Harold Bloom, "Afterword," *Frankenstein*, p. 215. It is worth noting that *Frankenstein* preceded *Prometheus Unbound* and was of course written in ignorance of the *Book of Urizen*.

[31] Oates, "Frankenstein's Fallen Angel," p. 552.

[32] Gilbert and Gubar, who focus much of their argument on Shelley's reading of *Paradise Lost,* connect that reading to the demon's reading of the poem, as well as connecting Shelley's listening to her husband and Byron with the demon's listening to the DeLaceys.

Alan Bewell (essay date 1988)

SOURCE: "An Issue of Monstrous Desire: *Frankenstein* and Obstetrics," in *The Yale Journal of Criticism,* Vol. 2, No. 1, Fall, 1988, pp. 105-28.

[*In the densely historical analysis in the essay that follows, Bewell considers the importance of late eighteenth-century obstetrics in relation to Shelley's composition. Returning to an earlier critical theory that the novel reflected Shelley's own experiences with childbirth, Bewell argues that it "represents Mary Shelley's deliberate attempt to introduce an ambiguously female-based theory of creation into the Romantic discourse on the imagination."*]

The amount of attention Mary Shelley gives to the process of creating a human being and to the "duties of a creator towards his creature"[1] makes **Frankenstein** quite unusual. Prior to the twentieth century, writers—though they seem to have found no end to the ways of describing, both literally and metaphorically, how children are made and brought into the world—have had very little to say about pregnancy or pregnant women. The nine-month period between conception and birth, when the child is formed in the womb of the mother, has been relatively ignored, especially given that pregnancy was the condition of a major portion of women's lives in those days before birth control.

Ellen Moers was first to argue that Mary Shelley's novel should be read as "a birth myth," expressing its author's painful experience as a young woman pregnant three times between her elopement with Percy Bysshe, in 1814, and the conclusion of the novel three years later. "Nothing so sets her apart from the generality of writers of her own time, and before, and for long afterward," Moers writes "than her early and chaotic experience, at the very time she became an author, with motherhood. Pregnant at sixteen, and almost constantly pregnant throughout the following five years; yet not a secure mother, for she lost most of her babies soon after they were born; and not a lawful mother, for she was not married—not at least when, at the age of eighteen, Mary Godwin began to write **Frankenstein**. So are monsters born."[2] Treating the novel as a displaced autobiography, Moers reads the birth of the monster as a metaphor, as a distraught young, middle-class woman's anxiety-ridden personal statement about the horrors of failed motherhood.

Perhaps because of the importance of Moers's essay for feminist studies, it has lately been much criticized. From what we know of the importance that Mary Shelley gave to the idea of domestic life, Moers's argument that the novel expresses a "revulsion against newborn life, and the drama of guilt, dread, and flight surrounding birth and its consequences," would seem to be less a description of the author's attitudes toward children, than those of her husband Percy Bysshe.[3] Recent feminists, interested less in female experience than in female authorship, have also been critical of Moers's reduction of the text to biology. "To insist," writes Mary Jacobus, "that **Frankenstein** reflects Mary Shelley's experience of the trauma of parturition and postpartum depression may tell us about women's lives, but it reduces the text itself to a monstrous symptom."[4] Critics such as Barbara Johnson continue to interpret the novel as autobiography, but in their flight from biological determinations of femaleness, they tend to translate the "monster-in-the-text" and the "monstrous text" into abstract metaphors, into the figure of woman-as-monster or the "*theory* of autobiography as monstrosity." Ironically, despite her concern with the absence of mothers in the novel, Johnson seems equally intent on enacting her own form of interpretive violence against mothers, as she seeks to rid **Frankenstein** of Mary Shelley the silent, and somewhat scandalous, pregnant mother, to replace her with a speaking female author. Johnson's claim that for Mary Shelley to give birth to herself on the page, she needed first to "figuratively repeat the matricide that her physical birth all too literally entailed"[5] may also be said to describe her own interpretive practice.

In her survey of recent feminist criticism and theory, Margaret Homans has noted a major problem with Moers's criticism in its tendency to present women's experiences as if they were universal, requiring only representation; consequently, it rarely attends to the ways in which these experiences have been historically and discursively constructed.[6] This is certainly the case when Moers reads the creation of the monster—"So are monsters born"—as a natural product of Mary Shelley's chaotic youth, her frequent pregnancies, her lack of domestic security, and her unmarried status. Moers unselfconsciously applies her own sexual mores to the creation of the novel in assuming that Mary Shelley shares her beliefs. Johnson's account of the novel, on the other hand, as a "textual dramatization" of "the monstrousness of selfhood,"[7] is equally ahistorical and abstract in its claims concerning the nature of male and female autobiography. Both critics rightly recognize the centrality of the question of the genesis of monsters to understanding **Frankenstein,** but neither makes any attempt to understand what Mary Shelley actually might have thought about these matters. Consequently, they leave unclear, except as analogy, the connection between biology and writing, monstrous texts and monstrous babies, Mary Shelley as pregnant woman and as female author. Mary Poovey and William Veeder do attempt to rethink in historical terms these relationships, and I would like here to develop this line of thinking further to argue that Mary Shelley's experience of pregnancy and loss was not simply a biological matter, but also a social and discursive event, which made her familiar, in ways that critics have not been, with the language of obstetrics and its extensive and long-standing discourse on the causes of monsters and abortions. Moers takes the presence of this language in **Frankenstein** as a sign that the novel is autobiographical; I would argue in addition that it represents Mary Shelley's deliberate attempt to introduce an ambiguously female-based theory of creation into the Romantic discourse on the imagination. Using sexual reproduction as a model for all modes of creation, she made obstetrics the mastercode of her aesthetics and applied its concrete arguments, about the creative power of a mother's psyche upon the fetus and the proper environment for human reproduction, to criticize and to curb the excesses of male Romantic imaginations, particularly her husband's.

The period between 1650 and 1800 saw a massive increase in the publication of books on midwifery. This spate of books is largely attributable to the appearance of man-midwives, who asserted their dominance over traditional midwives, first, by claiming that the profession required extensive medical expertise, and second, through their exclusive right to use surgical instruments, such as hooks, crotchets, extractors, and crutches, in delivery. Leaving this issue aside for the moment, I would note that the books generally follow a fairly standardized pattern. They all stress the importance of a knowledge of anatomy and physiology, so the structure and function of the organs of generation receive a good deal of attention. By the middle of the eighteenth century, artists and engravers such as George Stubbs were commissioned to do high-quality anatomical plates. Most of these books also give advice on the symptoms and diagnosis of pregnancy, the disorders peculiar to pregnant women, and various ways to determine the sex of an unborn child. Delivery methods are frequently dealt with in detail, often with plate illustrations of the different kinds of births that a midwife may confront. Remarks on the lying-in period and on the diseases that women and newborn infants are subject to during this period sometimes appear as well, and earlier books often include advice on choosing a midwife.

For my present purposes, I want to stress that these books tend to be very much concerned with discipline, with establishing rules of conduct for pregnant women who wished to be delivered of healthy and wellformed children. They are explicitly books on the "management" or "government" of pregnant wives. Where normally a woman's behavior was guided by moral, religious, familial, and economic restraints, pregnant women found themselves—then, as now—the subject of intensive medical scrutiny and advice. A brief mention of the titles of a few of these books will suffice to indicate their disciplinary character. The seventeenth-century midwife Jane Sharp wrote *The Midwives Book. Or the Whole Art of Midwifry Discovered. Directing Childbearing Women how to behave themselves; In their Conception, Breeding, Bearing, and Nursing of Children.* James Guillemeau's is entitled *Child-birth; or, The Happy Deliverie of Women. Wherein is set downe the Government of Women. In the Time: Of their Breeding Childe: Of their Travaile, both Naturall, and Contrary to Nature: And Of their Lying in.* The book includes two chapters, one entitled, "What dyet and order a woman with child ought to keepe," and another, "How a woman must governe her self the nine moneths she goeth with child." One of the most popular handbooks of the eighteenth century, *Aristotle's Compleat Master-Piece, In Three Parts; Displaying the Secrets of Nature in the Generation of Man* (1694?), includes a chapter on "How a woman should order herself that desires to conceive, and what she ought to do after conception," and another on "How child bearing women ought to govern themselves during the time of their pregnancy." The London physician John Clarke, who was summoned when Mary Wollstonecraft developed complications at the birth of her daughter, and who also arrived five minutes late for the birth of Mary's first child (in 1815), was famous for *Practical Essays on the Management of Pregnancy and Labour,* published by the radical bookseller Joseph Johnson.

This antenatal regimen generally revolved around the right use of the classical six "non-naturals": air, meat and drink, exercise and rest, sleeping and waking, fulness and emptiness, and the passions of the mind. Alexander Hamilton, in *Outlines of the Theory and Practice of Midwifery,* in the section entitled "Management during Pregnancy," sets down a typical list of rules of conduct. "The strictest temperance and regularity in diet, sleeping, exercise, and amusement," he argues, "are necessary to be observed by those who have reason to dread abortions." "Overheating, irregular passions, and costiveness" are also to be avoided, as are "the hazards of shocks, from falls in walking or riding, from bruises in crowds, or frights from bustle."[8] No extreme cures or actions regarding complaints are to be taken. The dress is to be loose and easy. Women are advised to frequent places where the air is pure and tempered. For this reason, as Hamilton argues in a later book, *The Family Female Physician,* they "should be strictly prohibited from crowded companies and public places. The impurity of the air, on such occasions, is sufficient, in the irritable state of pregnant women, to induce many very disagreeable complaints." Nevertheless, he stresses the equal importance of their avoiding being alone, because in solitary situations "they are apt to become melancholy; and it is well known that the depressing passions sometimes prove the source of the most dangerous disease which can occur during pregnancy."[9] The proper psychological environment for pregnant women, then, is neither public, nor private, but a domestic one, in which, through "cheerful company and variety of objects . . . their minds may be always composed and happy."[10] Eighteenth-century obstetric theory did not simply reflect the emerging ideological importance of the idea of domestic family life. It helped to shape it. It was a major element in the "entire medico-sexual regime" that, in Michel Foucault's words, "took hold of the family milieu."[11]

There remains another aspect of the obstetric management of pregnant wives, which is of major importance to *Frankenstein:* the striking emphasis placed on the power of a pregnant woman's imagination and desires to mark or deform a developing fetus. The midwifery books constituted an important early discourse on the female imagination, one that accorded it extraordinary powers. Central to this theory was the notion that a woman's imagination functioned mimetically: an image placed before her eyes and strongly impressed on her imagination would be reproduced on the body of the child. "The strong Attention of the Mother's Mind to a *Determined* Object," James Augustus Blondel comments, in summarizing this tradition, "can cause a *Determined* Impression upon the Body of the Child: As for Instance . . . her strong Desire of a *Peach,* or of an *Apricock* can cause the Colour and shape of a *Peach,* or of an *Apricock* upon a *Determined* part of the Child's Body."[12] This idea had a long-standing tradition, and can be traced back to classical medicine, notably to the work of Soranus, Aristotle, Galen, Avicenna, and to the works of some of Victor Frankenstein's favorite authors—Cornelius Agrippa, Paracelsus, and Pliny. It was also favored by the early Church Fathers, notably Saint Jerome, who saw a precedent in the story of Jacob and the rods:

> And Jacob took him rods of green poplar, and of the hazel and chestnut tree; and pilled white strakes in them, and made the white appear which *was* in the rods.

> And he set the rods which he had pilled before the flocks in the gutters in the watering troughs when the flocks came to drink, that they should conceive when they came to drink.

> And the flocks conceived before the rods, and brought forth cattle ring-straked, speckled, and spotted.

> (Gen. 30:37-39)

Ambroise Paré, in his account of the origin of monsters, supplies two other famous examples, in which an image brought before the eyes of a conceiving woman is transferred directly to the fetus:

> The Ancients having diligently sought into all the secrets of Nature, have marked and observed other causes of the generation of Monsters: for, understanding the force of imagination to be so powerful in us, as for the most part, it may alter the body of them that imagine, they soon persuaded themselves that the faculty which formeth the Infant may be led and governed by the firm and strong cogitation of the Parents begetting them (often deluded by nocturnal and deceitful apparitions) or by the mother conceiving them; and so that which is strongly conceived in the mind, imprints the force into the Infant conceived in the womb. . . . We have read in *Heliodorus,* that *Persia* Queen of *Aethiopia,* by her Husband *Hidustes,* being also an Ethiope, had a daughter of a white complexion, because in the embraces of her husband, by which she proved with child, she earnestly fixed her eye and mind upon the picture of the faire *Andromeda* standing opposite unto her. Damascene reports, that he saw a Maid hairy like a Bear, which had that deformity by no other cause or occasion than that her Mother earnestly beheld in the very instant of receiving and conceiving the seed, the image of St. *John* covered with a Camels skin, hanging upon the posts of the bed.[13]

In both these instances (and in the case of Jacob's sheep), monsters are produced at the moment of conception when a mother's ardent gaze on an image overpowers the form-making power of the seed, which, from Aristotle's *De generatione animalium* onward, was usually believed to originate in the male. In these texts, *sexual* possession and conception ("in the embraces of her husband") are linked to *mental* possession and conception ("she *earnestly* fixed her eye and mind," "her Mother *earnestly* beheld") because the sexual act was not viewed simply as a biological event, but one in which volition was linked to pleasure through the womb's active grasping of the seed. As the ambiguous description of St. John "hanging upon the posts of the bed" suggests, monsters are conceived when an image usurps the place of the biological father, if not in the bed, at least in the mind of his wife.[14] Traditional obstetric theory may have often allotted women a secondary or subordinate role in biological reproduction, their purpose frequently being that of a *tabula rasa* for the male seed, the "nutriment" for the developing "form" of the child. But a contrary, more feminist position, also developed, that reasserted the importance of the mother by admitting that the mother's imagination, if not fully satisfied with this arrangement, might intervene in this process, when not carefully regulated, to mar or deface the form provided by the father.

Though there was some controversy concerning whether "the firme and strong cogitation" of both parents, or only the mother, could mark the child at conception, few disagreed that during the subsequent nine months the fetus was particularly vulnerable to the dangerous force of a mother's imagination. Daniel Turner summarizes how this maternal "revision" was understood to take place. "We shall take Notice," he writes, "of some monstrous Births, or otherways deform'd and blemish'd by Marks from the strong Imagination or disappointed Longings of the Mother; which have had not only Power sufficient to pervert and disturb what the Ancients called the *Plastick,* or formative Faculty, in drawing forth the *prima Stamina,* or first Lines from the then ductile and pliable Matter, but to stamp its Characters, to dismember and dislocate, and to make large and bloody Wounds upon the Body of the *Foetus,* conceiv'd long since and formed compleatly."[15] An idea of bodily inscription is implied in these discussions: a mother's "strong Imagination" and "disappointed Longings" can "pervert" or "disturb" the proper form of the child, not only by erasing or "draw[ing] forth" the original "first Lines" of the child, "conceiv'd long since and formed compleatly," but also by actually impressing or stamping their own "Characters" on the living fetus. Monsters and monstrous marks thus represent the destructive intervention of female imagination and desire in the transference and reproduction of the human image. These monstrous features constituted the inscribed traces of a conflict, sometimes a life-and-death struggle, between female passion and the form-making powers of the male seed. They could thus be read as a history of a woman's imaginative life during those nine months, of the balance of power worked out between the male and the female, written out in living characters on the body of the child.

Among the many examples given of the power of a pregnant woman's imagination to revise the features of a child, two famous cases, recounted by Nicolas Malebranche in *The Search after Truth,* deserve mention. The first was of a woman who, "having attended too carefully to the portrait of Saint Pius on the feast of his canonization, gave birth to a child who looked exactly like the representation of the saint." Malebranche goes on to describe him:

> He had the face of an old man, as far as is possible for a beardless child; his arms were crossed upon his chest, with his eyes turned toward the heavens; and he had very little forehead, because the image of the saint being raised toward the vault of the church, gazing toward heaven, had almost no forehead. He had a kind of inverted miter on his shoulders, with many round marks in the places where miters are covered with gems. In short, this child strongly resembled the tableau after which its mother had formed it by the power of her imagination. This is something that all Paris has been able to see as well as me, because the body was preserved for a considerable time in alcohol.

Again we see how the mother, by looking too carefully and too long at an image, produces confusion, as her body impresses the image that she sees on the already established features of the fetus. The second case was of a child Malebranche had seen at the hospital for *Incurables,* "whose body," he said, "was broken in the same places in which those of criminals are broken. He had remained nearly twenty years in this state." The cause of this disastrous accident, Malebranche declared,

> was that his mother, having known that a criminal was to be broken, went to see the execution. All the blows given to this miserable creature forcefully struck the imagination of this mother and, by a sort of counterblow, the tender and delicate brain of her child . . . sweeping away the soft and tender parts of the child's bones.[16]

Here the mother's imagination re-enacts, "by a sort of counterblow," the terrible spectacle enacted before her eyes.

It may appear from the above cases that a woman's imagination is essentially passive in its attempt to reproduce what the mother sees. It should be stressed, however, that the major force behind this active attempt to refashion the features of the fetus is female passion. Women's longings and imaginings were generally considered dangerous, and this was especially true of pregnant women, because it was believed that pregnancy was an abnormal condition that gave rise not only to great bellies, but also to "great Loathings and . . . many different Longings."[17] As Jane Sharp noted, a sure sign of conception was that a woman would suddenly develop "a preternatural desire to something not fit to eat nor drink, as some women with child have longed to bite off a piece of their Husbands Buttocks."[18] This abnormal intensity and irregularity of imagination was seen as a major threat to the child, for it suggested that "the Marks and Deformities, Children bring into the World" were not only attributable to what a woman might have seen, but also were expressions of her unnatural desires, "the sad Effect of the Mother's irregular Fancy and Imagination." In short, pregnant women can and "do breed *Monsters* by the Wantonness of their *Imagination.*"[19]

Concerned about the assumed intensity and abnormality of a pregnant woman's imagination as well as the enormous effect that her unsatisfied desires and inexplicable loathings might have on the child, the authors of midwifery books developed an extensive discourse on the nature and functioning of her imagination, aimed at regulating and normalizing not only what she did, but what she looked at, thought about, and desired while pregnant. In addition to advice about proper physical activities, they also developed a psychic regimen that sought to curb her imagination and desires from excessive or unusual activity. Blondel in his criticism of what he calls "the imaginationists" summarizes what a woman in this condition should avoid:

1. A strong Longing for something in particular, in which Desire the Mother is either gratified, or disappointed. 2. A sudden Surprise. 3. The Sight and Abhorrence of an ugly and frightful Object. 4. The Pleasure of Looking on, and Contemplating, even for a long Time, a Picture, or whatsoever is delightful to the Fancy. 5. Fear, and Consternation, and great Apprehension of Dangers. 6. And lastly, An Excess of Anger, of Grief, or of Joy.[20]

This is a discipline that focuses on excesses. It matters little whether a desire is gratified or disappointed. And the indulgence in pleasurable sights or in the delights of Fancy can be just as damaging as the experience of horror. All sustained emotional or intellectual activities and any situation that might *impress* a woman in any way are to be avoided; pregnant women are "to take great care, that their imagination be pure and clear, that their children may be well formed."[21] Sheltered, yet limited by these rules of conduct, a woman's spiritual and physical life found its apt culminating expression in her literal "confinement" during the ninth month of pregnancy. Little wonder, then, that pregnant women appear so rarely in early literature, except as a subject of comic or satiric control.

James Guillemeau, in *Child-birth; or, The Happy Deliverie of Women,* gives a summary of the ideal environment for a pregnant woman:

> Now concerning the passions of the minde, a woman with child must be pleasant and merrie, shunning all melancholike and troublesome things that may vexe or molest her mind: for as *Aristotle* saith, A woman with child must have a setled and quiet mind, which *Avicen* also counselleth, that those which have conceived, ought to be preserved from all feare, sadnesse, and disquietnes of mind, without speaking or doing any thing that may offend or vexe them; so that discreet women, and such as desire to have children, will not give eare unto lamentable and fearefull tales or storyes, nor cast their eyes upon pictures or persons which are uglie or deformed, least the imagination imprint on the child the similitude of the said person or picture, which doing, women shall be sure to be well and happily delivered, and that (with the help of God) they shall beare their burthen to the full terme, which shall be sent into the world without much paine, promising them a happie and speedie deliverie."[22]

The midwifery handbooks provide a very powerful argument supporting the institution of marriage and the ideal of a domestic environment in which the woman is secure from "all feare, sadnesse, and disquietnes of mind." Her mind is to be "setled and quiet," and only the most foolhardy of women would give "eare unto lamentable and fearefull tales or storyes."

In most cultures, pregnant women are a marginalized population, dependent on others and frequently set apart from society. It should not surprise us then that they were subject to increased discursive and social control. And then, as now, it would have been hard for them to ignore medical advice, even when it had no experimental basis. It is difficult, then, to think of a more androcentric discourse, one more interested in the control of women's bodies and minds. One way of critically appraising this discourse might be to seek out female authors who were resistant to its dictates or who struggled to articulate a different sense of what it means to be pregnant. This approach, in this instance, is problematic for a number of reasons. First, it was not men alone who promulgated these obstetric ideas, but also women. In fact, one might argue that one significant reason why the discourse on the power of a female imagination largely disappeared by the end of the eighteenth century was that male-midwives, who at that time took control of the field from midwives, made it disappear. Further, to the extent that these ideas have continued beyond the eighteenth century, they have done so, not in the sphere of medicine, but in the stories that mothers pass on to their daughters. Another reason why this should not be seen as a univocal male discourse is a theoretical one: though languages, viewed abstractly, can limit the horizon of what can be said, no language is the exclusive property of any group or gender. Masters may dream of languages that would force servants to agree with them, but no language cannot be bent to a servant's needs. If viewed in concrete historical terms, all languages embody an ongoing struggle for power and meaning among social groups. From this perspective, though there can be little doubt that this obstetric theory was a language aimed at controlling a marginalized group of individuals, the manner in which this discourse talks about pregnant women—as it allots them enormous powers of imagination and dangerous desires—manifests a specific historical distribution of power between genders. The subsequent historical disappearance of these pregnant women from literature and medical discourse, rather than suggesting the disappearance of that gender conflict, suggests the emergence of new deployments of power.

When James Augustus Blondel first set out to criticize this theory, he was astonished that when "the sole and absolute Power of *Imagination* is settled upon the Mother . . . Women, to my great Surprise, are so weak, as to plead guilty to such an Accusation, groundless and contrary to their Interests."[23] Blondel's only explanation for why women were willing to accept this "groundless" theory, so opposed to "their Interests," was that they were "weak." If, instead, we view the female willingness to promote this discourse as a trade-off of one form of power for another, one interest for another, we can recognize that despite their social confinement, pregnant women did derive from this discourse a certain form of limited power. First, it reasserted, if only by negative example, the tacit cooperation of the female in reproduction, a creative role that was denied her by Aristotelian embryology. Ironically, the discourse on monsters provided women with a means of asserting their importance in the process of reproduction. Second, the pregnant mother, possessed by a despotic and diseased imagination, yet also possessing and seeking to protect a prospective male heir, could act as both hostage-taker and negotiator, working out suitable arrangements, over the course of her pregnancy, aimed at satisfying the two warring factions within herself. For instance, Win Littlewit, in Ben Jonson's *Bartholomew Fair,* claims that she is suffering "a natural disease of woman, called 'A longing to eat pig'" (I.vi.39) in order to force others to allow her to attend the Fair. Mrs. Pickle, in Smollett's *Peregrine Pickle,* also uses longing as a stratagem, first to rid herself of the attentions of Mrs. Grizzle, but later as playful diversion.[24] There is also evidence that women, who did not need to be pregnant to be socially confined, were at least partially amenable to a discourse that justified the demands of appetite, that insisted on the satisfaction of desires, and that allowed them to express an imaginative wantonness ("longings" and "loathings"), that would have been difficult to admit in other situations.[25] Rabelais's description of how Gargamelle, having carried Gargantua for eleven months, could not refrain from gorging herself on "sixteen quarters, two bushels, and six pecks" of tripe, may speak of the necessity for pregnant women to regulate their "immodest" desires.[26] Yet at the same time, we are given one of the most powerful of literary images of the demands and fulfillment of female bodily desire. In Rabelais's carnivalesque world, great bellies, as they emblematize the power of life, fertility and death, assert their own kind of order, even as they threaten conventional modes of control. From this perspective, the rejection of this obstetric theory by the end of the eighteenth century may have been an advance for science, but it also significantly diminished the sexual power of women, already eroded by the medical assertion that there was no link between conception and desire.[27] No wonder, then, that even though these ideas lost their medical authority, they remained popular among women throughout the nineteenth century.

Given the complex issues surrounding the employment of obstetric theory at the beginning of the nineteenth century, the simplest way of approaching a discussion of its role in *Frankenstein* is to analyze first its function in the novel, and then its significance in Mary Shelley's 1831 preface. As a cautionary obstetric tale that recounts how an individual who pays scant heed to either the biological or imaginative conditions of human reproduction gives birth to a monster, *Frankenstein* draws extensively on this discourse. Many readers have noted that Victor goes to great lengths, in Margaret Homans's words, "to circumvent the normal channels of procreation."[28] It should be added, how-

ever, that he also ignores the antenatal regimen proffered by midwifery handbooks. Irregular in diet, caring little for sleep as he engages in his "midnight labours . . . with unrelaxed and breathless eagerness" (49), taking in the dank and poisonous airs of graveyards, dissecting-rooms, and slaughter-houses, increasingly avoiding all contact with others because, as he says, "Company was irksome to me" (155), Victor shows by negative example what one should not do if one wants to create a healthy child. "My cheek had grown pale with study, and my person had become emaciated with confinement," Victor declares, as he unconsciously identifies himself with a woman in confinement (49). "Every night I was oppressed by a slow fever, and I became nervous to a most painful degree; my voice became broken, my trembling hands almost refused to accomplish their task; I became as timid as a love-sick girl, and alternate tremor and passionate ardour took the place of wholesome sensation and regulated ambition."[29] In the 1831 edition, Victor's nervous condition increases his susceptibility to "shocks" and "frights:" "the fall of a leaf startled me, and I shunned my fellow-creatures as if I had been guilty of a crime."[30] Yet, ever a procrastinator, Victor believes that this melancholy will be short-lived: "exercise and amusement would soon drive away such symptoms; and I promised myself both of these, when my creation should be complete" (51). Any person with even a moderate knowledge of contemporary obstetric theory might have told him that by then it would be too late.[31]

Shelley not only draws on obstetric recommendations regarding diet, sleep, exercise, and pure air, but also focuses explicitly on regulating the imagination in creation. Since monsters and monstrous marking constituted a document of the embryological conflicts caused by a mother's wanton or abnormal passion, Victor's monster can be read as the objectification of his own unregulated and contradictory desires. Victor Frankenstein draws our attention to this question when he attempts to recount the events that led up to the creation of the monster. Interestingly, he links the onset of this passion with the onset of puberty, when, at the age of thirteen, while "confined" to an inn, he discovered a volume of the works of Cornelius Agrippa:

> When I would account to myself for the birth of that passion, which afterwards ruled my destiny, I find it arise, like a mountain river, from ignoble and almost forgotten sources; but, swelling as it proceeded, it became the torrent which, in its course, has swept away all my hopes and joys.
>
> Natural philosophy is the genius that has regulated my fate. [32]

Victor would claim that his imagination was "regulated," that natural philosophy was "the genius," or deity of generation and birth, governing his actions. Yet his description of the "birth" of this passion is of a "swelling" that leads to an abortion, a "torrent" sweeping away his "hopes and joys." Just as in Paré's account of how the image of St. John interposed itself between the conceiving mother and her proper object of desire, Cornelius Agrippa comes to stand between Victor and Elizabeth: "she did not interest herself in the subject, and I was left by her to pursue my studies alone" (34). In his "ardour" to create, a word emphasized repeatedly throughout the novel, Victor shows little concern for a regimen of the imagination. "I had worked hard for nearly two years," he confesses, "for the sole purpose of infusing life into an inanimate body. For this I had deprived myself of rest and health. I had desired it with an ardour that far exceeded moderation" (52). Equally clear is his inability to turn his eyes away from this object of desire. "I was . . . forced," he says, "to spend days and nights in vaults and charnel houses. *My attention was fixed* upon every object the most insupportable to the delicacy of the human feelings" (47, my emphasis). He describes how his "eyeballs were starting from their sockets in attending to the details of my employment," and yet how, with the strange mixture of "loathing" and "eagerness"—so much a part of the discourse on pregnant women—he sought to bring his "work near to a conclusion." "I could not tear my thoughts from my employment, loathsome in itself, but which had taken an irresistible hold of my imagination," he declares. Obsessed with this single desire, he even begins to lose "all soul or sensation" in his body. He becomes "insensible to the charms of nature" and forgets "those friends who were so many miles absent, and whom I had not seen for so long a time" (50).

Because Western culture has traditionally understood sexual reproduction as a mode of representation—the transmission of the image of the father to his children—obstetric theory, in its emphasis on and attempt to limit the powers of women's imaginations, implicitly constituted a theory of representation, dealing with the conception and production, the expression and revision, of living (rather than sculptural or literary) forms. *Frankenstein* distinctively appropriates and extends this discourse on bodily creation to all aspects of human knowledge, and especially to literary creation. Where Wordsworth speaks of the imagination as passing through an educative discipline that socializes it and leads it to see itself in the calm and enduring forms of external nature, Mary Shelley achieves a similar goal by applying the laws of biological creation to human thought, claiming (through Victor) that "a human being in perfection ought always to preserve a calm and peaceful mind, and never to allow passion or a transitory desire to disturb his tranquillity. I do not think that the pursuit of knowledge is an exception to this rule. If the study to which you apply yourself has a tendency to weaken your affections, and to destroy your taste for those simple pleasures in which no alloy can possibly mix, then that study is certainly unlawful,

that is to say, not befitting the human mind" (51). The link between literary activity and sexual reproduction among the male characters is quite clear. *Frankenstein* is ostensibly the published manuscript, "the tale which I have recorded" (216), of the failed poet cum explorer Robert Walton. Because this narrative is composed over a nine-month period, between December 11, the date of his first letter to his sister Margaret Saville, and September 12th of the following year, it can thus be seen as the monstrous product of his own isolation, of his inability to find what he claims he greatly needs at the very beginning of his journey—a friend with "affection enough for me to endeavour to regulate my mind" (14). Victor also knows quite well that he is not only the creator of a monster, but also the author of "the strangest tale that ever imagination formed" (207). Through the monster, we learn that he recorded in detail the events leading up to the creation of the monster. "You minutely described in these papers every step you took in the progress of your work," comments the monster (126). Further, when Victor discovers that Robert Walton is making notes concerning this history, "he asked to see them, and then himself corrected and augmented them in many places; but principally in giving the life and spirit to the conversations he held with his enemy." For readers who may have missed the analogy between Victor's endeavor to reanimate these dead conversations (that is, Robert Walton's already aborted record of them) and his earlier efforts at "bestowing animation upon lifeless matter" (47), Mary Shelley adds the following comment. "'Since you have preserved my narration,' said he, 'I would not that a mutilated one should go down to posterity'" (207).

Mary Shelley's decision to write a novel in which creation takes the form of a birth myth should not be seen, then, as simply a form of personal therapy, a way of representing, as Moers first argued, maternal horror; nor is it simply an autobiographical depiction of the abstract notion of the self as monster. By drawing out the analogy between bodily and artistic reproduction, Shelley also found a way to argue for the importance of a domestic environment and a discipline of imagination in the creation of art. Agreeing with her mother that it was not women, but men who suffered most from excessive imaginations, from moral weakness, and from "appetites . . . more depraved by unbridled indulgence and the fastidious contrivances of satiety," Mary Shelley turns the discourse on the management of pregnant women back upon men, to argue that it is they who must learn to regulate their bodies and idealizing fantasies.[32] As William Veeder has suggested, Mary Shelley shares with nineteenth-century "domestic" feminists the ideal of extending "feminine virtues," such as modesty, to men, in order to "curb masculine excesses."[33] By making Victor "pregnant" with an idea, she is able to apply this complex discourse on the biological creation of monsters, one that had focused on female creation, to Romantic aesthetics. She was thus able to counter the prevailing idea of the poet, set forth by her husband in *Alastor,* as an isolated genius whose fixation on the ideal necessarily leads him into conflict with nature and society. By abrogating the laws of nature and reproduction, Victor destroys nature and himself.

I have so far restricted my comments to the manner in which Mary Shelley applied obstetric discourse to others, to the physical and psychic management of male Romantic conceptions. This still leaves the question of her own attitude toward this discourse unclear. To the extent that we read **Frankenstein** as an autobiography, we might see it as the expression of a contradictory sense of guilt on her own part and a reproach against her husband for his outright disregard of the emotional and physical needs of a pregnant woman. It is well known that the novel is closely bound up with Mary Shelley's intense anguish at the death of her first child, an unnamed daughter, born prematurely, who died shortly thereafter. It should be added, however, that it would have been difficult for any woman, having faced this painful loss, not to have also wondered whether her inability to carry this child for its full term was not caused by the physical, emotional, and financial strains that she had suffered from the moment she first eloped with Shelley. The death of this child, combined with the events surrounding the death of Clara in 1818, not only suggest that her husband gave little thought to the needs of pregnant women and children, but also make it clear that Mary's insistence on the importance of a domestic environment for the delivery of healthy children was not for her a set of abstract principles, but was deeply rooted in personal experience.

In the preface of 1831, a more complex idea of the relationship between Mary Shelley's aesthetics and obstetric theory emerges. Though ostensibly written to provide biographical facts concerning the creation of **Frankenstein,** the preface is actually largely a fiction, explicitly addressing the question of literary authority. From the moment that Shelley, punning on the word "dilate," announces that she will answer the frequently asked question, "How I, then a young girl, came to think of, and to dilate upon, so very hideous an idea?," we are given notice that the preface will equate, as Marc Rubenstein has observed, conceiving or *"think-ing of a story . . .* with producing a baby."[34] Obstetric theory reappears as the language with which she explains, often using double-entendres, the birth of this monstrous text. Having recounted the events surrounding the ghost-story contest (and we should remember that pregnant women, as James Guillemeau observed, were not to "give eare unto lamentable and fearefull tales or storyes"), she inserts what may, in fact, be her own fictional version of Polidori's tale:

> Poor Polidori had some terrible idea about a skull-headed lady, who was so punished for peeping

through a key-hole—what to see I forget—something very shocking and wrong of course; but when she was reduced to a worse condition than the renowned Tom of Coventry, he did not know what to do with her, and was obliged to despatch her to the tomb of the Capulets, the only place for which she was fitted.

> [225]

In this story, it is the woman, rather than the child, who is turned into a monster by what she sees—"something very shocking and wrong of course." Nevertheless, it shares with obstetric tales the emphasis on the need for a moral regimen, the pernicious effect of shocking sights, and the dangerous powers, which can only be alluded to obliquely, of sexual activity and desire.[35]

The reproductive metaphors structuring Mary Shelley's account of how she conceived the idea of **Franken-stein** are but thinly veiled. She describes how, like Victor, she initially set out to create the story single-handedly. But she confronted a "blank incapability of invention," and when asked each morning, *"Have you thought of a story?,"* was forced "to reply with a mortifying negative" (226). At this point, drawing explicitly on embryological metaphors, she addresses the question of aesthetic invention:

> Invention, it must be humbly admitted, does not consist in creating out of void, but out of chaos; the materials must, in the first place, be afforded: it can give form to dark, shapeless substances, but cannot bring into being the substance itself. In all matters of discovery and invention, even of those that appertain to the imagination, we are continually reminded of the story of Columbus and his egg. Invention consists in the capacity of seizing on the capabilities of a subject, and in the power of moulding and fashioning ideas suggested to it. [226]

In a very suggestive interpretation of the preface, with which I plan to disagree, Marc Rubenstein has argued that Mary Shelley accepts the traditional Classical notion that the female is passive in procreation and that this passage (along with others in the preface) shows the "great pains" that she took, in her aversion to bringing herself forward in print, "to disclaim any role for her own imagination" in the creation of **Frankenstein**. He goes on to argue that in the next paragraph, when she tells how she, a "nearly silent listener," overheard Shelley and Byron discussing Erasmus Darwin's experiments in bestowing life on a piece of vermicelli, "she is trying to draw for us a picture of her imagination as a passive womb, inseminated by those titans of romantic poetry, Byron and Shelley."[36] As further support, Rubenstein has insightfully noted that in *Zoönomia* Darwin had also taken up a radically male-oriented obstetric position by arguing "that the world has long been mistaken in ascribing great power to the imagination of the female, whereas . . . the real power of imagination, in the act of generation, belongs solely to the male." "Monstrous births" are to be attributed solely to "the imagination of the *male* parent."[37] Drawing on an essentially false analogy between reproduction in humans and in plant and birds, Darwin argues that since "the eggs in pullets, like the seeds in vegetables, are produced gradually, long before they are impregnated, it does not appear how any sudden effect of imagination of the mother at the time of impregnation can produce any considerable change in the nutriment already thus laid up for the expected or desired embryon. And that hence any changes of the embryon, except those uniform ones in the production of mules and mulattoes, more probably depend on the imagination of the male parent." Like his predecessors, Darwin was able to supply medical cases to support his position. One such example involved a man who had a child with dark hair and dark eyes, despite the fact that he and his wife were of light complexion:

> On observing this dissimilarity of one child to the others he assured me, that he believed it was his own imagination, that produced the difference; and related to me the following story. He said, that when his lady lay in of her third child, he became attached to a daughter of one of his inferior tenants, and offered her a bribe for her favours in vain; and afterwards a greater bribe, and was equally unsuccessful; that the form of this girl dwelt much in his mind for some weeks, and that the next child, which was the dark-ey'd young lady above mentioned, was exceedingly like, in both features and colour, to the young woman who refused his addresses.

Darwin thus felt confident that the form, and even the sex, of a child was determined by "the imagination of the male at the time of copulation, or at the time of the secretion of the semen . . . as the motions of the chissel of the turner imitate or correspond with those of the ideas of the artist." Males could be said to be the product of men who were thinking primarily about themselves and their own organs during sexual intercourse, while females were a likely result of men who were thinking about a female form, and her organs, during the sexual act. Darwin consequently concluded that *callipaedia,* the art of begetting beautiful children and of procreating either males or females could, indeed, be taught, though the subject could not "be unfolded with sufficient delicacy for the public eye." He nevertheless does hint that "the phalli, which were hung round the necks of the Roman ladies, or worn in their hair, might have effect in producing a greater proportion of male children."[38]

Darwin's theory of generation led a somewhat eccentric and short-lived life in medical history. It was nevertheless the kind of theory that would have interested Shelley and Byron, as it foregrounded the powers of the male imagination. Thus, it may also have been a topic of discussion at the Villa Diodati. If such was the case, then we can recognize the extent to which Mary Shelley, in *Frankenstein* and the preface, despite her assumption of the mask of a Proper Lady, actually resists this male usurpation of the powers of imagination traditionally reserved for women. If we return to the previously cited passage concerning Columbus's egg, it is clear that even as she evokes the Aristotelian idea of the male (Columbus) fashioning the "dark, shapeless substances" of the female (egg), the point of the passage is to reverse this relationship. Rather than presenting the female as passive, it insists that even if the male may provide the "incitement" (229) to create, the female does the inventing, because "invention consists in the capacity of seizing on the capabilities of a subject, and in the power of moulding and fashioning ideas suggested to it" (226). It is also hard to miss the slightly risqué satire operating in her description of the two men talking about Darwin's having "preserved a piece of vermicelli in a glass case, till by some extraordinary means it began to move with voluntary motion." Since vermicelli is the diminutive form of *verme,* or "worm," a word whose phallic meaning was conventional, it is not difficult to see in Mary Shelley's comment, "Not thus, after all, would life be given" (227), an outright rejection of Darwin's theory of generation as much as of his theory of life.[39]

Rubenstein rightly argues that Mary Shelley's account of how she overheard the two poets talking about creation is an account of verbal insemination. But when she describes the conception of the monster, she reasserts the power of the female imagination to create monsters:

> Night waned upon this talk, and even the witching hour had gone by, before we retired to rest. When I placed my head on my pillow, I did not sleep, nor could I be said to think. My imagination, unbidden, possessed and guided me, gifting the successive images that arose in my mind with a vividness far beyond the usual bounds of reverie. I saw—with shut eyes, but acute mental vision,—I saw the pale student of unhallowed arts kneeling beside the thing he had put together. I saw the hideous phantasm of a man stretched out, and then, on the working of some powerful engine, show signs of life, and stir with an uneasy, half vital motion. [227-28]

Here, as Mary Shelley, "possessed and guided" by her imagination, engenders, at the "witching hour," her own "hideous phantasm," which comes between her and her husband (who ostensibly sleeps beside her), there is no suggestion of passivity in the female imagination. Even the sexual metaphors tend to reassert the generative powers of the female, for what distinguishes the vermicelli that began "to move with voluntary motion" from the "powerful engine" that engenders on "a man stretched out . . . an uneasy, half vital motion" is the intervention of a woman's imagination.

Margaret Homans, in her recent study of nineteenth-century literature, has suggestively argued that women during the nineteenth century were viewed as the bearers of words as well as of children. *Frankenstein* suggests that the very question of whether women could be the true authors of these letters or could, through the power of their imaginations, revise and deface the words and children that they bore, was an issue fought out not only in the aesthetic sphere, but also in the theories of biological generation that it employs. *Frankenstein* provides a paradigm of the manner in which a female author could invert a disciplinary discourse to assert her own power and authority while also limiting the power and authority of others. In this sense, her willingness to "bid my hideous progeny go forth and prosper," constitutes, by its admission that the novel is her monster alone (which "did not owe the suggestion of one incident, nor scarcely of one train of feeling, to my husband" [229]) an assertion of her own imaginative authority, one that strangely was forced to proceed through the figure of a monstrous text. Yet it should equally be said that this criticism also implicitly extends to Mary Shelley herself, and indicates a conflict between her imaginative needs and her conception of her duty as a mother.

Since Mary Shelley, to assert this contradictory power, needed to appropriate an obsolescent medical discourse, we should also recognize that the novel stands in a somewhat ambivalent relationship to the obstetric theory of her time, which had become, by the 1820s, almost exclusively a male science. This ambivalence is part of the novel's criticism of the scientific and medical takeover of the sphere of human reproduction, the increasing control that obstetrics had taken over the workshop of creation through its claim, phrased in a typically masculine manner, that it could "penetrate into the recesses of nature, and shew how she works in her hiding places" (42). To place Mary Shelley's critique of obstetric theory in context, we should recognize that she was not the first woman to be critical of the rising power of this new science: for almost two centuries, women, for more reasons than simply modesty, had expressed concern about the views and practices of man-midwives. *Tristram Shandy* captures this controversy at its most strident phase, during the third quarter of the eighteenth century.[40] Certainly the most influential female voice was that of the midwife Elizabeth Nihell, whose *Treatise on the Art of Midwifery* (1760) constitutes a concerted polemic, generally against the male "usurpation" of the field, through scientific knowledge and instruments, and particularly against William Smellie. In this work of extraordinary rhetorical power, one of her best-known images has striking affinities with the story of *Frankenstein*:

> As to the reproach which Mr. Smellie makes to us of being interested, I can, for myself, prove that I have delivered gratuitously, and in pure charity, above nine hundred women. I doubt much, whether our critic can say as much, unless he reckons it for a charity, that which he exercised on his automaton or machine, which served him for a model of instruction to his pupils. This was a wooden statue, representing a woman with child, whose belly was of leather, in which a bladder full, perhaps, of small beer, represented the uterus. This bladder was stopped with a cork, to which was fastened a string of packthread to tap it, occasionally, and demonstrate in a palpable manner the flowing of the red-colored waters. In short, in the middle of the bladder was a wax-doll, to which were given various positions.

> By this admirably ingenious piece of machinery, were formed and started up an innumerable and formidable swarm of men-midwives, spread over the town and country. . . . Does it become a doctor to call us interested, who himself, for three guineas in nine lessons, made you a man-midwife, or a female one, by means of this most curious machine, this mock-woman?[41]

In this image of William Smellie "exercis[ing] on his automaton," his "mock-woman," with its leather belly, its bladder-uterus filled with beer, yet stopped with a cork, there is much that anticipates (and ironically undercuts) nineteenth-century male fantasies about the scientific elimination of the biological need for women.[42] Much too that suggests the ambiguous sexual and maternal bonding between Victor and his monster. The parallel is even more emphatic when one recalls the female monster that Victor decides to destroy, in fear that "a race of devils would be propagated upon the earth, who might make the very existence of the species of man a condition precarious and full of terror" (163). Yet what makes Mary Shelley's story of monstrous creation different from Nihell's is that Mary Shelley could not take up Nihell's cause without also recognizing that modern science had made this discourse, with its continuing assertion of the power of female imagination, obsolescent. "You have burdened your memory with exploded systems, and useless names. . . . These fancies, which you have so greedily imbibed, are a thousand years old, and as musty as they are ancient," declares squat Mr. Kempe, as he criticizes Victor's interest in occult science and gives him a bibliography of new books to read. In *Frankenstein,* if we listen carefully, we can hear the names and voices of this superseded female tradition, which Mary Shelley, like Victor, drew upon in order to assert her own ambiguous power as an author.

Notes

[1] Mary Wollstonecraft Shelley, *Frankenstein, or The Modern Prometheus,* edited by James Rieger (Chicago: University of Chicago Press, 1982), 97. All future citations to this edition will be incorporated in the text.

[2] Ellen Moers, "Female Gothic," in *Literary Women* (Garden City, N. Y.: Doubleday, 1976), 92.

[3] Moers, "Female Gothic," 81.

[4] Mary Jacobus, "Is There a Woman in This Text?," *New Literary History* 14 (1982): 138.

[5] Barbara Johnson, "My Monster/My Self," *Diacritics* 12 (1982): 10, 4.

[6] Margaret Homans, "Feminist Criticism and Theory. The Ghost of Creusa," *Yale Journal of Criticism* 1 (1987): 167.

[7] Johnson, "My Monster/My Self," 3.

[8] Alexander Hamilton, *Outlines of the Theory and Practice of Midwifery,* new ed. (Edinburgh: Charles Elliot, 1787), 188.

[9] Alexander Hamilton, *The Family Female Physician: or, a Treatise on the Management of Female Complaints, and of Children in Early Infancy* (Worcester, Mass.: Isaiah Thomas, 1793), 161-62.

[10] Hamilton, *Theory and Practice of Midwifery,* 189.

[11] Michel Foucault, *The History of Sexuality. Volume 1: An Introduction,* translated by Robert Hurley (New York: Pantheon, 1978), 42.

[12] James Augustus Blondel, *The Strength of Imagination in Pregnant Women Examin'd: And the Opinion that Marks and Deformations in Children Arise from Thence, Demonstrated to be a Vulgar Error* (London: J. Peele, 1727), 10-11.

[13] Ambroise Paré, *Of the Generation of Man, in The Works of that Famous Chirugeon Ambrose Parey,* translated by Thomas Johnson (London: Mary Clark, 1678), 596.

[14] The implicit rivalry between the father and these surrogate images is indicated in the story, attributed to Saint Jerome, of how Hippocrates saved a noblewoman from being punished as an adulteress, for giving birth to a child of dark complexion when she and her husband were both white. It is said that he had observed a picture hanging in the woman's chamber, "exactly resembling the Infant, and which he found she had been often very intently viewing" (Daniel Turner, *De Morbis Cutaneis. A Treatise of Diseases Incident to the Skin. In Two Parts* [London: R. Bonwicke, J. Walthoe, R. Wilkin, T. Ward, and S. Tooke, 1723], 169).

[15] Turner, *De Morbis Cutaneis,* 169.

[16] Nicolas Malebranche, *The Search after Truth,* translated by Thomas M. Lennon and Paul J. Olscamp (Columbus, Ohio: Ohio State University, 1980), 115-16.

[17] Aristotle [pseud.], *Aristotle's Compleat and Experienc'd Midwife: In Two Parts,* 7th ed. (London, 1740?), 28.

[18] Jane Sharp, *The Midwives Book. Or the Whole Art of Midwifry Discovered. Directing Childbearing Women how to behave themselves; In their Conception, Breeding, Bearing, and Nursing of Children* (1671; rpt. New York: Garland Publishing, 1985), 103.

[19] Blondel, *The Strength of Imagination in Pregnant Women Examin'd* i; Blondel, *The Power of the Mother's Imagination over the Foetus Examin'd* (London: John Brotherton, 1729), xi.

[20] Blondel, *The Power of the Mother's Imagination over the Foetus Examin'd,* 2.

[21] Aristotle [pseud.], *Aristotle's Compleat Master-Piece, In Three Parts; Displaying the Secrets of Nature in the Generation of Man,* 13th ed. (London: Zechariah Felding, 1766), 40.

[22] James Guillemeau, *Child-birth; or, The Happy Deliverie of Women. Wherein is set downe the Government of Women. In the Time: Of their Breeding Childe: Of their Travaile, both Naturall, and Contrary to Nature: And Of their Lying in* (London: A. Hatfield, 1612), 26.

[23] Blondel, *The Power of the Mother's Imagination over the Foetus Examin'd,* 8.

[24] Ben Jonson, *Bartholomew Fair,* edited by Eugene M. Waith (New Haven: Yale University Press, 1963). For an excellent discussion of obstetric theories of the imagination and eighteenth-century literature, see G. S. Rousseau, "Pineapples, Pregnancy, and *Peregrine Pickle,*" in *Tobias Smollett: Bicentennial Essays Presented to Lewis M. Knapp,* edited by G. S. Rousseau and P.-G. Boucé (New York: Oxford University Press, 1971), 79-109.

[25] For a perceptive study of what eighteenth-century women thought about their sexuality and the ways in which they sought to deny, repress, or control their passion, see Patricia Meyer Spacks, "Ev'ry Woman is at Heart a Rake," *Eighteenth Century Studies* 8 (1974): 27-46. In pointing out that "imagination is—or is understood by these woman writers to be—actually the source of sexual feeling," Spacks cites Mrs. Thrale's comments on the relationship between obsession and sexual passion: "'Tis this *Avarice* of mental Enjoyment, this *Hoarded* Folly; which now & then so blazes out of a sudden under the Name of Love; & I think the Reason

of that Furor being more violent among the Female Sex is chiefly because being less tolerated to *declare* their Passion, it preys upon the Mind till it burst all Reserve, & makes itself amends for their long Concealment" (38). Obstetric discourse, in its admission of the violence of female imagination and in its fear of the effect that the repression of desire might have on the child, explicitly addressed concerns that were otherwise generally left unspoken.

[26] François Rabelais, *The Histories of Gargantua and Pantagruel* (1955; rpt. Great Britain: Penguin, 1983), 48.

[27] Thomas Laqueur, "Orgasm, Generation, and the Politics of Reproductive Biology," *Representations* 14 (1986): 1-41.

[28] Margaret Homans, *Bearing the Word: Language and Female Experience in Nineteenth-Century Women's Writing* (Chicago: University of Chicago Press, 1986), 103.

[29] Shelley, *Frankenstein,* 51; the citation includes autograph variants from the Thomas copy of 1823.

[30] Shelley, *Frankenstein,* 242. In a more extensive study of the medical discourse on sexuality informing *Frankenstein,* it would be valuable to explore, as William Veeder has insightfully suggested, the ways in which contemporary descriptions of the physiological effects of masturbation provide an additional explanation for Victor's increasing nervousness and possible insanity. The major works in this area are the frequently reprinted anonymous book *Onania; or the Heinous Sin of Self-Pollution, and all its Frightful Consequences, in Both Sexes, Considered* (1707-8) and S. A. Tissot's *Onanism* (London, 1766). For secondary literature on this subject, see E. H. Hare, "Masturbatory Insanity: The History of an Idea," *Journal of the History of Medical Science* 108 (1962): 1-25; R. H. MacDonald, "The Frightful Consequences of Onanism," *Journal of the History of Ideas* 28 (1967): 423-31; and G. S. Rousseau, "Nymphomania, Bienville and the Rise of Erotic Sensibility," in *Sexuality in Eighteenth-Century Britain,* edited by Paul-Gabriel Boucé (Totowa, N.J.: Barnes and Noble, 1982), 95-119.

[31] It is worth noting that during the eighteenth century accounts of monstrous births began to appear with greater frequency in the proceedings of the Royal Academy. The subject matter of this genre of medical discourse, which G. S. Rousseau has discussed in illuminating detail (93-94), can be gleaned from a listing of the titles of some of these cases: "A Foetus of Thirteen Years"; "Fatal Accident: Woman Carry'd a Child Sixteen Years"; "Account of a Monstrous Boy"; "Account of a monstrous child born of a woman under sentence of transportation"; "An account of a mon-

strous foetus resembling an hooded monkey"; "Case of a child turned upside down"; "A remarkable conformation, or lusus naturae in a child"; "Part of a letter concerning a child of monstrous size"; "Account of a Child's being taken out of the abdomen after having lain there upwards of 16 years"; "A Letter concerning a child born with an extraordinary tumor near the anus, containing some rudiments of an embryo in it"; "An account of a praeternatural conjunction of two female children"; "Part of a letter concerning a child born with the jaundice upon it, received from its father's imagination, and of the mother taking the same distemper from her husband the next time of being with child"; or "An Account of a double child born at Hebus, near Middletown in Lancashire." It is clear that when Victor Frankenstein decided to give a scientific account of his own "monstrous birth," a child that took two years to create, he was not writing in a vacuum, but was contributing to an already well-established genre of scientific inquiry.

[32] Mary Wollstonecraft, *Vindication of the Rights of Woman,* edited by Miriam Brody (Harmondsworth, England: Penguin, 1975), 247.

[33] William Veeder, *Mary Shelley and "Frankenstein": The Fate of Androgyny* (Chicago: University of Chicago Press, 1986), 31. This argument was originally made by Mary Poovey, who suggests that the development of Mary Shelley's career reveals "the way that a certain kind of literary self-expression could accommodate a woman's unorthodox desires to the paradigm of the Proper Lady" (*The Proper Lady and the Woman Writer* [Chicago: University of Chicago Press, 1984], 116).

[34] Marc Rubenstein, "'My Accursed Origin': The Search for the Mother in *Frankenstein,*" *Studies in Romanticism* 15 (1976): 179.

[35] One of the more popular of obstetric cases, drawn from Fienus' *de viribus Imaginationis,* was that of the sister of Philip Meurs, Apostolical Pronotar and Canon of St. Peter's in Louvain, whose sister was in every way normal, except that she was without a head, "instead of which was joyned to Her Neck the Likeness of a Shell Fish, having two Valves which shut and open'd; and by which, from a Spoon, she took her Nourishment" (Daniel Turner, *De Morbis Cutaneis,* 175). It seems that the mother had a strong desire for mussels, which she was unable to procure at that instant. This girl lived to the age of eleven, when in a fit of anger, she angrily bit down on the spoon that fed her, which broke these valves, and she died shortly thereafter.

[36] Rubenstein, "My Accursed Origin," 178-81. Mary Poovey also argues that in the preface and in her 1831 revisions to the novel, Mary Shelley rejects the imagi-

nation in favor of notions of female passivity and propriety.

[37] Erasmus Darwin, *Zoönomia; or, the Laws of Organic Life,* 2 vols. (London: J. Johnson, 1794-96), 1:520, 1:516.

[38] *Zoönomia,* 1:515-24.

[39] U. C. Knoepflmacher sees "a faint note of resentment" in Mary Shelley's recital of "the two 'illustrious poets' who, 'annoyed by the platitude of prose, speedily relinquished their uncongenial task.' The seed they have so carelessly implanted in Mary (and 'poor Polidori') becomes a burden that is hers alone. It is she who has to give birth to a 'hideous progeny,' because she can better understand the pains of abandonment. Like the Monster, the author has been deserted" ("Thoughts on the Aggression of Daughters," in *The Endurance of Frankenstein: Essays on Mary Shelley's Novel,* edited by George Levine and U. C. Knoepflmacher [Berkeley and Los Angeles: University of California Press, 1979], 100).

[40] For a useful overview of the debate between Elizabeth Nihell and William Smellie, see I. H. Flack (pseud. Harvey Graham), *Eternal Eve; the History of Gynaecology and Obstetrics* (Garden City, N.Y.: Doubleday, 1951), 269-305. For the obstetric context of *Tristram Shandy,* see Arthur H. Cash, "The Birth of Tristram Shandy: Sterne and Dr Burton," in *Sexuality in Eighteenth-Century Britain,* edited by Paul-Gabriel Boucé, 198-224.

[41] Elizabeth Nihell, *A Treatise on the Art of Midwifery. Setting Forth various Abuses therein, especially as to the Practice with Instruments: the Whole Serving to put all Rational Inquirers in a fair Way of very safely forming their own Judgment upon the Question; Which is it best to employ, in Cases of Pregnancy and Lying-in, a Man-Midwife or, a Midwife* (London: A. Morley, 1760), 50-52.

[42] Mary Jacobus, in her exploration of the role of mimetic desire and rivalry in theoretical discourse, in "Is There a Woman in This Text?," examines in greater detail scientists' efforts to eliminate women from their creation myths.

Anne K. Mellor (essay date 1988)

SOURCE: "Problems of Perception," in *Mary Shelley: Her Life, Her Fiction, Her Monsters,* Methuen, 1988, pp. 127-40.

[*In the following chapter from her book-length study of Shelley's work, Mellor examines how Shelley depicts human nature in* Frankenstein. *Considering the novel in its intellectual context, Mellor determines that it "presents diametrically opposed answers": the Rousseauean* tabula rasa *on one hand and an Augustinian inherent evil on the other.*]

. . . How does Mary Shelley conceive of nature as such? In other words, what *is* nature, both the external world and human nature? *Frankenstein* insistently raises this question. It is the question that Victor is trying to answer, namely, "whence . . . did the principle of life proceed?" (46). And it is the question that haunts his creature, who repeatedly asks "Who was I? What was I? Whence did I come? What was my destination?" (124).

As the characters wrestle with this ontological problem, the novel presents diametrically opposed answers. The creature insists that his innate nature is innocent, benevolent, loving. He is Rousseau's noble savage, born free but everywhere in chains, a Blakean man of innocent energy. Confronting Frankenstein for the first time, he asserts "I was benevolent and good; misery made me a fiend" (95). At the end of his autobiographical narration, the creature repeats that "My vices are the children of a forced solitude that I abhor; and my virtues will necessarily arise when I live in communion with an equal" (143). Frankenstein, in opposition, claims that his creature is innately evil, a vile insect, a devil: "Abhorred monster! fiend that thou art! the tortures of hell are too mild a vengeance for thy crimes. Wretched devil!" (94). If the creature represents innate human nature, as Mary Shelley's persistent authorial denomination of him as "creature" and Percy Shelley's editorial revision of "creature" to "being" suggest, then is a human being innately good or innately evil, a romantic child of innocence or an Augustinian child of original sin?

The question is vividly focused in the symbolic scene when the creature first sees himself. "How was I terrified, when I viewed myself in a transparent pool! At first I started back, unable to believe that it was indeed I who was reflected in the mirror; and when I became fully convinced that I was in reality the monster that I am, I was filled with the bitterest sensations of despondence and mortification" (109). This important passage suggests that in this novel identity is a process not so much of knowing (re-cognition) as of *seeing.* Even though the creature is unable to recognize himself, "unable to believe it was indeed I," his eyes convince him that "I was in reality the monster that I am."

As a unique being, an original, the creature functions in the novel as the sign of the unfamiliar, the unknown. He is a sign detached from a visual or verbal grammar, without diachronic or synchronic context, without precursor or progeny.[1] As such, he poses the fundamental epistemological problem: how is he to be perceived? In the novel, all the characters impose a semiotic construction upon the creature. They read his features or interpret his appearance as having a determinate meaning. In effect, they endorse the contemporary theories of Johann Caspar Lavater and Franz Gall. Lavater's treatise on physiognomy argued that the innate soul or character of the individual manifested itself in the person's physical appearance. The properly trained physiognomist could therefore determine a person's moral nature by correctly reading the meaning of his or her physical characteristics. Dr. Gall and his English-based disciple Johann Christoph Spurzheim reversed Lavater's theory and argued instead that the actual physical formation of the newborn infant determined its later moral nature. One could therefore identify a person's character by correctly reading the shape of his or her skull and body. This new "science" of phrenology was familiar to Mary Shelley. She had herself been physiognomically diagnosed as a three-week-old infant and had learned the basic tenets of Dr. Gall's system in 1814 from her friend Henry Voisey.[2]

The creature's unfamiliar physiognomy is consistently interpreted by the characters in the novel as monstrous, threatening, or evil. Victor Frankenstein, already prejudiced by his youthful "invincible repugnance to new countenances" (40), immediately construes his animated creature as a "wretch": "I beheld the wretch—the miserable monster whom I had created" (53). As his creature, grinning, leans forward to embrace his father, Frankenstein sees the gesture as an attempt "seemingly to detain me" (53) and quickly "escapes" from "the demoniacal corpse to which I had so miserably given life," exclaiming that "no mortal could support the horror of that countenance" (53).

That Frankenstein's response is an *arbitrary* semantic construction is made clear when he next encounters his creature. Seeing his gigantic form approach across the Mer de Glace, Frankenstein observes that "his countenance bespoke bitter anguish, combined with disdain and malignity" (94). But the creature resists this consistently negative reading of his appearance. When Frankenstein again violently rejects his offspring—"Begone! relieve me from the sight of your detested form"—his creature responds: "'Thus I relieve thee, my creator,' he said, and placed his hated hands before my eyes" (96). The creature thus draws our attention to the possibility that Frankenstein is *misreading* his countenance, judging a mere appearance rather than the hidden reality.

Not only Frankenstein but all the other people the creature encounters immediately see his physiognomy as evil. The old man in his hut, "perceiving me, shrieked loudly, and, quitting the hut, ran across the fields with a speed of which his debilitated form hardly appeared capable" (100). The inhabitants of the nearby village "shrieked . . . fainted . . . attacked me, until, grievously bruised by stones and many other kinds of missile

weapons, I escaped to the open country" (101). When Felix, Agatha and Safie finally see him:

> Who can describe their horror and consternation on beholding me? Agatha fainted; and Safie, unable to attend to her friend, rushed out of the cottage. Felix darted forward, and with supernatural force tore me from his father, to whose knees I clung: in a transport of fury, he dashed me to the ground, and struck me violently with a stick. (131)

The rustic whose drowning girlfriend he saves both tears her from the creature's arms and then shoots the creature. And even the young eyes of William Frankenstein, as the creature embraces him, instantly see the creature as evil: "As soon as he beheld my form, he placed his hands before his eyes, and uttered a shrill scream . . . 'Let me go,' he cried; 'monster! ugly wretch! you wish to eat me, and tear me to pieces— You are an ogre'—"(139).

Only two characters in the novel do not immediately interpret the creature as evil. The first of course is blind. Father De Lacey, unable to see the creature kneeling at his feet, listens instead to his eloquent speech and *hears* truth in the creature's assertion that "I have good dispositions; my life has been hitherto harmless, and, in some degree, beneficial; but a fatal prejudice clouds their eyes, and where they ought to see a feeling and kind friend, they behold only a detestable monster" (130). Father De Lacey replies, "I am blind, and cannot judge of your countenance, but there is something in your words which persuades me that you are sincere" (130). Here Father De Lacey articulates the reader's own response. The reader (as opposed to the filmgoer) has not *seen* the Monster, but only *heard* descriptions of his appearance. At this point in the novel, the reader's sympathies have shifted away from the horrified Frankenstein and toward the speaking creature, whose language is at least as powerful as the words earlier spoken about him. Mary Shelley gives the reader—through Father De Lacey—the opportunity to choose between two competing sets of information: that provided by those characters who see the monster but don't listen to him and that provided by Father De Lacey who listens to the creature but can't see him. But whether the blind De Lacey reads the creature's character correctly, we as readers can never know, for he is ripped out of the novel by his prejudging son.

Walton, because he has listened to the creature's autobiography, does not immediately reject him on the basis of a first impression, a single reading of his face. Confronting the creature for the first time at Frankenstein's deathbed, Walton is both repulsed— "Never did I behold a vision so horrible as his face, of such loathsome, yet appalling hideousness. I shut my eyes involuntarily . . ."—and, because he has thus eliminated his visual image of the creature, attracted to him: "I called on him to stay" (216). Hearing the creature's remorse, Walton's "first impulses, which had suggested to me the duty of obeying the dying request of my friend, in destroying his enemy, were now suspended by a mixture of curiosity and compassion" (217). Walton's responses to the creature continue to veer between sympathy—"I was at first touched by the expressions of his misery"—and hostility—"when I again cast my eyes on the lifeless form of my friend, indignation was re-kindled within me" (218). But Walton's final judgement on the creature is mute. After the creature's impassioned apologia pro vita sua, Walton says nothing. In the last sentence of the manuscript, he significantly loses "sight" of the creature "in the darkness and distance."

This last sentence thus underlines the basic problem of perception in the novel: how are we to *see* the innate being of the creature? Walton, who of all the characters knows him best, has "lost sight" of him. The creature's self-analysis acknowledges that he is both good and evil, but perhaps like King Lear more sinned against than sinning:

> Once I falsely hoped to meet with beings, who, pardoning my outward form, would, love me for the excellent qualities which I was capable of bringing forth. I was nourished with high thoughts of honour and devotion. But now vice has degraded me beneath the meanest animal. No crime, no mischief, no malignity, no misery, can be found comparable to mine . . . the fallen angel becomes a malignant devil. . . . Am I to be thought the only criminal, when all human kind sinned against me? (219)

But neither Walton nor the author confirms the creature's self-analysis. At the end he remains lost "in darkness and distance."

The creature thus represents the confrontation of the human mind with an unknowable nature, with the experience that eighteenth-century philosophers called the sublime. The creature, in fact, inhabits those landscapes that Edmund Burke explicitly identified as the sources of the sublime. In his *A Philosophical Inquiry into the Origin of Our Ideas of the Sublime and the Beautiful* (1757), Burke characterised the sublime as "whatever is fitted in any sort to excite the ideas of pain and danger; that is to say, whatever is in any sort terrible, or is conversant about terrible objects, or operates in a manner analogous to terror, is a source of the *sublime*; that is, it is productive of the strongest emotions which the mind is capable of feeling."[3] A sublime landscape is one which seems to threaten the viewer's life. Burke defined the typical qualities of a sublime landscape as greatness of dimension (especially as contrasted with the finite limits of the human body) which gives rise to an idea of infinity; obscurity

(which blurs the definition of boundaries); profound darkness or intense light; and sudden, sharp angles. Confronted with such overwhelming objects as towering mountains, huge dark caves, gloomy architectural ruins, or sudden blinding light, the human mind first experiences terror or fear and then, as the instinct of self-preservation is gradually relaxed, astonishment ("that state of the soul in which all its motions are suspended with some degree of horror"[4]), admiration, reverence, and respect. For one thus receives, according to Burke, a sensible impression of the Deity by whose power these overwhelming scenes are created.

The appearances of the creature in the novel are simultaneous with the revelation of the sublime. Approaching Secheron as night encloses the Alps, Frankenstein encounters a violent storm: "thunder burst with a terrific crash over my head. It was echoed from Salêve, the Juras, and the Alps of Savoy; vivid flashes of lightning dazzled my eyes, illuminating the lake, making it appear like a vast sheet of fire; then for an instant every thing seemed of a pitchy darkness" (71). As lightning flashes, Frankenstein's terrified eyes recognize in this landscape of Satan's Pandemonium the creature he had abandoned, "hanging among the rocks," the creature who is again lost in obscurity as the scene is "enveloped in an impenetrable darkness" (72). Frankenstein first speaks to his creature on the Mer de Glace above Chamounix, a landscape defined by eighteenth-century travellers as the locus of the sublime. The creature then follows him to an equally threatening, desolate landscape, the remotest of the Orkneys, "a rock, whose high sides were continually beaten upon by the waves" (161). The sublime nature of this northern Scottish coast was captured by Turner in his drawings of mountain torrents, stormy seas, Ben Arthur, and Ailsa Rock for his "Scottish Pencils" series done in 1801. The creature finally ends his existence among "the mountainous ices of the ocean" at the North Pole, in that frozen wasteland imaged in Caspar David Friedrich's *The Wreck of the "Hope"* (1821) as the ultimate apocalyptic sublime, where he is "lost in darkness and distance" (221).

The creature himself embodies the human sublime. His gigantic stature, his physical strength (as great as "the winds" or "a mountain stream," acknowledges Frankenstein [74]), his predilection for desert mountains and dreary glaciers (where he alone finds "refuge" [95]), and above all his origin in the transgression of the boundary between life and death, all render him both "obscure" and "vast," the touchstones of the sublime. Moreover, the creature's very existence seems to constitute a threat to human life. His appearance throughout the novel rouses "the strongest emotion which the mind is capable of feeling," a Gothic *frisson* of pure terror.

But Mary Shelley's calculated association of the creature with Burke's sublime is intended to do more than rouse a powerful aesthetic response in the reader. Thomas Weiskel has drawn our attention to the semiotic significance of sublime landscapes.[5] Encountering such a landscape, the human mind attempts to determine the meaning of the image before it. Burke and Kant suggested that the meaning of such an immense landscape is the infinite and incomprehensible power of God or nature (the thing-in-itself). In this reading, what is signified (divine omnipotence or the *Ding-an-sich*) is greater than the signifier (the landscape and our linguistic descriptions of it). Weiskel has called this the "negative" sublime, since the human mind is finally overwhelmed or negated by a greater, even transcendent power. In contrast, Wordsworth in the Mount Snowdon episode of *The Prelude* or Coleridge in "This Lime-tree Bower My Prison" suggested that the meaning of a sublime landscape may lie in its capacity to inspire the poetic imagination to a conception of its own power as a "mighty mind" or "almighty spirit."[6] In this reading, what is signified (the landscape) is less than the signifier (the poetic language produced by the creative imagination). Weiskel has called this the "positive" sublime, since the human mind finally confronts its own linguistic power.

With this distinction in mind, we can see that in semiotic terms, Frankenstein's creature brilliantly represents both the negative and the positive modes of the sublime. On the one hand, he is a vast power beyond human linguistic control. Like the wrath of God on judgment day, his revenge is boundless, imageless. His physical appearance is only a metaphor for the havoc he can wreak on the entire human race. As he warns Frankenstein:

> Slave, I before reasoned with you, but you have proved yourself unworthy of my condescension. Remember that I have power; you believe yourself miserable, but I can make you so wretched that the light of day will be hateful to you. You are my creator, but I am your master;—obey! (165)

In this reading of the creature as the negative sublime, he signifies the power of universal human destruction, the unthinkable, unimaginable, unspeakable, experience of a deluge or a holocaust. He is the thing-in-itself, the elemental "chaos" of external nature, those "dark, shapeless substances" which precede and annihilate the forms of life.[7] As Mary Shelley reminded her readers in her Preface to the 1831 edition of *Frankenstein:* "Invention . . . does not consist in creating out of void, but out of chaos; the materials must, in the first place, be afforded: it can give form to dark, shapeless substances, but cannot bring into being the substance itself." (226) As the *Ding-an-sich,* the dark shapeless substance itself, the creature is forever displaced by the mind's own "inventions," its categorizing or structuring perceptual processes. In this sense, the creature represents the positive sublime, an arbitrary semantic

system, that invented meaning which the human mind imposes on the chaos of nature. The creature is that which is "always already" linguistically structured in visual or verbal signs, his countenance both "bespoke" and "expressed". Mary Shelley here relies on a Kantian anthropology even as she anticipates its most sophisticated modern revisions. Like Sapir, Whorf, Lévi-Strauss, and Derrida, she suggests that the basic Kantian categories which structure the mind's phenomenological perceptions of nature are not space, time, unity, and causality, but rather the conventions of visual and verbal languages. Victor Frankenstein construes the unknown in linguistic terms: his creature's countenance "bespoke bitter anguish, combined with disdain and malignity"; it "expressed the utmost extent of malice and treachery" (94, 164). In this novel, such linguistic readings become social realities. The interpretations of nature that human minds supply become ideologies, phenomenological constructions of their material existence.

The semiotic significance of *Frankenstein* was recognized in the first dramatic production of the novel. H. M. Milner's play bill for *Frankenstein: or, The Man and the Monster. A Romantic Melo-Drama, in Two Acts,* first performed at the Royal Cobourg Theatre in London on July 3, 1826, listed the monster in the dramatis personae thus: "*********** [played by] Mr. O. Smith." Milner thus drew attention to the unknowability, the purely fictive semantic significance, of the creature. Mary Shelley commented approvingly when she saw Thomas Cooke in the role on August 29 that "this nameless mode of naming the unnameable is rather good."[8] But Milner imposed his own reading upon the creature in his description of scene 2 as "Friendly Intentions of the Monster misinterpreted from his tremendous appearance, and met with Violence." Like most readings of Mary Shelley's text, this one radically simplifies the semiotic significance of the creature.

But Mary Shelley's purposes are primarily ethical rather than epistemological or aesthetic. She wishes us to see that human beings typically interpret the unfamiliar, the abnormal, and the unique as evil. In other words, humans use language, their visual and verbal constructions of reality, to name or image the human and the nonhuman and thus to fix the boundaries between us and them. In so doing, as Foucault has pointed out in *Madness and Civilization* and *Discipline and Punish,* we use language as an instrument of power, to define the borderline between reason and madness, between the socially acceptable and the criminal, and thus to control the terrors of the unknown.[9]

As Mary Shelley's novel illustrates, this linguistic process of naming or imaging becomes a discourse of power that results in the domination of the ideology of a ruling class and leads directly to the creation of evil.

By consistently seeing the creature's countenance as evil, the characters in the novel force him to *become* evil. Whether his innate nature might be, the creature becomes a monster because he, like Polyphemus before him,[10] has been denied access to a human community, denied parental care, companionship, love. His violent rage and malignant murders—of William, Justine, Clerval, Elizabeth, and finally, in consequence, of Alphonse and Victor Frankenstein—are the result of a humanly engendered semiotic construction of the creature as terrifying and horrible. Mary Shelley strikingly shows us that when we see nature as evil, we make it evil. What is now proved was once only imagined, said Blake. The moment Victor Frankenstein sees his creature again, he conceives him to be the murderer of his brother: "No sooner did that idea cross my imagination, than I became convinced of its truth" (71). Having conceived his creature as a "devil" and his "enemy," Frankenstein has made him so.

Moreover, because we can consciously know only the linguistic universes we have ourselves constructed, if we read or image the creature as evil, we write ourselves as the authors of evil. In Blake's pithy phrase, "we become what we behold." Victor Frankenstein becomes the monster he semiotically construes. As Victor confesses, "I considered the being whom I had cast among mankind . . . nearly in the light of my own vampire, my own spirit let loose from the grave, and forced to destroy all that was dear to me" (72). Frankenstein becomes the monster he names, just as in the popular imagination informed by the cinematic versions of Mary Shelley's novel, his name "Frankenstein" becomes the monster.

Victor's identification with his creature is underlined by the novel's persistent association of both men with the fallen Adam and with Satan. Reading Elizabeth's letter, Victor "dared to whisper paradisiacal dreams of love and joy; but the apple was already eaten, and the angel's arm bared to drive me from all hope" (186); "like the archangel who aspired to omnipotence," he confesses to Walton, "I am chained in an eternal hell" (208). The creature too is both Adam and Satan, as he explicitly reminds Victor: "I ought to be thy Adam; but I am rather the fallen angel, whom thou drivest from joy for no misdeed" (95). Increasingly, Victor resembles his creature: "When I thought of him, I gnashed my teeth, my eyes became inflamed" (87). Finally, the boundary between Victor and his creature is annihilated. In his nightmare, the creature literally enters his body. "I felt the fiend's grasp *in* my neck, and could not free myself from it; groans and cries rung *in* my ears" (181; italics mine). Metaphorically, the creature becomes Frankenstein's "own vampire" (72), cannibalistically devouring his creator.

During their final chase across the frozen Arctic wastes, Frankenstein and his creature are indistinguishable. Hunter and hunted blur into one consciousness, one spirit of revenge, one despair, one victim. Victor swears on the grave of William, Elizabeth, and his father to live in order "to execute this dear revenge": "Let the cursed and hellish monster drink deep of agony; let him feel the despair that torments me." He is immediately echoed by the loud and fiendish laugh of his creature: "I am satisfied: miserable wretch! you have determined to live, and I am satisfied" (200). Victor both pursues and is pursued by his creature. Not only does the monster leave marks to guide Frankenstein, but he enters Frankenstein's very soul. As Victor says, "I was cursed by some devil, and carried about with me my eternal hell" (201). Even those "good spirits" who leave food for Frankenstein and whom he had "invoked to aid" him are in fact his own monster, equally bent on revenge. Finally, both Frankenstein and his creature are lost in darkness among the frozen Arctic wastes. By the end of the novel, we cannot separate the wretched, solitary Frankenstein from the wretched, solitary monster. Even Frankenstein's passionate suffering, which has led at least one critic to hail him as a romantic hero,[11] has been more than shared by his creature. As the monster addresses the corpse of Victor, in the original manuscript, "Blasted as you wert, my agony is superior to yours; for remorse is the bitter sting that rankles in my wounds and tortures me to madness" (220:34-221:2). The creature has become his creator, the creator has become his creature.

Many readers have noticed that the monster becomes an alter-ego or double for Victor Frankenstein, a pattern of psychological mirroring that Mary Shelley borrowed from her father's doubles, Caleb Williams and Falkland. But to date these readings have focused on the monster as a manifestation of Frankenstein's repressed desires, whether Oedipal, egotistical, narcissistic, or masochistic.[12] It is true that the monster acts out Frankenstein's subliminal hostility to women by killing his bride on his wedding night. But such psychological interpretations do not account for the larger philosophical questions centrally at issue in the novel. What, finally, is being? Whence did the principle of life proceed? By reading his creation as evil, Frankenstein constructs a monster. The novel itself however leaves open the question of what the creature essentially *is*. Clearly, this being has the capacity to do good; equally clearly, it has the capacity to do evil. But whether it was born good and corrupted by society, or born evil and justly subjected to the condemnation of society, or neither, the novel does not tell us.

Instead *Frankenstein* shows us that in the world that human beings phenomenologically construct, the unknown is imaged, read, and written as "malignant." We thereby create the injustice and evil that we imagine. This is Mary Shelley's final critique of the Romantic ideology. By empowering the imagination as the final arbiter of truth and the poet as the (unacknowledged) legislator of the world, this ideology frees the imagination to construct whatever reality it desires. But the human imagination, left to its own devices, as the rationalist Theseus warned in *A Midsummer Night's Dream,* sees "more devils than vast hell can hold" or in the night, "imagining some fear," supposes every bush a bear. As *Frankenstein* illustrates, the abnormal is more likely to be seen as monstrous than with Titania's eyes of love which "can transpose to form and dignity . . . things base and vile, holding no quantity."

Mary Shelley's answer to the ontological and epistemological issues raised in *Frankenstein,* then, is a radical skepticism, a skepticism that she derived from David Hume and Immanuel Kant, whose ideas she had discussed with Percy Shelley. Since the human mind can never know the thing-in-itself, it can know only the constructs of its own imagination. As the creature says, "the human senses are insurmountable barriers to our union" (141). Because the mind is more likely to respond to the unknown with fear and hostility than with love and acceptance, an unfettered imagination is more likely to construct evil than good. Thus we can finally identify the monster with the poetic imagination itself, as Irving Massey has suggested: "the monster is the imagination, which reveals itself as a hideous construct of the dead parts of things that were once alive when it tries to realize itself, enter the world on the world's terms."[13] The liberation of the imagination advocated by the Romantic poets was regarded by Mary Shelley as both promiscuous and potentially evil. For imaginative creation is not necessarily identical with moral responsibility, as Walter Pater and Oscar Wilde later demonstrated, or closer to home, as Byron and Percy Shelley illustrated. Mary Shelley firmly believed that the romantic imagination must be consciously controlled by love, specifically a mothering love that embraces even freaks. As Victor Frankenstein admits: "If the study to which you apply yourself has a tendency to weaken your affections, and to destroy your taste for those simple pleasures in which no alloy can possibly mix, then that study is certainly unlawful, that is to say, not befitting the human mind" (51).

In advocating this ideal of self-control, of moderation and domestic decorum, Mary Shelley is endorsing an ideology grounded on the trope of the loving and harmonious bourgeois family. She is taking a considered ethical, political, and aesthetic position, a position that is essentially conservative. Human nature may not *be* evil, but human beings are more likely to *construe* it as evil than as good. Since the imagination is motivated by fears, frustrated desires, and fantasies of power, it must be curbed by a strenuous commitment to the preservation of a moral society. In Mary Shelley's view, that moral order traditionally based itself on a reading of nature as sacred. So long as human beings

see nature as a loving mother, the source of life itself, they will preserve organic modes of production and reproduction within the nuclear family and will respect the inherent rights of every life-form. They will, moreover, protect and nurture all the products of nature—the old, the sick, the handicapped, the freaks—with love and compassion.

At the aesthetic level, this ideology entails the privileging of the beautiful over the sublime and a reversal of the eighteenth-century ordering of the arts. For as Burke wrote, the sublime appeals to the instinct of self-preservation and rouses feelings of terror that result in a lust for power, domination, and continuing control. But the beautiful appeals to the instinct of self-procreation and rouses sensations of both erotic and affectional love. Significantly, in Mary Shelley's novel, the idealized figure of Clerval consistently prefers the gently undulating and brightly colored landscapes of the beautiful, as painted by Claude Lorraine and Richard Wilson, and the variegated picturesque landscapes celebrated by Uvedale Price and William Gilpin. In a moment of innocence regained, Frankenstein and Clerval find ecstasy in "a serene sky and verdant fields" and "the flowers of spring" (65). Clerval explicitly rejects the landscapes of the sublime (as painted by Salvator Rosa or John Martin):

> I have seen this lake agitated by a tempest, when the wind tore up whirlwinds of water, and gave you an idea of what the water-spout must be on the great ocean, and the waves dash with fury the base of the mountain, where the priest and his mistress were overwhelmed by an avalanche, and where their dying voices are still said to be heard amid the pauses of the nightly wind; I have seen the mountains of La Valais, and the Pays de Vaud: but this country, Victor, pleases me more than all these wonders. The mountains of Switzerland are more majestic and strange; but there is a charm in the banks of this divine river, that I never before saw equalled. Look at that castle which overhangs yon precipice; and that also on the island, almost concealed amongst the foliage of those lovely trees; and now that group of labourers coming from among their vines; and that village half-hid in the recess of the mountain. Oh, surely, the spirit that inhabits and guards this place has a soul more in harmony with man, than those who pile the glacier, or retire to the inaccessible peaks of the mountains of our own country. (153)

By valuing the picturesque and the beautiful above the sublime, Clerval affirms an aesthetic grounded on the family and the community rather than on the individual. Images of cooperation (between human beings—the village; between man and nature—the laborers among the vines) are of a higher aesthetic order than images of isolation and destruction (the dying priest and his forbidden mistress; the inaccessible mountain peaks).

Clerval thus prefers an aesthetic grounded on the female rather than on the male. Isaac Kramnick has shown us that a gender division is imbedded in Burke's descriptions of the sublime and the beautiful. The sublime is masculine, the beautiful is feminine. The sublime has the qualities Burke associated with his powerful, demanding, violent, unloving father. It is vast, dark, and gloomy; "great, rugged and negligent;" "solid and ever massive;" awesome in its infinite power; capable of arousing only fear, terror, and abject admiration. In contrast, the beautiful is associated with Burke's gentle, shy, devoted mother. It is "small," "smooth and polished," "light and delicate," gently undulating, regular. It produces in the beholder only feelings of affection and tenderness, a nurturant sense of well-being.[14] Clerval's aesthetic of the beautiful is thus grounded in a conscious sympathy between the human mind and a benevolent female nature.

When Mary Shelley first saw the Alps, an experience she recorded in her *History of a Six Weeks Tour* (1817), she responded to their grandeur, not with terror or a conviction of human finitude, but with a wholeness of vision that discovered the vital and life-giving among the frozen wastes, the beautiful within the sublime, the female within the male:

> The scenery of this days journey was divine, exhibiting piny mountains barren rocks, and spots of verdure surpassing imagination. After descending for nearly a league between lofty rocks, covered with pines, and interspersed with green glades, where the grass is short, and soft, and beautifully verdant, we arrived at the village of St. Sulpice. (41)

And at the "desolate" summit of Montanvert, her eyes passed over the barren ice-fields to seek out the life which struggled to survive in their midst:

> We went on the ice; it is traversed by irregular crevices, whose sides of ice appear blue, while the surface is of a dirty white. We dine on the mountain. The air is very cold, yet many flowers grow here, and, among others, the rhododendron, or *Rose des Alpes,* in great profusion.[15]

Even among the most conventionally sublime landscapes, Mary Shelley typically sought out the elements of the beautiful, systematically construing nature not as a punishing or death-dealing force but as a maternal, nurturing, life-giving power, just as, in *Frankenstein,* she construed Mont Blanc and the attendant Alps as mighty images of female fertility. Clerval's reading of mother nature is here, in 1818, her own.

Frankenstein promotes the belief that the moment we foreswear an ecological reading of mother earth, the moment we construe nature as Frankenstein does, as the dead mother or as inert matter, at that moment we set in motion an ideology grounded on patriarchal values of individualism, competition, aggression, egoism, sexism, and racism. We set in motion the imperialist ideology that, as Mary Shelley reminds us, enslaved Greece and destroyed Mexico and Peru (51). We legislate a society capable both of developing and of exploding an atomic bomb, of annihilating itself in a nuclear holocaust. "You are my creator, but I am your master!"

Significantly, at the end of Mary Shelley's novel, the monster is still alive. Victor Frankenstein has vowed to return his creature to the cemetery whence he came, but that vow is fulfilled by neither Frankenstein nor his double, Walton. We have only the monster's word that he will destroy himself on a fiery pile at the North Pole. To believe him may be to engage in a fantasy as deceptive as Walton's vision of a coming together of fire and ice, a tropical paradise, at the North Pole. Mary Shelley left the ending of her novel open. The creature is "lost sight of . . . in the darkness and distance," lost in the unnameable, yet still present as the power of the unknown. But she has taught us that if we do not consciously embrace the unknown with nurturing affection, we may unconsciously construe it as the Other—alien, threatening, sublime. The absence of a mothering love, as *Frankenstein* everywhere shows, can and does make monsters, both psychological and technological. Mary Shelley's mythic vision of a manmade monster reverberates even more frighteningly today than it did in 1818.

Notes

[1] On the epistemological issues raised by the monster, see L. J. Swingle, "Frankenstein's Monster and Its Romantic Relatives: Problems of Knowledge in English Romanticism," *Texas Studies in Literature and Language* 15 (1973): 51-65; and Joseph H. Gardner, "Mary Shelley's Divine Tragedy," *Essays in Literature* 4 (1977): 182-97. On the semiotic implications, see Peter Brooks, "'Godlike Science/Unhallowed Arts': Language, Nature and Monstrosity," *Endurance of Frankenstein,* ed. George Levine and U. C. Knoepflmacher (Berkeley and Los Angeles, and London: University of Chicago Press, 1979), pp. 205-20; and Jerrold E. Hogle, "Otherness in *Frankenstein:* The Confinement/Autonomy of Fabrication," *Structuralist Review* 2 (1980): 20-48.

[2] For Lavater's physiognomical theories, see Johann Caspar Lavater, *Essays on Physiognomy, Designed to Promote the Knowledge and Love of Mankind,* 4 Vols., trans. Henry Hunter (London, 1789-98). For the physiognomical analysis of the infant Mary Godwin, see R. Glynn Grylls, *Mary Shelley—A Biography* (London: Oxford University Press, 1938), pp. 10-11: the physiognomist Mr. Nicholson reported on September 18, 1797, that the three-week-old Mary Godwin's skull

"possessed considerable memory and intelligence," while her forehead, eyes and eyebrows manifested a "quick sensibility, irritable, scarcely irascible" and her "too much employed" mouth showed "the outlines of intelligence. She was displeased, and it denoted much more of resigned vexation than either scorn or rage." Franz Joseph Gall's phrenological system was expounded by Johann Christoph Spurzheim in *The Physiognomical System of Drs. Gall and Spurzheim* (London, 1815). For Mary Shelley's familiarity with Dr. Gall's system, see her *Journal*, ed. Frederick L. Jones (Norman, Oklahoma: University of Oklahoma Press, 1947), p. 15; and *The Journals of Claire Clairmont 1814-1827*, ed. Marion Kingston Stocking (Cambridge: Harvard University Press, 1968), p. 44.

[3] Edmund Burke, *A Philosophical Inquiry into the Origin of Our Ideas of the Sublime and the Beautiful* (London, 1757; repr. Philadelphia, 1806), p. 47.

[4] Edmund Burke, *The Sublime and the Beautiful*, p. 77.

[5] Thomas Weiskel, *The Romantic Sublime* (Baltimore: Johns Hopkins University Press, 1976).

[6] For further discussion of this point, see my "Coleridge's 'This Lime-Tree Bower My Prison' and the Categories of English Landscape," *Studies in Romanticism* 18 (1979): 253-270.

[7] We should recall here Mary Shelley's fascination with Poussin's *Deluge* (or *Winter*), the only painting she mentioned from her visit to the Louvre in 1814 (*Mary Shelley's Journal*, ed. Frederick L. Jones, p. 6). On the creature as an image of elemental Chaos, readers might wish to consult Frances Ferguson's "Legislating the Sublime," in *Studies in Eighteenth-Century British Art and Aesthetics*, ed. Ralph Cohen (Berkeley: University of California Press, 1985), pp. 128-47, which reaches rather different conclusions from mine.

[8] *The Letters of Mary Wollstonecraft Shelley*, ed. Betty T. Bennett (Baltimore: Johns Hopkins University Press, 1980, 1983), I:378.

[9] Michel Foucault, *Madness and Civilization*, trans. Richard Howard (New York: Vintage Books, 1961); *Discipline and Punish—The Birth of the Prison*, trans. Alan Sheridan (New York: Vintage Books, 1977, 1979).

[10] Mary Shelley described *Frankenstein* as a defense of Polyphemus. Replying to Leigh Hunt's remark that "Polyphemus . . . always appears to me a pathetic rather than a monstrous person, though his disappointed sympathies at last made him cruel," Mary Shelley commented, "I have written a book in defence of Polypheme—have I not?" (*Letters of Mary Shelley*, ed. Betty T. Bennet, I:91, dated April 6, 1819). The allusion is to the one-eyed, uncouth, giant Cyclops Polyphemus, whose passionate love for the beautiful nymph Galatea is rejected; the story is recounted in Book 12 of Ovid's *Metamorphoses*. The scorned Polyphemus, in jealousy and despair, murders Galatea's lover Acis. I owe this observation to Aija Ozolins, "Dreams and Doctrine: Dual Stands in *Frankenstein*," *Science-Fiction Studies* 6 (1975): 106.

[11] Robert Kiely, *The Romantic Novel in England* (Cambridge: Harvard University Press, 1972), p. 158. Kiely has been misled by the association of Victor Frankenstein with Percy Shelley into seeing the character of Frankenstein too positively, as a romantic "hero" whose "fault is more nature's than his." While Kiely acknowledges Frankenstein's egoism, he gives too much credit to Frankenstein's "superiority through suffering" and mistakenly identifies as a major theme in the novel the "idea that the genius, even in his failures, is unique, noble, and isolated from other men by divine right" (pp. 156, 158, 172).

[12] On the relation of *Frankenstein* to *Caleb Williams*, see Katherine Richardson Powers, *The Influence of William Godwin on the Novels of Mary Shelley* (New York: Arno Press, 1980); Gay Clifford, "*Caleb Williams* and *Frankenstein*: First-Person Narration and Things as They Are," *Genre* 10 (1977): 601-17; and A. D. Harvey, "*Frankenstein* and *Caleb Williams*," *Keats-Shelley Journal* 29 (1980): 21-27.

On Frankenstein and his creature as psychological doubles or alter-egos, see among others, Masao Miyoshi, *The Divided Self* (New York: New York University Press, 1969), pp. 79-89; Martin Tropp, *Mary Shelley's Monster* (Boston: Houghton, 1976); J. M. Hill, "*Frankenstein* and the Physiognomy of Desire," *American Imago* 32 (1975): 335-58; Harold Bloom, "Afterword" to *Frankenstein* (New York: New American Library, 1965), pp. 212-23; Paul A. Cantor, *Creator and Creature: Myth-making and English Romanticism* (New York: Cambridge University Press, 1984), pp. 115-24; and William Veeder, *Mary Shelley and Frankenstein—The Fate of Androgyny* (Chicago: University of Chicago Press, 1986), pp. 89-92, passim. Paul Sherwin both develops and criticizes such Freudian interpretations in "*Frankenstein*: Creation as Catastrophe," *PMLA* 96 (1981): 883-903.

[13] Irving Massey, *The Gaping Pig—Literature and Metamorphosis* (Berkeley and Los Angeles, and London: University of California Press, 1976), p. 129.

[14] On the gender division in Burke's aesthetic theory, see Isaac Kramnick, *The Rage of Edmund Burke—Portrait of an Ambivalent Conservative* (New York: Basic Books, 1977), pp. 92-98.

[15] *Mary Shelley's Journal*, ed. Frederick L. Jones, p. 53. I am indebted to Gary Harrison for bringing the importance of this passage to my attention.

Alan Rauch (essay date 1995)

SOURCE: "The Monstrous Body of Knowledge in Mary Shelley's *Frankenstein*," in *Studies in Romanticism*, Vol. 34, No. 2, Summer, 1995, pp. 227-53.

[*In the following essay, Rauch reads* Frankenstein *as "Shelley's critique of knowledge"—specifically of scientific knowledge as a discourse owned, shaped, and frequently misused by men.*]

> Glavanism . . . independently of other advantages, holds out such hopes of utility in regard to . . . mankind; a work containing a full account of the late improvements which have been made in it . . . cannot fail of being acceptable to the public in general, and in particular to medical men, to whose department, in one point of view, it more essentially belongs.
>
> Preface to Giovanni Aldini's *Improvements of Galvanism* (1803)[1]

> Death snatches away many blooming children, the only hopes of their doating parents
>
> Mary Shelley, *Frankenstein* (1818)

I. Knowledge and Culture

New perspectives on *Frankenstein* are hard to come by. Recent scholarship has provided a wide variety of insights into the novel, making it a central text in feminist studies, the history of the novel, psychoanalytical criticism, and, of course, the impact of science on the novel.[2] For reasons that aren't entirely clear, however, the issue of the nature of knowledge—as a cultural artifact—has not been rigorously pursued. Part of the problem may well be that while Shelley[3] explores Frankenstein's character, she is deliberately unspecific about the details of his scientific work. Aside from passing references to his techniques and to his instruments, there is little in the novel that actually describes Frankenstein's scientific activity, much less his scientific context. Moreover, the narrative structure of the novel renders the creature a *fait accompli*—large, apparently ugly, and periodically violent—thereby obscuring its ontological design and development.

Although the reader never learns the details of Frankenstein's science or the degree of the creature's "monstrosity," one thing is clear: the monster, whatever else it may be, represents a remarkable "body" of knowledge. The nature of that knowledge, how it was obtained, how it was implemented, and what resulted from it, are my primary concerns in this essay. These concerns will touch on a central question for readers of *Frankenstein:* To what extent was the creation of the monster transgressive, morally repugnant, or both? I will argue that the creature, as an embodiment of knowledge, is neither.[4] Frankenstein's conception of

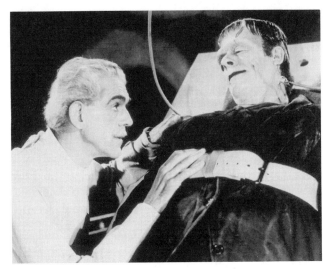

The monster, while his creator looks on.

the creature, however, is another story and what I hope to make clear is that, for Shelley, the moral integrity of the scientist has everything to do with the viability of knowledge. By ignoring the humane qualities that clearly make knowledge effective, particularly nurturing and caring, Frankenstein finds nothing admirable in what should be a remarkable creation.

Whatever else can be said about Frankenstein, there is no doubt that he possesses a remarkable amount of knowledge and, from a technical perspective at least, is enormously skillful. Moreover, Frankenstein's knowledge has no precedent; new and ambiguous, it represents both threat and promise to an uninformed public. What intensifies that double-edged nature of knowledge—as threat and promise—is the fact that "knowledge" was a male artifact in the nineteenth-century. Shelley's story, which revolves around the appropriation of reproduction by a man, underscores that concern. But I do not simply want to argue that *Frankenstein* is a transgressive tale about the usurpation of reproduction (from god or woman); rather it is about Frankenstein's seemingly willful misunderstanding of the value of the knowledge he gains in the context of reproduction.[5]

II. Knowledge and Narrative

Shelley's critique of knowledge permeates the novel as a whole. The intertwining male narratives in the novel are persuasive, but not always convincing or reliable. Shelley requires active readers who will question the coherence and the consistency of all the narratives as they develop throughout the book. The novel is thus self-consciously constructed as a kind of "knowledge text" that functions in the tradition of the "thought problem." The compilation of male narratives is, of course, the work of two women, two manuscripts overseen by two M.S.s: Margaret Saville and her creator

Mary Shelley. Together they silently preside over narratives that purport to be accurate and scientific. Their silence requires each reader, in a process that is similar to scientific discovery, to examine the narratives closely in an effort to determine their reliability.

Shelley's narrative technique is an inclusive one, conscripting the reader into a participatory process that is diametrically opposed to Frankenstein's isolationist and exclusionary methodology. As a representation of knowledge acquired by "M.S.," the text itself as some readers have pointed out, has a monstrous quality. Daniel Cottom argues persuasively that there is an intrinsic monstrosity to all representational forms, from monsters to novels. "The monster," he writes "figures as the text insofar as **Frankenstein** may be regarded as a pure work of art or of some other abstraction that conceals the labor of its origin."[6] But the author of this text has not only assembled a set of narratives for the reader, she has allowed the reader to become part of that structure; this revisionary approach to knowledge anticipates, as we will see, feminist critiques of science. The structure also serves as a constant reminder of Frankenstein's fear of knowledge's social context. The solitude and seclusion that Frankenstein seems to require for his work can only result in knowledge that can have neither context nor value. For Mary Shelley this is intended to be the most frightening aspect of her novel.

Shelley, of course, makes certain that the reader understands how extensive Frankenstein's knowledge must be—of physiology, surgery, medicine, and chemistry—in order to create his creature. Shelley's concern about the integrity of Frankenstein as scientist is particularly evident in Frankenstein's description of the events surrounding the construction of a female creature. Filled with inconsistencies and contradictions, this part of the narrative draws our attention to Frankenstein's shortcomings. Equally important here is the realization that Walton, who mediates the narratives of Frankenstein and the monster (in addition to his own), cannot be relied upon for much more than simple reportage. The reader, thus embedded in the logic of the narrative, is compelled to be observant and critical in spite of the text, and "learns" a critical skill necessary both to conduct science and to critique it.[7]

Though he makes an early claim for wanting to father a "new species," Frankenstein feigns astonishment at the monster's desire for a female companion. "I was bewildered," he tells Walton, "perplexed and unable to arrange my ideas sufficiently to understand the full extent of his proposition" (140).[8] Yet, clearly the proposition was as much a part of Frankenstein's original agenda, as it now seems to be part of the monster's. Frankenstein would have Walton believe that the idea of a female is completely new, when a female creature was fully anticipated at the very beginning of his work.

Walton here, as elsewhere, fails to object to this apparently obvious inconsistency. But his passive role as auditor does more than simply allow for Frankenstein's long narrative to continue; Walton's silence, frustrating as it is, engages our own sense of logic and inference.

Shelley's embedded critique does not end here; in the ensuing pages, she underscores Frankenstein's preternatural resistance to the monster's desire for a mate or, simply, for *his* companionship. Once Frankenstein decides that he cannot complete the female creature he has made at the monster's request, he tells Walton that he destroyed her by tearing "the thing" to pieces. Frankenstein is then able to persuade Walton and perhaps even himself that he would never have considered the project had it not been for the monster. But the monster's position is reasonable even in Frankenstein's account of the story.[9] "Instead of threatening," Frankenstein reports him as saying, "I am content to reason with you" (141). Needless to say the monster's ominous warning that "we may not part until you have promised to comply with my requisition" (140) is a threat, and by this time, he is already responsible for the deaths of William and Justine. But the fact of the matter is that the monster, in asking for a mate, is merely trying to find a social context for his own existence. "The monster's desire for his mate," writes Peter Brooks, "may itself be a substitute for his real, his absolute demand, which is for recognition by his creator."[10] Brooks recognizes the monster's essential need to be bound to Frankenstein if there is any chance for it to be situated in the world. The same, of course, ultimately holds true for Frankenstein himself who remains isolated and, in Brooks's sense, inarticulate, without the creature. Seeing that Frankenstein has rejected his own "society," the creature simply wants him to take responsibility for having created a social being artificially. That Frankenstein is unable to understand that he owes the creature companionship, in one way or another, is consistent with his inability to see any value in social exchange.

As a prerequisite to creating the female creature Frankenstein demands that the monster and his companion must "quit Europe forever, and every other place in the neighbourhood of man" (144). The agreement seems both fair and, in terms of Frankenstein's enlightenment context, rational; yet only pages later Frankenstein brutally dismembers the female ostensibly on the grounds of having been "struck senseless by fiendish threats." Frankenstein then describes his actions in a way that makes them seem a response to "malice and treachery." But it is irrationality that most marks Frankenstein's response in this frantic moment. When confronted with the very real problem of what to do with the knowledge that he has generated, Frankenstein is at a complete loss.

Frankenstein's violent treatment of the female creature is both disturbing and intriguing. If Frankenstein can be read, as Elissa Marder suggests, "as the attempt to forget the mother's legacy entirely," the female creature was certainly galling to Frankenstein for its potential to *re*appropriate the role of reproduction. Frankenstein, Marder writes, is driven by a compulsion "to circumvent the necessity of passing through the mother in order to give birth and be born."[11] It is worth arguing further that Frankenstein, as repulsed as he is by the creature he has created, is completely unable to contemplate the notion of a *female* embodiment of knowledge. Such a "natural" embodiment, Mary Ann Doane argues, would normally offer "a certain amount of epistemological comfort" since the biological role of the mother renders her "immediately knowable."[12] Because mothers offer at least "the possibility of certitude in historical knowledge," they are "aligned with the social function of knowledge." Doane's contention that without the mother, both "the story of origins" and narrative itself become unstable, helps explain much of the narrative tension in the novel.

The dismemberment of the female, as Ludmilla Jordanova points out, has a long history in medical conceptions of women's bodies.[13] The female body was frequently conceptualized as a fragmented form in terms of the way it was viewed and the knowledge that was derived from it. Thus when nineteenth century obstetrical procedure dealt with an unexpelled placenta by removing the placenta in fragments, it was consistent with the way women were perceived in general and with the way in which they were healed. The physicians who attended Mary Wollstonecraft, for example, interceded very quickly and worked assiduously to remove the placenta piece by piece. This process, which often disregarded the condition of the patient as a whole, was painful, dangerous, and frequently resulted in severe infections and many deaths,[14] as it did in the case of Wollstonecraft. This gruesome procedure, while not necessarily motivated by malice, surely retained an air of cruelty and violence that is evoked in Frankenstein's destruction of the female.

III. Product vs. Process

The events immediately following Frankenstein's destruction of the female creature are also worth looking at briefly, if only to underscore Shelley's interest in eroding Frankenstein's credibility. When he returns to his Scottish laboratory to dispose of the remains of the second monster, he places them in a basket with stones and drops them irretrievably into the sea. This act, according to Frankenstein, is consistent with a commitment to abandon the scientific practice and the scientific frame of mind that led to the creation of the monster. Yet while waiting for the cover of darkness to dispose of the "relics" of his work, Frankenstein passes the time in a revealing way: "In the mean time," he says offhandedly, "I sat upon the beach, employed in cleaning and arranging my chemical apparatus"

(168). If Frankenstein is indeed serious about his "solemn vow never to resume my labours," this pastime, which suggests that Frankenstein has plans for future scientific projects, is anything but idle or innocent; yet Walton and presumably most readers overlook this part of Frankenstein's narrative. The act of cleaning equipment, which under most circumstances would hardly seem worth noting, stands out here because it suggests a moment of honesty in an otherwise entirely fabricated narrative. Frankenstein's story is, ironically, belied by a moment of unguarded candor, an important moment, given the way it undermines the integrity of narrative and communication, which, for better or worse is the cornerstone of scientific practice.

Frankenstein, by undermining narrative, rejects the central tenets of scientific practice: application, dissemination, or exchange. Frankenstein, in hoarding knowledge and storing it, so to speak, in one creature, seems to be missing the apparent point of science. The comments of Shelley's parents, whose works she read closely, are telling on this score. "Truth," wrote Mary Wollstonecraft, "must be common to all, or it will be inefficacious with respect to its influence on general practice."[15] Godwin's sentiments, not surprisingly, are similar. "Knowledge and the enlargement of intellect," he argues in *Enquiry Concerning Political Justice* (1793), "are poor when unmixed with sentiments of benevolence and sympathy."[16] The link that Godwin sees between science and virtue suggests the posture that Frankenstein professes to assume, though certainly not the actual spirit of his enterprise:

> If I have conceived an earnest desire of being the benefactor of my race, I shall no doubt, find out a channel in which for [sic] my desire to operate, and shall be quick-sighted in discovering the defects, or comparative littleness, of the plan I may have chosen. (306)

Scientists, as John F. W. Herschel argues in his *Preliminary Discourse on the Study of Natural History* (1830), can only benefit by "a sense of common interest, of mutual assistance, and a feeling of sympathy in a common pursuit."[17] Knowledge, by the same token, can only be advanced if "it is diffused as widely and as rapidly as possible." Moved perhaps by a recognition of the growing professionalization, competitiveness, and insularity of science, Herschel argues forcefully that pursuit of knowledge must be a social endeavor. His *Discourse,* which came on the heels of much of his own work in chemistry, astronomy and related sciences, might serve in its own right as a strong indictment of Frankenstein as scientist.

That Frankenstein himself is unclear about the role of the scientist is attributable to his early reading in alchemy. The works of Paracelsus, Cornelius Agrippa, and Albertus Magnus, that so preoccupied the young

Frankenstein, are as M. Krempe explains, "useless names . . . in this enlightened and scientific age" (40). While Krempe redirects Frankenstein's reading, he is too late to alter the conception of science that has already shaped Frankenstein's thinking. The influence of the alchemists on Frankenstein is clear; from them he has come to understand science as a goal or product-oriented activity rather than process-oriented activity. In other words, for Frankenstein the scientist's objective is to transform one thing into another, rather than to investigate the ontological relationship between things.[18] The slow and step-wise process of science, of arranging facts in "connected classifications," is too mundane and has no attraction for Frankenstein.[19] Given his fascination with the "Elixir of Life," Frankenstein cannot overcome his "contempt for the uses of modern natural philosophy":

> It was very different, when the masters of science sought immortality and power; such views, although futile, were grand: but now the scene was changed. The ambition of the inquirer seemed to limit itself to the annihilation of those visions on which my interest in science was chiefly founded. I was required to exchange chimeras of boundless grandeur for realities of little worth. (41)[20]

The attitude that the efforts of modern science result in "realities of little worth" can only belong to an individual who has lived what Frankenstein himself describes as a "remarkably secluded" life. Having read the alchemists in seclusion, and followed their practice of working in seclusion, Frankenstein has no social context for his science. It is not surprising, then, that he should devalue advances in knowledge that have broad impact and widespread application for those that engage a very narrow audience. Herschel evokes Frankenstein's language when he warns, that in spite of their role in "the creation of experimental philosophy" (12), the work of the alchemists was too "remote" and ultimately not grounded in "the realities of nature." The pursuit of science, adds Herschel, should not be secretive or proprietary:

> Knowledge is not, like food, destroyed by use, but rather augmented and perfected. It acquires not, perhaps, a greater certainty, but at least a confirmed authority and a probable duration, by universal assent; and there is no body so complete, but that it may acquire accession, or so free from error but that it may receive correction in passing through the minds of millions. (69)

While Herschel would seek knowledge in the midst of millions, Frankenstein cannot pursue it unless alone. Even when he arrives at the university town of Ingolstadt, he is unable to appreciate the value of science to the community. Instead of finding the academic world inviting, he reports that even there he

could not overcome an "invincible repugnance to new countenances" (40). Aloof and out of touch with those around him, Frankenstein cannot help but use his science to create something that is as repugnant to society as society is to him.

The creation of life is thus, for Frankenstein, a purely intellectual challenge that is completely disconnected from the academic and the social worlds in which he exists. Nowhere in the process of creating the monster does he reflect on the potential value of each new scientific innovation that results in the creature. Yet to the scientific community, any one of the techniques that could result in the creation of a fully formed version of a human being, would surely have been a scientific triumph. Frankenstein's inability to see—quite literally—the parts for the whole is crucial here, not merely for what it owes alchemy, but for the way that it reflects the patriarchal practices of science in general. Such practices, according to Donna Haraway, not only posit a false objectivity, they assiduously avoid adjusting knowledge to contexts. Haraway's advocacy for "situated knowledges," which "are about communities, not about isolated individuals" (590), is particularly resonant in *Frankenstein*. Shelley's concerns about science anticipate feminist critiques in the way she challenges Frankenstein's method of practice, his "objective" claims, and finally, his understanding of what counts as knowledge.

IV. The Body of Knowledge

Frankenstein's shortcomings could not have gone undetected by Shelley's readers, who surely subscribed to the traditional view of scientific procedure. Frankenstein ignores the "slow, uncertain, and irregular" pattern, to use Herschel's language, by which science has traditionally contributed to knowledge. That, finally, he contributes no lasting achievement to science in the process is Shelley's clearest indictment of his work. By rejecting science's "realities of little worth," he has dismissed a long tradition in which small but useful discoveries accumulate to create what we call scientific knowledge, and what is more important he has dismissed the scientific community that validates that knowledge.[21] Instead, Frankenstein opts to direct all of his science in the creation of a separate and distinct body of knowledge. The monster as the incarnation of that knowledge enters the world without introduction and without precedent.

New and unfamiliar knowledge, however "good" or "bad," can only be troubling to those who are unacquainted with its origins. The scientist needs to recognize that all knowledge has a monstrous quality and the only way to introduce knowledge is to demonstrate it, that is, to display it and in doing so, to demystify it. The tension between the pursuit of knowledge and the communication of knowledge is surely as crucial as any epistemological dilemma faced in the scientific world. Science, according to Herschel,

> has its own peculiar terms, and, so to speak, its own idioms of language; and these it would be unwise, were it even possible, to relinquish; but everything that tends to clothe it in a strange and repulsive garb, and especially every thing that, to keep up an appearance of superiority over the rest of mankind, assumes an unnecessary guise of profundity and obscurity, should be sacrificed without mercy. Not to do this, is to deliberately reject the light which the natural unencumbered good sense of mankind is capable of throwing on every subject. (70)

The effective communication of knowledge, however, is predicated on a scientist's affinity for the knowledge that he or she has introduced. Frankenstein's failure as a scientist is due in great part, then, to his inability to recognize and perhaps even understand what the monster represents. Moreover, in an era when the public presentation of science had much to do with its value and its acceptability, Frankenstein's secretive approach to knowledge production can be taken as a sure sign that his discovery will be a disaster with respect to public understanding.[22]

V. Applied Knowledge

The compartmentalized nature of Frankenstein's scientific genius deserves close attention in terms of the way that it determines his actions. Schooled in the knowledge of the ancients, he has also learned the techniques of the moderns. Inspired by Professor Waldman, who encourages him to study "every branch of natural philosophy," he outstrips his colleagues in a matter of a few years. Frankenstein's encyclopedic knowledge seems to compare favorably to the polymathic genius of many late romantics, yet his knowledge is markedly limited by its sterility. The creature is emblematic of that sterility, but so is Frankenstein's fundamental understanding of what he has uncovered in his discovery of the principle of life. It is indeed remarkable that someone so obsessed by the force of life shows no insight into how to restore, lengthen, or preserve it.

This paradox is the most important irony in the novel. After having created the monster, that is after having created life itself, Frankenstein is plagued—because of the monster—by death. Frankenstein scavenges from the dead to create life, and the creature, in retribution, attacks the living to "create" death. That Frankenstein passively accepts the deaths of those around him is at first perplexing; but Frankenstein's fascination with the concept of life is wholly dependent on a parasitic devotion to death. Thus, the gray area between life and death, of restoring life to a being on the brink of death or only just recently dead, is a concept that Franken-

stein is unwilling to grasp. Are we to believe, for example, that the skills that created a monster from inorganic matter could not restore life to a previously living organism? Frankenstein makes the following claim, though given the context of his work, it seems self-serving and convenient:

> I thought, that if I could bestow animation upon lifeless matter, I might in process of time (although I now found it impossible) renew life where death had apparently devoted the body to corruption. (49)

From the perspective of nineteenth century scientific practice, Frankenstein's assertion is illogical and disingenuous. The notion of being able to instill life in an assemblage of human parts where it proved impossible in a whole cadaver would have struck Frankenstein's (and Shelley's) scientific contemporaries as absurd. The work of the renowned "electrician" Giovanni Aldini, a respected itinerant scientist and the nephew of Galvani, was based entirely on the hope of galvanic restoration of the fatally ill. "Numerous instances could be produced," Aldini contended in his *General Views on the Application of Galvanism,* "in which persons have been hurried to the grave before life was entirely extinct. I view with horror and indignation the haste with which a man, who appears to have drawn his last breath, is thus banished from society, and deprived of a chance of recovery."[23] To this end (with some entrepreneurial acumen), Aldini even proposed portable galvanic machines "weighing from 24 to 38 ounces"; these, he suggests, might be given to children who might "be taught its value from their tenderest years and afterwards learn to apply it in cases of suspended life" (41).

The surgeon, John Birch, in his 1802 *Essay on the Medical Application of Electricity,*[24] describes the reanimation of "a labouring man in a fit of despair" who, after hanging himself, could not be revived. The attending physician, reports Birch,

> passed an electric shock from one leg to the other, the effect of which was extremely surprising; the patient started, opened his eyes, and seemed very much frightened. . . . The shocks were repeated three or four times in the space of ten minutes; after the last, a kind of hysteric affection took place, and seemed further to relieve him; his feet became warm, a general perspiration ensued, [and] he became quite rational. (53)

"It is evident," Birch concludes, that "life, apparently suspended, was instantaneously called back by the shock." Needless to say, Birch's claims for the recuperative effect of electricity must be taken with a grain of salt, as must his reports that electricity can relieve constipation, the gout, mild paralysis, blindness, and impotence. Yet Birch's earnest application of this new technology in the service of his patients provides an interesting contrast to Frankenstein who shows none of Birch's ingenuity. Moreover, the parenthetical nature of Frankenstein's disclaimer—"although I now found it impossible"—about his knowledge of reanimation, renders it entirely suspect, given that Frankenstein does not recount even a single attempt to actually restore life. Even more important is the unmistakable subtext of the statement, that Frankenstein deliberately chose to pursue creation over restoration. It's hardly surprising then that Frankenstein never sees the obvious connection between the animation of the creature and the re-animation or restoration of the monster's victims.

Exactly what Frankenstein might be able to do with his knowledge is particularly interesting given that so many other characters manage to apply their knowledge in useful and productive ways. There is a consistent effort in the novel to demonstrate that scientific attentiveness can prolong and restore life. These are telling moments not only because they contrast so sharply with Frankenstein's patterns of behavior, but because they reveal Mary Shelley's concerns about how knowledge might be used to assist others.

Perhaps the most dramatic moment of reasoned intervention and assistance is the creature's effort to save a young girl from drowning. Although the monster has only just been rejected by the DeLaceys, he is still able to be alert and compassionate. Hidden in the woods, he sees a young girl running "in sport" from her companion. "She continued her course along the precipitous sides of the river," the monster tells Frankenstein,

> when suddenly her foot slipt, and she fell into the rapid stream. I rushed from my hiding place, and, with extreme labour from the force of the current, saved her, and dragged her to shore. She was senseless; and I endeavoured, by every means in my power, to restore animation . . . (137)

The enormous strength of the creature contributes to his success, but it isn't enough on its own. The monster must try "every means . . . to restore animation" and in doing so demonstrates a moral commitment to the application of knowledge in the service of humanity. The girl's companion, ignorant not only of the monster but of the method used to revive her, shoots the creature and thus provokes a vow of "deep and deadly revenge.[25] The contrast between the behavior of the untutored creature and his creator is striking. The monster, equipped only with the rudiments of scientific knowledge (gleaned perhaps from the notes on his own creation), makes the best use of it when it is needed.

Frankenstein, by contrast, demonstrates no similar commitment to the application of knowledge in the service of society. In his enthusiasm to discover "the principle of life," Frankenstein is indifferent to the problems that trouble the living. He shows no interest in making inquiries into the pragmatic issues of life and rejects the ugly workaday world of science. Frankenstein's lack of concern for pragmatism in science parallels his lack of sensitivity to the pragmatic product of his sublime conception. The monster must be fed, nurtured, and cared for, and it's no wonder, as Ellen Moers has pointed out, that Frankenstein is revolted by that prospect.[26] The daily routines of life—and death—are filled, as Mary Shelley knew very well, with unpleasant moments that require every bit as much skill and application as Frankenstein gave to his pursuit.

Frankenstein's own daily needs, medical or otherwise, are well taken care of in spite of his negligence toward others. Even in the rustic harbor town where he is arrested for the murder of Clerval, he is treated humanely. Though "on the point of death," Frankenstein is nursed back to health even though he is suspected of murder. Frankenstein characterizes the hired nurse sent to attend him as "indifferent," yet her tone betrays only a sense of deference and commitment that seem consistent with her responsibilities. "Are you better now, sir?" she asks politely of Frankenstein:

> I believe that it were better for you if you were dead, for I fancy it will go hard with you! . . . However, that's none of my business, I am sent to nurse you, and get you well; I do my duty with a safe conscience, it were well if every body did the same. (175)

The nurse's words should cut to the quick, but Frankenstein can only describe them as "unfeeling," particularly "to a person just saved, on the very brink of death." Frankenstein then accuses a local physician, who prescribes medication for him, of "carelessness" in spite of the fact that his very recovery is a testimonial to the care that he receives. The efforts of the local townspeople are also significant given their earnest but futile attempts to restore Clerval to life when his body is discovered.

The process of using galvanism in a restorative manner, that is to introduce electricity into objects living or dead was, as I have already indicated, familiar to scientists and scientific popularizers of the early nineteenth century. At Oxford, Percy Shelley was fascinated by galvanism and had an electrical machine in his rooms.[27] Although Mary Shelley's first exposure to the potential power of electricity may have taken place at the public lectures given by André-Jacques Garnerin in 1814, her extensive reading provided her with a variety of perspectives on the nature and uses of electricity.[28] Polidori, as Ann Mellor has pointed out, was probably trained in the therapeutic uses of galvanism when studying medicine at Edinburgh.[29]

Galvanism was touted by Aldini as a promising technique for the restoration of life. The technique would apparently have its greatest effect on subjects who had only recently died. For this reason Aldini was particularly interested in recently slaughtered animals and—more to the point—recently executed criminals. While such experiments had what might be called a Gothic undertone—particularly when a cadaver responded to the electricity by turning its head or rolling its eyes—the ostensible purpose of the experiment was to learn more about the resuscitation of recent victims of drowning, suffocation, and asphyxiation. The study of galvanism, as Aldini noted, was "undertaken for the advancement of the welfare of the human race."[30] The use of recently executed criminals, though ethically questionable, could be justified, in his view, if we recalled that "the bodies of valuable members of society are often found under similar circumstances, and with the same symptoms as those observed on executed criminals" (4). Many others, including William Nicholson, who discussed Aldini's experiments in his *Journal of Natural Philosophy, Chemistry and the Arts,* agreed:

> In the mean time the reader, will, doubtless, receive satisfaction from this short notice he [Aldini] has enabled me to give of his labour, on a subject which promises greatly to extend the limits of natural science and may be reasonably expected to add to the powers which man is enabled to exert for his own benefit over the numerous beings around him.[31]

The scientific talents of Frankenstein, evident in the unprecedented nature of his accomplishment are meant to be overwhelming; certainly, we are meant to understand that he has far surpassed real practitioners, such as Aldini. Yet Frankenstein, for all of his skill in creating the monster, does not attempt in the process of experimentation to revivify, as Aldini did, experimental corpses. More significantly he makes no effort to restore to life the individuals whom he supposedly loves when all of them have, in fact, died of asphyxiation and would, therefore, be perfect candidates for his technique. If we were to twist the plot of the novel by considering a Frankenstein who did restore the victims of the monster to life, the novel could have any number of absurd outcomes. In the direction of the Gothic, one can conjecture a variation of what Muriel Spark calls "a figure-eight 'macabresque,'" in a tedious chain of literally repetitive murders, where the victim is revived only to be murdered again.[32] A more romantic or comic ending, in the spirit of Victorian revisions of Shakespearean tragedy, might find Frankenstein in the midst of a revivified and happy family, while the frustrated monster, aware that Frankenstein has a context for his knowledge, slinks away.

My suggestions for alternative endings are intentionally absurd and clearly disrupt the tone of the novel,

yet they are not gratuitous.[33] Frankenstein, I would suggest, in neglecting his responsibility as a scientist, is oblivious to what seems obvious and humane to us and, I believe, to Mary Shelley as well. Frankenstein does not lack for knowledge, the monster is proof of that; but he is clearly unable to see how the application of that knowledge can be used in a way that is proper and judicious as well as humane and rational.

The lapses in Frankenstein's thinking are inevitably raised by first time readers of the novel, and their comments draw attention to some important issues. Frankenstein's fear of a "race of devils" resulting from the union of two monsters could, for example, be circumvented from the outset by making the initial creature infertile. This option, which students new to the novel almost always point out, is initially annoying because for more sophisticated readers it "misses the point."[34] But whether Frankenstein could or could not stitch together an infertile pair and send them on a one-way honeymoon to South America is not as preposterous as it may seem, since it represents an attempt to resolve the novel in a way that is consistent with Frankenstein's posture as a scientist and rationalist. That the reader is able to see the full potential and the possible applications of knowledge, where Frankenstein cannot, underscores the degree to which an obsessive desire has clouded his reason.

VI. Nurturing and Science

In the conclusion of *A Newton Among the Poets,* Carl Grabo suggests that for Percy Shelley, "Science, Knowledge, in which all share and contribute, is, like love, a way to the loss of the individual in the attainment of the larger self."[35] Grabo's evaluation of Percy Shelley's attitude toward science is, I think, accurate and helpful in understanding Mary Shelley's attitudes as well. The notion of the pursuit of knowledge, as a cooperative effort that operates in the service of a "larger self," is a perspective that Frankenstein lacks. But where Percy is interested in the more abstract implications of what he calls—in "Prometheus Unbound"—a "chain of linked thought," Mary Shelley is concerned with its practical implications.[36] In either case, "linked thought," as Grabo notes, underscores a belief "in the unity of knowledge" and the idea that an "individual adds his bit to the whole" (196).

The knowledge industry of the early nineteenth century introduced to the lay reader thousands of different directions into which the energies of science could be channeled. Some were of obvious benefit to mankind and others not. Itinerant lecturers had discovered the commercial potential of science and found large audiences wherever they spoke. Aldini was himself accused, perhaps justifiably, of using galvanism in a way that owed more to spectacle than to science. Frankenstein is a product of this tradition and it is not surprising that he acknowledges that much of his attraction to science stems from aspirations to glory, fame, and, to a lesser extent, riches:

> Wealth was an inferior object; but what glory would attend the discovery, if I could banish disease from the human frame, and render man invulnerable to any but a violent death! (34)

The hyperbole of Frankenstein's statement, relying as it does on terms like "banish" and "invulnerable," leaves little room for the practical applications of science that require patience and dedication. And while Galvanism was far from a mundane practice, the work of Aldini does suggest a wide range of potential applications in daily life. For Mary Shelley, the possible ramifications of Aldini's work must have been striking. Her vision, of revivifying her dead child in a way that eerily resembles Aldini's techniques, suggests how powerful a hold science seems to have had on her.

Mary Shelley's concern about her own health and the health of her family are crucial to our understanding of the novel.[37] The issue is not merely one of mothers in childbirth, but of the efficacy of human intervention in all forms of illness. Frankenstein's "big science," the creation of the monster, distracts us too easily from a paradigm of smaller science where knowledge is applied with great effect but without much ado. The novel is replete with scenes which emphasize the value of compassionate and nurturing behavior; even where professional medical attention seems ineffective, nurturing alone shows restorative and curative effects. These small moments of care and attention serve as a direct contrast to Frankenstein's science, and thus offer a moderated vision of how knowledge can and does work in social contexts.

The very first example of Shelley's alternative paradigm occurs even before Frankenstein's birth, when his mother, Caroline Beaufort, attends "with the greatest tenderness" her own ailing and destitute parent. Caroline takes on tedious and difficult work "to support life" but eventually the elder Beaufort dies and she is nearly overcome with grief. Her caring, however, clearly has an effect on Alphonse Frankenstein who, we learn, "came like a protecting spirit to the poor girl" (28). Though Frankenstein can narrate this history, he is unable to understand its significance or, for that matter, the way it foreshadows future events in his life. Just before Frankenstein leaves for university, Elizabeth, Frankenstein's beloved "sister," falls ill with scarlet fever. Frankenstein's mother, "when she heard that the life of her favourite was menaced," immediately attends to Elizabeth and "her watchful attentions triumphed over the malignity of the distemper."[38] "Elizabeth was saved," Frankenstein recounts dispassionately, but exposure to the illness proved "fatal to her preserver." Frankenstein demonstrates none of his

mother's zeal when it is her turn on the sickbed and reports her death in a way that is peculiarly detached. Even science proves helpless where Frankenstein's mother was successful; "the looks of the medical attendants," Frankenstein says, "prognosticated the worst event." The death of his mother, which haunts Frankenstein later in the novel, is interesting in that it underscores Frankenstein's own ineffectuality as a healer; the qualities that made his mother so successful a nurse are clearly missing in him. When Frankenstein uses his familiar passive voice to explain that "many arguments had been urged to persuade my mother to refrain from attending upon her [Elizabeth]," it is to rationalize the distance he maintained to avoid imperiling himself. The death of his mother does not elicit care or sympathy from him either, nor does it elicit the kind of scientific curiosity that one might expect in response to a tragic illness. Readers don't seem to know what to do with this relatively lengthy scene, which appears early in the novel, until it is rendered "Gothic" by Frankenstein's dream of his mother.[39] Yet it functions very effectively, if somewhat didactically, as a lesson in the efficacy of caring behavior. Critical inattention here seems to parallel Frankenstein's own behavior, in favoring the "monstrous" over the mundane. Caroline Beaufort, Justine Moritz, Clerval, Walton and the creature himself, all understand that knowledge, to be effective, must be applied responsibly and methodically.

As the "cause" of her own mother's death, Shelley surely conjectured about the circumstances surrounding Mary Wollstonecraft's death. Although Wollstonecraft was attended to by several doctors, none was able to save her. The question for Mary Shelley and virtually every woman of the period was not whether circumstances might have been different had galvanism been able to restore her mother to life, but whether science would ever learn how to protect mothers and their infants from death. Years after the writing of **Frankenstein,** Shelley suffered a miscarriage that threatened her life. In the intervening years she lost her favorite child, William Shelley (b. Jan. 24, 1816- d. June 17, 1819), and her daughter, Clara (b. Sept. 2, 1817-d. Sept. 24, 1818). After the death of her first child, an unnamed female born Feb. 22, 1815, she wrote, "'tis hard indeed for a mother to loose [sic] a child" (68) and later "stay at home net [sic] & think of my little dead baby—this is foolish I suppose yet whenever I am left alone to my own thoughts & do not read to divert them they always come back to the same point—that I was a mother & am so no longer" (69). One of the most frequently cited passages from the *Journals* follows several days later (March 19th):

> Dream that my little baby came to life again—that it had only been cold & that we rubbed it by the fire & it lived—I awake & find no baby—I think about the little thing all day. (70)

Shelley's dream is clearly important to readers of *Frankenstein,* particularly for those who are interested in interpreting the creation of the monster as a birth myth. The dream not only suggests how troubled Shelley was, but also how frustrated and helpless she felt. The mysterious death of her child, like the mysterious deaths of so many other children and mothers, was not a phenomenon that medical science could explain, much less prevent. The condition of pregnancy, as Claire Kahane has noted, makes sense as a "primary Gothic metaphor" given that in "this most definitively of female conditions potentially lie the most extreme apprehensions" (57). It is not surprising that Shelley in a crude way, but with scientific insight, should dream of a process of restoration and recovery for her dead infant.[40] Her imagination may have carried her beyond the current state of scientific knowledge, but it expresses a desperate longing for a time when senseless deaths could be avoided by human intervention. Frankenstein's entire narrative, in fact, is made possible by just such an intervention. Frankenstein, like the baby of Mary Shelley's dream, is cold and near death when he is discovered by Walton, who acts in a manner consistent with Shelley's reanimation dream. Walton brings the near frozen body of Frankenstein onto the deck and restores him to animation by rubbing him with brandy, and forcing him to swallow a small quantity. "As soon as he shewed signs of life," Walton writes to his sister, "we wrapped him up in blankets, and placed him near the chimney of the kitchen-stove. By slow degrees he recovered, and ate a little soup, which restored him wonderfully" (20). Though no physician himself, Walton is well acquainted enough with severe frostbite to take the appropriate steps to remedy it. His response, like the monster's reaction to the drowning girl, is immediate, focussed, and disciplined. Frankenstein's expression of gratitude to Walton for having "benevolently restored me to life" provides an instructive contrast for the remainder of his narrative, which shows no similar patterns of benevolence or, for that matter, restoration.

It is well worth remembering that while Mary Shelley was writing *Frankenstein* issues of childbirth and the medical treatment of mothers and infants assumed an unprecedented importance in the public mind. Several months after Clara was born, the English public was outraged when Princess Charlotte and her offspring—the long awaited heir—died during childbirth. The attending physician, Sir Richard Croft, committed suicide after a similar incident in the following year. The exact cause of Charlotte's death was not really understood and, according to Judith Schneid Lewis, continues to be the source of some debate.[41] Lewis suggests that the complications were associated with Charlotte's prolonged labor (over 50 hours) and indicates that a trend ensued, in the medical profession, to hasten deliveries. The death of Princess Charlotte, who received "the best" medical attention, underscores both the se-

verity of the problem shared by women throughout the nineteenth-century and the general concern about the inability of the medical sciences to improve the situation.[42] "It is hard to comprehend," write Elaine and English Showalter, "how little even scientists and doctors knew about human reproduction in the nineteenth century" (38).[43] The national disappointment at the death of so young a princess, not to mention that of the potential heir to the throne was, as one account put it, "a blow which the nation appears to really feel acutely."[44]

The months surrounding Charlotte's death were already hectic and stressful ones for Shelley, coming in the midst of her own pregnancy (with Clara), the publication of *Frankenstein,* a move to London, and preparations for a move to Italy. And though Italy had been recommended to the Shelleys for its recuperative powers, it had little to offer, from Shelley's perspective, in the way of good medical care. In a letter to Maria Gisborne she explains that they will be wintering in Pisa, "a place recomended [*sic*] particularly for Shelley's health":

> We would like of all things to have a house near you by the seaside at Livorno but the heat would frighten me for William who is so very delicate— and we must take the greatest possible care of him this summer—We shall at least be within reach of a good english physician & we have the most rooted contempt & in any case of illness the greatest dread of Italian Medicos. (98)

The doctor to whom Mary is referring is John Bell, an eminent surgeon from Edinburgh, who also moved to Italy for reasons of health. Bell had also established himself as something of a radical by opposing the move, made by the more socially prestigious physicians, to limit the attendance of surgeons at the Royal Infirmary. Over the course of time Bell became more than simply the Shelleys' family doctor; both he and his wife were frequent guests at the Shelley household. Bell's attraction for the Shelleys, as an eminent man of science and a man of conscience, must have been irresistible. Having stood firm in support of the surgeons against the elitist physicians, Bell's opposition to the tyranny within his profession could not help but elevate him in Percy's estimation.

In this capacity as a doctor Bell had not only "been of service" to Shelley, but he also treated William, who was ill with malaria. "Fortunately," Mary wrote, "he is attended by Mr. Bell who is reckoned even in London one of the first English Surgeons (99)." In spite of Bell's efforts William died on June 7, though the doctor clearly worked hard at trying to keep him alive. On June 5th Mary wrote "Yesterday he [William] was in the convulsions of death and he was saved from them" (99).

The close relationship that both Mary and Percy Shelley had with physicians, on both a personal and professional level, is important for an understanding of their attitudes toward science. That some of the doctors, like Bell, appeared in their lives well after the writing of *Frankenstein* is less important than the qualities that must have attracted the Shelleys to them. The pattern of Percy Shelley's illnesses left him constantly indebted to and on the lookout for good physicians, and Mary, always solicitous of Percy's health, her own health, and that of her children, incorporated them into her life as well.

The question of Percy Shelley's need for medical attention is less interesting here than the intellectual aspect of the doctor-patient relationship that was obviously very meaningful to him. One of the attractions for Percy was the fact that his physicians were men of science—people whom he could engage in scientific conversation. Another attraction was that many of the scientists, as Donald Reiman has pointed out, were liberal thinkers.[45] Shelley's first exposure to a doctor of this sort was at Eton when he struck up an acquaintance with Dr. James Lind.[46] Lind introduced Shelley to many radical and liberal works—perhaps even Godwin, and inspired in him a penchant for letter-writing and pamphleteering.

When Shelley's complaints grew serious many years later, he sought the advice of William Lawrence, whose medical reputation as one of London's finest doctors was already well established. But Lawrence gained particular notoriety as the author of *Lectures on Physiology, Zoology and the Natural History of Man* (1819), a materialist tract that, for a period, was banned. Lawrence's views, including the position that "vitality was a property of organized matter," were ones with which Percy could easily sympathize. Among the implications of Lawrence's immanentist position, as L. S. Jacyna has observed, is that moral and ethical responsibility "must arise from man's organic needs and aptitudes" rather than from a supreme being.[47] Although Shelley was already in Italy by the time the *Lectures* were published, it is certain that Shelley found as much of an ally in Lawrence as he did a physician. That Percy and Mary often found themselves in need of medical treatment is not unusual; what is striking is their knack for finding doctors who were not only accomplished in their fields, but scientifically curious, and—in some sense—radical or, at least, socially committed. These were people who viewed both practical and theoretical science in the context of social responsibility and who had a social and political agenda that Percy, at least, found admirable. Thus physicians had a substantially positive role in the lives of the Shelleys; in addition to attending to Mary, and to the Shelleys' children, they endeavored to learn more about the medical sciences and were willing, for the sake of that knowledge, to take positions that defied authority.

VII. *Demonstrating Knowledge in Society*

I have taken the time to discuss the doctors that the Shelleys knew because, as socially engaged physician/scientists, they helped elucidate Mary Shelley's conception of the moral obligations of the man of knowledge. Shelley is careful to make Frankenstein a master of many branches of knowledge, including medicine, and studiously avoids locating him in any one scientific tradition. The result is a "generic" scientist whose narrow obsession is expressed in the monster. Within the Christian tradition, such scientific "obsessions" were dangerous because they might either undermine the basis of faith, or simply distract the scientist from broader moral obligations. In a household permeated with Percy's atheism, cautionary religious proscriptions were nonsense. Shelley's enthusiasm for the radical ideas espoused by Percy was tempered and she adopted positions that suited her own inclination. Like Percy, she was interested in advocating and encouraging scientific inquiry, but where he was willing to trust the scientific community to participate in a "link'd chain of thought," she would have it answerable to a more familiar code of ethics. Thus her concern for the direction of science and for the moral responsibility of scientists does not stray too far from traditional Christian values, though it owes little to systems of belief. The hubris of Frankenstein's inquiry into the forces of life and death is secondary, in Mary's view, to the social hubris he commits by pursuing knowledge for the sake of no one but himself.

The familiar platitude, that Frankenstein is doomed because he transgresses into a realm of knowledge that is forbidden to humanity, needs to be put aside. Well before Frankenstein attempted to assume a God-like role, by creating a "new species," he broke faith with a tradition that was at once both moral and scientific. An alternative Frankenstein, cast in the mold of say, William Lawrence or John Bell would surely have directed his skills toward the "improvement" of mankind. Another Frankenstein might, like Edward Jenner, have taken his hard won knowledge to the provinces. Yet another Frankenstein, more important still, might have been a woman.[48] "Women," Wollstonecraft wrote in her *Vindication of the Rights of Woman,* "might certainly study the art of healing and be physicians as well as nurses" (261). Whatever the case, Frankenstein's life as a scientist would have been complete because of the moral quality guiding his pursuit of knowledge.

The choices available to Frankenstein are not merely a matter of speculation. Shelley invokes her own experiences and those of women like her to underscore the very real need for the knowledge that Frankenstein's science might have been able to offer. Her voice and her experience seem to inform Frankenstein's only moment of real awareness of the potential uses of his knowledge:

Death snatches away many blooming children, the
only hopes of their doating parents; how many brides
and youthful lovers have been one day in the bloom
of health and hope, and the next a prey for worms
and the decay of the tomb! (174)

Shelley allows Frankenstein to recognize, if only briefly,
the possibility that science might be able to have some
connection with its "object" of study. This kind of
approach, based on "respect rather than domination,"
hints at what Evelyn Fox Keller sees, in *Reflections on
Gender and Science,* as revisionary science.[49] Much of
Keller's critique emerges for the work of Barbara
McClintock, who posits, in terms that are meaningful
in *Frankenstein,* that the scientist must have a "feeling for the organism." Keller's critique of science is
similar to Shelley's in that it does not rely on a rejection of technology or of knowledge; nor does it invoke
traditional stereotypes of women as somehow more
sensitive or intuitive. Instead, it recognizes the scientific impulse to deny context and subjectivity in order
to impose the fictions "of disinterest, of autonomy,
[and] of alienation" (70). Knowledge produced under
this system, as Mary Shelley makes clear in *Frankenstein,* bears the heavy burden of these fictions. Shelley's
monster, unlike Frankenstein, understands that there
should be a way to situate himself in the discourse of
relationships.

Science, however, is structured to resist shifts in sensibility and, like Frankenstein himself, is destined to
generate knowledge without necessarily understanding
it. The monster, as the self-conscious product of science, simply wants to change what counts as knowledge and in doing so, be counted. Shelley wants the
reader to understand that if any constraints exist on
Frankenstein's knowledge, they are social rather than
supernatural. Because Frankenstein created the monster for his own benefit—to increase his own knowledge—rather than for the benefit of the community—
to contribute knowledge—the creature is inevitably
viewed by society as foreign and unacceptable. The
rationale behind that rejection is, of course, that the
monster represents a "species" of knowledge that has
not been contextualized. The monstrous creature, dwelling apart from a society that misunderstands it, is thus
the perfect embodiment of Frankenstein's knowledge
and finally of the scientist himself.

Notes

[1] The editor of this preface is not specified; the text is
a translation of Giovanni (John) Aldini's *An Account of
the Late Improvements of Galvanism with a series of
Curious and Interesting Experiments Performed Before
the Commissioners of the French National Institute and
Repeated Lately in the Anatomical Theatres of London*
(London: Cuthell and Martin, J. Murray, 1803).

[2] The literature on *Frankenstein* is extensive. Several
studies are worth noting here to give a sense of the
breadth of the work that has been done. Ann Mellor has
contributed significantly to feminist readings of the novel;
her study is strongly grounded in textual analysis as
well as close attention to contemporary events in science. Ellen Moers's early essay is a cornerstone of feminist thinking with respect to the novel. See also Mary
Poovey's *The Proper Lady and the Woman Writer* (Chicago: U of Chicago P, 1984) and Margaret Homans'
Bearing the Word (Chicago: U of Chicago P, 1986) for
analyses of Shelley and of the novel. For psychoanalytic readings of the text see William Veeder's *Mary
Shelley & Frankenstein: The Fate of Androgeny* and
Paul Sherwin's article "Frankenstein: Creation as Catastrophe" (*PMLA* 96.5 [1981]: 883-903). In *The Realistic
Imagination* (Chicago: U of Chicago P, 1981), George
Levine looks at the novel within the literary tradition of
realism; "the monster and his creator," Levine argues,
"reflect the culture's ambivalence about itself, the
realist's difficulty with the narrative conventions of realism" (24). Levine's "The Ambiguous Heritage of Frankenstein" is in George Levine and U. C. Knoepflmacher,
eds., *The Endurance of "Frankenstein"* (Berkeley: U of
California P, 1979) 3-30.

[3] I will refer to Mary Shelley throughout this essay by
either her full name or simply by "Shelley." Percy
Shelley will be referred to by either his full name or
his first name alone.

[4] In her analysis of *Frankenstein, Metropolis,* and "The
Birthmark," Ludmilla Jordanova pays close attention
to the representational element of knowledge. The
notion that knowledge is transgressive because it is an
"affront to nature and God" explains only part of the
story; knowledge can also be "profane because it is
inappropriate to the human condition" (*Sexual Visions*
[Madison: U of Wisconsin P, 1989] 127).

[5] Lester Friedman's reading of the novel as a parable
concerned with the "responsibility of medical research"
is helpful here ("Sporting with Life: Frankenstein and
the Responsibility of Medical Research," *Medical
Heritage* 1.3 [1985]: 181-85).

[6] Daniel Cottom, "'Frankenstein' and the Monster of
Representation," *Sub-Stance* 28 (1980): 67. Mary
Poovey, in *The Proper Lady and the Woman Writer,*
links the novel and the creature; both are the progeny
of the "unladylike" act of writing. In the symbolic
presentation of the creature, Poovey observes, we see
Shelley's attempt "to express and efface herself at the
same time and thus, at least partially, to satisfy her
conflicting desires for self-assertion and social acceptance" (131).

[7] Syndy Conger, in her brief essay, "Aporia and Radical Empathy: Frankenstein (Re)Trains the Reader" (in

Stephen Behrendt, ed., *Approaches to Teaching Shelley's "Frankenstein"* [New York: MLA Publications, 1990]), outlines the ways in which the reader must "determine right and wrong from experiencing, albeit vicariously, the lives of creator and creature" (66). Conger is right in pointing out that the various narratives of *Frankenstein* cannot be understood unless they are reread critically. Her own assertion, however, that Frankenstein's major flaw as a narrator is that he forgets "feelings," seems to underestimate the complexity of the text.

8 All citations will be from the first edition (1818) edited by James Rieger (Chicago: U of Chicago P, 1982), except where otherwise noted.

9 The notion that Frankenstein is operating within the confines of "scientific and rationalistic ambition" is advocated by Robert Wexblatt in "The Ambivalence of 'Frankenstein'" (*Arizona Quarterly* 36 [1980]: 101-17). Yet it seems clear that Shelley wants to alter our understanding of what defines "the rational" in scientific inquiry rather than simply, as Wexblatt wants to suggest, argue against it.

10 See Peter Brooks, "'Godlike Science / Unhallowed Arts': Language, Nature, and Monstrosity," in *The Endurance of "Frankenstein"* 205-20.

11 Elissa Marder, "The Mother Tongue in 'Phedre' and 'Frankenstein,'" *Yale French Studies* June 76 (1989): 68.

12 See Mary Ann Doane, "Technology, Representation, and the Feminine," in Mary Jacobus, Evelyn Fox Keller, and Sally Shuttleworth, eds., *Body/Politics: Women and the Discourses of Science* (New York: Routledge, 1990) 175.

13 In *Sexual Visions,* Ludmilla Jordanova traces three kinds of violence inherent in the "domain of natural sciences and medicine": "epistemological, actual, and representational" (60). The cultural impact of all three was substantial. In *Women and the Body: A Cultural Analysis of Reproduction* (Boston: Beacon, 1987), Emily Martin notes that "women are not only fragmented into body parts by the practices of scientific medicine . . . they are also profoundly alienated from science itself" (21). Thus women are dehumanized by being objectified and by being excluded, a process Frankenstein reenacts not only in this scene but in his general approach toward knowledge.

14 The "quality of obstetric teaching," Ornella Moscucci points out in *The Science of Woman* (Cambridge: Cambridge UP, 1990), was poor "even at mid-century." Moreover, gross incompetence in obstetrics and gynecology was common among both medical men and midwives. See also Alan Bewell's "An Issue of Mon-

strous Desire: 'Frankenstein' and Obstetrics" (*The Yale Journal of Criticism* 2.1 [1987]: 105-28) which draws on a history of obstetrics to argue that Shelley "made obstetrics the master code of her aesthetics" (107). For the circumstances surrounding the death of Mary Wollstonecraft see the biographies by Claire Tomalin (*The Life and Death of Mary Wollstonecraft* [London: Weidenfield and Nicholson, 1974]) and Eleanor Flexner (*Mary Wollstonecraft* [New York: Penguin, 1972]) as well as William St. Clair's study, *The Godwins and the Shelleys* (Baltimore: Johns Hopkins UP, 1989). Flexner accuses the attending physicians of gross medical incompetence aside from introducing an infection; St. Clair not only suggests that Dr. Poignand, the first attending physician, may have caused "severe damage" (177) but that Wollstonecraft "might have lived" had childbirth been "left to nature" (178). Whatever the case, what is absolutely clear is that medical knowledge, in the persons of Drs. Poignand, Clarke, Fordyce, and Carlisle, could do nothing to save her.

15 *A Vindication of the Rights of Woman* (1792) (Harmondsworth: Penguin, 1982) 86.

16 (Harmondsworth, Penguin, 1985) 306.

17 (Chicago: U of Chicago P, 1987) 351.

18 The notions of alchemy that I am referring to are the popular connotations of the discipline, focussing on transmutation and hermeticism. In contemporary terms, this regarding of alchemy is overly broad and overlooks the significant contributions it made to experimental science. See for example Thomas Goldstein's *The Dawn of Modern Science* (Boston: Houghton Mifflin, 1980) or Ian Hacking's *The Emergence of Probability* (Cambridge: Cambridge UP, 1975). Charles Mackay devotes a substantial section of his *Extraordinary Popular Delusions and the Madness of Crowds* (1841) (New York: Harmony Books, 1980) to alchemy, and while he recognizes its contribution to modern science, he derides it as an "unprofitable pursuit."

19 The notion of incremental additions to science can be found in Herschel, but is frequently associated with both Charles Lyell and Charles Darwin. For them, change in knowledge was similar to change in nature. Bruno Latour discusses the reliance, in contemporary science and engineering, on unproblematized systems, where process is not considered as important as product (*Science in Action* [Cambridge MA: Harvard UP, 1987]).

20 Shelley's "The Mortal Immortal" (1833) deals directly with the discovery of the elixir vitae as the product of alchemy. As in *Frankenstein,* the knowledge embodied in the elixir proves useless not only to its discoverer (Cornelius Agrippa) but to his student, Winzy, who has consumed the elixir. The elixir ren-

ders Winzy at least partly immortal and thus places him outside the context of human events. Like the monster, he pursues death to eradicate knowledge that can't be reconciled with reality. See Mary Shelley, *Collected Tales and Stories,* Charles Robinson, ed. (Baltimore: Johns Hopkins UP, 1976) 219-30.

[21] It is worth considering here Thomas Kuhn's notion, in *The Structure of Scientific Revolutions* (Chicago: U of Chicago P, 1972), of how science becomes "normal science" within a culture. "A New theory," writes Kuhn, "is always announced together with applications to some concrete range of natural phenomena; without them it would not even be a candidate for acceptance" (46).

[22] See Jan Golinski's *Science as Public Culture: Chemistry and Enlightenment in Britain, 1760-1820* (Cambridge: Cambridge UP, 1992) for the role of public science in the romantic period.

[23] See Aldini's *General Views on the Application of Galvanism to Medical Purposes Principally in cases of suspended Animation* (London: J. Callow, Princes Street and Burgess and Hill, Great Windmill Street, 1819) 17.

[24] Birch was "Surgeon Extraordinary" to the Prince of Wales and was affiliated with St. Thomas' Hospital where he almost certainly learned of Aldini's electrical experiments. Birch relied on static electricity, which was more convenient than the cumbersome Voltaic piles used in Galvanism. See Birch's *An Essay on the Medical Application of Electricity* (London: J. Johnson, 1802).

[25] I want here, and elsewhere, to avoid reification of the monster as essentially monstrous, i.e., that the creature must be frightening because it does not measure up to human standards of beauty or attractiveness. I also want to reject the notion, proposed by a number of readers including Sue Weaver Schopf, that the monster is "anti-social" or "misanthropic" ("'Of What a Strange Nature is Knowledge': Hartleian Psychology and the Creature's Arrested Moral Sense in Mary Shelley's 'Frankenstein,'" (*Romanticism Past and Present* 5.1 [1981]: 33-52). The monster's problem is quite the opposite; he is a social creature, who wants to engage other humans. As an embodiment of knowledge he understands that the appropriate context for him is a social one. That the monster recognizes himself as "ugly" when he looks at his reflection merely suggests the influence of social standards and the extent to which the monster himself is unaware of the knowledge he represents. The issue is not, as Robert Wexblatt argues, that the monster is "made to appear 'ugly' . . . because what he represents is 'bad'" (113). The impulse to reduce the monster and his actions to the level of the merely grotesque is problematic. By

accepting the creature as a conventional monster, in the most reductive way, readers elide the embedded context in which the creature exists. Stephanie Kiceluk, for example, has written persuasively that the monster demonstrates "Shelley's horrified recognition . . . of woman as she is culturally and socially constructed by man." Yet, in spite of her willingness to reinterpret the monster, she tacitly accepts the notion that the creature is responsible for "atrocity after atrocity" ("Made in His Image: Frankenstein's Daughters," *Michigan Quarterly Review* Winter 30.1 [1991]: 110-26). Kiceluk seems willing to judge the creature's "crimes" by traditional (patriarchal?) standards rather than seeing them as cultural and social constructions in their own right.

[26] See Ellen Moers, "Female Gothic" in *The Endurance of "Frankenstein"* 77-87.

[27] Richard Holmes, *Shelley: The Pursuit* (Harmondsworth: Penguin, 1974) 37-42.

[28] See the entry for Dec. 28, 1814 in *The Journals of Mary Shelley,* Vol. 1: 1814-1822, Paula R. Feldman and Diana Scott-Kilvert, eds. (Oxford: Oxford UP, 1987).

[29] See Mellor's "*Frankenstein:* A Feminist Critique of Science," in George Levine and Alan Rauch, eds., *One Culture: Essays in Science and Literature* (Madison: U of Wisconsin P, 1987) 305.

[30] Aldini, *Late Improvements in Galvanism* 78. Joseph Vanable, Jr. notes, in his brief survey of the medical uses of electricity, that it is "scarcely possible to overestimate the effect of Galvani's and Volta's experiments on the world of science and medicine" ("A History of Bioelectricity in Development and Regeneration," in Charles Dinsmore, ed., *A History of Regeneration Research* [Cambridge: Cambridge UP, 1991] 157). Vanable also credits Aldini's efforts, though the result of "ill-advised enthusiasm," as crucial to the dissemination of the practice of medical electricity.

[31] Excerpt from William Nicholson's *Journal of Natural Philosophy, Chemistry, and the Arts,* cited in Aldini's *A Late Account* iv.

[32] Muriel Spark, *Mary Shelley* (New York: E. P. Dutton, 1987) 162.

[33] The notion that amusement is among the potential responses (especially for the "common reader") to *Frankenstein* is examined by Philip Stevick in "*Frankenstein* and Comedy" in *The Endurance of "Frankenstein"* 221-39.

[34] And of course it does miss an important point because it grossly oversimplifies the notion of reproduction in the novel. Frankenstein is deeply resentful that

a fertile monster, in addition to everything else, will be able to reproduce without needing Frankenstein, thus rendering his "circumvention of the maternal" in Margaret Homans' words, pointless. The monster's true reproductive capacity, as Margaret Homans argues, is that he "emblematizes the literalization of literature that Shelley, through him, practices" (118). Nevertheless, such arguments may be useful in the process of recognizing both the book and the monster as instantiations of important but unfamiliar knowledge.

[35] *A Newton Among the Poets: Shelley's Use of Science in 'Prometheus Unbound'* (New York: Gordian P, 1968) 196.

[36] The quote, from "Prometheus Unbound" (IV. I. 394) (see *Shelley's Poetry and Prose,* Donald Reiman and Sharon Powers, eds. [New York: Norton, 1977] 205), describes an attitude toward knowledge that Frankenstein rejects. "Shelley seems to express here," Carl Grabo writes of this portion of the poem, "his belief in the unity of knowledge, his belief that the individual adds his bit to the whole" (196).

[37] Recent biographies, including Emily Sunstein's *Mary Shelley: Romance and Reality* (Boston: Little Brown and Company, 1989) discuss the medical treatment and the physician acquaintances of the Shelleys. Richard Holmes's biography of Percy also pays close attention to the subject. Kenneth Cameron describes Lind, who was physician to George III, as "a kindly man of Liberal ideas both in political and scientific thinking" (*Young Shelley* [New York: MacMillan, 1950] 13).

[38] I am quoting here from the 1831 version of the novel, ed. M. K. Joseph (New York: Oxford UP, 1969) 42-43. In the 1818 edition, Caroline Frankenstein impatiently waits until she hears that Elizabeth is recovering and then, finding "that she could no longer debar herself from her society . . . entered her bedchamber long before the danger of infection was past" (Rieger 37). The revision underscores Caroline Frankenstein's commitment to Elizabeth and makes her the active agent in Elizabeth's recovery. In both editions, Frankenstein recognizes the "fortitude and benignity" of his mother's actions, while making no effort to emulate them.

[39] See Marie Hélène-Huet's *Monstrous Imagination* (Cambridge, MA: Harvard UP, 1993) for a recent discussion of the significance of the kiss in Frankenstein's dream. Huet's reading of the novel, which relies on the role of Percy as Shelley's collaborator, is useful in considerations of the nature of monstrosity. Huet considers the monstrous in a long tradition of decontextualized art ("eikastiken" art), that is "art without art" (130).

[40] Linda Layne's studies of mothers' responses to the loss of children during pregnancy are extremely useful

in understanding *Frankenstein* from this perspective. Layne focuses on "fragmentation and integration in narratives of loss" and though many are linked to contemporary forms of technology, they are resonant in the context of Mary Shelley's own experiences with pregnancy and loss. See "Of Fetuses and Angels: Fragmentation and Integration in Narratives of Pregnancy Loss" (*Knowledge and Society* 9 [1992]: 29-58) and "Motherhood Lost: Cultural Dimensions of Miscarriage and Stillbirth in America" (*Women & Health* 16.3/4 [1990]: 69-98).

[41] See Lewis' *In the Family Way: Childbearing in the British Aristocracy, 1760-1860* (New Brunswick, NJ: Rutgers UP, 1986) 173.

[42] Susan Lawrence also notes that in the nineteenth century "the whole condition of pregnancy was obscure" ("'Desirous of Improvements in Medicine': Pupils and Practitioners in the Medical Societies at Guy's and St. Bartholomew's Hospitals, 1795-1815," *Bull. Hist. Med.* 59 [1985]: 99). William Arney's useful survey of obstetrics looks at some of the problems of the profession in Foucauldian terms of power and knowledge. Mary Poovey's *Uneven Developments* (Chicago: U of Chicago P, 1988) outlines the way in which early practices objectified the female body and appropriated it as a domain for male knowledge.

[43] See Elaine Showalter and English Showalter, "Victorian Women and Menstruation," in Martha Vicinus, ed., *Suffer and be Still: Women in the Victorian Age* (Bloomington: Indiana UP, 1972) 38-44.

[44] The loss of Charlotte and her child meant that succession, once again, was back in the disagreeable hands of George's aging and unappealing brothers. See Alison Plowden's *Caroline and Charlotte* (London: Sidgwick and Jackson, 1989) for a description of the events surrounding Charlotte's death. For a contemporary response, see "On the Late National Calamity" in *Blackwood's Edinburgh Magazine,* December 1817.

[45] See Donald Reiman, *Shelley and His Circle: Manuscripts Vol. VI* (New York: The Carl H. Pforzheimer Library, 1973) 652. Elsewhere in *Shelley and his Circle,* Kenneth Cameron argues that Lawrence's "antireligious views" may have attracted Shelley (Vol. 111: 483-84).

[46] See Desmond King-Hele's "Shelley and Dr. Lind," *Keats-Shelley Memorial Bulletin* 18 (1967): 1-6.

[47] Lawrence's controversial theories about the organization of life are examined by L. C. Jacyna ("Immanence or Transcendence. Theories of Life and Organization in Britain, 1790-1835," *Isis* 74 [1983]: 311-29) and Kentwood Wells ("Sir William Lawrence [1783-1867]: A Study of Pre-Darwinian Ideas on Heredity and Variation," *Journal of History of Biology* 4.2 [1971]: 319-61).

[48] Here again, Alan Bewell's reading of the novel as "an assertion of [Shelley's] imaginative authority" (124) is useful, situated as it is in the discourse of nineteenth-century obstetrics.

[49] See Evelyn Fox Keller's *Reflections on Gender and Science* (New Haven: Yale UP, 1985) and *A Feeling for the Organism* (New York: W. H. Freeman, 1983).

FURTHER READING

Bibliography

Frank, Frederick S. "Mary Shelley's *Frankenstein*: A Register of Research." *Bulletin of Bibliography* 40, No. 3 (1983): 163-88.

> Provides a brief critical overview and an exhaustive annotated bibliography of editions, biographies, and criticism both specific and general.

Biography

Sunstein, Emily W. *Mary Shelley: Romance and Reality.* Boston and Toronto: Little, Brown and Co., 1989, 478 p.

> Defining Shelley as an exemplary Romantic, seeks to provide an authoritative biography that cuts through the myths.

Criticism

Botting, Fred. "Reflections of Excess: *Frankenstein,* the French Revolution and Monstrosity." In *Reflections of Revolution: Images of Romanticism,* edited by Alison Yarrington and Kelvin Everest, pp. 26-38. London and New York: Routledge, 1993.

> Reads *Frankenstein* within the historical context of the French Revolution and its effect upon British culture.

————, ed. *New Casebooks: Frankenstein.* London: Macmillan, 1995, 271 p.

> Draws together essays representing the different critical approaches commonly employed in studying *Frankenstein.*

Goldberg, M. A. "Moral and Myth in Mrs. Shelley's *Frankenstein.*" *Keats-Shelley Journal* 8 (Winter 1959): 27-38.

> Explores the Promethean and Miltonic echoes in *Frankenstein* to reveal the novel's depiction of isolation and knowledge.

Hatlen, Burton. "Milton, Mary Shelley, and Patriarchy." In *Rhetoric, Literature, and Interpretation,* edited by Harry R. Garvin, pp. 19-47. Lewisburg, PA: Bucknell University Press, 1983.

> Contends that Shelley wrote from a radical political position, imbuing her novel with "egalitarian and libertarian motifs."

Hill-Miller, Katherine C. *"My Hideous Progeny": Mary Shelley, William Godwin, and the Father-Daughter Relationship.* Newark: University of Delaware Press, 1995, 249 p.

> Devotes attention to Godwin's influence on Shelley, particularly his influence as a literary predecessor; Hill-Miller focuses one chapter on *Frankenstein.*

Huet, Marie-Hélène. "Unwonted Paternity: The Genesis of *Frankenstein.*" In her *Monstrous Imagination,* pp. 129-62. Cambridge, MA: Harvard University Press, 1993.

> Within a historical study of discourses of procreation, argues that "rather than the prototype of a new genre, *Frankenstein* may be seen as the last and most powerful illustration of eikastiken art, art without art."

Kaplan, Morton, and Robert Kloss. "Fantasy of Paternity and the Doppelgänger: Mary Shelley's *Frankenstein.*" In *The Unspoken Motive: A Guide to Psychoanalytic Literary Criticism,* pp. 119-45. New York: Free Press, 1973.

> Demonstrates one of the classic psychoanalytic approaches to the novel, employing Freudian paradigms and the methods of dream analysis.

Ketterer, David. *Frankenstein's Creation: The Book, The Monster, and Human Reality.* British Columbia, Canada: English Literary Studies, 1979, 124 p.

> Contends that Shelley deliberately composed *Frankenstein* to convey a sense of apocalypse.

Levine, George, and U. C. Knoepflmacher, eds. *The Endurance of Frankenstein: Essays on Mary Shelley's Novel.* Berkeley and Los Angeles: University of California Press, 1979, 341 p.

> A collection of essays that, at the time of publication, both broke new ground in *Frankenstein* criticism and captured critical concerns driving the resurgence of interest in the novel. Critics include Ellen Moers, George Levine, Peter Brooks, and Judith Wilt.

London, Bette. "Mary Shelley, *Frankenstein,* and the Spectacle of Masculinity." *PMLA* 108, No. 2 (March 1993): pp. 253-67.

> Examines the presence of the male body in Shelley's novel, contending that it serves as "the site of an ineradicable materiality."

Lowe-Evans, Mary. *Frankenstein: Mary Shelley's Wedding Guest.* New York: Twayne Publishers, 1993, 97 p.

> Relates events in the novel directly to events in Shelley's life, seeking to shed light on the book, its author, and her era.

Marshall, David. "*Frankenstein,* or Rousseau's Monster: Sympathy and Speculative Eyes." In *The Surprising Effects of Sympathy: Marivaux, Diderot, Rousseau, and Mary Shelley,* pp. 178-227. Chicago: University of Chicago Press, 1988.

Considers *Frankenstein* in light of Shelley's readings of Rousseau, arguing that Shelley "presents detailed and complex readings of both the figure of Rousseau and Rousseau's writing about the problem of sympathy."

Poovey, Mary. "'My Hideous Progeny': The Lady and the Monster." In *The Proper Lady and the Woman Writer: Ideology as Style in the Works of Mary Wollstonecraft, Mary Shelley, and Jane Austen*, pp. 114-42. Chicago: University of Chicago Press, 1984.

> Examines the impact of gender-role demands on Shelley and her work, depicting her as torn between the desire for self-expression and the desire to conform.

Rieger, James, ed. *Frankenstein; or, the Modern Prometheus: The 1818 Text*, by Mary Shelley. Chicago: University of Chicago Press, 1974, 287 p.

> Supplements an authoritative reprint of the first edition of *Frankenstein* with an introduction, several appendices, and notes.

Rubenstein, Marc A. "'My Accursed Origin': The Search for the Mother in *Frankenstein*." *Studies in Romanticism* 15, No. 2 (Spring 1976): 165-94.

> Relying both on Shelley's biography and psychoanylitic methodology, analyzes *Frankenstein* as a struggle with "the problem of motherhood."

Small, Christopher. *Ariel Like a Harpy: Shelley, Mary, and Frankenstein*. London: Victor Gollancz, 1972, 352 p.

> Regards the novel as the product of direct and indirect "imaginative" influences at work in Shelley's immediate circumstances, her personal history, and her historical context.

Spark, Muriel. "*Frankenstein*." In her *Child of Light: A Reassessment of Mary Wollstonecraft Shelley*, pp. 128-49. Hadleigh, England: Tower Bridge Publications, 1951.

> Argues that *Frankenstein* constituted the beginning of "a new and hybrid fictional species," combining the conventions of the Gothic novel with philosophical depth.

Twitchell, James B. "*Frankenstein* and the Anatomy of Horror." *The Georgia Review* XXXVII, No. 1 (Spring 1983): 41-78.

> Discusses *Frankenstein* and its popular culture legacy as part of an effort to define the genre of "horror" and to discover its audience appeal.

Veeder, William. *Mary Shelley and Frankenstein: The Fate of Androgyny*. Chicago: University of Chicago Press, 1986, 277 p.

> Relying on the concepts of "androgyny" and "bifurcation," examines the presence of aggression in Shelley's work, considering in particular its relation to gender identity.

Additional coverage of Shelley's life and career is contained in the following sources published by Gale Research: *Nineteenth-Century Literature Criticism*, **Vol. 14;** *DISCovering Authors; DISCovering Authors Modules—Most Studied-Authors and Novelists modules; World Literature Criticism, 1500 to the Present; Dictionary of Literary Biography*, **Vols. 110, 116, and 159; and** *Concise Dictionary of British Literary Biography, 1789-1832.*

Alexander Smith

1829(?)-1867

Scottish poet and essayist.

INTRODUCTION

Smith is one of a small group of nineteenth-century writers recognized as Spasmodics, an affiliation that all but ended his poetic career. Spasmodic poets closely patterned their style after the Romantic poets, and were criticized for their excessive use of nature imagery and obscure allusions. This label plagued Smith for his entire life. Initially, Smith's combinations of urban and nature images in *A Life Drama* (1853) made him instantly popular. However, charges of plagiarism and criticisms of the Spasmodic style, along with a parody of his works, made him almost as instantly obscure. Once named a Spasmodic, Smith spent the rest of his life trying to disassociate himself from that group. After four failed attempts at poetry, he turned to writing essays, for which he received less attention but more favorable critiques. His essays and poems are recognized today as offering valuable insights into urban Victorian England.

Biographical Information

Smith was born in Kilmarnock, Scotland, and although the year is uncertain, it is generally stated as 1829 or 1830. Smith's family had hoped to school him for a career as a minister, but for unknown reasons, around the age of twelve he instead began work as a pattern designer with his father in Glasgow. Industrial Glasgow would prove to be a lasting positive influence on Smith's city poetry; the poem he later wrote about the city was considered by some critics to be one of his best pieces. Although his formal education ended at the primary level, Smith read a great deal while not at the factory. Byron and Shelley were his early favorites; later he turned to Keats and Tennyson. As a teenager he began writing his own poems, first publishing some little-noticed in 1850 in the Glasgow *Evening Citizen* under the name "Smith Murray." In 1851 Smith sent some poems to critic George Gilfillian, who was known for encouraging and critically supporting young poets. Gilfillian enthusiastically printed portions of Smith's poems in the *Eclectic Review* and the *London Literary Journal*, praising him for his "exquisite thoughts and imagery." After Gilfillian's review, readers were eager for more of Smith's works, and critics generally agree that this public demand, combined with pressure from Gilfillian, prompted Smith to fuse many of his smaller poems into a longer one,

which he named *A Life Drama*. This was the major piece published along with shorter selections in his first collection, *Poems* (1853). *Poems* was an immediate success with the public, and many critics claimed that Smith had the potential to become the next great poet. Smith subsequently quit his job as a pattern designer and in 1854 was appointed Secretary of Edinburgh University, a position which allowed him to spend more time on his poetry. In July of that same year, W. E. Aytoun, one of the first critics to label Smith a Spasmodic, published *Firmilian; or, The Student of Badajoz. A Spasmodic Tragedy*, a parody of the Spasmodic school and its proponent, Gilfillian. Aytoun criticized the Spasmodics for over-use of nature images, inclusion of lengthy passages that did not relate to the themes of their works, and lax morals. Criticism, and then public opinion, rapidly turned against Smith. His second work, *Sonnets on the War* (1855), a joint effort with fellow Spasmodic Sydney Dobell, was not well received and did nothing to relieve Smith of his derogatory label. By this time Smith, who had been acclaimed just two years before, was virtually forgotten and the book was generally ignored. Slightly more successful was *City Poems* (1857), which contains the poem "Glasgow". However, several critics brought charges of plagiarism against Smith, comparing his works to those by Tennyson and Keats. His last attempt at poetry was *Edwin of Deira* (1861), a story of England's first Christian king. This work was initially accepted by critics and could have rid Smith of the Spasmodic label if it had not been published soon after Tennyson's epic, *Idylls of the King.* (*Idylls of the King* is also based on a historical background—the story of King Arthur and the Knights of the Round Table—and comments on social problems of the time.) Cries of plagiarism were renewed, even though Smith had been working on *Edwin* before *Idylls* was published. The plagiarism charges again focused negative attention on Smith and the poem was not popularly received. Smith had married Flora Macdonald from Skye in 1857, and, in order to supplement his income from the university and support his growing family, he now turned to writing essays, contributing to magazines such as *Argosy*, *North British Review*, *Good Words*, and *West of Scotland*. His income was more consistent from the publication of his prose than it had been with the publication of his poetry, although biographers agree that prose did not provide Smith with the same personal satisfaction as poetry had. His first prose collection was *Dreamthorp* (1863), in which he commented on the role of an essayist; *A Summer in Skye* (1865), his second, contains essays about the island where his family spent their vacations. Smith became ill in 1865 but continued to write even as his condition deteriorated. He died in 1867 and a year later, friend Patrick P. Alexander published Smith's final collection of poetry and essays, *Last Leaves*.

Major Works

Although Smith often incorporated nature into his poetry, most of his poems contain urban backgrounds. His most popular poetic work, *A Life Drama*, is noted for its Spasmodic characteristics, including the autobiographical poet-hero who longs for fame. Additional Spasmodic elements, such as long allegorical digressions, oddly juxtaposed themes, and extreme emotional outbursts, are common in other works included in *Poems*, his first collection. From this point on, Smith, recognizing the negative effect that the Spasmodic label would have on his career, made efforts to tone down his poetic excesses in order to shake himself free of the title. *City Poems*, consequently, is simpler than previous works and includes the noted poem "Glasgow," which reflects the mixed feelings Smith had toward his hometown. This poem is often considered one of his best because of the balanced way in which he presents images he perceived as negative with those he found favorable. "Glasgow" also contains fewer nature allusions, reflecting his growing maturity as a poet. The nature references that he does include

are thought to be appropriate and to reflect an accurate sense of living in urban Scotland. Other evidence of maturity in his writing at this time is his poetic voice, which critics have found distinctly less English and more Scottish, as Smith began drawing more from his own Scottish experiences and less from the styles of the English poets. *Edwin of Deira*, with a historical background, was seen by the public as a conscious effort to avoid the Spasmodic style. However, critics suggest that in his struggle to change his form of writing, Smith lost his poetic voice and individuality. By this time he was again a little-known poet and the piece received little attention, save the charges of plagiarism. Smith did not totally abandon his poetic style when he began writing essays. In *Dreamthorp*, he wrote that an essay writer is a "kind of poet in prose" and stressed that style is the most important element to a writer. An essay, he explained, is a work of art and must be able to stand on its own as such. This poet-prose style also emerges in *A Summer in Skye*, which Smith offered not as a travel guide, but as a reflection of his observations on the culture and customs of the inhabitants on the island. Smith also wrote a novel in installments for *Good Words* magazine, titled *Alfred Hagart's Household* (1865). This, too, was autobiographical and was popular enough for the editor to ask Smith to extend it to two volumes. The follow-up, *Miss Oona McQuarrie: A Sequel to Alfred Hagart's Household*, was published serially in 1866.

Critical Reception

Smith was initially acclaimed for the images of nature in his poems and his ability to combine natural and urban images. It was over-use of these same devices, however, that caused his downfall. Smith was highly criticized for his displaced references to nature and for poetic digressions within digressions as well as for his lack of form. Moreover, critics questioned the morality of Spasmodic poetry in general pointing in particular to the hero of Smith's *A Life Drama*, who rapes a girl who is in love with him. Smith also suffered from charges of plagiarism—although early critics praised the young poet for admiring Keats and following Keats' style, within months, and for the rest of his career, critics argued over whether Smith patterned his style after influential poets or simply stole their ideas and structure. This led to a debate among contemporary critics, who began questioning whether any writer can possibly have a completely original thought. In the early twentieth century, critics revisited Smith's work and praised him not only for his essays, but also for his roles as a proponent of the essay as its own genre, and as a critic. Author Herbert B. Grimsditch wrote, "Smith can enter in to the spirit of a writer, giving a good interpretation of his work and his point of view, fulfilling one of the primary aims of criticism by arousing the desire to read the books criticised." In the last half of the century, critics returned to examining Smith's poetry, focusing both on plagiarism charges and on Smith's use of personal experience. Today, his work is viewed as a window to urban nineteenth-century life.

PRINCIPAL WORKS

*Poems (poetry) 1853
Sonnets on the War [with Sydney Dobell] (poetry) 1855
**City Poems (poetry) 1857
Edwin of Deira (poetry) 1861
Dreamthorp: A Book of Essays Written in the Country* (essays) 1863
*Alfred Hagart's Household (novel) 1865
A Summer in Skye (essays) 1865
Miss Oona McQuarrie: A Sequel to Alfred Hagart's Household (novel) 1866
Last Leaves: Sketches and Criticisms (poetry and essays) 1868
The Poetical Works of Alexander Smith (poetry) 1909*

*Includes *A Life Drama.*
**Includes the poem "Glasgow."

CRITICISM

George Gilfillian (essay date 1851)

SOURCE: "A New Poet in Glasgow," in *The Critic*, London, Vol. X, No. 256, December 1, 1851, pp. 567-68.

[*Gilfillian is the critic credited with discovering and encouraging Smith. The following article, the second on Smith by Gilfillian, introduced Smith to about six thousand readers before he had even published a book of poetry, and caused Smith's first volume to be eagerly anticipated. Here, Gilfillian favorably compares Smith to Keats, Shelley, and Coleridge, saying Smith has the potential to become a genius poet.*]

Discoverers are often a much injured class of men. Sometimes the worth of their object is denied, sometimes their claim to the fact of finding it out is contested, and sometimes, in the brilliance of the star, the astronomer who has first observed it is utterly eclipsed! Nevertheless it is a pleasant thing, "when a new planet swims into our ken," or when, to pursue the quotation, we happen to resemble—

> —Stout Cortez, when with eagle eyes
>   He stared at the Pacific, and all his men
> Gathered around him with a wild surmise,
>   Silent upon a peak in Darien.

This quotation is suggested, partly by the thought it embodies, and partly by the recollection of its author, both relevant to the subject before us. We—we first—we alone, claim the merit of discovering a new Poet in Glasgow, and a Poet, too, who in genius, circumstances, and present position, is not unlike John Keats. God forbid he should resemble him in his future destiny!

Some four months ago we received a packet of poetry from Glasgow, accompanied with a very modest note, signed "Alex. Smith." Encumbered with many duties, and with an immense mass of MS., good, bad, and indifferent, we allowed the volume to lie by us for a long time, till at last, lifting it up carelessly, we lighted upon some lines that pleased us, were tempted to read on—did so—and ere the end, were all but certain we had found a Poet—a new and real star in those barren Northern skies. We told the Poet our impressions; he in reply sent us two later effusions, which completely confirmed us; and we have now no hesitation in saying, that since Sidney Yendys, we have met with no more promising aspirant. He has not Yendys' intellect, nor art, nor culture, but his vein is equally true, and some of his verses are as sweet and tremblingly rich—like a rose shaken in the summer wind.

Poor fellow! at the age of ten he was sent from school to a commercial employment, where he has been engaged, ever since, ten hours a day, for the last eleven years. He is now, consequently, twenty-one. His principal, though not his best Poem, was written two years ago. It is entitled a "Life Fragment," and is, it seems, an attempt to set his "own life to music."

We may, without analysing the story, which is very slight, quote a few extracts from this powerful, though juvenile, unequal, and somewhat imitative Poem. These will speak for themselves, for their author, and for us! Hear this of certain books:

> They mingle gloom and splendour, as I've oft
> In thund'rous sunsets seen the thunder piles
> Seam'd with dull fire, and fiercest glory rents.
> They awe him to his knees, as if he stood
> In presence of a King. They give him tears,
> Such glorious tears as Eve's fair daughters shed
> When first they clasped a son of God, all bright
> With burning plumes and splendours of the sky
> *In zoning heaven of their milky arms.*
> How few read books aright! Most souls are shut
> By sense from their grandeurs, as the man who snores,
> Nightcapp'd and wrapt in blankets to the nose
> Is shut out from the Night, which, like a sea,
> *Breaketh for ever on a strand of stars.*

Again, of a Poet—

> His was not that love
> That comes on men with their beards; his soul
>   was rich
> And this his book unveils it, as the Night
> Her *panting wealth of stars.* The world was
>   cold,
> And he went down like a lone ship at sea;
> And now the fame which scorned him in life
> Waits on him like a menial.
> When the dark dumb Earth
> *Lay on her back and watch'd the shining
>   stars.* &c.

Hear this, too, of a Song—the Song itself we do not give:—

> I'll sing it to thee, 'tis a song of one,
> An image warm in his soul's caress,
> Like a sweet thought within a Poet's heart,
> Ere it is born in joy and golden words—
> Of one, whose *naked soul stood clad in love,*
> *Like a pale martyr in his shirt of fire.*

There is not a finer line than this last in literature! The combination of the thought, the image, and the picture formed from both, is perfect.

Let Mr. Smith be permitted again to speak of the Poet—of such as himself!

> The Poet was as far 'bove common men
> As a sun-steed, wild-eyed, and meteor-maned,
> Neighing the reeling stars, is 'bove a dray,
> With mud in its veins.
> Shaken with joy or sadness, tremulous
> As the soft star which in the azure East
> *Trembles with pity o'er bright bleeding
>   Day.*

But here is a higher voice:

> The soliloquy with which God broke
> The silence of the dead Eternities,—At which
>   ancient words,
> With *showery tresses like a child from sleep,*
> Uprose the splendid, mooned, and long-haired
>   Night,
> The loveliest born of God.

To this the lady well answers—

> Doubtless your first chorus
> Shall be the shoutings of the morning stars!
> What martial music is to marching men,
> Should Song be to Humanity. In bright Song
> The Infant Ages born and swathed are.

Thus he opens the Second Part; and is it not like the sound of a trumpet?

> Curl not thy grand lip with that scorn, O
>   World!
> Nor men with eyes of cold and cruel blue
> Wither my heart-strings with contemptuous
>   "Pooh!"
> Alas, my spirit sails not yet upfurled,
> Flap idly 'gainst the mast of my intent.
> Bagged Ledger men, with souls by Mammon
>   churl'd,
> What need of mocks or jeers from you or
>   yours,
> Since hope of Song is by Scorn's arrow shent!
> O Poesy, the glory of the lands,
> Of thee no more my thirsty spirit drinks.
> I seek the look of Fame! poor fool, so tries
> Some lonely wand'rer 'mong the desert sands,
> By shouts to *gain the notice of the Sphynx,*
> *Staring right on with calm eternal eyes.*

This last line should have been in Hyperion. It reminds us of

> Sate grey-haired Saturn, quiet as a stone.

Or,

> With solemn step an awful Goddess came!

Or,

> And plunged all noiseless into the deep Night.

but is, perhaps, finer than any of them. It is one of those lines which are *worlds* of self-contained power and harmony!

We give another laboured and very splendid passage:

> Ev'n as I write the ghost of one bright hour
> Comes from its grave and stands before me
>   now.
> "Twas at the close of a long summer's day,
> As we were standing on a grassy slope,
> The sunset hung before us like a dream
> That shakes a demon in his fiery lair.
> The clouds were standing round the setting
>   sun
> Like gaping caves, fantastic pinnacles;
> Wide castles throbbing in their own fierce
>   light;
> *Tall spires that went and came like spires of
>   flame,*
> Cliffs quivering with fire-snow, and sunset-
>   peaks
> Of piled gorgeousness, and rocks of fire
> A-tilt and poised; bare beaches crimson seas:
> All these were huddled in that dreadful West;
> All shook and trembled in unsteadfast light,
> And from the centre blazed the angry Sun,

Stern as the unlashed eye of God, a glare
O'er ev'ning city with its boom of sin.
Dost thou remember as we journeyed home,
(That dreadful sunset burnt into our brain)
With what a soothing came the naked Moon;
She, like a swimmer that has found his
    ground,
Came rippling up a silver strand of clouds,
And plunged from the other side into the
    Night.

Here is a fine thought in a softer vein:

O my Friend,
If thy rich heart is like a palace shattered,
Stand up amid the ruins of thy heart,
And with a calm brow front the solemn stars.
'Tis four o'clock already, see the Moon
Has climbed the eastern sky,
And sits and *tarries for the coming Night.*
So let thy soul be up and ready-armed,
In waiting till occasion comes like night,
As night to moons—to souls occasion comes.

Take another sweet image (perhaps suggested by that line in *Festus,* which David Scott pronounced the best in the poem

Friendship has passed me like a ship at sea.)—
We twain have met like ships upon the sea,
Who hold an hour's converse, so short, so
    sweet;
One little hour, and then away they speed
On lonely paths through mist and cloud and
    foam—
To meet no more.

Again, he says—

God is a worker. He has thickly sown
Wide space with rolling grandeurs. God is
    Love:
He yet shall wipe away Creation's tears,
And all the worlds shall summer in his smile.
Why work I not? the veriest *mote that* sports
Its one day life within the sunny beam,
Hath its *stern duties.* Wherefore have I none?

Listen, O world, to this picture of they weary self:

Methinks our darkened world doth wander
    lone,
A Cain-world, outcast from her peers in light;
Wild and curse driven. A poor maniac world,
Homeless and sobbing, through the deep she
    goes.

The following passage has obvious faults of rhythm and diction, but is quite equal to anything in *Festus* on the same theme. It is a picture of the poet of the coming time:

When ages flower, ages and bards are born;
My friend, a Poet must ere long arise,
And with a regal song sun-crown the age,
As a saint's head is with a glory crowned;
One who shall hallow Poetry to God
And to its own high uses—for poetry is
The grandest chariot in which king-thoughts
    ride;
One who shall fervent grasp the sword of
    song,
As a stern swordsman grasps his keenest blade
To gain the quickest passage to the heart.
A mighty Poet, whom this age shall choose
To be its spokesman to all coming times.
In the ripe full-blown season of his soul
He shall go forward in his spirit's strength
And grapple with the questions of all time
And wring from them their meanings. *As King
    Saul*
Called up the buried prophet from his grave
To speak his doom: so shall this Poet-King
Call up the dead Past from its awful grave
To tell him of our future. As the air
Doth sphere the world, so shall his heart of
    love—
Loving mankind, not peoples. As the lake
Reflects the flower, tree, rock, and bending
    heav'n,
Shall he reflect our great humanity.
And as the young Spring breathes with living
    breath
On a dead branch till it sprouts fragrantly,
Green leaves and sunny flowers shall he
    breathe life,
Through every theme he touch, making all
    Beauty
And Poetry for ever like the Stars.

There follows a noble rhapsody on the Stars, for which we have not room. We quote the closing passage of this **"Life-Fragment."**

As he wrote, his task the lovelier grew,
Like April into May, or as a child
A smile in the lap of life, by fine degrees
Orbs to a maiden walking with meek eyes
In atmosphere of beauty round her breath'd,
Over his work he flush'd and paled in room
Hallowed with glooms and books. Priests
    which have wed
Their makers unto Fame. Moons which have
    shed
Eternal halos around England's head;
Books dusky and thumbed *without, within* a
    sphere,
Smelling of Spring, as genial, fresh, and clear,

And beautiful as is the rainbow'd air
After May showers. Within this warm lair
He spent in writing all the winter moons.
But when May came with train of sunny
    noons,
He chose a leafy summer house within
The greenest nook of all his garden green.
Oft a fine thought, his face would flush
    divine,
As he had quaffed a cup of olden wine,
Which deifies the drinker: oft his face
Gleamed "like a spirit's" in that shady place,
When he saw *smiling upwards from the scroll*
The image of the thought within his soul,
As mid the waving shadows of the trees,
Mid garden odours and the hum of bees,
He wrote the last and closing passages.

'Tis truly a noble fragment of a **"Life"** this—the chip of a colossal block. We fervently trust that Mr. Smith's "life" may be long extended, his delicate health strengthened, and his circumstances so ameliorated, that he may fulfil the beautiful promise he has so unequivocally given.

We have a few sonnets from his pen. These are of various merit, some of them too much modelled on those of favourite authors such as Wordsworth. This fault of imitation is one with which Mr. Smith, like all young poets, is chargeable to some extent, and of which his detractors are certain bitterly to accuse him. His imitation, however, is occasional, not habitual; it is unconscious, not wilful; it fails to disguise the force and freshness of his own genius; it is not greater than was that of Shelley, Coleridge, and many others at the same period of life; and like them he has but to go on, and it will drop off like an old sandal, from his own naked and vigorous foot; that of one who pursues Poetry as a Pilgrimage, and feels that **"Life,"** even if a "fragment," should be a real, earnest and original one—the jagged splinter of an oak rent by lightning, and not the broken fraction of a mere bust or lay figure.

We quote three fine specimens of his Sonneteering vein. The first, though **"All in Honour"** is perhaps a little too luxurious in tone:

Last night my cheek was wetted with warm
    tears,
Each worth a world. They fell from eyes
    divine.
Last night a silken lip was pressed to mine,
And at its touch fled all the barren years.
And golden-couched on a bosom white,
Which came and went beneath me like a sea,
An Emperor I lay, in empire bright.
Lord of the beating heart! while tenderly
Love-words were glutting my love-greedy
    ears;

Kind Love, I thank thee for that happy night.
Richer this check for those warm tears of
    thine,
Than the vast midnight with its gleaming
    spheres:
Leander toiling through the midnight brine,
Kingdomless Antony were scarce my peers.

Like clouds or streams we wandered on at
    will,
Three glorious days, when, near our journey's
    end,
As down the moorland road we straight did
    wend,
To Wordsworth's "Inversneyd," talking to kill
The cold and cheerless drizzle in the air.
'Bove me I saw, at pointing of my friend,
An old fort, like a ghost upon the hill,
Stare in blank misery through the blinding
    rain;
So human like it seemed in its despair,
So stunned with grief, long gazed at it we
    twain,
Weary and damp we reached our poor abode,
I, warmly seated in the chimney nook,
Still saw that old fort on the moorland road,
Stare through the rain with strange woe-
    wildered look.

Beauty still walketh on the earth and air,
Our present sunsets are as rich in gold
As ere the Iliad's numbers were outrolled,
The roses of the spring are ever fair,
'Mong branches green still ring-doves coo and
    pair:
And the deep seas still foam their music old.
So if we are at all divinely souled,
This Beauty will unloose our bonds of care,
'Tis pleasant when blue skies are o'er us
    bending,
Within old starry-gated Poesy.
To meet a soul set to no earthly tune,
Like thine sweet friend! O dearer thou to me
Than are the dewy trees the sun, the moon,
Or noble music with a golden ending.

We have culled the previous extracts, and even the Sonnets, almost at random, and could easily have multiplied them by dozens. But we proceed now to give some extracts from a separate poem of his entitled the **"Page and the Lady,"** which we deem his finest *artistic* production.

The story of the Page and the Lady is simple—A lady of high birth and great beauty, hath an Indian Page, who falls in love with her, which love is betrayed in the course of a Conversation between them. The Conversation is the Poem. This confession she is at first disposed to treat with disdain, but ultimately she finds, by a very brief process of self-inquiry, that it is but the counterpart of a feeling towards him, which has long lurked in her own bosom. Let us take first the opening of the poem:

> On balcony, all summer, roofed with vines,
> A lady half-reclined amid the light,
> Golden and green, soft showering through the
>   leaves,
> Silent she sate one half the silent noon;
> At last she sank luxurious on her couch
> Purple and golden-fringed like the sun's,
> And stretch'd her white arms on the warm'd
>   air,
> As if to take some object where withal
> To ease the empty aching of her heart.

She is weary, because, although she has plenty of rich and noble suitors she has none she can love; and exclaims—

> O empty heart!
> O palace! rich and purple-chambered,
> When will thy Lord come home?

Then she bethinks herself in her weariness of her Page:

> My cub of Ind,—
> My sweetest plaything! He is bright and wild
> As is a gleaming panther of the hills.
> Lovely as lightning—beautiful as wild!
> His *sports and laughters are with fierceness
>   edged,*
> As I *were toying with a naked sword*
> Which starts within my veins the blood of
>   Earis.
> I fain would have the service of his voice,
> To kill with music this most languid noon.

She summons him accordingly to her presence and bids him sing a battle song, or better still:

> Some hungry lay of love,
> Like that you sung me on the eve you told
> How poor our English to your Indian darks,
> Shaken from od'rous hills what tender smells
> Pass like *fine pulses* through the mellow
>   nights,
> Your large round Moon, more beautiful than
>   ours—
> The showered stars—each hanging luminous,
> Like golden dewdrops in the Indian air.

He sings, as she bids, a very sweet, love song. At the close—

> Queenly the lady lay;
> One white hand hidden in a golden shoal
> Of ringlets, reeling down upon her couch,

> And heaving on the heavings of her breast,
> *The while her thoughts rose in her eyes like
>   stars,*
> *Rising and setting in the blue of night.*

Thus luxuriously rested, she begins to tell her Page of a rhyming cousin she had once. A strange person, truly!

> He went to his grave, not told what man he
>   was;
> He was unlanguaged, like the earnest sea,
> Which strives to gain an utterance on the
>   shore;
> But ne'er can *shape unto the listening hills*
> *The lore it gathered in its awful age,*
> The *crime* for which 'tis lashed by cruel
>   winds,
> To shrieks and spoomings to the frighted
>   stars,
> The thought, pain, grief within its lab'ring
>   breast.

Many strange things have been said about the sea. It has been called the "far resounding Main;" it has by an author of the day been boldly called "The Shadow and Mad Sister of the Earth." Thomson figures it as the "melancholy Main;" and well may it be both mad and melancholy, for Mr. Smith proclaims it a tongueless penitent, carrying in its bosom the memory of some Crime of Ages; lashed for its penance by the eternal winds; and yet unable to relieve itself by expressing its guilt, save in inarticulate shrieks, sobs, and "spoomings to the frighted stars." We think that we remember a similar thought in Mr. Gilfillian's *Second Gallery of Portraits,"* where he describes Mrs. Shelley, after her husband's death, wandering along the shore and asking vain questions at the sea, "which, like a dumb murderer, had done the deed, but was not able to utter the confession." Mr. Smith, however, improves upon this by making the crime a profound, old and general one, worthy of those long and fearful moanings which, even in calm, never altogether subside, and which in storm seem to express a divine desperation, as of a whole Synod of Gods plunged into Tartarus, and feeling the virgin fires on their immortal limbs.

The Lady, in her turn, condescends to sing a song, and proceeds in various measure to recount the history and character of those who in vain had loved her. She asks him, then, if he thinks that the power of Beauty is so great as is usually supposed, and he, in very glowing terms, affirms that it *is.*

> The lady dowered him with her richest look,
> Her arch head half-aside, her liquid eyes
> From 'neath their dim lids drooping,
>   slumbrous
> *Stood full* on his, and call'd the wild blood up
> All in a tumult to his sun-kissed cheek,

As if it wished to see her beauty too.
Then asked in dulcet tones "Dost think *me fair*."

We must omit his very eloquent reply, which is, of course, in the affirmative. She begins to suspect, from his language, that he has known by experience what love is. She asks him—

My lustrous Leopard, hast *thou* been in love?

What follows is admirable:

The Page's dark face flush'd the hue of wine
In crystal goblet, stricken by the sun,
His soul stood like a moon within his eyes,
Suddenly orbed, his passionate voice was shook,
By trembles into music *"Thee I love!"*
"Thou!" and the lady with a cruel laugh
(Each *silver throb* went through him like a sword,)
Flung herself back upon her fringed couch
From which she rose, upon him, like a queen,
She rose, and stabb'd him with her angry eyes.

We do not quote what she then says in words, unknowing her own heart; her laughter's "silver throbs" (what an exquisite expression!) had said it more eloquently before. Suffice it, she dismisses the crestfallen Page—

With arm sweep superb,
The light of scorn was cold within her eyes,
And withered his bloom'd heart, which like a rose
Had open'd timid to the noon of Love.

But mark now! After sitting alone for a season, she thus communes with her own soul, in a soliloquy worthy of any Poet or Dramatist:

It was my father's blood
That bore me, as a red and wrathful stream
Bears a shed leaf. I would recall my words,
And yet I would not.
Into what angry beauty rushed his face!
What lips! What splendid eyes! 'twas pitiful
To see such splendors ebb in utter woe.
His eyes half won me! Tush! I am a fool;
The blood that purples in these azure veins,
Rich'd with its long course thro' an hundred Earth,
Were foul'd and mudded if I stooped to him.
My father loves him for his free wild wit,
I for his beauty and sun-lighted eyes.
—To bring him to my feet, to lip my hand,
Had I it in my gift, I'd give the world—

Its panting fire—heart, diamonds, veins of gold,
Its rich strands, oceans, bells of cedar'd hills,
Whence summer smells are struck by all the winds.
But, whether I might lance him through the brain
With a proud look, or whether sternly kill
Him with a single deadly word of scorn,
Or—whether—yield me up,
And sink all tears and weakness in his arms,
And strike him blind with a *strong shock of joy*—
Alas! *I feel I could do each and all.*
I will be kind when next he brings me flowers,
Plucked from the shining forehead of the morn,
Ere they have ope'd their rich cores to the bee.
His wild heart with a ringlet will I chain,
And o'er him I will lean me like a heav'n,
And feed him with sweet looks and dew-soft word,
And beauty that might make a monarch pale;
And thrill him to the heart's core with a touch—
Smile him to Paradise at close of eve,
To hang upon my lip in silver dreams.

And thus is the story "left untold;" and yet what more is needed to tell us, that Love has triumphed over Rank, that the Lady has become the "Page" to the Page, and the Page the Lord to the Lady.

Charles Kingsley (review date 1853)

SOURCE: "Alexander Smith and Alexander Pope," in *Fraser's Magazine for Town & Country*, Vol. XLVIII, No. CCLXXXVL, October, 1853, pp. 452-66.

[*In the following excerpt, Kingsley derides Smith's works by saying that the shortcomings of* Poems *are the fault of Smith imitating too closely the works of other writers.*]

On reading this little book, [**Poems,** by Alexander Smith] and considering all the exaggerated praise and exaggerated blame which have been lavished on it, we could not help falling into many thoughts about the history of English poetry for the last forty years, and about its future destiny. Great poets, even true poets, are becoming more and more rare among us. There are those even who say that we have none; an assertion which, as long as Mr. Tennyson lives, we shall take the liberty of denying. But were he, which Heaven forbid, taken from us, whom have we to succeed him?

And he, too, is rather a poet of the sunset than of the dawn—of the autumn than of the spring. His gorgeousness is that of the solemn and fading year; not of its youth, full of hope, freshness, gay and unconscious life. Like some stately hollyhock or dahlia of this month's gardens, he endures while all other flowers are dying; but all around is winter—a mild one, perhaps, wherein a few annuals or pretty field weeds still linger on; but, like all mild winters, especially prolific in fungi, which, too, are not without their gaudiness, even their beauty, although bred only from the decay of higher organisms, the plagiarists of the vegetable world. Such is poetry in England; while in America, the case is not much better. What more enormous scope for new poetic thought than that which the new world gives? Yet the American poets, even the best of them, look lingeringly and longingly back to Europe and her legends; to her models, and not to the best of them—to her criticism, and not to the best of that—and bestow but a very small portion of such genius as they have on America and her new forms of life. If they be nearer to the spring than we, they are still deep enough in the winter. A few early flowers may be budding among them, but the autumn crop is still in somewhat shabby and rain-bedrabbled bloom. And for us, where are our spring flowers? What sign of a new poetic school? Still more, what sign of the healthy resuscitation of any old one?

'What matter, after all?' one says to oneself in despair, re-echoing Mr. Carlyle. 'Man was not sent into the world to write poetry. What we want is truth—what we want is activity. Of the latter we have enough in all conscience just now. Let the former need be provided for by honest and righteous history, and as for poets, let the dead bury their dead.' .... And yet, after all, man will write poetry, in spite of Mr. Carlyle: nay, beings who are not men, but mere forked radishes, will write it. Man is a poetry-writing animal. Perhaps he was meant to be one. At all events, he can no more be kept from it than from eating. It is better, with Mr. Carlyle's leave, to believe that the existence of poetry indicates some universal human hunger, whether after 'the beautiful,' or after 'fame,' or after the means of paying butchers' bills; and accepting it as a necessary evil which must be committed, to see that it be committed as well, or at least as little ill, as possible. In excuse of which we may quote Mr. Carlyle against himself, reminding him of a saying of Goethe once bepraised by him in print,—'We must take care of the beautiful, for the useful will take care of itself.'

And never, certainly, since Pope wrote his *Dunciad,* did the beautiful require more taking care of, or evince less capacity for taking care of itself; and never, we must add, was less capacity for taking care of it evinced by its accredited guardians of the press than at this present time, if the reception given to Mr. Smith's poems is to be taken as a fair expression of 'the public taste.'

Now, let it be fairly understood, Mr. Alexander Smith is not the object of our reproaches: but Mr. Alexander Smith's models and flatterers. Against him we have nothing whatsoever to say; for him, very much indeed.

Very young, as is said, self-educated, drudging for his daily bread in some dreary Glasgow prison-house of brick and mortar, he has seen the sky, the sun and moon—and, moreover, the sea, report says, for one day in his whole life; and this is nearly the whole of his experience in natural objects. And he has felt, too painfully for his peace of mind, the contrast between his environment and that of others—his means of culture and that of others—and, still more painfully, the contrast between his environment and culture, and that sense of beauty and power of melody which he does not deny that he has found in himself, and which no one can deny who reads his poems fairly; who reads even merely the opening page and key-note of the whole:—

> For as a torrid sunset burns with gold
> Up to the zenith, fierce within my soul
> A passion burns from basement unto
>   cope.
> Poesy, poesy, I'd give to thee
> As passionately my rich laden years,
> My bubble pleasures, and my awful joys,
> *As Hero gave her trembling sighs to find*
> *Delicious death on wet Leander's lip*
> Bare, bold, and tawdry, as a fingered
>   moth
> Is my poor life; but with one smile thou
>   canst
> Clothe me with kingdoms. Wilt thou
>   smile on me?
> Wilt bid me die for thee? Oh, fair and
>   cold!
> As well may some wild maiden waste her
>   love
> Upon the calm front of a marble Jove.

Now this scrap is by no means a fair average specimen of Mr. Smith's verse. But is not the self-educated man who could teach himself, amid Glasgow smoke and noise, to write such a distich as that exquisite one which we have given in italics, to be judged lovingly and hopefully?

What if he has often copied? What if, in this very scrap, chosen almost at random, there should be a touch from Tennyson's *Two Voices?* And what if imitations, nay, caricatures, be found in almost every page? Is not the explanation simple enough, and rather creditable than discreditable to Mr. Smith? He takes as his models Shelley, Keats, and their followers. Who is to blame for that? The Glasgow youth, or the public taste, which has been exalting these authors more and more for the last twenty years as the great poets of the nineteenth century? If they are the proper ideals of the day, who will blame him for following them as closely as possible—for saturating his memory so thoroughly with their words and thoughts that he reproduces them unconsciously to himself? Who will blame him for even consciously copying their images, if they have said better than he the thing which he wants to say, in the only poetical dialect which he knows? He does no more than all schools have done, copy their own masters; as the Greek epicists and Virgil copied Homer; as all succeeding Latin epicists copied Virgil; as Italians copied Ariosto and Tasso; as every one who can copies Shakspeare; as the French school copied, or thought they copied, 'The Classics,' and as a matter of duty used to justify any bold image in their notes, not by its originality, but by its being already in Claudian, or Lucan, or Virgil, or Ovid; as every poetaster, and a great many who were more than poetasters, twenty years ago, used to copy Scott and Byron, and as all poetasters now are copying the very same models as Mr. Smith, and failing while he succeeds.

We by no means agree in the modern outcry for 'originality.' Is it absolutely demanded that no poet shall say anything whatsoever that any other poet has said? If so, Mr. Smith may well submit to a blame, which he will bear in common with Shakespeare, Chaucer, Pope, and many another great name; and especially with Raphael himself, who made no scruple of adopting not merely points of style, but single motives and incidents, from contemporaries and predecessors. Who can look at any of his earlier pictures, the Crucifixion for instance, at present in Lord Ward's gallery at the Egyptian Hall, without seeing that he has not merely felt the influence of Perugino, but copied him; tried deliberately to be as like his master as he could? Was this plagiarism? If so, all education, it would seem, must be a mere training in plagiarism. For how is the student to learn, except by copying his master's models? Is the young painter or sculptor a plagiarist because he spends the first, often the best, years of his life in copying Greek statues; or the school-boy, for toiling at the reproduction of Latin metres and images, in what are honestly and fittingly called 'copies' of verses? And what if the young artist shall choose, as Mr. Smith has done, to put a few drawings into the exhibition, or to carve and sell a few statuettes? What if the school-boy, grown into a gownsman, shall contribute his share to a set of *Arundines', Cami* or *Prolusiones Etonienses?* Will any one who really knows what art or education mean complain of them for having imitated their models, however servilely? Will he not rather hail such an imitation as a fair proof, first of the student's reverence for authority—a more important element of 'genius' than most young folks fancy—and next, of his possessing any artistic power whatsoever? For, surely, if the greater contains the less, the power of creating must contain that of imitating. A young author's power of accurate imitation is, after all, the primary and in-

dispensable test of his having even the capability of becoming a poet. He who cannot write in a style which he does know, will certainly not be able to invent a new style for himself. The first and simplest form in which any metrical ear, or fancy, or imagination, can show itself, must needs be in imitating existing models. Innate good taste—that is, true poetic genius—will of course choose the best models in the long run. But not necessarily at first. What shall be the student's earliest ideal must needs be determined for him by circumstance, by the books to which he has access, by the public opinion which he hears expressed. Enough if he chooses, as Raphael did, the best models which he knows, and tries to exhaust them, and learn all he can from them, ready to quit them hereafter when he comes across better ones, yet without throwing away what he has learnt. 'Be faithful in a few things, and thou shalt become ruler over many things,' is one of those eternal moral laws which, like many others, holds as true of art as it does of virtue.

And on the whole, judging Mr. Alexander Smith by this rule, he has been faithful over a few things, and therefore we have fair hope of him for the future. For Mr. Smith does succeed, not in copying one poet, but in copying all, and very often in improving on his models. Of the many conceits which he has borrowed from Mr. Bailey, there is hardly one which he has not made more true, more pointed, and more sweet; nay, in one or two places, he has dared to mend John Keats himself. But his whole merit is by no means confined to the faculty of imitation. Though the **'Life Drama'** itself is the merest cento of reflections and images, without coherence or organization, dramatic or logical, yet single scenes, like that with the peasant and that with the fallen outcast, have firm self-consistency and clearness of conception; and these, as a natural consequence, are comparatively free from those tawdry spangles which deface the greater part of the poem. And, moreover, in the episode of 'The Indian and the Lady,' there is throughout a 'keeping in the tone,' as painters say, sultry and languid, yet rich and full of life, like a gorgeous Venetian picture, which augurs even better for Mr. Smith's future success than the two scenes just mentioned; for consistency of thought may come with time and training; but clearness of inward vision, the faculty of imagination, can be no more learnt than it can be dispensed with. In this, and this only, it is true that *poeta nascitur non fit;* just as no musical learning or practice can make a composer, unless he first possess an innate ear for harmony and melody. And it must be said that it is just in the passages where Mr. Smith is not copying, where he forgets for awhile Shelley, Keats, and the rest, and is content to be simply himself, that he is best; terse, vivid, sound, manly, simple. May he turn round some day, and deliberately pulling out all borrowed feathers, look at himself honestly and boldly in the glass, and we will warrant him, on the strength of the least gaudy, and as yet unpraised passages in his poems, that he will find himself after all more eagle than daw, and quite well plumed enough by nature to fly at a higher, because for him a more natural, pitch than he has yet done.

True, he has written a great deal of nonsense; nonsense in matter as well as in manner. But therein, too, he has only followed the reigning school. . . . As for manner, he does sometimes, in imitating his models, out-Herod Herod. But why not? If Herod be a worthy king, let him be by all means out-Heroded, if any man can do it. One cannot have too much of a good thing. If it be right to bedizen verses with metaphors and similes which have no reference, either in tone or in subject, to the matter in hand, let there be as many of them as possible. If a saddle is a proper place for jewels, then let the seat be paved with diamonds and emeralds, and Runjeet Singh's harness maker be considered as a lofty artist, for whose barbaric splendour Mr. Peat and his Melton customers are to forswear pigskin and severe simplicity—not to say utility and comfort. If poetic diction be different in species from plain English, then let us have it as poetical as possible, and as unlike English; as ungrammatical, abrupt, involved, transposed, as the clumsiness, carelessness, or caprice of man can make it. If it be correct to express human thought by writing whole pages of vague and bald abstract metaphysic, and then trying to explain them by concrete concetti, which bear an entirely accidental and mystical likeness to the notion which they are to illustrate, then let the metaphysic be as abstract as possible, the concetti as fanciful and far-fetched as possible. If Marino and Cowley be greater poets than Ariosto and Milton, let young poets imitate the former with might and main, and avoid spoiling their style by any perusal of the too-intelligible common sense of the latter. If Byron's moral (which used to be thought execrable) be really his great excellence, and his style (which used to be thought almost perfect) unworthy of this age of progress, then let us have his moral without his style, his matter without his form; or—that we may be sure of never falling for a moment into his besetting sins of terseness, grace, and completeness—without any form at all. If poetry, in order to be worthy of the nineteenth century, ought to be as unlike as possible to Homer or Sophocles, Virgil or Horace, Shakspeare or Spenser, Dante or Tasso, let those too idolized names be rased henceforth from the Calendar; let the *Ars Poetica* be consigned to flames by Mr. Calcraft, and Martinus Scriblerus's *Art of Sinking* placed forthwith on the list of the Committee of Council for Education, that not a working man in England may be ignorant that, whatsoever superstitions about art may have haunted the benighted heathens who built the Parthenon, *nous avons changés tout cela*. In one word, if it be best and most fitting to write poetry in the style in which almost every one has been trying to write it since Pope and plain sense went out, and Shelley and the seventh heaven came in, let it

be so written; and let him who most perfectly so 'sets the age to music,' be presented by the assembled guild of critics, not with the obsolete and too classic laurel, but with an electro-plated brass medal, bearing the due inscription, *Ars est nescire artem*. And when, in twelvemonths' time, he finds himself forgotten, perhaps decried, for the sake of the next aspirant, let him reconsider himself, try whether, after all, the common sense of the many will not prove a juster and a firmer standing-ground than the sentimentality and bad taste of the few, and read Alexander Pope. . . .

Hence it is, that as in all insincere and effete times the poetry of the day deals more and more with conceits, and less and less with true metaphors. In fact, *hinc illæ lachrymæ*. This is, after all, the primary symptom of disease in the public taste, which has set us on writing this review—that critics all round are crying, 'An ill-constructed whole, no doubt; but full of beautiful passages'—the word 'passages' turning out to mean, in plain English, conceits. The simplest distinction, perhaps, between an image and a conceit is this—that while both are analogies, the image is founded on an analogy between the essential properties of two things— the conceit on an analogy between its accidents. Images, therefore, whether metaphors or similes, deal with laws; conceits with private judgments. Images belong to the imagination, the power which sees things according to their real essence and inward life, and conceits to the fancy or phantasy, which only sees things as they appear.

To give an example or two from the *Life Drama:*—

> His heart holds a dead hope,
> As holds the wretched west the sunset's
> corse—
> Spit on, insulted by the brutal rains.
> The passion-panting sea
> Watches the unveiled beauty of the
> stars
> Like a great hungry soul.
> The moon,
> Arising from dark waves which plucked
> at her.
> Great spirits,
> Who left upon the mountain-tops of
> Death
> A light that made them lovely.

And hundreds, nay, thousands more in this book, whereof it must be said, that beautiful or not, in the eyes of the present generation—and many of them are put into very beautiful language, and refer to very beautiful natural objects—they are not beautiful really and in themselves; because they are mere conceits; the analogies in them are fortuitous, depending not on the nature of the things themselves, but on the private fancy of the writer, having no more real and logical coherence than a conundrum or a pun; in plain English, untrue; only allowable to Juliets or Othellos, while their self-possession, almost their reason, is in temporary abeyance under the influence of joy or sorrow. Every one must feel the exquisite fitness of Juliet's 'Gallop apace, ye fiery-footed steeds,' &c., for one of her character, in her circumstances: every one, we trust, and Mr. Smith among the number, will some day feel the exquisite impropriety of using such conceits as we have just quoted, or any other, page after page, for all characters and chances. For the West is not wretched; the rains never were brutal yet, and do not insult the sun's corpse, being some millions of miles nearer us than the sun, but only have happened once to seem to do so in the poet's eyes. The sea does not pant with passion, does not hunger after the beauty of the stars; Death has no mountain-tops, or any property which can be compared thereto; and 'the dark waves'—in that most beautiful conceit which follows, and which Mr. Smith has borrowed from Mr. Bailey, improving it marvellously nevertheless—do not 'pluck at the moon,' but only seem to do so. And what constitutes the beauty of this very conceit—far the best of those we have chosen—but that it looks so very like an image, so very like a law, from being so very common and customary an ocular deception to one standing on a low shore at night?

Or, again, in a passage which has been already often quoted as exquisite, and in its way is so:—

> The bridgroom sea
> Is toying with the shore, his wedded
>   bride;
> And in the fulness of his marriage joy
> He decorates her tawny brow with shells,
> Retires a pace, to see how fair she
>   looks,
> Then proud, runs up to kiss her.

Exquisite? Yes; but only exquisitely pretty. It is untrue—a false explanation of the rush and recoil of the waves. We learn nothing by these lines; we gain no fresh analogy between the physical and the spiritual world, not even between two different parts of the physical world. If the poetry of this age has a peculiar mission, it is to declare that such an analogy exists throughout the two worlds; then let poetry declare it. Let it set forth a real intercommunion between man and nature, grounded on a communion between man and God who made nature. Let it accept nature's laws as the laws of God. Truth, scientific truth, is the only real beauty. 'Let God be true, and every man a liar.'

Now, be it remembered that by far the greater proportion of this book consists of such thoughts as these; and that these are what are called its beauties; these are what young poets try more and more daily to in-

vent—conceits, false analogies. Be it remembered, that the affectation of such conceits has always marked the decay and approaching death of a reigning school of poetry; that when, for instance, the primæval forest of the Elizabethan poets dwindled down into a barren scrub of Vaughans, and Cowleys, and Herberts, and Crashawes, this was the very form in which the deadly blight appeared. . . .

Our task is ended. We have given as plainly as we can our reasons for the opinion which this Magazine has exprest several times already, that with the exception of Mr. Allingham and Mr. Meredith, our young poets are a very hopeless generation, and will so continue unless they utterly repent and amend. If they do not choose to awaken themselves from within, all that is left for us is to hope that they may be awakened from without, or by some radical revulsion in public taste be shown their own real value and durability, and compelled to be true and manly under pain of being laughed at and forgotten. A general war combining England, America, and Piedmont against the continental despots might, amid all its inevitable horrors, sweep away at once the dyspeptic unbelief, the insincere bigotry, the effeminate frivolity which now paralyses our poetry as much as it does our action, and strike from England's heart a lightning flash of noble deeds, a thunder peal of noble song. Such a case is neither an impossible nor a far-fetched one; let us not doubt that by some other means if not by that the immense volume of thought and power which is still among us will soon find its utterance, and justify itself to after ages by showing in harmonious and self-restrained poetry its kinship to the heroic and the beautiful of every age and clime. And till then; till the sunshine and the thaw shall come, and the spring flowers burst into bud and bloom, heralding a new golden year in the world's life, let us even be content with our pea-green and orange fungi; nay, even admire them, as not without their own tawdry beauty, their clumsy fitness; for after all they are products of nature, though only of her dyspepsia; and grow and breed—as indeed cutaneous disorders do— by an organic law of their own; fulfilling their little destiny, and then making, according to Professor Way, by no means bad manure. And so we take our leave of Mr. Alexander Smith, entreating him, if these pages meet his eye, to consider three things, namely, that in as far as he has written poetry, he is on the road to ruin by reason of following the worst possible models. That in as far as the prevailing taste has put these models before him he is neither to take much blame to himself, nor to be in anywise disheartened for the future. That in as far as he shall utterly reverse his whole poetic method, whether in morals or in æsthetics, leave undone all that he has done, and do all that he has not done, he will be, come what he evidently, by grace of God, can become if he will, namely, a lasting and a good poet.

Arthur Hugh Clough (review date 1853)

SOURCE: "Review of Some Poems by Alexander Smith and Matthew Arnold," in *Prose Remains of Arthur Hugh Clough*, edited by Mrs. Clough, Macmillan and Co., 1888, pp. 355-78.

[*Clough was an author, poet, and critic who wrote in both England and America during the late nineteenth century. Letters to his fiancé show that Clough originally liked Smith's work, especially* A Life Drama, *but lost enthusiasm for it before his first review of Smith was printed. The following excerpt is from a joint review of Matthew Arnold's and Smith's works, originally published in the* North American Review, *July, 1853. In it, Clough contends that despite "imperfections of style and taste," Smith's* Poems *is better than the average poet's first volume.*]

Poems by Alexander Smith, a volume recently published in London, and by this time reprinted in Boston, deserve attention. They have obtained in England a good deal more notice than is usually accorded there to first volumes of verse; nor is this by any means to be ascribed to the mere fact that the writer is, as we are told, a mechanic; though undoubtedly that does add to their external interest, and perhaps also enhances their intrinsic merit. It is to this, perhaps, that they owe a force of purpose and character which makes them a grateful contrast to the ordinary languid collectanea published by young men of literary habits; and which, on the whole, may be accepted as more than compensation for many imperfections of style and taste.

The models whom this young poet has followed have been, it would appear, predominantly, if not exclusively, the writers of his own immediate time, *plus* Shakspeare. The antecedents of the **Life-Drama,** the one long poem which occupies almost the whole of his volume, are to be found in the *'Princess,'* in parts of Mrs. Browning, in the love of Keats, and the *habit* of Shakspeare. There is no Pope, or Dryden,[1] or even Milton; no Wordsworth, Scott, or even Byron to speak of. We have before us, we may say, the latest disciple of the school of Keats, who was indeed no well of English undefiled, though doubtless the fountain-head of a true poetic stream. Alexander Smith is young enough to free himself from his present manner, which does not seem his simple and natural own. He has given us, so to say, his Endymion; it is certainly as imperfect, and as mere a promise of something wholly different, as was that of the master he has followed.

We are not sorry, in the meantime, that this Endymion is not upon Mount Latmos. The natural man does pant within us after *flumina silvasque*; yet really, and truth to tell, is it not, upon the whole, an easy matter to sit under a green tree by a purling brook, and indite pleasing stanzas on the beauties of Nature and fresh air? Or

is it, we incline to ask, so very great an exploit to wander out into the pleasant field of Greek or Latin mythology, and reproduce, with more or less of modern adaptation—

> the shadows
> Faded and pale, yet immortal, of Faunus, the
>   Nymphs, and the Graces?

Studies of the literature of any distant age or country; all the imitations and *quasi*-translations which help to bring together into a single focus the scattered rays of human intelligence; poems after classical models, poems from Oriental sources, and the like, have undoubtedly a great literary value. Yet there is no question, it is plain and patent enough, that people much prefer 'Vanity Fair' and 'Bleak House.' Why so? Is it simply because we have grown prudent and prosaic, and should not welcome, as our fathers did, the Marmions and the Rokebys, the Childe Harolds and the Corsairs? Or is it, that to be widely popular, to gain the ear of multitudes, to shake the hearts of men, poetry should deal, more than at present it usually does, with general wants, ordinary feelings, the obvious rather than the rare facts of human nature? Could it not attempt to convert into beauty and thankfulness, or at least into some form and shape, some feeling, at any rate, of content—the actual, palpable things with which our every-day life is concerned; introduce into business and weary task-work a character and a soul of purpose and reality; intimate to us relations which, in our unchosen, peremptorily appointed posts, in our grievously narrow and limited spheres of action, we still, in and through all, retain to some central, celestial fact? Could it not console us with a sense of significance, if not of dignity, in that often dirty, or at least dingy, work which it is the lot of so many of us to have to do, and which some one or other, after all, must do? Might it not divinely condescend to all infirmities; be in all points tempted as we are; exclude nothing, least of all guilt and distress, from its wide fraternisation; not content itself merely with talking of what may be better elsewhere, but seek also to deal with what *is* here? We could each one of us, alas, be so much that somehow we find we are not; we have all of us fallen away from so much that we still long to call ours. Cannot the Divine Song in some way indicate to us our unity, though from a great way off, with those happier things; inform us, and prove to us, that though we are what we are, we may yet, in some way, even in our abasement, even by and through our daily work, be related to the purer existence?

The modern novel is preferred to the modern poem, because we do here feel an attempt to include these indispensable latest addenda—these phenomena which, if we forget on Sunday, we must remember on Monday—these positive matters of fact, which people, who are not verse-writers, are obliged to have to do with.

> Et fortasse cupressum
> Scis simulare; quid hoc, si fractis enatat
>   exspes
> Navibus, ære dato qui pingitur?

The novelist does try to build us a real house to be lived in; and this common builder, with no notion of the orders, is more to our purpose than the student of ancient art who proposes to lodge us under an Ionic portico. We are, unhappily, not gods, nor even marble statues. While the poets, like the architects, are—a good thing enough in its way—studying ancient art, comparing, thinking, theorising, the common novelist tells a plain tale, often trivial enough, about this, that, and the other, and obtains one reading at any rate; is thrown away indeed to-morrow, but is devoured to-day.

We do not at all mean to prepare the reader for finding the great poetic desideratum in this present *Life-Drama*. But it has at least the advantage, such as it is, of not showing much of the *littérateur* or connoisseur, or indeed the student; nor is it, as we have said, mere pastoral sweet piping from the country. These poems were not written among books and busts, nor yet

> By shallow rivers, to whose falls
> Melodious birds sing madrigals.

They have something substantive and lifelike, immediate and first-hand, about them. There is a charm, for example, in finding, as we do, continual images drawn from the busy seats of industry; it seems to satisfy a want that we have long been conscious of, when we see the black streams that welter out of factories, the dreary lengths of urban and suburban dustiness,

> The squares and streets,
> And the faces that one meets,

irradiated with a gleam of divine purity.

There are moods when one is prone to believe that, in these last days, no longer by 'clear spring or shady grove,' no more upon any Pindus or Parnassus, or by the side of any Castaly, are the true and lawful haunts of the poetic powers; but, we could believe it, if anywhere, in the blank and desolate streets, and upon the solitary bridges of the midnight city, where Guilt is, and wild Temptation, and the dire Compulsion of what has once been done—there, with these tragic sisters around him, and with pity also, and pure Compassion, and pale Hope, that looks like despair, and Faith in the garb of doubt, there walks the discrowned Apollo, with unstrung lyre; nay, and could he sound it, those mournful Muses would scarcely be able, as of old, to respond and 'sing in turn with their beautiful voices.'

To such moods, and in such states of feeling, this *Life Drama* will be an acceptable poem. Under the guise of a different story, a story unskilful enough in its construction, we have seemed continually to recognise the ingenious, yet passionate, youthful spirit, struggling after somethings, like right and purity amidst the unnumbered difficulties, contradictions, and corruptions of the heated and crowded, busy, vicious, and inhuman town. Eager for action, incapable of action without some support, yet knowing not on what arm to dare to lean; not untainted; hard pressed; in some sort, at times, overcome—still we seem to see the young combatant, half combatant, half martyr, resolute to fight it out, and not to quit this for some easier field of battle—one way or other to make something of it.

The story, such as we have it, is inartificial enough. Walter, a boy of poetic temperament and endowment, has, it appears, in the society of a poet friend now deceased, grown up with the ambition of achieving something great in the highest form of human speech. Unable to find or make a way, he is diverted from his lofty purposes by a romantic love-adventure, obscurely told, with a 'Lady' who finds him asleep, Endymion-like, under a tree. The fervour and force of youth wastes itself here in vain; a quick disappointment—for the lady is betrothed to another—sends him back enfeebled, exhausted, and embittered, to essay once again his task. Disappointed affections, and baffled ambition, contending henceforward in unequal strife with the temptations of scepticism, indifference, apathetic submission, base indulgence, and the like; the sickened and defeated, yet only too strong, too powerful man, turning desperately off, and recklessly at last plunging in mid-unbelief into joys to which only belief and moral purpose can give reality; out of horror-stricken guilt, the new birth of clearer and surer, though humbler, conviction, trust, resolution; these happy changes met, perhaps a little prematurely and almost more than half-way, by success in the aims of a purified ambition, and crowned too, at last, by the blessings of a regenerate affection—such is the argument of the latter half of the poem; and there is something of a current and tide, so to say, of poetic intention in it, which carries on the reader (after the first few scenes), perforce, in spite of criticism and himself, through faulty imagery, turgid periods, occasional bad versification and even grammar, to the close. Certainly, there is something of a real flesh-and-blood heart and soul in the case, or this could not be so.

We quote from the later portion, when Walter returns to the home of his childhood:—

> 'Twas here I spent my youth, as far removed
> From the great heavings, hopes, and fears of
>   man,
> As unknown isle asleep in unknown seas.
> Gone my pure heart, and with it happy days;
> No manna falls around me from on high,
> Barely from off the desert of my life

I gather patience and severe content.
God is a worker. He has thickly strewn
Infinity with grandeur. God is Love;
He yet shall wipe away creation's tears,
And all the worlds shall summer in his smile.
Why work I not. The veriest mote that sports
Its one-day life within the sunny beam
Has its stern duties. Wherefore have I none?
I will throw off this dead and useless past,
As a strong runner, straining for his life,
Unclasps a mantle to the hungry winds.
A mighty purpose rises large and slow
From out the fluctuations of my soul,
As ghostlike from the dim and trembling sea
Starts the completed moon.

Here, in this determination, he writes his poem—attains in this spirit the object which had formerly been his ambition. And here, in the last scene, we find him happy, or peaceful at least, with Violet:—

Thou noble soul,
Teach me, if thou art nearer God than I!
My life was one long dream; when I awoke,
Duty stood like an angel in my path,
And seemed so terrible, I could have turned
Into my yesterdays, and wandered back
To distant childhood, and gone out to God
By the gate of birth, not death. Lift, lift me
  up
By thy sweet inspiration, as the tide
Lifts up a stranded boat upon the beach.
I will go forth 'mong men, not mailed in
  scorn,
But in the armour of a pure intent,
Great duties are before me, and great songs,
And whether crowned or crownless, when I
  fall,
It matters not, so as God's work is done.
I've learned to prize the quiet lightning deed,
Not the applauding thunder at its heels,
Which men call Fame. Our night is past;
We stand in precious sunrise; and beyond,
A long day stretches to the very end.

So be it, O young Poet; Poet, perhaps it is early to affirm; but so be it, at any rate, O young man. While you go forth in that 'armour of pure intent,' the hearts of some readers, be assured, will go with you. . . .

It is wonderful what stores of really valuable thought may lie neglected in a book, simply because they are not put in that form which serves our present occasions. But if we have been inclined to yield to a preference for the picture of simple, strong, and certain, rather than of subtle, shifting, and dubious feelings, and in point of tone and matter to go along with the young mechanic, in point of diction and manner, we

must certainly assign the palm to 'A,' in spite of a straining after the rounded Greek form, such as, to some extent, vitiates even the style of Milton. Alexander Smith lies open to much graver critical carping. He writes, it would almost seem, under the impression that the one business of the poet is to coin metaphors and similes. He tells them out as a clerk might sovereigns at the Bank of England. So many comparisons, so much poetry; it is the sterling currency of the realm. Yet he is most pleased, perhaps, when he can double or treble a similitude; speaking of A, he will call it a B, which is, as it were, the C of a D. By some maturer effort we may expect to be thus conducted even to Z. But simile within simile, after the manner of Chinese boxes, are more curious than beautiful; nor is it the true aim of the poet, as of the Italian boy in the street, to poise upon his head, for public exhibition, a board crowded as thick as they can stand with images, big and little, black and white, of anybody and everybody, in any possible order of disorder, as they happen to pack. *Tanquam scopulum, insolens verbum,* says the precept of ancient taste, which our author seems to accept freely, with the modern comment of—

In youth from rock to rock I went
With pleasure high and turbulent,—
  Most pleased when most uneasy.

The movement of his poem is indeed rapid enough; there is a sufficient impetus to carry us over a good deal of rough and 'rocky' ground; there is a real continuity of poetic purpose;—but it is so perpetually presumed upon; the attention, which the reader desires to devote to the pursuit of the main drift of what calls itself a single poem, *simplex et unum,* is so incessantly called off to look at this and look at that; when, for example, we would fain follow the thought and feeling of Violet and of Walter, we are with such peremptory and frequent eagerness summoned to observe how like the sky is to *x* and the stars are to *y,* that on the whole, though there *is* a real continuity of purpose, we cannot be surprised that the critic of the *London Examiner* failed to detect it. Keats and Shelley, and Coleridge, perhaps, before them, with their extravagant love for Elizabethan phraseology, have led to this mischief. Has not Tennyson followed a little too much in their train? Coleridge, we suppose, would have maintained it to be an excellence in the 'myriad-minded' dramatist, that he so often diverts us from the natural course of thought, feeling, and narrative, to see how curiously two trifles resemble each other, or that, in a passage of deep pathos, he still finds time to apprise us of a paronomasia. But faults which disfigure Shakspeare are not beauties in a modern volume.

I rot upon the waters when my prow
Should *grate* the golden isles,

may be a very Elizabethan, but is certainly rather a vicious expression. Force and condensation are good, but it is possible to combine them with purity of phrase. One of the most successful delineations in the whole poem is contained in the following passage, which introduces Scene VII.:—

[A balcony overlooking the sea.]

The lark is singing in the blinding sky,—
Hedges are white with May. The bridegroom sea
Is toying with the shore, his wedded bride,
And in the fulness of his marriage joy,
He decorates her tawny front with shells—
Retires a space to see how fair she looks,
Then proud, runs up to kiss her. All is fair,—
All glad, from grass to sun. Yet more I love
Than this, the shrinking day that sometimes comes
In winter's front, so fair 'mongst its dark peers,
It seems a straggler from the files of June,
Which in its wanderings had lost its wits,
And half its beauty, and when it returned,
Finding its old companions gone away,
It joined November's troop, then marching past;
And so the frail thing comes, and greets the world
With a thin crazy smile, then bursts in tears—
And all the while it holds within its hand
A few half-withered flowers;—I love and pity it.

It may be the fault of our point of view; but certainly we do not find even here that happy, unimpeded sequence which is the charm of really good writers. Is there not something incongruous in the effect of the immediate juxtaposition of these two images? We have lost, it may be, that impetuosity, that *élan*, which lifts the young reader over hedge and ditch at flying leaps, across country, or we should not perhaps entertain any offence, or even surprise, at being transferred *per saltum* from the one field to the other. But we could almost ask, was the passage, so beautiful, though perhaps a little prolonged, about the June day in November, written consecutively, and in one flow with the previous, and also beautiful, one about ocean and his bride? We dare say it was: but it does not read, somehow, in the same straight line with it—

Tantum series juncturaque pollet.

We venture, too, to record a perhaps hypercritical objection to 'the *blinding* sky' in this particular collocation. Perhaps in the first line of a scene, while the reader has not yet warmed to his duty, simplicity should be especially observed—a single image, without any repeated reflection, so to speak, in a second mirror, should suffice. The following, which open Scene XI., are better:—

Summer hath murmured with her leafy lips
Around my home, and I have heard her not;
I've missed the process of three several years
From shaking wind flowers to the tarnished gold
That rustles sere on Autumn's aged limbs.

Except the two last lines. Our author will not keep his eye steady upon the thing before him; he goes off, and distracts us, and breaks the impression he had begun to succeed in giving, by bidding us look now at something else. Some simpler epithets than *shaking,* and some plainer language than *tarnished gold* or *aged limbs,* would have done the work better. We are quite prepared to believe that these faults and these *disagreeables* have personally been necessities to the writer, are awkwardnesses of growth, of which the full stature may show no trace. He should be assured, however, that though the rude vigour of the style of his **Life-Drama** may attract upon the first reading, yet in any case, it is not the sort of writing which people recur to with pleasure and fall back upon with satisfaction. It may be a groundless fancy, yet we do fancy, that there is a whole hemisphere, so to say, of the English language which he has left unvisited. His diction feels to us as if between Milton and Burns he had not read, and between Shakspeare and Keats had seldom admired. Certainly there is but little inspiration in the compositions of the last century; yet English was really best and most naturally written when there was, perhaps, least to write about. To obtain a real command of the language, some familiarity with the prose writers, at any rate, of that period, is almost essential; and to write out, as a mere daily task, passages, for example, of Goldsmith, would do a verse-composer of the nineteenth century as much good, we believe, as the study of Beaumont and Fletcher.

Notes

[1] The word *spoom,* which Dryden uses as the verb of the substantive *spume,* occurs also in 'Beaumont and Fletcher.' Has Keats employed it? It seems hardly to deserve reimpatriation.

W. E. Aytoun (review date 1854)

SOURCE: "Alexander's Smith's Poems," in *Blackwood's Edinburgh Magazine,* Vol. LXXV, No. CCCCLXI, March, 1854, pp. 345-51.

[*In the review below, Aytoun became one of the first to label Smith a "Spasmodic" poet, a term that would remain with Smith his entire life. The critic characterized Spasmodic poetry as unoriginal and profane. In this essay, he criticizes Smith for using an excessive amount of imagery that does not further the thematic development of his poems. Several months after publishing this piece, Aytoun continued his attack on the Spasmodic poets by writing a parody of a Spasmodic tragedy (see following essay).*]

Some time ago a volume of poems appeared, over which there arose a great roar of critical battle, like the conflict over the dead Valerius, when "Titus pulled him by the foot, and Aulus by the head." Many hailed the author as a true poet, and prophesied his coming greatness; others fastened on obvious defects, and moused the book like Snug the joiner tearing Thisbe's mantle in his character of lion. Now that the hubbub has subsided, our still small voice may be heard.

The poet in question has at once deprecated and defied criticism in a sonnet, (p. 232).

> "There have been vast displays of critic wit
> O'er those who vainly flutter feeble wings,
> Nor rise an inch 'bove ground,—weak poet-
>   lings!
> And on them to the death men's brows are
>   knit.
> Ye men! ye critics! seems't so very fit
> They on a storm of Laughter should be blown
> O'er the world's edge to Limbo? Be it known,
> Ye men! ye critics! that beneath the sun
> The chiefest woe is this,—when all alone,
> And strong as life, a soul's great currents run
> Poesy-ward, like rivers to the sea,
> But never reach't. Critic, let that soul moan
> In its own hell, without a kick from thee.
> Kind Death, kiss gently, ease this weary one?"

Alexander Smith is partly right and partly wrong. It is true that, throned in his judicial chair, the critic, more intent on displaying his own powers than on doing justice to his subject, is apt to drop the mild and equal scales, and brandish the trenchant glittering sword. He ought to say in his heart, Peradventure there shall be found ten fine lines in this book—I will not destroy it for ten's sake.

But, on the other hand, there is a class to which forbearance would be misapplied and criminal. It would too much resemble our prison discipline, where Mr. William Sykes, after a long course of outrages on humanity, is shut up in a palace, treated like a prodigal son, and presently converted to Christianity. An absurd monomaniac, who, like Joanna Southcote, mistaking a dropsical disorder for the divine afflatus, and demanding worship on no better grounds than the greatness of his own blown conceit, may, by mere force of impudent pretension, induce a host of ignorant followers to have faith in him, ought to be exposed and ridiculed. Not savagely, perhaps, for the first offence; the pantaloons should be loosed with a paternal hand, and

the scourge mildly applied. If he still persists in misdoing, it should be laid on till the blood comes.

But Alexander Smith is far from coming under the latter denomination. A writer, especially a young writer, should be judged by his best; and there is enough excellence in the volume to cover many more sins than it contains, though they are numerous. And while it is a mistake to suppose that a fine poetic soul, however sensitive will "let itself be snuffed out by an article," yet there have been instances where undue severity has defrauded a writer of his just fame for many a long year; and though the critic in the end, has been compelled to render up the mesne profits of applause, yet that is small consolation for the sense of wrong, and the deprivation of merited influence and reputation.

While foreign writers sketch us as the most matter-of-fact and pudding-eating of peoples—while we pique ourselves on sturdy John Bullism, and cheerfully accept the portrait of an absurd old gentleman in a black coat, and a broad-brimmed hat and gaiters, with his hands in his well-filled breeches pockets, as a just impersonation of the genius of the nation, it is an obvious fact that a poet never had such a certainty of being appreciated in England as now. Fit audience is no longer few. Let him sound as high a note as he can for the life of him, he will yet find echoes enough to constitute fame. There are homes in England almost as common as hothouses, where fine criticism is nightly conversation—where appreciators, as true as any one who review in newspapers, hail a good and great writer as a personal friend. Here may be found all the elements necessary for the recognition of merit and the detection of imposture. Sturdy good sense refuses to believe in gaudy pretension; keen logic exposes emptiness; enthusiastic youth glows at the high thought, the splendid image; and the soft feminine nature responds, with ready tears and unsuppressed sighings, to all legitimate appeals to the heart.

With such tribunals more plentiful than county courts, a man is no longer justified in decrying fame, or appealing for justice to posterity. It must be an outward accident, indeed, that cheats an author of his due, when so many are eager to exchange praise for his fine gold. The demand for excellence in authorship exceeds the supply; and there are plenty of keen readers who, having traversed the realms of English poesy, yet thirst for fresh fields and pastures new. Therefore, if an ardent spirit finds the world deaf to his utterances, let him search uncomplainingly for the fault in his own mind, and never rashly conclude that for his fondly believed-in powers of thought and expression there is, as yet, no sympathetic public. Especially in poetry is the appetite of the time unsatisfied; mediocrity, which should be inadmissible, is indulgently received, and the poets of established reputation are on every shelf. Editions of Shakspeare appear in perplexing numbers, and the rusty armour in which a champion for his text appears, is contended for as if it were the heaven-forged panoply of Achilles.

Mr. Smith leaves his feelings on the subject of fame open to doubt. One might almost faney him a poet who, having desired fame too ardently in his hot youth, had discovered its emptiness in riper age. A sonnet is devoted to the depreciation of fame; whereas Walter, in the **Life-Drama** is more than enthusiastic to achieve it. We have no doubt the ardent wishes which Mr. Smith expresses through his hero are genuine, and that the philosophy of the sonnet is a philosophy he only fancies he has acquired. Combativeness may inspire the soldier to achievement, rivalry the statesman; both may be, in some measure, indifferent to other fame than the applause of their contemporaries. But it is in vain for the poet to express indifference to the opinion of the world and of posterity. Why has he written, except that thoughts bearing his impress may sound in the ears of the future, and that the echoes they arouse may convey to him, in his silent resting-place, tidings of the cheerful day, assuring him of a tenure in the earth he loved, and a lasting position among the race who were his brothers? What would not man do to secure remembrance after death? For this Erostratus burnt Diana's temple; for this the Pyramids were built, and built in vain; for this kings have destroyed nations; for this the care-worn money-getter gives his life to the founding of a wealthy name; and if a man may gain it more effectually by the simple publishing of thoughts, whose conception was to him a pleasure, let him be thankful that what all so ardently desire was granted to him on such easy terms, and that he may continue to be a real presence on this earth, when most of his contemporaries are as though they had never been.

Taking it for granted, then, that when a young poet publishes a work wherein the hero expresses an ardent desire for fame, the poet is himself speaking through the character, it will be interesting to see how he proposes to achieve it. Mr. Smith tells us, through his hero, that his plan for immortalising himself is "to set this age to music." That, he says, is the great work before the poet now.

To set this age to music!—'tis a phrase we have heard before of late years. Never was an age so intent upon self glorification as this. Like the American nation, it spends half its time looking in the glass; and, like it, always with the same loudly-expressed approbation of what the mirror reveals. It has long been its habit to talk its own praises, and now they must be sung. When polkas were first introduced, many familiar sounds were parodied, to give character to tunes of the new measure. Among these was the Railway-polka, in which the noise of the wheels and the clatter of machinery were admirably imitated; while a startling reality was given to the whole, by the occasional hoarse scream of the engine. Now, we fear that the effort of a poet to set the age to music would result in something resembling the railway polka—something more creditable as a work of ingenuity than of art, and embodying more appeals to the sense than to the heart or the imagination. To him who stands apart from the rush and roar, the many voices of the age convey a mingled sound that would scarcely seem musical even to the dreaming ear of a poet.

We see the spirit of the middle ages—the spirit of religious intolerance and superstitious faith—of deepest earnestness, and of bigotry springing out of that earnestness—reflected in Dante's page. Spenser shows us the days of the plume and the spear, when the beams of chivalry yet gilded the earth, when the motto of noble youth was—God and my lady. Another phase of the same era—the era of romantic discovery and adventure, when there were yet fairies on the green, and enchanted isles in the ocean—reappears in the works of Shakespeare. Pope has fixed for ever the time of courtliness, of external polish and artificial graces— the time when woman was no more divine—when Una had degenerated into Chloe—when love had given place to intrigue, devotion to foppery, faith to reasoning; yet a pleasant and graceful time. And it is no wonder that the poet, now, feeling that he too possesses "the vision and the faculty divine," should long to leave his name, not drifting over space, but anchored firmly on the times he lived in.

But none of these old poets went to work with the deliberate intention of setting his age to music. Where that, so far as we can see the meaning of the phrase, has been done, it is because the poet lived so much among the characteristic men and scenes of his age, that his mind, more impressionable and more true in its impressions than others, was imbued with its spirit, and moulded to its forms; so that, whatever his mind transmitted was coloured by those hues, and swayed by those outlines. The poet did not hunt about for the characteristics of his age, and then deliberately embody them: he chose a congenial theme when it offered itself, and it, unconsciously to him, became a picture of a phase of the time. When our age, too, is set to music, if ever, it will be in this way.

If ever—For ages of the world, as worthy of note perchance as this, and more rich in materials for poetry, have passed away without being set to music. Every great change of society, and of mankind's opinion, does not necessarily call for a poet to sing it. It may be more suitably reproduced through some other medium than verse—in newspapers, for instance, or in advertising vans. Of course, no man in his senses would say a word against this age of ours; he could expect nothing less than to be immediately bonneted, like an injudicious elector who has hissed the popular candidate: yet we would have liked Alexander Smith to indicate the direction in which he intends to seek his materials. Does he see anything heroic in an ardent desire to secure ease and comfort at the cost of many old and once respectable superstitions, such as honour and duty? Can he throw over the cotton trade "the light that never was on sea or shore?" Or is popular oratory distinguished by "thoughts that breathe and words that burn?" Will the railway station and the electric telegraph figure picturesquely in the poet's dream? Yet, when the age is set to music, these chords will be not the most subdued in the composition. Mr. Macaulay said about as much as could be said for the spirit of the age, when he drew a contrast in popular prose between the present and the past. Had he tried the subject in poetry, he would have found the task much less congenial than when he sung so manfully "how well Horatius kept the bridge, in the brave days of old."

Alexander Smith has one characteristic in common with Tennyson, the author of *Festus,* and some other poets of the time. All seem to have great power in the regions of the dreary. Their gaiety is spasmodic; when they smile, 'tis like Patience on a monument, as if Grief were sitting opposite. If this is their way of setting the age to music, 'tis, if most musical, yet most melancholy. Tennyson, who possesses the power of conveying the sentiment of dreariness beyond most poets that ever lived, generally selects some suitable subject for the exercise of it, such as *Mariana in the Moated Grange;* but Mr. Smith's hero, and Festus, are miserable from choice, and revel in their unaccountable woe, like the character in Peacock's novel, whose notion of making himself agreeable consists in saying, "Let us all be unhappy together." Not thus, O Alexander? sounds the keynote of the genial soul of a great poet.

Our author's notion of what constitutes a crushing affliction is altogether peculiar. A particular friend of his hero, after becoming quite blasphemous because he wanted "to let loose some music on the world," and couldn't (p. 137), commits suicide on a mountain, though whether by rope, razor, or prussic acid, we are not informed. However, being deranged, he no doubt received Christian burial. And Mr. Smith, speaking for himself in the sonnet already quoted, says that—

> "Beneath the sun
> The chiefest woe is this—When all alone,
> And strong as life, a soul's great currents run
> Posey-ward, like rivers to the sea,
> But never reach it."

The chiefest woe!—the chiefest, Alexander! Neither Job nor Jeremiah have enrolled it among human afflictions. Is there no starvation, nor pain, nor death in the world? Is the income-tax repealed? We appeal from Alexander in travail of a sonnet, with small hope of safe delivery to Alexander in the toothache, and we are confident he will change his opinion. Let him look at Hogarth's "Distressed Poet," and see what it is that moves his sympathy there. Not the perplexity of the poor poet himself—that raises only an irreverent smile—but the poor good pretty wife raising her household eyes meekly and wonderingly to the loud milkwoman, their inexorable creditor—the piece of meat that was to form their scanty dinner, abstracted by the felonious starveling of a cur,—these touch on deeper woes than the head-scratching distress of the unproductive poet.

To return to Mr. Smith's idea of setting the age to music. The first requisite clearly is, that the musician shall be pre-eminently a man of the age. It is at once evident that old-fashioned people, with any lingering remnants of the heroic or dark ages about their ideas, would be quite out of place here. None but liberals and progressionists need apply. These are so plentiful that there will be no difficulty in finding a great number who embody the most prominent characteristics of the time. Having got the man of the age, a tremendous difficulty occurs. We are very much afraid there will not only be nothing poetical in the cast of his ideas, but that he will be the embodiment of everything that is prosaic. Call to mind, O Alexander! the qualities essential to a poet—at the same time, picture to yourself a Man of the Age—and then fancy what kind of music you will extract from him. Set the age to music, quotha! Set the Stocks to music.

Having thus signally failed to point out how the thing is to be done, we will tell Alexander how it will not be done. Not by uttering unmeaning complaints against Fate and Heaven, and other names of similar import which we will not set down here, like a dog baying the moon. Not by uttering profane rant, which as it would not have been justified by the mad despair of a Lear or an Othello, is horribly nonsensical in the mouth of a young gentleman who ought to have taken a blue pill because his liver was out of order. Not by pouring forth floods of images and conceits which afford no perception of the idea their author would convey. Not by making the moon and the sea appear in such a variety of ridiculous characters that we shall never again stroll by moonlight on the shore without seeing something comical in the aspect of the deep and the heavenly bodies. Not by—But we have just lighted on a passage which proves that Mr. Smith knows what is right as well as anybody can tell him:—

> "Yet one word more—
> Strive for the poet's crown, but ne'er forget
> How poor are fancy's blooms to thoughtful
>   fruits."

And again—

"Poet he was not in the larger sense—
He could write pearls, but he could never
   write
A poem round and perfect as a star.

That is the point. Not to dismiss images unprotected on the world, like Mr. Winkle's shots—which, we are informed, were "unfortunate foundlings cast loose upon society, and billeted nowhere"—but to mature a worthy leading idea, waiting, watching, fostering it till it is full-grown and symmetrical in its growth; and from which the lesser ideas and images shall spring as naturally, necessarily, and with as excellent effect of adornment, as leaves from the tree.

Whether Alexander can do this, yet remains to be proved. Some of the requisites he possesses in a high degree. Force, picturesqueness of conception, and musical expression, all of which he has displayed, will do great things when giving utterance to a theme well chosen and well designed; but at present they only tell us, like a harp swept by the wind, of the melodies slumbering in the chords. Such is the Eolian character of the Life-drama—fitful, wild, melancholy, often suggestive of something exquisitely sweet and graceful, but faint, fugitive, and incoherent. When our poet sounds a strain worthy of the instrument, our pæans shall accompany and swell the chorus of applause.

The sonnets, as conveying tangible ideas, and such as excite interest and sympathy, have greatly exalted our opinion of the poet's powers. They have not been much quoted as yet by any of his discerning admirers, perhaps because there is little or nothing in them but what a plain man may understand, and they contain few allusions to the ocean or any of the planets. But here is one showing a fine picture—a picture that appeals to the imagination and the heart. It is at once manly and pathetic, representing a friendless, but independent and aspiring genius:—

"Joy, like a stream flows through the Christ-
   mas streets,
But I am sitting in my silent room—
Sitting all silent in congenial gloom.
To-night, while half the world the other
   greets
With smiles, and grasping hands, and drinks,
   and meats,
I sit and muse on my poetic doom.
Like the dim scent within a budded rose,
A joy is folded in my heart; and when
I think on poets nurtured 'mong the throes,
And by the lowly hearths of common men—
Think of their works, some song, some swell-
   ing ode,
With gorgeous music glowing to a close,
Deep-muffled as the dead-march of a god—
My heart is burning to be one of those."

As Mercutio says, "Is not this better, now, than groaning? Now art thou sensible—now art thou Romeo." We hope he will be "one of those," and think he may. Only he must believe that, however fine and rare the poetic faculties he has evinced, they cannot produce anything for posterity of themselves, but must build on a foundation of thought and art.

We are afraid, though we have not descended to verbal criticism, but have only indicated essential faults, that Alexander will think we have treated his book in an irreverent spirit; but, nevertheless, it is a truly paternal one. Even in such mood did we deal, of late, with our own beloved first-born, heir of his mother's charms and his father's virtues—a fine, clever fellow, in whom his parents take immense pride, though we judiciously conceal it for fear of increasing the conceit which is already somewhat conspicuous in his bearing. We rather think he had been led astray by the example of that young scoundrel Jones, who threatened to hang himself if his mother didn't give him five-and-twenty shillings to pay his score at the pastry cook's, and so terrified the poor lady into compliance. However that may be, our offspring, George, being denied of late, some unreasonable requests, straightway went into sulky heroics—spoke of himself as an outcast—stalked about with a gloomy air in dark corners of the shrubbery with his arms folded—smiled about twice a-day, in a withering and savage manner, though his natural disposition is cheerful and inclined to fun—and begged to decline to hold any further intercourse with his relatives. He kept up the brooding and injured character with great consistency (except that he always came regularly to meals, and eat them with his customary appetite, which is a very fine and healthy one), and was encouraged in it by his grandmother, who, between ourselves, reader, is a rather silly old woman, much given in her youth to maudlin sentimentalism, and Werterism, and bad forms of Byronism. She would take him aside, pat his head, kiss his cheek, and call him her poor dear boy, and slip money into his pocket, which he neither thanked her for, nor offered to refuse; and he became more firmly persuaded than ever, that he was one of the most ill-used young heroes that ever existed. This we were sorry to see—like Mrs. Quickly, we cannot abide swaggerers—and we bethought ourselves of a remedy. Some parents would have got in a rage and thrashed him—but he is a plucky young fellow, and this would only have caused him to consider himself a martyr; others would have mildly reasoned with him—but this would have given his fault too important and serious an air, so we treated him to a little irony and ridicule—caustic, not contemptuous, and more comical than spiteful. Just before beginning this course of treatment, we happened to overhear him making love, in the library, to Charlotte Jones (sister of the before-mentioned admirer of confectionary), a great, fat, lymphatic girl, who was spending a few days with her sisters, and who has no more sentiment or passion in her than so much calipee. However, he seemed to have quite enough for both, and poured forth his romantic devotion with a fervid fluency which I suspect must be the result of practice—for the young scamp is precocious, and conceived his first passion, at the age of nine, for a fine young woman of four-and-twenty. Charlotte, working away the white at a great cabbage-rose, not unlike herself, which she is embroidering in worsted, listened to his raptures with a lethargic calmness contrasting strongly with the impassioned air of the youth, who was no doubt ready, like Walter, Mr. Smith's hero, for the consideration of a kiss (if the placid object of his affections would have consented to such an impropriety), to "take Death at a flying-leap"—which is undoubtedly the most astonishing instance of agility on record since the cow jumped over the moon to the tune of "Hi, diddle, diddle." Our entrance, just when he had got on his knees, and was going to take her hand, somewhat disconcerted him; and we turned the incident to such advantage, that our very first jest at him in the presence of the family caused him (the boy has a fine sense of humour) to retire precipitately from the room, for fear he should compromise his dignity by exploding in laughter. He strove to preserve his gloomy demeanour for a day or two; but finding it of no effect to maintain a stern scowl on his forehead, while his mouth expanded in an unwilling grin, he gave up the attempt; and now greets any allusion to his former tragedy airs with as hearty a laugh as anybody.

Our impression is very strong that Mr. Smith is not himself satisfied with his work, and that the undiscriminating applause he has met with in some quarters will not deceive him. He must know that the ornaments of the *Life-Drama* are out of all proportion to the framework, and that the latter is too loosely put together to float far down the crowded stream of time. He has a strong leaning to mysticism, a common vice of the times, and should therefore exclude carefully all ideas which he cannot render clear to himself, and all expressions which fail to convey his meaning clearly to others. He should remember that, though a fine image may be welcomed for its own sake, yet, as a rule, similes and images are only admissible as illustrations, and if they do not render the parent thought more clear, they render it more cloudy. His great want is a proper root-idea, and intelligible theme which shall command the sympathies of other minds; these obtained, he will shake his faults like dewdrops from his mane; and he will find that his tropes, thus disciplined, will not only obtain double force from their fitness, but will also be intrinsically finer than the random growths of accident. It is true that Mr. Smith, through his spokesman, Walter, mentions a plan for a poem, his "loved and chosen theme," (p. 38). He says,

"I will begin in the oldest—Far in God,
When all the ages, and all suns and worlds,

And souls of men and angels lay in Him,
Like unborn forests in an acorn cup."

A prospect, the mere sketch of which fills us with concern. If we thought he would listen, we would say— No, Mr. Smith; don't begin in the oldest—leave the "dead eternities" alone, and don't let your "first chorus," on any account, be "the shouting of the morning stars." Rather begin, as you propose to end, with "silence," than in this melancholy way. Let your thoughts be based on the unalterable emotions of the heart, not on the wild driftings of the fancy. Observe all that strongly appeals to the feelings of others and of yourself—let art assist you to select and to combine—your warm imagination will give life to the conception, and your powers of fancy and language will vividly express it. Don't set down any odd conceit that may strike you about the relation of the sea and the stars, and the moon; but when you conceive an image which, besides being fine in itself, shall bear essential, not accidental, relation to some part of your theme, put it by till your main subject, in its natural expansion, affords it a fitting place.

Following this course, we trust that Alexander will prove worthy of the many illustrious scions of the house of Smith who have distinguished themselves since Adam, and maintain, its precedence over the houses of Brown, Jones, and Robinson. Sydney the Reverend— Horace and James of the Rejected Addresses—and William, of the modest and too obscure dramas (noticed by us before), might well become prouder of the patronymic to which they have already lent lustre, when Alexander, mellowed by time, and taught by thought and experience, shall have produced his next and riper work.

W. E. Aytoun (essay date 1854)

SOURCE: "Firmilian: A Tragedy," in *Blackwood's Edinburgh Magazine*, Vol. LXXV, No. CCCCLXIII, May, 1854, pp. 533-51.

[*Here, Aytoun continues his criticism of the Spasmodic poets. Claiming to have discovered a Spasmodic tragedy,* The Firmilian, *written by a hitherto unknown author. T. Percy Jones, Aytoun provides extensive quotes from the tragedy—which is in fact his own satire of the Spasmodic style—interspersed with an ironic commentary. While the essay does not mention Smith by name, by this time Aytoun had identified the few writers he considered Spasmodic, of which Smith was one. This parody further damaged Smith's reputation, and he was unable to shake the Spasmodic label even as his writing matured.*]

We have great pleasure in announcing to our readers the fact, that we have at last discovered that long-expected phenomenon, the coming Poet, and we trust that his light will very soon become visible in the literary horizon. We cannot, however, arrogate to ourselves any large share of merit in this discovery—indeed, we must confess, with a feeling akin to shame, that we ought to have made it at a much earlier date. *Firmilian* is not altogether new to us. We have an indistinct recollection of having seen the tragedy in manuscript well-nigh two years ago; and, if we remember aright, a rather animated correspondence took place on the subject of the return of the papers. We had, by some untoward accident, allowed them to find their way into the Balaam-box, which girnel of genius was at that particular time full up to the very hinges. We felt confident that *Firmilian* lay under the weight of some twenty solid layers of miscellaneous literature; and we should as soon have thought of attempting to disinter an icthyosaurus from a slate-quarry, as of ransacking the bowels of the chest for that treasury of rare delights. However, we took care, on the occasion of the next incremation, to make search for the missing article, and had the pleasure of returning it to Mr. Percy Jones, from whom we heard nothing further until we received his tragedy in print. Our first perusal having been rather of a cursory nature, we are not able to state with certainty whether the author has applied himself during the intervening period to the work of emendation; but we think it exceedingly probable that he has done so, as we now remark a degree of vivacity and force of expression, however extravagant many of the ideas may be, which had escaped our previous notice. We hope that, by a tardy act of justice, we shall offer no violence to that amiable modesty which has, in the mean time, restrained him from asking the verdict of the general public.

As to the actual amount of poetic genius and accomplishment which Mr. Percy Jones possesses, there may, even among the circle of his friends, be considerable difference of opinion. Those who admire spasmodic throes and writings may possibly be inclined to exalt him to a very high pinnacle of fame; for certainly, in no modern work of poetry—and there have been several recently published which might have borne the *imprimatur* of Bedlam—have we found so many symptoms of unmistakable lunacy. Still there is a method in his madness—a rapidity of perception and originality of thought, which contrasts very favourably with the tedious drivellings of some other writers of the same school. His taste is not one whit better than theirs, but he brings a finer fancy and a more vivid imagination to the task; nor is he deficient in a certain rude exaggerated dramatic power, which has more than once reminded us of the early style of Marlowe and the other predecessors of Shakespeare.

It is not very easy to comprehend the exact creed and method of the new school of poets, who have set themselves to work upon a principle hitherto unknown, or

at all events unproclaimed. This much we know from themselves, that they regard poetry not only as a sacred calling, but-as the most sacred of any—that, in their opinion, every social relation, every mundane tie, which can interfere with the bard's development, must be either disregarded or snapped asunder—and that they are, to the fainting race of Adam, the sole accredited bearers of the Amreeta cup of immortality. Such is the kind of nonsense regarding the nature of his mission which each fresh poetaster considers it his duty to enunciate; and as there is nothing, however absurd, which will not become credited by dint of constant repetition, we need not be surprised that some very extraordinary views regarding the "rights of genius" should of late years have been countenanced by men who ought to have known better. Poets are, like all other authors or artisans, valuable according to the quality of the article which they produce. If their handiwork be good, genuine, and true, it will pass at once into circulation and be prized—if the reverse, what title can they prefer to the name which they so proudly arrogate to themselves?

We do not, however, quarrel with a poet for having an exalted idea of his art—always supposing that he has taken any pains to acquire its rudiments. Without a high feeling of this kind, it would be difficult to maintain the struggle which must precede eminent success; nor would we have alluded to the subject but for the affectation and offensive swaggering of some who may indeed be rhymsters, but who never could be poets even if their days were to be prolonged to the extent of these of Methusaleh. When the painter of the tavern sign-post, whereon is depicted a beer-bottle voiding its cork, and spontaneously ejecting its contents right and left into a couple of convenient tumblers, talks to us of high art, Raphael, and the effects of *chiaroscuro* it is utterly impossible to control the action of the risible muscles. And, in like manner, when one of our young poetical aspirants, on the strength of a trashy duodecimo filled with unintelligible ravings, asserts his claim to be considered as a prophet and a teacher, it is beyond the power of humanity to check the intolerable tickling of the midriff.

But, apart from their exaggerated notions of their calling, let us see what is the practice of the poets of the Spasmodic School. In the first place, they rarely, if ever, attempt anything like a plot. After you have finished the perusal of their verses, you find yourself just as wise as when you began. You cannot tell what they would be at. You have a confused recollection of stars, and sunbeams, and moonbeams, as if you had been staring at an orrery; but sun, moon, and stars, were intended to give light to something—and what that something is, in the poet's page, you cannot, for the life of you, discover. In the second place, we regret to say that they are often exceedingly profane, not, we suppose, intentionally, but because they have not sense enough to see the limits which decency, as well as duty prescribes. In the third place, they are occasionally very prurient. And, in the fourth place, they are almost always unintelligible.

Now, although we cannot by any means aver that Mr. Percy Jones is entirely free from the faults which we have just enumerated, we look upon him as a decidedly favourable specimen of his tribe. There is, in *Firmilian,* if not a plot, at least some kind of comprehensible action; and in it he has portrayed the leading features of the poetical school to which he belongs with so much fidelity and effect, that we feel called upon to give an outline of his tragedy, with a few specimens from the more remarkable scenes.

The hero of the piece, Firmilian, is a student in the University of Badajoz, a poet, and entirely devoted to his art. He has been engaged for some time in the composition of a tragedy upon the subject of Cain, which is "to win the world by storm;" but he unfortunately discovers, after he has proceeded a certain length in his task, that he has not yet thoroughly informed himself, by experience, of the real nature of the agonies of remorse. He finds that he cannot do justice to his subject without steeping his own soul in guilt, so as to experience the pangs of the murderer; and as, according to the doctrines of the spasmodic school of poetry, such investigations are not only permitted, but highly laudable, he sets himself seriously to ponder with what victim he should begin. All our spasmodic poets introduce us to their heroes in their studies, and Mr. Percy Jones follows the tradition. He does not, however, like some of them, carry his imitative admission of Goethe's *Faust* so far, as personally to evoke Lucifer or Mephistopheles—an omission for which we are really thankful. Firmilian begins by a soliloquy upon his frame of mind and feelings; and states himself to be grievously perplexed and hindered in his work by his comparative state of innocence. He then meditates whether he should commence his course of practical remorse by putting to death Mariana, a young lady to whom he is attached, or three friends and fellow-students of his, with whom he is to dine next day. After much hesitation, he decides on the latter view, and, after looking up "Raymond Lullius" for the composition of a certain powder, retires to rest after a beautiful but somewhat lengthy apostrophe to the moon. There is nothing in this scene which peculiarly challenges quotation. The next is occupied by love-making; and certainly, if Mr. Percy Jones had intended to exhibit his hero throughout in the most amiable and romantic light, nothing could be better than his appearance in the bower of Mariana. If, here and there, we encounter an occasional floridness, or even warmth of expression, we attribute that in a great measure to the sunny nature of the clime; just as we feel that the raptures of Romeo and Juliet are in accordance with the temperament of the land that gave them birth. But we presently find that Firmilian, though a poet, is a hypo-

crite and traitor in love. The next scene is laid in a tavern, where he and his friends, Garcia Perez, Alphonzo D'Aguilar, and Alonzo Olivarez are assembled, and there is a discussion, over the wine-cup, on the inexhaustible subject of knightly love. Alphonzo, claiming to be descended from the purest blood of Castile, asserts the superiority of European beauty over the rest of the universe; to which Firmilian, though known to be betrothed to Mariana, makes the following reply—

FIRMILIAN

I knew a poet once; and he was young,
And intermingled with such fierce desires
As made pale Eros veil his face with grief,
And caused his lustier brother to rejoice.
He was as amorous as a crocodile
In the spring season, when the Memphian bank,
Receiving substance from the glaring sun,
Resolves itself from mud into a shore.
And—as the scaly creature wallowing there,
In its hot fits of passion, belches forth
The steam from out its nostrils, half in love,
And half in grim defiance of its kind;
Trusting that either from the reedy fen,
Some reptile-virgin coyly may appear,
Or that the hoary Sultan of the Nile
May make tremendous challenge with his jaws,
And, like Mark Antony, assert his right
To all the Cleopatras of the ooze—
So fared it with the poet that I knew.

He had a soul beyond the vulgar reach,
Sun-ripened, swarthy. He was not the fool
To pluck the feeble lily from its shade
When the black hyacinth stood in fragrance by.
The lady of his love was dusk as Ind,
Her lips as plenteous as the Sphinx's are,
And her short hair crisp with Numidian curl.
She was a negress. You have heard the strains
That Dante, Petrarch, and such puling fools
As loved the daughters of cold Japhet's race,
Have lavished idly on their icicles.
As snow melts snow, so their unhasty fall
Fell chill and barren on a pulseless heart.
But, would you know what noontide ardour is,
Or in what mood the lion, in the waste,
All fever-maddened, and intent on cubs,
At the oasis waits the lioness—
That shall you gather from the fiery song
Which that young poet framed, before he dared
Invade the vastness of his lady's lips.

Judging from the implied character of the ditty in question, we are not sorry that we cannot lay it before our

Glasgow Cathedral.

readers—indeed it does not appear in the volume, for D'Aguilar was so disgusted with the introduction that he openly reviled Firmilian as a pupil of Mahound, and bestowed a buffet on him, whereupon there was a flashing of swords. These, however were sheathed, and the students again sate down amicably to drink. Firmilian, being suddenly called away, entreats his friends to amuse themselves, during his absence, with a special bottle of "Ildefronso"—a vintage which we do not remember having seen in any modern list of wines. They comply—feel rather uncomfortable—and the scene concludes by the chant of a funeral procession beneath the window; an idea which we strongly suspect has been borrowed from Victor Hugo's tragedy of *Lucrece Borgia*.

The next scene exhibits Firmilian pacing the cloisters. His three friends have died by poison, but he is not able by any means to conjure up a feeling of adequate remorse. He does not see that he is at all responsible in the matter. If he had poured out the wine into their glasses, and looked upon their dying agonies, then, indeed, he might have experienced the desired sensations of guilt. But he did nothing of the kind. They

helped themselves, of their own free will and accord, and died when he was out of the way. On the whole, then, his first experiment was a blunder. During his reverie, an old preceptor of his, the priest of St. Nicholas, passes; and certain reminiscences of stripes suggest him as the next victim. The reader will presently see by what means this scheme is carried into execution. Suffice it to say, that the mere anticipation of it sheds a balm upon Firmilian's disappointed spirit, who, being now fully convinced that in a few days he will be able to realise the tortures of Cain, departs for an interview with Lilian, a young lady for whom he entertains a clandestine attachment. The next scene speaks for itself.

EXTERIOR OF THE CATHEDRAL OF ST. NICHOLAS.

Choir heard chaunting within.

Enter FIRMILIAN.

How darkly hangs yon cloud above the spire!
There's thunder in the air—
                    What if the flash

Should rend the solid walls, and reach the
   vault
Where my terrestrial thunder lies prepared,
And so, without the action of my hand,
Whirl up those thousand bigots in its blaze,
And leave me guiltless, save in the intent?

   That were a vile defraudment of my aim,
A petty larceny o' the element,
An interjection of exceeding wrong!
Let the hoarse thunder rend the vault of
   heaven,
Yea, shake the stars by myriads from their
   boughs,
As autumn tempests shake the fruitage
   down;—
Let the red lightning shoot athwart the sky,
Entangling comets by their spooming hair,
Piercing the zodiac belt, and carrying dread
To old Orion, and his whimpering hound;—
But let the glory of this deed be mine!

ORGAN *and* CHOIR

      Sublimatus ad honorem
        Nicholai presulis:
      Pietatis ante rorem
        Cunctis pluit populis:
      Ut vix parem aut majorem
        Habeat in seculis.

FIRMILIAN

Yet I could weep to hear the wretches sing!
There rolls the organ anthem down the aisle,
And thousand voices join in its acclaim.
All they are happy—they are on their knees;
Round and above them stare the images
Of antique saints and martyrs. Censers steam
With their Arabian charge of frankincense,
And every heart, with inward fingers counts,
A blissful rosary of pious prayer!
Why should they perish then? Is't yet too
   late?
   O shame, Firmilian, on thy coward soul?
What! thou, the poet!—thou, whose mission
   'tis
To send vibration down the chord of time,
Until its junction with eternity—
Thou, who hast dared and pondered and
   endured,
Gathering by piecemeal all the noble thoughts
And fierce sensations of the mind—as one
Who in a garden culls the wholesome rose,
And binds it with the deadly nightshade up;
Flowers not akin, and yet by contrast kind—
Thou, for a touch of what these mundane
   fools
Whine of as pity, to forego thine aim,

And never feel the gnawing of remorse,
Like the Promethean vulture on the spleen,
That shall instruct thee to give future voice
To the unuttered agonies of Cain!
Thou, to compare with that high consequence
The breath of some poor thousand knights and
   knaves,
Who soaring, in the welkin, shall expire!
Shame, shame, Firmilian! on thy weakness,
   shame!

ORGAN *and* CHOIR

      Auro dato violari
        Virgines prohibuit:
      Far in fame, vas in mari
        Servat et distribuit:
      Qui timebant naufragari
        Nautis opem tribuit.

FIRMILIAN.

A right good saint he seems, this Nicholas!
And over-worked too, if the praise be just,
Which these, his votaries, quaver as his claim.
Yet it is odd he should o'erlook the fact
That underneath this church of his are stored
Some twenty barrels of the dusky grain,
The secret of whose framing, in an hour
Of diabolic jollity and mirth,
Old Roger Bacon wormed from Belzebub!
He might keep better wardship for his friends;
But that to me is nothing. Now's the time!
Ha! as I take the matchbox in my hand,
A spasm pervades me, and a natural thrill
As though my better genius were at hand,
And strove to pluck me backwards by the
   hair.
I must be resolute. Lose this one chance,
Which bears me to th' Acropolis of guilt,
And this, our age, foregoes its noblest song.
I must be speedy—

ORGAN *and* CHOIR.

      A defunctis suscitatur
        Furtum qui commiserat:
      Et Judæus baptizatur
        Furtum qui recuperat:
      Illi vita restauratur,
        Hie ad fidem properat.

FIRMILIAN.

No more was needed to confirm my mind!
That stanza blows all thoughts of pity off,
As empty straws are scattered by the wind!
For I have been the victim of the Jews,
Who, by vile barter, have absorbed my means.

Did I not pawn—for that same flagrant stuff,
Which only waits a spark to be dissolved,
And, having done its mission, must disperse
As a thin smoke into the ambient air—
My diamond cross, my goblet, and my books?
What! would they venture to baptize the Jew?
The cause assumes a holier aspect, then;
And, as a faithful son of Rome, I dare
To merge my darling passion in the wrong
That is projected against Christendom!
Pity, avaunt! I may not longer stay.
  [*Exit into the vaults. A short pause, after
  which he reappears,*]

'Tis done! I vanish like the lightning bolt!

ORGAN *and* CHOIR.

        Nicholai sacerdotum
        Decus, honor, gloria:
        Plebem omnem, clerum totum—

  [*The Cathedral is blown up.*]

We back that scene, for intensity, against anything
which has been written for the last dozen of years.
Nay, we can even see in it traces of profound psychological observation. Firmilian, like Hamlet, is liable,
especially on the eve of action, to fits of constitutional
irresolution; and he requires, in order to nerve him to
the deed, a more direct and plausible motive than that
which originally prompted him. Hence we find him
wavering, and almost inclined to abandon his purpose,
until a casual passage in the choral hymn jars upon an
excitable nerve, and urges him irresistibly forward. We
shall presently find the same trait of character even
more remarkably developed in another scene.

We then come to the obsequies of the students, which,
being episodical, we may as well pass over. There are
two ways of depicting grief—one quiet and impressive,
the other stormy and clamorous. Mr. Percy Jones, as
might have been expected, adopts the latter method; and
we are bound to say that we have never perused anything in print so fearful as the ravings of the bereaved
Countess D'Aguilar, mother of the unfortunate Alphonzo.
She even forgets herself so far as to box the ears of the
confessor who is officiously whispering consolation.

Meanwhile, where is the hero of the piece—the successful Guy Fawkes of the cathedral? Perched on a
locality which never would have occurred to any but
the most exalted imagination.

SUMMIT OF THE PILLAR OF ST. SIMEON STYLITES.

FIRMILIAN.

'Twas a grand spectacle! The solid earth
Seemed from its quaking entrails to eruct

The gathered lava of a thousand years,
Like an imposthume bursting up from hell!
In a red robe of flame, the riven towers,
Pillars and altar, organ-loft and screen,
With a singed swarm of mortals intermixed,
Were whirled in anguish to the shuddering
  stars,
And all creation trembled at the din.
It was my doing—mine alone! and I
Stand greater by this deed than the vain fool
That thrust his torch beneath Diana's shrine.
For what was it inspired Erostratus
But a weak vanity to have his name
Blaze out for arson in the catalogue?
I have been wiser. No man knows the name
Of me, the pyrotechnist who have given
A new apotheosis to the saint
With lightning blast, and stunning thunder
  knell!
    And yet—and yet—what boots the sacrifice?
I thought to take remorse unto my heart,
As they young Spartan hid the savage fox
Beneath the foldings of his boyish gown,
And let it rive his flesh. Mine is not riven—
My heart is yet unscarred. I've been too
  coarse
And general in this business. Had there been
Amongst that multitude a single man
Who loved me, cherished me—to whom I
  owed
Sweet reciprocity for holy alms
And gifts of gentle import—had there been
Friend,—father,—brother, mingled in that
  crowd,
And I had slain him—then indeed my soul
Might have acquired fruition of its wish,
And shrieked delirious at the taste of sin!
But these—what were the victims unto me?
Nothing! Mere human atoms, breathing clods,
Uninspired dullards, unpoetic slaves,
The rag, and tag, and bobtail of mankind;
Whom, having scorched to cinders, I no more
Feel ruth for what I did, than if my hand
Had thrust a stick of sulphur in the nest
Of some poor hive of droning humble-bees,
And smoked them into silence!
            I must have
A more potential draught of guilt than this,
With more of wormwood in it!
            Here I sit,
Perched like a raven on old Simeon's shaft,
With barely needful footing for my limbs—
And one is climbing up the inward coil,
Who was my friend and brother. We have
  gazed
Together on the midnight map of heaven,
And marked the gems in Cassiopeia's hair—
Together have we heard the nightingale
Waste the exuberant music of her throat,

And lull the flustering breezes into calm—
Together have we emulously sung
Of Hyacinthus, Daphne, and the rest,
Whose mortal weeds Apollo changed to flowers.
Also from him I have derived much aid
In golden ducats, which I fain would pay
Back with extremest usury, were but
Mine own convenience equal to my wish.
Moreover, of his poems he hath sold
Two full editions of a thousand each,
While mine remains neglected on the
     shelves!
Courage, Firmilian! for the hour has come
When thou canst know atrocity indeed,
By smiting him that was thy dearest friend.
And think not that he dies a vulgar death—
'Tis poetry demands the sacrifice!
Yet not to him be that revealment made.
He must not know with what a loving hand—
With what fraternal charity of heart
I do devote him to the infernal gods!
I dare not spare him one particular pang,
Nor make the struggle briefer! Hush—he
     comes.

HAVERILLO *emerging from the staircase.*

How now, Firmilian!—I am scant of breath;
These steps have pumped the ether from my
     lungs,
And made the bead-drops cluster on my
     brow.
A strange, unusual rendezvous is this—
An old saint's pillar, which no human foot
Hath scaled this hundred years!

FIRMILIAN.

          Aye—it is strange!

HAVERILLO.

'Faith, sir, the bats considered it as such:
They seem to flourish in the column here,
And are not over courteous. Ha! I'm weary:
I shall sleep sound to-night.

FIRMILIAN.

          You *shall* sleep sound!

HAVERILLO.

Either there is an echo in the place,
Or your voice is sepulchral.

FIRMILIAN.

          Seems it so?

HAVERILLO.

Come, come, Firmilian—Be once more a man!
Leave off these childish tricks, and vapours bred
Out of a too much pampered fantasy.
What are we, after all, but mortal men,
Who eat, drink, sleep, need raiment and the like,
As well as any jolterhead alive?
Trust me, my friend, we cannot feed on
     dreams,
Or stay the hungry cravings of the maw
By mere poetic banquets.

FIRMILIAN.

          Say you so?
Yet have I heard that by some alchemy
(To me unknown as yet) you have transmuted
Your verses to fine gold.

HAVERILLO.

          And all that gold
Was lent to you, Firmilian.

FIRMILIAN.

          You expect,
Doubtless, I will repay you?

HAVERILLO.

          So I do.
You told me yesterday to meet you here,
And you would pay me back with interest.
Here is the note.

FIRMILIAN.

          A moment.—Do you see
Yon melon-vender's stall down i' the square?
Methinks the fruit that, close beside the eye,
Would show as largely as a giant's head,
Is dwindled to a heap of gooseberries!
If Justice held no bigger scales than those
Yon pigmy seems to balance in his hands,
Her utmost fiat scarce would weigh a drachm!
How say you?

HAVERILLO.

          Nothing—'tis a fearful height!
My brain turns dizzy as I gaze below,
And there's a strange sensation in my soles.

FIRMILIAN.

Ay—feel you that? Ixion felt the same
Ere he was whirled from heaven!

HAVERILLO.

    Firmilian!
You carry this too far. Farewell. We'll meet
When you're in better humour.

FIRMILIAN.

    Tarry, sir!
I have you here, and thus we shall not part.
I know your meaning well. For that same
    dross,
That paltry ore of Mammon's mean device
Which I, to honour you, stooped to receive,
You'd set the Alguazils on my heels!
What! have I read your thought? Nay, never
    shrink,
Nor edge towards the doorway! You're a
    scholar!
How was't with Phaeton?

HAVERILLO.

    Alas! he's mad.
Hear me, Firmilian! Here is the receipt—
Take it—I grudge it not! If ten times more,
It were at your sweet service.

FIRMILIAN.

    Would you do
This kindness unto me?

HAVERILLO.

    Most willingly

FIRMILIAN.

Liar and slave! There's falsehood in thine eye!
I read as clearly there, as in a book,
That, if I did allow you to escape,
In fifteen minutes you would seek the judge.
Therefore, prepare thee, for thou needs must
    die!

HAVERILLO.

Madman—stand off!

FIRMILIAN.

    There's but four feet of space
To spare between us. I'm not hasty, I!
Swans sing before their death, and it may be
That dying poets feel that impulse too:
Then, prythee, be canorous. You may sing
One of those ditties which have won you
    gold,

And my meek audience of the vapid strain
Shall count with Phœbus as a full discharge
For all your ducats. Will you not begin?

HAVERILLO.

Leave off this horrid jest, Firmilian!

FIRMILIAN.

Jest! 'Tis no jest! This pillar's very high—
Shout and no one can hear you from the
    square—
Wilt sing, I say?

HAVERILLO.

    Listen, Firmilian!
I have a third edition in the press,
Whereof the proceeds shall be wholly thine—
Spare me!

FIRMILIAN.

    A third edition! Atropos—
Forgive me that I tarried!

HAVERILLO.

    Mercy!—Ah!

[FIRMILIAN *hurls him from the column.*]

There is a grand recklessness and savage energy displayed in this scene, which greatly increases our admiration of the author's abilities. He seems, indeed, in the fair way of making the spasmodic school famous in modern literature. With the death of Haverillo an ordinary writer would have paused—not so Percy Jones, who, with a fine aptitude for destruction, makes his hero, Firmilian, kill two birds with one stone. The manner in which he accomplishes this feat is most ingenious. He maintains the unity of the design by a very slight alteration of the locality. Whilst the two poets are ominously conversing on the summit of the pillar, a critic, affected by an intolerable itch for notoriety, is prowling in the square beneath—

SQUARE BELOW THE PILLAR.

Enter APOLLODORUS, *a Critic.*

Why do men call me a presumptuous cur,
A vapouring blockhead, and a turgid fool,
A common nuisance, and a charlatan?
I've dashed into the sea of metaphor
With as strong paddles as the sturdiest ship
That churns Medusæ into liquid light,
And hashed at every object in my way.

My ends are public. I have talked of men
As my familiars, whom I never saw.
Nay—more to raise my credit—I have penned
Epistles to the great ones of the land,
When some attack might make them slightly
    sore,
Assuring them, in faith, it was not I.
What was their answer? Marry—shortly this:
"Who, in the name of Zernebock, are you?"
I have reviewed myself incessantly—
Yea, made a contract with a kindred soul
For mutual interchange of puffery.
Gods—how we blew each other! But, 'tis
    past—
Those halcyon days are gone; and, I suspect,
That, in some fit of loathing or disgust,
Mine ancient playmate hath deserted me.
And yet I am Apollodorus still!
I search for genius, having it myself,
With keen and earnest longings. I survive
To disentangle, from the imping wings
Of our young poets, their crustaceous slough.
I watch them, as the watcher on the brook
Sees the young salmon wrestling from its
    egg,
And revels in its future bright career.
Ha! what seraphic melody is this?

Enter SANCHO, *a Costermonger, singing.*

Down in the garden behind the wall,
    Merrily grows the bright-green leek;
The old sow grunts as the acorns fall,
    The winds blow heavy, the little pigs
        squeak.
Once for the litter, and three for the teat—
Hark to their music, Juanna my sweet!

APOLLODORUS.

Now, heaven be thanked! here is a genuine
    bard,
A creature of high impulse, one unsoiled
By coarse conventionalities of rule,
He labours not to sing, for his bright
    thoughts
Resolve themselves at once into a strain
Without the aid of balanced artifice.
All hail, great poet!

SANCHO.

Save you, my merry master! Need you any leeks or onions? Here's the primest cauliflower, though I say it, in all Badajoz. Set it up at a distance of some ten yards, and I'll forfeit my ass if it does not look bigger than the Alcayde's wig. Or would these radishes suit your turn? There's nothing like your radish for cooling the blood and purging distempered humours.

APOLLODORUS.

I do admire thy vegetables much.
But will not buy them. Pray you, pardon me
For one short word of friendly obloquy.
Is't possible a being so endowed
With music, song, and sun-aspiring thoughts,
Can stoop to chaffer idly in the streets,
And, for a huckster's miserable gain,
Renounce the urgings of his destiny?
Why, man, thine ass should be as Pegasus,
A sun-reared charger snorting at the stars,
And scattering all the Pleiads at his heels—
Thy cart should be an orient-tinted car,
Such as Aurora drives into the day,
What time the rosy-fingered Hours awake—
Thy reins—

SANCHO.

Look ye, master, I've dusted a better jacket than yours before now, so you had best keep a civil tongue in your head. Once for all, will you buy my radishes?

APOLLODORUS.

No!

SANCHO.

Then go to the devil and shake yourself!
                                      [*Exit.*]

APOLLODORUS.

The foul fiend seize thee and thy cauliflowers!
I was indeed a most egregious ass
To take this lubber clodpole for a bard,
And worship that dull fool. Pythian Apollo!
Hear me—O hear! Towards the firmament
I gaze with longing eyes; and, in the name
Of millions thirsting for poetic draughts,
I do beseech thee, send a poet down!
Let him descend, e'en as a meteor falls,
Rushing at noonday—
[*He is crushed by the fall of the body of*
HAVERILLO.]

We then find Firmilian wandering among the mountains, and lavishing a superfluity of apostrophe upon the rocks, forests, and cataracts around him. Whatever may be his moral deficiencies, we are constrained to admit that he must have studied the phenomena of nature to considerable purpose at the University of Badajoz, since he explains, in no fewer than twelve pages of blank verse, the glacier theory, entreating his own attention—for no one is with him—to the striated surface of rocks and the forcible displacement of boulders. He then, by way of amusement, works out a question in eonic sections. But, notwithstanding these exercitations, he is obviously not happy. He is still as far as ever from his grand object, the thorough appreciation of remorse—for he can assign a distinct moral motive for each atrocity which he has committed. He at last reluctantly arrives at the conclusion that he is not the party destined—

> To shrine that page of history in song,
> And utter such tremendous cadences,
> That the mere babe who hears them at the
>   breast,
> *Sans* comprehension, or the power of thought,
> Shall be an idiot to its dying hour!
> I deemed my verse would make pale Hecate's
>   orb
> Grow wan and dark; and into ashes change
> The radiant star-dust of the milky-way.
> I deemed that pestilence, disease, and death
> Would follow every strophe—for the power
> Of a true poet, prophet as he is,
> Should rack creation!

If this view of the powers of poets and poetry be correct, commend us to the continuance of a lengthened period of prose!

Firmilian then begins to look about him for a new subject, and a new course of initiative discipline. Magic first occurs to him—but he very speedily abandons that idea, from a natural terror of facing the fiend, and a wholesome dread of the Inquisition. He admits having made already one or two experiments in that line, and narrates, with evident horror, how he drew a chalk circle in his apartments, kindled a brazier, and began an incantation, when suddenly a lurid light appeared in the sockets of a skull upon the shelf, and so nearly threw him into convulsions that he could barely mutter the exorcism. (It appears, from another part of the poem, that this exploit had been detected by his servant, a spy of the Inquisition, in consequence of his having neglected to erase the cabalistic markings in chalk, and was of course immediately reported.) At last he determines to fall back upon sensuality, and to devote his unexampled talents to a grand poem upon the amours of the Heathen deities. He states, with much show of truth, that the tone of morals which an exclusively classical education is apt to give, cannot but be favourable to an extensive and sublime erotic undertaking—and that the youthful appetite, early stimulated by the perusal of the Pantheon, and the works of Ovid, Juvenal, and Catullus, will eagerly turn to anything in the vernacular which promises still stronger excitement. We shall not venture, at the present, to apply ourselves seriously to that question.

That Firmilian—for we shall not say Mr. Percy Jones—was well qualified for such an undertaking as he fi-

nally resolved to prosecute, must be evident to every one who has perused the earliest extract we have given; and we shall certainly hold ourselves excused from quoting the terms of the course of study which he now proposes to himself. Seriously, it is full time that the prurient and indecent tone which has liberally manifested itself in the writings of the young spasmodic poets should be checked. It is so far from occasional, that it has become a main feature of their school; and in one production of the kind, most shamefully bepuffed, the hero was represented as carrying on an intrigue with the kept-mistress of Lucifer! If we do not comment upon more recent instances of marked impurity, it is because we hope the offence will not be repeated. Meantime, let us back to Firmilian.

As he approaches the catastrophe, we remark, with infinite gratification, that Mr. Percy Jones takes pains to show that he is not personally identified with the opinions of his hero. Up to the point which we have now reached, there has been nothing to convince us that Jones did not intend Firmilian to be admired—but we are thankful to say that before the conclusion we are undeceived. Jones, though quite as spasmodic as the best of them, *has* a sense of morals; and we do not know that we ever read anything better, in its way, than the following scene:—

> A GARDEN.
>
> FIRMILIAN. MARIANA.
>
> FIRMILIAN.
>
> My Mariana!
>
> MARIANA.
>
>   O my beautiful!
> My seraph love—my panther of the wild—
> My moon-eyed leopard—my voluptuous lord!
> O, I am sunk within a sea of bliss,
> And find no soundings!
>
> FIRMILIAN.
>
>   Shall I answer back?
> As the great Earth lies silent all the night,
> And looks with hungry longing on the stars,
> Whilst its huge heart beats on its granite ribs
> With measured pulsings of delirious joy—
> So look I, Mariana, on thine eyes!
>
> MARIANA.
>
> Ah, dearest! wherefore are we fashioned thus?
> I cannot always hang around thy neck
> And plant vermilion kisses on thy brow;
> I cannot clasp thee, as yon ivy bush—

Too happy ivy!—holds, from year to year,
The stalwart oak within her firm embrace,
Mixing her tresses fondly up with his,
Like some young Jewish maid with
    Absalom's.
Nay, hold, Firmilian! do not pluck that rose!

FIRMILIAN.

Why not? it is a fair one.

MARIANA.

        Are fair things
Made only to be plucked? O fie on thee!
I did not think my lord a libertine!

FIRMILIAN.

Yet, sweetest, with your leave I'll take the
    rose,
For there's a moral in it.—Look you here.
'Tis fair, and sweet, and in its clustered leaves
It carries balmy dew: a precious flower,
And vermeil-tinctured, as are Hebe's lips,
Yet say, my Mariana, could you bear
To gaze for ever only upon this,
And fling the rest of Flora's casket by?

MARIANA.

No truly—I would bind it up with more,
And make a fitting posy for my breast.
If I were stinted in my general choice,
I'd crop the lily, tender, fresh, and white,—
The shrinking pretty lily—and would give
Its modest contrast to the gaudier rose.
What next? some flower that does not love
    the day—
The dark, full-scented night-stock well might
    serve
To join the other two.

FIRMILIAN.

        A sweet selection!
Think'st thou they'd bloom together on one
    breast
With a united fragrance?

MARIANA.

        Wherefore not?
It is by union that all things are sweet.

FIRMILIAN.

Thou speakest well! I joy, my Mariana,
To find thy spirit overleaps the pale

Of this mean world's injurious narrowness!
Never did Socrates proclaim a truth
More beautiful than welled from out thy
    lips—
"It is by union that all things are sweet."
Thou, darling, art my rose—my dewy rose—
The which I'll proudly wear, but not alone.
Dost comprehend me?

MARIANA.

        Ha! Firmilian—
How my eyes dazzle!

FIRMILIAN.

        Let me show you now
The lily I have ta'en to bind with thee.
[*He brings* LILIAN *from the summer-house.*]

MARIANA.

Is this a jest, Firmilian?

FIRMILIAN.

        Could I jest
With aught so fair and delicate as this?
Nay, come—no coyness! Both of you
    embrace.
Then to my heart of hearts—

MARIANA.

        Soft you a moment!
Methinks the posy is not yet complete.
Say, for the sake of argument, I share
My rights with this pale beauty—(for she's
    pretty;
Although so fragile and so frail a thing,
That a mere puff of April wind would mar
    her)—
Where is the night-stock?

    [FIRMILIAN *brings* INDIANA *from the tool-
    house.*]

        Here!

MARIANA.

        A filthy negress!
Abominable!

LILIAN.

Mercy on me! what blubber lips she has!

MARIANA, *furiously to* FIRMILIAN.

You nasty thing! Is this your poetry—
Your high soul-scheming and philosophy?
I hate and loathe you! (*To Indiana.*)—Rival of
　my shoe,
Go, get thee gone, and hide thee from the day
That loathes thine ebon skin! Firmilian—
You'll hear of this! My brother serves the
　king.

LILIAN.

My uncle is the chief Inquisitor,
And he shall know of this ere curfew tolls!
What! Shall I share a husband with a coal?

MARIANA.

Right, girl! I love thee even for that word—
The Inquisition makes most rapid work,
And in its books, that caitiff's name is down!

FIRMILIAN.

Listen one moment! When I was a babe,
And in a cradle puling for my nurse,
There fell a gleam of glory on the floor,
And in it, darkly standing, was a form—

MARIANA.

A negress, probably! Farewell awhile—
When next we meet—the faggot and the pile!
Come, Lilian!
　[*Exeunt.*]

INDIANA.

I shake from head to foot with sore affright—
What will become of me?

FIRMILIAN.

　　　Who cares? Good night!
[*Scene closes.*]

Bravo, Perey! The first part of that scene is managed
with a dexterity which old Dekker might have ap-
plauded, and the conclusion shows a perfect knowledge of womanly character and feeling. Firmilian is
now cast beyond the pale of society, and in imminent
danger, if apprehended, of taking a conspicuous part in
an *auto-da-fé.* An author of inferior genius would probably have consigned him to the custody of the Familiars, in which case we should have had a dungeon and
rack scene, if not absolute incremation as the catastrophe. But Jones knew better. He felt that such a cruel
fate might, by the effect of contrast, revive some kind
of sympathy in the mind of the reader for Firmilian,
and he has accordingly adopted the wiser plan of de-

picting him as the victim of his own haunted imagination. The closing scene is so eminently graphic and so
perfectly original, that we give it entire.

　　　A BARREN MOOR.

　　　Night—Mist and fog.

　　　Enter FIRMILIAN.

They're hot upon my traces! Through the mist
I heard their call and answer—and but now,
As I was crouching 'neath a hawthorn bush,
A dark Familiar swiftly glided by,
His keen eyes glittering with the lust of death.
If I am ta'en, the faggot and the pile
Await me! Horror! Rather would I dare,
Like rash Empedocles, the Etna gulf,
Than writhe before the slaves of bigotry.
Where am I? If my mind deceives me not,
Upon that common where two years ago,
An old blind beggar came and craved an alms,
Thereby destroying a stupendous thought
Just bursting in my mind—a glorious bud
Of poesy, but blasted ere its bloom!
I bade the old fool take the leftward path,
Which leads to the deep quarry, where he
　fell—
At least I deem so, for I heard a splash—
But I was gazing on the gibbous moon,
And durst not lower my celestial flight
To care for such an insect-worm as he!
　How cold it is! The mist comes thicker on.
Ha!—what is that? I see around me lights
Dancing and flitting, yet they do not seem
Like torches either—and there's music too!
I'll pause and listen.

Chorus of IGNES FATUI.

　　Follow, follow, follow!
　　　Over hill and over hollow;
　　It is ours to lead the way,
　　　When a sinner's footsteps stray—
　　Cheering him with light and song,
　　On his doubtful path along.
　　Hark! hark! The watchdogs bark.
There's a crash and a splash, and a blind
　man's cry,
But the poet looks tranquilly up at the sky!

FIRMILIAN.

Is it the echo of an inward voice,
Or spirit-words that make my flesh to creep,
And send the cold blood choking to my heart?
I'll shift my ground a little—

Chorus of IGNES FATUI.

Flicker, flicker, flicker!
Quicker still, and quicker.
Four young men sat down to dine,
And still they passed the rosy wine;
Pure was the cask, but in the flask
There lay a certain deadly powder—
Ha! his heart is beating louder!
Ere the day had passed away,
Gracia Perez lifeless lay!
Hark! his mother wails Alphonzo,
Never more shall strong Alonzo
Drink the wine of Ildefronso!

FIRMILIAN.

O horror! horror! 'twas by me they died!
I'll move yet farther on—

Chorus of IGNES FATUI.

In the vaults under
Bursts the red thunder;
Up goes the Cathedral,
Priest, people, and bedral!
    Ho! ho! ho! ho!

FIRMILIAN.

My brain is whirling like a potter's wheel!
O Nemesis!

Chorus of IGNES FATUI.

The Muses sing in their charmed ring,
And Apollo weeps for him who sleeps,
Alas! on a hard and stony pillow—
Haverillo! Haverillo!

FIRMILIAN.

I shall go mad!

Chorus of IGNES FATUI.

Give him some respite—give him some praise.
One good deed he has done in his days;
Chaunt it, and sing it, and tell it in chorus—
He has flattened the cockscomb of Apollodorus!

FIRMILIAN.

Small comfort that! The death of a shard-
    beetle,
Albeit the poorest and the paltriest thing
That crawls round refuse cannot weigh a
    grain
Against the ponderous avalanche of guilt
That hangs above me! O me miserable!
I'll grope my way yet further.

Chorus of IGNES FATUI.

Firmilian! Firmilian!
What have you done to Lilian?
There a cry from the grotto, a sob by the
    stream,
A woman's loud wailing, a little babe's
    scream!
    How fared it with Lilian,
    In the pavilion,
    Firmilian! Firmilian?

FIRMILIAN.

Horror! I'm lost!—

Chorus of IGNES FATUI.

Ho! ho! ho!
Deep in the snow
Lies a black maiden from Africa's shore!
    Hasten and shake her—
    You never shall wake her—
She'll roam through the glens of the Atlas no
    more!
    Stay, stay, stay,
    This way—this way—
There's a pit before, and a pit behind,
And the seeing man walks in the path of the
    blind!
            FIRMILIAN *falls into the quarry.*
    The IGNES FATUI *dance as the curtain
    descends.*

And so ends the tragedy of Firmilian.

It is rather difficult to give a serious opinion upon the merits of such a production as this. It is, of course, utterly extravagant; but so are the whole of the writings of the poets of the Spasmodic school; and, in the eyes of a considerable body of modern critics, extravagance is regarded as a proof of extraordinary genius. It is, here and there, highly coloured; but that also is looked upon as a symptom of the divine afflatus, and rather prized than otherwise. In one point of proclaimed spasmodic excellence, perhaps it fails. You can always tell what Percy Jones is after, even when he is dealing with "shuddering stars," "gibbous moons," "imposthumes of hell," and the like; whereas you may read through twenty pages of the more ordinary stuff without being able to discern what the writers mean— and no wonder, for they really mean nothing. They are simply writing nonsense-verses; but they contrive, by blazing away whole rounds of metaphor, to mask their absolute poverty of thought, and to convey the impression that there must be something stupendous under so heavy a canopy of smoke. If, therefore, unintelligibility, which is the highest degree of obscurity, is to be considered a poetic excellence, we are afraid that Jones must yield the palm to several of his contemporaries; if, on the contrary, perspicuity is to be regarded as a virtue, we do not hesitate in assigning the spasmodic prize to the author of *Firmilian.* To him the old lines on Marlowe, with the alteration of the name, might be applied—

> Next Percy Jones, bathed in the Thespian
>   Springs,
> Had in him those brave sublunary Things
> That your first Poets had; his Raptures were
> All Air and Fire, which made his Verses
>   clear;
> For that fierce Madness still he did retain,
> Which rightly should possess a Poet's Brain.

Matthew Arnold on Smith, in an 1853 letter to Arthur Hugh Clough:

As to Alexander Smith I have not read him—I shrink from what is so intensely immature—but I think the extracts I have seen most remarkable—and I think at the same time that he will not go far. I have not room or time for my reasons—but I think so. This kind does not go far: it dies like Keats or loses itself like Browning.

Matthew Arnold, in The Letters of Matthew Arnold to Arthur Hugh Clough, *edited by Howard Foster Lowry, Russell and Russell, 1932.*

The Athenæum (essay date 1857)

SOURCE: A review of *City Poems,* in *The Athenaeum,* No. 1556, August 22, 1857, pp. 1055-57.

[*Here, the anonymous critic claims that ideas in Smith's* City Poems *were taken from works of other authors, and that Smith has neither the "vision nor the faculty divine" to be a great poet.*]

A strange poetical propaganda came in a few years ago, with Apollodorus or Somebody Conqueror. The young gentlemen who followed his banner appeared to be by birth flighty, by education ungrammatical, by transmutation poets. They were all more or less subject to ethereal prospects, opinions, and starry influences. They saw strange visions and dreamt impossible similitudes. In whatever quarter of the world, or season of the year, they happened to light, they were always to be found in conjunction with the moon, and, as a matter of course, continually frothing about the sea, if not putting out the sun and making the earth dark with their own excessive brightness. Their partiality for daisies and skylarks implied an unfamiliarity with the localities and the seasons when those very pretty commonplaces of earth concur. Except with a

daisyrake, it was impossible to turn up so many shrivelled specimens of "the wee crimson-tipped flower" or to net so many larks out of place as the reader might catch without much trouble in any page of their poetry. Neither to lark nor to daisy was there generally such epithet or thought attached as justified the introduction. Among these young gentlemen Mr. Alexander Smith held rank as chief. His shield was bright, his plumage gay, his step assured. He announced himself a hero, and the busy world, that takes so much on trust, smiled on his burnished arms and dancing feathers. But time gave rise to doubts,—doubts whether the *meux chevalier* had forged the shining armour for himself or merely picked it up by the wayside—whether he were the true duke or only a comedian in a mask and cloak.

Our readers will remember that early this year a writer in the *Athenæum* drew attention to the system of composition adopted by the Apollodorus poets, as particularly exemplified in the verses of Mr. A. Smith. He showed by many examples that the easy system was, to take an image, an idea, or a passage from an acknowledged writer, change the order, or the passion, or the name, and then compose it into a new work. We venture to reproduce one of the examples given. Cyril Tourneur had written in his *Atheist's Tragedy:*—

> The weeping sea, like one
> Whose milder temper doth lament the death
> Of him whom in his rage he slew, runs up
> The shore, embraces him, kisses his cheek,
> Goes back again and forces up the sand.
> To bury him.

Out of this passage the reader sees how easy it must be to get the following lines, ostensibly by Mr. Smith:—

> The bridegroom sea
> Is toying with the shore, his wedded bride,
> And in the fulness of his marriage joy
> He decorates her tawny brow with shells,
> Retires a space to see how fair she looks,
> Then proud runs up to kiss her.

—Take away Tourneur's property from these lines— that is, the image, thought, action, word, and music— and what remains?

But everybody in our day has not read Cyril Tourneur, and those who did not know the original thought Mr. Smith's simile very fine, and even staked his claim as a poet on its beauty. The same principle of poetical compilation, we are very sorry to report, marks throughout the **City Poems** Even a rapid reading shows us this defect. Everywhere we find the mutilated property of other bards, strewn about like wrecks of noble vessels thrown upon a wild Scotch coast.

Mr. Wordsworth saw the shadow of a daisy, and Mr. Alexander Smith, too, sees it after him.—

> *The daisy, by the shadow that it casts,*
> Protects the lingering dew-drop from the sun.
> > *Wordsworth.*
> The dear old place is now before my eyes,
> Yea, to the daisy's shadow on the stone.
> > *Smith,* p. 91.

If Mr. Tennyson is partial to a pint of port, Mr. Smith imagines the effect of the same measure and liquid in poetry. Mr. Tennyson has a curlew, an empty house, and a moorland: 'Tis the place, and all around it, as of old, *the curlews call Dreary gleams about the moorland flying over Locksley Hall.* Mr. Smith (p. 11) thus transfers the landscape.—

> The empty house was left to whistling winds,
> In which *the curlew sailed with wavering cry,*
> *And flying sunny gleams.* . . . .
> *Six paces on the moor.*

Mr. Tennyson compares the sunbeam on Olivia's lips to a butterfly:—

> A second hovered round her lips
> Like a golden butterfly.—*'Talking Oak.'*

Apud Smith (p. 24):—

> A half-smile hovering round her happy lips
> Like a bright butterfly.

Here are two landscapes presented in similar forms and colours. Tennyson ("Gardener's Daughter") thus:—

> Washed by a slow, broad stream
> That stirred with languid pulses of the oar,
> Waves all its lazy lilies.

Mr. Smith (p. 88):—

> —a stream
> . . . slides lazy through the milky meads,
> And once a week the sleepy slow-trailed barge
> Rocks the broad water-lilies on its marge.

Wordsworth asserts the function of poetry to be to "apparel with celestial light," or glorify, "the common things of earth." Mr. Smith thus conveys the idea:—

> To put a something of celestial light
> Round the familiar face of every day.

The hero of the *Excursion* is thus pictured by Wordsworth:—

> What joy was his when from the naked
>   mountain top
> He saw the sun rise up and bathe the world
>   with light.

Mr. Smith (p. 118) thus adapts his figure:—

> What joy, when o'er the huddled chimney-
>   tops
> Rose the great yellow moon!

Byron enumerates the influences that affect the heart:—

> It may be a tone,
> A flower, a leaf.

Mr. Smith (p. 22) thus follows him:—

> That at a passing tone,
> The noiseless falling of an autumn leaf,
> It trembled into tears.

One of the never-to-be-forgotten lines of Philip Sydney is—

> A chamber deaf to noise and blind to light,
> A rosy garland.

Mr. Smith copies and corrupts one of the loveliest fancies in our national poetry (p. 114):

> Chamber of *de*light,
> Deaf to all noise, sweet as a rose's heart.

This touch of the spring in Mr. Smith's "A Boy's Poem"—

> Bliss
> Crept through my veins like that which stirs a tree
> From knotted root up to its slenderest spray
> Touched by the hand of Spring. (P. 179)

in Tennyson's original stands thus:—

> And even into mine inmost ring
> A pleasure I discerned,
> Like those blind motions of the spring
> That show the year is turned.—*Talking Oak.*

The lines—

> Shapes
> That haunt him with their beauty. (P. 34.)
> A haunting face
> Disturbed me with its beauty. (P. 179.)
> Her bliss disturbed her. (P. 24.)

combine and assuredly do *not* improve passages from Wordsworth's "Tintern Abbey"—

The cataract haunted me like a passion.
A sense subline
Disturbs me with the joy of elevated thoughts.

Wordsworth's

Consecration and the poet's dream,

Mr. Smith degrades into

Familiar things enough to you and me,
Take a strange glory from the poet's mind. (P. 34.)

The "Ode on Immortality" and "Tintern Abbey" may be reconstructed almost entirely by any one who has a little comparative industry and will pick the bits out of Mr. Smith's museum.

Here are two considerable, though mutilated, fragments:—

I've suffered much,
And known the deepest sorrow man can know.
That pain has fled upon the troubled years:
Although the world is darker than before,
There is a pathos round the daisy's head;
The common sunshine in the common fields,
The runnel by the road, the clouds that grow
Out of the blue abysses of the air,
*Do not as in my earlier days, oppress
Me with their beauty.*

And

You knew me when my fond and ignorant
youth
Was an unwindowed chamber of delight,
Deaf to all noise, sweet as a rose's heart:
A sudden earthquake rent it to the base,
And through the rifts of ruin sternly gleamed
An apparition of grey windy crag,
Black leagues of forest roaring like a sea,
And far lands dim with rain. *There* was my
world
And place for everymore. When forth I went
I took my gods with me, and set them up
Within my foreign home. What love I had,
What admiration and keen sense of joy,
Unspent in verse, has been to me a stream
Feeding the roots of being; living sap
That dwelt within the myriad boughs of life,
And kept the leaves of feeling fresh and
green.
Instead of sounding in the heads of fools,
Like wind within a ruin, it became
*A pious benediction and a smile
On all the goings on of human life;*

An incommunicable joy in day,
In lone waste places, and the light of stars.

For the originals of these verses—saving the patches obviously borrowed from Sydney, Coleridge, and Byron—read the lines in "Tintern Abbey," beginning

For I am
Not as in the hour of thoughtless youth,
. . . . . but feeling oftentimes
The still, sad music of humanity,

together with the passage in the Ode—

It is not now
As it hath been before;
Go where I may,
By night or day,
The things I once have seen
I now can see no more.
The rainbow comes and goes,
And lovely is the rose;
The sunshine is a glorious birth;
Yet still I know
When I go
That there hath passed a beauty from the earth.

We put together a string of passages with the original authorities:—

Could tell, Sir, if he would—yet never dared.
(P. 9.)

Imitated from 'Macbeth.'

Sleep in one room and at one table sit. (P. 21.)

Adapted from "King John."

The rain which I had heard so often weep
Alone, within the middle of the night,
Like a poor, beaten, and despised child
That has been thrust forth from its father's
door. (P. 118.)

Copied from Coleridge, almost word for word.

A lofty scorn I dared to shed
On human passions, hopes, and jars,
I—standing on the countless dead,
And pitied by the countless stars. (P. 100.)

Here is the original in Mrs. Browning:—

O man, thy hate with stars o'erhead,
They love with graves below.

Here is reproduced a well-remembered refrain from Mr. Tennyson's "Princess":—

Filled with the light of suns that are no more.
     (P. 112.)
But mock me with the days that are no more.
     (P. 113.)

Let these *City Poems* be opened at any page whatever, and there will be found glorious fragments of verse, which Mr. Smith has read somewhere, and has forgotten that others have read too—patches of seamless Milton, Shakspeare, Wordsworth, Shelley, Keats, Coleridge, the two Brownings, so turned, and padded, and tagged to breadths of home-spun inanity, that we scarcely know whether to be amazed at the impudence or to pity the poverty which makes such an attempt to cover its own nakedness.

The following beauties and elegances are Mr. Smith's own:—

     The belled landlord with his purple head,
     Like a red cabbage on December morn
     Crusted with snow.

     He seemed a mighty angel sent from God
     Standing before us—drunk.

                    I often sat
     At those wild drinking bouts, which seemed
          divine
     In a great flash of wit—*and rose next morn,
     Throat like the parched Sahara, and each ear
     Loud as a cotton mill.*

     O, rare to hear this Cotton-bag, with soul
     Scarce saucer-deep, rate Horton for his
          faults!

     True, as the monsoon breathing day and
          night
     To China and the Isles.

     *Here, black-eyed Richard ruins red-cheeked
     Moll,*
     Indifferent as a lord to her despair.

     Within the lake I see old Hodge's cows
     Stand in their shadows in a tranquil
          drowse.

     Men who at morning stood as prosperous
     As bearded autumn, were, ere sunset, poor
     As a worn scarecrow fluttering dingy rags
     Within the feeble wind.

          Round me standing in a marsh of
               doubt,
     She danced like elfin fire.

     A flood of pale green foam, that hissed and
     freathed.

     Like clouds of cherubs tiny cloudlets slept
     In soft and tender rose.

     Discourse burst from its melancholy
          weeds,
     As brilliant as a spangled dancing-girl.

In contrast to the *Life Drama* we are bound to say that Mr. Smith's imagination in these *City Poems* appears in very reduced circumstances, and to soar rather under the light of dips than the radiance of stars. Here are a few effects of candlelight.—

     She like a candle lit her father's hearth.
     The Lady Florence at the county ball,
     Quenching the beauties as the lightning dims
     The candles in a room.
     Joy stood like candles in her mother's eyes.

For charwomen—in England far from attractive society—Mr. Smith exhibits a strange preference. These, oyster-men and bellied landlords have supplanted moon-eyed panthers and cubs of Ind in his fancy. "The mighty pathos of the empty streets" is well pourtrayed throughout the poems. We give one of the best lyrics entire; and even in this the reader, will catch the music of other strings than those of Mr. Smith.—

     On the Sabbath-day,
     Through the churchyard old and grey,
     Over the crisp and yellow leaves, I held my
          rustling way;
     And amid the words of mercy, falling on my
          soul like balms,
     'Mid the gorgeous storms of music—in the
          mellow organ-calms,
     'Mid the upward streaming prayers, and the
          rich and solemn psalms,
     I stood careless, Barbara.

     My heart was otherwhere
     While the organ shook the air,
     And the priest, with outspread hands, blessed
          the people with a prayer;
     But, when rising to go homeward, with a mild
          and saint-like shine
     Gleamed a face of airy beauty with its
          heavenly eyes on mine—
     Gleamed and vanished in a moment—O that
          face was surely thine
     Out of heaven, Barbara!

     O pallid, pallid face!
     O earnest eyes of grace!
     When last I saw thee, dearest, it was in
          another place.
     You came running forth to meet me with my
          love-gift on your wrist:
     The flutter of a long white dress, then all was

lost in mist—
A purple stain of agony was on the mouth I kissed.
That wild morning, Barbara.

I searched, in my despair,
Sunny noon and midnight air;
I could not drive away the thought that you
    were lingering there.
O many and many a winter night I sat when
    you were gone,
My worn face buried in my hands, beside the
    fire alone—
Within the dripping churchyard, the rain
    plashing on your stone,
You were sleeping, Barbara.

'Mong angels, do you think
Of the precious golden link
I clasped around your happy arm while sitting
    by yon brink?
Or when that night of gliding dance, of
    laughter and guitars,
Was emptied of its music, and we watched,
    through latticed bars,
The silent midnight heaven creeping o'er us
    with its stars,
Till the day broke, Barbara?

In the years I've changed;
Wild and far my heart hath ranged,
And many sins and errors now have been on
    me avenged;
But to you I have been faithful, whatsoever
    good I lacked;
I loved you, and above my life still hangs that
    love intact—
Your love the trembling rainbow, I the
    reckless cataract—
Still I love you, Barbara.

Yet, love, I am unblest;
With many doubts opprest,
I wander like a desert wind, without a place
    of rest.
Could I but win you for an hour from off that
    starry shore,
The hunger of my soul were stilled, for Death
    hath told you more
Than the melancholy world doth know; things
    deeper than all lore
You could teach me, Barbara.

In vain, in vain, in vain,
You will never come again.
There droops upon the dreary hills a mournful
    fringe of rain;
The gloaming closes slowly round, loud winds
    are in the tree,
Round selfish shores for ever moans the hurt

and wounded sea,
There is no rest upon the earth, peace is with
    Death and thee,
Barbara!

And a few curious examples of rhyming.—

    On bank and brae how thick they grow,
    The self-same clumps, the self-same dyes,
    The primroses of long ago—
    But ah! the altered eyes!
    I dream they are the very flowers,
    Warm with the sun, wet with the showers,
    Which, years ago, I used to *pull*
    Returning from the murmuring *school*

This appears suitable for the 14th of February.—

    When first I saw your tender face,
        Saw you, loved you from afar,
    My soul was like forlornest space
        Made *sudden happy* by a star.

And here an example of music:—

    The sheep they leap in golden parks;
        My blood is bliss, my heart is pleasure;
    Then let my song flow like a lark's
        Above his nested treasure.

This is difficult to repeat fast:—

    Wat robbed a ruffled struggler of a kiss.

The sensitiveness of the hero's aural nerve is thus
represented:—

    He *heard* a spire start in its sleep.

Three of the six poems in this volume are not now new.
The opening poem, "Horton," we read some time ago in
the newspapers. "The Night before the Wedding" and
"The Change" appeared in the *National Magazine* not
long ago. The hero of "Horton" is evidently the author,
who sits in an office between two clerks:—one is "a moat
of dullness," the other, "all flame and air." The effect of
their association is alternately conveyed in the poem.

In this hasty reading we have sufficiently seen that Mr.
Smith is not one of Nature's poets—he possesses neither "the vision nor the faculty divine"; and that he has
not improved in the principle or the practice of his very
singular system of composition.

David Mason (essay date 1867)

SOURCE: "Alexander Smith," in *Macmillan's Magazine*, Vol. 15, February 15, 1867, pp. 342-52.

[In the following excerpt, written soon after Smith's death, Mason eulogizes Smith's writing career and refutes common criticisms of his work.]

On the 5th of last month Alexander Smith died in his house at Wardie, near Edinburgh, at the age of thirty-six. The degree of feeling evoked by this event in different quarters has varied, of course, with the different estimates that had been formed of the worth of the deceased—his place and likelihood in that portion of the British literature of our time to which he was a contributor, but the other contributors to which have been, and are, so numerous. By his personal friends, and those locally around him, the loss has been felt as hardly any other within that circle could have been. Nor is there a newspaper in the country that has not chronicled the event more or less emphatically as one of some public importance. Even among those London literary journals whose obituary notices in most cases are supposed to represent really central opinion, there has been, so far as we are aware, only one that has felt itself bound, in consistency with its peculiar relations to Mr. Smith while alive, to pursue him to his grave with words of slight. All this is of little consequence to him now, and will rectify itself without effort from anybody. In these pages, however, where Mr. Smith's own hand was not unknown from time to time, some memoir of him may well seem due.

Born, on the 31st of December, 1830, in the manufacturing town of Kilmarnock, in Ayrshire, where his father was a drawer of patterns, Alexander Smith passed his childhood and youth, first in that town, and then, successively, in Paisley and Glasgow. He received the ordinary Scottish school-education; and it was intended that he should go to Glasgow University, to qualify himself to be a minister in the religious denomination to which his parents belonged—one of the chief Protestant Dissenting bodies in Scotland. Circumstances preventing this, he was brought up to his father's occupation, and became, while yet a boy, a designer of patterns for Glasgow manufacturing firms. It was in the warehouse, amid the din of looms, or in his evening hours of release from his employment, that the passion for poetry seized him. Widely diffused as the faculty of verse-making now is among us—so widely diffused that there is not a district of England, Scotland, and Ireland that does not count its "poets" by the score— it would yet appear, on good evidence, that nowhere in the total area of the islands has the Muse of late troubled so many, touched so many into happiness or misery, as in and around money-making Glasgow. Alexander Smith used himself to tell with a kind of sly glee how, on one famous evening in Glasgow, he sat down to supper in the company of seventy other poets. Even these must have been but a selection from a much larger number latent among the ranks of operatives, clerks, and others in the great city and its adjacencies. At all events it was from a multitude of West-Scottish poets, some well known locally, and others slightly known or not at all, that Smith flashed out at length into preeminent distinction. He did so mainly by the higher power of his genius, but partly also in consequence of a peculiarity in the mode of its exercise.

There seems, for more than one generation, to have been an almost irresistible tendency among resident Scotch writers, whether in verse or in prose, to confine themselves to specially Scottish subjects, and, even in their treatment of such subjects, to traditional Scottish forms. Their themes have been taken from Scottish history, or from the circumstances and humours of contemporary Scottish life; and, even when they have not used the Scottish dialect, they have kept within a certain round of rhythms, metres, styles, and modes of conception, which precedent had established in connexion with their themes. The cause of this is the natural one—that people everywhere will write about what chiefly interests them, and in the forms of which custom has made them fondest; but the cause of this cause is, in great measure, the influence of Burns and Scott. The result, however, is that perhaps the majority of recent Scottish writers, resident within Scotland, have, without being themselves sufficiently aware of the fact, written wholly or mainly for a Scottish constituency. But, by some means or other, Alexander Smith from the first burst these bounds. Not, of course, that he was, or could be, an exception to the rule which provides that the scenery and circumstances amid which any one has been bred shall be transfused into his mind, and shall tinge its products to the last. In his earliest poems, as now in his completed writings, we can discern very definitely that district of actual British ground—from Glasgow, down the Firth of Clyde, to the West Highlands—the photographs from which had been the first furnishing of his memory, and the very meteorology of which had yielded him meanings and suggestions. This, as it was the ground over which his footsteps moved, was the immediate ground of his observations and experience. But, whether from the action in himself of that free imagination which tends everywhere through what is present to the elemental and conceivable, or from the effect upon him of readings in certain English poets of the rarer order, we can see that he had invented on this ground, or brought down over it and into it, a visionary world that was in no peculiar sense Scottish. While most of his local brothers in the craft of verse were keen in the hereditary Wallace-and-Bruce vein, or fervid *pro* and *con* the Covenanters, or singing variations of the old tunes to new Scottish streams and braes, incidents and maidens, this Glasgow poet was away in a less limited element, where the themes were love and friendship, birth and death, poverty and wealth, the hearts of poets passionate against the irony of fate and fact. While *they* were repeating the strains of Burns, Scott, and Tannahill, *he*, though loyal to these too, had constituted himself, for the purposes of his own poetry, the disciple rather of Shakespeare, Wordsworth, Keats, and Tennyson. There seems even to have been a fascination of his fancy for things English—a liking, generated in him by his readings, or perhaps by family incidents of which his childhood had heard reports, for the conception of the far-away Kentish downs, or rich English parks, or old English mansions quaint-gabled and deep in woods, as the scenes of his stories.

All this constituted a peculiarity in Smith, as compared with most of the other West-Scottish versifiers of fifteen years ago, from among whom he became conspicuous. By itself it would have been nothing; but, taken along with his superior genius, it increased the chance of his general recognition, should he ever get beyond that initial difficulty which is, was, and ever will be the despair of young poets without means—getting a volume published. The credit of having first sufficiently discerned Mr. Smith's worth in manuscript, and of having facilitated this necessary step for him, belongs to the Rev. George Gilfillian, of Dundee. Through his means specimens of Mr. Smith's as yet unpublished poems, with remarks on their merits, appeared in some London journals. Among those who were at once impressed by the specimens, and vividly interested in their unknown author, was Mr. G. H. Lewes. Frank, generous, and discriminating, then as now, Mr. Lewes used his literary position in the editorship of the *Leader* newspaper, and the whole power of his name, in aid of the new reputation. It is also within the knowledge of the present writer that among those who then, or immediately afterwards, helped, by their expressions of admiration, to secure for the new poet a high reception in good quarters, was Mr. Herbert Spencer. In short, so wide and strong was the interest created in Mr. Smith, before the actual appearance of his ***Life-Drama and other Poems*** in 1853, that, when the volume did appear, there was a rush for copies.

We have just been glancing again over this first volume, which introduced Mr. Alexander Smith's name to the public. It seems a duty, now that he is gone, to reproduce a few passages as specimens of the sort of things that roused readers of the volume and made them acknowledge the young author as a real poet and man of genius. Allowance must, of course, be made, for the injury done to mere passages by detaching them from their context.

> 'Tis not for me, ye Heavens! 'tis not for me
> To fling a Poem, like a comet, out,
> Far-splendouring the sleepy realms of night.
>
> That great and small, weakness and strength,
>   are nought;
> That, each thing being equal in its sphere,
> The May-night glowworm with its emerald
>   lamp

Is worthy as the mighty moon that drowns
Continents in her white and silent light:
This, this were easy to believe, were I
The planet that doth nightly wash the Earth's
Fair sides with moonlight; not the shining
      worm.

I seek the look of Fame! Poor fool! So tries
Some lonely wanderer 'mong the desert sands
By shouts to gain the notice of the Sphinx,
Staring right on with calm eternal eyes.

The fierce exulting worlds, the motes in rays,
   The churlish thistles, scented briers,
The wind-swept bluebells on the sunny braes,
      Down to the central fires,

Exist alike in love. Love is a sea,
   Filling all the abysses dim
Of lowest space, in whose deeps regally
      Suns and their bright broods swim.

This mighty sea of Love, with wondrous tides,
   Is sternly just to sun and grain:
'Tis laving at this moment Saturn's sides,
      'Tis in my blood and brain.

>   A grim old king,
> Whose blood leapt madly when the trumpets
>   brayed
> To joyous battle 'mid a storm of steeds,
> Won a rich kingdom on a battle-day;
> But in the sunset he was ebbing fast
> Ringed by his weeping lords. His left hand
>   held
> His white steed, to the belly splashed with
>   blood,
> That seemed to mourn him with its drooping
>   head;
> His right a broken brand; and in his ear
> His old victorious banners flap the winds.
> He called his faithful herald to his side:
> "Go! tell the dead I come!" With a proud
>   smile,
> The warrior with a stab let out his soul,
> Which fled, and shrieked through all the other
>   world,
> "Ye dead, my master comes!" And there
>   was pause
> Till the great shade should enter.

No sooner was he hence than critic-worms
Were swarming on the body of his fame;
And thus they judged the dead: "This Poet
   was
An April tree whose vermeil-loaded boughs
Promised to Autumn apples juiced and red,
But never came to fruit;" "He is to us
But a rich odour, a faint music-swell;"

"Poet he was not in the larger sense;
He could write pearls, but he could never
    write
A poem round and perfect as a star."

What martial music is to marching men
Should Song be to Humanity.

Oft, standing on a hill's green head, we felt
Breezes of love, and joy, and melody,
Blow through us, as the winds blow through
    the sky.
Oft with our souls in our eyes all day we fed
On summer landscapes, silver-veined with
    streams,
O'er which the air hung silent in its joy;
With a great city lying in its smoke,
A monster sleeping in its own thick breath;
And surgy plains of wheat, and ancient
    woods,
In the calm evenings cawed by clouds of
    rooks,
Acres of moss, and long black strips of firs,
And sweet cots dropt in green, where children
    played
To us unheard, till, gradual, all was lost
In distance-haze to a blue rim of hills,
Upon whose heads came down the closing
    sky.

That night the sky was heaped with clouds;
    Through one blue gulf profound,
Begirt with many a cloudy crag,
The moon came rushing like a stag,
    And one star like a hound.

How this mad old world
Reels to its burning grave, shouting forth
    names,
Like a wild drunkard at his frenzy's height,
And they who hear them deem such shoutings
    Fame!

My drooping sails
Flap idly 'gainst the mast of my intent;
I rot upon the waters when my prow
Should grate the golden isles.

I'll show you one that might have been an
    abbot
In the old time—a large and portly man,
With merry eyes, and crown that shines like
    glass.
No thin-smiled April he, bedript with tears,
But appled Autumn, golden-cheeked and tan;
A jest in his mouth feels sweet as crusted
    wine.
As if all eager for a merry thought,
The pits of laughter dimple in his cheeks;

His speech is flavorous; evermore he talks
In a warm, brown, autumnal sort of style.
A worthy man, Sir, who shall stand at compt
With conscience white, save some few stains
    of wine!

Old Mr. Wilmott; nothing in himself,
But rich as ocean! He has in his hand
Sea-marge and moor, and miles of stream and
    grove;
Dull flats, scream-startled as the exulting train
Streams like a meteor through the frighted
    night;
Wind-billowed plains of wheat, and marshy
    fens,
Unto whose reeds on midnights blue and cold
Long strings of geese come clanging from the
    stars.

'Twas late; for, as he reached the open roads,
The drowsy steeples tolled the hour of One.
The city now was left long miles behind;
A large black hill was looming 'gainst the
    stars;
He reached its summit. Far above his head,
Up there upon the still and mighty night,
God's name was writ in worlds. A while he
    stood,
Silent and throbbing like a midnight star;
He raised his hands. Alas! 'twas not in
    prayer;
He long had ceased to pray. "Father," he
    said,
"I wished to loose some music o'er Thy
    world,
"To strike from its firm seat some hoary
    wrong,
"And then to die in autumn, with the flowers
"And leaves and sunshine I have loved so
    well.
"Thou might'st have smoothed my way to
    some great end—
"But wherefore speak? Thou art the mighty
    God;
"This gleaming wilderness of suns and worlds
"Is an eternal and triumphant hymn
"Chanted by Thee unto Thine own great
    self!
"Wrapt in Thy skies, what were my prayers
    to Thee,
"My pangs, my tears of blood? They could
    not move
"Thee from the depths of Thine immortal
    dream.
"Thou hast forgotten me, God! Here, there-
    fore, here,
"To-night upon this bleak and cold hill-side
"Like a forsaken watch-fire will I die;
"And, as my pale corse fronts the glittering

night,
"It shall reproach Thee before all Thy
   worlds."
His death did *not* disturb that ancient Night.
Scornfullest Night! Over the dead there hung
Great gulfs of silence, blue and strewn with
   stars—
No sound, no motion, in the eternal depths.

I see a wretched isle, that ghostlike stands
   Wrapt in its mist-shroud in the wintry
      main:
And now a cheerless gleam of red-ploughed
   lands,
   O'er which a crow flies heavy in the rain.

         That largest Son of Time,
Who wandered singing through the listening
   world,
Will be as much forgot as the canoe
That crossed the bosom of a lonely lake
A thousand years ago.

Not bad, such passages as these, surely, from a youth who was not more than twenty-one years of age when they were written! Not bad? When have they been equalled by a beginner since? Critics of Mr. Smith, it is true—and some of them poets themselves, and therefore excellent judges—have been careful to warn the public against such mere images, flashes, bits of metrical rhetoric! They have been anxious to assure the public that such "passages" were not, and no amount of them could be, the real thing. All we can say is that, whether the real thing or not, it is to be wished we had more of them, and any young fellow that could give us more of them would, even at this time of day, be worth welcoming. To us they do seem to be poetry—genuine and most remarkable *particles* of poetry; but, whatever they are, we believe that the Laureate himself, if he encountered such passages now in a newly-published volume, would be pleasingly startled into curiosity about their author. Fourteen years ago, at all events, they did startle. They more than startled; they made a reputation. Much as depended on such individual passages, crude as was the structure of the poem in which they occurred, and possible as it was for the kindliest critic to point out here and there faults of taste, Mr. Smith's first volume was a great victory. Thousands of copies were sold in Great Britain and Ireland; there was an article on the volume in the *Revue des deux Mondes;* it was reviewed also in California, and lectured on in Australia. The young pattern-designer of Glasgow suddenly found himself famous. What was hardly less agreeable, he found himself appointed, by the Town Council of Edinburgh, on the 31st of January, 1854, to the post of secretary to Edinburgh University. The salary was only 150*l* a year, but with the prospect of literary leisure, and other social advantages.

Leaving Glasgow at the age of twenty-three, Mr. Smith became a resident in Edinburgh. The duties of his post consisted in his being present so many hours daily in his office within the walls of the University, and in there keeping the enrolment-books, receiving matriculation and graduation fees, writing business-letters, &c. He at once entered on these duties, and had not the least difficulty in adapting himself to them; and he discharged them to the end in the most quiet, easy, and punctual manner. From the moment of his coming to Edinburgh, he was, of course, an object of interest to many there, and very soon he had a new circle of attached friends to make up for the breaking of his Glasgow associations—if, indeed, compensation was necessary, with Glasgow still so near at hand. Among the first and most intimate of these new friends was Mr. Sydney Dobell, then on a long visit to Edinburgh. It was the time of the Crimean war, and the two friends jointly produced a volume of **War Sonnets** (1855), which was a good deal spoken of. It was not till 1857, however, that Mr. Smith gave the critics a distinct opportunity of reconsidering his claims to be called a poet, and trying to reverse, if they chose to do so, that previous verdict in his favour which had gone by acclamation. In that year he published his **City Poems**.

That previous verdict by acclamation in Mr. Smith's favour had been a sore subject with many. Naturally, there had been honest and reasonable dissentients from the verdict, or at least from the absoluteness of its terms, from the first. The feeling that splendid passages, or brilliant images, strewn through a poem, are not enough, was clearly a sound one; and there were some really careful critics not unfriendly to Mr. Smith, in whom the application of this feeling to him in particular had taken the form of a conviction that some abatement of the first *furore* in his favour might be desirable. Then, again, it had been pointed out that there were certain perpetually-recurring sources of Mr. Smith's images—that, to an unusual extent, he availed himself, in the production of his splendid passages, of a certain round of poetical *topics* or *places,* akin to the *topics* of the ancient teachers of oratory. The stars, seas kissing their shores, larks in the air, rainy skies— deprive Mr. Smith, it was said, of the power of allusion to these and a few more such leading phenomena of Nature; do this, and taboo for him also Mark Antony and Cleopatra among historical personages, and what would be left of him? It was a rude kind of test to propose, and showed a nature harsh as horse-hair in the critic who proposed it. What, pray, would be left of *anybody* on this principle of obliging him to think and feel without reference to these phenomena of Nature, or objects of history, which had first taught him to think and feel and with which, through thousands of hours, the highest actions of his spirit had been associated? And then the universality of some of the topics mentioned! Mark Antony may go, and larks may go, if it is desired; but for all men and all poets is there not a moral necessity based on a physical, why there should be frequency in their thoughts of the stars? Still the criticism held good against Mr. Smith to this extent, that he was detected in a kind of sameness, hardly to be avoided in so young a poet, but which it would need art and greater range of thinking to work off. Accordingly, this feeling, too, was lying in wait for Mr. Smith's second volume. Add the growing antipathy on the part of adherents of the older or direct school of poetry, the school of Scott and other straightforward narrative and lyrical poets—their growing antipathy to this new poetry of mystic raptures and exceptional spiritual states, this poetry all about poets, which seemed to be coming in upon the generation. Mr. Smith was by no means an especial representative of the new school, but he had his place in it. Hence, when Professor Aytoun's jocular phrase, "Spasmodic Poetry," got abroad, and began to serve, with clever people as well as with blockheads, as a convenient substitute for further inquiry into the thing it designated, Mr. Smith was necessarily included in the obloquy. The good-humoured Aytoun was far from having intended this, for he was one of Smith's most familiar Edinburgh friends.

Notwithstanding this composite accumulation of more or less reasonable critical feeling, lying in wait for Mr. Smith's *City Poems,* the volume, we believe, would have been successful, had there been nothing else. The volume seems to us to be Mr. Smith's best, and a decided advance on the previous volume in respect of art. But, unfortunately, there *was* something else. There may be unreasonable criticism as well as reasonable, criticism motived by ill-nature as well as criticism judiciously severe. However it happened, the publication of Mr. Smith's *City Poems* was the signal for bringing out an onslaught upon his poetry generally, more ill-natured than any critical attack we remember. The cue taken in this attack was not that Mr. Smith was one of the spasmodic poets, nor that he was a poet of few topics, nor that he was a poet of mere flashes and striking passages, but that he was a plagiary. By an elaborate compilation of parallel passages, which it must have taken the critic days and nights to prepare, the attempt was made to prove that every passage, line, or phrase in Mr. Smith's poems in which there was anything notable was a theft from some other poet, more or less disguised. Shakespeare, Milton, Wordsworth, Tennyson, with a dozen other well-known poets, were produced, chapter and verse, as his creditors for this or that; and, above all, a certain Cyril Tourneur, known to the antiquaries in our literature, was dug up from his grave, poor fellow, and confronted with his alleged appropriator. There was such evident animosity in the onslaught that it overleaped itself. None but the most leathery-minded person could have believed, if he had read a page of Mr. Smith's poems, that they or any poems like them could, by *à priori* possibility, have been composed on the principle put forward by the critic. As passage after

passage in any page of Milton might be decomposed, by the help of Todd's notes, into flakes from previous authors, so, in perhaps two per cent of the asserted cases of plagiarism by Mr. Smith, it was proved that he may have had recollections of the transmitted diction of previous poets. But there was nothing more. We have never yet met a competent reader of the criticism that thought there was anything more in it, and that did not speak of it with indignation. But the criticism appeared in a place of authority, and the public is a great sheep in these matters. Not from this cause alone, but from this cause in co-operation with others, Mr. Smith's *City Poems* did not secure nearly the amount of attention that was to be expected. Nay more, when, after four years of silence, Mr. Smith produced his little epic or idyll, called *Edwin of Deira,* it still seemed as if the public were under a reaction of feeling against him. He had thrown a great deal of care into this romance of Northumbria in the time of the Heptarchy; and the poem, if without the surprising flashes of its predecessors, is a most sunny and delightful piece of fantasia. Unfortunately, it came in the wake of Tennyson's *Idylls of the King,* and, being in blank verse and nearly coeval in its subject, seemed a resonance of *them.* Yet it had been in great part written before they were even announced.

Edwin of Deira (1861) was, with the exception of stray pieces in periodicals, the last of Mr. Smith's productions in the form of verse. Prose-writing, in which he had long been expert, and which he had practised in periodicals from the time of his coming to Edinburgh, became now his chief occupation. There were reasons for this, apart from his own inclination, in the comparative indifference with which his last poems had been received, taken in connexion with circumstances which made such indifference inconvenient. He had been for some years married—his wife being a lady of the Highland family of the Macdonalds of Skye, tracing their descent from the famous Flora Macdonald. A new world of delightful relationships was opened out to him by this marriage—periodical visits in the autumn-holidays to the island of Skye, and an acquaintanceship, by adoption, with half the Highlands. But, with a little family growing up around him, for the wants of which the salary for his Secretaryship to the University was not sufficient, there were calls upon him, when his poetry would not yield the required supplement, for other activity that should. In the easiest way in the world he acknowledged this necessity, and adjusted himself to it. In the evenings, or at leisure hours during the day, his pen was busy, meeting the demands upon it. He was such a silent person, so unobtrusive of himself or his own affairs, that there is probably no one living that could make an inventory of all he did in this way. He wrote anonymously in newspapers—but never, we believe, unworthily, and never on politics; and he contributed, under his name, to various periodicals. Out of his contributions to periodicals there grew a collection of essays, published under the title of *Dreamthorp* (1863). To this were added, partly by a similar course of previous production in periodicals, his two volumes entitled *A Summer in Skye* (1865), and consisting of descriptions of Highland and other Scottish scenery and manners, with interspersed legends and fancies, and his *Alfred Hagart's Household* (1866), a novel of simple elements, the scene of which is laid, with but a slight disguise, in Paisley and Glasgow, and in which one discerns an autobiographic tinge. A separate work of Mr. Smith, preceding the two last, was his edition of Burns, with a memoir, for Mr. Macmillan's Golden Treasury Series. Altogether, the amount of prose-writing which he had added, within a few years, to his three volumes of poems, was very considerable. In much of his prose, it will have been noted, he reverted to that specially Scottish ground, or circuit of themes and interests, which, as we have said, it is natural for resident Scottish writers to abide in, but which in his poetry he had instinctively left, or only let be seen through a general haze. In his *Summer in Skye,* indeed, which is perhaps his principal prose work, there is so much of the Celtic and the legendary, that the work is out of the usual native round, and no less adapted for English than for Scottish readers. It was, in fact, one of the most popular books of the season in both parts of the island.

By his prose-writings Mr. Smith had made for himself so distinct a new reputation, over and above his former one, that he probably felt it to be a matter of mere choice whether he would ever return to verse on any large scale, or go on producing more of those picturesque books of semi-poetical prose which people seemed to prefer. But the old love was strong. There *was* growing in him, we believe, the notion of a new attempt in pure poetry, and some new subject for such an attempt was shaping itself to his vision. But how insatiable is Death, and how capriciously it selects! There was probably no one in or about Edinburgh of any public mark the removal of whom in this year, or in any near term of years, appeared less likely. He had returned, at the close of last autumn, from his usual annual holiday in the Highlands, apparently in the best of health, and ready for his official duties at the University. These duties are somewhat heavier in the opening month of the session than at any other time, owing to the pressure of new matriculations. But Mr. Smith had nearly got through November, and was looking forward to the more leisurely portion of the winter. His house not being *in* Edinburgh, but in the suburb of Wardie, near Granton, on the Frith of Forth, he had a longish walk to the University in the mornings, but might, if he chose, exchange it for a few minutes of railway. One day he was unable to come. It was a cold, bronchitis, or something of that sort, and nothing serious was imagined. But it came to be diphtheria, and the diphtheria ended in typhus, and for weeks there was the greatest anxiety. He rallied so far, and passed his thirty-

sixth birthday, the last day of the year. But the hope was vain. On the morning of the 5th of January, 1867—at the beginning of that strange weather of snow-storm and fog for which the opening of 1867 will be long remembered—this too-short life came to a close.

Those who have in their minds a certain ideal of the look and physical appearance to be expected in poets, who fancy them as persons all weirdly, ecstatic, and wind-blown, would have had their ideal somewhat discomposed by their first sight of Alexander Smith. Even people who had no such ideal for all cases, but who had formed a preconception from Mr. Smith's early poems, found in him, when they came to know him, a very different sort of being from what they had pictured. He had a full sense of the fun of this himself. A tight-built, modest youth of middle stature, or nearer the short than the tall, with lightish-brown hair worn close, a round but nowise singular head, a placid and shrewd expression of face, and a distinct but not disagreeable cast in one of his eyes—such was the Alexander Smith one saw just after he had become famous. Latterly he had become stouter about the shoulders, and more manly-looking, with a tendency to baldness over the forehead, which gave a better impression of mental power. But the most remarkable thing about him was his wonderful quietness of demeanour. There was never a quieter man, one who could sit longer with others and obtrude himself less. People meeting him casually complained of this, and wanted more conversation, more of the poet. They might try him on this tack and that, but he foiled them, listening pleasantly to what was said, but keeping his own contributions to a minimum. When he was really known, one came to like this quietness as but the social form of a mind of the most perfect good sense, incapable of flummery or pretence, and sagacious in taking the measure of persons and things around it, but kindly-humorous and acquiescent rather than explosive or aggressive. There was something even formidable in this power of at least never, in the midst of other people's rubbish, saying anything that was silly or untrue. With his familiar friends, however, in a walk or in a snug room, he was, though still far from loquacious, chatty enough. He talked racily and simply, but generally with a flavour of shrewdness and humour. "So-and-so," he would say, "is the finest fellow in the world," and I "never come away from him without feeling rebuked by the contemplation of so lofty a standard; but then, you know, he's a great ass." Or, again, speaking of the reaction that had taken place against his own poetry, and of the ferocious onslaught upon him as a plagiary which had so much to do with this reaction, "One does feel these things," he said, "and it is queer to come out in the sunlight and walk along the street after you have read such a review of your book; but I find that all such chagrins pass off in exactly twenty-four hours." His fancy apparently was that every rotation of the earth brings things round again to the *status quo*. Nor was this mere talk. As the first sudden burst of applauses had never turned his head, so the contrary blast had no more than a twenty-four hours' effect upon his equanimity. He would have gone on to the end quietly, modestly, and like a man of the soundest sense.

Out of this very fact of Smith's personal quietness as a man, there might be evolved a criticism of his poetry more instructive, perhaps, than any that has yet been applied to it. Has not the notion been gaining ground of late that the poetry which the world most needs is such poetry as is the translation into imaginary forms of a mind itself tumultuous, rebellious, angry with the fierce seeds of future novelties, and feeling forward into the philosophy that may or may not be coming? In the past we have Shelley as an instance, and perhaps in the last new recognition of a poet in England this feeling has had part. One might convert this into a retrospective question respecting the poetry of Alexander Smith. Although the poets he himself conceives and describes in his poetry are beings of the kind mentioned, he does not seem to have been such a poet himself. Whatever storms of spirit he may have gone through, he had worked himself well through them, and nobody was troubled with any accounts of them. His opinions on all high matters had come, we daresay, to be very much those of his intellectual compeers of the present time, but he was a propagandist of no one or two speculations, and brandished no peculiar lance. Well, what of that? May we not fall back on the older idea of the poet, represented in the instance of Keats, and in still higher instances beyond him, which recognises in him one kind of poetic power, at all events, as lodged in a special organ, the connexions of which with the personal life of the poet, his philosophy and worldly manner, are too recondite to be easily traced? Are there not artists upon whom the power comes only when they are at their easel? Without denying that there may be artists of another kind, may we not regard Alexander Smith, in whose personal demeanour there was no little of tumult, and in whom quietness and modest shrewdness were the qualities that most endeared him to those about him, as an artist of a kind known of old, and for which there is still room? . . . .

Thomas Brisbane (essay date 1869)

SOURCE: "In Edinburgh," in *The Early Years of Alexander Smith*, Hodder & Stoughton, 1869, pp. 177-203.

[*In the following excerpt, Brisbane recounts the effects that criticism—particularly W. E. Aytoun's satire* Firmilian—*had on Smith both professionally and personally.*]

Elizabeth Barrett Browning on Smith, in an 1853 letter to Mr. Westwood:

Alexander Smith I know by copious extracts in reviews, and by some MSS. once sent to us by friends and readers. Judging from those he must be set down as a true poet in opulence of imagery, but defective, so far (he is said to be very young) in the intellectual part of poetry. His images are flowers thrown to him by the gods, beautiful and fragrant, but having no root either in Enna or Olympus. There's no unity and holding together, no reality properly so called, no thinking of any kind. I hear that Alfred Tennyson says of him: 'He has fancy without imagination.' Still, it is difficult to say at the dawn what may be written at noon. Certainly he is very rich and full of colour; nothing is more surprising to me than his favourable reception with the critics. I should have thought that his very merits would be against him.

Elizabeth Barrett Browning, in The Letters of Elizabeth Barrett Browning, Vol II, *edited by Frederic G. Kenyon, Smith, Elder, and Company, 1898.*

But as [Alexander Smith and I] were now both busily engaged in the work to which we had respectively devoted ourselves, our correspondence by letter became gradually less frequent; and I had not been favoured with an epistle from him for some considerable time, when the following, which explains itself, came to hand:—

MY DEAR BRISBANE,

I know I have acted very badly in not writing earlier; but for my sin I must plead, in extenuation, a multitude of good intentions and, fortunately, some little business. I have been arranging matters for a certain great event, which has, I confess, knocked all minor things out of my head. The wedding takes place on Monday first. To you and to all other friends of my bachelorhood I wave a farewell, and trust that in that other life I may know you all again.

I have but little news. I am in press again. This time my publishers are the Macmillans of Cambridge, who give me £250 for the book, the copyright to remain with me. When they make the same amount of profit, the profits are to be equally divided, so that if the thing is at all a success in a commercial point of view, I will gain more by it. I expect £100 or £50 from America also. The people who printed the *Life Drama* have been written on the subject, and I expect an answer soon. I think Macmillan's offer extremely liberal; and taking the time I have been in Edinburgh, in which the greater portion of the work has been done, and the little windfalls of money for other literary work, . . . in conjunction with my salary at college, there is a tolerable prospect that, with thriftiness and economy, Flora and I will be comfortable enough.

I can't tell you how strangely I feel in my present circumstances. Happy, of course; but happy with a kind or degree of fear and trembling at the heart of it that makes it more intense, while it troubles and shakes it. What the future is I do not know; and I cannot command it. When a man is alone, he does not care much: with the earth beneath his feet, the sky above his head, and a decent kind of conscience in him, he scrambles along pretty jollily; but when another nature is bound up with his own—who must accept the same fate, whether of bliss or bale, smile in the same sunshine, bow the head to the same storm of driving rain—why it *does* make one feel a little anxious. But hang it!—these ghosts ought to slink into their graves. What have *they* to do showing their empty sides and ugly faces among orange blossoms and the silver voices of the marriage bells?

I am sorry that our plans will not allow us to come round by Inverness, so that we shall not have the pleasure of seeing you, as I at one time hoped. We leave Skye on Tuesday by the steamer, and mean to stay a few days at Oban, and reach Edinburgh on Friday or Saturday night. F. has never been at the Trossachs, and I expect great delight in a trip there when the summer session closes; and I have also a desire to establish myself for some few weeks at Strone or Kilmun. Is there any chance of your being in Edinburgh soon?—With best wishes, I remain, yours affectionately,

A. SMITH.

His marriage, referred to in the above letter, took place in the spring of 1857. The lady to whom he was then united was Miss Flora Macdonald, daughter of Mr. Macdonald, of Ord, Skye, and related in blood to the heroine of that name; and connected also with Horatio Maculloch, the painter, between whom and Smith a very cordial friendship existed.

In the course of little more than a year after his marriage, he removed from Edinburgh to sweet Gesto Villa, at Wardie, near Granton, where on two occasions I had the pleasure of lodging over a night with him.

The above letter also makes reference to the publication of **City Poems** this same year. This, though to discerning readers the best of all Mr. Smith's poetical works, did not meet with such success as his first volume. From various causes the tide of popular sentiment had now ceased to run so strongly in his favour as it had once done. He had been accused of the sin of extensive plagiarism by some, and condemned by others as too sensational.

To the latter charge fullest expression was given in a satirical poem written by Professor Aytoun, and pub-lished in 1855, under the title—*Firmilian: a Spasmodic Tragedy, by T. Percy Jones*. That work proved a decided hit: it burst like a bomb in the circle of literature, and executed considerable damage on the reputation of several poets. This it did more, perhaps, on the ground of its being well-timed, than because of intrinsic poetic worth. It was certainly, however, characterized by great pungency and superlative smartness, in exposing what it termed the "spasmodic" school of poetry to unsparing ridicule. And no one in reading it could fail to perceive that Gilfillian, as a critic, and Bailey, Dobell, and Smith, as poets, were the chief *dramatis personæ;* while Carlyle and Ruskin, as prose writers, did not entirely escape being represented.

Smith was wont to laugh heartily over several passages of this book which most directly referred to himself; always spoke of it as a production of true genius, and never bore any malicious grudge against its author. But, at the same time, he did not altogether enjoy its allusions to himself: indeed, no man in his circumstances could do so. Nothing so prejudices the mass of men against a public man or author as, though excessive, deserved, and so successful, ridicule. And as this was achieved in *Firmilian* with superlative cleverness, public sentiment which had, perhaps, become already sated with its own over-rapturous applause at **A Life Drama,** began to look shy at its author.

While thus his popularity had commenced to decline, the other less just, and even less scrupulous and unmerciful attack upon his fame, told with far more effect than it would otherwise have done. The charge of plagiarism could happily be answered with the common weapon of fair argument, and not a few pens voluntarily fought powerfully thus in Smith's defence. While Shirley Brooks, in a smart characteristic paper in *Punch,* did him, perhaps, fully as much service as any or all others. Many generous friends, also, from different quarters, wrote consolingly and encouragingly to him private letters of assurance that this was only a passing cloud of infamy which would soon pass away.

The ridicule of *Firmilian,* however, though seemingly less harmless, could not be so well answered—first, from its very nature; and, further, because unfortunately it was in a good measure deserved;—and the felicitously conceived nickname of "Spasmodic" was a barbed arrow which, hitting, stuck. Smith bore this double attack with surprising equanimity and great fortitude, while it both injured him and did him good. Commercially, it marred the sale of his books, and so pecuniarily he suffered by it; while, at the same time, it sobered his poetic genius, and purged it of the sins of his youth. His own spirit had, indeed, of itself begun to recoil against the spasmodic character of his first book, but the chastising hand of Aytoun confirmed his repentance. Nor was he the only one who profited by *Firmilian*—that, though an unmerciful, was a well-timed and most salutary satire, which laughed out of popular favour a very unwholesome kind of poetry which had already received too much countenance, and was corrupting the literature of our age and country. The rising generation of poets were rapidly renouncing the simplicity of nature, and, if not spasmodic, were at least too sensational. Genius seemed too often intoxicated, or fevered, rather than inspired. The muse of song, forsaking ordinary human life, endeavoured to lure us away to a shadowy mist-magnifying land bordering on the realms of spiritual existence, where men that were not men, and women who were not women, but male and female demi-gods, or semi-demons—a mind-begotten hybrid race—now strutted rather than walked the stage of life, mouthing "great swelling words of vanity;" and anon endeavoured to scale the heavens and talk with the celestials familiarly as equals; or to dive into the abysmal depths of the nether world, where their eyes lighted up with an unusual kindly look. The life depicted in these poets' pages had neither the dignity of tragedy nor the sprightliness of pantomime; it often, however, partook more of the nature of the latter than of the former; was pantomime with pantaloon and clown,—the most human elements, after all, of that species of performance, left out. All the stars in the poetical firmament were spiritively threatening to become comets. To shine seemed nothing; to glare was grand. What matters might have come to under these pigmy Miltons and Dantes it is hard to say, had not Aytoun and others called them at length to a more sober mood.

Unfortunately, however, *Firmilian* happened to hit most heavily those who had transgressed least—Gilfillian and Smith. Aytoun seemed to reserve all his sharpest strokes for his own country-men. Gilfillian, especially, was both most cruelly and unjustly dealt with: while of Smith it might be said that he was not only the youngest and least guilty of the whole school, but the first, besides, who himself saw his error and resolved to abandon it. But treated as he was, he showed true nobleness of character in entertaining at the time no feelings of animosity towards his merciless reprover. And it is very pleasant indeed to read in his essay on "Sydney Dobell," published among *Last Leaves,* with how quiet and gentle a spirit he could, ten years afterwards, refer to *Firmilian*—its influence and its author; while it is not less pleasant to know that Aytoun, not very long after he so unsparingly lashed the author of *A Life Drama,* extended towards him a most generous, friendly hand, introducing him to the pages of *Blackwood,* and that a cordial friendship existed between them till the one followed the other with an interval of only a few months to the quiet grave.

City Poems, which appears to be presently out of print, has, if we mistake not, been gradually rising in public estimation, and is destined to rise still higher, and take the very first place among all Smith's poetical works. After its publication, he immediately devoted himself to the production of a historical poem, *Edwin of Deira*. But misfortune still followed him; for though he spent four years in its composition, Alfred Tennyson's *Idylls of the King*—a kindred subject—appeared before its publication, and so rendered Smith again liable to the suspicion of imitation, besides bringing him into unfortunate comparison with the laureate. Not that there were any genuine or great grounds for such comparison, however, being made; for the two works bear little or no resemblance to each other. Tennyson's is much the larger of the two poems, there is greater variety of character also in it, and he takes a firmer hold of his subject, and gives to it more depth and compactness; but Smith's **Edwin** sparkles more with gems than the *Idylls* do. But there was only occasion for comparison in the sequence of the two works—nothing more. And, after all, the want of acceptance by the public in Smith's case, did not, perhaps, result so much from the publication of Tennyson's book at this time, as from the fact that public favour had meanwhile, for a season at least, left him as a poet. It is very questionable, indeed, if at this period of his career any poem published by Smith would have met with a greater sale than **Edwin** did; unless it had been a veritable *Paradise Lost.* The work is not without great intrinsic merits. It is by far the most classical in construction and composition of all his poems. It breathes also a more healthy spirit than of any them. But in the literary as well as the physical world, when the tide recedes a man must just patiently wait its return. It was, however, perhaps, so far unfortunate that **Edwin of Deira,** notwithstanding all its merits, was, for immediate wide acceptance by the public, rather too unlike Mr. Smith's previous poetical productions. Those who had admired his earlier volumes so highly, could not all be expected to admire this one, in which the most peculiar traits of his original genius had almost entirely disappeared. But, further, notwithstanding its great merits, it does not, on the whole, equal *City Poems,* in poetic value. The most valuable thing in **Edwin of Deira** was the promise which it gave of what the author might yet have done, in this, to him, new domain of poesy, had years and leisure been allowed him. With such promise it was very rich indeed. That is an article in literature, however, which the general public have neither much discernment to perceive nor inclination to pay for. And it is still more to be regretted that neither his critics nor himself seemed to perceive this very clearly. So, as he neither gained pecuniarily, nor appeared to increase his fame by the publication of this book, he became, it is to be feared, a little disheartened—lost some measure of the passionate love for his harp which he once felt, and immediately turned his attention more to prose composition. **Edwin of Deira** was his last poetic production of any considerable length. He never abandoned poetry, however; nor could he do so,—

For it was his nature
To blossom into song, as 'tis a tree's
To leaf itself in April.

But his future poetical productions were confined to small pieces for the magazines, with the exception of a poem on **"Edinburgh"** which he had on hand, and which had only progressed a short way, when he died.

His chief prose work is **Dreamthorp,** a volume of essays having few equals in the English language. In it he celebrates the praises of the country, as in his poems he had done those of the town. It is by this volume that he will live longest as an exquisite prose writer, and on it his fame in that department of literature will mainly depend. It gained for him the name of Essayist.

In 1865 he published, next, *A Summer in Skye,* two volumes of very racy and graphic sketching of natural scenery and men and manners, which afford very pleasant reading. The work, however, is slightly marred in unity by extraneous matter at the beginning and close. These two parts constitute excrescences which it is desirable may be removed from future editions of this otherwise exquisite work.

In the same year also he edited an edition of Burns for Macmillan, with a memoir and glossary; and continued, from month to month to supply "Good Words" with his only prose tale, entitled *Alfred Hagart's Household,* which has since been published in a separate form in two volumes.

Numerous smaller articles from his pen had meantime graced the columns of several newspapers and the pages of sundry magazines and Encyclopedias. Some of the magazine articles have, since his death, been reprinted in the volume entitled **Last Leaves**. These works greatly increased his literary reputation. As a prose writer, in fact, he had now become a great and growing favourite with the public, and as a genial and wise moralist he was rapidly rising to a first place among British essayists. But the work performed by him during the last two years had been too great for any man regularly occupied, as he was, in an office daily from ten o'clock a.m. till four o'clock p.m.; and consequently, he began to suffer from an over-wrought brain. Indeed, during the greater part of these two years he was labouring under such a malady, without knowing what ailed him, or taking the only means of cure for this distemper—entire mental rest. As evidence of this, it is very painful now to read such reflections as the following in the second volume of *A Summer in Skye*:—"When I came up here a month or two ago, I was tired, jaded, ill at ease; I put spots in the sun, I flecked the loveliest blue of summer sky with bars of darkness; I felt the weight of the weary hours. Each morning called me as a slave-driver calls his slave. In sleep there was no refreshment; for in dream the weary day repeated itself yet

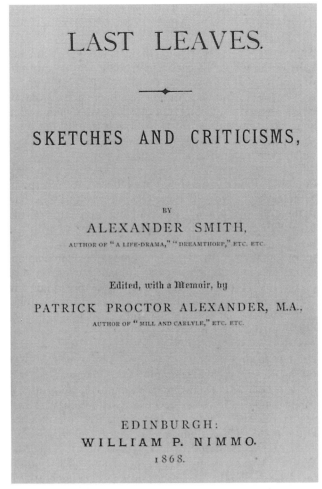

LAST LEAVES.

SKETCHES AND CRITICISMS,

BY

ALEXANDER SMITH,

AUTHOR OF "A LIFE-DRAMA," "DREAMTHORP," ETC. ETC.

Edited, with a Memoir, by

PATRICK PROCTOR ALEXANDER, M.A.,

AUTHOR OF "MILL AND CARLYLE," ETC. ETC.

EDINBURGH:
WILLIAM P. NIMMO.
1868.

Title page from a first edition of Smith's Last Leaves.

more wearily. I was nervous, apprehensive of evil, irritable—ill in fact." (p. 214). During all the following year, he continued more or less in this melancholy condition, and all the while was doing more mental work than previously. Surely none of his friends who knew this, but because he looked rosy all the while, "rather fleered at than sympathised with him," "thinking his complaint some form of mere hypochondria," had ever felt themselves the baneful effects of an exhausted brain. How one now wishes he had earlier told all to some experienced physician. For two years his holidays only tended to delay the fatal hour. It was a year of entire, and not two months of partial, rest he needed. At length the crisis came. And on November 20, 1866, he lay down upon his bed. His illness, which had now assumed the form of gastric fever, became complicated with diphtheria, and, after deceitful symptoms of recovery, lapsed into typhoid fever; so gradually sinking under the baneful influences of these malignant maladies, despite the skill of the best of the far-famed physicians of the Scottish capital, and the most assiduous care of those who loved him most, he breathed, at length, his last breath, in his house at Wardie, at nine o'clock on the morning of 5th, January, 1867, at the age of thirty-seven years and four days.

The news of his early death affected with unusual sorrow the whole literary and reading world. But still deeper far was he mourned by his relatives and numerous personal friends; for he had been a truly good, genial, generous, loving and most loveable man—such a friend as in this world is too rarely found, but once found can never be forgotten, and though lost by death must ever be missed and mourned.

On 10th January his body was borne to Warriston cemetery by sorrowing bereaved ones; and as they laid it there in the grave, "the cold but rich light of the early sunset seemed in melancholy harmony with the last scene of his bright and brief career;" but brief as, indeed, that career was, a sable company gathered again, about two months afterwards, around that grave, told of a briefer still, as they laid beside the father the remains of his first-born and much loved little daughter, of whose nativity he had sung most touchingly in his exquisite lyric of "Blaavin."

His last resting-place is now marked by a memorial of loving hearts. In the beginning of 1868, was erected there a beautiful Runic cross monument, with appropriate embellishments, the design of which was furnished as a tribute of affection by Mr. James Drummond, R.S.A., and containing a medallion likeness of the departed, which was executed by Mr. William Brodie, sculptor, another friend. This monument bears the simple inscription, "Alexander Smith, Poet and Essayist. Erected by some of his personal friends."

But, after all, his noblest monument is that which he himself erected—his life. Seldom if ever, indeed, has one so eminently gifted with a poetic temperament and genius, manifested such self-government, or lived a life so well balanced, beautiful, and blameless. That life is the best lesson he has taught us. It is a valuable legacy to all, but especially to aspiring young men and all candidates in literature. May many such profit by it!

Stephen Henry Thayer (essay date 1891)

SOURCE: "Alexander Smith," in *The Andover Review*, Vol. 15, No. LXXXVI, February, 1891, pp. 163-72.

[*Here, Thayer chronicles the development of maturity in Smith's writing, from his first labeling as a spasmodic poet, to the complex issues addressed in his essays.*]

When rare men die young, such as mark their way with presagings of genius, we cherish their work as we do the visions of the upland, while yet are denied to us the grander reaches from mountain heights. Much as we prize the impulse of these potential minds, age alone gives to their thought that ripe distinction and maturity which shall make them indisputable masters; hints of power, of resources, open glimpses of a scope and breadth that make us marvel at what might be the crowning fruition. There are instances of such genius, minds that have flashed as meteors across the literary sky, and then, without warning, have left us; tentative minds, yet, as signals, emitting such fire and beauty as make the world sad at the untimely taking off. Of this class, circumstances have much to do with the degree of brilliancy and attainment by which they are recognized. Byron, through the intensity of his individual traits, touched a popular chord, and suddenly rose to almost unexampled recognition. He was enabled through the glitter of his personality, and through the distinguishing features of his poetic creations, to draw the eyes of the reading world to himself; a certain audacious defiance allied to an abnormal dramatic, if not heroic attitude gave Byron a wide fame, and a perilous eminence. Keats and Shelley, with minds of finer grain, of more delicately poetic fibre, and of more exacting artistic feeling and spirit, lived and died with no such recognition or favor from the common voice; for the poetry of these, unlike Byron's, had but few readers while yet they lived. The three were contemporaneous, and all died young; Keats very young, misinterpreted, unsung, and broken-hearted. Byron's powers and tendency, it may be said, exemplified a nearer approach to maturity than did those of Shelley or Keats, but the three, respectively, left alike traces of marvelous poetic quality and distinction.

It is not, therefore, fair always to classify or to discriminate between writers by their limited and often fragmentary work, but by their high initiatory marks, which point unerringly to their possible range of thought and quality of genius. There are but few of such as these named whom the world can so confidently appropriate, but there is a larger group of writers (we speak of English authors) familiar to our minds, who, though having fallen short in promise, have yet, dying young, left some things so excellent and beautiful that men reverently cherish their excellence and beauty; of these, Alexander Smith is a noble, even an exceptionally noble example. Born and bred to laborious conditions, he won not only recognition, but an unmistakably eminent place in human letters. We need not discuss the determination and tendency of the will to master mean conditions and carve out the career that Nature forecasts in her endowments, nor need we dwell on the often-repeated experience of men with rare gifts, whom untoward fate has seemed to especially confront and contravene with harassment and defeat, for we never could, by any general survey, establish an order or theory that would meet, or adequately account for, vagaries and vicissitudes of this nature, nor that would challenge contradiction.

Alexander Smith's life had an interior conflict beyond any theory of accountability or compensations, and furnishes an instance of pathetic, poignant solicitude seldom experienced by one whose ambition was so free from offense, and whose nature and life were so rich in pure incentive and spirit. Art is an exacting mentor, and a noble stimulus; beauty and truth dwell in its temples; it has a religion of its own, and a service, as fitting as ever had creed, and it also bestows a freedom as wide as the dispensation of love itself. There never was artist or poet whosoever who did not feel need of its consecrating truth, though he might be a truant from its laws, defying their gentle insistence. Why should not the artistic sense have an excellence and righteousness of its own? The art precepts of a Ruskin, feeling, as they often did, tentatively and mistakingly for the right, yet breathing a loyalty unquestioned, give out an impulse toward rectitude in the religion of art as strenuous as ever a Milton's toward Puritanism. It was a misfortune of Alexander Smith that while his sensitive nature lent all its delicacy of feeling and soul-instinct to poetic impulse and poetic imagery, that it yet lacked that nice adjustment of this delicacy and this instinct in the assimilation of his poetic imagery to his creations, and in the fine blending of true tone and expression. It was this inaptitude, allied to a high ambition, bent on attaining what proved with him mostly unattainable, that wrought in his life, somewhat shattered in health as it was, a kind of perpetual heart-break, a tragic feeling of loss and bitterness akin to the deepest sadness, infinitely deeper than one might feel at a trick of fortune which should play him false, and which he might easily lay at the world's door; all the sentiment of his being, every fibre and pulsation seemed ready to add to the song he would sing, but yet, the ear, the touch, were below the inward gift, and made but partial response to the high spirit that felt it all. It is admitted by most who are familiar with the poetry of Alexander Smith that in the art and beauty of modulation, his untrained imagination was lacking in sure and effective balance, and that he, himself, felt keenly this blemish; these faulty, half utterances hindered and fettered his spirit. At first he did not surrender, he was brave; one has a right to test the full measure of faith which he may have in himself, to master the truth in his art; is it not as creditable in its way as to triumph, or essay to triumph, in any noble undertaking? The voice of the critics, the judgment of his fellow-craftsmen, when against him, spurred him, and served as a challenge; he was balked and thwarted, but, at first, not downcast; he knew he was a poet, as so many have known before and since. Can we not conceive that Carlyle must have felt to touch the harp of song more than once, with his great, deep nature, enrapt by the tides and swells of poetic emotion? Do we think it can be any consolation to the heart of him

who, steeped in poetry, breaks the silence only to find, alas, that there are lawless renderings of the rhythmic minstrelsy, when he knows that, at least, he has it *in* him? If it were immaturity only with Alexander Smith, his early volume, entitled **A Life Drama and Other Poems,** exhibited this, indeed, both in thought and art, but it exhibited more: there was a vagrant abandon of expression in his poetry, a persistent extravagance in the heedless huddling of thoughts and fancies, that could not have failed, as it did not, to challenge the critical and public taste, especially at a time when the exquisite lyrics of Tennyson, and his perfect idyls, like a magic flute, had captivated the poetic ear of the reading world; such tones as these, rendered so long, and without rival, made the minor songsters self-distrustful and chary. The English taste for the *music* of poetry was highly strung in those days, and felt the jarrings of untutored songsters, as it did, after the genius of Byron, of Shelley, of Keats, Scott, Campbell, and Moore had given to verse an almost matchless rhythmic euphony and beauty. Surely the sensitive nature of Alexander Smith must have felt keen misgivings when it resolved to cope with such as these.

His first volume was written while yet he labored as designer in one of the mills of Glasgow, but with all of its crudity and lavish exuberance it marked him for a higher place, and he was soon chosen Secretary of the Edinburgh University. The faults that appeared in this volume were not without precedent; do we forget "Endymion" of Keats, which was borne down by excess of classic lore and garment, and by an unrestrained wealth of imagery, the cruel condemnation of which broke his shattered life? Alexander Smith read the verdict of the critics, and, in a lesser degree than Keats, felt the burden of disappointment weighing his spirit down; at twenty-three years of age, however, men brought to sudden despair yet feel the warmth and see the light of morning suns. The day is mostly before them, and the buffer of their pride happily shields them from the lingering darkness and weariness of spirit which age brings. This frailty of health, of which I have intimated, had not, in this earlier period, asserted its mastery; unlike Keats and others who have lost their vital physical strength in the bloom of early manhood, Alexander Smith had not yet reached this crisis of his life; there was enough of success in his first poetic venture, and enough of flame and courage in his yet undaunted nature, to buoy his hope in a coming good fortune, which so often waits on faith and untiring industry. The public knew of him, the critics were ready to do him justice, the inexpressible longings which are only half breathed in the written song gave wings to his native purpose, and inspired his ardent love for poetry with a resolute will; four years only intervened between the coming of the first and second volume of his verse, four years of secret, tireless work, but work bound in love. During these he had written various prose essays; he had lost somewhat in health, and he had lavished his best resources on this new poetic advent, this volume entitled *City Poems.* Now he hoped for ample recognition, and not without encouragement. The reviewers, many of them, broke forth in almost unstinted praise. "Since Tennyson," said the *Literary Gazette,* "no poet has come before the public with the same promise as the author of this volume." The *Spectator* said: "It is to the earlier works of Keats and Shelley alone, that we can look for a counterpart in richness of fancy and force of expression." The *Westminster Review* added: "There is not a page of this volume on which we cannot find some Shakespearian felicity of expression, or some striking simile." And still another said: "Nearly every page is studded with striking metaphors." Yet, underlying these fair sayings, there seemed to lurk a negative verdict, the more extended reviews made marked qualifications, and there came from Tennyson himself a word that must have cast a heavy shadow over the young poet's dream. The laureate said that "Alexander Smith's poems show fancy, but not imagination." The quick sensibilities of his nature must have deeply felt these words, for who could better judge? And Tennyson was right. Simile, paradox, bold metaphor, quick invention, all children of a luxuriant fancy, were his in their wealth of vivid coloring, but there yet lacked a sustained spiritual imagination in carrying forward and amplifying in epic thought and dignity the higher order of creative verse. Striking passages there are in these poems, passages that easily, at first, arrest the attention, and captivate the sentiment of the reader, but a more critical study betrays marked unevenness; there is frequent and sudden falling away in movement and in quality; strained and unique fancies, introduced, lower the general motive and smite the nice, inward ear with a sense of incongruity. It is an instance of loose reins given to the wanton tricks of fancy, and another instance, resulting therefrom, of poetry overweighted with imagery, and thereby failing to answer the gentle, yet exacting demand of true art,— an art which holds the poet to the primal consideration of an harmonious entirety, and to the equally important condition of harmony in the parts. The author of *City Poems,* in spite of the reviewers, felt the sting of failure; his volume neither established nor confirmed its author as one of the choice few in the circle of English poets. The verdict was never reversed; it seems, now, to stand unshaken after thirty years. The effect wore on the author: the severe tension of feeling that such disheartenment left weighed on his sensitive nature; ill health came, stealthily, yet surely; he had written some essays, but they had given him but little fame. As the shadows seemed to gather, and he realized that the recognition for which he had labored and waited was as far remote from his grasp as ever, without tangible motive or aim, but simply as a passing consolation, he commenced a series of essays while, part of the time, journeying, if haply he might regain his lost strength. He alone who has met with such an

experience as this can enter into sympathy with the life that has passed through it. Possessed of one of the most exquisitely sensitive poetic temperaments, spurred by a noble ambition, raised by his own force of will and character, and the motives which they fostered, from a mean estate to one of comparative prominence wherein he could gain somewhat of the tuition and training which his mind needed; flushed with an aspiration and a promise which stirred within him visions of name and eminence in letters, and dreams of a niche in the temple of the immortals, he alone, I fancy, who has thus thought, with reason, to achieve an enviable place among men, and then feels his hold loosen, and himself fading from the world's sight, can participate in the bitterness of such an one as Alexander Smith, while, in utter misgiving, he breathed out the sweet, inimitable beauty and pathos that permeates, like a fine atmosphere, the spirit and sentiment of his prose poems in *Dreamthorp*.

Careless of repute now, indifferent to the listless public, bent only on disclosing to his own heart the exaltations, the reveries, that may raise him above sorrowings for a lost cause, he at last breathes a new freedom. With death not far away, he pours a wealth and warmth of spirit in this magic prose of his that gains for him all that, unseeking now, he had let slip as beyond him.

Dreamthorp, the half soliloquies, the unrestrained musings of a rich, disenthralled, idealized nature, heedless of praise or blame, won, without concern or purpose of its author, the now uncoveted prize, and made him famous in the world. No more notable essays in this rare vein, wherein the writer has made his reader a confidant, has told him of his foibles and weaknesses, of his fleeting moods and meditations, of his loves and aversions, of his vagrant delights and fancies, of a hundred and one impelling feelings and episodes, of reflections and observations that bear, with charming spirit and sincerity, on the motives and exigencies of human conduct and life, have been published since Lamb's "Elia," or Leigh Hunt's "Lear," and they gained, if anything, advantage over these, that they were doubly endowed with a beauty of imagery, a poetic flavor, and a philosophic elevation beyond either Lamb's or Hunt's.

This vein in prose writing I know, in this reportorial age, is out of date; the scientific and the journalistic vogues, in this latter day, for the time effectually kill prose-poetry in Human Letters. We classify our facts with nimble expertness, but seldom write our hearts. The eye and ear have great appetites, analysis stifles the emotion; we are detectives and epitomizers. We revel in Egyptology, anthropology, chronology, and all the ologies that can be tortured into scientific or metaphysical speculation, but think ourselves childish, if for an instant we pause to touch the springs of human sympathy, or interpret the impulses of emotive thought, save in our novels.

Irving is now old-fashioned; that fine humor which so leisurely plays through the mesh of his delightful romanticism has lost caste with the present race of astringent thinkers and writers. Every sentence takes deadly aim to-day; the expert, the specialist, is uppermost, and so it comes about that such as Lamb, Irving, and Alexander Smith are dusty; literature has run to facts, speculations, or polemics; positivism, agnosticism, and prehistoric research successively cudgel our tired brains. Modern society, with its prevailing mezzotints and neutralities in thought and enthusiasms, with its half-beliefs and relaxing sentiment, is compromising our story-tellers, while poetry is doing its best to smother itself in vague and misty meanings and metaphors, vexing itself with how not to say a simple thing in pure musical cadence and diction, laboring to wreck itself in words. In the midst of all this, however, and let us say grace for it, comes the voice of the good publisher, crying a "new edition of *Dreamthorp*," even though it be a poor one. Irving, too, is newly dressed, and newly heralded by more than one publisher, and the world is again buying these books. The protester and the publisher have joined hands, and are mutual friends. We have struck a clearing in this wilderness of literature, where the lights of these genuine spirits can impart their warmth once more; and how delightful! We have turned over and over the huge tomes on Evolution, have impaled our thousand darts in the targets of theory and doctrine, and again like thirsty children we return to these springs of feeling, fresh and pure, to authors who give us these human letters, themes personal, heart's-ease, consolations, in lieu of the "Gospel of dirt," as Carlyle dubs the latter-day materialistic writers. The human mind will always crave release, and is sure to call for its wings, sooner or later, and take to the wild wood. Men will love the epistolaries of human experience and of human sympathy better than the skillful thrusts of an intellectual sparring match, and so we are again, with infinite relish, reading *Dreamthorp*. And what is this famous volume? What does it contain? It is as beautiful in tone of thought as a veiled autumn sunset to the eye. This maturity came, in shadow, to Alexander Smith, hastened by the touch and pathos of gathering night; it came, too, with a wealth of fine spiritual consecration as healthful and native as it was tender and impressive; he lived in hearty and intimate relation with all that was noble and genuine. In his prose he possessed a singularly felicitous method, or no method of treatment, which was as fascinating as it was unconventional. He delighted in the roving spirit, blunt truth, and happy egotism of Montaigne, barring his vulgarity. Alexander Smith's thought of the essay was that, "as a literary form, it resembles the lyric, in so far as it is moulded by some central mood, whimsical, serious, or satirical." "Give the mood, and the essay, from

the first sentence to the last, grows around it as the cocoon grows around the silkworm." "The essay-writer is a chartered libertine, and a law unto himself." This is, indeed, the spirit and fashion of the old essayists after whom Alexander Smith patterned, if he patterned after anybody. It is the method and meaning of Montaigne, who wrote equally wise on trifling personal themes, and on the majesty of the king. His frankness was uncompromising, almost abandonment. As another has said, "He is serious on the most trifling subjects, and he trifles with the most serious." He is wayward, surprising, and, to most minds, without any logical sequence, but he is the prince of essayists. Alexander Smith loved him, and there came to his own style and mental vogue much of this famous author's liberty in art. Not all men can veil their seriousness under the guise of a light and airy invention or vein; not all can draw tears of tender sentiment from the eyes of laughter; not all, nay scarcely any writer, can treat great, ideal themes and issues in the same breath with innocent mockery and banter. Seriousness in Alexander Smith's mobile mind seems to go hand in hand with good fellowship and easy familiarity with the reader; he has the art of alternating between opposite and apparently discordant notes, but he has the rare genius of making his finest unity of feeling out of a medley of thought; "perilous moods, perilous art," you will say, but the result is all we have to consider, and when these gifts are native, how picturesque, how wise, withal, how Shakespearian!

Mr. Smith's *Summer in Skye* followed easily the first volume of essays, and possesses qualities suggesting the influence of the earlier and greater work. These were followed, in the year before his death, by an experimental novel, which did not in any way enhance the fame of the author; indeed, the beauty and inspiration so signal in the masterpiece is hardly sustained in his subsequent creation: his genius seemed to strike twelve in *Dreamthorp*.

There is more play for the fancy in prose than in poetry, and Mr. Smith employed it in a less spasmodic, and in a larger, more effective, more impartial way, and with a more sagacious purpose in his essays than in his poetry. His theory of human letters was somewhat unique; he believed that, in this field of literature, "It is not of as much consequence what you say, as how you say it," and, "that the charm of style is indefinable, yet all subduing, just as fine manners are in social life," and, finally, "that style, rather than thought, after all, is the immortal thing in literature." There was an illimitable range open to such a literary creed as these passages indicate; his subjects might be selected from a vast field. He discourses on the **"Importance of a Man to Himself,"** on **"Death and Dying,"** on **"Christmas,"** on **"Books and Gardens,"** on **"A Lark's Flight,"** on **"Vagabonds,"** subjects that are portentous of a wealth of description, of sentiment, of delicate satire, and of idiosyncratic treatment, such as, employed by him, marked his style as individually characteristic and distinguishable with a freshness of conception and a skill of mock egotism quite up to Lamb, and far excelling any contemporary. He was impatient of the monotonous world; he liked to write of odd men deflected from the common mould, and he lamented that they were now so rare to meet. The vagabond, to his mind, is a treat: "He chooses his friends neither for their fine houses nor their rare wines, but for their humors, their goodness of heart, their capacities of making a joke and of seeing one." "Tourists," he says, "would be few, if every inch of soil were drained, ploughed, manured;" personally, "he would detest a world all red and ruled with the ploughshare in spring, all covered with harvest in autumn;" he "desiderates moors and barren places, the copse where you can flush the wood-cock;" he says, "The fresh, rough, heathery part of human nature where the air is freshest, and where the linnets sing, is getting encroached upon by cultivated fields." "Every one is making himself and herself useful; every one is producing something; everybody is clever; everybody is a philanthropist; I don't like it, I love a little eccentricity." "It's high time, it seems to me," he says, "that a moral game law were passed for the preservation of the wild and vagrant feelings of human nature." These sayings of his epitomize the whole tenor of Alexander Smith's essays in **Dreamthorp**. They expose the touch by which his various coloring is made to produce most fascinating studies, wherein the shadings of thought, fancy, and spirit blend and interblend with the sure felicity and unpremeditated beauty of nature's own weaving. The vexing realities of conventional life confront him, he thinks we know it all now: "This world, the planet, is as familiar as the trodden pathway between towns." "Ah me," he adds, "what a world this was to live in two or three centuries ago, when it was getting itself discovered; when the sunset gave up America; when the Arabian Nights were commonplace."

There is a charming bearing of defiant freedom and abandon in the atmosphere and fibre of these prose poems, which give them a unique quality, and provoke a genuine relish for every word of them. There was a time, not very far gone, when these masters in human letters, from Montaigne to Goldsmith, Lamb, Hazlitt, Leigh Hunt, Irving, Alexander Smith, and their kind, commanded the heart of readers. Let us be wise and try if we can reclaim those days. The human mind palls and revolts from too deep and intricate soundings, such as the researches and polemics, that serve mainly to bore through the crustations of earth, or scale immeasurable heights, but have no power that moves and masters human emotions. Evolution has reached a point where a second Darwin is needed to make conjecture anywhere near fact. The Philosophy of Comte is taken in for repairs. The master debater in material and speculative science confesses that at the far edge of his circle he is gazing into an infinitude of veiled possibilities, which, at least, makes the promise and potency of matter still very questionable. Let these all rest and take breath, while this pure literature engages the mind, and brings into play the healthful and refreshing exercise of the more ideal conceptions of thought, so beneficent and wholesome as a foil and refuge to the human intellect in its feverish search among the complexities, perplexities, and problems of existence.

James Ashcroft Noble (essay date 1895)

SOURCE: "Mr. Stevenson's Forerunner," in *The Yellow Book*, Vol. IV, January, 1895, pp. 121-42.

[*In the following essay, Noble examines the autobiographical elements in Smith's prose as well as his use of picturesque detail.*]

For a long time—I can hardly give a number to its years—I have been haunted by a spectre of duty. Of late the visitations of the haunter have recurred with increasing frequency and added persistence of appeal; and though, like Hamlet, I have long dallied with the ghostly behest, like him I am at last compelled to obedience. Ghosts, I believe, have a habit of putting themselves in evidence for the purpose of demanding justice, and my ghost makes no display of originality: in this respect he follows the time-honoured example of his tribe, and if peace of mind is to return to me the exorcism of compliance must needs be uttered.

Emerson in one of his gnomic couplets proclaims his conviction that

"One accent of the Holy Ghost
This heedful world hath never lost"—

a saying which, shorn of its imaginative wings and turned into a pedestrian colloquialism, reads something like this—"What deserves to live the world will not let die." It is a comforting belief, yet there are times when Tennyson's vision of the "fifty seeds," out of which Nature "often brings but one to bear," seems nearer to the common truth of things; and all the world's heedfulness will not exclude Oblivion with her poppies from some spot which should have been sacred to Fame with her amaranth and asphodel. Still there will always be those who will stretch out a hand to repel or evict the intruder—even as in Mr. Watts's noble allegory Love would bar the door against Death—and I would fain play my little part in one not inglorious eviction.

I want to write of a wholly-forgotten prose-man (forgotten, that is, by all save a solitary enthusiast here and there), but I must first speak of a half-forgotten singer. Only people who are on the shady side of middle-age can remember the intense enthusiasm excited by the first work of the young Glasgow poet, Alexander Smith. He had been discovered by that mighty hunter of new poets, the Rev. George Gilfillian; and in the columns of Mr. Gilfillian's journal *The Critic* had been published a number of verses which whetted the appetite of connoisseurs in the early fifties for the maiden volume of a bard who, it was broadly hinted, might be expected to cast Keats into shadow. The prediction was a daring one; but the fifties, like the nineties, were a hey-day of new reputations; and when that brilliant though somewhat amorphous work, *A Life Drama,* saw the light, a good many people, not wholly indiscriminating, were more than half inclined to think that it had been fulfilled. The performance of the new poet, taken as a whole, might be emotionally crude and intellectually ineffective, but its affluence in the matter of striking imagery was amazing, and the critical literature of the day was peppered with quotations of Alexander Smith's "fine passages." Very few people open *A Life Drama* now, though much time is spent over books that are a great deal poorer; but if any reader, curious to know what kind of thing roused the admiration of connoisseurs in the years 1853-4, will spend an hour over the volume, he will come to the conclusion that it is a very remarkable specimen of what may be called the decorated style of poetic architecture.

> An opulent soul
> Dropt in my path like a great cup of gold,
> All rich and rough with stories of the gods.

> The sun is dying like a cloven king
> In his own blood; the while the distant moon,
> Like a pale prophetess that he has wronged,
> Leans eager forward with most hungry eyes
> Watching him bleed to death, and, as he
>   faints,
> She brightens and dilates; revenge complete
> She walks in lonely triumph through the
>   night.

> My drooping sails
> Flap idly 'gainst the mast of my intent;
> I rot upon the waters when my prow
> Should grate the golden isles.

> The bridegroom sea
> Is toying with the shore, his wedded bride,
> And, in the fulness of his marriage joy,
> He decorates her tawny brow with shells,
> Retires a space to see how fair she looks,
> Then, proud, runs up to kiss her.

These and such things as these were what the admiring critics loved to quote, and that they were indeed "fine passages" could not be denied even by people whose tastes were for something a little less gaudy. What was denied by those who were able to preserve some calmness of judgment amid the storm of enthusiasm was that this kind of fineness was the kind that goes to the making of great poetry. The special fine things were ingenious, striking, and sometimes beautiful conceits; they were notable *tours de force* of poetic fancy; but they bore little if any witness to that illuminating revealing imagination of which great poetry is all compact. The young writer's images were happy discoveries of external and accidental resemblances; not revelations of inherent and interpretative affinity. Howsoever graceful and pretty in its way were the figure which likened the sea and the shore to a bridegroom and his bride, it gave no new insight into the daily mystery of the swelling and ebbing tide—no such hint of a fine correspondence between the things of sense and of spirit as is given in the really imaginative utterance of Whitman:

> "Surely whoever speaks to me in the right
>   voice, him or her I shall follow,
> As the water follows the moon silently with
>   fluid steps anywhere around the globe."

What was most characteristic therefore in the verse of Alexander Smith was a winning or arresting quality of fancy; and, in poetry, fancy, though not to be despised, exercises a subordinate sway—"she is the second, not the first." It may be that Smith came to see this: it is more probable that he came to feel it, as a man feels many things which he does not formulate in a clearly outlined thought: at any rate, after the publication of *Edwin of Deira,* his third volume of verse, he ceased almost entirely from song, and chose as his favourite vehicle of expression a literary form in which his special gift counted for more, and carried greater weight of value, than it could ever count or carry in the poems by which he first caught the world's ear.

And yet, curiously enough, while Smith's reputation as a poet still lingers in a faint after-glow, the essays in which he expressed himself with so much more of adequacy and charm cannot be said to have won fame at all. They have had from the first their little circle of ardent admirers, but it has never widened; its circumference has never touched, never even approximated to, the circumference of that larger circle which includes all lovers of letters. To be unacquainted with Lamb or Hunt, Hazlitt or De Quincey, would be recognised as a regrettable limitation of any man's knowledge of English literature: non-acquaintance with Alexander Smith as a writer of prose is felt to be one of those necessary ignorances that can hardly be lamented because they are rendered inevitable by the shortness of life and the multiplicity of contending appeals. The fact that Smith as a poet achieved little more than a *succès d'estime* may have prejudiced his reputation as an essayist; but whatever theory be constructed to account for it, recent literary history presents no more curious instance of utter refusal to really admirable work of deserved recognition and far-reaching fame.

For it must be noted and insisted upon that the essays of Alexander Smith are no mere caviare literature. They have neither the matter nor the manner of coterie performance—the kind of performance which appeals to an acquired sense, and gives to its admirer a certain pleasing consciousness of aloofness from the herd. He is in the true line of descent from the great predecessors just named; and as they were his lineal forerunners, so are Mr. Robert Louis Stevenson and Mr. Richard Le Gallienne his lineal descendants. Indeed the name of Mr. Stevenson suggests, or rather re-suggests, a thought which is more or less familiar to most of us—that in the world of letters there are seasons uncongenial to certain growths of fame which in another spring and autumn might have blossomed and borne much fruit. Only by some such consideration is it possible to account for the curious fact that while *Virginibus Puerisque* and *Men and Books* found their audience at once, *Dreamthorp* and *Last Leaves* are still so largely unknown, and can now only be procured by diligent search of the catalogues of the second-hand booksellers. The fact is all the more curious because Alexander Smith may be roughly described as a Stevenson born out of due time. Roughly, of course, for the individuality of thinking and utterance which is so important in all pure literature is, in the essay, not only important but essential—the one thing needful, apart from which all other things are, comparatively speaking, of no account; and in both Smith's work and Mr. Stevenson's the note of personality always rings clear and true.

Their essays are what the essay in its purest form always tends to be—the prose analogue of the song of self-expression, with its explicit or implicit autobiography, that touches us as we are never touched by external splendours of epic or drama. In Montaigne, the father of the essay, the personal confession has an almost boyish incontinence of frankness: in Smith, as in all the modern men, it has more of reticence and reserve, but it is there all the time; and even when the thought seems most abstract and impersonal the manner of its utterance has not the coldness of disquisition, but the warmth of colloquy. We learn something of the secret of this quality of the work from a few sentences in which Smith discourses of his favourite craft and of his fellow-craftsmen. Just as two or three of our best sonneteers—Wordsworth and Rossetti to wit—have written admirable sonnets in celebration of the sonnet, so Alexander Smith is seldom seen to greater advantage than in the pages where he magnifies his office and makes himself the essayist of the essay.

> The essay, as a literary form, resembles the lyric, in so far as it is moulded by some central mood—whimsical, serious, or satirical. Give the mood, and the essay, from the first sentence to the last, grows around it as the cocoon grows around the silkworm. . . . The essayist is a kind of poet in prose, and if harshly questioned as to his uses, he might be unable to render a better apology for his existence than a flower might. The essay should be pure literature, as the poem is pure literature. The essayist wears a lance, but he cares more for the sharpness of its point than for the pennon that flutters upon it, than for the banner of the captain under whom he serves. He plays with death as Hamlet played with Yorick's skull, and he reads the morals—strangely stern, often, for such fragrant lodging—which are folded up in the bosoms of roses. He has no pride, and is deficient in a sense of the congruity and fitness of things. He lifts a pebble from the ground, and puts it aside more carefully than any gem; and on a nail in a cottage door he will hang the mantle of his thought, heavily brocaded with the gold of rhetoric.

It may be remarked in parenthesis that the above sentences were published in 1863, and they provide what is probably the first statement by an English writer with any repute of the famous doctrine "Art for art's sake" to which Smith seems to have worked his own way without the prompting of Gallican suggestion. Indeed, even in 1869, when Mr. Patrick Proctor Alexander edited Smith's posthumous volume, *Last Leaves,* he remarked in his introduction that he had thought of excluding the essay entitled **"Literary Work,"** in which the same doctrine was more elaborately advocated, apparently on the ground that it was a new heresy which might expose Smith to the pains and penalties of literary excommunication. How curious it seems. In ten years the essay which Mr. Alexander printed with an apology became the accepted creed of all or nearly all the younger men of letters in England, and now it is no longer either a dangerous luxury or an article of orthodox faith, but one of those uninteresting commonplaces which applied in one way is a truism, in another a fatuous absurdity. So does fortune turn her wheel for theories as well as for men and women.

In the passage just quoted Smith deals with the essay mainly as simple literature, but he loves and praises it not as literature only, but as autobiography; not merely as something that is in itself interesting and attractive, but as a window through which he can peer in upon something more interesting still—the master who built the house after his own design and made it an architectural projection of himself.

> You like to walk round peculiar or important men as you like to walk round a building, to view it from different points and in different lights. Of the essayist, when his mood is communicative, you obtain a full picture. You are made his contemporary and familiar friend. You enter into his humours and

his seriousness. You are made heir of his whims, prejudices, and playfulness. You walk through the whole nature of him as you walk through the streets of Pompeii, looking into the interior of stately mansions, reading the satirical scribblings on the walls. And the essayist's habit of not only giving you his thoughts, but telling you how he came by them, is interesting, because it shows you by what alchemy the ruder world becomes transmuted into the finer. We like to know the lineage of ideas, just as we like to know the lineage of great earls and swift racehorses. We like to know that the discovery of the law of gravitation was born of the fall of an apple in an English garden on a summer afternoon. Essays written after this fashion are racy of the soil in which they grow, as you taste the lava in the vines grown on the slopes of Etna, they say. There is a healthy Gascon flavour in Montaigne's Essays; and Charles Lamb's are scented with the primroses of Covent Garden.

In the first of these passages Alexander Smith speaks of the mantle of the essayist's thought "heavily brocaded with the gold of rhetoric," and he himself was a cunning embroiderer. It was a gift of nature, but he did not learn at once how he could best utilise it. He brocaded his poetry, and on poetry brocade even of gold is an impertinence, just as is paint—*pace* Gibson—on the white marble of the sculptured group or figure. In the essay he found a form which relies less exclusively upon body of imagination and perfectness of pure outline—which is more susceptible to legitimate adornment by the ornamentation of a passing fancy. It is a form in which even the conceit is not unwelcome: to use the language of science the conceit finds in the essay its fit environment. Thus, in Smith's pages Napoleon dies at St. Helena "like an untended watch-fire"; Ebenezer Elliot, the Corn Law rhymer, is "Apollo, with iron dust upon his face, wandering among the Sheffield knife-grinders"; the solitary Dreamthorp doctor has a fancy for arguing with the good simple clergyman, but though "he cannot resist the temptation to hurl a fossil at Moses," "he wears his scepticism as a coquette wears her ribbons—to annoy if he cannot subdue—and when his purpose is served, he puts aside his scepticism—as the coquette puts her ribbons." When the black funeral creeps into Dreamthorp from some outlying hamlet, the people reverently doff their hats and stand aside, for, as Smith puts it, "Death does not walk about here often, but when he does, he receives as much respect as the squire himself." There is, in this last sentence, a touch of quiet Addisonian irony; and, indeed, Smith reminds us at times of almost all his great predecessors in the art of essay-writing—of his prime favourites Montaigne and Bacon ("our earliest essayists and our best" is his own eulogium); and also of Addison, Steele, Lamb, Hazlitt, and Leigh Hunt. But it is never a reminder that brings with it a suggestion of imitation. The methods and graces of these distinguished forerunners are to be found in Smith's

pages only by patient analysis, and then never in their crude state, for his personality fuses them into a new amalgam and stamps them with a new hall-mark.

Perhaps the most purely individual qualities of Smith's work are given to it partly by his remarkable aptitude for the presentation of his thought in simile and metaphor; partly by his fine feeling for colour, and, indeed, for all the elements of picturesqueness; and partly by a native tendency to sombreness of reflection which makes such a theme as that of the essay, **"On Death and the Fear of Dying,"** attractive rather than repellent, or—to speak, perhaps, with greater accuracy—repellent, yet irresistibly fascinating, as is the eye of the rattlesnake to its prey. The image-making endowment makes itself manifest in almost every passage that it would be possible to quote as characteristic; and it may be noted that the associative habit of mind betrays itself not merely in the sudden simile which transfixes a resemblance on the wing, but in the numerous pages in which Smith showed his love for tracing the links of the chain that connects the near and the far, the present and the past, the seen and the unseen. Thus he writes in his Dreamthorp cottage:

> That winter morning when Charles lost his head in front of the banqueting-hall of his own palace, the icicles hung from the eaves of the houses here, and the clown kicked the snowballs from his clouted shoon, and thought but of his supper when at three o'clock the red sun set in the purple mist. On that Sunday in June, while Waterloo was going on, the gossips, after morning service, stood on the country roads discussing agricultural prospects, without the slightest suspicion that the day passing over their heads would be a famous one in the calendar. . . . The last setting sun that Shakspeare saw reddened the windows here, and struck warmly on the faces of the hinds coming home from the fields. The mighty storm that raged while Cromwell lay a-dying, made all the oak-woods groan round about here, and tore the thatch from the very roofs that I gaze upon. When I think of this I can almost, so to speak, lay my hand upon Shakspeare and upon Cromwell. These poor walls were contemporaries of both, and I find something affecting in the thought. The mere soil is, of course, full older than either, but *it* does not touch one in the same way. A wall is the creation of a human hand; the soil is not.

Smith's picturesqueness is fully in evidence here, though the passage was not quoted to illustrate it. Indeed, there are few writers who satisfy so largely the visual sense of the imagination. Even his literary appraisements—witness the essays on Dunbar and Chaucer, and that charming paper **"A Shelf in My Bookcase"**—have a pictorial quality, as if he must *see* something as well as *think* something. Here is Dreamthorp where the essayist, the transfigured Alexander Smith—"Smith's Smith" as the Autocrat of the Breakfast-table would put it—lives his ideal life:

This place suits my whim, and I like it better year after year. As with everything else, since I began to love it I find it growing beautiful. Dreamthorp—a castle, a chapel, a lake, a straggling strip of grey houses, with a blue film of smoke over all—lies embosomed in emerald. Summer with its daisies runs up to every cottage door. From the little height where I am now sitting I see it beneath me. Nothing could be more peaceful. The wind and the birds fly over it. A passing sunbeam makes brilliant a white gable-end, and brings out the colours of the blossomed apple-tree beyond, and disappears. I see figures in the street, but hear them not. The hands on the church clock seem always pointing to one hour. Time has fallen asleep in the afternoon sunshine. I make a frame of my fingers and look at my picture. On the walls of the next Academy's exhibition will hang nothing half so beautiful.

This is the *tout ensemble,* but every detail has its own pictorial charm. There is the canal—a prosaic unpicturesque thing is a canal; but this particular canal has "a great white water-lily asleep on its olive-coloured face," while to the picture-making eye "a barge trailing up through it in the sunset is a pretty sight; and the heavenly crimsons and purples sleep quite lovingly upon its glossy ripples. Nor does the evening star disdain it, for as I walk along I see it mirrored as clearly as in the waters of the Mediterranean itself."

The sombreness of reflection noted as one of the characteristic features of Smith's work as an essayist gives to that work a recognisable autumnal feeling. It is often difficult to think of it as the work of a young man full of the ordinary buoyant life of youth; though when the difficulty presents itself one may remember also that the young man was destined to die at thirty-seven—that fatal age for the children of imagination—and it is, perhaps, not too fanciful to indulge the thought that some presentiment of early doom may have given to Smith's mediatative moods much of their pensive seriousness. However this may be, it is certain that Alexander Smith, with a constancy which the most careless reader cannot fail to note, recurred again and again, both when opportunity offered and when opportunity had to be made, to the theme of death, its mystery, its fear, and its fascination. In one of his poems, which I quote from memory, he speaks of his life as a highway which, at some unknown point, has his grave cut across; and even in the joyous **"Spring Chanson"** the poet, addressing the singing merle, drops suddenly from the major into the minor key, and ends upon the note by which the key is dominated:

> Men live and die, the song remains; and when
> I list the passion of thy vernal breath
>   Methinks thou singest best to Love and Death—
> To happy Lovers and to dying Men.

Autumn and death must needs be naturally allied in human thought, though to the joyous-minded even autumn will be associated with its present fruitage rather than with its presage of dissolution; but this intrusion of death into a celebration of the life and growth of spring seems irrelevant, almost morbid: it may even seem artificial, as if the poet were deliberately striving after a strong literary effect by the expendient of an unnatural juxtaposition of incongruous ideas. To a man of Smith's mind and temperament it has certainly neither irrelevance nor artificiality; whether we can rightly call it morbid depends upon the meaning we attach to a word to which the personal feeling rather than the common reason gives a definition. Smith's habit was to endeavour to realise death that he might more fully and richly realise life. "To denude death of its terrible associations," he writes, "were a vain attempt, the atmosphere is always cold around an iceberg"; and yet in imagination he loves to draw near the iceberg for some shivering moments that he may enjoy more exquisitely the warmth of summer sun or piled-up winter fire. To his constant thought

> There are considerations which rob death of its ghastliness, and help to reconcile us to it. The thoughtful happiness of a human being is complex, and in certain moved moments which, after they have gone, we can recognise to have been our happiest, some subtle thought of death has been curiously intermixed. And this subtle admixture it is that gives the happy moment its character—which makes the difference between the gladness of a child, resident in mere animal health and impulse, and too volatile to be remembered, and the serious joy of a man who looks before and after, and takes in both this world and the next. Speaking broadly, it may be said that it is from some obscure recognition of the fact of death that life draws its final sweetness. . . . . This recognition does not always terrify. The spectre has the most cunning disguises, and often when near us, we are unaware of the fact of proximity. Unsuspected, this idea of death lurks in the sweetness of music; it has something to do with the pleasure with which we behold the vapour of morning; it comes between the passionate lips of lovers; it lives in the thrill of kisses. 'An inch deeper, and you will find the emperor.' Probe joy to its last fibre and you will find death.

To preserve always in the background of the mind some great thought or momentous interest, tends to ensure a certain fine justice in a man's estimate of the relative proportions of smaller things lying in the front of it, and Alexander Smith's essays have a restful quality of measure, balance, and sanity. In the **"Essay on an Old Subject,"** published in *Last Leaves,* the young man who had but recently gone into the thirties writes with imaginative prescience—or possibly from a premature experience—of the joys and gains of middle-age (by which he means the forty-fifth year or thereabouts); and there is in most of his essays, especially in the *Dreamthorp* papers which came earliest, a middle-aged maturity which charms and satisfies, and never disturbs. But it is not a middle-age which has ossified into routine and become dead to youth's enthusiasms—witness the fine ardour of the concluding sentence of the essay in which he "memorises" Carlyle's appearance at Edinburgh to deliver his Rectorial address: "When I saw him for the first time stand up amongst us the other day, and heard him speak kindly, brotherly, affectionate words. . . . I am not ashamed to confess that I felt moved towards him as I do not think, in any possible combination of circumstances, I could have felt moved towards any other living man." And yet, though he has not lost youth's ardour, he has freed himself from youth's arrogant impatience; he can be moved by enthusiasms, but not driven helplessly before them; he can project himself from himself and survey his own thought "in the round"; he has learned the lessons of Clough's pregnant words, "and yet—consider it again." At the same time his manner it never that tantalising, irritating manner of explicit guards, reserves, limitations—the manner of the writer who is always making himself safe by the sudden "but" or "nevertheless" or "notwithstanding." The due limitation is conveyed implicitly, in the primal statement of the thought—in the touch of irony or humorous extravagance which hints with sufficing clearness that this or that is not to be interpreted *au pied de la lettre*. The delightful essay **"On Vagabonds,"** at the close of the *Dreamthorp* volume, might be described roughly as a glorification of the life of Bohemia, and an impeachment, or at any rate a depreciation of commonplace Philistine respectability. In dealing with such a theme with such a bent of mind, the temptation to force the note, to overcharge the colour, would be to most men—to all young men, impatient of restricting conventions—well-nigh irresistible; but Smith resists it with no apparent effort of resistance. There is no holding of himself in lest he should speak unadvisedly with his tongue; on the contrary, he lets himself go with perfect abandonment. The "genuine vagabond," he says, "takes captive the heart," and he declares it "high time that a moral game law were passed for the preservation of the wild and vagrant feelings of human nature"; but just when we expect the stroke of exaggeration there comes instead the light touch of saving humour, and we know that the essayist is in less danger even than we of losing his head, or, as the expressive cant phrase has it, "giving himself away."

Some of the few (and if I could succeed in increasing their number I should be greatly content) who know Alexander Smith's prose well, and love it even as they know, have probably favourite papers or favourite groups. Some may feel especially drawn to the essays of pure reflection, such as **"Death and the Fear of Dying"** and **"The Importance of a Man to Himself"**; others to that delightful group in which the familiar simplicities of nature supply texts for tranquil meditation—**"Dreamthorp," "Christmas,"** and **"Books and**

Gardens," in which last there is also some delightful character-portraiture in the vignettes of the village doctor and clergyman; others to the essays in literary appreciation, such as **"Dunbar," "Geoffrey Chaucer," "Scottish Ballads,"** and **"A Shelf in My Bookcase."** In the words applied by Charles Lamb, with a certain free unscrupulousness to the whole world of books, I must say with regard to Alexander Smith's essays, "I have no preferences." To me they all have a charm which somewhat dulls the edge of discrimination, for the writer rather than the theme is the centre of interest; he is the hero of the play, and he is never off the stage. Still in some torture chamber of inquiry certain names might be extracted from me, and I think they would be **"Dreamthorp," "Books and Gardens,"** and **"A Lark's Flight."** This last study, which has not been previously named, is one of the most noteworthy of Smith's essays, and will be grateful to the more lazy readers inasmuch as it tells a story. It is the story of a murder and an execution, the murder vulgar and commonplace enough—a crime of brutal violence, the execution a sombrely picturesque function, with one striking incident which seized and held the imagination of the boy who witnessed it; and the story is told with an arresting vividness to which I know only one parallel in English literature, the narrative appendix to De Quincey's famous essay, "On Murder, considered as one of the Fine Arts." The execution took place, after the old custom in Scotland, on the spot where the crime had been committed—a lonely stretch of grassland, some distance outside the city of Glasgow. The criminals were Irish navvies, members of a large gang employed in the neighbourhood, and as there were some rumours of a rescue, a detachment of cavalry, supplemented by field-pieces, surrounded the scaffold. Of the scene itself, and the one occurrence round which its latent pathos crystallised, Smith gives the recollections of boyhood. The men were being brought in a cart to the place of execution, and when they reached the turn of the road where they could first see the black cross-beam with its empty halters, the boy noted the eager, fascinated gaze the doomed men cast upon it. At last the place was reached, and Smith writes:

> Around it a wide space was kept clear by the military; the cannon were placed in position; out flashed the swords of the dragoons; beneath and around on every side was the crowd. Between two brass helmets I could see the scaffold clearly enough, and when in a little while the men, bareheaded and with their attendants, appeared upon it, the surging crowd became stiffened with fear and awe. And now it was that the incident, so simple, so natural, so much in the ordinary course of things, and yet so frightful in its tragic suggestions, took place. Be it remembered that the season was early May, that the day was fine, that the wheatfields were clothing themselves in the green of the young crop, and that around the scaffold, standing on a sunny mound, a

wide space was kept clear. When the men appeared beneath the beam, each under his own proper halter, there was a dead silence,—every one was gazing too intently to whisper to his neighbour even. Just then, out of the grassy space at the foot of the scaffold, in the dead silence audible to all, a lark rose from the side of its nest, and went singing upward in its happy flight. O heaven! how did that song translate itself into dying ears? Did it bring, in one wild burning moment, father and mother, and poor Irish cabin, and prayers said at bedtime, and the smell of turf fires, and innocent sweet-hearting, and rising and setting suns? Did it—but the dragoon's horse has become restive, and his helmet bobs up and down and blots everything; and there is a sharp sound, and I feel the great crowd heave and swing, and hear it torn by a sharp shiver of pity, and the men whom I saw so near but a moment ago are at immeasurable distance, and have solved the great enigma,—and the lark has not yet finished his flight: you can see and hear him yonder in the fringe of a white May cloud. . . . . There is a stronger element of terror in this incident of the lark than in any story of a similar kind I can remember."

Gasps of admiration are amateurish, provincial, ineffective, but after reading such a passage as this, the words that come first—at any rate to me—are not in the least critical but simply exclamatory. It is wonderful writing! Then comes a calmer and more analytical moment in which one discovers something of the secret of the art in what has seemed at first not art at all but sheer nature. Mr. Pater, in one of his most instructive essays, has shown that the "classical" element in art is "the quality of order in beauty," and that "it is that addition of strangeness to beauty that constitutes the romantic character," romantic art at its best being moreover distinguished by a fine perfection of workmanship. This surely then is an impressive miniature example of romantic art with its combination of strangeness and beauty, and its flawless technique—its absolute saturation of the vehicle of expression with the very essence of the thing, the emotion that is to be expressed. Note the directness and simplicity of the early narrative sentences; they are a mere recital of facts, and their very baldness only mitigated by a single emotional phrase, "the surging crowd became stiffened with fear and awe," prepares the mind for what is to follow. And then, the sudden break in the second sentence beginning "Did it,"—how perfectly natural it seems, and yet how dexterous it really is; how it renders perfectly and at a single stroke what the best-chosen words of narrative would have rendered jumblingly, the brevity of the interval between the lark's rising and the consummation of doom—the sharp bewildering suddenness of the end. Then, lastly, the curious in these things may notice a certain peculiarity in the construction of the concluding sentence of the story—the penultimate sentence of the quotation. There are in the volume barely nine lines, and in these lines the word "and" occurs eleven times. All frequent and close repetitions of a single word are generally avoided by good writers, and the repetition of an insignificant conjunction such as "and" is, as a rule, something to be specially avoided. Smith habitually avoided as carefully as any of us, but here he had to give the feeling of impetuosity, of eager hurry to get the ghastly story told, and the "and" which rapidly accumulates detail upon detail recurs as naturally and inevitably as in the voluble speech of a little child bursting into her mother's room with some marvellous recital of adventure encountered in her morning walk. This is the high literary art which instinctively and perfectly adapts the means of language—of word, sound, pause, and cadence—to the end of absolute expression.

Alexander Smith himself is never wearisome; and it would ill become me to weary those whom I would fain interest by surplusage of comment; but I should like to add a word or two concerning those essays in which he appears as a critic of literature. Mr. Oscar Wilde has said that all good criticism is simply autobiography—that is, I suppose, a statement of personal preferences. I accept the definition if I may enlarge it by saying that criticism is not merely a statement of personal preferences but of justifications for such preferences presented with a view to persuasion. Of course even with this rider the definition still leaves autobiography the main element in criticism, and of such autobiographical appraisement Smith was a master. Whether he formulated the rule never to write of any authors whose work he did not enjoy I cannot say: he certainly acted upon it with the most delightful results. So keen in his gusto, so adequate and appetising his expression of it, that one may dare to say the next best thing to reading Montaigne, Bacon, Chaucer, and the Scottish Ballads, is to read what Alexander Smith has to say about them. His talk about books is always so human that it will delight people whom one would not think of calling literary. He discourses on *The Canterbury Tales* not as a man weighing and measuring a book, but as a wayfarer sitting in the inn-yard of the Tabard at Southwark, watching the crowd of pilgrims with the eye of an acute and good-natured observer, taking notes of their appearance, and drawing from it shrewd inferences as to habit and character. He has certain favourite volumes upon which he expatiates in the essay entitled **"A Shelf in my Bookcase";** and the principle of selection is obvious enough. They are books full of a rich humanity; beneath their paragraphs or stanzas he can feel the beating heart. The literary vesture is *simply* a vesture which half reveals and half conceals the objects of his love—the man or woman who lives and breathes behind. He reveals in the old Scotch ballads and German hymns, for in them the concealing veil is thin, and the thoughts and loves and pains of simple souls in dead centuries are laid open and bare. He prefers Hawthorne's *Twice-told Tales* to his longer and more elaborate works, such as *Transformation* and *The Scarlet Letter,* because he finds more of the man in them, the solitary author who had no public to think of, and who wrote because he must. He has a genuine catholicity, but it is not that uninteresting catholicity which lacks defined circumferences; and his general sensibility to excellence is emphasised by frank confession of his limitations. The author of *Paradise Lost* evidently lies a little outside the reach of Alexander Smith's tentacles of sympathy.

> Reading Milton is like dining off gold plate in a company of kings; very splendid, very ceremonious, and not a little appalling. Him I read but seldom, and only on high days and festivals of the spirit. Him I never lay down without feeling my appreciation increased for lesser men—never without the same kind of comfort that one returning from the presence feels when he doffs respectful attitude and dress of ceremony, and subsides into old coat, familiar arm-chair, and slippers. After long-continued organ-music the jangle of the Jew's harp is felt as an exquisite relief.

There is a trace of Philistinism here—the Philistinism which is not ashamed but rather complacent; and it may seem a strange whim on the part of one who loves Smith's work to choose as a final sample of it a passage which, some of the elect may think, does not show him at his best. But Danton's commendation of audacity, though not universally valid, is a word of wisdom to the advocate with a strong case. Alexander Smith's best is good with such a rare and delightful quality of goodness that his appreciator shows no great temerity in abandoning all reserves and concealments. He is not afraid of painting the wart, because it is overpowered by strength of feature and charm of expression. Alexander Smith, as he shows himself in his prose—in **Dreamthorp**, in *Last Leaves,* and in that entrancing book *A Summer in Skye*—is one of those writers concerning whom even a lover may tell not only the truth, but the whole truth. For myself, I read his essays when I was young and found them full of stimulation; I have read them again since I have become middle-aged, and have found them satisfyingly rest-giving. At no time have they been found wanting in something of rare and delicate delight. If criticism be indeed autobiography, no verdict upon the essays of Alexander Smith could well be at once more critical or more praiseful than this confession. I love Mr. Stevenson and my later contemporaries; but I think I must confess that I love my early contemporary, Mr. Stevenson's countryman and forerunner, better still.

Hugh Walker (essay date 1914)

SOURCE: Introduction to *Dreamthorp: With Selections from "Last Leaves,"* by Alexander Smith, Oxford University Press, 1914, pp. v-xxv.

[*In the essay below, Walker proposes that Smith should be considered among the greatest English prose writers.*]

Alexander Smith, the author of **Dreamthorp,** was born at Kilmarnock in Ayrshire on the last day of the year 1830, and died near Edinburgh on January 5, 1867. His whole life, therefore, covered little more than half the allotted span, and what we may call his effective life—deducting the years of immaturity—was considerably less than half of what is normal. Yet in these thirty-six years Smith touched almost the extreme heights and depths of obscurity, fame, and neglect; and this fact imparts an aspect of romance to a career which was in its outward circumstances eminently prosaic and commonplace.

Smith's father was a designer of patterns for lace-work; and at some period, vaguely referred to by the biographers of the poet as 'in his childhood' or in 'a few years' after Alexander's birth, he found it expedient to remove to Paisley, the centre in those days of the trade in a celebrated kind of shawl which required designs similar to those used by the lace-workers. Thence, 'in a short time', the family removed to Glasgow, with which city are associated Smith's youth and the opening of his literary career, and to which is dedicated the finest of his poems. The accounts of his education are equally vague. He is said to have received 'a good general education', and his friend Patrick Proctor Alexander says that it included 'some tincture of Latin and mathematics'. He adds that in English literature Smith was 'an unusually well-read man, even among men professedly literary'. But this doubtless was part of the education which Smith gave himself, and probably Alexander's conclusion is nearly correct—that the education which was given to him 'may perhaps have amounted to this, that he was thoroughly well taught to *read*'. It was the education imparted by a Scottish elementary school, which, in those days, for a boy of promise like Smith, would include the tincture of Latin and mathematics. As to the place where it was received, we know from **"A Lark's Flight"** that Smith was still a schoolboy after the removal to Glasgow. It was a schoolboy who saw the awful sight of the doomed men; and to the fact that the schoolboy was a poet in embryo we owe one of the most impressive passages in English prose.

We are told that Smith's parents thought of having him trained for the Church—the usual ambition of Scottish parents of their class for a promising son. No steps, however, seem to have been taken to realize it; certainly Smith never went to the University of the city in which he lived. In the end the line of least resistance was followed, and the boy learnt his father's trade. Pattern-designing is an occupation which has some smack of the artistic in it, and for that reason it might have appealed to the artistic soul of Smith. In point of fact it does not seem to have done so. His work is said to have been poor, he abandoned the trade as soon as he had an opportunity, and apparently he never afterwards drew a design, even for amusement. He drifted into literature, for which, as it proved, his surroundings were more favourable than they appeared to be. The editor of the Glasgow *Evening Citizen* was at that time James Hedderwick, whom Smith refers to in *A Summer in Skye* as a 'poet of no mean order'. He was certainly an accomplished man, and a good judge of literary excellence. He singled out Hugh Macdonald, the author of *Rambles Round Glasgow*, and made him his sub-editor. He encouraged Smith by printing his verses. Then, through George Gilfillan of Dundee (a man worthy of honourable remembrance for the generous help he gave to struggling genius), Smith was introduced to periodicals of higher literary standing, and pieces by him began to appear in the London *Critic* and the *Eclectic Review*. Finally, in 1853, he burst into full blossom with a volume of *Poems,* the principal item in which was *A Life-Drama*. It was received with applause so loud and unanimous that the morning when Byron awoke and found himself famous has been spoken of as the closest parallel. This encouragement, and the £100 he received for the volume, induced Smith to give up his trade of pattern-designing and throw himself upon the precarious one of literature. Fortunately he was not called upon long to depend solely on a resource so insecure. In 1854 he became secretary to the University of Edinburgh. For six hours' office work a day he received the modest sum of £150 a year; which was afterwards increased to £200 on his undertaking additional duties. Small as it was, this salary raised Smith above the danger of absolute want, and, indeed, so long as he remained a bachelor, provided adequately for his simple wants. But in 1857 he married a certain Flora Macdonald of Skye, who was akin to the celebrated heroine of the story of Prince Charlie. The marriage added greatly to his happiness, but also increased his cares; and it seems to have been overwork, induced by anxiety to provide for his wife and children, that brought him to his premature grave. He apparently had a kind of premonition of his fate. More than one of his critics has called attention to his brooding over death, and in his memorial notice Alexander Nicholson quotes as prophetic the lines,

> Before me runs a road of toil
> With my grave cut across.

During Smith's first winter in Edinburgh, Sydney Dobell, author of *The Roman* and *Balder,* was also resident there, and the two poets made acquaintance with one another and became friends. It was the opening year of the Crimean War, and they collaborated in a slender volume of *Sonnets on the War.* They were associated even before they met; for in May 1854 W. E. Aytoun had parodied them in *Blackwood's Magazine,* and when *Firmilian* appeared they passed from fame to notoriety as the Spasmodic Poets. The name happily hit their characteristic fault, and is still famil-

iar to many who have read neither the poems satirized nor the parody. The poets, who were both manly men, took Aytoun's jesting in excellent part. Aytoun on his side not only meant them no harm, but afterwards did all he could to promote Smith's interests. Nevertheless, it seems probable that *Firmilian* did Smith, and perhaps Dobell too, a permanent injury. The natural reaction after exaggerated praise had already set in. During the first enthusiasm for *A Life-Drama* Smith had been pronounced the greatest poet since Keats; nay, there were some who said that he was greater than Keats; among contemporaries Tennyson's was the only name that seemed to his admirers fit to place beside his; and comparison even with Shakespeare had been suggested. The feeling recorded by Mr. W. D. Howells was fairly common: 'I read this now dead-and-gone immortal with an ecstasy unspeakable; I raved of him by day, and dreamed of him by night; I got great lengths of his *Life-Drama* by heart, and can still repeat several gorgeous passages from it; I would almost have been willing to take the life of the sole critic who had the sense to laugh at him.' [The critic referred to was not Aytoun.] There is evidence here of a loss of balance. It is not good criticism to name Smith along with Shakespeare. The former certainly stood far below both Tennyson and Keats. But, as one excess is apt to beget another, many besides Mr. Howells came to feel that they had been befooled, and the satire of *Firmilian* was taken far too seriously. Smith's reputation as a poet never recovered from the blow. In *City Poems,* published in 1857, there is much finer poetry than any that is contained in the earlier volume. There are in particular the noble stanzas entitled **"Glasgow"**—stanzas in which the poet paints in words visions such as Turner put on canvas; and it is not easy to say who, besides Smith and Turner, has produced such effects. Yet this volume passed comparatively unnoticed, and achieved only a very partial success. *Edwin of Deira* (1861) was somewhat more favourably received than *City Poems,* but had by no means that warmth of welcome which had been given to the *Life-Drama.* The book had been published on the system of half profits; and the author's share amounted to just £15 5s. 3d. The effect of the natural reaction from excessive enthusiasm had been intensified by a charge of plagiarism, which was brought against each of Smith's three volumes of poetry in succession, and seemed to receive confirmation from the resemblance both in theme and in treatment between the latest of theme and the then recent *Idylls of the King.* Yet *Edwin of Deira* was written in great part before the *Idylls* appeared; and Patrick Proctor Alexander had seen at least half of it in manuscript before any hint of the precise nature of Tennyson's work had reached the public. The charge of plagiarism can seldom be justified. In Smith's case it is hardly more true than it would be if brought against Milton, and is less true than it would be if brought against Burns. There are many

The Irongate, Glasgow, Scotland

reminiscences of earlier poems in Smith's verse; but he was no literary thief, and none of his poems was stolen.

Smith had gone through one of the fieriest trials to which a man of letters could be subjected. Panegyric has turned many a head, and depreciation has embittered many a heart. Smith had not only to bear both, but defamation as well. His honour as a man of letters was assailed, and that in a way that was bound to tell upon his worldly fortunes. A 'spasmodic' person, such as he was supposed to be, could hardly be expected to bear well alternations so violent. Yet testimony is unanimous to the fact that he did bear every change with admirable equanimity and dignity. When the chorus of applause evoked by the *Life-Drama* burst upon him, a youth of twenty-two, it moved him not in the least. He did not foolishly affect indifference, says Alexander, but 'now, as always, his bearing was distinguished by a quiet and manly simplicity'. 'All the paeans of his admirers,' says Nicholson, 'had no effect whatever in disturbing the serene balance of his nature, resting as it did on a solid basis of common sense.' 'Serene balance' is hardly the phrase we expect to find

applied to a spasmodic poet; yet it must have been well chosen; for not only does Alexander's account confirm Nicholson's judgement, but Brisbane, in his *Early Years of Alexander Smith,* uses the very same word, and declares that seldom has a poetic genius 'lived a life so well *balanced,* beautiful and blameless'. He bore literary censure with the same equanimity with which he had borne praise. 'At the worst,' he said, 'it's only a ginger-beer bottle burst.' If he resented the charge of plagiarism, who can blame him? Even that he seems to have endured without complaint when it was brought against *A Life-Drama;* but when it was reiterated against *City Poems,* he did, according to Alexander, betray serious irritation. On no other occasion did his friend ever see evidence of such a feeling. The truth is that the 'spasmodic' element was only a youthful phase, and was superficial even in youth. After *A Life-Drama* there is nothing spasmodic in Alexander Smith's poetry.

The comparatively ill success of Smith's later volumes of verse, and the poor pecuniary recompense he won, forced him to turn to prose. His family was increasing, while his official salary was small and fixed. He therefore became an active contributor to all sorts of publications, from encyclopaedias to newspapers. A few of these contributions were gathered together by his friend Alexander in the posthumous *Last Leaves*. Prior to this, however, in 1863, had appeared *Dreamthorp*, a volume of essays mostly new. It is by these two collections that Smith must be judged in his rôle of essayist. In prose he wrote besides *A Summer in Skye,* a book which will hardly serve as a guide-book to the island, but one which, like Borrow's *Wild Wales,* seizes and fixes the poetry of the region with which it deals. Smith had the gift of sympathy and the insight which sympathy gives. He loved the Highlanders, and taught them to love him. A fanciful critic might explain this sympathy by reference to the strain of Highland blood that flowed in Smith's veins through his mother; but we are on safer ground in recalling that his wife was a Skye lady. The annual holiday spent after his marriage in her native island imbued him with the scenery of Skye and stamped it both on his prose and on his later verse. With the misty island he interwove his own spiritual life and the life of his family. In the concluding piece of his latest volume of verse he associates with the great Skye mountain of Blaavin the birth of that eldest daughter who died a few weeks after himself.

Throughout the nineteenth century, after Scott, whoever had to make his living by the pen was almost compelled, sooner or later, to turn to prose fiction. Alexander Smith was no exception to the rule. His last considerable publication was *Alfred Hagart's Household,* which first ran as a serial in *Good Words,* and then was published as a book in 1866. The story, though wholly destitute of excitement, is finely conceived and finely written, and has, moreover, that charm which is never absent from sincere autobiography; for, though we cannot safely go to *Alfred Hagart's Household* for facts, into it Smith put himself, and from it may be gathered not a few hints of events which had happened in the course of his life. The merit of the tale is of so quiet a sort that a revival of its popularity is hardly to be expected. At the time, however, it was so popular that the publishers urged Smith to expand it from one volume to two in a sequel, *Miss Oona McQuarrie,* which proved, as sequels are apt to prove, much inferior. The success of the first volume would probably have determined the course of Smith's literary life if he had survived a few years longer. At the time of his death he was meditating a novel which was to be written on the ordinary scale.

What we have principally to consider here is the character and value of Alexander Smith's work as an essayist, and that must be judged by the two volumes *Dreamthorp* and *Last Leaves;* for no one is ever likely again to turn over the pages of forgotten journals in order to identify his contributions. The mass of work buried in those journals must be very great; but specu-

lation as to its value is useless. What we know is that Patrick Proctor Alexander gathered what he considered the best of these remains into *Last Leaves,* and that, while some of the papers in it are excellent, others are only fairly good. It is not probable, therefore, that the most careful research would reveal much that would be calculated to raise Smith's reputation; we already possess enough to entitle the author to a high place among essayists, if the quality be rare.

First we may ask with regard to Smith how far he understood the literary form he handled in the essay. A clear theory of the essay is not indispensable to the writing of excellent essays; Lamb himself may have done his exquisite work half unconsciously. But, though not indispensable, it will be admitted to be, at least, a distinct advantage. Now in this respect the paper entitled **"On the Writing of Essays"** shows that Smith is unsurpassed. If we turn to the lexicographers, their definitions of the word essay give but little help. Johnson, himself one of the foremost essayists of his time, can only tell us that it is 'a loose sally of the mind, an irregular, indigested piece, not a regular and orderly performance'. That is to say, it is defined by what it is not, rather than by what it is, by defect rather than by merit, as if one tried to make the true character of the *Iliad* clearer by saying that it is 'not a veracious history'. Even the Oxford Dictionary is not very much more helpful. To explain what the essay really is requires an expansiveness which is denied to the lexicographer. The critic, however, has the opportunity, if he knows how to use it. Many have tried, but who with such success as Smith? The secret of his success is that he perceives quite clearly that there are really two quite disparate things which are called essays. Any comparatively short piece that does not pretend to be exhaustive may be called an essay. Even shortness is not absolutely essential: we have Locke's *Essay on the Human Understanding.* In this sense a paper on medicine, or one on the stars above, or on the mines in the bowels of the earth, may be entitled an essay; and the essay may no more be literature than *Bradshaw* is literature. In the other sense 'essay' is the name of a literary form, as real as that of the novel, or the epic, or the lyric. Smith has himself written essays in both senses of the word. His critical papers on Dunbar and on Chaucer are essays in the looser sense, differing from the imaginary ones on medicine or the stars or the mines in that they are literary. But when he writes **"On the Writing of Essays"** he seizes, as it were by instinct and without pausing to explain, on the inner meaning of the word; and what he describes is the essay *par excellence.* It is a matter of mood, he tells us. 'The essay-writer is a chartered libertine, and a law unto himself. A quick ear and eye, an ability to discern the infinite suggestiveness of common things, a brooding meditative spirit, are all that the essayist requires to start business with.' He is akin to the poet—and also to the lilies of the field: 'The essayist is a kind of poet in prose, and if questioned harshly as to his uses, he might be unable to render a better apology for his existence than a flower might.' He need not be markedly original, and he cannot arise at the beginning of literature. His business is not so much to coin new thoughts as to re-mint old ones. Hence his material is everywhere. Montaigne would have found his in Dreamthorp no less than in Gascony: 'Looking on, the country cart would not for nothing have passed him on the road to market, the setting sun would be arrested in its splendid colours, the idle chimes of the church would be translated into a thoughtful music.'

All this is both subtle and true. In Bacon, the earliest and weightiest of our English essayists, we can detect a certain flaw, because, although he followed Montaigne, he followed him with a Baconian stride—that is to say, the stride of a formal philosopher. Looking below the surface, we see that Bacon carried in his mind, perhaps only lurking there, an essentially negative conception of the essay, that conception which gave birth to Johnson's definition. To him the essay is a receptacle for 'dispersed meditations'. We feel that many of his essays might be expanded into treatises; they have not an organic completeness as they stand. But Montaigne's have this organic completeness; so have Charles Lamb's; so have all men's who are essayists in the esoteric sense of the word.

To which class does Smith belong? In a few of the papers of this volume, as has already been said, to that of essayists in the looser sense of the word; but in the majority, and essentially, to the class of essayists in the strictest sense. His place is in the group which contains Lamb, and the Thackeray of the *Roundabout Papers,* and R. L. Stevenson; and his position relatively to them must be determined by the quality of such pieces as **Dreamthorp** and **"A Lark's Flight"** and **"An Essay on an Old Subject"**. Merely *qua* essayist, he stands higher than men like Carlyle and Macaulay, who in other respects are much greater than he. Their papers are in the main essays by the accident that their authors did not choose or had not leisure to expand them into histories.

Perhaps the first and most indispensable characteristic of the writer who would be an essayist in this esoteric sense is that he be confidential. In the case of all the writers who have been named as examples of the class the reader feels that he is being admitted into the writer's intimacy, and no small part of the charm lies in the feeling of friendship so established. The essayist need tell us no facts about himself. He may mystify us, like Lamb, or record facts as trivial as the chalk-mark on Thackeray's door. It may almost be said that the less he has to do with facts the better. Certainly he must not use them in the manner the Autocrat of the Breakfast-Table condemns. The man who leads his ill-conditioned facts 'into decent company like so many

bull-dogs, ready to let them slip at every ingenious suggestion, or convenient generalization, or pleasant fancy', is the born enemy of the essayist, who draws the very breath of his being from such suggestions and fancies. What is indispensable is that the essayist must create an atmosphere which he himself pervades, as the odour of the flowers of summer fills the air. We feel Lamb in every one of the *Essays of Elia*; and we feel Alexander Smith all through **Dreamthorp**. The fact that he founds his greatest essay on an incident in his boyhood is trivial; but that **"A Lark's Flight"** throughout is full of the personality of the writer is not trivial. The title-essay **"Dreamthorp"** is charming because it gives a highly skilful description, or rather interpretation, of a place rich in associations of old Scottish history, but more charming still because it is so emphatically the place as seen with one particular pair of eyes. 'Come and see it *with me,*' is Smith's invitation to the reader; and the reader accompanies him and sees that which would probably be invisible to him if he took the canal-boat and got out at the wharf, for we are told that the railway does not come near. **"On Dreams and Dreaming"** is a subject that might be treated philosophically. So might Lamb's *Witches and other Night Fears*. But neither Lamb nor Smith professed to be a philosopher—Smith seems to have cherished a hostility to metaphysics unusual in a Scot,—and both essays give the impression of personal experience. The same impression of personality is conveyed by the essays on **"Death and the Fear of Dying,"** **"Vagabonds,"** **"Winter,"** and even sometimes by the critical essays, as by **"A Shelf in my Bookcase"**. This point is the more worth dwelling upon, because in himself Smith seems to have been reticent even among a reticent race. He was one of those men who can convey upon paper the confidences they are chary of uttering in speech. Intimate as Proctor Alexander was with him, for his friend's religion he had to turn to the essay on **"Christmas"**.

No human confidence can be entirely destitute of interest to humanity; but still, confidences vary widely in value. The gossip who whispers in the ear of another gossip her secret opinion of Mr. Blank or Mrs. Nobody, or her suspicion that the So-and-Sos are in a very bad way, is confidential, but not inspiring or elevating. But Alexander Smith's confidences are those of a poet. And a poet is, according to one of the greatest of the class in the nineteenth century,

> The general-in-chief,
> Thro' a whole campaign of the world's life
>   and death,
> Doing the King's work all the dim day long.

Browning is here thinking of the great poet; but, without claiming for Smith a rank so exalted, it is still true that the class is that to which he belongs. In prose as well as in verse his work is essentially poetic. He had that insight, more penetrating than the insight of common men, which marks the true poet; and therefore his confidences are light thrown upon dark places. This poetical element is revealed not only, nor even chiefly, by the use of metaphors and similes with a freedom that is more common in verse than in prose. 'The tea-urn purrs like a fondled cat,' is a phrase which might quite well appear in verse; and indeed it will scan. Prometheus, 'roofed by the keen crystals of the stars' is again poetic, both in conception and in expression. Poetic in a deeper sense is the implied comparison between death and an iceberg: it is as vain to deny the terrors of the one as the coldness of the other. But the poetic element in Smith's essays is not confined to phrases; it pervades whole passages and even essays. The picture of the village of Dreamthorp is poetic; so is the close of **"Christmas"**; so is the snow-storm in **"Winter"**; and in **"The Importance of a Man to Himself,"** how easily might the fine passage on spring, and its melancholy deeper than the melancholy of autumn, be turned into verse. A peculiar charm, therefore, and also a special value of the essays is that they afford the reader the companionship of a poet in undress; a companionship less austere than that which he offers in his singing-robes.

The reproach brought most frequently and with most truth against Smith's verse was that of excess of imagery. The style was turbid. It was a fault of youth, and even before *City Poems* appeared, the stream had flowed long enough to deposit much of the mud. Still, a tendency to ornament and a love of colour almost in excess were natural to Smith, and their effects are visible in his prose as well as in his verse. Another charge, which was also brought against his early work, causes a shock of surprise to the reader of his later verse and his prose. He was supposed to be more ignorant of nature than a poet has any right to be. Before he wrote *A Life-Drama* Smith's opportunities had been limited. He had been all his days a denizen of streets.

> Instead of shores where ocean beats,
> I hear the ebb and flow of streets,

he says in **"Glasgow"**. Yet that very poem contains the evidence that he had the heart of a poet of nature. Before *City Poems* was published opportunities of observation had multiplied. Smith had a keen eye, and accuracy of observation was instilled through his close companionship with Hugh Macdonald, an accomplished field-naturalist, whose railings at the errors of poets no doubt gave Smith a useful warning. Whatever may have been the case at the beginning of his career, afterwards he certainly wrote 'with his eye on the object'. An interesting example is given by Proctor Alexander. Speaking of Smith's close but usually silent observation in his walks, he says: 'Once in late autumn, as we lay, smoking and silent, on the hill above Bonaly—the

noble landscape stretched beneath, with the fretted outline of the city bounding it, and beyond, far reaches of shining sea, in dim distance wedded with the sky— he said suddenly: "Oh! look at those sprays of birch there between us and the tints of far sky; don't they look as if they would *drip purple wine on us?*"' The biographer adds that he looked and saw that Smith had photographed the effect in words, but he does not seem to have observed that this was either taken from or afterwards translated into his own verse by Smith. 'The beech is dipped in wine,' is a phrase in **"Glasgow"**. and at certain seasons the image is at least as true of the beech as of the birch.

By the time Smith came to write his prose, his apprenticeship to nature was served. The successive summers in Skye were an education to him, and few books in the language are more deeply impregnated with the spirit of scenery than that which he devotes to his favourite island. The essays, too, are full of this spirit. It is the essence of the title-essay of *Dreamthorp*, **"Winter"** is full of it, and it inspires the fine description of Duddingston in **"The Minister-Painter"**. But Smith's skill is shown more subtly in conveying an impression than in making a description. The description of the village of Dreamthorp is vague, but no one can read the essay without receiving an impression of deep unbroken peace. To tell the depth of the lake, the age of the castle, the length of the street and the number of houses in it, would be easy. That is a task within the competence of any guide-book compiler. But to produce the impression was difficult, and success in the attempt is evidence of literary genius.

Smith knew too that what interests man is not nature in herself, but nature in her relation with him. In *A Summer in Skye* the Highlanders and the mountains among which they live seem inextricably bound together. *Dreamthorp* blends past human history, and nature covering its traces with her ivies and lichens, with present human life moving slowly and uneventfully towards the graveyard beside the ruined castle. And if there are material ruins there are moral ones as well, which are more easily made. 'Human hearts get ruinous in so much less time than stone walls and towers.' These are the elements of the whole idyl: 'The generous, ungrudging sun, the melancholy ruin, like mad Lear, with the flowers and ivies of forgetfulness and grief, and between them, sweet and evanescent, human birth and love!' In **"Vagabonds"** again, imagery of nature is intertwined with human character. The vagabond Smith admires is the man who is not content to be wholly like other people; and he is compared with the rougher and less trimmed parts of the country. The burden of the essay is that 'the fresh, rough, heathery parts of human nature, where the air is freshest, and where the linnets sing, is getting encroached upon by cultivated fields'.

It remains to say a word about the more exoteric essays. They show—what is perhaps more conclusively proved elsewhere—that Smith was no inconsiderable critic. His introduction to the poems of Burns is one of the best of the many sketches of the poet's life. In the present volume, the papers on Dunbar and on Chaucer are very sound pieces of criticism, occasionally lit up with unexpected similes. Chaucer 'is like a cardinal virtue, a good deal talked about, a good deal praised, honoured by a vast amount of distant admiration, but with little practical acquaintance'. 'Not on the stage alone, in the world also, a man's real character comes out best in his asides.' The latter sentence is taken from the admirable concluding passage of the essay on Dunbar, where Smith speaks of the light thrown upon the poems of Burns by his letters and his recorded sayings, and of the disadvantage under which the student labours from the absence of all such aids in the case of Dunbar. So it is with Smith himself as critic. Sometimes a flood of light is thrown upon an author by an apparently casual phrase in an essay that does not profess to be critical. Thus, in the **"Essay on an Old Subject,"** we suddenly come upon the saying that Hawthorne 'was a middle-aged man from earliest boyhood'; and we feel at once that the paradox expresses a truth. This gift of illumination is Smith's heritage as a poet. In criticism, he shows it best in **"A Shelf in my Bookcase,"** where the personal predilections of the writer have the freest room and his friendliness is most intimately shown. His remarks on Hawthorne there are especially excellent, and those on Ebenezer Elliott are hardly less remarkable.

Smith was a critic not only of literature, but of art as well. Year after year, we are told, he contributed to the *Caledonian Mercury* papers on the pictures in the Royal Academy; and this phase of his activity is represented in *Last Leaves* by the essay entitled **"The Minister-Painter"** In that paper Smith explains the artistic poverty of earlier Scotland by her religion—'on Calvinism you can breed first-rate men, but not so easily first-rate artists'—and comments upon the awakening and the reaction. He himself is an example of the reaction; and it is interesting to note that his contemporary and fellow-citizen of Edinburgh, Dr. John Brown, is another example. Possibly, but for the repression of previous generations, neither Brown nor Smith would have written about pictures with such fresh zest and enjoyment. Apart from its merits as an essay, this paper is worthy of note as illustrating the very considerable range of Smith. Artistic criticism as well as literary—and in literature, from Chaucer to his own friend and collaborator Sydney Dobell; gardens as well as books; death as well as life; the joys of Christmas, but the sufferings entailed by winter as well: all these pass before his mind and become the subjects of his meditation. The general atmosphere is that of a gentle melancholy—the emotion of youth recollected in the chastened tranquillity of middle age.

It has sometimes been said that a man is to be judged by his supreme achievement. The test is not wholly satisfactory; at least it must not be taken alone, or Marlowe would rank not so very far below Shakespeare. Still, it is one test. And if he be judged by it, Smith's place is among the very greatest writers of English prose. His supreme achievement is the passage in **"A Lark's Flight"** which describes the soaring of the bird which gives its name to the essay. I have compared it elsewhere to the knocking at the gate in *Macbeth,* and I know not what to do but to repeat myself; for I have found nothing else in literature comparable to these two passages. If we keep in mind the circumstances of the knocking, with De Quincey's subtle interpretation of the incident, and then turn to Smith, it becomes plain that the latter passage is simply the realization of the thing that is imagined in the former. 'Ghastly' is the adjective by which Smith qualifies this lark's flight; and ghastly is the appropriate word to describe the contrast between the gory hands and the stained souls of Macbeth and Lady Macbeth, and, on the other hand, the trivial knocking which provokes the careless ribaldry of the porter. Smith has not only written a masterpiece of prose, but in doing so has shed a new glory on the name of Shakespeare. The great poet is a prophet as well. He foresaw in his imagination what was translated into fact before the eyes of a boy who was poet enough to understand it, and to reinterpret it for the nineteenth century.

[NOTE. In the preceding pages mention has occasionally been made, for the sake of illustration, of essays which will be found not in *Dreamthorp* but in *Last Leaves*.]

Herbert B. Grimsditch (essay date 1925)

SOURCE: "Alexander Smith: Poet and Essayist," in *The London Mercury*, Vol. XII, No. 69, July, 1925, pp. 284-94.

[*In the following essay, Grimsditch argues that while Smith's poetry is noteworthy because of its imagery, Smith deserves high regard as a prose writer because of the personal nature of and the humor found in his essays.*]

In literature, as in life, there is no fixed ratio between merit and reward, whether reward be taken to mean popularity and pecuniary gain or posthumous renown. Posterity, it is true, does sort out the authors who were undeniably great and relentlessly eliminates those who were undoubtedly little; but between these two extremes are placed a number of men whose status, in the eyes of the critics, is not definitely determined. Their reputations are reconsidered from time to time, and, not infrequently, as with Herman Melville and "Erewhon" Butler at the present time, the work of a writer who has been unduly neglected takes on a new lease of popularity.

G. Robert Stange comments on Smiths reflection of life in Glasgow:

The most striking scene in *A Life Drama* takes place on a city bridge at midnight (the passage may have suggested Clough's allusion to 'solitary bridges' thronged with personifications), but Smith's poems more often fall back on the stale theme of the desirability of escape from the evils of the city to the purity of the country. Only, I think, in a few fine passages in *City Poems* (1857) does Smith effectively express his own experience of life in the Glasgow slums. In **"A Boy's Poem"** he develops an impressive conceit of the slow, organic growth of the city:

> Slow the city grew,
> Like coral reef on which the builders die
> Until it stands complete in pain and death.
> Great bridges with their coronets of lamps
> Light the black stream beneath; rude ocean's
>   flock,
> Ships from all climes are folded in its docks;
> And every heart from its great central dome
> To farthest suburb is a darkened stage
> On which grief walks alone.

G. Robert Stange in The Victorian City, *Vol. 2, edited by H. J. Dyos and Michael Wolff, Routledge and Kegan Paul, 1973.*

Among these inhabitants of the middle state, who, like Mr. Kipling's Tomlinson, are neither good enough for heaven nor bad enough for hell, the Scottish poet and essayist, Alexander Smith, would seem to merit greater attention on the part of the present generation. "Lifted up" (as Carlyle said of Kotzebue) "on the hollow balloon of popular applause" long before his talents had reached maturity, his fall, on the deflation of that balloon, was a great one; and it would have been better for him in the end if he had made the ascent of Parnassus on foot. Yet among the minor poets and perhaps even among the major essayists he has real claims to recognition.

Smith was born at Kilmarnock on December 31st, 1830, son of a pattern-designer. No detailed accounts of his early years exist, but we are informed by his friend Patrick Proctor Alexander that his education included "some tincture of Latin and mathematics." It is improbable that he studied at all deeply along classical lines, since his works are almost entirely devoid of allusion to Greek and Roman fable at a time when such references were part of the regular poetical equipment. His family moved to Paisley and thence to Glasgow (the dates are not known) and in Glasgow Smith grew up, reading deeply in English prose and verse, astonishing the local literary and debating soci-

ety by the fine quality of his contributions, and eventually finding a place for some of his poems in the columns of a local newspaper. His parents thought of making him a minister, but for some reason the idea was abandoned. It is unlikely that it was any change of views on Smith's part which prevented the carrying-out of the first design, for, in spite of a certain rationalistic flavour in his thought, passages in *Edwin of Deira,* the essay on **"Christmas"** and elsewhere prove that his faith in the Christian religion remained unshaken: at all events, on leaving school he was not sent to a University, but became apprenticed to his father's trade.

Literature, however, was his main interest, and in the year 1850 he made his *début* as a poet with some verses *To a Friend* published in the *Glasgow Evening Citizen,* a paper which continued, from time to time, to offer him the hospitality of its pages, wherein a number of his poems appeared under the pseudonym of "Smith Murray." The next year he sent some specimens of his work for criticism to the Rev. George Gilfillian, of Dundee, who was known as a sponsor of young authors and a contributor to various critical reviews. Gilfillian was away from home when Smith's manuscripts arrived, so his reply was somewhat delayed; but when he did eventually read the poems he pronounced a very favourable opinion and followed it up with articles in the *Eclectic Review* and the *Critic,* praising Smith's work and quoting extracts therefrom. The result of this was a considerable interest in the young Scotsman on the part of literary people before he had published any work of outstanding importance. He made friends with Hugh Macdonald and Professor John Nichol, and his acquaintance was sought by many whose interest had been aroused by Gilfillian's articles.

From the age of eighteen Smith had been in the habit of spending his summer holiday in the Highlands and the Western Isles, where he composed a good deal of verse and recited it to his companion while tramping among the glens and mountains. In 1853 he gathered together some of these poems, including *A Life Drama* (which was strung together from a number of separate compositions) and submitted them to the publisher Bogue, who accepted them and paid a fee of £100. This volume of *Poems* called forth favourable reviews not only in England, but also in France and as far afield as the United States and Australia, selling in several thousands of copies and reaching a fourth edition by 1855. In the first flush of success Smith gave up his trade and set out for London with John Nichol, visiting Miss Martineau and Philip James Bailey on the way. In the Capital he met with sympathy and encouragement from G. H. Lewes, Sir Arthur Helps and Herbert Spencer, and subsequently he was the guest of the Duke of Argyle and of Lord Dufferin. However, he soon seems to have found the necessity of having a secure regular income, for we next find him (in 1854) in the post of Secretary to the University of Edinburgh at a salary of £150 per annum. At Edinburgh he met Sydney Dobell, with whom he collaborated in *Sonnets on the War* (1855); but already, in 1854, had appeared W. E. Aytoun's parody *Firmilian; or the Student of Badajoz: a spasmodic tragedy,* under the *nom de guerre* of "T. Percy Jones," which dealt a satirical blow at both Smith and Dobell before they had actually met. When Smith's *City Poems* were published in 1857 they encountered but a lukewarm reception: his marriage in the same year to a descendant of the famous Flora Macdonald increased his responsibilities and thenceforward his life was a constant struggle against poverty and overwork. His next volume, *Edwin of Deira* (1861) brought down on his head accusations of plagiarism—a charge which had already been levelled at *City Poems* by the *Athenæum* of December, 1857; and though Smith preserved his dignity under these attacks he deserted verse for prose, probably hoping that "the other harmony" would be more remunerative and less likely to give rise to calumny.

He contributed to numerous periodicals, and in 1863 collected a number of his essays in a volume called *Dreamthorp,* now deservedly the best known of his works, which was reprinted by the Oxford University Press in 1914 with an introduction by Professor Hugh Walker. Two years later appeared *A Summer in Skye* and an edition of Burns. Smith even essayed fiction, and a novel of his entitled *Alfred Hagart's Household* ran as a serial in *Good Words* and was issued in book form in 1866. He then wrote a sequel, *Miss Oona McQuarrie,* and one of his last literary tasks was the editing of J. W. S. Howe's *Golden Leaves from the American Poets,* in 1866, for towards the end of that year his health broke down, and he died of typhoid fever on January 5th, 1867. In 1868 Patrick P. Alexander made a selection from his periodical contributions and gave them to the world with the title *Last Leaves*.

It is easy but uncritical to dismiss Smith, Dobell and P. J. Bailey with the contemptuous epithet "Spasmodic." Such labels, attached to a group of men who are sincerely striving after artistic expression, are very harmful, however salutary they may be when affixed to obvious charlatans. A famous instance which comes to mind is Dr. Johnson's condemnation of the "Metaphysicals" in his *Life of Cowley* where he employed the term with a deprecatory connotation, and, in his haste to discover the faults of a type of work outside his ken, almost entirely overlooked its great and outstanding virtues. There is no need to put forward the untenable claim that Smith had the "grand style" in verse. We may search in vain for lines like

. . . magic casements opening on the foam
Of perilous seas in faery lands forlorn

or like

Thou dost preserve the stars from wrong;
And the most ancient heavens, through thee,
   are fresh and strong.

But none the less he possessed many of the qualities of a true poet and wrote much verse which deserves to live by virtue of the music of its cadences, the vivid beauty of its imagery and the delicate play of its imaginative power. In the medium of the essay his accomplishment was still greater, and the man who does not know *Dreamthorp,* **"A Lark's Flight"** and **"Christmas"** has denied himself some of the most delightful passages in English prose, second only to Lamb's excursions in the same kind.

A Life-Drama, Smith's first long poem, is, taken as a whole, an unsuccessful performance. It is a drama in name only, and, from the nature of its subject as well as from the looseness of its construction, cannot even be ranked with that literary genre of doubtful legitimacy, the unplayable poetic play. It deals with the soul-struggle of a young poet, Walter, who is seeking fame and ideal love and is baulked of the one by incapacity and of the other, first by the death of the earliest beloved and then by a moral lapse. Torn by remorse, Walter, after unburdening himself to an outcast woman on a city bridge at midnight and then grasping fame, only to find it dust and ashes, returns to his Violet and finds salvation in a love purified with suffering. Walter is too self-conscious and overmuch concerned with niceties of sentiment, toying with each pleasurable or painful emotion as it comes, unable to take a firm stand on any moral or intellectual principle. Smith was compared with Keats in the days of his success, and though to mention him at this hour in the same breath with the Keats of the *Odes* and *Hyperion* would be to display a total lack of sense of proportion, *A Life-Drama* does call to mind in parts the early work of that master. Edward's song in Scene 8, for instance, with its

O kiss me into faintness sweet and dim!

and

My heart, like moon-charmed waters, all unrest,

recalls the somewhat sickly lusciousness found in certain passages of *Endymion*. The poem is mainly in blank verse, for the most part unrelieved by feminine endings, and containing a very large proportion of end-stopped lines, so that the general effect inclines to monotony. Some of its lines are as flat and prosaic as the flattest of Wordsworth, for example:

The family went abroad.

and

> I shall go down to Bedfordshire to-morrow.

But when all this has been said there are many purple patches, and many instances of that power of evolving vivid and telling "images" which, so long ago as Longinus, was rightly considered a high poetic virtue. In such a simile as

> Her unpolluated corse doth sleep in earth
> Like a pure thought within a sinful soul

the transition from an unpleasant idea to a peaceful and gracious conception is skilfully effected. Equally apposite, in a different way, is the jovial Arthur's rough-and-ready piece of optimistic philosophy:

> . . . . The world's a tun,
> A gloomy tun, but he who taps the world
> Will find much sweetness in't. . . .

A Life-Drama is imbued with a rich feeling for nature, more especially under the glowing hues of sunset or the pale light of stars or moon. There is a singularly delicate beauty in many of Walter's speeches and soliloquies; and into his mouth are put some of the best lines in the poem:

> I saw the pale and penitential moon
> Rise from dark waves that plucked at her, and go
> Sorrowful up the sky. . . .

The exquisite lyrics of Beddoes give more than half their value to his plays, and the same is true, in lesser degree, of the lyrics scattered over the pages of this poem of Smith's; for example, the Lady's song (Scene 2), in simple ballad metre, which begins excellently—

> In winter when the dismal rain
>   Came down in slanting lines,
> And Wind, that grand old harper, smote
>   His thunder-harp of pines,
>
> A Poet sat in his antique room,
>   His lamp the valley kinged,
> 'Neath dry crusts of dead tongues he found
>   Truth, fresh and golden-winged.

This lacks something of the naïveté of the ballad, but it is in the old form and not far away from the old sentiment and falls pleasantly on the ear. Arthur's drinking-song in Scene 8 has the requisite rollicking metre and may bear comparison with Thomas Love Peacock's

> A heel-tap! A heel-tap! I never could bear it,

so far as versification is concerned. Walter has another lyric, in Scene 4, wherein an interesting metrical ex-

periment is made, depending largely on recurring rhyme through three ten-line stanzas. A further similarity with Beddoes may be detected in the occasional references to modern science.

Much of the questing after fame, expression and ideal love which plays so large a part in *A Life-Drama* is probably a reflection of the poet's own desires. We know that Keats gave voice to very similar longings for the fulfilment of his poetic purpose in *Hyperion: a Vision,* and if Smith had possessed as great a gift, his spiritual autobiography would have been better worth the reading.

In the same volume appear eight sonnets and three other pieces, **"An Evening at Home," "Lady Barbara"** and **"To—".** Of these, by far the most notable is **"Lady Barbara,"** in Spenserian stanzas, one of the best things Smith ever wrote in verse. Its language is distinguished and pregnant with romance, quite without conceits or straining after the unusual, but attaining that choice of the inevitable word which brings full realisation of what the late Sir Walter Raleigh meant, when he said in his essay on *Style* that there was no such thing as a synonym. What synonym could satisfactorily replace the adjective in this line from the mouth of a man doomed to sail the seas for ever?

> And onward I must float, through slow *moon-measured* years.

Pictures "flash upon that inward eye Which is the bliss of solitude"; pictures serene, or bizarre, like those conjured up by *Sir Eustace Grey.* The sonnets are not very good examples of the Petrarchan form, and the same is true of *Sonnets on the War,* written with Dobell two years later, wherein the regular sonnet-structure is scarcely ever employed, either in the sequence of the rhymes or the break in thought at the end of the octet, to the detriment of the general effect. **"An Evening at Home"** contains the sketch of the idea afterwards worked up into the long poem: *Edwin of Deira.* It also contains a line,

> A simple primrose on a grassy bank,

reminiscent of a famous verse in Wordsworth's *Peter Bell.* Accidental similarities of phrasing like this, and a passage in *Edwin of Deira,* Book I, on the bats,

> That skim the twilight on their leathern wings,

which recalls Collins's *Ode to Evening,* may have given rise to the accusations of plagiarism brought against Smith. But everything that we know of his private life, everything we can gather from his very self-revelatory work (apart from P. P. Alexander's detailed refutation of many of the charges in his note to *Last Leaves*) makes it extremely unlikely that he stooped to conscious borrowing from his predecessors.

Turning to *City Poems* it is evident that a great expansion of talent and a sensible progress in taste have taken place during the four years between the two volumes. The poet is still preoccupied with the subjects which occupied his mind when he wrote *A Life-Drama*. Like the central figure of "Horton,"

> . . . . His sin of sins
> Was ne'er to be the master of himself,

but he approaches considerably nearer to self-mastery than he has done before; his strength of character has increased and with it his command over his medium, which is still, in the main, blank verse. "Horton" contains a considerable amount of disquisition on the nature and purpose of poetry, and deals with the trials of yet another poet, maligned, misunderstood and driven to roistering by the tragic death of the woman he loves, a few days from the date fixed for marriage. His song, revealing the real soul, unknown to his boon-companions, gives voice to the great sorrow which weighs him down, and the name of Barbara, on which each stanza ends, forms a sad refrain. A verse may be given here:

> 'Mong angels do you think
> Of the precious golden link
> I clasped around your happy arm while sitting
>   by yon brink?
> Or when that night of gliding dance, of
>   laughter and guitars,
> Was emptied of its music, and we watched
>   through latticed bars,
> The silent midnight heaven, creeping o'er us
>   with its stars,
> Till the day broke, Barbara?

In *City Poems* the autobiographical element is strong, and a phrase in "A Boy's Poem": "It was the closing evening of the year, The night that I was born," slips out and reveals it beyond question, but, even were this not so, the dominant ideas of this poem, "Glasgow" and "Horton" accord so well with the known facts of the poet's life that no serious doubt can remain. In "Glasgow" we hear the song of the unwilling town-dweller, wistfully casting his mind back to days spent amid nature's splendour but nevertheless finding, as a true artist ever will find, that the city has a beauty of its own for him who has eyes to see it. "A Boy's Poem" is instinct with fine feeling for the moods and aspects of nature, and full of the tragedy of poverty and unrequited love, and an ever-present sense of the supremacy and inevitability of death. "Squire Maurice" seems to mark the stage at which Smith was at last able to project himself into another personality, and presents an interesting case of conscience—the problem before the Squire being that of the clash between his social status and preconceived ideals of feminine perfection and the deep love of a village girl. It is the kind of subject that

Crabbe delighted in, and to say that Smith's treatment of it has points of superiority to Crabbe's methods is to give him only his due allowance of praise.

This self-projection is carried a step further in *Edwin of Deira* wherein Smith not only escapes from his introspective Old Man of the Sea but achieves a certain amount of action and a concrete subject-matter which is lacking in his earlier work. Edwin, king of Deira, seeking refuge from his enemies at the court of King Redwald, falls in love with his daughter, Bertha. This love is reciprocated, but before they marry there is more fierce bloodshed provoked by Ethelbert; and Regner, favourite son of Redwald, is killed. There is an appealing description of the mourning, and then of the marriage between Edwin and Bertha. A child is born to them, and at last, by the instrumentality of a band of evangelists, the natives of Deira, after desecrating the shrines of their ancient faith and finding that no harm results, are baptised as Christians.

Edwin of Deira was in great part written before Tennyson's *Idylls* appeared, but it was unfortunate for Smith that his choice of a knightly theme should have occurred at this time, for it raised once more the outcry of plagiarism. For all their superficial similarity in certain particulars, however, *Edwin* and the *Idylls* are distinguished by differences of intention and method which ought to have been apparent to the critics. Smith's poem, however much it may fall short of Tennyson's wonderful pageant of the Arthurian legend, is, in a sense, the culmination of his poetic achievement. The vivid metaphor and simile, the keen perception of beauty, the transparent sincerity of sentiment which we find in the early poems are still there, but over and above these qualities are superadded a greater reticence, a more unaffected simplicity, and a surer ear for the harmony of verse.

The tale of Smith's work in metre (leaving aside such pieces as are buried in the files of the newspapers) is completed by "A Spring Chanson" (*Last Leaves*) and a few poems incorporated in *A Summer in Skye*. The "Chanson" recaptures some of the freshness of the Middle English lyric, and that section of it which runs off from the irregular four-beat measure into a trochaic cadence reminds one a little of Blake's *Auguries of Innocence*, but the auguries here are rather of spring:

> Ón all/hármless/créeping/thíngs
> Cómes de/síre of/páinted/wíngs.

On taking up the essays, one is struck immediately by the facility with which Smith seems to have attained an accomplished prose style without apparent gropings after a method. This is not to say that there are not certain passages which have a more immediate appeal and remain longer in the memory than others, but it would be difficult to trace any line of development from the early work to the later, showing definite gradations of progress. In the prose even more than in the verse there are rich jewels of imagery. "Youth," he says, in **"An Essay on an Old Subject"** (*Last Leaves*), "is a lyrical poet, middle age a quiet essayist, fond of recounting experiences, and of appending a moral to every incident." Or again, "Winter is like a Red Indian, noble in his forests and solitudes, deteriorated by cities and civilisation." (**"Winter"**: *Last Leaves*). Speaking of battered editions of classic literature in a village library he says: "The viands are celestial if set forth on a dingy tablecloth." (*Dreamthorp*). His sentences, in the main, are short, and on occasion he can strike clause on clause to drive home a contention, turning the subject round on every side but avoiding tautology. A passage from the essay on *Dunbar* (*Dreamthorp*) will exemplify this:

> In our theatres the pantomime, which was originally an adumbration of human life, has become degraded. Symbolism has departed from the boards, and burlesque reigns in its stead. The Lord Mayor's Show, the last remnant of the antique spectacular taste, does not move us now; it is held a public nuisance; it provokes the rude chaff of the streets. Our very mobs have become critical. Gog and Magog are dethroned. The knight feels the satiric comments through his armour. The very steeds are uneasy, as if ashamed.

Smith's breadth of reading is apparent not only from the definite references he makes to different authors, but in quotation, conscious like most of his Shakespearean phrases or unconscious like the obvious, unacknowledged echo of La Rochefoucauld which occurs in **"On the Importance of a Man to Himself"**: "Love and friendship are the discoveries of ourselves in others, and our delight in the recognition."

The essays in *Dreamthorp* and *Last Leaves* fall into two divisions—familiar notes and literary appreciations, while *A Summer in Skye* is more or less a series of the same two kinds loosely joined together by the recital of the actual tour. The English familiar essay is one of the most pleasing manifestations of the national genius. Its essence is that it shall be personal, discursive and good-humoured, without polemical purpose or violence of passion, a green oasis where the intellectually wearied may rest awhile from his labours. No better description of the genre could be found than the paper in *Dreamthorp*, **"On the Writing of Essays,"** which shows Smith not only a master-craftsman but a craftsman fully conscious of his own methods and literary lineage; while his remarks on Montaigne and his contrast of the Frenchman with Bacon prepare us for the exhibition of sound and penetrating criticism which is given in the *Dunbar*, the *Geoffrey Chaucer* and elsewhere.

In the title-essay and the others of the *Dreamthorp* volume Smith appears in the guise of a middle-aged philosopher living in the retirement of a small village, looking with a kindly eye upon the simple pursuits and amusements of the natives, recking nothing of the great world of cities, and discoursing with pleasant candour and humility on any subject which comes to his hand. There is a certain pathos in the assumption of this personality, for the placid country life mirrored in the pages of *Dreamthorp*, wherein a good-humoured argument between the doctor and the clergyman becomes worthy to be set down as an incident, is just the happy, carefree state to which the over-worked, town-dwelling secretary and literary free-lance never attained; and he died when only on the threshold of middle age. **"An Essay on an Old Subject"** (*Last Leaves*) gives voice to the praises of the "forties" as the time of life when the truest happiness can be tasted:

> On the whole, I take it that middle age is a happier period than youth. In the entire circle of the year there are no days so delightful as those of a fine October, when the trees are bare to the mild heavens, and the red leaves bestrew the road, and you can feel the breath of winter, morning and evening—no days so calm, so tenderly solemn, and with such a reverent meekness in the air. The lyrical upburst of the lark at such a time would be incongruous. The only sounds suitable to the season are the rusty caw of the homeward-sliding rook—the creaking of the wain returning empty from the farmyard. . . .

If in Smith's verse a hectic note at times intrudes and spoils the harmony, in the prose no such disturbing element is present. Mellowness of thought, ripeness of judgment, serenity of temper, make the author of *Dreamthorp* and *A Summer in Skye* a very different being from him whose lineaments can be discerned in Walter or Horton. Even such a subject as **"Death and the Fear of Dying"** is treated without a hint of morbidity: he begins with extracts from Montaigne and Bacon, acknowledging the bravery of their outlook, but commencing his own remarks by the statement that their words are ineffectual in the face of the mighty *fact*. The fact always claims Smith's highest respect. He can write sympathetically of superstitions and omens, but never for one moment does his own reason allow him to believe therein. He adverts to the recognition of the fact of death running through human consciousness, heightening pleasure by a sense of transience, and to the dignity conferred on the meanest beggar by its presence. He contrasts the shallowness of a line of Byron's with the depth of one of Hamlet's soliloquies, and, refusing to venture on any theological or metaphysical speculations, closes thus, simply, without dogmatism:

> It may not be so difficult, may not be so terrible, as our fears whisper. The dead keep their secrets, and in a little while we shall be as wise as they—and as taciturn.

The troubles and compensations of the literary life are discussed in **"Men of Letters"** (*Dreamthorp*), an essay full of thought, and of that wistfulness which is one of the most attractive qualities in Smith's writings—because it is sincere and not the pose of the sentimentalist. **"A Lark's Flight"** reveals another quality which has been hitherto unexpected—a dramatic gift of no mean order. Two criminals are being executed in public, and, just as the executioner is about to perform his task, a lark starts up from the grass by the scaffold and is still pursuing his singing flight heavenwards when the two men have passed into eternity. The passage which describes this incident has been likened by Professor Hugh Walker to the knocking at the gate in *Macbeth,* than which praise could no higher go.

Smith's literary likes and dislikes are difficult to account for, as will be seen on reading **"A Shelf from my Bookcase"** (*Dreamthorp*). Hawthorne's *Twice-Told Tales,* Aytoun's *Ballads of Scotland,* the *Lyra Germanica,* Boswell's *Johnson* and Ebenezer Elliott form a strange assortment. It is strange, too, to find Wordsworth expressly excluded from among his "intimates" along with Shakespeare and Milton, for it is part of Wordsworth's greatness that he can still be read in the "indolent, languid" mood of which Carlyle complained when writing of the Waverley Novels. Smith is well-read in the English essay, he knows his Chaucer, he delights in the old Scottish poetry and has something suggestive to say about each of them. He has a certain gift of throwing out a critical epigram, which, though it be not all-embracing (few epigrams can be that) yet gives a very fair idea of the author under discussion. Thus of Leigh Hunt he says: "He called one of his books *'A Book for the Parlour Window'*; all his books are for the parlour window." (**"Essayists Old and New"**: *Last Leaves*); and of Chaucer: "He is like a cardinal virtue, a good deal talked about, a good deal praised, honoured by a vast amount of distant admiration, but with little practical acquaintance." But apart from such *mots,* Smith can enter into the spirit of a writer, giving a good interpretation of his work and his point of view, fulfilling one of the primary aims of criticism by arousing the desire to read the books criticised.

No account of Smith's essays would be complete without some allusion to the delightful *Summer in Skye,* which, as has been said, is less a connected narrative of travel than a series of essays on the scenery, history, legend, manners and customs of the romantic island. Herein Smith shows that he is soaked in the traditional lore of the Hebrides; and furthermore that he can retail the feuds of the Macleods and the Macdonalds in such a manner that no whit of their interest is lost. Living before modern scholarship had knocked the bottom out of Macpherson's claims, he is a firm believer in the authenticity of "Ossian" and refers to him often, quoting him at some length. Association has great sway over his mind: he likes to visualise Johnson and Boswell

in the Hebrides (the Doctor alluding to the mountains as "protuberances"!), or to conjure up pictures of ancient, bloodthirsty heroes and deeds of treachery and strife. Above all, his faculty of scenic description here reaches its greatest excellence. Like most men of high imaginative power he endows nature with a personality, and conveys with great artistry the impression of gaunt and eerie majesty made by the stark mountains of Skye, the swift changes of weather and their effect on the character of the islanders, and the sense of inanimate nature frowning sternly on the puny race of men who draw a precarious livelihood from her soil. The personal character-sketches, too, are on a high level, and the picture we retain of Mr. M'Ian is clear in every feature and alive in every line.

Alexander Smith is an egotist, but of the kind whose egotism is delightful. In his essay **"On the Importance of a Man to Himself"** he distinguishes between the two types of egotism—

> The one is the offspring of a narrow and unimaginative personality; the other of a large and genial one.

This last was Smith's: his life was blameless and filled with untiring effort after art, whether in verse or prose. He was not destined to become a great poet, but as a prose-writer his place is high and secure, and in both mediums he has much to give the present age which it should not lightly reject.

Richard Murphy (essay date 1948)

SOURCE: "Alexander Smith on the Art of the Essay," in *If by Your Art: Testament to Percival Hunt,* edited by Agnes Lynch Starrett, University of Pittsburgh Press, 1948, pp. 239-50.

[*Here Murphy praises Smith for his work as an essayist and as "an illuminator of the essay as a literary genre."*]

Should you look up Alexander Smith's biography, as Christopher Morley once threatened to do in prefacing an edition of *Dreamthorp,*[1] you discover he was a "Scottish poet, one of [the] chief representatives of the spasmodic school,"[2] who lived from 1830[3] to 1867. So has the author of *Dreamthorp* been tagged and stored away by the literary classifiers. But meanwhile, in defiance of canon and syllabus, Smith's *prose* works have been widely reprinted and selected. *A Summer in Skye*[4] has been issued in half a dozen editions in this century, and *Dreamthorp*[5] in a dozen. His edition of Burns,[6] distinctive for its biographical essay, has been continuously in print since 1868. A voluminous collection[7] of Victorian prose includes Smith's essays among those of thirteen enduring writers of the period. *Eminent British Writers of the Nineteenth Century* draws upon Smith for parts of its eminence, and compares him with "Lamb, De Quincey and Stevenson."[8] If you would seek Smith's monument today, look in the prose anthologies. There one discovers not only the essays of Smith, but essays in appreciation of him.[9] A worthy essayist has been retrieved from the categorizers. Many readers of essays can say today what Professor George Carver said years ago: "When I read Smith the first time, I knew that for me a new name had appeared among the essayists whom I must reckon as the elect."[10]

If one seeks the vortex of Smith's distinction, it is to be found not in his skill as essayist, but in his ability as a critic, an illuminator of the essay as literary genre. It is in this realm that superlatives most abound. In the "theory of the essay," says Hugh Walker, "Smith is unsurpassed."[11] "No better view can be offered of the significance of the essay," declare Scott and Zeitlin.[12] "Alexander Smith's *Dreamthorp* contains the best definition of the personal essay," write Allen Tate and A. T. Johnson.[13] Frederick Mayer thought "no better introduction" could be found for his treatment of *Victorian Prose* than Smith's "essay upon essays."[14] Indeed, Smith's comments upon the essay have become so interwoven with critical theory that some authors draw upon him without acknowledgement.[15] A contemporary of Smith was puzzled that an essayist should be so introspective concerning his art. In reading "essays upon essayists by an essayist," he experienced "the sort of feeling we have in a room with mirrors upon opposite walls."[16] But today we appreciate Smith as a craftsman able to understand and articulate the theory of his art.

His theory comprehends the genesis, development, form and style of the essay. "The essayist does not appear early in the literary history of a country,"[17] he says. When the essayist emerges:[18]

> . . . the national temper has cooled down—men no longer stand blinded by the splendours of sunrise. The air has been emptied of wonder. The gods have deserted earth, and men only remain. . . . Before the Essayist can have free play, society must have existed long enough to have become self-conscious, introspective; to have brooded over itself and its perplexities. . . .

For the essay as we know it, we are indebted first of all to Montaigne, "the creator of a distinct literary form."[19] Montaigne demonstrated that personal experiences can be "employed to illustrate and set off . . . [a] subject."[20] Although he himself was the concern of his essays, he considered the events in his life as facts of nature.[21] He was "avowedly an egotist," but an egotist "consumed by a hunger for truth."[22] He wrote about himself because he had nothing else so interesting to write about, and because he had no public to please.[23] Montaigne is not only the first of the essayists, but

"the greatest of the garrulous and communicative."[24] Bacon contributed profundity; he is "the greatest of the serious and stately essayists."[25] The "satirists of society," Addison and Steele, "brought style to perfection."[26] In the nineteenth century, the scope of the essay was further enlarged. "Lamb extended the sphere of the essay, not so much because he dealt with subjects which till his day had been untouched, but because he imported into that literary form a fancy, humour, and tenderness."[27] Carlyle perfected the critical and biographical essay. He was an artist able to "brood over the abysses of being"; he revealed "that the poorest life is serious enough when seen against eternity."[28] Macaulay "is the creator of the Historical Essay." He contributed to the essay a pictorial quality; he painted "historical pictures" in a "wonderful splendor and pomp of colour"; "every figure . . . is finished down to the buttons and the fingernails." Unlike Carlyle, he could not "take hold of an individual and view him against immensity"; but he showed us how to delineate a man against the backdrop "of contemporary events."[29] So did Smith perceive the origins and the history of the essay to be: a literary form which began in Montaigne's introspective egoism, and developed and matured, as society became more complex and sophisticated, into the socially critical egoism of Macaulay and Carlyle.

Although Smith provided[30] for classification of essays by types, he sought not fine lines of demarcation, but rather the essential similarity in all forms. He excluded incidental aspects in searching for the essence. The essay is:[31]

> . . . neither a dissertation nor a thesis; . . . it is a work of art, and must conform to artistic rules. It requires not only . . . intellectual qualities, but unity, wholeness, self-completion. It must hang together. It must round itself off into a separate literary entity. When finished, it must be able to sustain itself and live.

The essay "bears the same relation to the general body of prose that the lyric bears to the general body of poetry."[32] In this comparison, Smith finds the key to the essay as form:[33]

> The essay, as a literary form, resembles the lyric, in so far as it is moulded by some central mood—whimsical, serious, or satirical. Give the mood, and the essay, from the first sentence to the last, grows around it as the cocoon grows around the silkworm.

In the author's mood we find the essay's intrinsic nature.

But not all men have the necessary intellectual qualities, the "constitutional turn of mind"[34] required for writing essays. The true essayist's "habit of mind is leisurely—he does not write from any special stress of passionate impulse";[35] he is not a pamphleteer. He must have "a quick ear and eye, an ability to discern the infinite suggestiveness of common things, a brooding meditative spirit."[36] If he wishes to follow Montaigne's example, the essayist must be frank, "perfectly tolerant of himself and of everybody else," but able to "laugh at himself and his reader."[37] If the essayist has these qualities, even a trivial subject will "lead him away to the great questions over which the serious imagination loves to brood."[38]

But to produce an artistic essay, the writer must have *style*. Since he is a "kind of poet in prose,"[39] he must depend upon style for his success. Although Smith makes style the final test, he shies away from any technical analysis of its elements:[40]

> To define the charm of style is as difficult as to define the charm of beauty or of fine manners. It is not one thing, it is the result of a hundred things. Everything a man has is concerned in it.

Consistently Smith maintains that an author's situations and responses, and the kind of man he is, determine style. "Emotion and utterance are twin-born, consentaneous, like sorrow and tears."[41] He calls attention to Bacon's sentence; it "bends beneath the weight of his thought, like a branch beneath the weight of its fruit."[42] Sentences worthy of a profound man. He cautions against mere "facility in writing."[43] As the literary skill of a man increases, so must his "intellectual resource increase at the same ratio."[44] One must beware "artifices to fillip the dull spirit of the reader."[45] If the writer resorts to tricks, he becomes a "'base mechanical,'"[46] and "his successes are not much higher than those of the acrobat or the ropedancer." The stylist is not "a lapidary coldly polishing a gem."[47] Style is the "amalgam and issue of all the mental and moral qualities in a man's possession."[48]

Although Smith exalted style, he also had profound respect for substance.[49] If he had to choose between weight of idea and *mere* form, he chose idea. He heard Mr. Gladstone, marvelled at his "clear and bell-like cadence," yet found him to be "an elocutionist" rather than "an orator or a thinker."[50] But he was moved by Carlyle's speech, though given in "low, wavering, melancholy tones," because he had "gone to the bottom of things and knows."[51] To the writer, thought and its expression are of one piece. For the essayist, "style [is] as much an element of his success as his thought."[52] But if the reader evaluates qualities in a finished literary work, style rather than content is the distinguishing element. Smith supported his position with two reasons. One, style not only gives life to ideas, but it gives to them immortality. It is true indeed that "thought is the material on which expression feeds,"[53] but:[54]

Thought, if left to itself, will dissolve and die. Style preserves it as balsams preserve Pharaoh. . . . The enamel of style is the only thing that can defy the work of time.

It is in this sense that "style, after all, rather than thought, is the immortal thing in literature."[55] Smith held it to be high literary service that:[56]

> . . . when thought grows old and worn with usage, it should, like current coin, be called in, and from the mint of genius, [be] reissued fresh and new.

Age does not invalidate a worthy idea, and it may gain by being recast:[57]

> To make a fine modern statue, there is a great melting down of old bronze.

Secondly, Smith venerated style as the personal, distinctive quality in literature. Style is:[58]

> . . . a secret window through which we can look in on the writer. A man may work with ideas which he has not originated, which do not in any special way belong to himself; but his style—in which is included his way of approaching a subject, and his method of treating it—is always personal and characteristic. We decipher a man by his style, find out secrets about him, as if we overheard his soliloquies, and had the run of his diaries. . . .

Because style gives life to thought, and because style is the personal, "peculiar"[59] element in literature, Smith could say in good conscience:[60]

> In reality, it is not of so much consequence what you say, as how you say it.

In regarding literature as "pure,"[61] Smith anticipated the aesthetic concepts of the later Victorians. His theories appeared in the 1850's and the early sixties, a time usually described in literary histories as one of high didactic purpose and social responsibility. As Hardin Craig and J. M. Thomas say, it was not at the mid-point, but "toward the close of the century" that literature came to be regarded as not "merely an instrument for instructing or moving men but an art which is to be exercised for the pleasure it gives both to the writer and to his readers."[62] *The Yellow Book,* in an article written by James Ashcroft Noble, hailed Smith as "a Stevenson born out of due time." Readers of *The Yellow Book* were told:[63] Smith provided

> . . . what is probably the first statement by an English writer with any repute of the famous doctrine "Art for art's sake" to which Smith seems to have worked his own way without the prompting of Gallican suggestion.

Although Smith was a precursor, he cannot accurately be classified among the advocates of *l'art pour l'art*. He disparaged neither social reform nor the study of human affairs. And he shunned aesthetic intensity. The essayist and the poet, he maintained, may "inform" and "cancel abuses," although reform is not their "duty."[64] He enjoyed Bunyan's "sermonising in disguise."[65] For Cowper's muse he had admiration: she "does not sit apart in sublime seclusion—she comes down into the ways of men, mingles in every-day concerns."[66] On his shelf of selected books, Smith had room for Ebenezer Elliott, "a monomaniac on the Corn-laws" and "poet of the poor."[67] Succinctly Smith put his theory on art:[68]

> What in a work of art is really valuable is the art. The statue that is only worth the weight of its metal is a very poor statue indeed.

Walter Pater's later phrase, "art for its own sake,"[69] revealed the trend toward aestheticism, and Oscar Wilde's "joy in art—the flawless beauty and perfect form of its expression,"[70] records its culmination.

Since Alexander Smith's theories are egoistic, they can best be understood in relation to the man himself. He was a simple man who read widely and recorded his appreciations. His father was a pattern designer in Kilmarnock when Alexander was born on December 31, 1829. His family hoped they might educate him for the ministry, but they were poor; so it seemed best that Alexander follow his father's vocation. At twelve Smith was a child-worker in a Glasgow warehouse, tracing designs on muslin.[71] As he developed into youth he turned to the world of books, that "finer world within the world,"[72] and the realm to which he devoted the rest of his days. He tried writing verse, and sent a packet of his youthful pieces to George Gilfillan of Dundee, then at the height of his influence in Scottish letters. Gilfillan encouraged Smith, hailed him as a "sun-buried Mercury," called upon all lovers of poesy to intervene lest Smith "pine away amid mechanical drudgery," and printed four pages of his verse.[73] In 1853, Bogue of London issued *Poems,* which, within three years, went through four London and twenty Boston[74] editions. At twenty-five Smith was famous, but needed a means of livelihood. The town council of Edinburgh, in 1854, responded by electing him Secretary of the University of Edinburgh, a position he held until his death.

With his induction as secretary, Smith began a regimen little varied through the rest of his life. Days went on university records, evenings in reading and writing. The holidays were spent at his wife's home in Skye. *City Poems*[75] and *Edwin of Deira*[76] were published but indifferently received. The charges of "spasmodity"[77] which had been brought against **A Life Drama,** in **Poems,** persisted, and a new attack, plagiarism,[78] was

raised. Sensitive to the charges made against his verse, Smith turned to writing reviews and essays. He had found his *metier*. At thirty-four, in retreat behind a full beard, he was the tolerant old gentleman of **Dreamthorp**. He wrote a novel, some tales, edited and reviewed as opportunity came his way. At thirty-seven he died, of typhoid. Fine phrases, he thought, are more desirable than banknotes, and the only fame he cared for was to be quoted occasionally.

Notes

[1] (Doubleday, Doran & Co., Garden City, 1934.) Morley has often sponsored Smith. One of the "writers in English who have given me the greatest pleasure in twenty years of mature reading," he testified [*Saturday Review of Literature,* VIII, No. 22 (Dec. 19, 1931), 394].

[2] *Webster's Biographical Dictionary* (1943).

[3] *Webster's* is in error on the date of birth, as are the *Dictionary of National Biography,* the *Cambridge History of English Literature,* and many other sources. Alexander Smith was born December 31, 1829. (For confirmation of the date, see the author's thesis, *Alexander Smith: Man of Letters,* University of Pittsburgh, 1939.)

[4] 2 volumes (London, Alexander Strahan, 1865).

[5] (London, Strahan & Co., 1863.) Both *Skye* and *Dreamthorp* were printed by Ballantyne in Edinburgh.

[6] *Poems, Songs and Letters,* being the *Complete Works of Robert Burns* (London, Macmillan, 1868); *Globe Edition*. This work is not to be confused with Smith's edition of *The Poetical Works of Robert Burns,* 2 volumes (Cambridge and London, Macmillan, 1865); *Golden Treasury Series.*

[7] Harrold, C. F. and Templeman, W. D., *English Prose of the Victorian Era* (New York, Oxford, 1938), p. 1743.

[8] Withington, R. and Van Winkle, C., 2 volumes (New York, 1934), I, xii.

[9] See, for example, B. C. Williams, *A Book of Essays* (Boston, 1931). The collection includes Smith's "On the Writing of Essays" and "In Praise of *Dreamthorp*" by Joseph J. Reilly.

[10] "Alexander Smith," *Of Essays and Essayists* (University of Pittsburgh, 1929).

[11] Introduction to *Dreamthorp with Selections from 'Last Leaves'* (*The World's Classics,* Oxford, 1914), p. xiv.

[12] Scott, F. W. and Zeitlin, Jacob, *Essays-Formal and Informal* (New York, 1930), p. 150.

[13] *America Through the Essay* (New York, 1938), p. i.

[14] (New York, 1935), p. 1. The essay reprinted is Smith's "On the Writing of Essays."

[15] Three samples follow: (1) A. C. Baugh, P. C. Kitchen, and M. W. Black, in *Writing by Types* (N. Y., 1925, p. 221) quote six lines by Smith, but identify them only as views of "an interesting essayist." (2) In *Modern Familiar Essays,* edited by W. M. and D. B. Tanner (Boston, 1927, p. 3 f.), Smith's ideas of the essay are used with and without quotation marks, but with no acknowledgment. (3) *Cf.* Smith's "The essayist . . . lies upon the idle grassy bank, like Jacques, letting the world flow past him, and from this thing and the other he extracts his mirth and his moralities" (*Dreamthorp,* p. 26); "The familiar essayist is a veritable Jacques upon a mossy bank, who, while he watches the world go jostling its way down the river of life, extracts from its seemingly confused and meaningless tumbling bits of living wisdom and quaint chuckles of fun" [Sister M. Eleanore, *The Literary Essay in English* (Boston, 1923, p. 199)].

[16] *London Quarterly Review,* XXI, No. 61 (Oct., 1868), 157. Reference is to Smith's "Essayists, Old and New," which was collected by Smith's friend, Patrick Proctor Alexander in *Last Leaves* (Edinburgh, W. P. Nimmo, 1868). The review, a very discerning one for the times, was by [James Smetham].

[17] "On the Writing of Essays," *Dreamthorp,* p. 30.

[18] "Essayists, Old and New," *Last Leaves,* p. 245 f.

[19] *Dreamthorp,* p. 39.

[20] *Op. cit.,* p. 37.

[21] *Ibid.,* p. 34.

[22] *Ibid.,* p. 35 f. Smith's meaning in *egotist* is akin to current usage of *egoist.*

[23] *Last Leaves,* p. 222 f.

[24] *Dreamthorp,* p. 39.

[25] *Loc. cit.*

[26] *Last Leaves,* p. 223 f.

[27] *Ibid.,* p. 227.

[28] *Ibid.,* p. 238 f.

[29] *Ibid.,* p. 240 f.

[30] See *Last Leaves,* p. 249.

[31] *Op. cit.,* p. 248.

[32] *Ibid.,* p. 247.

[33] *Dreamthorp,* p. 25.

[34] *Op. cit.,* p. 38.

[35] *Ibid.,* p. 30 f.

[36] *Ibid.,* p. 25.

[37] *Ibid.,* p. 34 f.

[38] *Ibid.,* p. 26.

[39] *Ibid.,* p. 25, 44.

[40] "Literary Work," *Last Leaves,* p. 131. The parallel with Buffon's "style is the man himself" (*Discours sur le Style,* 1753) is apparent, but Smith seems not to have read the earlier work.

[41] "Men of Letters," *Dreamthorp,* p. 165.

[42] *Dreamthorp,* p. 31.

[43] *Op. cit.,* p. 151.

[44] *Ibid.,* p. 150.

[45] "Scottish Ballads," *Last Leaves,* p. 14.

[46] *Dreamthorp,* p. 151. The phrase is from Shakespeare, *2 Henry VI,* I, iii, 196.

[47] *Last Leaves,* p. 18.

[48] *Dreamthorp,* p. 43.

[49] "You cannot make ideas; they must come unsought if they come at all" (*Dreamthorp,* p. 166).

[50] "Mr. Carlyle at Edinburgh," *Last Leaves,* p. 97 f.

[51] *Op. cit.,* p. 105 f.

[52] *Last Leaves,* p. 248.

[53] *Dreamthorp,* p. 151.

[54] *Last Leaves,* p. 130 f.

[55] *Dreamthorp*, p. 43.

[56] *Op. cit.*, p. 44.

[57] *Last Leaves*, p. 127.

[58] *Op. cit.*, p. 131 f.

[59] *Ibid.*, p. 230.

[60] *Dreamthorp*, p. 43.

[61] *Ibid.*, p. 25.

[62] *English Prose of the Nineteenth Century* (New York, 1929), p. 5 f.

[63] Vol. IV (January, 1895), 121-142. The highly appreciative article was titled "Mr. Stevenson's Forerunner." It was reprinted by Thomas Bird Mosher in his *fine* edition of *Dreamthorp* (Portland, Maine, 1913).

[64] *Dreamthorp*, p. 25.

[65] *Divine Emblems*, or *Temporal Things Spiritualized*-with Preface by Alexander Smith (London, Bickers and Son, [1867]), p. x.

[66] "William Cowper," by Alexander Smith, *Encyclopaedia Britannica*, 8th ed., VII (1854).

[67] "A Shelf in My Bookcase," *Dreamthorp*, p. 206 f.

[68] "Literary Work," *Last Leaves*, p. 128. This essay was first printed in *Good Words*, IV (1863), 740-742.

[69] "Conclusion," *The Renaissance* (dated 1868).

[70] "The English Renaissance of Art" (1882).

[71] The Rev. T. Brisbane, one of Smith's close friends in the warehouse days, has written intimately of him in *The Early Years of Alexander Smith* (London, Hodder and Stoughton, 1869).

[72] *Dreamthorp*, p. 144.

[73] *Eclectic Review*, II, *n. s.* (July-December, 1851), 447-462.

[74] The early American editions were by Ticknor, Reed, and Fields.

[75] (Cambridge, Macmillan, 1857.)

[76] (Cambridge and London, Macmillan, 1861.)

[77] The term was used by W. E. Aytoun to describe poets guilty of romantic excesses. Whatever the merits

of the word, it can apply to no more of Smith than his first youthful work.

[78] Time has dealt kindly with Smith in this regard. That his early work has echoes of the romantic poets is clear enough, but the charge of literary thievery soon ran itself out.

An anonymous critic describes Alexander Smith:

Perhaps our lady readers may be gratified by the information we are happily enabled to give them, that the young poet is rather slenderly built, with fair though not curly hair, like the hero of his drama; large blue eyes—one of them unfortunately cast, but the defect is lost sight of in the dreamy haze that in quiet moments seems to curtain his spirit; but when excited by mirth his eyes gleam like two of his much-loved stars. His temperament, it may be guessed, is nervous and susceptible: we may add, though conscious we tread on sacred ground, that the lines which grace our poetic corner to-day forms a key to much of the heart-poetry of the *Life Drama*.

An anonymous writer, in The Critic, *Vol. xiii, No. 321, August 15, 1854.*

Mary Jane W. Scott (essay date 1979)

SOURCE: "Alexander Smith: Poet of Victorian Scotland," in *Studies in Scottish Literature*, Vol. XIV, 1979, pp. 98-111.

[*Below, Scott maintains that Smith used his personal experience in mid-Victorian Scotland as the basis for his poetry.*]

"It ought . . . to be distinctly recognised that, whatever he is by birth, Mr. Smith is *not* a Scottish poet, if we understand by that a poet of a certain supposed national type. It is not Scottish scenery, Scottish history, Scottish character, and Scottish social humours that he represents or depicts," wrote David Masson in 1853.[1] Scots critic Masson must have held a very narrow definition of that "supposed national type," the Scottish poet, who presumably ought to limit himself to explicitly Scottish themes (and, probably, to Scots language as well). His critical motives in thus commenting on Alexander Smith's *A Life-Drama* (*Poems,* 1853) were perhaps nationalistic, more probably unimaginative. His conception of what the Scottish poet and Scottish poetry should be, was then (and still is) a common one, but clearly inadequate in failing to acknowledge the contributions of Anglo-Scots such as Smith. In his initial judgment of Alexander Smith, Masson was certainly premature.

A Life-Drama is in English, and was in fact heavily influenced by English and German Romantic literature and by Elizabethan drama. The poem's unevenness prompted Prof. W. E. Aytoun of Edinburgh to include Smith, along with English poets P. J. Bailey, Sydney Dobell, J. S. Bigg and J. W. Marston, in the infamous "Spasmodic School." But even the early *Life-Drama* incorporates much that is particularly Scottish in its most outstanding features, its strongly autobiographical theme and its abundant descriptive imagery. Alexander Smith's imagination fed primarily on his own mid-Victorian Scottish experience; his best poetry was always highly subjective, and his poetic representations could not help but reflect Scottish landscape, character and society. The Scottish description in the obsessively egocentric *Life-Drama* acts rather as pathetic fallacy (echoing the speaker's inner "spasms") than as realistic description for its own sake. But even here, Smith has transformed the borrowed attitudes and vocabulary of English Romantic poetry, to express his Scottish experience. Masson's early judgment would become particularly inappropriate after *A Life-Drama,* as Smith drew increasingly away from his English models and from the strident egocentricity of the "Spasmodic" style, to find his own poetic voice. He would develop the ability, hinted at in *Poems,* to place the Self within the Scottish context, and thus to strike a balance between subjective and objective, internal and environmental elements in his poetry. The Scottish landscape would achieve autonomy, separate identity from the poet's mind, in *City Poems* and in subsequent mature works. Thus can Alexander Smith's poetry, in addition to his abundant and strongly Scottish prose, tell us a great deal about Scotland in the mid-19th Century.

Alexander Smith was born in Kilmarnock, Ayrshire in 1829,[2] the son of a Lowland textile-pattern designer and his Highland wife. The Ayrshire birthplace was the first of many connections Smith would make between himself and Robert Burns; that he identified with Burns seems clear, from his essay on the poet, which he later used as the Preface for his edition of Burns.[3] Other implied parallels included: their background as laborer-poets; their self-education and wide reading; their "inspired" poetic vocation; their usual self-limitation to Scottish subject-matter and settings, as their most effective poetic material; their meteoric rise to fame and their distrust of public favor; their satirical wit (more often apparent in Smith's essays, but nonetheless present in the poetry); their deep love of nature, though always subordinate to the central human focus of the poetry; and the tragedy of their premature deaths (in 1865, when Smith adapted his Burns essay for the Preface, he was ill, and probably aware that he was dying). Smith wrote that Burns' grave was "dug too early—and yet too late," and this was sadly applicable to himself as well, since both poets suffered a loss of fame and favor prior to their early deaths.

After a series of removals to Paisley, and back to Kilmarnock, Smith's family settled in Glasgow, where the boy briefly attended primary school, his only formal education. Here he learnt to do elementary arithmetic and to read well. At the age of about twelve, "Daft Sandie" took up his father's trade as a pattern-designer, but continued to read voraciously, in English, Scottish and American literature. His early Scottish favorites included Burns, James Thomson, Thomas Campbell and Walter Scott. He probably also read, fairly early on, Hogg, Galt and Carlyle (all three of whom may have directly influenced *A Life-Drama*). He also seems to have been acquainted in youth with the Gaelic oral tradition of song and story, through his Mother and perhaps through a Highland friend or servant who reportedly entertained the family with Ossianic legends. His abiding interest in the Highlands would be reflected in his poetry and prose throughout his career.

It was during this period when, bored with tedious factory work in Glasgow, Smith began to write poetry and essays. He belonged to the Addisonian Literary Society, a group of fellow-laborers who met to practice the art of the English essay. His poetic "calling" he took especially seriously, telling only his closest friends of his endeavors. His first poems were published under the pseudonym "Smith Murray," in the *Glasgow Evening Citizen* (1850-51). Smith's early experience as a laborer in the harsh environment of industrial Glasgow was the main force which would shape his poetic imagination (much as it did Edwin Muir's in this century), for life.

Smith's young life was not without its pleasures, however. During his vacation from the factory each summer, he and his best friend Thomas Brisbane travelled to the Highlands and Islands. A great number of scenes and incidents in the poetry are specifically traceable to these visits, as Brisbane recorded; he also remarked on the extent to which Smith viewed the Highlands through a Romantic literary sensibility tutored by Walter Scott. Thus, while the urban poet Smith's appreciation of the Highlands (the land where "mythologies are bred," **"A Boy's Poem,"** 2. 664) was often romantic or idealizing, it was always grounded in personal experience. This was not the case with his portrayal of English scenes; Smith made only one trip to England (in 1853), and it remained for him remote. The few English settings in his poetry are sketchy and stylized, and usually distant in time as well as in place.

The young Smith spent much of his spare time in extensive walks along the Clyde and through the countryside near Glasgow, with such friends as Hugh Macdonald, who was an avid Scottish nationalist, naturalist, and aspiring Scots poet. Macdonald not only taught him much about the flora and fauna of the Clyde Valley, details of which appear frequently in the poet's imagery; he also counselled him to abandon English poetry, and write instead in Scots. Smith stood firm, however, and continued to write in English. Although he acknowledged the emotive power of Scots for those who grew up hearing it, "recalling infancy and the thousand instances of a love of a mother's heart, . . ."[4] he at this stage held an essentially Romantic attitude to his poetic art: he, the poet, was an inspired partaker in "divine" creation. Smith evidently felt that Scots, which had largely ceased to function on a formal literary level by mid-19th Century, and was used chiefly to evoke mirth or exaggerated sentimentality, was inappropriate to his higher calling, and so employed English from the beginning.

Smith was now leading an increasingly dual life, working in the factory all day and writing poetry late into the night. He produced many lyrics of varying quality, many of which dealt with a poet-persona like himself, who stood apart from the everyday life of the city, sometimes longing for involvement, but isolated, to a degree, by his calling. Smith eventually summoned the courage to send several of the lyrics to the Rev. George Gilfillan of Dundee, critic, reviewer and patron of struggling would-be Romantics. Gilfillan was highly impressed,[5] and urged Glaswegians to "neglect not one of the finest poets—perhaps, indeed, one promising to be the finest since Campbell—their good city had produced."[6] At Gilfillan's encouragement, Smith compiled his shorter, largely-autobiographical verses into a long poem in the fashionable monodrama format, *A Life-Drama*. This work formed the bulk of his first volume, *Poems* (1853). *A Life-Drama* is characterized by fitful action and a glut of sensuous, over-rich imagery; its poet-hero, the objectionably egocentric Walter, Smith modelled to an extent on Byron's *Manfred*, Bailey's *Festus,* and Goethe's *Faust* and *Werther* (possibly by way of Carlyle's translations). Primarily, however, Walter represents strong but distorted autobiography. W. E. Aytoun's "Spasmodic" label (a term of opprobrium first applied by Carlyle to Byron[7]), and his cruel parody *Firmilian,* severely damaged Smith's reputation at this crucial period; the "Spasmodic" label would cling to the poet of *A Life-Drama* despite his movement towards a better-balanced, more realistic and readable poetry.

In *A Life-Drama,* the hero Walter moves erratically through "crises" rather than "development" (the typical Spasmodic method[8]), but he ultimately affirms love and acceptance of Victorian "social responsibility."[9] Carlylean influence would seem to be strong: this climactic "Everlasting Yea," reinforced by Scottish Calvinistic work-ethic principles, as well as the use of abundant garment and textile imagery (central to *Sartor Resartus,* and strengthened by the poet's trade as pattern-designer), and an underlying concept of hero-worship, are characteristic of Smith's earlier, autobiographical poems.

Smith's descriptive method in *A Life-Drama* was simply to accumulate images in very great abundance ("our chief joy was to draw images from everything," *L-D,* Sc. IX). Of course, the use of copious natural imagery, mosaic-fashion, to compose a vivid picture had long been a feature of Scottish Gaelic descriptive poetry (of which Smith possibly knew, through his Mother, and through translations). In *A Life-Drama,* he used rich conventional Elizabethan and Romantic imagery in new combinations, and often with new concreteness and realistic impact, and also introduced fresh images to deal with complex psychological insights and responses to the environment of 19th-Century Scotland. While he described the countryside with great affection, his most striking and original imagery was that of the Industrial Revolution, essentially urban (Glasgow) inspired. Smith's **"Iron World"** (*L-D,* Sc. IV) is James Thomson's "iron times" (*Seasons,* "Spring," *2.* 274) of progressive society, fulfilled in Victorian Scotland.

While Smith's urban imagery is most plentiful and effective in the mature *City Poems* volume, it is nevertheless powerfully present in *A Life-Drama,* chiefly as it serves to reflect Walter's states of mind. Much of the Glasgow/Clyde description foreshadows the imagery of the lyric **"Glasgow."** An example of Smith's adaptation of conventional Romantic imagery, to express his vision of industrial Glasgow, might be this Shelleyan fire-personification, transformed:

> As slow he journeyed home, the wanderer saw
> The labouring fires come out against the dark,
> For with the light the country seemed on
>   flame:
> Innumerable furnaces and pits,
> And gloomy holds, in which that bright slave,
>   Fire,
> Doth pant and toil all day and night for man,
> Threw large and angry lustres on the sky,
> And shifting lights across the long black roads.
>   (*L-D,* Sc. VIII)

Such passages also recall Galt's *The Entail,* which portrays a similar vision of early 19th-Century, industrial Glasgow.[10] From the beginning, Smith was careful to incorporate the machinery of the Industrial Revolution into his urban vision; the foundry and factory, the railroad, the steamboat and the telegraph are as much a part of the Scottish landscape as the ancient Clyde itself, which runs through the city dark, deathly and Styx-like:

> This stream has turned
> The wheels of commerce, and come forth
>   distained;
> And now trails slowly through a city's heart,
> Drawing its filth as doth an evil soul
> Attract all evil things; putrid and black . . .
>   (*L-D,* Sc. X)

Smith's preoccupation with sin and evil, especially morbid in *A Life-Drama,* probably derived much from his Scottish Calvinistic upbringing, as well as from his reading of authors of moral-psychological emphasis such as Hogg, and his American counterpart Hawthorne; Walter of the "scarr'd heart, fed upon by hungry fires" (*L-D,* Sc. V) is in many ways a character worthy of either novelist.

A Life-Drama draws the significant contrast, developed with greater complexity in *City Poems* and later lyrics, between city and country. The poet-persona comes to accept his urban reality, to join in it, only in the poem's conclusion; acceptance of the city in any of the *Poems* is tentative, at best. In *A Life-Drama* the city, Glasgow, is vividly portrayed in terms of evil, darkness, and death; its atmosphere of murk, fog and smoke creates a particularly "northern" hell (compare hell's northern climate in Gavin Douglas's *Eneados*). By Smith's day, of course, industry had added greatly to the already grim atmosphere of the northern city. In contrast, the surrounding countryside is depicted, rather less realistically, in an atmosphere of brightness, clarity and color.

The passages in *A Life-Drama* which refer to the Highlands assume a Wordsworthian poetic voice, adapted to the Scottish scene; their simple, moving diction, quieter tone and more spiritual themes (love of nature, time and memory, the divinity of childhood) contrast sharply with Walter's usual urban intensity. These passages, recounting Walter's visit to Loch Lubnaig, contain a great deal of detailed description of places and incidents (for example, the graveyard scene and the eclipse, Sc. VI) which Brisbane would confirm as genuine, based on his visits with the poet to the Highlands.

A Highland reference of a different character occurs in Sc. VIII of *A Life-Drama;* it is the **"Drinking Song"** in praise of whiskey. The singer (Arthur) is English, and his song presents the typical mid-Victorian English picture of Scotland (complete with purple heather, deer-hunting parties, bagpipe music, "fresh ruddy lasses," and whiskey-quaffing stereotypes). The Scottish Highlands were opening up to English tourists during Victoria's reign as never before, and were frequently made the subject of English literature (such as, for example, Arthur Hugh Clough's *The Bothie,* 1848[11]). Smith's rollicking lyric seems, in fact, to have been a subtle parody, both of currently popular English notions of the Scottish Highlands, and of native Scottish sentimental or "kailyard" literature, which was an equally stereotyped product of the 19th Century. In his parody, Smith also hinted at the darker, more violent side of Scottish life ("hills stained with heather, like bloody footprints;" and, in general, the dangerous grip whiskey can take on men's souls). Like Burns, he was able to strike a satirical note without sacrificing the

lyrical delight or good humor of the song. Smith's skill at parody is a dimension of his talent which, unfortunately, has been overlooked or misinterpreted by his critics.

The language of *A Life-Drama* is, as might be expected, highly derivative of the English Romantics and their Elizabethan forebears in the "decorative" tradition. The poem does contain certain northern archaisms (such as "for aye") and even a few Scotticisms (such as Scots "aboon," and such localizing nouns as "braes" and the Gaelic "cairn"). Still, though a greater number of Scotticisms occur in *A Life-Drama* than in the later poems, they are nowhere particularly abundant in Smith's poetry (he used them more frequently to give "race"[12] to his prose works, to enhance local color, control tone, and exploit the unique connotative power of the dialect). His only Scots poem is also his only thoroughgoing satire; the late verse **"The Jubilation of Sergeant Major M'Turk in Witnessing the Highland Games"**[13] again attacks overly-sentimental views of Scotland, mocking the futility of modern Highland Games. It parodies such tartan-thumping nationalism as found in verses like John Imlah's "The Gathering."[14] In the final stanza, contrasting mock with real war, Smith employed the arresting Burnsian technique of turning from comic Scots verse to pure English, to make his serious point: "When bayonets next are levell'd/They may all be needed then."

Before considering *City Poems,* it is worth noting a further verse from the *Poems* volume, of an experimental nature. In **"Lady Barbara,"** departing from his usual autobiographical stance, Smith attempted to enter into the mind of an independent character. The verse is ballad-like, although it is not a ballad proper (Smith did not believe in the possibility of writing good modern ballad-imitations,[15] but chose rather to try to capture the psychological/emotional essence, the immediacy of ballad literature in his own new way). **"Lady Barbara"** has its experimental counterpart in this Browningesque, distancing mode in *City Poems,* **"Squire Maurice"** (whose plot, the difficult love of a nobleman for a peasant girl, recalls Ramsay's *Gentle Shepherd,* as well as the interpolated tale of Palemon and Lavinia in Thomson's *Seasons,* though without their simple, happy dénouements). It is interesting to note that both **"Lady Barbara"** and **"Squire Maurice"** are set in remote time, in a stylized and very English landscape, unlike Smith's more realistic Scottish settings for his autobiographical poems. These poems attempt to present, objectively, complex human situations, but neither is wholly successful, since they treat of themes outside the poet's own Scottish experience.

"The Change," an appropriately-titled autobiographical poem in his second volume, *City Poems* (1857), marks a number of important changes in Smith's life and art. He had given up his factory work in 1854, to take up an appointment as Secretary to Edinburgh University. He had married (his wife was a Highland girl, one Flora Macdonald from Skye, a descendant of the heroine), and had settled in the pleasant suburb of Wardie, near Edinburgh. **"The Change"** celebrates Smith's discovery of his own poetic voice. It signals the poet's longed-for return to the "real world," both in his life and in his poetry (a goal hinted at in **"Sonnet No. Three,"** *Poems*), and simultaneously refutes the lofty Romantic-Spasmodic concept of the poet's rôle which he had once assumed:[16]

> But mine is now a humbled heart,
> My lonely pride is weak as tears;
> No more I seek to stand apart,
> A mocker of the rolling years.
> Imprisoned in this wintry clime,
> I've found enough, O Lord of breath,
> Enough to plume the feet of time,
> Enough to hide the eyes of death.
> ("**The Change**," *ll.* 57-64)

In the "wintry clime" of Scotland, Smith had found new potential for a more outward-looking, true-to-nature poetry. His *City Poems* are far superior to *Poems,* and this is largely because they are on a human scale, grounded more realistically than ever in the poet's experience of life in mid-Victorian Scotland.

"Horton" opens *City Poems;* it is another monodrama, more carefully constructed than *A Life-Drama* and acting as a sequel to it. The character Horton was a poet-friend of the main speaker, representing Smith as he had been, a larger-than-life Romantic who strove too high and failed. Horton had died—just as Smith's youthful poetic Self had died. The main speaker is Smith himself, as he became, having cast off the impossible, Walter-like pretensions of youth. In addition to this central autobiographical situation, the poem is full of real details and incidents (for example, Horton's song, the refrain for the dead Barbara, which refers to Smith's lady-friend Barbara who drowned in the Glasgow and Paisley Canal in 1850). The poet's balancing of complex relationships in time and space, his skilful use of the internal monologue, and his bold and original urban imagery in the autobiographical **"Horton"** are typical of his mature, *City Poems* style.

"A Boy's Poem" is also strongly autobiographical, and built on Smith's personal recollections and impressions of Glasgow and the Highlands. It tells much of the young poet's own story, of his development in the context of 19th-Century Scotland, in contrast to the crisis-ridden, often obscure subjectivity of *A Life-Drama*. There is an abundance of rich and closely-detailed imagery (far less derivative than in the early *Poems*), describing the specifically-Scottish landscape, both urban and rural. The many images of the Industrial Revolution exist in the landscape without a trace

of awkwardness. The Highland descriptions, due to the poet's visits there with his wife, show renewed immediacy and affection. In many instances, **"A Boy's Poem"** parallels Smith's only novel, *Alfred Hagart's Household* (1866), which likewise portrays a Scottish childhood largely based on Smith's own. *Alfred Hagart's Household* might seem a rather pale limitation of Galt's novels of domestic life in the West of Scotland, but it makes pleasant reading, and is of some autobiographical interest. Smith had projected a full-scale Scottish novel, but never carried it out; he did, however, publish in periodicals several short-stories on Scottish themes.

Smith's poetic masterpiece is the lyric **"Glasgow."** It was not entirely original in concept, having followed the Glasgow pedlar-poet James Macfarlan's *City Songs* volume of Glasgow poetry (1855); Macfarlan had in turn, however, based much of his urban imagery on Smith's *A Life-Drama* and his other early poems. In **"Glasgow,"** Smith at last made the difficult assertion of *acceptance* of the city in all its aspects (an acceptance Edwin Muir was never able to make). Now, he could cry: "In thee, O City! I discern/Another beauty, sad and stern" (11.47-8). The ability to sustain such a central paradox, in a sort of "Negative Capability," is characteristic of his mature poetry; **"Glasgow"** is a superb illustration of the balance in his poetic vision, of subjective and objective views, good and evil elements which he achieved in *City Poems*. In **"Glasgow"** the speaker, clearly Smith himself, proclaims his love-hate relationship with the city, always aware that he belongs to it:

> "City! I am true son of thine" (*l.* 9);
>
> "I know the tragic hearts of towns" (*l.* 8);
>
> "I know thee as my mother's face" (*l.* 56);
>
> "Of me thou hast become a part—
> Some kindred with my human heart" (*ll.* 116-7);
>
> "For we have been familiar more
> Than galley-slave and weary oar" (*ll.* 119-120).

In **"Glasgow,"** rural life is known to the speaker only through small, second-hand messages like "A dropt rose lying in my way,/A butterfly that flutters gay/ Athwart the noisy street" (*ll.* 92-4). Deepest meanings for him are not found in the less-familiar country landscape, but in the city: "All raptures of this mortal breath,/Solemnities of life and death,/Dwell in thy noise alone." (*ll.* 113-5), and, "A sacredness of love and death/Dwells in thy noise and smoky breath" (*ll.* 135-6). The "sad and stern" images of the urban scene are closely detailed and realistic, in deliberate contrast to the more conventional, idealized rural descriptions. Likewise, the several urban personifications (the city

itself, the railroad, the Clyde) are dynamically portrayed, with concrete, sensuous images, while the rural
personifications (Summer, Autumn, the rainbow) are
stylized, emblematic. Glasgow is described, as in *A
Life-Drama,* in terms of hellish darkness, murk and
death, and the concise lyric form makes for even greater
immediacy. Such closely-observed description of the
particularly harsh aspects of the environment was a
Scottish literary commonplace by Smith's day (usually
applying to more realistic "winter," as opposed to stylized "spring," representations); Smith's application of
"winter" realism to industrial Glasgow added a new
dimension to the tradition. In *City Poems,* and especially in **"Glasgow,"** Smith broke away from his early
English Romantic models and proved himself a master
of that supremely Scottish talent, the poetry of realistic
natural description.

Smith's last poem of length is the historical-narrative
Edwin of Deira (1861). The story's germ had been
told as the interpolated tale in the poem **"An Evening
at Home"** (*Poems,* 1853), indicating Smith's early
interest in the myth of Edwin (King of Northumbria in
the 7th Century, who welcomed Christianity into Northern Britain and who was said to have founded
Edinburgh, or "Edwin's Burgh"). This Northern legend must have appealed to Smith in its connection
with Edinburgh, for he was by then living there, and
was forming a deep affection for the city. *Edwin* was
a failure in 1861, however, and remains so; while highly
polished and controlled, it lacks the fundamental in-
gredient of Smith's best work: personal experience. It
is remote from 19th-Century Scotland (as are **"Lady
Barbara"** and **"Squire Maurice"**) and from Smith's
own life. Unlike *A Life-Drama,* which is too subjective, *Edwin* is perhaps too objective, and likewise
unbalanced.

Two short lyrics were published in the *Edwin* volume,
which are more successful; they are both specifically
Highland in theme, and inspired by Smith's journeys
to Skye with his wife. **"Torquil and Oona"** is a ballad-like tale of death by drowning (a prominent theme
in Scottish literature, from the ballads, to Romantics
Falconer and Campbell, to the 20th-Century Orkney
poet George Mackay Brown). **"Blaavin"** is an intimate description of the speaker's love for a Highland
mountain, and his self-perceptions in relation to it. Such
affectionate personification of a mountain or other
natural object is a Gaelic literary convention[17] (adopted
recently, for example, by Norman MacCaig in his "A
Man in Assynt").[18] Smith's appreciation of Gaelic
poetry, at least in translations, was confirmed in his
critical comments on "Ossian," and translations of
"Ossianic" poetry by one Rev. Mr. Macpherson of
Inverary, which he published in *A Summer in Skye,*
1865. Both **"Torquil and Oona"** and **"Blaavin"** are
typical of Smith's later lyric poetry, in their quieter,
more philosophical approach, their more controlled yet

effective and carefully-chosen descriptive imagery, and
their ultimate spirit of optimism, or faith in nature.

The short, semi-autobiographical lyric remained Smith's
most congenial form, and although he published no
more volumes of poetry after *Edwin,* he continued to
write some worthwhile poetry, published in *A Summer in Skye,* and posthumously in *Last Leaves.* His
poetic output declined considerably, as he wrote more
and more popular prose to support a growing family.
His later poetry in general shows the influence of a
quieter, more comfortable life in Edinburgh than he
had known in Glasgow—Edinburgh, too, provided
poetic inspiration, but of a gentler sort. His imagery
became subdued, restrained; his attitude grew more
contemplative and spiritual. Harsh urban and industrial
imagery faded, and a more idealizing natural imagery
predominated. A typical such poem is **"Autumn"**
(*Summer in Skye*), set near Edinburgh. The pleasing
melancholy of the descriptive imagery shows the possible influence of Thomson's "Autumn," filtered
through his disciple in nature-poetry, Tennyson. The
poem's philosophy seems related to the Scottish Calvinistic work-ethic, implied in Smith's earlier poems,
and coming from the heart of a Scottish Victorian la-
borer-poet; here, the stern lesson of the necessity and
value of productive labor is taught by fruitful nature,
in an incantatory lyric.

By this time, the mid-1860's, Smith was feeling the
pressures of an increasingly onerous job; the Reform
Act of 1858 had added greatly to his duties as Secretary to the University. He began to dream of owning
a sheep-farm in Skye, but grew ill before he could
realize this dream. As his own death approached, his
poetry dwelt on his favorite themes of time and death
with particular poignancy. With these late, meditative
pieces he had come full circle, from the intensely subjective early poetry, through poetry of personal and
social "realism," to poetry of universal philosophical
significance. He had gained faith: not the orthodox
Presbyterian faith recommended to him by his mentor
Gilfillian many years before,[19] but a very personal faith
in nature's renewing power. Smith died in 1867, at age
37.

Smith left a poetic fragment when he died, entitled
"Edinburgh" (*Last Leaves*); it was intended as a com-
panion-piece to **"Glasgow,"** but he was unable to complete it. While **"Glasgow"** had been central to Smith's
mid-Victorian, socially-aware and immediate outlook,
in **"Edinburgh"** he went beyond the particulars of the
cityscape to create an imaginative, transcendant vision.
The two poems share the characteristic subjective
stance, but the subject himself had changed; Smith
described his adopted city, Edinburgh, as he might have
described his later poetry: "My later home is still and
fair / With mournfulness of sunset air" (*ll.* 7-8). With
subtlety the poet sifted Edinburgh's many appearances

and moods, including the added dimension of historical association, to try to discover the city's essence, its total reality. The delicately varied atmospheric imagery of light and color in **"Edinburgh"** is less concrete, more abstract and idealizing than that of grim **"Glasgow":** Smith did not mention Edinburgh's horrors of the Cowgate and Canongate slums in the poem (though he knew of them and described them in *A Summer in Skye*), and the poem's only violence is on the historical plane. Broadly, where Glasgow had been depicted in terms of "hell," Edinburgh was a "heaven," but each embraced infinite variations; Smith knew, accepted and belonged to both Scottish cities. Glasgow and Edinburgh were simply the most appropriate symbols the poet knew, to represent the dual nature of life, and of his own life in particular.

Although the great bulk of his prose has tended to overshadow the poetry, Alexander Smith would have wanted to be known primarily as a poet, and it remains true that as a poet he made his most original contributions to Scottish (and British) literature. He wrote, first and foremost, to express himself and his personal vision of mid-Victorian Scotland. Any specific literary influences, English or Scottish, are of secondary importance to the central, subjective and Scottish stance of the poet. Even David Masson was later to admit that Smith's poetry was grounded in his Scottish experience, though he held that Smith transformed this experience into "a visionary world that was in no particular sense Scottish." Masson was right in his final judgment of Smith, however, when he praised the poet's ability to *transcend* the bounds of Scottish language and subject-matter,[20] to create a poetry of universal import. Perhaps because he lived in Smith's own time, Masson did not realize just how much Smith's poetry would tell us, in the 20th Century, about the real life and the landscape of 19th-Century Scotland. The paradoxical beauty and the truth of Victorian Scotland itself, as the poet knew and accepted it, inspired the best of Alexander Smith's Anglo-Scottish poetry.

Notes

[1] [David Masson], "Theories of Poetry and a New Poet," *North British Review,* Vol. 19, No. 38 (August, 1853), p. 339.

[2] The date of Smith's birth has long been disputed (he was born Dec. 31st of either 1829 or 1830); most biographers have given 1829, though this has never been proven conclusively. The chief biographies of Smith, from which the biographical data in the present article is drawn, are: Thomas Brisbane, *The Early Years of Alexander Smith* (London, 1869), and Patrick Proctor Alexander, "Memoir" of Smith in his edition of Smith's *Last Leaves* (Edinburgh, 1868), pp. v-cxxiii.

[3] Alexander Smith, ed., *The Poetical Works of Robert Burns* (London, 1865).

[4] Alexander Smith, "Scottish Ballads," *Last Leaves,* pp. 26-7n.

[5] [George Gilfillian], "Recent Poetry," *Eclectic Review,* N.S. Vol. 2 (October, 1851), pp. 447-62; "A New Poet in Glasgow," *Critic,* Vol. 10 (December 1, 1851), pp. 567-8.

[6] Gilfillian, quoted by Brisbane, *Early Years,* pp. 123-4.

[7] P. P. Alexander, "Memoir," *Last Leaves,* p. 1xv.

[8] Jerome Hamilton Buckley, *The Victorian Temper* (London, 1966), p. 47.

[9] Mark A. Weinstein, *William Edmondstoune Aytoun and the Spasmodic Controversy* (New Haven, 1968), p. 90.

[10] John Galt's *The Entail* was first published in 1822. Note the similarity of Smith's portrayal of Walter, and of Glasgow in "pathetic fallacy" with him, to the character Claud, whose thoughts and feelings are likewise reflected by the industrial city, for example: "His [Claud's] whole bosom was a flaming furnace—raging as fiercely as those of the Muirkirk Iron Works that served to illuminate his path," John Galt, *The Entail,* ed. Ian A. Gordon (London, 1970), p. 245.

[11] For a discussion of this, see Editor's Notes to Arthur Hugh Clough's *The Bothie,* ed. Patrick Scott (Brisbane, 1976).

[12] Dr. Samuel Johnson used the vintner's term "race" to describe the unique flavor and descriptive force of James Thomson's language in *The Seasons,* in its earlier versions, before the revisions rid the poem of much of its Scottish expression (Johnson, "Thomson," *Lives of the Poets*).

[13] Alexander Smith, *A Summer in Skye* (London, 1865), I, 316-7.

[14] John Imlah, "The Gathering," *Whistle Binkie* (Glasgow, 1878), I, 43. It originally appeared in Series 4 (1853) of that collection.

[15] Smith, "Scottish Ballads," pp. 59-60.

[16] Smith's essay "Sydney Dobell" (*Last Leaves,* pp. 171-209) is the parallel in prose, of his rejection of the Romantic-Spasmodic poet's rôle in "The Change."

[17] A good example is "Praise of Ben Dorain" by the 18th-Century Gaelic poet, Duncan McIntyre, discussed

by Kurt Wittig, *The Scottish Tradition in Literature* (Edinburgh, 1958), pp. 188-9.

[18] Norman MacCaig, "A Man in Assynt," *Akros,* Vol. 3, No. 7 (March, 1968), pp. 11-17.

[19] George Gilfillian, *A Third Gallery of Literary Portraits* (Edinburgh, 1854), pp. 159-60.

[20] [David Masson], "Alexander Smith," *Macmillan's,* Vol. XV (February 15, 1867), pp. 343ff.

Richard Cronin (essay date 1990)

SOURCE: "Alexander Smith and the Poetry of Displacement," in *Victorian Poetry*, Vol. 28, No. 2, Summer, 1990, pp. 129-45.

[*In the following essay, Cronin asserts that* A Life Drama *reflects the life-long despair Smith felt at not being part of the exclusive poetic circle of England.*]

Bound up with **A Life Drama** in Alexander Smith's first volume is a poem called **"An Evening at Home."**[1] The title with its promise of cozy domesticities is glumly ironical. Forty miles to the South is Ayrshire where Smith was born, and a lost dream of peasant community, "The Cotter's Saturday Night."[2] Even farther away, is another dream, an evening party in an English country house, wine flowing, wit, poetry and song, and the daughter of the house looking with melting eyes on one of the guests, penetrating through the bitter world-weariness of his manner to the sensitive, passionate soul that subsists beneath.[3] Smith's evening at home is far removed from either of these. He has completed his ten hours of mindless labor tracing patterns onto strips of muslin, and has come back to the rented room in Charlotte Street, Glasgow, where he lives alone. It is the evening of November 18, 1852, and Smith's thoughts are of London and of Wellington's funeral:

> To-day a chief was buried—let him rest.
> His country's bards are up like larks, and fill
> With singing the wide heavens of his fame.
>   (p. 205)

Smith, sitting in his rented room, cannot join this chorus, and if there is a trace of contempt for the singers— early birds catching coffin worms—it is a contempt born of envy. Tennyson, the laureate, had been promptest of the larks. His great ode was published two days before the burial, in time to be hawked outside St. Paul's during the funeral service.[4] He was the chief singer in what is less an exaltation than a charm of larks. Smith admits the charm. What complicates his sense of it is that the larks form a charmed circle from which he knows himself excluded. His whole poem is dominated by his sense of his own isolation, his own exclusion.

Outside Smith's window there are "yellow fogs" and "misty rain" (p. 205) and grimy industrial buildings. He knows, like all poets of the mid-nineteenth century, that poetic inspiration is only to be found in Nature, in a "simple primrose on a grassy bank" (p. 207), but there is no Nature to be seen from his window. What is more, he has no great men to celebrate as the English bards celebrate Wellington. Glasgow with its "streets of warehouses" is ruled by hard-nosed merchants who want no poets to fill the heavens of their fame because the only heaven they can imagine is a "heaven of money-bags" (p. 208). Smith is a Scot, and it seems to him incongruous that a Scot should be writing poetry. Poetry happens in England: "Most brilliant star upon the crest of Time,/Is England" (p. 208). Smith has never been there. He cannot join the charm of larks and sing an elegy for Wellington, a dirge for a dead hero that will be at the same time a celebration of the sense of nationhood that for almost half a century Wellington had embodied. It is not Smith's nation, and, in any case, Smith carries with him a bitter knowledge that would make it hard to trill a song of simple gratitude for the life of a great man. He listens to the rain as it "Flings itself wildly on the window-panes,/Imploring shelter from the chasing wind" (p. 208). He hears the rain like that because he knows that the rain "beats on human limbs as well as walls." Glasgow is in the grip of the mid-century depression. Wages are low, unemployment is high, and in the streets there are homeless beggars.

So Smith does not write a poem about Wellington. Instead, he tells a little tale about a "lady" who lives on an island, and spends her time "feeding her petted swans" (p. 209). But she is not happy, because her "lord" is away from home. When he comes back he tells her that he has met some Christian missionaries and has been converted to Christianity. She is delighted, and the two of them paddle away together in a canoe to listen to the missionaries. The little story is absurd,[5] but it serves its turn: it distracts Smith from Charlotte Street and Glasgow and the muddle of the nineteenth century: "The Past is with me, and I scarcely hear / Outside the weeping of the homeless rain" (p. 218). But the last line is too strong: it is not the present but the past that is drowned out.

Smith begins his poem thinking of Wellington carried to his grave and the poets of England rising like larks to sing his praises. Death and larks are more curiously associated for Smith than the poem reveals. On May 14, 1841—Smith was only eleven but already a full-time factory worker—he had been one of a crowd of 150,000 who had followed behind the cart carrying two murderers, Dennis Doolan and Patrick Redding, to their place of execution.[6] The two men were Irish navvies who had killed their English overseer, whose appointment had been opposed by the navvies' union, the United Hibernian Labourers. Sir Archibald Alison,

The Broomielaw, Glasgow, looking west.

who organized the execution, thought it "a cold-blooded combination murder."[7] To enforce the example, it was decided that the hanging should take place some three miles from Glasgow, on the spot where the murder had taken place. Alison feared an attempt to rescue the condemned men, and called in 1,800 troops to safeguard the execution. In the event, all went smoothly. "My duty was done," writes Alison, "all felt there was a Government in the country." Not quite all, because Smith's feelings were quite other. What he noticed before his view of the execution was blocked by the brass helmet of a mounted dragoon, was "an incident so simple, so natural, so much in the ordinary course of things, and yet so frightful in its tragic suggestions":

> When the men appeared beneath the beam, each under his proper halter, there was a dead silence,— everyone was gazing too intently to whisper to his neighbour even. Just then, out of the grassy space at the foot of the scaffold, in the dead silence audible to all, a lark rose from the side of its nest, and went singing upward in its happy flight. (pp. 113-114)

Then the helmet came between Smith and the scaffold, he heard a sharp sound and felt the crowd heave, "torn

by a sharp shiver of pity," and still the lark was rising from its nest, still singing.

"An Evening at Home" might have been a better poem had the thought of Wellington's death prompted Smith to tell the story of the hanging of Doolan and Redding rather than a tale about pet swans and canoes and missionaries. But it was only after *A Life Drama* had made him famous, after he had given up his factory job and been appointed Secretary of the University of Edinburgh,[8] the position in which he remained for the rest of his short life, that Smith could bring himself to write directly about his early years. In two of the *City Poems,* published in 1857, Smith records his factory experience (**"Horton"** and **"A Boy's Poem"**), and in a third, **"Glasgow,"** he offers a benign tribute to the city where he grew up. But by then he is looking at Glasgow from the detached perspective of Edinburgh; he is remembering his factory years from a position of modest, middle-class respectability. By then, too, he has learned from Tennyson how to write an English idyll, that weird and wholly Victorian poetic kind that arrives at realism by way of Theocritus, subsumes jarring modern material within a gracefully easy blank verse, and thus contrives to bathe even the most un-likely subject matter in a nostalgic, pastoral glow. *City Poems* failed, and so did *Edwin of Deira,* the long narrative poem that Smith published four years later. After that Smith turned to prose. Here, too, both in *Dreamthorp,* a collection of essays, and in *A Summer in Skye,* a travel book, Smith records his earlier experience, but in prose he borrows a style from Lamb just as effective as the Tennysonian idyll in keeping himself at a safe distance from his subject matter.

Smith witnessed the Glasgow riots of 1848,[9] the most serious disturbances in all Britain in the year of revolutions. He was, he tells us, "a mere lad" who happened to be "in the streets at the time." He was not—he was eighteen—and his information seems curiously detailed for someone momentarily caught up in the crowd. Among much else he remembers "a begrimed collier with a rifle over his shoulder": "This worthy, more than two-thirds drunk, kept shouting at intervals, 'Vive la Republic! We'll hae Vive la Republic, an' naething *but* Vive la Republic!' to which intelligible political principle his followers responded with vociferous cheers." The facetiousness works to remove Smith from the scene, to place him at a safe, novelistic distance from the crowd. This is style working not so much to present experience as to offer an alibi.

After 1854 Smith uses style to hide behind. He is not a great poet. He is still of interest because there went into the making of his poems an interesting experience, but as the years go by and the subject matter is addressed more directly, the style becomes more detached. Smith believed that what we value in literature is its revelation of the writer's personality; "In truth, it is in the amount of this kind of personal revelation that the final value of a book resides." Predictably, he is an exponent of the expressivist aesthetic that dominated mid-Victorian poetics. But his development of the position is more interesting than we might except. First, it follows, for Smith, that "the style is even of more importance than the thought," because a writer's style reveals him most completely. Style is "a secret window through which we can look in on the writer" (*Last Leaves,* pp. 132, 126, 131). Second, Smith is not really interested in personalities in themselves. In an essay entitled **"A Shelf in My Bookcase"** (*Dreamthorp,* pp. 187-210), Smith disarmingly declares his preference for the lesser men of letters, writers that he can think of as belonging to himself rather than to the world. Of these his most surprising example is Ebenezer Elliott, the anti-Corn law rhymer, the Chartist turned free-trader, the author of the fiercest and most exuberant radical verse of the nineteenth century. Smith claims for Elliott's work "an historical value": "Evil times and embittered feelings, now happily passed away, are preserved in his books, like Pompeii and Herculaneum in Vesuvian lava" (p. 212). His verse is important not simply because it so nakedly reveals Elliott himself,

but because the self that the verse reveals is representative:

> Elliott is the poet of the English artizans—men who read newspapers and books, who are members of mechanics' institutes, who attend debating societies, who discuss political measures and political men, who are tormented by ideas. . . . I am amazed that the world does not hold [Elliott's poetry] in higher regard, if for nothing else than for its singularity. (p. 213)

I suspect that Smith is making a muted, indirect claim here for the value of his own early verse, in particular *A Life Drama.* In this one volume Smith can properly claim to be the poet of the Glasgow artisans, of those who had little schooling (Smith's ended when he was ten), who took menial jobs and pursued at nights and at weekends strenuous courses of self-education. These men met together in any one of dozens of Glasgow clubs (Smith's was the Addisonian), and there they talked literature, politics, natural science. Among these men, before 1848, the Chartists would have found their organizers, but after the 1848 riots Chartism died in Glasgow, and with it the possibility that the energies of such men might find a political outlet. *A Life Drama* is their poem.

This assertion will seem odd to those familiar with the work, which is entirely apolitical and is set for the most part in the English shires. Only two scenes take place in a city, and the first of them identifies the city as London. Walter, the hero of the poem, has a family estate in Kent, and is so secure in his class that he refers to a tenant as "one of my peasants" (p. 86). Walter is a poet, possessed by a frantic desire for fame. The plot manages at once to be very simple and utterly absurd. A lady taking her pet fawn for a walk comes across Walter sleeping under a tree, "Thick in the light of his own beauty" (p. 8). The two fall in love with each other, but when Walter declares his passion, the lady confesses that she is already betrothed and in a few weeks will become "a pale bride wedded to grey hair" (p. 79), a sacrifice to the financial interest of her family. Walter is plunged into despair and contemplates suicide, but when we next meet him he has reverted to his poetic ambitions, his disappointment has served only to give a more Byronic cast to his effusions. A friend, Edward, invites Walter to accompany him on a visit to a country house owned by a rich wine-bibber called Mr. Wilmott. There he meets Mr. Wilmott's beautiful daughter, Violet. She is immediately struck by Walter's fascinating pallor and is captivated when he tells her the story of his disappointment. She then declares her love to him, and he rapes her. Stricken with remorse, Walter takes himself off to a city. He stands at midnight on a deserted bridge, confesses himself to a passing prostitute and then rushes away. But when we next meet him he is still full of plans to write the poem that will make him famous, and in the following scene we learn from a conversation between two of Walter's friends that he has actually succeeded. The poem is written, published and has scored a huge hit. But success has not made Walter any happier. In the final scene Walter and Violet are reunited in Walter's ancestral home. Walter decides that love is more important than fame, and, secure in his love for Violet and his faith in God, decides to pursue his vocation without worrying about how the world receives his efforts.

To suggest that a ridiculous farrago such as this might have something to do with Glasgow artisans seems on the face of it improbable. In fact, the two most sensitive contemporary readers of Smith responded to *A Life Drama* in exactly this way. Arthur Hugh Clough relishes the poem because he glimpses in it "the black streams that welter out of factories, the dreary lengths of urban and suburban dreariness." Poetry, he argues, is now most likely to be found "in the blank and desolate streets, and upon the solitary bridges of the midnight city," and that is where, he assumes, Smith found it. He ascribes a valuable function to Smith's poem, a function connected with his class. Such poems "console us with a sense of significance, if not dignity, in that often dirty or at least dingy work, which it is the lot of so many of us to have to do, and which someone or other, after all, must do." Clough reviewed Smith's volume together with Arnold's 1850 and 1853 volumes.[10] To turn from *A Life Drama* to Arnold's poems is to travel between classes: it is to retreat from the city streets "and pass into a lighted sitting-room, and a family circle, with pictures and books, and literary leisure, and ornaments, and elegant small employments." Clough does not impute to *A Life Drama* any political bent, and yet, obscurely, he seems to feel it. Somewhat incongruously, he peoples Glasgow's solitary midnight bridges with a whole crowd of abstractions, among them "pale Hope that looks like despair." The echo of Shelley's *Mask of Anarchy* is obvious enough,[11] even though Clough is writing in March 1854, exactly six years after Glasgow's Peterloo. Trilling recognizes Clough's drift. Smith "had been a mechanic and this seems to have induced Citizen Clough to read into his pretentious work a democratic significance which is simply not there. Actually, no-one could have been of higher degree or greater elegance than the characters of *A Life Drama*; even *The Princess* was no more cozily swaddled in romantic arstocracy."[12] But Trilling is, I suspect, a more careful reader of Clough than of Smith.

The second witness is particularly powerful because his concern is to acquit Smith of charges to which, he assumes, *A Life Drama* leaves Smith vulnerable. Smith's biographer and the closest friend of his youth, the Rev. Thomas Brisbane, insists emphatically that *A Life Drama* is "unlike [Smith's] other work, unlike the man himself, and reflects his own spirit less than anything else that he has written" (p.142). It was composed "under the heat of unnatural and unhealthy excitement which several things had combined to effect." Brisbane identifies four of these unnatural stimulants. One is a short-lived enthusiasm for Bailey's *Festus*. Another has to do with the unusual circumstances of the composition of the poem. Smith had sent a batch of short poems to the Dundee minister and literary propagandist, the Rev. George Gilfillian immediately recognized in Smith "a second Keats," and proceeded to trumpet Smith's genius in articles in *The Eclectic Review* and *The Critic*.[13] So it was that Smith had the unique experience of finding himself famous almost before he could be said to have published any poems. With Gilfillian's encouragement he set about preparing his first volume. Gilfillian seems to have expected a conventional collection, but instead Smith embedded his existing poems within a single dramatic poem, *A Life Drama,* a poem that took as its primary subject Walter's pursuit of poetic fame and his achievment of it by the rapid and fevered composition of just such a poem as *A Life Drama*. In those heady months of 1852, as Smith welded together his lyrics, the subject of his poem became the process of its own composition.

The other two circumstances noted by Brisbane are rather different. Smith felt "often the disadvantage of a defective education." He resented the menial factory job that prevented him from pursuing "his favourite studies except in brief leisure hours." He saw "little or no visible prospect of bettering his circumstances," and "it was not wonderful that, patient as he was, his spirit should sometimes become despondent, fretful, and irritated" (p.144). He felt, it seems, like one of his own characters in *A Life Drama*:

> Dungeoned in poverty, he saw afar
> The shining peaks of fame that wore the sun,
> Most heavenly bright, they mocked him
>   through his bars. (p. 135)

To describe such feelings as "unhealthy and unnatural" seems harsh, but I take Brisbane's point to be that the tantalizing glimpse of fame that Gilfillian had offered him acted during the term of the composition of the poem to aggravate Smith's sense of the injustice of his social and economic and educational disadvantages. The final circumstance—last in my account, but Brisbane places it first—is interesting because it seems to make no sense. Brisbane is attempting to explain Smith's mood in 1852, and he begins his account by referring to events four years before:

> His youth had been passed in the very focus of Scottish chartism. In 1848 occurred the last French revolution, and the reflex of that movement had been felt in this country, as was manifest in riotous

risings in various parts of the kingdom, but especially in Glasgow. There the mob had at mid-day broken into shops in the very centre of the city; the military had been called out; and armed pensioners, too prompt to obey a hasty command, had fired upon the people, fatally shedding blood, which awakened the feeling of revenge in some, and alarm in all: so that the whole of the inhabitants were thrown for days into a state of ferment. And Smith had been a spectator of the most notable of these riots.

"No thoughtful and sensitive young man could be altogether unmoved or uninfluenced in spirit by the political agitation of these days," writes Brisbane and immediately begins to qualify his point very thoroughly. Smith was "no politician however, and still less a chartist," and by 1848 he was living, as far as he could, outside "the sphere of politics," "in a dreamland of poesy." The "riotous voices" of the mob "seemed only to disturb him, and engage his attention for a passing moment," leaving undisturbed "the deep current of his mind" (pp. 142-145). The riots, therefore, can scarcely be adduced in explanation of his mood some four years later.

I have no evidence that Smith was a Chartist in 1848, and, if he had been, it is extremely unlikely that he remained one in 1852. After fomenting the 1848 riots, and, as at least one historian suspects, organizing them,[14] the Chartists promptly disowned them, and the predictable consequence was that Chartism was extinguished as a political force in the city. But Smith's closest friend in 1852 was Hugh Macdonald—in his memoir of Smith, Patrick Proctor Alexander describes the two as "inseparable" (p. xiv)—and we have Smith's authority for believing Macdonald to have been at one time a Chartist. In a moving memorial to Macdonald, Smith writes:

> At this time [he can only mean the 1840s] the splendid promise of Chartism made glorious the horizon, and Macdonald, like so many of his class, conceived that the 'five pints' were the *avant-couriers* of the millenium. For him, in a very little while, Chartism went out like a theatrical sun. He no longer entertained the idea that he could to any perceptible extent aid in the regeneration of the race. Indeed, it is doubtful whether, in his latter days, he cared much whether the race would ever be regenerated.[15]

Again here we find the distancing so characteristic of Smith when handling these topics. Chartism is indulged as an amusing youthful folly. Macdonald responded "like so many of his class," and the phrase carefully avoids revealing that the class in question was precisely Smith's own. Macdonald, it seems, soon drifted into political quietism, and so, if he had ever shared his friend's enthusiasm, did Smith. Alexander can say of him at the end of his life that he responded to all

great political causes with an "indifference entire and contemptuous," and concludes: "I fear he was but a cool philanthropist in anything of the large and sublime sense." He retreated in the end into a defensively private life, arriving at the view that "man is a developed Mollusc" (pp. cv-cvi).

By the time he wrote *A Life Drama,* Smith had already given up politics, but what pervades the poem, what Brisbane and Clough both recognize in it, are political energies that have lost their object. Smith's hero may, just once, assert: "I wished to loose some music o'er Thy world, / To strike from its firm seat some hoary wrong" (p. 137). But this is an isolated instance. More usually, the fierce Promethean energies of the poem exist in a strange vacuum. Walter may be recommended to emulate "the great Corsican" (p. 81), but he is a Napoleon with no object except the frantic pursuit of his own fame. The poem is about the pursuit of fame and the pursuit of love, but fame is assaulted as if it were a Bastille, and Smith projects onto the women of the poem all the dreams and the anxieties of his class. He pictures them bewitched, "Won by the sweet omnipotence of song" (p. 56), or as responding to his advances with mocking laughter. He pictures himself forlorn and abandoned, and himself ripping aside maidenly modesties with passionate brutality. We should not look at the plot of the poem to locate its central activity but at its style. This everywhere reveals that the frenetic violence with which the hero pursues women and fame has its origin in displaced political enthusiasms. A kiss becomes a coup d'état:

> O untouched lips!
> I see them as a glorious rebel sees
> A crown within his reach. (p. 79)

Poets, like David's Horatii, "fervent grasp the sword of song" (p. 25). To think of writing good poems is to dream of emulating Tamburlaine rather than Tennyson:

> Ha! yet with a triumphant shout
> My spirit shall take captive all the spheres,
> And wring their riches out. (p. 12)

Two things characterize Smith's style in *A Life Drama*. Firstly, it is drawn entirely from books; secondly, the narrative is consistently subordinated to what Smith calls the "images." The plot is scarcely more than a string on which Smith threads his similes.

A Life Drama is an unusually literary poem, written in a language pillaged from books. The hero confesses as much: "Lady, in book-world have I ever dwelt, / This book has domed my being like a sky" (p. 18). He seems particularly to have in mind a book of Keats's poems,[16] and Keats is Smith's favorite resource, but he constructs this fabricated language of his by drawing on the other Romantics, too, on Bailey and Tennyson, and on Shakespeare and the Jacobean dramatists. *A Life Drama* is the production of a poet disconnected from the language of his poetry. Walter confesses that one of his tales is his own life story "tricked out in a quaint disguise" (p. 102). Poetic language at this stage in Smith's career can never be anything more than "a quaint disguise" making the poem transparent. As Violet tells Walter:

> you shine through each disguise;
> You are a masker in a mask of glass.
> You've such transparent sides, each casual eye
> May see the heaving heart. (p. 145)

The quaintness and the transparency are identical. Poetic language is the property of a nation and of a class from which Smith is excluded. It cannot clothe his thoughts; it can only disguise them quaintly, but it is a disguise through which any casual reader can look and see Smith revealed for what he is, for what Clough calls him, "the Glasgow mechanic."

This alienation is partly a matter of Smith's Scottishness. Smith held that the establishment of the *Edinburgh Review* and *Blackwood's Magazine* marked "the last distinct phase of Scotish intellectual life." Since then "Scotland and England have melted into each other," and the result is that Scotland "has no longer a separate existence in thought or geography" (*Last Leaves,* pp. 142-143). There can be no successor to Burns, no new national poet, because the nation that Burns addressed no longer exists. As a consequence, the poets who seem to be Burns's successors, poets such as Smith's friend Hugh Macdonald, or, to choose a stronger example, Tannahill, are not really like Burns at all. "These men are local poets," and that is all that they can be, for, since Burns, Scotland has disappeared as a nation, and no longer exists except as a collection of "localities." Tannahill is not a Scottish poet, but the poet of Glennifer hills, and Macdonald is the poet of "the country around Glasgow" (*A Summer in Skye,* p. 500). Smith has affection for these men. He looks kindly on the modesty of their ambition and relishes their modest achievement. But as a young man his own ambitions were quite other. His dream is Walter's:

> to hew his name out upon time
> As on a rock, then in immortalness
> To stand on time as on a pedestal. (p. 3)

He dreams of standing like Scott on some lofty column, freed from all merely local circumstances.[17] But Scotland can no longer support such ambitions. A poet who wishes to shine not like a "May-night glow-worm," but like "the mighty moon that drowns / Continents in her white and silent light" (p. 4) can only fulfil his ambitions if he first becomes English. The Scot who aspires to write major poetry must close his ears to the language he hears around him, and attend only to the language of books.

Smith's critics were quick to see this. In the *Athenaeum* in January, 1857,[18] Smith was exposed as a plagiarist. Smith had been praised, we are told, for having "painted English country life *without having been in England.*" But this was a less difficult enterprise than it might seem. Smith described the English countryside by stealing from the work of Wordsworth, Coleridge, Byron, Shelley, Keats, Bailey, and Tennyson. He could represent "the leafy luxuriance of our midland counties" even if he had not been there, because Keats had. The case is not well made, and Smith's friend, Patrick Proctor Alexander, is able to dispose of it without difficulty.[19] But it did great damage to Smith's reputation because, no matter how unconvincing the individual examples are, *A Life Drama* is, indeed, written in a language not Smith's own. Even a sympathetic critic like Clough notes as much: "He writes, it would almost seem, under the impression that the one business of a poet is to coin metaphors and similes. He tells them as a clerk might sovereigns at the Bank of England." Clough does not impute to Smith any felonious intent, but all the same he is careful to characterize Smith as a bank clerk—the coins he counts do not belong to him. In order to write poems Smith must first forget his own language, must make himself, like his own "earnest sea," "unlanguaged" (p. 62), because the kind of poetry he wants to write can only be written in the language of another country.

Smith's problem is twofold. He must free himself from Scotland, and he must also free himself from the city, because for him poetry has become localized not just in England, but in one part of England, the English shires in which *A Life Drama* is set. Smith worked at making himself a nature poet with the same energy that he read to make himself an English poet. He spent every evening at his books, and every Sunday he went on walks, out of Glasgow and all along the Clyde valley, looking for the scenery of Lincolnshire and of Kent.

To aspire to England, and the England of the shires, is to aspire towards a different class. The Glasgow mechanic has to make himself into Walter with his Kentish estate, its peacocks, its picturesquely crumbling fountains and ingratiating peasantry. These are the "aristocratic trappings" that Trilling finds in the poem, but there is nothing "cosy" about them. Smith's "quaint" disguises are fragile: their fragility distinguishes his poem. Keats and the Keatsian style may suddenly desert him, and his life will seem "Bare, bald, and tawdry, as a fingered moth" (p. 2), the memory of Keats's tiger-moth and its "deep-damasked wings" working only to oppress him with a sense of his own poverty-stricken existence laid bare by the contrast with the Keatsian richness. His claim to be a nature poet may collapse, and he be forced to confess that, "he was with Nature on the sabbath-days" (p. 133), only on the sabbath-days. And even then, nothing that he saw was as much his own as the "labouring fires," which, as he walked back to Glasgow in the gathering darkness, "came out against the dark." He watched them as they "Threw large and angry lustres in the sky, / And shifting lights across the long black roads" (p. 135). The story of Walter's life, as he tells it to Violet, has only the most fugitive connection with Walter's life as it is described elsewhere in the poem. Walter reveals himself here as someone who has not really inherited an estate in Kent, but as a quite different person, Alexander Smith: "Within a city One was born to toil / Whose heart could not mate with the common doom" (p. 131).

The energy of Smith's poem is generated by the gap between English and Scots, between Alexander Smith and Walter, between Glasgow and the Kent country-side. Smith's effort is to displace himself from Scotland, from Glasgow, from himself. But he is prey always to the fear that his best efforts may be ineffectual, and will meet with scornful rejection. Walter declares his love for the lady with a fawn by telling her a story of an Indian page who confessed his love to a white princess. She mocks his pretension: "My dusk Hyperion, Bacchus of the Inds!" And she dismisses him from her presence: "The light of scorn was cold within her eyes" (p. 75). All Smith's sense of national and social insecurity is quaintly disguised in the tale.

A Life Drama is a succession of "images," what Macdonald, Smith's friend, derisively called "whirly-was."[20] As always, Smith is transparent about it. His chief joy, Walter admits

> Was to draw images from everything:
> And images lay thick upon our talk,
> As shells on ocean sands. (p. 151)

Smith is "most pleased," writes Clough, "when he can double or treble a similitude; speaking of A, he will call it a B, which is, as it were, the C of D. By some maturer effort we may expect to be thus conducted even to Z." But this is not simply a stylistic tic. Simile works by displacement, by substitution, and to Smith these tactics are identical with the composition of poetry. Simile allows a gap between the thing and the thing that it is compared with, and Smith constructs his poem out of such gaps. Poetry for him is the art of displacement, of displacing himself from Glasgow, from Scotland, from his class. But it is an unstable art. Walter's speech opening Scene VII is representative:

> The lark is singing in the blinding sky
> Hedges are white with May. The bridegroom
>   sea
> Is toying with the shore, his wedded bride,
> And in the fulness of his marriage joy
> He decorates her tawny front with shells,
> Retires a space to see how fair she looks,

> Then proud, runs up to kiss her. All is fair—
> All glad, from grass to sun! Yet more I love
> Than this, the shrinking day, that sometimes
>   comes
> In Winter's front, so fair 'mong its dark peers,
> It seems a straggler from the files of June,
> Which in its wanderings had lost its wits,
> And half its beauty; and, when it returned,
> Finding its old companions gone away,
> It joined November's troop, then marching
>   past;
> And so the frail thing comes, and greets the
>   world
> With a thin crazy smile, then bursts in tears,
> And all the while it holds within its hand
> A few half-withered flowers. I love and pity
>   it! (pp. 111-112)

Clough offers this passage as an instance of what Smith can do at his best, but he regrets even here the absence of "that happy, unimpeded sequence which is the charm of really good writers." He finds "something incongruous in the effect of the immediate juxtaposition of these two images." The second image "does not read, somehow, in the same straight line" with the first. It is not hard to see why. The bridegroom sea performs a charming little charade with the beach. Sea-shells are the cameos, the necklaces and bracelets with which the affluent groom bedecks his prettily submissive bride. The sea acts out his part with graceful ease, secure in a sexual self-confidence that is the birthright of his class. In *A Life Drama* Smith has a tendency to credit the natural world with the social manners of the upper-classes. Poetry and nature share, as it were, the etiquette of the drawing-room. Smith's similitude can copy that confident grace, but it cannot really share it. The passage reads like pastiche, and the effect is wistful. Smith gazes in on an enclosed world like Heathcliff staring through the window of Thrushcross Grange: he is not a part of it. The second image has a different origin. Smith's maniac maid clutching her flowers claims kinship with Ophelia and the whole troop of crazed young women who patrol the poems of the Romantics. But her "thin crazy smile" allows a momentary glimpse of a quite different world, a city street crowded with dark-suited passers-by, and, in their midst, ignored by everyone around her, and in her turn ignoring them, a madwoman trapped in the endless rehearsal of some unknown, private grief.[21]

That madwoman is out of place in the city street. Clough finds the passage describing her out of place in Smith's poem. The hero, Walter, contrives to be at one and the same time a member of the landed gentry and a factory hand. Absurd as this is, of course, it produces one valuable result: no matter where Smith imagines Walter to be, whether enclosed in "the thousand-streeted and smoke-smothered town" or chatting with a lady and her pet deer in a Kentish wood he will always be out of place. *A Life Drama* is generated by Smith's sense of himself as displaced, and in the energy with which he expresses that displacement his poem achieves at any rate a historical interest. This energy creates the odd emotional complex that makes *A Life Drama* so distinctive. Long sections of the poem are concerned to build transparent wish-fulfilling fantasies in which Smith imagines himself become rich, famous, beloved, a privileged member of the exclusive circle of larks. But this dream is countered by a sullen suspicion that the English poets and the class from which they come form a closed circle from which he will always be excluded. Then, his poems become futile: "shouts to gain the notice of the Sphynx / Staring right on with calm eternal eyes" (p. 6), reducing him to "tears of impotence, and self-contempt" (p. 3). Self-contempt, guilt, self-disgust are recurrent emotions, and they attend equally Smith's ambition and its failure. He can feel himself a grubby interloper in the refined regions that he aspires to enter, staining them "as a lewd dream stains the holy sleep" (p. 169). At such moments he is one who finds his proper type not in the pure stream of the Kentish wood, but in the Clyde, "putrid and black" as it "trails slowly through a city's heart, / Drawing its filth" (pp. 169-170). But Smith is capable of being overcome with disgust not only by the thought of his own unworthiness but by the unworthiness of all that he aspires after. Then the ocean lapping on the sand, the image that embodies for Smith delicious visions of erotic refinement,[22] is transformed:

> Like a wild lover who has found his love
> Worthless and foul, our friend, the sea, has
>   left
> His paramour the shore; naked she lies,
> Ugly and black and bare. Hark how he
>   moans!
> the pain is in his heart. Inconstant fool!
> He will be up upon her breast tomorrow
> As eager as today. (p. 120)

These are not comfortable emotions, not, to use Trilling's term, cosy, but in its transparent expression of them *A Life Drama* achieves a real if limited value. We ought, I think, to value it in the same way that Smith valued the work of Ebeneezer Elliott, "if for nothing else than for its singularity."

Notes

[1] Alexander Smith, *Poems* (London, 1853), pp. 205-218. All subsequent page references are to this edition, which is dated 1853, but was, in fact, published at the end of 1852. See the Rev. Thomas Brisbane, *The Early Years of Alexander Smith* (London, 1869), p. 140.

Smith is a poet now largely forgotten, the enormous success of *A Life Drama* offered only as an instance of the vagaries of Victorian taste, his name rarely mentioned except as a member of the so-called spasmodic school of poetry. No-one could dispute that some early reviews of Smith's first volume (especially Gilfillian's, see note 13) praised him extravagantly, but it should be remembered that the volume was welcomed, if more guardedly, by the major Victorian poets. Tennyson thought Smith "a poet of considerable promise" (Hallam Tennyson, *Alfred Lord Tennyson: A Memoir* [London, 1897], 2:73). Elizabeth Barrett Browning claimed "none but a poet could write like this, and this, and this" (*The Letters of Elizabeth Barrett Browning,* ed. F. G. Kenyon [London, 1897], p. 120). Even Arnold, who might have been expected to be less charitable, wrote to Clough of *A Life Drama:* "I think the extracts I have seen most remarkable." It is true that he predicts Smith "will not go far," but he adds: "This kind does not go far: it dies like Keats or loses itself like Browning." This is less than damning. See *The Letters of Matthew Arnold to Arthur Hugh Clough,* ed. H. F. Lowry (London, 1932), p. 136. Clough's opinion is discussed in the body of my article.

The term "spasmodic school of poetry" was coined by W. E. Aytoun in his review of Smith's 1853 volume in *Blackwood's Magazine.* Aytoun continued the attack two months later by contributing extracts from a parody spasmodic tragedy, *Firmilian,* with commentary. See *Blackwood's Magazine* 76 (March 1854): 345-354, and 76 (May 1854): 533-551. Aytoun thought so well of his squib that he went on to publish it independently, and the term passed into general currency. As Smith himself remarks in his essay on his friend Sidney Dobell, the term "had a nickname's best prosperity— it stuck." See *Last Leaves: Sketches and Criticisms,* ed. with a Memoir by Patrick Proctor Alexander (Edinburgh, 1868), p. 171. Aytoun clearly identifies as members of the spasmodic school only two poets, Smith and Sidney Dobell, and the critic, George Gilfillian. Not until J. H. Buckley's essay, "The Spasmodic School," in his *The Victorian Temper* (London, 1966), pp. 41-65, did the term achieve any substantial content. Buckley identifies the spasmodic school as the group of poets championed in the 1840s and 1850s by the Dundee minister and literary propagandist, the Rev. George Gilfillian. Buckley is able to show close social relations between only two of the spasmodic poets, Smith and Dobell, who were intimates and who collaborated in a volume of poems on the Crimean War, *Sonnets on the War* (London, 1855). But, even in this case, he can claim the existence of a "school" only by some special pleading. He suggests, for example, that it was the success of Smith's *Life Drama* that "encouraged his friend Sidney Dobell to issue *Balder* (1853)" (p. 55), but it would seem that both poems were already published before the two men had met. Gilfillian writes to Dobell on July 22, 1853, congratulating him on the meeting. See *The Letters and Journals of George Gilfillian,* ed. Robert A. Watson and Elizabeth J. Watson (London, 1892), p. 155.

There are two recent articles on Smith. Mary Jane W. Scott's "Alexander Smith, Poet of Victorian England," *Studies in Scottish Literature* 14 (1979): 98-111, offers a sensible survey of Smith's career. Robert Crawford takes up Scott's suggestion that Smith's best known poem, "Glasgow," was influenced by the poems of James Macfarlan in his "Alexander Smith, James Macfarlan and City Poetry," *Scottish Literary Journal* 12 (November 1985): 35-52. There is a modern biography by Simon Berry that unfortunately remains unpublished. Berry gives notice of it in his "Alexander Smith, The Forgotten Enfant Terrible," *Scottish Book Collector* 7 (August-September 1988): 16-18. Following Berry's piece, pp. 19-20, is a provisional bibliography of works by and about Smith compiled by Hamish Whyte.

² According to Smith "the most exquisite of homely idylls" (*Last Leaves,* p. 141).

³ Not a banal novelette of my own, but a summary of *A Life Drama,* Scene VIII.

⁴ See Robert Bernard Martin, *Tennyson: The Unquiet Heart* (Oxford, 1984), p. 368.

⁵ Absurd in its context, but Smith's last published poem, *Edwin Of Deira* (London, 1861), the story of the first British king converted to Christianity, is only a grander version of the same tale. It is a story that expresses Smith's religious enthusiasm less than his fear of cultural isolation. Through Edwin's conversion a country "Parcelled into seven states" will be unified and become the "instrument" with which God will shape the world "For many a thousand years." The alternative is to remain a kingdom like one of those that God "hath thrown aside to rust / In a neglected corner." See *Edwin of Deira,* pp. 146-147.

⁶ Smith records this event in his most powerful essay, "A Lark's Flight," in *Dreamthorp* (1864; rpt. New York, 1972), pp. 98-117.

⁷ Alison gives his account of the execution in *Some account of my life and writings: an autobiography* (Edinburgh, 1883), 1:169-175. The estimate of the size of the crowd attending the execution is Alison's.

⁸ By no means so august a position then as now. Patrick Proctor Alexander remarks that Smith was called on to perform duties "for discharge of which a just taste would, perhaps, have ruled that the Porter at the gate was, on the whole, the more proper person." See Alexander's "Memoir," *Last Leaves,* p. cxvi.

⁹ *A Summer in Skye* (London, 1866), pp. 525-526.

¹⁰ *Prose Remains of Arthur Hugh Clough,* ed. Blanche Clough (London, 1888), pp. 355-378. Because of

Clough's discussion of *A Life Drama* in this review Smith's poem has retained a somewhat spectral life in the consciousness of students of Victorian poetry. Unfortunately, most commentators on Clough's review contrive explanations for it that free them from any need to consult Smith's poem. Carl Dawson suspects that the review is a "crowning insult" delivered by Clough to Arnold, and is motivated by a "personal animus" against his erstwhile friend. See *Victorian Noon: English Literature* in 1850 (Baltimore, 1979), p. 79. The slight on Arnold provokes Park Honan into a quite uncharacteristic outbreak of snobbery: "Alexander Smith (a lace-pattern designer of Glasgow and 'Spasmodic' poet)." See *Matthew Arnold: A Life* (London, 1981), p. 282. R. K. Biswas explains Clough's transgression as provoked by "personal pique" at Matthew Arnold, and by a desire to appease his fiancé after her "horrified reaction" to *Dipsychus* by publicly promoting more "conventional" attitudes. He is unable to say how championing *A Life Drama,* a poem that Aytoun castigates for its impiety and gross sensuality, might have been thought to have this reassuring effect. Biswas notes that on April 13, Clough enthusiastically recommended *A Life Drama* to Blanche Smith, but that already by May 17 he was writing, "I am rather sorry I recommended Master Alexander Smith to you." See *Arthur Hugh Clough: Towards a Reconsideration* (Oxford, 1972), pp. 197-199. If we recall that the pivotal event in *A Life Drama* is Walter's rape of Violet, then there seem other explanations possible for Clough's embarrassed volte-face than a sudden recovery of literary standards.

¹¹ Compare:

> And her name was Hope, she said,
> But she looked more like Despair. (*Mask of Anarchy,* ll. 87-88)

¹² Lionel Trilling, *Matthew Arnold* (London, 1939), pp. 146-147.

¹³ See George Gilfillian's "Recent Poetry," *Eclectic Review,* n.s. 2 (October 1851): 447-462, and "A New Poet in Glasgow," *Critic* 10 (December 1851): 567-568.

¹⁴ John P. McCaffrey in his "Irish Immigrants and Radical Movements in the West of Scotland in the Early Nineteenth Century," *Innes Review* 39 (1988): 44-60. McCaffrey disputes the point of view fostered by the Chartists themselves that the riots were an outbreak of mindless violence unconnected with Chartism. He notes that the riots were preceded by mass meetings addressed by at least one Chartist orator, that the rioters showed some signs of organization, concentrating their looting, for example, on gun shops, and that among those arrested were a number of skilled artisans in employment.

[15] *A Summer in Skye,* pp. 505-506. In the memoir of Macdonald prefixed to *Poems and Songs of Hugh Macdonald* (Glasgow, 1863) Smith's statement is confirmed. Macdonald's first poems appeared in the *Chartist Circular,* and at that time Fergus O'Connor was his political ideal. See the memoir, p. x. Again, the precision of Smith's statement is at odds with the lofty distance of his tone. He refers to the five, rather than the more conventional six, chartist demands. The sixth, the ballot, was consistently opposed by O'Connor and its omission from the Chartist petition of 1848 marked O'Connor's supremacy in the movement.

[16] Smith writes of this poet that he suffered in love, died young, and did not become famous until after his death. Also that "it was his nature / To blossom into song, as 'tis a tree's / To leaf itself in April" (p. 18). This seems to be a reminiscence of Keats's comment to Taylor, February 27, 1818: "If Poetry come not as naturally as the Leaves to a tree it had better not come at all."

[17] The foundation stone of the Scott column in Glasgow's George Square was laid in October, 1837. As a boy Smith could have watched the column being erected. The statue of the great writer raised high above the city is a powerful emblem of the possibility that literature might transcend all local and limiting circumstances, and would have been the more striking for its rarity. Smith notes that in the Scotland of the early nineteenth century "statues and public monuments were rare" (*Last Leaves,* p. 144).

[18] *Athenaeum* (January 3, 1857): 16-17.

[19] Alexander includes a defense of Smith against the charges of plagiarism in an appendix to *Last Leaves,* pp. 315-334.

[20] See Alexander's "Memoir," *Last Leaves,* p.xix. A whirly-wa is defined in the *Scottish National Dictionary* as a bauble, a gimcrack, or, in music, an unnecessary trill or a series of grace notes. In his *Epistle to Thomas Hogsitt, in answer to a Note of his on Music,* a poem in which he characteristically expresses his preference for traditional Scottish music over Italianate sophistications, Macdonald has the following stanza:

A' yon outlandish dons and hizzies,
Your Tamburinnis and your Grisis,
Wi' a' their whirly-was and graces
    I canna bide. (*Poems and Songs of Hugh Macdonald,* p. 93)

[21] In suggesting that Smith's image has its origin in a Glasgow street scene I have in mind Brisbane's comment on Smith's lyric "The Garden and the Child," *A Life Drama,* pp. 91-100. The poem was inspired, Brisbane tells us, when, while "returning from dinner along the Trongate to his work," Smith caught sight of "a bright, rosy, laughing little girl," "beautiful as heaven" (*The Early Life of Alexander Smith,* p. 74).

[22] In addition to the passage quoted above from p. 111, there are other versions of the same image on pp. 38, 43, and 127.

FURTHER READING

Biography

"Alexander Smith's *Last Leaves*." *London Quarterly Review* XXXI, No. 61 (October 1868): 142-59.
    Pays homage to Smith, concentrating on his posthumously published *Last Leaves.*

Hadden, J. Cuthbert. "A Forgotten Poet." *The Argosy* 70, No. 2 (February 1900): 196-206.
    Recounts Smith's personal life from 1851 to his death in 1867 in conjunction with his publications.

Criticism

Buckley, Jerome Hamilton. "The Spasmodic School." In *The Victorian Temper: A Study in Literary Culture,* pp. 41-65. Cambridge: Harvard University Press, 1951.
    Offers an overview of the development, reception, and fall of the Spasmodic poets.

Crawford, Robert. "Alexander Smith, James MacFarlan, and City Poetry." *Scottish Literary Journal* 12, No. 2 (November 1985): 35-52.
    Considers Smith's success as an "urban poet" and discusses possible influences on his city poetry, particularly James MacFarlan's *City Songs.*

Elton, Oliver. "Other Poets." In *A Survey of English Literature, 1830-1880* Vol. II, pp. 85-119. London: Edward Arnold, 1920.
    Includes discussion of the lives and works of Philip James Bailey, Sydney Dobell, and Alexander Smith.

Gilfillian, George. "Recent Poetry." *Eclectic Review* 2 (October 1851): 447-62.
    First review of Smith's work. Praises the poet for his "exquisite thoughts and images."

———. [as Apollodorus]. "Poetry and the Drama." *The Critic* XVI, No. 395 (15 September 1857): 413-15.
    Reviews Smith's *City Poems* and his literary growth since his first work. Argues that critics have been too harsh on Smith, and defends him against charges of plagiarism.

———. "A Cluster of New Poets." In *A Gallery of Literary Portraits,* edited by W. Robertson Nicoll, pp. 46-104.

Everyman's Library: Essays and Belles Lettres, edited by Ernest Rhys. London: J. M. Dent & Co., 1909.

   Reprints influential positive appraisals of Sydney Dobell, Alexander Smith, John Stanyan Bigg, and Gerald Massey that originally appeared in *Tait's Magazine*.

"The Last New Poet." *The Athenæum*, No. 1523 (3 January 1857): 16-18.

   Review of *A Life Drama*, asserting that Smith plagiarizes works of other authors, including Keats, Tennyson, and Shelley.

Meredith, George. "To Alex Smith, the 'Glasgow Poet': On His Sonnet to Fame." In *Poems* Vol. 1, p. 164. New York: Charles Scribner's Sons, 1910.

   A sonnet, first published in the 20 December 1851 *Leader*, in which Meredith expressed his admiration for Smith. This poem is frequently cited as evidence of the temporary but significant influence of Spasmodic poetry on Meredith's work.

Millar, J. H. "The Victorian Era: 1848-1880." In *A Literary History of Scotland*, pp. 586-644. London: T. Fisher Unwin, 1903.

   Includes discussion of Alexander Smith and W. E. Aytoun.

Poston, Lawrence. "Three Versions of Victorian Pastoral." *Genre* 13, No. 3 (Fall 1980): 305-35.

   Examines Smith's role in establishing the prose pastoral style of the nineteenth century.

Additional coverage of Smith's life and career is contained in the following source published by Gale Research: *Dictionary of Literary Biography*, Vols. 32 and 55. Additional coverage of the Spasmodic School can be found in *Nineteenth-Century Literature Criticism*, Vol. 24.

John Greenleaf Whittier

1807-1892

American poet, journalist, essayist, editor, and hymn writer.

For further discussion of Whittier's career, see *NCLC*, Volume 8.

INTRODUCTION

A noted abolitionist and social reformer, Whittier is chiefly remembered today for his poetry. In his most popular works, he used rural and biblical imagery to describe nineteenth-century New England life. With the favorable reception of poems such as *Snow-Bound: A Winter Idyl* (1866), Whittier joined the ranks of such other enduring American poets as William Cullen Bryant, Oliver Wendell Holmes, and Henry Wadsworth Longfellow. Whittier's reputation has suffered in the twentieth century because of the didacticism and dated nature of his works; his significant role in American literary history, however, is still acknowledged today.

Biographical Information

Whittier was born in Haverhill, Massachusetts, to Quaker parents. Though he had little formal education, he studied the Bible and the works of John Milton, Sir Walter Scott, Lord Byron, and Robert Burns. He was particularly impressed by the Scottish poet Burns, whose beautiful descriptions of rural farm scenes resonated strongly with the New England youth. Physically frail, Whittier was unsuited for farm work and dreamed of becoming a poet. In 1826 his sister Elizabeth anonymously sent his poem "The Exile's Departure" to the *Newburyport Free Press*. The poem so impressed editor and noted social reformer William Lloyd Garrison that he encouraged Whittier to contribute more of his work. He also helped Whittier attain his first literary position as editor of the political magazine the *American Manufacturer,* in 1829. A year later Whittier became editor of the widely read *New England Weekly Review*. Soon he published his first collection of tales and poems, *Legends of New England in Prose and Verse* (1831). Forced to resign his editorial responsibilities due to ill health and his father's death, Whittier returned to Haverhill in 1832. Influenced again by his mentor Garrison, Whittier wrote the first of many antislavery tracts, an essay entitled *Justice and Expediency; or, Slavery Considered with a View to Its Rightful and Effectual Remedy, Abolition* (1833). Aware that his abolitionist stance might jeopardize popular reception of his poetry, Whittier never-

theless chose to devote himself to what he considered a just and noble cause. For nearly twelve years he concentrated exclusively on abolitionist issues in his essays, prose, and poetry, while working for the Anti-Slavery Society. Whittier also worked for social change through political channels, campaigning extensively for candidates who proposed legislative answers to antislavery issues. ("Ichabod" [1850], considered one of Whittier's final abolitionist poems, reflected his shock and anger at the decision by his personal friend, the politician Daniel Webster, to support a compromise with Southern slaveholders.) In 1843, while continuing to work for abolition, Whittier resumed a more mainstream literary career, taking his themes primarily from everyday New England life. He continued examining these themes in his poetry and autobiographical sketches throughout the rest of his poetical career. He also contributed hymns to several popular hymnals. He reached his literary apex in 1866 with the publication of his most successful ballad, *Snow-Bound*. This work helped Whittier achieve renown as a literary figure. *Snow-Bound* was both a critical and a financial success, enabling its author to live comfortably until his death in 1892.

Major Works

The poetry and prose of Whittier's early years clearly reflect his social concerns and commitment to abolitionism, expressed in his pamphlet *Justice and Expediency*. The poems of these years, such as those published in *Poems* (1838), were generally propaganda pieces. With the publication of *Lays of My Home, and Other Poems* (1843), Whittier achieved a better-received balance of poetry and polemics, translating his social concerns into themes of regional pride, brotherly love, and religious ideals. Whittier employed New England imagery in his only novel, *Leaves from Margaret Smith's Journal in the Province of Massachusetts Bay* (1849). This work, in the form of a fictional journal, depicts life in the New England colonies through the eyes of a young English girl. In the following years Whittier composed many of his ballads, which show an increasing disengagement from political themes in favor of New England imagery, autobiographical sketches, and Quaker philosophy. The founding of the magazine *The Atlantic Monthly* in 1857 provided Whittier with a wide reading audience. Some of his finest poetic achievements were first published in the *Atlantic* during these years, including "Skipper Arisen's Ride" and "Telling the Bees" (1857). Whittier also wrote *Snow-Bound*, widely considered his best work, during this period. This poem, a nostalgic description of family interactions while snowbound by an unexpected winter storm, encapsulates Whittier's love of family, New England, and the past. The poem's emotional depth is thought to have derived from Whittier's grief over the deaths of his mother and sister. Today the work is considered as a precursor to the pastoral poems of such twentieth-century poets as Robert Frost.

Critical Reception

Critical appraisal of Whittier's work has passed through several phases over the years. His early critics, through the end of the Civil War, expressed admiration for the emotional impact and polemical effectiveness of his verse but pointed to numerous technical flaws, such as clumsy prose and faulty rhyme schemes. James Russell Lowell commended Whittier's boldness and sincerity, yet never considered him a first-rate poet. Similarly, Edgar Allan Poe called Whittier a "fine versifier," but would not include his name in the ranks of premier American poets. However, Whittier was a popular and respected writer, especially following the publication of *Snow-Bound*. The overwhelming popularity of this poem marked the beginning of the second phase of critical reaction, which lasted until the 1920s. During this period Whittier was esteemed as one of America's most admired literary figures. His personal life, described as saintly by biographers of the time, became inseparable from the evaluation of his work. His death prompted an outpouring of loving remembrances and fond memorials, few of which objectively assessed the quality of his work. Attitudes towards Whittier's poetry changed considerably beginning in the late 1920s, when critics took him to task for being overly moralistic and sentimental. Most commentators agreed, however, on his importance as a social reformer. His work subsequently received little critical attention until the 1950s, when interest in his poetry saw a modest revival. Many modern critics, such as John B. Pickard, consider the poet a paradoxical blend of success and failure and maintain that he should be remembered as a significant historical figure rather than for his contributions to literature. His early works survive mainly as historical documents that represent a turbulent era in American history, but a few of his best-loved pieces, such as *Snow-Bound*, endure as nostalgic pastorals and continue to be studied today. Recent critics tend to concur with Whittier's own appraisal of his place in history: "I am not one of the master singers and don't pose as one. By the grace of God, I am only what I am and don't wish to pass for more."

PRINCIPAL WORKS

"The Exile's Departure" (poetry) 1826; published in newspaper *Newburyport Free Press*

Legends of New England in Prose and Verse (stories and poetry) 1831

Moll Pitcher and the Minstrel Girl (poetry) 1832; revised, 1840

Justice and Expediency; or, Slavery Considered with a View to Its Rightful and Effectual Remedy, Abolition (essay) 1833

Mogg Megone (poetry) 1836

Poems Written during the Progress of the Abolition Question in the United States, Between the Years 1830 and 1838 (poetry) 1837; also published as *Poems* [revised edition] 1838

Lays of My Home, and Other Poems (poetry) 1843

The Stranger in Lowell (criticism) 1845

Voices of Freedom (poetry and essays) 1846

The Supernaturalism of New-England (poetry and prose) 1847

Leaves from Margaret Smith's Journal in the Province of Massachusetts Bay (novel) 1849

Old Portraits and Modern Sketches (poetry and biographical sketches) 1850

Songs of Labor, and Other Poems (poetry) 1850

The Chapel of the Hermit, and Other Poems (poetry) 1853

Literary Recreations and Miscellanies (prose) 1854

**The Panorama, and Other Poems* (poetry) 1856

The Poetical Works of John Greenleaf Whittier. 2 vols. (poetry) 1857

†*Home Ballads and Poems* (ballads and poetry) 1860

In War-Time, and Other Poems (poetry) 1863

Snow-Bound: A Winter Idyl (poetry) 1866

The Tent on the Beach, and Other Poems (poetry) 1867

Among the Hills, and Other Poems (poetry) 1868

Ballads of New-England (ballads) 1870

Child-Life: A Collection of Poems [editor; with Lucy Larcom] (poetry) 1872

The Pennsylvania Pilgrim, and Other Poems (poetry) 1872

Child Life in Prose [editor; with Lucy Larcom] (short stories) 1874

The Complete Works of John Greenleaf Whittier. 7 vols. (poetry, legends, essays, tales, biographical sketches, and historical sketches) 1876

‡*The Writings of John Greenleaf Whittier.* 5 vols. (poems, ballads, legends, essays, tales, biographical sketches, historical sketches, and criticism) 1888-9

At Sundown (poetry) 1890

The Complete Poetical Works of John Greenleaf Whittier (poetry) 1894

Whittier on Writers and Writing: The Uncollected Critical Writings of John Greenleaf Whittier (criticism) 1950

The Letters of John Greenleaf Whittier (letters) 1975

*This work includes the poem "Ichabod."

**This work includes the poem "Maud Muller" and "Barbara Frietchie."

†This work includes the poem "Skipper Ireson's Ride."

‡This work also includes poetry written by Elizabeth H. Whittier.

CRITICISM

Thomas Wentworth Higginson (essay date 1902)

SOURCE: "Whittier the Poet," in *John Greenleaf Whittier,* The Macmillan Company, 1907, pp. 150-70.

[*In the following excerpt, originally published in 1902, Higginson discusses the influence of religion and of moral and philosophical issues on Whittier's distinctive American style.*]

In . . . considering Whittier's more general claims as a poet, we must accept Lord Bacon's fine definition of poetry that "It hath something divine in it, because it raises the mind and hurries it into sublimity, by conforming the shows of things to the desires of the soul, instead of subjecting the soul to external things, as reason and history do." In this noble discrimination,—which one wonders not to have been cited among the rather inadequate arguments to prove that Lord Bacon was the real Shakespeare,—we have the key, so far as there is any, for the change from the boy Whittier, with his commonplace early rhymes, into the man who reached the sublime anthem of **"My Soul and I."** He also was "hurried into sublimity."

In the case of [Oliver Wendell] Holmes, it is a very common remark that his prose, especially "The Autocrat of the Breakfast Table," will outlast his poems, except perhaps "The Chambered Nautilus." No one can make any similar suggestion in regard to Whittier, whose best poetry wholly surpasses his best prose, in respect to grasp and permanence. It is, indeed, rather surprising to see how much of his prose he has thought it best to preserve, and by how little literary distinction it is marked. Earnestness and sound sense, it always has; and it always throws its stress on the side of manly sympathy and human progress, but more than this cannot be said. His few attempts at fiction are without marked life, and the little poems interspersed in them are better than the prose, which is rarely the case with authors. Much of this prose is simply in the line of reformatory journalism, and does not bear the test of the bound volume. Even in his narratives of real experience there is nothing to be compared with [James Russell] Lowell's "Moosehead Journal," or in general literary merit with his "On a Certain Condescension in Foreigners." On the other hand, Whittier escapes the pitfalls or tiresome side-paths into which both Lowell and Holmes were sometimes tempted; he may be prosaic, but never through levity, as sometimes happened to Lowell, or through some scientific whim, as in case of Holmes; and though his prose never has, on the literary side, the affluence of [Henry Wadsworth Longfellow's] *Hyperion,* it never shows the comparative poverty of [Longfellow's novel] "Kavanagh." It is, nevertheless, as a whole, so far inferior to his poems, that it is best at this day to give our chief attention to these.

No one can dwell much on Whittier without recognising him as the distinctively American poet of familiar life. More than any other he reaches the actual existence of the people, up to the time of his death. He could say of himself what Lowell said dramatically only, "We draw our lineage from the oppressed." Compared with him Longfellow, Holmes, and even Lowell, seem the poets of a class; Whittier alone is near the people; setting apart Emerson, who inhabited a world of his own, "so near and yet so far." His whole position was indeed characteristic of American society; had he lived in England, he would always have been, at his highest, in the position of some Corn-Law Rhymer, some Poet of the People; or at best, in the often degrading position of his favourite Burns himself, whereas in his own country this external difference was practically forgotten. Having gone thus far in fitting out this modest poet, nature gave to him, more directly than to either of the others, the lyric gift—a naturalness of song and flow, increasing with years and reaching where neither of the others attained. A few of Longfellow's poems have this, but Whittier it pervades; and beginning like Burns, with the very simplest form, the verse of four short lines, he gradually trained himself, like Burns, to more varied or at least to statelier measures.

Burns was undoubtedly his literary master in verse and Milton in prose. He said of Burns to Mrs. Fields, "He lives, next to Shakespeare, in the heart of humanity."[1] His contentment in simple measures was undoubtedly a bequest from this poet and was carried even farther, while his efforts were more continuous in execution and higher in tone. On the other hand, he drew from Milton his long prose sentences and his tendency to the florid rather than the terse. His conversation was terse enough, but not his written style. He said to Mrs. Fields: "Milton's prose has long been my favourite reading. My whole life has felt the influence of his writings."[2] He once wrote to Fields that Allingham, after Tennyson, was his favourite among modern British poets. I do not remember him as quoting Browning or speaking of him. This may, however, have been an accident. . . .

It was a natural result of his reticent habit and retired life that his maturer poems impress us, as we dwell upon them, with more sense of surprise as to their origin and shaping than exists in the case of any of his compeers, save only the almost equally reticent Emerson. In Longfellow's memoirs, in Lowell's letters, we see them discussing their purposes with friends, accepting suggestion and correction, while Whittier's poems come always with surprise, and even Mr. Pickard's careful labours add little to our knowledge. Mrs. Claflin and Mrs. Fields give us little as to the actual origins of his poems. I have never felt this deficiency more than in sitting in his house, once or twice, since his death, and observing the scantiness of even his library. Occasional glimpses in his notes help us a very little, as for instance what he says in the preface to his [short story collection] *Child Life in Prose,* published in 1873, as to his early sources of inspiration:—

> It is possible that the language and thought of some portions of the book may be considered beyond the comprehension of the class for which it is intended. Admitting that there may be truth in the objection, I believe, with Coventry Patmore in his preface to a child's book, that the charm of such a volume is increased rather than lessened by the surmised existence of an unknown element of power, meaning, and beauty. I well remember how, at a very early age, the solemn organ-roll of Gray's "Elegy" and the lyric sweep and pathos of Cowper's "Lament for the Royal George" moved and fascinated me with a sense of mystery and power felt rather than understood. "A spirit passed before my face, but the form thereof was not discerned." Freighted with unguessed meanings, these poems spake to me, in an unknown tongue, indeed, but like the wind in the pines or the waves on the beach, awakening faint echoes and responses, and vaguely prophesying of wonders yet to be revealed.

He was the Tyrtaeus or leading bard of the greatest moral movement of the age; and he probably gained in

all ways from the strong tonic of the antislavery agitation. This gave a training in directness, simplicity, genuineness; it taught him to shorten his sword and to produce strong effects by common means. It made him permanently high-minded also, and placed him, as he himself always said, above the perils and temptations of a merely literary career. Though always careful in his work, and a good critic of the work of others, he usually talked by preference upon subjects not literary—politics, social science, the rights of labour. He would speak at times, if skilfully led up to it, about his poems, and was sometimes, though rarely, known to repeat them aloud; but his own personality was never a favourite theme with him, and one could easily fancy him as going to sleep, like La Fontaine, at the performance of his own opera.

In his antislavery poetry he was always simple, always free from that excess or over-elaborateness of metaphor to be seen sometimes in Lowell. On the other hand he does not equal Lowell in the occasional condensation of vigorous thought into great general maxims. Lowell's "Verses suggested by the Present Crisis" followed not long after Whittier's **"Massachusetts to Virginia,"** and, being printed anonymously, was at first attributed to the same author. Whittier's poems had even more lyric fire and produced an immediate impression even greater, but it touched universal principles less broadly, and is therefore now rarely quoted, while Lowell's

> Truth forever on the scaffold, wrong forever
>   on the throne,

is immortal on the lips of successive orators.

Brought up at a period when Friends disapproved of music, Whittier had no early training in this direction, and perhaps no natural endowment. He wrote in a letter of 1882,—"I don't know anything of music, not one tune from another." This at once defined the limits of his verse, and restricted him to the very simplest strains. He wrote mostly in the four line ballad metre, which he often made not only very effective, but actually melodious. That he had a certain amount of natural ear is shown by his use of proper names, in which, after his early period of Indian experiments had passed, he rarely erred. In one of his very best poems, **"My Playmate,"** a large part of the effectiveness comes from the name of the locality:—

> The dark pines sing on Ramoth hill
>   The slow song of the sea.

He felt his own deficiency in regard to music, and had little faith in his own ear, the result being that even if he made a happy stroke in the way of sound, he was apt to distrust it at the suggestion of some prosaic friend with a foot rule, who convinced him that he was taking a dangerous liberty. Thus, in **"The New Wife and the Old,"** in describing the night sounds, he finally closed with—

> And the great sea waves below,
> Pulse o' the midnight beating slow.

This "pulse o' the midnight" was an unusual rhythmic felicity for him, but, on somebody's counting the syllables, he tamely submitted, substituting

> Like the night's pulse, beating slow,

which is spondaic and heavy; but he afterward restored the better line. In the same way, when he sang of the shoemakers in the very best of his *Songs of Labour,* he originally wrote:—

> Thy songs, Hans Sachs, are living yet,
>   In strong and hearty German,
> And Canning's craft and Gifford's wit,
>   And the rare good sense of Sherman.

Under similar pressure of criticism he was induced to substitute

> And patriot fame of Sherman,

and this time he did not repent. It is painful to think what would have become of the liquid measure of Coleridge's "Christabel" had some tiresome acquaintance, possibly "a person on business from Porlock," insisted on thus putting that poem in the stocks.

It shows the essential breadth which lay beneath the religious training of the Society of Friends, even in its most conservative wing, that Whittier, not knowing a note of music, should have contributed more hymns to the hymn-book than any other poet of his time, although this is in many cases through the manipulation of others, which furnished results quite unexpected to him. In a collection of sixty-six hymns prepared for the Parliament of Religions at Chicago in 1893, more were taken from Whittier's poems than from any other author, these being nine in all. The volume edited by Longfellow and Johnson, called *Hymns of the Spirit* (1864), has twenty-two from Whittier; the *Unitarian Hymn and Tune Book* of 1868, has seven, and Dr. Martineau's *Hymns of Praise* has seven. As has elsewhere been stated, Mr. and Mrs. Edwin D. Mead reported, after attending many popular meetings in England, in 1901, that they heard Whittier and Longfellow quoted and sung more freely than any other poets.

It is especially to be noticed that in Whittier's poems of the sea there is a salt breath, a vigorous companionship—perhaps because he was born and bred near it—not to be found in either of his companion authors. There is doubtless a dramatic movement, an onward

sweep in Longfellow's "Wreck of the Hesperus" and "Sir Humphrey Gilbert" such as Whittier never quite attained, and the same may be true of the quiet, emotional touch in Longfellow's "The Fire of Driftwood"; nor was there ever produced in America, perhaps, any merely meditative poem of the sea so thoughtful and so perfect in execution as Holmes's "The Chambered Nautilus." Among American poets less known, Brownlee Brown's "Thalatta" and Helen Jackson's "Spoken" were respectively beyond him in their different directions. But for the daily atmosphere and life, not so much of the sea as of the seaside, for the companionship of the sailor, the touch that makes the ocean like a larger and more sympathetic human being to those who dwell within its very sound, Whittier stands before them all; he is simply a companion to the sailor, as he is to the farmer and the hunter; and he weaves out of the life of each a poetry such as its actual child hardly knows. The **"Tent on the Beach"** will always keep us nearer to the actual life of salt water than can anything by Whittier's companion poets.

Probably no poet was ever more surprised by the success of a new book than was Whittier by that of this poem about which, as he wrote to a friend, he had great misgivings, as it was prepared under especial disadvantages. He was amazed when he saw in the *Boston Transcript* that a first edition of ten thousand copies had been printed, and thought it "an awful swindle" upon the public that a thousand copies a day should have been sold. This made more striking the fact that he put into it, perhaps, the best bit of self-delineation he ever accomplished in the following lines:—

> And one there was, a dreamer born,
>   Who, with a mission to fulfil,
> Had left the Muses' haunts to turn
>   The crank of an opinion mill,
> Making his rustic reed of song
> A weapon in the war with Wrong,
> Yoking his fancy to the breaking plough
> That beam-deep turned the soil for truth to
>   spring and grow.
>
> Too quiet seemed the man to ride
>   The winged Hippogriff, Reform;
> Was his a voice from side to side
>   To pierce the tumult of the storm?
> A silent, shy, peace-loving man,
> He seemed no fiery partisan
> To hold his way against the public frown,
> The ban of Church and State, the fierce mob's
>   bounding down.
>
> For while he wrought with strenuous will
>   The work his hands had found to do,
> He heard the fitful music still
>   Of winds that out of dreadland blew;

The din about him could not drown
What the strange voices whispered down;
Along his task-field weird processions swept,
The visionary pomp of stately phantoms
    stepped.

The uncertainty of an author's judgment of his own books was never better illustrated than by the fact that Whittier's poem **"Mabel Martin"** first published under the name of **"The Witch's Daughter"** in the *National Era* for 1857—erroneously described by Mr. Pickard as first published in 1866—was his greatest immediate financial success. It was somewhat enlarged as **"Mabel Martin"** in 1877, and he received for it $1000 at the first annual payment. Mr. Pickard pronounces it "charming," but I suspect that it is rarely copied, and hardly ever quoted—perhaps because the three-line measure is unfavourable to Whittier's style or to the public tastes. The absence of rhyme from one line in each three-line verse is not compensated by any advantage, while the four-line verse of the dedication of the whole work to the memory of his mother is very attractive.

He has defects of execution which are easily apparent. His poems, even to the latest, are apt to be too long, and to be laden with a superfluous moral, and come dangerously near to meriting the criticism of D'Alembert on Richardson's long-winded words, once so lauded: "Nature is a good thing, but do not bore us with it (*non pas à l'ennui*)." Whittier did not actually reach the point of ennui, but came very near it. As for his rhymes, though not so bad as those of Elizabeth Barrett Browning, they were, in his early years, bad enough. Mr. Linton, from the English point of view, or from any other, was justified in protesting against such rhymes as *worn* and *turn, joins* and *pines, faults* and *revolts, flood* and *Hood, even* and *Devon, heaven* and *forgiven.*[3] We can easily find in addition, *mateless* and *greatness, pearl* and *marl, women* and *trimming, scamper* and *Hampshire;* some of all this list, it must be remembered, being mere archaisms or localisms, and all tending in Whittier's case, as in Mrs. Browning's, to entire disappearance after middle life. No one complains of the rhymes in "Sonnets from the Portuguese."

Even when Whittier uses a mispronunciation or makes a slip in grammar, it has the effect of oversight or of whim, rather than of ignorance. Thus he commonly accents the word "romance" on the first syllable, as in—

Young Romance raised his dreamy eyes;

while at other times he places the stress more correctly on the last, as where he writes—

Where Tasso sang, let young Romance and
    Love.[4]

· · · · ·

In summing up the results of Whittier's twin career as poet and as file-leader, it may be safely said that his early career of reformer made him permanently high-minded, and placed him above the perils and temptations of a merely literary career. This he himself recognised from the first, and wrote it clearly and musically in a poem printed at the very height of conflict (1847), more than ten years before the Civil War. He took this poem as the prelude to a volume published ten years later, and again while revising his poems for a permanent edition in 1892. Unlike many of his earlier compositions, it is reprinted by him without the change of a syllable.

PROEM

I love the old melodious lays
Which softly melt the ages through,
    The songs of Spenser's golden days,
    Arcadian Sidney's silvery phrase,
Sprinkling our noon of time with freshest
    morning dew.

    Yet vainly in my quiet hours
To breathe their marvellous notes I try;
    I feel them, as the leaves and flowers
    In silence feel the dewy showers,
And drink with glad still lips the blessing of
    the sky.

    The rigour of a frozen clime,
The harshness of an untaught ear,
    The jarring words of one whose rhyme
    Beat often Labour's hurried time
On Duty's rugged march through storm and
    strife, are here.

    Of mystic beauty, dreamy grace,
No rounded art the lack supplies;
    Unskilled the subtler lines to trace
    Or softer shades of Nature's face.
I view her common forms with unanointed
    eyes.

    Nor mine the seer-like power to show
The secrets of the heart and mind;
    To drop the plummet-line below
    Our common world of joy and woe,
A more intense despair or brighter hope to
    find.

    Yet here at least an earnest sense
Of human right and weal is shown,
    A hate of tyranny intense
    And hearty in its vehemence
As if my brother's pain and sorrow were my
    own.

Undated photograph of a youthful Whittier.

> O Freedom! if to me belong
> Nor mighty Milton's gift divine,
>   Nor Marvell's wit and graceful song,
>   Still, with a love as deep and strong
> As theirs, I lay, like them, my best gifts on
>   thy shrine.

It is well to close this chapter with these words he wrote, at the Asquam House, in 1882, on the death of Longfellow, in a copy of the latter's poems, belonging to my sister:—

> Hushed now the sweet consoling tongue
> Of him whose lyre the Muses strung;
> His last low swan-song had been sung!

> His last! And ours, dear friend, is near;
> As clouds that rake the mountains here,
> We too shall pass and disappear,

> Yet howsoever changed or tost,
> Not even a wreath of mist is lost,
> No atom can itself exhaust.

> So shall the soul's superior force

Live on and run its endless course
In God's unlimited universe.

> And we, whose brief reflections seem
> To fade like clouds from lake and stream,
> Shall brighten in a holier beam.

Notes

[1] Fields's *Whittier*, p. 51.

[2] Fields's *Whittier*, p. 41.

[3] Linton's *Whittier*, p. 167.

[4] *Poetical Works*, IV. 38.

Lewis E. Weeks, Jr. (essay date 1964)

SOURCE: "Whittier Criticism Over the Years," in *Essex Institute Historical Collections*, Vol. C, No. 3, July, 1964, pp. 159-82.

[*In the following excerpt, the author contrasts the backgrounds and biases of various Whittier critics of the nineteenth and twentieth centuries.*]

From time to time it is interesting as well as profitable to review the course of the critical fortunes of our writers and to compare the evaluations of their contemporaries with those of a later generation. Such an examination is particularly interesting in the case of a writer like John Greenleaf Whittier, who enjoyed great popular acclaim.

The period of about one hundred and twenty years of Whittier criticism covered by this survey falls neatly in two parts divided roughly by Whittier's death at the turn of the century. The criticism in the first period has two disadvantages which that of the second does not have to face. When an author is still writing, the critic has only part of his ultimate production with which to deal. Furthermore, he is aware of the author himself, alive, responsive, and, in some part, influential as a personal force. This force, in the case of Whittier, was obviously much more powerful than is the case with many writers. Death probably makes it easier for the critic to be more objective. In addition, death generally terminates abruptly the likelihood that more material will have to be considered, making it possible for the critic to deal with the work as a whole. Taine suggested that the key to understanding an artist was his nationality, his times, and his environment. If we add to these the characteristic of temperament, we shall have a fairly complete set of criteria, which may be applied profitably both to the poet and to his critics.

In 1842 the Reverend Rufus W. Griswold, tireless anthologizer, literateur, champion of American writers, and infamous executor of Poe's literary remains, published the first edition of his *Poets and Poetry of America,* a monumental work and a mine of literary history devoted principally to biographical and bibliographical comment on the numerous poets whose works were included in the sizable tome. He felt that many of Whittier's best poems dealt with the slavery question, that they showed a manly vigor of thought and language, and a true spirit of liberty. Ironically enough, not one of the twelve poems by Whittier included in the collection dealt with the category Griswold felt represented Whittier's best verse, that devoted to the slavery question. In this volume, by comparison to Whittier, Longfellow had eleven poems and four pages; Whittier had twelve poems and twenty pages. *Mogg Megone* was included in its entirety. The eleventh edition, of 1853, was revised to include nine poems; but the number of pages dropped to eighteen through the omission of *Mogg.* Longfellow, in this edition, was allotted eight pages and fourteen poems. There were further revised editions, the final one brought up to date by R. H. Stoddard in 1873. The only change in the Whittier selections over the years, however, was the addition in 1855 of the poem **"Randolph of Roanoke."** This same edition paid tribute to the unusual vigor of invective and the honesty and courage of the Abolition poems. Boldness and energy are considered Whittier's chief characteristics; tenderness and grace are almost as important. Love for and faith in the republican form of government is needed to elevate the national character and literature; and Whittier provided them in good measure, according to the anthologist.

Whittier had published eight volumes of verse in the ten years between 1831, the date of his first book, and 1840, the date of *Moll Pitcher and the Minstrel Girl;* and though there must have been many reviews and notices in the newspapers and magazines of the day, the first review I have come across is of his volume, *Lays of My Home and Other Poems,* published in 1843. Strangely enough it appeared, of all places, in the *Southern Quarterly Review;*[1] and it is interesting for several reasons. The author states that the quality of Whittier's verse is "respectable" only and that "the sin of mediocrity lies at his doors." He is granted a "tolerable smoothness of flow" and "occasional energy of expression." However, his verses are "wondrously frigid." The reviewer goes on to say:

> He [Whittier] is called the Quaker poet, and his poetry is the very pink of broad brimism. It lacks very equally, tenderness and felicity. Its chief or only, merits are plain good sense, general correctness, and a very fair and commendable appreciation of morals and propriety. Beyond this, the volume is a blank. It possesses neither originality nor warmth—unless, indeed, when the author falls into a fury (as he does with Virginia) and for no better reason than we can see, but because our very excellent senior sister

thought proper to adopt certain measures to prevent philanthropic persons from the Bay State—Quakers, in all probability—from stealing and carrying back the slaves which they (or their ancestors) had previously sold her. This situation irritates Whittier and lets him show feeling, otherwise wanting in his poetry.

This critic was obviously shocked by the volume. He tells his readers that he was aware of the weakness critics have for exaggeration, and that he had allowed for the tendency of every Northerner to think every New England duckling a swan. But even making these concessions, he had expected, without knowing Whittier's work at first hand, that he was a true poet to some degree. But after reading the volume being reviewed, he realizes his error. Whittier does make verses that are not bad as verses go, but they lack "glow or inspiration" in any degree. Whittier's rhyme is good enough, but it is "frigid, very monotonous, and very commonplace."

The partisan quality of this review is quite obvious and is both understandable and typical of the general tendency of the Southern reviewers whenever the subject of slavery was involved. In addition, it seems to reveal the resentment that writers from both the South and West seemed to feel in response to a real or fancied note of superiority they detected on the part of the writers from the Northeast. It is interesting to note that these same writers of the Northeast had the same sensitiveness towards their literary brothers in Great Britain.

The next review,[2] of *Voices of Freedom,* published in 1846, did not appear until 1848; and the old problem of obscurity was very much in evidence. The reviewer praises the simple, sincere music of old and contrasts it with the unintelligibility of the present, allying Whittier with the former. The question that has been debated since Aristotle, whether the object of poetry is pleasure or knowledge, is also still alive in this review. In vigorous language, the writer commends Whittier for realizing that pleasure and instruction are possible at the same time, comments on the powers of literature to mould readers' actions for good or evil, and regrets that the devil seems to have a corner on the best literature at the present. More hopefully, he notes that even in France and among periodical readers, more substance is being demanded. He continues, "God be thanked that in this our free America we have at least one poet who seems thus to have understood the proper use of the 'gift and faculty divine.'" Unfortunately Whittier is not as well known as he deserves to be, and it is not strange that he does not find his way into the drawing rooms of our substantial citizens. He is too earnest, too loving, too full of tenderness for this class, which wants highly colored and artificial emotion. A mother who would weep to hear her daughter sing a ballad of love's despair in some distant land would be ashamed to hear her sing Whittier's **"Farewell of a Slave Mother to Her Daughter Sold into Southern Bondage."** Whittier's language is commended as vigorous, intelligible, truth-telling, and as chosen from the vital vocabulary of the heart. He is an example to other poets of the need to return to the matter-of-fact world which has ample subjects for poetry. Whittier deserves the highest praise because he deals with the shame and the glory of the real world rather than with the escape world of wishful thinking.

In 1849 a notable event in the history of Whittier publication occurred.[3] B. B. Mussey of Boston, possibly influenced by his enthusiasm in the cause of abolition and his desire to pay tribute to one of the cause's most ardent and effective workers, published an illustrated edition of Whittier's poems, including all previously printed poems and a single new one. More notable even than the publication of the volume was the fact that, in spite of the hostility of the South, the commercial interests of the North, and the indifference of the devotees of escapist romance, the volume became a best seller, the only one of Whittier's to be so honored, in spite of the great popularity of the later *Snowbound*. The fact that the sales were surprising to the publisher and that he had a strong sense of justice is shown by the fact that he paid Whittier considerably more than required by their agreement, giving him $500.00 for the copyright and a percentage of the sales.

It was this best seller of Whittier's that was reviewed in 1849 by a "Middle States" man, the editor of Littell's *Living Age*.[4] He speaks of having occasionally taken a poem of Whittier's from the newspapers and reprinted it in the magazine. On the other hand, many admirable ones were not chosen because of the fact that they were too strongly partisan to please some of the magazine's readers. Though Whittier is an ardent abolitionist, the editor does not find him malicious in his advocacy and wishes that the South had not condemned him out of hand as merely an abolitionist, for he has many other voices that the South could listen to and enjoy. The editor also reprints a notice of the volume from the *New York Albion,* which finds, contrary to the preceding view, that Whittier exhibits "vindictive intolerance." On the other hand, he is vigorous and original—qualities sadly lacking in current poetry. Paralleling the previous review, the critic refers disparagingly to the sentimental "Rosa Matilda school" as being so widespread that Whittier's "earnest, thoughtful, powerful" writing is all the more admirable and striking by contrast. He lacks "grace and finished liveliness" but makes up for it by bold simplicity. His rough appearance hides nobility. Though Whittier has a front rank as a poet, his vengeful intolerance as a lecturer carries over into some of his poetry and disfigures it. Refusing to illustrate by quotation Whittier's passion on the slavery issue and his lack of skill as a versifier, the reviewer concludes his notice by quoting several stanzas from **"Proem,"** his choice as the best poem in the volume, a memorable and highly finished poem in its alliteration, harmony, and metaphor.

This article highlights two of the barriers that Whittier faced early in his poetic career: the first was the fact that his abolition poems closed the minds of many readers, particularly in the South, to any of his other works, which they either did not know of or refused to read; secondly, the readers of romantic escape literature that was full of sugarplums, sentimental tears, and terror, rejected his treatment of everyday themes in a language simple, earnest, and earthy.

The most important piece of criticism resulting from the publication of the 1849 *Poems* was a long review article in the *Universalist Quarterly Review* by Henry Ballou, 2d.[5] As a considered judgment, he accorded Whittier a position as one of the two foremost American poets, Bryant being the other, if the better part of his work is used to judge him, although there are several others superior to him if technical excellence is the only basis. Here Whittier is occasionally lax. He does not fail for lack of ability, as the better work shows. This failure, whatever its reason, is regrettable; for he is a true poet with the eye, heart, and imagination more than any other American. The writer goes on to say that he knows of no other American who has

> the perfect truthfulness of conception that lies under his imaginative coloring together with his warm unaffected geniality of spirit, tempered with just enough of pensiveness to give it a romantic charm, and all brought out in so natural a freshness of expression and imagery. We say this only of the better class of his poems, for there is great inequality among them.

This lack of consistent quality is one of the most persistent charges made by the critics against Whittier throughout the years. Occasionally, Ballou suggests, the Quaker poet is too passionate, especially in the anti-slavery poems. What is meant seems to be that his feelings as a man run away with his control as an artist. Whittier's earnestness is prominent; and though he deals in sentiment, this quality of earnestness keeps him from being sentimental. He is particularly American in his "taste and manner" as well as his range. In his descriptions, there is a sense of naturalness and vitality that is not present in more analytical poets. Whittier's characters too have the air of reality and vitality; and more important, they are healthy and natural, no matter how unusual. One cannot help but wonder if this is an implied criticism of Poe and his morbid preoccupations. Although the reader is often surprised at the contrast between the Whittier of anger and passionate protest in the anti-slavery poems and the kindliness and geniality in others, Ballou feels that these are but two different manifestations of the same feeling of affection. Many of the poems are failures; yet the better ones "scattered the living coals of truth upon the nation's naked heart." However they may be regarded later, they did the work of the moment. The article concludes with the further suggestion that more care in technique and more concentration at the expense of nonessentials would make a great improvement on an already excellent product.

To do it justice, the next notice must be quoted in full, as no summary or paraphrase could be adequate:

> Mr. Whittier has some of the elements of a true poet, but his poems, though often marked by strength and tenderness, are our abomination. He is a Quaker, an infidel, an abolitionist, a philanthropist, a peace man, a Red Republican, a non-resistant, a revolutionist, all characters we hold in horror and detestation, and his poems are the echo of himself. God gave him noble gifts, every one of which he has used to undermine faith, to eradicate loyalty, to break down authority, and to establish the reign of anarchy, and all under the gentle mask of promoting love and good will, diffusing the Christian spirit, and defending the sacred cause of liberty. He approaches us in the gentle and winning form of an angel of light, and yet whether he means it or not, it is only to rob us of all that renders life worth possessing. If he believes himself doing the will of God, he is the most perfect dupe of the Evil One the Devil has ever been able to make. He is silly enough, after having denounced Pious the Ninth in the most savage manner, and canonized the assassins and ruffians who founded the Roman Republic, to think that he can pass with Catholics as not being their enemy, because, forsooth, he favored the Irish rebellion! Whoever denounces our Church or its illustrious chief is our enemy and we would much sooner hold the man who should seek to deprive us of life to be our friend, than the one who should undertake to deprive us of our religion. With this estimate of Mr. Whittier how can we praise his poems, or commend them to the public.[6]

The foregoing was taken from *Brownson's Quarterly Review* and was written six years after the editor's conversion to Catholicism. His pilgrimage, as Arthur M. Schlesinger, Jr. characterizes it in his biography of Brownson, had taken him from Calvinistic Presbyterianism into the pulpit of a Unitarian church and charter membership in the Transcendental Club, on to socialism and an attempt to found a Workingman's Party, and ultimately—and not without its logic—into the Catholic Church. It was from this position, not without its logic too, that the preceding article was written, illustrating, as it does, the problem of writing objective literary criticism when strong personal feelings and beliefs are involved. It is ironic and, from the point of view of the literary historian, regrettable that Brownson really did not review the book, the title of which was *Songs of Labor and Other Poems*. For in these poems, popular though they were and praised by many critics, Whittier did not come to

grips with the industrial revolution of his day and the problems of the working man, which Brownson himself had analyzed and penetrated so farsightedly.

In the first treatment of Whittier by the British press that I have come across, *Tait's Edinburgh Magazine* for February, 1855, had an article on the American poets Alice Carey, T. B. Read, Lowell, Holmes, and Whittier.[7] The author, who had saved Whittier for last, found that he had run out of space and had to dismiss him in a brief paragraph. He gently chides Whittier for referring to Watts' unmelodious psalms in *The Bridal of Pennacook,* the preface of which he feels is written in about the most unmusical blank verse ever penned. He further suggests that Whittier writes too much, but finds the poetry has vigor and feeling and appreciates it profoundly. He concludes the remarks with a further apology for the scanty treatment and a "kindly Godspeed."

Later in the year, the *Irish Quarterly Review*[8] in an article dealing with Whittier, Poe, Lowell, Read, and Willis, treated Whittier first and dealt quite thoroughly with him in a very high-flown style indeed. Whittier mirrors the grandeur of his country in majestic verse. The power and ambition of the people are reflected in his "nervous, ringing language." And there is all the "bold, lofty, and free aspirations of her statesmen, which in the unbending and devoted love of freedom, breathes through his work like the sighing of the wind through a forest of his native pine trees." Whittier is especially and foremost the American poet. Like Cooper, he sings of the land and the Indians; but particularly he concerns himself with what he conceives as the spirit of America, the ideas and the beliefs that have made her great and unique in commerce, morality, and philosophy. His work often lacks polish and concentration, but these are minor faults when compared with his vigor and noble simplicity. Yet all is not unvarnished praise, for Whittier is still a man of greater promise than performance. To fulfill that promise he must root out sectarian bitterness that will inevitably damage the reputation of anyone who supports it, in view of the inevitable direction America will take in this respect. One cannot help feeling that the author's prediction in history was not more discriminating than his enthusiastic approval of Whittier's poetry, especially when he held up *The Bridal of Pennacook* and *Mogg Megone* as among the most effective pieces. Yet this preference is understandable in view of the interest that the Europeans showed in almost any material dealing with the Indians or native American subjects. Many of the shorter poems are said to have "great descriptive beauty, dramatic incident and coloring, among which may be mentioned his fine lines on the Merrimac. . . ." The article concludes, "Freedom converts us if Whittier is an example of its effects in its gush of words, its vivid images, and its patriotism." This article is typical of a certain type of review from across the water, with its enthusiasm for the revolutionary and democratic experiment, an enthusiasm which was especially strong in Ireland for obvious reasons.

In a delightfully frank review of **Home Ballads** in the *North British Review*[9] for 1861, the author immediately strikes a note that is familiar to readers of Whittier when he says that with poetry, as with wine and friends, we cling to the familiar as we get older, though we realize that it is not absolutely better but only seems so to us. The result is a reluctance to read new poets and a subsequent injustice to those such as Whittier, who is a true poet with a tone that is native, wild and original. Far from being one of the current crop of poetic imitators who can toss off a clever likeness of whatever style is popular at the moment, he writes because he has to; and the music of his ideas and diction is as important a part of poetry as is "philosophy, theology, and the general omniscience of today's work." Whittier is preferred to all the rest of the moderns, and the only consolation for not having read him sooner is the fact that he has written a great deal that the reviewer has to look forward to. His best poems are the least ambitious. **"The Witch's Daughter"** is a lovely and moving tale; **"Skipper Ireson's Ride," "Telling the Bees," "My Playmate,"** and the **"Red River Voyager"** are better than **"Trinitas"** and **"The Preacher,"** though all have power and poetry in them.

In 1885, E. C. Stedman published his *Poets of America,* one of the first attempts to come to grips with the American poets and with the tradition of American literature as a unity. Analyzing Whittier, Stedman feels that he is preëminently the embodiment of the typical American qualities of the period, "domesticity, piety, freedom, loyalty to country and land." He goes on to speak of Whittier as the uncrowned laureate, the people's poet, full of faith, temperance, charity, virtue, democracy, a believer in the value of labor, freedom, and earnestness; and passionate in reform and having faith in its effectiveness. Whittier is more of a New England poet than a national one, may not appeal to all times and races, and probably will not influence later poets. However, he is the "singer of a significant time and people." His defects are numerous, according to Stedman; he lacks a sense of the moral duty the artist owes to his craft. His carelessness and occupation with other concerns, especially in the early works, is very apparent. After 1860 when he devoted himself to his poetry, considerable improvement is noticeable. His best work deals with country matters; *Snowbound* is his masterpiece. His slavery poems are the poorest; but his religious poetry evidences deep faith, a quality to which all times can respond.[10] Stedman probably represents the first critical treatment of Whittier from a strictly aesthetic point of view.

An Englishman, R. E. Prothero, writing in *Longman's Magazine* in 1886,[11] has some rather penetrating remarks to make on Whittier. He points out that, though Whittier was of the time and place that produced what was later to be called the New England Renaissance, he was without university training and was neither a Boston Brahmin nor a Transcendentalist. Yet he created a world of his own out of his personal circumstances. He was American in his subjects, settings, imagery, religion, politics, and in the practical nature of his poetry. Of the two periods of his work, the earlier reform period provides poetry that is still able to stir emotions, though, on the whole, it is repetitious, verbose, rhetorical, and piously excessive in its exhortation and ejaculation. The later poetry is much better. Whittier's descriptive powers are always great, fresh, and simple but not deep. He is a genuine story teller, though "mystic beauty, dreamy grace, rounded art, lofty imagination, are not his gifts."

As the century drew to a close, the criticism became increasingly elegiac; and at the same time, with Whittier's work obviously completed, the problem of fixing his position in American letters was seriously taken in hand. In 1887 F. H. Underwood, consul at Glasgow for several years, contributed, among many services for American literature, a series of papers on American authors to the magazine *Good Words.*[12] In the article on Whittier, he held **"The Barefoot Boy"** and *Snowbound* to be the best existing pictures of New England farm life and people, equal to Burns' "Cotter's Saturday Night." As a descriptive poet of nature, Whittier was particularly blessed by his native place. In his idylls, ballads, and narratives, he is the chief of the American poets, as no other is as close to the common people and so without intellectual pretensions that might separate him from them. There is no one in the United States "whose native poetical genius exceeds Whittier's." I suppose Underwood, who knew all the New England poets intimately, was thinking chiefly of Whittier's lack of education and cultural background when he refers to "native genius."

Whittier's death, in 1892, occasioned a number of articles, both in America and abroad. *The Nation*[13] pointed out that Whittier the man was characteristic of America in that there was "nothing to keep him from full identification with the most cultivated class, yet he was always able to remain in full sympathy with the least cultivated. In this respect he was more typically national than other bards." Of the three areas of his fame, his position as the poet of abolition and the creator of the New England legend is felt to be unique. His religious themes he shares with others. Lack of musical training is blamed for his limitations to the simplest forms of prosody. However, his natural ear for melody is apparent in his ballads. He is sometimes too diffuse and rambling; but in the anti-slavery poems and his later works, this tendency is curbed in favor of simplicity and directness. He soon outgrew his provincialism, and errors in grammar and pronunciation seem to the writer to be not the result of ignorance but of whim. Often to his detriment, he introduces direct and obvious moralizing that would be better left inherent in the structure of the poem itself. His birth placed him as one of the people; in this he is unlike most of the other New England greats. His Quaker background of oppression in the early New England period made him particularly sensitive to injustice and sympathetic to the downtrodden.

John V. Cheney, writing in the *Chataquan*[14] for December, 1892, sounds the democratic trumpet loudly. Contrary to the consensus, he finds that the anti-slavery poems by no means represent a waste of talent. They were needed, and Whittier was peculiarly fitted to write them. *The Songs of Labor* are unique and as such should be valued. Though Whittier is lacking the highest genius and is a bit "bald, crude, narrow, careless, he has sincerity, simplicity, sinew, enthusiasm, spontaneity, and directness." He is not only a representative American poet but one who is as sure as any to endure. Of the two widely read poets in America, Whittier—not Longfellow—attracts the sturdy class, the common man. Whittier's common sense, pith, and vigor is more effective than Long-fellow's greater art. As a lyricist, Whittier is a master of pathos and is second only to Longfellow as a story teller. His *Snowbound* and Lowell's *Bigelow Papers* hold first place in American Literature.

T. Cuthbert Hadden has an article in the British *Gentleman's Magazine* for October, 1892,[15] and says, " . . . if we cannot call him great, we can at least call him good." He then goes on to praise Whittier with discrimination. In speaking of the *Voices of Freedom* poems, he points out that they are powerful, if not always poetic, expressions of impassioned pleading and burning denunciation. Whittier's verses rank high among the world's satirical and critical poetry. He wrote much and should be judged only by his best, not by his mediocre work. His musical charm, lyrical passion, concentrated and exquisite expression of high poetical feeling are equal to anything which American poetry has produced. His character poems are excellent, individual, and graphic. The ballads are full of charm, pathos, and freshness. In them he did for America what Scott did for his country; the hymns are permanently fixed in English hymnology, and there is a religious feeling present in all of his poetry as in Cowper. The work is earnest and genuine, if not great, and will last.

In the *Westminster Review*[16] for January, 1893, there appeared an article whose author compared Whittier and Burns, his teacher. Inferior to Burns in "a certain farcical and virile sense of humor . . . and gentle hearted as he ever showed himself to his fellow creatures, he had not the exquisite sympathy with the animal race which distinguished his predecessor." Only once did Whittier reach the very highest quality possible in

poetry. Amusingly, the title of that piece which the writer feels to be the height of Whittier's poetic perfection appeared, with a very appropriate misspelling, as **"Skipper Treson's Ride."** This poem, along with **"Barbara Fritchie,"** is destined to survive in the anthology of the New World. The writer goes on to suggest that, though Whittier is inferior to Longfellow in "constructive faculty" in prosody and diction, he had all of Longfellow's gentle qualities and equaled him in the ballad, there being no better in this form among the American poets. The lack of intellectuality is considered unusual in such a fine poet, being apparent in his spontaneity, in his way of looking at life, and in his style. Whittier knew foreign literatures but did not assimilate them in the highest sense to make them a part of his art. It is his sincerity that frequently results in poetry superior to that of those who are technically better and who seem to have more intelligence.

The *London Quarterly Review*[17] in 1893 commented on the difficulty of fixing Whittier's permanent place in literature so close upon his death because of his tremendous popularity both as man and poet. In the last resort, however, his feeling for and expression of the universal elements in man are considered most important in establishing his place. The anti-slavery poetry that so much of his present fame rests upon will not be permanent. *Voices of Freedom* is mostly verse rather than poetry; yet **"Barbara Fritchie"** is spirited and should survive. **"Ichabod"** is cited as a fine example of occasional lyric. The writer also makes a point that is too often overlooked, it seems to me. He suggests that, because a specific name and occasion is associated with a particular poem, the feeling often persists that it lacks the universality or generalized application that is necessary if poetry is going to survive the immediate moment. He further points out that, though neither Webster nor the cause he represented concern us now, men we love and trust will from time to time betray us. Although it is hard to judge Whittier by strictly literary standards because he was such a personal force and because he wrote so much that is not excellent, his pictures of New England will live. In *Snowbound,* **"Among the Hills,"** and in the shorter lyrics and ballads, he has preserved vividly and movingly a way of life that is fast disappearing.

> As a mere man of letters, Whittier could hardly sustain a comparison with his compeers. He lacks the artist soul of Longfellow, the wit and fancy of Holmes, the keen satire and wide culture of Lowell; but there is an intensity of conviction, a white heat of enthusiasm, a trumpet note of courage and faith that cannot be paralleled in the works of his contemporaries.

The writer concludes that Whittier may live through his life and its influence. However, this critic fails to observe, when he sets up the division between Whittier's powerful feelings and the more cultivated and urbane qualities of his fellow poets, that frequently this feeling is given perfectly adequate artistic expression. His implication seems to be that it is a thing apart, one that is somehow a hindrance to poetic expression, as well it may be if not properly controlled, as in some of the anti-slavery poems.

In an article in *Lippincott's Magazine* for June, 1899,[18] R. H. Stoddard confirmed for the most part judgments expressed twenty-five years earlier, spoke of the great amount of material that had been written about Whittier, indicated he had read most of it without being much edified, and went on to state his distrust of contemporary opinion, a conclusion which this paper clearly refutes. Standing firmly with the historical critics, Stoddard pointed out that understanding of a poet required a knowledge of his life, background, and times, and that this was especially true in the case of Whittier. No American poet, he suggests, had so much to overcome by way of background as Whittier. It is interesting to note that when Stoddard objects to the quantity of Whittier's abolition verse, which he does not consider poetry, the editor inserted a conciliatory note, pointing out that many readers will not agree with this judgment. The *Voices of Freedom* Stoddard finds hasty, overlong in many cases, though spirited, vigorous, and rhetorical. His opinion of the Indian poems is that, while they do contain vivid and fine descriptions, they are not worthy of the telling as stories; nor are the characters any more than stock Indians of romance. He feels it to have been an advantage that Whittier read in the period, however; for this reading resulted in his interest in Colonial subjects and traditions that gave us **"Cassandra Southwick," "The Exiles,"** and other poems of Colonial days. His temperament and background led him to deal principally with those aspects of injustice and cruelty that disfigure the New England Puritan past. As the years passed, a more romantic and tender note became dominant in Whittier's poetry. Immediately after this comment, Stoddard speaks of Whittier as the laureate of labor, without realizing how his judgment of Whittier as increasingly romantic reveals both his own romanticism and Whittier's in the treatment of the labor poems. Stoddard gives them high praise and calls them spirited, picturesque, natural, and native. Critical of the ethical element in Whittier's poetry, he concludes, "Submission to his feelings was greater than . . . to his gifts, of which he caught a glimpse in some of his early ballads, which he discovered in *Songs of Labor,* and of which he had full possession when he wrote '**The Barefoot Boy,' 'Maud Muller,' 'Telling the Bees,'** and *Snowbound.*" These and **"Barbara Fritchie," "Skipper Ireson,"** and a few others are most American. Stoddard regrets there were not more of such poems and feels that Whittier will be read as Chaucer and Burns now are by students of social history as well as of literature.

In looking back over the criticism of the nineteenth century, one sees certain features clearly. Even during the period toward the close of the century when, by longevity and the impact of a strong and appealing personality, Whittier was certainly one of the most beloved of American poets, his contemporaries were aware of and implied, even when they did not actually state, the fact that his was not a major talent. Secondly, as the nation grew physically and in its complexity, it became increasingly evident that Whittier was more a poet of New England than of America. Thirdly, the poems of abolition, though popular, were in most cases recognized as inferior in spite of the fact that some of them rose to the level of poetry. Whittier's freshness, simplicity, earnestness, and sincerity are mentioned again and again; and the didactic element is increasingly criticized as the century draws to a close. One of the most interesting features of the criticism from across the water is its generosity and also its enthusiasm over Indians and native themes. Again there is little disagreement as to Whittier's carelessness and lack of range in form. Surprisingly Whittier's religious poetry, though mentioned frequently, does not receive the praise one would expect from the nineteenth century.

In the early years of the twentieth century, interest in Whittier held up quite well; and numerous articles were published. In 1907, Bliss Perry wrote an article titled "Whittier for Today" in the *Atlantic*.[19] He devotes a good deal of the article to Whittier's abolition activity and its influence on his poetry, finding, contrary to the generally held views, that it was not detrimental to the poet's art and that Whittier, more than either Byron or Wordsworth, influenced men's feelings and actions. In the process of the slavery struggle, he grew from a facile rhymer to a master of political poetry. There was no other like him in American literary history. "He found," Perry says, "in that absolute surrender to the claims of humanity the inspiration which transformed him into a poet." Like Byron, Whittier became a master of passionate declamation that was accepted without question as poetry by his age. A later age is apt to feel that it is mere oratory or pamphleteering; yet many of these efforts are more than that. Analyze Whittier, Perry suggests, and there is the ideal political poet, with a Quaker faith, an abstract love of justice, a warm sympathy and loyalty, a keen knowledge of the men of the times, a practical political eye, a simple, racy, and fervent speech,—and above all—courage. Perry points out how difficult it is even half a century later to recapture the overwhelming sense of opposition that Whittier had to face. Even fifteen years after his death, Perry feels that his audience is a thing of the past and has changed as definitely as his erstwhile neighbors have disappeared. There is a certain rusticity that, while it may endear him to many, makes him more local than Burns. His physical limitations, color blindness and tone deafness, were severe. His passion was always moral passion; and even in his religious

Whittier at his desk.

verse, his range was narrow and unoriginal. Perry concludes by standing firm on the proposition that there are two questions about which Whittier is always and forever right. The first is his insistence that there should not and must not be any race issue; we are all brothers. The second is that of international peace. Over fifty years have intervened to try and prove Perry wrong, but never has his insistence on these fundamental truths of Whittier's been more apparent or important than today.

In 1921 Percy H. Boynton[20] entered one of the few disclaimers to Whittier's position as a nature poet by suggesting that he was too close to nature as an unsuccessful farmer. And by 1925 in a volume called *Poets of America,* Clement Wood could dismiss Whittier in a single sentence: "As a poet, Whittier was a hardheaded Quaker; his flight brushed the ground."[21]

John Erskine and W. P. Trent, editing a volume called *Great Writers of America,* published in London in 1929,[22] try to assess Whittier in terms of world literature. They note that patriotic lyrics like **"Barbara Fritchie"** impressed the world and feel that it is as a poet of human freedom that Whittier must live if his reputation is to last. He wrote some good descriptive poetry of New England but not enough to hold his place. "He generally manages to attain a fair level of excellence. But on the whole, he displayed no great strength of intellect or of imagination, and little of that marked individuality of temperament which . . . is the chief mark of genius." His only realm of true mastery is in the anti-slavery poems.

> His hold upon unsophisticated readers who are docile to tradition and full of patriotism has doubtless continued fairly strong, and the teaching of American literature in the schools will undoubtedly help to maintain his reputation; but one is left wondering how the sophisticated public of two generations hence will regard him.

In 1931 Henry S. Canby was able to ignore Whittier in his *Classic Americans,*[23] although he included Irving, Cooper, Emerson, Thoreau, Hawthorne, Melville, Poe, and Whitman.

Winfield Scott,[24] a poet of note himself, in an article subtitled "A New Consideration of Whittier's Poetry," written in 1933, suggests that Whittier's best poetry came after the Civil War, beginning with *Snowbound* which fixed his eminent position as a poet in the hearts of a public that had already canonized him as a man. Among the reasons for his success as a poet is his intimate relationship to the life of the land and men, rather than through books, as was the case with Longfellow, Lowell, and Holmes. Whittier often fell into the trap of nineteenth-century sentimentality, although he knew the dangers it presented. Among the abolition poems, **"Laus Deo," "Ichabod,"** and attacks on hypocrisy were memorable. His success in the later poems involves nostalgia brought on by sadness, ill health, and loss of loved ones. These circumstances, Scott feels, caused him to turn to the past, whose people and land he loved. He shows a power of description of nature, sincere love, simplicity and directness. The swiftness of the pictures he was able to paint made his ballads succeed better than any others. **"Mabel Martin," "Kathleen," "The Countess," "Dead Feast of the Kol Folk," "The Brewing of Soma,"** and **"Skipper Ireson's Ride"** are among the best. His characters are not often successful, the exception being **"Abraham Davenport,"** which Scott sees as a forerunner of Robinson's character sketches. The use, particularly in the schools, of the more popular pieces like **"Barbara Fritchie"** and **"School Days"** has done Whittier a disservice, when there are things like **"The Last Walk in Autumn," "Abraham Davenport," "What the Birds Said,"** and **"The Henchman."** Scott suggests that the confusion of morality with art is still with us, causing the critics to neglect Whittier's religious verse, which includes some of the best hymns in American literature. His qualities may be summed up as descriptive accuracy, preciseness, and simplicity. Directness of ideas is present in the best work. His range of verse structure was limited, but within its limitations, skillful. His chief weakness Scott sees as a restriction of subject matter. He did not ride Milton's soaring Pegasus but the "farm wagon and buckboard of verse." In his search for materials, he dealt with labor before Whitman and with the New England past before Hawthorne. "All of it [his verse] is instinct with his honesty and his integrity; much of it shows his clearsightedness; the precious part of it is an American inheritance."

In 1937 Desmond Powell,[25] although judging Whittier as a minor and sectional poet whose descriptions rely considerably on the reader's local familiarity, did believe that Whittier had written poetry that would live. His weaknesses are seen as numerous. He wrote jogging verse, lacked concentration and the critical faculty, tacked morals on his poems, accepted the popular taste, and relied on the statement of a truth rather than its embodiment in a poem. Adapting his nature descriptions to the limitations of his red–green color

blindness, Whittier, Powell suggests, etched rather than painted scenes. *Snowbound* is artistry in black and white, as a consequence. One may be forgiven for wondering how in winter it could have been anything else. The fact that Whittier was unable to transmute the abolition experiences into poetry is explained, Powell feels, in the poem **"Amy Wentworth."** This failure was one of the intellect; for Whittier was a bad critic, accepting the function of art to be mere escape and leaving himself little scope in which to work this vein. He never realized that this theory failed to explain the great poetry that he admired most. His stories are poor, not because he lacked the narrative gift, but because he did not bother with character, which he could do well as *Snowbound* proves. The feelings of hate and scorn in the abolition poems were weakened by this theory of art as escape. Other passions were killed by it, too. The impression one ultimately receives from Whittier's work is not that he lacked passion but that he subdued it; for he is the warmest poet in the whole New England group. Sentimentality was not the cause of failure in many poems; they were merely bad poems. **"Telling the Bees"** is sentimental, but it achieves success because it is a good poem; we believe in it. Whittier became the poet of friendship and tenderness through this flight from stronger emotions. He is a poet of anthology scraps and would benefit from careful and drastic editing. As an example, Powell brings two stanzas together from **"The Henchman"** and quite rightly calls the result a perfect lyric.

> Oh, proud and calm!—she cannot know
> Where'er she goes with her I go.
> Oh, cold and fair!—she cannot guess
> I kneel to share her hound's caress!
>
> The hound and I are on her trail;
> The wind and I uplift her veil;
> As if a calm, cold moon she were
> And I the tide, I follow her.

Powell goes on to say that Whittier's humor is often neglected. **"My Old Schoolmaster,"** excerpts from **"A New England Legend,"** and **"The Double Headed Snake,"** are cited as examples. There is naturalism too, for Whittier knew that rural life was not always idyllic, though that is the way he presented it most often. In the **"Prelude"** to *Among the Hills* and in **"The Preacher,"** he presented the starkness of New England farm life.

Plaintive and rather appealing in its call to fling back the years, is the plea of W. Harvey-Jellie in the *Dalhousie Review*[26] for April, 1939. He suggests that poetry is being read again but that it is eternal shame to America that she is neglecting Whittier. Who is read today? Millay, Frost, Benet, Teasdale, Masters, Lindsay, Sandburg, Robinson, Dickinson, and MacLeish is the answer. Whittier is scarcely read at all: our age with its fears, Harvey-Jellie says, is foreign to that of Whittier with its calm faith. It is as mystic, in spite of his other fine poetry, that Whittier is greatest. **"The Eternal Goodness," "My Triumph," "My Soul and I,"** and **"The Mirror"** are among his best poems, according to Harvey-Jellie. Poetry, with the possible exception of Frost's is downright objective if not materialistic, and the ". . . barrier must be raised high against a suicidal national drift toward a soulless secularism. Back to Whittier!" is Mr. Harvey-Jellie's clarion call. This approach is perhaps explained when we learn that Mr. Harvey-Jellie is Professor of Hebrew at Presbyterian College in Montreal.

The most recent treatments of Whittier have appeared in 1957, when Howard Mumford Jones[27] wrote for the one hundred and fiftieth Whittier anniversary an article, "Whittier Reconsidered," published in the Essex Institute *Historical Collections,* and in 1959, when the same journal published Hyatt Waggoner's "What I Had I Gave: Another Look at Whittier."[28]

Jones suggests that Whittier's fate illustrates the changing values on the literary scene during the last half century. He says, "When Whittier died in 1892, there was small doubt that his was a major voice. Today it is a real question whether he is read at all except by children and students." On the contrary, it seems to me that the criticism already reviewed indicates that Whittier's contemporaries did not consider him a major poet. It is true, however, as Jones points out, that on the one hundred and fiftieth anniversary of his birth no critics were interested in him as they are in Whitman. No historian is concerned with placing him in the intellectual development of the country. Few scholars are at work on the text, unpublished material, or biography. Rather whimsically Mr. Jones notes that Whittier used to have four cards assigned to him in the Parker Brothers' game of "Authors;" for the record, he still does; and the poems on those four cards are *Snowbound,* **"The Eternal Goodness," "Laus Deo,"** and **"Among the Hills."** Their choice of poems is excellent. According to Jones, the abolition verse sounds like ranting, if it is not the genuine article, because Whittier failed to distinguish between having to write a poem and having a poem to write. This is one of his weaknesses; didacticism is another. Jones attributes this preachiness to the times that demanded it and to his experience as a newspaper poet and editor. Nevertheless, in spite of his faults, there is a small but permanent core of poetry in Whittier's nature poems, in his rare treatment of character, and in the poems of faith. He is honest in his response to nature and here anticipates Robert Frost. In this vein *Snowbound* is successful, but the subtitle should not be forgotten; the poem is an idyll. The poems of character are not **"Maud Muller"** and **"Barbara Fritchie"** but **"Rabbi Ishmael"** and—best of all—**"Abraham Davenport."** In his poems of faith, **"Our Master"** is perfect.

Hyatt Waggoner suggests, after reading the complete poems from cover to cover, that Whittier wrote about twenty-five poems which "are still very pleasurable to read and rewarding as poetry." Though he may be largely unread today, Whittier wrote enough good poetry to fill several volumes such as today's poets hang their reputations on. He is almost the exact counterpart of what the modern poets have taught us to like, and his own taste reveals his weakness. He loved the didactic. His admiration of Longfellow's "Psalm of Life" is a case in point. His contemporaries read him as a religious poet, and we must do so too. However, he is best when he is not explicitly religious; he is also best in the reform poems when he is strongly religious. In other words, when he writes of things seen and felt as resulting from faith, of love, and a sense of justice out of faith, then he is excellent. Invective out of this sort of feeling is also fine. **"Clerical Oppressors," "Official Piety," "The Gallows," "Lines on the Portrait of a Celebrated Publisher," "Letter from a Missionary,"** and **"On a Prayer Book"** are all examples. The best of these propaganda poems are not dated, for they present the fight for right and justice, freedom and brotherhood, and the vision of God's holy city on earth that is always pertinent. Whittier is not sentimental in his view of nature, for nature is never better than man. His faith in progress dates him, but it was God's progress, not man's. He distrusted the symbol, the talisman of the modern poet; but when fervor took hold of him as in some of the anti-slavery poems, an adequate symbol came to hand. Indeed, we should go on reading and teaching him. In two areas he never failed with emotions, ideas, and symbols: first, with the religious demands of conscience and, secondly, in the experiences of childhood. *Snowbound* is his best poem. Waggoner concludes by saying,

> I think we should decide that what he had was no major poetic talent, and the talent he had was weakened a good deal of the time by an outlook that made him distrust symbolization, but what he had was well worth the giving. Not just American life but American poetry too is richer because he lived and wrote.

Having surveyed a representative selection from over one hundred years of Whittier criticism, one can come to a number of conclusions. Relatively few of the nineteenth-century critics deal with Whittier's prose, and none from the twentieth do so. His prose style was generally felt to be clear, fresh, and pleasant, capable of effective nature descriptions and narrative force. The *Southern Literary Messenger,* in spite of its rejection of Whittier because of his abolition sentiments and activities, was the most generous of all in its praise, holding him to be, next to Hawthorne, America's most polished writer of prose. His geniality and humor are remarked from time to time; but his sense of justice, love of humanity, and sincerity are most frequently noted. None of the British articles refer to any of the prose works. Ironically, the most effective and interesting volume of prose, *Leaves from Margaret Smith's Journal,* the one prose work that perhaps really deserves to live as of more than scholarly interest, was not even noticed on its publication in any of the prominent journals.

As for the poetry, the general characteristics are often mentioned. Simplicity, directness, clarity, vigor, passion, sincerity, manliness, tenderness, melody, and imagery are all recognized and praised. He is outstanding as a nature poet and as a poet of human justice. Lack of careful planning occasionally results in faulty proportion and unity. Haste, rather than lack of ability, seems to cause faulty versification and rhyme from time to time. Objections to strong partisanship are raised, sometimes on the grounds of his position itself, and at other times because it is felt to weaken his art. The *Southern Quarterly Review,* in the most critical American reaction, very ungraciously rejects any claims for Whittier above mediocrity and curiously finds him frigid and lacking in tenderness. He is recognized as American to the marrow, though of that minority group concerned with justice, freedom, idealistic reform, and humanity, which has set the tone for the most admirable American vision, as opposed to American expediency and the materialism of the bustling and "sharp" Yankee variety.

In England, two general tendencies appear regarding Whittier first as an especially American poet and admirable, and second as an American and abolitionist, hence detestable and without merit as a poet. The *Athenaeum* represents the first point of view; *Blackwood's,* the only periodical to deny him any poetic ability, the second. A few American notices point out this cleavage in which the conservative and wealthy Americans reject Whittier as too radical, violent, and rude.

The difficulty of judging Whittier's passionate abolition verse as art is recognized by Ballou, who points out, however, that it did the intended job effectively by arousing the conscience of the North. The *Irish Quarterly Review* was very gaudy in its praise of Whittier as *the* American poet, revealing the physical grandeur of the country itself and singing and teaching the ideas and ideals that have made America both great and a democratic beacon for the rest of the world. Yet even this writer feels that Whittier is more a poet of promises than fulfillment as yet. Brownson presents the best example of criticism influenced by other factors than the work of the artist.

When the general tenor of the nineteenth-century material is assessed, in spite of the few extravagant claims, usually in partisan periodicals whose editors were friends and for which Whittier wrote, and a very few violently severe criticisms, Whittier is recognized as a poet who is not entitled to a place in the front ranks, in spite of admirable qualities as a man, champion of human rights, and poet. This consensus is remarkably close to today's judgment and speaks well for the perspicacity of the nineteenth-century critics when they were dealing with a person and forms they understood; indeed, Whittier's very understandability, in a day when obscurity was complained of, was a cause for praise. This opinion is supported by the fact that Whittier was not, a few claims to the contrary, nearly as popular and widely discussed in England as he was in America, probably because of the quality of his verse and his position as an advocate for a cause. Aside from *Blackwood's* violent rejection of him as poet and the *Irish Quarterly Review's* extreme admiration of his Americanism, the English notices are quite similar to the American, although they were fewer.

The twentieth-century critics, in spite of the variety of their tone, generally agree as to the scope of Whittier's talent and the areas in which it was successful. Even more important than this conclusion is the fact that, with few and obvious exceptions, these judgments are merely supplemental rather than counter to those of the nineteenth century, quite contrary to the popular belief, which held that Whittier was highly overrated by his contemporaries. The nineteenth-century critical opinion is particularly interesting because Whittier was so tremendously popular in his own day, because the American critics were accused of puffing their own, because Whittier's work was not completed when many of the critics judged him, and because these critics did not have the advantage of the longer perspective that the later critics enjoyed.

Notes

[1] *Southern Quarterly Review,* IV (October 1843), 516-519.

[2] *New Englander,* VI (January 1848), 58-66.

[3] For the story of this publication, see: C. M. Taylor, "The 1849 Best Seller," *Bulletin of the Friends Historical Association,* XXXVIII (Spring 1949), 36-37.

[4] *Littell's Living Age,* XX (13 Jan. 1849), 94-95.

[5] *Universalist Quarterly Review,* VI (April 1849), 142-160.

[6] *Brownson's Quarterly Review,* VII (October 1850), 540.

[7] *Tait's Edinburgh Magazine,* XXII (February 1855), 104.

[8] *Irish Quarterly Review,* V (September 1855), 561-590.

[9] *North British Review,* XXXIV (February 1861), 210-217.

[10] E. C. Stedman, *Poets of America* (Boston, 1885), pp. 93-107.

[11] *Longman's Magazine,* IX (December 1886), 182-189.

[12] F. H. Underwood, "John Greenleaf Whittier," *Good Words,* XXVIII (1887), 30-34.

[13] *Nation,* LV (September 1892), 199-200.

[14] John V. Cheney, "Whittier," *Chatauquan,* XVI (December 1892), 299-306.

[15] T. Cuthbert Hadden, "The Quaker Poet," *Gentleman's Magazine,* XLIX (October 1892), 408-417.

[16] *Westminster Review,* CXXXIX (January 1893), 7-11.

[17] *London Quarterly Review,* LXXIX (January 1893), 224-244.

[18] R. H. Stoddard, "John Greenleaf Whittier," *Lippincott's Magazine,* VII (March 1898), 808-816.

[19] Bliss Perry, "Whittier for Today," *Atlantic,* C (December 1907), 851-859.

[20] P. H. Boynton, *American Poetry* (New York, 1921), pp. 646-648.

[21] C. W. Wood, *Poets of America* (New York, 1925), p. 11.

[22] John Erskine and W. P. Trent, *Great Writers of America* (London, 1929), pp. 147-149.

[23] H. S. Canby, *Classic Americans* (New York, 1931).

[24] Winfield Scott, "Poetry in America: A New Consideration of Whittier's Verse," *New England Quarterly,* VII (June 1933), 258-275.

[25] Desmond Powell, "Whittier," *American Literature,* IX (November 1937), 335-342.

[26] W. Harvey-Jellie, "A Forgotten Poet," *Dalhousie Review,* XIX (April 1939), 91-100.

[27] Howard Mumford Jones, "Whittier Reconsidered," Essex Institute *Historical Collections,* XCIII (October 1957), 231-246.

[28] Hyatt H. Waggoner, "What I Had I Gave," Essex Institute *Historical Collections,* XCV (January 1959), 32-40.

Harry Hayden Clark (essay date 1968)

SOURCE: "The Growth of Whittier's Mind—Three Phases," in *Emerson Society Quarterly,* Vol. 50, 1968, First Quarter, pp. 119-26.

[*In the following excerpt, Clark traces the development of Whittier's themes from an early taste for "localistic sensationalism" through his championship of abolition to a broad concern for human welfare.*]

After one has analyzed Whittier's individual poems or fragments of his work, it is well to view him briefly in complete profile as a kind of man against the sky. Broadly speaking, he seems to have had three successive centers of emphasis—I say emphasis because there are of course minor exceptions which do not seriously invalidate this interpretation.

Up to 1833 Whittier was primarily concerned with the literary aspects of the sensational, the lurid, or the colorfully superstitious, usually approached from a localistic angle. The type is represented in **"The Demon's Cave"** (1831) in which he says there is in this actual New Hampshire cave "something to romance dear" since it is associated with "the restless phantoms of murdered men," the ghostly gibber and the demon's yell, although such superstitions have now passed "away at the glance of truth." Mary Pray's *A Study of Whittier's Apprenticeship* (1930) printed 109 of these early poems, and others have been printed by W. M. Merrill in the *Essex Institute Historical Collections,* XCI (1955), pp. 128-154. A glance at the titles in T. F. Currier's invaluable *Bibliography of John Greenleaf Whittier* (1937) will give one an idea of his cultivation, as in his Preface to **Legends of New England** (1831), of a "new" consciousness that "New England is rich in traditional lore—a thousand associations of superstition and manly daring and romantic adventure are connected with her green hills and her pleasant rivers." Such psychological "associationalism" of aesthetic feeling and actual historic places was in this period widespread, especially in the revered *North American Review* from 1815 on, as R. E. Streeter has shown.

Five of Whittier's early associates encouraged him in the trend suggested. Thus Joshua Coffin encouraged the boy's interest in local traditions and introduced him at the age of fourteen to the work of Burns who taught him to see the romance underlying the commonplace. A. W. Thayer urged him to continue his education and to write for publication. New Hampshire's Robert Dinsmoor (on whom Whittier wrote an appreciative essay) taught him that New England scenes could provide Yankee pastorals just as well as Scotland. And in editing the work of J. G. C. Brainard in 1832 Whittier centers his long Introduction on the fact that he "prefers the lowliest blossom of Yankee-land" to far-away exotics. "New England is full of Romance; and her writers would do well to follow the example of Brainard. The great forest which our fathers penetrated—the red men—their struggle and their disappearance—the Powwow and the War-dance—the savage inroad and the English sally—the tale of superstition, and the scenes of Witchcraft,—all these are rich materials of poetry." (This Introduction and about seventy other literary comments are reprinted in *Whittier on Writers and Writings,* ed. E. H. Cady and H. H. Clark, 1950.) The superstitions and witchcraft of Whittier's native state were made to seem suitable for poetic treatment by the fact that (as he said in reviews of Scott and his "Demonology and Witchcraft") such a famous author had showed a "bias" toward "the marvellous and the praeternatural" aroused by "Highland superstition." In his review of Scott's follower, Whittier's "old favorite Cooper" and his *Wept,* dealing with a New England Indian, Cooper is critical of improbabilities and of the "females," but he praises Cooper's sea novels for "rich and rare entertainment" as well as the earlier volumes of the Leatherstocking Series, celebrating manly daring and hair-breadth escapes in the localized forests. (See Cady and Clark, pp. 26-28).

II

If up to 1833 Whittier tended to emphasize localistic sensationalism of one kind or another, from 1833[1] to 1857 he tended to emphasize outward reformism or abolition which after 1843 shaded into a concern for more general brotherhood and mankind's common humanity as opposed to extremism. His reformism was a response to five influences. Garrison and other humanitarians fired Whittier's imagination as he dramatized his turn from the selfish quest of literary fame to a defiance (in the poem **"Ego"**) of "ermined robe and saintly gown" to the kind of "glorious martyrdom" for the rights of the lowly which he attributed to Garrison in his early (1833) poetic tribute. Especially important as an influence was Whittier's ancestral Quaker faith in equality and brotherhood and the stress on charity of heart associated with John Woolman whose work Whittier edited with a long eulogistic introduction. Milton and Puritan "defenders of English liberty, sowers of the seed, the fruits of which we are now reaping," (*Prose Works,* I, 288) were strong influences. (Milton of the great prose tracts such as *Areopagitica* came closest, Whittier said, to representing his ideal man at this time.) As one who believed in relying on persuasion and on ballots rather than on bullets, Whittier cherished the natural-rights tradition of Jefferson. In his prose tract, **"Justice and Expediency"** (1833), Whittier responded to the Yankee spirit of practical expediency in arguing that free men, sure of the fruits of their own labor, will have an incentive to work harder than slaves will. And finally British abolitionists and the visits of their spokesmen such as George Thompson helped to inspire Whittier in his crusade.

Three poems may be cited as representing various phases of his abolitionism. Perry Miller[2] was much impressed by his poem **"Toussaint L'Ouverture"** in Whittier's crisis year, 1833, which illustrates the way in which his earlier romantic sensationalism erupts in an abolitionist poem: "this phantasmagoric vision of the rebellion in Haiti . . . is stark violence, massacre, and, in the climax, rape of the white planter's wife by the black demon" driven to desperation. "The sexual passion, the fire, the volcano, erupt into a terminology of orgiastic destruction." **"A Sabbath Scene"** tells how Whittier's "brain took fire" when a clergyman, trying to help enforce the Fugitive Slave Law, ordered his Deacon to use the actual physical "holy tome" to trip and capture a trembling slave girl who sought to escape to the supposed sanctuary of a Christian church. Temporarily at least Whittier preferred to turn from such an abuse of the Scriptures to follow the guidance of God's word "interpreted by Nature." Less melodramatic is **"Massachusetts to Virginia"** which recalls how the latter's statesmen such as Patrick Henry joined northern revolutionists to achieve freedom from Britain; devoted to the traditions of their First Families, Jefferson's Virginians are in this poem taunted with having become "False to their fathers' memory, false to the faith they loved." **"Proem"** (1847-49) was written as a comprehensive introduction to all Whittier's abolition poems. In this he modestly claims he is unable to approach the "rounded art" and "mystic beauty, dreamy grace" of poets such as Spenser and Sidney whom he loves, but he will celebrate "our common world of joy and woe" and will lay his poems on the shrine of Freedom which he loves as ardently as did Milton.[3] Elsewhere Whittier said (in **"The Training,"** 1845) that "Milton approaches nearly to my conception of a true hero" as "the stern old republican," and "Milton's prose has long been my favorite reading. My whole life has felt the influence of his writings" (quoted in Pickard's *Life,* II, 506). Perhaps Whittier's most enduring and timely contribution to our political life is embodied in his editorial in the *Essex Gazette* for June 18, 1836, entitled **"Freedom of the Press"** claiming the right of dissent. (Governor Everett tried to get the legislature of Massachusetts to penalize spokesmen of abolition.) "We will yield to no laws whatever of our freedom of opinion, and the constitutional right of expressing that opinion. We are for giving Truth full play. We believe with Milton in his noble defence of the freedom of the Press." He argued that if the South managed to throttle freedom of expression and dissent, the South would enslave all white men as well as negroes, and would stagnate.

During the 1850's in poems such as **"Wordsworth"** Whittier holds that one can "read the world aright" who can "in its common forms discern / A beauty and a harmony," that one (like himself) whose ear is "pained / By strife of sect and party noise" finds especially welcome Wordsworth's "brook-like murmur . . . of nature's simple joys." (John Pickard and C. B. Williams have described the "schism" after 1843 within the abolitionist group and the split between the followers of Garrison and of Whittier. See Pickard, *NEQ,* XXXVII, 1964, 250-254; and Williams, *NEQ,* XXV, 1952, 248-254.) In **"Proem"** (1849) Whittier had coupled his reformist following of Milton in devoting his poems to liberty with his concern with "our common world of joy and woe." And in his **"Dedication to Songs of Labor"** (1850) he turns from "youth's enchanted forest" of his first period to "after-thoughts" associated with "life's autumnal lea" as he says that in his poems he seeks to "gladden duty's ways" by celebrating "the unsung beauty hid beneath life's common things." He tries to awaken not so much the reformist's unrest as "a manlier spirit of content," remembering that Christ was content to be "a poor man toiling with the poor, / In labor, as in prayer, fulfilling the same law." Remember, then, that Whittier's second period (as C. B. Williams helpfully suggests) has two phases—his Garrisonian abolition and concern with helping the helpless slave-labor, and (especially after 1843) an organic concern with the idea that "the strong hand makes strong the working brain" (cf. Thoreau) and a concern with the sanative "common things" and a manlier spirit of content with the life of the common man.

Taken as a whole, Whittier's prose essays in *Old Portraits and Modern Sketches* and *Literary Recreations* have two implications. First, wishing to give his personal reformism a broader basis, he tried to provide it with a broader temporal perspective by celebrating various now revered spokesmen of the Revolution of the seventeenth-century Puritans. Paradoxically, while he appeared to be dealing with the seventeenth-century Past, he singles out those spokesmen of the past who were iconoclasts, who pioneered in leading a revolt against bondage to throne and altar. But Whittier insists that Past, Present and Future are one, centered in the Now. Second, while Whittier's primary concern at the start in his prose portraits may have been a quest for examples of reformism, the heroic figures of the seventeenth century as he studied them led him to see that for the most part they stressed the inwardness of evil and sought to make men not masterless but selfmastered. (Milton who in the Second Sonnet on the Detraction said of his more radical opponents, license they mean when they cry liberty, for who loves that must first be wise and good, having overcome individual temptations.)

III

Let us now turn to Whittier's dominant emphases during his third period, during the last thirty-five years of his life, from 1857 when Mordell (p. 178) says "the work of Whittier as the poet of freedom and the singer of the oppressed really ended." (I should prefer to say

that he transcended his institutional reformism by including[4] it in a more proportionate synthesis involving the inward as well as the outward, organically related.)

As in **"Skipper Ireson's Ride"** on a rail while being externally tarred and feathered by the angry women whose husbands and brothers and sons the skipper had deserted, he turns in 1857 to the idea of the individual's inward conscience. Note the anguished cry of the physically tormented skipper to his persecutors:

> What is the shame that clothes the skin (*i.e.,* tar)
> To the nameless horror that lives within?

In his essay of 1862 introducing **"Dora Greenwell"** he hopes that "In the chaos of civil strife and the shadow of mourning which rests over the land, the contemplation of 'things unseen which are external' might not be unwelcome; . . . when the foundations of human confidence [in physical warfare] are shaken, and the trust in men proves vain, there might be glad listeners to a voice calling from the outward and the temporal to the inward and the spiritual" (VII, 303). In his many hymns such as **"The Eternal Goodness"** (1865-66) he acknowledges that past sages cannot paint too darkly the guilt and sin of which he as an individual is conscious "within." (For similar emphasis on the cause and cure of suffering as essentially within rather than outside the individual, see the Cambridge Edition of his poems, pp. 424; 433; 436; 438; 442; 448; 458; 460; 466.)

Institutional reform seemed impotent in the face of such afflictions as the death of his beloved mother in 1857, his two sisters in 1860 and 1864, and his own failing health at this time. He was also conscious of the fact that such masters as Milton and Emerson and Lowell had eventually turned from external reformism to a concern with inwardness. In 1870 he concluded, "The true life of a nation is in its personal morality, and no excellence of constitution and laws can avail much if the people lack purity and integrity" (VII, 432. See also VII, 228, where he says that "Unsupported by a more practical education, higher aims, and a deeper sense of the responsibilities of life and duty, it [women's exercise of the ballot] is not likely to prove a blessing [as a "remedy for all the evils"] in her hands any more than in man's." See also quote in S. T. Pickard's *Life,* II, 742, and VII, 356). Regardless of "outward" aids, he has become convinced that "no man his brother can redeem." In his long eulogy of Woolman he agrees with the Quaker sage that "all the varied growths of evil had their underlying root in human [individual] selfishness" (VII, 357). "There is something in the doctrine of total depravity and regeneration. We are born selfish. The discipline of [one's inward] life develops the higher qualities of character. . . . It is the [free-willed] conquering of innate selfish propensities that makes the saint; and the giving up unduly to impulses that in their origin are necessary to the preservation of life that makes the saint" (quoted in Pickard's *Life*, II, 629; see also VII, 232, 234). Whittier concluded that if the wrong-doer humbly repents breaking God's benign laws, such remorse may help to make evil educative, much as Milton did in his doctrine of the "fortunate fall" (*PL*, XII, 473-478).

During this period after 1857 Whittier urges that the Inner Light or the individual's intuition should be tested by a socially-mediated tradition such as that embodied in the Bible: The two revelations should test and reinforce one another. His **"Pennsylvania Pilgrim"** (1872) "read the Bible by the Inner Light." However, Whittier emphasized those aspects of his ancestral faith which accorded with other and older religious sects and he hoped that Catholics and Puritans and the Hindus would eventually come to understand that they were worshipping in the light of elemental truths at one[5] altar, just as he concluded that time is only an illusion, that past, present, and future are one.

"The Last Walk in Autumn" (1857) also illustrates Whittier's turn from the "dreams" of his earlier concern with either the luridly romantic or with utopian reform to a concern with poetic imagination which can find the universal in humble particulars, his work now being devoted to "the home and hearth" as in *Snowbound* (1867). "The beauty which old Greece or Rome / Sung, painted, wrought, lies close at home" and is discoverable by the imaginative "eye and ear / In all our daily walks" as well as in communion with his American friends Emerson (II, 105-112), Bayard Taylor, and Charles Sumner. He will now as a poet devote himself (in proceeding from kin to kind) to New England's "equal village schools," the "freeman's vote," religious freedom, her laborers' right to the rewards of their own efforts, and the "old home-bred virtues."

In place of his "hate of tyranny intense" and the tendency of the propagandist toward one-sidedness, Whittier in **"The Problem"** (1877) dividing management and labor argues that essentially "The interests of the rich man and the poor / Are one and same, inseparable evermore" and partisans of one or the other in their extremist panaceas offer but "catch-words of the blind / Leaders of the blind. / Solution there is none / Save in the Golden Rule of Christ alone," save in mediation and a peaceful recognition of the just claims of both sides in the controversy. Just as he regarded the Scripture as "a rule, not *the* rule of faith and practice," so Whittier urged his Quaker friends to find "no occasion to renew the disastrous quarrel of religion with science" (VII, 362) which men such as Swedenborg had used to show that objects in the "world of sense [are] only types and symbols of the world of spirit" (VII, 362). He also praised science as an agent of truth which had outmoded the cruel belief in witches. He praised the reverent Agassiz who was capable of

prayer. Indeed, Whittier derived reinforcement for his doctrine of charity as based on the scientific or Newtonian doctrine that "in the outward world all things [such as the planets] do mutually operate upon and affect each other; and that it is by the energy of this [centrifugal and centripetal balanced] principle that our solid earth is supported, and the heavenly bodies are made to keep the rhythmic harmonies of this creation." He had faith that "a law akin to this physical law had been ordained for the moral world," sanctioning social coherence and mutual charity drawing individuals together (V, 91). Like Thoreau, however, Whittier was sceptical of "poor Etzler" as a mere technologist who prophesied the coming of a "paradisiacal state by the sole agency of outward mechanics" (V, 353). (Whittier's over-all view of science deserves much more investigation.)

If in **"The Sabbath Scene"** the spokesmen of slavery had invoked the sanction of the Bible and consequently Whittier had briefly preferred to rely on outward nature rather than the Bible, his more characteristic later view is embodied in **"Andrew Rykman's Prayer"** (1864-65) where he concluded that all the external things of nature tend to "fluctuate and flow." In **"A Summer Pilgrimage"** (1883) he was confident that "Beyond this masquerade of shape and color, light and shade, / And dawn and set, dull wax and wane, / Eternal verities remain."

During Whittier's last period he repeatedly emphasized the idea that "in judging of my fellow-men, I can see no other standard than which our Lord and Master has given us, 'By their fruits ye shall know them.' The only orthodoxy that I am especially interested in is that of life and practice." (Quoted by Pickard, *Life*, I, 265.)

In **"The Last Walk in Autumn,"** in *Snowbound* and especially in **"The Pennsylvania Pilgrim"** Whittier does not so much discard his earlier two emphases as he transcended them by including them in a larger synthesis. Thus in the latter poem, which the poet prized as among his best (Pickard's *Life*, II, 575-576), the groundwork is obviously localistic, the colonial Quaker's life being set in Pennsylvania. The prose preface uses his benign life (in which Lewis Leary finds the central figure to be that of sowing seeds which flower in reform) as an example of the way in which Quaker influence "has been felt through two centuries in the amelioration of penal severities, the abolition of slavery, the reform of the erring, the relief of the poor and the suffering—felt, in brief, in every step of human progress." But of course the primary emphasis is on the individual (Pastorius) who read the Bible—was respectful of a socially-mediated tradition—by the Inner Light, by a reverent psychological awareness and responsiveness. If in the second period, Whittier's emphasis seems to have been essentially horizontal—man's concern with his fellow-men as in "The Poor

Voter on Election Day" (1848-52)—his emphasis in the third period is predominantly vertical, the Christian concern (cf. "Trinitas") for drawing one's fellowmen together being given deeper organic meaning by allegiance to the deity associated with perfection. In other words, as individuals are persuaded to approach the deity, to be responsive to the Inner Light, they will necessarily be drawn closer together in brotherhood.

In his final period Whittier increasingly deplored the divisions of sectarianism, and sought common ground between all sects devoted to the good of all predicated on making individuals not masterless but self-mastered. The extent to which his simple but not naive religious views have entered into the main stream of diverse religious groups is attested by the fact that nearly one hundred hymns have been extracted from poems (as Mr. Currier has shown in his *Bibliography*, p. 597). These hymns (some seventeen of which are still printed in standard *Hymnals* even in 1968) belie the claim of our avant-garde critics that Whittier is dead, since hundreds of thousands sing his hymns of tolerance and mercy who do not notice the poet's name.

His simple dependence on the individual's inner light safeguarded by traditional wisdom lends itself reasonably well to the uses of those who are not so much concerned with antiquarian historical facts about Christ as a person or about ritualism as with a recognition that one may think of the deity as revealed within the individual psychologically whenever he is aware of an impulse toward what generations of men have agreed to call goodness. Such an elementary belief is not likely to be outmoded.

Notes

[1] S. T. Pickard, *Life and Letters of John Greenleaf Whittier* (Boston, 1894, p. 131, says "There was a sudden, even startling change in the character of Whittier's poetry, when he made up his mind to champion the cause of the slave," beginning (Albert Mordell thinks) when in 1832 he met Garrison and read his abolitionist propaganda. Byron, whom Whittier associated with the Greek quest of freedom, appears to have served as a kind of bridge between Whittier's two periods, leading him to glorify Garrison as venturing close to "glorious martyrdom" as he braved "the dagger's point."

[2] Miller, "John Greenleaf Whittier: The Conscience in Poetry," *Harvard Review,* II (1964), 8-24. (This is the first printing of an address at Swarthmore in 1957.) The most detailed account of Whittier's reformist period is found in Albert Mordell's *Quaker Militant* (Boston, 1933), although the book as a whole reflects some Marxian and Freudian biases. Mordell concludes that the ardor of Whittier's "hate of tyranny intense"

places him on a level with our very greatest writers whom he identifies as Emerson, Thoreau and Hawthorne, and much above other American authors. On Whittier's political interests see also C. B. Williams, "Whittier's Relation to Garrison and the 'Liberator'," *NEQ,* XXV (1952), 248-255, and J. B. Pickard, "Whittier and the Abolition Schism of 1840," *NEQ,* XXXVII (1964), 250-254. See the bifurcated comments on Byron in the Cady-Clark volume, pp. 38-40, 93-103 and *passim.* Much as Whittier the moralist deplored Byron's licentiousness and impiousness, he could not help concluding in 1831 "We admire—we amost worship—the sublimity of Byron's genius," (pp. 70-71) for "no nobler heart" exists among the "laurel'd bards," and "he was the master spirit of his time" (p. 40).

[3] In a doctoral dissertation I was privileged to direct, Lester Zimmerman (*Milton's American Reputation to 1900,* 1949) has brought together Whittier's many quotations from and tributes to Milton as the spokesman of freedom (pp. 247-280).

[4] See quote in Pickard's *Life,* II, 513 and VII, 147, where he denies any "low esteem of his anti-slavery labors."

[5] See V, 113-114; VII, 353; V, 310; Mordell's quotation, 297-298; and the quotation in Pickard's *Life,* II, 632.

Robert Penn Warren (review date 1971)

SOURCE: "Whittier," in *The Sewanee Review,* Vol. LXXIX, No. 1, Winter, 1971, pp. 98-133.

[*Poet and novelist Robert Penn Warren won the Pulitzer Prize for his novel* All the King's Men. *In the following excerpt, he relates Whitter's maturation as a poet to his work as a journalist and political propagandist.*]

When Whittier, at the age of twenty-six, came to knock "Pegasus on the head", the creature he laid low was, indeed, not much better than the tanner's superannuated donkey. In giving up his poetry he gave up very little. Looking back on the work he had done up to that time, we can see little achievement and less promise of growth. He had the knack, as he put it in **"The Nervous Man"**, for making rhymes "as mechanically as a mason piles one brick above another", but nothing that he wrote had the inwardness, the organic quality, of poetry. The stuff, in brief, lacked content, and it lacked style. Even when he was able to strike out poetic phrases, images, or effects, he was not able to organize a poem; his poems usually began anywhere and ended when the author got tired. If occasionally we see a poem begin with a real sense of poetry, the poetry gets quickly lost in some abstract idea. Even a poem as late as **"The Last Walk in Autumn"** (1857) suffers in this way. It opens with a fine stanza like this:

> O'er the bare woods, whose outstretched
>   hands
>   Plead with the leaden heavens in vain,
>   I see beyond the valley lands,
>   The sea's long level dim with rain,
>   Around me, all things, stark and dumb,
>   Seem praying for the snows to come,
>   And for the summer bloom and greenness,
>   gone,
>   With winter's sunset lights and dazzling morn
>   atone.

But after five stanzas, the poem dies and the abstractions take over for some score of stanzas.

For a poet of natural sensibility, subtlety, and depth to dedicate his work to propaganda would probably result in a coarsening of style and a blunting of effects, for the essence of propaganda is to refuse qualifications and complexity. But Whittier had, by 1833, shown little sensibility, subtlety, or depth, and his style was coarse to a degree. He had nothing to lose, and stood to gain certain things. To be effective, propaganda, if it is to be more than random vituperation, has to make a point, and the point has to be held in view from the start; the piece has to show some sense of organization and control, the very thing Whittier's poems had lacked. But his prose had not lacked this quality, nor, in fact, a sense of the biting phrase; now his verse could absorb the virtues of his prose. It could learn, in addition to a sense of point, something of the poetic pungency of phrase and image, and the precision that sometimes marked the prose. He had referred to his poems as "fancies", and that is what they were, no more. Now he began to relate poetry, though blunderingly enough, to reality. The process was slow. It was ten years— 1843—before Whittier was able to write a piece as good as **"Massachusetts to Virginia"**. This was effective propaganda; it had content and was organized to make a point.

Whittier had to wait seven more years before, at the age of forty-three, he could write his first really fine poem. This piece, the famous **"Ichabod",** came more directly, and personally, out of his political commitment than any previous work. On March 7, 1850, Daniel Webster, senator from Massachusetts, spoke on behalf of the more stringent Fugitive Slave Bill that had just been introduced by Whittier's ex-idol Henry Clay; and the poem, which appeared in March in the *Washington National Era,*[1] a paper of the "political" wing of the Abolition movement, deals with the loss of the more recent and significant idol. "This poem," Whittier wrote years later, "was the outcome of the surprise and grief and forecast of evil consequences which I felt on reading the Seventh of March Speech by Daniel Webster. . . ."

But here the poet remembers his poem, which does dramatically exploit surprise and grief, better than he remembers the facts of its origin; he could scarcely have felt surprise at Webster's speech, for as early as 1847, in a letter to Sumner, Whittier had called Webster a "colossal coward" because of his attitude toward the annexation of Texas and the Mexican War.

Here is the poem:

> So fallen! so lost! the light withdrawn
>   Which once he wore!
> The glory from his gray hairs gone
>   Forevermore!
>
> Revile him not, the Tempter hath
>   A snare for all;
> And pitying tears, not scorn and wrath,
>   Befit his fall!
>
> Oh, dumb be passion's stormy rage,
>   When he who might
> Have lighted up and led his age,
>   Falls back in night.
>
> Scorn! would the angels laugh, to mark
>   A bright soul driven,
> Fiend-goaded, down the endless dark,
>   From hope and heaven!
>
> Let not the land once proud of him
>   Insult him now,
> Nor brand with deeper shame his dim,
>   Dishonored brow.
>
> But let its humbled sons, instead,
>   From sea to lake,
> A long lament, as for the dead,
>   In sadness make.
>
> Of all we loved and honored, naught
>   Save power remains;
> A fallen angel's pride of thought,
>   Still strong in chains.
>
> All else is gone; from those great eyes
>   The soul has fled;
> When faith is lost, when honor dies,
>   The man is dead!
>
> Then, pay the reverence of old days
>   To his dead fame;
> Walk backward, with averted gaze,
>   And hide the shame!

The effectiveness of **"Ichabod",** certainly one of the most telling poems of personal attack in English, is largely due to the dramatization of the situation. At the center of the dramatization lies a division of feeling on the part of the poet: the poem is not a simple piece of vituperation, but represents a tension between old trust and new disappointment, old admiration and new rejection, the past and the present. The Biblical allusion in the title sets this up: "And she named the child Ichabod, saying, the glory is departed from Israel" (*I Samuel* 4:21). The glory has departed, but grief rather than rage, respect for the man who was once the vessel of glory rather than contempt, pity for his frailty rather than condemnation—these are the emotions recommended as appropriate. We may note that they are appropriate not only as a generosity of attitude; they are also the emotions that are basically condescending, that put the holder of the emotions above the object of them, and that make the most destructive assault on the ego of the object. If Webster had been motivated by ambition, then pity is the one attitude unforgivable by his pride.

The Biblical allusion at the end offers a brilliant and concrete summary of the complexity of feeling in the poem. As Notley Sinclair Maddox has pointed out (*Explicator,* April, 1960), the last stanza is based on *Genesis* 9:20-25. Noah, in his old age, plants a vineyard, drinks the wine, and is found drunk and naked in his tent by his youngest son, Ham, who merely reports the fact to his brothers Shem and Japheth. Out of filial piety, they go to cover Noah's shame, but "their faces were backward, and they saw not their father's nakedness." Ham, for having looked upon Noah's nakedness, is cursed as a "servant to servants" to his "brethren".

The allusion works as a complex and precise metaphor: The great Webster of the past, who, in the time of the debate with Robert Young Hayne (1830), had opposed the slave power and thus established his reputation, has now become obsessed with ambition (drunk with wine) and has exposed the nakedness of human pride and frailty. The conduct of Shem and Japheth sums up, of course, the attitude recommended by the poet. We may remember as an ironical adjunct that the Biblical episode was used from many a pulpit as a theological defense of slavery; Ham, accursed as a "servant to servants", being, presumably, the forefather of the black race.

We may look back at the first stanza to see another complex and effective metaphor, suggested rather than presented. The light is withdrawn, and the light is identified, by the appositive construction, with the "glory" of Webster's gray hair—the glory being the achievement of age and the respect due to honorable age, but also the image of a literal light, an aureole about the head coming like a glow from the literal gray hair. This image fuses with that of the "fallen angel" of line 27 and the dimness of the "dim, / Dishonored brow" in lines 19 and 20. In other words, by suggestion, one of the things that hold the poem together (as contrasted with the logical sequence of the statement) is the im-

age of the angel Lucifer, the light-bearer, fallen by excess of pride. Then in lines 29 and 30, the light image, introduced in the first stanza with the aureole about the gray hair, appears as an inward light shed outward, the "soul" that had once shone from Webster's eyes (he had remarkably large and lustrous dark eyes). But the soul is now dead, the light "withdrawn", and we have by suggestion a death's-head with the eyes hollow and blank. How subtly the abstract ideas of "faith" and "honor" are drawn into this image, and how subtly the image itself is related to the continuing play of variations of the idea of light and dark.

From the point of view of technique this poem is, next to **"Telling the Bees"**, Whittier's most perfectly controlled and subtle composition. This is true not only of the dramatic ordering and interplay of imagery, but also of the handling of rhythm as related to meter and stanza, and to the verbal texture. For Whittier, in those rare moments when he could shut out the inane gabble of the sweet singers like Lydia Sigourney, and of his own incorrigible meter-machine, could hear the true voice of feeling. But how rarely he heard—or trusted—the voice of feeling. He was, we may hazard, afraid of feeling. Unless, of course, a feeling had been properly disinfected.

In the "war with wrong", Whittier wrote a number of poems that were, in their moment, effectively composed, but only two (aside from **"Ichabod"**) that survive to us as poetry. To one, **"Song of Slaves in the Desert"**, we shall return; but the other, **"Letter from a Missionary of the Methodist Episcopal Church South, in Kansas, to a Distinguished Politician"**, not only marks a high point in Whittier's poetic education but may enlighten us as to the relation of that education to his activity as a journalist and propagandist.

The **"Letter"** as the full title indicates, grew out of the struggle between the pro-slavery and the free-state forces for the control of "Bleeding Kansas". Though the poem appeared in 1854, four years after **"Ichabod"**, it shows us more clearly than the earlier piece how the realism, wit, and irony of Whittier's prose could be absorbed into a composition that is both polemic and poetry. The polemical element is converted into poetry by the force of its dramatization—as in the case of **"Ichabod"**: but here specifically by an ironic ventriloquism, the device of having the **"Letter"** come from the pen of the godly missionary:

> Last week—the Lord be praised for all His
>   mercies
> To His unworthy servant!—I arrived
> Safe at the Mission, *via* Westport; where
> I tarried over night, to aid in forming
> A Vigilance Committee, to send back,
> In shirts of tar, and feather-doublets quilted
> With forty stripes save one, all Yankee comers,

Uncircumcised and Gentile, aliens from
The Commonwealth of Israel, who despise
The prize of the high calling of the saints,
Who plant amidst this heathen wilderness
Pure gospel institutions, sanctified
By patriarchal use. The meeting opened
With prayer, as was most fitting. Half an
    hour,
Or thereaway, I groaned, and strove, and
    wrestled,
As Jacob did at Penuel, till the power
Fell on the people, and they cried "Amen!"
"Glory to God!" and stamped and clapped
    their hands;
And the rough river boatmen wiped their
    eyes;
"Go it, old hoss!" they cried, and cursed the
    niggers—
Fulfilling thus the word of prophecy,
"Cursed be Canaan."

By the ventriloquism the poem achieves a control of
style, a fluctuating tension between the requirements
of verse and those of "speech", a basis for the variations of tone that set up the sudden poetic, and ironic,
effect at the end:

    P.S. All's lost. Even while I write these
        lines,
    The Yankee abolitionists are coming
    Upon us like a flood—grim, stalwart men,
    Each face set like a flint of Plymouth Rock
    Against our institutions—staking out
    Their farm lots on the wooded Wakarusa,
    Or squatting by the mellow-bottomed Kansas;
    The pioneers of mightier multitudes,
    The small rain-patter, ere the thunder shower
    Drowns the dry prairies. Hope from man is
        not.
    Oh, for a quiet berth at Washington,
    Snug naval chaplaincy, or clerkship, where
    These rumors of free labor and free soil
    Might never meet me more. Better to be
    Door-keeper in the White House, than to
        dwell
    Amidst these Yankee tents, that, whitening,
        show
    On the green prairie like a fleet becalmed.
    Methinks I hear a voice come up the river
    From those far bayous, where the alligators
    Mount guard around the camping filibusters:
    "Shake off the dust of Kansas. Turn to
        Cuba—
    (That golden orange just about to fall,
    O'er-ripe, into the Democratic lap;)
    Keep pace with Providence, or, as we say,
    Manifest destiny. Go forth and follow
    The message of our gospel, thither borne
    Upon the point of Quitman's bowie-knife,

And the persuasive lips of Colt's revolvers.
There may'st thou, underneath thy vine and
    fig-tree,
Watch thy increase of sugar cane and negroes,
Calm as a patriarch in his eastern tent!"
Amen: So mote it be. So prays your friend.

Here quite obviously the ventriloquism is what gives
the poem a "voice", and the fact instructs us as to how
Whittier, less obviously, develops through dramatization a voice in **"Ichabod"**. The voice of a poem is
effective—is resonant—insofar as it bespeaks a life
behind that voice, implies a dramatic issue by which
that life is defined. We have spoken of the complexity
of feeling behind the voice of **"Ichabod"**, and in the
present case we find such a complexity in the character of the missionary himself. At first glance, we have
the simple irony of the evil man cloaking himself in
the language of the good. But another irony, and deeper,
is implicit in the poem: the missionary may not be
evil, after all; he may even be, in a sense, "good"—
that is, be speaking in perfect sincerity, a man good
but misguided; and thus we have the fundamental irony
of the relation of evil and good in human character,
action, and history. Whittier was a polemicist, and a
very astute one, as the **"Letter"** in its primary irony
exemplifies. But he was also a devout Quaker, and by
fits and starts a poet, and his creed, like his art, would
necessarily give a grounding for the secondary, and
deeper, irony, an irony that implies humility and forgiveness.

What we have been saying is that by repudiating poetry Whittier became a poet. His image of knocking
Pegasus on the head tells a deeper truth than he knew;
by getting rid of the "poetical" notion of poetry, he
was able, eventually, to ground his poetry on experience. In the years of his crusade and of the Civil War,
he was, bit by bit, learning this, and the process was,
as we have said, slow. It was a process that seems to
have been by fits and starts, trial and error, by floun-
dering, rather than by rational understanding. Whittier
was without much natural taste and almost totally devoid of critical judgment, and he seems to have had
only a flickering awareness of what he was doing—
though he did have a deep awareness, it would seem,
of his personal situation. As a poet he was trapped in
the automatism and compulsiveness that, in **"Amy
Wentworth"**, he defined as the "automatic play of pen
and pencil, solace in our pain"—the process that writing seems usually to have been for him. Even after a
triumph, he could fall back for another fifty poems
into this dreary repetitiveness.

The mere mass of his published work in verse between
1843 and the Civil War indicates something of this. In
1843 appeared *Lays of My Home,* in 1848 what
amounted to a collected edition, in 1850 *Songs of
Labor,* in 1853 *The Chapel of the Hermits, and Other*

Poems, in 1856 *The Panorama, and Other Poems,* in 1857 the *Poetical Works,* in two volumes, and in 1860, *Home Ballads, Poems and Lyrics.*

But in this massive and blundering production there had been a growth. In 1843 even poems like **"To My Old Schoolmaster"**, **"The Barefoot Boy"**, **"Maud Muller"**, **"Lines Suggested by Reading a State Paper"**, and **"Kossuth"** would have been impossible, not to mention **"Skipper Ireson's Ride"**, which exhibits something of the élan of traditional balladry and something of the freedom of living language of **"Ichabod"** and the **"Letter"**. But nothing short of miracle, and a sudden miraculous understanding of Wordsworth and the traditional ballad, accounts for a little masterpiece like **"Telling the Bees"**. There had been the technical development, but something else was happening too, something more difficult to define; Whittier was stumbling, now and then, on the subjects that might release the inner energy necessary for real poetry.

There was, almost certainly, a deep streak of grievance and undischarged anger in Whittier, for which the Abolitionist poems (and editorials) could allow a hallowed—and disinfected—expression; simple indignation at fate could become "right-eous indignation", and the biting sarcasm was redeemed by the very savagery of the bite. But there was another subject which released, and more deeply, the inner energy—the memory of the past, more specifically the childhood past, nostalgia, shall we say, for the happy, protected time before he knew the dark inward struggle, the outer struggle with "strong-willed men" (as he was to put it in **"To My Sister"**) to which he had to steel himself, the collapses, and the grinding headaches. Almost everyone has an Eden time to look back on, even if it never existed and he has to create it for his own delusion; but for Whittier the need to dwell on this lost Eden was more marked than is ordinary. If the simple indignation against a fate that had deprived him of the security of childhood could be transmuted into righteous indignation, both could be redeemed in a dream of Edenic innocence. This was the subject that could summon up Whittier's deepest feeling and release his fullest poetic power.

Furthermore, if we review the poems after 1850, we find a subsidiary and associated theme, sometimes in the same poem. In poems like **"Maud Muller"**, **"Kathleen"**, **"Mary Garvin"**, **"The Witch's Daughter"**, **"The Truce of Piscataqua"**, **"My Playmate"**, **"The Countess"**, and **"Telling the Bees"**, there is the theme of the lost girl, a child or a beloved, who may or may not be, in the course of a poem, recovered. Some of these poems, notably **"Maud Muller"** and **"Kathleen"**, raise the question of differences of social rank, as do **"The Truce of Piscataqua"** if we read "blood" for *social difference,* and **"Marguerite"** and **"Mary Garvin"** if we read the bar of religion in the

same way. This last theme, in fact, often appears; we have it in **"Amy Wentworth"**, **"The Countess"**, and **"Among the Hills"**, all of which belong to the mature period of Whittier's work, when he was looking nostalgically backward. But this theme of the lost girl, especially when the loss is caused by difference in social rank or the religious bar, even though it clearly repeats a theme enacted in Whittier's personal life, never really touched the spring of poetry in him except in **"Telling the Bees"**, where it is crossed with the theme of childhood to reduce the pang of the sexual overtones. The theme of the lost girl, taken alone, belonged too literally, perhaps, to the world of frustration. In life Whittier had worked out the problem and had survived, by finding the right kind of action for himself, a "sanctified" action, and this action could, as we have seen, contribute to some of his best poetry; but, more characteristically, his poetic powers were released by the refuge in assuagement, the flight into Eden, and this was at once his great limitation and the source of his success.

For the poems specifically of nostalgia for childhood, we have **"To My Old Schoolmaster"**, **"The Barefoot Boy"**, **"The Playmate"**, **"The Prelude"** (to **"Among the Hills"**), **"To My Sister, with a Copy of 'The Supernaturalism of New England'"**, **"School-Days"**, **"Telling the Bees"**, and, preeminently, *Snow-Bound.* It is not so much the number of poems involved that is significant, but the coherent quality of feeling and, by and large, the poetic quality in contrast to the other work. As Whittier puts it in **"The Prelude"**, he was more and more impelled to

> . . . idly turn
> The leaves of memory's sketch-book,
> dreaming o'er
> Old summer pictures of the quiet hills,
> And human life, as quiet, at their feet.

He was, as he shrewdly saw himself in **"Questions of Life"**, an "over-wearied child", seeking in "cool and shade his peace to find", in flight

> From vain philosophies, that try
> The sevenfold gates of mystery,
> And, baffled ever, babble still,
> Word-prodigal of fate and will;
> From Nature, and her mockery, Art
> And book and speech of men apart,
> To the still witness in my heart.

As a young man hot with passion and ambition, and later as a journalist, agitator, and propagandist, he had struggled with the world, but there had always been the yearning for the total peace which could be imaged in the Quaker meeting-house, but more deeply in childhood, as he summarized it in **"To My Sister"**:

And, knowing how my life hath been
A weary work of tongue and pen,
A long, harsh strife with strong-willed men,
    Thou wilt not chide my turning
To con, at times, an idle rhyme,
To pluck a flower from childhood's clime,
Or listen, at Life's noonday chime,
    For the sweet bells of Morning!

The thing which he fled from but did not mention was, of course, inner struggle, more protracted and more bitter than the outer struggle with "strong-willed men".

"To My Old Schoolmaster", which appeared in 1851, just after Whittier's great poetic break-through with **"Ichabod"**, is the germ of **Snow-Bound,** the summarizing poem of Whittier's basic impulse. It can be taken as such a germ not merely because it turns back to the early years, but because Joshua Coffin, the schoolmaster, was a person associated with certain of Whittier's rites of passage, as it were. It was Coffin who, when Whittier was a boy of fourteen, sat by the family fire and read aloud from Burns. It was Coffin who was with Whittier at the founding of the American Anti-Slavery Society in Philadelphia, in 1833. Furthermore, Coffin early encouraged Whittier's historical and antiquarian interests (a fact that explains certain passages in the poem), and shared in his religious sense of the world; and in this last connection it is logical to assume that when, late in life, Coffin, a sweet-natured and devout man, fell prey to the conviction that he was not among the "elect" and would be damned, the fact would stir the aging Whittier's deepest feelings about the meaning of his own experience. Be that as it may, when Coffin died, in June, 1864, just before the death of Whittier's sister Elizabeth, which provoked **Snow-Bound,** Whittier felt, as he said in a letter, that he had lost "one of the old landmarks of the past". This bereavement would be absorbed into the more catastrophic one about to occur, just as the figure of Coffin would be absorbed into that of the schoolmaster in the poem that is ordinarily taken to refer, as we shall see, to a certain George Haskell.

We have remarked that **"To My Old Schoolmaster"**, composed shortly after **"Ichabod"**, may in one sense be taken also as contributing to **Snow-Bound**. But an even earlier poem, **"Song of the Slaves in the Desert"** (1847), indicates more clearly the relation of the poems inspired by Whittier's "war on wrong" to the poems of personal inspiration. The **"Song"** is, as a matter of fact, the best poem done by Whittier up to that time; and here the homesickness of the slaves gives a clear early example of the theme of nostalgia. Furthermore, since the slaves are, specifically, female, here is the first example of the theme of the lost girl:

Where are we going? where are we going,
    Where are we going, Rubee?

Lord of peoples, lord of lands,
Look across these shining sands,
Through the furnace of the noon,
Through the white light of the moon.
Strong the Ghiblee wind is blowing,
Strange and large the world is growing!
Speak and tell us where we are going,
    Where are we going, Rubee?

Bornou land was rich and good,
Wells of water, fields of food,
Dourra fields, and bloom of bean,
And the palm-tree cool and green:
Bornou land we see no longer,
Here we thirst and here we hunger,
Here the Moor-man smites in anger:
    Where are we going, Rubee?

When we went from Bornou land,
We were like the leaves and sand,
We were many, we are few;
Life has one, and death has two:
Whitened bones our path are showing,
Thou All-seeing, thou All-knowing!
Hear us, tell us, where are we going,
    Where are we going, Rubee?

Moons of marches from our eyes
Bornou land behind us lies;
Stranger round us day by day
Bends the desert circle gray;
Wild the waves of sand are flowing,
Hot the winds above them blowing,—
Lord of all things! where are we going?
    Where are we going, Rubee?

We are weak, but Thou art strong;
Short our lives, but Thine is long;
We are blind, but Thou hast eyes;
We are fools, but Thou art wise!
Thou, our morrow's pathway knowing
Through the strange world round us growing,
Hear us, tell us, where are we going,
    Where are we going, Rubee?

The relation of **"Ichabod"** to the theme of nostalgia is somewhat more indirect and complex, but we may remember that, as the title declares, the theme is a lament for departed glory. Literally the glory is that of Webster, who has betrayed his trust, but also involved is the "glory" of those who trusted, who had trailed their own clouds of glory, not of strength and dedication, but of innocence, simplicity, and faith. The followers are betrayed by their natural protector, for, as the Biblical reference indicates, they are the sons of the drunken Noah. In the massiveness of the image, however, the father betrays the sons not only by wine but by death, for it is a death's-head with empty eyesockets that is the most striking fact of the poem.

Here the evitable moral betrayal is equated, imagistically, with the inevitable, and morally irrelevant, fact of death. But by the same token, as a conversion of the proposition, the fact of death in the morally irrelevant course of nature is, too, a moral betrayal. The child, in other words, cannot forgive the course of nature—the fate—that leaves him defenseless.

In connection with this purely latent content of the imagery, we may remark that Whittier, in looking back on the composition of the poem, claimed that he had recognized in Webster's act the "forecast of evil consequences" and knew the "horror of such a vision". For him this was the moment of confronting the grim actuality of life. It was, as it were, a political rite of passage. Here the protector has become the betrayer—has "died". So, in this recognition of the isolation of maturity, we have the beginning of the massive cluster of poems of the nostalgia of childhood.[2]

Let us glance at a later poem, **"The Pipes of Lucknow: An Incident of the Sepoy Mutiny"**, that seems, at first glance, even more unrelated to the theme of childhood than does **"Ichabod"**. But as **"Ichabod"** is associated with **"To My Old Schoolmaster"**, a more explicit poem of childhood, so **"Lucknow"** is associated with **"Telling the Bees"**. If we translate **"Lucknow"**, we have something like this: The Scots have left home (*i.e.,* grown up) and are now beleaguered.

> Day by day the Indian tiger
>   Louder yelled, and nearer crept;
> Round and round the jungle-serpent
>   Nearer and nearer circles swept.

The "Indian tiger" and the "jungle-serpent" are melodramatic versions of the "strong-willed men" and other manifestations of the adult world that Whittier had steeled himself to cope with, and had turned from, as the Scots turn now, on hearing the pipes, to seek assuagement in the vision of home. As another factor in this equation, we may recall that Whittier had early identified his father's rocky acres with the Scotland of Burns, and so the mystic "pipes o' Havelock" are the pipes of Haverhill.

With one difference: the pipes of Havelock announce not merely a vision of assuagement but also a vengeful carnage to be wrought on all those evil forces and persons that had robbed the child of "home", on the "strong-willed men" and the "Indian tiger" and the "jungle-serpent". Furthermore, since in the inner darkness, where its dramas are enacted, desire knows no logic or justice beyond its own incorrigible nature, we may see distorted in the dark face of the "Indian tiger" and the "jungle-serpent" the dark faces of those poor slaves in Dixie—for it was all their fault; they were the enemy—if it had not been for them Whittier would never have been drawn forth from the daydreams and neurotic indulgences of his youth into the broad daylight of mature and objective action.[3]

Whittier recognized in himself an appetite for violence. "I have still strong suspicions," he would write in the essay **"The Training"**, "that somewhat of the old Norman blood, something of the grim Berserker spirit, has been bequeathed to me." So, paradoxically, but in the deepest logic of his being, this strain of violence is provoked against these forces that would threaten the "peace" of childhood, and it is to the "air of Auld Lang Syne", rising above the "cruel roll of war-drums", that the vengeful slaughter is released and the gentle Quaker poet breaks out in warlike glee in such lines as:

> And the tartan clove the tartan
>   As the Goomtee cleaves the plain.

"Lucknow" in fact, seems nearer to Kipling than to the saint of Amesbury, the Abolitionist, and the libertarian poet who, in this very period, was writing poems deeply concerned with the freedom of Italians (**"From Perugia"**, 1858, and *"Italy"*, 1860), if not with that of Sepoys. But it is no mystery that in 1858, the year of **"Lucknow"**, Whittier should have written the gentle little masterpiece of nostalgia **"Telling the Bees"**, for both would seem to have been conditioned by the same traumatic event: the death of Whittier's mother, which occurred in December, 1857.

On February 16, 1858, Whittier sent **"Telling the Bees"** to James Russell Lowell, at the *Atlantic Monthly*, saying, "What I call simplicity may be only silliness." It was not silliness. It was a pure and beautiful little poem informed by the flood of feeling that broke forth at the death of his mother.

> Here is the place; right over the hill
>   Runs the path I took;
> You can see the gap in the old wall still,
>   And the stepping-stones in the shallow brook.
>
> There is the house, with the gate red-barred,
>   And the poplars tall;
> And the barn's brown length, and the cattle-yard,
>   And the white horns tossing above the wall.
>
> There are the beehives ranged in the sun;
>   And down by the brink
> Of the brook are her poor flowers, weed-o'errun,
>   Pansy and daffodil, rose and pink.
>
> A year has gone, as the tortoise goes,
>   Heavy and slow;

And the same rose blows, and the same sun
    glows,
    And the same brook sings of a year ago.

There's the same sweet clover-smell in the
    breeze;
    And the June sun warm
Tangles his wings of fire in the trees,
    Setting, as then, over Fernside farm.

I mind me how with a lover's care
    From my Sunday coat
I brushed off the burrs, and smoothed my hair,
    And cooled at the brookside my brow
        and throat.

Since we parted, a month had passed,—
    To love, a year;
Down through the beeches I looked at last
    On the little red gate and the well-sweep
        near.

I can see it all now,—the slantwise rain
    Of light through the leaves,
The sundown's blaze on her window-pane,
    The bloom of her roses under the eaves.

Just the same as a month before,—
    The house and the trees,
The barn's brown gable, the vine by the
    door,—
    Nothing changed but the hives of bees.

Before them, under the garden wall,
    Forward and back,
Went drearily singing the chore-girl small,
    Draping each hive with a shred of black.

Trembling, I listened: the summer sun
    Had the chill of snow;
For I knew she was telling the bees of one
    Gone on the journey we all must go!

Then I said to myself, "My Mary weeps
    For the dead to-day:
Haply her blind old grandsire sleeps
    The fret and the pain of his age away."

But her dog whined low; on the doorway sill,
    With his cane to his chin,
The old man sat; and the chore-girl still
    Sung to the bees stealing out and in.

And the song she was singing ever since
    In my ear sounds on:—
"Stay at home, pretty bees, fly not hence!
    Mistress Mary is dead and gone!"

The setting of the poem is a scrupulous re-creation of
the farmstead where Whittier spent his youth. The poem
was composed almost thirty years after Whittier had
gone out into the world, and some twenty-two years
after he had sold the home place and moved the family
to Amesbury. Not only is the same nostalgia that informs *Snow-Bound* part of the motivation of this poem,
but also the same literalism. But more than mere literalism seems to be involved in the strange fact that
Whittier keeps his sister Mary—or at least her name—
in the poem, and keeps her there to kill her off; and
there is, of course, the strange fact that he cast a shadowy self—the "I" of the poem—in the rôle of the lover
of Mary, again playing here with the theme of lost
love, of the lost girl, but bringing the story within the
family circle, curiously coalescing the youthful yearning for sexual love and the childhood yearning for love
and security within the family circle. And all this at a
time when Mary was very much alive.

Just as the shock of his mother's death turned Whittier's
imagination back to the boyhood home and released
the energy for **"Telling the Bees"**, so the death of his
sister Elizabeth lies behind *Snow-Bound*. The relation
of Whittier to this sister, who shared his literary and
other tastes, who herself wrote verses (often indistinguishable in their lack of distinction from the mass of
her brother's work), who was a spirited and humorous
person, and who, as a spinster, was a companion to his
bachelorhood, was of a more complex and intimate
kind than even that of Whittier to his mother. She was
"dear Lizzie, his sole home-flower, the meek lily-blos-
som that cheers and beautifies his life"—as was observed in the diary of Lucy Larcom, a poetess of some
small fame and one of the ladies who, along the way,
was in love, to no avail, with the poet himself. When
Elizabeth died, on September 3, 1864, Whittier said,
"The great motive of my life seems lost."

Shortly before Elizabeth's death there had been another crisis in Whittier's life, the end of his second and
final romance with Elizabeth Lloyd, whom we have
already mentioned. The relation with that lady was
something more than merely one among his numerous
frustrated romances. He had known her for some
twenty-five years, from the time when he was thirty.
She was good-looking, wrote verses, painted pictures,
believed ardently in Abolition, and was a Quaker to
boot. What could have been more appropriate? She
even fell in love with him, if we can judge from the
appeals in her letters toward the end of the first connection with her: "Spirit, silent, dumb and cold! What
hath possessed thee?" Or: "Do come, Greenleaf! I am
almost forgetting how thee looks and seems." But
Greenleaf was beating one of his strategic retreats; so
she cut her losses, got to work and made a literary
reputation of sorts, married a non-Quaker, and got "read
out of meeting".

After her husband's death, however, Elizabeth Lloyd,
now Howell, reappeared in Whittier's life. They be-

came constant companions. Both suffered from severe headaches, but they found that if they caressed each other's hair and massaged each other's brows, the headaches would go away. Or at least Whittier's headache would, and he proposed to her. She refused him, but not definitively, and the dalliance went on. Even a quarrel about Quakerism did not end it. But it did end; or perhaps it merely petered out. In any case, in later years the lady nursed a grievance, and spoke bitterly of the old sweetheart.

So in spite of Elizabeth Howell's healing hands, Whittier again took up his solitude, and if he still clung to the explanation that his bachelorhood had been due to "the care of an aged mother, and the duty owed a sister in delicate health", the last vestige of plausibility was, ironically enough, now to be removed by the sister's sudden death. He was now truly alone, with no landmarks left from the Edenic past except those of memory.

Before the end of the month in which Elizabeth died, Whittier sent to the *Atlantic* a poem which he said had "beguiled some weary hours". It was **"The Vanishers"**, based on a legend he had read in Schoolcraft's famous *History, Condition, and Prospects of the American Indians* about the beautiful spirits who fleetingly appear to beckon the living on to what Whittier calls "The Sunset of the Blest". To the Vanishers, Whittier likens the beloved dead:

> Gentle eyes we closed below,
>   Tender voices heard once more,
> Smile and call us, as they go
>   On and onward, still before.

The poem is, in its basic impulse, a first draft of ***Snow-Bound***.

In a very special way ***Snow-Bound*** summarizes Whittier's life and work. The poem gives the definitive expression to the obsessive theme of childhood nostalgia. As early as 1830, in **"The Frost Spirit"**, we find the key situation of the family gathered about a fire while the "evil power" of the winter storm (and of the world) goes shrieking by. Already, too, Whittier had long been fumbling toward his great question of how to find in the contemplation of the past a meaning for the future. In **"My Soul and I"**, (1847), the soul that turns in fear from the unknown future to seek comfort in the "Known and Gone" must learn that

> The past and the time to be are one,
>   And both are now.

The same issue reappears in **"The Garrison of Cape Ann"**:

> The great eventful present hides the past; but
>   through the din
> Of its loud life hints and echoes from the life
>   behind steal in;
> And the lore of home and fireside, and the
>   legendary rhyme,
> Make the task of duty lighter which the true
>   man owes his time.

And it appears again in **"The Prophecy of Samuel Sewall"** (1859).

As for the relation to the poet's personal life, *Snow-Bound* came after another manifestation of the old inhibition that forbade his seeking solace from Elizabeth Lloyd's healing hands (and this as he neared the age of sixty, when the repudiation of the solace must have seemed more nearly and catastrophically final). It came after the death of the sister had deprived him of the motive of his life. And it came, too, toward the end of the Civil War, when he could foresee the victory of the cause to which he had given his energies for more than thirty years and which had, in a sense, served as his justification for life, and as a substitute for other aspects of life. Now the joy of victory would, necessarily, carry with it a sense of emptiness. Furthermore, the victory itself was in terms sadly different, as Whittier recognized, from those that he had dreamed.

Snow-Bound is, then, a summarizing poem for Whittier; but it came, also, at a summarizing moment for the country. It came when the country—at least all the country that counted, the North—was poised on the threshold of a new life, the world of technology, big industry, big business, finance capitalism, and urban values. At that moment, caught up in the promises of the future, the new breed of American could afford to look back on his innocent beginnings; and the new breed could afford to pay for the indulgence of nostalgia—in fact, in the new affluence, paid quite well for it. Whittier's book appeared on February 17, 1866,' and the success was immediate. For instance, in April, J. T. Fields, the publisher, wrote to Whittier: "We can't keep the plaguey thing quiet. It goes and goes, and now, today, we are bankrupt again, not a one being in crib." The first edition earned Whittier ten thousand dollars—a sum to be multiplied many times over if translated into present values. The poor man was, overnight, modestly rich.

The scene of the poem, the "Flemish picture", as Whittier calls it, the modest genre piece, is rendered with precise and loving care, and this scene had its simple nostalgic appeal for the generation who had come to town and made it, and a somewhat different appeal, compensatory and comforting no doubt, for the generation that had stayed in the country and had not made it. But the poem is not simple, and it is likely that the appeals would have been far less strong and permanent if Whittier had not set the "idyl" in certain "perspectives" or deeper interpretations. In other words, it can be said of this poem, as of most poetry, that the effect does not depend so much on the thing looked at as on the way of the looking. True, if there is nothing to look at, there can be no looking, but the way of the looking determines the kind of feeling that fuses with the object looked at.

Before we speak of the particular "perspectives" in which the poem is set, we may say that there is a preliminary and general one. This general perspective, specified in Whittier's dedicatory note to his **"Winter Idyl"**,[5] denies that the poem is a mere "poem". The poem, that is, is offered as autobiography with all the validation of fact. In other words, the impulse that had appeared in **"The Vanishers"** as fanciful is here given a grounding in the real world, and in presenting that world the poem explores a complex idea—how different from the vague emotion of **"The Vanishers"**—concerning the human relation to Time.

The literalness of that world is most obviously certified by the lovingly and precisely observed details: the faces sharpened by cold, the "clashing horn on horn" of the restless cattle in the barn, the "grizzled squirrel" dropping his shell, the "board nails snapping in the frost" at night. The general base of the style is low, depending on precision of rendering rather than on the shock and brilliance of language or image; but from this base certain positive poetic effects emerge as accents and point of focus. For instance:

> A chill no coat, however stout,
> Of homespun stuff could quite shut out,
> A hard, dull bitterness of cold,
> That checked, mid-vein, the circling race
> Of life-blood in the sharpened face,
> The coming of the snow-storm told.
> The wind blew east; we heard the roar
> Of Ocean on his wintry shore,
> And felt the strong pulse throbbing there
> Beat with low rhythm our inland air.

Associated with this background realism of the style of the poem we find a firm realism in the drawing of character. Three of the portraits are sharp and memorable, accented against the other members of the group and at the same time bearing thematic relations to them: the spinster aunt, the schoolmaster, and Harriet Livermore.

The aunt, who had had a tragic love affair but who, as the poem states, had found reconciliation with life, bears a thematic relation to both Elizabeth Whittier and Whittier himself. The schoolmaster, whose name Whittier could not remember until near the end of his life, was a George Haskell, who later became a doctor, practiced in New Jersey and Illinois, and died in 1876

without even knowing, presumably, of his rôle in the poem; but as we have pointed out, there are echoes here, too, of Joshua Coffin. As for Harriet Livermore, Whittier's note identifies her. The fact that the "warm, dark languish of her eyes" might change to rage is amply documented by the fact that at one time, before the scene of **Snow-Bound,** she had been converted to Quakerism, but during an argument with another Quaker on a point of doctrine she asserted her theological view by laying out with a length of stove wood the man who was her antagonist. This action, of course, got her out of the sect. In her restless search for a satisfying religion, she represents one strain of thought in nineteenth-century America, and has specific resemblances to the characters Nathan and Nehemiah in Melville's *Clarel.* As a "woman tropical, intense", and at the same time concerned with ideas and beliefs, she is of the type of Margaret Fuller, the model for Zenobia in the *Blithedale Romance* of Hawthorne.

To return to the structure of the poem, there are three particular "perspectives"—ways in which the material is to be viewed—that can be localized in the body of the work. These perspectives operate as inserts that indicate the stages of the dialectic of this poem. The first appears in lines 175 to 211, the second in lines 400 to 437, and the third in lines 715 to the end.

The first section of the poem (up to the first perspective) presents a generalized setting: the coming of the storm, the first night, the first day, and the second night. Here the outside world is given full value in contrast to the interior, especially in the following passage, which is set between two close-ups of the hearthside, that Edenic spot surrounded by the dark world:

> The moon above the eastern wood
> Shone at its full; the hill-range stood
> Transfigured in the silver flood,
> Its blown snows flashing cold and keen,
> Dead white, save where some sharp ravine
> Took shadow, or the sombre green
> Of hemlocks turned to pitchy black
> Against the whiteness at their back.
> For such a world and such a night
> Most fitting that unwarming light,
> Which only seemed where'er it fell
> To make the coldness visible.

The setting, as we have said, is generalized; the individual characters have not yet emerged, the father having appeared in only one line of description and as a voice ordering the boys (John and his only brother, Matthew) to dig a path, with the group at the fireside only an undifferentiated "we". This section ends with the very sharp focus on the mug of cider simmering between the feet of the andirons and the apples sputtering—the literal fire, the literal comfort against the threat of literal darkness and cold outside.

Now the first perspective is introduced:

> What matter how the night behaved?
> What matter how the north-wind raved?
> Blow high, blow low, not all its snow
>   Could quench our hearth-fire's ruddy
>   glow.

But immediately, even as he affirms the inviolability of the fireside world, the poet cries out:

> O Time and Change!—with hair as gray
> As was my sire's that winter day,
> How strange it seems, with so much gone
> Of life and love, to still live on!

From this remembered scene by the fireside only two of the participants survive, the poet and his brother, who are now as gray as the father at that snowfall of long ago; for all are caught in Time, in this less beneficent snowfall that whitens every head, as the implied image seems to say. Given this process of the repetition of the pattern of Time and Change, what, the poet asks, can survive? The answer is that "love can never lose its own."

After the first perspective has thus grafted a new meaning on the scene of simple nostalgia by the fire, the poem becomes a gallery of individual portraits, the father, the mother, the uncle, the aunt, the elder sister (Mary), and the younger (Elizabeth), the schoolmaster, and Harriet Livermore. That is, each individual brings into the poem a specific dramatization of the problem of Time. In the simplest dimension, they offer continuity and repetition: they, the old, were once young, and now, sitting by the fire with the young, tell of youth remembered against the background of age. More specifically, each of the old has had to try to come to terms with Time, and their portraits concern this past.

When the family portraits have been completed, the second perspective is introduced; this is concerned primarily with the recent bereavement, with the absent Elizabeth, and with the poet's personal future as he walks toward the night and sees (as an echo from **"The Vanishers"**) Elizabeth's beckoning hand. Thus out from the theme of Time and Change emerges the theme of the Future, which is to be developed in the portraits of Haskell and Harriet Livermore.

The first will make his peace in Time, by identifying himself with progressive social good (which, as a matter of fact, George Haskell had done by 1866). Harriet Livermore, though seeking, by her theological questing, a peace out of Time, has found no peace in Time, presumably because she cannot seek in the right spirit; with the "love within her mute", she cannot identify herself with the real needs of the world about her (as

Aunt Mercy can and George Haskell will); she is caught in the "tangled skein of will and fate", and can only hope for a peace in divine forgiveness, out of Time. After the portrait of Harriet Livermore, we find the contrast in the mother's attitude at the goodnight scene: unlike Harriet she finds peace in the here-and-now, "food and shelter, warmth and health" and love, with no "vain prayers" but with a willingness to act practically in the world—an idea that echoes the theme of **"My Soul and I"**, which we have already mentioned. And this is followed with the peace of night and the "reconciled" dream of summer in the middle of the winter.

With dawn, the present—not the past, not the future—appears, with its obligations, joys, and promises. Here there is a lag in the structure of the poem. When the snow-bound ones awake to the sound of "merry voices high and clear", the poem should, logically, move toward its fulfilment. But instead, after the gay and active intrusion of the world and the present, we have the section beginning "So days went on", and then the dead "filler" for some twenty lines. Whittier's literalism, his fidelity to irrelevant fact rather than to relevant meaning and appropriate structure of the whole, here almost destroys both the emotional and the thematic thrust, and it is due only to the power of the last movement that the poem is not irretrievably damaged.

The third "perspective" (lines 715-759), which ends the poem, is introduced by the eloquence of these lines:

> Clasp, Angel of the backward look
>   And folded wings of ashen gray
>   And voice of echoes far away,
> The brazen covers of thy book . . .

Then follow certain new considerations. What is the relation between the dream of the past and the obligations and actions of the future? The answer is, of course, in the sense of continuity of human experience, found when one stretches the "hands of memory" to the "wood-fire's blaze" of the past; it is thus that one may discover the meaningfulness of obligation and action in Time, even as he discovers in the specific memories of the past an image for the values out of Time. The "idyl" is more than a "Flemish picture"; it is an image, and a dialectic, of one of life's most fundamental questions that is summed up in the haunting simplicity of the end:

> Sit with me by the homestead hearth,
> And stretch the hands of memory forth
>   To warm them at the wood-fire's blaze!
> And thanks untraced to lips unknown
> Shall greet me like the odors blown
> From unseen meadows newly mown,
> Or lilies floating in some pond,
> Wood-fringed, the wayside gaze beyond;

> The traveller owns the grateful sense
> Of sweetness near, he knows not whence,
> And, pausing, takes with forehead bare
> The benediction of the air.

As a corollary to the third "perspective" generally considered, Whittier has, however, ventured a specific application. He refers not merely to the action in the future, in general, in relation to the past, but also, quite clearly, to the Civil War and the new order with its "larger hopes and graver fears"—the new order of "throngful city ways" as contrasted with the old agrarian way of life and thought. He invites the "worldling"—the man who, irreligiously, would see no meaning in the shared experience of human history, which to Whittier would have been a form of revelation—to seek in the past not only a sense of personal renewal and continuity, but also a sense of the continuity of the new order with the American past. This idea is clearly related to Whittier's conviction, which we have already mentioned, that the course of development for America should be the fulfilling of the "implied intent" of the Constitution in particular, of the American revelation in general, and of God's will. And we may add that Whittier, by this, also gives another "perspective" in which his poem is to be read.

If we leave **Snow-Bound,** the poem, and go back again to its springs in Whittier's personal story, we may find that it recapitulates in a new form an old issue. The story of his youth is one of entrapments—and of his failure to break out into the world of mature action. In love, politics, and poetry, he was constantly being involved in a deep, inner struggle, with the self-pity, the outrage, the headaches, the breakdowns. He was, to no avail, trying to break out of the "past" of childhood into the "future" of manhood—to achieve, in other words, a self.

The mad ambition that drove him to try to break out of the entrapments, became in itself, paradoxically, another entrapment—another dead hand of the past laid on him. He cried out, "Now, now!"—not even knowing what he cried out for, from what need, for what reality. But nothing worked out, not love, nor politics, nor even poetry, that common substitute for success of a more immediate order. In poetry, in fact, he could only pile up words as a mason piles up bricks; he could only repeat, compulsively, the dreary clichés; his meter-making machine ground on, and nothing that came out was, he knew, real: his poems were only "fancies", as he called them, only an echo of the past, not his own present. And if he set out with the declared intention of being the poet of New England, his sense of its history was mere antiquarianism, mere quaintness—no sense of an abiding human reality. Again he was trapped in the past. All his passions strove, as he put it, "in chains". He found release from what he called "the pain of disappointment and the temptation to envy" only in repudiating the self, and all the self stood for, in order to save the self. He could find a cause that, because it had absorbed (shall we hazard?) all the inner forces of the "past" that thwarted his desires, could free him into some "future" of action.

So much for the story of the young Whittier.

But what of the old?

He had, in the end, fallen into another entrapment of the past. All action—and the possibility of action and continuing life—had been withdrawn: the solacing hands of Elizabeth Lloyd, the "great motive of . . . life" that the other Elizabeth represented, old friends such as Joshua Coffin, even the "cause" to which he had given his life and which had given his life meaning. Only memory—the past—was left. To live—to have a future—he had to re-fight the old battle of his youth on a new and more difficult terrain. He had to find a new way to make the past nourish the future.

It could not be the old way. The old way had been, in a sense, merely a surrender. By it, Whittier had indeed found a future, a life of action. But the victory had been incomplete, and the cost great; for we must remember that the grinding headaches continued and that the solacing hands of Elizabeth Lloyd had been, in the end, impossible for him.

The new way was more radical. That is, Whittier undertook to see the problem of the past and future as generalized rather than personal, as an issue confronting America, not only himself: furthermore, to see it *sub specie aeternitatis,* as an aspect of man's fate. And he came to see—how late!—that man's fate is that he must learn to accept and use his past completely, knowingly, rather than to permit himself to be used, ignorantly, by it.

Having struggled for years with the deep difficulties of his own life, Whittier at last found a way fruitfully to regard them, and **Snow-Bound** is the monument of this personal victory. No, it may be the dynamic image of the very process by which the victory itself was achieved. But there is another way in which we may regard it. It sets Whittier into relation to an obsessive and continuing theme in our literature, a theme that most powerfully appears in Cooper, Hawthorne, Melville, and Faulkner: what does the past mean to an American?

The underlying question is, of course, why a sense of the past should be necessary at all. Why in a country that was new—was all "future"—should the question have arisen at all? Cooper dealt with it in various dramatizations, most obviously in the figures of Hurry Harry and the old pirate in *Deerslayer* and of the squatter in *The Prairie,* who are looters, exploiters, and spoilers of man and nature: none of these men has a sense of the pride and humility that history may inculcate. How close are these figures to those of Faulkner's world who have no past, or who would repudiate the past, who are outside history—for example, the Snopeses (descendants of bushwhackers who had no "side" in the Civil War), Popeye of *Sanctuary,* Jason and the girl Quentin of *The Sound and the Fury* (who repudiate the family and the past), and of course poor Joe Christmas of *Light in August,* whose story is the pathetic struggle of a man who, literally, has no past, who does not know who he is or his own reality. Whittier, too, understood the fate of the man who has no past—or who repudiates his past. This is his "worldling" of ***Snow-Bound*** (whom we may also take as an image of what the past might have been had the vainglorious dreams of his youth been realized), whom he calls to spread his hands before the warmth of the past in order to understand his own humanity, to catch the sweetness coming "he knows not where", and the "benediction of the air".

But, on the other side of this question, Whittier understood all too well the danger of misinterpreting the past—in his own case the danger of using the past as a refuge from reality. Faulkner, too, fully understood this particular danger and dramatized it early in *Sartoris* and later in "The Odor of Verbena". But the theme appears more strikingly and deeply philosophized in characters like Quentin Compson in *The Sound and the Fury,* and Hightower in *Light in August.* But Faulkner understood other kinds of dangers of misinterpretation. Sutpen, with his "design" and no comprehension of the inwardness of the past, suggests, in spite of all differences, a parallel with Cooper's squatter in *The Prairie,* whose only link with the past is some tattered pages from the Old Testament that serve, in the end, to justify his killing of the brother-in-law (the pages having no word of the peace and brotherhood of the New Testament). But Faulkner's most complex instance of the misinterpretation of the past occurs with Ike McCaslin, who, horrified by the family crime of slavery and incest, thinks he can buy out simply by refusing his patrimony: he does not realize that a true understanding of the past involves both an acceptance and a transcendence of the acceptance.

If we turn to Melville, we find in *Pierre, or The Ambiguities* the story of a man trapped, as Whittier was, in the past and desperately trying to free himself for adult action, just as we find in *Battle-Pieces,* in more general terms, the overarching ironical idea of the vanity of human action set against man's need to validate his life in action. And, for a variation, in *Clarel* we find the hero (who has no "past"—who is fatherless and has lost his God, and who does not know mother or sister) seeking in history a meaning of life, this quest occurring in the Holy Land, the birthplace of

the spiritual history of the Western World; and it is significant that Clarel finds his only answer in the realization that men are "cross-bearers all"—that is, by identifying himself with the human community, in its fate of expiatory suffering—an answer very similar to, though in a different tonality from, that of ***Snow-Bound***.

With Hawthorne the same basic question is somewhat differently framed. We do not find figures with rôles like those of Hurry Harry, the squatter, Joe Christmas, Hightower, or Clarel, but we find, rather, a general approach to the meaning of the past embodied in Hawthorne's treatment of the history of New England. Nothing could be further than his impulse from the antiquarian and sentimental attitude of Whittier in his historical pieces or from that of Longfellow. What Hawthorne found in the past was not the quaint charm of distance but the living issues of moral and psychological definition. What the fact of the past meant to him was a perspective on the present which gives an archetypal clarity and a mythic force. The sentimental flight into an assuagement possible in the past was the last thing he sought. He could praise the ancestors, but at the same time thank God for every year that had come to give distance from them. In his great novel and the tales the underlying theme concerns "legend" as contrasted with "action", the "past" as contrasted with the "future", as in the works of Cooper, Melville, and Faulkner; and sometimes, most obviously in "My Kinsman, Major Molyneux", with this theme is intertwined the psychological struggle to achieve maturity, with the struggle seen as a "fate".

Whittier, though without the scale and power of Cooper, Hawthorne, Melville, and Faulkner, and though he was singularly lacking in their sense of historical and philosophic irony, yet shared their deep intuition of what it meant to be an American. Further, he shared their intuitive capacity to see personal fate as an image for a general cultural and philosophic situation. His star belongs in their constellation. If it is less commanding than any of theirs, it yet shines with a clear and authentic light.

Notes

[1] In which Whittier's only novel—or near-novel—*Margaret Smith's Journal,* had appeared the previous year, and in which *Uncle Tom's Cabin* was to appear.

[2] "Ichabod" has thematic parallels with Hawthorne's great story "My Kinsman, Major Molyneux". Both concern the degrading of a "father", Noah-as-Webster in his drunkenness and the Major at the hands of the mob. Both concern the son's involvement in the degrading: Whittier repudiates Webster even as Robin joins the mob in repudiating Molyneux. Both works concern a betrayal by the father: Webster of his politi-

cal trust, and Molyneux, less precisely, in being an agent of the King and not of the colonists (*i.e.,* children). Both concern what Hawthorne calls a "majesty in ruins", and in this connection involve deep ambivalences of the son toward the father. And in both the son is thrown back upon his own resources, Whittier as is implied in his comment on the poem, and Robin quite specifically when he is offered the chance of going home or staying in Boston to "rise" by his own "efforts."

There is probably one great difference between the two works. It is hard not to believe that Hawthorne was conscious of what is at stake in his work, and it is hard to believe that Whittier was not unconscious of certain implications in "Ichabod".

[3] The poem may be taken as a kind of racist nightmare, like that of Isaac McCaslin in Faulkner's story "Delta Autumn", when he lies shaking with horror at his vision of the wilderness ruined to make room for a world of "usury and mortgage and bankruptcy and measureless wealth, where a breed of Chinese and African and Aryan and Jew all breed and spawn together until no man has time to say which one is which nor cares". Needless to say, Whittier's nightmare, like Ike's, was conquered.

[4] Melville's book of poems on the Civil War, *Battle-Pieces,* appeared almost simultaneously, and was a crashing failure. As *Snow-Bound* seemed to dwell merely on the simplicity of the past, *Battle-Pieces* analyzed some of the painful complexities of the War and the present, and recognized some of the painful paradoxes in the glowing promises of the future: not what the public wanted to hear.

[5] Here is the beginning of the prefatory note: "The inmates of the family at the Whittier homestead who are referred to in the poem were my father, mother, my brother and two sisters, and my uncle and aunt, both unmarried. In addition, there was the district schoolmaster, who boarded with us. The 'not unfeared, half-welcome guest' was Harriet Livermore, daughter of Judge Livermore, of New Hampshire, a young woman of fine natural ability, enthusiastic, eccentric, with slight control over her violent temper, which sometimes made her religious profession doubtful. She was equally ready to exhort in school-house prayer-meetings and dance in a Washington ball-room, while her father was a member of Congress. She early embraced the doctrine of the Second Advent, and felt it her duty to proclaim the Lord's speedy coming. With this message she crossed the Atlantic and spent the greater part of a long life in traveling over Europe and Asia. She lived some time with Lady Hester Stanhope, a woman as fantastic and mentally strained as herself, on the slope of Mt. Lebanon, but finally quarrelled with her in regard to two white horses with red marks on their backs

which suggested the idea of saddles, on which her titled hostess expected to ride into Jerusalem with the Lord. A friend of mine found her, when quite an old woman, wandering in Syria with a tribe of Arabs, who, with the Oriental notion that madness is inspiration, accepted her as their prophetess and leader. At the time referred to in *Snow-Bound* she was boarding at the Rocks Village, about two miles from us."

Elsewhere, in a prefatory note to another poem. "The Countess", Whittier identifies the "wise old doctor" of *Snow-Bound* as Dr. Elias Weld of Haverhill, "the one cultivated man in the neighborhood", who had given the boy the use of his library.

Donald A. Ringe (essay date 1972)

SOURCE: "The Artistry of Whittier's *Margaret Smith's Journal,*" in *Essex Institute Historical Collections,* Vol. CVIII, No. 3, July, 1972, pp. 235-43.

[*In the following essay, Ringe contends that Whittier's major prose work,* Margaret Smith's Journal *in the Province of Massachusetts Bay, 1678-79, achieves artistic unity though the author's development of his narrator as a strong central consciousness in the work.*]

The major prose work of John Greenleaf Whittier, ***Margaret Smith's Journal in the Province of Massachusetts Bay, 1678-79,*** has evoked a critical response that has ranged from the lukewarm to the enthusiastic. Although most of the critics praise the accurate picture of colonial New England life that the book presents,[1] opinions about its artistic success have varied between Whitman Bennett's view that it is only "a pleasing little effort" that should not be considered "a truly notable achievement"[2] to Edward Wagenknecht's opinion that it is "one of the inexplicably neglected classics of American literature, . . . next to ***Snow-Bound,*** Whittier's unquestionable masterpiece."[3] Those critics who have discussed the work in detail tend to support the latter view. Lewis Leary thinks the novel a charming one and compares it briefly with *Huckleberry Finn* in the way the material is presented to the reader;[4] and John P. Pickard, in what is by far the best analysis of the work, points out the skill with which Whittier turned the journal form into a useful instrument for the presentation of his material, and praises the book for the fusion of form and theme that yielded Whittier "his one prose success."[5]

Yet for all the favorable criticism that the book has received, critics have yet to demonstrate that it is unequivocally a work of art. Some who praise it highly seem as much concerned with the content as with its mode of expression,[6] and few have approached the work in strictly literary terms. Even Pickard, who comes closest to demonstrating its artistic value, finds serious flaws in the novel. He objects to the sketchily treated "love plot centering on the disastrous romance of Rebecca Rawson and Thomas Hale and the happy marriage of Leonard Smith to Margaret Brewster," and he faults the book as well for the number of "unrelated tales," which, in his view, "expose the thinness of the plot."[7] These are serious charges to make if ***Margaret Smith's Journal*** is indeed the success that Pickard claims it to be, for they seem to assume that Whittier intended to write a sustained love plot which he somehow failed to realize. I wish to suggest, rather, that Whittier did not intend such a plot at all, but relied on the narrative voice to supply the focus of attention for his novel. None of the critics have treated the point of view as seriously as they should. As a result, they have failed to see that Margaret Smith is the central consciousness of the work and the means through which the various elements of the book are successfully unified.

To treat the character in any other way, as some of the critics have done,[8] is to violate the artistic integrity of the novel. Margaret Smith is the first person narrator in a work of historical fiction. As such, she provides our sole means of access to the materials through which the theme is expressed. Everything we see or hear in the book is filtered through Margaret's consciousness. She depicts the world as she sees it and reports what interests her most. To understand the book, therefore, we must understand the narrator, a unique individual whose personality and background provide the artistic control so necessary in a work that does not include a strong plot line. As an English traveler in America, she is in effect an innocent stranger, one who stands somewhat apart from the environment in which she finds herself, but who, as the niece of an important man in the colony, takes a personal interest in all that goes on about her, and who records her experience for the cousin in England for whom she is writing the journal. As a woman of twenty,[9] she is old enough to take part in serious discussions as they arise, and her sex gives her the freedom not only to associate with men in the normal course of society, but also to draw close to other women in the colony—women she could not relate to in the same way if she were a man.

Whittier never allows us to forget that Margaret is a stranger in New England, for throughout the first part of the novel, she compares what she finds in America with what she has experienced in her native land. A May morning near Agawam seems to her as "warm and soft as our summer days at home,"[10] but the American summer is hotter and drier than what she has been used to, and she thinks of the "summer season of old England" with its cool sea breezes, pleasant showers, and green fields (pp. 47-48). The colors of autumn amaze her "as unlike anything I had ever seen in old England" (p. 61), and the woods themselves are very different. The American forest, "tangled with

vines" and fallen boughs, is carpeted with a "thick matting of dead leaves," whereas the English woods "are kept clear of bushes and undergrowth, and the sward beneath [the trees] is shaven clean and close" (p. 82). Through allusions like these, Whittier keeps before the reader an awareness of Margaret Smith as an intelligent visitor who looks with fresh eyes on what she sees in the colonies.

Some of what she experiences is strange and unpleasant. On her trip to Rhode Island, for example, to visit her brother and his wife, the party is forced to stop overnight at an abandoned hut, where Margaret's companions make themselves at home and soon fall asleep. The strangeness of her situation, however, keeps Margaret "a long time awake." She lies on a bed of hemlock sprigs watching the stars through a hole in the roof and the moonlight that shines in the hut "through the seams of the logs." She listens to the sound of wind and waves and "the cry of wild animals in the depth of the woods" until she at last nods off (p. 170). She cannot stomach the dried meat and the "cakes of pounded corn" on which her companions breakfast the next morning, but she buys instead two cakes of maple sugar to eat (p. 171). Most of her experience in America, of course, is not so unfamiliar to her as this, but after nearly a year away from her native land, she begins to grow homesick for her friends in England (pp. 144, 167). Though she leaves America with some regrets, she is happy when the time comes for her to go home (p. 189). To the very end of the book, Whittier is consistent in maintaining the point of view. Margaret Smith remains an observant stranger who never becomes completely a part of what she sees.

Other aspects of Margaret's individuality are more subtly presented. From the very first entry in the journal, we learn some significant facts about her. She is not a member of the church (p. 11) and thus is free to view the Puritans in a much more objective fashion than if she were one of them.[11] She dresses more gaily than an aged magistrate approves of, and she seems to be somewhat less of a religious enthusiast than her brother. As they enter Boston harbor on the day of their arrival, he lifts up both hands and cries out with a verse of Scripture, whereas she merely says that she wept "for joy and thankfulness of heart, that God had brought us safely to so fair a haven" (p. 10). When she thinks that a wrong has been done, however, Margaret speaks out in no uncertain terms, as the following incident well illustrates. The aged magistrate's wife, she writes, "a quiet, sickly-looking woman, . . . seems not a little in awe of her husband," who "hath a very impatient, forbidding way with him, and . . . seemed to carry himself harshly at times towards her." When her Uncle Rawson says in his defense that "he has had much to try his temper" in the affairs of the colony, Margaret replies: "I told him it was no doubt true; but that I thought it a bad use of the Lord's chastenings to abuse one's best friends for the wrongs done by enemies; and, that to be made to atone for what went ill in Church or State, was a kind of vicarious suffering that, if I was in Madam's place, I should not bear with half her patience and sweetness" (pp. 11-12).

Because Margaret Smith is a strong and independent young woman with a mind of her own, she is able to observe intelligently the whole range of American life that presents itself to her senses and to learn from her experience. She arrives in America, for example, with certain fears and apprehensions, for thoughts of "the terrors of the wilderness" troubled her night and day. Yet when she awakens the first morning at her Uncle Rawson's plantation at Newbury, she asks herself: "Where be the gloomy shades, and desolate mountains, and the wild beasts, with their dismal howlings and rages! Here all looked peaceful, and bespoke comfort and contentedness" (pp. 19-20). A similar change in her views occurs when she meets the Indians, a change which shows her basically charitable nature. The first encounter startles her, and even to the end of her stay she can still be frightened by them. Yet Margaret needs only to meet the Indians on human terms to feel a sympathy for them as fellow creatures and to draw the appropriate conclusion. "These poor heathen people," she writes after a brief association with an Indian family, "seem not so exceeding bad as they have been reported; they be like unto ourselves, only lacking our knowledge and opportunities, which, indeed, are not our own to boast of, but gifts of God, calling for humble thankfulness, and daily prayer and watchfulness, that they be rightly improved" (p. 16).

Margaret goes through a similar experience in her other encounters with people. Her initial reaction to a Quaker girl named Margaret Brewster is to side with the Puritans against her (p. 26), but she quickly changes her mind. The gentleness of the girl and her kindness in performing acts of charity win Margaret over and probably help to influence her view of Quakers in general. To be sure, Margaret Smith is aware that some who call themselves Quakers are merely ranters (pp. 59, 180-181), and she knows that they have rudely interrupted the Puritan meetings. She does not like their "gravity and . . . staidness of deportment" (p. 172), and the "painful and melancholy look and . . . canting tone of discourse" that some of them affect (p. 179). But she notes that Rhode Island Quakers—"worthy and pious people"—were loving and kind to her when she spent some time among them (p. 172), and she cannot help but admire the "warmth and goodness of . . . heart" of Margaret Brewster (p. 179), nor does she regret that her brother married her. As she does with the Indians, Margaret Smith judges the Quakers not in terms of her own preconceptions, but rather on her own experience with them as human beings. To her mind, the goodness of Margaret Brewster and the acts of charity she has performed for others outweigh the sectarian beliefs that the Quaker girl holds.

The witchcraft excitement is the third important matter that comes to Margaret Smith's attention, and here her feelings are even more ambivalent than they are toward the Quakers. Although she believes that Caleb Powell, a suspected wizard, is only "a vain, talking man," and that a girl, supposed to be possessed, is "a vicious and spoiled child, delighting in mischief" (pp. 83-84), she does not dismiss the question of witchcraft out of hand. Though some may doubt the evidence that is presented against the accused witches, Margaret herself, as one would expect of a seventeenth-century girl, is so disturbed by what she has seen and heard at the bewitched house that she can hardly sleep (p. 101). But if Whittier maintains historical credibility by allowing Margaret Smith to be deeply troubled by the thought of witchcraft, he maintains the consistency of her charitable character by allowing her to sympathize with a condemned witch. When Goody Morse is reprieved by the governor and magistrates, Margaret writes: "For mine own part, I do truly rejoice that mercy hath been shown to the poor creature; for even if she is guilty, it affordeth her a season for repentance; and if she be innocent, it saveth the land from a great sin" (p. 187).

Margaret does not, of course, rely solely on her personal experience for the information she receives and records in her journal. She also hears the opinions of others, some of which confirm, and some contradict, the charitable attitude she usually shows toward others. These reports serve an important function in the book. The conflicting attitudes she records—and contradictory views are frequently juxtaposed in the journal—help lend an air of reality to the book and assure that the theme is presented in the most artistic fashion. Both sides of an issue are clearly presented—but presented in such a way as to confirm the views that Margaret Smith maintains. Thus, the charitable attitude of Elnathan Stone toward the Indians is strongly contrasted with his mother's bitterness toward them. He is dying as the result of wounds received in the Indian war and his suffering during captivity, yet he understands that the Indians have sometimes been provoked to warfare by the treatment they have received, and he even feels pity for them. His mother, however, "a poor widow, who had seen her young daughter tomahawked by the Indians" and is now watching her only son die, considers them simply children of the devil (pp. 28-29). Her attitude is, of course, perfectly understandable, but her son's is clearly the better one.

Other examples of the technique are found throughout the book. Margaret herself sees Deacon Dole's Indian "with blood running down his face, and much bruised and swollen" after he was punished by his master for being drunk and disorderly, yet the deacon himself says that "his servant Tom had behaved badly, for which he did moderately correct him" (pp. 49-50). When Margaret Brewster is fined for disturbing a Puritan meeting and then sentenced to the stocks for refusing to pay, some men step forward and pay the fine themselves, "so that she was set at liberty, whereat the boys and rude women were not a little disappointed, as they had thought to make sport of her in the stocks" (p. 42). There are even those who gain the reprieve for Goody Morse, the accused witch who is sentenced to death. Yet "many people, both men and women, coming in from the towns about to see the hanging, be sore disappointed, and do vehemently condemn the conduct of the Governor therein," and Goody Matson, "with half a score more of her sort," scolds and rails "about the reprieve of the witch, and [prophesies] dreadful judgments upon all concerned in it" (p. 187).

The most important example of the device, however, occurs near the middle of the book in a pair of contrasted sermons that clearly establish the theme. Mr. Richardson, a minister at Newbury, preaches against those "who have made a covenant with hell," and prays that they "may be speedily discovered in their wickedness, and cut off from the congregation" (p. 86). Dr. Russ, on the other hand, delivers a sermon on charity that urges the people to love one another. Margaret reports the second sermon at length "forasmuch as it hath given offence to some who did listen to it," and she mentions the harsh and vindictive people who find fault with it (pp. 96-97). Though Margaret herself makes no explicit comparison of the two sermons, it is clear to the reader that Whittier intended the sermon by Dr. Russ to be an important thematic statement. The great detail in which it is given provides a thematic weight that the other does not possess, and it states a view which, as we have seen, is strongly underscored elsewhere in the novel. Based on Paul's First Letter to the Corinthians, it preaches the need for Christian charity in one's dealings with his fellows and so provides the fundamental principle by which Margaret Smith, Margaret Brewster, Elnathan Stone, and others live and act.

The theme of Christian charity developed in this sermon, moreover, unifies the major elements that are included in the novel, especially the "love plot" and related incidents that Pickard objects to. Consider the most important one, the betrothal of Rebecca Rawson and Sir Thomas Hale. The particular verse on which Dr. Russ preaches states explicitly that charity is not selfish.[12] Yet the marriage is arranged for reasons of ambition and pride. Rebecca herself would seem to prefer the unpretentious Robert Pike, but her father in his pride has told this worthy young man "that he did design an alliance of his daughter with a gentleman of estate and family" (p. 39). Margaret believes at one point that "apart from the wealth and family of Sir Thomas, [her cousin] rather inclineth to her old friend and neighbor" (p. 23), but once Rebecca has made her

decision, she determines to go through with the wedding no matter what misgivings she may have. Only after she has been deserted in England by the impostor and bigamist that Sir Thomas turns out to be[13] does she finally admit that she allowed herself in "her pride and vanity . . . to discard worthy men for one of great show and pretensions, who had no solid merit to boast of" (p. 193). Rebecca's experience, then, is a variation on the main theme of the book. Her tragedy results when charity is forgotten and she bases her action on vanity, ambition, and pride.

The other romances in the book provide additional variations on the theme. When Margaret is in Maine, she meets a young Mr. Jordan, who is courting her cousin Polly. Margaret learns that he is about to give up a promising career as a Church of England minister to become a simple farmer, and she twits him on what he might be doing to the social prospects of his bride. "I told him," she writes, "that perhaps he might have become a great prelate in the Church, and dwelt in a palace, and made a great lady of our cousin; whereas now I did see no better prospect for him than to raise corn for his wife to make pudding of, and chop wood to boil her kettle" (pp. 76-77). But instead of following the path of ambition like Rebecca Rawson, Jordan and Polly dismiss such prospects, prospects which, they admit, might never be realized, and turn instead to the simple life they have chosen. Margaret, of course, who always had misgivings about Rebecca's course of action, is "exceedingly pleased" with her cousin Polly's choice and anticipates a happy life for her and her husband (p. 79).

Additional variations may be found in other romances that Margaret reports in her journal. She is much taken with the story of Sir Christopher Gardiner, who was separated from his betrothed at the instigation of her parents and who swore a vow to forsake marriage, only to encounter his beloved again in New England, where she had followed him. Margaret is deeply moved by their story, and although she never learns its outcome, she sympathizes with their plight. Whatever "their sins and their follies," she writes, "my prayer is, that they may be forgiven, for they loved much" (p. 76). In a similar fashion, she accepts the marriage of her brother Leonard to Margaret Brewster, though she would at one time have been very upset by his marrying a Quaker. She respects her brother's choice because she sees in Margaret Brewster a charitable attitude toward others that she cannot help but approve, and which she always tries to practice herself. When she learns, for example, of the sad plight of Rebecca Rawson after their voyage to England, Margaret Smith takes the unfortunate girl into her home and treats her with tender care. Each of these brief romances, therefore, develops an aspect of the theme of charity—or the unfortunate consequences that ensue when some other principle of action is followed.

Read in these terms, *Margaret Smith's Journal* is indeed a unified work of art, all major parts of which contribute to its central theme. Firmly grounded in the consciousness of Margaret Smith, who, as a consistently developed character, provides the major point of focus, the novel plays a series of important variations on the theme of charity. Margaret herself embodies a major part of this theme, for her actions and opinions well illustrate the operation of this principle in her own life. What she observes and reports, moreover, provides either confirmation of or a contrast to her view, and the interplay among the various incidents provides the major source of tension in the work. The sermon of Dr. Russ, of course, presents the Scriptural basis for the theme, and the several love affairs that Whittier includes exemplify further the need for Christian love as a basis for human action. So skillful, indeed, is Whittier in ringing his series of variations, that he can stand completely apart from his novel and let it speak for itself. His artistic control, solidly based in the central character, is firmly and consistently maintained to make his brief novel what Edward Wagenknecht takes it to be—a classic of American literature that deserves to be better known.

Notes

[1] That the work is indeed historically accurate has been amply demonstrated by Cecil B. Williams, *Whittier's Use of Historical Material in* Margaret Smith's Journal (Chicago, 1936).

[2] *Whittier: Bard of Freedom* (Chapel Hill, N.C., 1941), p. 216. See also George R. Carpenter, who thought the book "too slight in substance, too sober in style" to be widely read. *John Greenleaf Whittier* (Boston, 1903), p. 246.

[3] *John Greenleaf Whittier: A Portrait in Paradox* (New York, 1967), p. 7. See also Albert Mordell, who writes that "the book is a thing of beauty, a work of art." *Quaker Militant: John Greenleaf Whittier* (1933; rpt.: Port Washington, N.Y., 1969), p. 185.

[4] *John Greenleaf Whittier* (New York, 1961), pp. 127-129.

[5] *John Greenleaf Whittier: An Introduction and Interpretation* (New York, 1961), pp. 119-129.

[6] See especially Mordell, *Quaker Militant,* p. 185.

[7] *Whittier, Introduction and Interpretation,* p. 124. See also Lewis Leary, who, in "A Note on Whittier's Margaret Smith," *Emerson Society Quarterly,* No. 50, part 2, 75 (I Quarter 1968), considers the narrative threads too slender.

[8] Cecil B. Williams, for example, does not accept her as the central character in the work and considers the book disunified. *Whittier's Use of Historical Material,* p. 29. Mordell, on the other hand, transforms her into a mouthpiece for the author. *Quaker Militant,* p. 183.

[9] Though Margaret's exact age is not mentioned in the book, she writes in her first entry that she is "just about" her cousin Rebecca's age, and we know from one of Whittier's letters that Rebecca, a historical character, was "about twenty-one" at the time of her marriage, over a year after the narrative begins. See Samuel T. Pickard, *Life and Letters of John Greenleaf Whittier* (Boston, 1894), p. 340.

[10] *The Prose Works of John Greenleaf Whittier* (Boston, 1892), I, 13. Citations in my text are to page numbers in this volume.

[11] There is even evidence that Margaret Smith may have High Church leanings, for in the epilogue to the story, her grandson, a curate in England in 1747, points out that Rebecca "was not . . . a member of the church, having some scruples in respect to the rituals, as was natural from her education in New England, among Puritan schismatics" (pp. 194-195). The implication is strong that Margaret and Rebecca belong to different churches at least after they arrive in England.

[12] 1 Cor. xiii:5. The critic would do well to read the whole context of this verse, for it is very pertinent to both the sermon and the novel.

[13] Although Rebecca's story reads like a bit of sentimental fiction, it is nonetheless a true one. See Williams, *Whittier's Use of Historical Material,* p. 31.

James E. Rocks (essay date 1993)

SOURCE: "Whittier's *Snow-Bound*: The Circle of Our Hearth and the Discourse on Domesticity," in *Studies in the American Renaissance 1993,* edited by Joel Myerson, University Press of Virginia, 1993, pp. 339-53.

[*In the following excerpt, Rocks relates Whittier's poem* Snow-Bound *to nineteenth-century debates on home and family.*]

When John Greenleaf Whittier's younger sister Elizabeth, the companion of his mature years, died on 3 September 1864, he suffered a loss no less severe than if a wife of many years had died. More sociable than her shy brother, Elizabeth had been at the center of his life, the person whose support had helped nurture a public career of considerable success and fame and a private domestic life of exceptional warmth and security. Writing to his wide circle of friends, particularly to Gail Hamilton, Grace Greenwood, and Lydia Maria Child, he expressed the profound depression that her death had induced, but also his acceptance of the will of God that had determined the course of his sister's illness and death. To Annie Fields, his publisher's wife and among his closest women friends, he wrote: "I find it difficult even now to understand and realize all I have lost. But I sorrow without repining, and with a feeling of calm submission to the Will which I am sure is best."[1]

While acceptance of the divine ways distinguishes Whittier's letters to his consoling friends, Elizabeth's death brought about a major transition in his life. One consequence of this change was a temporary failure with language; the glib pen that had composed dozens of poems on national, political, and social topics was unable to express this personal loss. To Theodore Tilton, a New York journalist who supported abolition and women's rights, Whittier expressed his speechlessness in a terse, poetic line: "I cannot now write anything worthy of her memory."[2] Responding to his friends' condolences was painful but necessary; expressing the meaning of his sister's life as his companion and the domestic order and tranquility which she, like their parents before her, had sustained for him was far more difficult. Within a year the Civil War concluded, and one of his last, and best, anti-slavery poems **"Laus Deo"** put some finality on a lifetime of combatting slavery. And by October 1865 he finished the work that was "worthy of her memory." Published in February 1866, **Snow-Bound** became Whittier's most popular and famous—and his best—work, one of the important autobiographical writings of the nineteenth century. It was, as Robert Penn Warren has aptly called it, a "summarizing poem,"[3] because in it Whittier discovered the power of language again—the very weapon against the destructive, frightening natural world that his solitary family employs in the charmed circle around the hearth—and because the poem articulated the domestic and gender ideology of Whittier's time to an audience ready to be healed after the schism of the Civil War and responsive to a philosophy that linked home, hearth, and heaven into one vision of a unified past and future.

Readings of **Snow-Bound** have generally not placed the poem in the context of Whittier's whole life—why the poem came to be at a critical time in his personal life, his public career, and the post-Civil War period of anticipated reconciliation and the reuniting of the "house divided." Studies have recognized the complexity of his personality and the interrelationship of his work and his times and, more recently, his advocacy of women in the literary marketplace, but they have not examined sufficiently the domestic and gender ideological issues that give the poem its considerable relevance as a coalescence of the discourses on domestic economy during the first half of the nineteenth

century. **Snow-Bound** deserves to be reread for the wealth of its connections to the important discussions of the time on family and home. Whittier's definition of the masculine and the feminine in the poem reveals his long-held beliefs about his own gender identity, at a time when male writers often felt insecure about their masculinity in a commercial world, and discloses his traditional values regarding the family and women's role, which was defined in the writings of, among others, Catharine Beecher and her sister Harriet Beecher Stowe, as that of the dominant moral authority of society. While his portrayal of women in **Snow-Bound** does partake of the sentimental tradition of the time, his views in that poem, as well as in his letters, transcend the purely patriarchal and reflect his strong Quaker principle of human rights.

In an essay on the Scottish poet William Burleigh in the 9 September 1847 issue of the *National Era,* the anti-slavery paper of which he was for fifteen years a contributing editor and in which most of his literary works appeared until the founding of the *Atlantic Monthly* in 1857, Whittier described a poetic country very like the one he would create in **Snow-Bound**. The charm of the poetry of Scotland, he wrote, was "its simplicity, and genuine, affected sympathy with the common joys and sorrows of daily life. It is a home-taught, household melody." He also lamented that the poetry of home, nature, and the affections was lacking in America; there were no songs of American domestic life, "no Yankee pastorals."[4] By the time Whittier accomplished in **Snow-Bound** his call for a native form of the antique genre, there were already major examples of the pastoral, but by the mid-1860s the genre was rather played out (except of course for Whitman), and much of the appeal of **Snow-Bound** was its backward glance to a simpler world, to a time prior to the social and political upheaval of the 1830s to 1860s. Whittier's readers had always valued him for what James Russell Lowell, in the *North American Review* of January 1864, called his "intense home-feeling." Later, in a review of **Snow-Bound,** Lowell expressed the effect of the poem's nostalgia on a sentimental audience: "It describes scenes and manners which the rapid changes of our national habits will soon have made as remote from us as if they were foreign or ancient."[5] Lowell was correct in his assessment of the poem's appeal, but his future verb tense was mistaken; by the time of the publication of Whittier's major poem, those rapid social changes had already made the scenes and manners of the world of Whittier's boyhood farm remote and quaint for many of his readers.[6]

In **Snow-Bound** Whittier returned to his youthful past for two immediate, compelling, yet contradictory reasons. He wanted his niece Lizzie to know the family portrait, and he needed the money that a longer poem about the rural past could earn. But there were also other reasons, perhaps not so easily identified, that inspired his "winter idyl." Creating this poem would bring further healing to the recovery from his loss of Elizabeth and, unaware as he might have been of another consequence, it would contribute in a small way to the public appeals for national reconciliation after the Civil War. And most importantly *Snow-Bound* would characterize a domestic ideology of home and hearth that dated as it might have seemed to some readers in Whittier's time, was, however, a representation of the principal values that had defined the American family in the nineteenth century. Whittier's desire to recreate his home life served both his own practical and emotional needs and those of a nation seeking order once again; for Whittier the time could not have been more favorable.

On the flyleaf of a first edition of *Snow-Bound,* Whittier wrote some lines in 1888 expressing the faith and peace of his old age (he would die within two years). Thinking of the time when he composed his pastoral, he wrote about his sorrow then: "Lone and weary life seemed when / First these pictures of the pen / Grew upon my page."[7] The general dispiritendness and lack of confidence in his poetic ability, exacerbated by and contributing to his chronic ill health, are reflected in the letters he wrote, primarily to James T. Fields, during the several months (August to October 1865) while he was composing and revising the poem. Because Whittier tended to be self-effacing in his correspondence—and particularly so to other writers and his publisher—he refers to his manuscript only as "tolerably good" or "pretty good."[8] To Lucy Larcom, a close friend of Elizabeth and one of his "pupils" among the women authors he knew, Whittier wrote in a postscript to a letter in January 1866, a month before the poem's publication: "I'm not without my misgivings about it."[9] On the other hand, reading proofs of it in December 1865, he wrote Fields that he agreed with him and his wife Annie that the poem was "good"; furthermore, he took a particular interest in its physical make-up, engravings, and date of publication (a December distribution would make it a timely gift-book, he suggested), and fussed over some last-minute revisions. His anxieties were groundless: within two months of the February publication, *Snow-Bound* had sold 10,000 copies and by mid-summer 20,000 copies. Ultimately Whittier earned $10,000 from this one volume; its success provided him economic security and reaffirmed his poetic reputation.[10]

Whittier's uncertainty about the worth of his poem was typical of his general insecurity as a writer throughout his career; later, despite the critical and financial success of *Snow-Bound,* he would say that subsequent poems, however less inspired, were better. Scholars of Whittier's writings have always noted his lack of a keen critical insight, into both his own and others' writings, although he was an unpatronizing advocate and support of the many women authors who wrote

and visited him with accounts of their craft. This uncertainty about his own vocation—at once liking and not liking his compositions—is an example of the pattern of oppositions and contradictions that critics have found in his own life and in the imagery and themes of *Snow-Bound.* Whittier was torn between the quiet study and the fretful political scene, and his life can best be defined as an oscillation between the public and the private—a pattern of outside and inside that dominates the theme of *Snow-Bound,* as John B. Pickard and other critics have demonstrated, and reveals its autobiographical dimensions. Because Whittier identified an old teacher from his Haverhill past as the source of the character of the schoolmaster, scholars have not recognized an important autobiographical connection between the schoolmaster and an idealized young Whittier. The schoolmaster can be read as an artistic representation of the adolescent Whittier, because the schoolmaster depicts the youthful artistthinker, comfortable near the hearth but anxious to go outside into the world where he can make a reputation if not achieve fame. Manliness, for Whittier, as it was for many male writers during this period, could be experienced in the making of strong poetic verse, crafted in the cause of social and political change. The anxiety of manhood was overcome in the world outside the home, which was defined and controlled by women as a place of refuge from the active world of material gain and political turmoil.

Writing in 1882, Whittier looked back on his shy youth as a time of "vague dreams and ambitions and fancies interweaving with [his] common-place surroundings."[11] In an early poem, written in his teens, Whittier stated that he needed to seek out an education because he did not want to grow up a "fool."[12] Whittier's own statements—both early and late in his writings—confirm his commitment to a life that alternates action with repose, the life of the scholar in rhythm with that of the man of political and social involvement. Whenever he returned to the farm in the early decades of his life, he did so out of the necessity of family responsibility, money, or the too-intense activity of his political, journalistic, and abolitionist work. And when he came to write *Snow-Bound,* his poem of reconciliation with the past and future, he put himself into it not only as the first-person narrator but also as the schoolmaster, who was the man Whittier had hoped to become and the man who would guide the country into a new era of peace and renewal. Whittier's young schoolmaster characterizes the ideal blend of the artistic and the scholarly with masculine athleticism; like Whittier himself he was nurtured in the domestic setting and yet, through books and experience, went out to meet the future. The schoolmaster's father, exactly like Whittier's, was a yeoman who worked the land for a meager but adequate livelihood: "By patient toil subsistence scant, / Not competence and yet not want."[13] In the tradition of schoolmasters in American literature, Whittier's is a jovial, sociable type, attracted like Whittier to vivacious and charming women; also he is independent and self-reliant, one who combines the practical and abstract in clear-sighted balance: he "[c]ould doff at ease his scholar's gown / To peddle wares from town to town" (454-55). As a storyteller he could domesticate the antique and the exotic, bringing to the realm of the commonplace the great scenes of the historical past and interpreting for his audience those moments in terms it could easily associate with the homely and everyday: "dread Olympus at his will / Became a huckleberry hill" (478-79).

A major reason for the popularity of *Snow-Bound,* and one which critics have not adequately emphasized, is the poem's rhetoric of reconciliation and consolation for a future in which all wrongs will be righted and freedom will replace slavery. The schoolmaster is just such a man for that task, and in a major section of the poem (480-510) Whittier envisions the new America, a land that will be led by young apostles like the schoolmaster, who will eliminate pride, ignorance, prejudice, and treason, and restore wisdom, learning, equality, and peace. These powerful lines reveal Whittier's hope for the restoration of the American promise, and they look back to his own past when he envisioned his career committed to the abolition of slavery: "Large-brained, clear-eyed, of such as he / Shall Freedom's young apostles be" (485-86). The schoolmaster is the leader of a future America, reconciling the opposites of Yankee and Southerner, working inside and outside the family and uniting rural and urban. In the character of the schoolmaster Whittier defined some important traits of masculinity in the self-reliant scholar-poet, values of male gender ideology among writers of his time that he attempted to demonstrate in his own behavior and writing.[14]

Snow-Bound is as deeply connected to the period after the Civil War as it is to the time of Whittier's boyhood, because it offers consolation not only for the poet, who had lost a close relative, but also for the nation at large, which had lost many family members. The deaths of one million soldiers during the war required this need for reconciliation, which was reflected in the popular works of the time, among them, for example, *The Gates Ajar* (1868) by Elizabeth Stuart Phelps, another close friend among the many women writes Whittier mentored.[15] The sense of having survived so much loss after the war is pondered in a major passage of the poem as Whittier reflects on the change that comes with the passage of time. With everyone in his family dead except his brother, he thinks of how strange it seems "with so much gone / Of life and love, to still live on!" (181-82). Even though his sentiment refers to the changes in his own family, it opens out to include the whole American nation, which had suffered such a collective loss but still continued to live and needed to find through memory and faith

the connections to a meaningful past and a hopeful future. Just as during the war, in popular songs and poems, the image of the home as a haven of comfort and escape was kept alive for the homeless soldiers, so after the war the idea of home as a place of order and permanence—and as a setting for the remembrance of deceased family members and friends—took on for Americans an even more potent meaning. In the connections between the Civil War and domestic ideology, *Snow-Bound* reunites the "house divided" and sanctifies the "holy hearth" (Whittier's description in the poem **"To My Sister"**) as an anticipation of heaven.[16]

In the prominent passage on time and change Whittier states that the once living family members have left the familiar premises: "No step is on the conscious floor!" (199). The home, especially the farm, as a setting of familial love, connectedness, and identity is central to the ideology and imagery of the whole poem and especially to that important, if traditional, consolation section. To Whittier's readers during the first half of the nineteenth century, engaged as they were by the rhetoric of domesticity, the definition of home was a foremost cultural and social issue. The discourse on domesticity engaged a wide and important number of commentators, among them some of the women authors whom Whittier counted as his best friends and correspondents—Lydia Sigourney is a major example—not to mention a considerable group of both men and women authors whose works he did not necessarily know first hand (we have no evidence in his essays or letters, for instance) but whose ideology was so pervasive in the thinking of the time that it had at least an indirect influence on his own conceptualization of domestic values. As he was deeply involved in the anti-slavery discourse of the time, with its accompanying feminist commentaries on women's political rights, he was quite aware of the discussions on domestic ideology that characterized much of the writing of his peers. *Snow-Bound* brings together, and helps us to understand, the varied discourses on domesticity and gender during the first half of the century.

Whittier's Quaker upbringing and the life-long practice of his family faith engendered his fervent abolitionism, and they also explain the profound belief in domestic values that runs through his writings. The famous Quaker family scene in Chapter XIII of *Uncle Tom's Cabin* works an important intertextuality with *Snow-Bound* because in it Stowe characterizes the domestic economy that slavery destroyed; for Stowe black women needed and deserved the same domestic authority that white women could achieve.[17] Whittier was deeply moved by Stowe's novel, published in the *National Era* from June 1851 to April 1852, while he was a corresponding editor of the paper. In a letter to William Lloyd Garrison he called the novel "glorious" and twice after it was published he wrote his praises to

Stowe in equally religious terms, rhetoric that is rare in Whittier's often laudatory expressions of literary judgment or political commentary: "Ten thousand thanks for thy immortal book!"; "I bless God for it, as I look with awe and wonder upon its world moving mission."[18] The power of Stowe's novel resided in, among other ideas and images, the ideal domestic order in which each family member contributed to the general economic good, with no one segment of the human family subservient to another and denied the domestic circle.

Although the Quaker settlement depicted by Stowe is more sentimentalized than Whittier's boyhood home in *Snow-Bound,* it represents the domestic ideal of the time expounded in the popular handbooks on house design and on the nurturing ministrations of the capable wife, all of which were familiar to Whittier's audience. The opening paragraph of Chapter XIII describes the perfect kitchen design, neat, orderly, and comfortable, and features the "motherly," "persuasive," and "honest" rocking chair where Eliza sits, which like the Quaker mother Rachel's old rocker is the central symbol of this domestic paradise. Such possessions of the material culture, like the tea kettle, "a sort of censer of hospitality and good cheer," or the knives and forks, which "had a social clatter as they went on to the table," define and unite the home and the homemaker and are given human attributes; they make music to accompany Rachel's "loving words, and gentle moralities, and motherly loving kindness."[19] Rachel is the ideal Quaker mother, quite like Whittier's own mother and her representation in *Snow-Bound;* she is beautiful in her maturity and adept at all domestic and culinary tasks, both a healer of ills and a bringer of harmony and good fellowship. Most important, she is the maker of a home, a concept that George Harris, as a deracinated slave, has never been able to comprehend. Stowe's portrait of the home in this chapter emphasizes the Christian definition that prevailed during these antebellum decades; her language shares the rhetoric of Whittier's tributes to Stowe in his letters and reflects Whittier's own description of the family circle in *Snow-Bound.*

To combat slavery, alcoholism, and women's disenfranchisement, reform movements in the early nineteenth century sought support from the institution of the family, which was often defined in terms of the domestic economy represented in Stowe's famous novel and by the architecture and decoration of the houses wherein the family resided. Clifford E. Clark, Jr., summarizes this social phenomenon: "[The] influence of the temperance and anti-slavery movements together with the new outlook of Protestantism, the reaction against the pace of social change, the need for new housing, the expansion of the cities, and the vogue of romanticism all served to give the advocates of domestic housing reform an unprecedented influence on the

American public."[20] The number of handbooks that recommended house design and argued for the rural home as a place of seclusion from the activities of a material economy demonstrates the significance of appropriate housing as a key component in the discussions on domestic economy. Sara Josepha Hale, in *Godey's Lady's Book,* for example, wrote often about the ideal home, as did Andrew Jackson Downing, in *The Architecture of Country Houses,* and Catharine Beecher, in *Treatise on Domestic Economy,* two works that provide an important background to understanding the timely success of Whittier's pastoral poem on domestic and gender ideology.

Downing's essay on rural architecture first appeared in 1850 and went through nine printings and sold 16,000 copies by the end of the Civil War. Among the many such treatises and handbooks that were widely read in the period of the 1840s to the 1860s, Downing's popularized the current ideology of the house as a civilizing, moral force for the betterment of the genius and character of the family. For Downing, as for most of these writers, the rural cottage and farm house, closely connected to the soil, of an ample, solid design and built of enduring material, were the best environments for nurturing family values. The farmer's dwelling, he wrote, "ought to suggest simplicity, honesty of purpose, frankness, a hearty, genuine spirit of good-will, and a homely and modest, though manly and independent, bearing in his outward deportment."[21] Although Whittier was not familiar, so far as we can determine, with Downing's popular book, these sentiments on the farmhouse might well have been his own, phrased in language he would have used, especially the notion of the manliness of the house and its resident farmer.

Snow-Bound celebrates Downing's sturdy rural cottage, in a setting of pastoral harmony, that conforms to the landscape and unites the inner world of the hearth with the outer world of the barns, lands, and farm animals. In the essay cited earlier on the Scottish poet William Burleigh, Whittier commented on the numerous "great, unshapely, shingle structures, glaring with windows, which deform our landscape."[22] He recognized the need for an attractive, yet functional house, such as Downing and other commentators described, wherein the family could live harmoniously and communicate openly. Although Whittier's childhood home at Haverhill was built in the late seventeenth century, it possessed the qualities which later theorists on house design would advocate, in part to recapture the nostalgia of an earlier pioneer time, when the family unit was even stronger. Many of the writers on farmhouse architecture emphasized the need for sight lines from house to barn so that the farmer and his wife could keep watch over the activities of the whole farm. In those sections of *Snow-Bound* in which Whittier describes the barn activities during the snowstorm (19-30, 81-92)—passages which Robert Penn Warren mistakenly calls "dead filler"[23]—Whittier is connecting the inner and outer worlds in a rhythm that defines his own personal ideology of retreat from and action in society. His farm setting epitomizes the ideal rural home as fashioned and advocated by Downing and other popular writers on the architectural design of the time.[24]

Whittier was acquainted with probably the most popular of these writers on family values, Harriet Beecher Stowe. Her sister, Catharine Beecher, was the author of several works on female hegemony and the culture of the home, one of them co-authored with Stowe, *The American Woman's Home* (1869). *Treatise on Domestic Economy,* which first appeared in 1841 and was reprinted almost every year from 1841 to 1856, gained Beecher the reputation, as her biographer Kathryn Kish Sklar states, "as a national authority on the psychological state and the physical well-being of the American home."[25] Like *Uncle Tom's Cabin* Beecher's writing contextualizes Whittier's poem, because it expounds the female ideal portrayed in **Snow-Bound:** the wife who acquires her status and identity by creating the home setting that nurtures children and draws a circle of repose for the enterprising husband. In order to fulfill herself, argued Beecher, a woman must put the needs of others before her own desires; as Sklar writes, "Self-sacrifice, more than any other concept, informed both the triumph and tensions of nineteenth-century womanhood, and Catharine Beecher was its major theoretician."[26] She believed that the general good of society required women to be the moral foundation of a democratic society and the healer of social conflict, and in this role women could gain authority. Never could she be on an equal footing politically with men but her role as domestic ideologue would give her identity in a society dominated by men and commerce. "A woman, who is habitually gentle, sympathizing, forbearing, and cheerful," Beecher wrote, "carries an atmosphere about her, which imparts a soothing and sustaining influence, and renders it easier for all to do right, under her administration, than in any other situation."[27] Beecher attributed to women the responsibility for Christian nurture in the home, thus serving, ultimately, the welfare of the state by integrating domestic values with a reformed social and political morality.

Catharine Beecher's doctrine of female influence did not admit of true equality between the sexes but defended women's superior role as mistress of the household, wherein the family could attain Christian faith and moral rectitude. Because of his Quaker background, Whittier believed that women as well as men possessed the capacity for inner light, and throughout his career he appreciated and supported the intellectual and artistic talents of many women friends. On the other hand, however, Whittier never actively supported women's right to enfranchisement and political equality, and accepted the belief of Beecher and other writers that women's domestic tasks were her first and principal duties, although he demonstrated repeatedly in his letters that women could strive for literary recognition and economic prosperity. Furthermore, Whittier tended to accept the conventional notion that men's and women's responsibilities were distinctly separate.[28] In Stowe's Quaker family Rachel and Simeon Halliday respect one another as equals in a Christian family, but Stowe's chapter clearly portrays them as master and mistress of separate spheres, she of the kitchen and he of the political world outside. What gives her ultimate authority, as Beecher and Whittier would have it, is her capacity to inculcate Christian morality into her children so that they may make the right judgments in the complex moral dilemmas they will face in the political world outside the protection of the home.

Catharine Beecher's treatise and Stowe's Rachel define the model woman by what was then understood and has come to be known as the angel of the house, a metaphor that appropriates the religious rhetoric permeating all these domestic discourses during the nineteenth century. Of central interest to a reading of **Snow-Bound** is Whittier's treatment of the female gender ideology of the period in his portraits of the women of his childhood home; more than the men, even the schoolmaster with his future-oriented vision, they represent the central morality of a poem that drew a sizable audience because of its ideological resonances. Although the descriptions of the women of his family comprise only about twenty percent of the lines of the poem, the importance of these portraits is considerably greater than the proportion of lines assigned to them. These women define the benign piety and ministering goodness of the angel, particularly in the character of Whittier's mother, Abigail Whittier, from her first appearance in the poem turning her spinning wheel to one of the last references to her as an aid to and healer of the sick, the "Christian pearl of charity" (673), desiring that no one during those dark nights of "mindless wind" (102) and "[d]ead white" snow (147) will lack warmth and security. Whittier's mother universalizes the meaning of home in her story-telling; as a maker of words while spinning her thread, she casts a poet's spell of fact and fantasy to conquer nature's "spell" of fearsome weather. She defines a "simple life and country ways" (265) and unifies the home of the past with the homes of the present, her own and those of the readers' real and imagined homes: "She made us welcome to her home; / Old hearths grew wide to give us room" (267-68).[29] Abigail Whittier is the angel of light described in Cornelius Agrippa's occult writings, a passage of which serves as one epigraph to the poem; these angels come alive in the presence of the wood fire of the hearth, the earthly counterpart to the celestial fire of heaven, and transform the temporal home into a holy place.

Whittier's unmarried aunt, his mother's sister, Mercy Evans Hussey, is described as "homeless" (354) because, as Whittier expresses it, a "Fate / Perverse" (352-53) had denied her a husband. While she never had her own home, she, like so many unmarried women of her time, found a place of security and identity in her family's home. "[W]elcome wheresoe'er she went" (356), she epitomizes Beecher's code of female self-lessness and represents an untarnished innocence and virginity which Whittier praises even though her spinsterhood is out of the natural scheme of things, as he defines a woman's life. Like all of the women in the poem, except of course Harriet Livermore, his aunt is the angel whose "presence seemed the sweet income / And womanly atmosphere of home" (358-59). Domestic economy, represented in the play on the word "income," derives not only from the farmer in the field but from the woman at the hearth. Whittier admonishes the reader strongly not to judge ill of her innocence, as if to defend the single person, like himself, who can keep the ideal in an imperfect, changing world. Self-sacrifice as an attribute of feminine behavior is reflected even more fully in Mary Whittier, the oldest child, who had been an active support of her brother's poetic career but whose own domestic career failed for want of a happy marriage. A truthful, just, trusting, and impulsive woman, she "let her heart / Against the household bosom lean" (393-94). Whittier sees in her death the only consolation possible for a life of bitter regret; in this conventional response he acknowledges society's judgment of the irrevocable effects of a bad marriage on a woman's life and concedes only one option for his elder sister, a return to the first home and duty to the original family hearth.

Whittier's final portrait of the women in his youthful household is of Elizabeth, whom he remembers as an adult, not as a childhood contemporary. The poetic theme of the permanence of memory is represented in Elizabeth, whose death brought a "loss in all familiar things" (420) but a gain in the richness of a remembered past. He recognizes his own mortality more acutely and anticipates a reunion with her in paradise. The angel of their house has become an "Angel of the backward look" (715), or the spirit of memory, lately transformed into an angel of heaven. She is a guide, with her large eyes as beacons, leading the elder Whittier, known all his life for his own intense and penetrating eyes, from his earthly home to his divine home. The summer vision beginning with line 407 to the end of that section (437) articulates Whittier's religious philosophy, in a passage of traditional, yet intensely felt, Christian rhetoric of the hoped-for afterlife.

Although each of the women in Whittier's family—Elizabeth most fully—exemplifies the type of the nineteenth-century angel, Harriet Livermore contrasts dramatically with that ideal and sits outside the family circle. She may be characterized as the spirit of darkness in Cornelius Agrippa's polarity of light and dark-

ness; isolated in the farmhouse because of the weather, her "darkness" is not lightened by the wood fire of the family circle. She combines an uneasy mix of light and dark, her light described paradoxically as "dangerous" (527) and "sharp" (528). The portrait of Livermore is one of the longest in the poem and is separated from the portraits of the other family members by the highly autobiographical description of the schoolmaster, to whom she is more akin. Her delineation works a notable opposition to the values of the domestic ideology in the poem and complicates Whittier's depiction of the world outside, which the men must enter for their self-definition. Although clearly womanly in her appearance—one thinks of Hawthorne's Zenobia, who is at once more beguiling and less daunting—Livermore possesses traits that the ideology of the time would define as masculine. Whittier describes her passionate, bold, self-centered, wilful temperament combined with her womanly shape: "Her tapering hand and rounded wrist / Had facile power to form a fist" (538-39). Her personality and appearance define her contradictory nature, and because she can never join a conventional domestic circle, she succumbs to eccentric religious beliefs and fitful rambling. Whittier acknowledges his compassion for her solitary wanderings, her unrequited love, and her "outward wayward life" (565), which contrasts with the inward domestic life he celebrates. The "tumultuous privacy of storm" which rages outside in Emerson's "The Snow-Storm" (the second epigraph) describes the emotional turbulence of her unorthodox, anti-social behavior and her "unbent will's majestic pride" (518). The character of Harriet Livermore adds depth and complexity to *Snow-Bound* and compares with that of the schoolmaster, likewise an "outward" person. In Whittier's conceptualization of gender identities the schoolmaster has the privilege (indeed the necessity) to venture outside, but his quintessential self has been formed within the domestic circle and as a man he has the right to seek his individuality. Livermore's religious eccentricities are cause and effect of her drawing a circle around herself and excluding all others from those bounds. Because she possesses traits that are distinctly masculine according to the gender ideology of the time, she fails to live up to the eternal feminine and suffers accordingly.[30]

Whittier's interest in Harriet Livermore reveals a curious fascination with an unconventional woman who sacrifices her domestic role and becomes, by circumstance and choice, a homeless wanderer, the dreaded result of rejecting the charmed circle. Whittier's other women, who fulfill the responsibilities allotted to them by the ideology of the time, are never homeless; in fact, they define the place of their existence and sanctify it. Through the ministrations of women, the home, as the paradigm of a democratic society, fosters traditional values in children and tempers commercial and political assertiveness in men, thereby moving American society toward a higher realm of virtue. In *Snow-*

Bound Whittier affirms the domestic economy of his time and the personal values and family, history of his Quaker heritage and defines the redeemed American family, lately broken apart by the Civil War but now ready for consolation and renewal. In the poem he recreates his younger self in the schoolmaster, a healer no less than Whittier's mother Abigail, who is the maternal ideal for the schoolmaster as she was for her own son. The merit of ***Snow-Bound*** resides in its fusion of public philosophy and private creed; written at a timely moment both for the poet and his society, the poem unites the many discourses of its age into an intricate pattern of theme and metaphor.

Notes

[1] *The Letters of John Greenleaf Whittier,* ed. John B. Pickard, 3 vols. (Cambridge: Harvard University Press, 1975), 3:78.

[2] *Letters,* 3:77. Tilton became famous for his disastrous suit against Henry Ward Beecher for allegedly committing adultery with Tilton's wife. Whittier found it difficult not to support Beecher.

[3] *John Greenleaf Whittier: An Appraisal and a Selection* (Minneapolis: University of Minnesota Press, 1971), p. 47.

[4] *Whittier on Writers and Writing,* ed. Edwin Cady and Harry Hayden Clark (Syracuse: Syracuse University Press, 1950), p. 121.

[5] *Critical Essays on John Greenleaf Whittier,* ed. Jayne Kribbs (Boston: G. K. Hall, 1980), pp. 40, 42.

[6] Roland Woodwell, Whittier's most recent biographer, explains the effect on the reader in 1866 of Whittier's reminiscence of a moribund culture: "Deep in the American mind was a real or imagined love for the farm, often strongest in those who had never lived on a farm nor had their ancestors since the settlement of North America. Sitting in their warm homes, in the new luxury of a hot-air furnace and flaring gas chandeliers, they let their imagination give them a nostalgic delight in a life they had never known" (*John Greenleaf Whittier* [Haverhill, Mass.: Trustees of the John Greenleaf Whittier Homestead, 1985], p. 338). V. L. Parrington speaks of *Snow-Bound*'s "homely economy long since buried under the snows of forgotten winters." Whittier's economics, he says, have no relationship with "a scrambling free-soilism or a rapacious capitalism" (from his *Main Currents in American Thought* [1927-30], reprinted in *Critical Essays on Whittier,* p. 105). This is precisely the economic reality that domestic ideology in the nineteenth century was attempting to isolate; the home provided a haven from the marketplace. Whittier himself seemed to re-

alize that he was dealing with a distant past when he wrote to Fields in August 1865 that he was creating a "homely picture of *old* New England times" (*Letters,* 3:99).

[7] *The Complete Poetical Works of John Greenleaf Whittier* (Boston: Houghton, Mifflin, 1895), p. 525.

[8] *Letters,* 3:99, 102.

[9] *Letters,* 3:117. Whittier's long and complex half-century friendship with Lucy Larcom is chronicled in Shirley Marchalonis, "A Model for Mentors'?: Lucy Larcom and John Greenleaf Whittier," in *Patrons and Protégées: Gender, Friendship and Writing in Nineteenth-Century America,* ed. Marchalonis (New Brunswick: Rutgers University Press, 1988), pp. 94-121.

[10] *Letters,* 3:113, and Woodwell, *John Greenleaf Whittier,* p. 337.

[11] *Letters,* 3:444.

[12] *John Greenleaf Whittier's Poetry,* p. 4. Warren emphasizes Whittier's "almost pathological ambition" to find his position in the new American society of the nineteenth century. In one of his later poems, "My Namesake," Whittier speaks of the dichotomy of past and future that defines his career: "He reconciled as best he could / Old faith and fancies new" (*Complete Poetical Works,* p. 393).

[13] Lines 450-51; further line numbers will appear in the text; the 1895 *Complete Poetical Works* is the source.

[14] Whittier's portrait of Uncle Moses reveals an interesting treatment of male gender ideology; like Thoreau, his uncle was a student of nature and woodcraft, who lived only within his own parish. "Content to live where life began" (325), he was the opposite type of Whittier and the schoolmaster, and possessed characteristics that are more like feminine gender values than the male behavior Whittier characterizes in his father and the schoolmaster.

[15] Ann Douglas, "Heaven Our Home: Consolation Literature in the Northern United States, 1830-1880," in *Death in America,* ed. David E. Stannard (Philadelphia: University of Pennsylvania Press, 1975), p. 50.

[16] In "To My Sister," Whittier speaks of their childhood home as a sanctified place, an image that implies an anticipation of the final home in heaven. Frances Armstrong, in *Dickens and the Concept of Home* (Ann Arbor: UMI Research Press, 1990), writes of the connection between the past and future home; the childhood home is "the place to which one can return to die, sure of an acceptance and forgiveness which will act as an encouraging preliminary to or even substitute for entry to heaven" (p. 2).

[17] Gillian Brown, in *Domestic Individualism: Imagining Self in Nineteenth-Century America* (Berkeley: University of California Press, 1990), discusses the idea that in slavery the economic and personal status are never differentiated. She writes, concerning *Uncle Tom's Cabin:* "The call to the mothers of America for the abolition of slavery is a summons to fortify the home, to rescue domesticity from shiftlessness and slavery" (p. 16).

[18] *Letters,* 2:191, 201, 213.

[19] *Uncle Tom's Cabin,* in *Harriet Beecher Stowe: Three Novels,* sel. Kathryn Kish Sklar (New York: Library of America, 1982), pp. 162, 163, 165, 170.

[20] "Domestic Architecture as an Index to Social History: The Romantic Revival and the Culture of Domesticity in America, 1840-1870," *Journal of Interdisciplinary History,* 7 (Summer 1976): 47.

[21] *The Architecture of Country Houses* (New York: Dover, 1969 [1850]), p. 139.

[22] *Whittier on Writers and Writing,* ed. Cady and Clark, p. 121. In a letter several years before his death, Whittier commented that in the life of the farmer the best gains could be made in the creation of pleasant homes (*Letters,* 3:563).

[23] Warren, *John Greenleaf Whittier's Poetry,* p. 53.

[24] The extensive writing on the flourishing discourse on domestic architecture during the nineteenth century includes the following excellent essays and books: Clifford Edward Clark, Jr., *The American Family Home, 1800-1960* (Chapel Hill: University of North Carolina Press, 1986); Oscar P. Handlin, *The American Home: Architecture and Society, 1815-1915* (Boston: Little, Brown, 1979); Dolores Hayden, *The Grand Domestic Revolution: A History of Feminist Designs for American Homes, Neighborhoods, and Cities* (Cambridge: MIT Press, 1981); Sally McMurray, *Families and Farmhouses in Nineteenth-Century America: Vernacular Design and Social Change* (New York: Oxford University Press, 1988); Maxine Van de Wetering, "The Popular Concept of 'Home' in Nineteenth-Century America," *Journal of American Studies,* 18 (April 1984): 5-28; and Gwendolyn Wright, *Building the Dream: A Social History of Housing in America* (New York: Pantheon, 1981). Wright states: "To the majority of citizens in the early republic, the ideal American home was an independent homestead, attractive enough to encourage family pride yet unpretentious and economical" (p. 73). Gaston Bachelard's *The Poetics of Space* (trans. Maria Jolas [New York: Orion, 1964]) offers valuable commentary on the felicitous space of old houses, where dreams and the imagination invigorate memories of the past, particularly during a winter storm. Bachelard's discussion on the dialectic of outside and inside the house has significance to a reading of *Snow-Bound.*

[25] *Catharine Beecher: A Study in American Domesticity* (New Haven: Yale University Press, 1973), p. 151.

[26] *Catharine Beecher,* p. xiv.

[27] *Treatise on Domestic Economy for the Use of Young Ladies at Home and at School* (New York: Harpers, 1848), pp. 148-49.

[28] Gail Hamilton (the pen name of Mary Abigail Dodge) was one of his most ardent, humorous, and lively correspondents, frequently playing the coy role almost of a beloved. In a letter to him in October 1865, she writes about his "household idyls, in which I know there will be serving and women doing daintily all manner of pretty feminine doings" (*Letters,* 3:103).

[29] Thomas Wentworth Higginson confirmed Whittier's characterization of his mother as Beecher's ideal woman: "Mrs. Whittier was placid, strong, sensible, an exquisite housekeeper and 'provider'; it seems to me that I have since seen no whiteness to be compared to the snow of her table cloths and napkins" (quoted in Samuel T. Pickard, *Whittier-Land: A Handbook of North Essex* [Cambridge: Riverside Press, 1956 (1904)], p. 78). Mrs. Whittier's housekeeping talents are comparable to Rachel Halliday's in *Uncle Tom's Cabin.* Eliza looks in on supper preparations and sees the table with its "snowy cloth" (p. 168); all these references to white connect with the dreamy state of Eliza's post-sleep languor to suggest the power of domesticity, defined curiously in language with racial overtones.

[30] In a letter in 1879, Whittier recounted the subsequent history of Harriet Livermore and his later contacts with her; he states he did not exaggerate her personality in his poem and in this letter he describes her in more positive terms as "a brilliant darkeyed woman—striking in her personal appearance, and gifted in conversation." He does indicate, in a typical stereotyping of the time, that her peculiar behavior and fanaticism were the result of a failed love affair" (*Letters,* 3:412-13).

FURTHER READING

Bibliography

Currier, Thomas Franklin. *A Bibliography of John Greenleaf Whittier.* Cambridge, Mass.: Harvard University Press, 1937, 16 p.

Bibliography prepared by the early twentieth century's leading Whittier scholar.

Von Frank, Albert J. *Whittier: A Comprehensive Annotative Bibliography.* New York: Garland, 1976, 273 p.
Considered one of the most complete Whittier bibliographies.

Whittier, John Greenleaf. *The Complete Poetical Works of Whittier.* Boston: Houghton Mifflin Co., 1894, 542 p.
Includes an annotated bibliography with biographical sketch and introduction written by Whittier.

Biography

Pickard, Samuel T. *Life and Letters of John Greenleaf Whittier.* 2 vols. Boston: Houghton Mifflin and Co., Riverside Press, 1894.
The "official" biography sanctioned by Whittier before his death. Although Pickard's biography greatly romanticizes Whittier's political motivation, the work is still considered a standard source for its broad survey of Whittier's letters and memoirs.

Pollard, John A. *John Greenleaf Whittier: Friend of Man.* Boston: Houghton Mifflin Co., Riverside Press, 1949, 615 p.
A lengthy biography of Whittier which provides several helpful appendices. Pollard includes a bibliography as well as extensive notes concerning Whittier's lineage.

Wagenknecht, Edward. *John Greenleaf Whittier: A Portrait in Paradox.* New York: Oxford University Press, 1967, 262 p.
Describes Whittier in terms of various paradoxes that Wagenknecht believes to have shaped the poet's life, politics, and poetry.

Criticism

Boynton, H. W. "John Greenleaf Whittier: An Appreciation, Apropos of the Poet's Centenary." *Putnam's Monthly* III, No. 3 (December 1907): 274-80.
Suggests that Whittier be remembered and commended not for the quality of his poems, but for his song-like descriptions of nature and sentimental themes.

Budick, E. Miller. "The Immortalizing Power of Imagination: A Reading of Whittier's *Snow-Bound.*" *Emerson Society Quarterly* 31, No. 2 (2nd Quarter, 1985): 89-99.
Discusses how Whittier comes to terms with the problem of mortality in *Snow-Bound.*

Carey, George G. "Whittier's Roots in a Folk Culture." *Essex Institute Historical Collections* CIV, No. 1 (January 1968): 3-18.
Places Whittier and his poetry in the context of New England story-telling and folk traditions.

Kribbs, Jayne K. Introduction to *Critical Essays on John Greenleaf Whittier*, pp. xiii-xl. Boston: G. K. Hall & Co., 1980.
Provides a brief biography of Whittier's personal and literary life as well as an introduction to nineteenth- and twentieth-century critical reception of his works.

Leary, Lewis. "A Note on Whittier's *Margaret Smith.*" *Emerson Society Quarterly* 50 (1st Quarter, 1968): 75-8.
Describes Whittier's one novel as a "minor classic" and praises its celebration of the human spirit.

McEuen, Kathryn Anderson. "Whittier's Rhymes." *American Speech* XX, No. 1 (February 1945): 51-7.
By placing Whittier's rhymes in the context of regional New England pronunciation, refutes critics who label his rhyming "faulty."

Meek, Frederick M. "Whittier the Religious Man." *Emerson Society Quarterly* 50 (1st Quarter, 1968): 86-92.
Examines the deep religious roots of Whittier's life and the influence of his religious poetry on American literature and society.

Pickard, John B. "Whittier's Abolitionist Poetry." *Emerson Society Quarterly* 50 (1st Quarter, 1968): 105-15.
Suggests new ways of approaching Whittier's abolitionist poetry in terms of its artistic merit, rather than its biographical and historical significance.

Smythe, Daniel W. "Whittier and the New Critics." *Emerson Society Quarterly* 50 (1st Quarter, 1968): 22-6.
Defends Whittier's poetical skills against dismissive comments by proponents of the "New Criticism," a theoretical approach to literature, popular in the early twentieth century, that maintained works of literature or other artwork should be evaluated without reference to their historical, social, or biographical environments.

Additional coverage of Whittier's life and career is contained in the following sources published by Gale Research: *Dictionary of Literary Biography*, Vol. 1; and *Concise Dictionary of American Literary Biography, 1640-1865.*

How to Use This Index

Calvino, Italo
1923-1985.....CLC 5, 8, 11, 22, 33, 39,
73; SSC 3

list all author entries in the following Gale Literary Criticism series:

BLC = *Black Literature Criticism*
CLC = *Contemporary Literary Criticism*
CLR = *Children's Literature Review*
CMLC = *Classical and Medieval Literature Criticism*
DA = *DISCovering Authors*
DAB = *DISCovering Authors: British*
DAC = *DISCovering Authors: Canadian*
DAM = *DISCovering Authors Modules*
    DRAM: *Dramatists module*
    MST: *Most-studied authors module*
    MULT: *Multicultural authors module*
    NOV: *Novelists module*
    POET: *Poets module*
    POP: *Popular/genre writers module*

DC = *Drama Criticism*
HLC = *Hispanic Literature Criticism*
LC = *Literature Criticism from 1400 to 1800*
NCLC = *Nineteenth-Century Literature Criticism*
PC = *Poetry Criticism*
SSC = *Short Story Criticism*
TCLC = *Twentieth-Century Literary Criticism*
WLC = *World Literature Criticism, 1500 to the Present*

The cross-references

See also CANR 23; CA 85-88;
  obituary CA 116

list all author entries in the following Gale biographical and literary sources:

AAYA = *Authors & Artists for Young Adults*
AITN = *Authors in the News*
BEST = *Bestsellers*
BW = *Black Writers*
CA = *Contemporary Authors*
CAAS = *Contemporary Authors Autobiography Series*
CABS = *Contemporary Authors Bibliographical Series*
CANR = *Contemporary Authors New Revision Series*
CAP = *Contemporary Authors Permanent Series*
CDALB = *Concise Dictionary of American Literary Biography*
CDBLB = *Concise Dictionary of British Literary Biography*

DLB = *Dictionary of Literary Biography*
DLBD = *Dictionary of Literary Biography Documentary Series*
DLBY = *Dictionary of Literary Biography Yearbook*
HW = *Hispanic Writers*
JRDA = *Junior DISCovering Authors*
MAICYA = *Major Authors and Illustrators for Children and Young Adults*
MTCW = *Major 20th-Century Writers*
NNAL = *Native North American Literature*
SAAS = *Something about the Author Autobiography Series*
SATA = *Something about the Author*
YABC = *Yesterday's Authors of Books for Children*

Nineteenth-Century
Literature Criticism

Cumulative Indexes
Volumes 1-59

Literary Criticism Series
Cumulative Author Index

Alcala-Galiano, Juan Valera y
See Valera y Alcala-Galiano, Juan

Alcott, Amos Bronson 1799-1888 .. NCLC 1
See also DLB 1

Alcott, Louisa May
1832-1888 ..... NCLC 6, 58; DA; DAB;
DAC; DAM MST, NOV; WLC
See also CDALB 1865-1917; CLR 1, 38;
DLB 1, 42, 79; DLBD 14; JRDA;
MAICYA; YABC 1

Aldanov, M. A.
See Aldanov, Mark (Alexandrovich)

Aldanov, Mark (Alexandrovich)
1886(?)-1957 .... TCLC 23
See also CA 118

Aldington, Richard 1892-1962 ...... CLC 49
See also CA 85-88; CANR 45; DLB 20, 36,
100, 149

Aldiss, Brian W(ilson)
1925- .... CLC 5, 14, 40; DAM NOV
See also CA 5-8R; CAAS 2; CANR 5, 28;
DLB 14; MTCW; SATA 34

Alegria, Claribel
1924- .... CLC 75; DAM MULT
See also CA 131; CAAS 15; DLB 145; HW

Alegria, Fernando 1918- .... CLC 57
See also CA 9-12R; CANR 5, 32; HW

Aleichem, Sholom .... TCLC 1, 35
See also Rabinovitch, Sholem

Aleixandre, Vicente
1898-1984 .... CLC 9, 36; DAM POET;
PC 15
See also CA 85-88; 114; CANR 26;
DLB 108; HW; MTCW

Alepoudelis, Odysseus
See Elytis, Odysseus

Aleshkovsky, Joseph 1929-
See Aleshkovsky, Yuz
See also CA 121; 128

Aleshkovsky, Yuz .... CLC 44
See also Aleshkovsky, Joseph

Alexander, Lloyd (Chudley) 1924- .. CLC 35
See also AAYA 1; CA 1-4R; CANR 1, 24,
38, 55; CLR 1, 5; DLB 52; JRDA;
MAICYA; MTCW; SAAS 19; SATA 3,
49, 81

Alexie, Sherman (Joseph, Jr.)
1966- .... CLC 96; DAM MULT
See also CA 138; NNAL

Alfau, Felipe 1902- .... CLC 66
See also CA 137

Alger, Horatio, Jr. 1832-1899 ..... NCLC 8
See also DLB 42; SATA 16

Algren, Nelson 1909-1981 .... CLC 4, 10, 33
See also CA 13-16R; 103; CANR 20;
CDALB 1941-1968; DLB 9; DLBY 81,
82; MTCW

Ali, Ahmed 1910- .... CLC 69
See also CA 25-28R; CANR 15, 34

Alighieri, Dante 1265-1321 .... CMLC 3, 18

Allan, John B.
See Westlake, Donald E(dwin)

Allen, Edward 1948- .... CLC 59

Allen, Paula Gunn
1939- .... CLC 84; DAM MULT
See also CA 112; 143; NNAL

Allen, Roland
See Ayckbourn, Alan

Allen, Sarah A.
See Hopkins, Pauline Elizabeth

Allen, Woody
1935- .... CLC 16, 52; DAM POP
See also AAYA 10; CA 33-36R; CANR 27,
38; DLB 44; MTCW

Allende, Isabel
1942- .... CLC 39, 57, 97; DAM MULT,
NOV; HLC
See also AAYA 18; CA 125; 130;
CANR 51; DLB 145; HW; INT 130;
MTCW

Alleyn, Ellen
See Rossetti, Christina (Georgina)

Allingham, Margery (Louise)
1904-1966 .... CLC 19
See also CA 5-8R; 25-28R; CANR 4;
DLB 77; MTCW

Allingham, William 1824-1889 ... NCLC 25
See also DLB 35

Allison, Dorothy E. 1949- .... CLC 78
See also CA 140

Allston, Washington 1779-1843 .... NCLC 2
See also DLB 1

Almedingen, E. M. .... CLC 12
See also Almedingen, Martha Edith von
See also SATA 3

Almedingen, Martha Edith von 1898-1971
See Almedingen, E. M.
See also CA 1-4R; CANR 1

Almqvist, Carl Jonas Love
1793-1866 .... NCLC 42

Alonso, Damaso 1898-1990 .... CLC 14
See also CA 110; 131; 130; DLB 108; HW

Alov
See Gogol, Nikolai (Vasilyevich)

Alta 1942- .... CLC 19
See also CA 57-60

Alter, Robert B(ernard) 1935- ...... CLC 34
See also CA 49-52; CANR 1, 47

Alther, Lisa 1944- .... CLC 7, 41
See also CA 65-68; CANR 12, 30, 51;
MTCW

Altman, Robert 1925- .... CLC 16
See also CA 73-76; CANR 43

Alvarez, A(lfred) 1929- .... CLC 5, 13
See also CA 1-4R; CANR 3, 33; DLB 14,
40

Alvarez, Alejandro Rodriguez 1903-1965
See Casona, Alejandro
See also CA 131; 93-96; HW

Alvarez, Julia 1950- .... CLC 93
See also CA 147

Alvaro, Corrado 1896-1956 .... TCLC 60

Amado, Jorge
1912- .... CLC 13, 40; DAM MULT,
NOV; HLC
See also CA 77-80; CANR 35; DLB 113;
MTCW

Ambler, Eric 1909- .... CLC 4, 6, 9
See also CA 9-12R; CANR 7, 38; DLB 77;
MTCW

Amichai, Yehuda 1924- ...... CLC 9, 22, 57
See also CA 85-88; CANR 46; MTCW

Amiel, Henri Frederic 1821-1881 .. NCLC 4

Amis, Kingsley (William)
1922-1995 ..... CLC 1, 2, 3, 5, 8, 13, 40,
44; DA; DAB; DAC; DAM MST, NOV
See also AITN 2; CA 9-12R; 150; CANR 8,
28, 54; CDBLB 1945-1960; DLB 15, 27,
100, 139; INT CANR-8; MTCW

Amis, Martin (Louis)
1949- .... CLC 4, 9, 38, 62
See also BEST 90:3; CA 65-68; CANR 8,
27, 54; DLB 14; INT CANR-27

Ammons, A(rchie) R(andolph)
1926- .... CLC 2, 3, 5, 8, 9, 25, 57;
DAM POET; PC 16
See also AITN 1; CA 9-12R; CANR 6, 36,
51; DLB 5, 165; MTCW

Amo, Tauraatua i
See Adams, Henry (Brooks)

Anand, Mulk Raj
1905- .... CLC 23, 93; DAM NOV
See also CA 65-68; CANR 32; MTCW

Anatol
See Schnitzler, Arthur

Anaya, Rudolfo A(lfonso)
1937- .... CLC 23; DAM MULT, NOV;
HLC
See also CA 45-48; CAAS 4; CANR 1, 32,
51; DLB 82; HW 1; MTCW

Andersen, Hans Christian
1805-1875 .... NCLC 7; DA; DAB;
DAC; DAM MST, POP; SSC 6; WLC
See also CLR 6; MAICYA; YABC 1

Anderson, C. Farley
See Mencken, H(enry) L(ouis); Nathan,
George Jean

Anderson, Jessica (Margaret) Queale
.... CLC 37
See also CA 9-12R; CANR 4

Anderson, Jon (Victor)
1940- .... CLC 9; DAM POET
See also CA 25-28R; CANR 20

Anderson, Lindsay (Gordon)
1923-1994 .... CLC 20
See also CA 125; 128; 146

Anderson, Maxwell
1888-1959 ...... TCLC 2; DAM DRAM
See also CA 105; 152; DLB 7

Anderson, Poul (William) 1926- .... CLC 15
See also AAYA 5; CA 1-4R; CAAS 2;
CANR 2, 15, 34; DLB 8; INT CANR-15;
MTCW; SATA 90; SATA-Brief 39

Anderson, Robert (Woodruff)
1917- .... CLC 23; DAM DRAM
See also AITN 1; CA 21-24R; CANR 32;
DLB 7

Anderson, Sherwood
1876-1941 .... TCLC 1, 10, 24; DA;
DAB; DAC; DAM MST, NOV; SSC 1;
WLC
See also CA 104; 121; CDALB 1917-1929;
DLB 4, 9, 86; DLBD 1; MTCW

Andier, Pierre
See Desnos, Robert

Andouard
See Giraudoux, (Hippolyte) Jean

Andrade, Carlos Drummond de ...... **CLC 18**
See also Drummond de Andrade, Carlos

Andrade, Mario de 1893-1945 ..... **TCLC 43**

Andreae, Johann V(alentin)
1586-1654 .... **LC 32**
See also DLB 164

Andreas-Salome, Lou 1861-1937 ... **TCLC 56**
See also DLB 66

Andrewes, Lancelot 1555-1626 .... **LC 5**
See also DLB 151, 172

Andrews, Cicily Fairfield
See West, Rebecca

Andrews, Elton V.
See Pohl, Frederik

Andreyev, Leonid (Nikolaevich)
1871-1919 .... **TCLC 3**
See also CA 104

Andric, Ivo 1892-1975 .... **CLC 8**
See also CA 81-84; 57-60; CANR 43;
DLB 147; MTCW

Angelique, Pierre
See Bataille, Georges

Angell, Roger 1920- .... **CLC 26**
See also CA 57-60; CANR 13, 44; DLB 171

Angelou, Maya
1928- .... **CLC 12, 35, 64, 77; BLC; DA;
DAB; DAC; DAM MST, MULT, POET,
POP**
See also AAYA 7; BW 2; CA 65-68;
CANR 19, 42; DLB 38; MTCW;
SATA 49

Annensky, Innokenty Fyodorovich
1856-1909 .... **TCLC 14**
See also CA 110; 155

Annunzio, Gabriele d'
See D'Annunzio, Gabriele

Anon, Charles Robert
See Pessoa, Fernando (Antonio Nogueira)

Anouilh, Jean (Marie Lucien Pierre)
1910-1987 ...... **CLC 1, 3, 8, 13, 40, 50;
DAM DRAM**
See also CA 17-20R; 123; CANR 32;
MTCW

Anthony, Florence
See Ai

Anthony, John
See Ciardi, John (Anthony)

Anthony, Peter
See Shaffer, Anthony (Joshua); Shaffer,
Peter (Levin)

Anthony, Piers 1934- .. **CLC 35; DAM POP**
See also AAYA 11; CA 21-24R; CANR 28;
DLB 8; MTCW; SAAS 22; SATA 84

Antoine, Marc
See Proust, (Valentin-Louis-George-Eugene-)
Marcel

Antoninus, Brother
See Everson, William (Oliver)

Antonioni, Michelangelo 1912- ..... **CLC 20**
See also CA 73-76; CANR 45

Antschel, Paul 1920-1970
See Celan, Paul
See also CA 85-88; CANR 33; MTCW

Anwar, Chairil 1922-1949 .... **TCLC 22**
See also CA 121

Apollinaire, Guillaume
1880-1918 .... **TCLC 3, 8, 51;
DAM POET; PC 7**
See also Kostrowitzki, Wilhelm Apollinaris
de
See also CA 152

Appelfeld, Aharon 1932- .... **CLC 23, 47**
See also CA 112; 133

Apple, Max (Isaac) 1941- .... **CLC 9, 33**
See also CA 81-84; CANR 19, 54; DLB 130

Appleman, Philip (Dean) 1926- ..... **CLC 51**
See also CA 13-16R; CAAS 18; CANR 6,
29

Appleton, Lawrence
See Lovecraft, H(oward) P(hillips)

Apteryx
See Eliot, T(homas) S(tearns)

Apuleius, (Lucius Madaurensis)
125(?)-175(?) .... **CMLC 1**

Aquin, Hubert 1929-1977......... **CLC 15**
See also CA 105; DLB 53

Aragon, Louis
1897-1982 ..... **CLC 3, 22; DAM NOV,
POET**
See also CA 69-72; 108; CANR 28;
DLB 72; MTCW

Arany, Janos 1817-1882........ **NCLC 34**

Arbuthnot, John 1667-1735 .... **LC 1**
See also DLB 101

Archer, Herbert Winslow
See Mencken, H(enry) L(ouis)

Archer, Jeffrey (Howard)
1940- .... **CLC 28; DAM POP**
See also AAYA 16; BEST 89:3; CA 77-80;
CANR 22, 52; INT CANR-22

Archer, Jules 1915- .... **CLC 12**
See also CA 9-12R; CANR 6; SAAS 5;
SATA 4, 85

Archer, Lee
See Ellison, Harlan (Jay)

Arden, John
1930- ..... **CLC 6, 13, 15; DAM DRAM**
See also CA 13-16R; CAAS 4; CANR 31;
DLB 13; MTCW

Arenas, Reinaldo
1943-1990 ...... **CLC 41; DAM MULT;
HLC**
See also CA 124; 128; 133; DLB 145; HW

Arendt, Hannah 1906-1975 ..... **CLC 66, 98**
See also CA 17-20R; 61-64; CANR 26;
MTCW

Aretino, Pietro 1492-1556 .... **LC 12**

Arghezi, Tudor................... **CLC 80**
See also Theodorescu, Ion N.

Arguedas, Jose Maria
1911-1969 .... **CLC 10, 18**
See also CA 89-92; DLB 113; HW

Argueta, Manlio 1936-............ **CLC 31**
See also CA 131; DLB 145; HW

Ariosto, Ludovico 1474-1533........ **LC 6**

Aristides
See Epstein, Joseph

Aristophanes
450B.C.-385B.C......... **CMLC 4; DA;
DAB; DAC; DAM DRAM, MST; DC 2**

Arlt, Roberto (Godofredo Christophersen)
1900-1942 ..... **TCLC 29; DAM MULT;
HLC**
See also CA 123; 131; HW

Armah, Ayi Kwei
1939- .... **CLC 5, 33; BLC;
DAM MULT, POET**
See also BW 1; CA 61-64; CANR 21;
DLB 117; MTCW

Armatrading, Joan 1950- .... **CLC 17**
See also CA 114

Arnette, Robert
See Silverberg, Robert

**Arnim, Achim von (Ludwig Joachim von
Arnim)** 1781-1831 .... **NCLC 5**
See also DLB 90

Arnim, Bettina von 1785-1859.... **NCLC 38**
See also DLB 90

Arnold, Matthew
1822-1888 ..... **NCLC 6, 29; DA; DAB;
DAC; DAM MST, POET; PC 5; WLC**
See also CDBLB 1832-1890; DLB 32, 57

Arnold, Thomas 1795-1842 ...... **NCLC 18**
See also DLB 55

Arnow, Harriette (Louisa) Simpson
1908-1986 .... **CLC 2, 7, 18**
See also CA 9-12R; 118; CANR 14; DLB 6;
MTCW; SATA 42; SATA-Obit 47

Arp, Hans
See Arp, Jean

Arp, Jean 1887-1966.............. **CLC 5**
See also CA 81-84; 25-28R; CANR 42

Arrabal
See Arrabal, Fernando

Arrabal, Fernando 1932- ... **CLC 2, 9, 18, 58**
See also CA 9-12R; CANR 15

Arrick, Fran.................... **CLC 30**
See also Gaberman, Judie Angell

Artaud, Antonin (Marie Joseph)
1896-1948 ... **TCLC 3, 36; DAM DRAM**
See also CA 104; 149

Arthur, Ruth M(abel) 1905-1979.... **CLC 12**
See also CA 9-12R; 85-88; CANR 4;
SATA 7, 26

Artsybashev, Mikhail (Petrovich)
1878-1927 .... **TCLC 31**

Arundel, Honor (Morfydd)
1919-1973 .... **CLC 17**
See also CA 21-22; 41-44R; CAP 2;
CLR 35; SATA 4; SATA-Obit 24

Arzner, Dorothy 1897-1979........ **CLC 98**

Asch, Sholem 1880-1957 .... **TCLC 3**
See also CA 105

Ash, Shalom
See Asch, Sholem

Ashbery, John (Lawrence)
1927- . . . . . . **CLC 2, 3, 4, 6, 9, 13, 15, 25, 41, 77; DAM POET**
See also CA 5-8R; CANR 9, 37; DLB 5, 165; DLBY 81; INT CANR-9; MTCW

Ashdown, Clifford
See Freeman, R(ichard) Austin

Ashe, Gordon
See Creasey, John

Ashton-Warner, Sylvia (Constance)
1908-1984 . . . . **CLC 19**
See also CA 69-72; 112; CANR 29; MTCW

Asimov, Isaac
1920-1992 . . . . . . **CLC 1, 3, 9, 19, 26, 76, 92; DAM POP**
See also AAYA 13; BEST 90:2; CA 1-4R; 137; CANR 2, 19, 36; CLR 12; DLB 8; DLBY 92; INT CANR-19; JRDA; MAICYA; MTCW; SATA 1, 26, 74

Assis, Joaquim Maria Machado de
See Machado de Assis, Joaquim Maria

Astley, Thea (Beatrice May)
1925- . . . . **CLC 41**
See also CA 65-68; CANR 11, 43

Aston, James
See White, T(erence) H(anbury)

Asturias, Miguel Angel
1899-1974 . . . . **CLC 3, 8, 13; DAM MULT, NOV; HLC**
See also CA 25-28; 49-52; CANR 32; CAP 2; DLB 113; HW; MTCW

Atares, Carlos Saura
See Saura (Atares), Carlos

Atheling, William
See Pound, Ezra (Weston Loomis)

Atheling, William, Jr.
See Blish, James (Benjamin)

Atherton, Gertrude (Franklin Horn)
1857-1948 . . . . **TCLC 2**
See also CA 104; 155; DLB 9, 78

Atherton, Lucius
See Masters, Edgar Lee

Atkins, Jack
See Harris, Mark

Attaway, William (Alexander)
1911-1986 . . . . **CLC 92; BLC; DAM MULT**
See also BW 2; CA 143; DLB 76

Atticus
See Fleming, Ian (Lancaster)

Atwood, Margaret (Eleanor)
1939- . . . . . **CLC 2, 3, 4, 8, 13, 15, 25, 44, 84; DA; DAB; DAC; DAM MST, NOV, POET; PC 8; SSC 2; WLC**
See also AAYA 12; BEST 89:2; CA 49-52; CANR 3, 24, 33; DLB 53; INT CANR-24; MTCW; SATA 50

Aubigny, Pierre d'
See Mencken, H(enry) L(ouis)

Aubin, Penelope 1685-1731(?) . . . . **LC 9**
See also DLB 39

Auchincloss, Louis (Stanton)
1917- . . . . **CLC 4, 6, 9, 18, 45; DAM NOV; SSC 22**
See also CA 1-4R; CANR 6, 29, 55; DLB 2; DLBY 80; INT CANR-29; MTCW

Auden, W(ystan) H(ugh)
1907-1973 . . . . . **CLC 1, 2, 3, 4, 6, 9, 11, 14, 43; DA; DAB; DAC; DAM DRAM, MST, POET; PC 1; WLC**
See also AAYA 18; CA 9-12R; 45-48; CANR 5; CDBLB 1914-1945; DLB 10, 20; MTCW

Audiberti, Jacques
1900-1965 . . . . . . **CLC 38; DAM DRAM**
See also CA 25-28R

Audubon, John James
1785-1851 . . . . **NCLC 47**

Auel, Jean M(arie)
1936- . . . . **CLC 31; DAM POP**
See also AAYA 7; BEST 90:4; CA 103; CANR 21; INT CANR-21; SATA 91

Auerbach, Erich 1892-1957 . . . . . . **TCLC 43**
See also CA 118; 155

Augier, Emile 1820-1889 . . . . **NCLC 31**

August, John
See De Voto, Bernard (Augustine)

Augustine, St. 354-430 . . . . . . **CMLC 6; DAB**

Aurelius
See Bourne, Randolph S(illiman)

Aurobindo, Sri 1872-1950 . . . . **TCLC 63**

Austen, Jane
1775-1817 . . . . . **NCLC 1, 13, 19, 33, 51; DA; DAB; DAC; DAM MST, NOV; WLC**
See also AAYA 19; CDBLB 1789-1832; DLB 116

Auster, Paul 1947- . . . . **CLC 47**
See also CA 69-72; CANR 23, 52

Austin, Frank
See Faust, Frederick (Schiller)

Austin, Mary (Hunter)
1868-1934 . . . . **TCLC 25**
See also CA 109; DLB 9, 78

Autran Dourado, Waldomiro
See Dourado, (Waldomiro Freitas) Autran

Averroes 1126-1198 . . . . **CMLC 7**
See also DLB 115

Avicenna 980-1037 . . . . **CMLC 16**
See also DLB 115

Avison, Margaret
1918- . . . . **CLC 2, 4, 97; DAC; DAM POET**
See also CA 17-20R; DLB 53; MTCW

Axton, David
See Koontz, Dean R(ay)

Ayckbourn, Alan
1939- . . . . . . **CLC 5, 8, 18, 33, 74; DAB; DAM DRAM**
See also CA 21-24R; CANR 31; DLB 13; MTCW

Aydy, Catherine
See Tennant, Emma (Christina)

Ayme, Marcel (Andre) 1902-1967 . . . **CLC 11**
See also CA 89-92; CLR 25; DLB 72; SATA 91

Ayrton, Michael 1921-1975 . . . . **CLC 7**
See also CA 5-8R; 61-64; CANR 9, 21

Azorin . . . . **CLC 11**
See also Martinez Ruiz, Jose

Azuela, Mariano
1873-1952 . . . . . . **TCLC 3; DAM MULT; HLC**
See also CA 104; 131; HW; MTCW

Baastad, Babbis Friis
See Friis-Baastad, Babbis Ellinor

Bab
See Gilbert, W(illiam) S(chwenck)

Babbis, Eleanor
See Friis-Baastad, Babbis Ellinor

Babel, Isaac
See Babel, Isaak (Emmanuilovich)

Babel, Isaak (Emmanuilovich)
1894-1941(?) . . . . . . **TCLC 2, 13; SSC 16**
See also CA 104; 155

Babits, Mihaly 1883-1941 . . . . **TCLC 14**
See also CA 114

Babur 1483-1530 . . . . **LC 18**

Bacchelli, Riccardo 1891-1985 . . . . . **CLC 19**
See also CA 29-32R; 117

Bach, Richard (David)
1936- . . . . . . **CLC 14; DAM NOV, POP**
See also AITN 1; BEST 89:2; CA 9-12R; CANR 18; MTCW; SATA 13

Bachman, Richard
See King, Stephen (Edwin)

Bachmann, Ingeborg 1926-1973 . . . . . **CLC 69**
See also CA 93-96; 45-48; DLB 85

Bacon, Francis 1561-1626 . . . . **LC 18, 32**
See also CDBLB Before 1660; DLB 151

Bacon, Roger 1214(?)-1292 . . . . . . **CMLC 14**
See also DLB 115

Bacovia, George . . . . **TCLC 24**
See also Vasiliu, Gheorghe

Badanes, Jerome 1937- . . . . **CLC 59**

Bagehot, Walter 1826-1877 . . . . . . **NCLC 10**
See also DLB 55

Bagnold, Enid
1889-1981 . . . . . . **CLC 25; DAM DRAM**
See also CA 5-8R; 103; CANR 5, 40; DLB 13, 160; MAICYA; SATA 1, 25

Bagritsky, Eduard 1895-1934 . . . . . **TCLC 60**

Bagrjana, Elisaveta
See Belcheva, Elisaveta

Bagryana, Elisaveta . . . . **CLC 10**
See also Belcheva, Elisaveta
See also DLB 147

Bailey, Paul 1937- . . . . **CLC 45**
See also CA 21-24R; CANR 16; DLB 14

Baillie, Joanna 1762-1851 . . . . **NCLC 2**
See also DLB 93

Bainbridge, Beryl (Margaret)
1933- . . . . **CLC 4, 5, 8, 10, 14, 18, 22, 62; DAM NOV**
See also CA 21-24R; CANR 24, 55; DLB 14; MTCW

Baker, Elliott 1922- . . . . **CLC 8**
See also CA 45-48; CANR 2

Baker, Jean H. . . . . **TCLC 3, 10**
See also Russell, George William

Baker, Nicholson
1957- . . . . **CLC 61; DAM POP**
See also CA 135

Baker, Ray Stannard   1870-1946 . . . **TCLC 47**
See also CA 118

Baker, Russell (Wayne)   1925- . . . . . . **CLC 31**
See also BEST 89:4; CA 57-60; CANR 11, 41; MTCW

Bakhtin, M.
See Bakhtin, Mikhail Mikhailovich

Bakhtin, M. M.
See Bakhtin, Mikhail Mikhailovich

Bakhtin, Mikhail
See Bakhtin, Mikhail Mikhailovich

Bakhtin, Mikhail Mikhailovich
1895-1975 . . . . **CLC 83**
See also CA 128; 113

Bakshi, Ralph   1938(?)- . . . . **CLC 26**
See also CA 112; 138

Bakunin, Mikhail (Alexandrovich)
1814-1876 . . . . **NCLC 25, 58**

Baldwin, James (Arthur)
1924-1987 . . . . . . **CLC 1, 2, 3, 4, 5, 8, 13, 15, 17, 42, 50, 67, 90; BLC; DA; DAB; DAC; DAM MST, MULT, NOV, POP; DC 1; SSC 10; WLC**
See also AAYA 4; BW 1; CA 1-4R; 124; CABS 1; CANR 3, 24; CDALB 1941-1968; DLB 2, 7, 33; DLBY 87; MTCW; SATA 9; SATA-Obit 54

Ballard, J(ames) G(raham)
1930- . . . . **CLC 3, 6, 14, 36; DAM NOV, POP; SSC 1**
See also AAYA 3; CA 5-8R; CANR 15, 39; DLB 14; MTCW

Balmont, Konstantin (Dmitriyevich)
1867-1943 . . . . **TCLC 11**
See also CA 109; 155

Balzac, Honore de
1799-1850 . . . . **NCLC 5, 35, 53; DA; DAB; DAC; DAM MST, NOV; SSC 5; WLC**
See also DLB 119

Bambara, Toni Cade
1939-1995 . . . . . . **CLC 19, 88; BLC; DA; DAC; DAM MST, MULT**
See also AAYA 5; BW 2; CA 29-32R; 150; CANR 24, 49; DLB 38; MTCW

Bamdad, A.
See Shamlu, Ahmad

Banat, D. R.
See Bradbury, Ray (Douglas)

Bancroft, Laura
See Baum, L(yman) Frank

Banim, John   1798-1842 . . . . **NCLC 13**
See also DLB 116, 158, 159

Banim, Michael   1796-1874 . . . . . . **NCLC 13**
See also DLB 158, 159

Banjo, The
See Paterson, A(ndrew) B(arton)

Banks, Iain
See Banks, Iain M(enzies)

Banks, Iain M(enzies)   1954- . . . . **CLC 34**
See also CA 123; 128; INT 128

Banks, Lynne Reid . . . . **CLC 23**
See also Reid Banks, Lynne
See also AAYA 6

Banks, Russell   1940- . . . . **CLC 37, 72**
See also CA 65-68; CAAS 15; CANR 19, 52; DLB 130

Banville, John   1945- . . . . **CLC 46**
See also CA 117; 128; DLB 14; INT 128

Banville, Theodore (Faullain) de
1832-1891 . . . . **NCLC 9**

Baraka, Amiri
1934- . . . . **CLC 1, 2, 3, 5, 10, 14, 33; BLC; DA; DAC; DAM MST, MULT, POET, POP; DC 6; PC 4**
See also Jones, LeRoi
See also BW 2; CA 21-24R; CABS 3; CANR 27, 38; CDALB 1941-1968; DLB 5, 7, 16, 38; DLBD 8; MTCW

Barbauld, Anna Laetitia
1743-1825 . . . . **NCLC 50**
See also DLB 107, 109, 142, 158

Barbellion, W. N. P. . . . . **TCLC 24**
See also Cummings, Bruce F(rederick)

Barbera, Jack (Vincent)   1945- . . . . . . **CLC 44**
See also CA 110; CANR 45

Barbey d'Aurevilly, Jules Amedee
1808-1889 . . . . **NCLC 1; SSC 17**
See also DLB 119

Barbusse, Henri   1873-1935 . . . . **TCLC 5**
See also CA 105; 154; DLB 65

Barclay, Bill
See Moorcock, Michael (John)

Barclay, William Ewert
See Moorcock, Michael (John)

Barea, Arturo   1897-1957 . . . . **TCLC 14**
See also CA 111

Barfoot, Joan   1946- . . . . **CLC 18**
See also CA 105

Baring, Maurice   1874-1945 . . . . **TCLC 8**
See also CA 105; DLB 34

Barker, Clive   1952- . . . **CLC 52; DAM POP**
See also AAYA 10; BEST 90:3; CA 121; 129; INT 129; MTCW

Barker, George Granville
1913-1991 . . . . . **CLC 8, 48; DAM POET**
See also CA 9-12R; 135; CANR 7, 38; DLB 20; MTCW

Barker, Harley Granville
See Granville-Barker, Harley
See also DLB 10

Barker, Howard   1946- . . . . **CLC 37**
See also CA 102; DLB 13

Barker, Pat(ricia)   1943- . . . . **CLC 32, 94**
See also CA 117; 122; CANR 50; INT 122

Barlow, Joel   1754-1812 . . . . **NCLC 23**
See also DLB 37

Barnard, Mary (Ethel)   1909- . . . . **CLC 48**
See also CA 21-22; CAP 2

Barnes, Djuna
1892-1982 . . . **CLC 3, 4, 8, 11, 29; SSC 3**
See also CA 9-12R; 107; CANR 16, 55; DLB 4, 9, 45; MTCW

Barnes, Julian (Patrick)
1946- . . . . **CLC 42; DAB**
See also CA 102; CANR 19, 54; DLBY 93

Barnes, Peter   1931- . . . . **CLC 5, 56**
See also CA 65-68; CAAS 12; CANR 33, 34; DLB 13; MTCW

Baroja (y Nessi), Pio
1872-1956 . . . . **TCLC 8; HLC**
See also CA 104

Baron, David
See Pinter, Harold

Baron Corvo
See Rolfe, Frederick (William Serafino Austin Lewis Mary)

Barondess, Sue K(aufman)
1926-1977 . . . . **CLC 8**
See also Kaufman, Sue
See also CA 1-4R; 69-72; CANR 1

Baron de Teive
See Pessoa, Fernando (Antonio Nogueira)

Barres, Maurice   1862-1923 . . . . **TCLC 47**
See also DLB 123

Barreto, Afonso Henrique de Lima
See Lima Barreto, Afonso Henrique de

Barrett, (Roger) Syd   1946- . . . . **CLC 35**

Barrett, William (Christopher)
1913-1992 . . . . **CLC 27**
See also CA 13-16R; 139; CANR 11; INT CANR-11

Barrie, J(ames) M(atthew)
1860-1937 . . . . **TCLC 2; DAB; DAM DRAM**
See also CA 104; 136; CDBLB 1890-1914; CLR 16; DLB 10, 141, 156; MAICYA; YABC 1

Barrington, Michael
See Moorcock, Michael (John)

Barrol, Grady
See Bograd, Larry

Barry, Mike
See Malzberg, Barry N(athaniel)

Barry, Philip   1896-1949 . . . . **TCLC 11**
See also CA 109; DLB 7

Bart, Andre Schwarz
See Schwarz-Bart, Andre

Barth, John (Simmons)
1930- . . . . . . **CLC 1, 2, 3, 5, 7, 9, 10, 14, 27, 51, 89; DAM NOV; SSC 10**
See also AITN 1, 2; CA 1-4R; CABS 1; CANR 5, 23, 49; DLB 2; MTCW

Barthelme, Donald
1931-1989 . . . . . . **CLC 1, 2, 3, 5, 6, 8, 13, 23, 46, 59; DAM NOV; SSC 2**
See also CA 21-24R; 129; CANR 20; DLB 2; DLBY 80, 89; MTCW; SATA 7; SATA-Obit 62

Barthelme, Frederick   1943- . . . . **CLC 36**
See also CA 114; 122; DLBY 85; INT 122

Barthes, Roland (Gerard)
1915-1980 . . . . **CLC 24, 83**
See also CA 130; 97-100; MTCW

Barzun, Jacques (Martin)   1907- . . . . . **CLC 51**
See also CA 61-64; CANR 22

Bashevis, Isaac
See Singer, Isaac Bashevis

Bashkirtseff, Marie   1859-1884 . . . **NCLC 27**

Basho
See Matsuo Basho

Bass, Kingsley B., Jr.
See Bullins, Ed

Bass, Rick 1958-................. **CLC 79**
See also CA 126; CANR 53

Bassani, Giorgio 1916-............ **CLC 9**
See also CA 65-68; CANR 33; DLB 128;
MTCW

Bastos, Augusto (Antonio) Roa
See Roa Bastos, Augusto (Antonio)

Bataille, Georges 1897-1962 .... **CLC 29**
See also CA 101; 89-92

Bates, H(erbert) E(rnest)
1905-1974 .... **CLC 46; DAB;
DAM POP; SSC 10**
See also CA 93-96; 45-48; CANR 34;
DLB 162; MTCW

Bauchart
See Camus, Albert

Baudelaire, Charles
1821-1867 .... **NCLC 6, 29, 55; DA;
DAB; DAC; DAM MST, POET; PC 1;
SSC 18; WLC**

Baudrillard, Jean 1929-........... **CLC 60**

Baum, L(yman) Frank 1856-1919 ... **TCLC 7**
See also CA 108; 133; CLR 15; DLB 22;
JRDA; MAICYA; MTCW; SATA 18

Baum, Louis F.
See Baum, L(yman) Frank

Baumbach, Jonathan 1933-...... **CLC 6, 23**
See also CA 13-16R; CAAS 5; CANR 12;
DLBY 80; INT CANR-12; MTCW

Bausch, Richard (Carl) 1945- ...... **CLC 51**
See also CA 101; CAAS 14; CANR 43;
DLB 130

Baxter, Charles
1947- .... **CLC 45, 78; DAM POP**
See also CA 57-60; CANR 40; DLB 130

Baxter, George Owen
See Faust, Frederick (Schiller)

Baxter, James K(eir) 1926-1972 .... **CLC 14**
See also CA 77-80

Baxter, John
See Hunt, E(verette) Howard, (Jr.)

Bayer, Sylvia
See Glassco, John

Baynton, Barbara 1857-1929...... **TCLC 57**

Beagle, Peter S(oyer) 1939-........ **CLC 7**
See also CA 9-12R; CANR 4, 51;
DLBY 80; INT CANR-4; SATA 60

Bean, Normal
See Burroughs, Edgar Rice

Beard, Charles A(ustin)
1874-1948 .... **TCLC 15**
See also CA 115; DLB 17; SATA 18

Beardsley, Aubrey 1872-1898 ..... **NCLC 6**

Beattie, Ann
1947- .... **CLC 8, 13, 18, 40, 63;
DAM NOV, POP; SSC 11**
See also BEST 90:2; CA 81-84; CANR 53;
DLBY 82; MTCW

Beattie, James 1735-1803 .... **NCLC 25**
See also DLB 109

Beauchamp, Kathleen Mansfield 1888-1923
See Mansfield, Katherine
See also CA 104; 134; DA; DAC;
DAM MST

Beaumarchais, Pierre-Augustin Caron de
1732-1799 .... **DC 4**
See also DAM DRAM

Beaumont, Francis
1584(?)-1616 .... **LC 33; DC 6**
See also CDBLB Before 1660; DLB 58, 121

Beauvoir, Simone (Lucie Ernestine Marie
Bertrand) de
1908-1986 .... **CLC 1, 2, 4, 8, 14, 31, 44,
50, 71; DA; DAB; DAC; DAM MST,
NOV; WLC**
See also CA 9-12R; 118; CANR 28;
DLB 72; DLBY 86; MTCW

Becker, Carl 1873-1945 .... **TCLC 63:**
See also DLB 17

Becker, Jurek 1937-............ **CLC 7, 19**
See also CA 85-88; DLB 75

Becker, Walter 1950-............ **CLC 26**

Beckett, Samuel (Barclay)
1906-1989 ...... **CLC 1, 2, 3, 4, 6, 9, 10,
11, 14, 18, 29, 57, 59, 83; DA; DAB;
DAC; DAM DRAM, MST, NOV;
SSC 16; WLC**
See also CA 5-8R; 130; CANR 33;
CDBLB 1945-1960; DLB 13, 15;
DLBY 90; MTCW

Beckford, William 1760-1844 .... **NCLC 16**
See also DLB 39

Beckman, Gunnel 1910-........... **CLC 26**
See also CA 33-36R; CANR 15; CLR 25;
MAICYA; SAAS 9; SATA 6

Becque, Henri 1837-1899........ **NCLC 3**

Beddoes, Thomas Lovell
1803-1849 .... **NCLC 3**
See also DLB 96

Bede c. 673-735................ **CMLC 20**
See also DLB 146

Bedford, Donald F.
See Fearing, Kenneth (Flexner)

Beecher, Catharine Esther
1800-1878 .... **NCLC 30**
See also DLB 1

Beecher, John 1904-1980.......... **CLC 6**
See also AITN 1; CA 5-8R; 105; CANR 8

Beer, Johann 1655-1700............ **LC 5**
See also DLB 168

Beer, Patricia 1924-............. **CLC 58**
See also CA 61-64; CANR 13, 46; DLB 40

Beerbohm, Max
See Beerbohm, (Henry) Max(imilian)

Beerbohm, (Henry) Max(imilian)
1872-1956 .... **TCLC 1, 24**
See also CA 104; 154; DLB 34, 100

Beer-Hofmann, Richard
1866-1945 .... **TCLC 60**
See also DLB 81

Begiebing, Robert J(ohn) 1946-..... **CLC 70**
See also CA 122; CANR 40

Behan, Brendan
1923-1964 .... **CLC 1, 8, 11, 15, 79;
DAM DRAM**
See also CA 73-76; CANR 33;
CDBLB 1945-1960; DLB 13; MTCW

Behn, Aphra
1640(?)-1689 ...... **LC 1, 30; DA; DAB;
DAC; DAM DRAM, MST, NOV,
POET; DC 4; PC 13; WLC**
See also DLB 39, 80, 131

Behrman, S(amuel) N(athaniel)
1893-1973 .... **CLC 40**
See also CA 13-16; 45-48; CAP 1; DLB 7,
44

Belasco, David 1853-1931 .... **TCLC 3**
See also CA 104; DLB 7

Belcheva, Elisaveta 1893- .... **CLC 10**
See also Bagryana, Elisaveta

Beldone, Phil "Cheech"
See Ellison, Harlan (Jay)

Beleno
See Azuela, Mariano

Belinski, Vissarion Grigoryevich
1811-1848 .... **NCLC 5**

Belitt, Ben 1911-................ **CLC 22**
See also CA 13-16R; CAAS 4; CANR 7;
DLB 5

Bell, Gertrude 1868-1926........ **TCLC 67**
See also DLB 174

Bell, James Madison
1826-1902 .... **TCLC 43; BLC;
DAM MULT**
See also BW 1; CA 122; 124; DLB 50

Bell, Madison Smartt 1957-....... **CLC 41**
See also CA 111; CANR 28, 54

Bell, Marvin (Hartley)
1937- .... **CLC 8, 31; DAM POET**
See also CA 21-24R; CAAS 14; DLB 5;
MTCW

Bell, W. L. D.
See Mencken, H(enry) L(ouis)

Bellamy, Atwood C.
See Mencken, H(enry) L(ouis)

Bellamy, Edward 1850-1898 ...... **NCLC 4**
See also DLB 12

Bellin, Edward J.
See Kuttner, Henry

Belloc, (Joseph) Hilaire (Pierre Sebastien
Rene Swanton)
1870-1953 ... **TCLC 7, 18; DAM POET**
See also CA 106; 152; DLB 19, 100, 141,
174; YABC 1

Belloc, Joseph Peter Rene Hilaire
See Belloc, (Joseph) Hilaire (Pierre Sebastien
Rene Swanton)

Belloc, Joseph Pierre Hilaire
See Belloc, (Joseph) Hilaire (Pierre Sebastien
Rene Swanton)

Belloc, M. A.
See Lowndes, Marie Adelaide (Belloc)

Bellow, Saul
1915- ...... **CLC 1, 2, 3, 6, 8, 10, 13, 15,
25, 33, 34, 63, 79; DA; DAB; DAC;
DAM MST, NOV, POP; SSC 14; WLC**
See also AITN 2; BEST 89:3; CA 5-8R;
CABS 1; CANR 29, 53;
CDALB 1941-1968; DLB 2, 28; DLBD 3;
DLBY 82; MTCW

Belser, Reimond Karel Maria de 1929-
See Ruyslinck, Ward
See also CA 152

Bely, Andrey .... **TCLC 7; PC 11**
See also Bugayev, Boris Nikolayevich

Benary, Margot
See Benary-Isbert, Margot

Benary-Isbert, Margot 1889-1979... **CLC 12**
See also CA 5-8R; 89-92; CANR 4;
CLR 12; MAICYA; SATA 2;
SATA-Obit 21

Benavente (y Martinez), Jacinto
1866-1954 ..... **TCLC 3; DAM DRAM,**
                                            MULT
See also CA 106; 131; HW; MTCW

Benchley, Peter (Bradford)
1940- ..... **CLC 4, 8; DAM NOV, POP**
See also AAYA 14; AITN 2; CA 17-20R;
CANR 12, 35; MTCW; SATA 3, 89

Benchley, Robert (Charles)
1889-1945 .... **TCLC 1, 55**
See also CA 105; 153; DLB 11

Benda, Julien 1867-1956 .... **TCLC 60**
See also CA 120; 154

Benedict, Ruth 1887-1948 .... **TCLC 60**

Benedikt, Michael 1935- .... **CLC 4, 14**
See also CA 13-16R; CANR 7; DLB 5

Benet, Juan 1927-............... **CLC 28**
See also CA 143

Benet, Stephen Vincent
1898-1943 ...... **TCLC 7; DAM POET;**
                                            SSC 10
See also CA 104; 152; DLB 4, 48, 102;
YABC 1

Benet, William Rose
1886-1950 ...... **TCLC 28; DAM POET**
See also CA 118; 152; DLB 45

Benford, Gregory (Albert) 1941-.... **CLC 52**
See also CA 69-72; CANR 12, 24, 49;
DLBY 82

Bengtsson, Frans (Gunnar)
1894-1954 .... **TCLC 48**

Benjamin, David
See Slavitt, David R(ytman)

Benjamin, Lois
See Gould, Lois

Benjamin, Walter 1892-1940 ...... **TCLC 39**

Benn, Gottfried 1886-1956........ **TCLC 3**
See also CA 106; 153; DLB 56

Bennett, Alan
1934- ... **CLC 45, 77; DAB; DAM MST**
See also CA 103; CANR 35, 55; MTCW

Bennett, (Enoch) Arnold
1867-1931 .... **TCLC 5, 20**
See also CA 106; 155; CDBLB 1890-1914;
DLB 10, 34, 98, 135

Bennett, Elizabeth
See Mitchell, Margaret (Munnerlyn)

Bennett, George Harold 1930-
See Bennett, Hal
See also BW 1; CA 97-100

Bennett, Hal .... **CLC 5**
See also Bennett, George Harold
See also DLB 33

Bennett, Jay 1912-............... **CLC 35**
See also AAYA 10; CA 69-72; CANR 11,
42; JRDA; SAAS 4; SATA 41, 87;
SATA-Brief 27

Bennett, Louise (Simone)
1919- ..... **CLC 28; BLC; DAM MULT**
See also BW 2; CA 151; DLB 117

Benson, E(dward) F(rederic)
1867-1940 .... **TCLC 27**
See also CA 114; DLB 135, 153

Benson, Jackson J. 1930-......... **CLC 34**
See also CA 25-28R; DLB 111

Benson, Sally 1900-1972 .... **CLC 17**
See also CA 19-20; 37-40R; CAP 1;
SATA 1, 35; SATA-Obit 27

Benson, Stella 1892-1933......... **TCLC 17**
See also CA 117; 155; DLB 36, 162

Bentham, Jeremy 1748-1832 ..... **NCLC 38**
See also DLB 107, 158

Bentley, E(dmund) C(lerihew)
1875-1956 .... **TCLC 12**
See also CA 108; DLB 70

Bentley, Eric (Russell) 1916-....... **CLC 24**
See also CA 5-8R; CANR 6; INT CANR-6

Beranger, Pierre Jean de
1780-1857 .... **NCLC 34**

Berdyaev, Nicolas
See Berdyaev, Nikolai (Aleksandrovich)

Berdyaev, Nikolai (Aleksandrovich)
1874-1948 .... **TCLC 67**
See also CA 120

Berendt, John (Lawrence) 1939-.... **CLC 86**
See also CA 146

Berger, Colonel
See Malraux, (Georges-)Andre

Berger, John (Peter) 1926- ...... **CLC 2, 19**
See also CA 81-84; CANR 51; DLB 14

Berger, Melvin H. 1927- .... **CLC 12**
See also CA 5-8R; CANR 4; CLR 32;
SAAS 2; SATA 5, 88

Berger, Thomas (Louis)
1924- .... **CLC 3, 5, 8, 11, 18, 38;**
                                            DAM NOV
See also CA 1-4R; CANR 5, 28, 51; DLB 2;
DLBY 80; INT CANR-28; MTCW

Bergman, (Ernst) Ingmar
1918- .... **CLC 16, 72**
See also CA 81-84; CANR 33

Bergson, Henri 1859-1941....... **TCLC 32**

Bergstein, Eleanor 1938-.......... **CLC 4**
See also CA 53-56; CANR 5

Berkoff, Steven 1937-............. **CLC 56**
See also CA 104

Bermant, Chaim (Icyk) 1929- ...... **CLC 40**
See also CA 57-60; CANR 6, 31

Bern, Victoria
See Fisher, M(ary) F(rances) K(ennedy)

Bernanos, (Paul Louis) Georges
1888-1948 .... **TCLC 3**
See also CA 104; 130; DLB 72

Bernard, April 1956- .... **CLC 59**
See also CA 131

Berne, Victoria
See Fisher, M(ary) F(rances) K(ennedy)

Bernhard, Thomas
1931-1989 .... **CLC 3, 32, 61**
See also CA 85-88; 127; CANR 32;
DLB 85, 124; MTCW

Berriault, Gina 1926-............. **CLC 54**
See also CA 116; 129; DLB 130

Berrigan, Daniel 1921-............ **CLC 4**
See also CA 33-36R; CAAS 1; CANR 11,
43; DLB 5

Berrigan, Edmund Joseph Michael, Jr.
1934-1983
See Berrigan, Ted
See also CA 61-64; 110; CANR 14

Berrigan, Ted..................... **CLC 37**
See also Berrigan, Edmund Joseph Michael,
Jr.
See also DLB 5, 169

Berry, Charles Edward Anderson 1931-
See Berry, Chuck
See also CA 115

Berry, Chuck..................... **CLC 17**
See also Berry, Charles Edward Anderson

Berry, Jonas
See Ashbery, John (Lawrence)

Berry, Wendell (Erdman)
1934- .... **CLC 4, 6, 8, 27, 46;**
                                            DAM POET
See also AITN 1; CA 73-76; CANR 50;
DLB 5, 6

Berryman, John
1914-1972 ...... **CLC 1, 2, 3, 4, 6, 8, 10,**
                                            13, 25, 62; DAM POET
See also CA 13-16; 33-36R; CABS 2;
CANR 35; CAP 1; CDALB 1941-1968;
DLB 48; MTCW

Bertolucci, Bernardo 1940- .... **CLC 16**
See also CA 106

Bertrand, Aloysius 1807-1841 .... **NCLC 31**

Bertran de Born c. 1140-1215 ..... **CMLC 5**

Besant, Annie (Wood) 1847-1933 ... **TCLC 9**
See also CA 105

Bessie, Alvah 1904-1985........... **CLC 23**
See also CA 5-8R; 116; CANR 2; DLB 26

Bethlen, T. D.
See Silverberg, Robert

Beti, Mongo.... **CLC 27; BLC; DAM MULT**
See also Biyidi, Alexandre

Betjeman, John
1906-1984 .... **CLC 2, 6, 10, 34, 43;**
                                            DAB; DAM MST, POET
See also CA 9-12R; 112; CANR 33;
CDBLB 1945-1960; DLB 20; DLBY 84;
MTCW

Bettelheim, Bruno 1903-1990 ...... **CLC 79**
See also CA 81-84; 131; CANR 23; MTCW

Betti, Ugo 1892-1953 .... **TCLC 5**
See also CA 104; 155

Betts, Doris (Waugh) 1932-.... **CLC 3, 6, 28**
See also CA 13-16R; CANR 9; DLBY 82;
INT CANR-9

Bevan, Alistair
See Roberts, Keith (John Kingston)

Bialik, Chaim Nachman
1873-1934 .... **TCLC 25**

Bickerstaff, Isaac
See Swift, Jonathan

Bidart, Frank 1939- . . . . **CLC 33**
See also CA 140

Bienek, Horst 1930- . . . . **CLC 7, 11**
See also CA 73-76; DLB 75

Bierce, Ambrose (Gwinett)
1842-1914(?) . . . . . . **TCLC 1, 7, 44; DA;**
DAC; DAM MST; SSC 9; WLC
See also CA 104; 139; CDALB 1865-1917;
DLB 11, 12, 23, 71, 74

Biggers, Earl Derr 1884-1933 . . . . . **TCLC 65**
See also CA 108; 153

Billings, Josh
See Shaw, Henry Wheeler

Billington, (Lady) Rachel (Mary)
1942- . . . . **CLC 43**
See also AITN 2; CA 33-36R; CANR 44

Binyon, T(imothy) J(ohn) 1936- . . . . **CLC 34**
See also CA 111; CANR 28

Bioy Casares, Adolfo
1914- . . . . **CLC 4, 8, 13, 88;**
DAM MULT; HLC; SSC 17
See also CA 29-32R; CANR 19, 43;
DLB 113; HW; MTCW

Bird, Cordwainer
See Ellison, Harlan (Jay)

Bird, Robert Montgomery
1806-1854 . . . . **NCLC 1**

Birney, (Alfred) Earle
1904- . . . . **CLC 1, 4, 6, 11; DAC;**
DAM MST, POET
See also CA 1-4R; CANR 5, 20; DLB 88;
MTCW

Bishop, Elizabeth
1911-1979 . . . . . . **CLC 1, 4, 9, 13, 15, 32;**
DA; DAC; DAM MST, POET; PC 3
See also CA 5-8R; 89-92; CABS 2;
CANR 26; CDALB 1968-1988; DLB 5,
169; MTCW; SATA-Obit 24

Bishop, John 1935- . . . . **CLC 10**
See also CA 105

Bissett, Bill 1939- . . . . **CLC 18; PC 14**
See also CA 69-72; CAAS 19; CANR 15;
DLB 53; MTCW

Bitov, Andrei (Georgievich) 1937- . . . **CLC 57**
See also CA 142

Biyidi, Alexandre 1932-
See Beti, Mongo
See also BW 1; CA 114; 124; MTCW

Bjarme, Brynjolf
See Ibsen, Henrik (Johan)

Bjornson, Bjornstjerne (Martinius)
1832-1910 . . . . **TCLC 7, 37**
See also CA 104

Black, Robert
See Holdstock, Robert P.

Blackburn, Paul 1926-1971 . . . . . **CLC 9, 43**
See also CA 81-84; 33-36R; CANR 34;
DLB 16; DLBY 81

Black Elk
1863-1950 . . . . . **TCLC 33; DAM MULT**
See also CA 144; NNAL

Black Hobart
See Sanders, (James) Ed(ward)

Blacklin, Malcolm
See Chambers, Aidan

Blackmore, R(ichard) D(oddridge)
1825-1900 . . . . **TCLC 27**
See also CA 120; DLB 18

Blackmur, R(ichard) P(almer)
1904-1965 . . . . **CLC 2, 24**
See also CA 11-12; 25-28R; CAP 1; DLB 63

Black Tarantula
See Acker, Kathy

Blackwood, Algernon (Henry)
1869-1951 . . . . **TCLC 5**
See also CA 105; 150; DLB 153, 156

Blackwood, Caroline 1931-1996 . . . **CLC 6, 9**
See also CA 85-88; 151; CANR 32;
DLB 14; MTCW

Blade, Alexander
See Hamilton, Edmond; Silverberg, Robert

Blaga, Lucian 1895-1961 . . . . **CLC 75**

Blair, Eric (Arthur) 1903-1950
See Orwell, George
See also CA 104; 132; DA; DAB; DAC;
DAM MST, NOV; MTCW; SATA 29

Blais, Marie-Claire
1939- . . . . **CLC 2, 4, 6, 13, 22; DAC;**
DAM MST
See also CA 21-24R; CAAS 4; CANR 38;
DLB 53; MTCW

Blaise, Clark 1940- . . . . **CLC 29**
See also AITN 2; CA 53-56; CAAS 3;
CANR 5; DLB 53

Blake, Nicholas
See Day Lewis, C(ecil)
See also DLB 77

Blake, William
1757-1827 . . . . **NCLC 13, 37, 57; DA;**
DAB; DAC; DAM MST, POET; PC 12;
WLC
See also CDBLB 1789-1832; DLB 93, 163;
MAICYA; SATA 30

Blake, William J(ames) 1894-1969 . . . **PC 12**
See also CA 5-8R; 25-28R

Blasco Ibanez, Vicente
1867-1928 . . . . **TCLC 12; DAM NOV**
See also CA 110; 131; HW; MTCW

Blatty, William Peter
1928- . . . . **CLC 2; DAM POP**
See also CA 5-8R; CANR 9

Bleeck, Oliver
See Thomas, Ross (Elmore)

Blessing, Lee 1949- . . . . **CLC 54**

Blish, James (Benjamin)
1921-1975 . . . . **CLC 14**
See also CA 1-4R; 57-60; CANR 3; DLB 8;
MTCW; SATA 66

Bliss, Reginald
See Wells, H(erbert) G(eorge)

Blixen, Karen (Christentze Dinesen)
1885-1962
See Dinesen, Isak
See also CA 25-28; CANR 22, 50; CAP 2;
MTCW; SATA 44

Bloch, Robert (Albert) 1917-1994 . . . **CLC 33**
See also CA 5-8R; 146; CAAS 20; CANR 5;
DLB 44; INT CANR-5; SATA 12;
SATA-Obit 82

Blok, Alexander (Alexandrovich)
1880-1921 . . . . **TCLC 5**
See also CA 104

Blom, Jan
See Breytenbach, Breyten

Bloom, Harold 1930- . . . . **CLC 24**
See also CA 13-16R; CANR 39; DLB 67

Bloomfield, Aurelius
See Bourne, Randolph S(illiman)

Blount, Roy (Alton), Jr. 1941- . . . . . **CLC 38**
See also CA 53-56; CANR 10, 28;
INT CANR-28; MTCW

Bloy, Leon 1846-1917 . . . . **TCLC 22**
See also CA 121; DLB 123

Blume, Judy (Sussman)
1938- . . . **CLC 12, 30; DAM NOV, POP**
See also AAYA 3; CA 29-32R; CANR 13,
37; CLR 2, 15; DLB 52; JRDA;
MAICYA; MTCW; SATA 2, 31, 79

Blunden, Edmund (Charles)
1896-1974 . . . . **CLC 2, 56**
See also CA 17-18; 45-48; CANR 54;
CAP 2; DLB 20, 100, 155; MTCW

Bly, Robert (Elwood)
1926- . . . . **CLC 1, 2, 5, 10, 15, 38;**
DAM POET
See also CA 5-8R; CANR 41; DLB 5;
MTCW

Boas, Franz 1858-1942 . . . . **TCLC 56**
See also CA 115

Bobette
See Simenon, Georges (Jacques Christian)

Boccaccio, Giovanni
1313-1375 . . . . **CMLC 13; SSC 10**

Bochco, Steven 1943- . . . . **CLC 35**
See also AAYA 11; CA 124; 138

Bodenheim, Maxwell 1892-1954 . . . **TCLC 44**
See also CA 110; DLB 9, 45

Bodker, Cecil 1927- . . . . **CLC 21**
See also CA 73-76; CANR 13, 44; CLR 23;
MAICYA; SATA 14

Boell, Heinrich (Theodor)
1917-1985 . . . . **CLC 2, 3, 6, 9, 11, 15, 27,**
32, 72; DA; DAB; DAC; DAM MST,
NOV; SSC 23; WLC
See also CA 21-24R; 116; CANR 24;
DLB 69; DLBY 85; MTCW

Boerne, Alfred
See Doeblin, Alfred

Boethius 480(?)-524(?) . . . . **CMLC 15**
See also DLB 115

Bogan, Louise
1897-1970 . . . . **CLC 4, 39, 46, 93;**
DAM POET; PC 12
See also CA 73-76; 25-28R; CANR 33;
DLB 45, 169; MTCW

Bogarde, Dirk . . . . **CLC 19**
See also Van Den Bogarde, Derek Jules
Gaspard Ulric Niven
See also DLB 14

Brandes, Georg (Morris Cohen)
1842-1927 .... TCLC 10
See also CA 105

Brandys, Kazimierz 1916- .... CLC 62

Branley, Franklyn M(ansfield)
1915- .... CLC 21
See also CA 33-36R; CANR 14, 39;
CLR 13; MAICYA; SAAS 16; SATA 4,
68

Brathwaite, Edward Kamau
1930- .... CLC 11; DAM POET
See also BW 2; CA 25-28R; CANR 11, 26,
47; DLB 125

Brautigan, Richard (Gary)
1935-1984 .... CLC 1, 3, 5, 9, 12, 34, 42;
DAM NOV
See also CA 53-56; 113; CANR 34; DLB 2,
5; DLBY 80, 84; MTCW; SATA 56

Brave Bird, Mary 1953-
See Crow Dog, Mary (Ellen)
See also NNAL

Braverman, Kate 1950- .... CLC 67
See also CA 89-92

Brecht, Bertolt
1898-1956 ...... TCLC 1, 6, 13, 35; DA;
DAB; DAC; DAM DRAM, MST; DC 3;
WLC
See also CA 104; 133; DLB 56, 124; MTCW

Brecht, Eugen Berthold Friedrich
See Brecht, Bertolt

Bremer, Fredrika 1801-1865 ..... NCLC 11

Brennan, Christopher John
1870-1932 .... TCLC 17
See also CA 117

Brennan, Maeve 1917- .... CLC 5
See also CA 81-84

Brentano, Clemens (Maria)
1778-1842 .... NCLC 1
See also DLB 90

Brent of Bin Bin
See Franklin, (Stella Maraia Sarah) Miles

Brenton, Howard 1942- .... CLC 31
See also CA 69-72; CANR 33; DLB 13;
MTCW

Breslin, James 1930-
See Breslin, Jimmy
See also CA 73-76; CANR 31; DAM NOV;
MTCW

Breslin, Jimmy .... CLC 4, 43
See also Breslin, James
See also AITN 1

Bresson, Robert 1901- .... CLC 16
See also CA 110; CANR 49

Breton, Andre
1896-1966 ..... CLC 2, 9, 15, 54; PC 15
See also CA 19-20; 25-28R; CANR 40;
CAP 2; DLB 65; MTCW

Breytenbach, Breyten
1939(?)- ...... CLC 23, 37; DAM POET
See also CA 113; 129

Bridgers, Sue Ellen 1942- .... CLC 26
See also AAYA 8; CA 65-68; CANR 11,
36; CLR 18; DLB 52; JRDA; MAICYA;
SAAS 1; SATA 22, 90

Bridges, Robert (Seymour)
1844-1930 ...... TCLC 1; DAM POET
See also CA 104; 152; CDBLB 1890-1914;
DLB 19, 98

Bridie, James.................... TCLC 3
See also Mavor, Osborne Henry
See also DLB 10

Brin, David 1950- .... CLC 34
See also CA 102; CANR 24;
INT CANR-24; SATA 65

Brink, Andre (Philippus)
1935- .... CLC 18, 36
See also CA 104; CANR 39; INT 103;
MTCW

Brinsmead, H(esba) F(ay) 1922- .... CLC 21
See also CA 21-24R; CANR 10; MAICYA;
SAAS 5; SATA 18, 78

Brittain, Vera (Mary)
1893(?)-1970 .... CLC 23
See also CA 13-16; 25-28R; CAP 1; MTCW

Broch, Hermann 1886-1951 ...... TCLC 20
See also CA 117; DLB 85, 124

Brock, Rose
See Hansen, Joseph

Brodkey, Harold (Roy) 1930-1996 .. CLC 56
See also CA 111; 151; DLB 130

Brodsky, Iosif Alexandrovich 1940-1996
See Brodsky, Joseph
See also AITN 1; CA 41-44R; 151;
CANR 37; DAM POET; MTCW

Brodsky, Joseph .. CLC 4, 6, 13, 36, 50; PC 9
See also Brodsky, Iosif Alexandrovich

Brodsky, Michael Mark 1948- ..... CLC 19
See also CA 102; CANR 18, 41

Bromell, Henry 1947-............. CLC 5
See also CA 53-56; CANR 9

Bromfield, Louis (Brucker)
1896-1956 .... TCLC 11
See also CA 107; 155; DLB 4, 9, 86

Broner, E(sther) M(asserman)
1930- .... CLC 19
See also CA 17-20R; CANR 8, 25; DLB 28

Bronk, William 1918-............. CLC 10
See also CA 89-92; CANR 23; DLB 165

Bronstein, Lev Davidovich
See Trotsky, Leon

Bronte, Anne 1820-1849......... NCLC 4
See also DLB 21

Bronte, Charlotte
1816-1855 ..... NCLC 3, 8, 33, 58; DA;
DAB; DAC; DAM MST, NOV; WLC
See also AAYA 17; CDBLB 1832-1890;
DLB 21, 159

Bronte, Emily (Jane)
1818-1848 .... NCLC 16, 35; DA; DAB;
DAC; DAM MST, NOV, POET; PC 8;
WLC
See also AAYA 17; CDBLB 1832-1890;
DLB 21, 32

Brooke, Frances 1724-1789 .... LC 6
See also DLB 39, 99

Brooke, Henry 1703(?)-1783 .... LC 1
See also DLB 39

Brooke, Rupert (Chawner)
1887-1915 ...... TCLC 2, 7; DA; DAB;
DAC; DAM MST, POET; WLC
See also CA 104; 132; CDBLB 1914-1945;
DLB 19; MTCW

Brooke-Haven, P.
See Wodehouse, P(elham) G(renville)

Brooke-Rose, Christine 1926- ...... CLC 40
See also CA 13-16R; DLB 14

Brookner, Anita
1928- .... CLC 32, 34, 51; DAB;
DAM POP
See also CA 114; 120; CANR 37; DLBY 87;
MTCW

Brooks, Cleanth 1906-1994 ..... CLC 24, 86
See also CA 17-20R; 145; CANR 33, 35;
DLB 63; DLBY 94; INT CANR-35;
MTCW

Brooks, George
See Baum, L(yman) Frank

Brooks, Gwendolyn
1917- ...... CLC 1, 2, 4, 5, 15, 49; BLC;
DA; DAC; DAM MST, MULT, POET;
PC 7; WLC
See also AITN 1; BW 2; CA 1-4R;
CANR 1, 27, 52; CDALB 1941-1968;
CLR 27; DLB 5, 76, 165; MTCW;
SATA 6

Brooks, Mel..................... CLC 12
See also Kaminsky, Melvin
See also AAYA 13; DLB 26

Brooks, Peter 1938-............. CLC 34
See also CA 45-48; CANR 1

Brooks, Van Wyck 1886-1963...... CLC 29
See also CA 1-4R; CANR 6; DLB 45, 63,
103

Brophy, Brigid (Antonia)
1929-1995 .... CLC 6, 11, 29
See also CA 5-8R; 149; CAAS 4; CANR 25,
53; DLB 14; MTCW

Brosman, Catharine Savage 1934-.... CLC 9
See also CA 61-64; CANR 21, 46

Brother Antoninus
See Everson, William (Oliver)

Broughton, T(homas) Alan 1936- ... CLC 19
See also CA 45-48; CANR 2, 23, 48

Broumas, Olga 1949-.......... CLC 10, 73
See also CA 85-88; CANR 20

Brown, Charles Brockden
1771-1810 .... NCLC 22
See also CDALB 1640-1865; DLB 37, 59,
73

Brown, Christy 1932-1981........ CLC 63
See also CA 105; 104; DLB 14

Brown, Claude
1937- ..... CLC 30; BLC; DAM MULT
See also AAYA 7; BW 1; CA 73-76

Brown, Dee (Alexander)
1908- .... CLC 18, 47; DAM POP
See also CA 13-16R; CAAS 6; CANR 11,
45; DLBY 80; MTCW; SATA 5

Brown, George
See Wertmueller, Lina

Brown, George Douglas
1869-1902 .... TCLC 28

Brown, George Mackay
1921-1996 . . . . **CLC 5, 48**
See also CA 21-24R; 151; CAAS 6;
CANR 12, 37; DLB 14, 27, 139; MTCW;
SATA 35

Brown, (William) Larry 1951-. . . . . . **CLC 73**
See also CA 130; 134; INT 133

Brown, Moses
See Barrett, William (Christopher)

Brown, Rita Mae
1944- . . . . . **CLC 18, 43, 79; DAM NOV,
POP**
See also CA 45-48; CANR 2, 11, 35;
INT CANR-11; MTCW

Brown, Roderick (Langmere) Haig-
See Haig-Brown, Roderick (Langmere)

Brown, Rosellen 1939-. . . . . **CLC 32**
See also CA 77-80; CAAS 10; CANR 14, 44

Brown, Sterling Allen
1901-1989 . . . . **CLC 1, 23, 59; BLC;
DAM MULT, POET**
See also BW 1; CA 85-88; 127; CANR 26;
DLB 48, 51, 63; MTCW

Brown, Will
See Ainsworth, William Harrison

Brown, William Wells
1813-1884 . . . . **NCLC 2; BLC;
DAM MULT; DC 1**
See also DLB 3, 50

Browne, (Clyde) Jackson 1948(?)-. . . **CLC 21**
See also CA 120

Browning, Elizabeth Barrett
1806-1861 . . . . . **NCLC 1, 16; DA; DAB;
DAC; DAM MST, POET; PC 6; WLC**
See also CDBLB 1832-1890; DLB 32

Browning, Robert
1812-1889 . . . . **NCLC 19; DA; DAB;
DAC; DAM MST, POET; PC 2**
See also CDBLB 1832-1890; DLB 32, 163;
YABC 1

Browning, Tod 1882-1962 . . . . **CLC 16**
See also CA 141; 117

Brownson, Orestes (Augustus)
1803-1876 . . . . **NCLC 50**

Bruccoli, Matthew J(oseph) 1931- . . **CLC 34**
See also CA 9-12R; CANR 7; DLB 103

Bruce, Lenny . . . . **CLC 21**
See also Schneider, Leonard Alfred

Bruin, John
See Brutus, Dennis

Brulard, Henri
See Stendhal

Brulls, Christian
See Simenon, Georges (Jacques Christian)

Brunner, John (Kilian Houston)
1934-1995 . . . . . . **CLC 8, 10; DAM POP**
See also CA 1-4R; 149; CAAS 8; CANR 2,
37; MTCW

Bruno, Giordano 1548-1600. . . . . **LC 27**

Brutus, Dennis
1924- . . . . . **CLC 43; BLC; DAM MULT,
POET**
See also BW 2; CA 49-52; CAAS 14;
CANR 2, 27, 42; DLB 117

Bryan, C(ourtlandt) D(ixon) B(arnes)
1936- . . . . **CLC 29**
See also CA 73-76; CANR 13;
INT CANR-13

Bryan, Michael
See Moore, Brian

Bryant, William Cullen
1794-1878 . . . . . **NCLC 6, 46; DA; DAB;
DAC; DAM MST, POET**
See also CDALB 1640-1865; DLB 3, 43, 59

Bryusov, Valery Yakovlevich
1873-1924 . . . . **TCLC 10**
See also CA 107; 155

Buchan, John
1875-1940 . . . . **TCLC 41; DAB;
DAM POP**
See also CA 108; 145; DLB 34, 70, 156;
YABC 2

Buchanan, George 1506-1582 . . . . **LC 4**

Buchheim, Lothar-Guenther 1918-. . . **CLC 6**
See also CA 85-88

Buchner, (Karl) Georg
1813-1837 . . . . **NCLC 26**

Buchwald, Art(hur) 1925-. . . . . **CLC 33**
See also AITN 1; CA 5-8R; CANR 21;
MTCW; SATA 10

Buck, Pearl S(ydenstricker)
1892-1973 . . . . **CLC 7, 11, 18; DA; DAB;
DAC; DAM MST, NOV**
See also AITN 1; CA 1-4R; 41-44R;
CANR 1, 34; DLB 9, 102; MTCW;
SATA 1, 25

Buckler, Ernest
1908-1984 . . **CLC 13; DAC; DAM MST**
See also CA 11-12; 114; CAP 1; DLB 68;
SATA 47

Buckley, Vincent (Thomas)
1925-1988 . . . . **CLC 57**
See also CA 101

Buckley, William F(rank), Jr.
1925- . . . . **CLC 7, 18, 37; DAM POP**
See also AITN 1; CA 1-4R; CANR 1, 24,
53; DLB 137; DLBY 80; INT CANR-24;
MTCW

Buechner, (Carl) Frederick
1926- . . . . . . **CLC 2, 4, 6, 9; DAM NOV**
See also CA 13-16R; CANR 11, 39;
DLBY 80; INT CANR-11; MTCW

Buell, John (Edward) 1927-. . . . . **CLC 10**
See also CA 1-4R; DLB 53

Buero Vallejo, Antonio 1916- . . . **CLC 15, 46**
See also CA 106; CANR 24, 49; HW;
MTCW

Bufalino, Gesualdo 1920(?)-. . . . . **CLC 74**

Bugayev, Boris Nikolayevich 1880-1934
See Bely, Andrey
See also CA 104

Bukowski, Charles
1920-1994 . . . . **CLC 2, 5, 9, 41, 82;
DAM NOV, POET**
See also CA 17-20R; 144; CANR 40;
DLB 5, 130, 169; MTCW

Bulgakov, Mikhail (Afanas'evich)
1891-1940 . . . . **TCLC 2, 16;
DAM DRAM, NOV; SSC 18**
See also CA 105; 152

Bulgya, Alexander Alexandrovich
1901-1956 . . . . **TCLC 53**
See also Fadeyev, Alexander
See also CA 117

Bullins, Ed
1935- . . . . **CLC 1, 5, 7; BLC;
DAM DRAM, MULT; DC 6**
See also BW 2; CA 49-52; CAAS 16;
CANR 24, 46; DLB 7, 38; MTCW

Bulwer-Lytton, Edward (George Earle Lytton)
1803-1873 . . . . **NCLC 1, 45**
See also DLB 21

Bunin, Ivan Alexeyevich
1870-1953 . . . . **TCLC 6; SSC 5**
See also CA 104

Bunting, Basil
1900-1985 . . . . **CLC 10, 39, 47;
DAM POET**
See also CA 53-56; 115; CANR 7; DLB 20

Bunuel, Luis
1900-1983 . . . . **CLC 16, 80;
DAM MULT; HLC**
See also CA 101; 110; CANR 32; HW

Bunyan, John
1628-1688 . . . . . . **LC 4; DA; DAB; DAC;
DAM MST; WLC**
See also CDBLB 1660-1789; DLB 39

Burckhardt, Jacob (Christoph)
1818-1897 . . . . **NCLC 49**

Burford, Eleanor
See Hibbert, Eleanor Alice Burford

Burgess, Anthony
. **CLC 1, 2, 4, 5, 8, 10, 13, 15, 22, 40, 62,
81, 94; DAB**
See also Wilson, John (Anthony) Burgess
See also AITN 1; CDBLB 1960 to Present;
DLB 14

Burke, Edmund
1729(?)-1797 . . . . . . **LC 7, 36; DA; DAB;
DAC; DAM MST; WLC**
See also DLB 104

Burke, Kenneth (Duva)
1897-1993 . . . . **CLC 2, 24**
See also CA 5-8R; 143; CANR 39; DLB 45,
63; MTCW

Burke, Leda
See Garnett, David

Burke, Ralph
See Silverberg, Robert

Burke, Thomas 1886-1945 . . . . **TCLC 63**
See also CA 113; 155

Burney, Fanny 1752-1840 . . . . **NCLC 12, 54**
See also DLB 39

Burns, Robert 1759-1796. . . . . **PC 6**
See also CDBLB 1789-1832; DA; DAB;
DAC; DAM MST, POET; DLB 109;
WLC

Burns, Tex
See L'Amour, Louis (Dearborn)

Burnshaw, Stanley 1906-. . . . . . **CLC 3, 13, 44**
See also CA 9-12R; DLB 48

Burr, Anne 1937- . . . . **CLC 6**
See also CA 25-28R

Burroughs, Edgar Rice
    1875-1950 .... **TCLC 2, 32; DAM NOV**
    See also AAYA 11; CA 104; 132; DLB 8;
    MTCW; SATA 41

Burroughs, William S(eward)
    1914- .... **CLC 1, 2, 5, 15, 22, 42, 75;
        DA; DAB; DAC; DAM MST, NOV,
        POP; WLC**
    See also AITN 2; CA 9-12R; CANR 20, 52;
    DLB 2, 8, 16, 152; DLBY 81; MTCW

Burton, Richard F.   1821-1890 .... **NCLC 42**
    See also DLB 55

Busch, Frederick   1941- ... **CLC 7, 10, 18, 47**
    See also CA 33-36R; CAAS 1; CANR 45;
    DLB 6

Bush, Ronald   1946- .... **CLC 34**
    See also CA 136

Bustos, F(rancisco)
    See Borges, Jorge Luis

Bustos Domecq, H(onorio)
    See Bioy Casares, Adolfo; Borges, Jorge
    Luis

Butler, Octavia E(stelle)
    1947- ..... **CLC 38; DAM MULT, POP**
    See also AAYA 18; BW 2; CA 73-76;
    CANR 12, 24, 38; DLB 33; MTCW;
    SATA 84

Butler, Robert Olen (Jr.)
    1945- .... **CLC 81; DAM POP**
    See also CA 112; DLB 173; INT 112

Butler, Samuel   1612-1680 .... **LC 16**
    See also DLB 101, 126

Butler, Samuel
    1835-1902 ...... **TCLC 1, 33; DA; DAB;
        DAC; DAM MST, NOV; WLC**
    See also CA 143; CDBLB 1890-1914;
    DLB 18, 57, 174

Butler, Walter C.
    See Faust, Frederick (Schiller)

Butor, Michel (Marie Francois)
    1926- .... **CLC 1, 3, 8, 11, 15**
    See also CA 9-12R; CANR 33; DLB 83;
    MTCW

Buzo, Alexander (John)   1944- ...... **CLC 61**
    See also CA 97-100; CANR 17, 39

Buzzati, Dino   1906-1972 .... **CLC 36**
    See also CA 33-36R

Byars, Betsy (Cromer)   1928- .... **CLC 35**
    See also AAYA 19; CA 33-36R; CANR 18,
    36; CLR 1, 16; DLB 52; INT CANR-18;
    JRDA; MAICYA; MTCW; SAAS 1;
    SATA 4, 46, 80

Byatt, A(ntonia) S(usan Drabble)
    1936- ... **CLC 19, 65; DAM NOV, POP**
    See also CA 13-16R; CANR 13, 33, 50;
    DLB 14; MTCW

Byrne, David   1952- .... **CLC 26**
    See also CA 127

Byrne, John Keyes   1926-
    See Leonard, Hugh
    See also CA 102; INT 102

Byron, George Gordon (Noel)
    1788-1824 ..... **NCLC 2, 12; DA; DAB;
        DAC; DAM MST, POET; PC 16; WLC**
    See also CDBLB 1789-1832; DLB 96, 110

Byron, Robert   1905-1941 .... **TCLC 67**

C. 3. 3.
    See Wilde, Oscar (Fingal O'Flahertie Wills)

Caballero, Fernan   1796-1877 ..... **NCLC 10**

Cabell, Branch
    See Cabell, James Branch

Cabell, James Branch   1879-1958 ... **TCLC 6**
    See also CA 105; 152; DLB 9, 78

Cable, George Washington
    1844-1925 .... **TCLC 4; SSC 4**
    See also CA 104; 155; DLB 12, 74;
    DLBD 13

Cabral de Melo Neto, Joao
    1920- .... **CLC 76; DAM MULT**
    See also CA 151

Cabrera Infante, G(uillermo)
    1929- ..... **CLC 5, 25, 45; DAM MULT;
        HLC**
    See also CA 85-88; CANR 29; DLB 113;
    HW; MTCW

Cade, Toni
    See Bambara, Toni Cade

Cadmus and Harmonia
    See Buchan, John

Caedmon   fl. 658-680............ **CMLC 7**
    See also DLB 146

Caeiro, Alberto
    See Pessoa, Fernando (Antonio Nogueira)

Cage, John (Milton, Jr.)   1912- ..... **CLC 41**
    See also CA 13-16R; CANR 9;
    INT CANR-9

Cain, G.
    See Cabrera Infante, G(uillermo)

Cain, Guillermo
    See Cabrera Infante, G(uillermo)

Cain, James M(allahan)
    1892-1977 .... **CLC 3, 11, 28**
    See also AITN 1; CA 17-20R; 73-76;
    CANR 8, 34; MTCW

Caine, Mark
    See Raphael, Frederic (Michael)

Calasso, Roberto   1941- .... **CLC 81**
    See also CA 143

Calderon de la Barca, Pedro
    1600-1681 .... **LC 23; DC 3**

Caldwell, Erskine (Preston)
    1903-1987 .... **CLC 1, 8, 14, 50, 60;
        DAM NOV; SSC 19**
    See also AITN 1; CA 1-4R; 121; CAAS 1;
    CANR 2, 33; DLB 9, 86; MTCW

Caldwell, (Janet Miriam) Taylor (Holland)
    1900-1985 .... **CLC 2, 28, 39;
        DAM NOV, POP**
    See also CA 5-8R; 116; CANR 5

Calhoun, John Caldwell
    1782-1850 .... **NCLC 15**
    See also DLB 3

Calisher, Hortense
    1911- ..... **CLC 2, 4, 8, 38; DAM NOV;
        SSC 15**
    See also CA 1-4R; CANR 1, 22; DLB 2;
    INT CANR-22; MTCW

Callaghan, Morley Edward
    1903-1990 ..... **CLC 3, 14, 41, 65; DAC;
        DAM MST**
    See also CA 9-12R; 132; CANR 33;
    DLB 68; MTCW

Callimachus
    c. 305B.C.-c. 240B.C......... **CMLC 18**

Calvin, John   1509-1564 .... **LC 37**

Calvino, Italo
    1923-1985 ..... **CLC 5, 8, 11, 22, 33, 39,
        73; DAM NOV; SSC 3**
    See also CA 85-88; 116; CANR 23; MTCW

Cameron, Carey   1952- .... **CLC 59**
    See also CA 135

Cameron, Peter   1959-............. **CLC 44**
    See also CA 125; CANR 50

Campana, Dino   1885-1932........ **TCLC 20**
    See also CA 117; DLB 114

Campanella, Tommaso   1568-1639 .... **LC 32**

Campbell, John W(ood, Jr.)
    1910-1971 .... **CLC 32**
    See also CA 21-22; 29-32R; CANR 34;
    CAP 2; DLB 8; MTCW

Campbell, Joseph   1904-1987 .... **CLC 69**
    See also AAYA 3; BEST 89:2; CA 1-4R;
    124; CANR 3, 28; MTCW

Campbell, Maria   1940-....... **CLC 85; DAC**
    See also CA 102; CANR 54; NNAL

Campbell, (John) Ramsey
    1946- .... **CLC 42; SSC 19**
    See also CA 57-60; CANR 7; INT CANR-7

Campbell, (Ignatius) Roy (Dunnachie)
    1901-1957 .... **TCLC 5**
    See also CA 104; 155; DLB 20

Campbell, Thomas   1777-1844 .... **NCLC 19**
    See also DLB 93; 144

Campbell, Wilfred............... **TCLC 9**
    See also Campbell, William

Campbell, William   1858(?)-1918
    See Campbell, Wilfred
    See also CA 106; DLB 92

Campion, Jane................... **CLC 95**
    See also CA 138

Campos, Alvaro de
    See Pessoa, Fernando (Antonio Nogueira)

Camus, Albert
    1913-1960 .... **CLC 1, 2, 4, 9, 11, 14, 32,
        63, 69; DA; DAB; DAC; DAM DRAM,
        MST, NOV; DC 2; SSC 9; WLC**
    See also CA 89-92; DLB 72; MTCW

Canby, Vincent   1924-............ **CLC 13**
    See also CA 81-84

Cancale
    See Desnos, Robert

Canetti, Elias
    1905-1994 .... **CLC 3, 14, 25, 75, 86**
    See also CA 21-24R; 146; CANR 23;
    DLB 85, 124; MTCW

Canin, Ethan   1960-.............. **CLC 55**
    See also CA 131; 135

Cannon, Curt
    See Hunter, Evan

Cape, Judith
    See Page, P(atricia) K(athleen)

Cavanna, Betty .... **CLC 12**
See also Harrison, Elizabeth Cavanna
See also JRDA; MAICYA; SAAS 4;
SATA 1, 30

Cavendish, Margaret Lucas
1623-1673 .... **LC 30**
See also DLB 131

Caxton, William 1421(?)-1491(?)..... **LC 17**
See also DLB 170

Cayrol, Jean 1911- .... **CLC 11**
See also CA 89-92; DLB 83

Cela, Camilo Jose
1916- ..... **CLC 4, 13, 59; DAM MULT;**
HLC
See also BEST 90:2; CA 21-24R; CAAS 10;
CANR 21, 32; DLBY 89; HW; MTCW

Celan, Paul ...... **CLC 10, 19, 53, 82; PC 10**
See also Antschel, Paul
See also DLB 69

Celine, Louis-Ferdinand
.... **CLC 1, 3, 4, 7, 9, 15, 47**
See also Destouches, Louis-Ferdinand
See also DLB 72

Cellini, Benvenuto 1500-1571 .... **LC 7**

Cendrars, Blaise .... **CLC 18**
See also Sauser-Hall, Frederic

Cernuda (y Bidon), Luis
1902-1963 ...... **CLC 54; DAM POET**
See also CA 131; 89-92; DLB 134; HW

Cervantes (Saavedra), Miguel de
1547-1616 .... **LC 6, 23; DA; DAB;**
DAC; DAM MST, NOV; SSC 12; WLC

Cesaire, Aime (Fernand)
1913- .... **CLC 19, 32; BLC;**
DAM MULT, POET
See also BW 2; CA 65-68; CANR 24, 43;
MTCW

Chabon, Michael 1963- .... **CLC 55**
See also CA 139

Chabrol, Claude 1930- .... **CLC 16**
See also CA 110

Challans, Mary 1905-1983
See Renault, Mary
See also CA 81-84; 111; SATA 23;
SATA-Obit 36

Challis, George
See Faust, Frederick (Schiller)

Chambers, Aidan 1934- .... **CLC 35**
See also CA 25-28R; CANR 12, 31; JRDA;
MAICYA; SAAS 12; SATA 1, 69

Chambers, James 1948-
See Cliff, Jimmy
See also CA 124

Chambers, Jessie
See Lawrence, D(avid) H(erbert Richards)

Chambers, Robert W. 1865-1933... **TCLC 41**

Chandler, Raymond (Thornton)
1888-1959 .... **TCLC 1, 7; SSC 23**
See also CA 104; 129; CDALB 1929-1941;
DLBD 6; MTCW

Chang, Jung 1952- .... **CLC 71**
See also CA 142

Channing, William Ellery
1780-1842 .... **NCLC 17**
See also DLB 1, 59

Chaplin, Charles Spencer
1889-1977 .... **CLC 16**
See also Chaplin, Charlie
See also CA 81-84; 73-76

Chaplin, Charlie
See Chaplin, Charles Spencer
See also DLB 44

Chapman, George
1559(?)-1634 ..... **LC 22; DAM DRAM**
See also DLB 62, 121

Chapman, Graham 1941-1989 ...... **CLC 21**
See also Monty Python
See also CA 116; 129; CANR 35

Chapman, John Jay 1862-1933 ..... **TCLC 7**
See also CA 104

Chapman, Lee
See Bradley, Marion Zimmer

Chapman, Walker
See Silverberg, Robert

Chappell, Fred (Davis) 1936-.... **CLC 40, 78**
See also CA 5-8R; CAAS 4; CANR 8, 33;
DLB 6, 105

Char, Rene(-Emile)
1907-1988 .... **CLC 9, 11, 14, 55;**
DAM POET
See also CA 13-16R; 124; CANR 32;
MTCW

Charby, Jay
See Ellison, Harlan (Jay)

Chardin, Pierre Teilhard de
See Teilhard de Chardin, (Marie Joseph)
Pierre

Charles I 1600-1649 .... **LC 13**

Charyn, Jerome 1937- .... **CLC 5, 8, 18**
See also CA 5-8R; CAAS 1; CANR 7;
DLBY 83; MTCW

Chase, Mary (Coyle) 1907-1981 ...... **DC 1**
See also CA 77-80; 105; SATA 17;
SATA-Obit 29

Chase, Mary Ellen 1887-1973 .... **CLC 2**
See also CA 13-16; 41-44R; CAP 1;
SATA 10

Chase, Nicholas
See Hyde, Anthony

Chateaubriand, Francois Rene de
1768-1848 .... **NCLC 3**
See also DLB 119

Chatterje, Sarat Chandra 1876-1936(?)
See Chatterji, Saratchandra
See also CA 109

Chatterji, Bankim Chandra
1838-1894 .... **NCLC 19**

Chatterji, Saratchandra .... **TCLC 13**
See also Chatterje, Sarat Chandra

Chatterton, Thomas
1752-1770 .... **LC 3; DAM POET**
See also DLB 109

Chatwin, (Charles) Bruce
1940-1989 .. **CLC 28, 57, 59; DAM POP**
See also AAYA 4; BEST 90:1; CA 85-88;
127

Chaucer, Daniel
See Ford, Ford Madox

Chaucer, Geoffrey
1340(?)-1400 .... **LC 17; DA; DAB;**
DAC; DAM MST, POET
See also CDBLB Before 1660; DLB 146

Chaviaras, Strates 1935-
See Haviaras, Stratis
See also CA 105

Chayefsky, Paddy .... **CLC 23**
See also Chayefsky, Sidney
See also DLB 7, 44; DLBY 81

Chayefsky, Sidney 1923-1981
See Chayefsky, Paddy
See also CA 9-12R; 104; CANR 18;
DAM DRAM

Chedid, Andree 1920-............ **CLC 47**
See also CA 145

Cheever, John
1912-1982 ...... **CLC 3, 7, 8, 11, 15, 25,**
64; DA; DAB; DAC; DAM MST, NOV,
POP; SSC 1; WLC
See also CA 5-8R; 106; CABS 1; CANR 5,
27; CDALB 1941-1968; DLB 2, 102;
DLBY 80, 82; INT CANR-5; MTCW

Cheever, Susan 1943-.......... **CLC 18, 48**
See also CA 103; CANR 27, 51; DLBY 82;
INT CANR-27

Chekhonte, Antosha
See Chekhov, Anton (Pavlovich)

Chekhov, Anton (Pavlovich)
1860-1904 ..... **TCLC 3, 10, 31, 55; DA;**
DAB; DAC; DAM DRAM, MST; SSC 2;
WLC
See also CA 104; 124; SATA 90

Chernyshevsky, Nikolay Gavrilovich
1828-1889 .... **NCLC 1**

Cherry, Carolyn Janice 1942-
See Cherryh, C. J.
See also CA 65-68; CANR 10

Cherryh, C. J. .... **CLC 35**
See also Cherry, Carolyn Janice
See also DLBY 80

Chesnutt, Charles W(addell)
1858-1932 .... **TCLC 5, 39; BLC;**
DAM MULT; SSC 7
See also BW 1; CA 106; 125; DLB 12, 50,
78; MTCW

Chester, Alfred 1929(?)-1971....... **CLC 49**
See also CA 33-36R; DLB 130

Chesterton, G(ilbert) K(eith)
1874-1936 .... **TCLC 1, 6, 64;**
DAM NOV, POET; SSC 1
See also CA 104; 132; CDBLB 1914-1945;
DLB 10, 19, 34, 70, 98, 149; MTCW;
SATA 27

Chiang Pin-chin 1904-1986
See Ding Ling
See also CA 118

Ch'ien Chung-shu 1910-........... **CLC 22**
See also CA 130; MTCW

Child, L. Maria
See Child, Lydia Maria

Child, Lydia Maria 1802-1880 .... **NCLC 6**
See also DLB 1, 74; SATA 67

Child, Mrs.
See Child, Lydia Maria

Child, Philip 1898-1978 . . . . **CLC 19, 68**
See also CA 13-14; CAP 1; SATA 47

Childers, (Robert) Erskine
1870-1922 . . . . **TCLC 65**
See also CA 113; 153; DLB 70

Childress, Alice
1920-1994 . . . . **CLC 12, 15, 86, 96; BLC;**
DAM DRAM, MULT, NOV; DC 4
See also AAYA 8; BW 2; CA 45-48; 146;
CANR 3, 27, 50; CLR 14; DLB 7, 38;
JRDA; MAICYA; MTCW; SATA 7, 48,
81

Chislett, (Margaret) Anne 1943- . . . . **CLC 34**
See also CA 151

Chitty, Thomas Willes 1926- . . . . **CLC 11**
See also Hinde, Thomas
See also CA 5-8R

Chivers, Thomas Holley
1809-1858 . . . . **NCLC 49**
See also DLB 3

Chomette, Rene Lucien 1898-1981
See Clair, Rene
See also CA 103

Chopin, Kate
. . . . **TCLC 5, 14; DA; DAB; SSC 8**
See also Chopin, Katherine
See also CDALB 1865-1917; DLB 12, 78

Chopin, Katherine 1851-1904
See Chopin, Kate
See also CA 104; 122; DAC; DAM MST,
NOV

Chretien de Troyes
c. 12th cent. - . . . . **CMLC 10**

Christie
See Ichikawa, Kon

Christie, Agatha (Mary Clarissa)
1890-1976 . . . . . . **CLC 1, 6, 8, 12, 39, 48;**
DAB; DAC; DAM NOV
See also AAYA 9; AITN 1, 2; CA 17-20R;
61-64; CANR 10, 37; CDBLB 1914-1945;
DLB 13, 77; MTCW; SATA 36

Christie, (Ann) Philippa
See Pearce, Philippa
See also CA 5-8R; CANR 4

Christine de Pizan 1365(?)-1431(?) . . . . **LC 9**

Chubb, Elmer
See Masters, Edgar Lee

Chulkov, Mikhail Dmitrievich
1743-1792 . . . . **LC 2**
See also DLB 150

Churchill, Caryl 1938- . . . **CLC 31, 55; DC 5**
See also CA 102; CANR 22, 46; DLB 13;
MTCW

Churchill, Charles 1731-1764 . . . . **LC 3**
See also DLB 109

Chute, Carolyn 1947- . . . . **CLC 39**
See also CA 123

Ciardi, John (Anthony)
1916-1986 . . . . **CLC 10, 40, 44;**
DAM POET
See also CA 5-8R; 118; CAAS 2; CANR 5,
33; CLR 19; DLB 5; DLBY 86;
INT CANR-5; MAICYA; MTCW;
SATA 1, 65; SATA-Obit 46

Cicero, Marcus Tullius
106B.C.-43B.C. . . . . **CMLC 3**

Cimino, Michael 1943- . . . . **CLC 16**
See also CA 105

Cioran, E(mil) M. 1911-1995 . . . . . . **CLC 64**
See also CA 25-28R; 149

Cisneros, Sandra
1954- . . . . . **CLC 69; DAM MULT; HLC**
See also AAYA 9; CA 131; DLB 122, 152;
HW

Cixous, Helene 1937- . . . . **CLC 92**
See also CA 126; CANR 55; DLB 83;
MTCW

Clair, Rene . . . . **CLC 20**
See also Chomette, Rene Lucien

Clampitt, Amy 1920-1994 . . . **CLC 32; PC 17**
See also CA 110; 146; CANR 29; DLB 105

Clancy, Thomas L., Jr. 1947-
See Clancy, Tom
See also CA 125; 131; INT 131; MTCW

Clancy, Tom . . . . . **CLC 45; DAM NOV, POP**
See also Clancy, Thomas L., Jr.
See also AAYA 9; BEST 89:1, 90:1

Clare, John
1793-1864 . . . . **NCLC 9; DAB;**
DAM POET
See also DLB 55, 96

Clarin
See Alas (y Urena), Leopoldo (Enrique
Garcia)

Clark, Al C.
See Goines, Donald

Clark, (Robert) Brian 1932- . . . . **CLC 29**
See also CA 41-44R

Clark, Curt
See Westlake, Donald E(dwin)

Clark, Eleanor 1913-1996 . . . . **CLC 5, 19**
See also CA 9-12R; 151; CANR 41; DLB 6

Clark, J. P.
See Clark, John Pepper
See also DLB 117

Clark, John Pepper
1935- . . . . **CLC 38; BLC; DAM DRAM,**
MULT; DC 5
See also Clark, J. P.
See also BW 1; CA 65-68; CANR 16

Clark, M. R.
See Clark, Mavis Thorpe

Clark, Mavis Thorpe 1909- . . . . **CLC 12**
See also CA 57-60; CANR 8, 37; CLR 30;
MAICYA; SAAS 5; SATA 8, 74

Clark, Walter Van Tilburg
1909-1971 . . . . **CLC 28**
See also CA 9-12R; 33-36R; DLB 9;
SATA 8

Clarke, Arthur C(harles)
1917- . . . . **CLC 1, 4, 13, 18, 35;**
DAM POP; SSC 3
See also AAYA 4; CA 1-4R; CANR 2, 28,
55; JRDA; MAICYA; MTCW; SATA 13,
70

Clarke, Austin
1896-1974 . . . . . . **CLC 6, 9; DAM POET**
See also CA 29-32; 49-52; CAP 2; DLB 10,
20

Clarke, Austin C(hesterfield)
1934- . . . . **CLC 8, 53; BLC; DAC;**
DAM MULT
See also BW 1; CA 25-28R; CAAS 16;
CANR 14, 32; DLB 53, 125

Clarke, Gillian 1937- . . . . **CLC 61**
See also CA 106; DLB 40

Clarke, Marcus (Andrew Hislop)
1846-1881 . . . . **NCLC 19**

Clarke, Shirley 1925- . . . . **CLC 16**

Clash, The
See Headon, (Nicky) Topper; Jones, Mick;
Simonon, Paul; Strummer, Joe

Claudel, Paul (Louis Charles Marie)
1868-1955 . . . . **TCLC 2, 10**
See also CA 104

Clavell, James (duMaresq)
1925-1994 . . . . **CLC 6, 25, 87;**
DAM NOV, POP
See also CA 25-28R; 146; CANR 26, 48;
MTCW

Cleaver, (Leroy) Eldridge
1935- . . . . . **CLC 30; BLC; DAM MULT**
See also BW 1; CA 21-24R; CANR 16

Cleese, John (Marwood) 1939- . . . . . **CLC 21**
See also Monty Python
See also CA 112; 116; CANR 35; MTCW

Cleishbotham, Jebediah
See Scott, Walter

Cleland, John 1710-1789 . . . . **LC 2**
See also DLB 39

Clemens, Samuel Langhorne 1835-1910
See Twain, Mark
See also CA 104; 135; CDALB 1865-1917;
DA; DAB; DAC; DAM MST, NOV;
DLB 11, 12, 23, 64, 74; JRDA;
MAICYA; YABC 2

Cleophil
See Congreve, William

Clerihew, E.
See Bentley, E(dmund) C(lerihew)

Clerk, N. W.
See Lewis, C(live) S(taples)

Cliff, Jimmy . . . . **CLC 21**
See also Chambers, James

Clifton, (Thelma) Lucille
1936- . . . . **CLC 19, 66; BLC;**
DAM MULT, POET; PC 17
See also BW 2; CA 49-52; CANR 2, 24, 42;
CLR 5; DLB 5, 41; MAICYA; MTCW;
SATA 20, 69

Clinton, Dirk
See Silverberg, Robert

Clough, Arthur Hugh 1819-1861 . . **NCLC 27**
See also DLB 32

Clutha, Janet Paterson Frame 1924-
See Frame, Janet
See also CA 1-4R; CANR 2, 36; MTCW

Clyne, Terence
See Blatty, William Peter

Cobalt, Martin
See Mayne, William (James Carter)

Cobbett, William 1763-1835 . . . . . **NCLC 49**
See also DLB 43, 107, 158

Coover, Robert (Lowell)
        1932- .... **CLC 3, 7, 15, 32, 46, 87;**
                                                 DAM NOV; SSC 15
        See also CA 45-48; CANR 3, 37; DLB 2;
        DLBY 81; MTCW

Copeland, Stewart (Armstrong)
        1952- .... **CLC 26**

Coppard, A(lfred) E(dgar)
        1878-1957 .... **TCLC 5; SSC 21**
        See also CA 114; DLB 162; YABC 1

Coppee, Francois   1842-1908 ...... **TCLC 25**

Coppola, Francis Ford   1939-....... **CLC 16**
        See also CA 77-80; CANR 40; DLB 44

Corbiere, Tristan   1845-1875 ..... **NCLC 43**

Corcoran, Barbara   1911-.......... **CLC 17**
        See also AAYA 14; CA 21-24R; CAAS 2;
        CANR 11, 28, 48; DLB 52; JRDA;
        SAAS 20; SATA 3, 77

Cordelier, Maurice
        See Giraudoux, (Hippolyte) Jean

Corelli, Marie   1855-1924........ **TCLC 51**
        See also Mackay, Mary
        See also DLB 34, 156

Corman, Cid...................... **CLC 9**
        See also Corman, Sidney
        See also CAAS 2; DLB 5

Corman, Sidney   1924-
        See Corman, Cid
        See also CA 85-88; CANR 44; DAM POET

Cormier, Robert (Edmund)
        1925- .... **CLC 12, 30; DA; DAB; DAC;**
                                           DAM MST, NOV
        See also AAYA 3, 19; CA 1-4R; CANR 5,
        23; CDALB 1968-1988; CLR 12; DLB 52;
        INT CANR-23; JRDA; MAICYA;
        MTCW; SATA 10, 45, 83

Corn, Alfred (DeWitt III)   1943-.... **CLC 33**
        See also CA 104; CAAS 25; CANR 44;
        DLB 120; DLBY 80

Corneille, Pierre
        1606-1684 .... **LC 28; DAB; DAM MST**

Cornwell, David (John Moore)
        1931- .... **CLC 9, 15; DAM POP**
        See also le Carre, John
        See also CA 5-8R; CANR 13, 33; MTCW

Corso, (Nunzio) Gregory   1930-... **CLC 1, 11**
        See also CA 5-8R; CANR 41; DLB 5, 16;
        MTCW

Cortazar, Julio
        1914-1984 ..... **CLC 2, 3, 5, 10, 13, 15,**
               33, 34, 92; DAM MULT, NOV; HLC;
                                                 SSC 7
        See also CA 21-24R; CANR 12, 32;
        DLB 113; HW; MTCW

CORTES, HERNAN   1484-1547..... **LC 31**

Corwin, Cecil
        See Kornbluth, C(yril) M.

Cosic, Dobrica   1921- .... **CLC 14**
        See also CA 122; 138

Costain, Thomas B(ertram)
        1885-1965 .... **CLC 30**
        See also CA 5-8R; 25-28R; DLB 9

Costantini, Humberto
        1924(?)-1987 .... **CLC 49**
        See also CA 131; 122; HW

Costello, Elvis   1955-............. **CLC 21**

Cotter, Joseph Seamon Sr.
        1861-1949 .... **TCLC 28; BLC;**
                                                 DAM MULT
        See also BW 1; CA 124; DLB 50

Couch, Arthur Thomas Quiller
        See Quiller-Couch, Arthur Thomas

Coulton, James
        See Hansen, Joseph

Couperus, Louis (Marie Anne)
        1863-1923 .... **TCLC 15**
        See also CA 115

Coupland, Douglas
        1961- .... **CLC 85; DAC; DAM POP**
        See also CA 142

Court, Wesli
        See Turco, Lewis (Putnam)

Courtenay, Bryce   1933-........... **CLC 59**
        See also CA 138

Courtney, Robert
        See Ellison, Harlan (Jay)

Cousteau, Jacques-Yves   1910-...... **CLC 30**
        See also CA 65-68; CANR 15; MTCW;
        SATA 38

Coward, Noel (Peirce)
        1899-1973 .... **CLC 1, 9, 29, 51;**
                                                 DAM DRAM
        See also AITN 1; CA 17-18; 41-44R;
        CANR 35; CAP 2; CDBLB 1914-1945;
        DLB 10; MTCW

Cowley, Malcolm   1898-1989 .... **CLC 39**
        See also CA 5-8R; 128; CANR 3, 55;
        DLB 4, 48; DLBY 81, 89; MTCW

Cowper, William
        1731-1800 ...... **NCLC 8; DAM POET**
        See also DLB 104, 109

Cox, William Trevor
        1928- .... **CLC 9, 14, 71; DAM NOV**
        See also Trevor, William
        See also CA 9-12R; CANR 4, 37, 55;
        DLB 14; INT CANR-37; MTCW

Coyne, P. J.
        See Masters, Hilary

Cozzens, James Gould
        1903-1978 .... **CLC 1, 4, 11, 92**
        See also CA 9-12R; 81-84; CANR 19;
        CDALB 1941-1968; DLB 9; DLBD 2;
        DLBY 84; MTCW

Crabbe, George   1754-1832....... **NCLC 26**
        See also DLB 93

Craddock, Charles Egbert
        See Murfree, Mary Noailles

Craig, A. A.
        See Anderson, Poul (William)

Craik, Dinah Maria (Mulock)
        1826-1887 .... **NCLC 38**
        See also DLB 35, 163; MAICYA; SATA 34

Cram, Ralph Adams   1863-1942.... **TCLC 45**

Crane, (Harold) Hart
        1899-1932 ....**TCLC 2, 5; DA; DAB;**
                    DAC; DAM MST, POET; PC 3; WLC
        See also CA 104; 127; CDALB 1917-1929;
        DLB 4, 48; MTCW

Crane, R(onald) S(almon)
        1886-1967 .... **CLC 27**
        See also CA 85-88; DLB 63

Crane, Stephen (Townley)
        1871-1900 ...... **TCLC 11, 17, 32; DA;**
               DAB; DAC; DAM MST, NOV, POET;
                                                 SSC 7; WLC
        See also CA 109; 140; CDALB 1865-1917;
        DLB 12, 54, 78; YABC 2

Crase, Douglas   1944-............. **CLC 58**
        See also CA 106

Crashaw, Richard   1612(?)-1649...... **LC 24**
        See also DLB 126

Craven, Margaret
        1901-1980 .... **CLC 17; DAC**
        See also CA 103

Crawford, F(rancis) Marion
        1854-1909 .... **TCLC 10**
        See also CA 107; DLB 71

Crawford, Isabella Valancy
        1850-1887 .... **NCLC 12**
        See also DLB 92

Crayon, Geoffrey
        See Irving, Washington

Creasey, John   1908-1973.......... **CLC 11**
        See also CA 5-8R; 41-44R; CANR 8;
        DLB 77; MTCW

Crebillon, Claude Prosper Jolyot de (fils)
        1707-1777 .... **LC 28**

Credo
        See Creasey, John

Creeley, Robert (White)
        1926- ..... **CLC 1, 2, 4, 8, 11, 15, 36, 78;**
                                                 DAM POET
        See also CA 1-4R; CAAS 10; CANR 23, 43;
        DLB 5, 16, 169; MTCW

Crews, Harry (Eugene)
        1935- .... **CLC 6, 23, 49**
        See also AITN 1; CA 25-28R; CANR 20;
        DLB 6, 143; MTCW

Crichton, (John) Michael
        1942- .... **CLC 2, 6, 54, 90; DAM NOV,**
                                                 POP
        See also AAYA 10; AITN 2; CA 25-28R;
        CANR 13, 40, 54; DLBY 81;
        INT CANR-13; JRDA; MTCW; SATA 9,
        88

Crispin, Edmund .... **CLC 22**
        See also Montgomery, (Robert) Bruce
        See also DLB 87

Cristofer, Michael
        1945(?)- .... **CLC 28; DAM DRAM**
        See also CA 110; 152; DLB 7

Croce, Benedetto   1866-1952 ...... **TCLC 37**
        See also CA 120; 155

Crockett, David   1786-1836 .... **NCLC 8**
        See also DLB 3, 11

Crockett, Davy
        See Crockett, David

Crofts, Freeman Wills
        1879-1957 .... **TCLC 55**
        See also CA 115; DLB 77

Croker, John Wilson   1780-1857 .. **NCLC 10**
        See also DLB 110

Davies, Rhys 1903-1978.......... **CLC 23**
See also CA 9-12R; 81-84; CANR 4;
DLB 139

Davies, (William) Robertson
1913-1995 ..... **CLC 2, 7, 13, 25, 42, 75,**
91; DA; DAB; DAC; DAM MST, NOV,
POP; WLC
See also BEST 89:2; CA 33-36R; 150;
CANR 17, 42; DLB 68; INT CANR-17;
MTCW

Davies, W(illiam) H(enry)
1871-1940 .... **TCLC 5**
See also CA 104; DLB 19, 174

Davies, Walter C.
See Kornbluth, C(yril) M.

Davis, Angela (Yvonne)
1944- .... **CLC 77; DAM MULT**
See also BW 2; CA 57-60; CANR 10

Davis, B. Lynch
See Bioy Casares, Adolfo; Borges, Jorge
Luis

Davis, Gordon
See Hunt, E(verette) Howard, (Jr.)

Davis, Harold Lenoir 1896-1960.... **CLC 49**
See also CA 89-92; DLB 9

Davis, Rebecca (Blaine) Harding
1831-1910 .... **TCLC 6**
See also CA 104; DLB 74

Davis, Richard Harding
1864-1916 .... **TCLC 24**
See also CA 114; DLB 12, 23, 78, 79;
DLBD 13

Davison, Frank Dalby 1893-1970 ... **CLC 15**
See also CA 116

Davison, Lawrence H.
See Lawrence, D(avid) H(erbert Richards)

Davison, Peter (Hubert) 1928- ..... **CLC 28**
See also CA 9-12R; CAAS 4; CANR 3, 43;
DLB 5

Davys, Mary 1674-1732............. **LC 1**
See also DLB 39

Dawson, Fielding 1930- .... **CLC 6**
See also CA 85-88; DLB 130

Dawson, Peter
See Faust, Frederick (Schiller)

Day, Clarence (Shepard, Jr.)
1874-1935 .... **TCLC 25**
See also CA 108; DLB 11

Day, Thomas 1748-1789............. **LC 1**
See also DLB 39; YABC 1

Day Lewis, C(ecil)
1904-1972 .... **CLC 1, 6, 10;**
DAM POET; PC 11
See also Blake, Nicholas
See also CA 13-16; 33-36R; CANR 34;
CAP 1; DLB 15, 20; MTCW

Dazai, Osamu .... **TCLC 11**
See also Tsushima, Shuji

de Andrade, Carlos Drummond
See Drummond de Andrade, Carlos

Deane, Norman
See Creasey, John

de Beauvoir, Simone (Lucie Ernestine Marie
Bertrand)
See Beauvoir, Simone (Lucie Ernestine
Marie Bertrand) de

de Brissac, Malcolm
See Dickinson, Peter (Malcolm)

de Chardin, Pierre Teilhard
See Teilhard de Chardin, (Marie Joseph)
Pierre

Dee, John 1527-1608 .... **LC 20**

Deer, Sandra 1940-............... **CLC 45**

De Ferrari, Gabriella 1941-........ **CLC 65**
See also CA 146

Defoe, Daniel
1660(?)-1731 .... **LC 1; DA; DAB; DAC;**
DAM MST, NOV; WLC
See also CDBLB 1660-1789; DLB 39, 95,
101; JRDA; MAICYA; SATA 22

de Gourmont, Remy(-Marie-Charles)
See Gourmont, Remy (-Marie-Charles) de

de Hartog, Jan 1914-............. **CLC 19**
See also CA 1-4R; CANR 1

de Hostos, E. M.
See Hostos (y Bonilla), Eugenio Maria de

de Hostos, Eugenio M.
See Hostos (y Bonilla), Eugenio Maria de

Deighton, Len .... **CLC 4, 7, 22, 46**
See also Deighton, Leonard Cyril
See also AAYA 6; BEST 89:2;
CDBLB 1960 to Present; DLB 87

Deighton, Leonard Cyril 1929-
See Deighton, Len
See also CA 9-12R; CANR 19, 33;
DAM NOV, POP; MTCW

Dekker, Thomas
1572(?)-1632 ..... **LC 22; DAM DRAM**
See also CDBLB Before 1660; DLB 62, 172

Delafield, E. M. 1890-1943 ...... **TCLC 61**
See also Dashwood, Edmee Elizabeth
Monica de la Pasture
See also DLB 34

de la Mare, Walter (John)
1873-1956 .... **TCLC 4, 53; DAB; DAC;**
DAM MST, POET; SSC 14; WLC
See also CDBLB 1914-1945; CLR 23;
DLB 162; SATA 16

Delaney, Franey
See O'Hara, John (Henry)

Delaney, Shelagh
1939- .... **CLC 29; DAM DRAM**
See also CA 17-20R; CANR 30;
CDBLB 1960 to Present; DLB 13;
MTCW

Delany, Mary (Granville Pendarves)
1700-1788 .... **LC 12**

Delany, Samuel R(ay, Jr.)
1942- .... **CLC 8, 14, 38; BLC;**
DAM MULT
See also BW 2; CA 81-84; CANR 27, 43;
DLB 8, 33; MTCW

De La Ramee, (Marie) Louise 1839-1908
See Ouida
See also SATA 20

de la Roche, Mazo 1879-1961...... **CLC 14**
See also CA 85-88; CANR 30; DLB 68;
SATA 64

Delbanco, Nicholas (Franklin)
1942- .... **CLC 6, 13**
See also CA 17-20R; CAAS 2; CANR 29,
55; DLB 6

del Castillo, Michel 1933- .... **CLC 38**
See also CA 109

Deledda, Grazia (Cosima)
1875(?)-1936 .... **TCLC 23**
See also CA 123

Delibes, Miguel .... **CLC 8, 18**
See also Delibes Setien, Miguel

Delibes Setien, Miguel 1920-
See Delibes, Miguel
See also CA 45-48; CANR 1, 32; HW;
MTCW

DeLillo, Don
1936- ..... **CLC 8, 10, 13, 27, 39, 54, 76;**
DAM NOV, POP
See also BEST 89:1; CA 81-84; CANR 21;
DLB 6, 173; MTCW

de Lisser, H. G.
See De Lisser, H(erbert) G(eorge)
See also DLB 117

De Lisser, H(erbert) G(eorge)
1878-1944 .... **TCLC 12**
See also de Lisser, H. G.
See also BW 2; CA 109; 152

Deloria, Vine (Victor), Jr.
1933- .... **CLC 21; DAM MULT**
See also CA 53-56; CANR 5, 20, 48;
MTCW; NNAL; SATA 21

Del Vecchio, John M(ichael)
1947- .... **CLC 29**
See also CA 110; DLBD 9

de Man, Paul (Adolph Michel)
1919-1983 .... **CLC 55**
See also CA 128; 111; DLB 67; MTCW

De Marinis, Rick 1934-........... **CLC 54**
See also CA 57-60; CAAS 24; CANR 9, 25,
50

Dembry, R. Emmet
See Murfree, Mary Noailles

Demby, William
1922- ..... **CLC 53; BLC; DAM MULT**
See also BW 1; CA 81-84; DLB 33

Demijohn, Thom
See Disch, Thomas M(ichael)

de Montherlant, Henry (Milon)
See Montherlant, Henry (Milon) de

Demosthenes 384B.C.-322B.C. .... **CMLC 13**

de Natale, Francine
See Malzberg, Barry N(athaniel)

Denby, Edwin (Orr) 1903-1983 ..... **CLC 48**
See also CA 138; 110

Denis, Julio
See Cortazar, Julio

Denmark, Harrison
See Zelazny, Roger (Joseph)

Dennis, John 1658-1734............ **LC 11**
See also DLB 101

Dennis, Nigel (Forbes) 1912-1989 .... **CLC 8**
See also CA 25-28R; 129; DLB 13, 15;
MTCW

De Palma, Brian (Russell) 1940- .... **CLC 20**
See also CA 109

De Quincey, Thomas 1785-1859 ... **NCLC 4**
See also CDBLB 1789-1832; DLB 110; 144

Deren, Eleanora 1908(?)-1961
See Deren, Maya
See also CA 111

Deren, Maya .... **CLC 16**
See also Deren, Eleanora

Derleth, August (William)
1909-1971 .... **CLC 31**
See also CA 1-4R; 29-32R; CANR 4;
DLB 9; SATA 5

Der Nister 1884-1950 .... **TCLC 56**

de Routisie, Albert
See Aragon, Louis

Derrida, Jacques 1930- .... **CLC 24, 87**
See also CA 124; 127

Derry Down Derry
See Lear, Edward

Dersonnes, Jacques
See Simenon, Georges (Jacques Christian)

Desai, Anita
1937- .... **CLC 19, 37, 97; DAB;
DAM NOV**
See also CA 81-84; CANR 33, 53; MTCW;
SATA 63

de Saint-Luc, Jean
See Glassco, John

de Saint Roman, Arnaud
See Aragon, Louis

Descartes, Rene 1596-1650 ...... **LC 20, 35**

De Sica, Vittorio 1901(?)-1974 ..... **CLC 20**
See also CA 117

Desnos, Robert 1900-1945 .... **TCLC 22**
See also CA 121; 151

Destouches, Louis-Ferdinand
1894-1961 .... **CLC 9, 15**
See also Celine, Louis-Ferdinand
See also CA 85-88; CANR 28; MTCW

de Tolignac, Gaston
See Griffith, D(avid Lewelyn) W(ark)

Deutsch, Babette 1895-1982 .... **CLC 18**
See also CA 1-4R; 108; CANR 4; DLB 45;
SATA 1; SATA-Obit 33

Devenant, William 1606-1649 .... **LC 13**

Devkota, Laxmiprasad
1909-1959 .... **TCLC 23**
See also CA 123

De Voto, Bernard (Augustine)
1897-1955 .... **TCLC 29**
See also CA 113; DLB 9

De Vries, Peter
1910-1993 .... **CLC 1, 2, 3, 7, 10, 28, 46;
DAM NOV**
See also CA 17-20R; 142; CANR 41;
DLB 6; DLBY 82; MTCW

Dexter, John
See Bradley, Marion Zimmer

Dexter, Martin
See Faust, Frederick (Schiller)

Dexter, Pete
1943- .... **CLC 34, 55; DAM POP**
See also BEST 89:2; CA 127; 131; INT 131;
MTCW

Diamano, Silmang
See Senghor, Leopold Sedar

Diamond, Neil 1941- .... **CLC 30**
See also CA 108

Diaz del Castillo, Bernal 1496-1584 .. **LC 31**

di Bassetto, Corno
See Shaw, George Bernard

Dick, Philip K(indred)
1928-1982 .... **CLC 10, 30, 72;
DAM NOV, POP**
See also CA 49-52; 106; CANR 2, 16;
DLB 8; MTCW

Dickens, Charles (John Huffam)
1812-1870 ...... **NCLC 3, 8, 18, 26, 37,
50; DA; DAB; DAC; DAM MST, NOV;
SSC 17; WLC**
See also CDBLB 1832-1890; DLB 21, 55,
70, 159, 166; JRDA; MAICYA; SATA 15

Dickey, James (Lafayette)
1923- .... **CLC 1, 2, 4, 7, 10, 15, 47;
DAM NOV, POET, POP**
See also AITN 1, 2; CA 9-12R; CABS 2;
CANR 10, 48; CDALB 1968-1988;
DLB 5; DLBD 7; DLBY 82, 93;
INT CANR-10; MTCW

Dickey, William 1928-1994 ...... **CLC 3, 28**
See also CA 9-12R; 145; CANR 24; DLB 5

Dickinson, Charles 1951- .... **CLC 49**
See also CA 128

Dickinson, Emily (Elizabeth)
1830-1886 .... **NCLC 21; DA; DAB;
DAC; DAM MST, POET; PC 1; WLC**
See also CDALB 1865-1917; DLB 1;
SATA 29

Dickinson, Peter (Malcolm)
1927- .... **CLC 12, 35**
See also AAYA 9; CA 41-44R; CANR 31;
CLR 29; DLB 87, 161; JRDA; MAICYA;
SATA 5, 62

Dickson, Carr
See Carr, John Dickson

Dickson, Carter
See Carr, John Dickson

Diderot, Denis 1713-1784 .... **LC 26**

Didion, Joan
1934- .. **CLC 1, 3, 8, 14, 32; DAM NOV**
See also AITN 1; CA 5-8R; CANR 14, 52;
CDALB 1968-1988; DLB 2, 173;
DLBY 81, 86; MTCW

Dietrich, Robert
See Hunt, E(verette) Howard, (Jr.)

Dillard, Annie
1945- .... **CLC 9, 60; DAM NOV**
See also AAYA 6; CA 49-52; CANR 3, 43;
DLBY 80; MTCW; SATA 10

Dillard, R(ichard) H(enry) W(ilde)
1937- .... **CLC 5**
See also CA 21-24R; CAAS 7; CANR 10;
DLB 5

Dillon, Eilis 1920-1994 .... **CLC 17**
See also CA 9-12R; 147; CAAS 3; CANR 4,
38; CLR 26; MAICYA; SATA 2, 74;
SATA-Obit 83

Dimont, Penelope
See Mortimer, Penelope (Ruth)

Dinesen, Isak .... **CLC 10, 29, 95; SSC 7**
See also Blixen, Karen (Christentze
Dinesen)

Ding Ling .... **CLC 68**
See also Chiang Pin-chin

Disch, Thomas M(ichael) 1940- ... **CLC 7, 36**
See also AAYA 17; CA 21-24R; CAAS 4;
CANR 17, 36, 54; CLR 18; DLB 8;
MAICYA; MTCW; SAAS 15; SATA 54

Disch, Tom
See Disch, Thomas M(ichael)

d'Isly, Georges
See Simenon, Georges (Jacques Christian)

Disraeli, Benjamin 1804-1881 .. **NCLC 2, 39**
See also DLB 21, 55

Ditcum, Steve
See Crumb, R(obert)

Dixon, Paige
See Corcoran, Barbara

Dixon, Stephen 1936- ..... **CLC 52; SSC 16**
See also CA 89-92; CANR 17, 40, 54;
DLB 130

Dobell, Sydney Thompson
1824-1874 .... **NCLC 43**
See also DLB 32

Doblin, Alfred .... **TCLC 13**
See also Doeblin, Alfred

Dobrolyubov, Nikolai Alexandrovich
1836-1861 .... **NCLC 5**

Dobyns, Stephen 1941- .... **CLC 37**
See also CA 45-48; CANR 2, 18

Doctorow, E(dgar) L(aurence)
1931- ..... **CLC 6, 11, 15, 18, 37, 44, 65;
DAM NOV, POP**
See also AITN 2; BEST 89:3; CA 45-48;
CANR 2, 33, 51; CDALB 1968-1988;
DLB 2, 28, 173; DLBY 80; MTCW

Dodgson, Charles Lutwidge 1832-1898
See Carroll, Lewis
See also CLR 2; DA; DAB; DAC;
DAM MST, NOV, POET; MAICYA;
YABC 2

Dodson, Owen (Vincent)
1914-1983 .... **CLC 79; BLC;
DAM MULT**
See also BW 1; CA 65-68; 110; CANR 24;
DLB 76

Doeblin, Alfred 1878-1957 .... **TCLC 13**
See also Doblin, Alfred
See also CA 110; 141; DLB 66

Doerr, Harriet 1910- .... **CLC 34**
See also CA 117; 122; CANR 47; INT 122

Domecq, H(onorio) Bustos
See Bioy Casares, Adolfo; Borges, Jorge
Luis

Domini, Rey
See Lorde, Audre (Geraldine)

Dominique
See Proust, (Valentin-Louis-George-Eugene-) Marcel

Don, A
See Stephen, Leslie

Donaldson, Stephen R. 1947- .... **CLC 46; DAM POP**
See also CA 89-92; CANR 13, 55; INT CANR-13

Donleavy, J(ames) P(atrick) 1926- .... **CLC 1, 4, 6, 10, 45**
See also AITN 2; CA 9-12R; CANR 24, 49; DLB 6, 173; INT CANR-24; MTCW

Donne, John 1572-1631 .... **LC 10, 24; DA; DAB; DAC; DAM MST, POET; PC 1**
See also CDBLB Before 1660; DLB 121, 151

Donnell, David 1939(?)- .... **CLC 34**

Donoghue, P. S.
See Hunt, E(verette) Howard, (Jr.)

Donoso (Yanez), Jose 1924-1996 .... **CLC 4, 8, 11, 32; DAM MULT; HLC**
See also CA 81-84; 155; CANR 32; DLB 113; HW; MTCW

Donovan, John 1928-1992 .... **CLC 35**
See also CA 97-100; 137; CLR 3; MAICYA; SATA 72; SATA-Brief 29

Don Roberto
See Cunninghame Graham, R(obert) B(ontine)

Doolittle, Hilda 1886-1961 ..... **CLC 3, 8, 14, 31, 34, 73; DA; DAC; DAM MST, POET; PC 5; WLC**
See also H. D.
See also CA 97-100; CANR 35; DLB 4, 45; MTCW

Dorfman, Ariel 1942- .... **CLC 48, 77; DAM MULT; HLC**
See also CA 124; 130; HW; INT 130

Dorn, Edward (Merton) 1929-... **CLC 10, 18**
See also CA 93-96; CANR 42; DLB 5; INT 93-96

Dorsan, Luc
See Simenon, Georges (Jacques Christian)

Dorsange, Jean
See Simenon, Georges (Jacques Christian)

Dos Passos, John (Roderigo) 1896-1970 ...... **CLC 1, 4, 8, 11, 15, 25, 34, 82; DA; DAB; DAC; DAM MST, NOV; WLC**
See also CA 1-4R; 29-32R; CANR 3; CDALB 1929-1941; DLB 4, 9; DLBD 1; MTCW

Dossage, Jean
See Simenon, Georges (Jacques Christian)

Dostoevsky, Fedor Mikhailovich 1821-1881 ...... **NCLC 2, 7, 21, 33, 43; DA; DAB; DAC; DAM MST, NOV; SSC 2; WLC**

Doughty, Charles M(ontagu) 1843-1926 .... **TCLC 27**
See also CA 115; DLB 19, 57, 174

Douglas, Ellen .... **CLC 73**
See also Haxton, Josephine Ayres; Williamson, Ellen Douglas

Douglas, Gavin 1475(?)-1522 .... **LC 20**

Douglas, Keith 1920-1944 .... **TCLC 40**
See also DLB 27

Douglas, Leonard
See Bradbury, Ray (Douglas)

Douglas, Michael
See Crichton, (John) Michael

Douglas, Norman 1868-1952 ...... **TCLC 68**

Douglass, Frederick 1817(?)-1895 .... **NCLC 7, 55; BLC; DA; DAC; DAM MST, MULT; WLC**
See also CDALB 1640-1865; DLB 1, 43, 50, 79; SATA 29

Dourado, (Waldomiro Freitas) Autran 1926- .... **CLC 23, 60**
See also CA 25-28R; CANR 34

Dourado, Waldomiro Autran
See Dourado, (Waldomiro Freitas) Autran

Dove, Rita (Frances) 1952- .... **CLC 50, 81; DAM MULT, POET; PC 6**
See also BW 2; CA 109; CAAS 19; CANR 27, 42; DLB 120

Dowell, Coleman 1925-1985 .... **CLC 60**
See also CA 25-28R; 117; CANR 10; DLB 130

Dowson, Ernest (Christopher) 1867-1900 .... **TCLC 4**
See also CA 105; 150; DLB 19, 135

Doyle, A. Conan
See Doyle, Arthur Conan

Doyle, Arthur Conan 1859-1930 .... **TCLC 7; DA; DAB; DAC; DAM MST, NOV; SSC 12; WLC**
See also AAYA 14; CA 104; 122; CDBLB 1890-1914; DLB 18, 70, 156; MTCW; SATA 24

Doyle, Conan
See Doyle, Arthur Conan

Doyle, John
See Graves, Robert (von Ranke)

Doyle, Roddy 1958(?)- .... **CLC 81**
See also AAYA 14; CA 143

Doyle, Sir A. Conan
See Doyle, Arthur Conan

Doyle, Sir Arthur Conan
See Doyle, Arthur Conan

Dr. A
See Asimov, Isaac; Silverstein, Alvin

Drabble, Margaret 1939- .... **CLC 2, 3, 5, 8, 10, 22, 53; DAB; DAC; DAM MST, NOV, POP**
See also CA 13-16R; CANR 18, 35; CDBLB 1960 to Present; DLB 14, 155; MTCW; SATA 48

Drapier, M. B.
See Swift, Jonathan

Drayham, James
See Mencken, H(enry) L(ouis)

Drayton, Michael 1563-1631 .... **LC 8**

Dreadstone, Carl
See Campbell, (John) Ramsey

Dreiser, Theodore (Herman Albert) 1871-1945 .... **TCLC 10, 18, 35; DA; DAC; DAM MST, NOV; WLC**
See also CA 106; 132; CDALB 1865-1917; DLB 9, 12, 102, 137; DLBD 1; MTCW

Drexler, Rosalyn 1926- .... **CLC 2, 6**
See also CA 81-84

Dreyer, Carl Theodor 1889-1968.... **CLC 16**
See also CA 116

Drieu la Rochelle, Pierre(-Eugene) 1893-1945 .... **TCLC 21**
See also CA 117; DLB 72

Drinkwater, John 1882-1937...... **TCLC 57**
See also CA 109; 149; DLB 10, 19, 149

Drop Shot
See Cable, George Washington

Droste-Hulshoff, Annette Freiin von 1797-1848 .... **NCLC 3**
See also DLB 133

Drummond, Walter
See Silverberg, Robert

Drummond, William Henry 1854-1907 .... **TCLC 25**
See also DLB 92

Drummond de Andrade, Carlos 1902-1987 .... **CLC 18**
See also Andrade, Carlos Drummond de
See also CA 132; 123

Drury, Allen (Stuart) 1918-........ **CLC 37**
See also CA 57-60; CANR 18, 52; INT CANR-18

Dryden, John 1631-1700 .... **LC 3, 21; DA; DAB; DAC; DAM DRAM, MST, POET; DC 3; WLC**
See also CDBLB 1660-1789; DLB 80, 101, 131

Duberman, Martin 1930-........... **CLC 8**
See also CA 1-4R; CANR 2

Dubie, Norman (Evans) 1945-...... **CLC 36**
See also CA 69-72; CANR 12; DLB 120

Du Bois, W(illiam) E(dward) B(urghardt) 1868-1963 .... **CLC 1, 2, 13, 64, 96; BLC; DA; DAC; DAM MST, MULT, NOV; WLC**
See also BW 1; CA 85-88; CANR 34; CDALB 1865-1917; DLB 47, 50, 91; MTCW; SATA 42

Dubus, Andre 1936- .... **CLC 13, 36, 97; SSC 15**
See also CA 21-24R; CANR 17; DLB 130; INT CANR-17

Duca Minimo
See D'Annunzio, Gabriele

Ducharme, Rejean 1941- .... **CLC 74**
See also DLB 60

Duclos, Charles Pinot 1704-1772 ..... **LC 1**

Dudek, Louis 1918- .... **CLC 11, 19**
See also CA 45-48; CAAS 14; CANR 1; DLB 88

Equiano, Olaudah
    1745(?)-1797 . . . . LC 16; BLC;
                                    DAM MULT
    See also DLB 37, 50

Erasmus, Desiderius 1469(?)-1536. . . . LC 16

Erdman, Paul E(mil) 1932- . . . . CLC 25
    See also AITN 1; CA 61-64; CANR 13, 43

Erdrich, Louise
    1954- . . . . CLC 39, 54; DAM MULT,
                                    NOV, POP
    See also AAYA 10; BEST 89:1; CA 114;
        CANR 41; DLB 152; MTCW; NNAL

Erenburg, Ilya (Grigoryevich)
    See Ehrenburg, Ilya (Grigoryevich)

Erickson, Stephen Michael 1950-
    See Erickson, Steve
    See also CA 129

Erickson, Steve . . . . CLC 64
    See also Erickson, Stephen Michael

Ericson, Walter
    See Fast, Howard (Melvin)

Eriksson, Buntel
    See Bergman, (Ernst) Ingmar

Ernaux, Annie 1940- . . . . CLC 88
    See also CA 147

Eschenbach, Wolfram von
    See Wolfram von Eschenbach

Eseki, Bruno
    See Mphahlele, Ezekiel

Esenin, Sergei (Alexandrovich)
    1895-1925 . . . . TCLC 4
    See also CA 104

Eshleman, Clayton 1935- . . . . CLC 7
    See also CA 33-36R; CAAS 6; DLB 5

Espriella, Don Manuel Alvarez
    See Southey, Robert

Espriu, Salvador 1913-1985 . . . . CLC 9
    See also CA 154; 115; DLB 134

Espronceda, Jose de 1808-1842 . . . NCLC 39

Esse, James
    See Stephens, James

Esterbrook, Tom
    See Hubbard, L(afayette) Ron(ald)

Estleman, Loren D.
    1952- . . . . . . CLC 48; DAM NOV, POP
    See also CA 85-88; CANR 27;
        INT CANR-27; MTCW

Eugenides, Jeffrey 1960(?)- . . . . CLC 81
    See also CA 144

Euripides c. 485B.C.-406B.C. . . . . DC 4
    See also DA; DAB; DAC; DAM DRAM,
        MST

Evan, Evin
    See Faust, Frederick (Schiller)

Evans, Evan
    See Faust, Frederick (Schiller)

Evans, Marian
    See Eliot, George

Evans, Mary Ann
    See Eliot, George

Evarts, Esther
    See Benson, Sally

Everett, Percival L. 1956- . . . . CLC 57
    See also BW 2; CA 129

Everson, R(onald) G(ilmour)
    1903- . . . . CLC 27
    See also CA 17-20R; DLB 88

Everson, William (Oliver)
    1912-1994 . . . . CLC 1, 5, 14
    See also CA 9-12R; 145; CANR 20; DLB 5,
        16; MTCW

Evtushenko, Evgenii Aleksandrovich
    See Yevtushenko, Yevgeny (Alexandrovich)

Ewart, Gavin (Buchanan)
    1916-1995 . . . . CLC 13, 46
    See also CA 89-92; 150; CANR 17, 46;
        DLB 40; MTCW

Ewers, Hanns Heinz 1871-1943 . . . TCLC 12
    See also CA 109; 149

Ewing, Frederick R.
    See Sturgeon, Theodore (Hamilton)

Exley, Frederick (Earl)
    1929-1992 . . . . CLC 6, 11
    See also AITN 2; CA 81-84; 138; DLB 143;
        DLBY 81

Eynhardt, Guillermo
    See Quiroga, Horacio (Sylvestre)

Ezekiel, Nissim 1924- . . . . CLC 61
    See also CA 61-64

Ezekiel, Tish O'Dowd 1943- . . . . CLC 34
    See also CA 129

Fadeyev, A.
    See Bulgya, Alexander Alexandrovich

Fadeyev, Alexander . . . . TCLC 53
    See also Bulgya, Alexander Alexandrovich

Fagen, Donald 1948- . . . . CLC 26

Fainzilberg, Ilya Arnoldovich 1897-1937
    See Ilf, Ilya
    See also CA 120

Fair, Ronald L. 1932- . . . . CLC 18
    See also BW 1; CA 69-72; CANR 25;
        DLB 33

Fairbairns, Zoe (Ann) 1948- . . . . CLC 32
    See also CA 103; CANR 21

Falco, Gian
    See Papini, Giovanni

Falconer, James
    See Kirkup, James

Falconer, Kenneth
    See Kornbluth, C(yril) M.

Falkland, Samuel
    See Heijermans, Herman

Fallaci, Oriana 1930- . . . . CLC 11
    See also CA 77-80; CANR 15; MTCW

Faludy, George 1913- . . . . CLC 42
    See also CA 21-24R

Faludy, Gyoergy
    See Faludy, George

Fanon, Frantz
    1925-1961 . . . . CLC 74; BLC;
                                    DAM MULT
    See also BW 1; CA 116; 89-92

Fanshawe, Ann 1625-1680 . . . . LC 11

Fante, John (Thomas) 1911-1983 . . . CLC 60
    See also CA 69-72; 109; CANR 23;
        DLB 130; DLBY 83

Farah, Nuruddin
    1945- . . . . . CLC 53; BLC; DAM MULT
    See also BW 2; CA 106; DLB 125

Fargue, Leon-Paul 1876(?)-1947 . . . TCLC 11
    See also CA 109

Farigoule, Louis
    See Romains, Jules

Farina, Richard 1936(?)-1966 . . . . CLC 9
    See also CA 81-84; 25-28R

Farley, Walter (Lorimer)
    1915-1989 . . . . CLC 17
    See also CA 17-20R; CANR 8, 29; DLB 22;
        JRDA; MAICYA; SATA 2, 43

Farmer, Philip Jose 1918- . . . . CLC 1, 19
    See also CA 1-4R; CANR 4, 35; DLB 8;
        MTCW

Farquhar, George
    1677-1707 . . . . LC 21; DAM DRAM
    See also DLB 84

Farrell, J(ames) G(ordon)
    1935-1979 . . . . CLC 6
    See also CA 73-76; 89-92; CANR 36;
        DLB 14; MTCW

Farrell, James T(homas)
    1904-1979 . . . . CLC 1, 4, 8, 11, 66
    See also CA 5-8R; 89-92; CANR 9; DLB 4,
        9, 86; DLBD 2; MTCW

Farren, Richard J.
    See Betjeman, John

Farren, Richard M.
    See Betjeman, John

Fassbinder, Rainer Werner
    1946-1982 . . . . CLC 20
    See also CA 93-96; 106; CANR 31

Fast, Howard (Melvin)
    1914- . . . . CLC 23; DAM NOV
    See also AAYA 16; CA 1-4R; CAAS 18;
        CANR 1, 33, 54; DLB 9; INT CANR-33;
        SATA 7

Faulcon, Robert
    See Holdstock, Robert P.

Faulkner, William (Cuthbert)
    1897-1962 . . . . . CLC 1, 3, 6, 8, 9, 11, 14,
                            18, 28, 52, 68; DA; DAB; DAC;
                            DAM MST, NOV; SSC 1; WLC
    See also AAYA 7; CA 81-84; CANR 33;
        CDALB 1929-1941; DLB 9, 11, 44, 102;
        DLBD 2; DLBY 86; MTCW

Fauset, Jessie Redmon
    1884(?)-1961 . . . . CLC 19, 54; BLC;
                                    DAM MULT
    See also BW 1; CA 109; DLB 51

Faust, Frederick (Schiller)
    1892-1944(?) . . . . . TCLC 49; DAM POP
    See also CA 108; 152

Faust, Irvin 1924- . . . . CLC 8
    See also CA 33-36R; CANR 28; DLB 2, 28;
        DLBY 80

Fawkes, Guy
    See Benchley, Robert (Charles)

Fearing, Kenneth (Flexner)
    1902-1961 . . . . CLC 51
    See also CA 93-96; DLB 9

Fecamps, Elise
    See Creasey, John

Federman, Raymond 1928- ...... **CLC 6, 47**
See also CA 17-20R; CAAS 8; CANR 10, 43; DLBY 80

Federspiel, J(uerg) F. 1931- .... **CLC 42**
See also CA 146

Feiffer, Jules (Ralph)
1929- ...... **CLC 2, 8, 64; DAM DRAM**
See also AAYA 3; CA 17-20R; CANR 30; DLB 7, 44; INT CANR-30; MTCW; SATA 8, 61

Feige, Hermann Albert Otto Maximilian
See Traven, B.

Feinberg, David B. 1956-1994 ...... **CLC 59**
See also CA 135; 147

Feinstein, Elaine 1930- .... **CLC 36**
See also CA 69-72; CAAS 1; CANR 31; DLB 14, 40; MTCW

Feldman, Irving (Mordecai) 1928- .... **CLC 7**
See also CA 1-4R; CANR 1; DLB 169

Fellini, Federico 1920-1993 ..... **CLC 16, 85**
See also CA 65-68; 143; CANR 33

Felsen, Henry Gregor 1916- .... **CLC 17**
See also CA 1-4R; CANR 1; SAAS 2; SATA 1

Fenton, James Martin 1949- .... **CLC 32**
See also CA 102; DLB 40

Ferber, Edna 1887-1968 .... **CLC 18, 93**
See also AITN 1; CA 5-8R; 25-28R; DLB 9, 28, 86; MTCW; SATA 7

Ferguson, Helen
See Kavan, Anna

Ferguson, Samuel 1810-1886 ..... **NCLC 33**
See also DLB 32

Fergusson, Robert 1750-1774 .... **LC 29**
See also DLB 109

Ferling, Lawrence
See Ferlinghetti, Lawrence (Monsanto)

Ferlinghetti, Lawrence (Monsanto)
1919(?)- .... **CLC 2, 6, 10, 27; DAM POET; PC 1**
See also CA 5-8R; CANR 3, 41; CDALB 1941-1968; DLB 5, 16; MTCW

Fernandez, Vicente Garcia Huidobro
See Huidobro Fernandez, Vicente Garcia

Ferrer, Gabriel (Francisco Victor) Miro
See Miro (Ferrer), Gabriel (Francisco Victor)

Ferrier, Susan (Edmonstone)
1782-1854 .... **NCLC 8**
See also DLB 116

Ferrigno, Robert 1948(?)- .... **CLC 65**
See also CA 140

Ferron, Jacques 1921-1985 ... **CLC 94; DAC**
See also CA 117; 129; DLB 60

Feuchtwanger, Lion 1884-1958 ..... **TCLC 3**
See also CA 104; DLB 66

Feuillet, Octave 1821-1890 ...... **NCLC 45**

Feydeau, Georges (Leon Jules Marie)
1862-1921 ..... **TCLC 22; DAM DRAM**
See also CA 113; 152

Ficino, Marsilio 1433-1499 .... **LC 12**

Fiedeler, Hans
See Doeblin, Alfred

Fiedler, Leslie A(aron)
1917- .... **CLC 4, 13, 24**
See also CA 9-12R; CANR 7; DLB 28, 67; MTCW

Field, Andrew 1938- .... **CLC 44**
See also CA 97-100; CANR 25

Field, Eugene 1850-1895 .... **NCLC 3**
See also DLB 23, 42, 140; DLBD 13; MAICYA; SATA 16

Field, Gans T.
See Wellman, Manly Wade

Field, Michael .... **TCLC 43**

Field, Peter
See Hobson, Laura Z(ametkin)

Fielding, Henry
1707-1754 ...... **LC 1; DA; DAB; DAC; DAM DRAM, MST, NOV; WLC**
See also CDBLB 1660-1789; DLB 39, 84, 101

Fielding, Sarah 1710-1768 .... **LC 1**
See also DLB 39

Fierstein, Harvey (Forbes)
1954- ..... **CLC 33; DAM DRAM, POP**
See also CA 123; 129

Figes, Eva 1932- .... **CLC 31**
See also CA 53-56; CANR 4, 44; DLB 14

Finch, Robert (Duer Claydon)
1900- .... **CLC 18**
See also CA 57-60; CANR 9, 24, 49; DLB 88

Findley, Timothy
1930- ...... **CLC 27; DAC; DAM MST**
See also CA 25-28R; CANR 12, 42; DLB 53

Fink, William
See Mencken, H(enry) L(ouis)

Firbank, Louis 1942-
See Reed, Lou
See also CA 117

Firbank, (Arthur Annesley) Ronald
1886-1926 .... **TCLC 1**
See also CA 104; DLB 36

Fisher, M(ary) F(rances) K(ennedy)
1908-1992 .... **CLC 76, 87**
See also CA 77-80; 138; CANR 44

Fisher, Roy 1930- .... **CLC 25**
See also CA 81-84; CAAS 10; CANR 16; DLB 40

Fisher, Rudolph
1897-1934 .... **TCLC 11; BLC; DAM MULT**
See also BW 1; CA 107; 124; DLB 51, 102

Fisher, Vardis (Alvero) 1895-1968 .... **CLC 7**
See also CA 5-8R; 25-28R; DLB 9

Fiske, Tarleton
See Bloch, Robert (Albert)

Fitch, Clarke
See Sinclair, Upton (Beall)

Fitch, John IV
See Cormier, Robert (Edmund)

Fitzgerald, Captain Hugh
See Baum, L(yman) Frank

FitzGerald, Edward 1809-1883 .... **NCLC 9**
See also DLB 32

Fitzgerald, F(rancis) Scott (Key)
1896-1940 ...... **TCLC 1, 6, 14, 28, 55; DA; DAB; DAC; DAM MST, NOV; SSC 6; WLC**
See also AITN 1; CA 110; 123; CDALB 1917-1929; DLB 4, 9, 86; DLBD 1; DLBY 81; MTCW

Fitzgerald, Penelope 1916- ... **CLC 19, 51, 61**
See also CA 85-88; CAAS 10; DLB 14

Fitzgerald, Robert (Stuart)
1910-1985 .... **CLC 39**
See also CA 1-4R; 114; CANR 1; DLBY 80

FitzGerald, Robert D(avid)
1902-1987 .... **CLC 19**
See also CA 17-20R

Fitzgerald, Zelda (Sayre)
1900-1948 .... **TCLC 52**
See also CA 117; 126; DLBY 84

Flanagan, Thomas (James Bonner)
1923- .... **CLC 25, 52**
See also CA 108; CANR 55; DLBY 80; INT 108; MTCW

Flaubert, Gustave
1821-1880 .... **NCLC 2, 10, 19; DA; DAB; DAC; DAM MST, NOV; SSC 11; WLC**
See also DLB 119

Flecker, Herman Elroy
See Flecker, (Herman) James Elroy

Flecker, (Herman) James Elroy
1884-1915 .... **TCLC 43**
See also CA 109; 150; DLB 10, 19

Fleming, Ian (Lancaster)
1908-1964 ...... **CLC 3, 30; DAM POP**
See also CA 5-8R; CDBLB 1945-1960; DLB 87; MTCW; SATA 9

Fleming, Thomas (James) 1927- .... **CLC 37**
See also CA 5-8R; CANR 10; INT CANR-10; SATA 8

Fletcher, John 1579-1625 ...... **LC 33; DC 6**
See also CDBLB Before 1660; DLB 58

Fletcher, John Gould 1886-1950 ... **TCLC 35**
See also CA 107; DLB 4, 45

Fleur, Paul
See Pohl, Frederik

Flooglebuckle, Al
See Spiegelman, Art

Flying Officer X
See Bates, H(erbert) E(rnest)

Fo, Dario 1926- ..... **CLC 32; DAM DRAM**
See also CA 116; 128; MTCW

Fogarty, Jonathan Titulescu Esq.
See Farrell, James T(homas)

Folke, Will
See Bloch, Robert (Albert)

Follett, Ken(neth Martin)
1949- ...... **CLC 18; DAM NOV, POP**
See also AAYA 6; BEST 89:4; CA 81-84; CANR 13, 33, 54; DLB 87; DLBY 81; INT CANR-33; MTCW

Fontane, Theodor 1819-1898 ..... **NCLC 26**
See also DLB 129

Foote, Horton
1916- .... **CLC 51, 91; DAM DRAM**
See also CA 73-76; CANR 34, 51; DLB 26;
INT CANR-34

Foote, Shelby
1916- .... **CLC 75; DAM NOV, POP**
See also CA 5-8R; CANR 3, 45; DLB 2, 17

Forbes, Esther 1891-1967......... **CLC 12**
See also AAYA 17; CA 13-14; 25-28R;
CAP 1; CLR 27; DLB 22; JRDA;
MAICYA; SATA 2

Forche, Carolyn (Louise)
1950- .... **CLC 25, 83, 86; DAM POET;**
PC 10
See also CA 109; 117; CANR 50; DLB 5;
INT 117

Ford, Elbur
See Hibbert, Eleanor Alice Burford

Ford, Ford Madox
1873-1939 .... **TCLC 1, 15, 39, 57;**
DAM NOV
See also CA 104; 132; CDBLB 1914-1945;
DLB 162; MTCW

Ford, John 1895-1973............ **CLC 16**
See also CA 45-48

Ford, Richard 1944-.............. **CLC 46**
See also CA 69-72; CANR 11, 47

Ford, Webster
See Masters, Edgar Lee

Foreman, Richard 1937-.......... **CLC 50**
See also CA 65-68; CANR 32

Forester, C(ecil) S(cott)
1899-1966 .... **CLC 35**
See also CA 73-76; 25-28R; SATA 13

Forez
See Mauriac, Francois (Charles)

Forman, James Douglas 1932-...... **CLC 21**
See also AAYA 17; CA 9-12R; CANR 4,
19, 42; JRDA; MAICYA; SATA 8, 70

Fornes, Maria Irene 1930-...... **CLC 39, 61**
See also CA 25-28R; CANR 28; DLB 7;
HW; INT CANR-28; MTCW

Forrest, Leon 1937- .... **CLC 4**
See also BW 2; CA 89-92; CAAS 7;
CANR 25, 52; DLB 33

Forster, E(dward) M(organ)
1879-1970 ..... **CLC 1, 2, 3, 4, 9, 10, 13,**
15, 22, 45, 77; DA; DAB; DAC;
DAM MST, NOV; WLC
See also AAYA 2; CA 13-14; 25-28R;
CANR 45; CAP 1; CDBLB 1914-1945;
DLB 34, 98, 162; DLBD 10; MTCW;
SATA 57

Forster, John 1812-1876 .... **NCLC 11**
See also DLB 144

Forsyth, Frederick
1938- .. **CLC 2, 5, 36; DAM NOV, POP**
See also BEST 89:4; CA 85-88; CANR 38;
DLB 87; MTCW

Forten, Charlotte L. .... **TCLC 16; BLC**
See also Grimke, Charlotte L(ottie) Forten
See also DLB 50

Foscolo, Ugo 1778-1827.......... **NCLC 8**

Fosse, Bob .... **CLC 20**
See also Fosse, Robert Louis

Fosse, Robert Louis 1927-1987
See Fosse, Bob
See also CA 110; 123

Foster, Stephen Collins
1826-1864 .... **NCLC 26**

Foucault, Michel
1926-1984 .... **CLC 31, 34, 69**
See also CA 105; 113; CANR 34; MTCW

Fouque, Friedrich (Heinrich Karl) de la Motte
1777-1843 .... **NCLC 2**
See also DLB 90

Fourier, Charles 1772-1837 ...... **NCLC 51**

Fournier, Henri Alban 1886-1914
See Alain-Fournier
See also CA 104

Fournier, Pierre 1916-............ **CLC 11**
See also Gascar, Pierre
See also CA 89-92; CANR 16, 40

Fowles, John
1926- ...... **CLC 1, 2, 3, 4, 6, 9, 10, 15,**
33, 87; DAB; DAC; DAM MST
See also CA 5-8R; CANR 25; CDBLB 1960
to Present; DLB 14, 139; MTCW;
SATA 22

Fox, Paula 1923-................ **CLC 2, 8**
See also AAYA 3; CA 73-76; CANR 20,
36; CLR 1, 44; DLB 52; JRDA;
MAICYA; MTCW; SATA 17, 60

Fox, William Price (Jr.) 1926- ..... **CLC 22**
See also CA 17-20R; CAAS 19; CANR 11;
DLB 2; DLBY 81

Foxe, John 1516(?)-1587 .... **LC 14**

Frame, Janet
1924- .... **CLC 2, 3, 6, 22, 66, 96**
See also Clutha, Janet Paterson Frame

France, Anatole .... **TCLC 9**
See also Thibault, Jacques Anatole Francois
See also DLB 123

Francis, Claude 19(?)- .... **CLC 50**

Francis, Dick
1920- .... **CLC 2, 22, 42; DAM POP**
See also AAYA 5; BEST 89:3; CA 5-8R;
CANR 9, 42; CDBLB 1960 to Present;
DLB 87; INT CANR-9; MTCW

Francis, Robert (Churchill)
1901-1987 .... **CLC 15**
See also CA 1-4R; 123; CANR 1

Frank, Anne(lies Marie)
1929-1945 .... **TCLC 17; DA; DAB;**
DAC; DAM MST; WLC
See also AAYA 12; CA 113; 133; MTCW;
SATA 87; SATA-Brief 42

Frank, Elizabeth 1945-........... **CLC 39**
See also CA 121; 126; INT 126

Frankl, Viktor E(mil) 1905-........ **CLC 93**
See also CA 65-68

Franklin, Benjamin
See Hasek, Jaroslav (Matej Frantisek)

Franklin, Benjamin
1706-1790 ..... **LC 25; DA; DAB; DAC;**
DAM MST
See also CDALB 1640-1865; DLB 24, 43,
73

Franklin, (Stella Maraia Sarah) Miles
1879-1954 .... **TCLC 7**
See also CA 104

Fraser, (Lady) Antonia (Pakenham)
1932- .... **CLC 32**
See also CA 85-88; CANR 44; MTCW;
SATA-Brief 32

Fraser, George MacDonald 1925-.... **CLC 7**
See also CA 45-48; CANR 2, 48

Fraser, Sylvia 1935-.............. **CLC 64**
See also CA 45-48; CANR 1, 16

Frayn, Michael
1933- .... **CLC 3, 7, 31, 47;**
DAM DRAM, NOV
See also CA 5-8R; CANR 30; DLB 13, 14;
MTCW

Fraze, Candida (Merrill) 1945-..... **CLC 50**
See also CA 126

Frazer, J(ames) G(eorge)
1854-1941 .... **TCLC 32**
See also CA 118

Frazer, Robert Caine
See Creasey, John

Frazer, Sir James George
See Frazer, J(ames) G(eorge)

Frazier, Ian 1951-............... **CLC 46**
See also CA 130; CANR 54

Frederic, Harold 1856-1898...... **NCLC 10**
See also DLB 12, 23; DLBD 13

Frederick, John
See Faust, Frederick (Schiller)

Frederick the Great 1712-1786 ...... **LC 14**

Fredro, Aleksander 1793-1876..... **NCLC 8**

Freeling, Nicolas 1927- .... **CLC 38**
See also CA 49-52; CAAS 12; CANR 1, 17,
50; DLB 87

Freeman, Douglas Southall
1886-1953 .... **TCLC 11**
See also CA 109; DLB 17

Freeman, Judith 1946-........... **CLC 55**
See also CA 148

Freeman, Mary Eleanor Wilkins
1852-1930 .... **TCLC 9; SSC 1**
See also CA 106; DLB 12, 78

Freeman, R(ichard) Austin
1862-1943 .... **TCLC 21**
See also CA 113; DLB 70

French, Albert 1943- .... **CLC 86**

French, Marilyn
1929- .... **CLC 10, 18, 60;**
DAM DRAM, NOV, POP
See also CA 69-72; CANR 3, 31;
INT CANR-31; MTCW

French, Paul
See Asimov, Isaac

Freneau, Philip Morin 1752-1832 .. **NCLC 1**
See also DLB 37, 43

Freud, Sigmund 1856-1939 .... **TCLC 52**
See also CA 115; 133; MTCW

Friedan, Betty (Naomi) 1921-...... **CLC 74**
See also CA 65-68; CANR 18, 45; MTCW

Friedlander, Saul 1932-........... **CLC 90**
See also CA 117; 130

Friedman, B(ernard) H(arper)
1926- . . . . **CLC 7**
See also CA 1-4R; CANR 3, 48

Friedman, Bruce Jay   1930- . . . . **CLC 3, 5, 56**
See also CA 9-12R; CANR 25, 52; DLB 2, 28; INT CANR-25

Friel, Brian   1929- . . . . **CLC 5, 42, 59**
See also CA 21-24R; CANR 33; DLB 13; MTCW

Friis-Baastad, Babbis Ellinor
1921-1970 . . . . **CLC 12**
See also CA 17-20R; 134; SATA 7

Frisch, Max (Rudolf)
1911-1991 . . . . . **CLC 3, 9, 14, 18, 32, 44;
DAM DRAM, NOV**
See also CA 85-88; 134; CANR 32; DLB 69, 124; MTCW

Fromentin, Eugene (Samuel Auguste)
1820-1876 . . . . **NCLC 10**
See also DLB 123

Frost, Frederick
See Faust, Frederick (Schiller)

Frost, Robert (Lee)
1874-1963 . . . . **CLC 1, 3, 4, 9, 10, 13, 15,
26, 34, 44; DA; DAB; DAC; DAM MST,
POET; PC 1; WLC**
See also CA 89-92; CANR 33; CDALB 1917-1929; DLB 54; DLBD 7; MTCW; SATA 14

Froude, James Anthony
1818-1894 . . . . **NCLC 43**
See also DLB 18, 57, 144

Froy, Herald
See Waterhouse, Keith (Spencer)

Fry, Christopher
1907- . . . . . **CLC 2, 10, 14; DAM DRAM**
See also CA 17-20R; CAAS 23; CANR 9, 30; DLB 13; MTCW; SATA 66

Frye, (Herman) Northrop
1912-1991 . . . . **CLC 24, 70**
See also CA 5-8R; 133; CANR 8, 37; DLB 67, 68; MTCW

Fuchs, Daniel   1909-1993 . . . . **CLC 8, 22**
See also CA 81-84; 142; CAAS 5; CANR 40; DLB 9, 26, 28; DLBY 93

Fuchs, Daniel   1934- . . . . **CLC 34**
See also CA 37-40R; CANR 14, 48

Fuentes, Carlos
1928- . . . . . . **CLC 3, 8, 10, 13, 22, 41, 60;
DA; DAB; DAC; DAM MST, MULT,
NOV; HLC; SSC 24; WLC**
See also AAYA 4; AITN 2; CA 69-72; CANR 10, 32; DLB 113; HW; MTCW

Fuentes, Gregorio Lopez y
See Lopez y Fuentes, Gregorio

Fugard, (Harold) Athol
1932- . . . . **CLC 5, 9, 14, 25, 40, 80;
DAM DRAM; DC 3**
See also AAYA 17; CA 85-88; CANR 32, 54; MTCW

Fugard, Sheila   1932- . . . . **CLC 48**
See also CA 125

Fuller, Charles (H., Jr.)
1939- . . . . **CLC 25; BLC; DAM DRAM,
MULT; DC 1**
See also BW 2; CA 108; 112; DLB 38; INT 112; MTCW

Fuller, John (Leopold)   1937- . . . . . . **CLC 62**
See also CA 21-24R; CANR 9, 44; DLB 40

Fuller, Margaret . . . . **NCLC 5, 50**
See also Ossoli, Sarah Margaret (Fuller marchesa d')

Fuller, Roy (Broadbent)
1912-1991 . . . . **CLC 4, 28**
See also CA 5-8R; 135; CAAS 10; CANR 53; DLB 15, 20; SATA 87

Fulton, Alice   1952- . . . . **CLC 52**
See also CA 116

Furphy, Joseph   1843-1912 . . . . **TCLC 25**

Fussell, Paul   1924- . . . . **CLC 74**
See also BEST 90:1; CA 17-20R; CANR 8, 21, 35; INT CANR-21; MTCW

Futabatei, Shimei   1864-1909 . . . . . **TCLC 44**

Futrelle, Jacques   1875-1912 . . . . . . **TCLC 19**
See also CA 113; 155

Gaboriau, Emile   1835-1873 . . . . . . **NCLC 14**

Gadda, Carlo Emilio   1893-1973 . . . . **CLC 11**
See also CA 89-92

Gaddis, William
1922- . . . . . **CLC 1, 3, 6, 8, 10, 19, 43, 86**
See also CA 17-20R; CANR 21, 48; DLB 2; MTCW

Gage, Walter
See Inge, William (Motter)

Gaines, Ernest J(ames)
1933- . . . . **CLC 3, 11, 18, 86; BLC;
DAM MULT**
See also AAYA 18; AITN 1; BW 2; CA 9-12R; CANR 6, 24, 42; CDALB 1968-1988; DLB 2, 33, 152; DLBY 80; MTCW; SATA 86

Gaitskill, Mary   1954- . . . . **CLC 69**
See also CA 128

Galdos, Benito Perez
See Perez Galdos, Benito

Gale, Zona
1874-1938 . . . . . . **TCLC 7; DAM DRAM**
See also CA 105; 153; DLB 9, 78

Galeano, Eduardo (Hughes)   1940- . . . **CLC 72**
See also CA 29-32R; CANR 13, 32; HW

Galiano, Juan Valera y Alcala
See Valera y Alcala-Galiano, Juan

Gallagher, Tess
1943- . . **CLC 18, 63; DAM POET; PC 9**
See also CA 106; DLB 120

Gallant, Mavis
1922- . . . . **CLC 7, 18, 38; DAC;
DAM MST; SSC 5**
See also CA 69-72; CANR 29; DLB 53; MTCW

Gallant, Roy A(rthur)   1924- . . . . **CLC 17**
See also CA 5-8R; CANR 4, 29, 54; CLR 30; MAICYA; SATA 4, 68

Gallico, Paul (William)   1897-1976 . . . **CLC 2**
See also AITN 1; CA 5-8R; 69-72; CANR 23; DLB 9, 171; MAICYA; SATA 13

Gallo, Max Louis   1932- . . . . **CLC 95**
See also CA 85-88

Gallois, Lucien
See Desnos, Robert

Gallup, Ralph
See Whitemore, Hugh (John)

Galsworthy, John
1867-1933 . . . . . . **TCLC 1, 45; DA; DAB;
DAC; DAM DRAM, MST, NOV;
SSC 22; WLC 2**
See also CA 104; 141; CDBLB 1890-1914; DLB 10, 34, 98, 162

Galt, John   1779-1839 . . . . **NCLC 1**
See also DLB 99, 116, 159

Galvin, James   1951- . . . . **CLC 38**
See also CA 108; CANR 26

Gamboa, Federico   1864-1939 . . . . . **TCLC 36**

Gandhi, M. K.
See Gandhi, Mohandas Karamchand

Gandhi, Mahatma
See Gandhi, Mohandas Karamchand

Gandhi, Mohandas Karamchand
1869-1948 . . . . . **TCLC 59; DAM MULT**
See also CA 121; 132; MTCW

Gann, Ernest Kellogg   1910-1991 . . . . **CLC 23**
See also AITN 1; CA 1-4R; 136; CANR 1

Garcia, Cristina   1958- . . . . **CLC 76**
See also CA 141

Garcia Lorca, Federico
1898-1936 . . . **TCLC 1, 7, 49; DA; DAB;
DAC; DAM DRAM, MST, MULT,
POET; DC 2; HLC; PC 3; WLC**
See also CA 104; 131; DLB 108; HW; MTCW

Garcia Marquez, Gabriel (Jose)
1928- . . . . **CLC 2, 3, 8, 10, 15, 27, 47, 55,
68; DA; DAB; DAC; DAM MST,
MULT, NOV, POP; HLC; SSC 8; WLC**
See also AAYA 3; BEST 89:1, 90:4; CA 33-36R; CANR 10, 28, 50; DLB 113; HW; MTCW

Gard, Janice
See Latham, Jean Lee

Gard, Roger Martin du
See Martin du Gard, Roger

Gardam, Jane   1928- . . . . **CLC 43**
See also CA 49-52; CANR 2, 18, 33, 54; CLR 12; DLB 14, 161; MAICYA; MTCW; SAAS 9; SATA 39, 76; SATA-Brief 28

Gardner, Herb(ert)   1934- . . . . **CLC 44**
See also CA 149

Gardner, John (Champlin), Jr.
1933-1982 . . . . . **CLC 2, 3, 5, 7, 8, 10, 18,
28, 34; DAM NOV, POP; SSC 7**
See also AITN 1; CA 65-68; 107; CANR 33; DLB 2; DLBY 82; MTCW; SATA 40; SATA-Obit 31

Gardner, John (Edmund)
1926- . . . . **CLC 30; DAM POP**
See also CA 103; CANR 15; MTCW

Gardner, Miriam
See Bradley, Marion Zimmer

Gardner, Noel
See Kuttner, Henry

Gardons, S. S.
See Snodgrass, W(illiam) D(e Witt)

Garfield, Leon 1921-1996......... **CLC 12**
See also AAYA 8; CA 17-20R; 152;
CANR 38, 41; CLR 21; DLB 161; JRDA;
MAICYA; SATA 1, 32, 76;
SATA-Obit 90

Garland, (Hannibal) Hamlin
1860-1940 .... **TCLC 3; SSC 18**
See also CA 104; DLB 12, 71, 78

Garneau, (Hector de) Saint-Denys
1912-1943 .... **TCLC 13**
See also CA 111; DLB 88

Garner, Alan
1934- .... **CLC 17; DAB; DAM POP**
See also AAYA 18; CA 73-76; CANR 15;
CLR 20; DLB 161; MAICYA; MTCW;
SATA 18, 69

Garner, Hugh 1913-1979 .... **CLC 13**
See also CA 69-72; CANR 31; DLB 68

Garnett, David 1892-1981 .... **CLC 3**
See also CA 5-8R; 103; CANR 17; DLB 34

Garos, Stephanie
See Katz, Steve

Garrett, George (Palmer)
1929- .... **CLC 3, 11, 51**
See also CA 1-4R; CAAS 5; CANR 1, 42;
DLB 2, 5, 130, 152; DLBY 83

Garrick, David
1717-1779 .... **LC 15; DAM DRAM**
See also DLB 84

Garrigue, Jean 1914-1972 .... **CLC 2, 8**
See also CA 5-8R; 37-40R; CANR 20

Garrison, Frederick
See Sinclair, Upton (Beall)

Garth, Will
See Hamilton, Edmond; Kuttner, Henry

Garvey, Marcus (Moziah, Jr.)
1887-1940 .... **TCLC 41; BLC;**
DAM MULT
See also BW 1; CA 120; 124

Gary, Romain .... **CLC 25**
See also Kacew, Romain
See also DLB 83

Gascar, Pierre .... **CLC 11**
See also Fournier, Pierre

Gascoyne, David (Emery) 1916- .... **CLC 45**
See also CA 65-68; CANR 10, 28, 54;
DLB 20; MTCW

Gaskell, Elizabeth Cleghorn
1810-1865 .. **NCLC 5; DAB; DAM MST**
See also CDBLB 1832-1890; DLB 21, 144,
159

Gass, William H(oward)
1924- ... **CLC 1, 2, 8, 11, 15, 39; SSC 12**
See also CA 17-20R; CANR 30; DLB 2;
MTCW

Gasset, Jose Ortega y
See Ortega y Gasset, Jose

Gates, Henry Louis, Jr.
1950- .... **CLC 65; DAM MULT**
See also BW 2; CA 109; CANR 25, 53;
DLB 67

Gautier, Theophile
1811-1872 .... **NCLC 1, 59;**
DAM POET; SSC 20
See also DLB 119

Gawsworth, John
See Bates, H(erbert) E(rnest)

Gay, Oliver
See Gogarty, Oliver St. John

Gaye, Marvin (Penze) 1939-1984 ... **CLC 26**
See also CA 112

Gebler, Carlo (Ernest) 1954-....... **CLC 39**
See also CA 119; 133

Gee, Maggie (Mary) 1948-........ **CLC 57**
See also CA 130

Gee, Maurice (Gough) 1931-....... **CLC 29**
See also CA 97-100; SATA 46

Gelbart, Larry (Simon) 1923- ... **CLC 21, 61**
See also CA 73-76; CANR 45

Gelber, Jack 1932-........**CLC 1, 6, 14, 79**
See also CA 1-4R; CANR 2; DLB 7

Gellhorn, Martha (Ellis) 1908- .. **CLC 14, 60**
See also CA 77-80; CANR 44; DLBY 82

Genet, Jean
1910-1986 ...... **CLC 1, 2, 5, 10, 14, 44,**
46; DAM DRAM
See also CA 13-16R; CANR 18; DLB 72;
DLBY 86; MTCW

Gent, Peter 1942-................ **CLC 29**
See also AITN 1; CA 89-92; DLBY 82

Gentlewoman in New England, A
See Bradstreet, Anne

Gentlewoman in Those Parts, A
See Bradstreet, Anne

George, Jean Craighead 1919-...... **CLC 35**
See also AAYA 8; CA 5-8R; CANR 25;
CLR 1; DLB 52; JRDA; MAICYA;
SATA 2, 68

George, Stefan (Anton)
1868-1933 .... **TCLC 2, 14**
See also CA 104

Georges, Georges Martin
See Simenon, Georges (Jacques Christian)

Gerhardi, William Alexander
See Gerhardie, William Alexander

Gerhardie, William Alexander
1895-1977 .... **CLC 5**
See also CA 25-28R; 73-76; CANR 18;
DLB 36

Gerstler, Amy 1956-.............. **CLC 70**
See also CA 146

Gertler, T. .... **CLC 34**
See also CA 116; 121; INT 121

gfgg .... **CLC XvXzc**

Ghalib .... **NCLC 39**
See also Ghalib, Hsadullah Khan

Ghalib, Hsadullah Khan 1797-1869
See Ghalib
See also DAM POET

Ghelderode, Michel de
1898-1962 .... **CLC 6, 11; DAM DRAM**
See also CA 85-88; CANR 40

Ghiselin, Brewster 1903- .... **CLC 23**
See also CA 13-16R; CAAS 10; CANR 13

Ghose, Zulfikar 1935-............ **CLC 42**
See also CA 65-68

Ghosh, Amitav 1956-............ **CLC 44**
See also CA 147

Giacosa, Giuseppe 1847-1906 ...... **TCLC 7**
See also CA 104

Gibb, Lee
See Waterhouse, Keith (Spencer)

Gibbon, Lewis Grassic .... **TCLC 4**
See also Mitchell, James Leslie

Gibbons, Kaye
1960- .... **CLC 50, 88; DAM POP**
See also CA 151

Gibran, Kahlil
1883-1931 .... **TCLC 1, 9; DAM POET,**
POP; PC 9
See also CA 104; 150

Gibran, Khalil
See Gibran, Kahlil

Gibson, William
1914- ....**CLC 23; DA; DAB; DAC;**
DAM DRAM, MST
See also CA 9-12R; CANR 9, 42; DLB 7;
SATA 66

Gibson, William (Ford)
1948- .... **CLC 39, 63; DAM POP**
See also AAYA 12; CA 126; 133; CANR 52

Gide, Andre (Paul Guillaume)
1869-1951 .... **TCLC 5, 12, 36; DA;**
DAB; DAC; DAM MST, NOV; SSC 13;
WLC
See also CA 104; 124; DLB 65; MTCW

Gifford, Barry (Colby) 1946-....... **CLC 34**
See also CA 65-68; CANR 9, 30, 40

Gilbert, W(illiam) S(chwenck)
1836-1911 ..... **TCLC 3; DAM DRAM,**
POET
See also CA 104; SATA 36

Gilbreth, Frank B., Jr. 1911-....... **CLC 17**
See also CA 9-12R; SATA 2

Gilchrist, Ellen
1935- .... **CLC 34, 48; DAM POP;**
SSC 14
See also CA 113; 116; CANR 41; DLB 130;
MTCW

Giles, Molly 1942-.............. **CLC 39**
See also CA 126

Gill, Patrick
See Creasey, John

Gilliam, Terry (Vance) 1940-....... **CLC 21**
See also Monty Python
See also AAYA 19; CA 108; 113;
CANR 35; INT 113

Gillian, Jerry
See Gilliam, Terry (Vance)

Gilliatt, Penelope (Ann Douglass)
1932-1993 .... **CLC 2, 10, 13, 53**
See also AITN 2; CA 13-16R; 141;
CANR 49; DLB 14

Gilman, Charlotte (Anna) Perkins (Stetson)
1860-1935 .... **TCLC 9, 37; SSC 13**
See also CA 106; 150

Gilmour, David 1949-............. **CLC 35**
See also CA 138, 147

Gilpin, William 1724-1804....... **NCLC 30**

Gilray, J. D.
   See Mencken, H(enry) L(ouis)

Gilroy, Frank D(aniel) 1925-........ **CLC 2**
   See also CA 81-84; CANR 32; DLB 7

Ginsberg, Allen
   1926- ......**CLC 1, 2, 3, 4, 6, 13, 36, 69;**
      DA; DAB; DAC; DAM MST, POET;
      PC 4; WLC 3
   See also AITN 1; CA 1-4R; CANR 2, 41;
      CDALB 1941-1968; DLB 5, 16, 169;
      MTCW

Ginzburg, Natalia
   1916-1991 ....**CLC 5, 11, 54, 70**
   See also CA 85-88; 135; CANR 33; MTCW

Giono, Jean 1895-1970.........**CLC 4, 11**
   See also CA 45-48; 29-32R; CANR 2, 35;
      DLB 72; MTCW

Giovanni, Nikki
   1943- ......**CLC 2, 4, 19, 64; BLC; DA;**
      DAB; DAC; DAM MST, MULT, POET
   See also AITN 1; BW 2; CA 29-32R;
      CAAS 6; CANR 18, 41; CLR 6; DLB 5,
      41; INT CANR-18; MAICYA; MTCW;
      SATA 24

Giovene, Andrea 1904-............ **CLC 7**
   See also CA 85-88

Gippius, Zinaida (Nikolayevna) 1869-1945
   See Hippius, Zinaida
   See also CA 106

Giraudoux, (Hippolyte) Jean
   1882-1944 .... **TCLC 2, 7; DAM DRAM**
   See also CA 104; DLB 65

Gironella, Jose Maria 1917-....... **CLC 11**
   See also CA 101

Gissing, George (Robert)
   1857-1903 ....**TCLC 3, 24, 47**
   See also CA 105; DLB 18, 135

Giurlani, Aldo
   See Palazzeschi, Aldo

Gladkov, Fyodor (Vasilyevich)
   1883-1958 ....**TCLC 27**

Glanville, Brian (Lester) 1931-...... **CLC 6**
   See also CA 5-8R; CAAS 9; CANR 3;
      DLB 15, 139; SATA 42

Glasgow, Ellen (Anderson Gholson)
   1873(?)-1945 ....**TCLC 2, 7**
   See also CA 104; DLB 9, 12

Glaspell, Susan 1882(?)-1948.....**TCLC 55**
   See also CA 110; 154; DLB 7, 9, 78;
      YABC 2

Glassco, John 1909-1981 .... **CLC 9**
   See also CA 13-16R; 102; CANR 15;
      DLB 68

Glasscock, Amnesia
   See Steinbeck, John (Ernst)

Glasser, Ronald J. 1940(?)-........ **CLC 37**

Glassman, Joyce
   See Johnson, Joyce

Glendinning, Victoria 1937-........ **CLC 50**
   See also CA 120; 127; DLB 155

Glissant, Edouard
   1928- .... **CLC 10, 68; DAM MULT**
   See also CA 153

Gloag, Julian 1930- .... **CLC 40**
   See also AITN 1; CA 65-68; CANR 10

Glowacki, Aleksander
   See Prus, Boleslaw

Gluck, Louise (Elisabeth)
   1943- ....**CLC 7, 22, 44, 81;**
      DAM POET; PC 16
   See also CA 33-36R; CANR 40; DLB 5

Gobineau, Joseph Arthur (Comte) de
   1816-1882 ....**NCLC 17**
   See also DLB 123

Godard, Jean-Luc 1930-.......... **CLC 20**
   See also CA 93-96

Godden, (Margaret) Rumer 1907-... **CLC 53**
   See also AAYA 6; CA 5-8R; CANR 4, 27,
      36, 55; CLR 20; DLB 161; MAICYA;
      SAAS 12; SATA 3, 36

Godoy Alcayaga, Lucila 1889-1957
   See Mistral, Gabriela
   See also BW 2; CA 104; 131; DAM MULT;
      HW; MTCW

Godwin, Gail (Kathleen)
   1937- ....**CLC 5, 8, 22, 31, 69;**
      DAM POP
   See also CA 29-32R; CANR 15, 43; DLB 6;
      INT CANR-15; MTCW

Godwin, William 1756-1836...... **NCLC 14**
   See also CDBLB 1789-1832; DLB 39, 104,
      142, 158, 163

Goebbels, Josef
   See Goebbels, (Paul) Joseph

Goebbels, (Paul) Joseph
   1897-1945 ....**TCLC 68**
   See also CA 115; 148

Goebbels, Joseph Paul
   See Goebbels, (Paul) Joseph

Goethe, Johann Wolfgang von
   1749-1832 ....**NCLC 4, 22, 34; DA;**
      DAB; DAC; DAM DRAM, MST,
      POET; PC 5; WLC 3
   See also DLB 94

Gogarty, Oliver St. John
   1878-1957 ....**TCLC 15**
   See also CA 109; 150; DLB 15, 19

Gogol, Nikolai (Vasilyevich)
   1809-1852 ....**NCLC 5, 15, 31; DA;**
      DAB; DAC; DAM DRAM, MST; DC 1;
      SSC 4; WLC

Goines, Donald
   1937(?)-1974 ....**CLC 80; BLC;**
      DAM MULT, POP
   See also AITN 1; BW 1; CA 124; 114;
      DLB 33

Gold, Herbert 1924-.......**CLC 4, 7, 14, 42**
   See also CA 9-12R; CANR 17, 45; DLB 2;
      DLBY 81

Goldbarth, Albert 1948-........ **CLC 5, 38**
   See also CA 53-56; CANR 6, 40; DLB 120

Goldberg, Anatol 1910-1982 .... **CLC 34**
   See also CA 131; 117

Goldemberg, Isaac 1945-.......... **CLC 52**
   See also CA 69-72; CAAS 12; CANR 11,
      32; HW

Golding, William (Gerald)
   1911-1993 .... **CLC 1, 2, 3, 8, 10, 17, 27,**
      58, 81; DA; DAB; DAC; DAM MST,
      NOV; WLC
   See also AAYA 5; CA 5-8R; 141;
      CANR 13, 33, 54; CDBLB 1945-1960;
      DLB 15, 100; MTCW

Goldman, Emma 1869-1940...... **TCLC 13**
   See also CA 110; 150

Goldman, Francisco 1955-......... **CLC 76**

Goldman, William (W.) 1931-.... **CLC 1, 48**
   See also CA 9-12R; CANR 29; DLB 44

Goldmann, Lucien 1913-1970 ...... **CLC 24**
   See also CA 25-28; CAP 2

Goldoni, Carlo
   1707-1793 .... **LC 4; DAM DRAM**

Goldsberry, Steven 1949-......... **CLC 34**
   See also CA 131

Goldsmith, Oliver
   1728-1774 ...... **LC 2; DA; DAB; DAC;**
      DAM DRAM, MST, NOV, POET;
      WLC
   See also CDBLB 1660-1789; DLB 39, 89,
      104, 109, 142; SATA 26

Goldsmith, Peter
   See Priestley, J(ohn) B(oynton)

Gombrowicz, Witold
   1904-1969 ....**CLC 4, 7, 11, 49;**
      DAM DRAM
   See also CA 19-20; 25-28R; CAP 2

Gomez de la Serna, Ramon
   1888-1963 ....**CLC 9**
   See also CA 153; 116; HW

Goncharov, Ivan Alexandrovich
   1812-1891 ....**NCLC 1**

Goncourt, Edmond (Louis Antoine Huot) de
   1822-1896 ....**NCLC 7**
   See also DLB 123

Goncourt, Jules (Alfred Huot) de
   1830-1870 ....**NCLC 7**
   See also DLB 123

Gontier, Fernande 19(?)-.......... **CLC 50**

Goodman, Paul 1911-1972....**CLC 1, 2, 4, 7**
   See also CA 19-20; 37-40R; CANR 34;
      CAP 2; DLB 130; MTCW

Gordimer, Nadine
   1923- ....**CLC 3, 5, 7, 10, 18, 33, 51, 70;**
      DA; DAB; DAC; DAM MST, NOV;
      SSC 17
   See also CA 5-8R; CANR 3, 28;
      INT CANR-28; MTCW

Gordon, Adam Lindsay
   1833-1870 ....**NCLC 21**

Gordon, Caroline
   1895-1981 ... **CLC 6, 13, 29, 83; SSC 15**
   See also CA 11-12; 103; CANR 36; CAP 1;
      DLB 4, 9, 102; DLBY 81; MTCW

Gordon, Charles William 1860-1937
   See Connor, Ralph
   See also CA 109

Gordon, Mary (Catherine)
   1949- ....**CLC 13, 22**
   See also CA 102; CANR 44; DLB 6;
      DLBY 81; INT 102; MTCW

Gregory, Isabella Augusta (Persse)
1852-1932 . . . . TCLC 1
See also CA 104; DLB 10

Gregory, J. Dennis
See Williams, John A(lfred)

Grendon, Stephen
See Derleth, August (William)

Grenville, Kate 1950- . . . . CLC 61
See also CA 118; CANR 53

Grenville, Pelham
See Wodehouse, P(elham) G(renville)

Greve, Felix Paul (Berthold Friedrich)
1879-1948
See Grove, Frederick Philip
See also CA 104; 141; DAC; DAM MST

Grey, Zane
1872-1939 . . . . TCLC 6; DAM POP
See also CA 104; 132; DLB 9; MTCW

Grieg, (Johan) Nordahl (Brun)
1902-1943 . . . . TCLC 10
See also CA 107

Grieve, C(hristopher) M(urray)
1892-1978 . . . . CLC 11, 19; DAM POET
See also MacDiarmid, Hugh; Pteleon
See also CA 5-8R; 85-88; CANR 33;
MTCW

Griffin, Gerald 1803-1840 . . . . NCLC 7
See also DLB 159

Griffin, John Howard 1920-1980 . . . . CLC 68
See also AITN 1; CA 1-4R; 101; CANR 2

Griffin, Peter 1942- . . . . CLC 39
See also CA 136

Griffith, D(avid) Lewelyn W(ark)
1875(?)-1948 . . . . TCLC 68
See also CA 119; 150

Griffith, Lawrence
See Griffith, D(avid) Lewelyn W(ark)

Griffiths, Trevor 1935- . . . . CLC 13, 52
See also CA 97-100; CANR 45; DLB 13

Grigson, Geoffrey (Edward Harvey)
1905-1985 . . . . CLC 7, 39
See also CA 25-28R; 118; CANR 20, 33;
DLB 27; MTCW

Grillparzer, Franz 1791-1872 . . . . . . NCLC 1
See also DLB 133

Grimble, Reverend Charles James
See Eliot, T(homas) S(tearns)

Grimke, Charlotte L(ottie) Forten
1837(?)-1914
See Forten, Charlotte L.
See also BW 1; CA 117; 124; DAM MULT,
POET

Grimm, Jacob Ludwig Karl
1785-1863 . . . . NCLC 3
See also DLB 90; MAICYA; SATA 22

Grimm, Wilhelm Karl 1786-1859 . . NCLC 3
See also DLB 90; MAICYA; SATA 22

Grimmelshausen, Johann Jakob Christoffel
von 1621-1676 . . . . LC 6
See also DLB 168

Grindel, Eugene 1895-1952
See Eluard, Paul
See also CA 104

Grisham, John 1955- . . CLC 84; DAM POP
See also AAYA 14; CA 138; CANR 47

Grossman, David 1954- . . . . CLC 67
See also CA 138

Grossman, Vasily (Semenovich)
1905-1964 . . . . CLC 41
See also CA 124; 130; MTCW

Grove, Frederick Philip . . . . TCLC 4
See also Greve, Felix Paul (Berthold
Friedrich)
See also DLB 92

Grubb
See Crumb, R(obert)

Grumbach, Doris (Isaac)
1918- . . . . CLC 13, 22, 64
See also CA 5-8R; CAAS 2; CANR 9, 42;
INT CANR-9

Grundtvig, Nicolai Frederik Severin
1783-1872 . . . . NCLC 1

Grunge
See Crumb, R(obert)

Grunwald, Lisa 1959- . . . . CLC 44
See also CA 120

Guare, John
1938- . . . . CLC 8, 14, 29, 67;
DAM DRAM
See also CA 73-76; CANR 21; DLB 7;
MTCW

Gudjonsson, Halldor Kiljan 1902-
See Laxness, Halldor
See also CA 103

Guenter, Erich
See Eich, Guenter

Guest, Barbara 1920- . . . . CLC 34
See also CA 25-28R; CANR 11, 44; DLB 5

Guest, Judith (Ann)
1936- . . . . CLC 8, 30; DAM NOV, POP
See also AAYA 7; CA 77-80; CANR 15;
INT CANR-15; MTCW

Guevara, Che . . . . CLC 87; HLC
See also Guevara (Serna), Ernesto

Guevara (Serna), Ernesto 1928-1967
See Guevara, Che
See also CA 127; 111; DAM MULT; HW

Guild, Nicholas M. 1944- . . . . CLC 33
See also CA 93-96

Guillemin, Jacques
See Sartre, Jean-Paul

Guillen, Jorge
1893-1984 . . . . . . CLC 11; DAM MULT,
POET
See also CA 89-92; 112; DLB 108; HW

Guillen, Nicolas (Cristobal)
1902-1989 . . . . CLC 48, 79; BLC;
DAM MST, MULT, POET; HLC
See also BW 2; CA 116; 125; 129; HW

Guillevic, (Eugene) 1907- . . . . CLC 33
See also CA 93-96

Guillois
See Desnos, Robert

Guillois, Valentin
See Desnos, Robert

Guiney, Louise Imogen
1861-1920 . . . . TCLC 41
See also DLB 54

Guiraldes, Ricardo (Guillermo)
1886-1927 . . . . TCLC 39
See also CA 131; HW; MTCW

Gumilev, Nikolai Stephanovich
1886-1921 . . . . TCLC 60

Gunesekera, Romesh . . . . CLC 91

Gunn, Bill . . . . CLC 5
See also Gunn, William Harrison
See also DLB 38

Gunn, Thom(son William)
1929- . . . . CLC 3, 6, 18, 32, 81;
DAM POET
See also CA 17-20R; CANR 9, 33;
CDBLB 1960 to Present; DLB 27;
INT CANR-33; MTCW

Gunn, William Harrison 1934(?)-1989
See Gunn, Bill
See also AITN 1; BW 1; CA 13-16R; 128;
CANR 12, 25

Gunnars, Kristjana 1948- . . . . CLC 69
See also CA 113; DLB 60

Gurganus, Allan
1947- . . . . CLC 70; DAM POP
See also BEST 90:1; CA 135

Gurney, A(lbert) R(amsdell), Jr.
1930- . . . . CLC 32, 50, 54; DAM DRAM
See also CA 77-80; CANR 32

Gurney, Ivor (Bertie) 1890-1937 . . . TCLC 33

Gurney, Peter
See Gurney, A(lbert) R(amsdell), Jr.

Guro, Elena 1877-1913 . . . . TCLC 56

Gustafson, Ralph (Barker) 1909- . . . . CLC 36
See also CA 21-24R; CANR 8, 45; DLB 88

Gut, Gom
See Simenon, Georges (Jacques Christian)

Guterson, David 1956- . . . . CLC 91
See also CA 132

Guthrie, A(lfred) B(ertram), Jr.
1901-1991 . . . . CLC 23
See also CA 57-60; 134; CANR 24; DLB 6;
SATA 62; SATA-Obit 67

Guthrie, Isobel
See Grieve, C(hristopher) M(urray)

Guthrie, Woodrow Wilson 1912-1967
See Guthrie, Woody
See also CA 113; 93-96

Guthrie, Woody . . . . CLC 35
See also Guthrie, Woodrow Wilson

Guy, Rosa (Cuthbert) 1928- . . . . CLC 26
See also AAYA 4; BW 2; CA 17-20R;
CANR 14, 34; CLR 13; DLB 33; JRDA;
MAICYA; SATA 14, 62

Gwendolyn
See Bennett, (Enoch) Arnold

H. D. . . . . CLC 3, 8, 14, 31, 34, 73; PC 5
See also Doolittle, Hilda

H. de V.
See Buchan, John

Haavikko, Paavo Juhani
1931- . . . . CLC 18, 34
See also CA 106

Habbema, Koos
See Heijermans, Herman

Hacker, Marilyn
1942- . . . . **CLC 5, 9, 23, 72, 91;**
DAM POET
See also CA 77-80; DLB 120

Haggard, H(enry) Rider
1856-1925 . . . . **TCLC 11**
See also CA 108; 148; DLB 70, 156, 174;
SATA 16

Hagiosy, L.
See Larbaud, Valery (Nicolas)

Hagiwara Sakutaro 1886-1942 . . . . **TCLC 60**

Haig, Fenil
See Ford, Ford Madox

Haig-Brown, Roderick (Langmere)
1908-1976 . . . . **CLC 21**
See also CA 5-8R; 69-72; CANR 4, 38;
CLR 31; DLB 88; MAICYA; SATA 12

Hailey, Arthur
1920- . . . . **CLC 5; DAM NOV, POP**
See also AITN 2; BEST 90:3; CA 1-4R;
CANR 2, 36; DLB 88; DLBY 82; MTCW

Hailey, Elizabeth Forsythe 1938- . . . **CLC 40**
See also CA 93-96; CAAS 1; CANR 15, 48;
INT CANR-15

Haines, John (Meade) 1924- . . . . **CLC 58**
See also CA 17-20R; CANR 13, 34; DLB 5

Hakluyt, Richard 1552-1616 . . . . **LC 31**

Haldeman, Joe (William) 1943- . . . . . **CLC 61**
See also CA 53-56; CAAS 25; CANR 6;
DLB 8; INT CANR-6

Haley, Alex(ander Murray Palmer)
1921-1992 . . . . **CLC 8, 12, 76; BLC; DA;**
DAB; DAC; DAM MST, MULT, POP
See also BW 2; CA 77-80; 136; DLB 38;
MTCW

Haliburton, Thomas Chandler
1796-1865 . . . . **NCLC 15**
See also DLB 11, 99

Hall, Donald (Andrew, Jr.)
1928- . . **CLC 1, 13, 37, 59; DAM POET**
See also CA 5-8R; CAAS 7; CANR 2, 44;
DLB 5; SATA 23

Hall, Frederic Sauser
See Sauser-Hall, Frederic

Hall, James
See Kuttner, Henry

Hall, James Norman 1887-1951 . . . **TCLC 23**
See also CA 123; SATA 21

Hall, (Marguerite) Radclyffe
1886-1943 . . . . **TCLC 12**
See also CA 110; 150

Hall, Rodney 1935- . . . . **CLC 51**
See also CA 109

Halleck, Fitz-Greene 1790-1867 . . **NCLC 47**
See also DLB 3

Halliday, Michael
See Creasey, John

Halpern, Daniel 1945- . . . . **CLC 14**
See also CA 33-36R

Hamburger, Michael (Peter Leopold)
1924- . . . . **CLC 5, 14**
See also CA 5-8R; CAAS 4; CANR 2, 47;
DLB 27

Hamill, Pete 1935- . . . . **CLC 10**
See also CA 25-28R; CANR 18

Hamilton, Alexander
1755(?)-1804 . . . . **NCLC 49**
See also DLB 37

Hamilton, Clive
See Lewis, C(live) S(taples)

Hamilton, Edmond 1904-1977 . . . . . . **CLC 1**
See also CA 1-4R; CANR 3; DLB 8

Hamilton, Eugene (Jacob) Lee
See Lee-Hamilton, Eugene (Jacob)

Hamilton, Franklin
See Silverberg, Robert

Hamilton, Gail
See Corcoran, Barbara

Hamilton, Mollie
See Kaye, M(ary) M(argaret)

Hamilton, (Anthony Walter) Patrick
1904-1962 . . . . **CLC 51**
See also CA 113; DLB 10

Hamilton, Virginia
1936- . . . . **CLC 26; DAM MULT**
See also AAYA 2; BW 2; CA 25-28R;
CANR 20, 37; CLR 1, 11, 40; DLB 33,
52; INT CANR-20; JRDA; MAICYA;
MTCW; SATA 4, 56, 79

Hammett, (Samuel) Dashiell
1894-1961 . . . . **CLC 3, 5, 10, 19, 47;**
SSC 17
See also AITN 1; CA 81-84; CANR 42;
CDALB 1929-1941; DLBD 6; MTCW

Hammon, Jupiter
1711(?)-1800(?) . . . . **NCLC 5; BLC;**
DAM MULT, POET; PC 16
See also DLB 31, 50

Hammond, Keith
See Kuttner, Henry

Hamner, Earl (Henry), Jr. 1923- . . . **CLC 12**
See also AITN 2; CA 73-76; DLB 6

Hampton, Christopher (James)
1946- . . . . **CLC 4**
See also CA 25-28R; DLB 13; MTCW

Hamsun, Knut . . . . **TCLC 2, 14, 49**
See also Pedersen, Knut

Handke, Peter
1942- . . . . **CLC 5, 8, 10, 15, 38;**
DAM DRAM, NOV
See also CA 77-80; CANR 33; DLB 85,
124; MTCW

Hanley, James 1901-1985 . . . **CLC 3, 5, 8, 13**
See also CA 73-76; 117; CANR 36; MTCW

Hannah, Barry 1942- . . . . **CLC 23, 38, 90**
See also CA 108; 110; CANR 43; DLB 6;
INT 110; MTCW

Hannon, Ezra
See Hunter, Evan

Hansberry, Lorraine (Vivian)
1930-1965 . . . . . . **CLC 17, 62; BLC; DA;**
DAB; DAC; DAM DRAM, MST,
MULT; DC 2
See also BW 1; CA 109; 25-28R; CABS 3;
CDALB 1941-1968; DLB 7, 38; MTCW

Hansen, Joseph 1923- . . . . **CLC 38**
See also CA 29-32R; CAAS 17; CANR 16,
44; INT CANR-16

Hansen, Martin A. 1909-1955 . . . . . **TCLC 32**

Hanson, Kenneth O(stlin) 1922- . . . . **CLC 13**
See also CA 53-56; CANR 7

Hardwick, Elizabeth
1916- . . . . **CLC 13; DAM NOV**
See also CA 5-8R; CANR 3, 32; DLB 6;
MTCW

Hardy, Thomas
1840-1928 . . . . . . **TCLC 4, 10, 18, 32, 48,**
53; DA; DAB; DAC; DAM MST, NOV,
POET; PC 8; SSC 2; WLC
See also CA 104; 123; CDBLB 1890-1914;
DLB 18, 19, 135; MTCW

Hare, David 1947- . . . . **CLC 29, 58**
See also CA 97-100; CANR 39; DLB 13;
MTCW

Harford, Henry
See Hudson, W(illiam) H(enry)

Hargrave, Leonie
See Disch, Thomas M(ichael)

Harjo, Joy 1951- . . . **CLC 83; DAM MULT**
See also CA 114; CANR 35; DLB 120;
NNAL

Harlan, Louis R(udolph) 1922- . . . . . **CLC 34**
See also CA 21-24R; CANR 25, 55

Harling, Robert 1951(?)- . . . . **CLC 53**
See also CA 147

Harmon, William (Ruth) 1938- . . . . . **CLC 38**
See also CA 33-36R; CANR 14, 32, 35;
SATA 65

Harper, F. E. W.
See Harper, Frances Ellen Watkins

Harper, Frances E. W.
See Harper, Frances Ellen Watkins

Harper, Frances E. Watkins
See Harper, Frances Ellen Watkins

Harper, Frances Ellen
See Harper, Frances Ellen Watkins

Harper, Frances Ellen Watkins
1825-1911 . . . . **TCLC 14; BLC;**
DAM MULT, POET
See also BW 1; CA 111; 125; DLB 50

Harper, Michael S(teven) 1938- . . **CLC 7, 22**
See also BW 1; CA 33-36R; CANR 24;
DLB 41

Harper, Mrs. F. E. W.
See Harper, Frances Ellen Watkins

Harris, Christie (Lucy) Irwin
1907- . . . . **CLC 12**
See also CA 5-8R; CANR 6; DLB 88;
JRDA; MAICYA; SAAS 10; SATA 6, 74

Harris, Frank 1856-1931 . . . . **TCLC 24**
See also CA 109; 150; DLB 156

Harris, George Washington
1814-1869 . . . . **NCLC 23**
See also DLB 3, 11

Harris, Joel Chandler
1848-1908 . . . . **TCLC 2; SSC 19**
See also CA 104; 137; DLB 11, 23, 42, 78,
91; MAICYA; YABC 1

Harris, John (Wyndham Parkes Lucas)
Beynon 1903-1969
See Wyndham, John
See also CA 102; 89-92

Harris, MacDonald . . . . **CLC 9**
See also Heiney, Donald (William)

Heinlein, Robert A(nson)
    1907-1988 . . . . . . **CLC 1, 3, 8, 14, 26, 55;**
                                            DAM POP
    See also AAYA 17; CA 1-4R; 125;
    CANR 1, 20, 53; DLB 8; JRDA;
    MAICYA; MTCW; SATA 9, 69;
    SATA-Obit 56

Helforth, John
    See Doolittle, Hilda

Hellenhofferu, Vojtech Kapristian z
    See Hasek, Jaroslav (Matej Frantisek)

Heller, Joseph
    1923- . . . . **CLC 1, 3, 5, 8, 11, 36, 63; DA;**
        DAB; DAC; DAM MST, NOV, POP;
                                            WLC
    See also AITN 1; CA 5-8R; CABS 1;
    CANR 8, 42; DLB 2, 28; DLBY 80;
    INT CANR-8; MTCW

Hellman, Lillian (Florence)
    1906-1984 . . . . . . **CLC 2, 4, 8, 14, 18, 34,**
        44, 52; DAM DRAM; DC 1
    See also AITN 1, 2; CA 13-16R; 112;
    CANR 33; DLB 7; DLBY 84; MTCW

Helprin, Mark
    1947- . . . . **CLC 7, 10, 22, 32;**
                                            DAM NOV, POP
    See also CA 81-84; CANR 47; DLBY 85;
    MTCW

Helvetius, Claude-Adrien
    1715-1771 . . . . **LC 26**

Helyar, Jane Penelope Josephine   1933-
    See Poole, Josephine
    See also CA 21-24R; CANR 10, 26;
    SATA 82

Hemans, Felicia   1793-1835 . . . . . . **NCLC 29**
    See also DLB 96

Hemingway, Ernest (Miller)
    1899-1961 . . . . **CLC 1, 3, 6, 8, 10, 13, 19,**
        30, 34, 39, 41, 44, 50, 61, 80; DA; DAB;
        DAC; DAM MST, NOV; SSC 1; WLC
    See also AAYA 19; CA 77-80; CANR 34;
    CDALB 1917-1929; DLB 4, 9, 102;
    DLBD 1; DLBY 81, 87; MTCW

Hempel, Amy   1951- . . . . **CLC 39**
    See also CA 118; 137

Henderson, F. C.
    See Mencken, H(enry) L(ouis)

Henderson, Sylvia
    See Ashton-Warner, Sylvia (Constance)

Henley, Beth . . . . **CLC 23; DC 6**
    See also Henley, Elizabeth Becker
    See also CABS 3; DLBY 86

Henley, Elizabeth Becker   1952-
    See Henley, Beth
    See also CA 107; CANR 32; DAM DRAM,
    MST; MTCW

Henley, William Ernest
    1849-1903 . . . . **TCLC 8**
    See also CA 105; DLB 19

Hennissart, Martha
    See Lathen, Emma
    See also CA 85-88

Henry, O. . . . . **TCLC 1, 19; SSC 5; WLC**
    See also Porter, William Sydney

Henry, Patrick   1736-1799 . . . . **LC 25**

Henryson, Robert   1430(?)-1506(?). . . . **LC 20**
    See also DLB 146

Henry VIII   1491-1547 . . . . **LC 10**

Henschke, Alfred
    See Klabund

Hentoff, Nat(han Irving)   1925- . . . . . **CLC 26**
    See also AAYA 4; CA 1-4R; CAAS 6;
    CANR 5, 25; CLR 1; INT CANR-25;
    JRDA; MAICYA; SATA 42, 69;
    SATA-Brief 27

Heppenstall, (John) Rayner
    1911-1981 . . . . **CLC 10**
    See also CA 1-4R; 103; CANR 29

Herbert, Frank (Patrick)
    1920-1986 . . . . . . **CLC 12, 23, 35, 44, 85;**
                                            DAM POP
    See also CA 53-56; 118; CANR 5, 43;
    DLB 8; INT CANR-5; MTCW; SATA 9,
    37; SATA-Obit 47

Herbert, George
    1593-1633 . . . . **LC 24; DAB;**
                                DAM POET; PC 4
    See also CDBLB Before 1660; DLB 126

Herbert, Zbigniew
    1924- . . . . **CLC 9, 43; DAM POET**
    See also CA 89-92; CANR 36; MTCW

Herbst, Josephine (Frey)
    1897-1969 . . . . **CLC 34**
    See also CA 5-8R; 25-28R; DLB 9

Hergesheimer, Joseph
    1880-1954 . . . . **TCLC 11**
    See also CA 109; DLB 102, 9

Herlihy, James Leo   1927-1993 . . . . . . **CLC 6**
    See also CA 1-4R; 143; CANR 2

Hermogenes   fl. c. 175- . . . . **CMLC 6**

Hernandez, Jose   1834-1886 . . . . . . **NCLC 17**

Herodotus   c. 484B.C.-429B.C.. . . . . **CMLC 17**

Herrick, Robert
    1591-1674 . . . . . **LC 13; DA; DAB; DAC;**
                        DAM MST, POP; PC 9
    See also DLB 126

Herring, Guilles
    See Somerville, Edith

Herriot, James
    1916-1995 . . . . **CLC 12; DAM POP**
    See also Wight, James Alfred
    See also AAYA 1; CA 148; CANR 40;
    SATA 86

Herrmann, Dorothy   1941- . . . . **CLC 44**
    See also CA 107

Herrmann, Taffy
    See Herrmann, Dorothy

Hersey, John (Richard)
    1914-1993 . . . . **CLC 1, 2, 7, 9, 40, 81, 97;**
                                            DAM POP
    See also CA 17-20R; 140; CANR 33;
    DLB 6; MTCW; SATA 25;
    SATA-Obit 76

Herzen, Aleksandr Ivanovich
    1812-1870 . . . . **NCLC 10**

Herzl, Theodor   1860-1904 . . . . **TCLC 36**

Herzog, Werner   1942- . . . . **CLC 16**
    See also CA 89-92

Hesiod   c. 8th cent. B.C.- . . . . **CMLC 5**

Hesse, Hermann
    1877-1962 . . . . **CLC 1, 2, 3, 6, 11, 17, 25,**
        69; DA; DAB; DAC; DAM MST, NOV;
                                        SSC 9; WLC
    See also CA 17-18; CAP 2; DLB 66;
    MTCW; SATA 50

Hewes, Cady
    See De Voto, Bernard (Augustine)

Heyen, William   1940- . . . . **CLC 13, 18**
    See also CA 33-36R; CAAS 9; DLB 5

Heyerdahl, Thor   1914- . . . . **CLC 26**
    See also CA 5-8R; CANR 5, 22; MTCW;
    SATA 2, 52

Heym, Georg (Theodor Franz Arthur)
    1887-1912 . . . . **TCLC 9**
    See also CA 106

Heym, Stefan   1913- . . . . **CLC 41**
    See also CA 9-12R; CANR 4; DLB 69

Heyse, Paul (Johann Ludwig von)
    1830-1914 . . . . **TCLC 8**
    See also CA 104; DLB 129

Heyward, (Edwin) DuBose
    1885-1940 . . . . **TCLC 59**
    See also CA 108; DLB 7, 9, 45; SATA 21

Hibbert, Eleanor Alice Burford
    1906-1993 . . . . **CLC 7; DAM POP**
    See also BEST 90:4; CA 17-20R; 140;
    CANR 9, 28; SATA 2; SATA-Obit 74

Hichens, Robert S.   1864-1950 . . . . . **TCLC 64**
    See also DLB 153

Higgins, George V(incent)
    1939- . . . . **CLC 4, 7, 10, 18**
    See also CA 77-80; CAAS 5; CANR 17, 51;
    DLB 2; DLBY 81; INT CANR-17;
    MTCW

Higginson, Thomas Wentworth
    1823-1911 . . . . **TCLC 36**
    See also DLB 1, 64

Highet, Helen
    See MacInnes, Helen (Clark)

Highsmith, (Mary) Patricia
    1921-1995 . . . . **CLC 2, 4, 14, 42;**
                                            DAM NOV, POP
    See also CA 1-4R; 147; CANR 1, 20, 48;
    MTCW

Highwater, Jamake (Mamake)
    1942(?)- . . . . **CLC 12**
    See also AAYA 7; CA 65-68; CAAS 7;
    CANR 10, 34; CLR 17; DLB 52;
    DLBY 85; JRDA; MAICYA; SATA 32,
    69; SATA-Brief 30

Highway, Tomson
    1951- . . . . . **CLC 92; DAC; DAM MULT**
    See also CA 151; NNAL

Higuchi, Ichiyo   1872-1896 . . . . **NCLC 49**

Hijuelos, Oscar
    1951- . . . . **CLC 65; DAM MULT, POP;**
                                            HLC
    See also BEST 90:1; CA 123; CANR 50;
    DLB 145; HW

Hikmet, Nazim   1902(?)-1963 . . . . **CLC 40**
    See also CA 141; 93-96

Hildegard von Bingen
    1098-1179 . . . . **CMLC 20**
    See also DLB 148

Hope, Christopher (David Tully)
   1944- . . . . **CLC 52**
   See also CA 106; CANR 47; SATA 62

Hopkins, Gerard Manley
   1844-1889 . . . . . . **NCLC 17; DA; DAB;**
      DAC; DAM MST, POET; PC 15; WLC
   See also CDBLB 1890-1914; DLB 35, 57

Hopkins, John (Richard) 1931- . . . . . . **CLC 4**
   See also CA 85-88

Hopkins, Pauline Elizabeth
   1859-1930 . . . . **TCLC 28; BLC;**
      DAM MULT
   See also BW 2; CA 141; DLB 50

Hopkinson, Francis 1737-1791 . . . . . . **LC 25**
   See also DLB 31

Hopley-Woolrich, Cornell George 1903-1968
   See Woolrich, Cornell
   See also CA 13-14; CAP 1

Horatio
   See Proust, (Valentin-Louis-George-Eugene-)
   Marcel

Horgan, Paul (George Vincent O'Shaughnessy)
   1903-1995 . . . . . . **CLC 9, 53; DAM NOV**
   See also CA 13-16R; 147; CANR 9, 35;
   DLB 102; DLBY 85; INT CANR-9;
   MTCW; SATA 13; SATA-Obit 84

Horn, Peter
   See Kuttner, Henry

Hornem, Horace Esq.
   See Byron, George Gordon (Noel)

Hornung, E(rnest) W(illiam)
   1866-1921 . . . . **TCLC 59**
   See also CA 108; DLB 70

Horovitz, Israel (Arthur)
   1939- . . . . **CLC 56; DAM DRAM**
   See also CA 33-36R; CANR 46; DLB 7

Horvath, Odon von
   See Horvath, Oedoen von
   See also DLB 85, 124

Horvath, Oedoen von 1901-1938 . . . **TCLC 45**
   See also Horvath, Odon von
   See also CA 118

Horwitz, Julius 1920-1986 . . . . **CLC 14**
   See also CA 9-12R; 119; CANR 12

Hospital, Janette Turner 1942- . . . . . **CLC 42**
   See also CA 108; CANR 48

Hostos, E. M. de
   See Hostos (y Bonilla), Eugenio Maria de

Hostos, Eugenio M. de
   See Hostos (y Bonilla), Eugenio Maria de

Hostos, Eugenio Maria
   See Hostos (y Bonilla), Eugenio Maria de

Hostos (y Bonilla), Eugenio Maria de
   1839-1903 . . . . **TCLC 24**
   See also CA 123; 131; HW

Houdini
   See Lovecraft, H(oward) P(hillips)

Hougan, Carolyn 1943- . . . . **CLC 34**
   See also CA 139

Household, Geoffrey (Edward West)
   1900-1988 . . . . **CLC 11**
   See also CA 77-80; 126; DLB 87; SATA 14;
   SATA-Obit 59

Housman, A(lfred) E(dward)
   1859-1936 . . . . . **TCLC 1, 10; DA; DAB;**
      DAC; DAM MST, POET; PC 2
   See also CA 104; 125; DLB 19; MTCW

Housman, Laurence 1865-1959 . . . . . **TCLC 7**
   See also CA 106; 155; DLB 10; SATA 25

Howard, Elizabeth Jane 1923- . . . **CLC 7, 29**
   See also CA 5-8R; CANR 8

Howard, Maureen 1930- . . . . . **CLC 5, 14, 46**
   See also CA 53-56; CANR 31; DLBY 83;
   INT CANR-31; MTCW

Howard, Richard 1929- . . . . . . **CLC 7, 10, 47**
   See also AITN 1; CA 85-88; CANR 25;
   DLB 5; INT CANR-25

Howard, Robert Ervin 1906-1936 . . . **TCLC 8**
   See also CA 105

Howard, Warren F.
   See Pohl, Frederik

Howe, Fanny 1940- . . . . **CLC 47**
   See also CA 117; SATA-Brief 52

Howe, Irving 1920-1993 . . . . **CLC 85**
   See also CA 9-12R; 141; CANR 21, 50;
   DLB 67; MTCW

Howe, Julia Ward 1819-1910 . . . . . **TCLC 21**
   See also CA 117; DLB 1

Howe, Susan 1937- . . . . **CLC 72**
   See also DLB 120

Howe, Tina 1937- . . . . **CLC 48**
   See also CA 109

Howell, James 1594(?)-1666 . . . . **LC 13**
   See also DLB 151

Howells, W. D.
   See Howells, William Dean

Howells, William D.
   See Howells, William Dean

Howells, William Dean
   1837-1920 . . . . **TCLC 7, 17, 41**
   See also CA 104; 134; CDALB 1865-1917;
   DLB 12, 64, 74, 79

Howes, Barbara 1914-1996 . . . . **CLC 15**
   See also CA 9-12R; 151; CAAS 3;
   CANR 53; SATA 5

Hrabal, Bohumil 1914- . . . . **CLC 13, 67**
   See also CA 106; CAAS 12

Hsun, Lu
   See Lu Hsun

Hubbard, L(afayette) Ron(ald)
   1911-1986 . . . . **CLC 43; DAM POP**
   See also CA 77-80; 118; CANR 52

Huch, Ricarda (Octavia)
   1864-1947 . . . . **TCLC 13**
   See also CA 111; DLB 66

Huddle, David 1942- . . . . **CLC 49**
   See also CA 57-60; CAAS 20; DLB 130

Hudson, Jeffrey
   See Crichton, (John) Michael

Hudson, W(illiam) H(enry)
   1841-1922 . . . . **TCLC 29**
   See also CA 115; DLB 98, 153, 174;
   SATA 35

Hueffer, Ford Madox
   See Ford, Ford Madox

Hughart, Barry 1934- . . . . **CLC 39**
   See also CA 137

Hughes, Colin
   See Creasey, John

Hughes, David (John) 1930- . . . . **CLC 48**
   See also CA 116; 129; DLB 14

Hughes, Edward James
   See Hughes, Ted
   See also DAM MST, POET

Hughes, (James) Langston
   1902-1967 . . . . . **CLC 1, 5, 10, 15, 35, 44;**
      BLC; DA; DAB; DAC; DAM DRAM,
      MST, MULT, POET; DC 3; PC 1;
      SSC 6; WLC
   See also AAYA 12; BW 1; CA 1-4R;
   25-28R; CANR 1, 34; CDALB 1929-1941;
   CLR 17; DLB 4, 7, 48, 51, 86; JRDA;
   MAICYA; MTCW; SATA 4, 33

Hughes, Richard (Arthur Warren)
   1900-1976 . . . . . . **CLC 1, 11; DAM NOV**
   See also CA 5-8R; 65-68; CANR 4;
   DLB 15, 161; MTCW; SATA 8;
   SATA-Obit 25

Hughes, Ted
   1930- . . . . **CLC 2, 4, 9, 14, 37; DAB;**
      DAC; PC 7
   See also Hughes, Edward James
   See also CA 1-4R; CANR 1, 33; CLR 3;
   DLB 40, 161; MAICYA; MTCW;
   SATA 49; SATA-Brief 27

Hugo, Richard F(ranklin)
   1923-1982 . . . . **CLC 6, 18, 32;**
      DAM POET
   See also CA 49-52; 108; CANR 3; DLB 5

Hugo, Victor (Marie)
   1802-1885 . . . . **NCLC 3, 10, 21; DA;**
      DAB; DAC; DAM DRAM, MST, NOV,
      POET; PC 17; WLC
   See also DLB 119; SATA 47

Huidobro, Vicente
   See Huidobro Fernandez, Vicente Garcia

Huidobro Fernandez, Vicente Garcia
   1893-1948 . . . . **TCLC 31**
   See also CA 131; HW

Hulme, Keri 1947- . . . . **CLC 39**
   See also CA 125; INT 125

Hulme, T(homas) E(rnest)
   1883-1917 . . . . **TCLC 21**
   See also CA 117; DLB 19

Hume, David 1711-1776 . . . . **LC 7**
   See also DLB 104

Humphrey, William 1924- . . . . **CLC 45**
   See also CA 77-80; DLB 6

Humphreys, Emyr Owen 1919- . . . . . **CLC 47**
   See also CA 5-8R; CANR 3, 24; DLB 15

Humphreys, Josephine 1945- . . . . **CLC 34, 57**
   See also CA 121; 127; INT 127

Huneker, James Gibbons
   1857-1921 . . . . **TCLC 65**
   See also DLB 71

Hungerford, Pixie
   See Brinsmead, H(esba) F(ay)

Hunt, E(verette) Howard, (Jr.)
   1918- . . . . **CLC 3**
   See also AITN 1; CA 45-48; CANR 2, 47

Hunt, Kyle
   See Creasey, John

Hunt, (James Henry) Leigh
1784-1859 ...... **NCLC 1; DAM POET**

Hunt, Marsha 1946- .... **CLC 70**
See also BW 2; CA 143

Hunt, Violet 1866-1942 .... **TCLC 53**
See also DLB 162

Hunter, E. Waldo
See Sturgeon, Theodore (Hamilton)

Hunter, Evan
1926- .... **CLC 11, 31; DAM POP**
See also CA 5-8R; CANR 5, 38; DLBY 82;
INT CANR-5; MTCW; SATA 25

Hunter, Kristin (Eggleston) 1931-... **CLC 35**
See also AITN 1; BW 1; CA 13-16R;
CANR 13; CLR 3; DLB 33;
INT CANR-13; MAICYA; SAAS 10;
SATA 12

Hunter, Mollie 1922- .... **CLC 21**
See also McIlwraith, Maureen Mollie
Hunter
See also AAYA 13; CANR 37; CLR 25;
DLB 161; JRDA; MAICYA; SAAS 7;
SATA 54

Hunter, Robert (?)-1734............ **LC 7**

Hurston, Zora Neale
1903-1960 .... **CLC 7, 30, 61; BLC; DA;
DAC; DAM MST, MULT, NOV; SSC 4**
See also AAYA 15; BW 1; CA 85-88;
DLB 51, 86; MTCW

Huston, John (Marcellus)
1906-1987 .... **CLC 20**
See also CA 73-76; 123; CANR 34; DLB 26

Hustvedt, Siri 1955- .... **CLC 76**
See also CA 137

Hutten, Ulrich von 1488-1523....... **LC 16**

Huxley, Aldous (Leonard)
1894-1963 ..... **CLC 1, 3, 4, 5, 8, 11, 18,
35, 79; DA; DAB; DAC; DAM MST,
NOV; WLC**
See also AAYA 11; CA 85-88; CANR 44;
CDBLB 1914-1945; DLB 36, 100, 162;
MTCW; SATA 63

Huysmans, Charles Marie Georges
1848-1907
See Huysmans, Joris-Karl
See also CA 104

Huysmans, Joris-Karl.............. TCLC 7
See also Huysmans, Charles Marie Georges
See also DLB 123

Hwang, David Henry
1957- .... **CLC 55; DAM DRAM; DC 4**
See also CA 127; 132; INT 132

Hyde, Anthony 1946- .... **CLC 42**
See also CA 136

Hyde, Margaret O(ldroyd) 1917-... **CLC 21**
See also CA 1-4R; CANR 1, 36; CLR 23;
JRDA; MAICYA; SAAS 8; SATA 1, 42,
76

Hynes, James 1956(?)- .... **CLC 65**

Ian, Janis 1951- .... **CLC 21**
See also CA 105

Ibanez, Vicente Blasco
See Blasco Ibanez, Vicente

Ibarguengoitia, Jorge 1928-1983.... **CLC 37**
See also CA 124; 113; HW

Ibsen, Henrik (Johan)
1828-1906 .... **TCLC 2, 8, 16, 37, 52;
DA; DAB; DAC; DAM DRAM, MST;
DC 2; WLC**
See also CA 104; 141

Ibuse Masuji 1898-1993........... **CLC 22**
See also CA 127; 141

Ichikawa, Kon 1915- .... **CLC 20**
See also CA 121

Idle, Eric 1943- .... **CLC 21**
See also Monty Python
See also CA 116; CANR 35

Ignatow, David 1914- ...... **CLC 4, 7, 14, 40**
See also CA 9-12R; CAAS 3; CANR 31;
DLB 5

Ihimaera, Witi 1944- .... **CLC 46**
See also CA 77-80

Ilf, Ilya........................ TCLC 21
See also Fainzilberg, Ilya Arnoldovich

Illyes, Gyula 1902-1983........... **PC 16**
See also CA 114; 109

Immermann, Karl (Lebrecht)
1796-1840 .... **NCLC 4, 49**
See also DLB 133

Inclan, Ramon (Maria) del Valle
See Valle-Inclan, Ramon (Maria) del

Infante, G(uillermo) Cabrera
See Cabrera Infante, G(uillermo)

Ingalls, Rachel (Holmes) 1940-..... **CLC 42**
See also CA 123; 127

Ingamells, Rex 1913-1955 .... **TCLC 35**

Inge, William (Motter)
1913-1973 .. **CLC 1, 8, 19; DAM DRAM**
See also CA 9-12R; CDALB 1941-1968;
DLB 7; MTCW

Ingelow, Jean 1820-1897 .... **NCLC 39**
See also DLB 35, 163; SATA 33

Ingram, Willis J.
See Harris, Mark

Innaurato, Albert (F.) 1948(?)- .. **CLC 21, 60**
See also CA 115; 122; INT 122

Innes, Michael
See Stewart, J(ohn) I(nnes) M(ackintosh)

Ionesco, Eugene
1909-1994 .... **CLC 1, 4, 6, 9, 11, 15, 41,
86; DA; DAB; DAC; DAM DRAM,
MST; WLC**
See also CA 9-12R; 144; CANR 55;
MTCW; SATA 7; SATA-Obit 79

Iqbal, Muhammad 1873-1938 ..... **TCLC 28**

Ireland, Patrick
See O'Doherty, Brian

Iron, Ralph
See Schreiner, Olive (Emilie Albertina)

Irving, John (Winslow)
1942- ..... **CLC 13, 23, 38; DAM NOV,
POP**
See also AAYA 8; BEST 89:3; CA 25-28R;
CANR 28; DLB 6; DLBY 82; MTCW

Irving, Washington
1783-1859 ..... **NCLC 2, 19; DA; DAB;
DAM MST; SSC 2; WLC**
See also CDALB 1640-1865; DLB 3, 11, 30,
59, 73, 74; YABC 2

Irwin, P. K.
See Page, P(atricia) K(athleen)

Isaacs, Susan 1943- ... **CLC 32; DAM POP**
See also BEST 89:1; CA 89-92; CANR 20,
41; INT CANR-20; MTCW

Isherwood, Christopher (William Bradshaw)
1904-1986 .... **CLC 1, 9, 11, 14, 44;
DAM DRAM, NOV**
See also CA 13-16R; 117; CANR 35;
DLB 15; DLBY 86; MTCW

Ishiguro, Kazuo
1954- ...... **CLC 27, 56, 59; DAM NOV**
See also BEST 90:2; CA 120; CANR 49;
MTCW

Ishikawa, Hakuhin
See Ishikawa, Takuboku

Ishikawa, Takuboku
1886(?)-1912 .... **TCLC 15;
DAM POET; PC 10**
See also CA 113; 153

Iskander, Fazil 1929- .... **CLC 47**
See also CA 102

Isler, Alan .... CLC 91

Ivan IV 1530-1584 .... **LC 17**

Ivanov, Vyacheslav Ivanovich
1866-1949 .... **TCLC 33**
See also CA 122

Ivask, Ivar Vidrik 1927-1992....... **CLC 14**
See also CA 37-40R; 139; CANR 24

Ives, Morgan
See Bradley, Marion Zimmer

J. R. S.
See Gogarty, Oliver St. John

Jabran, Kahlil
See Gibran, Kahlil

Jabran, Khalil
See Gibran, Kahlil

Jackson, Daniel
See Wingrove, David (John)

Jackson, Jesse 1908-1983 .... **CLC 12**
See also BW 1; CA 25-28R; 109; CANR 27;
CLR 28; MAICYA; SATA 2, 29;
SATA-Obit 48

Jackson, Laura (Riding) 1901-1991
See Riding, Laura
See also CA 65-68; 135; CANR 28; DLB 48

Jackson, Sam
See Trumbo, Dalton

Jackson, Sara
See Wingrove, David (John)

Jackson, Shirley
1919-1965 .... **CLC 11, 60, 87; DA;
DAC; DAM MST; SSC 9; WLC**
See also AAYA 9; CA 1-4R; 25-28R;
CANR 4, 52; CDALB 1941-1968; DLB 6;
SATA 2

Jacob, (Cyprien-)Max 1876-1944 ... **TCLC 6**
See also CA 104

Jacobs, Jim 1942- .... **CLC 12**
See also CA 97-100; INT 97-100

Jacobs, W(illiam) W(ymark)
1863-1943 .... **TCLC 22**
See also CA 121; DLB 135

Jacobsen, Jens Peter 1847-1885 .. **NCLC 34**

Johnson, Uwe
1934-1984 . . . . **CLC 5, 10, 15, 40**
See also CA 1-4R; 112; CANR 1, 39;
DLB 75; MTCW

Johnston, George (Benson) 1913- . . . **CLC 51**
See also CA 1-4R; CANR 5, 20; DLB 88

Johnston, Jennifer 1930- . . . . **CLC 7**
See also CA 85-88; DLB 14

Jolley, (Monica) Elizabeth
1923- . . . . **CLC 46; SSC 19**
See also CA 127; CAAS 13

Jones, Arthur Llewellyn 1863-1947
See Machen, Arthur
See also CA 104

Jones, D(ouglas) G(ordon) 1929- . . . . **CLC 10**
See also CA 29-32R; CANR 13; DLB 53

Jones, David (Michael)
1895-1974 . . . . **CLC 2, 4, 7, 13, 42**
See also CA 9-12R; 53-56; CANR 28;
CDBLB 1945-1960; DLB 20, 100; MTCW

Jones, David Robert 1947-
See Bowie, David
See also CA 103

Jones, Diana Wynne 1934- . . . . **CLC 26**
See also AAYA 12; CA 49-52; CANR 4,
26; CLR 23; DLB 161; JRDA; MAICYA;
SAAS 7; SATA 9, 70

Jones, Edward P. 1950- . . . . **CLC 76**
See also BW 2; CA 142

Jones, Gayl
1949- . . . . **CLC 6, 9; BLC; DAM MULT**
See also BW 2; CA 77-80; CANR 27;
DLB 33; MTCW

Jones, James 1921-1977 . . . . **CLC 1, 3, 10, 39**
See also AITN 1, 2; CA 1-4R; 69-72;
CANR 6; DLB 2, 143; MTCW

Jones, John J.
See Lovecraft, H(oward) P(hillips)

Jones, LeRoi . . . . **CLC 1, 2, 3, 5, 10, 14**
See also Baraka, Amiri

Jones, Louis B. . . . . **CLC 65**
See also CA 141

Jones, Madison (Percy, Jr.) 1925- . . . **CLC 4**
See also CA 13-16R; CAAS 11; CANR 7,
54; DLB 152

Jones, Mervyn 1922- . . . . **CLC 10, 52**
See also CA 45-48; CAAS 5; CANR 1;
MTCW

Jones, Mick 1956(?)- . . . . **CLC 30**

Jones, Nettie (Pearl) 1941- . . . . **CLC 34**
See also BW 2; CA 137; CAAS 20

Jones, Preston 1936-1979 . . . . **CLC 10**
See also CA 73-76; 89-92; DLB 7

Jones, Robert F(rancis) 1934- . . . . **CLC 7**
See also CA 49-52; CANR 2

Jones, Rod 1953- . . . . **CLC 50**
See also CA 128

Jones, Terence Graham Parry
1942- . . . . **CLC 21**
See also Jones, Terry; Monty Python
See also CA 112; 116; CANR 35; INT 116

Jones, Terry
See Jones, Terence Graham Parry
See also SATA 67; SATA-Brief 51

Jones, Thom 1945(?)- . . . . **CLC 81**

Jong, Erica
1942- . . . . **CLC 4, 6, 8, 18, 83;
DAM NOV, POP**
See also AITN 1; BEST 90:2; CA 73-76;
CANR 26, 52; DLB 2, 5, 28, 152;
INT CANR-26; MTCW

Jonson, Ben(jamin)
1572(?)-1637 . . . . . . **LC 6, 33; DA; DAB;
DAC; DAM DRAM, MST, POET;
DC 4; PC 17; WLC**
See also CDBLB Before 1660; DLB 62, 121

Jordan, June
1936- . . . . . **CLC 5, 11, 23; DAM MULT,
POET**
See also AAYA 2; BW 2; CA 33-36R;
CANR 25; CLR 10; DLB 38; MAICYA;
MTCW; SATA 4

Jordan, Pat(rick M.) 1941- . . . . **CLC 37**
See also CA 33-36R

Jorgensen, Ivar
See Ellison, Harlan (Jay)

Jorgenson, Ivar
See Silverberg, Robert

Josephus, Flavius c. 37-100 . . . . . **CMLC 13**

Josipovici, Gabriel 1940- . . . . **CLC 6, 43**
See also CA 37-40R; CAAS 8; CANR 47;
DLB 14

Joubert, Joseph 1754-1824 . . . . **NCLC 9**

Jouve, Pierre Jean 1887-1976 . . . . . . **CLC 47**
See also CA 65-68

Joyce, James (Augustine Aloysius)
1882-1941 . . . . **TCLC 3, 8, 16, 35, 52;
DA; DAB; DAC; DAM MST, NOV,
POET; SSC 3; WLC**
See also CA 104; 126; CDBLB 1914-1945;
DLB 10, 19, 36, 162; MTCW

Jozsef, Attila 1905-1937 . . . . **TCLC 22**
See also CA 116

Juana Ines de la Cruz 1651(?)-1695 . . . **LC 5**

Judd, Cyril
See Kornbluth, C(yril) M.; Pohl, Frederik

Julian of Norwich 1342(?)-1416(?) . . . . **LC 6**
See also DLB 146

Juniper, Alex
See Hospital, Janette Turner

Junius
See Luxemburg, Rosa

Just, Ward (Swift) 1935- . . . . **CLC 4, 27**
See also CA 25-28R; CANR 32;
INT CANR-32

Justice, Donald (Rodney)
1925- . . . . **CLC 6, 19; DAM POET**
See also CA 5-8R; CANR 26, 54;
DLBY 83; INT CANR-26

Juvenal c. 55-c. 127 . . . . **CMLC 8**

Juvenis
See Bourne, Randolph S(illiman)

Kacew, Romain 1914-1980
See Gary, Romain
See also CA 108; 102

Kadare, Ismail 1936- . . . . **CLC 52**

Kadohata, Cynthia . . . . **CLC 59**
See also CA 140

Kafka, Franz
1883-1924 . . . . **TCLC 2, 6, 13, 29, 47, 53;
DA; DAB; DAC; DAM MST, NOV;
SSC 5; WLC**
See also CA 105; 126; DLB 81; MTCW

Kahanovitsch, Pinkhes
See Der Nister

Kahn, Roger 1927- . . . . **CLC 30**
See also CA 25-28R; CANR 44; DLB 171;
SATA 37

Kain, Saul
See Sassoon, Siegfried (Lorraine)

Kaiser, Georg 1878-1945 . . . . **TCLC 9**
See also CA 106; DLB 124

Kaletski, Alexander 1946- . . . . **CLC 39**
See also CA 118; 143

Kalidasa fl. c. 400- . . . . **CMLC 9**

Kallman, Chester (Simon)
1921-1975 . . . . **CLC 2**
See also CA 45-48; 53-56; CANR 3

Kaminsky, Melvin 1926-
See Brooks, Mel
See also CA 65-68; CANR 16

Kaminsky, Stuart M(elvin) 1934- . . . **CLC 59**
See also CA 73-76; CANR 29, 53

Kane, Francis
See Robbins, Harold

Kane, Paul
See Simon, Paul (Frederick)

Kane, Wilson
See Bloch, Robert (Albert)

Kanin, Garson 1912- . . . . **CLC 22**
See also AITN 1; CA 5-8R; CANR 7;
DLB 7

Kaniuk, Yoram 1930- . . . . **CLC 19**
See also CA 134

Kant, Immanuel 1724-1804 . . . . . . **NCLC 27**
See also DLB 94

Kantor, MacKinlay 1904-1977 . . . . . . **CLC 7**
See also CA 61-64; 73-76; DLB 9, 102

Kaplan, David Michael 1946- . . . . . . **CLC 50**

Kaplan, James 1951- . . . . **CLC 59**
See also CA 135

Karageorge, Michael
See Anderson, Poul (William)

Karamzin, Nikolai Mikhailovich
1766-1826 . . . . **NCLC 3**
See also DLB 150

Karapanou, Margarita 1946- . . . . **CLC 13**
See also CA 101

Karinthy, Frigyes 1887-1938 . . . . . . **TCLC 47**

Karl, Frederick R(obert) 1927- . . . . . **CLC 34**
See also CA 5-8R; CANR 3, 44

Kastel, Warren
See Silverberg, Robert

Kataev, Evgeny Petrovich 1903-1942
See Petrov, Evgeny
See also CA 120

Kataphusin
See Ruskin, John

Katz, Steve 1935- . . . . **CLC 47**
See also CA 25-28R; CAAS 14; CANR 12;
DLBY 83

Author Index

Kopit, Arthur (Lee)
1937- . . . . . **CLC 1, 18, 33; DAM DRAM**
See also AITN 1; CA 81-84; CABS 3;
DLB 7; MTCW

Kops, Bernard 1926-. . . . . **CLC 4**
See also CA 5-8R; DLB 13

Kornbluth, C(yril) M. 1923-1958. . . . **TCLC 8**
See also CA 105; DLB 8

Korolenko, V. G.
See Korolenko, Vladimir Galaktionovich

Korolenko, Vladimir
See Korolenko, Vladimir Galaktionovich

Korolenko, Vladimir G.
See Korolenko, Vladimir Galaktionovich

Korolenko, Vladimir Galaktionovich
1853-1921 . . . . **TCLC 22**
See also CA 121

Korzybski, Alfred (Habdank Skarbek)
1879-1950 . . . . **TCLC 61**
See also CA 123

Kosinski, Jerzy (Nikodem)
1933-1991 . . . . **CLC 1, 2, 3, 6, 10, 15, 53,
70; DAM NOV**
See also CA 17-20R; 134; CANR 9, 46;
DLB 2; DLBY 82; MTCW

Kostelanetz, Richard (Cory) 1940- . . **CLC 28**
See also CA 13-16R; CAAS 8; CANR 38

Kostrowitzki, Wilhelm Apollinaris de
1880-1918
See Apollinaire, Guillaume
See also CA 104

Kotlowitz, Robert 1924-. . . . . **CLC 4**
See also CA 33-36R; CANR 36

Kotzebue, August (Friedrich Ferdinand) von
1761-1819 . . . . **NCLC 25**
See also DLB 94

Kotzwinkle, William 1938- . . . **CLC 5, 14, 35**
See also CA 45-48; CANR 3, 44; CLR 6;
DLB 173; MAICYA; SATA 24, 70

Kozol, Jonathan 1936-. . . . . **CLC 17**
See also CA 61-64; CANR 16, 45

Kozoll, Michael 1940(?)-. . . . . **CLC 35**

Kramer, Kathryn 19(?)-. . . . . **CLC 34**

Kramer, Larry 1935- . . **CLC 42; DAM POP**
See also CA 124; 126

Krasicki, Ignacy 1735-1801 . . . . **NCLC 8**

Krasinski, Zygmunt 1812-1859 . . . . **NCLC 4**

Kraus, Karl 1874-1936. . . . . **TCLC 5**
See also CA 104; DLB 118

Kreve (Mickevicius), Vincas
1882-1954 . . . . **TCLC 27**

Kristeva, Julia 1941- . . . . **CLC 77**
See also CA 154

Kristofferson, Kris 1936-. . . . . **CLC 26**
See also CA 104

Krizanc, John 1956-. . . . . **CLC 57**

Krleza, Miroslav 1893-1981. . . . . **CLC 8**
See also CA 97-100; 105; CANR 50;
DLB 147

Kroetsch, Robert
1927- . . . . **CLC 5, 23, 57; DAC;
DAM POET**
See also CA 17-20R; CANR 8, 38; DLB 53;
MTCW

Kroetz, Franz
See Kroetz, Franz Xaver

Kroetz, Franz Xaver 1946- . . . . **CLC 41**
See also CA 130

Kroker, Arthur 1945-. . . . . **CLC 77**

Kropotkin, Peter (Aleksieevich)
1842-1921 . . . . **TCLC 36**
See also CA 119

Krotkov, Yuri 1917-. . . . . **CLC 19**
See also CA 102

Krumb
See Crumb, R(obert)

Krumgold, Joseph (Quincy)
1908-1980 . . . . **CLC 12**
See also CA 9-12R; 101; CANR 7;
MAICYA; SATA 1, 48; SATA-Obit 23

Krumwitz
See Crumb, R(obert)

Krutch, Joseph Wood 1893-1970. . . . **CLC 24**
See also CA 1-4R; 25-28R; CANR 4;
DLB 63

Krutzch, Gus
See Eliot, T(homas) S(tearns)

Krylov, Ivan Andreevich
1768(?)-1844 . . . . **NCLC 1**
See also DLB 150

Kubin, Alfred (Leopold Isidor)
1877-1959 . . . . **TCLC 23**
See also CA 112; 149; DLB 81

Kubrick, Stanley 1928-. . . . . **CLC 16**
See also CA 81-84; CANR 33; DLB 26

Kumin, Maxine (Winokur)
1925- . . . . . **CLC 5, 13, 28; DAM POET;
PC 15**
See also AITN 2; CA 1-4R; CAAS 8;
CANR 1, 21; DLB 5; MTCW; SATA 12

Kundera, Milan
1929- . . . . **CLC 4, 9, 19, 32, 68;
DAM NOV; SSC 24**
See also AAYA 2; CA 85-88; CANR 19,
52; MTCW

Kunene, Mazisi (Raymond) 1930-. . . **CLC 85**
See also BW 1; CA 125; DLB 117

Kunitz, Stanley (Jasspon)
1905-. . . . . **CLC 6, 11, 14**
See also CA 41-44R; CANR 26; DLB 48;
INT CANR-26; MTCW

Kunze, Reiner 1933-. . . . . **CLC 10**
See also CA 93-96; DLB 75

Kuprin, Aleksandr Ivanovich
1870-1938 . . . . **TCLC 5**
See also CA 104

Kureishi, Hanif 1954(?)-. . . . . **CLC 64**
See also CA 139

Kurosawa, Akira
1910- . . . . **CLC 16; DAM MULT**
See also AAYA 11; CA 101; CANR 46

Kushner, Tony
1957(?)- . . . . **CLC 81; DAM DRAM**
See also CA 144

Kuttner, Henry 1915-1958. . . . . **TCLC 10**
See also CA 107; DLB 8

Kuzma, Greg 1944-. . . . . **CLC 7**
See also CA 33-36R

Kuzmin, Mikhail 1872(?)-1936 . . . . **TCLC 40**

Kyd, Thomas
1558-1594 . . . . **LC 22; DAM DRAM;
DC 3**
See also DLB 62

Kyprianos, Iossif
See Samarakis, Antonis

La Bruyere, Jean de 1645-1696. . . . . . **LC 17**

Lacan, Jacques (Marie Emile)
1901-1981 . . . . **CLC 75**
See also CA 121; 104

**Laclos, Pierre Ambroise Francois Choderlos
de** 1741-1803 . . . . **NCLC 4**

La Colere, Francois
See Aragon, Louis

Lacolere, Francois
See Aragon, Louis

La Deshabilleuse
See Simenon, Georges (Jacques Christian)

Lady Gregory
See Gregory, Isabella Augusta (Persse)

Lady of Quality, A
See Bagnold, Enid

**La Fayette, Marie (Madelaine Pioche de la
Vergne Comtes** 1634-1693. . . . . . . **LC 2**

Lafayette, Rene
See Hubbard, L(afayette) Ron(ald)

Laforgue, Jules
1860-1887 . . . . **NCLC 5, 53; PC 14;
SSC 20**

Lagerkvist, Paer (Fabian)
1891-1974 . . . . **CLC 7, 10, 13, 54;
DAM DRAM, NOV**
See also Lagerkvist, Par
See also CA 85-88; 49-52; MTCW

Lagerkvist, Par . . . . **SSC 12**
See also Lagerkvist, Paer (Fabian)

Lagerloef, Selma (Ottiliana Lovisa)
1858-1940 . . . . **TCLC 4, 36**
See also Lagerlof, Selma (Ottiliana Lovisa)
See also CA 108; SATA 15

Lagerlof, Selma (Ottiliana Lovisa)
See Lagerloef, Selma (Ottiliana Lovisa)
See also CLR 7; SATA 15

La Guma, (Justin) Alex(ander)
1925-1985 . . . . **CLC 19; DAM NOV**
See also BW 1; CA 49-52; 118; CANR 25;
DLB 117; MTCW

Laidlaw, A. K.
See Grieve, C(hristopher) M(urray)

Lainez, Manuel Mujica
See Mujica Lainez, Manuel
See also HW

Laing, R(onald) D(avid)
1927-1989 . . . . **CLC 95**
See also CA 107; 129; CANR 34; MTCW

Lamartine, Alphonse (Marie Louis Prat) de
1790-1869 . . . . . **NCLC 11; DAM POET;
PC 16**

Lamb, Charles
1775-1834 . . . . **NCLC 10; DA; DAB;
DAC; DAM MST; WLC**
See also CDBLB 1789-1832; DLB 93, 107,
163; SATA 17

Lamb, Lady Caroline 1785-1828.. **NCLC 38**
See also DLB 116

Lamming, George (William)
1927- .... **CLC 2, 4, 66; BLC;
DAM MULT**
See also BW 2; CA 85-88; CANR 26;
DLB 125; MTCW

L'Amour, Louis (Dearborn)
1908-1988 .... **CLC 25, 55; DAM NOV,
POP**
See also AAYA 16; AITN 2; BEST 89:2;
CA 1-4R; 125; CANR 3, 25, 40;
DLBY 80; MTCW

Lampedusa, Giuseppe (Tomasi) di ... **TCLC 13**
See also Tomasi di Lampedusa, Giuseppe

Lampman, Archibald 1861-1899 .. **NCLC 25**
See also DLB 92

Lancaster, Bruce 1896-1963........ **CLC 36**
See also CA 9-10; CAP 1; SATA 9

Landau, Mark Alexandrovich
See Aldanov, Mark (Alexandrovich)

Landau-Aldanov, Mark Alexandrovich
See Aldanov, Mark (Alexandrovich)

Landis, Jerry
See Simon, Paul (Frederick)

Landis, John 1950-.............. **CLC 26**
See also CA 112; 122

Landolfi, Tommaso 1908-1979... **CLC 11, 49**
See also CA 127; 117

Landon, Letitia Elizabeth
1802-1838 .... **NCLC 15**
See also DLB 96

Landor, Walter Savage
1775-1864 .... **NCLC 14**
See also DLB 93, 107

Landwirth, Heinz 1927-
See Lind, Jakov
See also CA 9-12R; CANR 7

Lane, Patrick
1939- .... **CLC 25; DAM POET**
See also CA 97-100; CANR 54; DLB 53;
INT 97-100

Lang, Andrew 1844-1912........ **TCLC 16**
See also CA 114; 137; DLB 98, 141;
MAICYA; SATA 16

Lang, Fritz 1890-1976 .... **CLC 20**
See also CA 77-80; 69-72; CANR 30

Lange, John
See Crichton, (John) Michael

Langer, Elinor 1939- .... **CLC 34**
See also CA 121

Langland, William
1330(?)-1400(?) ...... **LC 19; DA; DAB;
DAC; DAM MST, POET**
See also DLB 146

Langstaff, Launcelot
See Irving, Washington

Lanier, Sidney
1842-1881 ...... **NCLC 6; DAM POET**
See also DLB 64; DLBD 13; MAICYA;
SATA 18

Lanyer, Aemilia 1569-1645 ...... **LC 10, 30**
See also DLB 121

Lao Tzu .... **CMLC 7**

Lapine, James (Elliot) 1949-....... **CLC 39**
See also CA 123; 130; CANR 54; INT 130

Larbaud, Valery (Nicolas)
1881-1957 .... **TCLC 9**
See also CA 106; 152

Lardner, Ring
See Lardner, Ring(gold) W(ilmer)

Lardner, Ring W., Jr.
See Lardner, Ring(gold) W(ilmer)

Lardner, Ring(gold) W(ilmer)
1885-1933 .... **TCLC 2, 14**
See also CA 104; 131; CDALB 1917-1929;
DLB 11, 25, 86; MTCW

Laredo, Betty
See Codrescu, Andrei

Larkin, Maia
See Wojciechowska, Maia (Teresa)

Larkin, Philip (Arthur)
1922-1985 .... **CLC 3, 5, 8, 9, 13, 18, 33,
39, 64; DAB; DAM MST, POET**
See also CA 5-8R; 117; CANR 24;
CDBLB 1960 to Present; DLB 27;
MTCW

Larra (y Sanchez de Castro), Mariano Jose de
1809-1837 .... **NCLC 17**

Larsen, Eric 1941- .... **CLC 55**
See also CA 132

Larsen, Nella
1891-1964 .... **CLC 37; BLC;
DAM MULT**
See also BW 1; CA 125; DLB 51

Larson, Charles R(aymond) 1938-... **CLC 31**
See also CA 53-56; CANR 4

Las Casas, Bartolome de 1474-1566.. **LC 31**

Lasker-Schueler, Else 1869-1945 .. **TCLC 57**
See also DLB 66, 124

Latham, Jean Lee 1902-.......... **CLC 12**
See also AITN 1; CA 5-8R; CANR 7;
MAICYA; SATA 2, 68

Latham, Mavis
See Clark, Mavis Thorpe

Lathen, Emma .... **CLC 2**
See also Hennissart, Martha; Latsis, Mary
J(ane)

Lathrop, Francis
See Leiber, Fritz (Reuter, Jr.)

Latsis, Mary J(ane)
See Lathen, Emma
See also CA 85-88

Lattimore, Richmond (Alexander)
1906-1984 .... **CLC 3**
See also CA 1-4R; 112; CANR 1

Laughlin, James 1914-........... **CLC 49**
See also CA 21-24R; CAAS 22; CANR 9,
47; DLB 48

Laurence, (Jean) Margaret (Wemyss)
1926-1987 .... **CLC 3, 6, 13, 50, 62;
DAC; DAM MST; SSC 7**
See also CA 5-8R; 121; CANR 33; DLB 53;
MTCW; SATA-Obit 50

Laurent, Antoine 1952- .... **CLC 50**

Lauscher, Hermann
See Hesse, Hermann

Lautreamont, Comte de
1846-1870 .... **NCLC 12; SSC 14**

Laverty, Donald
See Blish, James (Benjamin)

Lavin, Mary 1912-1996 .. **CLC 4, 18; SSC 4**
See also CA 9-12R; 151; CANR 33;
DLB 15; MTCW

Lavond, Paul Dennis
See Kornbluth, C(yril) M.; Pohl, Frederik

Lawler, Raymond Evenor 1922- .... **CLC 58**
See also CA 103

Lawrence, D(avid) H(erbert Richards)
1885-1930 .... **TCLC 2, 9, 16, 33, 48, 61;
DA; DAB; DAC; DAM MST, NOV,
POET; SSC 4, 19; WLC**
See also CA 104; 121; CDBLB 1914-1945;
DLB 10, 19, 36, 98, 162; MTCW

Lawrence, T(homas) E(dward)
1888-1935 .... **TCLC 18**
See also Dale, Colin
See also CA 115

Lawrence of Arabia
See Lawrence, T(homas) E(dward)

Lawson, Henry (Archibald Hertzberg)
1867-1922 .... **TCLC 27; SSC 18**
See also CA 120

Lawton, Dennis
See Faust, Frederick (Schiller)

Laxness, Halldor................. **CLC 25**
See also Gudjonsson, Halldor Kiljan

Layamon fl. c. 1200-............ **CMLC 10**
See also DLB 146

Laye, Camara
1928-1980 .... **CLC 4, 38; BLC;
DAM MULT**
See also BW 1; CA 85-88; 97-100;
CANR 25; MTCW

Layton, Irving (Peter)
1912- .... **CLC 2, 15; DAC; DAM MST,
POET**
See also CA 1-4R; CANR 2, 33, 43;
DLB 88; MTCW

Lazarus, Emma 1849-1887........ **NCLC 8**

Lazarus, Felix
See Cable, George Washington

Lazarus, Henry
See Slavitt, David R(ytman)

Lea, Joan
See Neufeld, John (Arthur)

Leacock, Stephen (Butler)
1869-1944 .. **TCLC 2; DAC; DAM MST**
See also CA 104; 141; DLB 92

Lear, Edward 1812-1888 .... **NCLC 3**
See also CLR 1; DLB 32, 163, 166;
MAICYA; SATA 18

Lear, Norman (Milton) 1922- ...... **CLC 12**
See also CA 73-76

Leavis, F(rank) R(aymond)
1895-1978 .... **CLC 24**
See also CA 21-24R; 77-80; CANR 44;
MTCW

Leavitt, David 1961-... **CLC 34; DAM POP**
See also CA 116; 122; CANR 50; DLB 130;
INT 122

Lester, Richard 1932-............ **CLC 20**

Lever, Charles (James)
1806-1872 .... **NCLC 23**
See also DLB 21

Leverson, Ada 1865(?)-1936(?) .... **TCLC 18**
See also Elaine
See also CA 117; DLB 153

Levertov, Denise
1923- ...... **CLC 1, 2, 3, 5, 8, 15, 28, 66;**
DAM POET; PC 11
See also CA 1-4R; CAAS 19; CANR 3, 29,
50; DLB 5, 165; INT CANR-29; MTCW

Levi, Jonathan.................... **CLC 76**

Levi, Peter (Chad Tigar) 1931- ..... **CLC 41**
See also CA 5-8R; CANR 34; DLB 40

Levi, Primo
1919-1987 .... **CLC 37, 50; SSC 12**
See also CA 13-16R; 122; CANR 12, 33;
MTCW

Levin, Ira 1929- ..... **CLC 3, 6; DAM POP**
See also CA 21-24R; CANR 17, 44;
MTCW; SATA 66

Levin, Meyer
1905-1981 .... **CLC 7; DAM POP**
See also AITN 1; CA 9-12R; 104;
CANR 15; DLB 9, 28; DLBY 81;
SATA 21; SATA-Obit 27

Levine, Norman 1924-............ **CLC 54**
See also CA 73-76; CAAS 23; CANR 14;
DLB 88

Levine, Philip
1928-.......... **CLC 2, 4, 5, 9, 14, 33;**
DAM POET
See also CA 9-12R; CANR 9, 37, 52;
DLB 5

Levinson, Deirdre 1931-........... **CLC 49**
See also CA 73-76

Levi-Strauss, Claude 1908- .... **CLC 38**
See also CA 1-4R; CANR 6, 32; MTCW

Levitin, Sonia (Wolff) 1934- .... **CLC 17**
See also AAYA 13; CA 29-32R; CANR 14,
32; JRDA; MAICYA; SAAS 2; SATA 4,
68

Levon, O. U.
See Kesey, Ken (Elton)

Levy, Amy 1861-1889........... **NCLC 59**
See also DLB 156

Lewes, George Henry
1817-1878 .... **NCLC 25**
See also DLB 55, 144

Lewis, Alun 1915-1944........... **TCLC 3**
See also CA 104; DLB 20, 162

Lewis, C. Day
See Day Lewis, C(ecil)

Lewis, C(live) S(taples)
1898-1963 ..... **CLC 1, 3, 6, 14, 27; DA;**
DAB; DAC; DAM MST, NOV, POP;
WLC
See also AAYA 3; CA 81-84; CANR 33;
CDBLB 1945-1960; CLR 3, 27; DLB 15,
100, 160; JRDA; MAICYA; MTCW;
SATA 13

Lewis, Janet 1899-.............. **CLC 41**
See also Winters, Janet Lewis
See also CA 9-12R; CANR 29; CAP 1;
DLBY 87

Lewis, Matthew Gregory
1775-1818 .... **NCLC 11**
See also DLB 39, 158

Lewis, (Harry) Sinclair
1885-1951 ..... **TCLC 4, 13, 23, 39; DA;**
DAB; DAC; DAM MST, NOV; WLC
See also CA 104; 133; CDALB 1917-1929;
DLB 9, 102; DLBD 1; MTCW

Lewis, (Percy) Wyndham
1884(?)-1957 .... **TCLC 2, 9**
See also CA 104; DLB 15

Lewisohn, Ludwig 1883-1955...... **TCLC 19**
See also CA 107; DLB 4, 9, 28, 102

Leyner, Mark 1956-.............. **CLC 92**
See also CA 110; CANR 28, 53

Lezama Lima, Jose
1910-1976 .... **CLC 4, 10; DAM MULT**
See also CA 77-80; DLB 113; HW

L'Heureux, John (Clarke) 1934-.... **CLC 52**
See also CA 13-16R; CANR 23, 45

Liddell, C. H.
See Kuttner, Henry

Lie, Jonas (Lauritz Idemil)
1833-1908(?) .... **TCLC 5**
See also CA 115

Lieber, Joel 1937-1971.............. **CLC 6**
See also CA 73-76; 29-32R

Lieber, Stanley Martin
See Lee, Stan

Lieberman, Laurence (James)
1935-...................... **CLC 4, 36**
See also CA 17-20R; CANR 8, 36

Lieksman, Anders
See Haavikko, Paavo Juhani

Li Fei-kan 1904-
See Pa Chin
See also CA 105

Lifton, Robert Jay 1926-.......... **CLC 67**
See also CA 17-20R; CANR 27;
INT CANR-27; SATA 66

Lightfoot, Gordon 1938-.......... **CLC 26**
See also CA 109

Lightman, Alan P. 1948- .... **CLC 81**
See also CA 141

Ligotti, Thomas (Robert)
1953-.............. **CLC 44; SSC 16**
See also CA 123; CANR 49

Li Ho 791-817.................... **PC 13**

Liliencron, (Friedrich Adolf Axel) Detlev von
1844-1909 .... **TCLC 18**
See also CA 117

Lilly, William 1602-1681 .... **LC 27**

Lima, Jose Lezama
See Lezama Lima, Jose

Lima Barreto, Afonso Henrique de
1881-1922 .... **TCLC 23**
See also CA 117

Limonov, Edward 1944-........... **CLC 67**
See also CA 137

Lin, Frank
See Atherton, Gertrude (Franklin Horn)

Lincoln, Abraham 1809-1865..... **NCLC 18**

Lind, Jakov .... **CLC 1, 2, 4, 27, 82**
See also Landwirth, Heinz
See also CAAS 4

Lindbergh, Anne (Spencer) Morrow
1906- .... **CLC 82; DAM NOV**
See also CA 17-20R; CANR 16; MTCW;
SATA 33

Lindsay, David 1878-1945 .... **TCLC 15**
See also CA 113

Lindsay, (Nicholas) Vachel
1879-1931 .... **TCLC 17; DA; DAC;**
DAM MST, POET; WLC
See also CA 114; 135; CDALB 1865-1917;
DLB 54; SATA 40

Linke-Poot
See Doeblin, Alfred

Linney, Romulus 1930- .... **CLC 51**
See also CA 1-4R; CANR 40, 44

Linton, Eliza Lynn 1822-1898.... **NCLC 41**
See also DLB 18

Li Po 701-763 .... **CMLC 2**

Lipsius, Justus 1547-1606 .... **LC 16**

Lipsyte, Robert (Michael)
1938-............. **CLC 21; DA; DAC;**
DAM MST, NOV
See also AAYA 7; CA 17-20R; CANR 8;
CLR 23; JRDA; MAICYA; SATA 5, 68

Lish, Gordon (Jay) 1934-.. **CLC 45; SSC 18**
See also CA 113; 117; DLB 130; INT 117

Lispector, Clarice 1925-1977....... **CLC 43**
See also CA 139; 116; DLB 113

Littell, Robert 1935(?)- .... **CLC 42**
See also CA 109; 112

Little, Malcolm 1925-1965
See Malcolm X
See also BW 1; CA 125; 111; DA; DAB;
DAC; DAM MST, MULT; MTCW

Littlewit, Humphrey Gent.
See Lovecraft, H(oward) P(hillips)

Litwos
See Sienkiewicz, Henryk (Adam Alexander
Pius)

Liu E 1857-1909................. **TCLC 15**
See also CA 115

Lively, Penelope (Margaret)
1933-......... **CLC 32, 50; DAM NOV**
See also CA 41-44R; CANR 29; CLR 7;
DLB 14, 161; JRDA; MAICYA; MTCW;
SATA 7, 60

Livesay, Dorothy (Kathleen)
1909- .... **CLC 4, 15, 79; DAC;**
DAM MST, POET
See also AITN 2; CA 25-28R; CAAS 8;
CANR 36; DLB 68; MTCW

Livy c. 59B.C.-c. 17 .... **CMLC 11**

Lizardi, Jose Joaquin Fernandez de
1776-1827 .... **NCLC 30**

Llewellyn, Richard
See Llewellyn Lloyd, Richard Dafydd
Vivian
See also DLB 15

Llewellyn Lloyd, Richard Dafydd Vivian
  1906-1983 . . . . **CLC 7, 80**
  See also Llewellyn, Richard
  See also CA 53-56; 111; CANR 7;
    SATA 11; SATA-Obit 37

Llosa, (Jorge) Mario (Pedro) Vargas
  See Vargas Llosa, (Jorge) Mario (Pedro)

Lloyd Webber, Andrew 1948-
  See Webber, Andrew Lloyd
  See also AAYA 1; CA 116; 149;
    DAM DRAM; SATA 56

Llull, Ramon c. 1235-c. 1316 . . . . . **CMLC 12**

Locke, Alain (Le Roy)
  1886-1954 . . . . **TCLC 43**
  See also BW 1; CA 106; 124; DLB 51

Locke, John 1632-1704 . . . . **LC 7, 35**
  See also DLB 101

Locke-Elliott, Sumner
  See Elliott, Sumner Locke

Lockhart, John Gibson
  1794-1854 . . . . **NCLC 6**
  See also DLB 110, 116, 144

Lodge, David (John)
  1935- . . . . **CLC 36; DAM POP**
  See also BEST 90:1; CA 17-20R; CANR 19,
    53; DLB 14; INT CANR-19; MTCW

Loennbohm, Armas Eino Leopold 1878-1926
  See Leino, Eino
  See also CA 123

Loewinsohn, Ron(ald William)
  1937- . . . . **CLC 52**
  See also CA 25-28R

Logan, Jake
  See Smith, Martin Cruz

Logan, John (Burton) 1923-1987 . . . . . **CLC 5**
  See also CA 77-80; 124; CANR 45; DLB 5

Lo Kuan-chung 1330(?)-1400(?) . . . . . . **LC 12**

Lombard, Nap
  See Johnson, Pamela Hansford

London, Jack . . **TCLC 9, 15, 39; SSC 4; WLC**
  See also London, John Griffith
  See also AAYA 13; AITN 2;
    CDALB 1865-1917; DLB 8, 12, 78;
    SATA 18

London, John Griffith 1876-1916
  See London, Jack
  See also CA 110; 119; DA; DAB; DAC;
    DAM MST, NOV; JRDA; MAICYA;
    MTCW

Long, Emmett
  See Leonard, Elmore (John, Jr.)

Longbaugh, Harry
  See Goldman, William (W.)

Longfellow, Henry Wadsworth
  1807-1882 . . . . . **NCLC 2, 45; DA; DAB;**
                 DAC; DAM MST, POET
  See also CDALB 1640-1865; DLB 1, 59;
    SATA 19

Longley, Michael 1939- . . . . **CLC 29**
  See also CA 102; DLB 40

Longus fl. c. 2nd cent. - . . . . **CMLC 7**

Longway, A. Hugh
  See Lang, Andrew

Lonnrot, Elias 1802-1884 . . . . **NCLC 53**

Lopate, Phillip 1943- . . . . **CLC 29**
  See also CA 97-100; DLBY 80; INT 97-100

Lopez Portillo (y Pacheco), Jose
  1920- . . . . **CLC 46**
  See also CA 129; HW

Lopez y Fuentes, Gregorio
  1897(?)-1966 . . . . **CLC 32**
  See also CA 131; HW

Lorca, Federico Garcia
  See Garcia Lorca, Federico

Lord, Bette Bao 1938- . . . . **CLC 23**
  See also BEST 90:3; CA 107; CANR 41;
    INT 107; SATA 58

Lord Auch
  See Bataille, Georges

Lord Byron
  See Byron, George Gordon (Noel)

Lorde, Audre (Geraldine)
  1934-1992 . . . . **CLC 18, 71; BLC;**
                 DAM MULT, POET; PC 12
  See also BW 1; CA 25-28R; 142; CANR 16,
    26, 46; DLB 41; MTCW

Lord Jeffrey
  See Jeffrey, Francis

Lorenzini, Carlo 1826-1890
  See Collodi, Carlo
  See also MAICYA; SATA 29

Lorenzo, Heberto Padilla
  See Padilla (Lorenzo), Heberto

Loris
  See Hofmannsthal, Hugo von

Loti, Pierre . . . . **TCLC 11**
  See also Viaud, (Louis Marie) Julien
  See also DLB 123

Louie, David Wong 1954- . . . . **CLC 70**
  See also CA 139

Louis, Father M.
  See Merton, Thomas

Lovecraft, H(oward) P(hillips)
  1890-1937 . . . . **TCLC 4, 22; DAM POP;**
                                         SSC 3
  See also AAYA 14; CA 104; 133; MTCW

Lovelace, Earl 1935- . . . . **CLC 51**
  See also BW 2; CA 77-80; CANR 41;
    DLB 125; MTCW

Lovelace, Richard 1618-1657 . . . . **LC 24**
  See also DLB 131

Lowell, Amy
  1874-1925 . . . . **TCLC 1, 8; DAM POET;**
                                         PC 13
  See also CA 104; 151; DLB 54, 140

Lowell, James Russell 1819-1891 . . **NCLC 2**
  See also CDALB 1640-1865; DLB 1, 11, 64,
    79

Lowell, Robert (Traill Spence, Jr.)
  1917-1977 . . . **CLC 1, 2, 3, 4, 5, 8, 9, 11,**
    15, 37; DA; DAB; DAC; DAM MST,
                           NOV; PC 3; WLC
  See also CA 9-12R; 73-76; CABS 2;
    CANR 26; DLB 5, 169; MTCW

Lowndes, Marie Adelaide (Belloc)
  1868-1947 . . . . **TCLC 12**
  See also CA 107; DLB 70

Lowry, (Clarence) Malcolm
  1909-1957 . . . . **TCLC 6, 40**
  See also CA 105; 131; CDBLB 1945-1960;
    DLB 15; MTCW

Lowry, Mina Gertrude 1882-1966
  See Loy, Mina
  See also CA 113

Loxsmith, John
  See Brunner, John (Kilian Houston)

Loy, Mina . . . . **CLC 28; DAM POET; PC 16**
  See also Lowry, Mina Gertrude
  See also DLB 4, 54

Loyson-Bridet
  See Schwob, (Mayer Andre) Marcel

Lucas, Craig 1951- . . . . **CLC 64**
  See also CA 137

Lucas, George 1944- . . . . **CLC 16**
  See also AAYA 1; CA 77-80; CANR 30;
    SATA 56

Lucas, Hans
  See Godard, Jean-Luc

Lucas, Victoria
  See Plath, Sylvia

Ludlam, Charles 1943-1987 . . . . . **CLC 46, 50**
  See also CA 85-88; 122

Ludlum, Robert
  1927- . . . **CLC 22, 43; DAM NOV, POP**
  See also AAYA 10; BEST 89:1, 90:3;
    CA 33-36R; CANR 25, 41; DLBY 82;
    MTCW

Ludwig, Ken . . . . **CLC 60**

Ludwig, Otto 1813-1865 . . . . **NCLC 4**
  See also DLB 129

Lugones, Leopoldo 1874-1938 . . . . . **TCLC 15**
  See also CA 116; 131; HW

Lu Hsun 1881-1936 . . . . . . **TCLC 3; SSC 20**
  See also Shu-Jen, Chou

Lukacs, George . . . . **CLC 24**
  See also Lukacs, Gyorgy (Szegeny von)

Lukacs, Gyorgy (Szegeny von) 1885-1971
  See Lukacs, George
  See also CA 101; 29-32R

Luke, Peter (Ambrose Cyprian)
  1919-1995 . . . . **CLC 38**
  See also CA 81-84; 147; DLB 13

Lunar, Dennis
  See Mungo, Raymond

Lurie, Alison 1926- . . . . **CLC 4, 5, 18, 39**
  See also CA 1-4R; CANR 2, 17, 50; DLB 2;
    MTCW; SATA 46

Lustig, Arnost 1926- . . . . **CLC 56**
  See also AAYA 3; CA 69-72; CANR 47;
    SATA 56

Luther, Martin 1483-1546 . . . . **LC 9, 37**

Luxemburg, Rosa 1870(?)-1919 . . . . **TCLC 63**
  See also CA 118

Luzi, Mario 1914- . . . . **CLC 13**
  See also CA 61-64; CANR 9; DLB 128

L'Ymagier
  See Gourmont, Remy (-Marie-Charles) de

Lynch, B. Suarez
  See Bioy Casares, Adolfo; Borges, Jorge
    Luis

Lynch, David (K.) 1946-.......... **CLC 66**
See also CA 124; 129

Lynch, James
See Andreyev, Leonid (Nikolaevich)

Lynch Davis, B.
See Bioy Casares, Adolfo; Borges, Jorge
Luis

Lyndsay, Sir David 1490-1555 ...... **LC 20**

Lynn, Kenneth S(chuyler) 1923-.... **CLC 50**
See also CA 1-4R; CANR 3, 27

Lynx
See West, Rebecca

Lyons, Marcus
See Blish, James (Benjamin)

Lyre, Pinchbeck
See Sassoon, Siegfried (Lorraine)

Lytle, Andrew (Nelson) 1902-1995 .. **CLC 22**
See also CA 9-12R; 150; DLB 6; DLBY 95

Lyttelton, George 1709-1773........ **LC 10**

Maas, Peter 1929- .... **CLC 29**
See also CA 93-96; INT 93-96

Macaulay, Rose 1881-1958 ..... **TCLC 7, 44**
See also CA 104; DLB 36

Macaulay, Thomas Babington
1800-1859 .... **NCLC 42**
See also CDBLB 1832-1890; DLB 32, 55

MacBeth, George (Mann)
1932-1992 .... **CLC 2, 5, 9**
See also CA 25-28R; 136; DLB 40; MTCW;
SATA 4; SATA-Obit 70

MacCaig, Norman (Alexander)
1910- ..... **CLC 36; DAB; DAM POET**
See also CA 9-12R; CANR 3, 34; DLB 27

MacCarthy, (Sir Charles Otto) Desmond
1877-1952 .... **TCLC 36**

MacDiarmid, Hugh
.... **CLC 2, 4, 11, 19, 63; PC 9**
See also Grieve, C(hristopher) M(urray)
See also CDBLB 1945-1960; DLB 20

MacDonald, Anson
See Heinlein, Robert A(nson)

Macdonald, Cynthia 1928-...... **CLC 13, 19**
See also CA 49-52; CANR 4, 44; DLB 105

MacDonald, George 1824-1905..... **TCLC 9**
See also CA 106; 137; DLB 18, 163;
MAICYA; SATA 33

Macdonald, John
See Millar, Kenneth

MacDonald, John D(ann)
1916-1986 .... **CLC 3, 27, 44;
DAM NOV, POP**
See also CA 1-4R; 121; CANR 1, 19;
DLB 8; DLBY 86; MTCW

Macdonald, John Ross
See Millar, Kenneth

Macdonald, Ross..... **CLC 1, 2, 3, 14, 34, 41**
See also Millar, Kenneth
See also DLBD 6

MacDougal, John
See Blish, James (Benjamin)

MacEwen, Gwendolyn (Margaret)
1941-1987 .... **CLC 13, 55**
See also CA 9-12R; 124; CANR 7, 22;
DLB 53; SATA 50; SATA-Obit 55

Macha, Karel Hynek 1810-1846 .. **NCLC 46**

Machado (y Ruiz), Antonio
1875-1939 .... **TCLC 3**
See also CA 104; DLB 108

Machado de Assis, Joaquim Maria
1839-1908 ..... **TCLC 10; BLC; SSC 24**
See also CA 107; 153

Machen, Arthur.......... **TCLC 4; SSC 20**
See also Jones, Arthur Llewellyn
See also DLB 36, 156

Machiavelli, Niccolo
1469-1527 .... **LC 8, 36; DA; DAB;
DAC; DAM MST**

MacInnes, Colin 1914-1976...... **CLC 4, 23**
See also CA 69-72; 65-68; CANR 21;
DLB 14; MTCW

MacInnes, Helen (Clark)
1907-1985 ..... **CLC 27, 39; DAM POP**
See also CA 1-4R; 117; CANR 1, 28;
DLB 87; MTCW; SATA 22;
SATA-Obit 44

Mackay, Mary 1855-1924
See Corelli, Marie
See also CA 118

Mackenzie, Compton (Edward Montague)
1883-1972 .... **CLC 18**
See also CA 21-22; 37-40R; CAP 2;
DLB 34, 100

Mackenzie, Henry 1745-1831 .... **NCLC 41**
See also DLB 39

Mackintosh, Elizabeth 1896(?)-1952
See Tey, Josephine
See also CA 110

MacLaren, James
See Grieve, C(hristopher) M(urray)

Mac Laverty, Bernard 1942-....... **CLC 31**
See also CA 116; 118; CANR 43; INT 118

MacLean, Alistair (Stuart)
1922-1987 .... **CLC 3, 13, 50, 63;
DAM POP**
See also CA 57-60; 121; CANR 28; MTCW;
SATA 23; SATA-Obit 50

Maclean, Norman (Fitzroy)
1902-1990 .... **CLC 78; DAM POP;
SSC 13**
See also CA 102; 132; CANR 49

MacLeish, Archibald
1892-1982 .... **CLC 3, 8, 14, 68;
DAM POET**
See also CA 9-12R; 106; CANR 33; DLB 4,
7, 45; DLBY 82; MTCW

MacLennan, (John) Hugh
1907-1990 .... **CLC 2, 14, 92; DAC;
DAM MST**
See also CA 5-8R; 142; CANR 33; DLB 68;
MTCW

MacLeod, Alistair
1936- ...... **CLC 56; DAC; DAM MST**
See also CA 123; DLB 60

MacNeice, (Frederick) Louis
1907-1963 ...... **CLC 1, 4, 10, 53; DAB;
DAM POET**
See also CA 85-88; DLB 10, 20; MTCW

MacNeill, Dand
See Fraser, George MacDonald

Macpherson, James 1736-1796 ...... **LC 29**
See also DLB 109

Macpherson, (Jean) Jay 1931-...... **CLC 14**
See also CA 5-8R; DLB 53

MacShane, Frank 1927-.......... **CLC 39**
See also CA 9-12R; CANR 3, 33; DLB 111

Macumber, Mari
See Sandoz, Mari(e Susette)

Madach, Imre 1823-1864........ **NCLC 19**

Madden, (Jerry) David 1933- .... **CLC 5, 15**
See also CA 1-4R; CAAS 3; CANR 4, 45;
DLB 6; MTCW

Maddern, Al(an)
See Ellison, Harlan (Jay)

Madhubuti, Haki R.
1942- .... **CLC 6, 73; BLC;
DAM MULT, POET; PC 5**
See also Lee, Don L.
See also BW 2; CA 73-76; CANR 24, 51;
DLB 5, 41; DLBD 8

Maepenn, Hugh
See Kuttner, Henry

Maepenn, K. H.
See Kuttner, Henry

Maeterlinck, Maurice
1862-1949 ...... **TCLC 3; DAM DRAM**
See also CA 104; 136; SATA 66

Maginn, William 1794-1842....... **NCLC 8**
See also DLB 110, 159

Mahapatra, Jayanta
1928- .... **CLC 33; DAM MULT**
See also CA 73-76; CAAS 9; CANR 15, 33

Mahfouz, Naguib (Abdel Aziz Al-Sabilgi)
1911(?)-
See Mahfuz, Najib
See also BEST 89:2; CA 128; CANR 55;
DAM NOV; MTCW

Mahfuz, Najib .... **CLC 52, 55**
See also Mahfouz, Naguib (Abdel Aziz
Al-Sabilgi)
See also DLBY 88

Mahon, Derek 1941-.............. **CLC 27**
See also CA 113; 128; DLB 40

Mailer, Norman
1923- ...... **CLC 1, 2, 3, 4, 5, 8, 11, 14,
28, 39, 74; DA; DAB; DAC; DAM MST,
NOV, POP**
See also AITN 2; CA 9-12R; CABS 1;
CANR 28; CDALB 1968-1988; DLB 2,
16, 28; DLBD 3; DLBY 80, 83; MTCW

Maillet, Antonine 1929-...... **CLC 54; DAC**
See also CA 115; 120; CANR 46; DLB 60;
INT 120

Mais, Roger 1905-1955 .... **TCLC 8**
See also BW 1; CA 105; 124; DLB 125;
MTCW

Maistre, Joseph de 1753-1821 .... **NCLC 37**

Maitland, Frederic 1850-1906 ..... **TCLC 65**

Maitland, Sara (Louise) 1950-...... **CLC 49**
See also CA 69-72; CANR 13

Major, Clarence
1936- .... **CLC 3, 19, 48; BLC;
DAM MULT**
See also BW 2; CA 21-24R; CAAS 6;
CANR 13, 25, 53; DLB 33

Major, Kevin (Gerald)
    1949- .... **CLC 26; DAC**
    See also AAYA 16; CA 97-100; CANR 21,
    38; CLR 11; DLB 60; INT CANR-21;
    JRDA; MAICYA; SATA 32, 82

Maki, James
    See Ozu, Yasujiro

Malabaila, Damiano
    See Levi, Primo

Malamud, Bernard
    1914-1986 ...... **CLC 1, 2, 3, 5, 8, 9, 11,
        18, 27, 44, 78, 85; DA; DAB; DAC;
        DAM MST, NOV, POP; SSC 15; WLC**
    See also AAYA 16; CA 5-8R; 118; CABS 1;
    CANR 28; CDALB 1941-1968; DLB 2,
    28, 152; DLBY 80, 86; MTCW

Malaparte, Curzio 1898-1957 ..... **TCLC 52**

Malcolm, Dan
    See Silverberg, Robert

Malcolm X .... **CLC 82; BLC**
    See also Little, Malcolm

Malherbe, Francois de 1555-1628 ..... **LC 5**

Mallarme, Stephane
    1842-1898 .... **NCLC 4, 41;
        DAM POET; PC 4**

Mallet-Joris, Francoise 1930- ...... **CLC 11**
    See also CA 65-68; CANR 17; DLB 83

Malley, Ern
    See McAuley, James Phillip

Mallowan, Agatha Christie
    See Christie, Agatha (Mary Clarissa)

Maloff, Saul 1922- .... **CLC 5**
    See also CA 33-36R

Malone, Louis
    See MacNeice, (Frederick) Louis

Malone, Michael (Christopher)
    1942- .... **CLC 43**
    See also CA 77-80; CANR 14, 32

Malory, (Sir) Thomas
    1410(?)-1471(?) ...... **LC 11; DA; DAB;
        DAC; DAM MST**
    See also CDBLB Before 1660; DLB 146;
    SATA 59; SATA-Brief 33

Malouf, (George Joseph) David
    1934- .... **CLC 28, 86**
    See also CA 124; CANR 50

Malraux, (Georges-)Andre
    1901-1976 ...... **CLC 1, 4, 9, 13, 15, 57;
        DAM NOV**
    See also CA 21-22; 69-72; CANR 34;
    CAP 2; DLB 72; MTCW

Malzberg, Barry N(athaniel) 1939-... **CLC 7**
    See also CA 61-64; CAAS 4; CANR 16;
    DLB 8

Mamet, David (Alan)
    1947- .... **CLC 9, 15, 34, 46, 91;
        DAM DRAM; DC 4**
    See also AAYA 3; CA 81-84; CABS 3;
    CANR 15, 41; DLB 7; MTCW

Mamoulian, Rouben (Zachary)
    1897-1987 .... **CLC 16**
    See also CA 25-28R; 124

Mandelstam, Osip (Emilievich)
    1891(?)-1938(?) ...... **TCLC 2, 6; PC 14**
    See also CA 104; 150

Mander, (Mary) Jane 1877-1949... **TCLC 31**

Mandeville, John fl. 1350- .... **CMLC 19**
    See also DLB 146

Mandiargues, Andre Pieyre de ...... **CLC 41**
    See also Pieyre de Mandiargues, Andre
    See also DLB 83

Mandrake, Ethel Belle
    See Thurman, Wallace (Henry)

Mangan, James Clarence
    1803-1849 .... **NCLC 27**

Maniere, J.-E.
    See Giraudoux, (Hippolyte) Jean

Manley, (Mary) Delariviere
    1672(?)-1724 .... **LC 1**
    See also DLB 39, 80

Mann, Abel
    See Creasey, John

Mann, (Luiz) Heinrich 1871-1950... **TCLC 9**
    See also CA 106; DLB 66

Mann, (Paul) Thomas
    1875-1955 .... **TCLC 2, 8, 14, 21, 35, 44,
        60; DA; DAB; DAC; DAM MST, NOV;
        SSC 5; WLC**
    See also CA 104; 128; DLB 66; MTCW

Mannheim, Karl 1893-1947 .... **TCLC 65**

Manning, David
    See Faust, Frederick (Schiller)

Manning, Frederic 1887(?)-1935... **TCLC 25**
    See also CA 124

Manning, Olivia 1915-1980 ...... **CLC 5, 19**
    See also CA 5-8R; 101; CANR 29; MTCW

Mano, D. Keith 1942- .... **CLC 2, 10**
    See also CA 25-28R; CAAS 6; CANR 26;
    DLB 6

Mansfield, Katherine
    .. **TCLC 2, 8, 39; DAB; SSC 9, 23; WLC**
    See also Beauchamp, Kathleen Mansfield
    See also DLB 162

Manso, Peter 1940- .... **CLC 39**
    See also CA 29-32R; CANR 44

Mantecon, Juan Jimenez
    See Jimenez (Mantecon), Juan Ramon

Manton, Peter
    See Creasey, John

Man Without a Spleen, A
    See Chekhov, Anton (Pavlovich)

Manzoni, Alessandro 1785-1873 .. **NCLC 29**

Mapu, Abraham (ben Jekutiel)
    1808-1867 .... **NCLC 18**

Mara, Sally
    See Queneau, Raymond

Marat, Jean Paul 1743-1793 .... **LC 10**

Marcel, Gabriel Honore
    1889-1973 .... **CLC 15**
    See also CA 102; 45-48; MTCW

Marchbanks, Samuel
    See Davies, (William) Robertson

Marchi, Giacomo
    See Bassani, Giorgio

Margulies, Donald .... **CLC 76**

Marie de France c. 12th cent. -.... **CMLC 8**

Marie de l'Incarnation 1599-1672.... **LC 10**

Marier, Captain Victor
    See Griffith, D(avid Lewelyn) W(ark)

Mariner, Scott
    See Pohl, Frederik

Marinetti, Filippo Tommaso
    1876-1944 .... **TCLC 10**
    See also CA 107; DLB 114

Marivaux, Pierre Carlet de Chamblain de
    1688-1763 .... **LC 4**

Markandaya, Kamala .... **CLC 8, 38**
    See also Taylor, Kamala (Purnaiya)

Markfield, Wallace 1926-.......... **CLC 8**
    See also CA 69-72; CAAS 3; DLB 2, 28

Markham, Edwin 1852-1940 ...... **TCLC 47**
    See also DLB 54

Markham, Robert
    See Amis, Kingsley (William)

Marks, J
    See Highwater, Jamake (Mamake)

Marks-Highwater, J
    See Highwater, Jamake (Mamake)

Markson, David M(errill) 1927-.... **CLC 67**
    See also CA 49-52; CANR 1

Marley, Bob .... **CLC 17**
    See also Marley, Robert Nesta

Marley, Robert Nesta 1945-1981
    See Marley, Bob
    See also CA 107; 103

Marlowe, Christopher
    1564-1593 ..... **LC 22; DA; DAB; DAC;
        DAM DRAM, MST; DC 1; WLC**
    See also CDBLB Before 1660; DLB 62

Marlowe, Stephen 1928-
    See Queen, Ellery
    See also CA 13-16R; CANR 6, 55

Marmontel, Jean-Francois
    1723-1799 .... **LC 2**

Marquand, John P(hillips)
    1893-1960 .... **CLC 2, 10**
    See also CA 85-88; DLB 9, 102

Marques, Rene
    1919-1979 ...... **CLC 96; DAM MULT;
        HLC**
    See also CA 97-100; 85-88; DLB 113; HW

Marquez, Gabriel (Jose) Garcia
    See Garcia Marquez, Gabriel (Jose)

Marquis, Don(ald Robert Perry)
    1878-1937 .... **TCLC 7**
    See also CA 104; DLB 11, 25

Marric, J. J.
    See Creasey, John

Marrow, Bernard
    See Moore, Brian

Marryat, Frederick 1792-1848 .... **NCLC 3**
    See also DLB 21, 163

Marsden, James
    See Creasey, John

Marsh, (Edith) Ngaio
    1899-1982 ...... **CLC 7, 53; DAM POP**
    See also CA 9-12R; CANR 6; DLB 77;
    MTCW

Marshall, Garry 1934-............ **CLC 17**
    See also AAYA 3; CA 111; SATA 60**

Marshall, Paule
  1929- . . . . **CLC 27, 72; BLC;**
                                DAM MULT; SSC 3
  See also BW 2; CA 77-80; CANR 25;
  DLB 157; MTCW

Marsten, Richard
  See Hunter, Evan

Marston, John
  1576-1634 . . . . **LC 33; DAM DRAM**
  See also DLB 58, 172

Martha, Henry
  See Harris, Mark

Martial c. 40-c. 104 . . . . **PC 10**

Martin, Ken
  See Hubbard, L(afayette) Ron(ald)

Martin, Richard
  See Creasey, John

Martin, Steve 1945- . . . . **CLC 30**
  See also CA 97-100; CANR 30; MTCW

Martin, Valerie 1948- . . . . **CLC 89**
  See also BEST 90:2; CA 85-88; CANR 49

Martin, Violet Florence
  1862-1915 . . . . **TCLC 51**

Martin, Webber
  See Silverberg, Robert

Martindale, Patrick Victor
  See White, Patrick (Victor Martindale)

Martin du Gard, Roger
  1881-1958 . . . . **TCLC 24**
  See also CA 118; DLB 65

Martineau, Harriet 1802-1876. . . . **NCLC 26**
  See also DLB 21, 55, 159, 163, 166;
  YABC 2

Martines, Julia
  See O'Faolain, Julia

Martinez, Jacinto Benavente y
  See Benavente (y Martinez), Jacinto

Martinez Ruiz, Jose 1873-1967
  See Azorin; Ruiz, Jose Martinez
  See also CA 93-96; HW

Martinez Sierra, Gregorio
  1881-1947 . . . . **TCLC 6**
  See also CA 115

Martinez Sierra, Maria (de la O'LeJarraga)
  1874-1974 . . . . **TCLC 6**
  See also CA 115

Martinsen, Martin
  See Follett, Ken(neth Martin)

Martinson, Harry (Edmund)
  1904-1978 . . . . **CLC 14**
  See also CA 77-80; CANR 34

Marut, Ret
  See Traven, B.

Marut, Robert
  See Traven, B.

Marvell, Andrew
  1621-1678 . . . . . . **LC 4; DA; DAB; DAC;**
                        DAM MST, POET; PC 10; WLC
  See also CDBLB 1660-1789; DLB 131

Marx, Karl (Heinrich)
  1818-1883 . . . . **NCLC 17**
  See also DLB 129

Masaoka Shiki. . . . . **TCLC 18**
  See also Masaoka Tsunenori

Masaoka Tsunenori 1867-1902
  See Masaoka Shiki
  See also CA 117

Masefield, John (Edward)
  1878-1967 . . . . **CLC 11, 47; DAM POET**
  See also CA 19-20; 25-28R; CANR 33;
  CAP 2; CDBLB 1890-1914; DLB 10, 19,
  153, 160; MTCW; SATA 19

Maso, Carole 19(?)- . . . . **CLC 44**

Mason, Bobbie Ann
  1940- . . . . **CLC 28, 43, 82; SSC 4**
  See also AAYA 5; CA 53-56; CANR 11,
  31; DLB 173; DLBY 87; INT CANR-31;
  MTCW

Mason, Ernst
  See Pohl, Frederik

Mason, Lee W.
  See Malzberg, Barry N(athaniel)

Mason, Nick 1945- . . . . **CLC 35**

Mason, Tally
  See Derleth, August (William)

Mass, William
  See Gibson, William

Masters, Edgar Lee
  1868-1950 . . . . . . **TCLC 2, 25; DA; DAC;**
                        DAM MST, POET; PC 1
  See also CA 104; 133; CDALB 1865-1917;
  DLB 54; MTCW

Masters, Hilary 1928- . . . . **CLC 48**
  See also CA 25-28R; CANR 13, 47

Mastrosimone, William 19(?)- . . . . . . **CLC 36**

Mathe, Albert
  See Camus, Albert

Matheson, Richard Burton 1926- . . . **CLC 37**
  See also CA 97-100; DLB 8, 44; INT 97-100

Mathews, Harry 1930- . . . . **CLC 6, 52**
  See also CA 21-24R; CAAS 6; CANR 18,
  40

Mathews, John Joseph
  1894-1979 . . . . . . **CLC 84; DAM MULT**
  See also CA 19-20; 142; CANR 45; CAP 2;
  NNAL

Mathias, Roland (Glyn) 1915- . . . . . . **CLC 45**
  See also CA 97-100; CANR 19, 41; DLB 27

Matsuo Basho 1644-1694. . . . . **PC 3**
  See also DAM POET

Mattheson, Rodney
  See Creasey, John

Matthews, Greg 1949- . . . . **CLC 45**
  See also CA 135

Matthews, William 1942-. . . . . **CLC 40**
  See also CA 29-32R; CAAS 18; CANR 12;
  DLB 5

Matthias, John (Edward) 1941-. . . . . . **CLC 9**
  See also CA 33-36R

Matthiessen, Peter
  1927- . . . . **CLC 5, 7, 11, 32, 64;**
                            DAM NOV
  See also AAYA 6; BEST 90:4; CA 9-12R;
  CANR 21, 50; DLB 6, 173; MTCW;
  SATA 27

Maturin, Charles Robert
  1780(?)-1824 . . . . **NCLC 6**

Matute (Ausejo), Ana Maria
  1925- . . . . **CLC 11**
  See also CA 89-92; MTCW

Maugham, W. S.
  See Maugham, W(illiam) Somerset

Maugham, W(illiam) Somerset
  1874-1965 . . . . **CLC 1, 11, 15, 67, 93;**
                          DA; DAB; DAC; DAM DRAM, MST,
                          NOV; SSC 8; WLC
  See also CA 5-8R; 25-28R; CANR 40;
  CDBLB 1914-1945; DLB 10, 36, 77, 100,
  162; MTCW; SATA 54

Maugham, William Somerset
  See Maugham, W(illiam) Somerset

Maupassant, (Henri Rene Albert) Guy de
  1850-1893 . . . . . **NCLC 1, 42; DA; DAB;**
                      DAC; DAM MST; SSC 1; WLC
  See also DLB 123

Maupin, Armistead
  1944- . . . . **CLC 95; DAM POP**
  See also CA 125; 130; INT 130

Maurhut, Richard
  See Traven, B.

Mauriac, Claude 1914-1996. . . . . **CLC 9**
  See also CA 89-92; 152; DLB 83

Mauriac, Francois (Charles)
  1885-1970 . . . . **CLC 4, 9, 56; SSC 24**
  See also CA 25-28; CAP 2; DLB 65;
  MTCW

Mavor, Osborne Henry 1888-1951
  See Bridie, James
  See also CA 104

Maxwell, William (Keepers, Jr.)
  1908- . . . . **CLC 19**
  See also CA 93-96; CANR 54; DLBY 80;
  INT 93-96

May, Elaine 1932- . . . . **CLC 16**
  See also CA 124; 142; DLB 44

Mayakovski, Vladimir (Vladimirovich)
  1893-1930 . . . . **TCLC 4, 18**
  See also CA 104

Mayhew, Henry 1812-1887 . . . . . . **NCLC 31**
  See also DLB 18, 55

Mayle, Peter 1939(?)-. . . . . **CLC 89**
  See also CA 139

Maynard, Joyce 1953-. . . . . **CLC 23**
  See also CA 111; 129

Mayne, William (James Carter)
  1928- . . . . **CLC 12**
  See also CA 9-12R; CANR 37; CLR 25;
  JRDA; MAICYA; SAAS 11; SATA 6, 68

Mayo, Jim
  See L'Amour, Louis (Dearborn)

Maysles, Albert 1926- . . . . **CLC 16**
  See also CA 29-32R

Maysles, David 1932-. . . . . **CLC 16**

Mazer, Norma Fox 1931- . . . . **CLC 26**
  See also AAYA 5; CA 69-72; CANR 12,
  32; CLR 23; JRDA; MAICYA; SAAS 1;
  SATA 24, 67

Mazzini, Guiseppe 1805-1872 . . . . **NCLC 34**

McAuley, James Phillip
  1917-1976 . . . . **CLC 45**
  See also CA 97-100

Meltzer, Milton 1915- . . . . **CLC 26**
See also AAYA 8; CA 13-16R; CANR 38;
CLR 13; DLB 61; JRDA; MAICYA;
SAAS 1; SATA 1, 50, 80

Melville, Herman
1819-1891 . . . . . **NCLC 3, 12, 29, 45, 49;**
DA; DAB; DAC; DAM MST, NOV;
SSC 1, 17; WLC
See also CDALB 1640-1865; DLB 3, 74;
SATA 59

Menander
c. 342B.C.-c. 292B.C. . . . . **CMLC 9;**
DAM DRAM; DC 3

Mencken, H(enry) L(ouis)
1880-1956 . . . . **TCLC 13**
See also CA 105; 125; CDALB 1917-1929;
DLB 11, 29, 63, 137; MTCW

Mercer, David
1928-1980 . . . . **CLC 5; DAM DRAM**
See also CA 9-12R; 102; CANR 23;
DLB 13; MTCW

Merchant, Paul
See Ellison, Harlan (Jay)

Meredith, George
1828-1909 . . **TCLC 17, 43; DAM POET**
See also CA 117; 153; CDBLB 1832-1890;
DLB 18, 35, 57, 159

Meredith, William (Morris)
1919- . . **CLC 4, 13, 22, 55; DAM POET**
See also CA 9-12R; CAAS 14; CANR 6, 40;
DLB 5

Merezhkovsky, Dmitry Sergeyevich
1865-1941 . . . . **TCLC 29**

Merimee, Prosper
1803-1870 . . . . **NCLC 6; SSC 7**
See also DLB 119

Merkin, Daphne 1954- . . . . **CLC 44**
See also CA 123

Merlin, Arthur
See Blish, James (Benjamin)

Merrill, James (Ingram)
1926-1995 . . . . **CLC 2, 3, 6, 8, 13, 18, 34,**
91; DAM POET
See also CA 13-16R; 147; CANR 10, 49;
DLB 5, 165; DLBY 85; INT CANR-10;
MTCW

Merriman, Alex
See Silverberg, Robert

Merritt, E. B.
See Waddington, Miriam

Merton, Thomas
1915-1968 . . **CLC 1, 3, 11, 34, 83; PC 10**
See also CA 5-8R; 25-28R; CANR 22, 53;
DLB 48; DLBY 81; MTCW

Merwin, W(illiam) S(tanley)
1927- . . . . . . **CLC 1, 2, 3, 5, 8, 13, 18, 45,**
88; DAM POET
See also CA 13-16R; CANR 15, 51; DLB 5,
169; INT CANR-15; MTCW

Metcalf, John 1938- . . . . **CLC 37**
See also CA 113; DLB 60

Metcalf, Suzanne
See Baum, L(yman) Frank

Mew, Charlotte (Mary)
1870-1928 . . . . **TCLC 8**
See also CA 105; DLB 19, 135

Mewshaw, Michael 1943- . . . . **CLC 9**
See also CA 53-56; CANR 7, 47; DLBY 80

Meyer, June
See Jordan, June

Meyer, Lynn
See Slavitt, David R(ytman)

Meyer-Meyrink, Gustav 1868-1932
See Meyrink, Gustav
See also CA 117

Meyers, Jeffrey 1939- . . . . **CLC 39**
See also CA 73-76; CANR 54; DLB 111

Meynell, Alice (Christina Gertrude Thompson)
1847-1922 . . . . **TCLC 6**
See also CA 104; DLB 19, 98

Meyrink, Gustav . . . . **TCLC 21**
See also Meyer-Meyrink, Gustav
See also DLB 81

Michaels, Leonard
1933- . . . . **CLC 6, 25; SSC 16**
See also CA 61-64; CANR 21; DLB 130;
MTCW

Michaux, Henri 1899-1984 . . . . . **CLC 8, 19**
See also CA 85-88; 114

Michelangelo 1475-1564 . . . . **LC 12**

Michelet, Jules 1798-1874 . . . . . . **NCLC 31**

Michener, James A(lbert)
1907(?)- . . . . **CLC 1, 5, 11, 29, 60;**
DAM NOV, POP
See also AITN 1; BEST 90:1; CA 5-8R;
CANR 21, 45; DLB 6; MTCW

Mickiewicz, Adam 1798-1855 . . . . . **NCLC 3**

Middleton, Christopher 1926- . . . . . . **CLC 13**
See also CA 13-16R; CANR 29, 54;
DLB 40

Middleton, Richard (Barham)
1882-1911 . . . . **TCLC 56**
See also DLB 156

Middleton, Stanley 1919- . . . . **CLC 7, 38**
See also CA 25-28R; CAAS 23; CANR 21,
46; DLB 14

Middleton, Thomas
1580-1627 . . . . . . **LC 33; DAM DRAM,**
MST; DC 5
See also DLB 58

Migueis, Jose Rodrigues 1901- . . . . . **CLC 10**

Mikszath, Kalman 1847-1910 . . . . . **TCLC 31**

Miles, Josephine (Louise)
1911-1985 . . . . **CLC 1, 2, 14, 34, 39;**
DAM POET
See also CA 1-4R; 116; CANR 2, 55;
DLB 48

Militant
See Sandburg, Carl (August)

Mill, John Stuart 1806-1873 . . **NCLC 11, 58**
See also CDBLB 1832-1890; DLB 55

Millar, Kenneth
1915-1983 . . . . **CLC 14; DAM POP**
See also Macdonald, Ross
See also CA 9-12R; 110; CANR 16; DLB 2;
DLBD 6; DLBY 83; MTCW

Millay, E. Vincent
See Millay, Edna St. Vincent

Millay, Edna St. Vincent
1892-1950 . . . . . **TCLC 4, 49; DA; DAB;**
DAC; DAM MST, POET; PC 6
See also CA 104; 130; CDALB 1917-1929;
DLB 45; MTCW

Miller, Arthur
1915- . . . . **CLC 1, 2, 6, 10, 15, 26, 47, 78;**
DA; DAB; DAC; DAM DRAM, MST;
DC 1; WLC
See also AAYA 15; AITN 1; CA 1-4R;
CABS 3; CANR 2, 30, 54;
CDALB 1941-1968; DLB 7; MTCW

Miller, Henry (Valentine)
1891-1980 . . . . **CLC 1, 2, 4, 9, 14, 43, 84;**
DA; DAB; DAC; DAM MST, NOV;
WLC
See also CA 9-12R; 97-100; CANR 33;
CDALB 1929-1941; DLB 4, 9; DLBY 80;
MTCW

Miller, Jason 1939(?)- . . . . **CLC 2**
See also AITN 1; CA 73-76; DLB 7

Miller, Sue 1943- . . . . . **CLC 44; DAM POP**
See also BEST 90:3; CA 139; DLB 143

Miller, Walter M(ichael, Jr.)
1923- . . . . **CLC 4, 30**
See also CA 85-88; DLB 8

Millett, Kate 1934- . . . . **CLC 67**
See also AITN 1; CA 73-76; CANR 32, 53;
MTCW

Millhauser, Steven 1943- . . . . **CLC 21, 54**
See also CA 110; 111; DLB 2; INT 111

Millin, Sarah Gertrude 1889-1968 . . **CLC 49**
See also CA 102; 93-96

Milne, A(lan) A(lexander)
1882-1956 . . . . **TCLC 6; DAB; DAC;**
DAM MST
See also CA 104; 133; CLR 1, 26; DLB 10,
77, 100, 160; MAICYA; MTCW;
YABC 1

Milner, Ron(ald)
1938- . . . . . . **CLC 56; BLC; DAM MULT**
See also AITN 1; BW 1; CA 73-76;
CANR 24; DLB 38; MTCW

Milosz, Czeslaw
1911- . . . . **CLC 5, 11, 22, 31, 56, 82;**
DAM MST, POET; PC 8
See also CA 81-84; CANR 23, 51; MTCW

Milton, John
1608-1674 . . . . . . **LC 9; DA; DAB; DAC;**
DAM MST, POET; WLC
See also CDBLB 1660-1789; DLB 131, 151

Min, Anchee 1957- . . . . **CLC 86**
See also CA 146

Minehaha, Cornelius
See Wedekind, (Benjamin) Frank(lin)

Miner, Valerie 1947- . . . . **CLC 40**
See also CA 97-100

Minimo, Duca
See D'Annunzio, Gabriele

Minot, Susan 1956- . . . . **CLC 44**
See also CA 134

Minus, Ed 1938- . . . . **CLC 39**

Miranda, Javier
See Bioy Casares, Adolfo

Mirbeau, Octave 1848-1917 . . . . . . **TCLC 55**
See also DLB 123

Morgan, Seth 1949(?)-1990 . . . . **CLC 65**
See also CA 132

Morgenstern, Christian
1871-1914 . . . . **TCLC 8**
See also CA 105

Morgenstern, S.
See Goldman, William (W.)

Moricz, Zsigmond 1879-1942 . . . . . **TCLC 33**

Morike, Eduard (Friedrich)
1804-1875 . . . . **NCLC 10**
See also DLB 133

Mori Ogai . . . . **TCLC 14**
See also Mori Rintaro

Mori Rintaro 1862-1922
See Mori Ogai
See also CA 110

Moritz, Karl Philipp 1756-1793 . . . . . . **LC 2**
See also DLB 94

Morland, Peter Henry
See Faust, Frederick (Schiller)

Morren, Theophil
See Hofmannsthal, Hugo von

Morris, Bill 1952- . . . . **CLC 76**

Morris, Julian
See West, Morris L(anglo)

Morris, Steveland Judkins 1950(?)-
See Wonder, Stevie
See also CA 111

Morris, William 1834-1896 . . . . **NCLC 4**
See also CDBLB 1832-1890; DLB 18, 35,
57, 156

Morris, Wright 1910- . . . **CLC 1, 3, 7, 18, 37**
See also CA 9-12R; CANR 21; DLB 2;
DLBY 81; MTCW

Morrison, Chloe Anthony Wofford
See Morrison, Toni

Morrison, James Douglas 1943-1971
See Morrison, Jim
See also CA 73-76; CANR 40

Morrison, Jim . . . . **CLC 17**
See also Morrison, James Douglas

Morrison, Toni
1931- . . . . **CLC 4, 10, 22, 55, 81, 87;**
BLC; DA; DAB; DAC; DAM MST,
MULT, NOV, POP
See also AAYA 1; BW 2; CA 29-32R;
CANR 27, 42; CDALB 1968-1988;
DLB 6, 33, 143; DLBY 81; MTCW;
SATA 57

Morrison, Van 1945- . . . . **CLC 21**
See also CA 116

Mortimer, John (Clifford)
1923- . . . . . . **CLC 28, 43; DAM DRAM,**
POP
See also CA 13-16R; CANR 21;
CDBLB 1960 to Present; DLB 13;
INT CANR-21; MTCW

Mortimer, Penelope (Ruth) 1918- . . . . **CLC 5**
See also CA 57-60; CANR 45

Morton, Anthony
See Creasey, John

Mosher, Howard Frank 1943- . . . . . . **CLC 62**
See also CA 139

Mosley, Nicholas 1923- . . . . **CLC 43, 70**
See also CA 69-72; CANR 41; DLB 14

Mosley, Walter
1952- . . . . . **CLC 97; DAM MULT, POP**
See also AAYA 17; BW 2; CA 142

Moss, Howard
1922-1987 . . . . **CLC 7, 14, 45, 50;**
DAM POET
See also CA 1-4R; 123; CANR 1, 44;
DLB 5

Mossgiel, Rab
See Burns, Robert

Motion, Andrew (Peter) 1952- . . . . . . **CLC 47**
See also CA 146; DLB 40

Motley, Willard (Francis)
1909-1965 . . . . **CLC 18**
See also BW 1; CA 117; 106; DLB 76, 143

Motoori, Norinaga 1730-1801 . . . . **NCLC 45**

Mott, Michael (Charles Alston)
1930- . . . . **CLC 15, 34**
See also CA 5-8R; CAAS 7; CANR 7, 29

Mountain Wolf Woman
1884-1960 . . . . **CLC 92**
See also CA 144; NNAL

Moure, Erin 1955- . . . . **CLC 88**
See also CA 113; DLB 60

Mowat, Farley (McGill)
1921- . . . . . . **CLC 26; DAC; DAM MST**
See also AAYA 1; CA 1-4R; CANR 4, 24,
42; CLR 20; DLB 68; INT CANR-24;
JRDA; MAICYA; MTCW; SATA 3, 55

Moyers, Bill 1934- . . . . **CLC 74**
See also AITN 2; CA 61-64; CANR 31, 52

Mphahlele, Es'kia
See Mphahlele, Ezekiel
See also DLB 125

Mphahlele, Ezekiel
1919- . . . . . **CLC 25; BLC; DAM MULT**
See also Mphahlele, Es'kia
See also BW 2; CA 81-84; CANR 26

Mqhayi, S(amuel) E(dward) K(rune Loliwe)
1875-1945 . . . . **TCLC 25; BLC;**
DAM MULT
See also CA 153

Mrozek, Slawomir 1930- . . . . **CLC 3, 13**
See also CA 13-16R; CAAS 10; CANR 29;
MTCW

Mrs. Belloc-Lowndes
See Lowndes, Marie Adelaide (Belloc)

Mtwa, Percy (?)- . . . . **CLC 47**

Mueller, Lisel 1924- . . . . **CLC 13, 51**
See also CA 93-96; DLB 105

Muir, Edwin 1887-1959 . . . . **TCLC 2**
See also CA 104; DLB 20, 100

Muir, John 1838-1914 . . . . **TCLC 28**

Mujica Lainez, Manuel
1910-1984 . . . . **CLC 31**
See also Lainez, Manuel Mujica
See also CA 81-84; 112; CANR 32; HW

Mukherjee, Bharati
1940- . . . . **CLC 53; DAM NOV**
See also BEST 89:2; CA 107; CANR 45;
DLB 60; MTCW

Muldoon, Paul
1951- . . . . **CLC 32, 72; DAM POET**
See also CA 113; 129; CANR 52; DLB 40;
INT 129

Mulisch, Harry 1927- . . . . **CLC 42**
See also CA 9-12R; CANR 6, 26

Mull, Martin 1943- . . . . **CLC 17**
See also CA 105

Mulock, Dinah Maria
See Craik, Dinah Maria (Mulock)

Munford, Robert 1737(?)-1783 . . . . **LC 5**
See also DLB 31

Mungo, Raymond 1946- . . . . **CLC 72**
See also CA 49-52; CANR 2

Munro, Alice
1931- . . . . . . **CLC 6, 10, 19, 50, 95; DAC;**
DAM MST, NOV; SSC 3
See also AITN 2; CA 33-36R; CANR 33,
53; DLB 53; MTCW; SATA 29

Munro, H(ector) H(ugh) 1870-1916
See Saki
See also CA 104; 130; CDBLB 1890-1914;
DA; DAB; DAC; DAM MST, NOV;
DLB 34, 162; MTCW; WLC

Murasaki, Lady . . . . **CMLC 1**

Murdoch, (Jean) Iris
1919- . . . . . . **CLC 1, 2, 3, 4, 6, 8, 11, 15,**
22, 31, 51; DAB; DAC; DAM MST,
NOV
See also CA 13-16R; CANR 8, 43;
CDBLB 1960 to Present; DLB 14;
INT CANR-8; MTCW

Murfree, Mary Noailles
1850-1922 . . . . **SSC 22**
See also CA 122; DLB 12, 74

Murnau, Friedrich Wilhelm
See Plumpe, Friedrich Wilhelm

Murphy, Richard 1927- . . . . **CLC 41**
See also CA 29-32R; DLB 40

Murphy, Sylvia 1937- . . . . **CLC 34**
See also CA 121

Murphy, Thomas (Bernard) 1935- . . . **CLC 51**
See also CA 101

Murray, Albert L. 1916- . . . . **CLC 73**
See also BW 2; CA 49-52; CANR 26, 52;
DLB 38

Murray, Les(lie) A(llan)
1938- . . . . **CLC 40; DAM POET**
See also CA 21-24R; CANR 11, 27

Murry, J. Middleton
See Murry, John Middleton

Murry, John Middleton
1889-1957 . . . . **TCLC 16**
See also CA 118; DLB 149

Musgrave, Susan 1951- . . . . **CLC 13, 54**
See also CA 69-72; CANR 45

Musil, Robert (Edler von)
1880-1942 . . . . **TCLC 12, 68; SSC 18**
See also CA 109; CANR 55; DLB 81, 124

Muske, Carol 1945- . . . . **CLC 90**
See also Muske-Dukes, Carol (Anne)

Muske-Dukes, Carol (Anne) 1945-
See Muske, Carol
See also CA 65-68; CANR 32

Nodier, (Jean) Charles (Emmanuel)
1780-1844 .... **NCLC 19**
See also DLB 119

Nolan, Christopher 1965- .... **CLC 58**
See also CA 111

Noon, Jeff 1957- .... **CLC 91**
See also CA 148

Norden, Charles
See Durrell, Lawrence (George)

Nordhoff, Charles (Bernard)
1887-1947 .... **TCLC 23**
See also CA 108; DLB 9; SATA 23

Norfolk, Lawrence 1963- .... **CLC 76**
See also CA 144

Norman, Marsha
1947- .... **CLC 28; DAM DRAM**
See also CA 105; CABS 3; CANR 41;
DLBY 84

Norris, Benjamin Franklin, Jr.
1870-1902 .... **TCLC 24**
See also Norris, Frank
See also CA 110

Norris, Frank
See Norris, Benjamin Franklin, Jr.
See also CDALB 1865-1917; DLB 12, 71

Norris, Leslie 1921- .... **CLC 14**
See also CA 11-12; CANR 14; CAP 1;
DLB 27

North, Andrew
See Norton, Andre

North, Anthony
See Koontz, Dean R(ay)

North, Captain George
See Stevenson, Robert Louis (Balfour)

North, Milou
See Erdrich, Louise

Northrup, B. A.
See Hubbard, L(afayette) Ron(ald)

North Staffs
See Hulme, T(homas) E(rnest)

Norton, Alice Mary
See Norton, Andre
See also MAICYA; SATA 1, 43

Norton, Andre 1912- .... **CLC 12**
See also Norton, Alice Mary
See also AAYA 14; CA 1-4R; CANR 2, 31;
DLB 8, 52; JRDA; MTCW; SATA 91

Norton, Caroline 1808-1877 ...... **NCLC 47**
See also DLB 21, 159

Norway, Nevil Shute 1899-1960
See Shute, Nevil
See also CA 102; 93-96

Norwid, Cyprian Kamil
1821-1883 .... **NCLC 17**

Nosille, Nabrah
See Ellison, Harlan (Jay)

Nossack, Hans Erich 1901-1978 ..... **CLC 6**
See also CA 93-96; 85-88; DLB 69

Nostradamus 1503-1566 .... **LC 27**

Nosu, Chuji
See Ozu, Yasujiro

Notenburg, Eleanora (Genrikhovna) von
See Guro, Elena

Nova, Craig 1945- .... **CLC 7, 31**
See also CA 45-48; CANR 2, 53

Novak, Joseph
See Kosinski, Jerzy (Nikodem)

Novalis 1772-1801 .... **NCLC 13**
See also DLB 90

Nowlan, Alden (Albert)
1933-1983 .. **CLC 15; DAC; DAM MST**
See also CA 9-12R; CANR 5; DLB 53

Noyes, Alfred 1880-1958 .... **TCLC 7**
See also CA 104; DLB 20

Nunn, Kem 19(?)- .... **CLC 34**

Nye, Robert
1939- .... **CLC 13, 42; DAM NOV**
See also CA 33-36R; CANR 29; DLB 14;
MTCW; SATA 6

Nyro, Laura 1947- .... **CLC 17**

Oates, Joyce Carol
1938- ...... **CLC 1, 2, 3, 6, 9, 11, 15, 19,
33, 52; DA; DAB; DAC; DAM MST,
NOV, POP; SSC 6; WLC**
See also AAYA 15; AITN 1; BEST 89:2;
CA 5-8R; CANR 25, 45;
CDALB 1968-1988; DLB 2, 5, 130;
DLBY 81; INT CANR-25; MTCW

O'Brien, Darcy 1939- .... **CLC 11**
See also CA 21-24R; CANR 8

O'Brien, E. G.
See Clarke, Arthur C(harles)

O'Brien, Edna
1936- .... **CLC 3, 5, 8, 13, 36, 65;
DAM NOV; SSC 10**
See also CA 1-4R; CANR 6, 41;
CDBLB 1960 to Present; DLB 14;
MTCW

O'Brien, Fitz-James 1828-1862 ... **NCLC 21**
See also DLB 74

O'Brien, Flann .... **CLC 1, 4, 5, 7, 10, 47**
See also O Nuallain, Brian

O'Brien, Richard 1942- .... **CLC 17**
See also CA 124

O'Brien, Tim
1946- ...... **CLC 7, 19, 40; DAM POP**
See also AAYA 16; CA 85-88; CANR 40;
DLB 152; DLBD 9; DLBY 80

Obstfelder, Sigbjoern 1866-1900 ... **TCLC 23**
See also CA 123

O'Casey, Sean
1880-1964 ...... **CLC 1, 5, 9, 11, 15, 88;
DAB; DAC; DAM DRAM, MST**
See also CA 89-92; CDBLB 1914-1945;
DLB 10; MTCW

O'Cathasaigh, Sean
See O'Casey, Sean

Ochs, Phil 1940-1976 .... **CLC 17**
See also CA 65-68

O'Connor, Edwin (Greene)
1918-1968 .... **CLC 14**
See also CA 93-96; 25-28R

O'Connor, (Mary) Flannery
1925-1964 .... **CLC 1, 2, 3, 6, 10, 13, 15,
21, 66; DA; DAB; DAC; DAM MST,
NOV; SSC 1, 23; WLC**
See also AAYA 7; CA 1-4R; CANR 3, 41;
CDALB 1941-1968; DLB 2, 152;
DLBD 12; DLBY 80; MTCW

O'Connor, Frank .... **CLC 23; SSC 5**
See also O'Donovan, Michael John
See also DLB 162

O'Dell, Scott 1898-1989 .... **CLC 30**
See also AAYA 3; CA 61-64; 129;
CANR 12, 30; CLR 1, 16; DLB 52;
JRDA; MAICYA; SATA 12, 60

Odets, Clifford
1906-1963 .... **CLC 2, 28, 98;
DAM DRAM; DC 6**
See also CA 85-88; DLB 7, 26; MTCW

O'Doherty, Brian 1934- .... **CLC 76**
See also CA 105

O'Donnell, K. M.
See Malzberg, Barry N(athaniel)

O'Donnell, Lawrence
See Kuttner, Henry

O'Donovan, Michael John
1903-1966 .... **CLC 14**
See also O'Connor, Frank
See also CA 93-96

Oe, Kenzaburo
1935- ..... **CLC 10, 36, 86; DAM NOV;
SSC 20**
See also CA 97-100; CANR 36, 50;
DLBY 94; MTCW

O'Faolain, Julia 1932- .... **CLC 6, 19, 47**
See also CA 81-84; CAAS 2; CANR 12;
DLB 14; MTCW

O'Faolain, Sean
1900-1991 .... **CLC 1, 7, 14, 32, 70;
SSC 13**
See also CA 61-64; 134; CANR 12;
DLB 15, 162; MTCW

O'Flaherty, Liam
1896-1984 .... **CLC 5, 34; SSC 6**
See also CA 101; 113; CANR 35; DLB 36,
162; DLBY 84; MTCW

Ogilvy, Gavin
See Barrie, J(ames) M(atthew)

O'Grady, Standish James
1846-1928 .... **TCLC 5**
See also CA 104

O'Grady, Timothy 1951- .... **CLC 59**
See also CA 138

O'Hara, Frank
1926-1966 .... **CLC 2, 5, 13, 78;
DAM POET**
See also CA 9-12R; 25-28R; CANR 33;
DLB 5, 16; MTCW

O'Hara, John (Henry)
1905-1970 .... **CLC 1, 2, 3, 6, 11, 42;
DAM NOV; SSC 15**
See also CA 5-8R; 25-28R; CANR 31;
CDALB 1929-1941; DLB 9, 86; DLBD 2;
MTCW

O Hehir, Diana 1922- .... **CLC 41**
See also CA 93-96

Okigbo, Christopher (Ifenayichukwu)
1932-1967 . . . . CLC 25, 84; BLC;
DAM MULT, POET; PC 7
See also BW 1; CA 77-80; DLB 125;
MTCW

Okri, Ben   1959- . . . . CLC 87
See also BW 2; CA 130; 138; DLB 157;
INT 138

Olds, Sharon
1942- . . . . . CLC 32, 39, 85; DAM POET
See also CA 101; CANR 18, 41; DLB 120

Oldstyle, Jonathan
See Irving, Washington

Olesha, Yuri (Karlovich)
1899-1960 . . . . CLC 8
See also CA 85-88

Oliphant, Laurence
1829(?)-1888 . . . . NCLC 47
See also DLB 18, 166

Oliphant, Margaret (Oliphant Wilson)
1828-1897 . . . . NCLC 11
See also DLB 18, 159

Oliver, Mary   1935-. . . . . CLC 19, 34, 98
See also CA 21-24R; CANR 9, 43; DLB 5

Olivier, Laurence (Kerr)
1907-1989 . . . . CLC 20
See also CA 111; 150; 129

Olsen, Tillie
1913- . . . . . CLC 4, 13; DA; DAB; DAC;
DAM MST; SSC 11
See also CA 1-4R; CANR 1, 43; DLB 28;
DLBY 80; MTCW

Olson, Charles (John)
1910-1970 . . . . . CLC 1, 2, 5, 6, 9, 11, 29;
DAM POET
See also CA 13-16; 25-28R; CABS 2;
CANR 35; CAP 1; DLB 5, 16; MTCW

Olson, Toby   1937- . . . . CLC 28
See also CA 65-68; CANR 9, 31

Olyesha, Yuri
See Olesha, Yuri (Karlovich)

Ondaatje, (Philip) Michael
1943- . . . . CLC 14, 29, 51, 76; DAB;
DAC; DAM MST
See also CA 77-80; CANR 42; DLB 60

Oneal, Elizabeth   1934-
See Oneal, Zibby
See also CA 106; CANR 28; MAICYA;
SATA 30, 82

Oneal, Zibby . . . . CLC 30
See also Oneal, Elizabeth
See also AAYA 5; CLR 13; JRDA

O'Neill, Eugene (Gladstone)
1888-1953 . . . . . . TCLC 1, 6, 27, 49; DA;
DAB; DAC; DAM DRAM, MST; WLC
See also AITN 1; CA 110; 132;
CDALB 1929-1941; DLB 7; MTCW

Onetti, Juan Carlos
1909-1994 . . . . CLC 7, 10; DAM MULT,
NOV; SSC 23
See also CA 85-88; 145; CANR 32;
DLB 113; HW; MTCW

O Nuallain, Brian   1911-1966
See O'Brien, Flann
See also CA 21-22; 25-28R; CAP 2

Oppen, George   1908-1984 . . . . CLC 7, 13, 34
See also CA 13-16R; 113; CANR 8; DLB 5,
165

Oppenheim, E(dward) Phillips
1866-1946 . . . . TCLC 45
See also CA 111; DLB 70

Origen   c. 185-c. 254. . . . . CMLC 19

Orlovitz, Gil   1918-1973 . . . . CLC 22
See also CA 77-80; 45-48; DLB 2, 5

Orris
See Ingelow, Jean

Ortega y Gasset, Jose
1883-1955 . . . . . TCLC 9; DAM MULT;
HLC
See also CA 106; 130; HW; MTCW

Ortese, Anna Maria   1914-. . . . . CLC 89

Ortiz, Simon J(oseph)
1941- . . . . CLC 45; DAM MULT,
POET; PC 17
See also CA 134; DLB 120; NNAL

Orton, Joe . . . . CLC 4, 13, 43; DC 3
See also Orton, John Kingsley
See also CDBLB 1960 to Present; DLB 13

Orton, John Kingsley   1933-1967
See Orton, Joe
See also CA 85-88; CANR 35;
DAM DRAM; MTCW

Orwell, George
. . . . . TCLC 2, 6, 15, 31, 51; DAB; WLC
See also Blair, Eric (Arthur)
See also CDBLB 1945-1960; DLB 15, 98

Osborne, David
See Silverberg, Robert

Osborne, George
See Silverberg, Robert

Osborne, John (James)
1929-1994 . . . . CLC 1, 2, 5, 11, 45; DA;
DAB; DAC; DAM DRAM, MST; WLC
See also CA 13-16R; 147; CANR 21;
CDBLB 1945-1960; DLB 13; MTCW

Osborne, Lawrence   1958- . . . . CLC 50

Oshima, Nagisa   1932- . . . . CLC 20
See also CA 116; 121

Oskison, John Milton
1874-1947 . . . . . TCLC 35; DAM MULT
See also CA 144; NNAL

Ossoli, Sarah Margaret (Fuller marchesa d')
1810-1850
See Fuller, Margaret
See also SATA 25

Ostrovsky, Alexander
1823-1886 . . . . NCLC 30, 57

Otero, Blas de   1916-1979. . . . . CLC 11
See also CA 89-92; DLB 134

Otto, Whitney   1955-. . . . . CLC 70
See also CA 140

Ouida . . . . TCLC 43
See also De La Ramee, (Marie) Louise
See also DLB 18, 156

Ousmane, Sembene   1923- . . . . CLC 66; BLC
See also BW 1; CA 117; 125; MTCW

Ovid
43B.C.-18(?) . . . CMLC 7; DAM POET;
PC 2

Owen, Hugh
See Faust, Frederick (Schiller)

Owen, Wilfred (Edward Salter)
1893-1918 . . . . . . TCLC 5, 27; DA; DAB;
DAC; DAM MST, POET; WLC
See also CA 104; 141; CDBLB 1914-1945;
DLB 20

Owens, Rochelle   1936-. . . . . CLC 8
See also CA 17-20R; CAAS 2; CANR 39

Oz, Amos
1939- . . . . CLC 5, 8, 11, 27, 33, 54;
DAM NOV
See also CA 53-56; CANR 27, 47; MTCW

Ozick, Cynthia
1928- . . . . CLC 3, 7, 28, 62; DAM NOV,
POP; SSC 15
See also BEST 90:1; CA 17-20R; CANR 23;
DLB 28, 152; DLBY 82; INT CANR-23;
MTCW

Ozu, Yasujiro   1903-1963 . . . . CLC 16
See also CA 112

Pacheco, C.
See Pessoa, Fernando (Antonio Nogueira)

Pa Chin . . . . CLC 18
See also Li Fei-kan

Pack, Robert   1929-. . . . . CLC 13
See also CA 1-4R; CANR 3, 44; DLB 5

Padgett, Lewis
See Kuttner, Henry

Padilla (Lorenzo), Heberto   1932-. . . CLC 38
See also AITN 1; CA 123; 131; HW

Page, Jimmy   1944-. . . . . CLC 12

Page, Louise   1955-. . . . . CLC 40
See also CA 140

Page, P(atricia) K(athleen)
1916- . . . . CLC 7, 18; DAC; DAM MST;
PC 12
See also CA 53-56; CANR 4, 22; DLB 68;
MTCW

Page, Thomas Nelson   1853-1922. . . . SSC 23
See also CA 118; DLB 12, 78; DLBD 13

Paget, Violet   1856-1935
See Lee, Vernon
See also CA 104

Paget-Lowe, Henry
See Lovecraft, H(oward) P(hillips)

Paglia, Camille (Anna)   1947-. . . . . . CLC 68
See also CA 140

Paige, Richard
See Koontz, Dean R(ay)

Pakenham, Antonia
See Fraser, (Lady) Antonia (Pakenham)

Palamas, Kostes   1859-1943 . . . . TCLC 5
See also CA 105

Palazzeschi, Aldo   1885-1974 . . . . CLC 11
See also CA 89-92; 53-56; DLB 114

Paley, Grace
1922- . . . . CLC 4, 6, 37; DAM POP;
SSC 8
See also CA 25-28R; CANR 13, 46;
DLB 28; INT CANR-13; MTCW

Palin, Michael (Edward)   1943-. . . . . CLC 21
See also Monty Python
See also CA 107; CANR 35; SATA 67

Palliser, Charles 1947-............. **CLC 65**
See also CA 136

Palma, Ricardo 1833-1919....... **TCLC 29**

Pancake, Breece Dexter 1952-1979
See Pancake, Breece D'J
See also CA 123; 109

Pancake, Breece D'J............... **CLC 29**
See also Pancake, Breece Dexter
See also DLB 130

Panko, Rudy
See Gogol, Nikolai (Vasilyevich)

Papadiamantis, Alexandros
1851-1911 .... **TCLC 29**

Papadiamantopoulos, Johannes 1856-1910
See Moreas, Jean
See also CA 117

Papini, Giovanni 1881-1956....... **TCLC 22**
See also CA 121

Paracelsus 1493-1541............. **LC 14**

Parasol, Peter
See Stevens, Wallace

Parfenie, Maria
See Codrescu, Andrei

Parini, Jay (Lee) 1948- .... **CLC 54**
See also CA 97-100; CAAS 16; CANR 32

Park, Jordan
See Kornbluth, C(yril) M.; Pohl, Frederik

Parker, Bert
See Ellison, Harlan (Jay)

Parker, Dorothy (Rothschild)
1893-1967 .... **CLC 15, 68;**
DAM POET; SSC 2
See also CA 19-20; 25-28R; CAP 2;
DLB 11, 45, 86; MTCW

Parker, Robert B(rown)
1932- ...... **CLC 27; DAM NOV, POP**
See also BEST 89:4; CA 49-52; CANR 1,
26, 52; INT CANR-26; MTCW

Parkin, Frank 1940-.............. **CLC 43**
See also CA 147

Parkman, Francis, Jr.
1823-1893 .... **NCLC 12**
See also DLB 1, 30

Parks, Gordon (Alexander Buchanan)
1912- ... **CLC 1, 16; BLC; DAM MULT**
See also AITN 2; BW 2; CA 41-44R;
CANR 26; DLB 33; SATA 8

Parnell, Thomas 1679-1718......... **LC 3**
See also DLB 94

Parra, Nicanor
1914- ...... **CLC 2; DAM MULT; HLC**
See also CA 85-88; CANR 32; HW; MTCW

Parrish, Mary Frances
See Fisher, M(ary) F(rances) K(ennedy)

Parson
See Coleridge, Samuel Taylor

Parson Lot
See Kingsley, Charles

Partridge, Anthony
See Oppenheim, E(dward) Phillips

Pascal, Blaise 1623-1662.......... **LC 35**

Pascoli, Giovanni 1855-1912...... **TCLC 45**

Pasolini, Pier Paolo
1922-1975 .... **CLC 20, 37; PC 17**
See also CA 93-96; 61-64; DLB 128;
MTCW

Pasquini
See Silone, Ignazio

Pastan, Linda (Olenik)
1932- .... **CLC 27; DAM POET**
See also CA 61-64; CANR 18, 40; DLB 5

Pasternak, Boris (Leonidovich)
1890-1960 ...... **CLC 7, 10, 18, 63; DA;**
DAB; DAC; DAM MST, NOV, POET;
PC 6; WLC
See also CA 127; 116; MTCW

Patchen, Kenneth
1911-1972 ... **CLC 1, 2, 18; DAM POET**
See also CA 1-4R; 33-36R; CANR 3, 35;
DLB 16, 48; MTCW

Pater, Walter (Horatio)
1839-1894 .... **NCLC 7**
See also CDBLB 1832-1890; DLB 57, 156

Paterson, A(ndrew) B(arton)
1864-1941 .... **TCLC 32**
See also CA 155

Paterson, Katherine (Womeldorf)
1932- .... **CLC 12, 30**
See also AAYA 1; CA 21-24R; CANR 28;
CLR 7; DLB 52; JRDA; MAICYA;
MTCW; SATA 13, 53

Patmore, Coventry Kersey Dighton
1823-1896 .... **NCLC 9**
See also DLB 35, 98

Paton, Alan (Stewart)
1903-1988 ...... **CLC 4, 10, 25, 55; DA;**
DAB; DAC; DAM MST, NOV; WLC
See also CA 13-16; 125; CANR 22; CAP 1;
MTCW; SATA 11; SATA-Obit 56

Paton Walsh, Gillian 1937-
See Walsh, Jill Paton
See also CANR 38; JRDA; MAICYA;
SAAS 3; SATA 4, 72

Paulding, James Kirke 1778-1860.. **NCLC 2**
See also DLB 3, 59, 74

Paulin, Thomas Neilson 1949-
See Paulin, Tom
See also CA 123; 128

Paulin, Tom...................... **CLC 37**
See also Paulin, Thomas Neilson
See also DLB 40

Paustovsky, Konstantin (Georgievich)
1892-1968 .... **CLC 40**
See also CA 93-96; 25-28R

Pavese, Cesare
1908-1950 ..... **TCLC 3; PC 13; SSC 19**
See also CA 104; DLB 128

Pavic, Milorad 1929-............. **CLC 60**
See also CA 136

Payne, Alan
See Jakes, John (William)

Paz, Gil
See Lugones, Leopoldo

Paz, Octavio
1914- ...... **CLC 3, 4, 6, 10, 19, 51, 65;**
DA; DAB; DAC; DAM MST, MULT,
POET; HLC; PC 1; WLC
See also CA 73-76; CANR 32; DLBY 90;
HW; MTCW

p'Bitek, Okot
1931-1982 .... **CLC 96; BLC;**
DAM MULT
See also BW 2; CA 124; 107; DLB 125;
MTCW

Peacock, Molly 1947-............. **CLC 60**
See also CA 103; CAAS 21; CANR 52;
DLB 120

Peacock, Thomas Love
1785-1866 .... **NCLC 22**
See also DLB 96, 116

Peake, Mervyn 1911-1968....... **CLC 7, 54**
See also CA 5-8R; 25-28R; CANR 3;
DLB 15, 160; MTCW; SATA 23

Pearce, Philippa .... **CLC 21**
See also Christie, (Ann) Philippa
See also CLR 9; DLB 161; MAICYA;
SATA 1, 67

Pearl, Eric
See Elman, Richard

Pearson, T(homas) R(eid) 1956- .... **CLC 39**
See also CA 120; 130; INT 130

Peck, Dale 1967-............... **CLC 81**
See also CA 146

Peck, John 1941-................ **CLC 3**
See also CA 49-52; CANR 3

Peck, Richard (Wayne) 1934-...... **CLC 21**
See also AAYA 1; CA 85-88; CANR 19,
38; CLR 15; INT CANR-19; JRDA;
MAICYA; SAAS 2; SATA 18, 55

Peck, Robert Newton
1928- .. **CLC 17; DA; DAC; DAM MST**
See also AAYA 3; CA 81-84; CANR 31;
JRDA; MAICYA; SAAS 1; SATA 21, 62

Peckinpah, (David) Sam(uel)
1925-1984 .... **CLC 20**
See also CA 109; 114

Pedersen, Knut 1859-1952
See Hamsun, Knut
See also CA 104; 119; MTCW

Peeslake, Gaffer
See Durrell, Lawrence (George)

Peguy, Charles Pierre
1873-1914 .... **TCLC 10**
See also CA 107

Pena, Ramon del Valle y
See Valle-Inclan, Ramon (Maria) del

Pendennis, Arthur Esquir
See Thackeray, William Makepeace

Penn, William 1644-1718.......... **LC 25**
See also DLB 24

Pepys, Samuel
1633-1703 ..... **LC 11; DA; DAB; DAC;**
DAM MST; WLC
See also CDBLB 1660-1789; DLB 101

Percy, Walker
1916-1990 .... **CLC 2, 3, 6, 8, 14, 18, 47,**
65; DAM NOV, POP
See also CA 1-4R; 131; CANR 1, 23;
DLB 2; DLBY 80, 90; MTCW

Plimpton, George (Ames) 1927-..... **CLC 36**
See also AITN 1; CA 21-24R; CANR 32;
MTCW; SATA 10

Plomer, William Charles Franklin
1903-1973 .... **CLC 4, 8**
See also CA 21-22; CANR 34; CAP 2;
DLB 20, 162; MTCW; SATA 24

Plowman, Piers
See Kavanagh, Patrick (Joseph)

Plum, J.
See Wodehouse, P(elham) G(renville)

Plumly, Stanley (Ross) 1939- ...... **CLC 33**
See also CA 108; 110; DLB 5; INT 110

Plumpe, Friedrich Wilhelm
1888-1931 .... **TCLC 53**
See also CA 112

Poe, Edgar Allan
1809-1849 .... **NCLC 1, 16, 55; DA;
DAB; DAC; DAM MST, POET; PC 1;
SSC 1, 22; WLC**
See also AAYA 14; CDALB 1640-1865;
DLB 3, 59, 73, 74; SATA 23

Poet of Titchfield Street, The
See Pound, Ezra (Weston Loomis)

Pohl, Frederik 1919- .... **CLC 18**
See also CA 61-64; CAAS 1; CANR 11, 37;
DLB 8; INT CANR-11; MTCW;
SATA 24

Poirier, Louis 1910-
See Gracq, Julien
See also CA 122; 126

Poitier, Sidney 1927- .... **CLC 26**
See also BW 1; CA 117

Polanski, Roman 1933- .... **CLC 16**
See also CA 77-80

Poliakoff, Stephen 1952- .... **CLC 38**
See also CA 106; DLB 13

Police, The
See Copeland, Stewart (Armstrong);
Summers, Andrew James; Sumner,
Gordon Matthew

Polidori, John William
1795-1821 .... **NCLC 51**
See also DLB 116

Pollitt, Katha 1949- .... **CLC 28**
See also CA 120; 122; MTCW

Pollock, (Mary) Sharon
1936- .... **CLC 50; DAC; DAM DRAM,
MST**
See also CA 141; DLB 60

Polo, Marco 1254-1324 .... **CMLC 15**

Polonsky, Abraham (Lincoln)
1910- .... **CLC 92**
See also CA 104; DLB 26; INT 104

Polybius c. 200B.C.-c. 118B.C. .... **CMLC 17**

Pomerance, Bernard
1940- .... **CLC 13; DAM DRAM**
See also CA 101; CANR 49

Ponge, Francis (Jean Gaston Alfred)
1899-1988 .... **CLC 6, 18; DAM POET**
See also CA 85-88; 126; CANR 40

Pontoppidan, Henrik 1857-1943 ... **TCLC 29**

Poole, Josephine .... **CLC 17**
See also Helyar, Jane Penelope Josephine
See also SAAS 2; SATA 5

Popa, Vasko 1922-1991 .... **CLC 19**
See also CA 112; 148

Pope, Alexander
1688-1744 ..... **LC 3; DA; DAB; DAC;
DAM MST, POET; WLC**
See also CDBLB 1660-1789; DLB 95, 101

Porter, Connie (Rose) 1959(?)- ..... **CLC 70**
See also BW 2; CA 142; SATA 81

Porter, Gene(va Grace) Stratton
1863(?)-1924 .... **TCLC 21**
See also CA 112

Porter, Katherine Anne
1890-1980 ...... **CLC 1, 3, 7, 10, 13, 15,
27; DA; DAB; DAC; DAM MST, NOV;
SSC 4**
See also AITN 2; CA 1-4R; 101; CANR 1;
DLB 4, 9, 102; DLBD 12; DLBY 80;
MTCW; SATA 39; SATA-Obit 23

Porter, Peter (Neville Frederick)
1929- .... **CLC 5, 13, 33**
See also CA 85-88; DLB 40

Porter, William Sydney 1862-1910
See Henry, O.
See also CA 104; 131; CDALB 1865-1917;
DA; DAB; DAC; DAM MST; DLB 12,
78, 79; MTCW; YABC 2

Portillo (y Pacheco), Jose Lopez
See Lopez Portillo (y Pacheco), Jose

Post, Melville Davisson
1869-1930 .... **TCLC 39**
See also CA 110

Potok, Chaim
1929- .... **CLC 2, 7, 14, 26; DAM NOV**
See also AAYA 15; AITN 1, 2; CA 17-20R;
CANR 19, 35; DLB 28, 152;
INT CANR-19; MTCW; SATA 33

Potter, Beatrice
See Webb, (Martha) Beatrice (Potter)
See also MAICYA

Potter, Dennis (Christopher George)
1935-1994 .... **CLC 58, 86**
See also CA 107; 145; CANR 33; MTCW

Pound, Ezra (Weston Loomis)
1885-1972 ...... **CLC 1, 2, 3, 4, 5, 7, 10,
13, 18, 34, 48, 50; DA; DAB; DAC;
DAM MST, POET; PC 4; WLC**
See also CA 5-8R; 37-40R; CANR 40;
CDALB 1917-1929; DLB 4, 45, 63;
MTCW

Povod, Reinaldo 1959-1994 .... **CLC 44**
See also CA 136; 146

Powell, Adam Clayton, Jr.
1908-1972 .... **CLC 89; BLC;
DAM MULT**
See also BW 1; CA 102; 33-36R

Powell, Anthony (Dymoke)
1905- .... **CLC 1, 3, 7, 9, 10, 31**
See also CA 1-4R; CANR 1, 32;
CDBLB 1945-1960; DLB 15; MTCW

Powell, Dawn 1897-1965 .... **CLC 66**
See also CA 5-8R

Powell, Padgett 1952-............. **CLC 34**
See also CA 126

Power, Susan .... **CLC 91**

Powers, J(ames) F(arl)
1917- .... **CLC 1, 4, 8, 57; SSC 4**
See also CA 1-4R; CANR 2; DLB 130;
MTCW

Powers, John J(ames) 1945-
See Powers, John R.
See also CA 69-72

Powers, John R. .... **CLC 66**
See also Powers, John J(ames)

Powers, Richard (S.) 1957- .... **CLC 93**
See also CA 148

Pownall, David 1938-............. **CLC 10**
See also CA 89-92; CAAS 18; CANR 49;
DLB 14

Powys, John Cowper
1872-1963 .... **CLC 7, 9, 15, 46**
See also CA 85-88; DLB 15; MTCW

Powys, T(heodore) F(rancis)
1875-1953 .... **TCLC 9**
See also CA 106; DLB 36, 162

Prager, Emily 1952- .... **CLC 56**

Pratt, E(dwin) J(ohn)
1883(?)-1964 .... **CLC 19; DAC;
DAM POET**
See also CA 141; 93-96; DLB 92

Premchand...................... **TCLC 21**
See also Srivastava, Dhanpat Rai

Preussler, Otfried 1923-.......... **CLC 17**
See also CA 77-80; SATA 24

Prevert, Jacques (Henri Marie)
1900-1977 .... **CLC 15**
See also CA 77-80; 69-72; CANR 29;
MTCW; SATA-Obit 30

Prevost, Abbe (Antoine Francois)
1697-1763 .... **LC 1**

Price, (Edward) Reynolds
1933- .... **CLC 3, 6, 13, 43, 50, 63;
DAM NOV; SSC 22**
See also CA 1-4R; CANR 1, 37; DLB 2;
INT CANR-37

Price, Richard 1949- .... **CLC 6, 12**
See also CA 49-52; CANR 3; DLBY 81

Prichard, Katharine Susannah
1883-1969 .... **CLC 46**
See also CA 11-12; CANR 33; CAP 1;
MTCW; SATA 66

Priestley, J(ohn) B(oynton)
1894-1984 .... **CLC 2, 5, 9, 34;
DAM DRAM, NOV**
See also CA 9-12R; 113; CANR 33;
CDBLB 1914-1945; DLB 10, 34, 77, 100,
139; DLBY 84; MTCW

Prince 1958(?)- .... **CLC 35**

Prince, F(rank) T(empleton) 1912- .. **CLC 22**
See also CA 101; CANR 43; DLB 20

Prince Kropotkin
See Kropotkin, Peter (Aleksieevich)

Prior, Matthew 1664-1721.......... **LC 4**
See also DLB 95

Pritchard, William H(arrison)
1932- .... **CLC 34**
See also CA 65-68; CANR 23; DLB 111

Rand, Ayn
        1905-1982 ..... **CLC 3, 30, 44, 79; DA;**
                DAC; DAM MST, NOV, POP; WLC
        See also AAYA 10; CA 13-16R; 105;
        CANR 27; MTCW

Randall, Dudley (Felker)
        1914- ...... **CLC 1; BLC; DAM MULT**
        See also BW 1; CA 25-28R; CANR 23;
        DLB 41

Randall, Robert
        See Silverberg, Robert

Ranger, Ken
        See Creasey, John

Ransom, John Crowe
        1888-1974 .... **CLC 2, 4, 5, 11, 24;**
                DAM POET
        See also CA 5-8R; 49-52; CANR 6, 34;
        DLB 45, 63; MTCW

Rao, Raja   1909- ... **CLC 25, 56; DAM NOV**
        See also CA 73-76; CANR 51; MTCW

Raphael, Frederic (Michael)
        1931- .... **CLC 2, 14**
        See also CA 1-4R; CANR 1; DLB 14

Ratcliffe, James P.
        See Mencken, H(enry) L(ouis)

Rathbone, Julian   1935- .... **CLC 41**
        See also CA 101; CANR 34

Rattigan, Terence (Mervyn)
        1911-1977 .... **CLC 7; DAM DRAM**
        See also CA 85-88; 73-76;
        CDBLB 1945-1960; DLB 13; MTCW

Ratushinskaya, Irina   1954- .... **CLC 54**
        See also CA 129

Raven, Simon (Arthur Noel)
        1927- .... **CLC 14**
        See also CA 81-84

Rawley, Callman   1903-
        See Rakosi, Carl
        See also CA 21-24R; CANR 12, 32

Rawlings, Marjorie Kinnan
        1896-1953 .... **TCLC 4**
        See also CA 104; 137; DLB 9, 22, 102;
        JRDA; MAICYA; YABC 1

Ray, Satyajit
        1921-1992 ... **CLC 16, 76; DAM MULT**
        See also CA 114; 137

Read, Herbert Edward   1893-1968.... **CLC 4**
        See also CA 85-88; 25-28R; DLB 20, 149

Read, Piers Paul   1941- ...... **CLC 4, 10, 25**
        See also CA 21-24R; CANR 38; DLB 14;
        SATA 21

Reade, Charles   1814-1884 .... **NCLC 2**
        See also DLB 21

Reade, Hamish
        See Gray, Simon (James Holliday)

Reading, Peter   1946- .... **CLC 47**
        See also CA 103; CANR 46; DLB 40

Reaney, James
        1926- ...... **CLC 13; DAC; DAM MST**
        See also CA 41-44R; CAAS 15; CANR 42;
        DLB 68; SATA 43

Rebreanu, Liviu   1885-1944 .... **TCLC 28**

Rechy, John (Francisco)
        1934- .... **CLC 1, 7, 14, 18;**
                DAM MULT; HLC
        See also CA 5-8R; CAAS 4; CANR 6, 32;
        DLB 122; DLBY 82; HW; INT CANR-6

Redcam, Tom   1870-1933 .... **TCLC 25**

Reddin, Keith.................... **CLC 67**

Redgrove, Peter (William)
        1932- .... **CLC 6, 41**
        See also CA 1-4R; CANR 3, 39; DLB 40

Redmon, Anne.................... **CLC 22**
        See also Nightingale, Anne Redmon
        See also DLBY 86

Reed, Eliot
        See Ambler, Eric

Reed, Ishmael
        1938- .... **CLC 2, 3, 5, 6, 13, 32, 60;**
                BLC; DAM MULT
        See also BW 2; CA 21-24R; CANR 25, 48;
        DLB 2, 5, 33, 169; DLBD 8; MTCW

Reed, John (Silas)   1887-1920 ...... **TCLC 9**
        See also CA 106

Reed, Lou...................... **CLC 21**
        See also Firbank, Louis

Reeve, Clara   1729-1807 .... **NCLC 19**
        See also DLB 39

Reich, Wilhelm   1897-1957....... **TCLC 57**

Reid, Christopher (John)   1949-..... **CLC 33**
        See also CA 140; DLB 40

Reid, Desmond
        See Moorcock, Michael (John)

Reid Banks, Lynne   1929-
        See Banks, Lynne Reid
        See also CA 1-4R; CANR 6, 22, 38;
        CLR 24; JRDA; MAICYA; SATA 22, 75

Reilly, William K.
        See Creasey, John

Reiner, Max
        See Caldwell, (Janet Miriam) Taylor
        (Holland)

Reis, Ricardo
        See Pessoa, Fernando (Antonio Nogueira)

Remarque, Erich Maria
        1898-1970 .... **CLC 21; DA; DAB; DAC;**
                DAM MST, NOV
        See also CA 77-80; 29-32R; DLB 56;
        MTCW

Remizov, A.
        See Remizov, Aleksei (Mikhailovich)

Remizov, A. M.
        See Remizov, Aleksei (Mikhailovich)

Remizov, Aleksei (Mikhailovich)
        1877-1957 .... **TCLC 27**
        See also CA 125; 133

Renan, Joseph Ernest
        1823-1892 .... **NCLC 26**

Renard, Jules   1864-1910 .... **TCLC 17**
        See also CA 117

Renault, Mary.............. **CLC 3, 11, 17**
        See also Challans, Mary
        See also DLBY 83

Rendell, Ruth (Barbara)
        1930- .... **CLC 28, 48; DAM POP**
        See also Vine, Barbara
        See also CA 109; CANR 32, 52; DLB 87;
        INT CANR-32; MTCW

Renoir, Jean   1894-1979 .... **CLC 20**
        See also CA 129; 85-88

Resnais, Alain   1922-............. **CLC 16**

Reverdy, Pierre   1889-1960 .... **CLC 53**
        See also CA 97-100; 89-92

Rexroth, Kenneth
        1905-1982 ...... **CLC 1, 2, 6, 11, 22, 49;**
                DAM POET
        See also CA 5-8R; 107; CANR 14, 34;
        CDALB 1941-1968; DLB 16, 48, 165;
        DLBY 82; INT CANR-14; MTCW

Reyes, Alfonso   1889-1959 .... **TCLC 33**
        See also CA 131; HW

Reyes y Basoalto, Ricardo Eliecer Neftali
        See Neruda, Pablo

Reymont, Wladyslaw (Stanislaw)
        1868(?)-1925 .... **TCLC 5**
        See also CA 104

Reynolds, Jonathan   1942-....... **CLC 6, 38**
        See also CA 65-68; CANR 28

Reynolds, Joshua   1723-1792 .... **LC 15**
        See also DLB 104

Reynolds, Michael Shane   1937- .... **CLC 44**
        See also CA 65-68; CANR 9

Reznikoff, Charles   1894-1976 .... **CLC 9**
        See also CA 33-36; 61-64; CAP 2; DLB 28,
        45

Rezzori (d'Arezzo), Gregor von
        1914- .... **CLC 25**
        See also CA 122; 136

Rhine, Richard
        See Silverstein, Alvin

Rhodes, Eugene Manlove
        1869-1934 .... **TCLC 53**

R'hoone
        See Balzac, Honore de

Rhys, Jean
        1890(?)-1979 .... **CLC 2, 4, 6, 14, 19, 51;**
                DAM NOV; SSC 21
        See also CA 25-28R; 85-88; CANR 35;
        CDBLB 1945-1960; DLB 36, 117, 162;
        MTCW

Ribeiro, Darcy   1922- .... **CLC 34**
        See also CA 33-36R

Ribeiro, Joao Ubaldo (Osorio Pimentel)
        1941- .... **CLC 10, 67**
        See also CA 81-84

Ribman, Ronald (Burt)   1932- .... **CLC 7**
        See also CA 21-24R; CANR 46

Ricci, Nino   1959-............... **CLC 70**
        See also CA 137

Rice, Anne   1941- ..... **CLC 41; DAM POP**
        See also AAYA 9; BEST 89:2; CA 65-68;
        CANR 12, 36, 53

Rice, Elmer (Leopold)
        1892-1967 .... **CLC 7, 49; DAM DRAM**
        See also CA 21-22; 25-28R; CAP 2; DLB 4,
        7; MTCW

Rice, Tim(othy Miles Bindon)
1944- .... CLC 21
See also CA 103; CANR 46

Rich, Adrienne (Cecile)
1929- .... CLC 3, 6, 7, 11, 18, 36, 73, 76;
DAM POET; PC 5
See also CA 9-12R; CANR 20, 53; DLB 5,
67; MTCW

Rich, Barbara
See Graves, Robert (von Ranke)

Rich, Robert
See Trumbo, Dalton

Richard, Keith.................... CLC 17
See also Richards, Keith

Richards, David Adams
1950- .... CLC 59; DAC
See also CA 93-96; DLB 53

Richards, I(vor) A(rmstrong)
1893-1979 .... CLC 14, 24
See also CA 41-44R; 89-92; CANR 34;
DLB 27

Richards, Keith   1943-
See Richard, Keith
See also CA 107

Richardson, Anne
See Roiphe, Anne (Richardson)

Richardson, Dorothy Miller
1873-1957 .... TCLC 3
See also CA 104; DLB 36

Richardson, Ethel Florence (Lindesay)
1870-1946
See Richardson, Henry Handel
See also CA 105

Richardson, Henry Handel......... TCLC 4
See also Richardson, Ethel Florence
(Lindesay)

Richardson, John
1796-1852 .... NCLC 55; DAC
See also DLB 99

Richardson, Samuel
1689-1761 ...... LC 1; DA; DAB; DAC;
DAM MST, NOV; WLC
See also CDBLB 1660-1789; DLB 39

Richler, Mordecai
1931- .... CLC 3, 5, 9, 13, 18, 46, 70;
DAC; DAM MST, NOV
See also AITN 1; CA 65-68; CANR 31;
CLR 17; DLB 53; MAICYA; MTCW;
SATA 44; SATA-Brief 27

Richter, Conrad (Michael)
1890-1968 .... CLC 30
See also CA 5-8R; 25-28R; CANR 23;
DLB 9; MTCW; SATA 3

Ricostranza, Tom
See Ellis, Trey

Riddell, J. H.   1832-1906 .... TCLC 40

Riding, Laura................... CLC 3, 7
See also Jackson, Laura (Riding)

Riefenstahl, Berta Helene Amalia   1902-
See Riefenstahl, Leni
See also CA 108

Riefenstahl, Leni................ CLC 16
See also Riefenstahl, Berta Helene Amalia

Riffe, Ernest
See Bergman, (Ernst) Ingmar

Riggs, (Rolla) Lynn
1899-1954 ..... TCLC 56; DAM MULT
See also CA 144; NNAL

Riley, James Whitcomb
1849-1916 ...... TCLC 51; DAM POET
See also CA 118; 137; MAICYA; SATA 17

Riley, Tex
See Creasey, John

Rilke, Rainer Maria
1875-1926 .... TCLC 1, 6, 19;
DAM POET; PC 2
See also CA 104; 132; DLB 81; MTCW

Rimbaud, (Jean Nicolas) Arthur
1854-1891 ..... NCLC 4, 35; DA; DAB;
DAC; DAM MST, POET; PC 3; WLC

Rinehart, Mary Roberts
1876-1958 .... TCLC 52
See also CA 108

Ringmaster, The
See Mencken, H(enry) L(ouis)

Ringwood, Gwen(dolyn Margaret) Pharis
1910-1984 .... CLC 48
See also CA 148; 112; DLB 88

Rio, Michel   19(?)-................ CLC 43

Ritsos, Giannes
See Ritsos, Yannis

Ritsos, Yannis   1909-1990..... CLC 6, 13, 31
See also CA 77-80; 133; CANR 39; MTCW

Ritter, Erika   1948(?)-............. CLC 52

Rivera, Jose Eustasio   1889-1928... TCLC 35
See also HW

Rivers, Conrad Kent   1933-1968...... CLC 1
See also BW 1; CA 85-88; DLB 41

Rivers, Elfrida
See Bradley, Marion Zimmer

Riverside, John
See Heinlein, Robert A(nson)

Rizal, Jose   1861-1896........... NCLC 27

Roa Bastos, Augusto (Antonio)
1917- ..... CLC 45; DAM MULT; HLC
See also CA 131; DLB 113; HW

Robbe-Grillet, Alain
1922- ...... CLC 1, 2, 4, 6, 8, 10, 14, 43
See also CA 9-12R; CANR 33; DLB 83;
MTCW

Robbins, Harold
1916- .... CLC 5; DAM NOV
See also CA 73-76; CANR 26, 54; MTCW

Robbins, Thomas Eugene   1936-
See Robbins, Tom
See also CA 81-84; CANR 29; DAM NOV,
POP; MTCW

Robbins, Tom................ CLC 9, 32, 64
See also Robbins, Thomas Eugene
See also BEST 90:3; DLBY 80

Robbins, Trina   1938-............. CLC 21
See also CA 128

Roberts, Charles G(eorge) D(ouglas)
1860-1943 .... TCLC 8
See also CA 105; CLR 33; DLB 92;
SATA 88; SATA-Brief 29

Roberts, Elizabeth Madox
1886-1941 .... TCLC 68
See also CA 111; DLB 9, 54, 102;
SATA 33; SATA-Brief 27

Roberts, Kate   1891-1985 .... CLC 15
See also CA 107; 116

Roberts, Keith (John Kingston)
1935- .... CLC 14
See also CA 25-28R; CANR 46

Roberts, Kenneth (Lewis)
1885-1957 .... TCLC 23
See also CA 109; DLB 9

Roberts, Michele (B.)   1949-........ CLC 48
See also CA 115

Robertson, Ellis
See Ellison, Harlan (Jay); Silverberg, Robert

Robertson, Thomas William
1829-1871 .... NCLC 35; DAM DRAM

Robinson, Edwin Arlington
1869-1935 .... TCLC 5; DA; DAC;
DAM MST, POET; PC 1
See also CA 104; 133; CDALB 1865-1917;
DLB 54; MTCW

Robinson, Henry Crabb
1775-1867 .... NCLC 15
See also DLB 107

Robinson, Jill   1936-.............. CLC 10
See also CA 102; INT 102

Robinson, Kim Stanley   1952- ...... CLC 34
See also CA 126

Robinson, Lloyd
See Silverberg, Robert

Robinson, Marilynne   1944-........ CLC 25
See also CA 116

Robinson, Smokey................. CLC 21
See also Robinson, William, Jr.

Robinson, William, Jr.   1940-
See Robinson, Smokey
See also CA 116

Robison, Mary   1949-.......... CLC 42, 98
See also CA 113; 116; DLB 130; INT 116

Rod, Edouard   1857-1910 .... TCLC 52

Roddenberry, Eugene Wesley   1921-1991
See Roddenberry, Gene
See also CA 110; 135; CANR 37; SATA 45;
SATA-Obit 69

Roddenberry, Gene................ CLC 17
See also Roddenberry, Eugene Wesley
See also AAYA 5; SATA-Obit 69

Rodgers, Mary   1931-............. CLC 12
See also CA 49-52; CANR 8, 55; CLR 20;
INT CANR-8; JRDA; MAICYA;
SATA 8

Rodgers, W(illiam) R(obert)
1909-1969 .... CLC 7
See also CA 85-88; DLB 20

Rodman, Eric
See Silverberg, Robert

Rodman, Howard   1920(?)-1985..... CLC 65
See also CA 118

Rodman, Maia
See Wojciechowska, Maia (Teresa)

Rodriguez, Claudio   1934-......... CLC 10
See also DLB 134

Roelvaag, O(le) E(dvart)
1876-1931 .... TCLC **17**
See also CA 117; DLB 9

Roethke, Theodore (Huebner)
1908-1963 ...... CLC **1, 3, 8, 11, 19, 46;**
DAM POET; PC 15
See also CA 81-84; CABS 2;
CDALB 1941-1968; DLB 5; MTCW

Rogers, Thomas Hunton 1927- ..... CLC **57**
See also CA 89-92; INT 89-92

Rogers, Will(iam Penn Adair)
1879-1935 ...... TCLC **8; DAM MULT**
See also CA 105; 144; DLB 11; NNAL

Rogin, Gilbert 1929-.............. CLC **18**
See also CA 65-68; CANR 15

Rohan, Koda .... TCLC **22**
See also Koda Shigeyuki

Rohmer, Eric.................... CLC **16**
See also Scherer, Jean-Marie Maurice

Rohmer, Sax .... TCLC **28**
See also Ward, Arthur Henry Sarsfield
See also DLB 70

Roiphe, Anne (Richardson)
1935-..................... CLC **3, 9**
See also CA 89-92; CANR 45; DLBY 80;
INT 89-92

Rojas, Fernando de 1465-1541 ...... LC **23**

Rolfe, Frederick (William Serafino Austin
Lewis Mary) 1860-1913...... TCLC **12**
See also CA 107; DLB 34, 156

Rolland, Romain 1866-1944....... TCLC **23**
See also CA 118; DLB 65

Rolle, Richard c. 1300-c. 1349 ... CMLC **21**
See also DLB 146

Rolvaag, O(le) E(dvart)
See Roelvaag, O(le) E(dvart)

Romain Arnaud, Saint
See Aragon, Louis

Romains, Jules 1885-1972......... CLC **7**
See also CA 85-88; CANR 34; DLB 65;
MTCW

Romero, Jose Ruben 1890-1952 ... TCLC **14**
See also CA 114; 131; HW

Ronsard, Pierre de
1524-1585 .... LC **6; PC 11**

Rooke, Leon
1934-........ CLC **25, 34; DAM POP**
See also CA 25-28R; CANR 23, 53

Roper, William 1498-1578 .... LC **10**

Roquelaure, A. N.
See Rice, Anne

Rosa, Joao Guimaraes 1908-1967... CLC **23**
See also CA 89-92; DLB 113

Rose, Wendy
1948- .... CLC **85; DAM MULT; PC 13**
See also CA 53-56; CANR 5, 51; NNAL;
SATA 12

Rosen, Richard (Dean) 1949-....... CLC **39**
See also CA 77-80; INT CANR-30

Rosenberg, Isaac 1890-1918....... TCLC **12**
See also CA 107; DLB 20

Rosenblatt, Joe .... CLC **15**
See also Rosenblatt, Joseph

Rosenblatt, Joseph 1933-
See Rosenblatt, Joe
See also CA 89-92; INT 89-92

Rosenfeld, Samuel 1896-1963
See Tzara, Tristan
See also CA 89-92

Rosenstock, Sami
See Tzara, Tristan

Rosenstock, Samuel
See Tzara, Tristan

Rosenthal, M(acha) L(ouis)
1917-1996 .... CLC **28**
See also CA 1-4R; 152; CAAS 6; CANR 4,
51; DLB 5; SATA 59

Ross, Barnaby
See Dannay, Frederic

Ross, Bernard L.
See Follett, Ken(neth Martin)

Ross, J. H.
See Lawrence, T(homas) E(dward)

Ross, Martin
See Martin, Violet Florence
See also DLB 135

Ross, (James) Sinclair
1908- ...... CLC **13; DAC; DAM MST;**
SSC 24
See also CA 73-76; DLB 88

Rossetti, Christina (Georgina)
1830-1894 ..... NCLC **2, 50; DA; DAB;**
DAC; DAM MST, POET; PC 7; WLC
See also DLB 35, 163; MAICYA; SATA 20

Rossetti, Dante Gabriel
1828-1882 .... NCLC **4; DA; DAB;**
DAC; DAM MST, POET; WLC
See also CDBLB 1832-1890; DLB 35

Rossner, Judith (Perelman)
1935-................... CLC **6, 9, 29**
See also AITN 2; BEST 90:3; CA 17-20R;
CANR 18, 51; DLB 6; INT CANR-18;
MTCW

Rostand, Edmond (Eugene Alexis)
1868-1918 ..... TCLC **6, 37; DA; DAB;**
DAC; DAM DRAM, MST
See also CA 104; 126; MTCW

Roth, Henry 1906-1995 ...... CLC **2, 6, 11**
See also CA 11-12; 149; CANR 38; CAP 1;
DLB 28; MTCW

Roth, Joseph 1894-1939 .... TCLC **33**
See also DLB 85

Roth, Philip (Milton)
1933- ...... CLC **1, 2, 3, 4, 6, 9, 15, 22,
31, 47, 66, 86; DA; DAB; DAC;
DAM MST, NOV, POP; WLC**
See also BEST 90:3; CA 1-4R; CANR 1, 22,
36, 55; CDALB 1968-1988; DLB 2, 28,
173; DLBY 82; MTCW

Rothenberg, Jerome 1931-....... CLC **6, 57**
See also CA 45-48; CANR 1; DLB 5

Roumain, Jacques (Jean Baptiste)
1907-1944 .... TCLC **19; BLC;**
DAM MULT
See also BW 1; CA 117; 125

Rourke, Constance (Mayfield)
1885-1941 .... TCLC **12**
See also CA 107; YABC 1

Rousseau, Jean-Baptiste 1671-1741 ... LC **9**

Rousseau, Jean-Jacques
1712-1778 ...... LC **14, 36; DA; DAB;**
DAC; DAM MST; WLC

Roussel, Raymond 1877-1933 ..... TCLC **20**
See also CA 117

Rovit, Earl (Herbert) 1927-........ CLC **7**
See also CA 5-8R; CANR 12

Rowe, Nicholas 1674-1718.......... LC **8**
See also DLB 84

Rowley, Ames Dorrance
See Lovecraft, H(oward) P(hillips)

Rowson, Susanna Haswell
1762(?)-1824 .... NCLC **5**
See also DLB 37

Roy, Gabrielle
1909-1983 .... CLC **10, 14; DAB; DAC;**
DAM MST
See also CA 53-56; 110; CANR 5; DLB 68;
MTCW

Rozewicz, Tadeusz
1921- .... CLC **9, 23; DAM POET**
See also CA 108; CANR 36; MTCW

Ruark, Gibbons 1941- .... CLC **3**
See also CA 33-36R; CAAS 23; CANR 14,
31; DLB 120

Rubens, Bernice (Ruth) 1923-... CLC **19, 31**
See also CA 25-28R; CANR 33; DLB 14;
MTCW

Rubin, Harold
See Robbins, Harold

Rudkin, (James) David 1936- ...... CLC **14**
See also CA 89-92; DLB 13

Rudnik, Raphael 1933-............. CLC **7**
See also CA 29-32R

Ruffian, M.
See Hasek, Jaroslav (Matej Frantisek)

Ruiz, Jose Martinez .... CLC **11**
See also Martinez Ruiz, Jose

Rukeyser, Muriel
1913-1980 .... CLC **6, 10, 15, 27;**
DAM POET; PC 12
See also CA 5-8R; 93-96; CANR 26;
DLB 48; MTCW; SATA-Obit 22

Rule, Jane (Vance) 1931-......... CLC **27**
See also CA 25-28R; CAAS 18; CANR 12;
DLB 60

Rulfo, Juan
1918-1986 .... CLC **8, 80; DAM MULT;**
HLC
See also CA 85-88; 118; CANR 26;
DLB 113; HW; MTCW

Rumi, Jalal al-Din 1297-1373 .... CMLC **20**

Runeberg, Johan 1804-1877...... NCLC **41**

Runyon, (Alfred) Damon
1884(?)-1946 .... TCLC **10**
See also CA 107; DLB 11, 86, 171

Rush, Norman 1933-.............. CLC **44**
See also CA 121; 126; INT 126

Rushdie, (Ahmed) Salman
1947- ..... CLC **23, 31, 55; DAB; DAC;**
DAM MST, NOV, POP
See also BEST 89:3; CA 108; 111;
CANR 33; INT 111; MTCW

Rushforth, Peter (Scott) 1945- ..... CLC **19**
See also CA 101

Scott, Joanna 1960- . . . . CLC 50
See also CA 126; CANR 53

Scott, Paul (Mark) 1920-1978. . . . CLC 9, 60
See also CA 81-84; 77-80; CANR 33;
DLB 14; MTCW

Scott, Walter
1771-1832 . . . . NCLC 15; DA; DAB;
DAC; DAM MST, NOV, POET; PC 13;
WLC
See also CDBLB 1789-1832; DLB 93, 107,
116, 144, 159; YABC 2

Scribe, (Augustin) Eugene
1791-1861 . . . . NCLC 16; DAM DRAM;
DC 5

Scrum, R.
See Crumb, R(obert)

Scudery, Madeleine de 1607-1701 . . . . . LC 2

Scum
See Crumb, R(obert)

Scumbag, Little Bobby
See Crumb, R(obert)

Seabrook, John
See Hubbard, L(afayette) Ron(ald)

Sealy, I. Allan 1951- . . . . CLC 55

Search, Alexander
See Pessoa, Fernando (Antonio Nogueira)

Sebastian, Lee
See Silverberg, Robert

Sebastian Owl
See Thompson, Hunter S(tockton)

Sebestyen, Ouida 1924- . . . . CLC 30
See also AAYA 8; CA 107; CANR 40;
CLR 17; JRDA; MAICYA; SAAS 10;
SATA 39

Secundus, H. Scriblerus
See Fielding, Henry

Sedges, John
See Buck, Pearl S(ydenstricker)

Sedgwick, Catharine Maria
1789-1867 . . . . NCLC 19
See also DLB 1, 74

Seelye, John 1931- . . . . CLC 7

Seferiades, Giorgos Stylianou 1900-1971
See Seferis, George
See also CA 5-8R; 33-36R; CANR 5, 36;
MTCW

Seferis, George . . . . CLC 5, 11
See also Seferiades, Giorgos Stylianou

Segal, Erich (Wolf)
1937- . . . . CLC 3, 10; DAM POP
See also BEST 89:1; CA 25-28R; CANR 20,
36; DLBY 86; INT CANR-20; MTCW

Seger, Bob 1945- . . . . CLC 35

Seghers, Anna . . . . CLC 7
See also Radvanyi, Netty
See also DLB 69

Seidel, Frederick (Lewis) 1936- . . . . . CLC 18
See also CA 13-16R; CANR 8; DLBY 84

Seifert, Jaroslav
1901-1986 . . . . CLC 34, 44, 93
See also CA 127; MTCW

Sei Shonagon c. 966-1017(?) . . . . . . CMLC 6

Selby, Hubert, Jr.
1928- . . . . CLC 1, 2, 4, 8; SSC 20
See also CA 13-16R; CANR 33; DLB 2

Selzer, Richard 1928- . . . . CLC 74
See also CA 65-68; CANR 14

Sembene, Ousmane
See Ousmane, Sembene

Senancour, Etienne Pivert de
1770-1846 . . . . NCLC 16
See also DLB 119

Sender, Ramon (Jose)
1902-1982 . . CLC 8; DAM MULT; HLC
See also CA 5-8R; 105; CANR 8; HW;
MTCW

Seneca, Lucius Annaeus
4B.C.-65. . . . . . . CMLC 6; DAM DRAM;
DC 5

Senghor, Leopold Sedar
1906- . . . . . CLC 54; BLC; DAM MULT,
POET
See also BW 2; CA 116; 125; CANR 47;
MTCW

Serling, (Edward) Rod(man)
1924-1975 . . . . CLC 30
See also AAYA 14; AITN 1; CA 65-68;
57-60; DLB 26

Serna, Ramon Gomez de la
See Gomez de la Serna, Ramon

Serpieres
See Guillevic, (Eugene)

Service, Robert
See Service, Robert W(illiam)
See also DAB; DLB 92

Service, Robert W(illiam)
1874(?)-1958 . . . . . . TCLC 15; DA; DAC;
DAM MST, POET; WLC
See also Service, Robert
See also CA 115; 140; SATA 20

Seth, Vikram
1952- . . . . CLC 43, 90; DAM MULT
See also CA 121; 127; CANR 50; DLB 120;
INT 127

Seton, Cynthia Propper
1926-1982 . . . . CLC 27
See also CA 5-8R; 108; CANR 7

Seton, Ernest (Evan) Thompson
1860-1946 . . . . TCLC 31
See also CA 109; DLB 92; DLBD 13;
JRDA; SATA 18

Seton-Thompson, Ernest
See Seton, Ernest (Evan) Thompson

Settle, Mary Lee 1918- . . . . CLC 19, 61
See also CA 89-92; CAAS 1; CANR 44;
DLB 6; INT 89-92

Seuphor, Michel
See Arp, Jean

Sevigne, Marie (de Rabutin-Chantal) Marquise
de 1626-1696 . . . . LC 11

Sexton, Anne (Harvey)
1928-1974 . . . . CLC 2, 4, 6, 8, 10, 15, 53;
DA; DAB; DAC; DAM MST, POET;
PC 2; WLC
See also CA 1-4R; 53-56; CABS 2;
CANR 3, 36; CDALB 1941-1968; DLB 5,
169; MTCW; SATA 10

Shaara, Michael (Joseph, Jr.)
1929-1988 . . . . CLC 15; DAM POP
See also AITN 1; CA 102; 125; CANR 52;
DLBY 83

Shackleton, C. C.
See Aldiss, Brian W(ilson)

Shacochis, Bob . . . . CLC 39
See also Shacochis, Robert G.

Shacochis, Robert G. 1951-
See Shacochis, Bob
See also CA 119; 124; INT 124

Shaffer, Anthony (Joshua)
1926- . . . . CLC 19; DAM DRAM
See also CA 110; 116; DLB 13

Shaffer, Peter (Levin)
1926- . . . . . . CLC 5, 14, 18, 37, 60; DAB;
DAM DRAM, MST
See also CA 25-28R; CANR 25, 47;
CDBLB 1960 to Present; DLB 13;
MTCW

Shakey, Bernard
See Young, Neil

Shalamov, Varlam (Tikhonovich)
1907(?)-1982 . . . . CLC 18
See also CA 129; 105

Shamlu, Ahmad 1925- . . . . CLC 10

Shammas, Anton 1951- . . . . CLC 55

Shange, Ntozake
1948- . . . . CLC 8, 25, 38, 74; BLC;
DAM DRAM, MULT; DC 3
See also AAYA 9; BW 2; CA 85-88;
CABS 3; CANR 27, 48; DLB 38; MTCW

Shanley, John Patrick 1950- . . . . CLC 75
See also CA 128; 133

Shapcott, Thomas W(illiam) 1935- . . CLC 38
See also CA 69-72; CANR 49

Shapiro, Jane . . . . CLC 76

Shapiro, Karl (Jay) 1913- . . CLC 4, 8, 15, 53
See also CA 1-4R; CAAS 6; CANR 1, 36;
DLB 48; MTCW

Sharp, William 1855-1905 . . . . TCLC 39
See also DLB 156

Sharpe, Thomas Ridley 1928-
See Sharpe, Tom
See also CA 114; 122; INT 122

Sharpe, Tom . . . . CLC 36
See also Sharpe, Thomas Ridley
See also DLB 14

Shaw, Bernard . . . . TCLC 45
See also Shaw, George Bernard
See also BW 1

Shaw, G. Bernard
See Shaw, George Bernard

Shaw, George Bernard
1856-1950 . . . TCLC 3, 9, 21; DA; DAB;
DAC; DAM DRAM, MST; WLC
See also Shaw, Bernard
See also CA 104; 128; CDBLB 1914-1945;
DLB 10, 57; MTCW

Shaw, Henry Wheeler
1818-1885 . . . . NCLC 15
See also DLB 11

Shaw, Irwin
1913-1984 . . . . **CLC 7, 23, 34;**
DAM DRAM, POP
See also AITN 1; CA 13-16R; 112;
CANR 21; CDALB 1941-1968; DLB 6,
102; DLBY 84; MTCW

Shaw, Robert 1927-1978 . . . . **CLC 5**
See also AITN 1; CA 1-4R; 81-84;
CANR 4; DLB 13, 14

Shaw, T. E.
See Lawrence, T(homas) E(dward)

Shawn, Wallace 1943- . . . . **CLC 41**
See also CA 112

Shea, Lisa 1953- . . . . **CLC 86**
See also CA 147

Sheed, Wilfrid (John Joseph)
1930- . . . . **CLC 2, 4, 10, 53**
See also CA 65-68; CANR 30; DLB 6;
MTCW

Sheldon, Alice Hastings Bradley
1915(?)-1987
See Tiptree, James, Jr.
See also CA 108; 122; CANR 34; INT 108;
MTCW

Sheldon, John
See Bloch, Robert (Albert)

Shelley, Mary Wollstonecraft (Godwin)
1797-1851 . . . . **NCLC 14, 59; DA; DAB;**
DAC; DAM MST, NOV; WLC
See also CDBLB 1789-1832; DLB 110, 116,
159; SATA 29

Shelley, Percy Bysshe
1792-1822 . . . . **NCLC 18; DA; DAB;**
DAC; DAM MST, POET; PC 14; WLC
See also CDBLB 1789-1832; DLB 96, 110,
158

Shepard, Jim 1956- . . . . **CLC 36**
See also CA 137; SATA 90

Shepard, Lucius 1947- . . . . **CLC 34**
See also CA 128; 141

Shepard, Sam
1943- . . . . **CLC 4, 6, 17, 34, 41, 44;**
DAM DRAM; DC 5
See also AAYA 1; CA 69-72; CABS 3;
CANR 22; DLB 7; MTCW

Shepherd, Michael
See Ludlum, Robert

Sherburne, Zoa (Morin) 1912- . . . . . . **CLC 30**
See also AAYA 13; CA 1-4R; CANR 3, 37;
MAICYA; SAAS 18; SATA 3

Sheridan, Frances 1724-1766 . . . . **LC 7**
See also DLB 39, 84

Sheridan, Richard Brinsley
1751-1816 . . . . **NCLC 5; DA; DAB;**
DAC; DAM DRAM, MST; DC 1; WLC
See also CDBLB 1660-1789; DLB 89

Sherman, Jonathan Marc . . . . **CLC 55**

Sherman, Martin 1941(?)- . . . . **CLC 19**
See also CA 116; 123

Sherwin, Judith Johnson 1936- . . . **CLC 7, 15**
See also CA 25-28R; CANR 34

Sherwood, Frances 1940- . . . . **CLC 81**
See also CA 146

Sherwood, Robert E(mmet)
1896-1955 . . . . . **TCLC 3; DAM DRAM**
See also CA 104; 153; DLB 7, 26

Shestov, Lev 1866-1938 . . . . **TCLC 56**

Shevchenko, Taras 1814-1861 . . . . **NCLC 54**

Shiel, M(atthew) P(hipps)
1865-1947 . . . . **TCLC 8**
See also CA 106; DLB 153

Shields, Carol 1935- . . . . **CLC 91; DAC**
See also CA 81-84; CANR 51

Shields, David 1956- . . . . **CLC 97**
See also CA 124; CANR 48

Shiga, Naoya 1883-1971 . . . **CLC 33; SSC 23**
See also CA 101; 33-36R

Shilts, Randy 1951-1994 . . . . **CLC 85**
See also AAYA 19; CA 115; 127; 144;
CANR 45; INT 127

Shimazaki, Haruki 1872-1943
See Shimazaki Toson
See also CA 105; 134

Shimazaki Toson . . . . **TCLC 5**
See also Shimazaki, Haruki

Sholokhov, Mikhail (Aleksandrovich)
1905-1984 . . . . **CLC 7, 15**
See also CA 101; 112; MTCW;
SATA-Obit 36

Shone, Patric
See Hanley, James

Shreve, Susan Richards 1939- . . . . . . **CLC 23**
See also CA 49-52; CAAS 5; CANR 5, 38;
MAICYA; SATA 46; SATA-Brief 41

Shue, Larry
1946-1985 . . . . . . **CLC 52; DAM DRAM**
See also CA 145; 117

Shu-Jen, Chou 1881-1936
See Lu Hsun
See also CA 104

Shulman, Alix Kates 1932- . . . . . . **CLC 2, 10**
See also CA 29-32R; CANR 43; SATA 7

Shuster, Joe 1914- . . . . **CLC 21**

Shute, Nevil . . . . **CLC 30**
See also Norway, Nevil Shute

Shuttle, Penelope (Diane) 1947- . . . . . **CLC 7**
See also CA 93-96; CANR 39; DLB 14, 40

Sidney, Mary 1561-1621 . . . . **LC 19**

Sidney, Sir Philip
1554-1586 . . . . . **LC 19; DA; DAB; DAC;**
DAM MST, POET
See also CDBLB Before 1660; DLB 167

Siegel, Jerome 1914-1996 . . . . **CLC 21**
See also CA 116; 151

Siegel, Jerry
See Siegel, Jerome

Sienkiewicz, Henryk (Adam Alexander Pius)
1846-1916 . . . . **TCLC 3**
See also CA 104; 134

Sierra, Gregorio Martinez
See Martinez Sierra, Gregorio

Sierra, Maria (de la O'LeJarraga) Martinez
See Martinez Sierra, Maria (de la
O'LeJarraga)

Sigal, Clancy 1926- . . . . **CLC 7**
See also CA 1-4R

Sigourney, Lydia Howard (Huntley)
1791-1865 . . . . **NCLC 21**
See also DLB 1, 42, 73

Siguenza y Gongora, Carlos de
1645-1700 . . . . **LC 8**

Sigurjonsson, Johann 1880-1919 . . . **TCLC 27**

Sikelianos, Angelos 1884-1951 . . . . **TCLC 39**

Silkin, Jon 1930- . . . . **CLC 2, 6, 43**
See also CA 5-8R; CAAS 5; DLB 27

Silko, Leslie (Marmon)
1948- . . . . **CLC 23, 74; DA; DAC;**
DAM MST, MULT, POP
See also AAYA 14; CA 115; 122;
CANR 45; DLB 143; NNAL

Sillanpaa, Frans Eemil 1888-1964 . . . **CLC 19**
See also CA 129; 93-96; MTCW

Sillitoe, Alan
1928- . . . . **CLC 1, 3, 6, 10, 19, 57**
See also AITN 1; CA 9-12R; CAAS 2;
CANR 8, 26, 55; CDBLB 1960 to
Present; DLB 14, 139; MTCW; SATA 61

Silone, Ignazio 1900-1978 . . . . **CLC 4**
See also CA 25-28; 81-84; CANR 34;
CAP 2; MTCW

Silver, Joan Micklin 1935- . . . . **CLC 20**
See also CA 114; 121; INT 121

Silver, Nicholas
See Faust, Frederick (Schiller)

Silverberg, Robert
1935- . . . . **CLC 7; DAM POP**
See also CA 1-4R; CAAS 3; CANR 1, 20,
36; DLB 8; INT CANR-20; MAICYA;
MTCW; SATA 13, 91

Silverstein, Alvin 1933- . . . . **CLC 17**
See also CA 49-52; CANR 2; CLR 25;
JRDA; MAICYA; SATA 8, 69

Silverstein, Virginia B(arbara Opshelor)
1937- . . . . **CLC 17**
See also CA 49-52; CANR 2; CLR 25;
JRDA; MAICYA; SATA 8, 69

Sim, Georges
See Simenon, Georges (Jacques Christian)

Simak, Clifford D(onald)
1904-1988 . . . . **CLC 1, 55**
See also CA 1-4R; 125; CANR 1, 35;
DLB 8; MTCW; SATA-Obit 56

Simenon, Georges (Jacques Christian)
1903-1989 . . . . **CLC 1, 2, 3, 8, 18, 47;**
DAM POP
See also CA 85-88; 129; CANR 35;
DLB 72; DLBY 89; MTCW

Simic, Charles
1938- . . . . **CLC 6, 9, 22, 49, 68;**
DAM POET
See also CA 29-32R; CAAS 4; CANR 12,
33, 52; DLB 105

Simmel, Georg 1858-1918 . . . . **TCLC 64**

Simmons, Charles (Paul) 1924- . . . . . **CLC 57**
See also CA 89-92; INT 89-92

Simmons, Dan 1948- . . . **CLC 44; DAM POP**
See also AAYA 16; CA 138; CANR 53

Simmons, James (Stewart Alexander)
1933- . . . . **CLC 43**
See also CA 105; CAAS 21; DLB 40

Smollett, Tobias (George) 1721-1771 . . **LC 2**
See also CDBLB 1660-1789; DLB 39, 104

Snodgrass, W(illiam) D(e Witt)
1926- . . . . **CLC 2, 6, 10, 18, 68;**
DAM POET
See also CA 1-4R; CANR 6, 36; DLB 5;
MTCW

Snow, C(harles) P(ercy)
1905-1980 . . . . . . **CLC 1, 4, 6, 9, 13, 19;**
DAM NOV
See also CA 5-8R; 101; CANR 28;
CDBLB 1945-1960; DLB 15, 77; MTCW

Snow, Frances Compton
See Adams, Henry (Brooks)

Snyder, Gary (Sherman)
1930- . . **CLC 1, 2, 5, 9, 32; DAM POET**
See also CA 17-20R; CANR 30; DLB 5, 16,
165

Snyder, Zilpha Keatley 1927- . . . . . . **CLC 17**
See also AAYA 15; CA 9-12R; CANR 38;
CLR 31; JRDA; MAICYA; SAAS 2;
SATA 1, 28, 75

Soares, Bernardo
See Pessoa, Fernando (Antonio Nogueira)

Sobh, A.
See Shamlu, Ahmad

Sobol, Joshua. . . . . **CLC 60**

Soderberg, Hjalmar 1869-1941 . . . . **TCLC 39**

Sodergran, Edith (Irene)
See Soedergran, Edith (Irene)

Soedergran, Edith (Irene)
1892-1923 . . . . **TCLC 31**

Softly, Edgar
See Lovecraft, H(oward) P(hillips)

Softly, Edward
See Lovecraft, H(oward) P(hillips)

Sokolov, Raymond 1941- . . . . **CLC 7**
See also CA 85-88

Solo, Jay
See Ellison, Harlan (Jay)

Sologub, Fyodor . . . . **TCLC 9**
See also Teternikov, Fyodor Kuzmich

Solomons, Ikey Esquir
See Thackeray, William Makepeace

Solomos, Dionysios 1798-1857 . . . **NCLC 15**

Solwoska, Mara
See French, Marilyn

Solzhenitsyn, Aleksandr I(sayevich)
1918- . . . . . . **CLC 1, 2, 4, 7, 9, 10, 18, 26,**
34, 78; DA; DAB; DAC; DAM MST,
NOV; WLC
See also AITN 1; CA 69-72; CANR 40;
MTCW

Somers, Jane
See Lessing, Doris (May)

Somerville, Edith 1858-1949 . . . . . **TCLC 51**
See also DLB 135

Somerville & Ross
See Martin, Violet Florence; Somerville,
Edith

Sommer, Scott 1951- . . . . **CLC 25**
See also CA 106

Sondheim, Stephen (Joshua)
1930- . . . . **CLC 30, 39; DAM DRAM**
See also AAYA 11; CA 103; CANR 47

Sontag, Susan
1933- . . . . **CLC 1, 2, 10, 13, 31;**
DAM POP
See also CA 17-20R; CANR 25, 51; DLB 2,
67; MTCW

Sophocles
496(?)B.C.-406(?)B.C. . . . . . **CMLC 2; DA;**
DAB; DAC; DAM DRAM, MST; DC 1

Sordello 1189-1269 . . . . **CMLC 15**

Sorel, Julia
See Drexler, Rosalyn

Sorrentino, Gilbert
1929- . . . . **CLC 3, 7, 14, 22, 40**
See also CA 77-80; CANR 14, 33; DLB 5,
173; DLBY 80; INT CANR-14

Soto, Gary
1952- . . . . **CLC 32, 80; DAM MULT;**
HLC
See also AAYA 10; CA 119; 125;
CANR 50; CLR 38; DLB 82; HW;
INT 125; JRDA; SATA 80

Soupault, Philippe 1897-1990 . . . . . . **CLC 68**
See also CA 116; 147; 131

Souster, (Holmes) Raymond
1921- . . . **CLC 5, 14; DAC; DAM POET**
See also CA 13-16R; CAAS 14; CANR 13,
29, 53; DLB 88; SATA 63

Southern, Terry 1924(?)-1995 . . . . **CLC 7**
See also CA 1-4R; 150; CANR 1, 55;
DLB 2

Southey, Robert 1774-1843 . . . . **NCLC 8**
See also DLB 93, 107, 142; SATA 54

Southworth, Emma Dorothy Eliza Nevitte
1819-1899 . . . . **NCLC 26**

Souza, Ernest
See Scott, Evelyn

Soyinka, Wole
1934- . . . . **CLC 3, 5, 14, 36, 44; BLC;**
DA; DAB; DAC; DAM DRAM, MST,
MULT; DC 2; WLC
See also BW 2; CA 13-16R; CANR 27, 39;
DLB 125; MTCW

Spackman, W(illiam) M(ode)
1905-1990 . . . . **CLC 46**
See also CA 81-84; 132

Spacks, Barry (Bernard) 1931- . . . . . **CLC 14**
See also CA 154; CANR 33; DLB 105

Spanidou, Irini 1946- . . . . **CLC 44**

Spark, Muriel (Sarah)
1918- . . . . . **CLC 2, 3, 5, 8, 13, 18, 40, 94;**
DAB; DAC; DAM MST, NOV; SSC 10
See also CA 5-8R; CANR 12, 36;
CDBLB 1945-1960; DLB 15, 139;
INT CANR-12; MTCW

Spaulding, Douglas
See Bradbury, Ray (Douglas)

Spaulding, Leonard
See Bradbury, Ray (Douglas)

Spence, J. A. D.
See Eliot, T(homas) S(tearns)

Spencer, Elizabeth 1921- . . . . **CLC 22**
See also CA 13-16R; CANR 32; DLB 6;
MTCW; SATA 14

Spencer, Leonard G.
See Silverberg, Robert

Spencer, Scott 1945- . . . . **CLC 30**
See also CA 113; CANR 51; DLBY 86

Spender, Stephen (Harold)
1909-1995 . . . . . . **CLC 1, 2, 5, 10, 41, 91;**
DAM POET
See also CA 9-12R; 149; CANR 31, 54;
CDBLB 1945-1960; DLB 20; MTCW

Spengler, Oswald (Arnold Gottfried)
1880-1936 . . . . **TCLC 25**
See also CA 118

Spenser, Edmund
1552(?)-1599 . . . . **LC 5; DA; DAB; DAC;**
DAM MST, POET; PC 8; WLC
See also CDBLB Before 1660; DLB 167

Spicer, Jack
1925-1965 . . . . **CLC 8, 18, 72;**
DAM POET
See also CA 85-88; DLB 5, 16

Spiegelman, Art 1948- . . . . **CLC 76**
See also AAYA 10; CA 125; CANR 41, 55

Spielberg, Peter 1929- . . . . **CLC 6**
See also CA 5-8R; CANR 4, 48; DLBY 81

Spielberg, Steven 1947- . . . . **CLC 20**
See also AAYA 8; CA 77-80; CANR 32;
SATA 32

Spillane, Frank Morrison 1918-
See Spillane, Mickey
See also CA 25-28R; CANR 28; MTCW;
SATA 66

Spillane, Mickey . . . . **CLC 3, 13**
See also Spillane, Frank Morrison

Spinoza, Benedictus de 1632-1677 . . . . **LC 9**

Spinrad, Norman (Richard) 1940- . . . **CLC 46**
See also CA 37-40R; CAAS 19; CANR 20;
DLB 8; INT CANR-20

Spitteler, Carl (Friedrich Georg)
1845-1924 . . . . **TCLC 12**
See also CA 109; DLB 129

Spivack, Kathleen (Romola Drucker)
1938- . . . . **CLC 6**
See also CA 49-52

Spoto, Donald 1941- . . . . **CLC 39**
See also CA 65-68; CANR 11

Springsteen, Bruce (F.) 1949- . . . . . . **CLC 17**
See also CA 111

Spurling, Hilary 1940- . . . . **CLC 34**
See also CA 104; CANR 25, 52

Spyker, John Howland
See Elman, Richard

Squires, (James) Radcliffe
1917-1993 . . . . **CLC 51**
See also CA 1-4R; 140; CANR 6, 21

Srivastava, Dhanpat Rai 1880(?)-1936
See Premchand
See also CA 118

Stacy, Donald
See Pohl, Frederik

465

Stoppard, Tom
1937- ...... **CLC 1, 3, 4, 5, 8, 15, 29, 34, 63, 91; DA; DAB; DAC; DAM DRAM, MST; DC 6; WLC**
See also CA 81-84; CANR 39; CDBLB 1960 to Present; DLB 13; DLBY 85; MTCW

Storey, David (Malcolm)
1933- ..... **CLC 2, 4, 5, 8; DAM DRAM**
See also CA 81-84; CANR 36; DLB 13, 14; MTCW

Storm, Hyemeyohsts
1935- .... **CLC 3; DAM MULT**
See also CA 81-84; CANR 45; NNAL

Storm, (Hans) Theodor (Woldsen)
1817-1888 .... **NCLC 1**

Storni, Alfonsina
1892-1938 ..... **TCLC 5; DAM MULT; HLC**
See also CA 104; 131; HW

Stout, Rex (Todhunter) 1886-1975 ... **CLC 3**
See also AITN 2; CA 61-64

Stow, (Julian) Randolph 1935- .. **CLC 23, 48**
See also CA 13-16R; CANR 33; MTCW

Stowe, Harriet (Elizabeth) Beecher
1811-1896 ..... **NCLC 3, 50; DA; DAB; DAC; DAM MST, NOV; WLC**
See also CDALB 1865-1917; DLB 1, 12, 42, 74; JRDA; MAICYA; YABC 1

Strachey, (Giles) Lytton
1880-1932 .... **TCLC 12**
See also CA 110; DLB 149; DLBD 10

Strand, Mark
1934- .. **CLC 6, 18, 41, 71; DAM POET**
See also CA 21-24R; CANR 40; DLB 5; SATA 41

Straub, Peter (Francis)
1943- .... **CLC 28; DAM POP**
See also BEST 89:1; CA 85-88; CANR 28; DLBY 84; MTCW

Strauss, Botho 1944- .... **CLC 22**
See also DLB 124

Streatfeild, (Mary) Noel
1895(?)-1986 .... **CLC 21**
See also CA 81-84; 120; CANR 31; CLR 17; DLB 160; MAICYA; SATA 20; SATA-Obit 48

Stribling, T(homas) S(igismund)
1881-1965 .... **CLC 23**
See also CA 107; DLB 9

Strindberg, (Johan) August
1849-1912 ...... **TCLC 1, 8, 21, 47; DA; DAB; DAC; DAM DRAM, MST; WLC**
See also CA 104; 135

Stringer, Arthur 1874-1950 ...... **TCLC 37**
See also DLB 92

Stringer, David
See Roberts, Keith (John Kingston)

Strugatskii, Arkadii (Natanovich)
1925-1991 .... **CLC 27**
See also CA 106; 135

Strugatskii, Boris (Natanovich)
1933- .... **CLC 27**
See also CA 106

Strummer, Joe 1953(?)- .... **CLC 30**

Stuart, Don A.
See Campbell, John W(ood, Jr.)

Stuart, Ian
See MacLean, Alistair (Stuart)

Stuart, Jesse (Hilton)
1906-1984 .... **CLC 1, 8, 11, 14, 34**
See also CA 5-8R; 112; CANR 31; DLB 9, 48, 102; DLBY 84; SATA 2; SATA-Obit 36

Sturgeon, Theodore (Hamilton)
1918-1985 .... **CLC 22, 39**
See also Queen, Ellery
See also CA 81-84; 116; CANR 32; DLB 8; DLBY 85; MTCW

Sturges, Preston 1898-1959 ...... **TCLC 48**
See also CA 114; 149; DLB 26

Styron, William
1925- .... **CLC 1, 3, 5, 11, 15, 60; DAM NOV, POP**
See also BEST 90:4; CA 5-8R; CANR 6, 33; CDALB 1968-1988; DLB 2, 143; DLBY 80; INT CANR-6; MTCW

Suarez Lynch, B.
See Bioy Casares, Adolfo; Borges, Jorge Luis

Su Chien 1884-1918
See Su Man-shu
See also CA 123

Suckow, Ruth 1892-1960 .... **SSC 18**
See also CA 113; DLB 9, 102

Sudermann, Hermann 1857-1928 .. **TCLC 15**
See also CA 107; DLB 118

Sue, Eugene 1804-1857 .... **NCLC 1**
See also DLB 119

Sueskind, Patrick 1949- .... **CLC 44**
See also Suskind, Patrick

Sukenick, Ronald 1932- ..... **CLC 3, 4, 6, 48**
See also CA 25-28R; CAAS 8; CANR 32; DLB 173; DLBY 81

Suknaski, Andrew 1942- .... **CLC 19**
See also CA 101; DLB 53

Sullivan, Vernon
See Vian, Boris

Sully Prudhomme 1839-1907 ...... **TCLC 31**

Su Man-shu .... **TCLC 24**
See also Su Chien

Summerforest, Ivy B.
See Kirkup, James

Summers, Andrew James 1942- ..... **CLC 26**

Summers, Andy
See Summers, Andrew James

Summers, Hollis (Spurgeon, Jr.)
1916- .... **CLC 10**
See also CA 5-8R; CANR 3; DLB 6

Summers, (Alphonsus Joseph-Mary Augustus) Montague 1880-1948 .... **TCLC 16**
See also CA 118

Sumner, Gordon Matthew 1951- .... **CLC 26**

Surtees, Robert Smith
1803-1864 .... **NCLC 14**
See also DLB 21

Susann, Jacqueline 1921-1974 ...... **CLC 3**
See also AITN 1; CA 65-68; 53-56; MTCW

Su Shih 1036-1101 .... **CMLC 15**

Suskind, Patrick
See Sueskind, Patrick
See also CA 145

Sutcliff, Rosemary
1920-1992 .... **CLC 26; DAB; DAC; DAM MST, POP**
See also AAYA 10; CA 5-8R; 139; CANR 37; CLR 1, 37; JRDA; MAICYA; SATA 6, 44, 78; SATA-Obit 73

Sutro, Alfred 1863-1933 .... **TCLC 6**
See also CA 105; DLB 10

Sutton, Henry
See Slavitt, David R(ytman)

Svevo, Italo .... **TCLC 2, 35**
See also Schmitz, Aron Hector

Swados, Elizabeth (A.) 1951- ...... **CLC 12**
See also CA 97-100; CANR 49; INT 97-100

Swados, Harvey 1920-1972 .... **CLC 5**
See also CA 5-8R; 37-40R; CANR 6; DLB 2

Swan, Gladys 1934- .... **CLC 69**
See also CA 101; CANR 17, 39

Swarthout, Glendon (Fred)
1918-1992 .... **CLC 35**
See also CA 1-4R; 139; CANR 1, 47; SATA 26

Sweet, Sarah C.
See Jewett, (Theodora) Sarah Orne

Swenson, May
1919-1989 .... **CLC 4, 14, 61; DA; DAB; DAC; DAM MST, POET; PC 14**
See also CA 5-8R; 130; CANR 36; DLB 5; MTCW; SATA 15

Swift, Augustus
See Lovecraft, H(oward) P(hillips)

Swift, Graham (Colin) 1949- .... **CLC 41, 88**
See also CA 117; 122; CANR 46

Swift, Jonathan
1667-1745 ...... **LC 1; DA; DAB; DAC; DAM MST, NOV, POET; PC 9; WLC**
See also CDBLB 1660-1789; DLB 39, 95, 101; SATA 19

Swinburne, Algernon Charles
1837-1909 ...... **TCLC 8, 36; DA; DAB; DAC; DAM MST, POET; WLC**
See also CA 105; 140; CDBLB 1832-1890; DLB 35, 57

Swinfen, Ann .... **CLC 34**

Swinnerton, Frank Arthur
1884-1982 .... **CLC 31**
See also CA 108; DLB 34

Swithen, John
See King, Stephen (Edwin)

Sylvia
See Ashton-Warner, Sylvia (Constance)

Symmes, Robert Edward
See Duncan, Robert (Edward)

Symonds, John Addington
1840-1893 .... **NCLC 34**
See also DLB 57, 144

Symons, Arthur 1865-1945 .... **TCLC 11**
See also CA 107; DLB 19, 57, 149

Symons, Julian (Gustave)
1912-1994 . . . . **CLC 2, 14, 32**
See also CA 49-52; 147; CAAS 3; CANR 3,
33; DLB 87, 155; DLBY 92; MTCW

Synge, (Edmund) J(ohn) M(illington)
1871-1909 . . . . **TCLC 6, 37;**
DAM DRAM; DC 2
See also CA 104; 141; CDBLB 1890-1914;
DLB 10, 19

Syruc, J.
See Milosz, Czeslaw

Szirtes, George 1948- . . . . **CLC 46**
See also CA 109; CANR 27

T. O., Nik
See Annensky, Innokenty Fyodorovich

Tabori, George 1914- . . . . **CLC 19**
See also CA 49-52; CANR 4

Tagore, Rabindranath
1861-1941 . . . . **TCLC 3, 53;**
DAM DRAM, POET; PC 8
See also CA 104; 120; MTCW

Taine, Hippolyte Adolphe
1828-1893 . . . . **NCLC 15**

Talese, Gay 1932- . . . . **CLC 37**
See also AITN 1; CA 1-4R; CANR 9;
INT CANR-9; MTCW

Tallent, Elizabeth (Ann) 1954- . . . . . **CLC 45**
See also CA 117; DLB 130

Tally, Ted 1952- . . . . **CLC 42**
See also CA 120; 124; INT 124

Tamayo y Baus, Manuel
1829-1898 . . . . **NCLC 1**

Tammsaare, A(nton) H(ansen)
1878-1940 . . . . **TCLC 27**

Tan, Amy (Ruth)
1952- . . . . **CLC 59; DAM MULT, NOV,**
POP
See also AAYA 9; BEST 89:3; CA 136;
CANR 54; DLB 173; SATA 75

Tandem, Felix
See Spitteler, Carl (Friedrich Georg)

Tanizaki, Jun'ichiro
1886-1965 . . . . . . **CLC 8, 14, 28; SSC 21**
See also CA 93-96; 25-28R

Tanner, William
See Amis, Kingsley (William)

Tao Lao
See Storni, Alfonsina

Tarassoff, Lev
See Troyat, Henri

Tarbell, Ida M(inerva)
1857-1944 . . . . **TCLC 40**
See also CA 122; DLB 47

Tarkington, (Newton) Booth
1869-1946 . . . . **TCLC 9**
See also CA 110; 143; DLB 9, 102;
SATA 17

Tarkovsky, Andrei (Arsenyevich)
1932-1986 . . . . **CLC 75**
See also CA 127

Tartt, Donna 1964(?)- . . . . **CLC 76**
See also CA 142

Tasso, Torquato 1544-1595 . . . . **LC 5**

Tate, (John Orley) Allen
1899-1979 . . . . **CLC 2, 4, 6, 9, 11, 14, 24**
See also CA 5-8R; 85-88; CANR 32;
DLB 4, 45, 63; MTCW

Tate, Ellalice
See Hibbert, Eleanor Alice Burford

Tate, James (Vincent) 1943- . . . **CLC 2, 6, 25**
See also CA 21-24R; CANR 29; DLB 5,
169

Tavel, Ronald 1940- . . . . **CLC 6**
See also CA 21-24R; CANR 33

Taylor, C(ecil) P(hilip) 1929-1981 . . . **CLC 27**
See also CA 25-28R; 105; CANR 47

Taylor, Edward
1642(?)-1729 . . . . **LC 11; DA; DAB;**
DAC; DAM MST, POET
See also DLB 24

Taylor, Eleanor Ross 1920- . . . . **CLC 5**
See also CA 81-84

Taylor, Elizabeth 1912-1975 . . . **CLC 2, 4, 29**
See also CA 13-16R; CANR 9; DLB 139;
MTCW; SATA 13

Taylor, Henry (Splawn) 1942- . . . . . . **CLC 44**
See also CA 33-36R; CAAS 7; CANR 31;
DLB 5

Taylor, Kamala (Purnaiya) 1924-
See Markandaya, Kamala
See also CA 77-80

Taylor, Mildred D. . . . . **CLC 21**
See also AAYA 10; BW 1; CA 85-88;
CANR 25; CLR 9; DLB 52; JRDA;
MAICYA; SAAS 5; SATA 15, 70

Taylor, Peter (Hillsman)
1917-1994 . . . . . **CLC 1, 4, 18, 37, 44, 50,**
71; SSC 10
See also CA 13-16R; 147; CANR 9, 50;
DLBY 81, 94; INT CANR-9; MTCW

Taylor, Robert Lewis 1912- . . . . **CLC 14**
See also CA 1-4R; CANR 3; SATA 10

Tchekhov, Anton
See Chekhov, Anton (Pavlovich)

Teasdale, Sara 1884-1933 . . . . **TCLC 4**
See also CA 104; DLB 45; SATA 32

Tegner, Esaias 1782-1846 . . . . **NCLC 2**

Teilhard de Chardin, (Marie Joseph) Pierre
1881-1955 . . . . **TCLC 9**
See also CA 105

Temple, Ann
See Mortimer, Penelope (Ruth)

Tennant, Emma (Christina)
1937- . . . . **CLC 13, 52**
See also CA 65-68; CAAS 9; CANR 10, 38;
DLB 14

Tenneshaw, S. M.
See Silverberg, Robert

Tennyson, Alfred
1809-1892 . . . . **NCLC 30; DA; DAB;**
DAC; DAM MST, POET; PC 6; WLC
See also CDBLB 1832-1890; DLB 32

Teran, Lisa St. Aubin de . . . . **CLC 36**
See also St. Aubin de Teran, Lisa

Terence 195(?)B.C.-159B.C. . . . . . . **CMLC 14**

Teresa de Jesus, St. 1515-1582 . . . . . . **LC 18**

Terkel, Louis 1912-
See Terkel, Studs
See also CA 57-60; CANR 18, 45; MTCW

Terkel, Studs . . . . **CLC 38**
See also Terkel, Louis
See also AITN 1

Terry, C. V.
See Slaughter, Frank G(ill)

Terry, Megan 1932- . . . . **CLC 19**
See also CA 77-80; CABS 3; CANR 43;
DLB 7

Tertz, Abram
See Sinyavsky, Andrei (Donatevich)

Tesich, Steve 1943(?)-1996 . . . . . . **CLC 40, 69**
See also CA 105; 152; DLBY 83

Teternikov, Fyodor Kuzmich 1863-1927
See Sologub, Fyodor
See also CA 104

Tevis, Walter 1928-1984 . . . . **CLC 42**
See also CA 113

Tey, Josephine . . . . **TCLC 14**
See also Mackintosh, Elizabeth
See also DLB 77

Thackeray, William Makepeace
1811-1863 . . . . **NCLC 5, 14, 22, 43; DA;**
DAB; DAC; DAM MST, NOV; WLC
See also CDBLB 1832-1890; DLB 21, 55,
159, 163; SATA 23

Thakura, Ravindranatha
See Tagore, Rabindranath

Tharoor, Shashi 1956- . . . . **CLC 70**
See also CA 141

Thelwell, Michael Miles 1939- . . . . . **CLC 22**
See also BW 2; CA 101

Theobald, Lewis, Jr.
See Lovecraft, H(oward) P(hillips)

Theodorescu, Ion N. 1880-1967
See Arghezi, Tudor
See also CA 116

Theriault, Yves
1915-1983 . . **CLC 79; DAC; DAM MST**
See also CA 102; DLB 88

Theroux, Alexander (Louis)
1939- . . . . **CLC 2, 25**
See also CA 85-88; CANR 20

Theroux, Paul (Edward)
1941- . . . . **CLC 5, 8, 11, 15, 28, 46;**
DAM POP
See also BEST 89:4; CA 33-36R; CANR 20,
45; DLB 2; MTCW; SATA 44

Thesen, Sharon 1946- . . . . **CLC 56**

Thevenin, Denis
See Duhamel, Georges

Thibault, Jacques Anatole Francois
1844-1924
See France, Anatole
See also CA 106; 127; DAM NOV; MTCW

Thiele, Colin (Milton) 1920- . . . . **CLC 17**
See also CA 29-32R; CANR 12, 28, 53;
CLR 27; MAICYA; SAAS 2; SATA 14,
72

Thomas, Audrey (Callahan)
1935- . . . . **CLC 7, 13, 37; SSC 20**
See also AITN 2; CA 21-24R; CAAS 19;
CANR 36; DLB 60; MTCW

Thomas, D(onald) M(ichael)
1935- . . . . **CLC 13, 22, 31**
See also CA 61-64; CAAS 11; CANR 17,
45; CDBLB 1960 to Present; DLB 40;
INT CANR-17; MTCW

Thomas, Dylan (Marlais)
1914-1953 . . . **TCLC 1, 8, 45; DA; DAB;
DAC; DAM DRAM, MST, POET;
PC 2; SSC 3; WLC**
See also CA 104; 120; CDBLB 1945-1960;
DLB 13, 20, 139; MTCW; SATA 60

Thomas, (Philip) Edward
1878-1917 . . . . . . **TCLC 10; DAM POET**
See also CA 106; 153; DLB 19

Thomas, Joyce Carol 1938- . . . . **CLC 35**
See also AAYA 12; BW 2; CA 113; 116;
CANR 48; CLR 19; DLB 33; INT 116;
JRDA; MAICYA; MTCW; SAAS 7;
SATA 40, 78

Thomas, Lewis 1913-1993 . . . . **CLC 35**
See also CA 85-88; 143; CANR 38; MTCW

Thomas, Paul
See Mann, (Paul) Thomas

Thomas, Piri 1928- . . . . **CLC 17**
See also CA 73-76; HW

Thomas, R(onald) S(tuart)
1913- . . . . **CLC 6, 13, 48; DAB;
DAM POET**
See also CA 89-92; CAAS 4; CANR 30;
CDBLB 1960 to Present; DLB 27;
MTCW

Thomas, Ross (Elmore) 1926-1995 . . **CLC 39**
See also CA 33-36R; 150; CANR 22

Thompson, Francis Clegg
See Mencken, H(enry) L(ouis)

Thompson, Francis Joseph
1859-1907 . . . . **TCLC 4**
See also CA 104; CDBLB 1890-1914;
DLB 19

Thompson, Hunter S(tockton)
1939- . . . . **CLC 9, 17, 40; DAM POP**
See also BEST 89:1; CA 17-20R; CANR 23,
46; MTCW

Thompson, James Myers
See Thompson, Jim (Myers)

Thompson, Jim (Myers)
1906-1977(?) . . . . **CLC 69**
See also CA 140

Thompson, Judith . . . . **CLC 39**

Thomson, James
1700-1748 . . . . . **LC 16, 29; DAM POET**
See also DLB 95

Thomson, James
1834-1882 . . . . . **NCLC 18; DAM POET**
See also DLB 35

Thoreau, Henry David
1817-1862 . . . . . **NCLC 7, 21; DA; DAB;
DAC; DAM MST; WLC**
See also CDALB 1640-1865; DLB 1

Thornton, Hall
See Silverberg, Robert

Thucydides c. 455B.C.-399B.C. . . . **CMLC 17**

Thurber, James (Grover)
1894-1961 . . . . **CLC 5, 11, 25; DA; DAB;
DAC; DAM DRAM, MST, NOV; SSC 1**
See also CA 73-76; CANR 17, 39;
CDALB 1929-1941; DLB 4, 11, 22, 102;
MAICYA; MTCW; SATA 13

Thurman, Wallace (Henry)
1902-1934 . . . . **TCLC 6; BLC;
DAM MULT**
See also BW 1; CA 104; 124; DLB 51

Ticheburn, Cheviot
See Ainsworth, William Harrison

Tieck, (Johann) Ludwig
1773-1853 . . . . **NCLC 5, 46**
See also DLB 90

Tiger, Derry
See Ellison, Harlan (Jay)

Tilghman, Christopher 1948(?)- . . . . . **CLC 65**

Tillinghast, Richard (Williford)
1940- . . . . **CLC 29**
See also CA 29-32R; CAAS 23; CANR 26,
51

Timrod, Henry 1828-1867 . . . . **NCLC 25**
See also DLB 3

Tindall, Gillian 1938- . . . . **CLC 7**
See also CA 21-24R; CANR 11

Tiptree, James, Jr. . . . . **CLC 48, 50**
See also Sheldon, Alice Hastings Bradley
See also DLB 8

Titmarsh, Michael Angelo
See Thackeray, William Makepeace

**Tocqueville, Alexis (Charles Henri Maurice
Clerel Comte)** 1805-1859 . . . . . **NCLC 7**

Tolkien, J(ohn) R(onald) R(euel)
1892-1973 . . . . **CLC 1, 2, 3, 8, 12, 38;
DA; DAB; DAC; DAM MST, NOV,
POP; WLC**
See also AAYA 10; AITN 1; CA 17-18;
45-48; CANR 36; CAP 2;
CDBLB 1914-1945; DLB 15, 160; JRDA;
MAICYA; MTCW; SATA 2, 32;
SATA-Obit 24

Toller, Ernst 1893-1939 . . . . **TCLC 10**
See also CA 107; DLB 124

Tolson, M. B.
See Tolson, Melvin B(eaunorus)

Tolson, Melvin B(eaunorus)
1898(?)-1966 . . . . **CLC 36; BLC;
DAM MULT, POET**
See also BW 1; CA 124; 89-92; DLB 48, 76

Tolstoi, Aleksei Nikolaevich
See Tolstoy, Alexey Nikolaevich

Tolstoy, Alexey Nikolaevich
1882-1945 . . . . **TCLC 18**
See also CA 107

Tolstoy, Count Leo
See Tolstoy, Leo (Nikolaevich)

Tolstoy, Leo (Nikolaevich)
1828-1910 . . . . . . **TCLC 4, 11, 17, 28, 44;
DA; DAB; DAC; DAM MST, NOV;
SSC 9; WLC**
See also CA 104; 123; SATA 26

Tomasi di Lampedusa, Giuseppe 1896-1957
See Lampedusa, Giuseppe (Tomasi) di
See also CA 111

Tomlin, Lily . . . . **CLC 17**
See also Tomlin, Mary Jean

Tomlin, Mary Jean 1939(?)-
See Tomlin, Lily
See also CA 117

Tomlinson, (Alfred) Charles
1927- . . . . **CLC 2, 4, 6, 13, 45;
DAM POET; PC 17**
See also CA 5-8R; CANR 33; DLB 40

Tonson, Jacob
See Bennett, (Enoch) Arnold

Toole, John Kennedy
1937-1969 . . . . **CLC 19, 64**
See also CA 104; DLBY 81

Toomer, Jean
1894-1967 . . . . . . **CLC 1, 4, 13, 22; BLC;
DAM MULT; PC 7; SSC 1**
See also BW 1; CA 85-88;
CDALB 1917-1929; DLB 45, 51; MTCW

Torley, Luke
See Blish, James (Benjamin)

Tornimparte, Alessandra
See Ginzburg, Natalia

Torre, Raoul della
See Mencken, H(enry) L(ouis)

Torrey, E(dwin) Fuller 1937- . . . . **CLC 34**
See also CA 119

Torsvan, Ben Traven
See Traven, B.

Torsvan, Benno Traven
See Traven, B.

Torsvan, Berick Traven
See Traven, B.

Torsvan, Berwick Traven
See Traven, B.

Torsvan, Bruno Traven
See Traven, B.

Torsvan, Traven
See Traven, B.

Tournier, Michel (Edouard)
1924- . . . . **CLC 6, 23, 36, 95**
See also CA 49-52; CANR 3, 36; DLB 83;
MTCW; SATA 23

Tournimparte, Alessandra
See Ginzburg, Natalia

Towers, Ivar
See Kornbluth, C(yril) M.

Towne, Robert (Burton) 1936(?)- . . . . **CLC 87**
See also CA 108; DLB 44

Townsend, Sue 1946- . . **CLC 61; DAB; DAC**
See also CA 119; 127; INT 127; MTCW;
SATA 55; SATA-Brief 48

Townshend, Peter (Dennis Blandford)
1945- . . . . **CLC 17, 42**
See also CA 107

Tozzi, Federigo 1883-1920 . . . . **TCLC 31**

Traill, Catharine Parr
1802-1899 . . . . **NCLC 31**
See also DLB 99

Trakl, Georg 1887-1914 . . . . **TCLC 5**
See also CA 104

Transtroemer, Tomas (Goesta)
1931- . . . . **CLC 52, 65; DAM POET**
See also CA 117; 129; CAAS 17

Transtromer, Tomas Gosta
  See Transtroemer, Tomas (Goesta)

Traven, B. (?)-1969 . . . . **CLC 8, 11**
  See also CA 19-20; 25-28R; CAP 2; DLB 9,
  56; MTCW

Treitel, Jonathan 1959- . . . . **CLC 70**

Tremain, Rose 1943- . . . . **CLC 42**
  See also CA 97-100; CANR 44; DLB 14

Tremblay, Michel
  1942- . . . . . . **CLC 29; DAC; DAM MST**
  See also CA 116; 128; DLB 60; MTCW

Trevanian . . . . **CLC 29**
  See also Whitaker, Rod(ney)

Trevor, Glen
  See Hilton, James

Trevor, William
  1928- . . . . . **CLC 7, 9, 14, 25, 71; SSC 21**
  See also Cox, William Trevor
  See also DLB 14, 139

Trifonov, Yuri (Valentinovich)
  1925-1981 . . . . **CLC 45**
  See also CA 126; 103; MTCW

Trilling, Lionel 1905-1975 . . . . **CLC 9, 11, 24**
  See also CA 9-12R; 61-64; CANR 10;
  DLB 28, 63; INT CANR-10; MTCW

Trimball, W. H.
  See Mencken, H(enry) L(ouis)

Tristan
  See Gomez de la Serna, Ramon

Tristram
  See Housman, A(lfred) E(dward)

Trogdon, William (Lewis) 1939-
  See Heat-Moon, William Least
  See also CA 115; 119; CANR 47; INT 119

Trollope, Anthony
  1815-1882 . . . . . **NCLC 6, 33; DA; DAB;
  DAC; DAM MST, NOV; WLC**
  See also CDBLB 1832-1890; DLB 21, 57,
  159; SATA 22

Trollope, Frances 1779-1863 . . . . . **NCLC 30**
  See also DLB 21, 166

Trotsky, Leon 1879-1940 . . . . **TCLC 22**
  See also CA 118

Trotter (Cockburn), Catharine
  1679-1749 . . . . **LC 8**
  See also DLB 84

Trout, Kilgore
  See Farmer, Philip Jose

Trow, George W. S. 1943- . . . . **CLC 52**
  See also CA 126

Troyat, Henri 1911- . . . . **CLC 23**
  See also CA 45-48; CANR 2, 33; MTCW

Trudeau, G(arretson) B(eekman) 1948-
  See Trudeau, Garry B.
  See also CA 81-84; CANR 31; SATA 35

Trudeau, Garry B. . . . . **CLC 12**
  See also Trudeau, G(arretson) B(eekman)
  See also AAYA 10; AITN 2

Truffaut, Francois 1932-1984 . . . . **CLC 20**
  See also CA 81-84; 113; CANR 34

Trumbo, Dalton 1905-1976 . . . . **CLC 19**
  See also CA 21-24R; 69-72; CANR 10;
  DLB 26

Trumbull, John 1750-1831 . . . . . . **NCLC 30**
  See also DLB 31

Trundlett, Helen B.
  See Eliot, T(homas) S(tearns)

Tryon, Thomas
  1926-1991 . . . . . **CLC 3, 11; DAM POP**
  See also AITN 1; CA 29-32R; 135;
  CANR 32; MTCW

Tryon, Tom
  See Tryon, Thomas

Ts'ao Hsueh-ch'in 1715(?)-1763 . . . . . . **LC 1**

Tsushima, Shuji 1909-1948
  See Dazai, Osamu
  See also CA 107

Tsvetaeva (Efron), Marina (Ivanovna)
  1892-1941 . . . . **TCLC 7, 35; PC 14**
  See also CA 104; 128; MTCW

Tuck, Lily 1938- . . . . **CLC 70**
  See also CA 139

Tu Fu 712-770 . . . . **PC 9**
  See also DAM MULT

Tunis, John R(oberts) 1889-1975 . . . **CLC 12**
  See also CA 61-64; DLB 22, 171; JRDA;
  MAICYA; SATA 37; SATA-Brief 30

Tuohy, Frank . . . . **CLC 37**
  See also Tuohy, John Francis
  See also DLB 14, 139

Tuohy, John Francis 1925-
  See Tuohy, Frank
  See also CA 5-8R; CANR 3, 47

Turco, Lewis (Putnam) 1934- . . . **CLC 11, 63**
  See also CA 13-16R; CAAS 22; CANR 24,
  51; DLBY 84

Turgenev, Ivan
  1818-1883 . . . . **NCLC 21; DA; DAB;
  DAC; DAM MST, NOV; SSC 7; WLC**

Turgot, Anne-Robert-Jacques
  1727-1781 . . . . **LC 26**

Turner, Frederick 1943- . . . . **CLC 48**
  See also CA 73-76; CAAS 10; CANR 12,
  30; DLB 40

Tutu, Desmond M(pilo)
  1931- . . . . . **CLC 80; BLC; DAM MULT**
  See also BW 1; CA 125

Tutuola, Amos
  1920- . . . . **CLC 5, 14, 29; BLC;
  DAM MULT**
  See also BW 2; CA 9-12R; CANR 27;
  DLB 125; MTCW

Twain, Mark
  . . . . . **TCLC 6, 12, 19, 36, 48, 59; SSC 6;
  WLC**
  See also Clemens, Samuel Langhorne
  See also DLB 11, 12, 23, 64, 74

Tyler, Anne
  1941- . . . . **CLC 7, 11, 18, 28, 44, 59;
  DAM NOV, POP**
  See also AAYA 18; BEST 89:1; CA 9-12R;
  CANR 11, 33, 53; DLB 6, 143; DLBY 82;
  MTCW; SATA 7, 90

Tyler, Royall 1757-1826 . . . . **NCLC 3**
  See also DLB 37

Tynan, Katharine 1861-1931 . . . . **TCLC 3**
  See also CA 104; DLB 153

Tyutchev, Fyodor 1803-1873 . . . . . **NCLC 34**

Tzara, Tristan
  1896-1963 . . . . **CLC 47; DAM POET**
  See also Rosenfeld, Samuel; Rosenstock,
  Sami; Rosenstock, Samuel
  See also CA 153

Uhry, Alfred
  1936- . . . . . **CLC 55; DAM DRAM, POP**
  See also CA 127; 133; INT 133

Ulf, Haerved
  See Strindberg, (Johan) August

Ulf, Harved
  See Strindberg, (Johan) August

Ulibarri, Sabine R(eyes)
  1919- . . . . **CLC 83; DAM MULT**
  See also CA 131; DLB 82; HW

Unamuno (y Jugo), Miguel de
  1864-1936 . . . **TCLC 2, 9; DAM MULT,
  NOV; HLC; SSC 11**
  See also CA 104; 131; DLB 108; HW;
  MTCW

Undercliffe, Errol
  See Campbell, (John) Ramsey

Underwood, Miles
  See Glassco, John

Undset, Sigrid
  1882-1949 . . . . **TCLC 3; DA; DAB;
  DAC; DAM MST, NOV; WLC**
  See also CA 104; 129; MTCW

Ungaretti, Giuseppe
  1888-1970 . . . . **CLC 7, 11, 15**
  See also CA 19-20; 25-28R; CAP 2;
  DLB 114

Unger, Douglas 1952- . . . . **CLC 34**
  See also CA 130

Unsworth, Barry (Forster) 1930- . . . . **CLC 76**
  See also CA 25-28R; CANR 30, 54

Updike, John (Hoyer)
  1932- . . . . . . **CLC 1, 2, 3, 5, 7, 9, 13, 15,
  23, 34, 43, 70; DA; DAB; DAC;
  DAM MST, NOV, POET, POP;
  SSC 13; WLC**
  See also CA 1-4R; CABS 1; CANR 4, 33,
  51; CDALB 1968-1988; DLB 2, 5, 143;
  DLBD 3; DLBY 80, 82; MTCW

Upshaw, Margaret Mitchell
  See Mitchell, Margaret (Munnerlyn)

Upton, Mark
  See Sanders, Lawrence

Urdang, Constance (Henriette)
  1922- . . . . **CLC 47**
  See also CA 21-24R; CANR 9, 24

Uriel, Henry
  See Faust, Frederick (Schiller)

Uris, Leon (Marcus)
  1924- . . . . **CLC 7, 32; DAM NOV, POP**
  See also AITN 1, 2; BEST 89:2; CA 1-4R;
  CANR 1, 40; MTCW; SATA 49

Urmuz
  See Codrescu, Andrei

Urquhart, Jane 1949- . . . . **CLC 90; DAC**
  See also CA 113; CANR 32

Ustinov, Peter (Alexander) 1921- . . . . **CLC 1**
  See also AITN 1; CA 13-16R; CANR 25,
  51; DLB 13

Vaculik, Ludvik 1926- .... **CLC 7**
See also CA 53-56

Valdez, Luis (Miguel)
1940- ..... **CLC 84; DAM MULT; HLC**
See also CA 101; CANR 32; DLB 122; HW

Valenzuela, Luisa
1938- ... **CLC 31; DAM MULT; SSC 14**
See also CA 101; CANR 32; DLB 113; HW

Valera y Alcala-Galiano, Juan
1824-1905 .... **TCLC 10**
See also CA 106

Valery, (Ambroise) Paul (Toussaint Jules)
1871-1945 .... **TCLC 4, 15;**
　　　　　　　　　　　　　　DAM POET; PC 9
See also CA 104; 122; MTCW

Valle-Inclan, Ramon (Maria) del
1866-1936 ..... **TCLC 5; DAM MULT;**
　　　　　　　　　　　　　　　　　　　HLC
See also CA 106; 153; DLB 134

Vallejo, Antonio Buero
See Buero Vallejo, Antonio

Vallejo, Cesar (Abraham)
1892-1938 .... **TCLC 3, 56;**
　　　　　　　　　　　　　DAM MULT; HLC
See also CA 105; 153; HW

Vallette, Marguerite Eymery
See Rachilde

Valle Y Pena, Ramon del
See Valle-Inclan, Ramon (Maria) del

Van Ash, Cay 1918- .... **CLC 34**

Vanbrugh, Sir John
1664-1726 .... **LC 21; DAM DRAM**
See also DLB 80

Van Campen, Karl
See Campbell, John W(ood, Jr.)

Vance, Gerald
See Silverberg, Robert

Vance, Jack .... **CLC 35**
See also Vance, John Holbrook
See also DLB 8

Vance, John Holbrook 1916-
See Queen, Ellery; Vance, Jack
See also CA 29-32R; CANR 17; MTCW

Van Den Bogarde, Derek Jules Gaspard Ulric
Niven 1921-
See Bogarde, Dirk
See also CA 77-80

Vandenburgh, Jane .... **CLC 59**

Vanderhaeghe, Guy 1951- .... **CLC 41**
See also CA 113

van der Post, Laurens (Jan)
1906-1996 .... **CLC 5**
See also CA 5-8R; 155; CANR 35

van de Wetering, Janwillem 1931- .. **CLC 47**
See also CA 49-52; CANR 4

Van Dine, S. S. .... **TCLC 23**
See also Wright, Willard Huntington

Van Doren, Carl (Clinton)
1885-1950 .... **TCLC 18**
See also CA 111

Van Doren, Mark 1894-1972..... **CLC 6, 10**
See also CA 1-4R; 37-40R; CANR 3;
DLB 45; MTCW

Van Druten, John (William)
1901-1957 .... **TCLC 2**
See also CA 104; DLB 10

Van Duyn, Mona (Jane)
1921- .... **CLC 3, 7, 63; DAM POET**
See also CA 9-12R; CANR 7, 38; DLB 5

Van Dyne, Edith
See Baum, L(yman) Frank

van Itallie, Jean-Claude 1936- .... **CLC 3**
See also CA 45-48; CAAS 2; CANR 1, 48;
DLB 7

van Ostaijen, Paul 1896-1928 ..... **TCLC 33**

Van Peebles, Melvin
1932- .... **CLC 2, 20; DAM MULT**
See also BW 2; CA 85-88; CANR 27

Vansittart, Peter 1920-........... **CLC 42**
See also CA 1-4R; CANR 3, 49

Van Vechten, Carl 1880-1964 ...... **CLC 33**
See also CA 89-92; DLB 4, 9, 51

Van Vogt, A(lfred) E(lton) 1912-..... **CLC 1**
See also CA 21-24R; CANR 28; DLB 8;
SATA 14

Varda, Agnes 1928- .... **CLC 16**
See also CA 116; 122

Vargas Llosa, (Jorge) Mario (Pedro)
1936- .... **CLC 3, 6, 9, 10, 15, 31, 42, 85;**
　　DA; DAB; DAC; DAM MST, MULT,
　　　　　　　　　　　　　　NOV; HLC
See also CA 73-76; CANR 18, 32, 42;
DLB 145; HW; MTCW

Vasiliu, Gheorghe 1881-1957
See Bacovia, George
See also CA 123

Vassa, Gustavus
See Equiano, Olaudah

Vassilikos, Vassilis 1933-........ **CLC 4, 8**
See also CA 81-84

Vaughan, Henry 1621-1695 .... **LC 27**
See also DLB 131

Vaughn, Stephanie. .... **CLC 62**

Vazov, Ivan (Minchov)
1850-1921 .... **TCLC 25**
See also CA 121; DLB 147

Veblen, Thorstein (Bunde)
1857-1929 .... **TCLC 31**
See also CA 115

Vega, Lope de 1562-1635.......... **LC 23**

Venison, Alfred
See Pound, Ezra (Weston Loomis)

Verdi, Marie de
See Mencken, H(enry) L(ouis)

Verdu, Matilde
See Cela, Camilo Jose

Verga, Giovanni (Carmelo)
1840-1922 .... **TCLC 3; SSC 21**
See also CA 104; 123

Vergil
70B.C.-19B.C...... **CMLC 9; DA; DAB;**
　　　　　　　　DAC; DAM MST, POET; PC 12

Verhaeren, Emile (Adolphe Gustave)
1855-1916 .... **TCLC 12**
See also CA 109

Verlaine, Paul (Marie)
1844-1896 .... **NCLC 2, 51;**
　　　　　　　　　　　　　DAM POET; PC 2

Verne, Jules (Gabriel)
1828-1905 .... **TCLC 6, 52**
See also AAYA 16; CA 110; 131; DLB 123;
JRDA; MAICYA; SATA 21

Very, Jones 1813-1880........... **NCLC 9**
See also DLB 1

Vesaas, Tarjei 1897-1970......... **CLC 48**
See also CA 29-32R

Vialis, Gaston
See Simenon, Georges (Jacques Christian)

Vian, Boris 1920-1959 .... **TCLC 9**
See also CA 106; DLB 72

Viaud, (Louis Marie) Julien 1850-1923
See Loti, Pierre
See also CA 107

Vicar, Henry
See Felsen, Henry Gregor

Vicker, Angus
See Felsen, Henry Gregor

Vidal, Gore
1925- ..... **CLC 2, 4, 6, 8, 10, 22, 33, 72;**
　　　　　　　　　　　　　DAM NOV, POP
See also AITN 1; BEST 90:2; CA 5-8R;
CANR 13, 45; DLB 6, 152;
INT CANR-13; MTCW

Viereck, Peter (Robert Edwin)
1916- .... **CLC 4**
See also CA 1-4R; CANR 1, 47; DLB 5

Vigny, Alfred (Victor) de
1797-1863 ...... **NCLC 7; DAM POET**
See also DLB 119

Vilakazi, Benedict Wallet
1906-1947 .... **TCLC 37**

Villiers de l'Isle Adam, Jean Marie Mathias
Philippe Auguste Comte
1838-1889 .... **NCLC 3; SSC 14**
See also DLB 123

Villon, Francois 1431-1463(?) .... **PC 13**

Vinci, Leonardo da 1452-1519...... **LC 12**

Vine, Barbara .... **CLC 50**
See also Rendell, Ruth (Barbara)
See also BEST 90:4

Vinge, Joan D(ennison)
1948- .... **CLC 30; SSC 24**
See also CA 93-96; SATA 36

Violis, G.
See Simenon, Georges (Jacques Christian)

Visconti, Luchino 1906-1976....... **CLC 16**
See also CA 81-84; 65-68; CANR 39

Vittorini, Elio 1908-1966...... **CLC 6, 9, 14**
See also CA 133; 25-28R

Vizinczey, Stephen 1933-.......... **CLC 40**
See also CA 128; INT 128

Vliet, R(ussell) G(ordon)
1929-1984 .... **CLC 22**
See also CA 37-40R; 112; CANR 18

Vogau, Boris Andreyevich 1894-1937(?)
See Pilnyak, Boris
See also CA 123

Vogel, Paula A(nne) 1951-........ **CLC 76**
See also CA 108

Warner, Susan (Bogert)
　1819-1885 . . . . **NCLC 31**
　See also DLB 3, 42

Warner, Sylvia (Constance) Ashton
　See Ashton-Warner, Sylvia (Constance)

Warner, Sylvia Townsend
　1893-1978 . . . . **CLC 7, 19; SSC 23**
　See also CA 61-64; 77-80; CANR 16;
　DLB 34, 139; MTCW

Warren, Mercy Otis 1728-1814. . . **NCLC 13**
　See also DLB 31

Warren, Robert Penn
　1905-1989 . . . . **CLC 1, 4, 6, 8, 10, 13, 18,
　39, 53, 59; DA; DAB; DAC; DAM MST,
　NOV, POET; SSC 4; WLC**
　See also AITN 1; CA 13-16R; 129;
　CANR 10, 47; CDALB 1968-1988;
　DLB 2, 48, 152; DLBY 80, 89;
　INT CANR-10; MTCW; SATA 46;
　SATA-Obit 63

Warshofsky, Isaac
　See Singer, Isaac Bashevis

Warton, Thomas
　1728-1790 . . . . **LC 15; DAM POET**
　See also DLB 104, 109

Waruk, Kona
　See Harris, (Theodore) Wilson

Warung, Price 1855-1911. . . . . **TCLC 45**

Warwick, Jarvis
　See Garner, Hugh

Washington, Alex
　See Harris, Mark

Washington, Booker T(aliaferro)
　1856-1915 . . . . **TCLC 10; BLC;
　DAM MULT**
　See also BW 1; CA 114; 125; SATA 28

Washington, George 1732-1799. . . . . . **LC 25**
　See also DLB 31

Wassermann, (Karl) Jakob
　1873-1934 . . . . **TCLC 6**
　See also CA 104; DLB 66

Wasserstein, Wendy
　1950- . . . . **CLC 32, 59, 90;
　DAM DRAM; DC 4**
　See also CA 121; 129; CABS 3; CANR 53;
　INT 129

Waterhouse, Keith (Spencer)
　1929- . . . . **CLC 47**
　See also CA 5-8R; CANR 38; DLB 13, 15;
　MTCW

Waters, Frank (Joseph)
　1902-1995 . . . . **CLC 88**
　See also CA 5-8R; 149; CAAS 13; CANR 3,
　18; DLBY 86

Waters, Roger 1944- . . . . **CLC 35**

Watkins, Frances Ellen
　See Harper, Frances Ellen Watkins

Watkins, Gerrold
　See Malzberg, Barry N(athaniel)

Watkins, Gloria 1955(?)-
　See hooks, bell
　See also BW 2; CA 143

Watkins, Paul 1964- . . . . **CLC 55**
　See also CA 132

Watkins, Vernon Phillips
　1906-1967 . . . . **CLC 43**
　See also CA 9-10; 25-28R; CAP 1; DLB 20

Watson, Irving S.
　See Mencken, H(enry) L(ouis)

Watson, John H.
　See Farmer, Philip Jose

Watson, Richard F.
　See Silverberg, Robert

Waugh, Auberon (Alexander) 1939- . . **CLC 7**
　See also CA 45-48; CANR 6, 22; DLB 14

Waugh, Evelyn (Arthur St. John)
　1903-1966 . . . . . . **CLC 1, 3, 8, 13, 19, 27,
　44; DA; DAB; DAC; DAM MST, NOV,
　POP; WLC**
　See also CA 85-88; 25-28R; CANR 22;
　CDBLB 1914-1945; DLB 15, 162; MTCW

Waugh, Harriet 1944- . . . . **CLC 6**
　See also CA 85-88; CANR 22

Ways, C. R.
　See Blount, Roy (Alton), Jr.

Waystaff, Simon
　See Swift, Jonathan

Webb, (Martha) Beatrice (Potter)
　1858-1943 . . . . **TCLC 22**
　See also Potter, Beatrice
　See also CA 117

Webb, Charles (Richard) 1939- . . . . . . **CLC 7**
　See also CA 25-28R

Webb, James H(enry), Jr. 1946- . . . . **CLC 22**
　See also CA 81-84

Webb, Mary (Gladys Meredith)
　1881-1927 . . . . **TCLC 24**
　See also CA 123; DLB 34

Webb, Mrs. Sidney
　See Webb, (Martha) Beatrice (Potter)

Webb, Phyllis 1927- . . . . **CLC 18**
　See also CA 104; CANR 23; DLB 53

Webb, Sidney (James)
　1859-1947 . . . . **TCLC 22**
　See also CA 117

Webber, Andrew Lloyd. . . . . **CLC 21**
　See also Lloyd Webber, Andrew

Weber, Lenora Mattingly
　1895-1971 . . . . **CLC 12**
　See also CA 19-20; 29-32R; CAP 1;
　SATA 2; SATA-Obit 26

Webster, John
　1579(?)-1634(?) . . . . . . **LC 33; DA; DAB;
　DAC; DAM DRAM, MST; DC 2; WLC**
　See also CDBLB Before 1660; DLB 58

Webster, Noah 1758-1843 . . . . **NCLC 30**

Wedekind, (Benjamin) Frank(lin)
　1864-1918 . . . . . . **TCLC 7; DAM DRAM**
　See also CA 104; 153; DLB 118

Weidman, Jerome 1913- . . . . **CLC 7**
　See also AITN 2; CA 1-4R; CANR 1;
　DLB 28

Weil, Simone (Adolphine)
　1909-1943 . . . . **TCLC 23**
　See also CA 117

Weinstein, Nathan
　See West, Nathanael

Weinstein, Nathan von Wallenstein
　See West, Nathanael

Weir, Peter (Lindsay) 1944- . . . . **CLC 20**
　See also CA 113; 123

Weiss, Peter (Ulrich)
　1916-1982 . . . . **CLC 3, 15, 51;
　DAM DRAM**
　See also CA 45-48; 106; CANR 3; DLB 69,
　124

Weiss, Theodore (Russell)
　1916- . . . . **CLC 3, 8, 14**
　See also CA 9-12R; CAAS 2; CANR 46;
　DLB 5

Welch, (Maurice) Denton
　1915-1948 . . . . **TCLC 22**
　See also CA 121; 148

Welch, James
　1940- . . . . . **CLC 6, 14, 52; DAM MULT,
　POP**
　See also CA 85-88; CANR 42; NNAL

Weldon, Fay
　1933- . . . . **CLC 6, 9, 11, 19, 36, 59;
　DAM POP**
　See also CA 21-24R; CANR 16, 46;
　CDBLB 1960 to Present; DLB 14;
　INT CANR-16; MTCW

Wellek, Rene 1903-1995. . . . . **CLC 28**
　See also CA 5-8R; 150; CAAS 7; CANR 8;
　DLB 63; INT CANR-8

Weller, Michael 1942- . . . . **CLC 10, 53**
　See also CA 85-88

Weller, Paul 1958- . . . . **CLC 26**

Wellershoff, Dieter 1925- . . . . **CLC 46**
　See also CA 89-92; CANR 16, 37

Welles, (George) Orson
　1915-1985 . . . . **CLC 20, 80**
　See also CA 93-96; 117

Wellman, Mac 1945- . . . . **CLC 65**

Wellman, Manly Wade 1903-1986 . . **CLC 49**
　See also CA 1-4R; 118; CANR 6, 16, 44;
　SATA 6; SATA-Obit 47

Wells, Carolyn 1869(?)-1942 . . . . . . **TCLC 35**
　See also CA 113; DLB 11

Wells, H(erbert) G(eorge)
　1866-1946 . . . . **TCLC 6, 12, 19; DA;
　DAB; DAC; DAM MST, NOV; SSC 6;
　WLC**
　See also AAYA 18; CA 110; 121;
　CDBLB 1914-1945; DLB 34, 70, 156;
　MTCW; SATA 20

Wells, Rosemary 1943- . . . . **CLC 12**
　See also AAYA 13; CA 85-88; CANR 48;
　CLR 16; MAICYA; SAAS 1; SATA 18,
　69

Welty, Eudora
　1909- . . . . . . **CLC 1, 2, 5, 14, 22, 33; DA;
　DAB; DAC; DAM MST, NOV; SSC 1;
　WLC**
　See also CA 9-12R; CABS 1; CANR 32;
　CDALB 1941-1968; DLB 2, 102, 143;
　DLBD 12; DLBY 87; MTCW

Wen I-to 1899-1946 . . . . **TCLC 28**

Wentworth, Robert
　See Hamilton, Edmond

Werfel, Franz (V.) 1890-1945 . . . . . . **TCLC 8**
　See also CA 104; DLB 81, 124

Wilder, Samuel 1906-
See Wilder, Billy
See also CA 89-92

Wilder, Thornton (Niven)
1897-1975 ..... **CLC 1, 5, 6, 10, 15, 35,**
82; DA; DAB; DAC; DAM DRAM,
MST, NOV; DC 1; WLC
See also AITN 2; CA 13-16R; 61-64;
CANR 40; DLB 4, 7, 9; MTCW

Wilding, Michael 1942- .... **CLC 73**
See also CA 104; CANR 24, 49

Wiley, Richard 1944- .... **CLC 44**
See also CA 121; 129

Wilhelm, Kate .... **CLC 7**
See also Wilhelm, Katie Gertrude
See also CAAS 5; DLB 8; INT CANR-17

Wilhelm, Katie Gertrude 1928-
See Wilhelm, Kate
See also CA 37-40R; CANR 17, 36; MTCW

Wilkins, Mary
See Freeman, Mary Eleanor Wilkins

Willard, Nancy 1936- .... **CLC 7, 37**
See also CA 89-92; CANR 10, 39; CLR 5;
DLB 5, 52; MAICYA; MTCW;
SATA 37, 71; SATA-Brief 30

Williams, C(harles) K(enneth)
1936- .... **CLC 33, 56; DAM POET**
See also CA 37-40R; DLB 5

Williams, Charles
See Collier, James L(incoln)

Williams, Charles (Walter Stansby)
1886-1945 .... **TCLC 1, 11**
See also CA 104; DLB 100, 153

Williams, (George) Emlyn
1905-1987 ...... **CLC 15; DAM DRAM**
See also CA 104; 123; CANR 36; DLB 10,
77; MTCW

Williams, Hugo 1942- .... **CLC 42**
See also CA 17-20R; CANR 45; DLB 40

Williams, J. Walker
See Wodehouse, P(elham) G(renville)

Williams, John A(lfred)
1925- ... **CLC 5, 13; BLC; DAM MULT**
See also BW 2; CA 53-56; CAAS 3;
CANR 6, 26, 51; DLB 2, 33;
INT CANR-6

Williams, Jonathan (Chamberlain)
1929- .... **CLC 13**
See also CA 9-12R; CAAS 12; CANR 8;
DLB 5

Williams, Joy 1944- .... **CLC 31**
See also CA 41-44R; CANR 22, 48

Williams, Norman 1952- .... **CLC 39**
See also CA 118

Williams, Sherley Anne
1944- ..... **CLC 89; BLC; DAM MULT,**
POET
See also BW 2; CA 73-76; CANR 25;
DLB 41; INT CANR-25; SATA 78

Williams, Shirley
See Williams, Sherley Anne

Williams, Tennessee
1911-1983 ..... **CLC 1, 2, 5, 7, 8, 11, 15,**
19, 30, 39, 45, 71; DA; DAB; DAC;
DAM DRAM, MST; DC 4; WLC
See also AITN 1, 2; CA 5-8R; 108;
CABS 3; CANR 31; CDALB 1941-1968;
DLB 7; DLBD 4; DLBY 83; MTCW

Williams, Thomas (Alonzo)
1926-1990 .... **CLC 14**
See also CA 1-4R; 132; CANR 2

Williams, William C.
See Williams, William Carlos

Williams, William Carlos
1883-1963 .... **CLC 1, 2, 5, 9, 13, 22, 42,**
67; DA; DAB; DAC; DAM MST, POET;
PC 7
See also CA 89-92; CANR 34;
CDALB 1917-1929; DLB 4, 16, 54, 86;
MTCW

Williamson, David (Keith) 1942- .... **CLC 56**
See also CA 103; CANR 41

Williamson, Ellen Douglas 1905-1984
See Douglas, Ellen
See also CA 17-20R; 114; CANR 39

Williamson, Jack .... **CLC 29**
See also Williamson, John Stewart
See also CAAS 8; DLB 8

Williamson, John Stewart 1908-
See Williamson, Jack
See also CA 17-20R; CANR 23

Willie, Frederick
See Lovecraft, H(oward) P(hillips)

Willingham, Calder (Baynard, Jr.)
1922-1995 .... **CLC 5, 51**
See also CA 5-8R; 147; CANR 3; DLB 2,
44; MTCW

Willis, Charles
See Clarke, Arthur C(harles)

Willy
See Colette, (Sidonie-Gabrielle)

Willy, Colette
See Colette, (Sidonie-Gabrielle)

Wilson, A(ndrew) N(orman) 1950- .. **CLC 33**
See also CA 112; 122; DLB 14, 155

Wilson, Angus (Frank Johnstone)
1913-1991 .. **CLC 2, 3, 5, 25, 34; SSC 21**
See also CA 5-8R; 134; CANR 21; DLB 15,
139, 155; MTCW

Wilson, August
1945- .... **CLC 39, 50, 63; BLC; DA;**
DAB; DAC; DAM DRAM, MST,
MULT; DC 2
See also AAYA 16; BW 2; CA 115; 122;
CANR 42, 54; MTCW

Wilson, Brian 1942- .... **CLC 12**

Wilson, Colin 1931- .... **CLC 3, 14**
See also CA 1-4R; CAAS 5; CANR 1, 22,
33; DLB 14; MTCW

Wilson, Dirk
See Pohl, Frederik

Wilson, Edmund
1895-1972 .... **CLC 1, 2, 3, 8, 24**
See also CA 1-4R; 37-40R; CANR 1, 46;
DLB 63; MTCW

Wilson, Ethel Davis (Bryant)
1888(?)-1980 .... **CLC 13; DAC;**
DAM POET
See also CA 102; DLB 68; MTCW

Wilson, John 1785-1854 .... **NCLC 5**

Wilson, John (Anthony) Burgess 1917-1993
See Burgess, Anthony
See also CA 1-4R; 143; CANR 2, 46; DAC;
DAM NOV; MTCW

Wilson, Lanford
1937- ..... **CLC 7, 14, 36; DAM DRAM**
See also CA 17-20R; CABS 3; CANR 45;
DLB 7

Wilson, Robert M. 1944- .... **CLC 7, 9**
See also CA 49-52; CANR 2, 41; MTCW

Wilson, Robert McLiam 1964- ..... **CLC 59**
See also CA 132

Wilson, Sloan 1920- .... **CLC 32**
See also CA 1-4R; CANR 1, 44

Wilson, Snoo 1948- .... **CLC 33**
See also CA 69-72

Wilson, William S(mith) 1932- ..... **CLC 49**
See also CA 81-84

Winchilsea, Anne (Kingsmill) Finch Counte
1661-1720 .... **LC 3**

Windham, Basil
See Wodehouse, P(elham) G(renville)

Wingrove, David (John) 1954- ...... **CLC 68**
See also CA 133

Winters, Janet Lewis .... **CLC 41**
See also Lewis, Janet
See also DLBY 87

Winters, (Arthur) Yvor
1900-1968 .... **CLC 4, 8, 32**
See also CA 11-12; 25-28R; CAP 1;
DLB 48; MTCW

Winterson, Jeanette
1959- .... **CLC 64; DAM POP**
See also CA 136

Winthrop, John 1588-1649......... **LC 31**
See also DLB 24, 30

Wiseman, Frederick 1930- .... **CLC 20**

Wister, Owen 1860-1938 .... **TCLC 21**
See also CA 108; DLB 9, 78; SATA 62

Witkacy
See Witkiewicz, Stanislaw Ignacy

Witkiewicz, Stanislaw Ignacy
1885-1939 .... **TCLC 8**
See also CA 105

Wittgenstein, Ludwig (Josef Johann)
1889-1951 .... **TCLC 59**
See also CA 113

Wittig, Monique 1935(?)- .... **CLC 22**
See also CA 116; 135; DLB 83

Wittlin, Jozef 1896-1976 .... **CLC 25**
See also CA 49-52; 65-68; CANR 3

Wodehouse, P(elham) G(renville)
1881-1975 ... **CLC 1, 2, 5, 10, 22; DAB;**
DAC; DAM NOV; SSC 2
See also AITN 2; CA 45-48; 57-60;
CANR 3, 33; CDBLB 1914-1945;
DLB 34, 162; MTCW; SATA 22

Woiwode, L.
See Woiwode, Larry (Alfred)

Woiwode, Larry (Alfred) 1941-... **CLC 6, 10**
See also CA 73-76; CANR 16; DLB 6;
INT CANR-16

Wojciechowska, Maia (Teresa)
1927-...................... **CLC 26**
See also AAYA 8; CA 9-12R; CANR 4, 41;
CLR 1; JRDA; MAICYA; SAAS 1;
SATA 1, 28, 83

Wolf, Christa 1929-........ **CLC 14, 29, 58**
See also CA 85-88; CANR 45; DLB 75;
MTCW

Wolfe, Gene (Rodman)
1931-........... **CLC 25; DAM POP**
See also CA 57-60; CAAS 9; CANR 6, 32;
DLB 8

Wolfe, George C. 1954-.......... **CLC 49**
See also CA 149

Wolfe, Thomas (Clayton)
1900-1938 ..... **TCLC 4, 13, 29, 61; DA;
DAB; DAC; DAM MST, NOV; WLC**
See also CA 104; 132; CDALB 1929-1941;
DLB 9, 102; DLBD 2; DLBY 85; MTCW

Wolfe, Thomas Kennerly, Jr. 1931-
See Wolfe, Tom
See also CA 13-16R; CANR 9, 33;
DAM POP; INT CANR-9; MTCW

Wolfe, Tom .... **CLC 1, 2, 9, 15, 35, 51**
See also Wolfe, Thomas Kennerly, Jr.
See also AAYA 8; AITN 2; BEST 89:1;
DLB 152

Wolff, Geoffrey (Ansell) 1937-..... **CLC 41**
See also CA 29-32R; CANR 29, 43

Wolff, Sonia
See Levitin, Sonia (Wolff)

Wolff, Tobias (Jonathan Ansell)
1945-.................... **CLC 39, 64**
See also AAYA 16; BEST 90:2; CA 114;
117; CAAS 22; CANR 54; DLB 130;
INT 117

Wolfram von Eschenbach
c. 1170-c. 1220 .... **CMLC 5**
See also DLB 138

Wolitzer, Hilma 1930-............ **CLC 17**
See also CA 65-68; CANR 18, 40;
INT CANR-18; SATA 31

Wollstonecraft, Mary 1759-1797...... **LC 5**
See also CDBLB 1789-1832; DLB 39, 104,
158

Wonder, Stevie .... **CLC 12**
See also Morris, Steveland Judkins

Wong, Jade Snow 1922-.......... **CLC 17**
See also CA 109

Woodcott, Keith
See Brunner, John (Kilian Houston)

Woodruff, Robert W.
See Mencken, H(enry) L(ouis)

Woolf, (Adeline) Virginia
1882-1941 ...... **TCLC 1, 5, 20, 43, 56;
DA; DAB; DAC; DAM MST, NOV;
SSC 7; WLC**
See also CA 104; 130; CDBLB 1914-1945;
DLB 36, 100, 162; DLBD 10; MTCW

Woollcott, Alexander (Humphreys)
1887-1943 .... **TCLC 5**
See also CA 105; DLB 29

Woolrich, Cornell 1903-1968...... **CLC 77**
See also Hopley-Woolrich, Cornell George

Wordsworth, Dorothy
1771-1855 .... **NCLC 25**
See also DLB 107

Wordsworth, William
1770-1850 .... **NCLC 12, 38; DA; DAB;
DAC; DAM MST, POET; PC 4; WLC**
See also CDBLB 1789-1832; DLB 93, 107

Wouk, Herman
1915- .. **CLC 1, 9, 38; DAM NOV, POP**
See also CA 5-8R; CANR 6, 33; DLBY 82;
INT CANR-6; MTCW

Wright, Charles (Penzel, Jr.)
1935- .... **CLC 6, 13, 28**
See also CA 29-32R; CAAS 7; CANR 23,
36; DLB 165; DLBY 82; MTCW

Wright, Charles Stevenson
1932- .... **CLC 49; BLC 3;
DAM MULT, POET**
See also BW 1; CA 9-12R; CANR 26;
DLB 33

Wright, Jack R.
See Harris, Mark

Wright, James (Arlington)
1927-1980 .... **CLC 3, 5, 10, 28;
DAM POET**
See also AITN 2; CA 49-52; 97-100;
CANR 4, 34; DLB 5, 169; MTCW

Wright, Judith (Arandell)
1915- .... **CLC 11, 53; PC 14**
See also CA 13-16R; CANR 31; MTCW;
SATA 14

Wright, L(aurali) R. 1939-......... **CLC 44**
See also CA 138

Wright, Richard (Nathaniel)
1908-1960 .... **CLC 1, 3, 4, 9, 14, 21, 48,
74; BLC; DA; DAB; DAC; DAM MST,
MULT, NOV; SSC 2; WLC**
See also AAYA 5; BW 1; CA 108;
CDALB 1929-1941; DLB 76, 102;
DLBD 2; MTCW

Wright, Richard B(ruce) 1937-...... **CLC 6**
See also CA 85-88; DLB 53

Wright, Rick 1945-............... **CLC 35**

Wright, Rowland
See Wells, Carolyn

Wright, Stephen Caldwell 1946-.... **CLC 33**
See also BW 2

Wright, Willard Huntington 1888-1939
See Van Dine, S. S.
See also CA 115

Wright, William 1930-............ **CLC 44**
See also CA 53-56; CANR 7, 23

Wroth, LadyMary 1587-1653(?) ..... **LC 30**
See also DLB 121

Wu Ch'eng-en 1500(?)-1582(?)........ **LC 7**

Wu Ching-tzu 1701-1754 .... **LC 2**

Wurlitzer, Rudolph 1938(?)-.. **CLC 2, 4, 15**
See also CA 85-88; DLB 173

Wycherley, William
1641-1715 ..... **LC 8, 21; DAM DRAM**
See also CDBLB 1660-1789; DLB 80

Wylie, Elinor (Morton Hoyt)
1885-1928 .... **TCLC 8**
See also CA 105; DLB 9, 45

Wylie, Philip (Gordon) 1902-1971... **CLC 43**
See also CA 21-22; 33-36R; CAP 2; DLB 9

Wyndham, John. .... **CLC 19**
See also Harris, John (Wyndham Parkes
Lucas) Beynon

Wyss, Johann David Von
1743-1818 .... **NCLC 10**
See also JRDA; MAICYA; SATA 29;
SATA-Brief 27

Xenophon
c. 430B.C.-c. 354B.C......... **CMLC 17**

Yakumo Koizumi
See Hearn, (Patricio) Lafcadio (Tessima
Carlos)

Yanez, Jose Donoso
See Donoso (Yanez), Jose

Yanovsky, Basile S.
See Yanovsky, V(assily) S(emenovich)

Yanovsky, V(assily) S(emenovich)
1906-1989 .... **CLC 2, 18**
See also CA 97-100; 129

Yates, Richard 1926-1992 ..... **CLC 7, 8, 23**
See also CA 5-8R; 139; CANR 10, 43;
DLB 2; DLBY 81, 92; INT CANR-10

Yeats, W. B.
See Yeats, William Butler

Yeats, William Butler
1865-1939 ..... **TCLC 1, 11, 18, 31; DA;
DAB; DAC; DAM DRAM, MST,
POET; WLC**
See also CA 104; 127; CANR 45;
CDBLB 1890-1914; DLB 10, 19, 98, 156;
MTCW

Yehoshua, A(braham) B.
1936- .... **CLC 13, 31**
See also CA 33-36R; CANR 43

Yep, Laurence Michael 1948-...... **CLC 35**
See also AAYA 5; CA 49-52; CANR 1, 46;
CLR 3, 17; DLB 52; JRDA; MAICYA;
SATA 7, 69

Yerby, Frank G(arvin)
1916-1991 .... **CLC 1, 7, 22; BLC;
DAM MULT**
See also BW 1; CA 9-12R; 136; CANR 16,
52; DLB 76; INT CANR-16; MTCW

Yesenin, Sergei Alexandrovich
See Esenin, Sergei (Alexandrovich)

Yevtushenko, Yevgeny (Alexandrovich)
1933- .... **CLC 1, 3, 13, 26, 51;
DAM POET**
See also CA 81-84; CANR 33, 54; MTCW

Yezierska, Anzia 1885(?)-1970 ..... **CLC 46**
See also CA 126; 89-92; DLB 28; MTCW

Yglesias, Helen 1915-.......... **CLC 7, 22**
See also CA 37-40R; CAAS 20; CANR 15;
INT CANR-15; MTCW

Yokomitsu Riichi 1898-1947 ...... **TCLC 47**

Yonge, Charlotte (Mary)
1823-1901 .... **TCLC 48**
See also CA 109; DLB 18, 163; SATA 17

York, Jeremy
See Creasey, John

Literary Criticism Series
Cumulative Topic Index

This index lists all topic entries in Gale's *Classical and Medieval Literature Criticism, Contemporary Literary Criticism, Literature Criticism from 1400 to 1800, Nineteenth-Century Literature Criticism,* and *Twentieth-Century Literary Criticism.*

Topic Index

Topic Index

Topic Index

NCLC Cumulative Nationality Index

Nationality Index

NCLC-59 Title Index

Title Index

ISBN 0-8103-7106-5

90000

9 780810 371064